ART AT AUCTION
IN
AMERICA

1994 EDITION

The comprehensive, up-to-date annual art
price guide to over 10,000 artists and 20,000 works
of art sold at America's major auction houses
from August 1992 through August 1993.

KREXPRESS
10169 New Hampshire Ave./Suite 195
Silver Spring, MD 20903

Library of Congress   ISSN 1046-4999
ISBN 0-9624926-4-7

If additional copies of this valuable art collecting tool are needed they can be ordered directly from the publisher at $39.50 per copy plus $2.50 handling and shipping. For quantity orders of 5 or more copies please contact the publisher by mail or phone.

KREXPRESS
10169 New Hampshire Ave./# 195
Silver Spring, MD 20903
(301) 445-6009

Cover reproduction: Aldro T. Hibbard (American 1886 - 1972)
Winter, Mt. Mansfield, Vermont
Oil on Canvas
18″ x 26″

PRINTED IN THE UNITED STATES OF AMERICA

TABLE OF CONTENTS

INTRODUCTION

The art market began to show new life during the 1992-1993 auction year. Unsold lots decreased dramatically at most auction houses and new, fresh material has begun to appear again. Some of the major auction houses used this opportunity to increase their buyer's commissions from 10% to 15% of the hammer price but it does not appear that this change impacted demand to any great degree. Hopefully, we can now look forward to an exciting and active 1994 art auction season.

In a continuing effort to broaden our coverage, we have added another auction house to our listings - **Frank H. Boos** of Bloomfield Hills, Michigan.

If you are unfamiliar with this important publication, ART AT AUCTION IN AMERICA is designed to give both the novice and the expert the power of portable knowledge so that they can be more informed and confident art collectors. The listings contain the key data pertinent to each work's value with the exception of subjective aspects such as condition and attractiveness or quality of the piece.

The art sales information has been collected from major auction houses in the United States and Canada, and includes both foreign and American artists. Much art, of course, is also sold through dealers, galleries and brokers. These sales represent the art retail market and actual selling prices are rarely available to the public. The auction market, on the other hand, represents the art wholesale market to a large degree. This being said, it is important that beginning collectors and investors understand that prices paid at auction for a particular artists work are only a guide and can be somewhat different than those quoted by a dealer. These reasons include: 1) The auction market is generally less susceptible to (but not immune from) artificial manipulation of prices—particularly for the works of contemporary artists. 2) Dealers and brokers obviously must make a profit on a sale, whereas an auction house automatically receives a commission on each painting sold ranging from 20% to 30% of the selling price. Also, many dealers guarantee the authenticity of their inventory, in effect providing you insurance. Most auction houses do too, but have many disclaimers in their terms of sale. 3) The auction market will often reflect up and down price swings in an artist's value before the retail market shows a similar trend. Many a dealer has run back to his gallery to reprice stock immediately after auction results have set new records.

It is not practical or possible to provide the novice a complete background with regard to art values in the limited space available here. However, it is important to briefly review some general observations about how certain factors affect the value of a work of art. Although it may not be new information for experienced dealers and collectors, it will be of value to most others.

Disclaimer

Every effort has been made to assure the accuracy of the information included here. However, in a mass of data this large, all of it initially compiled by auction houses outside our control, a few errors are inevitable. If you question any information, please contact us or the auction house involved for corroboration before relying on it. We do, in fact, encourage you to notify us of any errors you may find since this information will all be retained in an historical data bank.

Additionally, as is explained in more detail in the text of this guide, many factors may contribute to the value of a particular artwork. Therefore, you should not rely upon these ranges to purchase a particular piece of artwork, but should instead obtain an appraisal from a reputable dealer or art professional. The Publisher and Writer accept no responsibility and/or liability for any purchase of a work of art which is later appraised at a value less than the values set forth in this guide. This guide is provided for informational purposes only.

IMPORTANT FEATURES OF
ART AT AUCTION IN AMERICA

ART AT AUCTION IN AMERICA is the most comprehensive portable guide available.

Any work by any artist which sells for twenty-five dollars or more is included.

ART AT AUCTION IN AMERICA is easy to use.

Prioritizes works of art within each artist's listing by descending price which allows you to see what effect variables such as medium, size, subject, auction house and date of sale may have on a painting's value.

ART AT AUCTION IN AMERICA includes only practical information.

Artists are listed alphabetically without regard to nationality or painting style. However, nationalities and birth and death dates are indicated whenever available. Paintings identified by subjective attributions such as "attributed to," "circle of," "style of," "manner of," or "school of" are not included.

ART AT AUCTION IN AMERICA is user friendly.

A key to the abbreviations in the listings is included in two places, near the end of the introductory material, and also on the inside of the back cover.

ART AT AUCTION IN AMERICA retains all original titles of art work.

Titles provided by the auction house in the language of the artist, usually French, Spanish, German or Italian, are retained as referenced in the original auction catalogue.

Each succeeding edition of ART AT AUCTION IN AMERICA will include an expanded list of artists.

If there are no current sales of works by an important artist who was listed in a previous edition, the artist's name will still be included in the 1994 Edition, with a notation of which edition to check for information. There are well over 3000 such artists listed this year.

ART AT AUCTION IN AMERICA lists all sales prices in U.S. Dollars.

Canadian auction prices have already been converted for you at 1.0 Canadian Dollars = 0.80 U.S. Dollars.

ART AT AUCTION IN AMERICA includes private sales of auction houses.

Occasionally, auction house price lists indicate that some paintings, which did not sell at auction, were sold privately after the sale. These sales, while not strictly an auction price, are of useful reference value and have been included in this book.

IMPORTANT FACTORS AFFECTING ART VALUES

Most popular collectibles such as prints, stamps, coins, furniture, toys, etc., are produced in multiples with no discernable difference between like items. This produces a market and values which usually reflect simple supply and demand for each given item, and the resultant confidence that an item can be bought or sold for a certain price.

Fine arts, on the other hand, are more complicated to value because each item is unique. There can be no absolute value because no two items are exactly alike. The best that can be done is to look at similar items to get a feel for the approximate value of a particular piece. It is this subjectivity and inherent uncertainty which intimidates many would-be art collectors. ART AT AUCTION IN AMERICA provides specific information about each individual work which then can be compared to similar items in question. This can significantly increase the confidence of the buyer and seller of art.

The following key factors generally determine art values (in no particular order):

1. The Artist (name, nationality and dates of activity)
2. The Mediums Used (e.g., oil on canvas, watercolor on paper)
3. The Size of the Work
4. The Subject Matter
5. The Date Painted (if known)
6. The Auction House (or dealer) selling the work and its location
7. The Date of Sale
8. The Condition of the Piece
9. The Authenticity
10. The "Attractiveness" or General Quality of Work
11. Provenance
12. Historical Considerations

1. The Artist

This can often be the most important factor in art values. A painting by Renoir, for example, will be worth considerably more than an otherwise similar painting by a relatively minor impressionist artist simply because of the name. Like all artists, however, Renoir produced some works I'm sure he would like to have forgotten.

In this guide artist's names are listed alphabetically. Occasionally, paintings resulted from the collaborative efforts of two artists. In these cases, the paintings are included under both artists' listings. Among some Old Masters particularly, and occasionally others, artists went by a pseudonym, as did Tiziano Vecellio, better known as Titian. In these cases, the paintings are listed under both names. Paintings described as "attributed to," "circle of," "style of," or "manner of" a particular artist and "School" paintings such as "American School," are not included in this catalogue. There is little value in listing this information because of its subjectivity.

For example, a Hudson River Scene, unsigned and described as "American School" could be worth anything from $25 to $10,000 or more depending on the overall size, artistic quality and attractiveness of the painting. In any guide such as this, without a photo of each painting, the information would be useless to a buyer or seller.

We have also provided nationality information and dates of activity where possible. Nationalities can be hard to pin down since many artists emigrated during their lifetimes and others lived and painted in distant lands. We have tried to follow the precedent of others in assigning nationality but some variations are inevitable. Among the lesser-known European artists, so little may be known they are simply described as European or Continental.

The birth and death dates of artists are included where available. Obviously, among living artists only the birth date is listed, but sometimes even among older artists only one date is known. In some cases, if neither their birth nor death dates are known, but all their known paintings fall into a particular range of dates, they are described by their active dates (in which case the dates in the catalogue are preceded by the letter "a."). The artists of whom even less is known, are assigned a century which corresponds to what little may be known about them or their painting style.

2. The Mediums Used

This factor includes both the material applied to convey an artistic idea and the material or substrate onto which it is applied. Prior to the 20th Century, there were only a limited number of mediums used with oil paints, watercolor, tempera, charcoal, chalk, and ink, typical examples applied to such materials as canvas, linen, panel, board, or paper. The advent of so-called modern art has expanded the available mediums dramatically (and I might add complicated the cataloguing of these works). The mediums are thus divided into two categories, a) the classical painting mediums, and b) the modern/contemporary mediums. This will simplify using the key to abbreviations.

Abbreviations for the material(s) applied are always listed first on the left, followed by a slash (/), which can be translated as meaning "on." The material or substrate onto which they are applied is listed to the right of the slash (again in abbreviated form). If that substrate is laid onto another substrate, another slash follows with that second substrate listed. For those readers familiar with normal convention of listing mediums, those conventions are followed as much as possible. The limited space available, however, requires some changes to be made. The abbreviations are still done as logically and mnemonically as possible.

Some typical examples of classical mediums:

O/C	oil on canvas
W/Pa	watercolor on paper
O/C/B	oil on canvas laid down on board
Pe&W/Pa	Pencil and Watercolor on paper

Some typical examples of modern mediums:

Mk/Pa	Marker on paper
L/C	Collage on canvas
Sp Ss/C	Synthetic Polymer Silkscreened on canvas

The mediums used often have a major effect on value. In general, oil paintings by a given artist command higher prices than watercolors, which in turn command higher prices than the ink drawings. There are plenty of exceptions, however, so it's important that an entire artist's listing be reviewed before developing any conclusions. If the medium is omitted from a specific listing, it means this information was not included in the auction catalogue.

3. The Size of the Work

The size of a piece often has a significant effect on its value. Everything else being equal, larger typically means more expensive. If paintings get too large, however, the size of the market that can accommodate such a painting shrinks dramatically, another factor that affects value. Paintings produced in horizontal format, where the width (horizontal dimension) exceeds the height (vertical dimension), are more common and apparently more desirable for many collectors than paintings produced in a vertical format, where height exceeds the width.

This guide states dimensions in inches rounded to the nearest whole inch, with the vertical dimension the first number and the horizontal dimension the second number. Round paintings are described with a single number followed by the abbreviation "dia" for diameter. The only exception to the use of inches is in the listing of some Old Master drawings which are more commonly described in millimeters (mm). (Dividing the mm number by 25 will give you a close approximation in inches.)

If the size dimension is missing from a listing, that means it was omitted from the auction catalogue.

4. The Subject Matter

The subject may range from a brief description of the painting by the auction house to an actual title assigned by the artist. We have been as descriptive as possible given the limited space available.

We opted not to simply list the paintings by category such as still life, landscape, portrait, etc. The title usually indicates its general category and provides additional useful information. For example, if a portrait of George Washington by Rembrandt Peale were to be listed simply as Portrait, it wouldn't explain to the reader why it went for what may appear to be a very high price.

Among modern art works, some are simply "Untitled" and an apt verbal description impossible. Those works are usually of the abstract genre. Some foreign works, particularly French, German and Latin American, are often titled in the artist's language. Many of these are not translated into English in this guide.

It is also important to be aware that while many artists painted a variety of subjects, often one or more of those subject areas is considered more desirable by collectors and/or experts and hence may command a higher price. A variety of reasons for these differences apply. It may be that the artist simply painted a particular type of subject better. It also may be that a particular subject area may be more desirable in today's market. An example of this is the current popularity of beach scenes. Any beach scene by an artist like Edward Potthast (Am 1857-1927) will usually sell for more than his other landscapes. In his case, Potthast has become well known for his impressionistic beach scenes, which in turn creates additional demand for the type of scene he is famous for.

John F. Francis (Am 1808-1886) is known as a major 19th Century American still-life painter but he also did many studio portraits of average people. Since this subject area is not popular today, his still lifes bring significantly higher prices than his portraits.

The point is to be aware that the subject area, or even a subgrouping within the subject area, can have a great impact on the price of an individual work of art. The way prices are prioritized in any artist's listing in this guide allows one to see how and to what extent the subject can affect prices. Another item of note is that American painters often generate higher prices for paintings of American scenes than foreign scenes, although the gap seems to be closing.

A review of general subject areas includes:

Landscape - Outdoor vistas which may or may not contain figures, buildings, etc.

Marine - Subjects relating to ships and/or the sea.

Genre - Scenes of everyday life from some time period.

Still Lifes - Picked fruit or flowers, dead game, pottery, etc.

Trompe l'oeil - "Fool the eye" images created on a flat surface appearing to be three-dimensional.

Figure - Single person or groups of people.

Hunting/Sporting - Typically fox-hunting scenes, horses.

Wildlife - Wild animals in native habitat.

Illustrations - Pieces produced for ads, magazine covers, etc.

Primitives (folk art) - Art done by amateurs without any training.

Modern - Avant-garde, abstract, non-traditional.

There are, of course, gray areas, and paintings that don't easily fit into one subject or are combinations of two or more areas.

5. The Date Painted

Some works are dated by the artist and, if so, that date is provided in the catalogue following the title or description. This factor, while usually of less importance than other variables, can identify during which period of the artist's life the work was done. For artists who went through distinct periods of changing style—for example, George Inness and Pablo Picasso—the time periods can have an impact on value.

The majority of works, however, are not dated by the artist.

Dating can also provide valuable information for those researching a particular artist. For example, dated landscapes can sometimes help determine when the artist may have traveled to certain locations or worked with other artists.

6. The Auction House Selling the Painting

The auction house often impacts prices. For important paintings, this difference is usually not significant. For middle-range and less expensive paintings, however, prices are often higher in large metropolitan areas, New York City being the most notable. There is more money there, a higher concentration of collectors, and more contact with the general art-buying public particularly because of their name recognition and the sheer mass of art which is traded. The larger auction houses included in this price guide also have a reputation to protect, can afford larger staffs, and are able to do more research in cataloguing paintings and determining authenticity. "Local" artists, who are not well known nationally, usually sell more easily and at higher prices in auction houses nearer their home base where they are better known. For example, many early- to mid-20th Century "California Artists" sell best in California.

This price guide includes most major auction houses from coast to coast. There are scores of additional smaller auction houses and while each could add a couple of "local" artists to the overall listings, this advantage is outweighed by our efforts to keep the book relatively small and portable.

7. The Date of Sale

Like much of business and commerce, art sales and auctions slow during the summer months. Competing diversions, like vacations, contribute to this trend. For the buyer, this can mean some bargains at auction since there are fewer people to compete with. The seller, however, should stick to the prime auction season of October to May if intending to consign paintings for sale. It is rare for any major works to be auctioned in the summer months.

This price guide lists the month and year of sales following the abbreviated name of the auction house. If there has been an increase in value for a particular artist's work during the year, the trend may be seen by comparing prices to dates sold.

The date also allows the reader the opportunity to find the catalogue of the actual sale cited and perhaps see a photo of a painting of interest if reproduced in that catalogue.

_____

The next five key factors, Numbers 8 through 12, all relatively subjective, are often not available and thus are not included among the data in this price guide. However, they still should be considered important factors. _____

8. The Condition of the Piece

Obviously, condition can have a major effect on anything you buy. The more pristine and nearly flawless, the better—and often more expensive. It's not any different with works of art. Examples of less-than- perfect condition can range from paint loss for oil paintings to "foxing" of watercolors to outright damage such as holes in canvas or paper tears. The extent of damage and the difficulty of repair are most important. A small bit of paint loss and expert restoration in the sky, say, of a large landscape will have little effect on value. The same loss and restoration in a key part of the painting, such as figures or buildings, can have a more significant impact. A qualified restorer can repair almost any damage, but, the costs can be quite high. For your sake, never let an unqualified person touch any work of art!

Condition is a variable not included in most auction catalogues and hence is not included in this guide. It can usually be provided by the auction house for a specific piece if you request it and any buyer should always do so before bidding. If restoration has been done well, it will be invisible to the naked eye. An ultraviolet (black) light will often show up restored areas and other problems with a painting. It can be a useful tool for collectors and dealers alike.

9. The Authenticity

The question of authenticity of a piece is always a problem. I've found it to be one of the biggest deterrents to collectors entering the fine arts field.

There is no way for a guide such as this to guarantee authenticity. Signed works generally are safer choices for any buyers but even signatures are obviously not foolproof. This guide does not indicate whether works are signed or unsigned due to space limitations and also because most works (with the exception of Old Masters) are signed.

Large and reputable dealers are probably the safest choice here for the newer collector, and although you may pay more for this "insurance" it's a good way to get started. This price guide can still help the collector and dealer determine if the prices asked or offered are at least reasonable. Once one becomes more knowledgeable and confident, auctions can become an enjoyable and useful alternative. My feeling is that the major auction houses, at least, do the best job they can in assuring the authenticity of pieces they sell.

Among lower-priced works, the question of authenticity becomes far less important. There just isn't much incentive to counterfeit works that sell for under $1000 to $2000. Anyone talented enough to forge such works probably could sell his or her own works for at least that much or would likely forge more valuable pieces. Analogously, counterfeiters do not produce bogus paper money in denominations smaller than $20 or $50 dollar bills.

10. The "Attractiveness" or General Quality of the Work

As discussed in the section about artists, even the best has days when everything works out and days when nothing seems to work out. This, "quality" of a work is very subjective and obviously cannot be catalogued or reported in a guide such as this. Only if you look at enough art, especially enough works by a particular artist, will you be able to differentiate between the exceptional, the average, and the terrible. Experienced dealers and collectors can tell the difference, which may help explain drastic contrast in the listings in this guide for certain artists with similar paintings in the same auction.

The "attractiveness" can also relate to the subject matter. There are numerous examples of "pretty" pictures by obscure artists reaching prices ten times or more their projected value. This is often not because they were particularly well painted but because they were pleasant, "pretty" pictures of romantic scenes at the park or beach, both popular subjects today.

11. Provenance

Provenance is defined as the origin or source. In art, it is essentially the history of ownership or lineage from as near to the artist's hand as possible. This really could be included within the review of authenticity since it serves to authenticate by tracing backward.

Major works of art sometimes have a clear provenance but most works do not. It is not available for most paintings and hence is not included in this price guide.

12. Historical Significance

Most works of art have no historical significance but a painting such as Monet's "Impression Sunrise" obviously does, at least within the field of art history. Other paintings with true historical significance are some of the paintings of the American West produced in the 19th Century, and of famous statesmen like George Washington.

Sometimes, the historical significance can affect value and other times it may just be interesting—how interesting determines the effect on value.

The painting by James Hamilton, reproduced on the cover of the 1990 Premiere Edition, for example, has an interesting history which could affect it's value. It was one of several small paintings purchased by the U.S. Government and presented by Abraham Lincoln to Charlotte Saunders Cushman, the leading American actress of her day, in appreciation for her work with the fledgling American Red Cross during the Civil War.

In other cases, paintings were reproduced as popular engraved prints and thus became far more famous than would ever occur otherwise. Here, the actual original painting may have a higher value than normally expected.

Other Suggested Resources Relating to the Auction Market

A well developed and more detailed background and review of art value considerations for the novice can be found in *Curriers Art Price Guides*. These guides also contain a general price range for each artist but no specific information on individual paintings sold. [Currier Publications, P. O. Box 2098, Brockton, MA 02403]

For keeping abreast of the market between editions of ART AT AUCTION IN AMERICA...

Art and Auction Magazine provides monthly updates of both the American and foreign auction markets. Its coverage tends to be focused on the higher priced more newsworthy happenings, but it includes interesting inside information on the art market in general. [Art & Auction, 250 W. 57th St., New York, NY 10107]

Maine Antique Digest, published monthly, and *Antiques and the Arts Weekly* are large tabloid publications which are read by many collectors and professionals in the collectibles business. Both publications contain information about upcoming auctions as well as highlights of those just past. They are not limited in scope to New England, but are nationwide in coverage. [Maine Antique Digest, P. O. Box 645, Waldoboro, ME 04572] [Antiques & the Arts Weekly, The Bee Publishing Co., 5 Church Hill Rd., Newtown, CT 06470]

There are many more regional antique and arts publications in each area of the country and these can also often be of great value to collectors.

EXPLANATION OF PRICING

The prices listed in this guide are all in U.S. dollars, rounded to the nearest dollar. The lower cutoff point is $25; i.e., paintings selling for less than $25 are not included. There is no maximum. Works selling for one million dollars or more are priced using the capital letter M to signify millions; e.g., 3.0M would be $3,000,000 and 3.025M would be $3,025,000. Canadian dollars have been converted to U.S. dollars at a rate of 1.0 CD = 0.80 USD.

Nearly all auction houses add their own commission to the hammer price. Some of the auction houses include this in their published prices, some do not. It is usually easy to determine if any price listed includes the commission. If the prices are simple round numbers like $4,000 or $20,000, the commissions are probably not included. On the other hand, if the prices listed are $4,400 or $22,000, then the commissions probably are included. The following reviews which auction houses include commissions in their price lists and which do not:

NOTE: Several major auction houses increased their buyers commissions from 10% to 15% in mid-year.

Auction Houses Listed with 10% or 15% commissions Included in their prices

Barridoff
Butterfield & Butterfield
Christie's/Christie's East
Dolye
Eldred's
Mystic
Skinner's
Sotheby's/Sotheby's Arcade
Sotheby's Toronto
Weschler's

Auction Houses Listed with Commissions Not Included in their prices

Alderfer
Boos
Bourne
DuMouchelles
Freeman/Fine Arts
Hanzel Galleries
Illustration House
Leslie Hindman
Louisiana Auction Exchange
John Moran
Selkirk's
C. G. Sloan
Wolf's
Young Fine Arts

Arguments can be made as to whether it is more accurate to include the commissions paid or not. However, it is felt that the 10-15 percent difference is not important enough to be too concerned about given the subjectivity of art valuations anyway. Therefore, to reiterate, the prices listed in this guide include the commission where the auction house includes it in their published prices and it is not included where they do not.

The prices are listed in descending price order independent of the other variables. There are several other ways to organize the data, but this is a *price* guide, and the simplest way for the user to determine which variables have the most significant affect on the price of a particular artist's work is through prioritization by descending price. Any other method of organization would be useful in looking at that one variable; e.g., date sold, but it would be very difficult to draw any other conclusions.

Again, it is important to note that the prices come from the auction houses and are entered into our database. Thus errors, although rare, are undoubtedly inevitable. In fact, we have questioned a few suspicious numbers on the price lists and have, indeed, gotten corrections. If any information looks questionable, please contact us or the auction house before relying on it.

KEYS TO USING THIS GUIDE

The key to the abbreviations used in ART AT AUCTION IN AMERICA, and included below, is also reproduced on inside of the back cover so the user does not have to flip back and forth in this book.

Artist's Name

Artist's names are listed alphabetically irrespective of nationality or dates of activity. Some names are difficult to alphabetize such as Willem De Kooning and Vincent Van Gogh. Van Gogh is listed under Van, and De Kooning is listed under De. French surnames which contain de are usually listed following convention, e.g., Diaz de la Pena is listed under Diaz....

Artists who used or were known by a pseudonym are usually listed under both their family name and pseudonym.

Artist's Nationality

Am	American	Hun	Hungarian
Arg	Argentinean	In	Indian
Aut	Australian	Irs	Irish
Aus	Austrian	Isr	Israeli
Bel	Belgian	It	Italian
Bol	Bolivian	LA	Latin American
Brz	Brazilian	Jap	Japanese
Br	British	Mex	Mexican
Bul	Bulgarian	Nz	New Zealander
Can	Canadian	Nic	Nicaraguan
Chl	Chilean	Nor	Norwegian
Chi	Chinese	Per	Peruvian
Col	Columbian	Phi	Philippino
Con	Continental	Pol	Polish
Cos	Costa Rican	Por	Portuguese
Cub	Cuban	PR	Puerto Rican
Czk	Czechoslovakian	Rom	Romanian
Dan	Danish	Rus	Russian
Dut	Dutch	Saf	South African
Ecu	Ecuadorian	Scn	Scandinavian
Eng	English	Sco	Scottish
Eur	European	Spa	Spanish
Fin	Finnish	Swd	Swedish
Flm	Flemish	Sws	Swiss
Fr	French	Tha	Thai
Ger	German	Tur	Turkish
Grk	Greek	Uru	Uruguayan
Hai	Haitian	Ven	Venezuelan
		Yug	Yugoslavian

Artist's Dates

1) If:
    a) Birth and Death Dates are known   1810-1888
    b) Only Birth Date known or still living   1810-
    c) Only Death Date known   -1888
2) If only Active Dates known   a 1830-1848
3) If only Century known   19C

Reference to other editions

Such a reference under an artist's name indicates there were no sales of that artist's work during the 1992-1993 auction year, but sales information can be found in the noted edition of ART AT AUCTION IN AMERICA.

Size of Work

In inches rounded to the nearest whole inch.
    First Dimension = height of work (vertical dimension)
                    x = by
    Second Dimension = width of work (horizontal dimension)
    Round Paintings = a number followed by "dia" indicating diameter

Mediums Used in the Work

In the interest of accuracy and completeness, we have included more mediums than most similar publications. Please do not be intimidated by the size of the listings as most actually occur infrequently, and the common ones are easily committed to memory.

Traditional Mediums

Q	Aquatint	Et	Egg Tempera	Pnc	Peinture a la Colle
Bc	Body Color	E	Enamel	Pal	Peinture a l'essence
Br	Brush	Gd	Gold Leaf/Gold Paint	Pl	Pen and Ink
K	Chalk	G	Gouache	Pe	Pencil
C	Charcoal	H	Graphite	B	Sepia
Cw	Chinese White	R	Grisaille	T	Tempera
Kc	Colored Chalk	I	Ink	V	Varnish
Y	Crayon	O	Oil	S	Wash
D	Drypoint	P	Pastel	W	Watercolor

Modern Mediums

A	Acrylic	Os	Oil Stick
Ar	Air Brush	Pt	Paint
Bp	Ball Point Pen	Pts	Paint Stick
Cs	Casein	Pp	Petroplastic
Cg	Chromogesso	Ph	Photograph
L	Collage	Pg	Pigment
Cp	Colored Pencil	Pol	Politec
Ct	Copper Paint	Pr	Polyester Resin
Det	Detrempe	Py	Polymer
Dis	Dispersion	Px	Proxylin
Du	Duco	Rn	Resin
Em	Emulsion	Rs	Rubber Stamp
N	Encaustic	Sd	Sand
Fx	Fax	Sg	Sanguine
Fp	Felt Pen	Ss	Silkscreen
Gp	Gun Powder	Sv	Silverpoint
Lx	Latex	Slt	Solvent Transfer
Lq	Liquitex	Sp	Synthetic Polymer
Mg	Magna	Vy	Vinylite
Mk	Marker	Wx	Wax
MM	Mixed Media		

Mediums Applied To

Ab	Academy Board/Artist's Board	L	Linen
A	Acetate	Mb	Marble
Al	Aluminum	M	Masonite
B	Board	Me	Metal
Bu	Burlap	My	Mylar
C	Canvas	Pn	Panel
Cb	Canvas Board	Pa	Paper
Cd	Cardboard	Pb	Paperboard
Cel	Celluloid	Ph	Parchment
Clx	Celotex	Pl	Plaster
Ce	Cement	Pls	Plastic
Cer	Ceramic	Pw	Plywood
Cl	Cloth	Por	Porcelain
Cp	Copper	Rb	Ragboard
Cot	Cotton	S	Silk
F	Fabric	Sl	Slate
Fg	Fibreglass	St	Steel
Frs	Fresco	Tn	Tin
Gl	Glass	Wd	Wood
Iv	Ivory	Wb	Woodboard
Ju	Jute	V	Vellum
Lh	Leather	Vl	Vinyl

Auction House

Ald	**Sanford A. Alderfer Auction Co.** 501 Fairgrounds Road, Hatfield, PA 19440	(215) 368-5477
Brd	**Barridoff Galleries** P.O. Box 9715, Portland, ME 04104	(207) 772-5011
Bor	**Richard A. Bourne Co.** P. O. Box 141, Hyannisport, MA 02647	(508) 775-0797
But	**Butterfield and Butterfield** 220 San Bruno Avenue, San Francisco, CA 94103	(415) 861-7500
Chr	**Christie's** 502 Park Avenue, New York, NY 10022	(212) 546-1000
	Christie's East 219 East 67th Street, New York, NY 10021	(212) 606-0400
Doy	**William Doyle Galleries** 175 East 87th Street, New York, NY 10128	(212) 427-2730
Dum	**DuMouchelles Art Galleries Co.** 409 E. Jefferson Avenue, Detroit, MI 48226	(313) 963-6255
Eld	**Robert C. Eldred Co.** Route 6A, East Dennis, MA 02641	(508) 385-3116
Fhb	**Frank H. Boos** 420 Enterprise Court, Bloomfield Hills, MI 48302	(313) 332-1500
Fre	**Freeman/Fine Arts of Philadelphia, Inc.** 1808-10 Chestnut Street, Philadelphia, PA 19103	(215) 563-9275
Hnd	**Leslie Hindman Auctioneers** 215 W. Ohio St., Chicago, IL 60610	(312) 670-0010
Hnz	**Hanzel Galleries** 1220 South Michigan Avenue, Chicago, IL 60605	(312) 922-6234
Ilh	**Illustration House, Inc.** 96 Spring Street, New York, NY 10012	(212) 966-9444
Lou	**Louisiana Auction Exchange, Inc.** 2031 Government Street, Baton Rouge, LA 70806	(504) 924-1803
Mor	**John Moran Auctioneers** 3202 E. Foothill Blvd., Pasadena, CA 91107	(818) 793-1833
Mys	**Mystic Fine Arts** 47 Holmes Street, Mystic CT 06355	(203) 572-8873
Sel	**Selkirk's** 4166 Olive Street, St. Louis, MO 63108	(314) 533-1700
Skn	**Skinner, Inc.** 357 Main Street, Bolton, MA 01740	(508) 779-6241
Slo	**C. G. Sloan & Co., Inc.** 4920 Wyaconda Road, North Bethesda, MD 20852	(301) 468-4911
Sby	**Sotheby's** 1334 York Avenue, New York, NY 10021	(212) 606-7000
	Sotheby's Arcade 1334 York Avenue, New York, NY 10021	(212) 606-7516
Sbt	**Sotheby's Toronto** 9 Hazelton Ave., Toronto, Ontario M5R2E1, Canada	(416) 926-1774
Wes	**Weschler's** 909 E Street, N.W., Washington, DC 20004	(202) 628-1281
Wlf	**Wolf's** 1239 West 6th Street, Cleveland, OH 44113	(216) 575-9653
Yng	**Young Fine Arts Gallery, Inc.** P. O. Box 313, North Berwick, ME 03906	(207) 676-3104

Title or Description of work

Self-explanatory, though some titles are in the language of the artist. Some modern works are untitled.

Date Painted

The year date as actually inscribed on the work. May be complete such as 1864 or partial such as 64. Occasionally, only part of a date may be legible and may be listed as 186?.

Date of Auction

Month and year of auction.

Prices

All in U.S. dollars in descending price order. Some include ten percent buyer's commission, some do not, depending on auction house. M means million; e.g., 4.05M =$4,050,000. Canadian dollars are converted at 1.0 CD = 0.80 USD.

SEE HOW EASY IT IS TO FIND JUST THE INFORMATION YOU NEED

Artist's full name (listed alphabetically)

Artist's nationality

Medium

Size in inches

Description or title of the work

Artist's birth and death date or century

Date of work (if artist dated it)

Auction house

Date of auction

Prices realized in dollars and in descending price order

John, Augustus Eng 1878-1961
  Pe/Pa 13x8 Seated Female Nude Skn 11/88........................ 250
Johns, Jasper Am 1930-
  O/C 68x53 False Start Spb 11/88.................................. 17.05M
  N/C 60x60 Gray Rectangles Spb 11/88............................. 4.29M
  O/C 72x50 Screen Piece II 1968 Spb 11/88........................ 1.37M
Johnson, David Am 1827-1908
  O/C 10x18 Ocean Beach, New Jersey 1877 Chr 9/88........ 13200
  O/B 6x9 On Esopus Creek 1876 Chr 9/88............................ 3850
Johnson, Jonathan Eastman Am 1824-1906
  O/C 40x33 Honorable Morgan O'Brian Wes 10/88............... 2000
Johnson, Marshall Am 1850-1921
  O/C 18x24 Beating to Windward Bor 8/88........................... 2900
Johnson, Roy Am 1890-1963
  W/Pa 14x11 Dutch Girl By Window Wes 10/88.................... 225
  O/M 20x16 Lady In Garden Wes 10/88................................ 125
  O/CB 16x12 Woman Holding Fan Wes 10/88......................... 75
Jones, Hugh Bolton Am 1848-1907
  O/C 14x20 A Lush Spring Chr 9/88................................... 4400

25

Abades, E. Martinez   Con 20C
  * See 1992 Edition ....

Abades, Juan Martinez   Spa 1862-
  * See 1993 Edition ....

Abakanowicz, Magdalena   1930-
  * See 1993 Edition ....

Abbatt, Agnes Dean   Am 1847-1917
  * See 1993 Edition ....

Abbema, Louise   Fr 1858-1927
  O/C 33x40 Portrait Madame Lucien Guitry 76 Chr 5/93 ... 41,400

Abbett   Am 20C
  O/M 18x24 A Turkey Eld 8/93 3,300

Abbett, Robert K.   Am 1926-
  G/Pa 19x14 Summer Camp Ih 11/92 650
  G/Pa 20x16 Nude in Picture Frame Ih 5/93 600

Abbey, Edwin Austin   Am 1852-1911
  W&G/Pa 10x12 Woman in the Woods 1879 Sby 12/92 ... 18,700
  G&Pe/B 28x21 Study for a Figure Sby 1/93 2,070

Abbott, Meredith Brooks   Am 20C
  O/C 14x11 Milk Can But 6/93 575

Abbott, Samuel Nelson   Am 1874-1953
  * See 1993 Edition ....

Abbott, Yarnall   Am 1870-1938
  * See 1993 Edition ....

Abdy, Rowena Meeks   Am 1887-1945
  * See 1993 Edition ....

Abel-Boulineau, N.   Fr 20C
  * See 1990 Edition ....

Abercrombie, Gertrude   Am 1909-
  O/M 4x5 Interior with Still Life Hnd 5/93 2,200
  O/M 8x10 Surrealist Composition '54 Hnd 3/93 1,900

Ableta, James   Am 20C
  * See 1991 Edition ....

Abrams, Lucien   Am 1870-1941
  O/Pn 7x9 Three Bathers Brd 8/93 1,320

Abreu, Mario   Ven 1918-
  * See 1990 Edition ....

Abry, Leon Eugene Auguste   Bel 1857-1905
  * See 1990 Edition ....

Absolon, John   Eng 1815-1895
  * See 1992 Edition ....

Abularach, Rodolfo
  * See 1992 Edition ....

Accard, Eugene   Fr 1824-1888
  * See 1993 Edition ....

Accardi, Carla   1924-
  O/C 53x25 Untitled Chr 2/93 7,700
  O/C 24x36 Labirinto 1957 Chr 2/93 6,600

Acconci, Vito   1940-
  Y&Ph/Pa 30x40 Directions (2-Hr Activity) 1971 Sby 11/92 . 8,800
  Y&Ph/Pa 12x18 Line Drawing I, II, III 1973 Sby 2/93 ... 3,163
  C/Pa 20x28 Study for Intermediaries 1974 Sby 5/93 2,300

Aceves, Gustavo   Spa 19C
  O/Pn 9x7 Courtyard Scene Mys 12/92 550

Acheff, William   Am 1947-
  * See 1993 Edition ....

Achenbach, Andreas   Ger 1815-1910
  O/C 24x19 Goats Grazing by a Cliff 1855 Chr 10/92 8,800

Achenbach, Anna Thomson   Am 20C
  O/C 24x20 Portrait of a Boy Fre 10/92 1,300
  O/C 22x32 Saturday Fights Fre 10/92 1,250
  O/C 24x28 Manayunk '56 Fre 10/92 325
  O/C 22x34 Blossom in the Snow Fre 4/93 150
  O/C 22x28 Still Life Oranges Fre 4/93 150
  O/C 24x20 Still Life with Pineapple Fre 10/92 140

Achenbach, Oswald   Ger 1827-1905
  * See 1993 Edition ....

Achille-Fould, Mlle. Georges   Fr 1865-
  * See 1993 Edition ....

Achtschellinck, Lucas   Flm 1626-1699
  * See 1990 Edition ....

Adam, Albrecht   Ger 1786-1862
  O/C 9x8 Mounted Cavalry Officer 1856 Chr 10/92 12,100

Adam, Benno   Ger 1812-1892
  O/Pn 19x25 Farm Animals 1838 Chr 5/93 4,025

Adam, Emil   Ger 1843-1924
  O/C 23x30 Dark Bay in a Loose Stall 1884 Doy 5/93 2,750

Adam, Franz   Ger 1815-1886
  * See 1991 Edition ....

Adam, Joseph Denovan   Br 1842-1896
  * See 1993 Edition ....

Adam, Julius   Ger 1826-1874
  O/C 12x16 Playful Kittens Sby 10/92 28,600

Adam, Julius   Ger 1852-1913
  O/C 12x16 Kittens in a Toy Wagon Sby 5/93 18,400

Adam, Richard Benno   Ger 1873-1936
  O/C 26x34 The Rider Cap.Zsnk on a Hunt 1906 Chr 10/92 . 3,520

Adam, William   Am 1846-1931
  O/C 10x15 Monterey Dunes But 3/93 1,650
  O/B 12x15 California Sand Dunes Lou 12/92 800
  O/B 16x20 Church with Palms Hnd 9/92 130

Adams, Charles Partridge   Am 1858-1942
  O/C 12x16 Sunset Behind the Trees But 6/93 3,162
  O/C 40x61 Misty Morning Sby 9/92 2,420
  O/C 14x18 Mountainous Landscape Chr 5/93 2,300
  W&G/B 10x14 Hazy Afternoon, Estes Park Sby 9/92 2,200
  O/C 20x24 Moonrise at Laguna Beach Mor 6/93 1,870
  O/C 20x24 Moonrise at Laguna Beach But 10/92 1,650
  O/C 18x14 Afternoon on Convict Lake But 10/92 1,100
  W/Pa 5x7 Head of Moraine Park-Estes Park, CO Mor 11/92 . 700
  W/Pa 7x10 Mountain Landscape Mor 11/92 650
  W/Pa 5x7 San Miguel Mountains Mor 2/93 500

Adams, John Clayton   Br 1840-1906
  O/C 30x48 Going to Market Sby 2/93 36,800
  O/C 12x18 River Landscape 1895 Dum 4/93 1,600

Adams, John Ottis   Am 1851-1927
  * See 1993 Edition ....

Adams, John Quincy   Aus 1874-1933
  * See 1991 Edition ....

Adams, John W.   Am 1874-1925
  Pl/Pa 8x6 Colonial Woman in Front of House Ih 11/92 900

Adams, Wayman   Am 1883-1959
  O/Pn 15x12 A Carriage Ride Chr 12/92 3,520

Adams, Willis Seaver   Am 1842-1921
  * See 1992 Edition ....

Adamson, Dorothy   Br -1934
  * See 1992 Edition ....

Adamson, Harry Curieux   Am 20C
  * See 1992 Edition ....

Adamson, John
  * See 1991 Edition ....

Adamson, Sydney   Am a 1892-1914
  O/C 27x40 The Rebel Charge 1899 Chr 12/92 4,400
  I&Cw/Pa 21x14 Pekin 1900 Chr 12/92 1,045

Adan, Louis Emile   Fr 1839-1937
  O/Pn 25x37 The Suitor Sby 10/92 16,500
  O/C 21x29 Little Scissors Grinder But 5/93 6,325

Addams, Charles   Am 1912-1988
  I&S/Pa 11x12 Women Having Tea Ih 11/92 1,900
  I&S/Pa 12x13 Policeman Warning Tunnel Traffic Ih 11/92 .. 1,700
  I&W/Pa 14x12 Soviet Soldiers Doing Calisthentics Ih 11/92 . 1,600
  I&W/Pa 10x10 Waiter Seagulls Rockefeller Center Ih 5/93 . 1,200

Addey, Joseph-Poole   Irs 19C
  W/Pa 19x28 Irish Landscape with Mountains 1881 Dum 1/93 . 600

Addison, Robert   Am 20C
  T/B 16x25 Forsaken 56 Hnd 5/93 2,200

Addy, Alfred   Am 20C
  O/Pn 12x20 Landscape Mys 3/93 385

Adler, Edmund   Ger 1871-1957
  O/C 27x22 Ready for School Sby 2/93 11,500
  O/C 22x27 Preparing the Flag Chr 5/93 9,200

Adler, Jankel   Pol 1895-1949
  * See 1991 Edition ....

Adler, Jules   Fr 1865-1952
  * See 1991 Edition ....

Adolphe, Albert Jean   Am 1865-1940
  * See 1991 Edition ....

Adomeit, George   Am 1879-
O/B 6x6 Landscape Wlf 4/93 250
Adriani, Camille   Am 20C
O/C 24x30 Winter Landscape Hnd 12/92 700
O/C 20x16 Woman with Parasol Sel 12/92 400
Adrion, Lucien   Fr 1889-1953
O/Pn 23x29 Place de l'Opera, Paris 1924 Hnd 5/93 4,000
O/C 37x43 Paris Street Scene Sby 6/93 2,070
Aerni, Franz Theodor   Ger 1853-1918
O/C 17x29 Road with Passing Travelers Wlf 9/92 4,600
Aertsen, Pieter   1507-1575
* See 1992 Edition . . . .
Affleck, William   Br 1869-
* See 1993 Edition . . . .
Africano, Nicholas   1948-
O,A&Mg/M 49x84 Let Me Help You 1981 Sby 5/93 12,650
O/M 12x23 Oysters in Vinegar Again! 1981 Sby 5/93 4,600
O&L/C 20x17 Flesh, Armor 1986 Chr 11/92 3,300
Pl/Pa 8x11 I Get Hurt Chr 11/92 660
Afro (Basaldella)   1912-1976
W&Y/Pa 19x13 Hourglass 48 Chr 11/92 14,300
Agam, Yaacov   1928-
G&Pe/Pa 21x21 Dalia 71 Sby 6/93 4,140
A/C 15x18 Maquette of First 4 days Creation 1961 Chr 11/92 3,850
Agard, Charles Jean   Fr 1866-
O/C 11x16 Soleil Levant sur la Riviere Sby 10/92 1,650
Agnew, Clark   Am 19C
* See 1990 Edition . . . .
Agnew, J. F.   Am 19C
O/C 22x17 Sailboats in Harbor Wlf 3/93 650
Agostini, Tony   It 1916-
O/C 29x21 Les Roses Rouges Sby 10/92 1,650
O/C 18x15 Le Chevalet du Peintre Sby 10/92 1,430
O/C 29x21 Les Roses Rouges Sby 2/93 1,150
Agrasot Y Juan, Joaquin   Spa 1836-1907
O/Pn 16x11 The Collector's Cabinet 1871 Sby 5/93 17,250
Agthe, Curt   Ger 1862-
* See 1992 Edition . . . .
Aguilar, Homero
* See 1990 Edition . . . .
Aguste, Phillipe   Hai 20C
* See 1992 Edition . . . .
Ahl, Henry Curtis   Am 1905-
* See 1991 Edition . . . .
Ahl, Henry Hammond   Am 1869-1953
O/B 8x10 Girl by a River Yng 2/93 250
Ahlborn, August Wilhelm   Ger 1796-1857
* See 1991 Edition . . . .
Ahn, Miriam   Am 20C
O/C 67x65 Flower Message But 10/92 1,210
Ahrendt, William   Am 20C
O/C 31x23 The Grand Canyon Sby 3/93 1,610
Aid, George Charles   Am 1872-1938
O/C 45x57 The Bridge Players Chr 5/93 23,000
Aiken, Charles A.   Am 1872-1965
O/C 21x17 Woman Holding Rose Mys 12/92 204
Aime   20C
O/C 18x24 Rooftops Yng 2/93 80
Ainsley, Dennis   Am 1880-1952
O/C 24x31 Italian Village Scene Wes 5/93 440
O/C 24x36 Market Scene Mys 12/92 275
Aitken, John E.   Br 1881-1957
W/Pa 14x20 Pair: Dutch Scenes Sel 12/92 1,250
Aivasovsky, Ivan Constantin.   Rus 1817-1900
* See 1992 Edition . . . .
Aizenberg, Roberto   Arg 1928-
O/C/M 59x25 Torre 1971 Chr 11/92 17,600
Aizpiri, Paul   Fr 1919-
O/Pn 39x26 Pichet de Fleurs Chr 2/93 20,900
O/C 45x36 Portrait de Femme Chr 11/92 19,800
O/C 39x29 Clown Aux Oiseaux Chr 2/93 17,600
O/C 32x26 Clown Sby 2/93 17,250
O/C 26x21 Le Clown Chr 11/92 13,200
O/C 32x22 Nature Morte Chr 2/93 6,600

G&W/Pa 22x19 Still Life Sby 6/93 5,175
O/C 14x11 Nature Morte aux Fruits Chr 11/92 3,520
Ajdukiewicz, Zygmund   Pol 1861-1917
* See 1992 Edition . . . .
Akers, Vivian Milner   Am 1886-1966
O/C 30x36 Summer Splendor, Maine 1928 Brd 8/93 8,800
O/C 30x34 Landscape w/Mountains 1928 Dum 1/93 2,500
Akkeringa, Johannes Evert   Dut 1894-
* See 1993 Edition . . . .
Akkersdijk, Jacob   Dut 1815-1862
O/C 24x33 Outside the Stables 1847 Chr 5/93 2,300
Alajalov, Constantin   Am 1900-1987
* See 1993 Edition . . . .
Alban, Vicente   Ecu 18C
O/C 32x42 Set of Four Castes Chr 11/92 154,000
Albee, Percy   Am 1883-1959
W/B 22x30 Free Enterprise Sby 3/93 748
Alberici, Augusto   It 1846-
* See 1992 Edition . . . .
Alberola, Jean-Michel   1953-
O/C 79x79 Suzanne et Les Vieillards 83 Chr 11/92 6,050
Albers, Josef   Am 1888-1976
O/B 48x48 Homage to the Square: Sudden Yes But 4/93 101,500
O/M 24x24 Homage to Square: w/Safron 1962 Chr 11/92 . 46,200
O/M 16x16 Homage to the Square: Neutral 1969 Sby 11/92 20,900
O/Pa 15x22 Vice Versa C Sby 2/93 9,775
Albert De Gesne, Jean Victor   Fr 1834-1903
* See 1991 Edition . . . .
Albert, Adolphe   Fr 20C
* See 1992 Edition . . . .
Albert, E. Maxwell   Am 19C
* See 1993 Edition . . . .
Albert, Ernest   Am 1857-1946
O/C 25x30 Evening Hour 1937 Hnd 5/93 10,000
O/C 25x30 Winter Eve Skn 11/92 8,250
O/C 25x30 Golden Day Chr 5/93 4,600
Albert, Jeannine   Fr 1939-
O/C 31x27 Still Life of Flowers in Vase Sel 9/92 1,300
Albert, Karl   Am 1911-
O/C 20x30 Ebb Tide Mor 11/92 750
O/M 12x16 Desert Edge Mor 11/92 500
Alberti, C.   Con 19C
O/C 21x26 Floral Still Life Hnd 12/92 1,000
Alberti, Giuseppe Vizzotto   It 19C
* See 1992 Edition . . . .
Albertinelli, Mariotto   1474-1515
O/Pn 34 dia Mary and Joseph Adoring Christ Sby 1/93 . . 57,500
Albina, Luca   It 20C
* See 1993 Edition . . . .
Albinson, Dewey Ernest   Am 1898-
* See 1993 Edition . . . .
Albotto, Francesco   1721-1753
* See 1992 Edition . . . .
Albricci, Enrico   1714-1775
O/C 26x36 Wedding Feast of the Dwarves Sby 1/93 18,400
Albright, Adam Emory   Am 1862-1957
O/C 24x16 Two Boys in Meadow 1901 But 6/93 5,750
Albright, Gertrude Partington   Am 1883-1959
* See 1993 Edition . . . .
Albright, Henry   Am 1887-1951
O/C 21x17 Fluteplayer But 12/92 2,750
Albright, Ivan Le Lorraine   Am 1897-1985
Bp/Pa 4x5 I Am Chained Hnd 9/92 275
Alcazar Y Ruiz, Manuel   Spa 19C
* See 1991 Edition . . . .
Aldin, Cecil   Eng 1870-1935
* See 1992 Edition . . . .
Aldine, Marc   Fr 1917-
O/C 24x32 Doge's Palace and the Grand Canal Skn 5/93 . 2,970
O/C 24x32 Grand Canal, Doge's Palace Skn 5/93 2,750
Aldrich, George Ames   Am 1872-1941
O/C 30x36 The Creek, Winter Hnd 6/93 5,400
O/C 25x30 Winter Landscape Sby 3/93 5,290

O/C 19x25 Country Stream Cottage, Normandy Hnd 10/92 . 4,400
O/C 31x38 Winter Scene with Village Dum 10/92 3,500
O/B 20x25 Nude by a Brook Brd 8/93 1,430
O/C 18x20 White House Fre 4/93 1,300
O/C 30x28 A Castle on a Hillside Chr 5/93 1,265
O/Wd 16x24 River Scene with Boatman Hnd 10/92 1,000
O/C 18x22 Houses by a River Wes 10/92 880

Alechinsky, Pierre   Bel 1927-
A/Pa/C 39x25 Interdependant 1985 Chr 11/92 17,600

Alegiani, Francesco   It 19C
O/C 39x29 Trompe L'Oeil of Pair of Roosters 1869 Sby 5/93 9,488

Alexander, Clifford Grear   Am 1870-1954
* See 1990 Edition

Alexander, Eveline Marie ((Lady))   Can a 1841-1851
O/C 10x14 Two-Horse Sleigh Crossing River 1851 Sbt 5/93   4,180

Alexander, Francesca   Am 1837-1917
* See 1991 Edition . . . .

Alexander, Francis   Am 1800-1880
O/C 25x22 Portrait Mrs. Esther Dresser 1821 Sel 4/93 450

Alexander, Henry   Am 1860-1895
* See 1991 Edition . . . .

Alexander, John   1945-
O/C 78x84 Hiding from the Hunters Sby 11/92 8,800

Alexander, John White   Am 1856-1915
C/B 20x18 Portrait Sketch Drawn from Lift 86 Chr 12/92 . . 1,100

Alexejeff, Alexandre   Rus 1811-1878
O/Pn 17x14 Portrait of Bejeweled Woman But 5/93 3,450

Alexieff, Alexander I.   Rus 1842-
* See 1993 Edition . . . .

Alfani, Domenico   It 16C
* See 1990 Edition . . . .

Alfonzo, Carlos   Cub 1950-1991
A/C 84x84 Sin Titulo Sby 5/93 31,050
O/C 84x60 Birth 89 Chr 11/92 16,500

Alizone, H.   Fr 20C
O/C 18x24 The Close of Day at Martain Slo 4/93 700

Aiken, Henry Thomas (Jr.)   Br 1785-1851
O/C 13x17 Going to; and Returning (2) Chr 10/92 10,450
O/C 12x26 York to London Royal Mail Chr 2/93 7,700

Aiken, Samuel (Jr.)   Br 1784-1825
* See 1993 Edition . . . .

Aiken, Samuel Henry   Br 1810-1894
O/C 10x14 Full Cry; The Kill: Four Sby 6/93 12,075
O/C 12x24 York-London Mail in Snowstorm Sby 6/93 6,900
O/C 20x16 Fighting Cock Sby 6/93 4,600

Allan, Robert Weir   Am 1851-1942
W/Pa 16x22 Village and Barges: Pair 1900 Sby 1/93 2,875
O/C 14x20 Two: Apple Picking; The Beach 1914 Skn 11/92 1,650

Allan, Sir William   Br 1782-1850
K&Cw/Pa 6x7 Study of Hands Chr 10/92 550

Allan, William   Am 1936-
W&H/Pa 32x30 Unlike the Magician '69 But 10/92 660

Alleaume, Ludovic   Fr 1859-
* See 1991 Edition . . . .

Allegrini, Flaminio   a 1625-1635
K,Pl&S/Pa 13x10 Gymnasts in Costumes 1529 Chr 1/93 . . . 9,350

Allen, A.   Am 20C
O/C 24x30 Bouquet Hnd 12/92 100

Allen, Charles Curtis   Am 1886-1950
O/Cb 18x24 Mountain in Winter Skn 3/93 660

Allen, Courtney   Am 1896-1969
O/C 32x31 Sinister Doctor and Patient Ilh 5/93 1,400
O/C 31x42 Aviators Starting Fire in Snow Ilh 11/92 950

Allen, Greta   Am 1881-
O/C 30x25 Portrait of C. G. Hutchison 1914 Mys 3/93 110

Allen, Junius   Am 1896-1962
* See 1993 Edition . . . .

Allen, Marion Boyd   Am 1862-1941
O/C 50x35 Young Woman in White 1917 Brd 2/93 6,600
O/C 26x18 Woman in a Cap Yng 2/93 175

Allen, Thomas   Am 20C1849-1924
O/B 8x5 American Landscape 1894 Slo 5/93 475

Allen, Willard   Am 20C
O/C 30x40 Landscape 19 Hnd 10/92 800

Allievi, Fernando   Arg 1954-
* See 1992 Edition . . . .

Allis, Arthur S.   Am 1904-1973
W,Y,G&H/Pa 12x10 Election Time Boston '28 Skn 9/92 715

Allis, C. Harry   Am 1876-1938
* See 1992 Edition . . . .

Allori, Alessandro   It 1535-1607
* See 1991 Edition . . . .

Allori, Cristofano   It 1577-1621
* See 1992 Edition . . . .

Alma-Tadema, Lady Laura (Epps)   Br 1852-1909
* See 1992 Edition . . . .

Alma-Tadema, Sir Lawrence   Br 1836-1912
O/C 60x38 The Baths of Caracalla Sby 5/93 . . . . 2.5325M
O/Pn 44x29 The Coliseum (A Roman Holiday) Chr 2/93 . 462,000
O/Pn 31x23 A Picture Gallery Sby 2/93 233,500

Almanza, Cleofas   Mex 1850-1915
* See 1993 Edition . . . .

Almaraz, Carlos   1941-
K/Pa 26x20 Two Drawings Chr 11/92 4,620

Alonso, Carlos   Arg 1929-
* See 1993 Edition . . . .

Alott, Robert   Aus 19C
O/Pn 7x15 Peasants Strolling 1872 Wes 3/93 880

Alott, Rudolf   Fr 19C
* See 1990 Edition . . . .

Alpuy, Julio   Uru 1919-
Cp/Pa 6x7 Ciudad Sby 11/92 2,475

Alsina, J.   Fr 20C
* See 1992 Edition . . . .

Alston, Charles   Am 20C
W&S/Pa 12x16 Abstractions: Pair 60 Sby 9/92 440

Alt, Franz   Aus 1821-1914
* See 1992 Edition . . . .

Alt, Otmar
* See 1993 Edition . . . .

Altamirano, Arturo Pacheco   Chl 20C
O/C 39x39 Escena de Puerto Chr 11/92 4,400
O/C 23x28 La Cosecha Chr 11/92 2,860

Alten, Mathias   Am 1871-1938
O/C 22x18 Portrait of Lady in Black Hat Dum 7/93 1,200

Altmann, Alexander   Rus 1885-1932
* See 1992 Edition . . . .

Altoon, John   Am 1925-1969
I,W&Ab/Pa 30x40 Harper Series, 1966 66 But 4/93 2,587
MM/Pa 30x36 Study for a Painting But 10/92 1,540
Pl/B 30x40 Two Women But 4/93 690

Altrui, E.   It 19C
O/Pn 9x12 Sorrento 1878 Brd 8/93 1,760

Altson, Abbey   Br a 1890-1899
* See 1993 Edition . . . .

Alvardi, Carlo
* See 1993 Edition . . . .

Alvarez, Jean   Spa 19C
O/C 12x17 Two Rug Merchants But 11/92 1,760

Alvarez, Luis Catala   Spa 1841-1901
O/C 19x25 Tea Time Tease 1875 Chr 5/93 34,500
O/C 17x12 Her First Portrait But 5/93 11,500
O/Pn 11x7 Naples 79 Chr 10/92 6,600

Alvarez, Mabel   Am 1891-1985
O/C 25x30 Floral-Black Vase Mor 11/92 4,250
O/B 18x14 Bouquet in White Vase But 3/93 2,475
O/B 14x11 Woman at Window Mor 2/93 1,700
O/Cb 18x14 Portrait of Girl Mor 11/92 1,300
O/C 20x16 Hawaiian Woman But 6/93 1,150
O/B 10x14 5 Figures Under a Tree Mor 2/93 1,000
O/Cb 12x16 Fruit Stand Mor 6/93 825
W/Pa 9x5 Design for Mural Decorations 1913 Mor 11/92 . . . 750
O/Cb 20x16 Haitian Woman Mor 11/92 700
O/Cb 16x12 Nude at Beach Mor 11/92 700
W/Pa 9x6 Design for Mural Decorations 1913 Mor 11/92 . . . 650
W/Pa 11x6 Design for Mural Decorations 1913 Mor 11/92 . . 450

29

Alvarez-Dumont, Eugenio   Spa 1864-1927
O/C 35x45 En La Tarde En Biarritz 1909 Sby 2/93   79,500
Aman-Jean, Edmond   Fr 1860-1935
O/B 26x32 Woman with Vase of Flowers Chr 5/93   2,990
O/C 13x12 Idle Moment Doy 5/93   2,310
Amaral, Antonio Henrique   Brz 1935-
* See 1993 Edition . . . .
Amato, Sam
O/C 48x58 Morning Stillness '57 Sby 6/93   518
Amberg, Wilhelm   Ger 1822-1899
* See 1993 Edition . . . .
Ambramovic, Ulay & Marina   20C
* See 1993 Edition . . . .
Ambrogiani, Pierre   1907-1985
O/C 20x39 La Ferme Briancon a Gault Chr 5/93   3,680
Ameglio, Mario   Fr 1897-1970
O/C 18x22 Montmartre Sby 2/93   1,955
O/C 18x21 Place Pigalle 1953 Sby 2/93   1,955
O/C 18x22 Place Pigalle Sby 2/93   1,840
O/C 18x21 Le Moulin Rouge Chr 5/93   1,725
O/C 18x22 Paris-Vue du Montmartre (Nord) Sby 10/92   1,650
Amen, Irving   Am 1918-
* See 1993 Edition . . . .
Amenoff, Gregory   1948-
* See 1993 Edition . . . .
Ames, Ezra   Am 1768-1836
O/Pn 20x24 Woman Wearing Eye Glasses Eld 4/93   660
Amick, Robert Wesley   Am 1879-1969
O/C 30x40 The Palomino Horse Hnz 5/93   550
W/Pa 22x27 Harbor Scene Lou 3/93   375
Amigoni, Jacopo   It 1675-1752
* See 1992 Edition . . . .
Amisani, Giuseppe
O/C 30x36 Princess Ostheim Sby 6/93   4,600
Amorosi, Antonio   It 1660-1738
* See 1993 Edition . . . .
Amorsolo, Fernando   Phi 1892-1972
O/Cb 20x26 Maiden Resting in a Rice Paddy 1935 But 10/92 9,900
O/Cb 20x26 Igorot Men and Dogs 1935 But 10/92   9,350
O/Cb 15x20 Man with Fighting Rooster 1938 But 10/92   7,150
O/Cb 13x19 After a Day of Fishing 1936 But 4/93   6,325
O/Cb 14x18 Man with Fighting Rooster 1938 But 4/93   5,462
Amsden, Mary E.
H/Pa Size? Three Drawings 1864 Wlf 3/93   100
Anastasi, William   1933-
H/Pa 11x12 Two Subway Drawings 1990 Chr 11/92   1,650
Ancelet, Gabriel-Auguste   Fr 19C
* See 1992 Edition . . . .
Ancillotti, Torello   It 1844-1899
O/Pn 9x7 A Cavalier Reading Sby 10/92   1,980
Ancinelli, Dagli   1621-1661
* See 1992 Edition . . . .
Ancker, A.   Con 19C
W/Pa 12x9 Matador 1889 Slo 4/93   125
Anders, Ernst   Ger 1845-1911
* See 1991 Edition . . . .
Andersen, Carl Christian   Dan 1849-1906
* See 1991 Edition . . . .
Andersen, Johannes
O/B 39x29 The Bather Wlf 3/93   1,200
Anderson, C.   Am 20C
O/B 22x32 Autumnal Landscape Fre 10/92   200
Anderson, Doug   Am 1954-
O/C 48x96 Tape on the Face 1982 Skn 5/93   1,045
O/C 36x48 Brains in the Pocket 1982 Skn 5/93   660
Anderson, I. K.   Am 29C
O/C 12x16 Oriental Still Life 1879 Hnd 12/92   160
Anderson, John   Am 20C
O/C 20x24 Interior (2) 48 Hnd 3/93   1,600
Anderson, Karl J.   Am 1874-1956
O/C 48x36 Woman Knitting/Man with Hoe 1901 Ald 9/92 . .   1,300
Anderson, Lennart   Am 1928-
* See 1991 Edition . . . .
Anderson, Oscar   Am 1873-1941
O/C 16x20 Deep Forest Yng 2/93   200

Anderson, Percy   Am 1881-1934
W&G/Pa 10x7 Costume: Girdle of Venus Hnz 5/93   50
W&G/Pa 11x9 Costume Girdle of Venus Hnz 5/93   30
Anderson, Percy   Eng a 1880-1889
W/Pa 18x12 Thespian 1888 Fre 10/92   200
Anderson, Ronald   1886-1926
P/Pa 16x13 Girl in Sailor Suit Yng 2/93   80
Anderson, Ruth A.   Am 1884-1939
O/C 21x17 Through the Trees 1916 Slo 4/93   700
O/C/B 16x20 Floral Still Life Slo 4/93   450
Anderson, Sophie   Br 1823-1903
O/C 24x20 The Young Weaver Chr 5/93   5,750
Anderson, Victor C.   Am 1882-1937
O/C 18x12 Sailor Sitting on Plough 1929 Ih 11/92   1,300
Anderson, W. Lingston   Br 19C
O/C 27x48 Grand Canal, Venice 1899 But 5/93   5,750
O/C 20x30 Pont-y-Pair, Bettws-y-Coed Fre 4/93   650
Anderson, Walter   Br a 1856-1886
* See 1993 Edition . . . .
Anderson, William   Br 1757-1837
* See 1992 Edition . . . .
Anderson, William   Br 1856-1893
O/C 12x24 Bringing Home the Flock: Pair But 11/92   4,400
Ando, C.   Jap 20C
O/C 42x30 Inside a Japanese Temple 1893 Sby 2/93   10,350
Andoe, Joe   1955-
O/L 40x48 Untitled (Tulip) Chr 10/92   2,750
O/L 20x24 Untitled Sby 11/92   2,200
O/L 36x46 Untitled Chr 2/93   2,200
O/C 20x24 Untitled (Olive Branch) Chr 11/92   2,200
O/C 20x24 Untitled (White Wreath) Chr 11/92   2,200
Andre   Fr 19C
O/C 22x18 Walk Through the Woods 1889 Chr 5/93   518
Andre, Albert   Fr 1869-1954
O/C 15x18 Lady Sewing Doy 5/93   17,050
O/C 22x18 Femme a sa Toilette Sby 2/93   9,200
O/C 15x18 Vue de Rochefort Garse, l'orage Chr 11/92   4,400
O/C 13x16 Paysage Chr 2/93   3,300
Andre, Carl
* See 1992 Edition . . . .
Andre, Charles Hippolyte   Fr a 1877-1913
* See 1992 Edition . . . .
Andrejevic, Milet   Yug 1925-
* See 1991 Edition . . . .
Andreotti, Federigo   It 1847-1930
O/C 41x30 Flirtation Chr 5/93   43,700
O/C 32x27 The Love Letter Sby 5/93   31,050
O/C 15x12 Seated Lady with Parasol Sby 10/92   8,800
Andrews, A.   Am 19C
O/B 19x12 Figures Beside a Campfire Sel 9/92   325
Andrews, Ambrose   Am 1824-1859
* See 1993 Edition . . . .
Andrews, Benny   Am 1930-
O/C 25x18 Crow Mys 12/92   600
Andrews, Eliphalat F.   Am 19C
* See 1991 Edition . . . .
Andrews, George Henry   Br 1816-1898
* See 1992 Edition . . . .
Andrews, Henry   Br 1816-1869
O/C/B 25x37 Party on Horseback 1839 Sby 5/93   5,750
Andrews, J.   20C
O/B 20x30 Lobster Yng 2/93   60
Andrews, J.   Br 19C
O/C 24x36 A Serenade Chr 2/93   1,540
Andriaenssen, Alexander   Flm 1587-1661
O/Pn 19x15 Still Life Dead Fowl But 5/93   3,730
Andriessen, Hendrick   Bel 1607-1655
* See 1991 Edition . . . .
Andriessen, Jurriaan   1742-1819
K,Pl&W/Pa 16x13 Landscape with Figures 1794 Chr 1/93 . .   2,860
Andyrson, W. Livingston   Sco 19C
O/C 20x30 Kilshurn Castle, Scotland Hnd 9/92   300
Anesi, Carlos   Arg 1965-
O/C 36x41 Galgo 1990 Chr 11/92   12,650

30

Anesi, Paolo It 1700-1761
* See 1991 Edition . . . .
Anfosso, Pierre It 20C
O/C 32x21 Plage Hnd 3/93   325
Anfrei, Jegorov Rus 1878-1954
G/Pa 9x13 Russian Horse Drawn Sled But 10/92   550
Angelis, Pieter 1685-1735
* See 1993 Edition . . . .
Angermeyer, Johann-Adalbert 1674-1740
O/Me 5x6 Pears, Cherries and Grapes 1733 Chr 1/93   10,450
Anglada-Camarasa, Hermen Spa 1873-1959
* See 1993 Edition . . . .
Anglade, Gaston Fr 1854-
O/C 20x29 Purple Heather Chr 2/93   1,540
Ango, Jean-Robert Fr a 1760-1769
* See 1993 Edition . . . .
Anguiano, Raul Mex 1915-
O/M 16x24 Taxco But 4/93   2,875
Annenkoff, Georges Rus 1890-1971
* See 1992 Edition . . . .
Annigoni, Pietro It 1900-
Fp/Pa 10x7 Self-Portrait and Two Men Hnd 5/93 . . .   600
I/Pa 14x13 Three Lobsters Hnd 5/93   500
Fp/Pa 10x7 Three Female Studies Hnd 5/93   400
Fp/Pa 10x7 Studies of Heads and Figures Hnd 5/93   350
Anquetin, Louis
* See 1992 Edition . . . .
Ansdell, Richard Br 1815-1885
* See 1993 Edition . . . .
Anshutz, Thomas Pollock Am 1851-1912
W/Pa 13x20 The Summer House Sby 12/92   7,425
C/Pa/Pa 25x19 Male Nude Study 1891 Chr 3/93   3,220
O/C 12x18 Grandmother Sewing Fre 4/93   1,500
W/Pa/B 10x13 Horse and Boat Sby 9/92   990
P/B 14x10 Sea, House, Landscape, Woman (5) Chr 5/93 . . .   288
Antes, Horst Ger 1936-
A/C 48x40 Agnath 1968 Sby 5/93   47,150
A/C 28x24 Portrait Landschaft Gartner 1968 Sby 2/93 . . .   31,625
Anthonis, Victor Dut 19C
O/C 57x71 Cavaliers Throwing Dice Wes 5/93   1,650
Antigna, Alexandre Fr 1817-1878
O/Pn 16x13 Scene D'Atelier Sby 2/93   9,775
Antonissen, Henri-Joseph Dut 1734-1794
* See 1993 Edition . . . .
Antrobus, Edmond G. 19C
* See 1993 Edition . . . .
Antunez, Nemesio Chl 1918-
* See 1993 Edition . . . .
Antwerp, Henry Loos Am
* See 1992 Edition . . . .
Anuszkiewicz, Richard Am 1930-
A/C 60x60 Untitled 1972 Chr 11/92   6,600
Lq/M 48x48 Complementary Fission 1964 Sby 2/93   5,750
Anvitti, Filippo It 1876-
* See 1993 Edition . . . .
Aoyama, Yoshio Jap 1894-
* See 1993 Edition . . . .
Appel, Charles P. Am 1857-
* See 1993 Edition . . . .
Appel, Karel Dut 1921-
O/C 51x77 Vluchtende Hoofden 61 Chr 2/93   85,800
O/C 51x77 Matin d'ete 61 Chr 10/92   52,800
O/C 42x27 Untitled Sby 5/93   37,950
O/C 60x48 The Storyteller No. I 1983 Chr 11/92   29,700
O/C 26x31 Personnage et Oiseau Sby 11/92   28,600
A/C 18x18 Looking into Space Sby 2/93   25,875
O/C 36x19 Impatient Lady 71 Sby 5/93   25,300
O/C 96x76 The Island 1986 Chr 2/93   23,100
O/C 76x66 Fish and Head 1980 Chr 10/92   22,000
O&L/B 39x30 Untitled 75 Chr 11/92   17,600
Y&G/Pa 22x30 Paysage Imagioneue 1959 Chr 10/92   11,550
G&L/Pa 25x20 Harlequin Boy 1962 Sby 2/93   9,775
G/Pa 20x20 Le Tete '59 But 10/92   7,150
Br&I/Pa 36x47 Untitled '80 Chr 11/92   6,050

Aquilara, Floranio
O/C 38x57 Harbor Night Scene Dum 5/93   2,000
O/C 15x22 Town Landscape Dum 5/93   600
P/Pa 11x15 Town Harbor Scene Dum 5/93   500
Aquillo 20C
O/Pa 20x14 Rose in a Glass Yng 2/93   100
Arakawa, Shusaku Jap 1936-
A/C 66x98 Twelve O'Clock Sby 11/92   88,000
MM/C 85x52 1/2 Inch/Chain of Confusion 1962 Sby 5/93 .   76,750
O/C 93x62 Untitled 64 Sby 5/93   43,125
Aralica, Stojan
O/C 40x32 Mrs. Duchich's Daughter 1931 Sby 2/93   1,380
Arana, Alfonso
* See 1992 Edition . . . .
Aranda, Jose Jimenez Spa 1837-1903
* See 1993 Edition . . . .
Arapoff, Alexis P. Rus 1904-1948
O/C 25x18 A Young Woman Yng 5/93   200
Araujo, Carlos Brz 1950-
O/C/Pn 71x63 Figura Chr 11/92   14,300
Arbuckle, George Franklin Can 1909-
O/B 12x16 Quebec Village Sbt 5/93   1,584
O/B 12x16 Norwood, Ontario '87 Sbt 5/93   968
O/B 18x24 Winter Birch and Poplars 1984 Sbt 5/93   880
Archipenko, Alexander Rus 1887-1964
* See 1993 Edition . . . .
Arcieri, Charles F. Am 1885-
O/C 26x20 Woman Wearing Paisley Shawl Mys 12/92   3,080
Ardissone, Yolande Fr 1872-
O/C 32x26 Les Grandes Voliers Sby 2/93   2,875
O/C 22x26 Two Paintings Sby 2/93   2,530
O/C 26x32 Bateaux Dans la Port Wes 10/92   1,430
O/C 32x16 Nature Morte Lou 6/93   1,000
Ardon, Mordecai
* See 1992 Edition . . . .
Arellano Mex a 1690-1720
O/C 99x111 Celebridad De Nochebuena 1720 Sby 5/93 .   497,500
Arends, Jan 1728-1805
* See 1992 Edition . . . .
Areno, Joseph Am 1950-
O/C 22x30 Vineyard, California But 6/93   3,162
O/B 19x14 Mexican Street Scene 91 But 10/92   2,750
P/Pa 24x18 Chinatown, Los Angeles 93 But 6/93   1,725
Arentino, Spinello It
* See 1991 Edition . . . .
Arias, J. Spa 19C
O/Pn 12x9 Mosque Interior Wes 10/92   880
O/Pn 12x7 Woman in Courtyard Wes 10/92   522
Arias, Miguel Cub 19C
* See 1993 Edition . . . .
Arikha, Avigdor 20C
Pe/Pa 14x20 Nude Studies: Two Drawings 82 Sby 10/92 . .   2,090
Pe/Pa 30x22 Nude Studies: Two Drawings 82 Sby 10/92 . .   1,320
Ariza, Gonzalo Col 1912-
O/C/Pn 27x17 Catleya, Rana y Cardenal Chr 11/92   13,200
Arlt, Paul Theodore Am 1914-
O/C 22x28 Monhegan Harbor in a Storm Sby 9/92   220
Arman (Pierre Fernandez) Fr 1928-
MM/C 46x35 Accumulation of Tubes Sby 2/93   20,700
MM/Pa 38x50 Plaster Violin Sby 11/92   7,700
MM 50x30 Fantomatic Chr 10/92   4,950
L/Pn 57x46 Untitled Chr 2/93   4,180
Armand, A. 19C
Pl&S/Pa 6x5 Library with Antiquities Chr 1/93   880
Armenise, Raffaelo It 1852-1925
O/B 15x21 Courtyard Scene Hnd 3/93   1,500
Armet Y Portanel, Jose Spa 1843-1911
* See 1993 Edition . . . .
Armfield, Edward Br 19C
O/C 12x16 Helping Themselves to Dinner Chr 5/93   1,610
Armfield, George Br 1808-1893
O/C 18x22 Terriers Ratting: Pair 1850 Sby 6/93   5,175
O/C 17x21 Terriers: Pair Sby 6/93   4,600
O/C 12x16 Suppertime Fre 10/92   1,800

31

Armfield, Maxwell   Am 20C
  * See 1991 Edition . . . .
Armfield, Maxwell Ashby   Br 1882-1972
  T/Pn 29x14 Day-Evening Chr 2/93   8,250
**Armington, Franklin Milton   Can
1876-1941**
  O/C 29x36 Rue Royale, Paris 1923 Sbt 11/92   9,240
  O/Pn 9x11 Boulevard St. Michel, Paris 1934 Sbt 11/92   2,552
  O/Pn 9x11 Marly-Le-Roi 1923 Sbt 11/92   1,144
Armitage, Thomas Liddall   Br 19C
  * See 1990 Edition . . . .
Armor, Charles   Am 1844-1911
  O/B 14x18 Still Life with Blackberries Wes 10/92   468
Armour, Mary Nicol Neill   1902-
  * See 1992 Edition . . . .
Armstrong   Am 20C
  O/C 28x23 Couple Hnd 9/92   170
Armstrong, David   Am 1836-1918
  * See 1993 Edition . . . .
Armstrong, Rolf   Am 1881-1960
  O/C 84x48 Standing Nude with Black Veil 1921 Ih 5/93 . .   27,000
  O/C 84x48 Enchantment 1921 Skn 9/92   15,400
Armstrong, William   Can 1822-1914
  W/Pa 10x14 High Rock Portage - Nipigon '97 Sbt 5/93 . . .   2,860
Arnald, George   Br 1763-1841
  * See 1992 Edition . . . .
Arnau, Francisco Pons   Spa 1886-
  O/C 40x32 Confidencias 1925 Sby 10/92   27,500
Arnautoff, Victor M.   Am 1896-1979
  O/Cb 22x28 City Hall, San Francisco But 10/92   1,650
Arndt, Franz-Gustav   Ger 1842-1905
  O/C 26x19 Mediterranian Foot Path Doy 11/92   1,540
Arndt, Paul Wesley   Am 1881-
  O/C 24x30 Beech and Oaks Dum 8/93   225
Arnegger, Alois   Aus 1879-1967
  O/C 29x40 Spring Landscape Sby 10/92   4,400
  O/C 25x37 Playing on the Garden Steps Doy 5/93   3,740
  O/C 35x48 View Along the Italian Riviera Sby 1/93   2,875
  O/C 28x40 Snowy Mountains Chr 5/93   2,760
  O/C 27x42 Water's Edge, Capri Sby 1/93   2,300
Arnesen, Vilhelm   Dan 1865-1948
  O/B 14x20 Anchored off a Lighthouse 1879 Chr 2/93   528
Arneson, Robert
  W/Pa 19x26 Monument to be at 1303 Alice St. Sby 6/93 . . .   748
Arnholt, Waldon Sylvester   Am 1909-
  O/M 26x18 Mohawk Indian Chief Joseph Brant 1968 Sby 3/93   460
Arno, Peter   Am 1904-1968
  W&R/Pa 18x14 Groom and Entranced Woman Ih 5/93 . . .   1,100
  W&R/Pa 15x12 Little Boy Watching Couple Embrace Ih 5/93   650
Arnold, Carl Johann   Ger 1829-1916
  * See 1992 Edition . . . .
Arnold, Ralph   Am 1928-
  L 18x7 Untitled 60 Hnd 12/92   70
Arnold, Reginald Ernest   Eng 1853-1938
  * See 1992 Edition . . . .
Arnold, S.   20C
  O/B 12x16 North Shore Town Yng 2/93   500
Arnold-Kaiser, Bernita
  * See 1990 Edition . . . .
Arnoldi, Charles   1946-
  * See 1993 Edition . . . .
Arnolt, Gustav Muss   Am 1858-1927
  * See 1993 Edition . . . .
Arnosa, Jose Gallegos   Spa 1859-1917
  * See 1993 Edition . . . .
Arnot, Paul   Am 20C
  O/C 24x36 Stream in Winter Fre 4/93   300
Arnull, George   Br 19C
  * See 1990 Edition . . . .
Arp, Jean   Fr 1887-1966
  O/M 32x24 Fantome Flairant Un Nombril Sby 11/92   275,000
  Pt/Wd 33x24 Constellation de Formes Sby 11/92   137,500
Arpa Y Perea, Jose   Spa 1862-1903
  * See 1990 Edition . . . .

Arpard, Migl de Kasnozy   Fr 1863-
  O/C 24x20 A Farewell Kiss Hnd 5/93   1,700
Arrieta, Jose Agustin   Mex 1802-1879
  * See 1993 Edition . . . .
Arrighi, S.   It 19C
  * See 1993 Edition . . . .
Arriolla, Fortunato   Am 1827-1872
  * See 1992 Edition . . . .
Arsenius, Johann Georg   Swd 1818-1903
  * See 1993 Edition . . . .
Art & Language
  Book 12x8 Theories of Ethics 71 pages Sby 11/92   6,050
Arter, J. Charles   Am 1859-1923
  O/C Size? Woman with Bouquet 1895 Dum 6/93   3,250
Arthur, Reginald   Br 19C
  * See 1991 Edition . . . .
Arthurs, Stanley Massey   Am 1877-1950
  O/C 18x12 Going to Church Mys 3/93   770
Artigue, Albert-Emile   Fr a 1875-1901
  O/Pn 14x11 An Arabian Vendor Sby 10/92   6,600
Artschwager, Richard   Am 1924-
  A/Clx 50x62 Double Portrait Sby 11/92   88,000
  A/Clx 32x15 Untitled Sby 11/92   36,300
  A/Clx 58x41 Accelerator II Chr 10/92   33,000
  Pe/Clx 19x19 Untitled 66 Sby 11/92   20,900
  C/Pa 25x19 Dinner and Wait '83 Chr 11/92   6,050
  C/Pa 19x25 Untitled 87 Sby 10/92   3,575
Artz, Constant   Dut 1870-1951
  * See 1993 Edition . . . .
Artz, David Adolf Constant   Dut 1837-1890
  * See 1993 Edition . . . .
Asada, Takashi
  * See 1993 Edition . . . .
Ascenzi   Con 20C
  * See 1992 Edition . . . .
Ashley, Frank N.   Am 1920-
  W&Pl/Pa 28x22 Paris, Afternoon But 12/92   3,300
  O/C 28x36 Lonely '47 Hnz 5/93   375
Ashton, Ethel V.   Am 20C
  * See 1993 Edition . . . .
**Askenazy, Mischa (Maurice)   Am
1888-1961**
  O/C 46x36 Japanese Sketch Book But 6/93   9,200
  O/B 17x15 Interior Artist's Daughter & Friend 1938 But 3/93   8,250
  O/C 26x18 Through a Window 1930 But 3/93   7,700
  O/C 28x34 House on an Island But 10/92   6,050
  O/C 32x26 Ballerina Mor 2/93   6,000
  O/C 20x24 Chavez Ravine-Los Angeles Mor 6/93   4,675
  O/C 42x32 Mother and Child But 6/93   4,600
  O/C 40x27 My Daughter But 6/93   4,600
  O/C 18x30 Chioggia, Italy But 3/93   3,300
  O/C 36x32 Boats in Venice Mor 2/93   3,250
  O/C 32x26 Boats in Venice Mor 6/93   3,025
  O/C 26x29 Florence Mor 11/92   2,500
  O/C 14x11 Girl with Red Ribbon Mor 11/92   2,000
  O/C 20x24 Rooftops But 6/93   1,950
  O/C/B 32x25 Portrait of Jenny But 6/93   1,720
  O/C 20x24 Cabins in Winter Mor 11/92   1,700
  O/C 36x28 Seated Woman Lou 12/92   1,700
  P,W&Pe/Pa 26x21 Nude; Venetian Canal: Double But 3/93 .   1,650
  MM/Pa 23x17 Portrait of Woman Mor 11/92   1,200
  O/C 17x13 Connie Mor 2/93   1,100
  W/Pa 22x27 Figures Near House Mor 2/93   1,100
  O/C 26x18 Ballerina Mor 11/92   1,000
  O/C 19x25 Snow in Venice Mor 2/93   700
  O/C 16x20 Dorothy & Mother Mor 11/92   650
  O/B 6x8 House in Landscape Mor 2/93   550
**Askevold, Anders Monsen   Swd
1834-1900**
  * See 1991 Edition . . . .
Askew, John   Br 19C
  O/C 25x42 Ship Off the Kent Coast Sby 6/93   6,900
Asoma, Tadashi   Jap 1923-
  O/C 40x40 Yoko Reading '69 Wlf 4/93   2

32

Aspell, Peter
O/Pa 13x9 Centesse 86 Sby 2/93 403
Asplund, Tore Am 20C
O/B 17x31 Chicago Skyline Wes 5/93 1,100
Asselbergs, Alphonse Bel 1839-1916
O/C 18x30 Pastoral Landscape Sel 12/92 650
Asselijn, Jan Dut 1610-1652
O/Pn 13x13 Travellers Fording a River Sby 5/93 25,300
Asselin, Maurice
O/C 24x29 Clearing Trees Outside the Village Sby 10/92 . . . 1,320
Assereti, G**vo 18C
  * See 1992 Edition . . . .
Assereto, Gioacchino It 1600-1649
  * See 1990 Edition . . . .
Asther, Nils
  * See 1992 Edition . . . .
Asti, Angelo Fr 1847-1903
O/C 24x18 Girl with Auburn Hair Dum 2/93 7,000
O/C 18x13 Italian Girl But 11/92 4,675
O/C 10x8 Red Headed Beauty Sby 1/93 1,035
Astrup, Nikolai Nor 1880-1928
  * See 1992 Edition . . . .
Atalaya, Enrique Spa -1914
  * See 1993 Edition . . . .
Atamian, Charles Garabed Tur 1872-
  * See 1993 Edition . . . .
Atkins, Arthur Am 1873-1899
O/C/B 14x18 Eze from the Villa St. Hospice But 3/93 1,980
Atkins, Lee Am 1913-1987
  * See 1993 Edition . . . .
Atkinson, Jacob Am 1864-1938
  * See 1992 Edition . . . .
Atl, Dr. Mex 1875-1964
C&H/B 18x23 Paricutin Sby 11/92 11,000
C/Pa 8x9 Paisaje con Volcan Sby 11/92 4,400
Atlan, Jean Fr 1913-1960
P/Pa 10x13 Untitled Sby 10/92 16,500
Attendu, Antoine Ferdinand Fr 19C
  * See 1993 Edition . . . .
Atwood, C. Am 20C
  * See 1992 Edition . . . .
Aubert, Jean Ernest Fr 1824-1906
  * See 1990 Edition . . . .
Aubin, Barbara Am 20C
O/C 48x37 Cape Cod Fishermen Hnz 5/93 200
Aublet, Albert Fr 1851-1938
O/C 34x55 Sur les Galets; Le Treport 1883 Sby 5/93 . . . 387,500
Audubon, John James Am 1785-1851
Pl&W/B 21x17 Eastern Grey Squirrel Chr 9/92 49,500
Audubon, John Woodhouse Am
1812-1868
O/C 25x30 Cat Stalking a Butterfly 1861 Sby 5/93 31,050
Audy, Jonny Fr a 1872-1976
  * See 1991 Edition . . . .
Auerbach, Frank 1931-
  * See 1993 Edition . . . .
Auerbach-Levy, William Am 1889-1964
O/B 20x16 Portrait Man in a Blue Shirt Sby 3/93 575
O/C 25x30 Free Parking/City Scene Skn 3/93 385
Aufray, Joseph Fr 1836-
O/Pn 11x8 Afternoon of Playtime Chr 10/92 2,200
Auge, Philippe Fr 1935-
  * See 1992 Edition . . . .
Augusta, George Am 20C
O/M 20x24 At the Beach Skn 9/92 660
Auguste, Clervaux Hai
  * See 1993 Edition . . . .
Ault, George Copeland Am 1891-1948
O/C 17x13 Where the Road Turns 1939 Sby 12/92 17,600
G/Pa 11x21 Woodstock Nocturne '40 Chr 9/92 3,300
Pe/Pa 14x10 Iris '32 Chr 9/92 2,640
H/Pa 13x8 St. Luke's, N.Y. '25 Sby 3/93 1,035
Aumond, Jean
W&Gd/Pa 10x8 Two Costume Designs Sby 10/92 1,100
W&Gd/Pa 10x8 Two Costume Designs Sby 10/92 770

Aumonier, James Br 1832-1911
O/C 24x36 Sunlight on the Downs Yng 5/93 650
Aumont, Louis Auguste Francois Dan
1805-1879
O/C 8x6 Portrait of a Man Yng 2/93 650
Aureli, Giuseppe It 1858-1929
W/Pb 16x10 In the Harem Sby 1/93 2,875
W/Pa 21x15 Pleasant Peasant Pastime 1882 Brd 2/93 1,100
W/Pa 16x11 Il Concerto Hnz 5/93 700
W/Pa 17x10 Cavalier by a Doorway 1880 Chr 10/92 660
W/Pa 21x15 Tavern Scene 1882 Hnd 5/93 375
Aussandon, Joseph Nicolas H. Fr 1836-
O/C 22x18 Little Girl Eating Porridge 69 Hnd 10/92 1,100
Austen, A. Eur 19C
O/C 18x14 Darby and Joan Slo 5/93 375
Austrian, Ben Am 1870-1921
  * See 1993 Edition . . . .
Aved, Jacques Andre Fr 1702-1766
  * See 1990 Edition . . . .
Avedisian, Edward 1936-
W&G/Pa 13x13 Untitled Chr 2/93 550
Avercamp, Barent Dut 1612-1679
  * See 1992 Edition . . . .
Avercamp, Hendrick Dut 1585-1663
  * See 1992 Edition . . . .
Avery, Kenneth Newell Am 1882-
  * See 1990 Edition . . . .
Avery, Milton Am 1893-1965
O/C 26x42 Porch Sitters--Sally and March 1952 Chr 5/93 244,500
O/C 36x28 Girl Drawing 1951 Sby 5/93 101,500
G&Pe/Pa 23x31 Green Sea 1948 Chr 5/93 51,750
W/Pa 23x31 Sun Bather and Sea Watcher 1948 Sby 5/93 . 40,250
W&Pe/Pa 22x31 Pines and Meadows Sby 12/92 34,100
W/Pa 15x22 The Bathers Sby 12/92 30,800
O/C 36x24 Woman in a Feathered Hat Sby 12/92 24,200
O/C 11x6 Orange Flowers 1958 Sby 9/92 23,100
O/Cb 22x28 Lilacs 1961 Chr 9/92 20,900
O/Cb 12x9 Pool Shark 1955 Sby 12/92 20,900
O/Cb 20x16 Pink Turtleneck (Self Portrait) 1963 Chr 5/93 . 17,250
O/C 30x25 Portrait of George Constant Chr 3/93 14,950
O/B 9x7 Bouquet by Sea 1955 But 6/93 12,650
O/Cb 24x18 Sleeping Figure Chr 9/92 12,100
O/Cb 18x24 Strange Bird 1953 Chr 9/92 10,000
G/Pa 11x17 Sally Reclining: Double Hnd 10/92 9,000
O/Cb 14x26 Siesta 1931 FHB 5/93 4,500
Fp/Pa 14x17 Two Seated Female Nudes Sby 9/92 3,575
Avitabile, Gennaro It 1864-
  * See 1993 Edition . . . .
Axentowicz, Theodor Pol 1859-1938
P/Pa 30x18 Zadumana Sby 1/93 2,875
Aycock, Alice 1946-
Cp/Pls 95x105 The New China Drawing 1984 Chr 10/92 . . . 6,600
Ayotte, Leo Can 1909-1977
  * See 1992 Edition . . . .
Baadsgaard, Alfrida Dan 1839-
  * See 1991 Edition . . . .
Babb, John Staines Br 1870-1900
  * See 1991 Edition . . . .
Babbage, H. I. Am 20C
O/B 11x13 Alpine Winter Scene Mys 3/93 82
Babbidge, James Gardner Am 1844-1919
O/C 24x36 Merchant Ship William H. Allison Slo 4/93 4,000
Baber, Alice
O/C 30x50 The Rain That Hears the Jaguar 1977 Sby 2/93 . 1,610
Baboulene, Eugene Fr 1905-
O/C 15x22 Maison a Toulon 1956 Chr 11/92 4,620
Bacardy, Don 20C
  * See 1991 Edition . . . .
Bacci, Edmondo It 1913-
O,Pls&Sd/C 28x28 Composition 57 Hnd 10/92 1,200
Bach, Elvira 20C
A,G&P/Pa 17x12 Untitled 84 Sby 10/92 1,265
Bache, Otto Dan 1839-1914
  * See 1990 Edition . . . .

Bachelier, Jean-Jacques   Fr 1724-1806
O/C 14x38 Still Lifes Game Poultry Figs: Four Sby 1/93 .. 90,500
Bacher, Thomas   Am 20C
A/C 42x54 Times Square Series - Fuji '85 Fre 4/93 450
Bachmann, Otto
T/M 24x39 Figures on Deck 1958 Sby 2/93 2,415
Backhuysen, Ludolf   Dut 1631-1708
O/C 17x22 Ferry Boat Reaching Shore Sby 1/93 10,063
Backus, Standish   Am 1910-
W/Pa 14x21 Landscape & With Train: Double Mor 6/93 770
Backvis, Francois   Bel 19C
* See 1990 Edition ....
Bacon, Charles Roswell   Am 1868-1913
* See 1990 Edition ....
Bacon, Francis   Am 1909-
* See 1992 Edition ....
Bacon, Henry   Am 1839-1912
O/C 16x13 Artist Painting Mys 12/92 2,640
W&Pe/Pa 13x20 Village Near Cairo Wes 10/92 330
P/Pa 15x22 Arab Scene Mys 12/92 220
Bacon, Peggy   Am 1895-1987
* See 1993 Edition ....
Badger, Samuel Finley Morse   Am 19C
O/C 36x23 American Bark "H.G. Johnson" '98 Eld 7/93 ... 8,250
Badura, Ben
O/C 20x18 Still Life Ald 9/92 2,600
O/B 14x16 Winter Landscape Ald 5/93 400
Badura, Faye Swengel
O/B 10x12 Pansies Ald 3/93 850
O/C 16x18 Spring Wedding at Church Ald 9/92 225
Baechler, Donald   Am 1956-
A&L/C 111x111 Plague of Responsibility 86 Sby 11/92 . 55,000
A/C 111x66 Untitled (Zagreb) 82 Chr 2/93 24,200
O,A&L/C 58x40 Green Carnation 90 Sby 5/93 19,550
O&L/C 42x42 The Onion Eater 88 Sby 11/92 7,150
A&L/C 42x42 Untitled (Head) 1983 Sby 10/92 4,950
G&L/Pa 17x14 Green Heart 90 Sby 10/92 1,980
Baeder, John   Am 1938-
* See 1991 Edition ....
Baer, Fritz   Ger 1850-1919
* See 1993 Edition ....
Baer, Jo   Am 1929-
O/C 72x72 Untitled (Korean) '62 Chr 11/92 8,800
O/C 60x86 Untitled '66 Chr 2/93 3,300
O/C 104x72 Untitled '68 Chr 2/93 3,080
Baer, William J.   Am 1860-1941
O/C 12x20 Salter's Point, Roundhill Sby 9/92 2,420
Baes, Emile   Bel 1879-1953
* See 1992 Edition ....
Baez, Salvador Martinez
O/B 20x24 Orquideas 1946 Chr 11/92 13,200
Bahieu, Jules G.   Bel 19C
* See 1993 Edition ....
Baierl, Theodor   Ger 1881-1932
O/Pn 18x15 Woman Strewing Flowers Dum 4/93 2,000
Bail, Franck Antoine   Fr 1858-1924
* See 1992 Edition ....
Bail, Joseph   Fr 1862-1921
O/C 29x24 Polishing Coppers Sby 10/92 8,800
O/C 30x25 Copper Bucket with Apples Wlf 9/92 1,900
O/C/B 32x27 Copper Pitcher with Apples Fre 4/93 1,700
Bailey, Frederick Victor   Br 20C
* See 1992 Edition ....
Bailey, T.   Am 1866-1961
O/C 24x32 Unnamed Clipper Ship Eld 7/93 275
O/C 16x12 Ship in Full Sail Lou 6/93 225
Bailey, William   Am 1930-
H/Pa 15x11 Nude in Armchair 1967 Chr 10/92 3,300
Pl/Pa 15x11 Two Untitled Drawings 1983 Chr 11/92 2,750
Baillio, R.   Fr a 1790-1810
* See 1993 Edition ....
Baird, Nathaniel Hughes   Br 1865-1936
O/C 29x37 Horses Watering Sby 6/93 2,875
Baird, Victor   Eng 1857-1924
O/Pn 7x9 Roosters Slo 5/93 600

Baird, William Baptiste   Am 1847-
O/C 10x13 Mother Hen and Her Chicks Sby 6/93 2,530
O/Pn 9x13 Cottage and Cow Stable 1900 Chr 12/92 1,320
Baj, Enrico   It 1924-
MM/B 28x20 Bird But 10/92 3,575
O/C 7x9 Abstract Composition But 10/92 1,980
Bak, Janos P.   1913-
O/C 24x30 Scene with Figures Dum 7/93 275
Bakalowicz, Ladislaus   Pol 1833-
O/C 30x20 Courtship Wlf 3/93 3,600
Baker, Elizabeth Gowdy   Am -1927
* See 1993 Edition ....
Baker, Ernest   Am 19C
* See 1992 Edition ....
Baker, F.   20C
O/C 18x40 South Bridge at Concord Yng 5/93 450
Baker, George A.   Am 1821-1880
O/B 10x8 Dolly But 12/92 2,750
Baker, Joe   Am 1946-
O/C 78x66 Frankie in a Blue Blanket But 10/92 4,400
Bakhuyzen, Alexandre H.   Dut 1830-
* See 1990 Edition ....
Bakhuyzen, G. J. Van De Sande   Dut 1826-1895
* See 1992 Edition ....
Bakhuyzen, Hendrik Van De Sand   Dut 1795-1860
O/Pn 11x15 Cattle and Sheep Sby 1/93 3,738
Bakhuyzen, Julius Van De Sande   Dut 1835-1925
* See 1991 Edition ....
Bakhuyzen, Ludolf   Dut 1631-1708
* See 1991 Edition ....
Bakos, Jozef G.   Am 1891-1976
O/C 18x24 Western Landscape Chr 9/92 4,950
Bakst, Leon   Rus 1866-1924
G/Pa 13x10 Six Costume Designs Sby 10/92 1,870
G/Pa 13x10 Six Costume Designs Sby 2/93 1,610
Balande, Gaston   Fr 1880-1971
* See 1992 Edition ....
Balassi, Mario   It 1604-1667
* See 1991 Edition ....
Baldessari, John   1931-
A/Ph 76x36 Cutting Ribbon Man in Wheelchair Chr 10/92 . 24,200
O&Ph/B 59x33 Man w/Arrow Piercing Chest Chr 11/92 .. 14,300
Ph&Pt/B 54x48 Body and Soul Sby 2/93 13,800
Balducci, Giovanni   It 1560-1631
* See 1993 Edition ....
Baldwin, Clifford P.   Am 1889-1961
O/C 20x24 In the Pines Mor 2/93 325
Bale, Charles Thomas   Eng a 1868-1875
O/C 17x14 Still Life Grapes, Apples, Plum 1889 Sby 1/93 .. 2,070
O/C 20x30 Tabletop Still Life Wes 12/92 1,430
Balestra, Antonio   It 1660-1740
* See 1992 Edition ....
Balestrieri, Lionello   It 1872-1958
O/C 29x21 Snowy Village Street Sby 1/93 3,450
Pe,W&G/Cd 11x16 I Giardini di Lussemburgo Sby 10/92 ... 3,300
W&G/Pa 18x11 A Parisian Cafe Chr 10/92 1,980
Balink, Henry C.   Am 1882-1963
O/C 10x12 Navajo Canyon, New Mexico Hnd 3/93 450
O/C 12x14 Ship Rock, New Mexico Hnd 3/93 375
Ball, Adrien Joseph Verhoeven   Bel 1824-1882
* See 1990 Edition ....
Ball, Alice Worthington   Am -1929
O/C 30x24 Canadian Village Street Skn 3/93 715
Ball, Arthur   Br 19C
* See 1993 Edition ....
Ball, L. Clarence   Am 1858-1915
W/Pa 14x21 Interior with Fireplace 1878 Yng 2/93 475
Ball, Thomas Watson   Am 1863-1934
O/C 22x30 Hilly Landscape Mys 3/93 495
O/C 24x30 "J" Boats Mys 3/93 220

34

Balla, Giacomo   It 1871-1958
* See 1993 Edition ....
Ballavoine, Jules Frederic   Fr 1855-1901
O/C 11x14 Au Bord de le Riviere Chr 5/93 4,370
O/Pn 13x10 Admiring the Bird Chr 10/92 1,320
O/C 18x15 Lady with Red Velvet Ribbon Chr 2/93 660
Ballesio, Federico   It 19C
W/Pa 21x28 Harem Musician's Repose Sby 10/92 6,325
W/Pa 21x14 Harem Beauty with a Tambourine Chr 10/92 . 4,180
Ballesio, G.   It 19C
* See 1992 Edition ....
Ballin, Hugo   Am 1879-1956
O/C 40x50 Mexican Party But 6/93 3,162
Ballin, Robert   Fr -1915
O/Pn 5x7 Roosters Feeding: Pair Slo 5/93 550
Balogh, Bela   Rus 20C
O/Cb 23x30 Still Life Lou 9/92 175
Balthus (Balthasar Klossowski)   Fr 1908-
O/C 39x32 Etude Pour "Les trois soeurs" 1954 Chr 11/92 517,000
O/C 36x29 Colette de Profil 54 Sby 5/93 288,500
O/C 40x32 Nu debout 54 Chr 11/92 275,000
O/B 24x21 Etude de trois personnages Chr 11/92 55,000
W/Pa 17x22 Portrait de Frederique 54 Chr 11/92 34,100
Pe/Pa 11x9 Femme nue allongee Chr 11/92 19,800
Pe/Pa 16x12 Portrait de Sheila Pickering 1935 Chr 11/92 . 11,000
Y/Pa 9x8 Portrait de Tamara Leibowitz Chr 11/92 10,450
Pe/Pa 10x12 Etudes 48 Chr 10/92 4,400
Bama, James E.   Am 1926-
* See 1993 Edition ....
Bamberger, Fritz   Ger 1814-1873
* See 1991 Edition ....
Bamfylde, Copleston Warre   -1791
* See 1992 Edition ....
Banchi, Giorgio   It 1789-1853
* See 1992 Edition ....
Bancroft, Milton Herbert   Am 1867-1947
* See 1992 Edition ....
Bandeira, Antonio   Brz 1922-
O/C 18x22 City in Black and Red 62 Chr 11/92 13,200
G&Br/Pa 19x14 Abstract in Pink 56 Chr 11/92 3,850
G&Pl/Pa 10x15 Abstract in Brown 56 Chr 11/92 2,200
Bandinelli, Baccio   It 1493-1560
* See 1991 Edition ....
Bando, Toshio
O/Pn 10x13 Still Life with Peaches Sby 2/93 1,093
Banks, Thomas J.   Br 19C
* See 1993 Edition ....
Bannard, Walter Darby
O/C 66x99 Grover Coast Sby 2/93 1,840
Bannatyne, John James   Br 1836-1911
O/C 21x30 Anchored Fishing Boat Chr 2/93 1,980
O/C 14x24 Holland River Landscape Sel 12/92 1,600
Bannister, Thaddeus   Am 1915-
* See 1993 Edition ....
Banting, Sir Frederick Grant   Can 1891-1941
O/Pn 9x11 Cobalt 1932 Sbt 11/92 3,960
Bantzer, Carl Ludwig Noah   Ger 1857-
* See 1993 Edition ....
Baptista Da Costa, Joao   Brz 1865-1926
* See 1993 Edition ....
Baquero, Mariano   Spa 19C
* See 1991 Edition ....
Barauss, Emile   Fr 1851-1930
* See 1992 Edition ....
Barbaglia, Giuseppe   It 1841-
O/C 63x36 Andromeda Sby 5/93 9,200
Barbarini, Emil   Aus 1855-1930
* See 1993 Edition ....
Barbarini, Ernst   Ger 20C
* See 1993 Edition ....
Barbasan, Mariano   Spa 1864-1924
* See 1993 Edition ....
Barbeau, Christian Marcel   Can 1925-
G/Pa 25x20 Abstract Composition '72 Sbt 11/92 1,144

Barber, Alfred R.   Br a 1879-1893
* See 1992 Edition ....
Barber, C. A.   20C
W/Pa 10x7 Best Friends Slo 5/93 375
Barber, Charles Burton   Br 1845-1894
* See 1992 Edition ....
Barber, John   Am 1898-1965
O/C 15x18 Provincetown Scene Skn 11/92 1,540
Barber, Thomas   1768-1843
O/C 65x54 Portrait of Two Boys Sby 5/93 20,700
Barbier, George   Fr 1882-1932
W,I&Pt/Pa 10x9 Two Costume Designs 1920 Sby 10/92 ... 2,750
W/Pa 11x8 Standing Woman and Bird on Perch Ih 5/93 ... 2,600
W/Pa 11x7 Folio of Watercolors (12) 1924 Wlf 5/93 1,600
W,I&Gd/Pa 10x9 Costume The Charleston 1925 Sby 10/92 . 1,540
I,W&Gd/Pa 10x9 Costume Design A Flower Sby 10/92 990
Barbieri, Giovanni Francesco   It 1591-1666
Pl&S/Pa 12x9 Executioner Holding Head St. John Chr 1/93 85,800
Pl/Pa 10x7 Mars, His Sword Drawn Chr 1/93 52,800
O/C 26x22 Mary Magdalene Contemplating Nails Chr 1/93 49,500
Pl/Pa 10x8 Woman Turned to the Left Chr 1/93 30,800
Pl/Pa 10x16 Hilly Landscape with Huntsman Chr 1/93 12,100
K/Pa 12x8 Saint Jerome in Penitence Chr 1/93 12,100
Barbudo, Salvador Sanchez   Spa 1858-1919
* See 1993 Edition ....
Barcelo, Miguel   1957-
* See 1993 Edition ....
Barcelo, Miguel   Spa 17C
* See 1991 Edition ....
Barchus, Eliza   Am 1857-1959
O/C 16x24 Mountain River But 6/93 1,150
O/C 30x50 Mountain Lake Dum 12/92 700
O/B 12x17 Mt. Hood Mys 3/93 440
Barclay, McClelland   Am 1891-1943
O&R/C 28x26 Man Asking a Woman Directions FHB 5/93 . 1,400
O/C 35x30 A Horse and Rider 1933 Chr 5/93 1,150
W&Pl/Pa 9x6 Ships (2) 1921 Mor 11/92 225
Bard, James   Am 1815-1897
* See 1992 Edition ....
Bardone, Guy   Fr 1927-
O/C 29x37 Citronniers Devant le Mer-Sicile Sby 10/92 3,850
O/C 32x26 Le Petit Pecheur Sby 10/92 2,640
O/C 20x24 Campagne A Nauplie, Greece Slo 4/93 1,500
Bardot, E.   19C
O/C 16x13 Elderly Scholar Reading Dum 4/93 450
Bardwell, Thomas   Eng a 1735-1780
* See 1990 Edition ....
Barella, Jose Puigdengolas
* See 1992 Edition ....
Barend, Johannes Hermanus   Dut 1840-1912
* See 1993 Edition ....
Barenger, James   Br 1745-1813
* See 1991 Edition ....
Bargheer, Eduard   Ger 1901-1979
H&W/Pa 9x11 The Crowd But 4/93 690
Bargue, Charles   Fr 1825-1883
* See 1993 Edition ....
Barilari, Enrique   Arg 1931-
* See 1990 Edition ....
Barile, Xavier   Am 1891-1981
O/M 20x24 Beyond Artist Drive, Death Valley Chr 5/93 ... 1,035
Barillot, Leon   Fr 1844-1929
* See 1992 Edition ....
Bark, Jared   1944-
A&MM/B 36x16 Untitled 1980 Chr 11/92 220
Barker of Bath, Benjamin   Br 1776-1836
* See 1992 Edition ....
Barker, George   Am 1882-1965
W/Pa 28x19 Crashing Waves Mys 3/93 110
Barker, John   Br 19C
O/C 31x24 Young Girl Drawing Water Mys 12/92 990

Barker, Thomas Jones   Br 1769-1847
* See 1991 Edition . . . .
Barlach, Ernst   Ger 1870-1938
* See 1991 Edition . . . .
Barland, Adam   Br a 1843-1885
  O/C 20x30 On the Thames, Oxford 84 Hnd 12/92 750
Barlow, Myron   Am 1873-1937
  O/C 40x40 A Cup of Tea Sby 5/93 13,800
  O/C 40x40 Hospitality Sby 5/93 8,050
  O/C/M 32x26 The Sisters 1907 Sby 3/93 2,990
  O/C 31x26 French Landscape Lou 6/93 900
Barnabe, Duilio   It 1914-1961
  O/C 21x40 Nature Morta Sel 12/92 2,200
Barnard, A.   19C
  O/C 20x27 Strawberries 1881 Yng 5/93 900
Barnard, Edward Herbert   Am 1855-1909
  * See 1991 Edition . . . .
Barnes, Archibald Georges   Br 1887-1972
  O/C 40x34 Still Life Sbt 11/92 704
Barnes, Ernest   Am 1873-
  O/C 30x36 Football Players But 10/92 1,320
Barnes, Frank   Nz 19C
  * See 1991 Edition . . . .
Barnes, Matthew Rackham   Am 1880-1951
  O/C 20x24 Emerald Night 1942 But 10/92 1,870
Barnet, Wil   Am 1911-
  MM/B 27x28 Girl on Bicycle 1971 Sby 3/93 4,313
  O/C 45x38 Abstract 1975 Chr 12/92 3,850
Barnett, Thomas P.   Am 1870-1929
  * See 1993 Edition . . . .
Barnoin, Henri Alphonse   Fr 1882-1935
  O/C 16x12 Village Street Mys 12/92 770
Barnsley, James MacDonald   Can 1861-1929
  O/Pn 13x8 Autumn, Near Dampierre, Normandy '86 Sbt 5/93 2,200
Baron, Henri Charles Antoine   Fr 1816-1885
  * See 1990 Edition . . . .
Barone, Antonio   Am 1889-1971
  O/C 20x24 The Street Vendor Chr 3/93 8,050
  W/Pa 10x13 Beach Scene with Grazia Sby 12/92 6,600
  W/Pa 10x14 View From Under the Pier Brd 8/93 3,300
Barr, William   Am 1867-1933
  * See 1992 Edition . . . .
Barraband, Jacques   Fr 1767-1809
  * See 1993 Edition . . . .
Barrable, George Hamilton   Br 19C
  O/C 46x30 Sisters Sby 1/93 7,475
Barradas, Rafael   Uru 1890-1929
  O/C 12x11 La Fiesta de Los Negros Sby 5/93 37,375
  W&H/Pa 14x11 Marinero en Libertad 1928 Sby 11/92 3,850
Barralet, John James   Am 1747-1815
  * See 1993 Edition . . . .
Barrau, Laureano   Spa 1864-1957
  O/C 77x41 Despues Del Bano '913 Sby 5/93 51,750
Barraud, Francois   Sws 1899-1934
  * See 1991 Edition . . . .
Barraud, Henry   Br 1811-1874
  O/C 28x36 Portrait of Thormanby 1860 Sby 6/93 11,500
Barraud, William   Br 1810-1850
  * See 1993 Edition . . . .
Barreda, Ernesto   Fr 1927-
  * See 1991 Edition . . . .
Barrel-Botti   Am 20C
  O/C 36x36 Girl in Garden Sel 12/92 1,150
  O/C 24x36 Sunlight on the Cover Sel 12/92 675
  O/C 36x36 Cross Country Skiers Sel 12/92 375
Barrera, Antonio   Col 1948-
  * See 1992 Edition . . . .
Barrera, Antonio   It 1889-
  * See 1993 Edition . . . .
Barreres, Domingo   Am 20C
  A/C 40x67 Costa Brava '82 Skn 5/93 880

Barret, George (Sr.)   Br 1728-1784
  * See 1993 Edition . . . .
Barret, Marius Antoine   Fr 1865-
  * See 1992 Edition . . . .
Barrett, J.   Br 19C
  * See 1992 Edition . . . .
Barrett, Mildred   Am 20C
  O/C 36x24 Flower Vendors Slo 4/93 180
Barrett, William S.   Am 1854-1927
  O/B 8x11 Moonlit Waters Yng 5/93 750
Barrios, Armando   Ven 1920-
  * See 1991 Edition . . . .
Barron, Hugh   Br 1745-1791
  * See 1992 Edition . . . .
Barry, Robert   1936-
  I/Pa 12x10 Basic Format for Hanging String 68 Sby 5/93 . . 3,163
  I&Pe/Pa 10x12 Wire Sculpture 1968 Sby 2/93 2,875
  I/Pa 7x6 Untitled Chr 11/92 770
Barse, George B. (Jr.)   Am 1861-1938
  O/C 27x35 The Oasis Sby 9/92 17,600
Barsotti, Hercules   Brz 1914-
  * See 1992 Edition . . . .
Bartezago, Enrico   Sws 19C
  O/Pn 7x10 Children at Play: Eight Sby 5/93 28,750
  O/Pn 10x13 The Wagon Ride Sby 5/93 4,313
Barth, Jack   1946-
  C/Pa/C 89x61 Altar of Good Fortune 82 Chr 10/92 2,090
Barth, Karl   Ger 1787-1853
  * See 1993 Edition . . . .
Bartholdi, Frederic-Auguste   Fr 19C
  * See 1991 Edition . . . .
Bartholomew, Gerard
  O/C 50x43 Untitled 1984 Sby 2/93 8,050
Bartlett, Dana   Am 1878-1957
  O/C 20x24 Autumn Sycamores Mor 6/93 5,500
  O/C 20x24 Rolling Hills But 3/93 4,400
  O/C 20x24 Laguna Hills Mor 2/93 4,000
  O/C 20x24 Early Summer Mor 11/92 3,750
  O/C 16x20 California Hills Mor 2/93 3,250
  O/B 34x33 Mountain Glacier But 6/93 2,875
  O/C 24x30 Ranch Hill Mor 6/93 2,475
  O/B 8x10 Paris - 1924 - Tuilleries Gardens Mor 11/92 . . 1,200
  O/C 20x24 Desert & Mountains Palm Springs Mor 11/92 . 1,100
  O/C 24x20 Sunset on the Pacific Lou 3/93 800
Bartlett, Frederic Clay   Am 1873-
  * See 1992 Edition . . . .
Bartlett, Gray   Am 1885-1951
  * See 1992 Edition . . . .
Bartlett, James W. Bo   Am 20C
  O/C 22x18 Eleanor Waking 1983 Fre 10/92 475
Bartlett, Jennifer   Am 1941-
  O/C 60x36 At Sands Point #31 Sby 5/93 51,750
  O/C 48x48 At Sands Point #25 Chr 11/92 33,000
  O/C 24x72 View of Sands Point #13 Sby 11/92 33,000
  P/Pa 20x26 In the Garden #63 Sby 5/93 8,050
  I/Pa 26x20 In the Garden #72 Sby 5/93 4,600
  O/C 10x14 Blue House Chr 10/92 3,850
  C&H/Pa 20x26 In the Garden #75 Chr 5/93 3,450
Bartlett, William Henry   Am 1809-1854
  * See 1992 Edition . . . .
Bartolena, Giovanni
  O/B 20x12 Still Life Flowers in Vase Sby 2/93 3,738
Bartoli, Jacques   Fr 1920-
  O/C 58x45 Le Bal Masque Hnd 3/93 5,200
  O/C 26x32 Cagnes: Depart de Courses Hnd 3/93 3,800
Bartolini, Frederico   It 20C
  W/Pa 21x15 North African Street Sby 1/93 5,175
  W/Pa/B 22x15 North African Street with Merchants Sby 1/93 3,738
Barton, Loren R.   Am 1893-1975
  O/C 26x34 Spring Flowers Mor 11/92 500
Bartsch, Walter   Am a 1966-1968
  O/C 48x34 Crowded Subway Mys 12/92 220
Barucci, Pietro   It 1845-1917
  O/C/B 24x44 Fisherfolk mending their Nets Chr 10/92 . . . 11,000
  O/C 32x20 Down the Mountain with Flock Chr 5/93 3,680

Barwolf, Georges Bel 1872-1935
* See 1992 Edition . . . .
Barye, Antoine Louis Fr 1795-1875
P&W/Pa 10x13 Lion Dans le Desert Sby 5/93 37,375
Basaldella, Afro It 1912-1976
W/Pa 9x7 Abstract Composition 57 But 4/93 1,380
Baselitz, Georg Ger 1938-
O/C 92x70 Damm 1975 Sby 5/93 112,500
I&S/Pa 24x17 Untitled 81 Sby 5/93 7,475
O,Br&/Pa 24x17 Baume 26, VII 76 Chr 11/92 4,950
I&C/Pa 24x17 Untitled 78 Sby 5/93 4,600
Basing, Charles Am 1865-1933
O/Cb 18x14 Archway into Village Chr 12/92 1,100
Baskin, Leonard Am 1922-
W&I/Pa 31x24 New Year; Antonement: (2) 1976 Chr 12/92 . 1,650
Basoli, Antonio It 1774-1848
* See 1991 Edition . . . .
Basquiat, Jean-Michel Fr 1961-1988
A&H/C 80x167 Jughead Chr 11/92 187,000
MM/C 96x146 Luna Park Sby 11/92 132,000
A,E&Os/C 50x50 Banker 82 Chr 11/92 110,000
A&Os/M 72x48 Untitled 1981 Chr 11/92 104,500
MM/C 56x34 Number 1 Sby 2/93 85,000
A&Os/C 52x74 Untitled Sby 2/93 71,250
A&Os/C 60x40 Untitled 85 Sby 2/93 68,500
A/C 72x72 Figure Four 1982 Chr 10/92 66,000
A,Ss&Os/C 60x48 Logo Chr 11/92 63,800
O,A&Os/C 69x64 Red Rabbit 1982 Sby 5/93 60,250
A,O&Os/C 60x60 Eating Birds Chr 11/92 55,000
A,E&Os/Wd 90x46 Untitled 85 Chr 10/92 49,500
Pe/Pa 40x50 Untitled 1986 Sby 11/92 38,500
A/Tn 37x13 Untitled Chr 11/92 11,000
Os/Pa 14x11 Untitled Chr 5/93 9,200
Os/Pa 14x11 Untitled Chr 5/93 9,200
Os/Pa 30x22 Untitled Chr 11/92 8,800
Os/Pa 30x24 Did the First Man Eat Pig? 1982 Chr 11/92 . . . 6,050
A&L/Cb 20x24 Untitled Chr 11/92 5,500
W,Fp&Y/Pa 22x15 Untitled Chr 11/92 5,500
Os/Pa 18x15 Untitled Chr 10/92 4,400
Os/Pn 20x20 Untitled Chr 2/93 3,850
I/Pa 34x44 Untitled (Torso) Sby 10/92 1,980
Y/Pa 18x12 Untitled Chr 11/92 1,650
Bassano, Francesc (the Younger) It 1549-1592
* See 1993 Edition . . . .
Bassano, Gerolamo 1566-1621
O/C 32x36 The Entombment Chr 5/93 6,325
Bassano, Jacopo It 1510-1592
* See 1992 Edition . . . .
Bassano, Leandro It 1557-1622
* See 1992 Edition . . . .
Basseporte, Madeleine-Francois Fr 1701-1780
* See 1990 Edition . . . .
Bassford, Wallace Am 1900-
O/C 35x45 Provincetown by Moonlight Skn 9/92 1,760
O/C 24x20 Zephyr Blown Eld 8/93 1,265
Bastiani, Lazzaro Di Jacopo It a 1425-1512
* See 1990 Edition . . . .
Bastien, Alfred Bel 1873-1955
O/C 43x37 Still Life of Red and White Roses Sel 12/92 . . . 5,500
Bastien-Lepage, Jules Fr 1848-1884
O/C 36x26 Les Enfants Pecheurs 1881 Sby 2/93 7,475
Baston Con 19C
O/C/B 23x27 Market Scene Slo 5/93 275
Batcheller, Frederick S. Am 1837-1889
O/C 10x14 Group of Pears Mys 3/93 1,760
O/C 30x18 Nasturtium Skn 11/92 825
Batchelor, Clarence D. Am 1888-1977
O/C 24x34 Nude at the Piano Mys 12/92 660
Pe&I/Pa 16x12 Artist Showing Painting Ih 11/92 225
Bateman, Charles Am 1890-
O/C 18x22 The Day's Catch Sby 6/93 4,025

Bateman, James Br 1814-1849
* See 1993 Edition . . . .
Bateman, Robert Br 19C
* See 1991 Edition . . . .
Bates, David 1952-
O/C 16x24 Woman by Creek Ald 5/93 650
Bates, David Br 1841-1921
* See 1993 Edition . . . .
Bates, Dewey Am 1851-1891
* See 1991 Edition . . . .
Bates, Kenneth Am 1895-1973
O/C 30x36 Madera Canyon Mys 3/93 275
Baton, Claude Am 20C
* See 1992 Edition . . . .
Battaglia, G. Bompiani It 19C
W/Pa 21x14 Flower Sellers of the Steps Hnz 5/93 1,100
Battaglie, Oracolo Delle It 1600-1658
* See 1993 Edition . . . .
Battista Dossi 1474-1548
O/C 21x14 The Flight Into Egypt Sby 1/93 31,625
Battista, Giovanni It 1858-1925
* See 1993 Edition . . . .
Battistello It 17C
* See 1990 Edition . . . .
Bauchant, Andre Fr 1873-1958
O/C 29x39 Santa Maria 1939 Chr 10/92 49,500
O/C 26x23 Fleurs 1929 Sby 11/92 35,750
O/C 34x39 Jeunes Filles a la Crique 1928 Chr 5/93 27,600
O/M 19x13 Portrait De Femme Sby 6/93 12,075
O/B 12x18 Le Porteur de Nouvelles 1939 Sby 6/93 5,750
Baude, Francois Charles Fr 1880-1953
O/C 102x79 Women Mending Fishing Nets 1924 But 11/92 . 3,300
Baudet, *
* See 1992 Edition . . . .
Baudit, Amedee Sws 1825-1890
* See 1993 Edition . . . .
Baudry, Paul Fr 1828-1886
* See 1991 Edition . . . .
Bauer, Carl Ferdinand Aus 1879-1954
* See 1990 Edition . . . .
Bauer, Johann Balthasar Ger 1811-1883
* See 1992 Edition . . . .
Bauer, Rudolf Ger 1889-1953
O/C 39x39 Fugue Chr 10/92 24,200
O/C 28x23 Titel Unbekannt Sby 2/93 21,850
O/C 32x48 Presto VIII Sby 10/92 17,600
O/B 29x41 Pizzicato Sby 10/92 15,400
G&W/Pa 20x26 Abstrakte Komposition Chr 5/93 5,175
W,Y&I/Pa 13x8 Untitled Sby 10/92 2,750
Bauer, William Am 1888-
O/C 16x12 Woodland Stream Wlf 5/93 150
Bauerle, Carl Wilhelm F. Ger 1831-1912
* See 1992 Edition . . . .
Bauermeister, Mary Am 1934-
* See 1993 Edition . . . .
Bauernfeind, Gustave Aus 1848-1904
* See 1993 Edition . . . .
Bauffe, V. Dut 20C
W/Pa 24x18 Sailboat Hnd 9/92 600
Baugin, Lubin Eur 1612-1633
* See 1990 Edition . . . .
Baugniet, Charles Bel 1814-1886
O/Pn 26x30 Les Confidantes Sby 10/92 20,900
Bauhofer, L. Aus 19C
O/B 5x4 Portrait of the Artist 1835 Wlf 9/92 1,800
Baum, Charles Am 1812-1878
* See 1992 Edition . . . .
Baum, Paul Ger 1859-1932
* See 1992 Edition . . . .
Baum, Walter Emerson Am 1884-1956
O/C 30x36 Winter Brook 1925 Chr 5/93 9,200
O/C 25x30 House, Road, and Trees Ald 3/93 5,200
O/B 12x14 Snowscape (2) 1926 Ald 9/92 3,300
O/B 25x30 Snowscape with River Ald 9/92 2,900
O/C 32x40 Of the Hill (Easton) Ald 3/93 2,750

O/C/B 16x20 Town and Creek 1927 Ald 5/93 2,750
O/C 21x28 In the Village Ald 5/93 2,500
O/C 25x30 Red Barn in Spring Ald 5/93 2,300
O/B 27x36 The Creeks Meet 1923 Ald 9/92 2,000
O/B 12x16 Old Lenape Lake 1929 Ald 3/93 1,800
O/B 14x17 Winter Scene Mys 12/92 1,760
O/B 10x8 House Blooming Trees by Creek Ald 9/92 1,700
O/C 16x20 Winter Landscape with Church Fre 4/93 1,400
O/B 12x16 Wile St. Manyunk 1946 Ald 9/92 1,050
G/Pa 8x12 Small Village Ald 5/93 1,000
O/B 16x20 River Hills Ald 3/93 950
O/C 16x20 Trumbauersville Road Ald 3/93 950
O/B 16x20 Poetic Snow Ald 9/92 900
O/B 16x20 Penna. Blossom Time Ald 3/93 800
O/B 16x20 Road to Town Ald 9/92 800
O/B 16x20 Spring Landscape Fre 4/93 700
O/B 3x5 Mauch Chunk Ald 9/92 650
O/M 26x34 The Frozen Stream 1932 Skn 11/92 605
MM/Pa 15x22 The Joining of Creeks Ald 9/92 500
O/B 10x12 Cat Hill Country Ald 9/92 350
O/B 3x5 Village Street Ald 9/92 250
W/Pa 3x6 Christmas Card Ald 5/93 115

Baumann, Karl Herman Am 1911-1984
W/Pa 16x13 Tropical River 40 But 10/92 1,100
Baumeister, Willi Ger 1889-1955
* See 1991 Edition . . . .
Baumes, Amedee Fr 1820-
* See 1991 Edition . . . .
Baumgartner, H. Ger 19C
* See 1992 Edition . . . .
**Baumgartner, Johann Wolfgang
1712-1761**
* See 1993 Edition . . . .
Baumgartner, Peter Ger 1834-1898
* See 1993 Edition . . . .
Baumgartner, Warren Am 1894-1963
W/Pa 14x20 Clock Lighthouse on the Clyde Mys 3/93 247
Baumhofer, Walter M. Am 1904-
* See 1991 Edition . . . .
Baur, H.
O/C 12x16 Kittens Dum 6/93 500
Baure, Albert Fr -1930
O/C 18x13 Promenade in the Park Sby 1/93 1,610
Baxter, Martha Wheeler Am 1869-1955
O/Cb 14x18 Near Palm Springs Cathedral City Lou 12/92 . . . 50
Bayard, Emile Antoine Fr 1837-1891
O/Pn 14x12 Monsieur dans le Salon But 11/92 2,200
Bayes, A. W. Eng 19C
O/C 24x18 Courting Scene Mys 3/93 935
Bayeu, Ramon
* See 1990 Edition . . . .
Bayne, Walter McPherson Am 1795-1859
O/C 12x18 Ponkapog Brook, Canton, Mass. 1817 Sby 3/93 1,725
Bazaine, Jean Fr 1904-
* See 1990 Edition . . . .
Bazile, Alberoi Hai 20C
O/M 24x20 Barnyard Scene Skn 9/92 302
Bazile, Castera Hai 20C
O/M 24x30 Women by the River 56 Sby 5/93 5,750
Baziotes, William A. Am 1912-1963
O/C 36x41 The Balcony Sby 2/93 28,750
I/Pa 13x18 Untitled Sby 10/92 6,600
Bazzani, Giuseppe It 1690-1769
* See 1991 Edition . . . .
Bazzani, Luigi
* See 1993 Edition . . . .
Bazzaro, Leonardo It 1853-1937
* See 1993 Edition . . . .
Beach, Thomas Br 1738-1806
* See 1993 Edition . . . .
Beal, Gifford Am 1879-1956
O/B 20x24 Bass Rocks, Gloucester Chr 5/93 79,500
O/Pn 24x36 Park Riders '20 Sby 5/93 35,650
O/B 12x18 Round Up at the Circus Sby 12/92 6,600
O/B 6x16 Beach at Provincetown 20 Chr 3/93 5,175

O/C 20x27 Circus Scene Mys 3/93 4,620
O&MM/B 20x24 Scene from Rosenkavalier '35 Mor 6/93 . . 3,300
G&Pe/Pa 10x15 Old Houses Chr 12/92 1,430
W/Pa 10x13 Circus at Newburgh Hnd 12/92 550
W/Pa 14x19 Sword Fisherman Skn 11/92 220
Beal, Jack Am 1931-
O/C 66x78 Sandra on a Sofa Sby 10/92 16,500
O/C 26x22 Bouquet of Tulips Sby 2/93 5,750
O/C 50x52 The Chair Doy 11/92 2,640
Beal, Reynolds Am 1867-1951
O/B 25x34 Boat Marina at Provincetown 1917 Sby 12/92 . 23,100
Y,W&Pe/Pa 11x14 Circus Scene w/Animals 1929 Sby 9/92 . 3,575
Cp/Pa 13x16 Gorham Bros. Circus 1936 Sby 9/92 3,575
Cp/Pa 13x19 Circus Scene with Ferris Wheel Sby 3/93 . . . 2,070
Y&MM/Pa 16x18 Circus Girls 1936 Brd 2/93 1,980
Cp/Pa Size? Sparks Circus 1930 Sby 9/92 1,760
Pe/Pa 12x12 Carnival in Gloucester 1948 Sby 9/92 1,430
Y/Pa 10x14 Pagliacci Circus 1918 Slo 7/93 1,400
Y/Pa 13x15 Circus Roustabouts 1924 Hnd 5/93 1,000
O/B 12x16 Sailboats 1935 Hnd 5/93 800
P&Y/Pa 8x10 Rockport, September 1941 Yng 5/93 600
Pe/Pa 7x10 Three Sketches of Sailboats Yng 5/93 175
Beal, William T.
* See 1991 Edition . . . .
Beale, J. B. Br 19C
O/C/M 32x17 Male Academy Sby 1/93 1,610
Beale, Mary 1633-1697
* See 1992 Edition . . . .
Beall, Cecil Calvert Am 1892-1967
W/Pa 18x12 Couple Embracing Ih 5/93 900
O/B 14x11 Man Rehearsing Speech Ih 5/93 250
Bean, Ainslie Br a 1880-1890
W/Pa 19x13 Mending the Nets Brd 2/93 550
Bean, Carolina Van Hook Am 1880-1970
K/Pa 18x11 Dorothea Morgan and Mrs. Robinson Slo 4/93 . . 100
Beard, Alice Am 20C
O/C 32x39 The Carrousel 1928 Sby 9/92 2,530
Beard, James Henry Am 1812-1893
O/C 15x12 Resting Pups 1872 Doy 5/93 2,750
O/C 30x25 Portrait of a Young Boy 1857 Sby 9/92 605
Beard, William Holbrook Am 1824-1900
O/C 38x59 The Witches Convention 1876 Sby 5/93 79,500
C/Pa 35x47 The Witches' Ride 1870 Sby 5/93 10,350
Bearden, Romare Am 1914-1988
A&L/B 45x51 Kansas City Sby 2/93 71,250
L/B 19x15 The Tenement World 1969 Sby 2/93 16,100
W&L/B 15x9 Untitled Sby 11/92 12,100
L/Pb 9x11 Untitled (Church) Sby 5/93 9,200
W&Pl/Pa/B 26x20 Untitled Chr 10/92 8,800
MM&L/M 9x12 Untitled Sby 10/92 8,800
L/B 17x11 Two Figures in a Landscape Sby 10/92 7,425
W/Pa 30x22 Northern Shore Chr 2/93 4,180
W/Pa 8x11 Morning Cul de Sac Sby 10/92 3,080
W&Pe/Pa 9x13 Vere's Garden Sby 10/92 2,420
Beardsley, George O. Am 20C
W/Pa 8x17 Rocky Mountain View Yng 3/93 60
Beare, George Eng a 1744-1749
O/C 35x27 Portrait Capt G B Rodney 1744 Sby 10/92 . . . 19,800
Beaton, Cecil
W,Pe&G/Pa 18x13 Portrait of Queen Alexandra Sby 2/93 . 1,380
G/Pa/B 14x11 Costume Design for La Traviata Sby 2/93 748
Beattie, George Eng 19C
O/C 24x42 English Squire at Gypsy Camp Slo 5/93 650
Beattie-Brown, William Br 1831-1909
O/C 15x22 Loch Cor-Arder, Inverness-Shire Sby 1/93 1,495
Beatty, John William Can 1869-1941
O/Pn 11x14 Pickerel Lake, Haliburton Sbt 5/93 1,980
O/B 9x11 Cottage on a Lane Sbt 5/93 1,320
O/Pn 11x9 Forest Interior Sbt 11/92 1,320
Beauchamp, Robert Am 20C
O/C 60x60 Rainbow Sby 3/93 1,840
H/Pa 37x80 Foot Sby 3/93 1,265
O/B 28x39 Harpy Sby 2/93 690
Beaudin, Andre Fr 1895-1979
O/C 17x24 Femme Nue Allongee 1932 Chr 5/93 4,025

38

Beauduin, Jean   Bel 1851-1916
O/C 24x29 A Summer's Eve Sby 10/92 7,150
O/C 24x29 An Afternoon on the Veranda 1899 Chr 2/93 ... 5,500
O/C 24x29 Printemps 1900 Sby 1/93 4,600
Beaugureau, Francis Henry   Am 1920-
A/C 30x43 Military Drill Chr 12/92 3,520
Beaulieu, Paul Vanier   Can 1910-
* See 1993 Edition ....
Beaumont, Arthur   Am 1879-1978
* See 1992 Edition ....
Beauquesne, Wilfrid Constant   Fr 1847-1913
O/C 26x33 Battle Scene 1891 But 5/93 2,300
O/C 26x33 A Cavalry Encounter Chr 10/92 1,650
Beauvais, Armand   Fr 1840-1911
* See 1992 Edition ....
Beauverie, Charles Joseph   Fr 1839-1924
O/Pn 18x15 Faggot Gatherers 1874 Sel 9/92 850
O/Pn 18x15 Faggot Gatherers 1874 Sel 12/92 800
Beaux, Cecilia   Am 1855-1942
O/C 67x34 Portrait of Alice Davison Chr 12/92 363,000
O/C 36x29 Dressing Dolls Hnd 3/93 76,000
O/C 74x39 Portrait Mrs. Robert Abbe Sby 3/93 57,500
Beavis, Richard   Br 1824-1896
* See 1992 Edition ....
Beccafumi, Domenico   It 1486-1551
* See 1993 Edition ....
Beccaria, Angelo   It 1820-1897
* See 1992 Edition ....
Becher, Arthur E.   Am 1877-1960
* See 1993 Edition ....
Becher, Bernd and Hilla   20C
Ph/B 48x37 Spherical Gas Tanks 1984 Chr 11/92 42,900
Ph/B 60x48 Winding Towers 1967-1978 Chr 2/93 35,200
Ph 16x12 Winding Towers Germ. France Britain Chr 10/92 16,500
Ph 59x43 Cooling Towers (Wood) (B) 1976 Chr 11/92 ... 15,400
Ph 36x42 Preparation Plants (Germany) Sby 11/92 7,700
Ph 24x20 Storage Gas Tank; Water Tower: 2 Sby 5/93 .. 5,463
Ph/Cd 16x12 Cooling Tower Sby 5/93 2,875
Bechi, Luigi   It 1830-1919
O/C 33x48 Musical Respite Sby 5/93 31,050
O/C 38x27 The Comforting Shepherd Sby 5/93 12,075
Bechtle, Robert   Am 1932-
* See 1993 Edition ....
Beck, A. R.   Am 20C
O/B 11x18 Caravan 1886 Hnd 10/92 425
Beck, Dunbar D.   Am 1902-1986
* See 1992 Edition ....
Beck, I. F.   Scn 19C
* See 1990 Edition ....
Beck, Jacob Samuel   1715-1778
* See 1992 Edition ....
Beck, John Augustus   Am 1831-1918
W&G/Pa 14x14 Coastal Views: Two 1882 Slo 4/93 250
Beck, Otto Walter   Am 1864-
P/B 43x33 Portrait of a Woman 1916 Sby 3/93 3,300
Becker, Carl   Ger 1862-1926
O/C 35x27 Karneval von Venedig But 5/93 3,450
Becker, Carl Ludwig Friedrich   Ger 1829-1900
O/C 50x38 Die Schmollenden 1861 Sby 10/92 17,050
Becker, Charlotte   Am 1907-
O/C 24x17 Baby in Rocking Chair Ih 11/92 1,700
Becker, Ludwig Hugo   Ger 1833-1868
O/C 43x62 Going to Church 1867 Sby 5/93 8,625
Becker, Maurice   Am 1889-
W&Pe/Pa 19x23 Bathers 38 Sby 9/92 825
Beckett, Charles E.   Am 1814-1856
* See 1993 Edition ....
Beckhoff, Harry   Am 1901-1979
I&W/Pa 15x11 Fishermen Astounded Ih 11/92 1,300
Beckman, Ford   1952-
MM/C/Pn 88x125 Black Wall Chair Painting 1989 Chr 2/93 . 1,210
Beckman, William   20C
* See 1991 Edition ....

Beckmann, Max   Am 1884-1950
* See 1993 Edition ....
Beckwith, Arthur   Am 1860-1930
* See 1993 Edition ....
Beckwith, James Carroll   Am 1852-1917
O/C 24x19 Under the Lilacs 1879 Sby 3/93 8,050
Bectles, E. F.
O/Pn 10x15 Ships on Rough Seas Dum 3/93 550
Beeb, E.   20C
O/C 60x42 Girl in Riding Attire 1921 Sel 2/93 750
Beechey, Richard Brydges   Br 1808-1895
* See 1990 Edition ....
Beechey, Sir William   Br 1753-1839
* See 1993 Edition ....
Beeldmaker, Adriaen-Cornelisz.   1625-1701
O/C 18x24 Cocker Spaniels in a Landscape 1692 Chr 10/92 3,520
Beelt, Cornelis   Dut 1660-1702
* See 1991 Edition ....
Beer, Wilhelm-Amandus   Ger 1837-1890
O/B 15x19 Russian Troika 1872 Wlf 3/93 4,000
Beerstraten, Jan   Dut 1622-1666
* See 1992 Edition ....
Beert I, Osias   Flm 1570-1624
* See 1990 Edition ....
Beert, Osias   Flm 1622-1678
* See 1990 Edition ....
Bega, Cornelis   Dut 1631-1664
* See 1990 Edition ....
Beggs, Helene Warder   Am 20C
O/B 18x12 Pair: Abstract Compositions Hnd 3/93 900
Behrens, Howard   Am 20C
* See 1993 Edition ....
Beich, Joachim Franz   1665-1748
* See 1993 Edition ....
Beigel, Peter   Br 1913-
* See 1990 Edition ....
Beinke, Fritz   Ger 1842-1907
* See 1993 Edition ....
Bel-Geddes, Norman   20C
* See 1991 Edition ....
Belanger, Francois-Joseph   Fr 1744-1818
I&S/Pa 12x8 Design for an Urn Slo 7/93 1,300
Belanger, Louis   Fr 1736-1816
* See 1993 Edition ....
Belarski, Rudolph   Am 1900-1983
O/B 25x19 Native Woman Whipping Cowering Man Ih 11/92 1,100
Belknap, Zedekiah   Am 1781-1858
* See 1992 Edition ....
Bell, Cecil C.   Am 1906-1970
O/M 30x40 Getting Acquainted Chr 12/92 11,000
Bell, Charles   1935-
O/C 50x66 Bunny Cycle Sby 5/93 60,250
G,K&H/B 32x40 A Study for the Journey '83 Chr 11/92 .. 16,500
Bell, Charles   Am 1874-1935
* See 1991 Edition ....
Bell, Edward August   Am 1862-1953
* See 1992 Edition ....
Bell, Larry   Am 1939-
A/Pa 52x36 Vapor Drawing 82 But 4/93 2,070
A/Pa 28x21 Vapor Drawing 78 But 4/93 690
Pg/Pa 51x36 Elipse But 10/92 660
Bell, Leland   Am 1922-
O/B 29x15 Self-Portrait Sby 3/93 1,150
Bell, Phillip   Am 1907-
* See 1993 Edition ....
Bell-Smith, Frederic Marlett   Can 1846-1923
O/Pn 5x4 Carlton Street; Church Street: Pair Sbt 11/92 3,872
O/B 9x11 Dusk, Westminster Bridge, London Sbt 5/93 2,860
W/Pa 7x11 The Strand, London, 1898 Sbt 11/92 2,464
W/Pa 24x16 View in the Rockies Sbt 11/92 2,200
W/Pa 18x24 Canadian Deep Sea Fishing Sbt 5/93 1,496
W/Pa 23x16 Gorge in the Rockies Sbt 11/92 1,408
W/Pa 8x12 Village Scene with Figures 1913 Sbt 5/93 1,408

W/Pa 19x13 Fraser Canyon '06 Sbt 5/93 1,056
W/Pa 10x15 Mountain Cabin Sbt 5/93 880
O/Pa 10x8 Birches Sbt 5/93 704
W/Pa 8x13 Rowboat on River '92 Dum 8/93 500
Bellandi, E.   It 1842-
O/C 17x14 Old Man Having a Midday Snack Chr 2/93 1,320
Bellange, Joseph Louis Hippoly   Fr 1800-1866
O/C 18x11 Soldiers Mys 3/93 1,320
Bellanger, Camille Felix   Fr 1853-1923
* See 1993 Edition . . . .
Bellanger, Georges   Fr 1847-1918
* See 1991 Edition . . . .
Bellefleur, Leon   Can 1910-
O/C 20x24 Trinidad '69 Sbt 5/93 6,160
Bellei, Gaetano   It 1857-1922
O/C Size? The Winning Hand Sby 2/93 24,150
Bellei, Jean Joseph Francois   Fr 1816-1898
* See 1992 Edition . . . .
Bellenge, Michel-Bruno   Fr 1726-1793
O/C 11x9 Still Life Flowers in Crystal Vase Sby 5/93 . . . 21,850
Bellerman, Ferdinand   Ger 1814-1889
* See 1990 Edition . . . .
Bellevois, Jacob Adriaensz.   Dut 1621-1675
* See 1993 Edition . . . .
Belli, A***
* See 1992 Edition . . . .
Belli, Giovacchino   It 1756-1882
* See 1990 Edition . . . .
Bellias, Richard   Fr 1921-1974
O/C 22x15 Anemones Skn 5/93 467
Bellini, Giovanni   It 1430-1516
* See 1991 Edition . . . .
Bellis, Hubert   Bel 1831-1902
O/C 60x40 Fall Flowers Chr 10/92 8,800
O/C 26x19 Still Life Wine and Fruit Sel 9/92 2,200
Bellmer, Hans   Fr 1902-1975
Pe&G/Pa/B 6x4 Sade 46 Chr 10/92 2,860
Belloli, Andrei Franzowitsch   Rus -1881
* See 1992 Edition . . . .
Bellon, Jean   Fr 1941-
* See 1992 Edition . . . .
Bellotti, Pietro   It 1627-1700
* See 1991 Edition . . . .
Bellotto, Bernardo   1721-1780
O/C 19x28 Rome Along the Tiber Chr 5/93 . . . . 1.1025M
Bellows, Albert Fitch   Am 1829-1883
O/C 20x30 Country Life Chr 12/92 46,200
O/C 10x18 Landscape with Seated Figure Wlf 9/92 1,800
Bellows, George Wesley   Am 1882-1925
O/Pn 20x24 Sanctuario 1917 Chr 12/92 198,000
O/Pn 15x19 West Wind Sby 12/92 85,250
O/C 20x24 Trout Stream and Mountains Sby 5/93 43,125
O/Pn 20x24 Mountain Orchard Chr 12/92 33,000
Y/Pa/B 11x14 Nude Reclining Chr 12/92 5,280
Pe/Pa 9x6 Jean Chr 3/93 4,830
C&Y/Pa/B 12x9 The Prisoner Sby 12/92 1,760
Pe/Pa 8x6 Fur Cuffs and Boa Hnz 5/93 275
Bellucci, Antonio   It 1654-1726
O/C 51x39 Allegory of Charity Sby 1/93 14,375
Beloff, Angelina   Rus 1884-1967
* See 1993 Edition . . . .
Beltran-Masses, Frederico   Spa 1885-1949
* See 1992 Edition . . . .
Bemelmans, Ludwig   Am 1898-1963
O/C 42x30 Sacre Coeur and Nun Sby 3/93 4,025
Bemish, T. Hills   Am 20C
W/Pa 20x29 Shepherdess with Sheep Sel 9/92 170
Benard, Jean-Baptiste   18C
* See 1992 Edition . . . .
Benassit, Louis Emile   Fr 1833-1902
* See 1992 Edition . . . .

Benedetti, Andrea   It 1615-1649
* See 1991 Edition . . . .
Benedikter, Alois Josef   Ger 1843-1931
O/C 15x21 Interior Genre Scene 1881 Skn 3/93 3,300
O/C 11x13 Monastery on Hill Sel 12/92 150
Beneker, Gerrit A.   Am 1882-1934
O/C 24x20 Portrait of Artist's Daughter Mys 3/93 770
Benezit, Emmanuel Charles   1887-1975
O/C 29x36 Cote Mediterranee, France 1920 Chr 11/92 . . 1,760
Benfatti, Alvise   It 1550-1609
* See 1993 Edition . . . .
Bengston, Billy Al   Am 1934-
A/C 44x78 Punta Entrada Draculas I & II (2) Chr 2/93 6,050
W/Pa 42x29 August Watercolor Sby 12/92 2,200
Benites
O/Cp 15x13 La Sagrada Trinidad Sby 5/93 9,775
Benlliure Y Gil, Jose   Spa 1855-1914
O/C 18x28 The Generosity of the Church Chr 10/92 63,800
O/Pn 21x15 Unconscious Sinners Chr 10/92 60,500
Benlliure Y Gil, Mariano   Spa 1862-
* See 1993 Edition . . . .
Benlliure Y Ortiz, Jose   Spa 1884-1916
* See 1993 Edition . . . .
Benn, Ben   Am 1884-1983
O/C 14x18 Sunset '53 '53 Fre 4/93 500
Bennett, Francis I.   Am 1876-
O/C 25x30 Boats at Martiques Hnd 5/93 3,200
Bennett, Frank Moss   Br 1874-1953
O/C 14x20 At the Wig Shop 1933 Chr 10/92 3,300
O/C 20x16 Drs. Johnson Bogdwell & Garrick 1946 Chr 5/93 3,220
O/C 15x12 Serenading the Yellow Canary 1903 Chr 5/93 . . 1,035
O/C 14x20 After the Hunt 1925 Chr 10/92 990
O/C 15x12 Serenading the Yellow Canary 1903 Chr 10/92 . . 825
Bennett, J. Maynard   Am 20C
N/C 12x9 Hollywood, French, Roma (4) Hnd 12/92 750
Bennett, Joseph   Am 1899-
O/C 30x40 Ceaseless Attack, West Coast But 10/92 1,650
Benois, Alexander Nikolaevich   Rus 1870-1960
Pe,I&G/Pa 13x9 Le Roi Nu: Costume Design Sby 10/92 990
W&Pe/Pa 19x13 Costume Design 1923 Sby 6/93 920
W/Pa 8x10 View of Lake Lugano 1908 Yng 2/93 700
Benois, Nicolai   Rus 1902-
* See 1992 Edition . . . .
Benoit, Rigaud   Hai 20C
O/M 30x24 La Duchesse Noire Chr 11/92 29,700
O/M 28x33 Sansive Pas Joue 60 Sby 11/92 17,600
O/M 24x30 The Shipwreck 74 Chr 11/92 12,100
Benoit-Levy, Jules   Fr 1866-
* See 1993 Edition . . . .
Bensell, George Frederick   Am 1837-1879
O/C 24x42 River Landscape with Indians Fre 10/92 2,800
O/C 28x16 Rapids and Rocks Fre 4/93 375
Benson, Frank Weston   Am 1862-1951
O/C 30x24 Portrait Emily V. Binney 1894 Sby 12/92 55,000
W&H/Pa 21x14 Camden Hills '23 Skn 3/93 6,600
W&R/Pa 12x20 Flying Geese 1903 Sby 9/92 3,520
O/Pn 7x5 Shore Landscape Hnz 5/93 800
Pe/Pa 11x8 Herons Brd 2/93 660
Benson, Townley   Am 20C
O/C 13x9 Desert Dwellings Yng 2/93 100
Benson, W.   Am 20C
O/C 18x28 Interior of a Barn with Sheep Sel 9/92 200
Bentivoglio, Ceasare
O/Pn 20x28 Coastal City in Italy Eld 8/93 412
Bentley, Claude   Am 1915-
O/M 12x36 Composition '52 Hnd 3/93 400
G/Pa 10x15 Abstraction '58 Hnd 5/93 200
Bentley, John William   Am 1880-1951
O/C 16x20 Winter Symphony Fre 4/93 2,100
O/C 24x32 Early Snow and Sunlight Sby 3/93 1,840
O/Cb 16x12 Old Colonial Church Sby 3/93 403
Benton, Dwight   Am 1834-
* See 1993 Edition . . . .

Benton, Fletcher Am 1931-
* See 1993 Edition . . . .
Benton, Thomas Hart Am 1889-1975
O/Cb 12x16 Loading Cotton '44 Sby 12/92 71,500
A/Pa 18x24 On Menemsha Pond '71 Sby 12/92 66,000
W&Pe/B 22x26 Fishermen's Camp, Buffalo River Chr 5/93 57,500
O/C 16x20 Waiting Sby 5/93 51,750
Pe/Pa 10x13 Study for Poker Night 48 Chr 12/92 30,800
O/C/B 16x12 The Crapshooters Chr 12/92 28,600
O/Cb 8x10 Study for the Changing West Sby 9/92 26,400
Pl&Pe/Pa 11x15 Sugar Mill A Chr 5/93 14,950
Pl&W/Pa 15x10 Cotton Pickers with Windmill Chr 12/92 . . 13,200
O/Pa 10x7 Landscape with Trees Sby 3/93 9,200
Pl,W&Pe/Pa 15x10 Cotton Pickers Chr 12/92 8,800
W&I/Pa 10x15 Cotton Pickers Sby 9/92 7,150
Pl&S/Pa 19x14 Study Apple of Discord: (2) '47 Chr 5/93 . . 6,325
W&P/Pa 19x16 Pine Trees Chr 9/92 5,500
O&R/Pa 10x7 King Philip Chr 9/92 4,400
O&I/B 8x9 Farm Scene Chr 12/92 3,300
Pe/Pa 11x9 Figures, Hills and Port Chr 5/93 1,380
Pe/Pa 4x9 Torso, Horses, Coal Mine (4) Chr 12/92 825
Benvenuti, Eugenio It 19C
W/Pa 10x16 Venice Fre 10/92 325
W/Pa 15x27 Grand Canal, Venice Hnd 3/93 300
W/Pa 10x15 Venetian Canal View Slo 4/93 300
W/Pa 10x15 Venice Fre 10/92 250
W/Pa 16x10 Canal in Venice Fre 10/92 190
Benwell, Austin Joseph Br 19C
* See 1991 Edition . . . .
Berard, Christian Fr 1902-1949
O/B 42x33 Personnage en rouge et vert 30 Chr 11/92 . . 17,600
Berard, Desire Honore Fr 1845-
* See 1992 Edition . . . .
Beraud, Jean Fr 1849-1936
O/Pn 9x6 The Music Hall Singer Chr 10/92 38,500
Berchem, Nicolaes Pietersz. Ger 1620-1683
* See 1993 Edition . . . .
Berchere, Narcisse Fr 1819-1891
* See 1992 Edition . . . .
Berchmans, Emile Bel 1867-
O/C 36x24 Assorted Roses in an Imari Vase 1910 Chr 2/93 7,150
Berczy, William Von Moll Can 1744-1813
* See 1991 Edition . . . .
Berea, Dimitri Am 1908-1975
O/C 36x29 Le Jardin Japonais Sby 6/93 3,163
O/C 22x18 Bouquets de Fleurs Dans L'Atelier 49 Chr 5/93 . 1,380
Berentz, Christian Ger 1658-1722
* See 1993 Edition . . . .
Beresford, Frank Ernest Eng 1881-1962
O/Pn 8x11 Maarken '24 Wes 5/93 440
Berg, Fred* Dut 19C**
O/Pn 8x10 Cows Grazing by Lake Sby 1/93 1,093
Berg, George Louis Am 1870-1941
* See 1992 Edition . . . .
Bergamann, Julius Hugo Ger 1861-1940
* See 1990 Edition . . . .
Bergamini, Francesco It 1815-1883
O/C 33x20 Thirsty Traveller's Respite Sby 1/93 9,775
O/C 18x27 Tavern Scene Fre 4/93 8,500
O/C 12x19 Flirtation Sby 10/92 5,500
Bergen, Claus Ger 20C
* See 1992 Edition . . . .
Berger, Ernst Aus 1857-1919
* See 1991 Edition . . . .
Berger, Hans Sws 1882-
* See 1993 Edition . . . .
Berger, Ronald Aus 1943-
O/B 4x5 Still Life Dum 6/93 800
O/B 5x6 Still Life Dum 7/93 800
O/B 5x6 Still Life Dum 7/93 750
Bergeret, Denis Pierre Fr 1846-1910
* See 1993 Edition . . . .
Bergey, Earle K. Am 1901-1952
* See 1993 Edition . . . .

Bergier, Joseph Dut 1753-1829
* See 1991 Edition . . . .
Bergmann, Julius H. Ger 1861-1940
* See 1993 Edition . . . .
Berhas, Frans Bel 1827-1897
* See 1990 Edition . . . .
Beringuier, Eugene Fr 1874-1949
* See 1993 Edition . . . .
Berjon, Antoine Fr 1754-1843
* See 1993 Edition . . . .
Berk, Henrietta Am 20C
O/C 33x38 Summer Landscape But 4/93 1,035
O/C 52x42 Wheat Sby 6/93 690
Berke, Ernest Am 1921-
O/Cb 12x16 Reclining Nude '81 Sby 3/93 863
Berke, Troy Am 20C
* See 1992 Edition . . . .
Berkeley, Stanley Br 1855-1909
* See 1992 Edition . . . .
Berkey, Ben Am 20C
W/Pa 21x29 The Antagonist Wlf 5/93 150
Berkhammer
O/C 14x20 Dutch Landscape Eld 8/93 440
Berkowitz, Leon Am 20C
O/C 52x60 Untitled (Stripe) 1966 Wes 3/93 3,520
A/C 57x75 Circular I '82 Wes 3/93 2,310
Berlant, Tony Am 1941-
MM&L/Pn 49x61 Steering Wheel But 4/93 6,325
E/Me 27x27 The Queen of Clubs Chr 11/92 3,080
Berman, Eugene Am 1889-1972
O/C 40x26 L'Eglise Santa Giustina 1931 Sby 2/93 13,800
O/C 36x29 Vue Imaginaire 1928 Sby 6/93 5,463
O/C 40x28 Lady from Parma 1942 Sby 2/93 4,600
O/C 16x12 Trio 1954 Sby 2/93 3,335
O/C 18x12 Antique Fragments 1954 Sby 2/93 2,300
G&I/B 17x14 El Volcano 1949 Sby 6/93 1,840
G&I/Pa 16x11 Ballet Imperial: Costume 1949 Sby 10/92 . . 1,760
O/C/B 29x36 Coucher de Soleil 1931 But 12/92 1,760
G&I/Pa 14x11 Design Les Ballets: Double 1950 Sby 10/92 . 1,100
I&Pe/Pa 13x10 Two Program Designs 1950 Sby 10/92 880
Pl/Pa 12x9 Fountain Design (2) 1949 Sby 2/93 690
Berman, Leonid Am 1896-1976
O/C 22x32 Calfatage 36 Sby 10/92 1,980
Berman, Wallace Am 1926-1976
* See 1991 Edition . . . .
Bermudez, Cundo Cub 1914-
O/B 18x14 Jimaguas Sby 5/93 29,900
G/Pa 35x25 Hombre En Rojo Sby 5/93 18,400
H,O&G/Pa 29x23 Los Danzoneros 54 Sby 5/93 17,250
Bernadotte, Prins Eugen Swd 20C
* See 1991 Edition . . . .
Bernara, L. Fr 19C
O/Pn 21x17 Arab Marketplace Chr 10/92 1,100
Bernard, Emile Fr 1868-1941
O/C 25x32 Les Baigneuses Chr 5/93 8,050
W/Pa 11x16 Constantinople '43 But 11/92 2,475
Bernard, Jean Joseph Fr 1864-1933
O/Pn 21x10 Psyche But 11/92 2,200
Bernardo, Monsu Dan 1624-1687
* See 1992 Edition . . . .
Bernath, Sandor Am 1892-
W/Pa 16x21 Yachting Skn 9/92 1,210
W&I/Pa 15x20 Two Marine Scenes Skn 5/93 935
Berndtson, Gunnar Swd 1854-1895
* See 1992 Edition . . . .
Berne-Bellecour, Etienne P. Fr 1838-1910
O/Pn 20x14 Climbing over the Stone Wall Chr 5/93 12,650
O/Pn 18x24 Officer's Repast Sby 10/92 11,550
O/C 10x15 Infantry Men Chr 5/93 2,760
O/Pn 15x10 Momento of Battle Sby 10/92 2,530
O/Pn 12x16 Military Manoeuvres 1897 Chr 10/92 2,420
O/Pn 15x11 Sailor by the Sea But 5/93 862
Berneker, Louis Frederick Am 1876-1937
O/C 24x20 Woman Sewing in an Interior Chr 5/93 1,840

Berni, Antonio   Arg 1905-
O/B 32x39 Paisaje con Silos 53 Chr 11/92   19,800
O/C 24x32 Paisaje Sby 5/93   10,350
Berninger, Edmund   Ger 1843-
* See 1993 Edition
Berninger, John E.
O/B 12x15 Winter Landscape 1927 Ald 9/92   150
Berninghaus, Charles   Am 1905-1971
* See 1993 Edition
Berninghaus, Oscar E.   Am 1874-1952
O/C 16x20 On the Trail, Winter Chr 12/92   22,000
O/Cb 16x20 After the Storm Chr 3/93   14,950
W/Pa 15x20 Hills of Taxco Sby 12/92   9,350
O/B 9x13 Resting in the Shade Sby 3/93   7,475
Bernstein, Theresa   Am 1890-
O/C 28x36 Hawthorne Inn '15 Sby 9/92   13,200
O/C 27x35 The Art Party 23 Skn 11/92   9,350
O/C 30x39 Preparedness Parade 1916 Skn 5/93   8,250
O/C 23x25 Suffrages Parade 12 Skn 5/93   4,950
O/C 19x23 Coney Island Beach Scene 15 Skn 11/92   4,400
O/C 27x36 Spuyten Duyvil 23 Chr 9/92   3,300
O/C 22x25 Suffrage Parade 1912 Skn 11/92   3,025
O/B 15x20 Folley Cove, Gloucester, MA 1920 Lou 9/92 . . .   2,500
O/B 14x20 Gloucester/Norman's Woe 18 Skn 5/93   2,310
O/B 12x16 Folley Cove Point 16 Chr 5/93   1,380
O/B 9x8 Window Shopping 14 Skn 5/93   1,320
O/B 8x6 Purple Landscape Skn 5/93   440
Beronneau, Andre   1905-
O/C 20x26 Port de Saint-Tropez 1931 Chr 5/93   1,495
Beroud, Louis   Fr 1852-1910
* See 1993 Edition
Bert, Emile   Bel 1814-1847
* See 1992 Edition
Bertauld, P.   Fr 19C
* See 1992 Edition
Bertaux, Jacques   Fr 1745-1818
* See 1991 Edition
Berthelemy, Jean-Simon   Fr 1743-1811
* See 1990 Edition
Berthelsen, Johann   Am 1883-1969
O/C 24x36 Brooklyn Bridge 1902 Slo 7/93   5,500
O/C 24x30 Washington Square Park Wes 12/92   4,730
O/Cb 24x20 Times Square, New York Chr 9/92   3,850
O/C/B 20x16 The Red Cross Building Wes 10/92   2,970
O/C 16x12 Fifth Avenue, New York City Wes 10/92   2,420
O/C 20x24 Skating in Central Park Sby 9/92   1,870
O/Cb 20x16 Madison Square Wes 12/92   1,650
O/C 16x12 St. Paul's Chapel, New York Lou 3/93   1,650
O/Cb 16x12 Winter Snow Scene Sby 3/93   1,150
P/Pa/B 16x12 City Nocturne Skn 9/92   880
Berthot, Jake   Am 1939-
* See 1993 Edition
Bertin, Jean Victor   Fr 1775-1842
* See 1993 Edition
Bertin, Roger   Fr 1915-
* See 1990 Edition
Bertini, G.
W/Pa 18x29 Venetian Canal Scene Dum 2/93   900
Bertini, Gianni   It 1913-
W/Pa 18x29 Venetian Canal Scene Sel 9/92   750
Berton, Louis   Fr 19C
O/C 23x32 Leaving the Oasis Sby 1/93   3,163
Bertoni, Mae   Am 1929-
W/Pa 14x20 Fishing Cove Fre 10/92   160
Bertrand, James   Fr 1823-1887
* See 1993 Edition
Bertrand, Paulin Andre   Fr 1852-1940
* See 1993 Edition
Bertrand, Pierre-Philippe   Fr 1884-
* See 1993 Edition
Bertzy   Con 19C
* See 1992 Edition
Berwin, V.
O/C 14x11 Interior Scene with Girl FHB 6/93   125

Berzevizy, Julius   Hun 1875-
O/Cb 12x16 New England Harbor; Artist: (2) Chr 12/92   99
Beschey, Balthasar   Flm 1708-1776
* See 1991 Edition
Besnard, Paul Albert   Fr 1849-1934
O/C 32x26 Nude Bather 1930 Wes 12/92   4,95
O/C 29x23 Paul Wes 12/92   4,95
O/Pa 23x16 Portrait of an Ingenue 1889 Sby 2/93   3,45
Bess, Forrest   Am 1911-1977
* See 1993 Edition
Besser, Arne   20C
* See 1993 Edition
Bessinger, Frederick   Am 1886-1975
* See 1993 Edition
Bessire, Dale Philip   Am 1892-
* See 1992 Edition
Bessonot, Boris   Rus 19C
* See 1990 Edition
Best, Arthur William   Am 1859-1935
O/C 12x16 Lake Tahoe But 3/93   2,09
O/C 12x16 Cattle in Landscape Mor 2/93   1,40
O/B 10x14 Field of Flowers Dum 8/93   25
O/C 11x14 Bald Mountain, Marin County Hnd 9/92   22
Best, David   Am 1945-
MM/Pa 24x18 Tracing Michelangelo's Notte '80 But 10/92 . .   27
Best, Harry Cassie   Am 1863-1936
O/C 30x24 Riders in Yosemite Lou 12/92   2,25
O/C 30x36 Riders in Yosemite Lou 3/93   80
Best, John   Br a 1750-1792
O/C 36x50 Four Horses in Landscape Chr 6/93   10,35
Bethell, James   Br 19C
* See 1993 Edition
Bethune, Gaston   Fr 1857-1897
W/Pa 15x22 Une Route a Menton Chr 5/93   48
Betts   Am 19C
W/Pa 11x15 In a Chinese Port Brd 8/93   22
Betts, Ethel-Franklin   Am 20C
* See 1993 Edition
Betts, Harold Harrington   Am 1881-
O/C 30x33 Taos Nights Lou 12/92   1,05
Betts, Louis   Am 1873-1961
O/C 40x30 Seated Nude Yng 5/93   1,80
Beulas, Jose   Spa 20C
O/C 38x58 View of Avila FHB 3/93   20
Beuys, Joseph   Ger 1921-1986
MM 42x31 Show Your Wound Sby 11/92   24,75
O,Pl&Rs/Pa 13x8 Haupstraum Blatt I-II Chr 11/92   24,20
Fp&H/B 26x20 Ventilplastik 1948 Chr 10/92   13,75
I/Pa 39x9 Untitled 1975 Chr 11/92   9,35
Pe/Pa 8x17 Untitled 1960 Sby 5/93   6,32
Lh 13x9 Three Untitled Works Chr 11/92   1,76
Ss/Wd 4x6 Holzpostkart Sby 5/93   46
Bevans, Marjorie Torre
I&W/Pa 8x13 Two: Children Outdoors Ilh 11/92   50
Beyle, Pierre Marie   Fr 1838-1902
* See 1992 Edition
Beyschlag, Robert   Ger 1838-1903
* See 1993 Edition
Bezombes, Roger   1913-
O/F/B 39x39 Le Vase Syrien Chr 2/93   3,52
Bezzi, Bartolomeo   It 1851-1925
* See 1993 Edition
Bezzuoli, Giuseppe   It 1784-1855
O/C 8x18 Roman Warrior and Statesmen Slo 7/93   3,75
Biala, Janice   Am 1903-
O/C 35x46 Boat on Seine (Grey) 69 Sby 9/92   77
O,G&L/C 18x32 Coastal View Slo 4/93   8
Bianchi, C.   It 20C
* See 1992 Edition
Bianchi, Isidoro   It 1602-1690
* See 1991 Edition
Bianchi, Mose   It 1840-1904
* See 1991 Edition
Bianchini, Antonio   It 20C
* See 1992 Edition

anchini, E. It 20C
O/C 12x16 The Coast of Capri Wes 12/92 495
anchini, V. It 20C
O/C 24x31 La Caccia al Topo 76 Chr 5/93 1,955
O/C 24x32 Regalo al Priore 76 Chr 5/93 1,150
ard, Francois Auguste Fr 1799-1882
O/C 18x24 The Artist's Studio Sby 5/93 11,500
arke, F. Con 19C
O/Pn 17x12 Arab Musician Fre 4/93 800
O/Pn 17x12 Middle Eastern Musicians Fre 4/93 700
blena, Giuseppe Galli It 1696-1756
* See 1993 Edition . . . .
ckerstaff, George S. Am 1893-1954
O/C 28x32 Mountain Landscape with Lake Hnd 10/92 1,000
icknell, Albion Harris Am 1837-1915
O/C 25x30 Fishing Boat, Venice Brd 8/93 4,950
O/C 9x19 Bar Rocks, Annisquam 1864 Wes 3/93 660
icknell, Frank Alfred Am 1866-1943
O/Pa 10x8 A Windy Day Chr 12/92 1,760
dau, Eugene Fr 19C
O/Pn 15x21 Les Colombes 1886 Sby 5/93 8,338
dauld, Jean-Joseph-Xavier Fr
758-1846
O/Pn 15x20 Mountainous Landscape 1758 Sby 1/93 4,025
idlo, Mike Am 1954-
O&E/C 37x109 Arabesque Chr 2/93 13,200
O/C 52x111 Watery Ways, 1950 Chr 5/93 4,370
idner, Robert
A/Pn 60x48 Rolls Royce DKB 559 76 Sby 6/93 1,150
iederman, James 1947-
A,C&K/Pa 53x37 Roz-Ah 1982 Chr 11/92 3,300
O&K/C/Pn 31x89 Storyline 1984 Chr 11/92 2,200
iedermann, Eduard Am
* See 1992 Edition . . . .
iedermann-Arendts, Hermine Ger 1855-
O/C 27x37 Litter of Dachsunds Sby 6/93 2,070
iegel, Peter Br 1913-1988
O/C 16x20 Through the Paddocks Sby 6/93 3,738
W/Pa 8x16 At the Races Chr 6/93 1,380
iehle, August F. Am 1885-1979
W/Pa 16x10 Cuisii Crown Wlf 5/93 150
iehn, Joshua (Joseph) Can a 1891-1899
* See 1992 Edition . . . .
ieler, Andre Charles Can 1896-1989
A&O/C 12x16 La Berline 1976 Sbt 5/93 1,408
iennourry, Victor Francois E. Fr
823-1893
* See 1992 Edition . . . .
ienvetu, Gustav Fr 20C
* See 1992 Edition . . . .
ierhals, Otto Am 1879-1935
* See 1993 Edition . . . .
ierstadt, Albert Am 1830-1902
O/C 13x19 An Indian Encampment '61 Sby 5/93 695,500
O/C 30x44 Jenny Lake, Wyoming Sby 5/93 266,500
O/Pa/C 14x19 In the Foothills of the Rockies Chr 12/92 . . 45,100
O/C 30x44 View of the Grindelwald Sby 5/93 35,650
O/Pa/M 19x14 Palm Tree, Nassau Chr 5/93 29,900
O/B 4x6 Figures in Hudson River Landscape Sby 5/93 . . . 25,300
O/Pa/B 14x18 Western Landscape Sby 12/92 19,800
O/Pa 14x19 Wasatch Mountains, Utah Sby 5/93 18,400
O/B 6x9 Coastal Scene Chr 9/92 16,500
O/Pa 14x19 The Grand Tetons Chr 3/93 14,950
O/C 14x21 Village and Church Brd 8/93 12,100
O/Pa/B 8x15 Campfire, Yosemite Valley Chr 3/93 11,500
O/Pa/M 14x19 Western Mountain Lake Sby 9/92 10,450
O/Pa/C 12x19 Cows Grazing Doy 11/92 7,480
O/Pa/B 13x20 Yellowstone Park Dum 12/92 7,000
O/B 6x5 Snow Peaked Mountains Mys 3/93 5,775
O/Pa/B 11x15 Grand Tetons and Snake River Brd 8/93 5,500
O/Pa 8x13 Ruins Roman Campagna 1867 Sby 9/92 5,500
O/Pa 11x11 White Mountains Brd 8/93 5,500
O&Pe/Pa/B 8x12 Butterfly Chr 3/93 5,175
O/B 14x19 Moonlight Reflections Skn 5/93 3,850
O/Pa 13x12 Trees, Rocks, and Moss Brd 8/93 3,850

O/M 13x19 Cloud Study over Mountains Chr 12/92 2,420
O/Pa/B 19x14 Mountain by the Sea Dum 12/92 2,400
O/Pa/B 11x15 Mountainside Dum 12/92 2,400
Biessy, Marie-Gabriel Fr 1854-1935
* 1992 Edition . . . .
Bigaud, Wilson Hai 20C
O/M 24x30 Chickens 1965 Chr 11/92 3,300
O/M 24x48 Central Market Chr 11/92 2,750
O/M 24x36 Carnival Chr 11/92 2,640
O/M 24x16 Going to Mass Sby 6/93 1,150
Bigelow, Daniel Folger Am 1823-1910
* See 1993 Edition . . . .
Biggs, Walter Am 1886-1968
W/Pa 21x25 Floral Bouquet with Bowl and Vase Ilh 5/93 . . 2,400
G/Pa 13x28 Child in Snow, Wolf in Distance 1943 Ilh 11/92 . 550
Bigler, Maryann
W/Pa 15x20 Rooster and Chickens FHB 6/93 80
Bignoli, Antonio It 1812-1886
W/Pa 8x10 Seated Outdoors by a Veranda Chr 10/92 715
Bigordi, Davide 1452-1525
T/Pn 10x16 The Pieta, with Saints Chr 1/93 66,000
Bigot, Trophime Fr 1579-1650
O/C 39x52 Cupid and Psyche Chr 5/93 18,400
Bihan, D. L. Br a 1850-
* See 1991 Edition . . . .
Bihet, G. Fr 19C
* See 1992 Edition . . . .
Bill, Max Am 20C
* See 1992 Edition . . . .
Bille, Carl Dan 1815-1898
* See 1993 Edition . . . .
Billet, Etienne Fr 1821-1881
* See 1993 Edition . . . .
Billet, Pierre Fr 1837-1922
* See 1993 Edition . . . .
Billing, Frederick W. Am 1835-1914
O/C 12x30 Roof of the World--The Alps 1893 Hnz 5/93 . . . 200
O/Pa 7x10 Clouds at Sunset Hnz 5/93 170
O/Pa 7x10 Deserted Beach Hnz 5/93 160
Billmyer, James & Charlotte Am 20C
W&Pe/Pa 13x12 Couple in the Moonlight Ilh 11/92 325
Billou, Paul Fr 1821-
O/C/B 5x9 French Lovers Reading Dum 2/93 450
Bills, A. M. Am 20C
O/B 15x12 Cascading Stream Yng 2/93 80
Biltius, Jacobus Dut 1633-1681
* See 1991 Edition . . . .
Bimmermann, Caesar Ger 19C
* See 1991 Edition . . . .
Binder, Jacob Ger 20C
* See 1992 Edition . . . .
Binet, Adolphe Gustave Fr 1854-1897
* See 1992 Edition . . . .
Binet, Georges Fr 1865-1949
* See 1992 Edition . . . .
Binet, Victor Baptiste B. Fr 1849-1924
O/C 18x15 Le Toit Rouge Sby 2/93 6,900
O/C 26x37 Field with Cattle But 11/92 4,125
Binford, Julien Am 1909-
* See 1993 Edition . . . .
Bing, V. & Schmid, Rudolf Am 20C
O/B 43x41 Telephone Workers 1929 Wes 3/93 1,018
Bingham, George Caleb Am 1811-1879
O/C 27x22 Portraits Mary & Elisha Brown: Pair Sel 9/92 . . 8,200
Binks, Reuben Ward Br 1860-1940
* See 1993 Edition . . . .
Binolt, Peter Ger 1590-1632
* See 1993 Edition . . . .
Biondetti, A. It 19C
W/Pa 12x7 Venetian Scene Wlf 4/93 100
Birch, Samuel John Lamorna Br
1869-1955
* See 1990 Edition . . . .
Birch, Thomas Am 1779-1851
O/C 17x28 The Carriage Ride Home Chr 12/92 16,500

Birch, William   Am 1755-1834
Pe&W/Pa 5x4 Portrait of a Man Eld 11/92 495
Birchall, William Minshall   Eng 1884-1940
* See 1993 Edition . . . .
Bird, Isaac F.   Eng 19C
O/C 47x36 Portrait of a Young Boy Wes 3/93 1,760
Birkhammer, Axel   Dan 1871-
* See 1993 Edition . . . .
Birkmeyer, Fritz   Ger 1848-1897
* See 1993 Edition . . . .
Birley, Sir Oswald   Nz 1880-1979
* See 1990 Edition . . . .
Birney, William Verplanck   Am 1858-1909
O/C 14x12 Relaxation Sby 3/93 6,900
O/C 8x10 Lighting his Pipe Chr 5/93 2,530
W&H/Pa/B 16x12 Feeding the Baby Sby 3/93 633
Biro, Geza   Hun 1919-
* See 1990 Edition . . . .
Birolli, Renato   It 1906-1959
* See 1993 Edition . . . .
Birren, Joseph P.   Am 1865-1933
O/B 24x28 A Rock of Ages But 10/92 4,125
O/B 32x38 Yosemite But 10/92 1,650
Bisbing, Henry Singlewood   Am 1849-1919
P/Pa 14x10 Hickory and Maples Yng 2/93 100
Biscaino, Bartolommeo   It 1632-1657
* See 1992 Edition . . . .
Bischoff, Elmer   Am 1916-1991
O/C/B 59x59 Two Women in a Landscape Sby 5/93 96,000
O/C 47x47 Landscape with Bare Tree Sby 5/93 33,350
Bischoff, Franz A.   Am 1864-1929
O/C 24x34 San Pedro Fishing Boats But 6/93 23,000
O/C 30x40 Pasadena Arroyo Landscape Mor 6/93 22,000
O/C 30x40 Dancing Reflections But 3/93 13,200
O/C 12x15 At the Table But 3/93 8,250
O/Pa 13x16 Oak Creek But 3/93 7,700
O/C 19x24 Hilltop Vista But 10/92 6,050
O/C/B 13x16 California Coastline But 10/92 3,300
O/B 13x19 Landscape with Trees Sby 3/93 3,105
O/B 13x17 Sierra Landscape Mor 11/92 3,000
O/B 13x19 California Blue Bonnets But 10/92 2,090
O/B 8x10 California Landscape But 6/93 1,955
O/B 16x20 Southern California Desert Scene Dum 2/93 . . . 1,600
O/B 13x19 Landscape and Ocean: Pair Sby 3/93 1,380
Bischoff, Friedrich   Ger 1819-1873
* See 1992 Edition . . . .
Bishop, Isabel   Am 1902-1988
O/C 33x40 Nude in Repose Doy 5/93 11,550
Pl&S/Pa 9x9 Woman with Child Sby 9/92 880
Bishop, Richard Evett   Am 1887-1975
* See 1993 Edition . . . .
Bisogno, V.   It 19C
W/Pa 5x15 Putti with Reindeer Hnd 10/92 375
Bison, Giuseppe Bernardino   It 1762-1844
K,Pl&S/Pa 9x7 Head of an Oriental Chr 1/93 770
K,Pl&S/Pa 5x4 Venus and Cupid Chr 1/93 770
Bispham, Henry Collins   Am 1841-1882
O/C 20x36 A Family of Deer 1891 Chr 5/93 2,300
Bisschop, Abraham   1670-1731
* See 1991 Edition . . . .
Bissi, Sergio Cirno   It 1902-
* See 1993 Edition . . . .
Bissier, Jules   Sws 1893-1965
O&T/L 17x21 Rondine 62 Sby 5/93 29,900
O&T/L 8x9 Rondine 61 Sby 5/93 19,550
T/L/B 9x10 4 Febr. 61 61 Chr 2/93 15,400
O&T/L 9x10 Variation (II) 22 62 Sby 5/93 14,950
G/C/C 7x10 14.Dec.58H Chr 10/92 13,200
T,Br&l/C 7x11 Dies Ditez 60 Chr 10/92 12,100
Bissiere, Roger   Fr 1886-1964
* See 1992 Edition . . . .
Bissolo, Francesco Di Vittore   a 1492-1554
* See 1992 Edition . . . .

Bisson, Edouard   Fr 1856-
* See 1992 Edition . . . .
Bisttram, Emil   Am 1895-1976
G&Pe/Pa 23x17 Domingo Chorus 36 Chr 5/93 13,
Pe/Pa 18x16 The Mother 31 Sby 3/93 3,
W/Pa 7x9 Abstract Lou 6/93 . . . .
Bittar, Antoine   Can 1957-
O/C 24x30 Harbour Front, Toronto 1988 Sbt 11/92 1,
O/Pn 8x6 Street Scene, Montreal 1992 Sbt 5/93 . . . .
Bittar, Pierre   Fr 20C
* See 1991 Edition . . . .
Bittinger, Charles   Am 1879-1970
O/M 32x25 The Lamp 1911 Chr 12/92 1,
O/C 16x20 The Old Homestead Sby 9/92 1,
Biva, Henri   Fr 1848-1928
O/C 40x28 Nature Morte Pivoines et Myosotis Sby 2/93 . . . 9,
O/C 26x32 Cascade a Villeneuve L'Etang Sby 5/93 3,
Biva, Paul   Fr 1851-1900
O/C 25x36 Corbeille de Fleurs Sby 5/93 13,
Bjulf, Soren Christian   Dan 1890-1958
O/C 22x19 The Flower Market Eld 8/93 1,
Black, LaVerne Nelson   Am 1887-1938
O/C 32x42 Ration Days Sby 3/93 23,0
Black, Norman   Am 20C
A/B 16x12 Surrealist Composition Hnd 12/92 . . . .
Black, Olive Parker   Am 1868-1948
O/C 14x20 Summer Landscape with Stream Sby 3/93 2,0
Black, Paul   Am 20C
* See 1993 Edition . . . .
Blackburn, Morris   Am 1902-1979
* See 1993 Edition . . . .
Blacklock, Thomas Bromley   Br 19C
O/C 16x21 Landscape with Figure & Haystacks But 5/93 . . 2,8
Blackman, E. W.   Am 20C
W/Pa 11x15 Saybrook Point Lighthouse Brd 8/93 . . . .
Blackman, Robert   Am 20C
* See 1993 Edition . . . .
Blackman, Walter   Am 1847-1928
* See 1993 Edition . . . .
Blackwood, David Lloyd   Can 1941-
W/Pa 27x41 View of Newton 1981 Sbt 5/93 2,4
Blaine, Mahlon   Am 1894-1970
W/Pa 14x12 Girl Comes to Big City Ih 11/92 1,3
Blair, Lee Everett   Am 1911-
W/Pa 14x22 Anacostia 1944 Mor 6/93 4,4
Blairat, Marcel   Fr 19C
W/Pa 8x10 Camels: Pair But 11/92 6
Blais, Jean-Charles   1956-
* See 1993 Edition . . . .
Blaize, Candide   Fr 1795-1885
* See 1992 Edition . . . .
Blake, Peter
* See 1992 Edition . . . .
Blakelock, Ralph Albert   Am 1847-1919
O/C 35x56 Jamaican Coastal Scene 1875 Sby 5/93 76,7
O/C 27x23 Teepees in the Moonlight Chr 5/93 55,2
O/C 37x22 Deep Woods Sby 3/93 17,2
O/C 18x32 Mountain Watershed Sby 12/92 14,3
O/C/C 27x35 Walking Along the River But 12/92 7,1
O/C 18x32 The Old Mill Chr 3/93 6,3
O/C 5x6 Landscape, Twilight Chr 9/92 3,5
O/Pn/Pn 5x7 Landscape with Clouds Chr 3/93 3,4
O/C 12x14 Moonlight Lou 9/92 3,0
O/Pn 6x8 Indian Encampment Chr 12/92 1,8
O/C 9x12 Clearing with Indian Camp Hnd 3/93 1,4
O/C 10x5 Landscape Dum 9/92 1,1
Blampied, Edmund   Br 1886-1966
* See 1992 Edition . . . .
Blanch, Arnold   Am 1896-1968
O/B 12x36 Green Field 57 But 6/93 1,4
O/C 15x22 Bearsville Hnd 10/92 7
Blanchard, Antoine   Fr 1910-1988
O/C 18x22 Boulevard la Madeleine 1900 Doy 11/92 7,7
O/C 18x22 La Madeleine Doy 11/92 7,7
O/C 13x18 Arc de Triomphe Hnd 3/93 7,5

44

O/C 13x18 Palais Royale But 11/92 6,050
O/C 13x18 Parisian Boulevard Wes 5/93 4,620
O/C 13x18 Porte St. Denis But 11/92 4,400
O/C 13x18 Cafe de la Paix Hnd 9/92 2,600
O/C 13x18 Place de la Concorde, Paris Wes 5/93 2,530
O/C 12x16 Piccadilly Circus Wes 5/93 2,310
O/C 24x36 Paris Street Scene Lou 9/92 2,300
O/C 18x20 Cafe de la Paix But 10/92 2,200
O/C 12x16 The Empire Theater, London Wes 5/93 2,200
O/C 13x18 Bookstalls Along the Seine Hnd 9/92 2,000
O/C 16x20 Paris Street Scene Lou 9/92 1,800
O/C 24x20 Paris Street Scene Lou 12/92 1,600
O/C 13x18 Bookstalls Along the Seine Hnd 5/93 1,000

Blanchard, Maria   Fr 1881-1932
  * See 1991 Edition . . . .

Blanchard, Remy   1958-
A&E/C 87x57 Cracheur de Feu Chr 11/92 330

Blanche, Jacques Emile   Fr 1861-1942
  * See 1993 Edition . . . .

Blanco, Dionisio   20C
O/C 30x40 Fantasias Oniricas de Sembradores 90 Sby 11/92 3,300

Blanes, Juan Manuel   Uru 1830-1901
O&H/B 14x9 Boceto Para El Caballo Sby 5/93 17,250

Blaney, Dwight   Am 1865-1944
W/Pa/B 13x16 Hollyhocks 1890 Skn 3/93 3,740

Blashfield, Edwin Howland   Am 1848-1936
  * See 1993 Edition . . . .

Blatas, Arbit   1908-
G/Cd 64x48 Mistress Quickly; John Falstaff: Pr Sby 2/93 . . 1,495

Blauvelt, Charles F.   Am 1824-1900
O/C 10x8 The Helping Hand Sby 9/92 2,090
O/C 30x40 Tasting the Broth '50 Slo 7/93 1,500

Blazey, Lawrence   Am 1902-
A/B 20x16 Raindrops on a Leaf Wlf 5/93 125
P/Pa 11x14 A Tenacled Sycamore Wlf 5/93 75
A/B 15x19 Brown Bag Lunch Wlf 5/93 75
W/Pa 24x18 Clay Rabbit Contemplating Dinner Wlf 5/93 50

Blechen, Carl   Ger 1798-1840
  * See 1993 Edition . . . .

Bleckner, Ross   Am 1949-
O/C 76x62 Twelve Nights 1986 Chr 11/92 132,000
O/C 108x72 Ellipse of Us Sby 11/92 77,000
O/C 108x72 Burning Trees 1986 Sby 5/93 51,750
O/C 102x76 Untitled 81 Sby 5/93 28,750
O/C 24x24 Untitled 1986 Sby 5/93 10,350
O/C 16x20 Untitled 1984 Chr 11/92 9,350
O/L 18x16 The Sense of Ending Chr 11/92 6,050
O/C 10x8 Untitled 1985 Chr 11/92 6,050
O/Pn 14x14 Pieces of Months 1987 Chr 2/93 4,400

Bleger, Paul-Leon   Fr 20C
  * See 1992 Edition . . . .

Bleker, Dirck   Dut 1622-1672
  * See 1990 Edition . . . .

Blenner, Carle John   Am 1864-1952
  * See 1993 Edition . . . .

Bles, David Joseph   Dut 1821-1899
O/C 16x22 Serenading with a Flute 53 Chr 10/92 4,400

Bleser, August (Jr.)   Am
  * See 1993 Edition . . . .

Bleuler, Johann Ludwig   Sws 1792-1850
  * See 1993 Edition . . . .

Blinks, Thomas   Br 1860-1912
O/C 44x60 Lament for the Master Chr 5/93 89,400
O/C 19x22 Setting Out 98 Chr 5/93 16,100
O/C 12x18 Hunting Scene 98 Skn 11/92 6,600

Bliss, Robert   Am 20C
  * See 1993 Edition . . . .

Bloch, Albert
O/C 54x40 Gruppe Andaechtiger Gestalten 1914 Sby 2/93 17,250

Bloch, Julius Thiengen   Am 1888-1966
O/C 24x20 Floral Still Life 1920 Fre 10/92 1,000

Bloch, Lucienne   Am 1909-
Et/M 20x14 Flint Flood '48 Sby 9/92 5,500

Bloemaert, Abraham   Dut 1564-1651
  * See 1992 Edition . . . .

Bloemaert, Hendrick   Dut 1601-1672
O/C 29x26 Boy Playing the Flute Sby 1/93 68,500

Bloemaert, The Pseudo-Hendrick   Dut 17C
  * See 1991 Edition . . . .

Bloemers, Arnoldus   Dut 1786-1844
O/C 26x21 Still Life with Assorted Flowers Chr 5/93 66,300

Blommers, Bernardus Johannes   Dut 1845-1914
  * See 1993 Edition . . . .

Blondel, Merry-Joseph   Fr 19C
  * See 1990 Edition . . . .

Blondin, Charles   Fr 20C
O/C 13x18 Paris Opera House Wes 3/93 440

Bloodgood, Morris Seymour   Am 1845-1920
O/C 12x20 Autumn Landscape 1882 Slo 5/93 375
O/B 14x20 Seascape Yng 2/93 100

Bloom, William
O/Pn 9x6 Standing Man in Derby Ilh 5/93 450

Bloomer, Hiram Reynolds   Am 1845-1911
O/Cb 14x21 Figure in Landscape Mor 11/92 650

Bloomfield, Harry   Am 20C
  * See 1992 Edition . . . .

Bloore, Ronald   Can 1925-
MM/Wd 5x7 Composition Sbt 5/93 616

Bloos, Richard   Ger 1878-1956
O/C 28x39 Le Bal Bullier a Paris 1909 Sby 5/93 17,250

Blouser, Florence Parker   Am 1889-1935
O/C 24x30 Figures - Olvera St. Mor 2/93 750
O/C 22x30 Laguna Coastal Mor 2/93 350

Blower, David H.   Am 1901-1976
  * See 1993 Edition . . . .

Bluemner, Oscar Florianus   Am 1867-1938
W&Pe/Pa/B 5x7 The Azure and Reflections Chr 12/92 . . . 24,200
W&Y/Pa 7x5 Five Works Sby 3/93 4,025
C&Pe/Pa 5x7 Four Drawings 18 Sby 9/92 3,740
C/Pa 5x8 Country and City Views: Ten Sby 9/92 3,575
C&Pe/Pa 5x6 Landscape Views: Ten Sby 9/92 3,025
C&Pe/Pa 5x6 Landscape Views: Ten Sby 9/92 2,860
I/Pa 5x8 German Valley and California: Pair 15 Sby 9/92 . . 2,750
C&Pe/Pa 5x8 Five Drawings 15 Sby 9/92 2,200
Y/Pa 5x8 Three Drawings Sby 3/93 1,725
C/Pa 5x6 Ten Drawings Sby 3/93 1,380
C&Pe/Pa 5x6 Bloomfield Plain; Bloomfield: Pair 18 Sby 9/92 1,210
C/Pa 5x8 New York Cityscape Chr 9/92 990
Y/Pa 5x8 Four Drawings Sby 3/93 575

Bluhm, Norman   Am 1920-
O/C 102x86 White Light 1958 Chr 2/93 18,150
W&G/Pa 36x60 Untitled Chr 11/92 7,150
O/C 36x29 Untitled 53 Chr 2/93 4,180
O/C 39x65 Smuggler's Notch '62 Sby 2/93 3,450
O/C 24x20 Carry On 60 Sby 6/93 2,875

Bluhm, Oscar   Ger 20C
G/Pa 16x12 Two Men and a Lady 1902 Hnd 3/93 1,900

Blum, Jerome S.   Am 1884-1956
  * See 1993 Edition . . . .

Blum, Robert Frederick   Am 1857-1903
P/Pa 18x15 Filipino Woman '89 Sby 12/92 77,000
W/Pa 8x12 In the Cathedral 1882 But 6/93 1,150

Blum, Yvonne   Fr 20C
P/Pa 166x13 Breton Woman 09 Hnd 10/92 275

Blume, Peter   Am 1906-
W,C&Pe/Pa 19x15 Suburban Houses 1926 Sby 9/92 2,750

Blumenschein, Ernest L.   Am 1874-1960
  * See 1993 Edition . . . .

Blumenschein, Helen Green   Am 1909-
  * See 1993 Edition . . . .

Blunt, John Samuel   Am 1798-1835
O/C 28x36 Niagara Falls, Down River 1831 Chr 5/93 23,000

Blyth, E.   Br 19C
O/C 19x23 Fruit of the Sea 1846 Chr 10/92 1,540

Blythe, David Gilmour Am 1815-1865
  * See 1992 Edition ....
Boardman, William Am 1815-1895
  * See 1991 Edition ....
Bobak, Bruno Can 1923-
  O/C 16x24 Evening Landscape Sbt 5/93 1,320
Bobak, Molly Joan Lamb Can 1922-
  O/C 22x30 Queen's Visit to Fredericton Sbt 11/92 4,400
Boccacci, Marcello 1914-
  O/Pn 32x11 Ritrato di donna Chr 5/93 920
Boccherini Am 20C
  * See 1992 Edition ....
Boccioni, Umberto It 1882-1916
  * See 1992 Edition ....
Bochner, Mel Am 1940-
  O/C 91x89 Implode 1984 Chr 10/92 9,900
  C/Pa 38x50 Three, Five, Four (Step) 1973 Sby 11/92 9,900
  P/Pa 38x50 Duple 1975 Sby 5/93 9,200
  G/Pa 12x16 First Fulcrum (Study) 1975 Sby 2/93 3,450
  W/Pa 20x27 Second Double Italic #3 1975 Sby 2/93 3,450
  W/Pa 10x14 Axes (Study) 1979 Sby 11/92 2,750
  H&Pe/Pa 10x24 Untitled 1982 Chr 2/93 1,430
Bockhorst, Johann 1604-1668
  O/C 48x38 Saint John the Baptist Sby 5/93 8,050
Boddington, Henry John Br 1811-1865
  O/C 15x11 The Fall of the Mawddock Chr 5/93 2,530
  O/C 25x32 Angling at the Old Bridge Dum 11/92 2,250
Bodeman, Willem Dut 1806-1880
  * See 1992 Edition ....
Bodenmuller, Frederich Ger 1845-
  * See 1993 Edition ....
Bodis, F. Con 20C
  O/C 20x16 Study of Bearded Man Sel 9/92 260
Bodmer, Karl Am 1809-1893
  O/C 14x22 Mountain Lake But 12/92 5,500
Bodwell, D. V. Am 20C
  O/B 13x14 Winter Snow Scene 1932 Mys 3/93 330
Boe, Franz Didrik Nor 1820-1891
  O/C 23x29 Still Life Rabbit and Rooster Sby 6/93 12,650
Boehm, Edouard Aus 1830-
  O/C 27x42 Pausing on a Woodland Path Sby 10/92 3,300
  O/C 27x42 Landscape with Figures and Lake But 5/93 2,300
  O/C 14x22 River Landscapes: Pair Sby 1/93 2,300
  O/C 19x25 Wooden Landscape with River Sby 1/93 1,035
Boemm, Ritta Hun 1868-1948
  O/C 24x30 Still Life Dum 7/93 285
  O/C 24x30 Still Life Dum 7/93 275
Boers, Marianne
  W&Pe/Pa 9x9 Model Ship 1971 Sby 2/93 460
Boers, Sebastian Theodoros V. Dut 1828-1893
  * See 1992 Edition ....
Boese, Henry Am 1847-1863
  O/C 24x42 Near the Hudson, Duchess County Sby 9/92 .. 11,000
  O/C 30x58 Cows Watering Chr 5/93 4,025
Boesen, Johannes Dan 1847-1916
  * See 1993 Edition ....
Boething, Marjory A. Am 1891-1972
  O/C 24x26 Floral Still Life Mor 2/93 600
Boetti, Alighiero E. 20C1940-
  A&Bp/Pa/C 40x110 Untitled 1979 Chr 11/92 15,400
Bogaert, Hendrik Dut 1627-1672
  * See 1993 Edition ....
Bogdani, Jacob Hun 1660-1724
  O/C 39x50 Poultry, A Blue-Ringed Dove Chr 10/92 41,800
Bogdanov-Bjelsky, Nikolai P. Rus 1868-1945
  O/C 51x40 An Afternoon Fishing 1917 Sby 2/93 20,700
Bogdanove, Abraham J. Am 1888-1946
  * See 1992 Edition ....
Bogert, George Hirst Am 1864-1944
  O/C 28x40 The Grand Canal at Night Chr 12/92 3,520
  O/C 28x40 Venice Hnd 10/92 1,000
  O/B 14x20 Sunset Yng 5/93 900
  O/C 55x36 Landscape at Dusk Chr 5/93 748

Boggio, Emilio Fr 1857-1920
  O/C/Pn 13x20 View of a Park Sby 1/93 2,300
Boggs, Frank Myers Am 1855-1926
  O/C 26x32 Along the Seine Sby 5/93 17,250
  O/C 11x16 Trafalgar Square Doy 11/92 3,575
  O/C 18x20 Street Scene Wtf 12/92 2,000
  O/C 22x17 Brooklyn Bridge from the River Doy 5/93 1,210
  K&W/Pa 10x16 Parisian Street Scene Wtf 9/92 750
  C/Pa 15x20 A Harbor Chr 12/92 550
Bogh, Carl Henrik Dan 1827-1893
  O/C 18x24 Piglets at Play 1877 Sby 6/93 8,050
Bohatsch, Erwin 1951-
  * See 1993 Edition ....
Bohm, Max Am 1868-1923
  O/C 13x10 Garden of Max Bohm Home at Etaples Yng 2/93 . 900
Bohm, Pal Hun 1839-1905
  * See 1992 Edition ....
Bohmen, Karl Ger 20C
  * See 1993 Edition ....
Bohrod, Aaron Am 1907-1992
  O/B 31x23 The Torso Hnz 5/93 2,800
  O/C 36x40 Doll Shop Ald 9/92 2,600
  O/B 14x10 Room with a View 1978 Hnd 9/92 2,200
  T/Pa 12x17 Burlesque Show '32 Hnd 12/92 1,500
  O/Pn 14x11 Cherub and Cherries 1974 Hnd 9/92 950
  G&R/Pa 15x15 Execution of Garcia Lorca 1939 Hnd 10/92 . 700
  G&R/Pa 15x12 Making a Smoke Screen 1943 Hnd 10/92 .. 700
  MM/Pb 15x10 Self Portrait of Artist Painting '32 Lou 9/92 .. 450
  G&W/Pa 11x8 Female Nude and Male Studies Hnd 9/92 ... 300
  I&W/Pa 5x7 Fantasy Horses Hnd 5/93 250
  Pl/Pa 10x8 Figural Studies Wtf 9/92 225
  W&I/Pa 9x12 Soldiers Washing Clothes 1943 Wtf 9/92 ... 200
  G&I/Pa 10x7 Winter Landscape Hnd 5/93 140
Boille, Luigi 1926-
  * See 1993 Edition ....
Boilly, Jules Fr 1796-1874
  * See 1993 Edition ....
Boilly, Louis-Leopold Fr 1761-1845
  O/C 21x17 Suitor Rejected Slo 7/93 19,000
Boisrond, Francois 1959-
  A/Cd 62x56 Redoublement 82 Chr 11/92 308
Boisselier, Felix Fr 1776-1811
  * See 1992 Edition ....
Boissier, Gaston Maurice E. Fr 19C
  * See 1990 Edition ....
Boizot, Antoine Honore Louis 1744-1800
  * See 1993 Edition ....
Bol, Ferdinand Dut 1616-1680
  * See 1991 Edition ....
Bol, Hans Dut 1534-1593
  * See 1991 Edition ....
Boland, Charles Con 20C
  * See 1992 Edition ....
Boldini, Giovanni It 1842-1931
  O/C 22x14 The Summer Stroll Chr 5/93 607,500
  K/Pa 14x10 Portrait of Madame X Chr 10/92 22,000
Bolduc, David Can 1945-
  * See 1992 Edition ....
Bole, Comtesse Jeanne Fr a 1870-1883
  * See 1992 Edition ....
Bolles, Enoch
  * See 1993 Edition ....
Bolotowsky, Ilya Am 1907-1981
  G&Pe/Pa 12x18 Study for Mural Sby 2/93 4,313
  Y&L/Pa 8x11 Untitled Sby 2/93 2,875
Bolt, M. C.
  * See 1991 Edition ....
Bolt, Ron Can 1938-
  * See 1993 Edition ....
Boltanski, Christian 1944-
  A&Y/Ph 40x28 Le Repas Refuse Chr 10/92 9,350
Bolton, Hale William Am 1885-1920
  * See 1992 Edition ....
Boltraffio, Giovanni Antonio It 1467-1516
  * See 1990 Edition ....

Bombled, Louis Charles   Fr 1862-1927
  * See 1993 Edition . . . .
Bombois, Camille   Fr 1883-1970
  O/C 29x24 Les Bas Noir Avec Journal Sby 11/92 93,500
  O/C 32x26 La Maison en Bourgogne Chr 11/92 60,500
  O/C 40x29 La Ruelle Du Moulin Sby 10/92 38,500
  O/C 26x20 L'Arbre Abattu Sby 11/92 34,100
  O/C 26x21 La Riviere Sby 5/93 11,500
  O/C 10x14 Au Bord de la Riviere Doy 11/92 11,000
  O/C 6x9 Summer Landscape Sby 2/93 5,750
  O/C 8x11 Paysage au Moulin Wlf 12/92 4,800
Bompard, Maurice   Fr 1857-1936
  O/C 34x27 Still Life Flowers in Vase Sby 1/93 1,380
  G/B 7x10 Windmills on a Canal Chr 5/93 690
Bompiani, Roberto   It 1821-1908
  * See 1992 Edition . . . .
Bompiani-Battaglia, Cecilia   It 1847-1927
  W&G/Pa 21x14 Two Views of Rome Skn 9/92 5,170
Bonati, Dante   Arg 1894-
  O/B/M 23x27 At the Quarry 1922 Lou 12/92 700
Bonavia, Carlo   It a 1740-1786
  * See 1991 Edition . . . .
Bondoux, Jules Georges   Eur -1920
  * See 1991 Edition . . . .
Bone, Robert Trewick   Br 1790-1840
  O/Pn 6x5 Portrait of Dr. Donne Hnd 5/93 400
Bonelli, James   Am 1916-
  O/C 30x36 Rooftops Fre 4/93 1,500
Bonevardi, Marcelo   Arg 1929-
  MM/C 70x86 The Supreme Instrument 65 Sby 5/93 18,400
  O/C&Wd 50x44 Box with Shadows II 69 Sby 5/93 6,900
  O/Wd 12x10 Facade 69 Chr 11/92 1,650
  MM 25x39 Figure in a Landscape 65 But 4/93 1,035
Bonfield, William Van De Velde   Am 19C
  * See 1990 Edition . . . .
Bonfils, Gaston   Fr 19C
  O/C 22x19 An Elegant Lady Bust Length Chr 5/93 1,150
Bongart, Sergei   Am 1918-1985
  * See 1992 Edition . . . .
Bonham, Horace   Am 1835-1892
  * See 1991 Edition . . . .
Bonheur, Auguste   Fr 1824-1884
  * See 1993 Edition . . . .
Bonheur, Rosa   Fr 1822-1899
  O/C 46x79 Spanish Crossing Pyrenees 1857 Chr 10/92 . . 99,000
  O/C 25x41 Wild Horses on Open Plains 1890 Sby 6/93 . . 57,500
  O/C 30x59 Le Labourage Nivernais Sby 2/93 20,700
  O/C 21x26 Studies Cows, Hens, Roosters Chr 2/93 10,450
  O/C 24x42 Vaches a L'Abreuvoir Sby 6/93 8,050
  O/C 21x31 Le Cerf, Effet du Matin Chr 10/92 4,620
  O/C 16x20 Sheep Grazing 1900 Hnd 10/92 3,400
  O/C 20x20 A Bull, The Chief Dum 5/93 1,600
Bonhomme, Leon   Fr 1870-1924
  O&G/Pa 7x9 Woman on Couch 1910 But 10/92 1,650
  P,W&C/Pa 8x6 Women of the Demi-Monde 1907 Sby 10/92 . 275
Boni, E.   It 19C
  W/Pa 15x25 Venice from the Canal Wlf 9/92 950
  W&Pe/Pa 25x16 Piazza San Marco, Venice Wlf 9/92 550
Bonifazio Veronese   It 1487-1553
  O/C 41x60 Holy Family with Saint Dorothy Sby 1/93 57,500
Bonington, Richard Parkes   Eng 1801-1828
  * See 1993 Edition . . . .
Bonirote, Pierre   Fr 1811-1891
  * See 1990 Edition . . . .
Bonito, Giuseppe   It 1707-1789
  * See 1992 Edition . . . .
Bonnal, Felicie Palade   Fr 19C
  * See 1993 Edition . . . .
Bonnar, James King   Am 1885-1961
  O/C 20x24 Autumn Yng 2/93 800
  O/B 16x20 Winter Snow Scene Mys 3/93 688
  W&G/Pa 10x13 Winter in a New England Village Yng 5/93 . . 650
  W/Pa 8x11 First Frost Yng 2/93 125

Bonnard, Pierre   Fr 1867-1947
  O/C 25x20 Les Fraises 1910 Chr 11/92 462,000
  O/B/Pn 24x16 Le Moulin Rouge 96 Sby 11/92 440,000
  O/Pn 12x12 Au Cafe Sby 11/92 396,000
  O/C 15x13 Mere et Enfant 1893 Sby 11/92 220,000
  O/C 16x19 Nature morte aux fruits Chr 11/92 198,000
  Pnc/B/Pn 15x13 Petit Nu, Bras Leves Sby 11/92 66,000
  Pe/Pa 6x5 Une Table Servie Pour Petit Dejeune Sby 10/92 . 9,900
Bonnat, Leon Joseph Florentin   Fr 1834-1922
  O/C 55x41 Arab Plucking a Thorn Chr 10/92 46,200
Bonnefond, Claude   Fr 1796-1860
  O/C 21x17 Une Pellerine Soutenue Sby 1/93 1,725
Bontecou, Lee   1931-
  * See 1993 Edition . . . .
Bonvin, Francois   Fr 1817-1887
  * See 1993 Edition . . . .
Bonvin, Leon   Fr 1834-1866
  * See 1991 Edition . . . .
Boog, Carle Michel   Am 1877-1967
  * See 1993 Edition . . . .
Boogaard, Willem-Jacobus   Dut 1842-1887
  O/Pn 7x10 Stable Interior: Pair But 11/92 4,400
Bookatz, Samuel   Am 1910-
  O/C 16x22 City Street Scene Wlf 5/93 25
Bookbinder, J.   Am 1911-
  O/B 16x20 Backstage Hnz 5/93 350
Booth, Franklin   Am 1874-1948
  PI/Pa 13x9 Shepherd, Sheep, Mythic Figure Ih 11/92 . . . 3,000
  PI/Pa 10x9 Man Seated on Steps Ih 5/93 1,600
Boothe, Power
  S&Pe/Pa 14x13 Untitled '74 Sby 2/93 403
Borchand, Edmund   Fr 1848-1922
  O/C 13x20 After the Brawl But 5/93 1,035
Bordignon, Noe   It 1834-1920
  * See 1991 Edition . . . .
Bordone, Paris   It 1500-1571
  * See 1993 Edition . . . .
Borduas, Paul-Emile   Can 1905-1960
  * See 1993 Edition . . . .
Borein, Edward   Am 1873-1945
  W/Pa 7x10 The Round Up Sby 9/92 7,150
  G/Pa Size? Tied Patience 1915 Fre 4/93 2,300
  PI/Pa 8x7 Running Indian But 12/92 2,200
  PI/Pa 7x13 Herd of Cows Lou 6/93 925
  I/Pa 4x4 Charging Steer Mor 6/93 385
Boren, James   Am 1921-
  * See 1991 Edition . . . .
Borenstein, Samuel   Can 1908-1969
  O/B 24x20 Mount Orford, Eastern Townships 1949 Sbt 5/93 4,180
Bores, Francisco   Spa 1898-1972
  O/C 18x22 Nature Morte 55 Chr 5/93 23,000
  O/C 13x16 Nature Morte a la Tasse 47 Sby 2/93 6,325
  O/C 11x14 Femme Nue Allongee 48 Chr 2/93 6,050
Borg, Carl Oscar   Am 1879-1947
  W/Pa 21x23 Canyon de Chelly/Indian Mor 6/93 9,350
  O/C 80x89 Padre Blessing Indians at Mission Mor 6/93 . . . 7,700
  G&Pe/Pa 10x14 Hopi Ruins Mor 2/93 2,750
  W/Pa 20x15 Mission San Luis Rey But 10/92 2,475
  I&W/Pa 3x5 Indian on Horseback 1946 Mor 2/93 2,250
  W,H&Cw/Pa 16x28 Rhyolite, Nevada But 6/93 1,955
  W/Pa 11x10 Western Landscape Lou 12/92 1,600
  O/C/B 8x10 The Doorway, Santa Fe But 3/93 1,540
  G/Cd 5x7 Harbor Entrance Mor 6/93 1,100
  MM/Pa 7x5 Illustration/Buccaneer Mor 11/92 500
  W/Pa 7x10 Stagecoach Ambush Yng 2/93 325
Borges, Jacobo   Ven 1931-
  * See 1993 Edition . . . .
Borglum, John Gutzon   Am 1867-1941
  O/C 16x25 Sheep in California Landscape 1891 But 6/93 . . 3,162
Borgord, Martin   Am 1869-1935
  O/Pn 20x16 Clisonne Vase Fre 4/93 850
Borie, Adolphe   Am 1877-1934
  O/C 30x22 Portrait of a Sportsman Ald 9/92 125

Borione, Bernard Louis   Fr 1865-
  * See 1993 Edition . . . .
Borman, Johannes   Dut a 1653-1659
  * See 1991 Edition . . . .
Borman, Leonard   Am 20C
  O/M 8x10 Coastals (2) Mor 11/92 75
Borofsky, Jonathan   Am 1942-
  O/C 45x51 Stone Head Sby 11/92 30,250
Borrani, Odoardo   It 1834-1905
  * See 1991 Edition . . . .
Borstein, Elena   20C
  * See 1991 Edition . . . .
Bortnyik, Sandor
  * See 1990 Edition . . . .
Bos, Hendrik   Dut 1901-
  * See 1992 Edition . . . .
Bosa, Louis   Am 1905-1981
  W/Pa 15x25 Central Park 1939 Lou 3/93 2,050
  O/Cb 10x16 Couple Seated by Venetian Canal Wlf 5/93 . . . 1,200
  O/C 10x16 Rural Scene with Figures Lou 3/93 1,100
  I&S/Pa 17x22 Figural Studies of Monks Wlf 5/93 300
Bosboom, Johannes   Dut 1817-1891
  Pe&S/Pa 8x11 Church Interior Chr 10/92 715
Bosc, Henriette   Fr 20C
  O/M 21x24 Still Life Lou 6/93 150
Boschetto, Giuseppe   It 1841-
  O/C 25x17 The Baptism Skn 3/93 7,150
Boscoli, Andrea   It 1560-1607
  * See 1993 Edition . . . .
Boshamer, Johannes Willem   Dut 1802-1857
  O/Pn 24x28 Harbor with Ships Sby 1/93 3,450
Boshier, Derek
  * See 1992 Edition . . . .
Bosley, Frederick A.   Am 1881-1942
  * See 1993 Edition . . . .
Bosman, Richard   Am 1944-
  O/C 29x36 Study for the River '88 Sby 6/93 2,875
Bosschaert, Jean-Baptiste   Flm 1667-1746
  * See 1993 Edition . . . .
Bossoli, Carlo   It 1815-1874
  W/Pa 7x20 Harbor Scene Hnz 5/93 450
Bossuet, Francois Antoine   Bel 1800-1889
  * See 1992 Edition . . . .
Boston, Frederick James   Am 1855-1932
  O/C 24x20 Reading Under the Wisteria Doy 5/93 1,870
Boston, Joseph H.   Am 1860-1954
  O/C 10x16 Cows Watering in a Wooded Stream Skn 5/93 . . . 495
  O/C 30x25 Portrait of a Woman Ald 9/92 260
  O/C 25x30 Seascape Mys 12/92 248
Botello, Angel   Spa 1913-1986
  O/Pw 30x24 Nina con Jaula de Pajaro Chr 11/92 . . . 17,600
  O/Pn 24x18 Nina con Peine Chr 11/92 13,200
  O/Pn 16x12 Still Life Chr 11/92 4,950
  O/Pn 36x31 Seated Nude Sby 6/93 3,450
  MM 15x13 Two Heads Brd 8/93 2,200
Botero, Fernando   Col 1932-
  O/C 90x74 La Casa de Las Gemelas Arias 73 Sby 11/92 . . . 1.54M
  O/C 81x75 Cuatro Mujeres 87 Sby 5/93 717,500
  O/C 70x72 Still Life Sandia y Naranjas 70 Chr 11/92 . . . 528,000
  O/C 50x37 La Madre Superiora 74 Chr 11/92 220,000
  O/C 16x78 El Secuestro 66 Chr 11/92 198,000
  W/pa 72x44 Primera Dama 81 Sby 11/92 170,500
  W/pa 72x44 Presidente 81 Sby 11/92 154,000
  O/C 51x59 Naturaleza Muerta 78 Chr 11/92 132,000
  Sg/Pa 19x14 Desnudo Fumando Chr 11/92 35,200
  H/Pa 17x14 Man with a Bowler Hat 80 Sby 5/93 . . . 24,150
  Pe/Pa 17x14 El Patron 1971 Chr 11/92 22,000
  H/Pa 17x14 Femme Assise 81 Sby 5/93 18,975
Both, Andries Dirksz.   Dut 1611-1641
  * See 1992 Edition . . . .
Both, Jan   Dut 1615-1652
  * See 1990 Edition . . . .

Bothwell, Dorr   Am 1902-
  O/B 24x24 For National Defense '40 Sby 9/92 3,575
Botke, Cornelius   Am 1887-1954
  O/C/B 16x20 Santa Paula Canyon But 6/93 3,162
  O/Pw 14x18 Landscape Mor 6/93 880
Botke, Jessie Arms   Am 1883-1971
  G/Pa 15x13 Flamingos But 6/93 1,955
  G/Pa/B 16x12 San Gabriel But 3/93 880
  W/Pa 10x12 House in Forest Landscape Mor 2/93 450
Botkin, Henry Albert   Am 1896-1983
  O/B 14x14 Celebration Sby 9/92 715
  O/Pb 28x39 Horizon in Green Lou 3/93 250
Bott, Emil   Am 19C
  * See 1993 Edition . . . .
Bottex, Jean-Baptiste   Hai 20C
  * See 1993 Edition . . . .
Botticelli, Sandro   It 1445-1510
  * See 1993 Edition . . . .
Botticini, Francesco   It 1446-1497
  * See 1991 Edition . . . .
Bottini, Georges   Fr 1874-1907
  * See 1993 Edition . . . .
Bottschild, Samuel   1640-1707
  K/Pa 15x10 Head of Bearded Man 1670 Chr 1/93 880
Boucart, Gaston H.   Fr 1878-1962
  O/C 24x29 Woman Knitting 1909 Sby 1/93 1,840
Bouchard, Lorne Holland   Can 1913-1978
  O/M 12x18 Farm - St. Placide - Quebec 1969 Sbt 11/92 . . . 1,320
  O/Pn 12x16 Morin Heights, P.Q. 1950 Sbt 5/93 528
Bouchard, Pierre Francois   Fr 1831-1889
  O/C 45x29 The Flower Girl Chr 2/93 13,200
Bouche, Louis   Am 1896-1969
  O/C 16x20 Urban Renewal Sby 3/93 805
Bouche, Louis Alexandre   Fr 1838-1911
  O/C 14x11 La Route de Village Sby 2/93 2,875
  O/C 10x10 Harlem River 1944 Skn 3/93 715
Bouchene, Dimitri
  O/C/B 18x13 View of the Seine Sby 10/92 935
Boucher, Alfred   Fr 1850-1934
  * See 1990 Edition . . . .
Boucher, Francois   Fr 1703-1770
  O/C 26x21 L'Heureuse Fecondite 1764 Sby 5/93 . . . 800,000
  O/C 26x31 Joseph presenting Father to Pharaoh Chr 10/92 77,000
Bouchet, Jules Frederic   Fr 1799-1860
  * See 1992 Edition . . . .
Bouchot, Francois   Fr 1800-1842
  * See 1992 Edition . . . .
Boucie, Pierre   Flm 1610-1673
  * See 1991 Edition . . . .
Boudat, Louis
  O/C 38x41 Vista de la Havana 1864 Sby 11/92 . . . 15,400
Boudet, Pierre   Fr 1925-
  * See 1992 Edition . . . .
Boudewijns, Adriaen & Bout, P.   1644-1711
  O/C 22x28 Hilly Landscape with Travellers Sby 10/92 6,600
Boudewijns, Adriaen Frans   Flm 1644-1711
  * See 1993 Edition . . . .
Boudin, Eugene   Fr 1824-1898
  O/C 20x26 Trouville, Scene de Plage Soleil Chr 11/92 . . . 715,000
  O/C 18x25 Villefrance, La Rades 92 Sby 5/93 . . . 200,500
  O/C 16x22 Trouville, vue prise de Deauville 96 Chr 11/92 137,500
  O/C 18x25 Camaret 70 Sby 5/93 123,500
  O/C 20x30 La riviere morte a Deauville 90 Chr 11/92 . . . 60,500
  O/Pn 16x13 Le port de Trouville 94 Chr 11/92 57,200
  O/C 18x26 Saint-Vaast-La-Hougue 90 Sby 5/93 . . . 51,750
  O/Pn 7x10 Trois-Mats Dans Un Port Sby 5/93 . . . 43,125
  O/Pn 6x9 Le Havre L'Avant-Port Sby 2/93 40,250
  O/Pn 11x8 Bateaux Echoues Sby 2/93 35,650
  P/Pa 8x11 Rivage Normand, Maree Basse Sby 11/92 . . . 35,200
  P/Pa/Pa 4x5 Le Treport Chr 11/92 23,100
  O/Pn 7x9 Chevaux a L'Attache Sby 5/93 12,650
  O/Pa/B 8x12 Bords De La Touques Sby 2/93 6,900
  C,K&Sg/Pa 10x8 Male Figure Fre 4/93 1,100

Boudry, Alois Bel 1851-1938
* See 1993 Edition . . . .
Bouel, Louis Francois Numance Fr 19C
* See 1992 Edition . . . .
**Bougereau, William Adolphe Fr
1825-1905**
W/Pa 20x14 La Guipier Mys 12/92 330
Bough, Samuel Sco 1822-1878
* See 1993 Edition . . . .
Boughton, George Henry Am 1833-1905
O/C 40x64 New Year's New Amsterdam 1870 Sby 12/92 . . 22,000
O/Pn 10x13 Christmas Eve Chr 12/92 2,420
W&G/Pa 10x8 Portrait of a Woman in White Chr 12/92 2,090
**Bouguereau, Elizabeth Jane G. Am
1837-1922**
Pl/Pa 36x25 Rudyard Kipling's Daughter 1907 Sby 5/93 . . 16,675
O/C 32x25 Philome and Procne Fre 4/93 3,100
**Bouguereau, William Adolphe Fr
1825-1905**
O/C 79x48 La Vierge, L'Enfant Jesus 1875 Sby 5/93 . . . 690,000
O/C 52x35 Le Coquillage 1871 Sby 10/92 528,000
O/C 79x43 Petites Maraudeuses 1872 Sby 2/93 222,500
O/C 96x69 Canephore Chr 2/93 203,500
O/C 40x21 Innocence Sby 10/92 198,000
O/C 33x25 Idylle Chr 2/93 110,000
O/C 51x35 Lady Maxwell 1890 Chr 10/92 88,000
O/C 71x32 Beaute Romane 1904 Chr 2/93 77,000
O/C 24x20 Portrait of a Young Girl Chr 5/93 28,750
O/C 16x11 Etude Pour La Vierge Aux Anges Sby 5/93 . . . 14,950
Bouilion, Michel Fr 17C
* See 1991 Edition . . . .
Bouillier, Amable Fr 1867-
* See 1992 Edition . . . .
Boulanger, Graciela Rodo Bol 1935-
* See 1993 Edition . . . .
Boulet, Cyprien-Eugene Fr 1877-1927
* See 1993 Edition . . . .
Boulier, Lucien Fr 1882-1963
O/M 11x14 Still Life: Pair Sby 2/93 4,255
O/C 14x11 Before the Dance Sby 6/93 690
Boult, F. Cecil Br 19C
* See 1993 Edition . . . .
Boundey, Burton S. Am 1879-1962
O/C 24x30 Bank of My Lake But 10/92 7,150
Bouquet, Andre 1897-
O/C 13x18 Rue de Village 1975 Chr 11/92 880
Bourdon, Sebastian Fr 1616-1671
* See 1992 Edition . . . .
Bourgain, Gustave Fr -1921
* See 1992 Edition . . . .
Bourgeois, J. C. Fr 20C
O/B 11x14 Rural Landscapes: Pair Sel 9/92 140
Bourgeois, Louise Am 1911-
Pl&H/Pa 11x9 Untitled 47 Chr 2/93 9,900
Br&V/Pa 11x8 Untitled Chr 2/93 9,900
Pl/Pa 19x12 Untitled 50 Chr 10/92 4,400
Bourgogne, Pierre Fr 1838-1904
* See 1992 Edition . . . .
Bourlard, Antoine Joseph Bel 1826-1899
* See 1992 Edition . . . .
Bourne, Jean Baptiste C. Fr a 1815-1900
* See 1992 Edition . . . .
Bout, Pieter Flm 1658-1719
* See 1993 Edition . . . .
Bout, Pieter & Boudewijns, A. 1658-1719
O/C 22x28 Hilly Landscape with Travellers Sby 10/92 6,600
Boutelle, Dewitt Clinton Am 1820-1884
O/C 10x8 Sunset in the Catskills 1871 Chr 9/92 6,600
Bouter, Cornelis Dut 1888-1966
O/C 24x30 Kitchen Chores Dum 1/93 3,500
O/C 28x32 Mother and Children in an Interior But 11/92 . . . 2,750
O/C 16x14 The Letter Sby 1/93 2,645
O/C 14x20 Children Picking Flowers Chr 10/92 2,200
O/C 20x24 Interior Scene Mother and Children But 5/93 . . . 2,070

Bouterwek, Friedrich Ger 1806-1876
* See 1990 Edition . . . .
**Boutibonne, Charles Edouard Fr
1816-1897**
O/Pn 22x15 An Indecisive Moment 1869 Sby 10/92 13,200
Boutigny, Paul Emile Fr 1854-1929
* See 1993 Edition . . . .
**Bouttats, Frederik (the Elder) Flm a
1612-1661**
* See 1990 Edition . . . .
Bouttats, Johann Baptiste a 1706-1735
O/C 32x50 Cranes Flying by Ruins 1731 Sby 5/93 5,750
Bouvard, Antoine
O/C 24x32 Doge's Palace, Venice Sby 10/92 7,700
O/C 14x11 Venetian Canal Sby 1/93 3,738
O/C 24x32 Doge's Palace and the Grand Canal Skn 5/93 . . 2,970
O/C 24x32 Grand Canal, Doge's Palace Skn 5/93 2,750
Bouvard, J* Fr 19C**
O/C 18x24 Venetian Canal Sby 1/93 4,888
Bouyssou, Jacques Fr 1926-
O/C 29x36 Plage Normande Chr 5/93 3,220
O/C 32x39 Paris, Les Abbesses Chr 5/93 2,530
O/C 29x36 Paris, Le Pont du Carrousel Chr 5/93 2,185
O/C 13x16 Grandcamp Chr 11/92 1,210
Bowen, Benjamin James Am 1859-1930
O/C 22x18 Girl with Roman Lamp Yng 2/93 80
Bowen, John T. Am 1801-1856
W/Pa 10x7 Natural Bridge, Virginia Sby 12/92 3,300
Bower, Alexander Am 1875-1952
O/C 40x40 Autumn Show 1925 Brd 8/93 10,725
W/Pa 14x20 Maine River View Brd 2/93 110
Bower, L. Scott Am 20C
O/C 25x30 Port Scene Fre 10/92 90
Bowers, George Newall Am 1849-1909
* See 1992 Edition . . . .
Bowes, David 20C
* See 1993 Edition . . . .
Bowie, Frank Louville Am 1857-1936
O/C 17x21 Trees and Rocks 1919 Hnd 6/93 300
Bowman, John 1953-
O/Pn 36x84 Harvest 1985 Chr 11/92 4,180
Bowser, David Bustill Am 1820-1900
* See 1991 Edition . . . .
Boxer, Stanley Robert Am 1926-
O/L 80x65 Slenderfallweepedlackingvale 78 But 4/93 2,875
K,H&Pl/Pa 19x26 Darknessdarknessohsopleasant '76 Chr 5/93 345
Boyce, George Price
* See 1991 Edition . . . .
Boyce, Thomas Nicholas Br 19C
W/Pa 12x19 Ships at Sea 1896 Hnd 5/93 475
Boyd, Fiske Am 1895-1975
O/C 28x34 Staten Island Mys 3/93 330
Boyd, Rutherford Am 1884-1951
W/Pa 18x26 Shanghai Express Sby 12/92 23,100
Boyer-Breton, Marthe Marie L. Fr 19C
* See 1992 Edition . . . .
Boyle, Charles Wellington Am 1861-1925
* See 1992 Edition . . . .
Boynton, Raymond Am 1864-1929
O/Pa 15x19 Gold Country 1939 But 10/92 440
Boynton, Raymond Am 1883-1951
O/C 24x18 Manoa Valley, Honolulu 1938 But 3/93 3,300
O/C 20x24 Ranch Near the Foothills 1947 But 6/93 1,380
Boze, Honore Br 1830-1908
* See 1990 Edition . . . .
Bozzalla, Giuseppe It 1874-1958
* See 1992 Edition . . . .
**Brabazon, Hercules Brabazon Br
1821-1906**
S/Pa 7x10 Grand Canal Venice Chr 10/92 1,760
S/Pa 7x11 Campanile Chr 10/92 880
W/Pa 9x11 Val Rosegg Chr 10/92 440
Bracho Y Murillo, Jose Maria Spa 19C
* See 1992 Edition . . . .

Brack, Emil   Ger 1860-1905
* See 1992 Edition ....
Brackenburg, Richard   Dut 1650-1702
* See 1991 Edition ....
Brackett, Sidney Lawrence   Am 19C
O/C 10x14 Boston Harbor - Governor's Island 1884 Eld 7/93 1,760
Brackett, Walter M.   Am 1823-1919
* See 1993 Edition ....
Brackman, David   Br 19C
* See 1991 Edition ....
Brackman, Robert   Am 1898-1980
O/C 20x12 Two Figure Study Chr 5/93 3,680
P/Pa 24x18 Two Peasant Women Doy 5/93 2,970
P/Pb 30x25 Washing her Hair Chr 12/92 2,090
P/Pa 19x25 Seated Woman with Staff Hnd 3/93 1,900
P/Pa 27x22 Two Figures Sby 3/93 1,840
P/Pa 20x26 Study of Two Female Nudes Sby 3/93 .. 1,265
P/Pa 18x24 Two Peasant Women Doy 11/92 1,210
Bradbury, Bennett   Am 20C
* See 1993 Edition ....
Bradbury, Gideon Elden   Am 1837-1904
* See 1993 Edition ....
Bradford, William   Am 1823-1892
O/C 18x30 Among the Icebergs, Labrador Chr 9/92 .. 35,200
O/C 18x30 Fishermen off Labrador 1881 Sby 5/93 ... 24,150
O/C 18x30 Summer Evening in the Arctic 75 Chr 5/93 .. 16,100
O/C 18x30 Perce Rock, Belle Isle Straits Sby 9/92 ... 4,950
W&R/Pa 6x10 End of the Day '74 Eld 7/93 1,540
Bradley, Anne Cary   Am 1884-
O/C 22x20 Corner Albion Perry's Garden Chr 12/92 .. 4,180
O/C 24x20 Monday Afternoon Skn 9/92 302
Bradley, Charles   Am 1883-
O/B 16x20 Desert Scene Mys 3/93 352
Bradley, William   Br 1801-1857
* See 1992 Edition ....
Bradshaw, Eva Theresa   Am 20C
O/C 12x24 Still Life Yellow Roses Skn 3/93 770
Bradstreet, Julia E.   Am 19C
O/B 9x14 Three Paintings Yng 5/93 150
Brady, Mary   Am a 1880-1913
* See 1993 Edition ....
Brail, Achille Jean Theodore   Fr 19C
* See 1991 Edition ....
Braley, Clarence E.   Am 1858-1925
P/Pa 13x23 Twilight Scene Acushnet River Eld 8/93 .. 248
Bramer, Leonard   Dut 1594-1674
* See 1990 Edition ....
Bramley, Frank   Eng 1857-1915
O/B 16x12 Fisherman with Pipe Dum 5/93 800
Bramtot, Alfred Henri   Fr 1852-1894
* See 1992 Edition ....
Brancaccio, Carlo   It 1861-1920
* See 1993 Edition ....
Branchard, Emile Pierre   Am 1881-1938
* See 1992 Edition ....
Brancusi, Constantin   Rom 1876-1957
* See 1991 Edition ....
Brandani, Enrico   It 1914-
* See 1993 Edition ....
Brandao-Giono, Wilson   20C
* See 1992 Edition ....
Brandeis, Antonietta   Aus 1849-1920
O/Pn 9x13 Spanish Steps, Rome Sby 1/93 16,100
O/Pn 13x9 Outing at the Pitti Palace Wes 12/92 7,700
O/Pn 9x6 Ca Foscari, Venice Sby 5/93 5,175
Brandi, Giacinto   It 1623-1691
* See 1992 Edition ....
Brandner, Karl C.   Am 1898-1961
O/C 20x24 Castle Rock Hnd 9/92 325
O/B 12x16 Landscape '20 Hnd 9/92 225
**Brandriff, George Kennedy   Am
1890-1936**
O/B 18x14 Children of the Mission But 6/93 3,162
O/M 18x15 Children of the Mission Wes 10/92 2,200
O/Ab Size? Waves crashing against rocks Wlf 12/92 1,700

Brandt, Carl L.   1831-1905
O/C 30x17 Classical Figures (2) Chr 2/93 3,300
Brandt, Rexford Elson   Am 1914-
W/Pa 15x21 Fishing Off the Point But 3/93 2,750
W/Pa 13x21 Salton Sea State Park But 10/92 2,750
W/Pa 11x20 Morning Wave 60 Mor 2/93 750
Brandtner, Fritz   Can 1896-1969
O/B 8x10 No Title - No. 2 '68 Sbt 5/93 2,200
MM 10x13 Abstract Composition Sbt 5/93 1,980
I/Pa 17x22 Georgian Bay Sbt 5/93 1,496
MM 9x8 City View - #48 Sbt 11/92 1,452
I/Pa 10x14 Abstract Composition Sbt 11/92 1,056
W/Pa 12x16 View of the Gaspe Sbt 5/93 704
Brangwyn, Sir Frank   Br 1867-1956
* See 1993 Edition ....
Branner, Martin   Am 1888-1970
Pl/Pa 6x20 Three Daily Comic "Winnie Winkle" Ih 11/92 ... 225
Bransom, Paul   Am 1885-1979
W/Pa 30x22 Portrait of a Gentlemen '06 Fre 10/92 ... 100
Brant, C.   Am 20C
W/Pa 16x21 Ships at Sea 1901 Mys 3/93 138
Braquaval, Louis   Fr 1856-1919
O/B 14x19 Campagne le Soir Doy 5/93 2,640
O/Pn 19x12 La Vieille Ville Sby 5/93 2,300
Braque, Georges   Fr 1882-1963
O/B 10x16 Barques au Sec Sby 11/92 110,000
**Brascassat, Jacques Raymond   Fr
1804-1867**
* See 1993 Edition ....
Brasher, Rex   Am 1869-1960
W/Pa 15x21 Flamingos Nesting 1909 Mys 12/92 ... 1,320
W/Pa 15x21 Shore Birds on the Rocks 1910 Mys 12/92 .. 660
Brasilier, Andre   Fr 1929-
O/C 24x29 Cavaliers sur la Neige 1977 Sby 2/93 36,800
O/C 29x36 Bruyeres-sur-Fere, Tardenois Chr 11/92 .. 13,200
Brathey, Bennett   Am 20C
O/C 29x46 Rocky Seashore Hnd 5/93 100
Brauer, Erik
W/Pa 20x15 A Joyful Shout of Triumph Sby 11/92 .. 3,850
W/Pa 20x15 For Two Zuzin Sby 11/92 3,850
Braun, Maurice   Am 1877-1941
O/C 14x18 Summer Landscape But 3/93 8,250
O/C 25x30 Hill Country But 3/93 7,150
O/B 6x9 Landscape Mor 6/93 6,050
O/C 36x40 Early Springtime Mor 6/93 5,500
O/C 20x26 Sunset But 10/92 1,760
Brauner, Victor   Rom 1903-1966
* See 1993 Edition ....
Brauntuch, Troy   1954-
* See 1993 Edition ....
Bravo, Claudio   Chl 1936-
O/C 63x59 Requiem for a Soprano Chr 11/92 181,500
P&Pe/Pa/Pn 30x43 El Enigma Chr 11/92 41,800
Sg&C/Pa 15x13 Mujer con Rosa Chr 11/92 35,200
C&Pe/Pa/M 39x28 Gato con Clavel Chr 11/92 33,000
P&H/Pa 20x26 Tin Cans 1971 Sby 11/92 31,900
Sg&C/Pa 29x40 Still: Lemons and Seashells 1943 Sby 5/93 25,300
C,Pe&Sg/Pa 39x28 Gato Chr 11/92 24,200
C&Pe/Pa 26x20 Legs and Hands Chr 11/92 14,300
P&O/Pa 3x3 Mariposa 1970 Sby 5/93 3,738
Bray, Arnold   Am 1892-1972
O/Cb 12x16 Reclining Nude Lou 6/93 450
Brayer, Yves   Fr 1907-1990
O/C 26x32 Printemps En Provence 1961 Sby 6/93 ... 14,950
O/C 32x39 Les Cabanes du Peintre en Camargue But 5/93 9,200
O/C 21x26 Le Maisons du Pont-Neuf 1956 Chr 11/92 .. 8,250
Brebiette, Pierre   Fr 1598-1650
* See 1993 Edition ....
Breck, John Leslie   Am 1861-1899
O/C 18x22 The River Chr 5/93 29,900
**Breckenridge, Hugh Henry   Am
1870-1937**
* See 1993 Edition ....
Bredin, Rae Sloan   Am 1881-1933
O/C 12x14 Gray Day/Delaware Valley Scene Skn 11/92 ... 8,800

Breen, Marguerite   Am 1885-1964
* See 1993 Edition . . . .
Breenbergh, Bartholomeus   Dut 1598-1657
* See 1993 Edition . . . .
Breham, Paul Henri   Fr 1850-1933
* See 1992 Edition . . . .
Brehm, George   Am 1878-1966
C/Pa 27x35 Men Trying to Hoise Cornerstone Ih 5/93 550
Brehm, Worth   Am 1883-1928
C/Pa 23x16 Boy Listening Ih 5/93 950
Breitbach, Carl   Ger 1833-1904
* See 1992 Edition . . . .
Breitmayle, M. V.   Am 20C
O/B 11x9 Landscape Hnd 9/92 150
Breitner, George Hendrik   Dut 1857-1923
* See 1991 Edition . . . .
Bremer, A.
O/C 24x20 Still Life Zinnias and Delphiniums Wlf 9/92 750
Brendekilde, Andersen   Dan 1857-1920
* See 1993 Edition . . . .
Brenner, Carl C.   Am 1838-1888
* See 1992 Edition . . . .
Brent, Adalie Margules   Am 1920-1992
Et/Pn 24x16 Boy Peeling Corn 1945 Lou 6/93 950
Brereton, J.   Br 19C
O/C 30x43 Horse in Country Landscape 1834 Hnd 3/93 . . . 9,600
Bresdin, Rodolphe   Fr 1825-1885
Pl/Pb 3x5 Fishermen in a Landscape 1868 Chr 5/93 5,175
Pl&S/Pa 4x3 Figures in a Landscape Chr 5/93 3,450
Pl/Pa 5x6 Figures in a Medieval Town Chr 5/93 1,610
Pl/Pa 2x3 Joseph and Potiphar's Wife Chr 5/93 1,093
Pl/Pa 1x3 Soldiers on Horseback Chr 5/93 1,035
Pl/Pa 2x2 Four Mounted Horsemen Chr 5/93 978
O/Pn 6x4 Portrait of Young Man Lou 6/93 225
Bressin, F.   Fr 19C
O/B 9x8 Horse Portraits Negofol & Oversight Chr 2/93 2,420
Bressler, Emile Alois Lucien   Sws 1886-1966
O/C 25x31 Plowing the Field 36 But 5/93 2,875
Bret, Paul   Br 1902-
O/B 15x18 Le Cap 1926 Yng 5/93 1,200
Bretland, Thomas   Br 1802-1874
* See 1992 Edition . . . .
Breton, Andre   Fr 20C
* See 1990 Edition . . . .
Breton, Jules Adolphe   Fr 1827-1906
O/C 37x32 La Mauvaise Herbe 1901 Sby 5/93 46,000
O/C 15x12 Petite glaneuse assise dans champ Chr 5/93 . . 25,300
O/C/Pn 8x10 The Return Home Chr 10/92 12,100
Pe/Pa 7x5 Woman Praying Wlf 12/92 325
Brett, Dorothy Eugenie   Am 1882-1977
* See 1991 Edition . . . .
Brett, Harold Mathews   Am 1880-1955
S/Pa 25x16 Woman in Rocking Chair Hnd 9/92 150
Breuer, Henry Joseph   Am 1860-1932
O/C 16x20 View of Mt. Tamalpais 1917 But 6/93 4,025
O/C 20x26 Pacific Sunset But 6/93 575
Breul, Hugo   Am 1854-1910
W/Pa 9x6 Girl and Cat 1904 Yng 2/93 425
Brevoort, James Renwick   Am 1832-1918
O/C 14x28 Late Summer Fishing 68 Chr 12/92 9,900
O/C 11x20 Farmington, Connecticut 67 Sby 3/93 6,900
O/C 15x22 Fishing on the Pond Chr 9/92 6,600
O/C 14x11 Figures in Wooded Landscape Wlf 5/93 1,300
Brewer, Bessie   Am 1883-1952
O/C 21x17 Copper Pot and Fruit Mys 12/92 165
Brewer, Nicholas Richard   Am 1857-1949
O/B 15x19 Desert Patchwork Fre 4/93 375
Brewerton, George Douglas   Am 1827-1901
P/Pa 28x22 Majestic View Across a River 1873 But 10/92 . . 660
Brewster, Amanda   Am 1859-
* See 1993 Edition . . . .

Brewster, Anna Richards   Am 1870-1952
O/Pn 4x7 Trafalgar Square Wlf 5/93 375
Brewtnall, Edward Frederick   Eng 1846-1902
W&Cw/Pa 31x19 The Frog-Prince 1880 Chr 10/92 4,400
O/C 36x61 Bailiff's Daughter of Islington 1879 Sby 10/92 . . 3,850
Breydel, Karel   Flm 1678-1733
O/Pn 7x10 Cavalry Skirmishes Chr 10/92 7,150
Brianchon
O/B 6x9 Landscape Ald 5/93 350
Brianchon, Maurice   Fr 1899-1979
O/C 21x26 Le Page Sby 5/93 32,200
O/C 32x39 Nature morte aux poires Chr 11/92 24,200
W&Pe/Pa 12x19 Campagne d'Ile de France Chr 2/93 1,980
Briante, Ezelino   It 1901-1970
O/C 25x37 After the Snowfall in the City Chr 2/93 1,045
O/Cb 16x20 A Busy Street Chr 2/93 352
O/B 13x20 A Harbor Scene Chr 2/93 220
Brice, William   Am 1921-
* See 1992 Edition . . . .
Bricher, Alfred Thompson   Am 1837-1908
O/Pn 12x20 Afternoon at the Shore Sby 3/93 65,750
O/C 20x42 New England in Autumn '85 Sby 12/92 63,250
O/C 15x33 Evening at Scituate-Low Tide Sby 5/93 60,250
O/C 22x32 Summer Afternoon, Long Island Sby 5/93 37,375
W&G/Pa 14x21 Low Tide 1880 Chr 12/92 22,000
W&Pe/Pa/B 10x21 Far Rockaway Beach Chr 5/93 11,500
W/Pa 23x15 Drying the Main at Anchor Sby 12/92 9,350
O/C 7x12 Autumn on the Lake 66 Chr 5/93 9,200
O/B 9x7 A Wintry Day 62 Chr 3/93 8,625
W/Pa 9x21 Seashore with Rocky Point Lou 12/92 3,900
O/C 10x8 River Landscape 64 But 12/92 3,850
W&Pe/Pa/B 10x26 Rocky Coast Sby 3/93 2,990
O/B 9x13 Ships Off a Rocky Coast Sby 9/92 2,090
W&G/Pa 13x20 Morning Calm/Shore View Skn 9/92 880
W/Pa 10x21 Steamer at Sea Fre 4/93 800
Bricknell, William Harry W.   Am 1860-
O/C 30x40 Jerome Bonaparte Squire, Violin Hnd 5/93 . . . 13,000
Bridges, Fidelia   Am 1835-1923
W/Pa 15x10 Birds and Nest on Branch Hnd 10/92 60
Bridgman, Frederick Arthur   Am 1847-1928
O/C 33x46 In a Village at El Biar, Algiers Chr 5/93 63,000
O/C 24x37 Domestic Interior Scene Chr 10/92 41,800
O/C 16x22 The First Steps 1878 Chr 5/93 40,250
O/C 30x20 Young Moorish Girl 188 Chr 10/92 22,000
O/C 21x36 Last Glow: Tangiers Sby 10/92 14,300
O/C 22x45 Calm Coast of Algiers Sby 10/92 11,000
O/C 18x35 At the Running Brook Chr 5/93 10,350
O/C 20x29 Arab Women at the Town Wall 1925 Sby 2/93 . . 9,775
O/C 21x26 Rue Droite, Dans le Vieux Nice Sby 5/93 6,900
O/C 41x21 La Cigale 1882 Sby 9/92 4,950
O/C 18x35 Relaxing Among Trees and Flowers But 12/92 . . 4,675
O/C 22x38 Entrance to a Mosque Sby 2/93 4,600
O/B 11x17 Caravan A Bou-Saada 1920 Wes 10/92 880
O/C 15x13 Brittany Peasant Lou 6/93 800
Briedly, George   Am 20C
W&G/Pa 13x26 Sheep by a Blossom Tree Fre 10/92 170
Briganti, Nicolas P.   Am 1895-1989
O/C 28x40 Doges Palace, Venice Chr 5/93 2,760
O/C 18x41 The Grand Canal, Venice Sby 3/93 2,645
O/C 24x36 Mediterranean Coast Sby 3/93 2,013
O/C 24x36 Venetian Canal Sby 3/93 1,495
O/C 24x18 Venetian Canal Hnd 5/93 850
O/C 24x36 River Landscape with Figures FHB 6/93 450
Brigden, Frederick Henry   Can 1871-1956
O/B 12x16 Old Mill; Sun Gleams: Pair Sbt 11/92 1,496
O/B 12x16 Landscape with Elm Sbt 11/92 704
W/Pa 14x12 Woodland Stream Sbt 11/92 660
Briggs, Austin   Am 1909-1973
O/B 12x11 Boy Standing Over Cowering Woman Ih 5/93 . . . 750
Pl&Pe/Pa 6x20 Four Daily Comics "Flash Gordon" Ih 5/93 . . 425
Briggs, Lamar   Am 20C
W/Pa 42x30 Untitled Hnd 9/92 200

Briggs, Lela Am 1896-
O/B 19x15 Still Life Lou 12/92 275
Briggs, Warren C. Am 1867-1903
  * See 1993 Edition ....
Bright, Hy Br 19C
W/Pa 16x12 Birds in Floral Landscape FHB 3/93 350
Brignoni, Sergio 20C
  * See 1991 Edition ....
Bril, Paul Flm 1554-1626
O/Pn 31x41 Allegories Months of Jan/Feb: Pair Sby 1/93 266,500
Brinkley, Nell Am -1944
Pl/Pa 13x16 Happy Image of Home Ih 5/93 700
Briscoe, Franklin Dulin Am 1844-1903
O/C 30x51 Returning with the Catch Sby 9/92 6,600
O/Pn 5x7 On the Fishing Banks 1885 Chr 5/93 4,830
O/B 9x13 Off for the Wreck 97 Chr 3/93 4,600
O/C 30x50 Fisherfolk on the Shore 1894 Skn 11/92 3,520
O/C/B 10x20 Sailors Caught in Gale 96 Sby 3/93 3,450
O/C 20x36 Grand Canal, Venice Chr 5/93 2,070
O/B 7x11 Ships at Sea Mys 12/92 1,100
O/Ab 7x11 The Surf at the Bar: Pair 1901 FHB 6/93 1,000
Brispot, Henri Fr 1846-1928
O/C 14x18 The Cardinal's Dinner Guest Sby 5/93 4,888
Brissaud, Pierre
W&Pe/B 10x7 The Chess Game Sby 10/92 550
Brissot De Warville, Felix S. Fr 1818-1892
  * See 1993 Edition ....
Bristol, John Bunyan Am 1826-1909
O/C 12x9 Fishing in the Wilds Mys 3/93 522
Bristow, Edmund Eng 1787-1876
O/C 18x16 The Old Horse Skn 3/93 3,300
O/B 8x10 Still Life with Game Bird Slo 7/93 950
Brito, Luis Rocca Ven 1964-
O/C 63x79 El Estranque 1990 Chr 11/92 8,800
Brito, Ramon Vasquez 20C
  * See 1991 Edition ....
Brittain, Miller Gore Can 1912-1968
O/B 24x16 Floating Blue Figure '54 Sbt 5/93 1,848
Broadhead, W. Smithson Br 19C
  * See 1992 Edition ....
Brock, C. E. Am 1870-1938
Pl/Pa 9x7 People on Line 1900 Ih 5/93 700
Brock, Richard H. Br 20C
  * See 1991 Edition ....
Broderson, Morris Am 1928-
O/C 55x72 Reimei Kurama Yama 1962 Sby 9/92 1,430
Brodie, Gandy 1924-
O/C 48x72 Untitled 1963 Chr 2/93 2,640
Broe, Vern Am 20C
O/B 12x16 Catboats Eld 7/93 908
O/M 18x14 Two Girls in a Garden Eld 11/92 440
Broedelet, Andre Dut 1872-1936
  * See 1993 Edition ....
Broemel, Carl W. Am 1891-
W/Pa 15x19 Bermuda Wtf 5/93 300
Broge, Alfred Dan 1870-1955
  * See 1993 Edition ....
Bromley, Frank C. Am 1860-1890
O/C 14x20 Morning L. Is. Sound 1884 Skn 3/93 1,320
Bromley, John Mallord Br 20C
W/Pa 14x21 Bosham Mill Sby 1/93 1,725
Bromley, William Br 19C
  * See 1992 Edition ....
Bronkhorst, Johannes 1587-1617
Bc/V 12x17 Pheasants, Parrot, Cockatoo Chr 1/93 13,200
Broodthaers, Marcel 1924-1976
E/Pls 47x32 Minuit 69 Chr 11/92 14,300
Brook, Alexander Am 1898-1980
O/C 13x9 View of the Savannah River Chr 9/92 2,200
O/C 30x24 Still Life Flowers, Fruit, Um 1927 Chr 12/92 1,980
O/C 11x9 Figure 40 Sby 3/93 748
Brooke, E. Adveno Br 19C
  * See 1992 Edition ....

Brooker, Harry Br a 1876-1902
O/C 28x36 Afternoon Games 1894 Sby 10/92 24,200
O/C 28x36 The Archers 1894 Sby 10/92 17,600
Brookes, Samuel Marsden Am 1816-1892
O/B 14x11 Still Life of Birds 1868 Wes 3/93 1,045
Brooks, Allan Can 1869-1946
G/Pa/B 11x15 Garganey Teal Doy 11/92 1,430
G/Pa/B 11x15 Tuffed Duck Doy 11/92 1,320
G/Pa/B 11x14 Falcated Teal Doy 11/92 1,210
G/Pa/B 11x15 Bronze Winged Duck Doy 11/92 935
G/Pa/B 11x15 Madagascan White Back Duck 1920 Doy 11/92 880
Brooks, Henry Howard Am
  * See 1991 Edition ....
Brooks, James Am 1906-1992
A/C 60x72 Token 81 Sby 2/93 21,850
A/C 60x36 Ipswich 80 Sby 2/93 13,800
A/C 14x35 Tryon 1969 Chr 11/92 3,190
Brf/Y&A/Pa 15x20 Untitled 64 Chr 11/92 2,200
Brooks, Leonard Frank Can 1911-
A&L/C 31x23 Thema Japones 1977 Sbt 11/92 1,760
Brooks, Maria Br a 1869-1890
  * See 1991 Edition ....
Brooks, Nicholas Alden Am 1849-1904
O/C 9x7 Sailboats on Moon Lit Waters Lou 9/92 300
Brooks, Romaine
O/C 14x11 Contesse Anna de Noailles Chr 9/92 3,850
Brooks, Thomas Br 1818-1892
  * See 1991 Edition ....
Broulliet, Pierre Andre Fr 1857-1914
  * See 1990 Edition ....
Brouwer, Glen Dut 20C
O/C 24x36 Spring Landscape Lou 9/92 600
Browere, Alburtus Del Orient Am 1814-1887
  * See 1993 Edition ....
Brown, Abigall Keyes Am 1891-
O/C 30x36 The Old Timers Skn 9/92 880
Brown, Alexander Kellock Br 1849-1922
O/C 39x34 Woman Near a Cottage Fre 10/92 1,050
Brown, Arthur W. Am 1881-1966
Pe&S/Pa 14x23 Men in Canoe Paddling 1936 Ih 5/93 1,400
Y&S/Pa 15x13 Ladies And Gentlemen '28 Sel 4/93 150
Brown, Benjamin Chambers Am 1865-1942
O/Cb 12x16 Near Elsinore, Dark Canyon But 3/93 4,125
O/C 16x20 Golden Evening Sel 9/92 4,000
O/B 12x16 Near Arcadia, California Mor 6/93 1,870
W/Pa 9x13 Venetian Scene But 3/93 1,210
Brown, Byron Am 1907-1961
  * See 1992 Edition ....
Brown, C. Emerson Am 1869-
O/C 14x20 Newburyport Marshes Yng 2/93 1,050
Brown, Carlyle Am 1919-1964
  * See 1992 Edition ....
Brown, Christopher Am 1951-
O/C 65x80 Swimmer But 10/92 2,750
Brown, Fred C. Am 19C
O/Ab 9x11 Apples, Grapes, Pears Wtf 3/93 750
Brown, George Elmer Am 1871-1946
  * See 1993 Edition ....
Brown, George Loring Am 1814-1889
O/C 22x36 Stormy Day Mys 3/93 1,980
Brown, Harrison Bird Am 1831-1915
O/C 13x25 Portland Brd 2/93 7,700
O/C 25x48 Surf and Cliffs 75 Brd 8/93 4,400
O/C 14x24 Mt. Washington Yng 5/93 3,750
O/C 25x29 The Falls Brd 8/93 3,520
O/C 13x23 Sunlit Cliffs Brd 2/93 1,760
O/C 10x18 Sailing on Casco Bay Brd 2/93 1,650
O/C 13x25 Salvaging the Old Wreck Brd 8/93 1,650
O/C 13x23 Saco Rapids Brd 2/93 1,430
W/Pa 6x10 Casco Bay Brd 2/93 715
Brown, Horace Am 1876-
  * See 1993 Edition ....

Brown, James Am 1951-
E&H/C 84x78 Horse Shoes and Crosses Chr 2/93 26,400
E,O&H/C 60x54 Untitled 1983 Chr 11/92 24,200
E/C 90x78 Untitled Sby 2/93 17,250
O/C 40x40 Scene from the Life of Achilles 1985 Chr 11/92 . 6,050
Brown, James Francis Am 1862-1935
O/C 25x18 Viewing an Auction Exhibition '90 Chr 12/92 990
Brown, Joan Am 1938-1991
O/C 74x72 Things in Landscape 59 Sby 2/93 35,650
O/C 72x96 People and Eye Trees in the Park 61 Sby 5/93 28,750
G/Pb 30x40 Reclining Nude Sby 5/93 25,300
O/C 78x96 Running at McAteer Track 1976 But 10/92 9,900
A/Pa 29x45 Figure Study 73 But 10/92 6,600
MM/Pa/B 40x26 Untitled But 4/93 4,312
O/C 56x52 Chicken at Jack's 1960 Hnd 12/92 4,000
O/C 36x30 Portrait of Modesto 1978 But 10/92 1,870
P/Pa 11x15 Vandarecca 76 But 10/92 1,320
Brown, John Appleton Am 1844-1902
O/C 25x35 Old Road Near Paris But 6/93 6,900
P/Pa/B 14x19 The Sheep Meadow Skn 3/93 3,025
P/Pa 16x21 Sunlight and Shadows Brd 2/93 935
O/Pa 16x21 Sunlight and Shadows 1870 Ald 9/92 600
Brown, John George Am 1831-1913
O/C 40x60 Heels Over Head 1894 Sby 5/93 195,000
O/C 30x25 Blackberry Picking Sby 5/93 35,650
O/C/B 25x30 We Can't Be Caught But 12/92 30,250
O/C 30x25 The Study Hour 1905 Sby 12/92 25,300
O/C 18x12 The Berry Picker 1877 Sby 12/92 19,800
O/C 24x17 Don't Move 1904 Chr 3/93 19,550
O/C 24x16 Teasing the Pup Sby 3/93 16,100
O/C 25x20 Can't Be Coaxed Chr 9/92 15,400
O/C 30x20 He Toils at Eighty 1884 Sby 5/93 13,800
O/C 25x20 Only a Nickel, Joe 1906 Chr 9/92 13,200
O/C 23x15 Have a Game? Chr 12/92 11,000
O/C 24x18 Shoe Shine Boy Wes 10/92 11,000
O/B 8x6 Fishin' 1872 Skn 9/92 5,500
O/C 25x20 Self Portrait 1897 Fre 10/92 4,250
O/C 7x6 Two Children in Woods Sby 3/93 2,185
Brown, John Lewis Fr 1829-1890
* See 1993 Edition
Brown, Manneville Ellihu D. Am 1810-1896
* See 1990 Edition ....
Brown, Mather Am 1761-1831
* See 1992 Edition ....
Brown, Paul Am 1893-1960
* See 1992 Edition ....
Brown, Reynold Am 1917-1991
MM&G/Pa 13x29 Poster "Revenge of Creature" Ih 5/93 .. 15,000
Brown, Robert Woodley Br 19C
O/C 20x24 A Punt in a Rural Scene Hnz 5/93 475
Brown, Roger Am 1941-
A/C 54x72 Interlocken mit Clouden 1976 Hnd 5/93 17,000
O/C 47x59 Trailer Park, Truck Stop Sby 5/93 8,625
O/C 72x52 Land O'Lakes Chr 10/92 8,250
Brown, Roy H. Am 1879-1956
O/C 21x26 View of a Sheltered Cottage Skn 9/92 1,210
O/C 20x24 New Hampshire Valley Yng 5/93 1,200
Brown, Samuel Joseph Am 1907-
O/C 30x21 Apples for Sale Wes 5/93 385
O/C 30x21 Old Man with a Pipe Wes 5/93 330
Brown, Walter Francis Am 1853-1929
O/B 7x9 Bridge Over the Seine Yng 2/93 400
Brown, William Beattie Br 1831-1909
* See 1993 Edition ....
Brown, William Mason Am 1828-1898
O/C 30x25 Still Life with Fruit and Vase Sby 5/93 42,550
O/C 12x18 October on Great Otter Creek, VT Chr 12/92 .. 17,600
O/C 14x12 Still Life with Fruits and Nuts Skn 9/92 16,500
O/C 10x12 Strawberries Chr 3/93 9,775
O/B 12x11 Hints of Autumn Sby 3/93 8,625
O/B/B 10x12 Summer Haze Chr 9/92 6,600
Brown, William Theophilus Am 1919-
O/Pn 12x18 Masquerade '61 But 4/93 3,737

Browne Am 19C
O/C 23x32 Frontiersman Firing Eld 4/93 880
Browne, Byron Am 1907-1961
O/C 28x24 Head of a Woman 1937 Chr 5/93 17,250
O/C 38x30 Sword Swallower 1946 Chr 5/93 9,775
O/C 14x12 Head of a Clown 1947 Chr 5/93 2,990
O/C 26x20 Harlequin 1960 Sby 9/92 2,200
I&G/Pa 26x20 Moonlight Aura 1954 Sby 3/93 1,840
I&G/Pa 26x20 Cyclops 1950 Sby 3/93 1,725
G/Pa 26x20 Kouros 1950 Sby 3/93 1,725
W,G&I/Pa 20x26 Beach at Sunrise 1954 Sby 9/92 1,430
G&I/Pa 26x17 The Acrobat 1948 Sby 9/92 1,210
O/C 6x15 Provincetown Beach 1958 Skn 5/93 1,100
I,W&G/Pa 19x25 Docked Boats 1953 Slo 5/93 800
Browne, Charles Francis Am 1859-1920
O/C 16x24 Cushings Island, Maine Hnd 10/92 1,700
Browne, Edward Br 19C
O/C 17x24 A Mare and Foal Chr 10/92 3,850
Browne, George Elmer Am 1871-1946
O/B 14x14 By the Shore Wlf 5/93 2,100
O/B 14x16 Blue Water, White Sails Lou 9/92 1,700
O/C 24x20 Fishing Harbor Wes 5/93 660
O/Pn 11x14 Big Sky/A Cloud Study Skn 9/92 358
Browne, Haviot Knight (Phiz) Br 1815-1882
W/Pa 8x7 Spanish Soldier with Sword Lou 9/92 150
Browne, Henriette Fr 1829-1901
* See 1993 Edition ....
Browne, Margaret Fitzhugh Am 1884-1972
* See 1993 Edition ....
Browne, Matilda Am 1869-1947
O/C 18x25 Playing in the Garden 1914 Skn 3/93 30,800
O/C 14x16 Cow's Heads Mys 12/92 385
Brownell, Charles De Wolf Am 1822-1909
* See 1991 Edition ....
Brownell, Peleg Franklin Can 1857-1946
O/B 10x16 By Ward Market, Ottawa '24 Sbt 5/93 11,880
O/B 13x16 Skiers in Snowy Landscape Sbt 5/93 1,980
P/Pa 11x15 Boats on the Shore Wes 10/92 880
Browning, Robert Barrett Br 1846-
O/C 83x51 Before the Mirror 1887 Chr 10/92 33,000
Brownlow, George Washington Br 19C
O/C 25x30 The Newborn Lamb 1863 Chr 2/93 5,500
Brownscombe, Jennie Augusta Am 1850-1936
O/C 20x29 An Unexpected Visitor Doy 11/92 3,300
O/C 30x40 Governor Morris Addressing Assembly Eld 8/93 . 1,650
O/C 10x13 Woman Reading 1881 Dum 9/92 1,600
W/Pa 28x21 Young Woman Bouquet of Roses Sby 9/92 . 1,540
W/Pa 11x8 Young Girl Mys 3/93 935
Brozik, Wencelas Von Vacslaw Czk 1851-1901
O/C 31x19 A Standing Cavalier Chr 10/92 2,420
Bruandet, Lazare Fr 1755-1804
G/Pa 13 dia Paysage avec Riviere Slo 7/93 1,200
Bruce, Edward Am 1879-1943
* See 1993 Edition ....
Bruce, Matt Br 20C
O/B 16x20 Cattle in Sunlit Landscape Sel 9/92 300
Bruce, Patrick Henry Am 1881-1936
* See 1992 Edition ....
Bruce, William Am 19C
* See 1991 Edition ....
Bruce, William Blair Can 1859-1906
* See 1993 Edition ....
Brueghel, Abraham & Courtois Flm 1631-1690
* See 1993 Edition ....
Brueghel, Jan (the Elder) Flm 1568-1625
O/Pn 15x23 The Adoration of the Magi 1617 Sby 5/93 .. 332,500
O/Pn 7 dia Flight into Egypt 1600 Sby 5/93 134,500
Brueghel, Jan (the Younger) Flm 1601-1678
O/Pn 19x14 Still Life Flowers Elaborate Pokal Sby 1/93 . 123,500

Brueghel, Jan & Van Balen, H. **1601-1678**
O/Cp 14x18 Allegory of Love Chr 10/92 60,500
Brueghel, Pieter (III) **Flm 1589-**
  * See 1991 Edition ....
Brueghel, Pieter (the Younger) **Flm 1564-1638**
O/Pn 17x23 Village Wedding Dance Sby 1/93 387,500
O/Pn/Pn 18x26 Hurdy-Gurdy Player 1610 Chr 5/93 167,500
O/Pn 7 dia Peasant Seated; Holding Staff: (2) Chr 5/93 . 107,000
Bruestle, Bertram G. **Am 1902-**
W/Pa 9x12 Winter River Scene Mys 12/92 138
Bruestle, George M. **Am 1872-1939**
O/C 22x30 New England Barns Sby 3/93 2,645
O/B 12x16 CT Farm Scene Mys 3/93 1,017
Brugairolles, Victor **Fr 1869-1936**
O/Pn 25x20 Venetian Canal Scene Hnd 10/92 450
Brugo, Giuseppe **It 20C**
O/C 27x17 The Curious Maid 1894 Chr 10/92 10,450
Bruls, Louis Joseph **Ger 1803-1882**
  * See 1993 Edition ....
Brumback, Louise Upton **Am 1872-1929**
W/Pa 19x15 Red Boat, Gloucester Wes 12/92 715
Brun, Guillaume Charles **Fr 1825-1908**
  * See 1993 Edition ....
Brunel De Neuville, Alfred A. **Fr 1852-1941**
O/C 21x32 Overturned Basket of Grapes Plums Chr 5/93 . 4,600
O/C/B 26x22 Kittens Playing w/Spool of Thread Chr 2/93 . 3,300
O/C 15x18 Les Petits Chats Sby 10/92 2,200
Brunelleschi, Umberto **It 1879-**
G,Pe&Gd/Pa 16x12 Two Costume Designs Sby 10/92 ... 2,420
W&Pe/Pa 13x10 Two Costume Designs Sby 10/92 2,310
G,Pe&Gd/Pa 15x11 Costume Design for Flower Sby 10/92 . 2,200
W,G&Gd/Pa 15x11 Costume Design for a Rose Sby 10/92 . 2,200
G,Pe&Gd/Pa 19x13 Costume Van Dongen Woman Sby 10/92 1,980
G,Pe&Gd/Pa 12x19 Two Costume Designs Sby 10/92 ... 1,980
G,Pe&Gd/Pa 12x18 Costume Pheasant Mistress Sby 10/92 . 1,320
G,Pe&Gd/Pa 19x13 Costume Painter's Woman Sby 10/92 . 1,100
W,G&Pe/Ab 14x21 Decor Design Pearl Fisherman Sby 10/92 990
G,W&Pe/Ab 14x21 Decor Design Pearl Fisherman Sby 10/92 990
G&Gd/Pa 10x6 Lady with Pigeons (2) Fre 4/93 700
W&Pe/Ab 14x21 Decor Design Pearl Fisherman Sby 10/92 . 660
G/Pa 10x7 Lady of Leisure (2) Fre 4/93 650
G/Pa 11x6 Two Ladys (2) Fre 4/93 650
Brunery, Francois **It 1845-**
O/Pn 22x15 News of the Day Sby 2/93 4,025
Brunery, Marcel **Fr 20C**
  * See 1993 Edition ....
Brunner, Ferdinand **Aus 1870-**
O/C 19x11 Village Street Sby 1/93 10,350
Brunner, Harry D.
O/B 18x14 Abstract Cityscape Ald 5/93 50
Brunner, Josef **Ger 1826-1893**
O/B 10x17 Thatched Cottage by a Lake 863 Chr 10/92 . 2,310
Brunning, William Allen **Br 19C**
O/C 39x34 Fisherfolk by the Sea Chr 10/92 2,200
Brunoni, Serge **Can 1930-**
O/C 30x40 L'Instant D'Avant Sbt 11/92 1,496
Brush, George De Forest **Am 1855-1941**
O/C 31x40 A Family Group 1907 Sby 12/92 242,000
O/C/B 10x9 Woman in Renaissance Dress 1910 Chr 12/92 28,600
Bruton, Helen **Am 1898-1985**
C/Pa 19x25 The Mackay House, Spring But 10/92 440
Bruton, Margaret **Am 1894-1983**
O/C 24x30 Taxco Tots (Mexico) But 10/92 1,430
O/C 30x24 Taxco, Mexico But 10/92 1,320
W/Pa 18x19 Mining Mountain Landscape But 10/92 935
O/Pa 17x23 New Roof, Mexico But 10/92 880
O/C 34x28 Girl in the Orchard But 6/93 575
O/B 22x18 Mexico Scene Mor 6/93 302
Bruyere, Elise **Fr 1776-1842**
  * See 1991 Edition ....
Bruzzi, Stefano **It 1835-1911**
  * See 1991 Edition ....

Bryant, Everett Lloyd **Am 1864-1945**
O/M 22x18 Floral Still Life Wes 5/93 1,10
G/Pa 8x19 Winter Snow Scene Mys 3/93 35
Brymner, William **Can 1855-1925**
  * See 1991 Edition ....
Bryson, Hope Mercereau **Am 20C**
  * See 1991 Edition ....
Bucci, *** **18C**
  * See 1993 Edition ....
Buchbinder, Simeon **Pol 19C**
  * See 1990 Edition ....
Buche, Joseph **Aus 1848-**
O/Pa 16x10 The Peddler Skn 9/92 24
Buchheister, Carl **Ger 1890-1964**
  * See 1992 Edition ....
Buchholz, Erich **1891-1972**
  * See 1993 Edition ....
Buchner, Georg **Ger 1858-1914**
  * See 1992 Edition ....
Buck, Charles Claude **Am 1890-1974**
O/B 14x34 Nude with Butterfly But 3/93 7,70
O/B 16x20 Boiling Clouds But 3/93 2,20
O/B 30x22 The Wave Spirit 1939 Mor 6/93 1,98
O/B 32x45 Family Hnd 5/93 1,00
O/B 22x18 Portrait of a Young Man But 10/92 55
Buckland, August P. **Am 1879-1927**
O/C 14x18 Landscape Mor 6/93 46
Buckler, Charles E. **Am 1869-**
O/C 28x38 The Mountain Valley Pool Lou 3/93 90
O/C 28x38 Winter Landscape Hnd 12/92 55
Buckley, Stephen **Am 1944-**
  * See 1992 Edition ....
Budelot, Philippe **Fr 19C**
O/C 16x22 A Stag Hunt Chr 5/93 3,45
Buehr, Karl A. **Am 1866-1952**
O/C 24x44 Yosemite Yng 5/93 90
O/B 18x22 Landscape Hnd 6/93 85
Buel, Hubert **Am 1915-1984**
W/Pa 15x21 Laguna Beach/Hotel/Coast Highway Mor 6/93 . 770
Buell, Alfred **Am 1910-**
W&O/Pa 16x13 Kissing Couple Ih 5/93 350
Bueno, Antonio **It 1918-1984**
  * See 1991 Edition ....
Bueno, Xavier **It 1915-1979**
O/C 28x20 Ragazzo Chr 5/93 8,625
MM/C 28x20 Donna in Piedi Chr 11/92 6,600
Buergerniss, Carl **Am 1877-1956**
O/C 24x20 Rear View of a Female Nude 1914 Fre 10/92 . 250
O/C 18x14 Woman in the Field Fre 10/92 250
O/C 27x20 Portrait Artist's Daughters 1924 Fre 10/92 240
O/C 24x18 Woman in Black Fre 10/92 170
O/C 14x18 Catboat Fre 4/93 90
O/C 14x18 Nude by the Water Fre 4/93 80
O/C 14x18 Boy in Woods 1910 Fre 4/93 70
O/C 18x24 Farm Buildings and Clouds 1925 Fre 4/93 60
P/Pa 9x11 Westmont Fre 10/92 60
Buff, Conrad **Am 1886-1975**
O/Cd 10x18 Desert Landscape Mor 2/93 2,750
Buffet, Bernard **Fr 1928-**
O/C 58x46 Vase de dahlias 64 Chr 11/92 99,000
O/C 35x58 Compo Santo, Pisa 59 Sby 10/92 88,000
O/C 35x58 Compo Santo, Pisa 59 Sby 5/93 79,500
O/C 36x26 Portrait de Femme 49 Sby 11/92 49,500
O/C 26x32 Compotier 54 Sby 5/93 48,875
O/C 32x51 Scene de Village avec Eglise 60 Hnd 5/93 48,000
O/C 26x18 Delphiniums bleus 64 Chr 11/92 44,000
O/C 26x40 Saint-Quai Portrieux '68 But 4/93 40,250
O/C 29x24 Vase de Coquelicots 64 Chr 10/92 38,500
O/C 21x26 Fleurs fond jaune 59 Hnd 5/93 28,000
O/Pa/M 26x20 Vase de Fleurs 63 Sby 2/93 20,700
Pl/Pa/C 20x26 Nature Morte 50 Chr 10/92 16,500
O/Cb 9x6 L'insecte Chr 11/92 6,050
Buffin, Carlos **Fr 19C**
  * See 1991 Edition ....

54

Bugiardini, Giuliano It 1475-1555
* See 1992 Edition . . . .
Buhler, Augustus W. Am 1853-1920
* See 1993 Edition . . . .
Buhot, Felix Hilaire Fr 1847-1898
* See 1992 Edition . . . .
Buizard, A. Con 19C
* See 1992 Edition . . . .
Buland, Jean Eugene Fr 1852-1927
* See 1991 Edition . . . .
Bull, Charles Livingston Am 1874-1932
MM 14x11 Wolf Studies Mys 12/92 110
Bull, Rene Am -1942
Pl/Pa 3x8 Fairy Emerging from Inkwell Ilh 11/92 325
Bulleid, George Lawrence Br 1858-
* See 1991 Edition . . . .
Bulman, Orville Am 20C
O/C 43x36 Mes Amis 1973 Sby 6/93 2,300
O/C 20x18 The Beginner/Caribbean Scene 1957 Skn 5/93 . . . 990
Bulmer, Lionel
* See 1992 Edition . . . .
Bunce, William Gedney Am 1840-1916
O/Pn 14x25 Distant View of Venice Sby 3/93 2,415
O/C 16x24 Lagoon with San Giorgio Maggiore Sby 3/93 . . . 1,265
O/Pn 13x9 Venetian View Sby 3/93 690
O/B 9x13 Venice at Sunset Yng 5/93 350
Bundy, John E. Am 1853-1933
O/C 10x14 Farm Scene 1901 Dum 10/92 800
Bunker, Dennis Miller Am 1861-1890
O/C 22x18 Portrait of a Woman Sby 5/93 29,900
Bunker, Ida May Am 20C
O/C 20x24 Eucalypti Hollywood Hills 1931 Mor 11/92 425
Bunner, Andrew Fisher Am 1841-1897
O/C 21x16 Venetian Canal Scene Skn 11/92 1,320
W/Pa 8x15 The Lagoon in Venice Sby 3/93 805
Bunnett, Henry Richard S. Can a 1880-
* See 1991 Edition . . . .
Bunny, Rupert Charles Wulsten Aut
1864-1947
* See 1991 Edition . . . .
Bunol, Laureano Barrau Spa 1863-1950
O/C 36x48 Return of the Fisherman Chr 10/92 60,500
Buono, Leon Guiseppe It 1888-
* See 1992 Edition . . . .
Burbank, Elbridge Ayer Am 1858-1949
* See 1993 Edition . . . .
Burce, William Gedney Am 1840-1916
O/Pn 9x13 Venetial Scene Mys 12/92 248
Burch, Alice Am 1909-
O/C 19x24 Marguerite Lou 9/92 100
Burchard, Pablo Chl 1876-
* See 1990 Edition . . . .
Burchfield, Charles Ephraim Am
1893-1967
W/Pa 39x33 Cicada Song in September 1956 Sby 5/93 . . 90,500
W&G/Pa/Pb 22x17 Sun Setting/Smoke 1917 Sby 12/92 . . . 88,000
W/Pa/B 30x40 Pussywillows in the Rain Sby 12/92 38,500
W&Pe/Pa/B 21x30 The Haymow Chr 12/92 34,100
W/Pa 22x17 Between Two Willows 1918 Sby 12/92 19,800
W/B 15x21 Winter Afternoon, Salem 1920 Sby 3/93 11,500
W&Pa/B 15x21 Clouds at Sunset 1917 Sby 9/92 8,800
W&C/Pa 18x27 Old Cottage in May 1933 Chr 5/93 7,425
Pe/Pa 14x20 Road to the Casino Brd 8/93 2,640
Pe/Pa 6x8 Untitled: Two Drawings Sby 9/92 770
W/Pa 6x4 Stylized Flowers 1933 Wlf 9/92 650
Burd, Clara Miller Am
* See 1993 Edition . . . .
Burden, Chris 1946-
MM/B 30x36 Two Drawings 1977 Chr 11/92 22,000
MM/B 32x40 Peace (From Devil Drawings) 1982 Chr 2/93 . 13,200
Mk&L/B 30x40 Man of the Seventies 1975 Sby 11/92 . . . 12,100
L,Ph&l/Pa 32x40 Thank You 1979 Sby 11/92 11,000
Bp,l&Rs/Pa 30x36 Full Financial Disclosure 1977 Chr 5/93 . 5,750
Buren, Daniel 1938-
A/F 57x53 Blanc et Noir Chr 2/93 12,100

Burg, Copeland Am 1895-
O/C 24x28 Cat and Vase 1938 Hnd 9/92 400
Burgariiko, J. Ger 19C
O/Cd 18x27 Huntsmen Leaving the Castle Wlf 9/92 700
Burgdorff, Ferdinand Am 1883-1975
O/B 24x30 Field of Poppies and Lupines 1939 But 3/93 . . . 2,750
O/B 20x24 San Francisco Peaks, Flagstaff, AZ Lou 12/92 . . . 850
O/C 18x21 Tropical Sky, Bay of Manila 1919 Hnd 5/93 600
O/M 22x30 Landscape 1933 Mor 6/93 550
O/C 16x24 Venus and Maria de la Salute 1915 Hnd 5/93 . . . 450
O/Pn 8x10 Two: Desert Scenes; Cloud Study Lou 9/92 250
Burgerniss, Carl Am 20C
O/C 14x20 Cornfields and Cottages 1926 Fre 4/93 60
Burgers, Hendricus Jacobus Dut
1834-1899
* See 1992 Edition . . . .
Burgess, Arthur James Aut 1879-1957
* See 1992 Edition . . . .
Burgess, J. H. Br 19C
O/C 9x12 Coastal Scene Hnd 12/92 80
Burgess, John Bagnold Eng 1830-1897
O/C 21x28 East Meets West 1874 Sby 5/93 16,100
Burgin, Victor 20C
Ph 40x61 St. Laurent Demands New Lifestyle Sby 2/93 . . . 1,725
Burke, Ainslee Am 20C
* See 1993 Edition . . . .
Burkel, Heinrich Ger 1802-1869
O/C 18x23 Travelers at an Alpine Tavern 1843 Skn 11/92 . 60,500
Burkhardt, Emerson C. Am 1905-1969
O/Cb 28x39 San Marco, Venice '60 Wlf 5/93 1,500
Burkhardt, Hans Gustav Am 1904-
O/C 16x20 Red and White Striped Barrier 1945 But 10/92 . . 1,760
P/Pa 24x18 Two Female Nudes 1940 Sby 3/93 1,380
Burlando, Leopoldo It 1841-
O/C 33x23 Ambrosian Library, Milan Hnd 12/92 4,600
Burleigh, Charles H. H. Br 1875-1956
* See 1990 Edition . . . .
Burleigh, Sidney R. Am 1853-1931
W/Pa 7x10 Cloudy Day Mys 3/93 605
W/Pa 5x7 Mountainous Landscape Mys 3/93 165
Burlin, Paul Harry Am 1886-1969
O/C 25x30 Houses in the Hills Chr 12/92 1,320
Burlingame, Dennis Meighan Am 1901-
* See 1992 Edition . . . .
Burliuk, David Am 1882-1967
O/C 39x50 Mural Landscape Sby 3/93 8,625
O/C 48x36 Dahlias and Mums in Autumn 1964 Sby 3/93 . . 5,175
O/C 32x52 La Siesta Sby 9/92 4,675
O/C 17x22 Southampton Sby 9/92 4,675
O/C 11x9 Cafe Scene Sby 3/93 2,875
O/C 20x16 Floral Still Life and Strawberries Sby 3/93 2,750
O/C 18x13 The Duet Sby 9/92 2,530
O/C 23x36 Positano Sby 9/92 2,310
O/Pn 19x15 Still Life Flowers in a Vase 1907 Chr 5/93 . . . 2,300
O/Cb 11x16 Bradenton Beach, Florida 1946 Chr 5/93 2,070
O/B 14x18 Capri 1949 Sby 3/93 1,840
O/C 27x19 Still Life with Photograph 1854 Sby 9/92 1,760
O/C 12x16 New Mexico Sby 9/92 1,650
MM/Pa 12x15 Tea Time But 4/93 1,610
O/M 11x16 Winter in Ural Mountain Town Sby 3/93 1,495
O/Pn 6x12 Friends Sby 9/92 1,430
O/Pn 8x10 Woman with White Goat Sby 3/93 1,380
G/M 9x12 Figures on a Dock Sby 9/92 1,320
O/M 13x14 The Card Players Sby 9/92 1,320
O/Cb 8x10 New Mexico But 4/93 1,265
MM/C/Pn 12x22 Marussia 1951 But 10/92 1,210
O/C 12x12 Woman Leading a Cow Sby 9/92 1,210
O/C/B 12x16 Portugal 1954 Sby 3/93 1,150
O/B 6x6 Vase of Flowers on a Bench Sby 3/93 863
W,P&l/Pa 11x15 A Farm in Hampton Bays Sby 3/93 690
W/Pa 11x17 Beach Scene Sby 3/93 575
O/Pn 12x5 Nude by a Waterfall Mys 12/92 358
Burmann, Fritz
* See 1993 Edition . . . .

Burmester, Georg
* See 1992 Edition ....
Burne-Jones, Sir Edward Coley Br 1833-1898
* See 1993 Edition ....
Burnett, Calvin W. Am 1921-
* See 1993 Edition ....
Burnett, William Hickling Br a 1844-1860
W/Pa 5x7 Tivoli 1838 Yng 2/93 100
Burnham, Anita Willets Am 1880-
O/C 18x12 Portrait of a Woman 1913 Wes 5/93 1,100
Burns, James Am 19C
* See 1993 Edition ....
Burns, Maurice K. Am 20C
* See 1993 Edition ....
Burpee, William Partridge Am 1846-1940
* See 1993 Edition ....
Burr, Alexander Hohenlohe Br 1837-1899
* See 1990 Edition ....
Burr, George Brainerd Am 1876-1950
O/C 25x19 Story Hour Chr 3/93 10,350
Burr, George Elbert Am 1859-1939
* See 1992 Edition ....
Burr, John Sco 1831-1893
* See 1993 Edition ....
Burras of Leeds, Thomas Br 19C
* See 1991 Edition ....
Burrell, Alfred Ray Am 1877-1952
O/Cb 16x18 Near Monterey, A Calm Day But 3/93 550
Burri, Alberto It 1915-
* See 1993 Edition ....
Burrington, Arthur Alfred Br 1856-1925
* See 1991 Edition ....
Burroughs, Bryson Am 1868-1934
MM/Pa 12x12 Two: Europa; Embarkation Skn 11/92 330
Burrows, F.
O/B 16x20 Old Farm Ald 5/93 60
Burt, Charles Thomas Br 1823-1902
* See 1992 Edition ....
Burton, Richmond 1960-
O/L&Wd 81x24 Untitled 1989 Sby 5/93 6,325
O/Pa/C 16x20 Untitled Sby 5/93 4,025
Busch, J. A. H. Dut 19C
* See 1992 Edition ....
Busch, Wilhelm Ger 1832-1908
* See 1993 Edition ....
Bush, Jack Hamilton Can 1909-1977
A/C 44x19 Sketch for Banner 1968 Sbt 5/93 8,360
O/C 36x40 September 1932 '32 Sbt 11/92 5,280
O/B 16x20 La Maison de Mme. Robitaille 1943 Sbt 11/92 .. 3,520
O/C 25x33 Saturday Afternoon on the Don '30 Sbt 5/93 .. 3,080
Bush, Norton Am 1834-1894
O/C 22x36 Tropical River Scene 1891 Sby 5/93 32,200
O/C 14x24 Boats on the River '74 Sby 5/93 8,050
O/Pa 16x8 Napa Falls 81 But 3/93 3,850
O/B 26x11 Pair of Tropical Landscapes But 10/92 2,200
Bushmiller, Ernest Am 1905-
Pl/Pa 15x23 Sunday Comic "Nancy" Ih 11/92 400
Bussiere, Gaston Fr 1862-1929
* See 1991 Edition ....
Busson, Charles Fr 1822-1908
* See 1992 Edition ....
Busson, Georges Fr 1859-1933
W&K/Pa 23x36 The Stag Hunt 1917 Chr 6/93 1,955
W/Pa 33x26 Le Relance: Rallye et Anjou 1899 Chr 6/93 .. 1,725
Bustos, Hermenegildo LA 1832-1907
* See 1992 Edition ....
Bustrov, Alexander Kirovich Rus 1956-
O/C 32x30 Still Life 89 Skn 9/92 550
Butcher, Laura Page Am 20C
* See 1993 Edition ....
Buthe, Michael
* See 1992 Edition ....
Butinone, Bernardino 1450-1507
O/Pn 10x9 The Crucifixion Chr 5/93 200,500

Butler, Charles E. Am 20C
O/B 9x12 The Fishing Hole 01 Skn 11/92 1,100
Butler, Edward Brugess Am 1853-1928
O/C 25x30 Landscape 1907 Mor 6/93 1,320
Butler, Howard Russell Am 1856-1934
O/C 42x52 Zion Canyon, Utah Sby 3/93 16,100
O/C/B 14x20 Cliffs on the Coast But 6/93 2,588
P/Pa 9x6 Mountain Landscape Eld 11/92 193
P/Pa 6x9 Sunrise Eld 11/92 176
Butler, Joseph Swd 1825-1885
* See 1992 Edition ....
Butler, Joseph Niklaus Ger 1822-1885
* See 1993 Edition ....
Butler, Mary Am 1865-1946
O/C 24x32 Harborside Fre 10/92 1,000
O/C 20x28 Purple Mountains Fre 10/92 700
O/C 20x28 Along the Coast Fre 10/92 600
O/C 20x28 Mountain Landscape Fre 10/92 600
O/C 24x30 Animated Landscape Fre 10/92 475
O/C 20x28 Landscape with Houses Fre 10/92 450
O/C 24x32 October in Scotland Wes 10/92 412
O/C 20x28 Jagged Rocks Fre 10/92 325
O/B 10x12 Maine Coast Yng 5/93 200
Butler, Philip Am 19C
O/C 14x24 Commercial Wharf, Nantucket Brd 8/93 880
Butler, Rozel Oertle Am 20C
O/C 39x30 Mexican Flower Market Lou 6/93 800
O/C 26x38 Taos Pueblo at Night Lou 9/92 600
Butler, Theodore Earl Am 1876-1937
O/C 24x29 French Landscape '06 Chr 12/92 27,500
O/C 32x25 William Howard Hart, Giverny Brd 8/93 13,200
Butler, Thomas Br a 1750-1759
* See 1990 Edition ....
Butman, Frederick A. Am 1820-1871
O/C 12x20 Landscape with Children But 10/92 6,050
O/C 18x30 The River Bridge But 10/92 2,750
O/C 16x24 Cattle by a Mountain Stream Mys 12/92 385
Butteri, Giovanni Maria It -1606
* See 1991 Edition ....
Buttersach, Bernhard Ger 1858-1909
* See 1990 Edition ....
Buttersworth, James Edward Am 1817-1894
O/C 17x27 Picking Up the Pilot Isle of Shoals Chr 5/93 . 123,500
O/C 20x30 Pilot Boats Sby 12/92 82,500
O/C 12x20 The Yacht Race Chr 5/93 23,000
O/C 14x22 Yachting in Baltimore Harbor Chr 5/93 20,700
O/C 20x30 Clipper in Heavy Seas Sby 12/92 17,600
O/Pn 8x12 View of Nassau Bahamas Chr 12/92 17,600
O/C 8x14 New York Harbor Chr 3/93 7,475
Buttersworth, Thomas Br 1768-1842
O/C 12x18 Clipper Ships Riding Rough Sea Sby 6/93 17,250
O/C 12x17 His Majesty's Ships off Bugio Light Hnd 10/92 16,000
O/C 12x17 His Majesty's Ships off Tower Belem Hnd 10/92 11,000
O/C 15x21 Stormy Seascape Hnd 5/93 6,200
Butting, Edwin Br 19C
O/B 8x13 Valley with Fisherman Hnd 9/92 500
Buttner, Werner 1954-
O/C 47x79 Machine Painting/5 Spare Parts 84 Sby 11/92 .. 5,500
Button, Albert Prentice Am 1872-
W/Pa 9x3 Arched Bridge, Staten Island Yng 2/93 325
Buzzi, A. It 19C
O/C 21x16 The Love Letter But 11/92 4,675
W/Pa 21x14 Street Music Skn 11/92 1,210
W/Pa/B 13x10 Italian Peasant Women Chr 2/93 330
Buzzi, Achille It 19C
W/Pa 20x13 Picking Grapes Chr 5/93 1,265
Bye, Ranulph Am 20C
W/Pa 14x21 Bay Scene Ald 9/92 575
W/Pa 12x19 Winter Field Ald 9/92 450
Byer, Samuel Am 20C
O/C 24x30 Alaskan Huskies Fre 4/93 220
Bygrave, William Am 19C
* See 1993 Edition ....

Byles, William Hounsom   Br a 1890-1916
  * See 1993 Edition . . . .
Byron, Bourmond   Hai 1923-
  * See 1993 Edition . . . .
Byron, Michael   1954-
  * See 1993 Edition . . . .
Caballero, Jorge Mantilla
  O/C 39x39 Untitled 71 Sby 11/92   4,125
Caballero, Luis   Spa 1943-
  O/C 57x45 Figura 88 Chr 11/92   16,500
Caballero, Maximo   Spa 19C
  * See 1991 Edition . . . .
Cabanel, Alexandre   Fr 1824-1889
  O/C 35x58 Cleopatre essayante des poisons Chr 2/93 . .   440,000
Cabie, Louis-Alexandre   Fr 1853-1939
  O/Pn 12x10 A Rocky Outcrop 1890 Chr 5/93   1,150
Cabot, Edward Clarke   Am 1818-1901
  W/Pa 5x8 Two Maine Lake Scenes Yng 5/93   475
Cabre, Manuel   Ven 1890-
  * See 1993 Edition . . . .
Cabrera, Miguel   Mex 1695-1786
  O/C 29x22 Nuestra Senora del Rosario 1768 Chr 11/92 . .   46,200
  O/C 29x23 San Juan Nepomuceno 1766 Chr 11/92   29,700
  O/Cp 11x8 San Jose 1737 Sby 11/92   13,200
Cacciarelli, V*   It 19C**
  * See 1993 Edition . . . .
Cachoud, Francois Charles   Fr 1866-1943
  O/C 26x32 A Starry Night Sby 10/92   11,000
  O/C 28x32 Neige et Lune Chr 5/93   2,300
Caddy, John Herbert   Can 1801-1883
  W/Pa 16x24 View of Hamilton Sbt 5/93   2,112
Cadell, Francois Campbell B.   Br 1883-
  * See 1992 Edition . . . .
Cadenasso, Giuseppe   Am 1858-1918
  P/Pa 11x14 Sunset on the Marsh But 10/92   1,870
Cades, Giuseppe   It 1750-1799
  * See 1992 Edition . . . .
Cadmus, Paul   Am 1904-
  ET/M 21x36 Hommage a Reynaldo Hahn Chr 9/92   35,200
  T/Pa 8x12 Mask with False Noses Chr 12/92   23,100
  K&C/Pa 13x20 Sleeping Figure Sby 9/92   4,950
  K&C/Pa 13x20 Male Nude Sby 9/92   4,400
  W&Pe/Pa 13x15 Seated Male Nude Chr 12/92   3,850
  C&K/Pa 7x9 Maggie the Bulldog (5) Chr 12/92   2,640
  Pl/Pa 9x7 Male Torso Chr 12/92   2,420
Cadora, E.   It 20C
  W/Pa 15x9 Venetian Canal Fre 4/93   100
Cady, Fred   Am 1855-1960
  * See 1993 Edition . . . .
Cady, Harrison   Am 1877-1970
  O,G&V/B 18x24 The Moonlight Sonata 1962 Sby 5/93 . . .   36,800
  Pl/W/Pa 26x20 Peter has a Plan Ih 5/93   550
  W,H&W/Pa 19x14 Beach at Pelican Bay Skn 3/93   495
Cady, Henry   Am 1849-
  W/Pa 15x23 Seascape Lou 9/92   475
Cady, Sam
  * See 1990 Edition . . . .
Caffe, Nino   It 1909-1975
  O/Pn 5x11 Five Paintings Chr 11/92   7,700
  O/Pn 12x26 Il Povero Novizio Chr 5/93   6,325
  O/Pn 8x24 Libera Uscita Slo 4/93   3,250
  O/Pn 12x14 I Curiosi Slo 4/93   2,250
  O/C 8x13 Interno di Cucina Slo 4/93   2,250
  O/Pn 8x11 Una Giornata di Pioggia Chr 5/93   2,185
  O/Cb 6x8 Red Hoops But 4/93   1,150
Cafferty, James H.   Am 1819-1869
  O/C 28x22 Portrait Gentleman w/Red Feather 1860 Brd 2/93 .   660
Caffi, Margherita   It 17C
  * See 1993 Edition . . . .
Caffieri, Hector   Br 1847-1932
  * See 1991 Edition . . . .
Caffyn, Walter Wallor   Br -1898
  * See 1992 Edition . . . .
Cage, John   20C
  K/Sp 30x42 Mesostic Tribute Sby 5/93   11,500

Cagnacci, Guido   It 1601-1663
  * See 1992 Edition . . . .
Cagniart, Emile   Fr 1851-1911
  * See 1992 Edition . . . .
Cagnoni, Amerino   It 1853-
  * See 1992 Edition . . . .
Cahill, William   Am 1878-1924
  O/C 28x42 Grandmother, Mother and Child But 12/92   6,050
Cahoon, Charles Drew   Am 1861-1951
  O/C 12x18 Girl at a Gate Eld 8/93   550
Cahoon, Martha   Am 1905-
  * See 1993 Edition . . . .
Cahoon, Ralph   Am 1910-1982
  O/M 15x19 Mermaids, Fisherman, Balloon, Ship Eld 8/93 .   17,600
  O/M 14x15 Sailors Watching Mermaids Eld 8/93   4,730
  W/Pa 8x6 Mermouse Holding Fishing Rod 1973 Eld 11/92 .   825
  Pe/Pa 12x8 Fisherman and Mermaid Eld 11/92   308
  Pe/Pa 12x9 Mermaids at a Lighthouse 1965 Eld 11/92 . . .   253
  Pe/Pa 9x8 Sailor and Mermaid Eld 11/92   121
Caille, Leon Emile   Fr 1836-1907
  O/Pn 10x7 The Spinning Wheel 1882 Chr 10/92   2,200
Caillebotte, Gustave   Fr 1848-1894
  O/C 36x29 Soleils au Bord de la Seine Sby 11/92   715,000
Cain, Georges-Jules-Auguste   Fr 1856-1919
  * See 1993 Edition . . . .
Caironi, Luigi   It 19C
  * See 1992 Edition . . . .
Caiserman-Roth, Ghitta   Can 1923-
  I/Pa 11x14 The Painter Sbt 5/93   748
Calame, Alexander   Sws 1810-1864
  * See 1993 Edition . . . .
Calbet, Antoine   Fr 1860-1944
  O/C 29x24 La Danse Aux Castagnettes Sby 10/92   6,050
  C,W&G/Pa 10x13 Reclining Nude with Poppies Chr 10/92 . .   3,080
Calder, Alexander   Am 1898-1976
  G/Pa 23x31 Untitled '47 Sby 2/93   20,700
  G/Pa 23x31 Untitled '47 Sby 2/93   10,925
  G/Pa 29x43 Striped Face with Red Nose 69 Sby 5/93 . . .   9,200
  W/Pa 29x41 Untitled 62 Sby 5/93   9,200
  I/Pa 9x10 Three Drawings Sby 10/92   8,250
  Br&I/Pa 30x43 Untitled 74 Chr 11/92   7,700
  G/Pa 29x43 Sheres Behind the Sun 71 Sby 2/93   7,475
  G/Pa 30x43 Untitled 70 Sby 2/93   7,475
  G/Pa 30x44 Untitled 75 Sby 6/93   7,475
  G/Pa 42x29 Untitled 66 Sby 2/93   6,900
  G/Pa 43x29 Two Starfish 72 Sby 2/93   6,325
  G/Pa 23x31 Untitled '47 Sby 2/93   6,325
  G&I/Pa 30x43 Flags 69 Chr 2/93   6,050
  G/Pa 30x44 Untitled 73 Sby 10/92   6,050
  G&I/Pa 23x31 Untitled 66 Chr 2/93   6,050
  G/Pa 30x41 Untitled (Sunrise) 75 Sby 10/92   6,050
  W&G/Pa 29x42 Emerging Forms 61 Sby 2/93   5,750
  W&I/Pa 19x16 Running Woman '46 Sby 6/93   5,750
  G,Br&I/Pa 30x43 Equilibre 73 Chr 2/93   4,950
  G,Br&I/Pa 30x43 Mistral 71 Chr 5/93   4,830
  G,Br&I/Pa 43x30 Pavots 71 Chr 5/93   4,830
  G/Pa 29x43 Color Field: Yellow is Dominant 69 Sby 2/93 .   4,600
  Br,I&G/Pa 31x23 Tapestry 74 Chr 11/92   4,400
  G/Pa 43x30 Red and Blue Wave 73 Sby 2/93   4,313
  G/Pa 29x43 Untitled 67 Sby 2/93   4,025
  G,Br&I/Pa 43x30 Christaux 72 Chr 5/93   3,450
  G/Pa 16x12 Untitled 73 Sby 10/92   3,300
  G,Br&I/Pa 30x43 Untitled Chr 5/93   3,220
  G/Pa 7x10 Abstract 49 Sby 6/93   3,163
  G&Pe/Pa 7x10 Untitled 49 Sby 2/93   3,163
  G/Pa 29x43 Untitled 68 Sby 6/93   3,163
  G/Pa 7x10 Untitled 49 Sby 2/93   2,760
  G/Pa 29x22 Untitled 65 Sby 10/92   2,530
Calderini, Marco   It 1850-
  * See 1992 Edition . . . .
Calderon, Charles-Clement   Fr 20C
  * See 1993 Edition . . . .

**Calderon, Philip Hermogenes   Br
1833-1898**
O/C 12x9 The Young Model Wlf 9/92   850
Calderon, William Frank   Br 1865-1943
O/C 33x27 A Pearl of Great Price 1884 Chr 10/92   24,200
Caldwell, Edmund   Br 1852-1930
* See 1992 Edition . . . .
Cale, George Viscont   Eng 19C
* See 1992 Edition . . . .
Caliari, Paolo   It 1528-1588
* See 1993 Edition . . . .
Califano, John   Am 1864-1924
O/C 14x20 Mountain Landscape with River Sby 3/93   1,380
O/C 22x28 Still Life with Fruit Hnd 12/92   950
O/C 24x36 Bridge and Water Dum 3/93   600
O/C 12x18 California Coast Lou 12/92   600
O/C 14x22 Landscape with Sheep Fre 10/92   450
Califano, John Edmund   Am 1862-1946
O/C 29x42 Woman with Herd of Goats Fre 4/93   2,100
Caliga, Isaac Henry   Am 1857-
* See 1993 Edition . . . .
Caligo, Domenico   It 19C
O/C 24x30 Interior of a Cathedral Fre 4/93   2,200
**Calixto De Jesus, Benedito   Brz
1853-1927**
* See 1993 Edition . . . .
Callari, Paolo   It
* See 1991 Edition . . . .
Calliano, Antonio Rafaelle   It 1785-1824
* See 1993 Edition . . . .
Calliyannis, Manolis
O/C 23x28 La Petite Colline 1956 Sby 6/93   1,035
Callot, Jacques   Fr 1592-1635
* See 1991 Edition . . . .
Callow, John   Br 1822-1878
* See 1993 Edition . . . .
Callow, William   Eng 1812-1908
* See 1992 Edition . . . .
Calogero, Jean   It 1922-
O/C 29x24 The Fantastic Hat Sby 2/93   3,565
O/B 12x16 Scene de Coulisse Hnd 12/92   1,000
O/C 22x18 Young Woman Sby 2/93   920
O/B 15x22 Clowns Hnd 3/93   500
O/B 12x16 La Fete Hnd 3/93   475
O/C 22x18 Lady with a Lamp Hnd 12/92   70
Calvaert, Dionisio   Flm 1540-1619
* See 1993 Edition . . . .
Calvi, Ercole   It 1824-1900
* See 1992 Edition . . . .
Calvi, Paolo   It a 1830-1866
O/B 8x11 Sailing Near a Rocky Coast Wes 5/93   1,760
Calyo, Nicolino   Am 1799-1884
G/Pa 12x17 Napoli da Mare Wlf 12/92   925
Camacho, Jorge   Cub 1934-
* See 1991 Edition . . . .
**Camarasa, Hermengild Anglada   Spa
1873-1959**
* See 1993 Edition . . . .
Camarroque, Charles   Fr 19C
* See 1993 Edition . . . .
Cambello, G*
O/C 30x25 Floral Still Life Sby 10/92   550
Cambiaso, Luca   It 1527-1585
O/C 42x33 Venus Blindfolding Cupid Chr 1/93   22,000
O/Pn 18x12 Madonna and Child Sby 5/93   20,700
Cambier, Guy   Fr 1923-
O/C 16x13 Tete Du Femme 1954 Sby 6/93   1,150
Camerarius, Adam   a 1650-1689
* See 1993 Edition . . . .
Cameron, Duncan   Br 1837-1916
O/C 20x30 Harvesting Near Lampyet Fre 4/93   1,300
Cameron, Robert Hartly   Am 1909-
O/C 29x29 Summer Beach Outing Doy 11/92   2,090
O/C 30x39 Children Playing in the Surf Fre 10/92   1,900
O/C 31x31 Tea time Under Parasols Fre 4/93   1,700

**Caminade, Alexandre Francois   Fr
1789-1862**
* See 1993 Edition . . . .
Camino, Guiseppe   It 1818-1890
O/C 32x46 Allevatori di Pecore 1888 Sby 10/92   6,600
Camoin, Charles   Fr 1879-1965
O/C 20x29 Elise au hamac, Cassis Chr 11/92   44,000
O/C 25x33 Le Brusc Hnd 10/92   15,000
O/C 26x32 Paysage Chr 10/92   11,000
P/Pa/B 18x13 Portrait de Femme Chr 5/93   5,175
O/C 18x15 La Femme en Robe Blanche Hnd 3/93   3,000
Camoir, Ch.
O/C 18x23 Landscape 1934 Ald 9/92   3,750
Camos, H.   Fr 19C
O/B 10x8 Chickens Dum 12/92   600
Campbell, Hugh
O/C 30x40 Katz Road 1948 Ald 9/92   500
O/C 30x40 Mill Dam on the Rancocas Ald 9/92   375
O/C 20x24 Orange House Ald 5/93   250
O/C 28x36 White Horses Ald 9/92   75
Campbell, Lang   Am 20C
I/Pa 8x10 Five Images for Uncle Wiggily 1920 Skn 5/93   770
I/Pa 8x10 Five Images for Uncle Wiggily 1920 Skn 5/93   467
Campbell, Laurence A.   Am 1940-
O/C 24x20 The Rose Garden Lou 9/92   1,700
Campbell, Orville A.   Am 20C
O/C 30x40 Blue Bonnets Hnd 12/92   950
Campbell, Paul Zane   20C
* See 1991 Edition . . . .
Campbell, Stephen   20C
O/C 89x94 Pursuit of Mediocrity/House 1988 Sby 10/92 . .   15,400
O/C 108x105 Topiary Gardeners Sby 6/93   4,600
O/C 98x107 Chain of Events 83 Sby 6/93   3,163
Camphausen, Wilhelm   Ger 1815-1885
* See 1992 Edition . . . .
Campigli, Massimo   It 1895-1971
* See 1993 Edition . . . .
Campio, H.   It 19C
* See 1993 Edition . . . .
Campion, George B.   Br 1796-1870
* See 1992 Edition . . . .
Campolmi, S.   It 19C
O/C 21x25 The Happy Family 1878 Chr 2/93   12,650
Camporeale, Sergio   Arg 1937-
* See 1993 Edition . . . .
Campos, Florencio Molina   Arg 1891-1964
O/C/B 16x20 El Cortejo 1942 Chr 11/92   7,150
G/Pa 8x13 Jinete Sby 2/93   1,265
G/Pa/B 8x11 Gaucho 1940 Sby 2/93   575
Campriani, Alceste   It 1848-1933
O/C 12x16 Still Life Grapes and Figs Chr 2/93   12,100
Camprubi, Leontine   Am 1916-
O/C 25x30 Spanish Festival Mys 3/93   192
W/Pa 16x14 Subway Crowd Mys 12/92   110
Camus, Blanche Augustine   Fr 19C
* See 1990 Edition . . . .
Canal, Giovanni Antonio   It 1697-1768
O/C 23x37 Riva Degli Schiavoni, Venice Sby 5/93 . . . . .   2.6425M
Canaletto   It 1697-1768
O/C 23x37 Riva Degli Schiavoni, Venice Sby 5/93 . . . . .   2.6425M
Canas, Benjamin   Brz 1933-
* See 1992 Edition . . . .
Canaveral Y Perez, Enrique   Spa 19C
* See 1990 Edition . . . .
Candia, Domingo   Arg 1896-
* See 1991 Edition . . . .
Candido, Peitro   Dut 1548-1628
* See 1991 Edition . . . .
Canet, Marcel   Fr 1875-
O/C/B 17x39 Napoleonic Military Scenes: Pair Slo 7/93   750
Canevari, Carlo   It 1922-
O/Pn 11x6 Whimsical Scenes: Three Paintings Sby 10/92 . . .   990
O/Pn 10x14 Whimsical Nuns Lou 12/92   300
O/Pn 6x11 High Winds Lou 9/92   125

Caniff, Milton   Am 1907-1988
P/Pa 6x20 Two Daily Comic "Terry and Pirates" llh 11/92 . . . 400
Canjura, Noe   Fr 1924-
O/C 13x18 Apres le Repas Hnd 9/92 325
O/C 18x13 Conversation Hnd 9/92 325
O/C 29x24 Petit Etudiant Hnd 9/92 300
O/C 29x24 Bouquet Hnd 3/93 160
Cannella, Pizzi   1955-
* See 1992 Edition . . . .
Cantagallina, Remigio   It 1582-1630
* See 1992 Edition . . . .
Cantarini, Simone   1612-1648
O/C 22x15 The Rest on the Flight into Egypt Chr 10/92 . . 37,400
Canter, Albert M.   Am 1892-
O/C 18x24 Landscape 1916 Ald 5/93 70
Canton, Gustav Jakob   Ger 1813-1885
* See 1993 Edition . . . .
Cantu, Federico   Mex 1908-1989
O/C 21x15 Harlequin 35 Sby 11/92 13,200
MM/Pa 19x24 Desnuda Rosada con Caracoles '45 But 10/92 2,750
H,l&W/Pa 26x20 Cuatro Jinetes 1944 Sby 5/93 1,725
P/Pa 20x26 Desert Study '48 But 4/93 920
Canu, Yvonne   Fr 1921-
O/C 20x26 La Rochelle Chr 5/93 6,325
O/C 24x32 St. Tropez et Les Pins Chr 5/93 5,750
O/C 18x22 Le Pique-Nique Chr 5/93 4,370
Canuti, Domenico Maria   It 1620-1684
I/Pa 4x2 Justice Slo 7/93 475
Caparn, Thos. J.
* See 1993 Edition . . . .
Capella, Francesco   1714-1787
* See 1992 Edition . . . .
Capon, George Emile   Fr 1890-1980
O/C 29x24 Woman Reading 1930 Hnd 5/93 2,000
Capone, Gaetano   It 1845-1920
O/C 20x12 Women by a Doorway Mys 12/92 1,210
O/Pn 8x10 Moonlight at Big Indian Slo 7/93 650
O/B 8x10 Autumn in the Catskills Slo 5/93 375
O/Cb 6x9 Afternoon in the Catskills Slo 7/93 200
Capp, Al   Am 1909-1979
* See 1993 Edition . . . .
Cappelli, Pietro   It -1924
* See 1991 Edition . . . .
Capuletti, Jose Manuel   Spa 20C1925-
O/C 18x15 Esquisse Wes 10/92 1,430
O/C 16x22 Nu Dans Un Paysage Fre 4/93 900
Caputo, Ulisse   It 1872-1948
O/C 34x26 The Mask 1911 Sby 1/93 6,613
Carabain, Jacques Francois   Bel 1834-1892
O/C 17x22 Vue De Eldfeld Sby 10/92 14,300
Caracciolo, Giovanni Battista   It 19C
* See 1991 Edition . . . .
Caracciolo, L.   It 20C
O/C 24x30 Portrait of a Woman Wtf 9/92 325
Caraud, Joseph   Fr 1821-1905
O/C 32x41 Marie-Antoinette et Fille 1870 Sby 10/92 26,400
O/C 38x29 L'Abbe Complaisant 1877 Sby 10/92 17,600
Caraud, R.   Fr 19C
* See 1993 Edition . . . .
Carbonell, Santiago   Spa 1960-
O/C 51x43 Tres Mujeres Chr 11/92 30,800
Carbonero, Jose Moreno   Spa 1860-
O/Pn 10x16 Religious Pageantry 98 Chr 10/92 22,000
Carchoune, Serge   20C
* See 1991 Edition . . . .
Cardenas, Juan   Col 1939-
* See 1993 Edition . . . .
Cardenas, Santiago   Col 1933-
A/C 43x39 Autorretrato Sby 5/93 7,188
Cardi, Ludovico   It 1559-1613
O/C 36x29 Adoration of the Shepherds Sby 5/93 8,050
Cardona, Juan   Spa 19C
* See 1990 Edition . . . .

Carducci, Adolfo   It 1903-1981
O/C 19x26 Flaneurs au Bois de Boulogne Wes 3/93 935
O/C 19x27 Promenade a Cheval Wes 12/92 825
O/C 19x26 Depart Pour Longchamp Wes 3/93 770
Carelli, A*   It 19C**
* See 1993 Edition
Carelli, Consalave   It 1818-1900
O/Pn 10x17 Bay of Naples from Posillipo Chr 10/92 13,200
O/Pn 9x17 Neapolitan Seascape Chr 10/92 7,150
Carelli, Giuseppe   It 1858-1921
O/C 10x18 Bay of Naples (2) Chr 10/92 8,800
O/Pn 10x19 Fishermen on the Bay Sby 2/93 5,750
O/C 11x19 Harbor and Fishing Boats Chr 5/93 5,175
Carena, Felice   It 1879-1966
* See 1993 Edition
Cargnel, V. Antonio   It 1872-1931
O/C 19x27 Street Scene Wtf 9/92 750
Cariani   It 1485-1547
* See 1993 Edition
Carillo, Lilla   Mex 1930-
* See 1990 Edition
Carlandi, Onorato   It 1848-1939
O/C 40x39 View of the Villa Adriana Sby 10/92 7,700
W/Pb 18x24 Villa Adriana Sby 1/93 4,025
Carles, Arthur Beecher   Am 1882-1952
O/C 30x30 Abstract Composition Fre 4/93 3,600
O/Cb 10x8 On the Canal, Venice Sby 9/92 1,430
O/Pn 7x10 Thatched Cottage and Seascape: Two Sby 9/92 . 1,430
Carlevarijs, Luca   It 1663-1727
* See 1992 Edition
Carlier, M.   Bel 20C
O/C 27x36 Still Life Peaches, Grapes Chr 10/92 3,850
Carlier, Max   Bel 1872-1938
O/C 36x24 Still Life Roses, Anemone Chr 10/92 7,150
Carlier, Modeste   Bel 1820-1878
O/C 47x36 Still Life Peonies, Gladiolas Sby 10/92 13,200
O/C 40x30 Still Life Assorted Flowers Fruit Sel 9/92 8,000
O/C 36x24 Still Life of Roses, Lilacs, Dahlia Lou 6/93 7,300
O/C 36x26 Still Life with Flowers Sby 10/92 4,950
O/C 35x24 Still Life Multi-Colored Roses Sel 12/92 3,500
Carlieri, Alberto   It 1672-1720
O/C 19x26 Classical Ruins with Man Preaching Chr 5/93 . . 18,400
Carlin, James   Am 1910-
O/C 24x36 Tavern Interior Sby 9/92 1,320
Carlisle, B.
O/C 19x27 Courting Couple Dum 7/93 375
Carlo, Chiostri   It 19C
O/C 20x31 Rotterdam Harbor Slo 4/93 1,400
O/C 20x31 Rotterdam Harbour Mys 12/92 990
Carlos, Ernest Stafford   Br 1883-1917
O/C 14x10 Boy Scout Playing the Bugle Sby 1/93 1,035
Carlsen, Dines   Am 1901-1966
O/C 29x27 The Mandarin Coat 1932 Chr 9/92 22,000
O/C 25x22 The Black Bottle Chr 9/92 11,000
O/B 12x15 Rapids and Rocks Hnd 12/92 300
O/B 15x12 Tree on the Cliff Hnd 12/92 300
Carlsen, E.   Am 20C
O/C 30x40 Seascape Lou 3/93 550
Carlsen, Soren Emil   Am 1853-1932
O/C 35x25 Mums 93 But 12/92 49,500
O/C 50x40 Green Trees 1928 Sby 5/93 40,250
O/C 30x35 Still Life Squash Pitcher '93 Sby 9/92 16,500
O/C 30x44 Still Life with Fish 1897 Sby 5/93 14,950
O/B 30x28 Still Life with Black Bottle 1929 Dum 7/93 . . . 12,000
O/C 48x54 Still Life with Game 1894 Chr 9/92 9,900
O/B 15x18 The French Fan 1922 But 12/92 9,900
O/C 20x24 Still Life Teapot and Onion Chr 12/92 8,800
O/C 27x36 Surf Breaking on Rocks Doy 5/93 7,700
O/Pn 12x10 Still life Chinese Objects 1901 Chr 12/92 4,400
O/C 14x10 Seated Woman Sby 3/93 3,680
O/B 5x10 Sand Dunes Chr 3/93 2,760
W/Pa 10x24 Still Life Green Vase, Fan, Glass Chr 12/92 . . . 1,870
O/Pn 8x9 Morning Sunlight Sby 3/93 1,265
O/C 12x16 Landscape 1931 Lou 3/93 1,250
O/C 17x24 Landscape Dum 1/93 1,250

O/C 14x18 Still Life Pitcher and Onions Doy 11/92 1,100
O/C 4x5 Group of Nine Oils Sby 3/93 1,093
W&H/Pa 5x11 29 Drawings Sby 3/93 690
O/C/B 12x10 Seated Woman in Green Sby 3/93 690
O/C 12x16 Rocky Coast Sby 3/93 575

Carlson, John Fabian   Am 1875-1945
O/C/B 31x40 Winter in the Forest Sby 12/92 9,350
O/B 12x16 Sunny Groves Sby 9/92 2,860
O/C 12x16 Gathering Shadows Sby 3/93 2,300
O/C 14x18 Winter Landscape Ald 9/92 950
W/Pa 8x14 Man Launching a Rowboat Dum 7/93 225

Carlyle, Florence   Can 1864-1923
  * See 1993 Edition . . . .

Carmagnolle, Adolphe   Am 19C
O/C 40x32 Children with Trumpet and Bird 1867 Chr 5/93 . . 3,220

Carme, Felix   Fr 19C
O/C 18x26 Grapes, Peaches, Figs & Pumpkin 97 Chr 5/93 . 1,150

Carmichael, Franklin   Can 1890-1945
O/B 12x10 La Cloche Hills, 1921 Sbt 11/92 14,960

Carmichael, James Wilson   Br 1800-1868
  * See 1993 Edition . . . .

Carmienke, Johann Hermann   Am 1810-1867
O/C 51x64 View Castle of Chillon 1858 Sby 9/92 12,100
O/C 36x52 Mt. Vesuvius/Bay of Naples 1860 Chr 5/93 . . . 10,925
O/C 16x24 River and Cottage 1889 Sby 9/92 1,430

Carneo, Antonio   It 1637-1692
O/C 31x28 The Holy Family Sby 1/93 29,900
O/C 50x38 Two Angels Supporting Dead Christ Sby 1/93 . 13,800

Carnicero, Antonio   It 1748-1814
  * See 1991 Edition . . . .

Carnier, Henri   Fr 20C
O/Pn 7x12 Pair: Italian Scenes Sel 4/93 1,050
O/C 20x12 Arab Street Scene Wes 10/92 632

Carnwath, Squeak   Am 1947-
O/Pa 23x30 Look 1989 But 10/92 1,870

Caro, Domenic   Am 1889-1968
O/C 20x27 Bay of Naples (2) Lou 6/93 100

Caro-Delvaille, Henry   Fr 1876-1926
G&O/B 25x21 Meditation 1924 Sby 1/93 1,150

Carolus, Jean   Bel a 1867-1872
O/Pn 28x22 The Introduction Sby 10/92 8,800

Carolus-Duran, Emile Auguste   Fr 1838-1917
  * See 1993 Edition . . . .

Caron, Antoine   Fr 1521-1599
  * See 1991 Edition . . . .

Caron, Paul Archibald   Can 1874-1941
  * See 1992 Edition . . . .

Caroselli, Angelo   It 1585-1652
  * See 1992 Edition . . . .

Carpaccio, Vittore   It 1450-1522
  * See 1993 Edition . . . .

Carpeaux, Jean-Baptiste   Fr 1827-1875
C/Pa 13x10 Portrait of Miss Boudin Chr 5/93 2,760

Carpenter, Ann
O/C 20x24 Norristown Street Scene Ald 9/92 225

Carpenter, Fred Green   Am 1882-1965
  * See 1992 Edition . . . .

Carpentero, Henri Joseph G.   Bel 1820-1874
O/Pn 17x22 Gentleman in a Library 1850 Sby 1/93 6,613

Carpentier, Evariste   Bel 1845-1922
  * See 1993 Edition . . . .

Carpioni, Giulio   It 1611-1674
  * See 1993 Edition . . . .

Carr, Henry   Br 1894-1970
  * See 1992 Edition . . . .

Carr, Lyell   Am 1857-
  * See 1993 Edition . . . .

Carr, M. Emily   Can 1871-1945
O/C 25x18 Brittany Scene Sbt 5/93 49,280
O/C 24x18 At Nootka, B.C. Sbt 11/92 39,600
O/Pa/Pn 22x16 Bole of a Tree-Autumn 1930 Sbt 11/92 . . . 23,760
W/Pa 25x18 Study of Totem Figure Sbt 5/93 19,800

O/C 16x22 Spring Wave Sbt 5/93 18,480
W/Pa 14x11 China Boy 1907 Sbt 5/93 7,040

Carr, Samuel S.   Am 1837-1908
O/C 22x36 School's Out '89 Sby 9/92 24,200
O/C 12x10 Playing Hooky Chr 5/93 6,900
O/C/B 17x24 Landscape with Sheep Lou 9/92 2,500
O/C 14x20 Sheep Grazing Lou 6/93 2,450

Carra, Carlo   It 1881-1966
O/C 16x20 Paesaggio But 10/92 49,500

Carracci, Annibale   It 1560-1609
K&P/Pa 8x7 Study for an Altar Frontal Chr 1/93 1,980

Carracci, Lodovico   It 1555-1619
  * See 1993 Edition . . . .

Carre, Georges Henri   Fr 1878-1945
O/Pn 16x10 Women in Garden Lou 12/92 200

Carree, Michiel   Dut 1657-1747
  * See 1991 Edition . . . .

Carreno, Mario   Cub 1913-
O/C 41x31 Paisaje 43 Sby 11/92 220,000
G/Pa 21x25 La Iniciacion 44 Sby 5/93 36,800
O/C/M 24x20 Mythological Rider 43 Sby 11/92 36,300
O/C 47x66 Geografia De La Angustia 77 Sby 5/93 28,750
T&I/B 17x21 Fondo Marino 48 Sby 11/92 16,500
T&I/B 17x21 Antillas 48 Sby 5/93 12,650
O/C 24x20 La Pescadora Pescada 79 Chr 11/92 12,100
T&I/B 11x15 Piedra Magica 48 Sby 11/92 9,350
O/C 31x41 Untitled '57 Sby 2/93 5,463
T&I/B 16x11 Figuras 48 Sby 5/93 4,600
G/Pa 21x30 Sin Titulo '69 Sby 5/93 4,025
Pl/Pa 8x11 Naturaleza Muerta 45 Sby 11/92 3,850

Carrick, John Mulcaster   Br a 1854-1878
  * See 1993 Edition . . . .

Carrier-Belleuse, Albert E.   Fr 1824-1887
  * See 1992 Edition . . . .

Carrier-Belleuse, Louis Robert   Fr 1848-1913
O/C 24x32 Workers at Noontime But 11/92 14,300
P/Pa/C 36x29 On the Beach Chr 2/93 11,000

Carrier-Belleuse, Pierre   Fr 1851-1932
P/C 26x42 Nu Sous Un Parasol 1890 Sby 10/92 55,000
P/C 64x39 La Danseuse 1897 Sby 2/93 19,550
P/C 46x36 Portrait de Femme But 5/93 5,175
O/C 18x13 Nature Morte aux Fromage et Fruits Sby 5/93 . 4,600

Carriere, Alphonse   Fr 1808-
O/C/M 17x22 Woman Seated at Table But 5/93 2,875

Carriere, Eugene   Fr 1849-1906
  * See 1993 Edition . . . .

Carrington, Leonora   Br 1917-
O/C 26x44 El Bano 1957 Sby 11/92 170,500
O/C 28x24 Ab Eo, Quod 1956 Sby 11/92 159,500
O/C 47x24 Dark Night of Aranoe 1976 Chr 11/92 143,000
O/C 36x48 Expedition of Dr. Ramsbottom 1961 Chr 11/92 125,000
O/Pn 16x35 El Grito 1951 Sby 5/93 101,500
O/C 26x15 Autorretrato 1973 Sby 5/93 74,000
O/C 24x20 A Warning to Mother 1973 Sby 5/93 65,750
O/C 22x22 The God Mother 1970 Sby 5/93 54,625
C&G/Pa 30x22 Mr. Pierre and Family Sby 5/93 10,350
Pe/Pa 9x9 Figura Chr 11/92 4,400

Carroll, John   Am 1892-1959
O/C 21x29 Three Figures Dum 11/92 4,750
O/C 24x20 First Orchid Dum 12/92 600

Carroll, Lawrence   1954-
MM/C/Wd 97x16 Untitled 1989 Sby 10/92 3,300

Carrothers, Grace Neville   Am 20C
O/B 10x12 The House by the Road: Pair 1927 Hnd 5/93 . . . 425

Carse, Alexander   Br 19C
  * See 1993 Edition . . . .

Carson, Robert   Am 20C
O/C 22x28 Violin & Various Objects 1946 Mys 12/92 192

Carson, W. A.
O/C 24x15 Rocky Mountains: Pair Dum 1/93 250

Carstensen, A.   Dan 1844-
O/B 14x24 Shipping Off the Coast 1880 Eld 7/93 770

Carte, Antoine   Bel 1886-1954
  * See 1992 Edition . . . .

Carter, Clarence H. Am 1904-
MM/Pa 15x22 Cricket in the Woodpile '36 Lou 3/93 3,700
O/C 14x14 Over and Above Series '68 Wlf 9/92 2,200
O/C 36x18 Over and Above No. 19 65 Sby 9/92 1,320
MM/Pa 22x30 Allegory of the Church III 62 But 10/92 1,210
Pe/Pa 8x10 Coal Mining Mys 3/93 357
Carter, Dennis Malone Am 1827-1881
* See 1990 Edition . . . .
Carter, Gary Am 1939-
* See 1990 Edition . . . .
Carter, H. M. Am 20C
O/C 24x30 Spring Reflections Fre 4/93 550
Carter, Pruett Am 1891-1955
O/C 11x16 Shopkeeper and Bookkeeper Ih 5/93 850
O/B 10x13 Town and Water's Edge Ald 3/93 625
Carter, Sydney Br 19C
* See 1990 Edition . . . .
Cartier, Jacques Fr 20C
* See 1991 Edition . . . .
Cartwright, Isabel Branson Am 1885-
* See 1992 Edition . . . .
Cary, William de la Montagne Am
1840-1922
* See 1993 Edition . . . .
Carzou, Jean Fr 1907-
O/Pa/M 20x25 Paysage Bourguignon Sel 12/92 2,250
O/Pa/M 20x25 Paysage Bourguignon Sel 2/93 500
Casagemas, Carlos 1881-1901
C/Pa 8x6 Portrait d'Homme Chr 5/93 1,380
Casali, Andrea It 1720-1783
* See 1992 Edition . . . .
Casanoday, Arcadio Spa 19C
* See 1991 Edition . . . .
Casanova, Francois-Joseph It 1727-1802
* See 1993 Edition . . . .
Casanovas, Enrique Spa 19C
* See 1992 Edition . . . .
Casanove, Francesco Spa
* See 1990 Edition . . . .
Casas, Ramon Spa 1866-
C&K/Pa 20x16 Gentleman Smoking a Pipe 09 Chr 5/93 . . . 9,200
Cascella, Michele It 1892-
O/C 36x25 Spring Flowers But 4/93 4,600
W&I/B 18x26 Pastorale 1923 Sby 2/93 2,875
W&I/B 18x26 Seated Woman in Landscape Sby 2/93 2,875
Cascella, Tommaso It 1890-1968
* See 1991 Edition . . . .
Casciaro, Giuseppe It 1863-1941
O/Pn 8x12 Village Path Sby 1/93 3,335
Case, Edmund E. Am 1840-1919
* See 1991 Edition . . . .
Case, Frank E. Am 20C
* See 1993 Edition . . . .
Case, Richard Am 1913-
O/C 28x26 Horseman Near Lantern Shooting Ih 5/93 3,300
Caseoro, Guido It 20C
O/C 21x35 Marina Grande Capri 1925 Hnd 9/92 700
Casenelli, Victor Am 1867-1961
O/B 13x18 Indian with Pack Horse Hnd 12/92 1,900
Caser, Ettore It 1880-1944
O/B 19x24 Apples, Plums and Grapes Yng 5/93 225
Casile, Alfred Fr 1847-1909
* See 1991 Edition . . . .
Casilear, John William Am 1811-1893
O/C 20x17 A Woodland Path '59 Chr 5/93 8,625
O/C 16x15 Trees Chr 9/92 3,850
O/C 12x18 Afternoon Near Lake George '82 Lou 9/92 2,000
Casissa, Nicola -1731
O/C 75x56 Still Life Sculpted Urn Flowers Sby 1/93 40,250
Cass, George Nelson Am -1882
O/C 20x30 River Fishing, Sunrise 69 Skn 5/93 3,520
O/C 12x18 Two Landscapes Skn 5/93 1,320
Cass, Kae Dorn Am 1901-1971
O/C 40x30 Standing Female Nude Wlf 5/93 350
W/Pa 18x24 Abandoned Victorian Mansion Wlf 5/93 70

Cassana, Giovanni Agostino 1658-1720
O/C 37x46 Rabbits, Poultry and Pigeon Chr 1/93 9,900
Cassatt, Mary Stevenson Am 1844-1926
P&G/Pa 26x22 Young Lady in a Loge Sby 11/92 . . . . 2.53M
P/Pa 14x19 Looking at a Picture Book (No. 1) Sby 5/93 . 90,500
Pe&K/Pa 14x11 Drawing "Afternoon Tea Party" Sby 5/93 . 76,750
P&Pe/Pa 24x19 Young Woman in Green Sby 5/93 74,000
O/Pn 19x16 Portrait Madame Cordier 1874 Sby 5/93 46,000
P/Pa 27x21 Young Girl Sby 5/93 17,250
Casselli, Henry Am 20C
O/Pa 20x29 Afro-American '73 Hnz 5/93 300
Cassidy, Ira Diamond Gerald Am
1879-1934
O/C 10x17 Cliff Dwellings 1914 But 12/92 2,750
O/C 10x17 Ruins in Utah 1914 But 12/92 2,750
G/Pa 23x19 Skiing to the Campsite But 6/93 1,150
Cassigneul, Jean Pierre Fr 1935-
O/C 21x25 La Plage a Deauville Chr 5/93 10,925
Casson, Alfred Joseph Can 1898-1992
O/B 30x36 Summer Parade Sbt 11/92 29,040
O/C 34x40 Massey Ferguson World War II Sbt 5/93 26,400
O/B 12x15 Heathcoat Road 1972 Sbt 11/92 7,040
W/Pa 11x14 Summer, Lake Mazinaw, Ontario 1952 Sbt 5/93 6,160
O/B 12x15 Farm on Lake Kamaniskeg 1945 Sbt 5/93 5,720
O/B 12x15 Autumn - Grenville, Quebec 1968 Sbt 5/93 4,400
Ss/Wd 10x11 Woodflowers Sbt 5/93 1,056
Ss/L 12x12 Four Flower Studies Sbt 5/93 352
Ss/Wd 10x11 Lady's Slipper; Wild Roses (2) Sbt 5/93 352
Castagneto, Giovanni Brz 1851-1900
O/Pn 18x13 Navios de Vela 1897 Chr 11/92 8,800
Castagnola, Gabriele It 1828-1883
O/C Size? Filippo Lippi and the Nun Bruti 1873 Wlf 12/92 . . 6,250
O/C 28x44 The Seduction 1877 Sby 5/93 5,750
Castaigne, J. Andre Fr 1861-
* See 1993 Edition . . . .
Castan, Pierre Jean Edmond Fr
1817-1892
O/Pn 10x7 The Toy Sailboat 1862 Chr 5/93 10,350
O/Pn 13x10 The Little Mother 1873 Chr 5/93 9,775
O/C/B 14x11 Resting in the Shade 1862 Skn 11/92 3,850
Castaneda, Alfredo Spa 1938-
H&Cp/Cd 10x12 Vidente 84 Sby 11/92 4,950
Casteels, Peeter (III) Flm 1684-1749
O/C 29x24 Still Life Tulips, Peonies, Iris 1733 Sby 5/93 . . 33,350
O/C 24x29 Ducks by a Pond Sby 1/93 17,250
O/C 32x26 Roses, Tulips, Morning Glory Chr 5/93 15,525
Castelan, A. G.
O/C 14x21 Still Life Fruit on Table Sel 9/92 160
Castellanos, Carlos Alberto Uru
1881-1945
O/B 16x13 Guaranies en el Bosque Sby 11/92 7,150
Castelli, Bartolomeo It 18C
* See 1991 Edition . . . .
Castelli, Giovanni Paolo It 1659-1731
* See 1993 Edition . . . .
Castelli, Luciano
* See 1992 Edition . . . .
Castello, Battista It 1545-1639
* See 1993 Edition . . . .
Castello, Valerio It 1625-1659
* See 1991 Edition . . . .
Castellon, Federico Am 1914-1971
* See 1993 Edition . . . .
Castelucho, Claudio Spa 1870-1927
O/C 26x21 Cafe Cantale a Barcelonne But 10/92 2,475
Castex-Degrange, Adolphe Louis Fr
1840-
* See 1992 Edition . . . .
Castiglione, Giovanni Benedett It
1609-1665
* See 1992 Edition . . . .
Castiglione, Giuseppe It 1829-1908
O/C 28x40 Court Presentation Chr 5/93 28,750
O/C 27x41 Sitting for his Portrait Chr 2/93 22,000
O/C 23x21 Two Women in a Garden Sel 9/92 6,000

Castillo Y Saavedra, Antonio Spa 1603-1668
* See 1992 Edition ....
Castillo, Jorge 1933-
A/C 70x60 Blue and Pink Interior 83 Sby 10/92 24,200
Castoldi, Guglieimo It 1852-
* See 1991 Edition ....
Castres, Edouard Sws 1838-1902
* See 1993 Edition ....
Castro Y Velasco, Antonio A. Spa 1655-1726
O/C 50x36 Archangel Michael Casting Satan Sby 1/93 ... 46,000
Catala, Luis Alvarez Spa 1836-1901
* See 1993 Edition ....
Catalan, Ramos Chi 20C
O/C 17x16 Mountain Landscape Wes 10/92 495
O/C 23x31 Andes Mountain Landscape Slo 7/93 425
O/C 20x24 Mountain Landscape Yng 5/93 300
Catano, F. It 19C
O/C 18x48 Fishing Village Chr 2/93 1,100
Cathelin, Bernard Fr 1919-
* See 1993 Edition ....
Catlin, George Am 1796-1872
W&G/Pa 21x27 Ambush for Flamingos Sby 12/92 27,500
Catti, Michele It 1855-1914
* See 1993 Edition ....
Cauchois, Eugene Henri Fr 1850-1911
O/C 26x32 Nature Morte Aux Chrysanthemes Sby 10/92 .. 23,100
O/C 18x15 Still Life (2) Chr 2/93 16,500
O/C 36x20 Les Deux Bouquets Sby 10/92 13,200
O/C 21x26 Jardiniere de Fleurs Sby 5/93 10,350
O/C 22x26 Assorted Flowers in Oriental Bowl Chr 5/93 .. 9,200
O/C 21x26 Nature Morte Des Fleurs Sby 10/92 8,800
O/C 21x26 Bouquet de Fleurs Des Champs Sby 2/93 8,625
O/C 24x20 A Summer Bouquet Chr 2/93 7,150
O/C 17x21 Still Life Pomegranates and Daisies Chr 10/92 .. 4,180
Caula, Sigismondo 1637-1713
* See 1992 Edition ....
Cavailles, Jean Jules Louis Fr 1901-1977
O/C 26x18 Femme a la Fenetre, Honfleur 36 Doy 5/93 3,850
Cavaliere D'Arpino It 1560-1640
O/C 19x28 Christ in Garden of Gethsemane Sby 1/93 82,250
Cavalieri, Luigi It 19C
* See 1992 Edition ....
Cavallino, Bernardo It 1616-1656
* See 1990 Edition ....
Cavallon, Giorgio Am 1904-
O/C/Pn 18x12 Untitled 1964 Chr 11/92 7,700
Cave, Jules Cyrille Fr 1859-
* See 1993 Edition ....
Cavedone, Giacomo It 1577-1660
O/C 15x12 Head of an Old Man Chr 1/93 7,150
Cavi, Romeo It 1862-1908
W/B 7x14 Courtyard Garden Wes 3/93 220
Cavilles, Jules Fr 1901-
* See 1991 Edition ....
Cawthorne, Neil Br 1936-
O/C 20x28 After the Race Sby 6/93 4,888
O/C 20x28 At the Start, Cheltenham Sby 6/93 4,370
O/C 20x26 A Furlong Out Sby 6/93 2,588
O/C 18x30 Over the Water, Newbury Sby 6/93 2,530
O/C 20x24 Two Horse Racing Scenes Skn 3/93 1,980
Cazassus Fr 1932-
O/C 25x21 Floral Still Life FHB 6/93 40
O/C 22x15 Village Scene with Worker FHB 6/93 30
Cazes, Romain Fr 1810-1881
* See 1992 Edition ....
Cazin, Jean Charles Fr 1841-1901
Pe/Pa 14x9 Canal Scene Hnd 10/92 400
O/B 5x8 Mountain Landscape Ald 5/93 275
Ceccarelli, Naddo It 14C
* See 1991 Edition ....
Cecchino Salviati 1510-1563
O/Pn 25x21 Portrait of a Young Boy Sby 5/93 25,875

Cecco Bravo It 1601-1661
* See 1993 Edition ....
Ceccobelli, Bruno 1952-
O,Wx&Y/Pa 29x21 Eudoxia 1985 Sby 10/92 2,750
Cecconi, Eugenio It 1842-1903
* See 1993 Edition ....
Cecconi, Lorenzo It 1867-
* See 1993 Edition ....
Cederberg, S. 19C
O/C 24x16 Street Urchin Slo 4/93 95
Celentano, Daniel Ralph Am 1902-
O/C 26x24 Auto Accident (2) Sby 3/93 12,075
O/C 24x28 Pitching Pennies 48 Sby 3/93 11,500
O/C 22x23 Convalescing Sby 3/93 2,18
Celesti, Andrea It 1637-1712
* See 1993 Edition ....
Celis, Perez 20C
* See 1992 Edition ....
Celmins, Vija 20C
* See 1991 Edition ....
Celommi, Pasquale It 1860-
* See 1993 Edition ....
Celommi, Raffaello It 1883-
* See 1993 Edition ....
Celoni, A. Con 19C
* See 1992 Edition ....
Cemin, Saint Clair 1951-
H/Pa 17x9 Candelabro Angelico 84 Chr 2/93 88
Centurion, Emilio Arg 1894-1970
* See 1993 Edition ....
Ceramano, Charles Ferdinand Bel 1829-1909
* See 1993 Edition ....
Cercone, Ettore It 1850-1896
* See 1990 Edition ....
Cerny, Charles 1892-1965
O/C 32x26 Mere et Fillette Espagne 1940 Sby 10/92 88
O/C 9x11 Still Life with Globe 1957 Eld 11/92 41
O/C 16x13 Nature Morte 1946 Chr 5/93 28
Cerrone, Edouardo It 1928-
O/B 5x7 Ducks Dum 8/93 1,30
O/B 5x7 Ducks Dum 8/93 70
O/B 5x7 Kitten with Baby Chick Dum 8/93 65
O/B 5x7 Kitten with Baby Chick Dum 8/93 45
O/B 5x7 Kitten with Baby Chick Dum 7/93 45
O/B 5x7 Kitten with Baby Chick Dum 7/93 37
Ceruti, Giacomo It 1698-1767
O/C 24x20 Young Woman Holding a Mask Sby 5/93 10,92
Cesari, Giuseppe It 1560-1640
O/C 19x28 Christ in Garden of Gethsemane Sby 1/93 82,25
Cesi, Bartolomeo 1583-1649
K/Pa 11x6 Young Man Wearing Cape Chr 1/93 24,20
Cezanne, Paul Fr 1839-1906
O/C 21x29 Arbres au Jas de Bouffan 1875 Chr 11/92 .. 1.6775M
W&Pe/Pa 13x19 Paysage Montagneux Sby 5/93 189,50
W&Pe/Pa 12x17 Arbres et Rochers a Bibemus Sby 5/93 .. 74,00
Chab, Victor Arg 1930-
* See 1990 Edition ....
Chabaud, Auguste 1882-1955
O/B 30x42 Laboureur pres des cypres, Provence Chr 11/92 10,45
Chabellard, J. Charles Fr 19C
* See 1991 Edition ....
Chabod, Emile Delphes Fr 19C
O/C 52x39 Vase de Fleurs Sby 10/92 15,40
Chadeayne, Robert Osbourne Am 1897-
* See 1992 Edition ....
Chadwick, Lynn Br 1914-
* See 1992 Edition ....
Chadwick, William Am 1879-1962
O/C 24x20 Mildred in an Interior Chr 12/92 19,80
O/C 24x30 A Stream by the Farm Chr 5/93 17,25
O/C 30x30 A Connecticut Autumn Chr 5/93 8,80
Chaffee, Samuel R. Am 20C
W/Pa 10x23 Country Lane at Sunset Dum 5/93 42
W/Pa 7x10 House in Landscape Mys 12/92 22

W/Pa 20x12 Forest Interior Mys 12/92 192
W/Pa 12x20 Autumn Scene Mys 3/93 165
W/Pa 5x18 Winter Snow Scene Mys 3/93 137

Chagall, Marc   Fr 1887-1985
O/C 32x24 L'Atelier de L'Artiste Sby 5/93 442,500
O&G/Pa 22x28 Les Armoureux a Paris Sby 11/92 440,000
G/Pa 26x20 L'Homme Au Parapluie Sby 11/92 374,000
W,P&Pe/Pa 30x22 Amoureux sous un bouquet Chr 11/92 . 319,000
G/Pa 26x20 Le violoniste bleu Chr 11/92 275,000
O/C 16x11 Le village russe Chr 11/92 242,000
G/Pa 19x27 Le Reve Sby 5/93 222,500
G/Pa 8x11 Le Soldat Sby 5/93 178,500
W&I/Pa 20x26 Musicien et Artiste 1981 Sby 11/92 170,500
G,Pl&Y/Pa 26x21 Coq au Petit Clown 1958 Sby 11/92 . . . 129,000
G&P/Pa 27x21 Couple et bouquet Chr 11/92 99,000
G,Pl&Pe/Pa 12x9 Homme a Cheval et Maternite Sby 5/93 . 90,500
P&S/Pa 25x19 Peonies 1950 Sby 11/92 82,500
L,P&Pl/Pa 13x10 Personnages au Cirque Sby 11/92 71,500
G,P,Y&I/Pa 8x12 Les Maries Sby 11/92 66,000
P,W&S/Pa 11x13 Le Mariage Sby 5/93 59,700
W&Pe/Pa/B 18x13 Bouquet Devant Une Fenetre Sby 5/93 . 57,500
G&W/Pa/B 19x18 Le lion et le moucheron Chr 11/92 57,200
Br&Pl/Pa 25x20 Amoureux sous un arbre Chr 11/92 33,000
IBr&Y/Pa/B 10x15 L'Autoportrait 1965 Sby 5/93 19,550
K&Pe/Pa 18x13 Moise Chr 5/93 5,175
Pl/Pa 11x9 L'Artiste 1948 Chr 2/93 1,980
Chagniot, Jean Alfred   Fr 1905-
O/C 19x22 Village Harbor Sby 2/93 978
Chalfant, Jefferson David   Am 1856-1931
Pe/Pa 12x10 The Horn Blower Sby 5/93 26,450
Pe/Pa 15x12 The Clock Tinker Sby 5/93 18,400
Challener, Frederick Sproston   Can 1869-1959
* See 1992 Edition . . . .
Chalon, Henry Bernard   Br 1770-1849
* See 1993 Edition . . . .
Chamberlain, John
MM/B 10x11 Untitled 62 Sby 2/93 9,200
Chamberlain, Norman Stiles   Am 1887-1961
O/B 16x20 Mission San Gabriel '21 Mor 6/93 935
Chamberlin, B. B.   19C
O/C 8x11 Harlem Bridge Eld 7/93 99
Chamberlin, Frank Tolles   Am 1873-1961
O/Cb 24x20 Oriental Still Life Blue Jardiniere Mor 6/93 . . . 1,980
Chambers, C. Bosseron   Am 1883-
O/C 36x25 Portrait Peggy Hopkins Joyce Hnd 9/92 500
Chambers, Charles E.   Am 1883-1941
O/C 24x36 Bride and Groom in the Kitchen Ilh 5/93 4,250
O/B 32x21 Group of People Gathered Around Ilh 11/92 . . . 3,500
O/C 33x22 Blonde Woman Getting Manicure Ilh 11/92 . . . 3,250
O/C 30x30 Guitar Player Dum 5/93 3,000
O&R/C 30x21 Couple in the Park Ilh 5/93 2,500
Chambers, George W.   Eng 19C
O/Pn 11x15 Sketch in Missouri Sel 4/93 425
Chambers, Joseph K.   Am -1916
O/C 10x12 Blue Hills at Sunset Eld 4/93 275
Chambers, Richard E. E.   Am 1863-1944
* See 1993 Edition . . . .
Champion, T.   Fr 19C
O/C 16x23 Village on Winding River Chr 5/93 345
Champion, Theo   Ger 1887-1952
O/C 16x23 Village on a Winding River Chr 10/92 2,200
Champney, Benjamin   Am 1817-1907
O/C 30x48 Lake George with Black Mountain 78 Doy 5/93 . 7,700
O/C 30x45 In the Mountains 1872 Brd 8/93 6,600
O/C 30x25 In the White Mountains 1881 Yng 5/93 3,750
O/C 12x10 Cattle and Sheep Grazing Skn 11/92 1,430
O/C 18x13 Rest Under the Birches Skn 5/93 1,100
Champney, James Wells   Am 1843-1903
O/C 22x18 Sealed with Affection Chr 12/92 8,800
O/Pn 5x8 View Through a Wood Skn 11/92 495
Chancrin, Rene
O/C 29x24 Trompe L'Oeil Sby 2/93 1,380

Chandler, John
A/C 72x45 Untitled 1976 Sby 2/93 575
A/C 72x45 Untitled 84 Sby 2/93 575
Chaney, Lester Joseph   Am 1907-
O/C 30x36 Seascape Hnz 5/93 200
Chapelain-Midy, Roger   Fr 1904-
O/C 24x32 Paysage de Fournes (Gard) 1949 Sby 10/92 . . . 1,870
Chaperon, Eugene   Fr 1857-
O/C 45x64 La Douche Au Regiment 1887 Sby 5/93 51,750
O/C 29x36 Glorious Trophies 1903 Sby 10/92 18,700
Chapin, Bryant   Am 1859-1927
O/C 10x20 Melon and Grapes Yng 2/93 1,100
O/C 8x12 Still Life with Fruit Lou 6/93 800
W/Pa 9x13 Grand Manan 1907 Mys 3/93 137
Chapin, C. H.   Am 19C
* See 1993 Edition . . . .
Chapin, Francis   Am 1899-1965
W/Pa 15x21 Reclining Nude Hnd 5/93 500
Chapin, James Ormsbee   Am 1887-1975
W/Pa 13x10 The Musicians '23 Sby 9/92 4,950
Chaplin, Arthur   Fr 1869-
* See 1992 Edition . . . .
Chaplin, Charles   Fr 1825-1891
O/C 19x12 Femme Aux Oiseaux Sby 10/92 11,550
O/C 11x19 Sleeping Nude Chr 2/93 4,620
Chapman, Carlton Theodore   Am 1860-1926
O/C 14x20 A Snowy Winter Stream Chr 5/93 1,495
Chapman, Charles J.   Am 20C
O/B 40x30 Deer by the River Fre 10/92 200
Chapman, Conrad Wise   Am 1842-1910
O/C 9x19 Valle de Mexico 1902 Sby 5/93 46,000
O/Pn 6x9 Scene de Plage en Normandie 1880 Sby 3/93 . . 12,650
W/B 11x8 Campesina Sby 11/92 10,450
W/B 12x8 Campesino Sby 11/92 10,450
Chapman, John Gadsby   Am 1808-1889
* See 1993 Edition . . . .
Chapman, John Linton   Am 1839-1905
* See 1993 Edition . . . .
Chapman, Minerva Josephine   Am 1858-1947
O/C 7x11 Teh Copper Kettle 1910 Wes 10/92 880
Chapman, William Ernst   Am 20C
O/C 20x28 Coastal Scene 1934 Lou 3/93 250
Chappel, Alonzo   Am 1828-1887
O/C 30x25 The Frontiersmen Chr 3/93 7,475
Charchoune, Serge   Rus 1888-1975
* See 1993 Edition . . . .
Chard, Daniel
A/M 15x34 Whig Lane '84 Sby 10/92 1,760
Chardin, Jean-Baptiste-Simeon   Fr 1699-1779
O/C 16x13 Ray-Fish, Basket Onions, Green Jug Chr 1/93 . 44,000
Charlemont, Eduard   Aus 1848-1906
O/Pn 17x13 Cavalier Studying a Map 1885 But 11/92 4,400
Charlemont, Hugo   Aus 1850-1939
O/C 25x35 Still Life Lilies, Peonies Sby 10/92 5,500
O/C 22x18 Blumenfenster Hnd 10/92 2,800
O/Pn 8x13 Wasservogel Hnd 10/92 2,100
O/Pn 10x15 Allee Hnd 10/92 2,000
Charlet, Frantz   Bel 1862-1928
O/C 32x32 Le Retour de Vainqueur Doy 11/92 8,525
Charlet, Nicholas Toussaint   Fr 1792-1845
* See 1993 Edition . . . .
Charlot, Jean   Fr 1898-1979
O/C 24x20 Madre con Hijo 37 Sby 11/92 16,500
O/C 11x8 Coiffure 30 Sby 5/93 5,175
Charlton, John   Br 1849-1917
O/C 55x78 Exercising the Horses 1890 Chr 5/93 6,900
Charnay, Armand   Fr 1844-1916
* See 1991 Edition . . . .
Charpentier, Georges   Fr 20C
* See 1993 Edition . . . .

Charpentier, Jean-Baptiste   Fr 1728-1806
* See 1991 Edition ....

Charpin, Albert   Fr 1842-1924
O/Pn 10x15 Hors Concours Hnd 10/92 950
O/Pn 9x13 Three Goats in Barn Hnd 3/93 650

Charreton, Victor   Fr 1864-1936
O/Cl 24x29 Landscape with Tree But 10/92 8,800
O/C 24x29 Town Scene But 10/92 8,800
O/B 12x14 Automne a Auvergne Sby 2/93 8,050

Charton, Ernest   Fr 1813-1905
* See 1993 Edition ....

Chartrand, Esteban   Spa 1825-1889
O/C 28x38 La Vallee de Coliseo, Cuba 1865 Chr 11/92 .. 12,000
O/C 10x20 Paisaje Sby 11/92 7,700
O/Pn 11x15 Paisaje Tropical 1878 Sby 11/92 7,700

Chase, Adelaide Cole   Am 1868-1944
* See 1993 Edition ....

Chase, E. M.   Am 20C
O/B 18x24 Three Paintings 1939 Yng 2/93 60

Chase, Frank Swift   Am 1886-1958
O/C 18x24 Blue Woodstock Hills But 6/93 575

Chase, Henry (Harry)   Am 1853-1889
O/C 20x30 European Coastline w/Ships 1870 Sel 12/92 10,000
O/C 16x20 European Coastal Scene 1877 Sel 9/92 6,500
O/C 16x10 Sailboat in Rough Seas Sel 4/93 900
O/C 15x22 Seascape 1878 Sby 3/93 690

Chase, Louisa   Am 1951-
N/C 72x78 St. Sabastion 79 Chr 11/92 3,850
O/C 70x90 Tulip 1980 Sby 6/93 3,450
O/Pa 23x30 Untitled Chr 11/92 825

Chase, Marian   Br 1844-1905
O/C 24x18 Dockers on the Thames Eld 8/93 165

Chase, Sidney M.   Am
* See 1990 Edition ....

Chase, Susan Miller   Am 20C
O/B 10x12 Figures on a Beach Yng 5/93 1,600
O/B 10x8 Seated Girls in White Dresses FHB 6/93 1,000
O/B 14x10 The Parasol Skn 3/93 935

Chase, William Merritt   Am 1849-1916
P/Pa 48x48 Peonies Sby 5/93 .... 3.9625M
O/C 28x24 Portrait Virginia Gerson Sby 5/93 101,500
O/Pn 7x9 Shinnecock Landscape Sby 12/92 82,500
O/Pn 15x9 The Jester Sby 5/93 57,500
O/Pn 8x13 Gowanus Pier Sby 9/92 35,200
O/C 25x19 Lady in a White Dress Sby 5/93 32,200
O/C 22x17 The Old Book Chr 12/92 28,600
O/Pn 8x12 Shinnicock Bay Dum 4/93 22,500
O/C 29x42 Still Life with Fish Sby 5/93 18,400
O/C 24x19 Miss Mary Margaret Sweeney Sby 5/93 12,650
O/C 26x21 Portrait of a Gentleman '77 Sby 12/92 10,450
O/C 26x16 Street Dancer, Italy Sby 12/92 8,250

Chasseriau, Theodore   Fr 1819-1856
* See 1992 Edition ....

Chat, A. A.   Am a 1890-1910
* See 1993 Edition ....

Chataud, Marc-Alfred   Fr 1833-1908
* See 1992 Edition ....

Chateaux, R*   Fr 19C**
* See 1993 Edition ....

Chatelain, James   Am 1947-
O/C 36x37 Untitled 1977 '77 FHB 3/93 800
O/C 30x46 Untitled 1974 '74 FHB 3/93 600
O/C 80x56 T-Top '84 FHB 3/93 500

Chatelet, Claude-Louis   Fr 1753-1794
* See 1991 Edition ....

Chatterton, Clarence K.   Am 1880-1973
O/B 12x16 Regatta at Kennebunkport Chr 5/93 11,500
G&Pe/Pa/B 13x19 Snake Hill '06 Sby 12/92 3,300

Chaves Y Ortiz, Jose   Spa 19C
* See 1993 Edition ....

Chavez, Gerardo   Per 1937-
* See 1993 Edition ....

Che, Chuang
MM&A/C 58x58 Abstract Collage 1967 Dum 9/92 1,300

Checa Y Sanz, Ulpiano   Spa 1860-1916
O/C 28x19 Piazza San Marco Sby 10/92 28,600

Chelminski, Jan Van   Pol 1851-1925
* See 1990 Edition ....

Chelmonski, Josef   Pol 1849-1914
* See 1991 Edition ....

Chemetou, Boris   Fr 1908-1982
* See 1993 Edition ....

Chemiakine, Mikhail   Rus 1943-
O/C 20x16 Portrait of a Woman 69 Chr 11/92 2,860
O/C 20x16 Portrait of a Woman 69 Chr 5/93 1,725

Chemielinski, W. T.   Pol 20C
O/C 16x20 Bustling Street Scene Chr 10/92 2,640
O/C 20x24 Troika Scene Hnz 5/93 850

Chen, Hilo   Am 1942-
O/C 54x80 Ying Yang 74 Sby 6/93 5,750
A/C 40x56 Bedroom-20 Chr 11/92 3,300

Cheney, Russell   Am 1881-1945
O/C 20x26 Cheney Residence, Kittery Point, ME Brd 8/93 .. 1,100

Chenoweth, Joseph G.
O/C 20x48 Eight Waiting Gangsters Ih 11/92 2,000

Cheret, Jules   Fr 1836-1932
O/Pn 11x8 Sur la Plage 87 Sby 2/93 7,763
O/C 19x11 Elegant Lady Chr 10/92 6,050
O/C 18x11 Woman with a Mandolin Chr 10/92 2,750

Cherkes, Constantine   Am 1919-
* See 1992 Edition ....

Cherry, Kathryn   Am 1880-1931
O/C 24x22 Road to Sea But 6/93 4,025
O/Cb 18x25 Still Life Fruit on a Table Sel 9/92 1,150
O/M 11x14 Rural Street Scene Sel 2/93 950
O/B 10x15 The Sea Beyond Sel 9/92 950

Chestnut, Billy Dohlman   Am 20C
* See 1992 Edition ....

Chevalier, Peter   1953-
O/C 32x39 Ideale Landschaft IX 85 Sby 2/93 1,265

Cheviot, Lillian   Br 20C
* See 1991 Edition ....

Chia, Sandro   1946-
O/C 78x92 Boy and Dog Sleeping Chr 11/92 71,500
O/C 61x61 Sculpture and Dust 1981 Sby 10/92 71,500
O/C 77x63 Dance of the Chairs with Flies Sby 2/93 43,125
O&Y/Pa 52x39 Mann mit Hirsch 82 Chr 11/92 18,700
O/Pa/B 42x37 Poison Chr 11/92 13,200
O&Pt/C 40x28 Untitled 75 Sby 10/92 9,900
O,OsH&L/Pa 16x12 Untitled 81 Chr 11/92 9,350

Chiapory, Bernard Charles   Fr 19C
* See 1993 Edition ....

Chiari, Guiseppe   It 1654-1727
* See 1992 Edition ....

Chichester, Cecil   Am 1891-1963
O/C 40x50 October Glory 1913 Skn 11/92 1,980

Chierici, Gaetano   It 1838-1920
O/C 23x19 Gioia and Dolore: Pair 1871 Sby 5/93 145,500
O/C 19x23 Baby & Grandfather: Pair 1867 Sby 2/93 17,250

Child, C. C.
W/Pa 10x12 River Landscape '25 Sel 12/92 60

Chillida, Eduardo
* See 1992 Edition ....

Chinnery, George   Br 1774-1852
* See 1993 Edition ....

Chintreuil, Antoine   Fr 1816-1873
* See 1991 Edition ....

Chiriacka, Ernest   Am 1920-
* See 1993 Edition ....

Chirico, L.   It 19C
O/C 39x25 Baptismal Procession Hnd 10/92 15,000

Chittenden, Alice Brown   Am 1859-1944
O/C 24x40 Chrysanthemums 1889 But 10/92 16,500
O/C 22x18 Roses and Daffodils But 10/92 4,950
O/C/B 18x24 Roses Bouquet But 10/92 3,575
O/Pa 18x12 Wild Peach Blossoms But 10/92 880
O/Cb 7x9 Summer Landscape Mor 6/93 825
O/B 7x9 Eucalyptus Landscape Mor 11/92 650

Chiu, Teng-Hiok   Chi 1903-
O/C 24x30 Street in Tangier, Morocco, 1937 Skn 9/92 770
O/B 16x20 Lake; Sun; Study (3) Lou 6/93 675
O/C 18x24 Morocco Lou 3/93 500
O/M 20x24 Summer Isles Lou 6/93 500
O/C 25x28 Ullapool, Scotland, 1936 Skn 9/92 440
O/Cb 20x24 Fisherman '36 Lou 6/93 400
O/Pa/M 16x23 Poolside, Miami Beach Lou 6/93 400
O/Pn 20x16 Tangiers '36 Lou 3/93 375
O/M 20x24 Manhattan Skyline Lou 6/93 325
O/Pn 23x16 Street Scene in Tangiers 1937 Lou 3/93 275
O/Cb 16x20 Tangiers '37 Lou 3/93 275
O/Cb 16x20 Tangiers '37 Lou 3/93 275
O/C 20x28 Farmfields No. 1 (2) Lou 6/93 225
O/B 8x11 The Picnic Lou 6/93 150
O/Cb 16x20 City Buildings Lou 6/93 100

Chivers, H. C.   Br 20C
O/C 16x20 Roses and Forget-Me-Nots 1935 Hnd 5/93 800

Chmielinski, Jean   Pol 20C
O/B 10x7 Winter Day in Warsaw: (2) Dum 8/93 1,100

Chmielinski, W. T.   Pol 20C
O/C 14x20 Sleigh Leaving Town Square But 11/92 3,025
O/B 10x13 In Old Warsaw Yng 2/93 325

Chocarne-Moreau, Paul Charles   Fr 1855-1931
* See 1993 Edition . . . .

Choubrac, Alfred   Fr 1853-1902
O/C 37x26 Oriental Fantasy Sby 10/92 11,000

Chouinard, Nelbert M.   Am 1879-1969
O/C 24x20 Street Scene Mor 2/93 400

Choukhaieff, Vassili I.
O/C 35x29 Still Life with Teapot 1921 Sby 2/93 8,050

Choultse, Ivan Fedorovich   Rus a 1880-1920
O/C 21x26 Sunlit Snowy Path Chr 2/93 10,450
O/C 21x25 Path Through Snow Covered Mountains Chr 2/93 7,700
O/C 26x37 November Evening Chr 10/92 6,600
O/C 26x26 Sheep Grazing in the Alps Chr 2/93 5,500
O/C 26x32 Early Morning Winter Walk Chr 10/92 3,080
O/C 32x43 Rocky Coast Hnd 3/93 1,000

Chouquet, Rene   20C
* See 1991 Edition . . . .

Christ, Pieter Casper   Dut 1822-
O/C 17x21 Road Through the Woods 1879 Hnd 5/93 1,300

Christensen, Anthonore   Dan 1849-1926
O/C 30x25 Lillies, Poppies and Bluebells 1870 Sby 5/93 . . 28,750

Christensen, Dan   Am 1942-
O/C 71x80 Amram Sby 2/93 2,415

Christensen, Florence   Am 20C
* See 1993 Edition . . . .

Christman, Reid   Am 20C
O/C 30x36 Spring Landscape, Sag Harbor 1948 Wlf 9/92 . . 2,000

Christmas, Ernst William   Am 1856-1918
* See 1993 Edition . . . .

Christo   Bul 1935-
H,Pe&Y/Pa 50x36 Trees (Champs Elysees) 1969 Sby 5/93 48,875
MM/B 22x28 Trees (Champs Elysees) 1969 Chr 11/92 . . . 38,500
C/Pa 36x96 Running Fence (Sonoma) 1974 Sby 5/93 37,950
L/B 28x22 Allied Chemical Tower-Packed 1968 Sby 11/92 29,700
MM&L/Pb 22x28 Islands (Biscayne Bay) 1982 Sby 2/93 . . 27,600
H,P&L/Pb 30x38 The Umbrellas 1987 Sby 5/93 26,450
H,P&L/Pb 30x38 The Umbrellas 1988 Sby 5/93 25,300
H&Y/B 28x22 Packed Tower, Spoleto 1968 Chr 10/92 . . . 6,600

Christy, Howard Chandler   Am 1873-1952
O/Cb 20x16 Peek-A-Boo! 1924 Chr 9/92 18,700
O/C 44x34 Landscape with Woman Skn 5/93 8,800
O/C 44x34 Forest Interior Scene 1944 Skn 5/93 6,600
O/Cb 20x16 Her Little Red Book Chr 3/93 6,325
C&P/B 20x24 Reclining Nude with Boa Ih 5/93 5,000
W/Pa 7x20 Woman in Red Dress Lou 3/93 850

Chumley, John   Am 1928-1984
G&Pe/Pa/B 30x40 Kathy Sby 3/93 5,463

Church, F. J.   Am 20C
* See 1993 Edition . . . .

Church, Frederic Edwin   Am 1826-1900
O/C 27x44 Mt Katahdin frm Millinocket 1895 Sby 12/92 . 159,500
O/Pa 14x21 View from Olana in the Snow Sby 5/93 . . . 129,000
O/C 11x16 Twilight in the Adirondacks Sby 12/92 82,500
O/Pa 10x6 Autumn Landscape, Vermont Sby 5/93 42,550
O/Pa 8x10 Winter on the Hudson River Sby 5/93 34,500
Pe/Pa 6x8 Sketch of a Landscape Sby 9/92 1,320

Church, Frederick Stuart   Am 1842-1923
O/C 20x30 Dancing Girl But 12/92 3,300
O/C 33x39 Nymph and Waterlilies 84 But 12/92 2,750
O/C 16x40 The Spring Song 1908 But 12/92 2,200
O/C 18x43 A Young Lioness 1906 But 12/92 1,870
G/Pa 9x14 A Jolly Time But 12/92 1,320

Chwala, Adolf   Czk 1836-1900
O/C 29x40 Austrian Mountains Dum 2/93 1,200

Ciampanti, Ansano   It 16C
* See 1992 Edition . . . .

Ciappa, Carlo   It 19C
* See 1993 Edition . . . .

Ciappa, F. A.   It 19C
* See 1992 Edition . . . .

Ciardi, Beppe   It 1875-1932
O/Pn 9x15 Paesaggio Hnd 9/92 1,400

Ciardi, Emma   It 1879-1933
O/B 15x20 Venezia 1923 Sby 2/93 20,125

Ciardi, Guglielmo   It 1842-1917
O/C 20x31 A View of Venice from Laguna 1892 Chr 5/93 . 90,500
O/C/Pn 14x25 Laguna a Chioggia Hnd 3/93 12,000

Ciardiello, Michel   It 1839-
* See 1991 Edition . . . .

Ciceri, Eugene   Fr 1813-1890
O/Pn 10x18 Figures in a River Landscape Chr 2/93 5,500
O/Pn 10x15 River Scene 76 Chr 10/92 3,520
W/Pa 10x17 Fishing on the River Chr 2/93 1,320
O/Pn 10x8 Wooded Forest Chr 5/93 1,150

Cignaroli, Gianbettino   It 1706-1772
* See 1993 Edition . . . .

Cikovsky, Nicolai   Am 1894-1934
O/Cb 13x17 Docked Sailboat Chr 12/92 770
O/M 7x10 Still Lifes: Pair Sby 9/92 660
P&W/Pa 13x20 Goat Island Yng 2/93 425
O/B 10x8 Flowers in a Vase Yng 2/93 375
G/Pa 17x23 Cows Grazing by the Coast 45 Chr 12/92 352
O/B 10x8 Still Life with Mandolin Yng 2/93 325

Cimaroli, Giambattista   It 1687-1757
* See 1993 Edition . . . .

Cimiotti, Gustave   Am 1875-1934
O/B 16x20 Stormy Sea Yng 2/93 1,300
O/B 16x20 Ocean Point Yng 5/93 950
O/Pb 8x11 City View Lou 6/93 425
O/Pb 10x12 Landscape Lou 6/93 200
O/Pb 8x11 Landscape Lou 6/93 200
O/C/Pb 8x11 Landscape with Lake Lou 6/93 150
O/Pn 8x11 Spring Landscape Lou 9/92 110

Cipolla, Fabius   It 1854-
* See 1993 Edition . . . .

Cipper, Giacomo Francesco   a 1706-1736
O/C 29x24 Laughing Boy Holding Paper & Garlic Sby 1/93 11,500

Cirino, Antonio   Am 1889-1983
O/B 8x10 Fishing Boats, Rockport Harbor Skn 5/93 1,430
O/C 20x24 Country House Yng 2/93 1,400
O/Cb 15x13 The Yellow House Skn 5/93 770
O/C 10x8 Street Scene Slo 5/93 400

Ciry, Michel   Fr 1919-
* See 1992 Edition . . . .

Cisilia, Jose Maria   20C
* See 1990 Edition . . . .

Citron, Minna
O/B 18x24 Insect Carnival 50 Sby 6/93 2,300

Civetta
* See 1991 Edition . . . .

Civita, Vincenzo   It 19C
* See 1991 Edition . . . .

Claeissins, Anthonie   Flm 1536-1613
* See 1993 Edition . . . .

Claes, Constant Guillaume   Bel 1826-1905
O/Pn 21x17 Genre Scene Two Young Women 1863 Skn 5/93 1,760
Claesz., Aert   Dut 1498-1564
* See 1991 Edition ....
Claesz., Anthony   Dut 1592-1635
* See 1990 Edition ....
Claesz., Pieter   Dut 1597-1661
O/Pn 16x24 Roemer, Jug, Olives, Lemon 1635 Chr 1/93   770,000
Claghorn, Joseph C.   Am 1869-1947
W/Pa 12x18 Couple with Horse Wes 3/93 330
Clair, Charles   Fr 1860-1930
O/C 16x14 Sheep and Rooster Fre 4/93 1,600
O/C 16x13 Stable Scene with Sheep Wes 10/92 962
Claire, Marie   Can 1939-
* See 1991 Edition ....
Clairin, Georges Jules Victor   Fr 1843-1919
O/C 32x52 The Royal Entourage Chr 2/93 31,900
O/C 32x24 Entrance to the Temple Sby 10/92 13,200
Clapp, Clinton W.   Am 19C
* See 1992 Edition ....
Clapp, William Henry   Am 1879-1954
O/C 30x36 Country Road '43 But 10/92 22,000
O/B 24x20 Houses and Trees But 3/93 18,700
O/C 20x24 Cuban Landscape 1916 Sbt 11/92 3,520
O/Pn 10x13 Abandoned Farm & Farm in Spring 45 Mor 6/93 3,300
Clapsaddle, Jerry   Am 20C
O/C 70x92 Slot 1975 Slo 4/93 600
Clare, C.   Br 19C
O/C 8x10 The Card Game; Refreshments: Pair Hnd 10/92 ... 500
Clare, George   Br a 1860-1900
* See 1993 Edition ....
Clare, Oliver   Eng 1853-1927
O/C 7x10 Still Life Robin's Nest with Eggs Sby 1/93 4,313
O/C 7x10 Still Life Grapes, Raspberries Sby 1/93 3,335
O/C 10x8 Grapes & Plums on a Mossy Bank (2) Chr 10/92 2,640
O/C 14x12 Plums and Raspberries But 5/93 2,300
O/B 6x8 Peaches, Plums and Strawberries Chr 5/93 1,610
O/C 8x14 Eggs in a Basket and Flowers Mys 12/92 880
Clare, Vincent   Eng 1855-1930
* See 1993 Edition ....
Clark, Alson Skinner   Am 1876-1949
O/C 32x26 Salon de L'Oeil de Boeuf Versailles But 10/92 .. 9,350
O/C 26x32 Arguello Adobe Near San Diego But 10/92 5,225
O/C 26x32 La Jolla Cove Mor 6/93 5,225
O/C 26x32 Near Palm Springs, California But 10/92 4,950
O/B 8x10 Luxembourg Gardens But 10/92 4,400
O/C/C 26x32 Fall in Olancha Mor 6/93 4,125
O/C 26x31 Luxembourg Gardens But 10/92 4,125
O/Pn 8x10 Church on the Seine, Paris But 6/93 3,738
O/C/B 7x9 Autumn Landscape But 3/93 1,650
O/Pn 17x12 Viola But 6/93 1,150
Clark, Benton H.   Am 1895-1964
O/C 25x30 Frontiersmen in Field With Oxen Ih 11/92 1,700
O/C 37x19 Introduction at a Carriage 38 Ih 5/93 1,300
Clark, C. Myron   Am 1876-1925
O/C 20x28 Springtime Landscape Wes 3/93 550
Clark, Dane   Am 20C
* See 1993 Edition ....
Clark, Eliot Candee   Am 1883-1980
O/C 26x26 New Lynchburg 1934 Lou 9/92 1,500
O/C 20x27 Autumn Meadow Lou 6/93 1,450
O/C 16x20 Creek in a Spring Landscape Chr 5/93 1,150
G/Pa 6x9 Three Works Wes 10/92 440
A/C 7x10 Winter Scene Fre 4/93 200
O/B 9x12 Field Landscape Ald 9/92 150
Clark, James   Br 1858-1943
O/C 20x24 Steer in Landscapes: Pair 192 Sby 6/93 9,200
O/C 17x27 Full Cry Sby 6/93 2,530
Clark, Matt   Am 1903-1972
O/Pn 22x25 Man on Horseback 1951 Ih 5/93 350
Clark, Octavius T.   Br 1850-1921
O/C 20x30 Near Frome Hnz 5/93 525

Clark, Paraskeva   Can 1898-1986
O/B 18x16 Algonquin Morning '53 Sbt 5/93 1,980
Clark, Rances   Am 20C
O/B 14x17 The Blue Ridge of ...(?) Mor 11/92 950
Clark, Roland   Am 1874-1957
* See 1993 Edition ....
Clark, S. Joseph   Br 19C
O/C 20x30 Landscape with Milkmaid and Cows But 5/93 .. 2,185
Clark, W.   Br 19C
* See 1992 Edition ....
Clark, Walter A.   Am 1848-1917
O/C 15x20 Pasture with Flowering Tree Fre 4/93 450
Clark, William   Br a 1827-1841
* See 1990 Edition ....
Clark, William Albert   Br 20C
O/C 17x21 Black Stallion Gentleman John 1914 Chr 2/93 .. 2,200
Clarke, A.   Eng 19C
O/C 16x21 Dogs Dum 12/92 450
Clarke, J. W.   Am 1861-1943
P/Pa 11x31 Mountainous Lake Scene FHB 6/93 45
Clarke, John Clem   Am 1937-
O/C 80x66 Group of Bathers Sby 10/92 5,225
Clary-Baroux, Adolphe   1865-1933
* See 1993 Edition ....
Claude, Eugene   Fr 1841-1923
O/C 18x23 Pansies Spilling from a Basket Doy 5/93 4,180
Claude, Jean Maxime   Fr 1824-1904
Pe&K/Pa 10x17 Pointer 1901 Chr 6/93 805
Claus, Emile   Bel 1849-1924
* See 1993 Edition ....
Clausell, Joaquin   Mex 1866-1935
O/B 14x22 Paisaje Marino Chr 11/92 44,000
O/C/Pn 18x38 Marina Sby 5/93 24,150
Clausen, Sir George   Br 1852-1944
* See 1991 Edition ....
Clave, Antoni   Spa 1913-
O&L/Pa/C 22x30 Le roi Chr 11/92 25,000
G,W&Pl/Pa 15x23 Marche du Village Chr 2/93 8,250
I,S&W/Pa 13x10 Portrait Tete D'Enfant Sby 10/92 4,125
Claveau, Antoine   Am a 1854-1872
O/C 36x48 Falls, Yosemite 1858 Sby 3/93 18,400
Claver, Francois   Fr 1918-
O/C 15x18 La Madeleine Wes 10/92 660
O/C 15x18 Place de la Concorde Wes 10/92 440
Clays, Paul Jean   Bel 1819-1900
O/Pn 27x39 Sailing Ships But 11/92 11,000
O/C 33x27 Passengers Disembarking Doy 11/92 9,350
O/C/B 10x16 Sailboats and Sunset Hnd 10/92 2,600
Clayton, Harold   Br 1896-1979
* See 1993 Edition ....
Cleenewerck, Henry   Am a 1880-1905
O/C 10x18 Boats on a River at Sunset But 3/93 2,200
Clegg and Guttman
* See 1992 Edition ....
Clemens, Paul   Fr 20C
* See 1992 Edition ....
Clemens, Paul Lewis   Am 1911-
* See 1992 Edition ....
Clement, Marie-Louise   Fr 20C
* See 1991 Edition ....
Clement, Serge
O/C 26x21 Girl in Meditation 60 Sby 2/93 920
Clemente, Francesco   1952-
G/L 143x178 My World War III 1983 Sby 10/92 137,500
MM/Pa 96x30 Four Seasons in One Day: Two Sby 5/93 .. 51,750
O&H/C 117x78 Etruscan China Chr 11/92 44,000
O/C 38x33 Untitled (Orange and Green) Sby 11/92 44,000
P/Pa 24x18 Three Points 1981 Sby 10/92 19,800
P/Pa 19x17 Untitled Sby 5/93 14,950
P/Pa 26x19 Rice Grains Sby 5/93 11,500
K&W/Pa 12x9 Fonetica Interiore Chr 2/93 7,150
Frs 10x16 Corda 1981 Sby 10/92 5,500
Ph/Pn 38x32 Untitled 1974 Chr 2/93 5,500
Clements, Grace   Am 1905-1969
* See 1992 Edition ....

Clemins, Vija
* See 1990 Edition . . . .

Cleminson, Robert   Br 19C
O/C 34x28 Hunting Dogs and Dead Game Sby 6/93 2,300
O/C 16x24 Two Hunting Dogs Dum 12/92 1,300

Clerisseau, Jacques-Louis   Fr 1722-1820
* See 1991 Edition . . . .

Clime, Winfield Scott   Am 1881-1958
O/M 9x12 Valley Under a Blanket of Snow Skn 5/93 825

Clinedinst, Benjamin West   Am 1859-1931
O/C 45x43 The Remedy 1886 Sby 9/92 6,050

Clint, Alfred   Br 1807-1883
O/C 24x42 An Extensive Coastal Landscape 1843 Chr 2/93 . 2,750

Clonney, James Goodwyn   Am 1812-1867
W/Pa 11x14 A Day Fishing Sby 5/93 14,950

Close, Chuck   Am 1940-
O/C 72x60 Cindy II 1988 Sby 11/92 231,000
l/Pa 58x41 Phyllis 1981 Chr 11/92 93,500
W/Pa 30x23 Linda/Eye Series I-V 1977 Sby 10/92 55,000

Closson, William Baxter   Am 1848-1926
* See 1993 Edition . . . .

Clough, Arthur   Am 20C
W/Pa 13x16 Catalina Channel 1934 Mor 2/93 850

Clough, George L.   Am 1824-1901
O/C 24x36 Passing Shower on the Hudson Chr 9/92 7,150

Clowes, Daniel   Br 1774-1829
O/C 24x35 Racehorse with Jockey Up 1821 Sby 6/93 4,600

Clusmann, William   Am 1859-1927
O/C 14x20 Winter Landscape Hnd 3/93 950

Clymer, John Ford   Am 1907-1989
O/C 34x27 Family Walking Along Mountain Trail 52 llh 11/92 7,500
O/B 26x21 Snowshoeing in Back Country Skn 11/92 4,620
O/Pn 12x28 Confederates Boarding Union Ship llh 11/92 . . 2,100
O/B 29x40 Paris-London Court Fashions Sby 3/93 1,610
O/B 28x40 Fashion Premiere at the Court Sby 3/93 1,495
O/C 24x36 A Bustling Harbor Chr 12/92 1,320

Coale, Griffith Baily   Am 1890-1950
* See 1993 Edition . . . .

Coarding, Gerald   Am 20C
O/C 30x24 The Egyptians But 12/92 3,300

Coates, Edmund C.   Am 1816-1871
O/C 29x42 Sailing off New York Harbor Sby 3/93 19,550
O/C 14x20 Figures Overlooking a River 62 Sby 3/93 690

Coates, George James   Br 1869-1930
O/C 30x20 Spanish Dancer Hnd 3/93 700

Cobb, Darius   Am 1834-1919
* See 1991 Edition . . . .

Cobbett, Edward John   Eng 1815-1899
* See 1993 Edition . . . .

Cobelle, Charles   Fr 1902-
O/C 30x40 Les Champs Elysses Lou 9/92 1,800
O/C 20x24 Paris Fantasy Dum 3/93 1,400
O/C 16x20 Paris Fantasy Dum 6/93 1,300
O/C 16x20 French Scene Dum 2/93 1,150
O/C 20x24 Paris Fantasy Dum 7/93 1,100
W/Pa 18x24 Paris Fantasy Dum 4/93 1,000
O/C 24x30 Paris Street Scene Lou 9/92 1,000
O/C 20x24 Street Scene with Figures Dum 6/93 900
O/C 20x24 View of Montmartre Sby 10/92 550
W/Pa 22x27 Paris Scene Dum 8/93 500
O/C 15x30 Colorful Parisian Street Scene Sel 9/92 375
O/C 16x20 La Femme a Place de la Concorde Hnd 3/93 275

Cobo, Chema   1952-
* See 1993 Edition . . . .

Coburn, Frank   Am 1866-1931
O/C 24x20 Los Angeles Park Scene But 10/92 8,250
O/B 17x14 Riany Chicago City Street Mor 2/93 7,000
O/B 10x14 Summer Landscape But 10/92 1,760
O/Pn 12x17 Beachscape at Dusk Wlf 9/92 1,000

**Coburn, Frederick Simpson   Can
1871-1960**
O/C 22x32 Logging Team, Winter '45 Sbt 11/92 11,440

Coccapani, Sigismondo   It 1583-1642
* See 1992 Edition . . . .

Coccorante, Leonardo   It a 1700-1750
O/C 79x101 Ships Foundering in Stormy Sea Chr 1/93 . . . 82,500
O/C 39x52 Ruins on the Shore Chr 1/93 28,600

**Cochin, Charles-N (the Younger)
1715-1790**
* See 1992 Edition . . . .

Cochran, Allen Dean   Am 1888-1935
* See 1992 Edition . . . .

**Cockburn, James Pattison   Can
1778-1848**
* See 1991 Edition . . . .

Cocteau, Jean   Fr 1889-1963
Pe/Pa/B 13x17 La Petite Fille Due Reve: Pair Sby 6/93 2,185
I&P/Pa 11x8 Mythical Face Dum 2/93 1,200
Pe/Pa 11x8 Portrait de L'Artiste 1959 Chr 5/93 920
Y/Pa 12x11 Portrait of a Young Man 1953 Fre 10/92 725

Codaro, V.   It 19C
* See 1992 Edition . . . .

Codazzi, Niccolo Viviano   It 1648-1693
* See 1992 Edition . . . .

Codazzi, Viviano   It 1603-1672
* See 1993 Edition . . . .

**Codazzi, Viviano & Cerquozzi   It
1603-1672**
* See 1992 Edition . . . .

**Codazzi, Viviano & Gargiulio   It
1603-1672**
* See 1993 Edition . . . .

Codde, Pieter Jacobsz   Dut 1599-1678
O/Pn 12x15 Elegant Figures in an Interior Sby 5/93 10,925

**Codino Y Langlin, Victoriano   Spa
1844-1911**
O/C 18x10 Monkey Business Chr 10/92 8,250

Codman, Charles   Am 1800-1842
* See 1993 Edition . . . .

Codron, Jef   Fr 19C
* See 1993 Edition . . . .

Coe, Sue
A/Pa 132x95 Killing Fields 87 Sby 2/93 4,600

Coedes, Louis Eugene   Fr 1810-1906
* See 1993 Edition . . . .

Coello, Alonso Sanchez   1515-1590
O/C 40x31 Child, Caterina, Aged 1 Sby 5/93 40,250

Coene, Jean Henri   Flm 1798-1866
* See 1991 Edition . . . .

Coene, Jean-Baptiste   Bel 1805-
* See 1993 Edition . . . .

**Coessin De La Fosse, Charles A   Fr
1829-1900**
* See 1990 Edition . . . .

Coffee, William John   Am 1872-1969
O/C 21x29 River Landscape Fre 10/92 375

Coffermans, Marcellus   Flm 1535-1575
* See 1993 Edition . . . .

Coffin, William Anderson   Am 1855-1925
* See 1993 Edition . . . .

Coffin, William Haskell   Am 1878-1941
P/Pa 14x10 Bust of Beautiful Brunette llh 11/92 700
O/C 8x12 Winter Twilight Yng 5/93 400

Coggeshall, John I.   Am 1856-1927
O/C 28x40 Harbor Scene 1896 Sby 3/93 2,530

Coggeshall-Wilson, J.   Br 20C
* See 1993 Edition . . . .

Cogniet, Leon   Fr 1794-1880
* See 1990 Edition . . . .

Cohen, Frederick E.   Am -1858
* See 1993 Edition . . . .

Cohen, Lois   Am 20C
* See 1993 Edition . . . .

Cohn, Harold   Am 1908-
O/C 30x14 The Mirror '52 Yng 2/93 675

Cohn, Max Arthur   Am 1903-
* See 1993 Edition . . . .

Coignard, James   Fr 1925-
O/C 22x26 Le Maison Chr 2/93 1,320

Col, Jan David Bel 1822-1900
* See 1992 Edition . . . .
Colacicco, Salvatore Am 20C
O/Pn 11x16 Two American Sailing Portraits Skn 11/92 1,650
Colahan, Colin
* See 1993 Edition . . . .
Colburn, Elanor Am 1866-1939
O/Cb 8x10 Coastal Mor 2/93 400
Cole, Alphaeus Philemon Am 1876-1900
O/C 12x16 Still Life with Peaches 1969 Eld 8/93 378
Cole, Charles Octavius Am 1814-
* See 1993 Edition . . . .
Cole, Fern Am 20C
O/C 24x29 Isn't He Precious Wlf 5/93 100
Cole, George Vicat Br 1810-1883
O/C 30x48 Near Newton, Lincolnshire 1856 Chr 10/92 . . 7,700
O/C 10x14 Cattle on a Country Road 1872 But 11/92 1,100
Cole, Joseph Foxcroft Am 1837-1892
* See 1993 Edition . . . .
Cole, T. Casilear Am 1888-1976
O/C 25x20 Portrait of a Young Man Mys 3/93 330
Cole, Thomas Am 1801-1848
O/C/Pn 32x48 The Good Shepherd 1848 Sby 5/93 255,500
O/C 25x20 Head of a Roman Woman Sby 12/92 19,800
H/Pa 11x13 In the Adirondacks Hnz 5/93 425
Coleman, Charles Caryl Am 1840-1928
O/Pn 16x10 Garden of Villa Castello 1904 Chr 9/92 2,860
Coleman, Enrico It 1846-1911
W/Pa 15x23 Grooming the Horses Sby 2/93 7,475
W/Pa 11x14 Character Studies Sby 2/93 4,600
Coleman, Glenn O. Am 1887-1932
O/B 18x24 Distant View of New York Sby 3/93 4,140
G&H/B 17x12 Patchin Place Sby 3/93 1,380
Coleman, Marion Am -1925
* See 1993 Edition . . . .
Coleman, Mary Darter Am 1894-1956
O/B 16x20 Boats in Harbor Yng 2/93 175
Coleman, Michael Am 1946-
G/Pa 10x15 Indian Encampment 1976 Chr 3/93 5,520
G/B 10x14 Winter Encampment Chr 3/93 4,025
Coleman, Ralph P. Am 1892-1968
* See 1993 Edition . . . .
Coleman, William Stephen Br 1829-1904
* See 1993 Edition . . . .
Colescott, Robert Am 1925-
W&C/Pa 23x18 Old Crow 78 But 10/92 880
Colinson, J. Eng 19C
O/C 10x14 Hay Barge in Thames Wlf 3/93 375
Coll, Giovanni It 1636-1681
* See 1991 Edition . . . .
Coll, Joseph Clement Am 1881-1921
Pl/Pa 11x13 Swordfight in Tavern Ih 5/93 1,600
Collazo, Guillermo Cub 1850-1896
O/Pn 9x5 En La Terraza 1889 Sby 5/93 5,175
Colle Am 20C
O/C 24x30 Harbor Scene Sel 12/92 170
Colle, Michel-Auguste Fr 1872-1949
* See 1990 Edition . . . .
Colley, Rus Am 20C
W/Pa 17x24 Still Life Beach Comber's Loot Wlf 5/93 50
Collier, Alan Caswell Can 1911-1990
O/C 24x36 Morning Hush Sbt 5/93 2,200
O/Pn 12x16 Fort Amherst, Newfoundland Sbt 5/93 836
O/B 12x16 Fox Harbour, Placentia Bay Sbt 5/93 660
O/B 12x16 Skeena River at Kitsegucla Sbt 5/93 616
O/Pn 12x16 Cape Breton Island Sbt 5/93 375
Collier, Evert Dut -1702
* See 1992 Edition . . . .
Collier, John Br 1708-1786
* See 1991 Edition . . . .
Collier, The Hon. John Br 1850-1934
* See 1993 Edition . . . .
Collignon a 1762-
* See 1992 Edition . . . .

Collin, Raphael Fr 1850-1916
* See 1993 Edition . . . .
Collins, Arthur G. Am 1866-
O/B 9x11 Sunrise Over a Forest Yng 2/93 275
Collins, Charles Eng 1851-1921
* See 1992 Edition . . . .
Collins, Earl Am 1925-
* See 1992 Edition . . . .
Collins, Hugh Br 19C
* See 1993 Edition . . . .
Collins, William Br 1788-1847
O/C 20x24 Figures Along the Coast Fre 10/92 2,000
O/Pn 16x21 Mending Nets 1827 Dum 11/92 1,900
Collinson, James Con 19C
* See 1991 Edition . . . .
Collomb, Paul 1921-
* See 1992 Edition . . . .
Colman, Roi Clarkson Am 1884-1945
O/C 28x36 Surf at Arch Beach But 3/93 1,100
Colman, Samuel Am 1832-1920
W&G/Pa 8x15 Puebla, Mexico '92 Sby 12/92 4,125
Pe/Pa 10x16 On the Ellis River 1857 Brd 8/93 55
Colomanus, J. Con 20C
O/Pn 9x12 Fox Hunt Fre 4/93 500
Colonelli-Sciarra, Salvatore It a 1729-1736
* See 1991 Edition . . . .
Colt, James Am 20C
O/M 20x24 A One Dog Town Mor 11/92 425
Coltman, Ora Am 1858-
P/Pa 14x10 Canal River Scene 1909 Wlf 5/93 200
Colucci, Gio It 20C
O&I/Pa 11x10 Village Church: Pair Sby 2/93 740
Colunga, Alejandro Mex 1948-
O&P/Pa 25x19 El Burro 84 Chr 11/92 4,400
Colville, Alexander Can 1920-
O/B 12x16 Barn, New Brunswick '46 Sbt 11/92 4,225
Coman, Charlotte Buell Am 1833-1924
O/C 21x24 Mountain Hamlet Dum 1/93 1,000
Comba, Pierre Fr -1934
W/Pa 30x21 Soldiers Resting on Mountain Path Yng 5/93 . . . 700
Combas, Robert 1957-
A/Pa 42x48 Dr. Martin's Shoe 82 Chr 11/92 2,640
Comerre, Leon Francois Fr 1850-1934
* See 1993 Edition . . . .
Comerre-Paton, Jaqueline Fr 1859-
* See 1993 Edition . . . .
Commere, Jean Yves 1920-1986
O/C 6x10 Paysage: Two Chr 2/93 4,180
Compte-Calix, Francois C. Fr 1813-1880
* See 1993 Edition . . . .
Compton, Edward Harrison Br 1881-1960
* See 1993 Edition . . . .
Compton, Edward Theodore Br 1849-1921
W/Pa 10x14 Views in the Alps: Pair Sby 1/93 2,875
Compton, T. C. Eng 19C
O/C/B 15x13 Girl Feeding the Chickens Hnd 6/93 700
Comradt, Johannes Ludvig Dan 1779-1849
O/C 23x17 Still Life Melon, Snails, Grapes 1839 Sby 10/92 15,400
Comte De Grimberghe, Edmond Ger 1865-1920
* See 1990 Edition . . . .
Comte de Montpezat, Henri D'A. Fr 1817-1859
O/C 17x24 Hunting Party Sby 5/93 6,325
Conca, Sebastiano It 1680-1764
* See 1992 Edition . . . .
Conca, Tommaso 1735-1822
Pl&S/Pa 9x27 Design for a Ceiling (2) Chr 1/93 1,760
Conconi, Luigi It 1852-1917
* See 1993 Edition . . . .
Condo, George 1957-
O,Pl,L&Y/C 98x118 Big White One 87 Chr 11/92 46,200

O/L 63x77 Dream Sequence and Big Sur 91 Chr 11/92 . . . 27,500
O/C 60x48 Untitled Chr 11/92 20,900
O,P&L/C 48x60 Chapeau 89 Sby 5/93 17,250
O/C 67x51 Yellow Fool 86 Sby 2/93 17,250
O/C 36x48 Surrealist Landscape 83 Chr 2/93 13,200
O&L/C 59x32 Spotted Stain 1989 Sby 5/93 9,200
O/C 33x22 Untitled (Portrait) Chr 2/93 8,800
K/Pa 32x23 Untitled Chr 2/93 3,850
O/L 7x5 Untitled 85 Sby 2/93 1,438
O/C 9x6 Mouth 85 Sby 2/93 1,150

Cone, Marvin D.   Am 1891-1964
O/C 18x20 Landscape Sby 9/92 6,600

Conely, William Brewster   Am 1830-1911
O/C 30x25 Portrait Richard Storrs Willis 1887 Dum 5/93 . . . 1,100

Congdon, Thomas Raphael   Am 1862-1917
* See 1992 Edition . . . .

Connard, Philip   Br 1875-1958
* See 1991 Edition . . . .

Connavale, Robert
O/C 24x30 Winter Landscape 1943 Ald 5/93 100

Connaway, Jay Hall   Am 1893-1970
* See 1993 Edition . . . .

Connelly, Chuck   1955-
* See 1993 Edition . . . .

Conner, Bruce   20C
* See 1991 Edition . . . .

Conner, John Anthony   Am 1892-1971
O/B 9x12 Flowered Hillside Mor 2/93 1,400
O/Cb 9x12 Landscape Mor 6/93 825
O/C 25x30 Marine - Southern California Mor 2/93 475
O/C 16x24 Edge of the Desert Mor 2/93 450

Conner, Paul   Am 1881-1968
O/B 23x30 Desert Flowers Verbena Dum 6/93 950

Connor, Charles   20C
* See 1991 Edition . . . .

Conradi, H.   Eur 19C
O/C 15x30 Venetian View Slo 7/93 1,100

Constable, John   Eng 1776-1837
* See 1990 Edition . . . .

Constable, William   Am 1783-1861
* See 1991 Edition . . . .

Constant, Benjamin   Fr 1845-1902
O/C 13x16 Un Envoi de Serbie 1876 Fre 4/93 6,750
O/C 37x30 Lady with Ribbon '95 Lou 6/93 1,500

Constant, George   Am 1892-1978
W/Pa 21x16 Seated Woman 1931 Mys 12/92 154

Constantin, S*   It 19C
O/C 17x21 The Discussion Wes 12/92 550

Constantinescu, Constantin   Rom 20C
O/M 21x16 Seascapes: Four Slo 5/93 300

Conti, Primo   20C
* See 1991 Edition . . . .

Conti, Tito   It 1842-1924
O/C 38x55 At the Cardinal's 1880 Chr 5/93 40,250
O/C 33x27 Italian Peasant Girl with Grapes 1876 Chr 2/93 . 7,150

Conway, Fred   Am 1900-1972
O/C 40x48 Shadynook 1931 Sel 4/93 1,200
A/M 48x24 Dancer '54 Sel 12/92 1,100
O/Cb 10x14 Caddies Sel 9/92 775
O/Cb 10x14 Lost Ball Sel 12/92 500
W/Pa 15x22 Street Scene in an Old Neighborhood '54 Sel 9/92 250
O/B 9x9 Still Life of Flowers Sel 9/92 210

Conway, John S.   Am 1852-1925
* See 1993 Edition . . . .

Conwell, Averil   Am 20C
O/C 30x26 Floral Still Life Hnd 5/93 190

Cook, A. R.   Eng 19C
P/Pa Young Victorian Girl Wlf 5/93 200

Cook, Ebenezer Wake   Br 1843-1926
* See 1991 Edition . . . .

Cook, Gladys Emerson   Am 1901-
W/Pa 17x15 Costume Design for Ziegfield Slo 5/93 275

Cook, Gordon   Am 1927-1985
O/C 15x18 Soft Cheese Box But 10/92 4,950

O/C 25x18 Large Delta Tower But 10/92 2,200
W/Pa 10x14 Sailing But 10/92 1,870
W/Pa 9x10 Watertower But 10/92 1,870
W/Pa 9x8 House in the Trees But 10/92 1,760
W/Pa 8x9 Sailboat But 10/92 1,650
W/Pa 9x8 Top But 10/92 1,320

Cook, Howard   Am 1901-1980
* See 1992 Edition . . . .

Cook, John A.   Am 1870-1936
W/Pa 10x19 Country Road Wes 10/92 522
W/Pa 7x10 Gloucester Harbor Eld 8/93 220

Cook, Otis   Am 1900-
O/C 20x24 Winter Snow Scene Mys 3/93 1,540

Cook, William Edwards   Am 1881-
W&C/Pa 10x12 Lakeviews, Boats, Houses 1913 Chr 5/93 . . 1,150

Cooke, Edward William   Eng 1811-1880
* See 1991 Edition . . . .

Cooke, George   Am 1793-1849
* See 1991 Edition . . . .

Cooke, H. Lester   Am 20C
W/Pa 13x31 Whaling Fleet 1963 Wes 10/92 330

Cooke, John   Br a 1887-1903
* See 1991 Edition . . . .

Cookesley, Margaret Murray   Eng -1927
O/C 25x30 In Captivity 1908 Sby 5/93 11,500

Cooley, Ben   Am 19C
* See 1993 Edition . . . .

Coolidge, Cassius Marcellus   Am 1844-1934
O/C 23x33 The Poker Game Wes 10/92 17,600
O/C 24x34 Summit Conference Wes 3/93 14,300
O/C 20x26 Eating His Words Wes 3/93 6,270
O/C 22x28 Sick in Bed Wes 5/93 5,060
O/C 24x34 A Monarch Wes 10/92 2,200

Coolidge, Mary Rosamond   Am 1884-
O/C 32x26 Portrait of Edna Hathaway Mys 3/93 880
O/Cb 16x20 Lumber Yard Skn 5/93 770

Coomans, Diana   Con 19C
* See 1993 Edition . . . .

Coomans, Heva   Bel 19C
O/C 20x28 Classical Beauties Chr 10/92 13,200

Coomans, Pierre Olivier Joseph   Bel 1816-1889
O/Pn 27x22 The Emperor's Children 1879 Chr 10/92 15,400

Coombs, Delbert Dana   Am 1850-1938
O/C 18x24 At the Blacksmith Shop, Winter 1885 Brd 8/93 . 5,500

Cooper, Abraham   Br 1787-1868
* See 1993 Edition . . . .

Cooper, Alexander Davis   Am 1837-1888
* See 1993 Edition . . . .

Cooper, Alfred Egerton   Br 1883-
O/C 20x16 Portrait of a Young Man Hnd 10/92 275

Cooper, Astley D. M.   Am 1856-1924
O/C 84x128 Indian Encampment/Tetons 1905 But 10/92 . . 10,450
O/C/B 32x52 Buffalo with Fallen Indian 1888 But 3/93 5,500
O/C 14x17 Cheyenne Autumn 1914 But 6/93 2,300

Cooper, Colin Campbell   Am 1856-1937
O/C 26x20 The Flatiron Building Doy 5/93 19,800
W&G/Pa/B 18x22 Balboa Park, San Diego 1916 Sby 9/92 . 10,450
O/C 23x29 Happy Days 1903 But 10/92 7,700
O/B 14x11 Broadway from the Post Office Chr 3/93 4,600
O/Cb 14x18 Nantucket Street at Night Chr 12/92 3,850
W&G/Pa 7x10 View of Rochester But 6/93 3,450
O/B 7x12 View of Notre Dame But 6/93 2,875
O/M 12x16 House in Summer Landscape Mor 2/93 1,900
W/Pa 17x14 Manhattan Business District Lou 12/92 1,600
O/Cb 8x13 Coastal View at Dawn Slo 5/93 1,500
P/Pa 20x26 California Landscape Lou 6/93 1,400
O/C 24x20 Church Interior Fre 4/93 1,400
O/B 5x7 Paris 1900 Mor 11/92 850
O/B 5x7 Harbor Mor 6/93 750
O/B 5x7 Florence from A...(?) 1912 Mor 11/92 650
W/Pa 15x18 Castle in a Landscape Fre 10/92 500
O/B 5x7 Atmospheric Landscape Mor 2/93 475
G/Pa 4x7 Near Oatman, Arizona Mor 11/92 375

Pe/Pa 14x10 Cityscape with Triumphal Arch Dum 7/93 250

Cooper, Edwin   Br 1785-1833
* See 1993 Edition . . . .

Cooper, Emma Lampert   Am 1860-1920
O/C 26x32 Chickens Feeding Outside the Barn Chr 12/92 . . 4,620
O/C 22x18 Delhi Fruit Stand FHB 6/93 900
O/B 11x9 Courtyard Mor 11/92 300

Cooper, J. D.
* See 1992 Edition . . . .

Cooper, T. F.
O/B 16x20 Boatyard, East Gloucester Dum 5/93 375

Cooper, Thomas Sidney   Br 1803-1902
O/C 30x40 Cow and Sheep in Pasture 1897 Hnd 6/93 6,800

Cooper, W. Savage   Br a 1880-1926
O/C 50x30 Roses Softly Blooming 1906 Sby 2/93 40,250

Cooper, William Sidney   Br 1854-1927
O/C 24x20 The Highlands 1876 Chr 10/92 1,650
O/C 24x20 The Highlands 1876 Slo 7/93 1,400
O/C 16x24 Sunset with Cows 1914 Fre 4/93 900

Coopse, Pieter   Dut 17C
* See 1991 Edition . . . .

Coosemans, Alexander   Flm 1627-1689
* See 1992 Edition . . . .

Cope, Charles West   Eng 1811-1890
O/C Size? Parting of Lord & Lady Russell 1861 Wtf 3/93 . . 3,900

Cope, George   Am 1855-1929
O/C 51x32 The Hunter's Equipment 1891 Sby 12/92 . . . 209,000

Cope, Gordon Nicholson   Am 1906-1970
* See 1992 Edition . . . .

Copeland, Alfred Bryant   Am 1840-1909
O/C 27x46 The Birth of Venus 1887 Chr 10/92 14,300

Copeland, Charles G.   Am 1840-1909
W/Pa 18x28 Autumn with Moose Hunters Skn 11/92 550

Copley, John Singleton   Am 1737-1815
P/Pa/C 23x18 Greg/Lucretia Townsend (2) 1756 Sby 12/92 41,250

Copley, Robert   20C
* See 1991 Edition . . . .

Copley, William   Am 1919-
O/C 32x26 Saysme No. 6 57 Chr 2/93 5,280
A&Sd/C 29x24 Quatuoir 59 Chr 11/92 4,180
A&C/C 42x25 Untitled 82 Chr 2/93 3,850

Coppedge, Fern Isabel   Am 1883-1951
O/C 24x20 Gloucester Port Ald 9/92 14,000
O/C 24x24 House Along Delaware River Ald 9/92 10,500
O/C 24x24 Yellow Houses Across the River Ald 9/92 . . . 10,500
O/B 16x14 Winter Afternoon Ald 9/92 7,000
O/C 30x30 Harbor Entrance Ald 9/92 5,000
O/B 14x16 Late Summer No. 12 Brd 8/93 2,970
O/Ab 25x30 Early Winter Pennsylvania Wtf 9/92 2,700
O/B 10x12 House and Winter River Landscape Ald 5/93 . . 1,500
O/B 9x9 Houses on Hill Ald 9/92 1,250
O/B 7x8 Houses by River Ald 9/92 1,100
O/C 16x20 Landscape Ald 9/92 375

Copperman, Mildred Tuner   Am 20C
* See 1992 Edition . . . .

Coppimi, C.   It
O/B 7x9 Trompe-L'Oeil Dead Song Birds: Four Eld 4/93 . . 1,210

Coppin, John A.   Am 1904-
* See 1993 Edition . . . .

Coppin, John Stevens   Am 1904-1986
O/M 26x22 The Gallery '65 FHB 3/93 550
O/M 16x22 Rclining Female Nude '67 FHB 3/93 500
O/C 24x24 Eskimos on a Snowy Beach '55 FHB 3/93 200
O/M 30x38 Two Pheasants in Flight '52 FHB 3/93 200
O/M 24x20 Bust Length Self Portrait '64 FHB 3/93 190
Pe/Pa 14x9 Three Drawings FHB 3/93 165

Coppini, Eliseo Fausto   It 1870-
O/C 20x14 Reverie 17 Sby 2/93 3,220

Coppola, Antonio   It 1839-
G/B 11x17 Boaters w/Mount Vesuvius Erupting Wes 5/93 . . . 495

Coques, Gonzales   Flm 1614-1684
* See 1993 Edition . . . .

Corazzi, Giulietta   It 19C
O/C 25x20 Portrait of a Child 1886 FHB 6/93 400
O/C 25x20 Portrait of a Child 1886 FHB 6/93 350

Corbellini, Luigi   It 1901-1968
O/C 25x17 Seated Nude Woman But 5/93 2,300
O/C 11x9 Helenitta Sby 2/93 920
O/C 14x11 La Robe Sby 2/93 920
O/C 18x13 Child with Birdcage Sby 6/93 805

Corbino, Jon   Am 1905-1964
O&H/M 10x8 Halloween Party Skn 3/93 1,320
O/C 20x15 Nude Study Wtf 12/92 900
O/C 16x12 Ballet Dancers Hnz 5/93 675
Pe&I/M 16x12 Pensive Woman Hnz 5/93 625

Corbit, George Cecil   Am 1892-1944
* See 1993 Edition . . . .

Corbitt, Harriet   Am 20C
W/Pa 11x14 Cats Hnz 5/93 50

Corbould, Aster R. Chantrey   Eng -1920
I,G&R/Pa 7x10 Horse Race Wes 3/93 330

Corchon Y Diaque, Federico   Spa 19C
* See 1993 Edition . . . .

Corcos, Vittorio Matteo   It 1859-1933
O/C 42x26 The Rendezvous 88 Sby 5/93 37,375

Cordero, Francisco   Mex 19C
* See 1991 Edition . . . .

Cordier, Charles Pierre M.   Fr 1848-1909
O/C 51x77 Chemin du bord de mer Chr 5/93 18,400

Cordrey, Earl   Am 1902-1977
G/Pa 17x16 Senorita Gambling Ih 5/93 250

Corelli, Augusto   It 1853-1910
W/Pa 19x11 Young Peasant Girl Wes 5/93 1,100

Corelli, G.   It 19C
O/C 23x32 Bay of Naples 1860 Slo 5/93 500

Corinth, Lovis   Ger 1858-1925
* See 1993 Edition . . . .

Corley, Philip   Am 20C
O/Pn 26x32 Cafe de Tertre Hnz 5/93 700

Corneille (C. G. Van Beverloo)   Spa 1922-
ASs/C 59x111 La Monde Des Fables '75 Chr 11/92 3,300

Corneille, Michel   Fr 1642-1708
* See 1993 Edition . . . .

Cornell, Joseph   Am 1903-1972
Pt,Pe&L/Pa 12x15 Untitled Sby 2/93 13,800

Corner, Thomas C.   Am 1865-1938
* See 1992 Edition . . . .

Cornet, Alphonse   Fr 1814-1874
O/C 16x18 He Loves me He Loves me not 1880 Chr 10/92 2,640

Cornil, Gaston   Fr 1883-
* See 1990 Edition . . . .

Cornish, William Permeanus   Eng 20C
W/Pa/Pn 30x46 The Old Print Shop 1898 Chr 10/92 5,500

Cornoyer, Paul   Am 1864-1923
O/C 22x26 Washington Square Chr 12/92 88,000
O/C 18x24 Street Scene Chr 9/92 27,500
O/C 22x27 Flatiron Building Sby 9/92 25,300
O/C 22x27 New England House Moonlight Sby 9/92 9,350
O/C 27x20 Urban Nocturne Chr 5/93 5,750
O/C 12x16 Parisian Winter Lou 9/92 3,000
O/C 22x18 Venetian Street Scene Sel 4/93 3,000
O/C 12x16 Busy New York Street Scene Sel 4/93 2,600
O/C 12x16 Nocturnal River Landscape Sel 12/92 1,350
O/C 13x16 Sunlit Italian Courtyard Sel 4/93 925

Cornwell, Dean   Am 1892-1960
O/C 30x28 The Cafe Table '20 Chr 9/92 26,400
O/C 36x28 Waiting 20 Chr 3/93 21,850
O/C 21x31 Bullet Train Hnd 3/93 7,800
O/B 17x27 Mary and Joseph Riding Donkey Ih 11/92 . . . 4,750
O/B 11x38 Figures and Stagecoach 1918 Ih 5/93 2,750
O/C 15x18 The Pot Seller of Bethlehem Lou 9/92 600

Coronel, Pedro   Mex 1923-1985
O/C 47x32 La Sonadora 1974 Chr 11/92 28,600

Coronel, Rafael   Mex 1932-
O/C 59x49 Anciana Chr 11/92 55,000
O/C 50x60 La Espera Chr 11/92 46,200
O/C 40x51 La Ficcion Chr 11/92 33,000
O/C 32x40 Personaje Chr 11/92 33,000
O/C 39x47 Escena Del Circo Sby 5/93 23,000
O/C 47x47 El Viego y la Foca '67 But 10/92 15,400

O/B 20x20 Dark Heads in Profile Sby 6/93 9,775
O/B 20x20 La Pantomima Sby 6/93 9,775
O/C 40x26 The Ice Cream Vendor '73 Dum 5/93 5,500
H&A/B 40x30 El Buscador 1969 Sby 11/92 4,400
O/M 16x22 El Payaso Chr 11/92 4,400

Corot, Jean Baptiste Camille Fr 1796-1875
O/C 32x43 Smyrne-Bournabat Sby 11/92 .... 1.32M
O/C 22x32 Ville d'Avray Chr 5/93 475,500
O/C 18x22 Les Ramasseuses De Pissenlits Sby 5/93 ... 365,500
O/C 13x18 Un Verger a l'Epoque Chr 5/93 365,500
O/C 23x32 Le Marais au Grande Arbre Chr 5/93 332,500
O/C 18x22 Le Batelier au Bord de L'Etang Sby 5/93 145,500
O/Pn 13x18 La berge d'une riviere Chr 5/93 134,500
O/C 16x22 La Vachere au bord de l'eau Chr 5/93 96,000
O/C 11x16 Vue Prise a Rive (Tyrol Italien) Sby 2/93 85,000
O/C 15x18 La Vallee de la Solle Sby 5/93 63,000
O/Pn 8x6 Portrait of Daumier Chr 2/93 44,000

Corpora, Antonio It 1919-
* See 1993 Edition ....

Correa, Benito Rebolledo Chl 1880-1964
O/C 22x18 Los Cabrios Chr 5/93 2,300
O/C 27x33 Goats Grazing on a Hillside Chr 5/93 2,070
O/C 17x28 El Huaso Chr 5/93 1,495

Correa, Juan Mex 17C
O/C 67x44 The Guardian Angel Chr 11/92 30,800

Corrodi, Hermann David Salomon It 1844-1905
O/C 29x18 Bank of the Nile But 5/93 9,775
O/C 14x11 Italian Sunset Slo 5/93 1,300

Corrodi, Salomon Sws 1810-1892
W/Pa 16x25 Shepherds Grazing Flocks 1874 Wes 10/92 .. 5,500
W/Pb 18x26 Reflections on a Lake 1875 Chr 10/92 3,300

Corsi, Sante It 19C
* See 1990 Edition ....

Corson Am 20C
O/C 20x24 Pekinese Hnd 9/92 300

Cortes, Edouard-Leon Fr 1882-1969
O/C 26x37 Boulevard Madeleine, Paris Chr 10/92 46,200
O/C 26x36 Twilight, Place de la Republique Sby 5/93 ... 31,050
O/C 36x29 Twilight Near Notre Dame Sby 5/93 27,600
O/C 18x22 L'Arc de Triomphe Sby 2/93 21,850
O/C 13x18 Boulevard des Italiens Sby 5/93 20,125
O/C 24x20 Rue de Madeleine Hnd 12/92 20,000
O/C 13x18 Boulevard St. Denis Chr 2/93 19,800
O/C 15x24 Les Grands Boulevards, Le Soir Sby 2/93 19,550
O/C 24x20 Boulevard St. Martin Hnd 12/92 19,000
O/C 13x18 Boulevard St. Denis Chr 10/92 18,700
O/C 15x18 Place de la Republique Chr 11/92 18,700
O/C 20x26 L'Obelisk, Place Vendome But 5/93 18,400
O/C 18x22 Parisian Street But 5/93 18,400
O/C 18x22 Le Port St. Denis Chr 10/92 17,600
O/C 13x18 Parisian Street But 11/92 17,600
O/C 18x22 La Place de L'Opera en Hiver Sby 5/93 17,250
O/C 13x18 Place Pigalle in Winter Chr 2/93 16,500
O/C 13x18 La Gare de L'Est Sby 2/93 15,525
O/C 13x18 La Madeleine Sby 6/93 15,525
O/C 13x18 L'Opera But 11/92 15,400
O/C 13x18 L'Arc de Triomphe Chr 5/93 14,950
O/C 13x18 Parisian Street But 5/93 14,950
O/C 13x18 Porte St. Denis Sby 2/93 14,950
O/C 18x22 La Madeleine Sby 10/92 14,300
O/C 13x18 Notre Dame But 11/92 14,300
O/C 13x19 Place de l'Opera Chr 11/92 14,300
O/C 13x18 Le Rue Royale Madeleine Sby 2/93 13,800
O/C 10x13 Marche aux Fleurs, Madeleine Chr 2/93 13,750
O/C 18x22 Paris Street Scene Hnd 3/93 13,500
O/C 18x22 Place Vendome Sby 6/93 13,225
O/C 11x18 Boulevard de Madeleine Chr 2/93 13,200
O/C 11x14 Les Champs Elysees l'Arc de Triomph Chr 11/92 13,200
O/C 13x18 Place Clichy Chr 11/92 13,200
O/C 18x22 Theatre du Gymnase Sby 10/92 13,200
P/Pa 25x36 Paris Sous la Neige '08 Sby 5/93 12,650
O/C 13x18 Arc de Triomphe Hnd 3/93 12,500
O/C 13x18 La Madeleine Chr 10/92 12,100

O/C 13x18 Paris in Winter Sby 10/92 12,100
O/C 13x18 Les Champs Elysee Sby 5/93 12,075
O/C 13x18 Cafe de la Paix Hnd 10/92 12,000
O/C 13x18 Place de l'Opera Hnd 3/93 12,000
O/C 13x18 Paris Street Scene Hnd 12/92 11,500
O/C 13x18 La Madeleine Hnd 10/92 11,000
O/C 13x18 Bookstalls Along the Seine Hnd 10/92 10,500
O/C 13x18 Place Vendome Sby 10/92 10,450
O/C 13x18 Rue Royale, Concorde Chr 2/93 10,450
O/C 13x18 Vue de la Place de la Concorde Sby 5/93 ... 10,350
O/C 15x22 Notre Dame But 5/93 9,775
O/C 13x18 Porte Saint Martin Sby 2/93 9,775
O/C 13x18 Place de l'Opera Hnd 10/92 9,500
O/C 20x26 Arc de Triomphe Hnd 10/92 9,400
G/Pa 10x18 Les Grands Boulevards/La Neige Sby 10/92 . 9,350
G/Pa 11x22 Porte Saint Denis Sby 10/92 9,350
O/C 13x18 Cafe de la Paix, L'Opera Chr 5/93 9,200
O/C 13x18 Parisian Boulevard Doy 11/92 8,250
O/C 13x18 Parisian Street at Dusk Doy 11/92 7,975
O/C 18x22 Place Vendome, Paris Slo 4/93 7,500
O/C 13x18 Paris Street Scene Dum 6/93 7,000
O/C 18x22 Place de la Bastille Sby 5/93 6,900
G/Pa/B 8x13 Notre Dame et La Quais Chr 5/93 5,175
G/Pa/B 8x13 Rue Royale et La Concorde Chr 5/93 ... 5,175
O/C 18x22 Parisian Plaza Scene Hnz 5/93 4,100
O/C 13x18 Flower Vendor Parisian Skn 11/92 3,575
G/Pa 8x13 Place de la Republique Sby 2/93 2,760

Cortez, Jenness Am 1945-
* See 1993 Edition ....

Corwin, Charles Abel Am 1857-1938
* See 1992 Edition ....

Corzas, Francisco Mex 1936-
O/C 47x40 El Burgues 1979 Chr 11/92 55,000
O/C 53x44 Desnudo 76 Sby 5/93 46,000

Cosenza, Guiseppe It 1847-
* See 1993 Edition ....

Cosgrove, Stanley Morel Can 1911-
O/C 20x24 Winter Scene '74 Sbt 11/92 7,920
O/C 16x24 Grove of Trees Sbt 5/93 4,840
O/C/B 16x20 Trees with River Sbt 11/92 4,840
O/Pn 12x16 Landscape of Trees Sbt 5/93 3,960
O/B 16x12 Landscape Sbt 5/93 3,740
O/B 12x16 Still Life Apples and Pitcher '59 Sbt 5/93 ... 3,520

Cosileto, T. It 19C
O/C 22x31 A Kiss Goodbye Chr 5/93 1,610

Cosimi It 20C
O/C 9x12 Sheep in a Barn Sel 9/92 225

Cossaar, Cornelius-Johannis Bel 1874-1966
O/C 36x28 Notre Dame Hnd 3/93 500

Cossar, Jan Dut 1879-1966
O/C 18x13 Cathedral Interior Dum 9/92 600

Cosson, Marcel Fr 1878-1956
* See 1993 Edition ....

Costa, Emmanuele It 1875-
O/C 11x18 Italian Coastal Scene Lou 6/93 900

Costa, Giovanni It 1833-1903
O/C 21x12 Woman with Basket of Berries Hnd 3/93 1,200
O/C 21x12 Woman with Bunch of Fruit Hnd 3/93 1,100

Costa, Olga Mex 1913-
* See 1993 Edition ....

Costa, Oreste It 1851-1901
O/C 32x25 Still Life Game and Fruit 1873 Sby 1/93 1,955

Costantini, Giuseppe It 1850-
O/Pn 9x14 Game of Cards 1879 Chr 2/93 13,750

Costantini, Virgil It 1882-1940
O/C 40x32 The Model's Repose Sby 2/93 107,000
O/C 39x25 The Seamstress Sby 5/93 23,000

Costantini, Virgil It 20C
O/C 40x33 Coccinelle 1925 Chr 2/93 18,700

Costanzi, Placido It a 1590-1659
* See 1991 Edition ....

Coster 17C
* See 1993 Edition ....

Costigan, John E.   Am 1888-1972
W/Pa 22x29 Milking the Cow Sby 12/92 2,475
Cosway, Richard   Br 1742-1841
* See 1990 Edition . . . .
Cotanda, Vicente Nicolau   Spa 1852-1899
* See 1993 Edition . . . .
Cotes, Francis   Eng 1725-1770
O/C 47x39 Portrait Mrs. Macrae, Nee Roche Sby 5/93 . . . 40,250
Cottavoz, Andre   Fr 1922-
* See 1993 Edition . . . .
Cottet, Charles   Fr 1863-1924
O/Pn 9x14 Cows Watering Chr 10/92 825
Cottingham, Robert   Am 1935-
O/C 78x78 Dr. Gibson 1971 Sby 10/92 16,500
Cotton, William   Am 1880-1958
* See 1991 Edition . . . .
Coubine, Otakar
* See 1992 Edition . . . .
Coubine, Othon   1883-1969
O/C 21x26 Still Life with Peaches Sby 2/93 6,038
O/C 20x24 Summer Landscape Sby 2/93 2,875
O/C 24x29 Landscape Chr 11/92 1,100
Couder, Gustave-Emile   Fr -1903
O/C 21x28 Jete de Fleurs Sby 5/93 29,900
Couldery, Horatio H.   Br 1832-1893
O/C 7x9 Two Cats Stalk a Toad Eld 8/93 2,310
Coulter, Mary   Am 1880-1966
* See 1992 Edition . . . .
Coulter, William Alexander   Am 1849-1936
O/C 25x21 A Black Ball Liner But 3/93 4,950
O/C 25x16 At Angel Island 1889 But 10/92 2,750
O/B 12x10 In Tow But 10/92 1,980
Courant, Maurice Francois A.   Fr 1847-1925
O/C 18x22 Port au Crepescule 1901 Wes 10/92 2,090
Courbet, Gustave   Fr 1819-1877
O/C 30x38 Cascade, Chevreuil, Biche et Faun Chr 10/92 . 220,000
O/C 18x22 Marine 74 Chr 10/92 88,000
Courbet, Gustave & Ordinaire,M   Fr 1819-1877
* See 1992 Edition . . . .
Courbet, Gustave & Pata, C.   Fr 1819-1877
O/C 17x20 Le Puits Noir a Ornans Chr 5/93 28,750
Courtat, Louis   Fr -1909
* See 1993 Edition . . . .
Courtens, Hermann   Bel 1884-1956
O/C 31x42 Pink and Yellow Roses in Vase Chr 2/93 1,375
Courter, F.   Am 20C
O/B 16x12 Portrait Abraham Lincoln Hnd 9/92 275
Courtice, Rody Kenny   Can 1895-1973
O/B 20x16 The Mine Head Sbt 5/93 1,408
Courtois, Guillaume & Brueghel   Fr 1628-1679
* See 1993 Edition . . . .
Courtois, Gustave Claude Etien   Fr 1853-1924
* See 1990 Edition . . . .
Courtois, Jacques   1621-1675
O/C 37x50 Military Skirmish Sby 10/92 20,900
Couse, Eanger Irving   Am 1866-1936
O/C 46x35 Flute Player at the Spring Sby 5/93 178,500
O/C 35x46 San Juan Pottery Sby 5/93 129,000
O/C 24x29 Warming Hands by the Stream Chr 5/93 57,500
O/C 25x29 The Sacred Rain Bowl Sby 12/92 41,250
O/B 12x16 A Pueblo Fireplace Sby 9/92 25,300
O/B 16x12 Juan, Pueblo Indian 1927 Chr 9/92 16,500
W/Pa 7x10 Adobe House Lou 12/92 750
Pe/Pa 6x4 Double Self-Portrait Yng 5/93 150
Couse, William Percy   Am 1898-
O/C 12x30 Boom Town 1921 But 12/92 5,225
Cousin, Charles   Fr 20C
O/C 20x26 Ville Franche (Riviera) Sby 2/93 1,150

Coutau, Hippolyte   Fr 1866-
O/Pn 8x10 Parade for King of Sweden 1908 Chr 10/92 385
Coutaud, Lucien   Fr 1904-
* See 1993 Edition . . . .
Coutts, Alice   Am 1880-1973
* See 1993 Edition . . . .
Coutts, Gordon   Am 1880-1937
O/C 36x48 La Fiesta-Old Mexico Mor 6/93 2,750
O/C/B 20x28 Tangiers Mor 6/93 1,870
O/Cb 16x10 View of Chinatown Lou 12/92 1,150
O/C 18x27 Near Indio Mor 11/92 800
Couture, Thomas   Fr 1815-1879
* See 1991 Edition . . . .
Couturier, *   Fr 20C**
O/C 14x18 Comme il la Voit Wes 10/92 908
Couturier, Philibert Leon   Fr 1823-1901
* See 1993 Edition . . . .
Covarrubias, Miguel   Mex 1904-1957
G/Pa 12x9 Mujer Sentada Sby 6/93 2,300
W/Pa 11x8 Indio Chamula Sby 11/92 1,100
I&Pe/Pa 11x8 Urchin Sby 2/93 805
Covell, Janet E.   Am 20C
W/Pa 14x10 Desert Tree Yng 2/93 100
Coventry, Robert McGowan   Br 1855-1914
O/C 24x36 Gathering Mussels But 11/92 3,300
Covert, John   Am 1882-1960
O/C 38x30 Moorish Warrior '06 Sby 3/93 2,185
Coward, Sir Noel   Br
* See 1993 Edition . . . .
Cowdery, Jennie Van Fleet   Am 20C
O/B 15x23 Afternoon Hnd 12/92 200
Cowles, Fleur
* See 1992 Edition . . . .
Cowles, Russell   Am 1887-1979
* See 1993 Edition . . . .
Cowper, Frank Cadogan   Br 1877-1958
* See 1993 Edition . . . .
Cox, *   Br 19C
* See 1993 Edition . . . .
Cox, Allyn   Am 1896-1982
O/C 52x40 Faggot Carrier and Woman 1922 Hnd 5/93 90
O/C 25x21 Woman with a Mirror Hnd 5/93 15
Cox, David (Jr.)   Br 1809-1885
W/Pa 14x22 Holwood Park Sby 1/93 1,150
Cox, Jan   Am 20C
O&Gd/Pls Size? Bird and Hand 1963 Sby 10/92 77
O/B 8x10 House in a Landscape 1948 Mys 12/92 16
Cox, Kenyon   Am 1856-1919
O/C Size? September Sunshine 1884 Fre 10/92 15,00
Coypel, Charles Antoine   Fr 1694-1752
P/Pa/C 17x13 Head of Venus Urania Chr 1/93 7,70
Cozza, Francesco   It 1605-1682
* See 1991 Edition . . . .
Cozzens, Frederick Schiller   Am 1856-1928
I,G&Pe/Pa 12x10 Close Hauled 87 Sby 6/93 3,70
W/Pa 14x22 Breakwater at Low Tide '95 Sby 12/92 1,60
W&Pe/Pa/B 14x22 Ships Sailing 1901 Sby 9/92 80
W/Pa 12x14 War Ships '05 Wes 5/93 50
Cozzi, Fiora   20C
O/C 24x36 Summer Scene by Brook Slo 4/93 20
Crabeels, Florent Nicolas   Bel 1829-1896
* See 1993 Edition . . . .
Crabeth, Wouter (II)   Flm 1595-1644
* See 1993 Edition . . . .
Crafty, Victor   Fr 1840-1906
* See 1993 Edition . . . .
Cragg, Tony   1949-
O/MM 97x93 Palette Chr 11/92 28,60
Craig, Charles   Am 1846-1931
O/C 24x36 River Valley Dusk 1902 Slo 7/93 8,00
W/Pa 23x19 Geronimo Slo 7/93 7,50
O/C 24x35 Lonely Road Dusk 1902 Slo 7/93 4,30
Craig, Frank   Br 1874-1918
G&R/Pa 17x29 At a Fancy Restaurant 1903 Ilh 5/93 3,00

72

Craig, Henry Robertson   Irs 1916-1984
* See 1993 Edition ....

Craig, Thomas Bigelow   Am 1849-1924
O/C/M Size? Figures Ashore Watching Sailboat Fre 10/92 . . 4,750
W/Pa 15x25 Cows in Landscape Dum 1/93 3,000
O/C 20x30 Cows Watering in a River Sby 3/93 2,530
O/C 20x30 Midsummer 1897 Eld 4/93 1,980
O/C 10x14 Late Afternoon Sunshine But 6/93 1,725
O/C 10x14 Spring Ploughing 1900 Wlf 3/93 1,300
O/C 30x25 Autumn Afternoon Sby 9/92 1,210
O/C 20x30 Cows in a Landscape Wlf 9/92 1,200
O/C 12x16 Cattle on Hillside Lou 3/93 750
W/Pa 10x14 A Rainy Day Landscape Eld 4/93 143
W/Pa 10x14 A Forest Path Eld 8/93 66

Craig, William Marshall   Br 1788-1828
* See 1992 Edition ....

Cram, Allen Gilbert   Am 1886-1947
* See 1992 Edition ....

Cramer, Helene   Ger 1844-
* See 1991 Edition ....

Cramer, Konrad   Am 1888-1963
I,Y&H/Pa 11x17 16 4/10 Cents a Gallon Sby 3/93 920

Cramer, S. J.   Am 19C
O/C 19x28 River Ferry 1890 Sel 9/92 175

Cranach, Lucas (the Elder)   Ger 1472-1553
* See 1990 Edition ....

Cranach, Lucas (the Younger)   Ger 1515-1586
* See 1992 Edition ....

Cranch, Christopher Pearse   Am 1813-1892
* See 1993 Edition ....

Crandell, Bradshaw   Am 1896-1966
O/C 40x30 Seated Female Bather Hnd 12/92 1,300

Crane, Bruce   Am 1857-1937
O/C 25x30 Winter on Long Island Chr 12/92 30,800
O/C 46x45 The Hills Sby 3/93 28,750
O/C 28x36 February Thaw Sby 3/93 23,000
O/C 18x24 After the Storm Sby 12/92 11,000
O/C 25x30 Peace and Quiet But 12/92 9,900
O/C 20x30 Harvest Sby 9/92 6,875
O/C 18x24 Stream, Indian Summer Skn 5/93 4,400
O/C 14x20 Gray October Chr 5/93 3,450
O/C 14x20 Countryside in Autumn Sby 9/92 3,300
O/C 14x18 River Landscape FHB 5/93 1,900
O/Cb 8x10 Mohawk Hills Chr 12/92 1,650
W/Pa 9x18 Stream in Winter Fre 4/93 225

Crane, F.   Eng 20C
O/C 30x40 Herdsman and Sheep Slo 4/93 220

Crane, Frederick   Am 1847-1915
* See 1992 Edition ....

Crane, Stanley   Am 1905-
O/C Size? Houses in a Landscape Mys 12/92 319

Crane, Walter   Br 1845-1915
W/Pa 14x11 Cleopatra's Needle '95 Fre 4/93 1,350

Crary, Robert Fulton   Am 19C
O/C 10x12 Still Life Pipe, Tobacco, Cigar 1879 Chr 12/92 . . 1,100

Craven, Edgar Malin   Am 20C
O/C 20x30 Autumnal Landscape Sel 9/92 450

Crawford, Esther Mabel   Am 1872-1958
* See 1992 Edition ....

Crawford, John   Am a 1850-
* See 1993 Edition ....

Crawford, Ralston   Am 1906-1978
W&Pe/Pa 16x20 Buffalo Grain Elevators Sby 12/92 15,400
W,I&Pe/Pa 11x16 Tampa-St. Petersburg Sby 12/92 8,250

Crawford, Robert C.   Br 1842-1924
O/C 19x31 Children Playing 1897 Chr 5/93 1,725

Crawford, Will
R/Pa 12x9 A Terrific Thunderstorm Eld 8/93 99

Crawley/Atkinson Productions   Can 20C
G/Cel 12x15 Two: Babar Skn 3/93 605
G/Cel 12x15 Two: Babar Skn 3/93 220

Creifelds, Richard   Am 1853-1939
O/B 10x8 Portrait of Isabel 1919 Sby 9/92 303

Creixams, Pierre   Spa 1893-1965
* See 1992 Edition ....

Cremonini, Leonardo   It 1925-
O/C 32x43 I cavalli che urlano 55 Chr 11/92 44,000
O/C 46x35 Le Bagnanti Viste Sott'Acqua 53 Chr 2/93 8,250

Crespi, Giuseppe Maria   It 1665-1747
* See 1990 Edition ....

Cresswell, William Nicoll   Can 1818-1888
O/C 18x30 Sheep Resting in Landscape 1876 Sbt 11/92 . . 2,640
W/Pa 15x21 Thumb Rock 1881 Sbt 5/93 1,408
W/Pa 5x11 Rocky Shore with Boats Sbt 5/93 616

Cressy, Susan   Am -1942
* See 1993 Edition ....

Creswick, Thomas   Br 1811-1869
O/B 29x39 Landscape with Windmill Wlf 12/92 1,100
O/C 20x16 Peasant Woman by Fence Chr 5/93 1,093

Creti, Donato   It 1671-1749
* See 1992 Edition ....

Criley, Theodore   Am 1880-1930
O/C 40x44 Weston Beach, South Shore Point But 10/92 . . 5,500
O/C 40x48 North Shore: Point Lobos But 10/92 4,675
O/C 38x49 Road Through Fremont But 10/92 4,125
O/C 32x40 Jameses Rocks, Bird Island But 10/92 3,575
O/C 30x36 On Point Lobos North Shore, Carmel But 10/92 . 3,575
O/C 32x40 Arizona Canyon But 10/92 3,025
O/C 26x32 San Jose Beach But 6/93 2,875
O/C 30x36 Weston Beach, South Shore Point But 6/93 . . 2,587
O/C 32x40 Carmel River Near Fish Ranch But 10/92 . . 2,475
O/C 30x36 Canyon Landscape But 10/92 2,090
O/B 32x26 China Cove, Point Lobos But 6/93 1,840
O/C 30x36 Cove at Jamses But 6/93 1,840
O/C 32x40 Oak Tree on Spring Hill But 10/92 1,760
O/C 32x26 Portrait John O'Shea But 3/93 1,540
O/C 26x32 Coast Hills, Monterey County But 6/93 1,495
O/C 32x40 Rocky Point from North of Sobrantes But 10/92 . 1,430
O/C 24x29 Blossoming Orchard But 6/93 1,150
O/C 18x22 Point Aven But 6/93 748

Crippa, Roberto   It 1921-1972
* See 1992 Edition ....

Crisp, Arthur Watkins   Am 1881-
O/Cb 9x6 Katri by the River Skn 11/92 302

Criss, Francis   Am 1901-1975
* See 1993 Edition ....

Crite, Allan Rohan   Am 1910-
O/Cb 16x20 Boston Street Scene 1939 Sby 9/92 990

Crivelli, Angelo Maria   It -1760
* See 1992 Edition ....

Crivelli, Vittorio   It a 1481-1501
* See 1990 Edition ....

Croato, Bruno   1875-1948
* See 1993 Edition ....

Crochepierre, Andre-Antoine   Fr 1860-
* See 1993 Edition ....

Crocker, John Denison   Am 1823-1879
* See 1993 Edition ....

Crockwell, Spencer Douglass   Am 1904-1968
O/B 30x23 Dad's Off at War Ilh 11/92 4,000
O/B 17x24 Couple Carving a Pumpkin Ilh 5/93 2,000

Croegaert, Georges   Fr 1848-1923
O/Pn 13x9 Portrait of a Woman Mys 3/93 522

Crompton, James Shaw   Br 1853-1916
W/Pb 11x15 The Naughty Parrot Chr 10/92 825

Cromwell, Joane   Am -1966
* See 1992 Edition ....

Cropsey, Jasper Francis   Am 1823-1900
O/C 36x59 Sunset at Greenwood Lake 1888 Sby 5/93 . . 189,500
O/C 18x38 The Saw Mill River Chr 5/93 79,500
O/C 18x38 Autumn by the Lake 1890 Sby 5/93 54,625
O/C 22x27 View on the Hudson River 1852 Chr 12/92 . . 38,500
O/C 12x20 Autumn Landscape 1873 Brd 2/93 31,900
O/C/Pn 15x24 Winter in Switzerland 1860 Chr 9/92 . . 28,600
O/C 12x20 View of the Hudson in Autumn Brd 2/93 25,300

O/C 12x20 Foggy Morning, Long Island 1873 Brd 2/93 . . . 22,000
O/C 10x8 The Pond in Springtime 1879 Chr 12/92 17,600
O/C 14x21 Autumn on the Hudson 1884 Sby 5/93 13,800
O/C 10x8 Rowing at Sunset 1873 Chr 12/92 13,200
O/C 10x15 Autumn by the Brook 1855 Chr 9/92 12,100
O/C 18x30 Anne Hathaway's Cottage Sby 3/93 10,925
W,Pe&Cw/Pa 15x25 On the Docks 1886 Chr 3/93 10,925
O/C 8x6 A Study, The Brook 1881 Chr 3/93 9,200
O/B 3x5 Sunset 1875 Chr 9/92 5,500
O/C 8x10 Cows Watering in Autumn Sby 9/92 4,125

Crosby, William   Br 19C
* See 1992 Edition . . . .

Crosio, Luigi   It 1835-1915
* See 1991 Edition . . . .

Crosland, Enoch   Eng 19C
* See 1992 Edition . . . .

Cross, Henri-Edmond   Fr 1856-1910
* See 1993 Edition . . . .

Cross, Henry H.   Am 1837-1918
O/C 28x42 Bay Pacer on Racetrack Sby 6/93 11,500
O/B 16x22 The Bay 1889 Hnz 5/93 425

Cross, Roy   Am 20C
W&G/Pb 7x12 West Indies Trading Sloop Mediator Skn 3/93 . 880

Crosthwaite, Paul   Am 20C
O/B 30x24 Picnic Yng 2/93 325

Crow, Gonzalo Endara   Ecu 1936-
* See 1993 Edition . . . .

Crowe, Eyre   Br 1824-1910
* See 1992 Edition . . . .

Crowley, Nicholas Joseph   1813-1857
O/C 81x52 Portrait Mother and Child Sby 10/92 9,350
O/C 87x59 Portrait of a Gentleman Sby 10/92 7,700

Cruess, Maris   Am 1890-
O/B 20x20 Old Barn But 6/93 374

Cruikshank, George   Br 1792-1878
* See 1993 Edition . . . .

Cruikshank, William   Eng 1848-1922
W/Pa 9x13 Still Life Grapes, Apples Hnd 5/93 600

Cruys, Cornelis   dut a 1644-1660
* See 1990 Edition . . . .

Cruz-Diez, Carlos   Ven 1923-
MM/Pn 24x24 Physiochromie No. 437 1968 Chr 11/92 4,400

Csot   Hun 1930-
* See 1992 Edition . . . .

Cuartas, Gregorio   Col 1938-
* See 1993 Edition . . . .

**Cubells Y Ruiz, Enrique M.   Spa
1874-1917**
* See 1992 Edition . . . .

Cucchi, Enzo   1950-
O/C 110x141 Pin Vicino Agli Dei 1983 Chr 11/92 110,000
O&MM/C 114x154 Untitled 1986 Chr 2/93 79,200
O/C 71x44 Santo Santo 1981 Chr 11/92 49,500
O&N/C 16x20 Untitled 1981 Sby 5/93 19,550

Cucuel, Edward   Am 1875-1951
O/C 32x32 Woman Picking Flowers Sby 9/92 29,700
O/C 25x31 House by the River Chr 3/93 10,350
O/C 48x37 Gitta Cucuel, the Dancer Chr 3/93 9,200

Cuevas, Jose Luis   Mex 1934-
* See 1993 Edition . . . .

Cugat, Delia   Arg 1935-
O/C 38x51 Mujer en el Muelle Chr 11/92 8,800

Cuixart, Modesto   20C
* See 1993 Edition . . . .

Cullen, Maurice Galbraith   Can 1866-1934
O/C/B 29x66 Moonlight Landscape Sbt 11/92 19,360
O/C 17x21 Venice 1902 Sbt 11/92 12,320
O/C/B 18x22 Mediterranean View Sbt 11/92 6,160
P/Pa/Pn 22x18 Montreal River, Early Winter 1925 Sbt 11/92 5,280
O/B 11x14 Early Spring Sbt 11/92 4,048
O/Pn 10x14 Grand Canal, Venice Sbt 5/93 3,520

Cullin, Isaac J.   Br 19C
O/C 30x41 Jockeys Weighing In Prior Waterloo Sby 6/93 . 28,750

Culver, Charles   Am 1908-1967
W/Pa 19x25 Seated Antelope FHB 5/93 2,200

W/Pa 11x14 African Porcupine FHB 5/93 . . . . 1,2▪
W/Pa 11x9 Zebra Licking Flank FHB 5/93 . . . . 1,2C
W&G/Pa 15x22 Depicting a Loon Dum 3/93 . . . . 9C
W/Pa 14x10 Standing Buck Rearing Head FHB 3/93 . . . . . . 4C
W/Pa 6x10 City Scene 1949 FHB 5/93 . . . . 3▪
W/Pa 9x5 Winter Tree FHB 3/93 11

**Culverhouse, Johann Mongels   Am
1820-1891**
O/C 28x44 The Blacksmith Shop 1868 Skn 3/93 . . . . 4,4▪
O/C 22x30 School Room Scene 1867 Skn 3/93 . . . . 3,8▪
O/C 30x54 Moonlight Boating Party 1870 Fre 10/92 . . . . . 3,0C

**Cumming, Constance Frederica G   Aut
19C**
W,G&Pe/Pa 19x27 Sequoia South Grove 1878 Sby 3/93 . . 2,5▪
W,G&Pe/Pa 20x26 Grizzly Giant-Sequoia 1878 Sby 3/93 . . 69

Cunaeus, Conradyn   Dut 1828-1895
O/Pn 20x28 Before the Hunt Sby 6/93 11,21

Cuneo, Jose   Uru 1889-1977
O/C 36x36 Luna Menguante 1931 Sby 11/92 . . . . 41,2▪

Cuneo, Rinaldo   Am 1877-1939
* See 1993 Edition . . . .

Cunningham, Fern
O/B 20x24 Glouster Harbor Dum 4/93 . . . . 8▪

Cuprien, Frank W.   Am 1871-1948
O/C 18x28 The Shadow of the Cliff-Cal Mor 2/93 . . . . . . 2,7▪
O/C 10x13 The New Moon 1916 Mor 11/92 . . . . 1,3C
O/C 14x20 Coastal Mor 11/92 . . . . 6▪

Curling, P.   Am 20C
S/Pa 15x20 Steeple Chase Rider 75 Hnd 3/93 . . . . 2C

Curran, Charles Courtney   Am 1861-1942
O/C 30x30 The Cabbage Field 1914 Chr 12/92 . . . . 38,5C
O/C 20x30 May Afternoon 1916 Chr 12/92 . . . . 28,6▪
O/M 30x30 The West Wind 1918 Sby 5/93 . . . . 24,1▪
O/C 16x8 Gathering Flowers '94 Chr 9/92 . . . . 5,5C
O/C 20x12 Portrait of a Young Girl 83 But 1/2 . . . . 2,2C
O/M 9x12 On the Crest of the Mountain Chr 9/92 . . . . . . 2,0▪

Currie, Sidney   Br a 1892-1930
O/C 20x30 Fishing by the Riverbank Chr 5/93 2,18

Currier, Joseph Frank   Am 1843-1909
* See 1993 Edition . . . .

Currier, Mary Ann   Am 20C
* See 1991 Edition . . . .

Currier, Walter Barron   Am 1879-1934
O/C 20x24 Rip Tide 1925 Mor 6/93 . . . . 6C

Curry, John Steuart   Am 1897-1946
W,G&Pe/Pa 14x11 The Mississippi Flood 1937 Sby 12/92   15,4C
O/B/B 15x22 The Freeing of the Slaves 193* Chr 9/92 . . . 14,3C
G/B 8x17 Children and School Sleigh Chr 5/93 . . . . 2,3C

Curry, Robert   Am 1872-1945
O/C 28x22 Stream in Autumn Skn 5/93 . . . . 8▪

Curtis, Calvin   Am 1822-1893
* See 1993 Edition . . . .

Curtis, George   Am 1826-1881
* See 1992 Edition . . . .

Curtis, George Vaughan
O/C 18x22 Still Life Ald 9/92 . . . . 1▪

Curtis, Jenny C.   Am
* See 1992 Edition . . . .

Curtis, Leland   Am 1897-
O/C 30x40 Desert and Mountains But 3/93 . . . . 2,2C
O/C 18x24 Oasis But 6/93 1,72

Curtis, Philip Campbell   Am 1907-
* See 1993 Edition . . . .

Curtis, Ralph   Am 1854-1902
O/Pn 6x9 Still Life Chr 12/92 . . . . 9▪

Cusachs Y Cusachs, Jose   Spa 1851-1908
O/C 22x18 Soldiers on Horseback 1905 Chr 2/93 . . . . . . 38,5C

Cushing, Otho   Am 1871-1942
Pe/Pa 20x14 Four Illustrations Ih 11/92 22

Cusi Y Ferret, Manuel   Spa 1857-
O/C 42x46 Balcony View of the Ball 1908 Doy 5/93 17,60

Custis, Eleanor Parke   Am 1897-1983
* See 1993 Edition . . . .

Cutbert, R.   Eng 19C
W/Pa 8x11 Town Scene Mys 3/93 . . . . 1▪

74

Cutrone, Ronnie   1948-
A&O/C 72x72 Beauty in Eye of the Beholder 1984 Chr 11/92 4,400
Cutting, Francis H.   Am 1872-1964
O/C 16x20 Mission Interior 1946 Mor 11/92 250
Cutts, Gertrude Spurr   Can 1858-1941
O/B 7x10 Path to the Farm Sbt 5/93 792
Cuyp, Aelbert   Dut 1620-1691
* See 1993 Edition ....
Cuyp, Benjamin Gerritsz.   Dut 1612-1652
* See 1993 Edition ....
Cyndo, Jose Rico   Spa 1864-
* See 1992 Edition ....
Cyr, Henri De Gouvion Saint   Fr 1888-
* See 1993 Edition ....
Czernus, Tibor
* See 1991 Edition ....
D'Acosta, Hy. Walker   Spa 19C
* See 1990 Edition ....
D'Amico, Peter
O/C 36x40 Sea Gate Sby 2/93 1,380
D'Andrea, Bernard   Am 1923-
G/Pa 9x6 Woman in Green Sports Car Ih 5/93 125
D'Anna, Alessandro   It a 1800-
G/Pa 16x25 Bay of Naples: Pair 1795 Sby 1/93 24,150
D'Anty, Henry   Fr 1910-
O/C 26x32 Toits Rouges Sby 10/92 1,540
O/C 36x29 Breton Sby 10/92 1,320
O/C 24x48 Ships in a Harbor Sby 6/93 805
D'Anville, Hubert-Francois
* See 1991 Edition ....
D'Arcangelo, Alan   Am 1930-
A/C 38x43 Landscape 1968 Sby 10/92 2,640
Pg/C 48x48 Constellation #114 1971 Sby 2/93 1,035
Pg/C 48x48 Constellation #114 1971 Sby 6/93 460
D'Arcy, Andre-Marie   Fr 20C
O/M 9x6 L'Arc de Triomphe; Sacre-Coeur (2) 1951 Lou 6/93   100
D'Arles, Jean Henry   1734-1784
O/C 43x63 Ports Morning/Evening: Pair 1767 Sby 5/93 .. 189,500
D'Arthois, Jacques   Flm 1613-1686
O/C 45x72 Landscape w/Rainbow, Palace Sby 5/93 37,375
D'Ascenzo, Nicola   Am 1871-1954
O/C 12x8 Sketch of a Fountain Chr 12/92 935
W/Pa 10x12 Fireplace Room 1896 Ald 9/92 125
D'Auria, V*   Con 20C**
O/C 23x47 Fisherman's Return, Capri Sby 1/93 1,380
D'Avino
* See 1993 Edition ....
D'Entraygues, Charles Bertrand   Fr 1851-
O/C 13x16 Interior Genre Scene Children 1881 Skn 3/93 .. 5,225
D'Espagnat, Georges   Fr 1870-1950
O/C 32x26 Vase de Fleurs Sby 2/93 19,550
O/C 32x26 Nu De Dos Sby 5/93 17,250
O/C 24x19 Vase de Fleurs et Livres sur Table Sby 10/92 . 12,100
O/C 24x20 Repos a la Campagne Sby 2/93 9,775
O/Pn 18x15 Bouquet de Fleurs Sby 2/93 7,475
O/C/B 14x17 Still Life with Fruits Sby 2/93 5,750
O/C 16x13 Portrait de femme Chr 10/92 5,500
D'Espic, Christian
* See 1992 Edition ....
D'Esposito, Vincenzo   a 1890-1920
* See 1993 Edition ....
D'Este, N.   Con 19C
* See 1992 Edition ....
D'Hondecoeter, Gillis Claesz.   Dut 1575-1638
* See 1991 Edition ....
D'Leon, Omar   Nic 1935-
O&Wx/C 20x24 Melons and Pomegranites 1989 Doy 11/92 . 2,750
Da *, Livinio   a 1596-**
* See 1990 Edition ....
Da Carussi, Jacopo   It 1494-1556
* See 1990 Edition ....
Da Castello, Francesco   1540-
O/C 56x42 Saint Sebastian Sby 1/93 25,300

Da Costa, Milton   20C
* See 1991 Edition ....
Da Costa, Zeferino
O/C 33x25 Jeanne D'Arc Chr 11/92 13,200
Da Cotignola, Francesco Z.   It 1470-1532
* See 1993 Edition ....
Da Imola, Innocenzo   1485-1548
O/Pn 38x30 Madonna and Child w/Infant St. John Chr 5/93 81,500
Da Lodi, Calisto Piazza   It 1500-1562
* See 1993 Edition ....
Da Lugano, Zoppo   1590-1660
* See 1992 Edition ....
Da Molin, Oreste   It 1856-1912
* See 1992 Edition ....
Da Perugia, Benedetto Di Bonf.   It a 1445-1496
* See 1992 Edition ....
Da Ponte, Francesco   It 1549-1592
* See 1993 Edition ....
Da Ponte, Jacopo   It 1510-1592
* See 1992 Edition ....
Da Ponte, Leandro   It 1557-1622
* See 1992 Edition ....
Da Rios, Luigi   It 1844-1892
O/C 21x17 Bellina Hnd 3/93 3,400
Da Salerno, Sabbatini   It 1487-1530
* See 1991 Edition ....
Da Santa Croce, Girolamo
* See 1991 Edition ....
Da Tivoli, Rosa   Ger 1657-1706
O/C 38x58 Landscape Shepherd Cows Sheep Dogs Sby 1/93 6,900
Da Treviso, Girolamo (the Elder)   1450-1496
O/C 59x26 Madonna and Child Enthroned Sby 1/93 40,250
Da Visso, Paolo   It
* See 1990 Edition ....
Dabo, Leon   Am 1868-1960
O/C 30x34 Summer Idyll '16 Sby 5/93 12,650
O/C 34x29 Hudson River View 1911 Skn 5/93 4,400
O/C 15x21 Luminous Seascape Small Boats Skn 11/92 .. 3,025
O/B 6x7 Landscapes and Still Lifes: Eight '39 Sby 9/92 .. 2,970
O/Cb 20x17 Trees and Rocks Chr 12/92 2,200
O/C 24x30 Shades of a Fall Afternoon Sby 3/93 2,070
O/B 20x16 Still Life of Flowers Chr 5/93 1,495
Dabo, Theodore Scott   Am 1877-
O/C 21x28 Nocturne But 12/92 3,025
Dado (Miodrag Djuric)   1933-
* See 1993 Edition ....
Daggiu   1714-1787
* See 1992 Edition ....
Dagn, Karl   Ger 20C
O/C 11x8 Self-Portrait 1908 Hnd 12/92 130
Dagnan-Bouveret, Pascal A.   Fr 1852-1929
* See 1993 Edition ....
Dagnaux, Albert Marie Adolphe   Fr 1861-1933
* See 1990 Edition ....
Dahl, Hans   Nor 1849-1937
O/C 15x22 Tending to the Fire on the Lake Chr 2/93 1,210
Dahl, Michael   Swd 1656-1743
O/C 52x54 Portrait of a Lady Chr 1/93 6,600
Dahlager, Jules   Am 20C
* See 1990 Edition ....
Dahlgreen, Charles W.   Am 1864-1955
O/B 52x39 White River, Ozarks Hnd 3/93 2,200
O/M 22x26 Landscape Hnd 3/93 950
O/B 18x22 Autumn in Brown County Hnz 5/93 850
O/B 22x26 Creek in Autumn Hnd 3/93 750
Dahlgren, Carl Christian   Am 1841-1920
O/C 20x24 Wooded Passage But 6/93 1,840
O/C 20x14 Resting on the Shore But 3/93 1,045
G/Pa 9x12 California Wildflowers But 6/93 632
O/C 13x24 Landscape Chr 5/93 299

Dahn, Walter 1954-
O&Pt/C 98x59 Man is Crying 1984 Sby 5/93 9,200
O/C 99x79 Untitled (Jewel) 86 Chr 11/92 8,800
O&E/C 79x59 Painter Drawing in Switzerland 83 Chr 11/92 . 6,600
A&E/C 14x59 Against Unification 89 Chr 10/92 6,050
Ss&MM/C 50x21 Ears Which Can Hear 89 Chr 5/93 3,450
O/C 98x98 Karthago 1984 Chr 5/93 1,840
Daingerfield, Eliott Am 1859-1932
* See 1993 Edition . . . .
Daini, Augusto It 19C
O/C 21x30 The Recital Sby 1/93 4,313
Daiwaille, Alexander Joseph Dut 1818-1888
* See 1993 Edition . . . .
Daken, Sydney Tilden Am 1876-1935
* See 1992 Edition . . . .
Dal Friso, Alvise It 1550-1609
* See 1993 Edition . . . .
Dal Sole, Giovanni Gioseffo It 1654-1719
* See 1992 Edition . . . .
Dalberg, G* Ger 19C**
O/C 31x24 River Landscape with Figures Sby 1/93 5,463
Dalby of York, David Br 1794-1836
* See 1991 Edition . . . .
Dalby, John Br a 1838-1853
O/B/Pn 9x12 Going Away Chr 6/93 3,450
Dalby, Joshua Br a 1838-1893
* See 1991 Edition . . . .
Dalens, Dirck (the Elder) Dut 1600-1677
* See 1993 Edition . . . .
Daley, Robert W. Am 1922-
W/Pa 23x23 Still Life of Daisies with Cyclamen Slo 4/93 . . . 225
Dali, Louis Fr 20C
O/C 20x24 French Street Scene Hnd 10/92 350
Dali, Salvador Spa 1904-1989
C,W&P/Pa 29x21 Gondole Surrealiste Sby 11/92 242,000
O/C 28x22 Josephine Hartford Bryce Chr 11/92 84,700
G,W,PI&L/B 20x15 Allegorie de soie 1950 Chr 11/92 79,200
LWBr&PI/B 30x20 La soie est une femme Chr 11/92 79,200
I/Pa 39x28 Horse and Rider 1935 Sby 11/92 52,250
G&I/Pa 30x24 Interior 1939 Sby 10/92 46,750
I&Pe/Pa 20x18 Melacolia 1934 Sby 11/92 30,800
G&Fp/Pa 12x11 St. Jude Sby 2/93 20,700
PI&S/Pa/B 22x28 Gift of Apollo 1943 Sby 10/92 15,400
W&PI/B 13x19 Study for Don Quixote 1964 Sby 10/92 . . . 14,300
I&S/Ab 5x6 Clowns in Clover Sby 2/93 8,050
PI/Pa 7x6 Les Deux Chasseurs Chr 2/93 3,850
Fp/Pa 17x23 Homme Debout Chr 5/93 3,680
I/Pa 10x14 On the Verge: Dedication Page 1950 Sby 2/93 . . 2,645
I/Pa 10x13 Michel de Montaigne Sby 2/93 2,530
Dallaire, Jean Philippe Can 1916-1965
G&Pe/Pa 12x9 Conditional Mood Sbt 11/92 6,160
Dalmau, Emilio Poy Spa 1876-1933
O/C 36x30 The Church Dance Chr 2/93 3,300
Dam, Vu Cao Vnm 1908-
O/C 24x20 Les Kakis '65 Dum 6/93 750
O/C 14x10 Composition '69 Hnd 9/92 200
O/C 11x9 La Deessee '69 Hnd 9/92 200
Damartin, Jose Miralles Spa 1851-
* See 1993 Edition . . . .
Dameron, Emile Charles Fr 1848-1908
* See 1993 Edition . . . .
Damm, Johan Frederik Dan 1820-1894
* See 1991 Edition . . . .
Damoye, Pierre Emmanuel Fr 1847-1916
* See 1993 Edition . . . .
Damrow, Charles Am 1916-
O/B 24x30 Elk in Autumn Mountains Lou 9/92 900
O/C 30x40 Crossing the Creek Sby 3/93 288
Damschroder, Jan Jac Matthys Ger 1825-1905
* See 1993 Edition . . . .
Dana, Edmund T. Am 19C
* See 1993 Edition . . . .

Danby, James Francis Br 1816-1875
* See 1991 Edition . . . .
Danby, Kenneth Edison Can 1940-
W/Pa 11x15 The Blue Truck '76 Sbt 5/93 1,320
Dande, Y. Fr 1892-
O/C 24x36 Winter Forest Scene Hnz 5/93 375
Dandini, Cesare It 1595-1658
O/C 45x39 Allegory of Charity Sby 10/92 24,200
Daneri, Eugenio Arg 1891-1970
* See 1990 Edition . . . .
Dangon, Jeanne Fr 1873-
* See 1991 Edition . . . .
Danhauser, Joseph Aus 1805-1845
* See 1992 Edition . . . .
Daniel, Matthew Am 1938-1990
O/B Size? Coal Mine Wlf 5/93 75
O/C 26x20 Still Life with Game Wlf 5/93 50
O/C 35x28 Abandoned Mine 1944 Wlf 5/93 25
Daniell, Thomas Br 1749-1840
* See 1993 Edition . . . .
Danloux, Henri-Pierre Fr 1753-1809
* See 1992 Edition . . . .
Dann, Frode N. 20C
* See 1991 Edition . . . .
Dannenberg, Alice Fr 1861-
* See 1993 Edition . . . .
Danner, Sara Kolb Am 1894-1969
O/B 28x30 The Art Fair But 10/92 1,650
O/Cb 20x24 Boats in Harbor Mor 6/93 522
O/C 16x20 Still Life Glasses & Grapes Mor 6/93 385
W/Pa 14x19 The Outdoor Market Mor 6/93 220
Dansaert, Leon Bel 1830-1909
* See 1992 Edition . . . .
Danton, F. (Jr.) Am 19C
* See 1991 Edition . . . .
Danz, Robert Ger 1841-
* See 1991 Edition . . . .
Daphnis, Nassos 1914-
PI/C 84x84 #6-68 68 Chr 11/92 3,520
Dapra, R. Con 20C
O/M 18x20 Auf Wiedersehen in Salzburg Regine Slo 4/93 . . . 475
Darboven, Hanna 20C
I/Pa 63x9 Variant 59 Sby 11/92 12,650
Pe/Pa 42x50 [7/5 Index, Tafel] Sby 10/92 8,250
Darby, Henry F. Am 1831-
O&Gd/Pn 5x7 Adam and Eve Fre 10/92 750
Darby, Louise Am 20C
O/B 10x14 Grey Morning-LaJolla 1924 Mys 12/92 110
Dargelas, Andre Henri Fr 1828-1906
O/C 30x19 Mademoiselle X Wes 12/92 6,600
O/Pn 13x9 Girl in Snowy Village Street Sby 1/93 4,313
Dargent, Jean E. (Yan'Dargent) Fr 1824-1889
O/Pn 24x15 The Young Cow Herder Chr 10/92 6,380
Darley, Felix Octavius Carr Am 1822-1888
W/Pa 11x9 Four Watercolors Sby 3/93 3,738
PI&S/Pa 9x13 Fishing on the Shore But 6/93 1,495
I&S/Pa 9x11 Feeding the Pigs Slo 4/93 300
Darling, J. N. "Ding" Am 1876-1962
PI/Pa 20x14 People's Relationship to Airplane Ih 11/92 175
Darling, William S. Am 1882-1963
O/C/B 24x30 June in Palm Springs But 6/93 1,725
O/C/M 20x30 Dunes in Bloom Mor 6/93 1,430
O/M 14x18 Landscape Mor 6/93 825
O/M 10x12 Landscape Mor 2/93 600
O/Cb 14x16 Cabin in Fall Landscape Mor 2/93 550
Darmanin, Jose Miralles Spa 1851-
* See 1993 Edition . . . .
Darr, Bill
W/Pa 15x23 Spring Path 1947 Ald 5/93 55
Darrah, Ann Sophia Towne 1819-1881
O/C 26x40 Figures Near Shore Yng 5/93 2,500
Darrieux, Charles Rene Fr 1879-1958
* See 1992 Edition . . . .

Dasburg, Andrew Michael Am 1887-1979
 * See 1993 Edition.............................
Dash, Robert Am 1932-
 O/C 60x60 Garden Path Doy 5/93 3,740
Datz, A. Mark Am 20C
 O/C 10x14 On the Hudson Sby 9/92 2,310
Daubigny, Charles Francois Fr 1817-1878
 O/C 31x46 Les Bords de L'Oise Sby 2/93 118,000
 O/C 69x44 Enfants Dans Le Jardin Sby 2/93 32,200
 O/Pn 7x13 Fishing on a Riverbank 1873 Chr 10/92 23,100
 O/C 20x32 Figures on a River Bank Chr 10/92 16,500
 O/C 28x20 Soleil Couchant Pres D'Une Mare Sby 10/92 . . 14,300
 O/Pn 11x12 Paysanne Chr 5/93 13,800
 O/Pn 9x16 Les Iles Vierges a Bezons Sby 10/92 12,650
 O/Pn 9x16 River Landscape at Sunset Sby 10/92 7,700
 O/Pn 12x18 The Pool of Gylien But 11/92 7,700
 O/Pn 10x14 Four Figures by a House 1940 Lou 3/93 3,750
Daubigny, Karl-Pierre Fr 1846-1886
 * See 1993 Edition.............................
Dauchot, Gabriel Fr 1927-
 O/C 32x16 Portrait of a Man Sby 6/93 1,035
 O/C 16x32 Figures on a Path Sby 2/93 920
Daufin, Jacques
 * See 1992 Edition.............................
Daugherty, James Henry Am 1889-1974
 O/C 36x44 The Wilderness Road Chr 9/92 16,500
 O/C 16x32 The Comforter Sby 3/93 1,150
 P/Pa 24x36 Untitled 71 Sby 9/92 770
Daumier, Honore Fr 1808-1879
 Pl&S/Pa 9x6 Deux Saltimbanques Sby 5/93 85,000
Daux, Charles Edmond Fr 19C
 * See 1990 Edition.............................
Dauzats, Adrien Fr 1804-1868
 O/C 21x26 Monastery of Saint Catherine, Sinai Chr 2/93 . . 19,800
Davenport, Carlson 1908-1972
 O/C 27x60 Century of Progress 1939 Doy 11/92 8,525
Davenport, Henry Am 1882-
 O/C 26x32 End of Summer Skn 5/93 3,080
 O/Ab 20x24 Entering the Mediterranean Eld 8/93 1,100
Davenport, Rebecca Am 1943-
 O/C 18x24 Fragment 1983 Slo 4/93 1,300
Davenport, W. S. Am 19C
 O/C 25x32 French Church Scene Eld 8/93 .. 55
Davey, Randall Am 1887-1964
 P/Pa 17x23 Horses and Jockeys Hnd 12/92 1,200
 W,G&H/Pa 8x12 Polo Match Skn 9/92 770
David, Gerard
 * See 1990 Edition.............................
David, Giovanni 1743-1790
 K,Pl&S/Pa 8x12 Poet Inspired by Nymph Chr 1/93 2,860
David, Hermine Fr 1886-1970
 * See 1993 Edition.............................
David, Jacques Louis Fr 1748-1825
 * See 1991 Edition.............................
David, Michael 1954-
 * See 1993 Edition.............................
David, Norman
 O/C 18x19 Creek Landscape 1947 Ald 9/92 180
David, Stanley S. Am 1847-1898
 * See 1991 Edition.............................
Davidson, Alexander Sco 1838-1887
 * See 1992 Edition.............................
Davidson, Charles Grant Am 1866-1945
 W/Pa Var Four Works Wes 3/93 385
 W/Pa Var Four Works Wes 3/93 302
 O/B 15x23 Rocks and Surf, Marblehead, MA Lou 9/92 300
Davidson, Charles Grant Eng 1824-1902
 W/Pa 7x13 Blossom Tree Fre 4/93 100
Davie, Alan Br 1920-
 * See 1993 Edition.............................
Davies, Arthur Bowen Am 1862-1928
 O/C 40x26 Protest Against Violence Sby 12/92 12,100
 O/C 22x17 Nymphs and Satyrs Sby 12/92 7,150
 O/C 23x28 Breathing Sacrifice Sby 9/92 6,875
 O/C 30x18 Indian Enchantment Sby 9/92 4,675

 O/C 26x40 Mountain Landscape with Village Sby 3/93 3,335
 C/Pa 12x15 Sixteen Drawings Sby 9/92 2,420
 O/B 8x16 Fleecy Arcady Sby 3/93 2,300
 O/C 26x40 Iris and Aeolis Bandying Showers Sby 9/92 ... 2,200
 O/C 22x17 Mermaid on the Dunes Hnd 3/93 2,000
 K&C/Pa 13x18 Studies Nude Female Model: 25 Sby 9/92 . . 1,870
 O/C 14x12 Two Figures by the Sea Chr 12/92 1,540
 P/Pa 10x13 Carrara and Rhone Valley: Pair 1924 Sby 9/92 . 1,430
 C/Pa 13x18 Studies Nude Female Model: 24 Sby 9/92 . . . 1,430
 P/Pa 14x11 The Dancer Chr 12/92 1,430
 O/C 10x12 Dancing Bacchantes Sby 3/93 1,380
 G/Pa/B 12x9 Day at the Beach But 12/92 1,100
 O/C 12x14 Lady in a Landscape Hnd 10/92 1,000
 O/Pn 5x10 California Sby 3/93 891
 W&H/Pa 13x10 Landscapes: Two Drawings Sby 3/93 748
 W/Pa 9x12 La Belle Endormita Skn 11/92 660
 W&G/Pa 9x12 The Country House Skn 11/92 660
 C&Y/Pa 17x13 Standing Nude Model Wes 10/92 440
 W/Pa 7x6 Dancer Lou 6/93 325
 S/Pa 6x8 Man on Beach Lou 6/93 150
Davies, Harold Christopher Am 1891-1976
 O/C 23x26 Third Street Bridge, San Francisco 1930 But 10/92 1,650
Davies, Kenneth Southworth Am 1925-
 * See 1993 Edition.............................
Davies, William Br 1826-1910
 O/C 17x23 Loch Eck, Argylshire 1893 Chr 10/92 2,420
 O/C 14x20 Glen Orchy Argylshire 1893 Chr 10/92 1,980
Davila, Fernando 20C
 * See 1992 Edition.............................
Davila, Jose Antonio Am 1935-
 A/C 40x48 El Decimotercer Encuentro 1984 Sby 2/93 9,200
Davis Am 20C
 P/Pa 24x18 Fourth of July Parade '56 Lou 3/93 325
Davis, Ann Am 19C
 O/C 31x22 Primitive Winter Scene Eld 4/93 770
Davis, Arthur Alfred Eng 19C
 O/C 24x36 Hunter and Hounds 1887 Wes 10/92 1,210
Davis, Charles Harold Am 1856-1933
 O/C 28x36 The Valley, September Afternoon Brd 2/93 . . . 24,200
 O/C 17x21 Afternoon Shadows, Mystic Skn 9/92 4,510
 O/M 25x30 Passing Fre 4/93 3,000
 O/C 16x13 The Road Skn 3/93 2,200
 O/Cb 9x14 Two: Sheep Meadow; Across the Field Skn 3/93 1,870
 O/B 12x18 Country Road, Amesbury Skn 3/93 1,210
Davis, Cornelia Cassady Am 1870-1920
 * See 1992 Edition.............................
Davis, Floyd M. Am 1896-1966
 I,S&R/Pa 19x25 Country Hoedown Ilh 11/92 1,300
Davis, Gene Am 1920-1985
 A/C 70x90 Dolphin 1975 Chr 2/93 6,050
 O/C 36x42 Green Giant 1978 Sby 10/92 2,750
Davis, Gladys Rockmore Am 1901-1967
 O/C 24x20 Portrait Female Nude Sby 9/92 2,200
 O/C 12x16 View in Cadiz Brd 2/93 1,100
Davis, Jack Am 1926-
 Pl&W/Pa 16x26 Groucho Marx/Love thru Ages Ilh 11/92 .. 1,000
 I&Pe/Pa 14x13 Hillbilly at School Meeting Ilh 11/92 550
Davis, John Scarlett Br 1804-1845
 * See 1991 Edition.............................
Davis, M.
 O/C 24x29 Untilled Farm Ald 9/92 300
Davis, Phil Am 1906-1964
 Pl/Pa 5x21 Daily Comic "Mandrake the Magician" Ilh 11/92 . . 400
Davis, Richard Barrett Eng 1782-1854
 O/C 16x24 Full Cry Chr 6/93 1,495
Davis, Roger Am 1898-1935
 O/C 14x11 Head of a Young Girl Dum 2/93 750
Davis, Ronald Am 1937-
 * See 1992 Edition.............................
Davis, S. C. Am 20C
 W/Pa 29x22 Venice Yng 2/93 225
Davis, Stark Am 1885-
 O/B 12x12 Peacock Hnd 5/93 900
 O/B 18x11 Two Peacocks with Urn of Flowers 1927 Ilh 11/92 275

Davis, Stuart   Am 1894-1964
O/C 9x12 Synthetic Souvenir 1941 Chr 12/92 110,000
G/Pa 13x12 Study for Package Deal Sby 12/92 60,500
O/C 37x30 Chinatown 1912 Sby 12/92 57,750
W,Pl&G/Pa 12x9 Snowy Night 1911 Chr 9/92 8,250
Davis, Theodore Russell   Am 1840-1894
* See 1992 Edition . . . .
Davis, W. H.   Br 19C
O/C 18x24 Hereford Bull Hnd 6/93 800
Davis, Warren B.   Am 1865-1928
O/C 16x22 New York Crossing Chr 5/93 10,925
O/B 7x6 The Dancers Dum 1/93 1,200
P/Pa 15x11 Seated Nude Yng 2/93 200
O/C 14x11 Meditation 1901 Dum 1/93 150
Davis, William M.   Am 1829-1920
* See 1991 Edition . . . .
Davis, William R.   Am 20C
* See 1993 Edition . . . .
Davisson, Homer Gordon   Am 1866-
W/Pa 20x30 Dutch Scene Mys 3/93 550
Dawes, Edwin M.   Am 1872-1945
O/C 24x30 Landscape Hnd 5/93 700
Dawson, Arthur   Br 1857-1922
O/C 36x28 Autumn Wooded Landscape Sel 4/93 1,300
Dawson, Manierre   Am 1887-1969
O/B 18x21 Malta '13 Sby 12/92 14,300
Dawson, Montague   Br 1895-1973
O/C 40x51 High Seas Sby 6/93 76,750
O/C 40x50 The Rising Moon-The Golden Fleece Sby 6/93 . 74,000
O/C 24x36 The Sprinkled Foam Chr 5/93 25,300
O/C 24x36 Winging Along the Solent Sby 6/93 25,300
O/C 24x36 Queen of the Clippers Off Cornwall FHB 3/93 . 25,000
O/C 20x30 Dawn and a West Wind in China Sea FHB 3/93 . 24,000
O/C 20x30 The Bostonian FHB 3/93 16,000
O/C 29x42 High Noon Doy 11/92 11,000
Dawson, Terry   Eng 20C
O/C 20x30 The Ship "Sussex" Hnz 5/93 275
Dawson-Watson, Dawson   Am 1864-1939
O/C 36x22 Elk in a Snowy Field 01 Skn 9/92 1,100
Day, James Francis   Am 1863-1942
* See 1993 Edition . . . .
Day, John   Am 1932-
O/B 24x30 Spring Thaw/Rhode Island Skn 9/92 302
Day, Larry   Am 20C
Pe&G/Pa 38x50 Study for Cocktail Party Fre 10/92 225
Dayez, Georges   Fr 1907-
* See 1993 Edition . . . .
Daynes-Grassot-Solin, Suzanne   Fr 1884-
* See 1990 Edition . . . .
De Alcibar, Jose   1751-1803
* See 1992 Edition . . . .
De Andreis, Alex   Bel 19C
O/C 32x26 A Cavalier Wlf 12/92 2,300
O/C 32x26 A Cavalier Chr 2/93 1,650
O/C 32x26 Cavalier with a Halberd But 11/92 1,650
O/C 26x22 L'Arquebuse Sby 1/93 1,265
De Antonio, Cristobal   Spa 19C
O/Pn 14x11 The Eavesdropper Sby 1/93 2,300
De Arellano, Juan   Spa 1614-1676
O/C 32x41 Still Life Tulips, Roses, Anemone Sby 5/93 . . 1.1025M
O/C 21x16 Still Life Flowers in Glass Vase Sby 1/93 . . . 178,500
De Arrieta, Pedro
* See 1992 Edition . . . .
De Backer, Franois Joseph Thom   Flm 1812-1872
* See 1991 Edition . . . .
De Backer, Jacob (the Elder)   1560-1589
O/Pn 26x19 Last Judgement Sby 5/93 25,300
De Baen, Jan   Dut 1633-1702
* See 1992 Edition . . . .
De Bar, Alexandre   Fr 1821-1901
* See 1992 Edition . . . .
De Beaumont, Charles Edouard   Fr 1812-1888
* See 1993 Edition . . . .

De Belay, Pierre   1890-1947
O/C 21x25 Le Pont Chr 11/92 4,95
De Bergh, Gillis Gillisz.   1600-1669
O/Pn 23x28 Sprig Plums, Peaches and Pears Chr 10/92 . . 55,00
De Bergue, Tony Francois   Fr 1820-
O/Pn 19x15 Une Dame a sa Toilette Wlf 3/93 1,60
De Berrio, Gaspar Miguel   Mex 18C
O/C 34x27 Virgen del Carmen 1761 Chr 11/92 23,10
O/C 33x40 Adoration of the Shepherds Chr 11/92 14,30
De Beul, Franz   Bel 1849-1919
* See 1993 Edition . . . .
De Beul, Henri   Bel 1845-1900
* See 1993 Edition . . . .
De Bie, Cornelis   Dut 1621-1654
* See 1993 Edition . . . .
De Bievre, Marie   Bel 1865-
* See 1993 Edition . . . .
De Blaas, Eugene   Aus 1843-1931
O/C 40x24 Le Billet Doux 1901 Chr 5/93 79,50
O/Pn 32x21 Return from Market 1882 Chr 5/93 70,70
O/C 40x58 The Recital Chr 5/93 68,50
O/Pn 32x16 Rest from Washing 1895 Sby 5/93 46,00
O/Pn 31x18 The Grape Picker 1902 Sby 10/92 38,50
De Bles, Herri Met   Flm 1480-1550
* See 1991 Edition . . . .
De Bloot, Pieter   Dut 1602-1658
* See 1993 Edition . . . .
De Bock, Theophile Emile A.   Dut 1851-1904
* See 1993 Edition . . . .
De Bondt, Jan   Flm a 17C
* See 1993 Edition . . . .
De Bonnemaison, Jules   Fr 1809-
* See 1991 Edition . . . .
De Botton, Jean   Fr 1898-1978
O/B 18x25 Musique de Chambre 1937 Sby 6/93 2,53
O/Cb 16x20 Still Life with Fruit 1961 Sby 6/93 69
O/C 21x32 Tezzes en Fleurs 58 Sby 6/93 69
O/C 16x16 Bouquet des Champs '34 Fre 10/92 50
De Boullogne, Louis   Fr
* See 1991 Edition . . . .
De Boulogne, Valentin   1591-1632
* See 1993 Edition . . . .
De Braekeleer, Adrien F.   Bel 1818-1904
* See 1992 Edition . . . .
De Braekeleer, Ferdinand   Bel 1792-1883
O/C 27x35 An Unwelcome Visitor 1864 Chr 10/92 26,40
De Braekeleer, Henri   Br 1840-1888
* See 1992 Edition . . . .
De Brantz, A.   19C
* See 1992 Edition . . . .
De Breanski, Alfred   Br 19C
* See 1993 Edition . . . .
De Breanski, Alfred (Jr.)   Br 1877-1945
O/C 24x36 The Mountains at Argyll But 11/92 6,050
O/C 16x24 On the Venetian Lagoon But 5/93 4,312
O/C 20x30 Evening, Thirlmere Hnd 12/92 750
De Breanski, Alfred (Sr.)   Br 1852-1928
O/C 26x44 Stepping Stones - Keston, Kent 1873 Chr 5/93 . 8,625
O/C 24x36 A Lane Near Windsor Chr 5/93 6,900
W/Pa 5x9 Highland Landscape Wes 10/92 495
De Breanski, Alfred Fontville   Br 19C
* See 1993 Edition . . . .
De Breanski, Gustave   Br 1856-1898
O/C 20x36 Ships in Rough Seas Mys 12/92 935
O/C 24x36 Southampton Water Sel 4/93 700
De Bree, Anthony   Eng 19C
* See 1991 Edition . . . .
De Brinant, Jules Ruinart   Fr 1838-1898
* See 1993 Edition . . . .
De Broczik, Wenceslas   Ger 1851-1901
* See 1990 Edition . . . .
De Brusse   Dut 20C
O/C 16x20 Landscape Lou 9/92 200

**De Bruyn, Cornelis-Johannes Dut a
1763-1828**
* See 1990 Edition ....
De Buel, L. Bel 19C
O/C 10x14 Sheep and Chickens in a Manger Skn 9/92 330
De Buncey, Marie Abraham R. Fr -1876
O/C 16x14 La Petite Escarpolette Sby 1/93 748
De Caceres, Ruiz Spa 19C
O/C 11x9 The Lute Player 1872 Chr 2/93 3,520
De Camp, Joseph Rodefer Am 1858-1923
O/C 25x30 Trees Along the Coast Chr 5/93 55,200
O/C 27x24 La Penserosa Chr 12/92 26,400
**De Carmontelle, Louis Carrogis
1717-1806**
K/Pa 10x7 Portrait Madmoiselle Grimperel 1758 Chr 1/93 . 60,500
K/Pa 10x6 Portrait Madmoiselle de la Perriere Chr 1/93 8,800
De Carolis, Jacopo It a 15C
* See 1993 Edition ....
De Carruci, Jacopo It 1493-1558
* See 1992 Edition ....
De Casorati, V. P. It 19C
* See 1993 Edition ....
De Casteras, Charles
O/C 18x24 Les Fleurs Pour L'Enfant 1916 Ald 5/93 85
De Caullery, Louis Flm a 1594-1620
* See 1992 Edition ....
De Cavalcanti, Emiliano Brz 1897-1967
* See 1990 Edition ....
**De Chamaillard, Ernest Ponth. Fr
1862-1930**
* See 1993 Edition ....
De Chatillon, Charles 1777-1844
* See 1992 Edition ....
**De Chavannes, Pierre Puvis Fr
1824-1898**
O/Pa/C 54x30 Sainte Genevieve enfant en priere Chr 2/93 418,000
K/Pa 13x9 Men Walking Sby 2/93 2,875
De Chavez, Jose Spa 19C
* See 1991 Edition ....
De Chirico, Giorgio It 1888-1978
O/C 15x19 Piazza d'Italia Chr 11/92 148,500
O/C 16x25 Cavalli antichi spaventati 1935 Chr 11/92 ... 132,000
O/C 16x20 Vita Silente Di Frutta Sby 10/92 66,000
G/Pa/B 13x18 Cavalli sulla spiaggia Chr 11/92 39,600
O/C 14x10 Nuda a Piedi Sby 10/92 28,600
G/Pa 13x10 Paessaggio Della Campagna Sby 11/92 25,300
W/Pa 7x10 Cavallo 1944 Chr 10/92 24,200
De Clausades, Pierre Fr 1910-
O/C 13x16 Sur L'Etang Wes 3/93 522
De Cock, Cesar Flm 1823-1904
* See 1993 Edition ....
De Coninck, David Flm 1636-1701
O/C 46x31 Melon, Grapes, Peaches Chr 10/92 27,500
De Cool, Delphine Fr 1830-
* See 1990 Edition ....
De Correa, Juan Mex a 1674-1739
O/C 60x77 Santa Teresa y el Nino Jesus Sby 11/92 27,500
De Corsi, Nicolas It 1882-1956
* See 1993 Edition ....
De Coster, Adam Flm 1586-1643
* See 1993 Edition ....
De Courten, Angelo It 1848-
O/C 26x33 Diana and the Lion Sby 2/93 6,900
De Crayer, Gaspas Flm 1584-1669
* See 1991 Edition ....
De Creeft, Jose Am 1884-
I/Pa 12x18 Sleeping Nude Sby 6/93 575
De Curzon, Paul Alfred Fr 1820-1895
* See 1991 Edition ....
De Czachorski, Ladislas Pol 1850-1911
* See 1990 Edition ....
De Diego, Julio Am 1900-1979
O/M 11x24 Bridge and Blue Horizon Brd 8/93 468
De Dominici, A* It 20C**
O/C 41x30 Una Signorina Coglie Verdura Sby 1/93 4,600

De Dominicis, Achille It a 1881-1884
W/Pa 14x10 The Minstrel 45 Sby 1/93 460
De Dramard, Georges Fr 1839-1900
* See 1993 Edition ....
De Dreux, Alfred Fr 1810-1860
O/C 36x29 Le Lad Blanc Sby 10/92 49,500
De Egusquiza, Rogelio Spa 1845-
* See 1992 Edition ....
De Erderly, Francis Am 1904-1959
O/B 20x16 Men in Boat Dum 3/93 850
O/C 18x28 Man at Table 1942 Dum 6/93 800
O/B 10x14 Prone Nude Dum 3/93 750
G/Pa 20x17 Religious Meeting Dum 9/92 700
Pe/Pa 27x23 Seated Nude Female FHB 5/93 600
O/C 11x9 Man in Blue Cap '42 Dum 3/93 550
C/Pa 16x11 Female Nude 1932 FHB 5/93 115
C/Pa 15x12 Bust of a Woman 1932 FHB 5/93 75
Pe/Pa 9x11 Group of People FHB 5/93 75
De Espinosa, Jeronimo Jacinto 16C
* See 1991 Edition ....
De Fleury, A. Fr 20C
O/C/B 16x20 Two Paris Street Scenes Lou 3/93 700
De Fleury, J. Vivien Br a 1845-1870
* See 1993 Edition ....
De Forest, Lockwood Am 1850-1932
O/C/B 29x48 Sunset Beyond a Valley 1878 But 3/93 7,150
De Forest, Roy Am 1930-
Fp/Pa 29x23 Untitled But 10/92 1,045
De Forestier, Henri Joseph Fr 1787-1868
O/C 45x58 Ulysse Massacrant Sby 10/92 44,000
De Framschi, M.
O/C 20x30 Arabian City Scene with Camels Eld 8/93 3,300
De Franceschi, Mariano It 1849-1896
W/Pa 14x20 An Arab Caravan Chr 10/92 715
De Fromantiou, Hendrik Dut 1633-1694
* See 1990 Edition ....
De Garay, M. Fr 19C
O/Pn 9x14 Elegant Party in a Park Chr 5/93 3,450
De Gelder, Aert Dut 1645-1727
* See 1991 Edition ....
De Gempt, Bernard
* See 1991 Edition ....
De Gheyn, Jocob (II) Flm 1565-1629
* See 1993 Edition ....
De Glehn, Wilfrid Gabriel Br 1870-1951
* See 1993 Edition ....
De Gobbis, Giuseppe It a 1772-1783
* See 1992 Edition ....
De Goeje, Pieter Dut 1779-1859
O/C 17x20 Pastoral Landscape Horse, Cows But 5/93 3,738
De Grailly, Victor Fr 1804-1899
O/C 17x24 Lake George But 11/92 2,200
**De Grandmaison, Nicholas Can
1892-1978**
P/Pa 18x14 Portrait of an Indian Sbt 11/92 6,600
O/C 20x16 Portrait of an Indian Sbt 5/93 4,400
**De Groot, Frans Arnold Breuhau Dut
1824-1872**
* See 1990 Edition ....
De Gros, Baron Jean Louis Fr 1793-1879
* See 1991 Edition ....
De Guastavino, Clement Pujol Fr 19C
* See 1991 Edition ....
De Gyselaer, Nicolaes 1590-1654
* See 1992 Edition ....
De Haas, Mauritz F. H. Am 1832-1895
O/C 53x95 Ship Breaking up on Rocks 1874 But 12/92 .. 24,200
O/C 20x34 Fisherfolk on the Shore Skn 11/92 11,000
O/C 24x34 Sunset, New York Harbor 1881 Chr 3/93 9,200
W&G/Pa 13x19 Off the Coast Chr 12/92 5,500
O/C 12x20 Ship Off Coast of Massachusetts Lou 6/93 ... 2,750
**De Haas, William Frederick Am
1830-1880**
O/C 22x36 October Day Off Mt. Desert 74 Chr 12/92 20,900

De Haes, Carlos   Spa 1829-1898
  * See 1993 Edition ....
De Hamilton, Karl-Wilhelm
  * See 1991 Edition ....
De Haven, Franklin   Am 1856-1934
  O/C 24x30 Seascape with Tornado Sby 9/92 990
  O/C 12x14 River and Country Road: Two Sby 9/92 825
  O/C 20x24 Autumn Landscape Wlf 5/93 600
  O/C 16x12 Gold and Turquoise Fre 10/92 190
De Haven, Hugh   Am 20C
  O/B 25x30 Dawn on the Harbour Mys 3/93 330
De Heem, Cornelis   Dut 1631-1695
  * See 1991 Edition ....
De Heem, David Davidsz.   Dut a 1610-1669
  * See 1990 Edition ....
De Heem, Jan Davidsz   Dut 1606-1684
  O/Pn 16x19 Still Life Grapes, Peaches, Oysters Sby 1/93 1.5425M
  O/C/Pn 28x37 Grapes Walnuts Plates 1626 Sby 5/93 51,750
De Heere, Lukas   Dut 1534-1584
  * See 1992 Edition ....
De Heusch, Jacob   Dut 1657-1701
  * See 1991 Edition ....
De Heuvel, Theodore Bernard   Flm 1817-1906
  * See 1992 Edition ....
De Hondecoeter, Gillis Claesz.   Dut 1604-1653
  * See 1992 Edition ....
De Hondecoeter, Melchior   Dut 1639-1695
  * See 1991 Edition ....
De Hooch, David   Dut a 1650-
  * See 1991 Edition ....
De Hooch, Pieter   Dut 20C
  W/Pa 18x24 Woman on the Beach with Net Hnd 10/92 650
De Hooch, Pieter   Dut 1629-1681
  O/C 26x23 Woman with Lute, Man with Violin Sby 1/93 .. 55,200
De Hoog, Bernard   Dut 1867-1943
  O/C 50x38 Mother and her Children Seated Chr 2/93 15,400
  O/C 20x16 Still Life with Roses But 5/93 6,325
  O/C 31x41 Nursing the Baby Slo 5/93 5,500
  O/C 23x19 Returning from Church Slo 10/92 3,300
  O/C 16x20 Mother and Child Dum 8/93 3,000
  O/C 8x6 Woman Sewing by Window But 5/93 2,875
  O/C 16x13 Two Ladies Having Tea Eld 8/93 1,760
De Hory, Elmyr   Hun 20C
  * See 1993 Edition ....
De Iturria, Ignacio   It
  O/C 24x29 Cadaques Sby 11/92 10,450
De Ivanowski, Sigismund   Pol 1875-1944
  * See 1993 Edition ....
De Jankowski, Cheslas Bois
  * See 1991 Edition ....
De Jimenez, Jose
  O/C 61x38 Divina Pastora Sby 5/93 23,000
De Jode, Pieter (I)   1570-1634
  * See 1993 Edition ....
De Joncieres, Leonce J. V.   Fr 1871-
  * See 1992 Edition ....
De Jongh, Claude   -1663
  O/Pn 7x9 Figures in Ferry Boat 1634 Sby 1/93 10,925
De Jongh, Gabriel   SAf 20C
  O/C 18x24 Cottage in Mountain Landscape Slo 7/93 350
De Jongh, Oene Romkes   Dut 1812-1896
  O/Pn 13x18 Dutch Street Scene Fre 10/92 3,100
De Jonghe, Gustave Leonhard   Bel 1829-1893
  O/Pn 22x18 Mother and Child 1864 But 5/93 9,775
De Jouderville, Isaac   1613-1648
  * See 1992 Edition ....
De Kerdrouet, Gustave Edouard   Fr 1802-
  * See 1992 Edition ....
De Koninck, Andries   Dut 17C
  * See 1991 Edition ....

De Kooning, Elaine   Am 1919-1989
  O/B 48x60 Southwestern Landscape 57 Sby 6/93 5,750
  Medium? 15x19 Rio Grande 1959 Sby 2/93 805
  W,P&L/Pa 15x11 Basketball '80 Sby 2/93 690
  H/Pa 14x15 Untitled '43 Chr 11/92 550
De Kooning, Willem   Dut 1904-
  E/Pa 22x30 Untitled (Black and White Abstract) Sby 5/93 985,000
  O/C 80x70 Flowers, Mary's Table 1971 Chr 11/92 907,500
  MM/Pa/B 24x36 Abstraction Chr 11/92 440,000
  O/Pa/C 58x43 Two Figures in Devon 71 Sby 11/92 126,500
  O/Pa/M 29x22 Untitled Sby 2/93 118,000
  P/Pa 16x20 Woman Sby 11/92 104,500
  O&P/Ph 24x25 Study for Stenographer Sby 5/93 68,500
  H/Pa 9x12 Untitled (Two Women) Chr 11/92 55,000
  H/Pa 9x12 Two Women Sby 11/92 38,500
  C/Pa 24x19 Untitled Chr 11/92 20,350
  C/Pa 10x8 Woman Chr 11/92 8,250
De L'Abadia, Juan   a 1473-1500
  * See 1992 Edition ....
De L'Aubiniere, C* A***   Can a 1880-1888**
  O/Cd 10x14 Niagara Fall, Spring Sbt 11/92 616
De La Bastida, Jose Marie   a 1783-
  * See 1992 Edition ....
De La Brely, August   Fr 1838-1906
  * See 1993 Edition ....
De La Corte, Gabriel   1648-1694
  * See 1990 Edition ....
De La Fosse, Charles   1636-1716
  * See 1993 Edition ....
De La Fosse, Charles Alexander   Fr 1829-
  * See 1991 Edition ....
De La Fresnaye, Roger   Fr 1885-1925
  O/C 29x36 Le Diabolo Sby 11/92 176,000
  Pe/Pa 8x6 L'Infirmiere de Bellejeune Wlf 9/92 325
De La Fuente, Virgilio Mattoni   Spa 1842-
  * See 1992 Edition ....
De La Haye, Reinier   1640-1695
  * See 1991 Edition ....
De La Hyre, Laurent   1606-1656
  O/C 25x35 Women at Fountain, Cows 1653 Sby 5/93 .. 415,000
De La Patelliere, Amedee   Fr 1890-1932
  * See 1991 Edition ....
De La Porte, Henri-Horace R.   1725-1793
  * See 1993 Edition ....
De La Serna, Ismael   Spa 1887-1968
  G&W/Pa/B 12x19 Carnaval 28 Chr 5/93 3,450
De La Torre, Martin Fernandez   Spa 1888-1938
  * See 1990 Edition ....
De La Touche, Gaston   Fr 1854-1913
  Pl/Pa 8x11 Group of Figures 1881 Wlf 9/92 600
De La Tour, Maurice Quentin   Fr
  * See 1991 Edition ....
De La Vega, Jorge   Arg 1930-1971
  MM&O/C 28x24 La Bestia Y La Bestia 62 Sby 5/93 2,875
De La Villeon, Emmanuel   Fr 1858-1944
  * See 1993 Edition ....
De Lacroix, Charles Francois G   Fr 1720-1782
  O/C 41x57 Mediterranean Harbors: Pair 1776 Sby 1/93 .. 123,500
  O/C 45x64 Coastline w/Figures Standing Chr 1/93 33,000
  O/C 11x17 Shipwreck Stormy Seas Sby 1/93 9,488
  O/C 8x10 Mediterranean Harbour Scene Sby 5/93 9,200
De Lairesse, Gerard   Flm 1641-1711
  * See 1993 Edition ....
De Lajoue, Jacques   Fr 1687-1761
  * See 1991 Edition ....
De Lall, Oscar   Can 1903-1971
  O/C 22x28 Canadian Autumn Yng 5/93 600
  O/B 12x16 Winter in Laurentians Yng 5/93 250
De Lara, Carlos Pascual   Spa 20C
  O/C 23x36 Concierto '48 Slo 4/93 350
De Largillierre, Nicolas   Fr 1656-1746
  * See 1992 Edition ....

De Laszlo De Lombos, Philip A.   Br 1869-1937
O/C 39x29 Tibor de Scitovszky/Wife: Pair 1927 Sby 5/93 . . 14,950
De Latoix, Gaspard   Am a 19C
* See 1992 Edition . . . .
De Latouche, Gaston   Fr 1854-1913
* See 1992 Edition . . . .
De Lavigerie, Samuel Marie C.   Fr 19C
* See 1992 Edition . . . .
De Leeuw, Alexis   Bel 19C
O/C 30x50 In Winter Time Sel 9/92 3,500
O/Pn 9x12 The Sleigh Ride Sel 9/92 1,300
De Lempicka, Tamara   Pol 1898-1980
O/C 39x29 Les Deux Fillettes Aux Rubans Bleus Sby 11/92 148,500
O/B 19x13 Still Life Mask, Plume and Cards Sby 2/93 . . . 23,000
O/C 24x18 Self Portrait at the Wheel 1954 Dum 5/93 20,000
O/C 16x20 Still Life Milk and Loaf Sby 2/93 19,550
O/C 20x16 Still Life Lemons on Red Chair Sby 2/93 16,100
O/C 24x18 Etude pour Le Couple Chr 11/92 14,300
O/C 16x13 Woman at the Theater Sby 2/93 11,500
O/Cb 14x11 Ville Des Rochers Sby 2/93 10,925
O/C 20x16 Abstract Composition 35 Sby 2/93 9,200
O/C 14x11 Femme au Turban Rouge et Blanc Chr 11/92 . . 6,600
H&W/Pa 13x10 Two Female Nudes Sby 2/93 2,415
Pe/Pa 11x9 Three Drawings Chr 11/92 2,090
Pe/Pa 15x11 Two Drawings 1923 Chr 11/92 2,090
Pe/Pa 11x8 Portrait 1925 Chr 11/92 880
De Leon Y Escosura, Ignacio   Spa 1834-1901
O/Pn 16x22 The Rude Parrot 1876 Hnd 3/93 29,000
O/Pn 16x22 Interior Scene 1875 Hnd 3/93 26,000
De Leon, Francisco Diaz   20C
* See 1991 Edition . . . .
De Lilie, Watteau   Fr 1731-1798
* See 1991 Edition . . . .
De Lisio, Arnaldo   It 1869-
W/Pa 21x13 Peasant Woman Dum 8/93 175
De Longpre, Paul   Am 1855-1911
W&Pe/B 19x13 Rhododendron 1895 Chr 5/93 8,050
W/Pa 20x15 Poppies in Oriental Vase 1900 Mor 2/93 3,000
W/Pa 12x9 Apple Blossoms Bumble Bees Sby 9/92 1,980
W&G/Pa 10x36 Chrysanthemums But 10/92 1,650
De Longpre, Raoul M.   Am 19C
W&G/Pa 21x29 Lilacs But 3/93 8,800
G/Pb 26x20 Red Roses and White Lilacs Chr 12/92 1,320
G/Pa 11x8 Roses Mys 12/92 440
De Looper, Willem   Am 1932-
O/C 48x49 Untitled '75 Slo 7/93 500
O/C 69x49 Untitled 1974 Slo 7/93 500
De Loose, Basile   Dut 1809-1885
O/C 33x28 A Painful Lesson But 11/92 12,100
De Lorimier, Etienne Chevalier 1759-1813
O/C 47x36 Villa Borghese; Temple Diana (2) 1810 Sby 5/93 68,500
De Loutherbourg, Philippe   Fr 1740-1812
* See 1993 Edition . . . .
De Luce, Percival   Am 1847-1914
* See 1992 Edition . . . .
De Lummen, Emile Van Marcke   Fr 1827-1890
O/C 28x36 Peasant Tending His Animals Chr 10/92 11,000
O/C 21x31 Going to Pasture Chr 10/92 4,400
O/Pn 11x14 Cattle Resting Chr 10/92 4,180
De Lutero, Giovanni-Dosso Dos   It
* See 1990 Edition . . . .
De Lyon, Corneille   1500-1575
O/Pn 7x5 Portrait of a Gentleman Chr 10/92 36,300
De Madrazo Y Garreta, Raimundo   Spa 1841-1920
* See 1993 Edition . . . .
De Madrazo Y Garreta, Ricardo   Spa 1852-1917
* See 1992 Edition . . . .
De Maghellen, Alfred   Fr 1871-
* See 1992 Edition . . . .

De Maine, Harry   Am 1880-
O/C 25x30 Twilight Brd 8/93 990
De Man, Cornelis   1621-1706
O/C 30x24 Couple seated at a draped Table Chr 10/92 . . . 55,000
De Maria, Nicola   1954-
O&L/Pa/C 80x120 Angeli 1982 Chr 10/92 19,800
De Maria, Walter   Am 1935-
* See 1992 Edition . . . .
De Marseille, Lacroix   Fr 1720-1782
* See 1993 Edition . . . .
De Martini, Joseph   Am 1896-
O/C 28x37 Rockport Quarry 1939 Sby 3/93 4,313
De Matteis, Paolo   It 1662-1728
K,Pl&S/Pa 9x7 Angels Revealing an Image Chr 1/93 1,980
De Mattos, Francisco Vieira (II) 1699-1778
K/Pa 10x18 Saint Francis Entering the Church Chr 1/93 . . . 1,045
De Mers, Joseph   Am 1910-1984
G/Pa 18x9 Couple by Open Car Door Ih 11/92 700
G/Pa 14x11 Girl Sewing Pants of Raggedy Andy Ih 11/92 . . 650
De Metz, F. Louis Lanfant   Fr 1814-1892
O/Pn 16x13 Naughty Child; New Nanny (2) Sby 2/93 25,300
O/Pn 13x9 A Busy Marketplace Chr 10/92 6,600
O/Pn 6x10 Busy Street in a Port Town Chr 10/92 6,050
O/C 13x16 Portrait d'Une Jeune Fille Sby 1/93 4,888
De Meyer, Hendrick (the Elder)   a 1637-1683
O/Pn 35x49 Beach at Scheveningen Fishing Boats Sby 1/93 14,950
De Meza, William   Am 19C
* See 1993 Edition . . . .
De Miranda, Juan   Mex 17C
O/C 81x57 Virgen de Guadalupe 1704 Sby 11/92 66,000
De Molijn, Pieter   Dut 1595-1661
* See 1993 Edition . . . .
De Momper, Frans   Flm 1603-1660
* See 1993 Edition . . . .
De Momper, Frans & Vrancx, S.   Flm 1603-1660
* See 1992 Edition . . . .
De Momper, Joos   Flm 1564-1635
O/Pn 10x7 Rocks with Parrots and Ducks Sby 1/93 17,250
De Momper, Phillip (I)   Flm
* See 1990 Edition . . . .
De Monfreid, Georges Daniel   Fr 1856-1929
* See 1993 Edition . . . .
De Montalant, I. O.   Fr 19C
* See 1993 Edition . . . .
De Montpezat, Henri D'Ainecy   Fr 1817-1859
O/C 17x24 Elegant Figures in a Courtyard Chr 2/93 2,750
De Moys, Rolan   a 1571-1592
O/Pn 17x13 The Descent from the Cross Sby 5/93 13,800
De Mura, Francesco   It 1696-1782
O/C 30x41 The Tribute Money Chr 1/93 19,800
De Nagy, Ernest   Ger 20C
O/B 14x18 Pigeon Cove Cape Ann, Mass. 1939 Ald 5/93 . . . 250
De Neuse, B.   Eur 20C
W/Pa 11x8 Mosque Hnz 5/93 60
De Neuville, Alphonse Marie   Fr 1835-1885
W&Pe/Pa 13x9 Madamoiselle Bausseil 1870 Fre 4/93 500
De Neuville, Brunel   Fr 20C
* See 1992 Edition . . . .
De Neyn, Pieter   Dut 1597-1639
O/Pn 17x23 River with Boors Conversing 1629 Chr 1/93 . 31,900
O/Pn 19x25 Herdsmen Resting by Dune Chr 5/93 13,800
De Niccolo, Lorenzo   It
* See 1990 Edition . . . .
De Nierman, Leonardo   Mex 20C
O/B 31x24 Autumn Flight Hnd 3/93 1,300
O/C 24x16 Night Flight Hnd 3/93 600
De Niro, Robert   Am 1922-
O/C 46x32 Still Life with Red Cloth Sby 2/93 3,163
O/Pa 22x30 Table with Roses and Eggs '62 Sby 2/93 920

C/Pa 25x19 Mother and Child Reading '57 Sby 2/93 805
C/Pa 19x25 Portrait of a Woman '57 Sby 2/93 690

De Nittis, Giuseppe It 1846-1884
O/C 13x17 At the Racetrack 74 Chr 10/92 715,000

De Nome, Francois It 1593-1640
O/C 36x34 Stoning of Saint Stephen Sby 10/92 5,500

De Notar, David Emil Joseph Bel 1825-1912
O/C 16x24 Flowers, Fruit and Fowl Chr 10/92 6,600

De Paez, Jose Mex 1715-
O/Cp 8 dia Virgen De Guadalupe Sby 5/93 21,850
O/C 32x25 Santa Rose de Lima Sby 11/92 3,575

De Paredes, Vincenta Spa 1857-
O/C 20x29 The Ultimatum Chr 10/92 7,700

De Penne, Charles Olivier Fr 1831-1897
O/Pn 22x18 Hunting Dogs Resting Chr 2/93 7,150
O/Pn 11x8 Brace of Gordon Setters Sby 6/93 6,038
O/Pn 13x10 Hounds at Rest Sby 6/93 5,175
O/Pn 10x8 Hunting Dogs by the River Mys 12/92 2,970
O/C 13x10 Huntsman and His Hounds Skn 3/93 2,200
WPe&G/Pa/B 11x15 Sportsman and his Hounds 90 Chr 6/93 633

De Pietro, Giovanni It a 1432-1479
* See 1993 Edition . . . .

De Pietro, Sano It 1406-1481
* See 1990 Edition . . . .

De Pisis, Filippo It 1896-1956
O/C 26x20 Bouquet de Fleurs Sby 2/93 65,750
G/Pa/B 20x15 Seated Man 48 Sby 2/93 1,840

De Pitati, Bonifazio It 1487-1553
O/C 41x60 Holy Family with Saint Dorothy Sby 1/93 . . . 57,500

De Poorter, Willem Dut 1608-1648
* See 1992 Edition . . . .

De Porcia, Francesco It 16C
* See 1990 Edition . . . .

De Prades, Alfred F. Br a 1844-1883
* See 1993 Edition . . . .

De Pratere, Edmond Joseph Bel 1826-1888
O/C 29x40 Cows in Pasture Slo 7/93 550

De Quiroz, Cesario Bernaldo Arg 1881-1968
O/M 24x30 Huerta Chr 11/92 20,900

De Reyna, Antonio Maria Spa 1859-1937
O/C 14x29 A Boathouse in Venice Sby 2/93 19,550
O/C 17x29 Venezia 84 Sby 5/93 11,500

De Ribcowski, Dey Am 1880-1936
O/C 24x40 Sunrise Over the Shore Sby 9/92 3,300
O/C 14x36 Sunset, Half Moon Bay But 6/93 1,610
O/C 20x24 Sailing in the Moonlight 1912 But 6/93 862
O/C 30x40 Night Fishermen Mor 11/92 500
O/C 20x16 Venetial Canal Scene Sel 4/93 400

De Ribera, Jusepe Spa 1588-1656
O/C 40x32 Portrait Philosopher or Architect Sby 1/93 96,000
O/C/Pn 70x51 Saint Jerome Chr 1/93 77,000

De Ring, Pieter Dut 1615-1660
* See 1990 Edition . . . .

De Rome, Albert Am 1885-1959
O/Cb 10x14 Monterey Bay But 10/92 1,760
W/Pa 12x8 Bright Angel Canyon But 6/93 632

De Roore, Jacobus Ignatius 1686-1747
O/Pn 21x25 Flora, seated beside a sculpted Urn Chr 10/92 35,200

De Rose, Anthony Lewis Am 1803-1839
* See 1992 Edition . . . .

De Saint-Andre, Simon Renard Fr 1613-1677
* See 1990 Edition . . . .

De Saint-Aubin, Augustin Fr 1736-1807
* See 1993 Edition . . . .

De Saint-Aubin, Gabriel-J. Fr 1724-1780
* See 1992 Edition . . . .

De Saint-Martin, Francisque M. Fr 1793-1867
* See 1993 Edition . . . .

De Saint-Memin, Charles B. F. Am 1770-1852
* See 1992 Edition . . . .

De Santa Maria, Andres Col 1869-1945
* See 1992 Edition . . . .

De Schryver, Louis Marie Fr 1862-1942
O/C 22x19 Marchande de Fleurs L'Elysee 1896 Sby 5/93 140,000
O/C 28x41 L'Avenue du Bois de Boulogne 1902 Chr 10/92 132,000
O/C 14x10 Marchande de Fleurs 95 Chr 5/93 34,500

De Silvestre, Louis (II) Fr 1675-1760
* See 1993 Edition . . . .

De Simone, A. J. It 19C
O/C 20x16 At Dusk Hnd 10/92 500

De Simone, Tommaso It 19C
O/C 18x26 H.M.S. Revenge Off Naples 1862 Sby 6/93 8,050

De Smet, Gustave Bel 1877-1943
* See 1991 Edition . . . .

De Smet, Henri Bel 1865-1940
* See 1992 Edition . . . .

De Smet, Leon Bel 1881-
* See 1991 Edition . . . .

De Soria, Martin It a 1475-
* See 1993 Edition . . . .

De Spinny, Guillaume Jean Jos. 1721-1785
* See 1993 Edition . . . .

De Stael, Nicolas Fr 1913-1955
O/C 51x35 Fleurs sur fond rouge 1953 Chr 11/92 682,000
O/C 39x29 Fleurs a Fontenay 1954 Chr 11/92 297,000
O/C 15x24 Paysage Chr 11/92 242,000
O/B 5x9 Ivry 1952 Chr 11/92 99,000
L 20x25 Volliers a Antibes Sby 5/93 23,000

De Steenhuyssen, W. Dut 20C
O/Pn 9x13 Plassen te Best 1915 Slo 7/93 400

De Stomme, Maerten Boelema Dut a 1642-1664
* See 1991 Edition . . . .

De Szyszlo, Fernando Per 1925-
A/C 79x79 Sol Negro 91 Chr 11/92 28,600
A/C 59x59 Recinto 90 Chr 11/92 24,200
A/C 59x47 Runa Macii 71 Chr 11/92 20,900
A/C 64x45 Yawar Mayus (Un Rio De Sangre) 63 Sby 5/93 20,700
A/C 59x47 Interior IV 72 Chr 11/92 18,700
A/C 51x63 Love Letter 1959 Sby 5/93 18,400
A/C 40x40 Mesa Ritual (Los Instrumentos) 1986 Chr 11/92 14,300

De Thomas, J.
O/B 16x22 Beethovan Ald 9/92 75

De Thoren, Otto Aus 1828-1889
O/Pn 14x23 Going to Market Wlf 3/93 3,600

De Thulstrup, Thure Am 1848-1930
* See 1992 Edition . . . .

De Tirtoff, Romain (Erte) Fr 1892-1990
G/Pa 13x9 Les Travaux D'Hercule 1934 Sel 12/92 3,500
G/Pa 13x10 La Chaleur Les Nuages 1926 Hnd 12/92 3,000
G/Pa 17x12 Fine Feathers Make Fine Birds Lou 3/93 1,500

De Tonnancour, Jacques G. Can 1917-
O/B 24x31 Blue Lake '63 Sbt 11/92 11,440
O&L/B 36x36 Cibles Pour Mousquetaires 1973 Sbt 5/93 . . 3,520
O/C 26x36 Rio '46 Sbt 5/93 3,520

De Torres, Antonio Mex 1666-1754
* See 1993 Edition . . . .

De Torres, Julio Romero Spa 1879-1930
O/C 25x21 Portrait of a Lady Sby 5/93 26,450

De Troy, Francois 1645-1730
O/C 36x46 Fete Aux Porcherons Sby 5/93 360,000
O/C 31x26 Portrait of a Lady 1717 Chr 5/93 29,900

De Troy, Jean-Francois Fr 1679-1752
* See 1991 Edition . . . .

De Vadder, Lodewyk Flm 1605-1655
* See 1991 Edition . . . .

De Valk, Kendrik Dut 17C
* See 1993 Edition . . . .

De Vigne, Edouard Bel 1806-1866
O/Pn 19x27 A Mountain Pass Chr 5/93 9,775

De Vlieger, Simon   Dut 1500-
* See 1991 Edition . . . .
De Villalpando, Cristobal   Mex 1649-1714
O/C 70x44 Sagrada Familia y Santa Trinidad Sby 11/92 . . 36,300
De Vity, Antonio   It 1901-
O/C 20x16 Paris Street Scene Lou 12/92 100
De Vlaminck, Maurice   Fr 1876-1958
O/C 21x25 Paysage D'Hiver Sby 11/92 101,750
O/C 24x29 Rue de Village Sby 5/93 101,500
O/C 26x32 La Maison Rouge Sby 11/92 93,500
O/C 21x26 Village Anime Sous la Neige Sby 10/92 79,750
O/C 21x26 Village Anime Sous la Neige Sby 5/93 72,900
O/C 22x29 Paysage au Champ de Ble Sby 5/93 71,250
O/C 22x29 Paysage Au Champ De Ble Sby 10/92 63,250
O/C 26x32 Marine Sby 11/92 57,750
O/C 22x26 Paysage D'Automne Sby 10/92 49,500
O/C 13x15 Maisons au Bord de l'Eau Sby 11/92 46,750
O/C 24x29 La foret Chr 11/92 44,000
O/C 18x22 La Gare D'Auvers-Sur-Oise Sby 10/92 44,000
O/C 24x29 Les Meules Sby 2/93 43,700
O/C 13x16 La Ferme Aux Arbres Sby 10/92 42,900
O/C 13x18 Paysage de Neige Sby 11/92 41,250
O/C 24x32 La Mer Sby 2/93 40,250
O/C 21x26 L'Eglise Sby 11/92 38,500
O/C 18x13 Les Fleurs Sby 2/93 27,600
G&Pl/Pa 15x18 Champ de bles Chr 11/92 19,800
WBr&l/Pa/B 14x17 L'Hiver Sby 2/93 13,225
W&l/Pa 15x19 Eglise Dans Les Bois Sby 10/92 13,200
Pl&S/Pa 7x4 Scene de Village 1924 Hnd 12/92 3,800
Pl&Br/Pa 9x13 Paysage Chr 5/93 2,875
De Voll, F. Usher   Am 1873-1941
O/C 12x16 April Showers/City Scene Skn 3/93 1,650
De Vos, Florence Marie   Am 1892-
* See 1993 Edition . . . .
De Vos, Marten   Flm 1532-1603
* See 1992 Edition . . . .
De Vos, Simon   Flm 1603-1676
O/Cp 22x29 Christ Crucified 1639 Hnd 5/93 9,000
De Vos, Vincent   Bel 1829-1875
* See 1993 Edition . . . .
De Vries, Dirck   Dut a 1590-1592
* See 1992 Edition . . . .
De Vries, Paul Vredemann   Dut a 1567-1630
* See 1990 Edition . . . .
De Vuillefroy, Georges Jean E.   Fr 19C
O/C 16x13 Pink Roses in a Glass Vase Chr 10/92 1,045
De Wael, Cornelis   Flm 1592-1667
* See 1992 Edition . . . .
De Waroquier, Henry   Fr 1881-1970
* See 1993 Edition . . . .
De Warville, Felix-Saturnin B.   Fr 1818-1892
O/C 11x15 Sheep in Landscape Fre 4/93 3,300
De Wet, Jacob Willemsz.   Dut 1610-1671
O/Pn 19x15 Annuciation to the Shepherds Sby 1/93 3,738
De Wilde, Frans   Bel 1840-1918
* See 1993 Edition . . . .
De Witte, Emanuel   Dut 1617-1692
* See 1992 Edition . . . .
De Yong, Joe   Am 1894-1975
W,G&Pe/Pb 10x15 Indians on Horseback 1937 But 12/92 . . 1,650
De Young, Harry   Am 20C
O/C 18x21 Wild Flowers Hnd 10/92 160
De Zamora, Jose
Pt,W&l/Pa 14x10 Chez Poiret 1912 Sby 10/92 1,980
W,Pe&Pt/Pa 13x10 Costume Design The Albatross Sby 10/92 440
W,Pe&Pt/Pa 13x10 Cloud Costume Sby 10/92 330
De Zubiaurre, Valentin   Spa 1879-
* See 1992 Edition . . . .
De Zubiaurre, Ramon   Spa 1882-
* See 1991 Edition . . . .
De Zurbaran, Francisco   Spa 1598-1664
* See 1992 Edition . . . .

De'Busi, Giovanni   It 1485-1547
* See 1993 Edition . . . .
De'Ferrari, Lorenzo   It 1644-1726
* See 1990 Edition . . . .
De'Rossi, Francesco   It 1510-1563
* See 1990 Edition . . . .
Deakin, Edwin   Am 1838-1923
O/C 36x18 St. Etienne Du Mont, Paris 1898 But 10/92 1,980
O/C 14x17 Grapes Spilling From a Basket Doy 11/92 1,870
O/C 30x20 Mill near Chillon Castle 1897 But 3/93 1,870
Dean, Walter Lofthouse   Am 1854-1912
O/C 9x14 Two Harbor Views 1901 Skn 3/93 1,650
O/C 14x18 Looking Across Gloucester Harbor Yng 5/93 . . . 475
Deandries, Alex
O/C 22x15 Armed Muskateer Dum 11/92 1,400
O/C 32x26 Cavalier in Red Dum 1/93 1,200
Deane, William Wood   Br 1825-1873
* See 1992 Edition . . . .
Dearth, Henry Golden   Am 1864-1918
* See 1992 Edition . . . .
Deas, Charles   Am 1818-1867
* See 1992 Edition . . . .
Debat-Ponson, Edouard Bernard   Fr 1847-1913
Pe/Pa 24x19 3 Figural Studies 1898 Wlf 12/92 200
Pe/Pa 25x19 3 Nude Figure Studies 1898 Wlf 12/92 200
Debertiz, Per   Nor 1880-1945
* See 1993 Edition . . . .
Deblois, Francois B.   Can 1829-1913
* See 1993 Edition . . . .
Debre, Olivier   Fr 1920-
O/C 51x64 Nature Morte 1956 Chr 5/93 27,600
O/C 45x58 Les Musiciens 48 Sby 10/92 2,640
Debucourt, Philibert-Louis   Fr 1755-1832
* See 1993 Edition . . . .
DeCamp, Ralph Earl   Am 1858-1936
O/C 16x36 Blaze in the Forest Hnd 3/93 400
Decamps, Albert   Fr 1862-1908
* See 1990 Edition . . . .
Decamps, Gabriel Alexandre   Fr 1803-1860
W/Pa 8x7 Un Grec Sby 5/93 2,588
O/Pn 8x7 The Wise Old Man Chr 2/93 1,320
O/C 15x20 Bay of Algiers Mys 12/92 302
Decamps, Maurice
O/C 24x29 Promenade des Anglais, Nice Sby 10/92 3,080
Dechar, Peter
* See 1992 Edition . . . .
Decker, Cornelis Gerritsz   1623-1678
O/Pn 21x17 Farmhouse Under Stormy Skies Sby 1/93 . . . 12,075
Decker, Joseph   Am 1853-1924
* See 1991 Edition . . . .
Decorchemont, Francois-Emile   Fr 1880-1971
* See 1992 Edition . . . .
Dedina, Jean   Czk 1870-
* See 1993 Edition . . . .
Defaux, Alexandre   Fr 1826-1900
* See 1993 Edition . . . .
Defaux, J.   Con 19C
O/C 15x18 Rivertown and a Village Path 1855 Chr 10/92 . . 2,200
Deforest, Henry J.   Can 1860-1924
O/C 23x36 Washington River in the Evening 1842 But 11/92 1,980
DeForest, Roy   Am 1930-
Pt/C 73x85 Attack of the Big Foot, 1987 But 4/93 23,000
MM/C 64x69 Thousand Miles Across the Pampas But 4/93 18,400
DeForrest, Lockwood   Am 1850-1932
O/B 10x14 Three Palms; Indio Landscape (2) 09 But 6/93 . 2,070
O/B 11x14 Landscape Mor 11/92 750
O/B 10x14 Santa Ynez Mission 06 But 6/93 690
O/B 7x9 Landscape Mor 11/92 550
Degas, Edgar   Fr 1834-1917
O/C 55x32 Danseuses en Jupes Vertes 1895 Chr 11/92 . . 7.15M
P/Pa 24x18 Toilette Matinale 94 Chr 11/92 . . . . 2.97M
O/C 11x9 Fillette en Robe Blanche Sby 11/92 550,000

P/Pa/B 27x33 Femme se Coiffant Sby 11/92 264,000
C&P/Pa/B 24x11 Quatre Danseuses Sby 11/92 187,000
C/Pa 18x11 Homme Nu Sby 2/93 9,200
Deglume, Henri
O/Cb 21x29 Birches on Hillside Sby 2/93 1,265
Degottex, Jean   1918-1988
* See 1993 Edition . . . .
Degrose
O/C 12x9 Landscape with Creek Ald 9/92 120
DeHaven, Frank   Am 1856-1934
O/C 12x16 The Fallen Tree Lou 3/93 600
Dehesghues, Leon   Fr 1852-1910
O/C 50x80 Fete de Neuilly 1884 Sby 10/92 30,250
Dehn, Adolf Arthur   Am 1895-1968
W/Pa 15x23 Jazz Horns Chr 3/93 14,950
W&Pe/Pa 16x23 My Heart Belongs to Daddy '41 Chr 9/92   14,300
G&Pe/Pa 15x22 The Breakers, Palm Beach 1951 Sby 3/93 . 1,840
O/B 32x44 Haitian Gala 1956 But 6/93 1,380
W/Pa 13x21 Strollers Chr 12/92 1,320
W/Pa 20x28 Inlet Mys 3/93 1,210
W&G/Pa 20x28 Florida Seascape Chr 12/92 528
W/Pa 12x18 Island Air Base Wlf 4/93 250
W/Pa 10x14 Jungle Airfield '43 Hnd 12/92 200
W/Pa 9x12 Loading a Plane, South Pacific Hnd 12/92 150
Dehner, Walt   Am 20C
* See 1992 Edition . . . .
Dehory, Elmyr   Fr 1905-1978
O/C 24x20 Two Figures Seated by a Window But 10/92 . . 1,320
DeHospodar, Stephen   Am 1902-1959
O/C 27x20 Winter River Mor 6/93 770
Dei Crocifissi, Simone   It a 1330-1339
* See 1990 Edition . . . .
Dei Fiori, Carlo   It 1653-1695
O/C 26x21 Still Life Poppies, Anemones Sby 5/93 10,925
Dei Fiori, Gasparo   It 1650-1732
* See 1993 Edition . . . .
Dei Pietri, Pietro Antonio   It 1663-1716
* See 1992 Edition . . . .
Deike, Clara   Am 20C
* See 1993 Edition . . . .
Deiker, Johannes Christian   Ger 1822-1895
* See 1993 Edition . . . .
Dejuinne, Francois Louis   Fr 1786-1844
* See 1991 Edition . . . .
Del Biondo, Giovanni   It 15C
* See 1991 Edition . . . .
Del Brina, Francesco   1540-1586
* See 1993 Edition . . . .
Del Buono, Marco & Di Giovanni 1402-1489
T/Pn 16x19 3 Panels from a Cassone Chr 10/92 39,600
Del Campo, Federico   Per a 1881-1889
O/C 24x14 Bridge of Sighs, Venice 1896 Chr 5/93 25,300
O/C 14x9 Leaving the Church 1900 Sby 2/93 6,900
Del Campo, Francisco Peralta   Spa 1837-1897
* See 1992 Edition . . . .
Del Casentino, Jacopo   It 1297-1358
* See 1993 Edition . . . .
Del Drago, Antonio   It a 18C
* See 1993 Edition . . . .
Del Fiore, Jacobello   It a 1370-1439
* See 1993 Edition . . . .
Del Garbo, Raffaelino   It 1466-1524
* See 1993 Edition . . . .
Del Ghirlandaio, Michele Di R.   1503-1577
O/Pn 38x30 Virgin and Child w/Infant St. John Sby 1/93 . . 68,500
Del Landini, Jacopo   It 1297-1358
* See 1993 Edition . . . .
Del Moro, Battista   It 1514-1575
* See 1992 Edition . . . .
Del Po, Giacomo   It 1652-1726
* See 1992 Edition . . . .

Del Rio, Jose Lapayese   1926-
O/C 29x40 Avila Chr 11/92 1,650
Del Sellaio, Jacopo   It 1441-1493
* See 1993 Edition . . . .
Del Torre, Giulio   It 1856-1932
* See 1993 Edition . . . .
Delachaux, Leon   Sws 1850-1919
O/C 16x22 Fairy Tales Sby 10/92 7,150
Delacroix, Auguste   Fr 1809-1868
O/C 24x20 Awaiting the Fishermen Wes 10/92 2,475
O/C 15x13 An Afternoon Break 1835 Chr 10/92 1,650
Delacroix, Eugene   Fr 1798-1863
* See 1993 Edition . . . .
Delacroix-Garnier, Pauline   Fr 1863-1912
* See 1992 Edition . . . .
Delafontaine, Pierre-Maximilie 1774-1860
K,PI&S/Pa 13x10 Design for a Medal Chr 1/93 2,420
Delahaye, Ernest Emile
O/C 22x15 Girl with Geese Dum 1/93 1,700
Delahaye, Ernest Jean   Fr 1855-
* See 1992 Edition . . . .
Delance, Paul Louis   Fr 1848-1924
O/C 28x23 Elegante Accoudee 1882 Sby 10/92 17,600
Delano, William Adams   Am 20C
W,G&Pe/Pa 4x6 Summer Pleasures (4) 1920 But 12/92 . . . 2,200
Delanoy, Jacques   Fr 1820-1890
* See 1991 Edition . . . .
Delapp, Terry   Am 1934-
A/C 24x32 Two Palms But 3/93 2,750
A/C 24x32 Orange Branch But 3/93 1,980
Delaroche, Paul   Fr 1797-1856
O/Pn 6x5 Salome Sby 2/93 6,325
Delarue   Fr 20C
O/C 25x31 Paysage Hnd 6/93 160
Delaunay, Robert   Fr 1885-1941
G/Pa/Pn 20x34 Air, Fer et Eau, Etude 1936 Chr 11/92 . . 143,000
Delaunay, Sonia   Fr 1885-1979
* See 1993 Edition . . . .
Delbos, Julius   Am 1879-1970
W/Pa 20x30 Boats in a Harbor Yng 5/93 300
Delff, Willem Jacobsz.   1580-1638
* See 1993 Edition . . . .
Delfosse, Georges Marie Joseph   Can 1869-1939
O/C 27x36 Vieille Maison Sbt 11/92 4,400
Delft, Cornelis Jacobsz.   Dut
* See 1990 Edition . . . .
Delhogue, A Lexis-Aguste   Fr 1867-1930
* See 1993 Edition . . . .
Dell'Abbate, Niccolo   It 1509-1571
K&PI/Pa 7x11 Scenes Life of Tarquinus Superbus Chr 1/93 22,000
Dell'Acqua, Cesare-Felix-G.   Aus 1821-1904
* See 1992 Edition . . . .
Della Questa, Francesco   1652-1723
O/C 19x25 Roses, Carnations, Narcissi Chr 1/93 7,700
Della Rovere, Giovanni Mauro   It 1575-1640
* See 1992 Edition . . . .
Della Vecchia, Pietro   It 1605-1678
O/C 45x39 Saul and David with Head of Goliath Chr 10/92 15,400
O/C 33x40 Warrior with Severed Head Chr 1/93 5,500
Dellenbaugh, Frederick Samuel   Am 1853-1935
* See 1990 Edition . . . .
Dellepiane, Davide   Fr 19C
O/C 55x75 L'Embarquement Sby 2/93 34,500
Delmotte, Marcel   Bel 1901-1984
* See 1993 Edition . . . .
Delobbe, Francois Alfred   Fr 1835-1920
O/C 26x22 Feeding the Chicks 1879 Chr 2/93 8,800
Delobre, Emile Victor Augustin   Fr 1873-1956
O/C 16x13 Cypresses by the Sea Sby 2/93 7,475

O/B 13x16 Manzanares a El Pardo, Espagne Chr 5/93 6,900
O/B 14x11 Vue du Golfe Chr 2/93 6,820
O/Pn 16x13 Red Sails, Concarneau, Brittany Sby 10/92 ... 6,325
O/Pn 13x16 Rowers at la Marne 43 Sby 10/92 5,500

Delooper, William   Am 1932-
* See 1992 Edition ....

Delort, Charles Edouard   Fr 1841-1895
* See 1993 Edition ....

Delpy, Hippolyte Camille   Fr 1842-1910
O/Pn 16x28 River Landscape at Sunset 1900 Chr 10/92 .. 17,600
O/Pn 10x18 Les Lavandeuses 71 Sby 10/92 7,150
O/Pn 9x16 Punt in a River Landscape Chr 2/93 6,600
O/C 33x53 Le Sechage des Filets Chr 2/93 5,500
O/Pn 13x18 A River at Dusk Chr 10/92 4,620
O/Pn 13x23 Figures Near Cottages Fre 10/92 3,500
O/Pn 9x13 River Landscape Chr 5/93 1,955

Delpy, Jacques-Henry   Fr 1877-1957
O/Pn 15x24 Resting by a River Chr 10/92 3,300
O/Pn 18x32 Man in a Punt Chr 2/93 3,080
O/C 13x18 River Landscape at Sunset Chr 10/92 2,420

Deluermoz, Henri   Fr 1876-1943
* See 1990 Edition ....

Delvaux, Paul   Bel 1897-
* See 1993 Edition ....

Delville, Jean   Bel 1867-1953
O/C 14x18 Ascension 1934 Sby 1/93 2,070

Delyen, Jacques-Francois   1684-1761
O/C 36x29 Portrait of the Artist Chr 1/93 44,000

Demachy, Pierre-Antoine   Fr 1723-1807
* See 1991 Edition ....

Demarle   Fr 19C
O/Pn 11x9 Le Soldat Slo 4/93 250

Demarne, Jean-Louis   Fr 1744-1829
* See 1993 Edition ....

Demarnette   Fr 1744-1829
* See 1993 Edition ....

Demel, F.   Aus 19C
O/C 32x29 St. Stephen's Cathedral Hnd 10/92 2,300

Deming, Edwin Willard   Am 1860-1942
O/M 24x48 Heading Home from a Successful Hunt Sby 3/93 1,610
O/B 12x16 Recital of the Ancient Myths Chr 5/93 1,150
W/Pa 6x5 Depicting Two American Indians Eld 8/93 440

Demont-Breton, Virginie   Fr 1859-1935
* See 1992 Edition ....

Demoutier, P.   Con 20C
W/Pa 14x8 Tunisian Alley Slo 4/93 135

Demuth, Charles Henry   Am 1883-1935
O/C 25x20 Welcome to Our City 1921 Sby 12/92 825,000
W/Pa 11x16 Pears and Plate Sby 12/92 110,000
W&Pe/Pa 11x9 Man/Woman, Provincetown '34 Chr 5/93 . 34,500
W/Pa 14x10 Still Life with Tulips 1917 Sby 12/92 27,500
W/Pa 8x11 Floral Still Life 1915 Sby 12/92 25,300
Pe/Pa 6x7 Male Studies and Paquebot (4) Chr 12/92 1,100

Denby, Edwin Hooper   Am 1873-
W/Pa 8x13 Chabarnet '97 Yng 5/93 150

Denes, Agnes   20C
* See 1991 Edition ....

Deneux, Gabriel Charles   Fr 1856-
O/C 55x70 The Wedding Sby 10/92 35,750

Denis, H.   Con 19C
* See 1992 Edition ....

Denis, Jose   Spa 19C
O/C 20x28 An Afternoon on the Patio 73 Sby 5/93 4,600

Denis, Louise   Bel 19C
O/C 27x41 Poppies and Daisies in Basket Chr 2/93 4,180

Denis, Maurice   Fr 1870-1943
O/C 23x18 Souvenir de Soir I Sby 5/93 156,500
O/C 46x45 Bethsabee au Bain Dans Les Jardins Sby 5/93 . 48,875

Dennis, James Morgan   Am 1891-
P/C 25x30 Mountains with River Dum 3/93 325

Dennis, Roger Wilson   Am 1902-
O/C 27x33 Morning At Noank 1985 Doy 11/92 2,530

Denny, Gideon Jacques   Am 1830-1886
O/B 12x18 Square Rigger Foundering 1879 But 3/93 3,025

Denslow, William Wallace   Am 1856-1915
Pe/Pa 10x14 Card Mill & Williams Point: Two 1900 Sby 9/92   440

Depero, Fortunato   It 1892-1960
O/Pn 28x36 Il Motociclista Sby 11/92 55,000
L/Cd 17x13 Veglia Sby 6/93 5,750

Der Garabedian, Giragos   Am 1892-1980
O/C 24x30 Pigeon Cove 1938 Skn 9/92 522

Derain, Andre   Fr 1880-1954
O/C 13x16 Environs de Chatou Sby 5/93 57,500
O/C 23x21 Femme au Chale Sby 5/93 46,000
O/C 32x26 Paysage aux arbres Chr 11/92 30,800
O/Pn 11x9 Nature Morte Sby 11/92 16,500
O/C 14x13 Tete Chr 10/92 7,700
O/C 14x12 Tete de Jeune Femme Chr 10/92 6,600
O/C 10x9 Tete de Jeune Garcon Chr 11/92 4,950
O/Wd 10x8 Head of a Girl Dum 7/93 3,750
S/Pa 14x11 Interior Scene with Figures But 4/93 1,725
Pe/Pa 23x17 Nu debout Chr 11/92 1,430

Dericks, Louis   Fr 19C
* See 1990 Edition ....

DeRome, Albert Thomas   Am 1885-1959
O/M 18x24 Spring Flowers Near Asilomar Mor 2/93 2,500
W/Pa 6x8 Kern River Canyon Mor 11/92 1,600
W/Pa 8x12 Bear Buttes, Eel River, Garberville 1920 Mor 2/93 1,300
W/Pa 12x8 Half Dome, Yosemite 1920 Mor 2/93 1,300
O/Cb 10x14 Veils of Light, Santa Cruz Mountain Mor 2/93 . 1,300
W/Pa 12x8 Gull Lake-No. of Bishop...1921 Mor 2/93 ... 1,200
W/Pa 8x9 Lone Pine Peak-Inyo County 1927 Mor 2/93 ... 1,000
O/C 6x8 Cannery Cove-May '46 Mor 11/92 600

Derrick, William Rowell   Am 1858-1941
W&H/Pb 9x7 Genre Scene with Girl, Lamb and Cat Skn 9/92   605

Derval, G.   Fr 19C
O/C 22x27 Serenade But 11/92 2,750

Des Clayes, Berthe   Can 1887-1968
O/Pn 10x14 Schooners in Harbour, Halifax Sbt 5/93 1,980

Des Fontaines, Andre   Fr 1869-
* See 1990 Edition ....

Des Gobelins, LeClerc   1734-1785
* See 1992 Edition ....

Des Jeux, Le Maitre   Fr 17C
* See 1992 Edition ....

Descubes, A*   Fr 20C**
* See 1993 Edition ....

Desflaches   Con 19C
* See 1990 Edition ....

Desgoffe, Alexandre   Fr
* See 1991 Edition ....

Desgoffe, Blaise   Fr 1830-1901
* See 1993 Edition ....

Deshayes, Charles Felix E.   Fr 1831-1895
* See 1993 Edition ....

Deshayes, Eugene   Fr 1828-1890
O/Pn 18x22 Le Campement Nomade Hnd 10/92 1,900

Deshays, Jean-Baptiste   Fr 1729-1756
* See 1991 Edition ....

Desnoyer, Francois   1894-1972
O&K/Pa 24x17 Femme Nue Devant Un Miroir 1961 Chr 2/93 . 880

Despallargues, Pedro   Spa 15C
* See 1991 Edition ....

Despeaux, Howard   Am 20C
* See 1992 Edition ....

Despiau, Charles   Fr 1874-1946
K/Pa 22x17 Femme Nue Allongee Chr 2/93 770
K/Pa/B 14x9 Nu debout Chr 11/92 770

**Desportes, Alexandre-Francois   Fr
1661-1743**
* See 1993 Edition ....

Dessar, Louis Paul   Am 1867-1952
O/C 24x30 Figure and Cart at Sunset Fre 10/92 1,400

Dessoulavy, Thomas   Br a 1829-1848
* See 1992 Edition ....

**Desubleo, Michele Di Giovanni   It
1601-1676**
* See 1993 Edition ....

Desvarreux, Raymond   Fr 1876-1963
O/C 20x21 Napoleon and His Entourage 1906 But 5/93 ... 1,725
Detaille, Jean Baptiste E.   Fr 1848-1912
O/C 19x25 Fallen Soldiers But 5/93 2,875
Detmold, Edward Julian   Br 1883-1957
Pl/Pa 9x16 Baghdad Lou 12/92 400
Detreville, Richard   Am 1864-1929
O/B 20x15 Boats Lou 3/93 275
Detroy, Leon
O&l/Pa/C 16x20 Red Tray with Fruit Sby 10/92 3,080
Detti, Cesare Auguste   It 1847-1914
O/C 19x29 Galileo at Court 78 Chr 5/93 51,750
O/C 36x29 The New Piece Chr 5/93 36,800
O/Pn 11x9 In the Garden '82 Sby 10/92 22,000
O/Pn 13x16 A Hawking Party Chr 5/93 10,350
O/C 29x21 The Recital Chr 2/93 5,500
O/C 14x11 Light Entertainment 1895 Sby 5/93 4,370
Deturck, Henri   Fr 1858-1898
* See 1993 Edition ....
Deully, Eugene   Fr 1860-
O/C 17x11 Hilltop Villa by Waterfall 1891 Slo 5/93 325
Deutsch, Boris   Rus 1892-1978
* See 1990 Edition ....
Deutsch, David   1943-
Br&l/Pa/C 84x60 Untitled Chr 10/92 5,500
Devaux, Jules Ernest   Fr 1837-
* See 1991 Edition ....
Devedeux, Louis   Fr 1820-1874
O/C 24x20 Admiring the Parrot Chr 2/93 7,700
Devieux, Henri   Fr 1839-1898
O/C 14x26 View of Venice '67 But 11/92 3,300
O/C 14x26 Venetian Scene But 11/92 1,870
Devine, Bernard   Am 1884-
O/C 30x36 Fanueil Hall, Boston 19?? Sby 3/93 3,220
Devis, Anthony   Br 1729-1817
W/Pa 11x15 Castle Over Looking River Hnz 5/93 260
Devis, Arthur   Br 1711-1787
* See 1992 Edition ....
Devis, Arthur William   1763-1822
* See 1993 Edition ....
Devos, Florence Marie   Am 1892-
O/Ab 11x14 Pastoral Landscape Eld 8/93 330
Devrient, Wilhelm   Ger 1799-
O/C 13x17 Grooming the Family Dog 1864 Chr 2/93 4,400
Dewasne, Jean   Fr 1921-
* See 1993 Edition ....
Dewey, Charles Melville   Am 1841-1937
G/Pa 21x15 The Hillside Pasture Eld 8/93 165
Dewing, Thomas Wilmer   Am 1851-1938
* See 1993 Edition ....
Dews, John Steven   Br 1949-
O/C 20x30 Ranger and Endeavour II Racing Sby 6/93 ... 68,500
Deyrolle, Theophile Louis   Fr 1844-1923
O/C 26x36 Washerwomen by a Stream Chr 5/93 8,050
O/C 29x20 Summer Afternoon in the Country Wlf 9/92 ... 4,000
Di Bartolo, Andrea   It a 1389-1428
* See 1990 Edition ....
Di Benedetto, Steve   1958-
A/C 60x60 Domestic Paralysis 1988 Chr 2/93 2,090
A/C 72x72 Gary Floyd 1990 Chr 2/93 1,760
Di Benvenuto, G. & Di Giovanni   It 1470-1524
T/Pn 8x23 Saint John the Evangelist Chr 1/93 49,500
Di Bicci, Neri   It 1419-1491
* See 1993 Edition ....
Di Bindo, Benedetto   It a 1411-1417
* See 1993 Edition ....
Di Bonaiuto, Andrea   It -1377
* See 1992 Edition ....
Di Bonaventura, Segna   It a 1298-1327
* See 1992 Edition ....
Di Cavalcanti, Emiliano   Brz 1897-
O&G/Pa/Pn 21x30 Maternidad Sby 11/92 31,900
O/C 24x20 Casal no Paisagem Chr 11/92 30,800
T/Pa/Pa 28x22 Mulher Perto do Balcao Chr 11/92 18,700

l/Pa 9x13 Luxuria Sby 11/92 2,090
Di Chirico, Giacomo   It 1845-1884
O/C 39x25 The Christening Chr 2/93 33,000
Di Cola Da Camerino, Arcangelo   It a 1416-1429
* See 1990 Edition ....
Di Cristofano, Mariotto   It 1393-1457
* See 1993 Edition ....
Di Donna, Porfirio   Am 1942-1986
O/C 24x22 Untitled 1977 1977 FHB 3/93 1,100
O/C 36x30 Center Shift 1977 FHB 3/93 900
Di Francesco, Domenico   It 1417-1491
* See 1993 Edition ....
Di Fredi, Bartolo   It
* See 1990 Edition ....
Di Ghese Vanni, Arcangelo   It a 1416-1429
* See 1991 Edition ....
Di Giovanni Del Guasta, Girola   It
* See 1990 Edition ....
Di Giovanni, Apol. & Del Buono   1415-1465
T/Pn 16x19 3 Panels from a Cassone Chr 10/92 39,600
Di Giovanni, B. & Di Benvenuto   It 1436-1518
T/Pn 8x23 Saint John the Evangelist Chr 1/93 49,500
Di Giovanni, Bartolommeo   It a 1487-1511
* See 1991 Edition ....
Di Giovanni, Benvenuto   It 1436-1518
* See 1993 Edition ....
Di Giuseppe, Mose Bianchi   It 1836-1900
* See 1993 Edition ....
Di Jacopo, Zenobio   1418-1479
* See 1992 Edition ....
Di Jongh, Tinus   SAf 20C
O/C 25x36 Between Caledon and Hermanus Slo 7/93 ... 1,300
O/C 14x23 The Karroo Slo 7/93 700
Di Leone, Andrea   It 1610-1685
* See 1992 Edition ....
Di Michelino, Domenico   It 1417-1491
* See 1993 Edition ....
Di Nardo, Mariotto   It a 1394-1424
* See 1993 Edition ....
Di Nerio, Ugolino   It a 1317-1349
* See 1993 Edition ....
Di Niccolo, Andrea   It a 1470-1512
* See 1993 Edition ....
Di Paolo, Giovanni   1403-1483
T&Gd/Pn 14x17 Head of Christ: Piece of Cross Sby 1/93 . 87,750
Di Piero, Alvaro   It
* See 1990 Edition ....
Di Pietro, Giovanni   1450-1528
O,T&Gd/Pn 13x9 The Madonna and Child Sby 1/93 43,125
Di Pietro, Sano   It 1406-1481
Gd&T/Pn 25x18 Madonna and Child Sby 5/93 167,500
Di Ridolfo, Michele   It 1503-1577
* See 1991 Edition ....
Di Rosa, Herve   20C
* See 1993 Edition ....
Di Rosselli, Bernardo Di S.   It 1450-1526
* See 1993 Edition ....
Di San Marzano, Pasquale R.   It 1851-1916
* See 1993 Edition ....
Di Simone, Giovanni di Ser G.   It 1407-1486
* See 1993 Edition ....
Di Suvero, Mark   Am 1933-
* See 1993 Edition ....
Di Tito, Santi   1536-1603
O/Pn 30x21 Personification of Natural Law Chr 5/93 74,000
Di Tomme, Luca   It 1330-1389
* See 1992 Edition ....
Diago, Roberto   Cub 1920-1957
l/Pa 11x15 Abstracto 48 Sby 11/92 4,400

G/Pa 10x10 Dos Musicos Chr 11/92 2,750
W&I/Pa 12x18 Sin Titulo 1942 Sby 5/93 1,380
Diamond, Jessica   1957-
PI&L/Pa 24x39 Those Who Dream and Do (2) Chr 2/93 . . . 1,650
Diaz De La Pena, Narcisse V.   Fr
1807-1876
O/C 24x33 Ciel D'Orage Termine '69 Sby 2/93 23,000
O/C 16x24 Faggot Gatherer in Wood 67 Chr 10/92 19,800
O/C 20x12 Une Femme Mythologique 31 Sby 10/92 18,700
O/Pn 10x15 Forest Path Sby 5/93 17,250
O/C 14x11 The Jewel Box Sby 5/93 16,100
O/Pn 18x27 Gathering Faggots, Fontainebleau 56 Chr 5/93 14,950
O/Pn 16x11 Nymphs in the Forest Chr 5/93 14,950
O/Pn 14x9 Toilet of Venus Chr 5/93 12,650
O/Pn 9x11 Faggot Gatherer Chr 5/93 11,500
O/C 22x17 Chemin en Foret Avec Bucheronne Sby 2/93 . . 10,925
O/Pn 10x13 La Foret de Fontainebleau Sby 2/93 8,050
O/C 7x10 Oriental Women in Landscape Sby 5/93 6,900
O/Pn 10x8 Meute de Chiens en Foret 53 Sby 2/93 5,750
O/C 16x20 In the Forest '54 Lou 9/92 3,900
O/C 22x19 Clearing in the Forest '53 Eld 8/93 3,850
O/Pn 6x9 Faggot Gatherer in Forest Clearing Chr 5/93 1,955
Diaz, Huertas Angel   Spa 19C
O/Cb 12x10 Still Life with Grapes Fre 10/92 850
Diaz, N.
O/C 11x16 Women and Cherub Ald 3/93 2,300
Dibbets, Jan   20C
W,Pe&Ph/Pa 30x40 Construction for a Grasspol Sby 11/92 . 3,850
Dickey, Dan   Am 1910-1961
* See 1993 Edition . . . .
Dickey, Robert Livingston   Am 1861-1944
C&W/Pa 11x17 Dogs Represent France, Britain, US Ilh 11/92   250
Dickinson, Edwin W.   Am 1891-1978
O/M 8x10 Vuillet's House 1946 Sby 9/92 8,250
Pe/Pa 10x8 Schooner; Greece: Two 24 Sby 9/92 5,225
Pe/Pa 8x5 Concert Touche Sby 9/92 1,980
O/C 26x30 Judith 1937 Sby 3/93 1,380
Dickinson, Preston   Am 1891-1930
O/B 6x4 Still Life 24 Chr 9/92 12,100
C&I/Pa 22x10 High Bridge Chr 9/92 7,700
Dickman, Charles   Am 1863-1943
* See 1993 Edition . . . .
Dicksee, Frank (Sir)   Eng 1853-1928
O/C 38x47 The Mirror 1896 Sby 2/93 800,000
Dicksee, Herbert Thomas   Br 1862-
* See 1991 Edition . . . .
Dicksee, Thomas Francis   Br 1819-1895
* See 1993 Edition . . . .
Dickson, Jane   20C
* See 1991 Edition . . . .
Dickson, William   Am 20C
O/C 29x39 Low Tide '92 Hnd 10/92 1,300
Didier, Jules   Fr 1831-1892
* See 1991 Edition . . . .
Didier-Pouget, William   Fr 1864-1959
O/C 18x26 Bruyeres en Fleurs But 5/93 4,600
O/C 20x26 Vallee de la Dordogne But 11/92 1,980
Diebenkorn, Richard   Am 1922-
G&L/Pa 38x25 Untitled 84 Sby 5/93 101,500
O/C 31x25 Reclining Nude - Pink Stripe 1962 Sby 11/92 . . 82,500
I&Pe/Pa 14x17 Sleeping Nude 61 Sby 5/93 51,750
I/Pa 16x13 Untitled 64 Sby 10/92 45,100
I&Pe/Pa 17x14 Untitled 65 Sby 10/92 27,500
Y/Pa 17x14 Seated Nude with Necklace 66 Sby 5/93 16,100
Pe&C/Pa 13x17 Untitled 65 Sby 10/92 8,800
Diedricksen, Theodore   Am 20C
O/C 44x38 Egyptian Fantasy 1912 Sby 3/93 10,925
Diefenbach, Anton Heinrich   Ger
1831-1914
O/C 20x15 The Young Shepherdess Sby 1/93 8,050
Diehl, Arthur Vidal   Am 1870-1929
O/B 12x18 Sunny Day, Provincetown 1927 Eld 8/93 4,180
O/Cd 11x31 A Trophy Fish 1917 Sby 6/93 4,025
O/C 20x40 Dunes at Provincetown 1914 Skn 9/92 1,320
O/B 20x40 Dunes, Late Afternoon 1918 Skn 5/93 990

O/B 17x17 Fishing Boats and Figures Skn 11/92 880
O/B 20x29 Oriental Street 1922 Skn 3/93 880
O/C 12x18 Venetian Port 1919 Fre 4/93 750
O/C 12x18 Seascape Eld 4/93 715
O/C 12x24 Harbor Scene with Fishing Boats 1915 Eld 8/93 . . 660
O/C 9x18 Harbor Scene with Fishermen Eld 7/93 605
O/C 12x25 Cape Cod Scene Eld 11/92 550
O/C 9x18 Seascape with Dunes 1925 Eld 8/93 550
O/B 6x13 Ocean Dunes Wes 3/93 495
O/C 10x14 Provincetown Dunes Skn 5/93 275
O/Ab 14x12 North African Street Scene at Night FHB 3/93 . . . 225
O/C 18x36 Off Race Point, 1912 Eld 4/93 220
Dielman, Frederick   Am 1847-1935
O/C 16x11 Feeding the Dog Chr 5/93 4,025
O/C 36x16 The Scholar Sby 3/93 1,150
Dielmann, Jacob Friedrich F.   Ger
1809-1885
PI/Pa 9x8 The Hunter's Return But 5/93 1,150
Diem, Peter Karl   Am 1890-1956
* See 1992 Edition . . . .
Dier, Erhard Amadeus   Aus 1893-1969
O/Por 10x12 Nude 1939 Lou 3/93 400
Dierckx, Pierre Jacques   1854-1947
O/C 27x33 Family at Breakfast Chr 5/93 1,380
Dieterle, Marie   Fr 1856-1935
O/C 24x20 Cows Drinking Chr 5/93 3,220
O/C 15x11 Cows Wading Chr 5/93 2,760
Dietrich, Adelheid   Am 1827-
O/C 15x17 Grapes, Peaches, Flowers 1867 Sby 12/92 . . . 46,750
O/C 23x19 Autumn Still Life with Blueberries 1874 But 6/93 18,400
O/C 23x19 Autumn Still Life 1874 But 6/93 17,250
Dietrich, Adolf
* See 1991 Edition . . . .
Dietrich, Christian Wilhelm E.   Ger
1712-1774
* See 1991 Edition . . . .
Dietz, H. R.   Am 1860-
* See 1990 Edition . . . .
Dietzsch, Barbara Regina   Ger 1706-1783
* See 1990 Edition . . . .
Dieudonne, Eugene Paul   Fr 1825-
O/C 41x26 Lady in a White Lace Dress Chr 10/92 8,800
Diez, Carlos Cruz   Ven 1923-
* See 1993 Edition . . . .
Diezler, Jakob   Ger a 1826-1850
O/C 17x44 Castle Stolzen Fels on Rhine 1845 Sby 10/92 . 12,100
Diezmann, F.
H&W/Pa 13x20 Indian Camp, Punta Arenas Sby 5/93 1,150
H&W/Pa 12x21 View From Colorado 1867 Sby 5/93 1,150
DiGemma, Joseph P.   Am 1910-
O/M 24x37 View of Rockport Harbor Skn 5/93 990
O/M 24x37 Rockport Harbor in Winter Skn 5/93 550
Dike, Phil   Am 1906-
* See 1993 Edition . . . .
Dill, Laddie John   Am 1943-
O/C 49x85 Untitled, 1982 But 10/92 3,300
MM/Wd 42x84 Untitled 1977 But 4/93 1,725
A/C 24x48 Untitled, 1985 But 4/93 1,035
O/Cot 29x21 Hand Painted T-Shirt '83 But 10/92 550
Dill, Otto   Ger 1884-1957
O/C 28x40 A Close Finish 1925 Chr 5/93 23,000
Dillaway, Theodore M.
O/B 20x24 Spring-New Hope Backyards 1942 Ald 5/93 400
Dillens, Adolphe Alexandre   Bel
1821-1877
* See 1990 Edition . . . .
Dillens, Hendrick Joseph   Bel 1812-1972
O/Pn 18x14 Flower Girl Outside a Cottage 1850 Chr 5/93 . . 4,830
Diller, Burgoyne   Am 1906-1964
* See 1993 Edition . . . .
Dillon, C. J.   Am 20C
O/C 22x18 Seated Woman Mys 3/93 220
Dillon, F.
O/B 11x18 Still Life Ironstone Sugar Bowl '96 Eld 11/92 176

Dinckel, George W. Am 1890-
O/C/B 24x30 Seascape Lou 3/93 950
Dine, Jim Am 1935-
Pe,H&C/Pa 60x36 Untitled 1974 Sby 5/93 28,750
W/Pa 13x13 Four Hearts 1970 But 10/92 7,150
Dineen, Alice
O/C 18x22 Leopard and Peacock 1936 Ald 3/93 400
Dinet, Etienne Fr 1861-1929
* See 1992 Edition . . . .
Dingle, John Darley (Adrian) Can 1911-1974
O/B 20x26 April's Temperament 1958 Sbt 5/93 440
Diranian, Serkis Tur 19C
* See 1991 Edition . . . .
Discart, Jean
* See 1991 Edition . . . .
Discepoli, Giovanni Battista 1590-1660
* See 1992 Edition . . . .
Disler, Martin 1949-
O/C 102x77 Das Gesicht Chr 11/92 12,100
Pt&l/Pa 62x103 Untitled 80 Sby 10/92 3,300
Os/Pa 16x20 Untitled 85 Chr 11/92 990
Disney Studios Am 20C
G/Cel 9x10 Mickey/Sorcerer's Apprent. 1940 Skn 9/92 . . . 4,400
G/Cel 11x12 Two Scenes from Fantasia, 1940 Skn 9/92 . . . 3,300
Cel 17x10 Lady & The Tramp Dum 4/93 2,750
Cel 11x8 Shere Kahn, The Jungle Book Dum 4/93 1,500
G/Cel 9x9 Goofy from the Art of Skiing Skn 9/92 990
G/Cel 8x8 Donald and Tootsie 1938 Skn 11/92 880
G/Cel 7x6 Dumbo from Dumbo, 1941 Skn 9/92 880
G/Cel 8x10 Jiminy Cricket Skn 3/93 522
G/Cel 6x5 Jiminy from Pinocchio, 1939 Skn 9/92 522
Cel 9x6 Donald Duck Dum 4/93 400
W&Pe/Pa 4x5 Thumper Dum 4/93 250
Pe/Pa 16x13 Brian Rose, Sleeping Beauty Dum 4/93 120
Pe/Pa 16x13 Brian Rose, Sleeping Beauty Dum 4/93 110
Cel 12x10 Casey Bats Again Dum 4/93 110
Cel 16x13 Hound Dog, Aristocats Dum 4/93 70
Distelboom 1653-1695
O/C 26x21 Still Life Poppies, Anemones Sby 5/93 10,925
Diteren, Vince Dut 20C
O/Pn 12x16 Dutch Scene Fre 4/93 110
Ditscheiner, Adolf Gustav Ger 1846-1904
* See 1990 Edition . . . .
Diveria, Achille Fr 1800-1857
l/Pa 2x3 Hunt; Offering Alms: Four Slo 4/93 450
Dix, Harry Am 20C
O/C 10x12 Downtown New York Fre 10/92 400
Dix, Otto Ger 1891-1969
S&W/Pa 20x15 Greisin Sby 2/93 70,700
W&Y/Pa/B 27x19 Kind im Mohnfeld 55 Chr 2/93 12,100
Pl&Br/Pa 16x16 Homunculus Sby 2/93 10,925
Pe/Pa 17x13 Schwangere Frau 1921 Sby 2/93 8,050
Y/Pa 11x10 Relaisposten Sby 2/93 4,888
Pe/Pa 19x14 Studie Zu Einem Selbstportrait; Dbl 24 Sby 2/93 4,025
W&Pe/Pa 19x15 Studie Schlafende Traumende Sby 2/93 . . 2,530
K/Pa 18x14 Sklave 15 Sby 6/93 2,070
Dixon, Francis Fitzroy Can 1856-1914
Pl/Pa 9x24 La Normandie 1881 Sbt 11/92 1,848
Dixon, Francis Stillwell Am 1879-1967
O/C 20x26 View of Point Lobos, California Skn 5/93 2,200
O/M 8x10 Cottage by the Stone Bridge Skn 9/92 495
Dixon, Maynard Am 1875-1946
O/C/B 12x16 Peak and Clouds 1945 But 3/93 16,500
O/Cb 9x6 The Lone Rider 15 Skn 3/93 16,500
O/C/B 12x16 Promise of Spring 1942 But 3/93 14,300
G&Pe/Pa 25x14 Indian Encampment 1940 Sby 3/93 9,775
O/B 10x14 Skies of New Mexico 1931 But 10/92 7,700
G/Pa 12x10 Desert Clouds But 6/93 7,475
G/Pa 9x19 Saguaro Landscape But 6/93 7,475
Pl&S/Pa 8x11 Youapai County, Arizona 1900 But 6/93 5,750
C/Pa 5x3 Diner 04 But 3/93 1,870
Pe/Pa 5x5 San Francisco Character #5 1904 But 3/93 1,870
Pe/Pa 4x4 Black Bucker 1942 But 6/93 1,495
Pl/Pa 4x4 Indians on Horseback 1942 But 6/93 1,380

P,Pe&l/Pa 6x5 Riders and Burros, Guadalajara 05 But 6/93 . 1,320
Pe/Pa 3x6 Figures in Desert 1937 But 6/93 1,265
Pa/Pa 5x6 Roundup at Flathead 09 But 6/93 1,265
H/Pa 4x4 Two Studies: Grazing Horse; Cloud But 10/92 605
Diziani, Antonio It 1737-1797
* See 1992 Edition . . . .
Do, Giovanni It 17C
* See 1990 Edition . . . .
Doane, Henry W. Am 1905-
* See 1993 Edition . . . .
Dobbin, John Eng 1815-1888
W/Pa 17x24 Canal View, Amsterdam 1877 Slo 5/93 500
Dobkowski, Jan Pol 1942-
Pe/Pa 20x29 Genesis XXXVII and Genesis CXII (2) Hnd 3/93 . 50
Doboujinski, Mstislav
G&Pe/Pa 8x10 La Dame aux Piques 1925 Sby 10/92 770
Dobrotka, Edward Am 20C
O/C 30x20 King, Queen, Court Tudor Wtf 9/92 750
W/Pa 12x23 Cleveland Flats (3) Wtf 9/92 250
W/B 15x20 World's Fair Exposition Wtf 9/92 225
W/Pa 12x19 Cleveland Fire (2) Wtf 9/92 170
W/B Var Four Watercolors Wtf 9/92 150
W/B 15x22 Steamer Ship Coming into Dock Wtf 9/92 150
W/B 20x7 Ice Skaters (2) Wtf 9/92 30
Dobrowsky, Josef Aut 1889-1962
* See 1991 Edition . . . .
Dobson, William Charles Thomas Br 1817-1898
* See 1991 Edition . . . .
Docharty, James Br 1829-1878
O/C 12x18 The Isle of Shoals 74 Skn 3/93 1,430
Dockree, Mark Edwin Br 19C
* See 1992 Edition . . . .
Dodd, Louis Br -1943
O/Pn 18x30 Occupation of Rhode Island by Brit. Sby 6/93 . 8,625
Dodge, M. DeLeftwich Am 20C
O/C 36x29 Louise and Baby Hnz 5/93 400
Dodge, Ozias Am 1868-1925
O/C 24x32 Winter Landscape Mys 3/93 302
O/B Var On the Wharf; Pasture Near Beach: 2 Mys 12/92 . . 162
Dodge, William DeLeftwich Am 1867-1935
O/C 41x24 Golden Glow Sby 3/93 6,038
W/Pa 9x12 Two Watercolors '99 Fre 4/93 120
Dodson, Frank Eng 1888-1963
C&K/Pa 21x14 Seated Nude 1953 Eld 8/93 440
Doeming, John Carl Am 20C
O/C 26x32 Rockaneck Street, Gloucester Hnz 5/93 725
Doemling, John C. Am 20C
O/Cb 16x20 Barn in Landscape Mor 2/93 400
Dogherty, Felix Am 19C
W/Pa 9x12 Washington on Horseback 1810 Sby 3/93 1,495
Dohanos, Stevan Am 1907-
G/Pa 22x20 Waiting in Line at Grocery Store Ih 5/93 26,000
O&H/M 8x10 A Day at the Fair Skn 3/93 825
O/M 20x24 Logs in Winter 48 Chr 5/93 805
W/Pa 23x30 Steps of New York Public Library Chr 5/93 805
W/Pa 16x33 Sandbagged French Foeign Legion Ih 5/93 700
Dohlmann, Augusta Johanne H. Dan 1847-1914
* See 1993 Edition . . . .
Dokoupil, Jiri Georg 1954-
O/C 83x83 The Post Nuclear Mother 1983 Chr 11/92 7,700
O/C 79x59 Untitled 81 Chr 11/92 7,700
MM/Cd 33x25 Untitled Chr 5/93 2,875
Dolan, A. Am a 1881-1883
O/C 14x11 White Mountain View '81 Skn 11/92 275
Dolci, Carlo It 1616-1686
* See 1990 Edition . . . .
Dolinsky, Nathan Am 1889-
* See 1993 Edition . . . .
Doll, Anton Ger 1826-1887
O/C 11x16 Peasants on a Frozen Pond Chr 10/92 9,900
Dollond, W. Anstey Br a 1879-1889
W/B 18x8 Day Dreams Sby 1/93 2,990

Dolph, John Henry   Am 1835-1903
O/C 22x30 Baby Playing with Kittens Chr 5/93 6,900
O/C 9x12 Asleep by the Fireplace Chr 12/92 1,870
Domela, Jan   Am 1894-1973
O/B 16x20 Old Mammoth Road But 3/93 2,090
O/B 12x16 Farm and Fields But 6/93 748
O/B 12x16 Farm Near Morro Bay But 6/93 632
O/Cb 12x16 Houses and Boats, Summer But 6/93 488
Domergue, Jean-Gabriel   Fr 1889-1962
O/C 46x35 Portrait of Jenny Dolly 28 Sby 2/93 17,250
O/C 46x35 Portrait of Rosie Dolly 28 Sby 2/93 17,250
O/C 22x18 Seated Ballerina Sby 6/93 8,050
O/C 26x18 L'elegante Chr 11/92 7,700
O/C 22x18 Society Beauty Sby 2/93 7,475
O&Pe/C/M 16x13 Lady in Evening Dress Sby 2/93 4,600
O/C 13x10 Portrait of a Lady Sby 10/92 3,300
O/C 18x15 Portrait of Young Woman Sby 6/93 3,163
O/C 11x9 Portrait de Femme Chr 2/93 1,650
O/Cb 9x8 Head of Young Woman Sby 6/93 1,610
Domingo Y Marques, Francisco   Spa 1842-1920
O/C 15x18 Grapes and Apples and Straw Basket Mys 3/93 . 1,100
O/C 11x18 Toro de Carreta 1874 Hnd 12/92 1,000
Domingo, Roberto Y Fallola   Spa 1883-1956
I,H&W/Pa 6x9 Bullfighters (Four) But 4/93 1,725
I&H/Pa 5x8 Bullfighters (Pair) But 4/93 518
W&G/Pa 12x6 Toros But 4/93 431
Dominguez, Oscar   Spa 1906-1958
Pl/Pa 9x12 Untitled: Album of 14 Drawings 50 Sby 2/93 . . 18,400
Dominique, John A.   Am 1893-
O/C 28x36 Mountains Near Matilya Dam 1960 But 3/93 . . . 3,300
Dommersen, William   Dut 1850-1927
O/C 11x15 Gathering at a Town Square 1880 Chr 10/92 . . . 2,420
O/C 16x24 Dutch Scene Hnd 5/93 1,300
Dommershuizen, Cornelis C.   Dut 1842-1928
* See 1993 Edition
Dommerson, Pieter Christian   Dut 1834-1908
* See 1992 Edition
Dommerson, William Raymond   Dut -1927
O/C 12x18 Harbor Scene Dum 1/93 1,800
Domoto, Hisao   Jap 1928-
O/C 77x60 Solution de Continuite #29 1964 Chr 11/92 . . . 82,500
Donald, John Milne   Br 1819-1858
* See 1993 Edition
Donaldson, Andrew Benjamin   Br 1840-1919
* See 1991 Edition
Donat, Frederick Reginald   Bel 1830-1870
O/Pn 16x21 Enjoying the Spirits Lou 3/93 2,000
Donati, Enrico   Am 1909-
O&Sd/C 35x45 Fossil Series 3000 B.C. 62 Chr 11/92 6,050
Donati, Lazzaro   It 1926-
O/Wd 20x30 Il Mattino 54 Sby 6/93 690
O/B 27x19 Le Nuvole Sby 2/93 575
O/B 14x16 Sotto La Neve Sby 2/93 575
Donducci, Giovanni Andrea   1575-1655
O/C 15x18 The Flight into Egypt Sby 10/92 9,350
Donelson, Earl   Am 20C
O/C 25x30 Nude with Black Slippers Fre 10/92 500
Donnelly, Thomas   Am 1893-
O/C 28x36 Progress of Industry 1938 Doy 5/93 1,210
Donoho, Gaines Ruger   Am 1857-1916
* See 1993 Edition
Donouy, Alexandre-Hyacinthe   Fr 1757-1841
* See 1990 Edition
Dorazio, Piero   It 1927-
* See 1993 Edition
Dore, Gustave   Fr 1832-1883
O/C 104x123 The Murder of Riccio Chr 10/92 4,400
Doret, E.   Con 19C
* See 1992 Edition

Dorne, Albert   Am 1904-1965
* See 1993 Edition
Dorset, Gerald
* See 1992 Edition
Dorsey, William   Am 20C
O/C 24x36 Big Sur Coastline But 3/93 1,980
O/C 40x30 Eucalyptus Coastal Mor 6/93 1,210
O/C 24x36 Santa Barbara Beach But 6/93 1,150
O/C 16x20 Eucalyptus Coastal Mor 6/93 1,100
O/C 48x26 Eucalyptus Pathway with Blue Iris Mor 6/93 . . . 1,100
O/C 40x50 Landscape by Stream Mor 6/93 990
O/M 26x34 Panoramic Landscape Mor 11/92 600
O/C 24x20 Edge of an Orange Grove But 3/93 550
O/C 28x22 Under the Avocado Tree Mor 6/93 495
O/C 12x9 Sycamore Canyon Mor 6/93 358
Doskow, Israel   Am 1881-
* See 1993 Edition
Doss, Galen W.   Am 1873-1957
O/Cb 14x11 The Flower Vendor Mor 2/93 600
Dosso Dossi   It 1517-1548
O/C 32x53 Figures on Country Road Sby 1/93 200,500
Dou, Gerrit   Dut 1613-1675
* See 1990 Edition
Doucet, Henri Lucien   Fr 1856-1895
O/C 18x14 A Harem Beauty Chr 10/92 4,400
Dougherty, James   Am 20C
* See 1993 Edition
Dougherty, Parke Custis   Am 1867-
* See 1993 Edition
Dougherty, Paul   Am 1877-1947
O/C 26x36 Crashing Surf But 3/93 13,200
O/C 27x36 A Freshening Gale Chr 9/92 6,600
O/C 24x29 Rocks and Surf But 10/92 6,600
O/C 36x34 Rocky Coast 1901 But 10/92 6,050
O/C 26x36 Pounding Breakers Yng 5/93 1,750
O/B 20x30 Night on the Baltic 1902 Yng 2/93 550
Doughty, Thomas   Am 1793-1856
O/C/M 43x56 Early Winter Chr 3/93 46,000
O/C 21x29 Landscape by the Dam Sby 12/92 11,000
O/C 20x28 A Southern Swamp Chr 5/93 10,925
Douglas, Edward Algernon S.   Br 19C
O/C 14x28 Four Hunt Scenes 1878 Skn 11/92 16,500
O/C 24x12 A Good Day; A Blank Day (2) 1907 Chr 6/93 . . 13,800
Douglas, Edwin   Br 1848-1914
* See 1993 Edition
Douglas, Haldane   Am 1893-1980
* See 1993 Edition
Douglas, Robert   Am 20C
* See 1992 Edition
Douglass, Robert W.
O/C 20x15 Kneeling Man with Gun & Diamonds Ih 5/93 . . . 250
Doutreleau, Pierre   Fr 1938-
O/C 24x36 Untitled Wlf 12/92 650
Douven, Jan Frans   1656-1727
* See 1993 Edition
Dove, Arthur Garfield   Am 1880-1946
O/B 30x40 Brick Barge with Landscape 1930 Sby 12/92 . 242,000
O/C 20x28 Barn Next Door Chr 12/92 176,000
W/Pa 5x9 Pier and Boathouses Doy 5/93 9,900
W&Pl/Pa/B 5x7 Abstraction, Autumn Leaves Chr 9/92 8,800
Dow, Arthur Wesley   Am 1857-1922
O/Cb 14x20 June Morning/View of Ipswich Skn 5/93 8,800
Dow, Jane Margaret   Am 1946-
L&O/C 54x72 Soul Song 1981 Slo 4/93 600
Dow, William J.   Am 1891-1973
W/Pa 10x14 Surf Yng 2/93 100
Dowalskoff, J. A.   Rus 19C
* See 1990 Edition
Dowd, Robert   Am 20C
O/C 28x40 Twenty Dollar Bill But 4/93 3,737
O/C 32x38 Inverted Jenny 68 But 10/92 2,750
W&C/Pa 11x16 Mail Train But 10/92 1,760
Downes, Rackstraw   Am 20C
* See 1993 Edition

Downey   Eng 20C
O/C 38x28 King Edward VII Slo 5/93 900
Downie, John P.   Eng 1871-1945
* See 1991 Edition . . . .
Downing, Thomas   Am 1928-
* See 1991 Edition . . . .
Doyen, Gustave   Fr
* See 1993 Edition . . . .
Draegert, Joe   Am 1945-
P/Pa 30x15 Irises 86 But 10/92 522
Draper, Herbert James   Br 1864-1920
* See 1992 Edition . . . .
Draper, William Franklin   Am 1912-
O/B 13x15 At the Circus But 12/92 1,430
Draver, O.
O/C 16x20 River Scene Dum 10/92 400
Drayton, Grace   Am 1875-1936
Pl&W/Pa 24x18 Dimples Runs Away 1914 Ih 5/93 1,100
W/Pa 14x14 Tessa Fre 4/93 900
I&W/Pa 24x18 Sunday Comic "Dimples" 1914 Ih 11/92 . . 850
Dreier, Katherine Sophie   Am 1877-1952
O/C 16x30 Improvisation 1938 Chr 5/93 6,900
Dressler, Edward James   Am 1859-1907
O/C 30x40 Summer Landscape 1901 Sby 3/93 2,760
Drew, Clement   Am 1808-1889
O/C 18x26 Outward Bound Off Boston Light 1863 Eld 7/93 . 3,520
O/C 14x22 Boston Light Southeast Gale Eld 7/93 3,410
O/B 9x12 Thacher Island Lights Yng 5/93 1,100
O/B 11x13 Marshfield Beach 1864 Eld 11/92 550
Drew, George W.   Am 1875-1968
O/C 18x36 Day of Yachting 1938 Skn 11/92 1,100
O/C 20x30 Summer Landscape 1941 Sby 9/92 880
O/Pn 7x11 Sunset Over the Marsh Mys 12/92 385
O/C 10x14 House on a River Fre 10/92 150
Drewes, Werner   Am 1899-1965
W/Pa 6x9 Abstraction 35 Sby 9/92 1,320
W&Pe/Pa 8x7 Cubist Abstraction Sby 9/92 1,100
W&Pe/Pa 8x7 Abstraction Chr 9/92 770
O/C 4x6 Abstract Composition '43 Wes 5/93 660
W/Pa 9x8 Composition Wes 10/92 660
C/Pa 8x6 Abstract Composition Wes 5/93 248
Driben, Peter   Am 20C
O/Pn 20x14 Man Smoking a Pipe Lou 6/93 175
Driggs, Elsie   Am 1898-1992
W&Pe/Pa 15x20 Hark, Hark, The Dogs Do Bark 1937 Sby 3/93 978
W&Pe/Pa 17x15 Soul Selects Her Own Society 1938 Sby 9/92 715
W&Pe/Pa 15x14 Apollo and Daphne Chr 3/93 460
P&O/C 30x40 C. S. Convertables Inc. 1985 Ald 5/93 400
P&O/C 24x47 Woman with Vase of Flowers 1984 Ald 5/93 . . 225
P&O/C 32x36 The Director 1987 Ald 5/93 195
P&O/C 47x29 Carytide and Stickball 1985 Ald 5/93 115
Driscole, M. A.   Am 19C
O/C 14x20 Mackerel Wlf 5/93 175
Driskell, Eleanore Johnson   Am 20C
* See 1993 Edition . . . .
Drolling, Martin   Fr 1752-1817
* See 1992 Edition . . . .
Droochsloot, Cornelisz.   Dut 1630-1673
* See 1992 Edition . . . .
Droochsloot, Joost Cornelisz.   Dut 1586-1666
O/Pn 16x34 Winter: Elegant Figures Promenading Chr 1/93 85,800
O/Pn 16x34 Summer: Figures Promenading 1624 Chr 1/93 44,000
Drost, Willem   Dut -1678
* See 1991 Edition . . . .
Drown, William Staples   Am -1915
O/C 11x15 Street Scene St. Augustine, Florida Sby 3/93 . . 345
Druet, Antoine   Fr 1857-
* See 1993 Edition . . . .
Drumaux, Angelina
O/C 46x32 Lilas Pourpre Sby 2/93 2,415
Drummond, Arthur   Br 1871-1951
* See 1993 Edition . . . .
Dryander, Johann Friedrich   1756-1812
* See 1993 Edition . . . .

Dryden, Helen   Am 1887-
W&G/Pa 18x14 Two Women Hoisting Umbrella Ih 11/92 . . 3,000
Dryer, Moira   1957-1992
A/Pn 48x61 Box Plaid 1990 Chr 11/92 6,600
Drysdale, Alexander John   Am 1870-1934
O&S/Pb 22x27 On the Bayou 1916 Lou 3/93 1,700
G/Pa 20x30 Southern Landscape with Willow Tree Sby 3/93 1,150
O/B 20x30 Swamp Scene 1917 Lou 9/92 600
Du Bois, Guy Pene   Am 1884-1958
O/B 26x20 Waiting for the Train 1917 Sby 12/92 68,750
O/C 36x29 Class Reunion 1924 Sby 12/92 55,000
O/C 24x20 Sunday Walkers '36 Sby 5/93 48,875
O/C 30x40 Race Day, Saratoga Sby 5/93 48,300
O/C 23x15 Study for Emancipation Mural 36 Chr 12/92 . . 20,900
O/Pa 15x22 Summer Landscape Sby 9/92 3,300
W&I/Pa 17x13 In God's Country Sby 9/92 1,100
I&H/Pa 12x9 Seated Artist with Model 05 Sby 3/93 863
PI/Pa 14x10 Wind Blown Tree Chr 12/92 770
Du Bois, Yvonne Pene   Am 1913-
* See 1993 Edition . . . .
Du Frenes, Rudolf Hirth   Ger 1846-1916
* See 1993 Edition . . . .
Du Paty, Leon & Poilpot, Theo.   Fr 19C
* See 1993 Edition . . . .
Du Pavillon, Isidore Pean   Fr 1790-1856
* See 1993 Edition . . . .
Du Puigaudeau, Ferdinand   Fr 1864-1930
* See 1993 Edition . . . .
Dubbels, Hendrik-Jacobsz.   1621-1707
O/C 45x61 Dutch Man-of-War at Anchor 1654 Chr 5/93 . 266,500
Dube, Mrs. Mattie   Am 1861-
* See 1993 Edition . . . .
Dubert, J. J.   Eur 19C
O/C 8x10 Fete Champetre: Pair But 5/93 3,450
Dubois
T/C 39x55 Lady Holding Mandolin Dum 6/93 500
Dubois, Arsene   Fr 19C
* See 1991 Edition . . . .
Dubois, Charles Edouard   Am 1847-1885
O/C 34x52 Evening at East Hampton, L.I. Sby 9/92 1,210
Dubois, Gaston   Con 19C
* See 1991 Edition . . . .
Dubois, Maurice Pierre   Fr 20C
* See 1991 Edition . . . .
Dubord, Jean Pierre   Fr 1949-
O/C 30x35 Le Jardin en Automne Wes 3/93 2,200
O/C 21x26 Ste. Marguerite Sur Duclair Wes 12/92 1,650
O/C 16x13 La Rue Sous la Neige a Maromme Wes 12/92 . . 880
Dubos, Angele   Fr 1844-
O/C 30x24 Heureux Age 1877 Sby 5/93 14,950
Dubourjal, Savinien Edme   Fr 1795-1853
P/Pa 17x13 Portrait of Mary Seager 1844 Wes 10/92 138
Dubreuil, Victor   Am a 1880-1910
* See 1992 Edition . . . .
Dubufe, Edouard Louis   Fr 1820-1883
* See 1993 Edition . . . .
Dubuffet, Jean   Fr 1901-1985
A/C 39x32 Passe l'heure 80 Chr 11/92 225,500
O/C 37x29 Noeud dans cheveux 55 Chr 11/92 198,000
A/C 39x32 Empressements 80 Chr 10/92 159,500
O&L/C 32x26 Paysage au ciel clair 56 Chr 11/92 143,000
G/Pa 15x21 Oasis 48 Chr 11/92 44,000
A&L/Pa 14x10 Sequence XXV 79 Sby 11/92 34,100
L&G/Pa 25x18 Topographie aux six pierres 58 Chr 11/92 . 26,400
Pnc/Pa/B 10x12 Arabe en Priere 48 Sby 11/92 19,800
I/Pa 10x13 Personnage Dans Un Paysage 60 Sby 5/93 . . 19,550
PI/Pa 9x12 Personnage dans un Paysage 60 Chr 11/92 . . 16,500
G&Mk/Pa 11x17 Texte Logologique X 67 Sby 11/92 16,500
Mk/Pa 10x7 La Tasse de The 66 Sby 11/92 14,300
G/Pa/B 10x13 Palmeraie Aux Roses 48 Sby 5/93 13,800
Mk/Pa 10x7 L'Arbre V 66 Sby 11/92 12,100
Bp&Mk/Pa 11x8 Maison de Province 64 Sby 10/92 9,900
Mk&L/Pa 9x11 Chien 73 Sby 2/93 9,775
Mk/Pa 10x7 La Tasse de The 66 Sby 2/93 9,200
Mk/Pa 11x8 Personnage (Buste en Profil) 67 Sby 5/93 . . . 8,050

Mk/Pa 10x7 Figure Enseigne VI (M199) 66 Sby 10/92 3,575
Dubuis, George S.   Am 20C
  * See 1992 Edition ....
Dubuisson, Alexander   Fr 1805-1870
  * See 1993 Edition ....
Ducaire-Roque, Maryse   Fr 20C
  * See 1992 Edition ....
Ducat, A.   Fr 19C
  O/B 8x13 Moonlit Landscape Lou 6/93 150
Duchamp, Marcel   Fr 1887-1968
  * See 1992 Edition ....
Duchamp, Suzanne   Fr 1889-1963
  * See 1993 Edition ....
Duck, Jacob   Dut 1600-1660
  * See 1991 Edition ....
Dudley, Charles
  O/C 12x16 Hunting Dogs Dum 7/93 850
Dudley, Frank V.   Am 1868-1957
  O/C 27x30 The Trail to Arcady Hnd 9/92 3,200
Duena, Victor   Phi 1888-1966
  G/Pa 12x17 Lady with Poodle 64 But 10/92 330
Duesberry, Joellyn   20C
  * See 1991 Edition ....
Duessel, H. A.   20C
  O/C 8x16 Landscapes: Pair Eld 8/93 550
Dufaug, G. A.   Fr 19C
  * See 1990 Edition ....
Duff, John   1943-
  H&A/Pa 23x19 Untitled 81 Chr 2/93 1,210
Duffaut, Prefete   Hai 1929-
  O/M 30x24 Tresors de Reine Herzulie 1955 Chr 11/92 . 5,720
  O/M 24x16 Imaginary Landscape Sby 6/93 1,495
  O/C 16x20 Haitian Hill Town Hnd 3/93 600
  O/C 8x10 City by the Sea 46 Skn 3/93 550
Duffield, William   Br 1816-1863
  O/C 21x12 Fruit and Stoneware Jug 1862 But 5/93 4,025
Dufner, Edward   Am 1872-1957
  O/C/B 26x31 Morning Sunshine Chr 12/92 57,200
  W&G/Pb 25x30 Summer Noon Skn 5/93 8,800
  W/Pa/B 15x20 Coastal Inlet Sby 9/92 660
Dufour, Bernard
  O/C 32x40 Untitled 56 Sby 10/92 1,650
Dufour, P.   Con 20C
  * See 1992 Edition ....
Dufresne, Charles   Fr 1876-1934
  O&P/Pa/C 14x18 La Petite Chasse Chr 5/93 3,105
Dufy, Jean   Fr 1888-1964
  O/C 28x36 Le Havre, Bateaux au Port Sby 11/92 46,750
  O/C 20x24 Ile de la cite Chr 11/92 39,600
  O/C 25x31 Interieur au Bouquet de Roses Sby 11/92 .. 39,600
  O/C 22x26 Paris, Champ de Courses Sby 5/93 37,950
  O/C 20x24 Le Champ de Courses Sby 5/93 35,650
  O/C 18x24 Au Cirque, Parade Equestre Sby 2/93 29,900
  O/C 18x22 Paris, La Seine Sby 11/92 28,600
  O/C 24x32 La Ferme Sby 11/92 27,500
  O/C 13x16 Vue de Paris Sby 5/93 26,450
  O/C 18x22 Elegantes et Cavaliers au Bois 29 Sby 2/93 . 25,300
  O/C 22x18 Bois de Boulogne Chr 10/92 24,200
  O/C 18x15 Nature Morte a la Bouteille 24 Sby 11/92 ... 22,000
  O/C 32x39 Paysage a Boussay 1922 Chr 11/92 22,000
  O/C 18x22 Le Cirque Sby 5/93 21,850
  O/C 18x25 Preuilly Sur Claisse Sby 10/92 19,800
  O/C 20x29 Voiliers a Maree Basse Chr 10/92 18,700
  G/Pa 15x25 Danseuse Mexicaine et Orchestre Chr 10/92 . 17,600
  O/C 15x18 Scene de Chasse a Courre Sby 10/92 17,600
  O/C 19x22 La Seine Doy 11/92 16,500
  O/C 14x17 La Seine (Heavenly Music) Wes 5/93 16,500
  W&G/Pa 19x25 Au Bois de Boulogne Sby 10/92 15,400
  O/C 13x16 Paris, Les Champs-Elysees Sby 10/92 14,300
  G/Pa 25x19 La Tour Eiffel Doy 5/93 12,650
  G&W/Pa/B 18x24 Paris, La Seine et la Tour Eiffel Sby 2/93 . 12,650
  G&W/Pa 13x20 Le Bois de Boulogne Chr 2/93 9,900
  G&W/Pa/B 18x24 Le Pont Alexandre III Sby 2/93 9,200
  G/Pa 19x24 Vu De Seine et Notre Dame Doy 11/92 ... 9,075
  G&W/Pa 18x24 Bouquet de Fleurs Chr 10/92 8,800

O/C 18x26 Une Vue de Paris Sby 10/92 8,800
G/Pa 16x12 Bouquet de Tulipes Chr 10/92 8,250
O/C 13x16 Bord Du Port Doy 11/92 7,425
W&G/Pa 20x24 La Jetee Lou 3/93 7,000
W/Pa 17x23 Villa in a Country Landscpae Wes 5/93 6,600
G&W/Pa 15x11 Vase de Fleurs Chr 11/92 6,050
G&W/Pa/B 22x18 Vase de Fleurs Sby 2/93 5,750
G/Pa 17x23 Vu Du Port Doy 11/92 4,675
O/C 8x12 Paysage Hnd 10/92 4,500
O/C 14x10 Riders in a Street Scene But 4/93 3,737
G/Pa 6x9 Tower Bridge 58 Chr 2/93 3,300
O/C 5x9 Seashells Skn 3/93 1,650
W,G&Pe/Pa 10x12 Coquille Chr 5/93 1,495
W&G/Pa/C 12x9 Portrait de Femme Chr 11/92 1,045
I&Pe/Pa/B 14x16 La Danseuse Russe Sby 2/93 1,035
Dufy, Raoul   Fr 1877-1953
  O/C 48x35 Etude Pour Un Grand Orchestre Sby 11/92 . 198,000
  O/C 18x22 Le Sechage Des Voiles Sby 11/92 104,500
  O/C 11x28 Les jetees Trouville et Deauville Chr 11/92 .. 88,000
  G/Pa/Pe 19x26 Hyde Park 1933 Chr 11/92 66,000
  W/Pa/B 19x23 Taormina Chr 11/92 35,200
  W/Pa 19x25 Beach Scene Hnd 12/92 26,500
  W/Pa/B 20x26 Coucher de Soleil Sby 2/93 25,300
  G,Br&I/Pa 17x16 Napoleon et Alexandre I Chr 10/92 .. 6,600
  Pe/Pa 11x15 Vue de village 24 Chr 11/92 2,200
  Pl/Pa/B 8x11 Le Pont de fer a Marseilles Chr 5/93 1,380
  P&I/Pa 9x12 Nice Wlf 5/93 500
Dughet, Gaspard   Fr 1615-1675
  * See 1992 Edition ....
Dujardin, Karel   Dut 1622-1678
  * See 1991 Edition ....
Duke, Alfred   Br 19C
  * See 1993 Edition ....
Duke, S. P.   Am 20C
  O/C 20x27 River Landscape Fre 10/92 475
Dulac, Edmund   Fr 1882-1953
  W&G/Pa 7x7 The Wizard 1906 Sby 10/92 10,450
  PeIW&G/Pa 12x11 Education of Achilles 18 Sby 10/92 .. 7,700
  W&P/Pa 15x11 Dreamland #21 12 Sby 2/93 920
Dull, Christian L.   Am 1902-
  O/C 30x24 Port Scene Fre 4/93 180
Dull, Christopher L.
  O/C 24x20 Evergreen Forest Ald 5/93 350
Dull, John J.   Am 1862-
  P/B 21x18 Bridge and Houses Ald 5/93 900
Duluard, Hippolyte Francois L.   Fr 1871-
  * See 1992 Edition ....
Dumm, Edwina   Am 1893-1990
  PI&W/Pa 16x12 Sinbad is Left Alone for the Day Ih 5/93 ... 800
Dumond, Frank Vincent   Am 1865-1951
  O/C 25x30 Stream, Nova Scotia 1933 Sby 3/93 6,900
  O/C Size? The Dancing Children 55 Chr 5/93 4,600
  O/C 24x31 Lilacs Skn 3/93 1,980
Dumont, Francois   Fr 19C
  * See 1992 Edition ....
Dumont, Henri   Fr 19C
  O/C 29x36 La Place de la Concorde Chr 10/92 4,400
Dumont, Pierre   Fr 1884-1936
  * See 1992 Edition ....
Dumont, R.   Con 19C
  * See 1992 Edition ....
Dunbar, Harold C.   Am 1882-1953
  O/B 10x14 Cape Dunes Yng 5/93 325
Duncan, Audrey
  * See 1992 Edition ....
Duncan, F.
  O/C 24x36 Waterfall Landscape Ald 3/93 110
Duncan, Gregor
  W&Pe/Pa 17x13 Man and Woman Sitting in Tree Ih 11/92 . 200
Duncan, James D.   Can 1805-1881
  W/Pa 6x9 Ottawa River at Les Chats Sbt 5/93 2,860
Duncan, John   Am 1866-1945
  T&Pe/Pa 19x28 Queen of Sheba & Her Entourage Sby 9/92 . 1,760
Duncan, Scott M.   Am
  O/C 12x16 Little Girl Dum 8/93 600

O/C 12x16 Dog Dum 6/93 500
Duncanson, Robert S. Am 1821-1872
  O/C 26x49 Vale of Kashmir 1870 Chr 12/92 35,200
  O/C 10x16 The Fisherman Sby 3/93 10,350
  O/C 31x26 Seated Man Holding Cane Eld 8/93 1,100
Dunet, Alfred 1889-1939
  O/C 24x18 Pichet de Fleurs Chr 5/93 1,725
Dunham, Carroll 1949-
  MM/Wd 91x61 American Walnut 1984 Chr 2/93 35,200
  OCsl&H/Wd 53x19 Untitled 1987 Chr 11/92 13,200
  MM/Wd 30x21 Secondary 1986 Chr 11/92 12,100
  Y/Pa 9x6 Untitled 82 Sby 6/93 575
Dunington, A. Eng 1830-1890
  O/Ab 9x12 Goatfell, Brodick, Arran 1897 Slo 5/93 750
Dunlap, Eugene Am 1916-
  O/C 30x35 Autumn Landscape Mor 6/93 165
Dunlap, Helena Am 1876-1955
  * See 1991 Edition . . . .
Dunlay, Thomas R. Am
  * See 1993 Edition . . . .
Dunlop, Ronald Ossory Br 1894-1973
  O/C 18x13 Portrait of Miss Davies Yng 2/93 150
Dunn, Harvey T. Am 1884-1952
  O/C 30x38 The Tea Party 16 Chr 12/92 30,800
  O/C 36x24 The Woodsman 1908 Sby 9/92 20,900
Dunning, Lois Am 19C
  * See 1993 Edition . . . .
Dunning, Robert Spear Am 1829-1905
  O/C 9x13 Fishing the Stream 1892 But 12/92 1,870
Dunoyer De Segonzac, Andre Fr 1884-1974
  W/Pa 23x31 Bouquet d'Anemones Doy 5/93 42,900
  W&Pl/Pa 23x31 Saint-Tropez Chr 11/92 36,300
  W&Pl/Pa 22x30 Nature morte a la bouteille Chr 11/92 22,000
  Pl&Br/Pa/M 16x23 Le Vignoble Chr 2/93 2,750
  O/Pn 16x13 Seated Cabaret Dancer Dum 2/93 2,750
  Pl/Pa 10x12 Cows in a Landscape Wlf 9/92 125
  Pl&S/Pa 6x7 Sebasto Wearing a Hat Eld 8/93 77
Dunoyer, Pierre 1949-
  * See 1993 Edition . . . .
Dunsmore, John Ward Am 1856-1945
  O/Pn 11x8 Attack at Fort Washington Mys 3/93 275
Dunstan, Bernard Br 1920-
  * See 1993 Edition . . . .
Dunton, William Herbert Am 1878-1936
  * See 1993 Edition . . . .
Duntze, Johannes Bertholomaus Ger 1823-1895
  * See 1990 Edition . . . .
Dupain, Edmond Louis Fr 1847-
  O/C 46x36 Courtship by the Sea But 11/92 9,350
  O/C 39x28 Chasing after the Flower Chr 5/93 4,600
  O/Pn 18x15 Lady with a Fan Hnd 3/93 2,000
Duplessis, C. Michel H. 18C
  O/Pn 15x20 Encampment at a Fort Sby 10/92 15,400
Dupont, Gainsborough Br 1754-1797
  * See 1992 Edition . . . .
Dupont, W. F. Am 19C
  O/C 24x36 Cows Grazing Before a Farmhouse Sby 3/93 . . . 575
Dupray, Henri Louis Fr 1841-1909
  O/C 21x32 A Cavalry Charge Chr 5/93 4,830
Dupre, Jules Fr 1811-1889
  O/C 11x17 Cows at Pasture Chr 10/92 22,000
  O/C 19x22 L'Ete Chr 5/93 16,100
  O/Pn 12x18 Paysage Sby 10/92 11,550
  O/C 10x13 Cottage in a Wooded Landscape Chr 5/93 3,680
  O/Pn 5x6 Quiet Pool in Wooded Landscape Chr 5/93 2,990
  O/Pn 7x11 Peasant by Quiet Pond Chr 5/93 2,760
  W/Pa 7x10 Figure in a Mountainous Landscape Mys 12/92 . . 358
Dupre, Julien Fr 1851-1910
  O/C 18x15 The Gleaner Sby 10/92 17,600
  O/C 15x22 The Milkmaid Sby 10/92 11,000
Dupre, Leon Victor Fr 1816-1879
  O/C 18x25 Cows Watering 74 Chr 5/93 5,520

Dupre, Louis Fr 1789-1837
  * See 1992 Edition . . . .
Dupuis, Pierre Fr 1610-1682
  * See 1992 Edition . . . .
Dupuy, Paul Michel Fr 1869-1949
  * See 1993 Edition . . . .
Dura, Alberto Uru 1888-1971
  O/C 31x26 Jardin 1920 Sby 5/93 9,200
  O/M 24x19 Cascada 1936 Sby 5/93 6,900
Dura, Gaetano It 19C
  * See 1992 Edition . . . .
Duran, A. Am a 1886-1900
  * See 1992 Edition . . . .
Duran, Charles Emile Carolus Fr 1837-1917
  O/B 17x14 Elegant Man Dum 2/93 3,000
Duran, Paul
  W&I/Pa 4x4 Twelve Drawings 96 Sby 6/93 403
Durand, Asher B. Am 1796-1886
  O/C 22x17 Landscape 1869 Sby 9/92 11,550
Durand, Elias W. Am a 1846-1857
  O/C 17x21 Cows Watering Eld 4/93 275
  O/C 18x24 Connecticut River Valley Eld 11/92 220
Duranti, Fortunato It 1787-1851
  * See 1993 Edition . . . .
Durck, Frederick Ger 1809-1884
  * See 1991 Edition . . . .
Duren, Terrence Romaine Am 1907-
  O/C 24x30 The Terrace Sby 9/92 990
  W/Pa 19x14 Mexican Lady with Vegetables FHB 6/93 250
Durenne, Eugene Antoine Fr 1860-1944
  * See 1992 Edition . . . .
Durfee, Bradford V. Am a 1879-1887
  * See 1993 Edition . . . .
Durig, Rolf Sws 1926-1985
  O/C 21x29 Fruit on a Tabletop '58 Wes 12/92 935
  O/B 20x24 Nature Morte '53 Wes 12/92 770
  O/B 24x20 Flowers 1960 Wes 5/93 330
Durrie, George Henry Am 1820-1863
  * See 1993 Edition . . . .
Durrie, John
  * See 1990 Edition . . . .
Durst, August Fr 1842-
  O/C 23x32 Jeune Fille Sur Un Pont Sby 2/93 7,763
Durston, Arthur Am 1897-1938
  * See 1992 Edition . . . .
Duru, Jean-Baptiste Fr 18C
  * See 1991 Edition . . . .
Dusart, Cornelis Dut 1660-1704
  O/Pn 9x8 Man Reading Letter Chr 1/93 9,900
Dusi, Cosroe It 1808-1859
  * See 1992 Edition . . . .
Duvall, Fannie Eliza Am 1861-1934
  O/C/B 15x19 Still Life Violets But 3/93 3,575
Duveneck, Frank Am 1848-1919
  O/Pn 15x10 Potted Tree Brd 8/93 5,060
Duvent, Charles Jules Fr 1867-1940
  * See 1990 Edition . . . .
Duverger, Theophile Emmanuel Fr 1821-1901
  * See 1993 Edition . . . .
Duvernois, L. Con 19C
  O/C 26x40 Calling for Boatman Slo 5/93 400
Duvieux, Henri Fr a 1880-1882
  O/C 16x26 View of Constantinople Chr 2/93 7,700
  O/B 20x30 Venetian Harbor Dum 6/93 750
Duxa, Karl Aus 1871-1937
  O/C 20x16 Spring Sby 1/93 1,150
Dvorak, Franz Aus 1862-
  O/C 74x108 The Concert, Saratoga 1890 Sby 2/93 79,500
Dwight, Thomas Eng 19C
  O/C 27x22 The Cumberland Valley Slo 5/93 275
Dwyer, Nancy 1959-
  A/C 79x90 Rich Chr 11/92 4,950

Dybsky, Evgeni
O/C 59x79 Landscape Falling Stars 1985 Sby 10/92 4,400
Dyco, William   Br 1806-1864
* See 1993 Edition ....
Dye, Charlie   Am 1906-1973
O/C 24x36 Open Range Branding 1960 Sby 9/92 27,500
Dye, Clarkson   Am 1869-1955
O/C 18x24 Landscape Mor 2/93 400
Dyer, Hezekiah Anthony   Am 1872-1943
G/Pa 11x9 Cottage Scene Mys 12/92 275
W&G/Pa 7x10 Alpine Lake Yng 5/93 225
Dyer, Nancy   Am 20C
G/Pa 9x12 Market Scenes (2) Mys 3/93 578
Dyf, Marcel   Fr 1899-1985
O/C 26x21 Fleurs Lou 3/93 11,000
O/C 29x36 L'Amandier du Jardin D'Arles Doy 11/92 8,800
O/C 29x24 Fleurs Sby 6/93 6,325
O/C 15x18 Day at the Beach Sby 10/92 4,950
O/C 18x22 Summer Town Along Stream 1974 Sby 10/92 .. 4,950
O/C 22x18 Seated Girl with Cat Sby 2/93 4,888
O/C 22x18 Jeune Fille Avec Chaton Hnd 3/93 4,200
O/C 22x18 Femme a sa Toilette Chr 11/92 4,180
O/C 22x18 Nu a sa Toilette Chr 11/92 4,180
O/C 26x22 Landscape with House But 5/93 3,450
O/C 18x22 Afternoon at the Park Sby 10/92 3,300
O/C 26x22 Portrait of a Gypsy Sby 10/92 3,300
O/C 22x18 Young Girl Writing at Her Desk Sby 6/93 3,220
O/C 22x26 Bateaux Echoues 1957 Sby 10/92 3,080
O/C 22x18 Parc Monceau 1957 Sby 10/92 2,750
C&O/P 9x11 Figures in a Park Wlf 9/92 2,000
O/C 24x20 Still Life with Roses Wes 10/92 1,650
O/C 28x23 Paysage Hnd 12/92 1,300
Dyke, Phil   Am 1906-
MM/Pa 23x14 Abstract '52 Mor 6/93 1,045
Dyke, Samuel P.   Am a 1855-1870
* See 1992 Edition ....
Dysselhof, G. Willem   Dut 20C
O/C 43x60 School of Fish Wlf 12/92 2,700
Dzigurski, Alexander   Am 1910-
O/C 23x36 Mediterranean Sea Dum 3/93 1,500
O/C 28x37 Seascape Dum 4/93 1,500
O/C 24x36 Seascape Hnd 5/93 1,200
O/C 23x30 Cipresge Hnd 9/92 500
O/C 24x36 Landscape Hnd 9/92 500
Dzubas, Friedel   Am 1915-
A/C 72x72 Cross River 1986 Sby 11/92 20,900
O/C 36x34 Late Fire 65 Chr 11/92 5,280
Pa 34x34 Untitled, 1915 '81 But 10/92 2,090
MM/F 11x6 Untitled 1957 Sby 2/93 460
E., Josep Antonio   18C
* See 1993 Edition ....
Eakins, Thomas   Am 1844-1916
* See 1992 Edition ....
Eames, G.   Eng 20C
O/C 16x20 British Cruiser "H.M.S. Hawke" 1905 Slo 7/93 .. 500
Earl, George   Br a 1856-1883
* See 1993 Edition ....
Earl, Maud   Br 1864-1943
O/C 61x95 Three Wall Panels Skn 3/93 9,900
Earl, Percy   Br a 1900-1930
W&G/Pa 15x22 Colours and Jockeys 1900 Sby 6/93 4,025
Earl, Thomas P.   Br a 1900-1935
* See 1992 Edition ....
Earle, Eyvind   Am 1916-
* See 1992 Edition ....
**Earle, Lawrence Carmichael   Am
1845-1921**
O/C 36x49 Marsh '08 Sby 3/93 6,900
W/Pa 16x20 Still Life with Game Lou 12/92 650
O/B 19x16 Fisherman at Rest Eld 8/93 605
Earp, Henry   Eng 1831-1914
O/C 15x12 Lane in Midhurst Dum 2/93 450
East, Sir Alfred   Br 1849-1913
O/C/M 10x15 View at Kettering Chr 10/92 1,760

Eastman, Charlotte Fuller   Am 1878-1965
P/Pa 11x16 On the Beach Yng 2/93 300
Eastman, Seth   Am 1808-1875
W&l/Pa 5x8 View in Texas 1849 Sby 12/92 5,500
Eastman, William Joseph   Am 1881-1950
W/Pa 20x15 Autumn Landscape Wlf 5/93 350
Eaton, Charles Harry   Am 1850-1901
O/B 16x22 Autumn Landscape 87 Sby 9/92 2,090
Eaton, Charles Warren   Am 1857-1937
O/C 12x22 Distant Cottages, Dusk Skn 11/92 2,200
O/C 18x16 River in the Woods Hnd 6/93 1,500
Eaton, Dorothy   Am
* See 1992 Edition ....
Ebatarinja, Walter   Eur 19C
W/Pa 20x13 Western Landscape Fre 4/93 50
Eberhard, Heinrich   20C
* See 1993 Edition ....
Eberle, Adolf   Ger 1843-1914
O/Pn 17x21 The New Puppies Sby 5/93 40,250
Eberle, Otto   Am 20C
O/B 15x12 Flowers in a Bowl 1919 Yng 5/93 600
Ebert, Anton   Aus 1845-1896
* See 1993 Edition ....
Ebert, Charles H.   Am 1873-1959
O/C 36x36 Ebert's Pond Chr 9/92 4,950
Ebert, Mary Roberts   Am 1873-1956
* See 1993 Edition ....
Ebner, Lajos Deak   Hun 1850-1934
O/Pn 12x16 The Cabbage Seller Wlf 3/93 3,300
Echlimann, Y.   Am 20C
O/C 48x48 Trompe L'Oeil '79 Slo 4/93 2,000
Eck, Jacques   Fr 1812-1887
* See 1993 Edition ....
Eckart, Christian   1959-
MM Var Odyssey #2: Three Panels 1986 Chr 5/93 3,220
Eckart, Christian   Dan 1832-1914
* See 1992 Edition ....
**Eckersberg, Christoffer W.   Dan
1783-1853**
* See 1992 Edition ....
Eckersberg, Hansine Kern   Dan 19C
O/C 23x18 Roses and Lilies Sby 10/92 6,600
Eckert, Henri-Ambrose   Ger 1807-1840
* See 1991 Edition ....
Eddis, Eden Upton   Br 1812-1901
* See 1992 Edition ....
Eddy, Don   Am 20C
A/C 48x66 Private Parking IV 71 Sby 11/92 14,300
Eddy, Henry Stephens   Am 1878-1944
O/C 16x20 October Day Skn 11/92 550
Eddy, W.
O/B 11x15 Schooner Race 1885 Eld 7/93 880
Ede, Frederic   Am 1865-1909
O/C 24x32 A Bend in the River Sby 9/92 3,850
O/C 15x18 Summer Landscape with Stream Sby 3/93 3,565
O/C 20x24 Cottage by a Rushing Stream Sby 9/92 1,430
Edgar, William   Am a 1870-1918
O/C 20x30 Koko Head at Sea But 3/93 3,300
Edgerly, Beatrice E.   Am 20C
* See 1991 Edition ....
Edlich, Stephen   Am 1944-
* See 1991 Edition ....
Edmonds, Francis William   Am 1806-1863
W/Pa 3x5 Figure with Sheep in Landscape Lou 12/92 ... 525
Edmondson, Edward   Am 19C
O/C 16x13 Cherries 1864 Mys 12/92 1,100
Edson, Aaron Allan   Can 1846-1888
O/C 22x15 The Berry Picker Sbt 11/92 1,320
W/Pa 8x12 Piling Grass Sbt 5/93 704
Eduardo, Jorge   Brz 1936-
* See 1992 Edition ....
Edwards, Ethel   Am 20C
T/Pa 19x13 Gion Festival Lou 3/93 65
Edwards, George Wharton   Am 1869-1950
O/C 24x20 Alcazar Palace Gardens, Seville Chr 5/93 5,750

O/C 30x30 Venetian Cathedral Mys 12/92 2,760
O/C 30x30 The Watch Store Mys 12/92 1,650
O/C 30x30 Avila Spain Mys 12/92 1,430
O/C 24x18 Old Fashioned Treasures Mys 12/92 1,420
O/B 18x24 Mending the Nets Mys 3/93 495

Edwards, Lionel Am 1874-1954
O/C 24x26 Houses in the Hills But 10/92 1,320

Edwards, Lionel Br 1878-1966
W&G/Pa 18x13 Remounts at Sea 1915 Sby 6/93 7,475
W/Pa 14x10 The First Whip Chr 6/93 3,450

Edwards, Marjorie
* See 1993 Edition . . . .

Edzard, Dietz Ger 1893-1963
O/M 30x42 Reclining Nude '45 Wes 12/92 8,800
O/C 32x26 Prima Ballerina Doy 5/93 8,250
O/C 40x32 White Evening Gown Lou 6/93 5,750
O/C 32x26 Ballerinas Sby 10/92 4,950
O/C 36x26 Still Life Flowers, Music Score 1956 Sby 2/93 . . 4,600
O/C 32x26 Two Ballerinas Sby 2/93 3,450
O/C 18x22 La Parade Chr 2/93 3,300
O/C 29x24 Portrait of Barclay Douglas Chr 11/92 3,080
O/C 26x21 Les Danseuses Chr 2/93 2,860
O/C 40x32 Girl on Balcony '51 Sel 12/92 2,750
O/C 16x13 View from the Cafe Sby 6/93 2,300
O/C 24x20 Danseuse Chr 2/93 1,760
O/C 11x14 Il Canale Grande, Venise Chr 2/93 1,430
O/C 6x16 Flute sur fond mauve Chr 11/92 1,100
O/Pn 11x11 Vase de Fleurs Chr 2/93 1,100

Eeckhout, Jakob Joseph Flm 1793-1861
* See 1993 Edition . . . .

Eerelman, Otto Dut 1839-1926
* See 1991 Edition . . . .

Egan, Eloise Am 1874-1967
O/C 40x32 Tenements N.Y.C. Mys 12/92 1,430
O/C 25x30 Slave Quarters, Charleston Chr 5/93 920
O/C 25x30 Street Scene at Sunset Mys 12/92 440
O/C 32x40 Winter in Westport Mys 12/92 330
O/C 25x30 Mon Atelier Mys 12/92 220
O/B 20x24 Dock Scene Mys 12/92 165
O/B 16x20 Fisherman on a Boat Mys 12/92 138
O/C 50x60 After the Hurricane, Florida Mys 12/92 110
O/C 25x30 Row of Palms Mys 12/92 82
O/C 20x24 Winter Morning Mys 12/92 55
O/C 25x30 French Street Scene Mys 12/92 28

Egerton, Daniel Thomas Eng 1797-1842
O/B 13x16 El Iztaccihuatl Desde Chalco Sby 11/92 165,000
O/C 16x21 San Joaquin Rd to Tlanepantla 1833 Sby 5/93 57,500

Eggenhofer, Nick Am 1897-1985
G&Pl/B 9x15 Stagecoach 1981 Chr 3/93 2,530
Pl&Pe/Pb 12x18 Jig Time But 12/92 1,100
P/Pa 18x24 Cattle Drive Wtf 5/93 700

Eggert, Sigmund Ger 1839-1896
O/C/B 33x27 The Pretty Tavern Maid Sby 5/93 6,900

Egginton, Frank J. Eng 1908-
W/B 11x15 Three Watercolors Sby 6/93 2,070

Eglau, Max Am 1825-
O/C 8x13 Southern Landscape with Figures Mys 12/92 550

Egner, Marie Aus 1850-1940
* See 1993 Edition . . . .

Ehehardt, Paul W. Con 20C
O/C 28x32 The Artist's Still Life Chr 10/92 440

Ehlinger, M. Am 20C
O/C 21x25 Kathie Hnd 9/92 850

Ehrig, Frances Belle Am 1912-
O/C 30x40 Maine Encounter Yng 2/93 275

Ehrig, William Am 1892-1969
O/C 28x38 Seascape Yng 2/93 550

Eichens, Friedrich Eduard Dut 1804-1877
* See 1992 Edition . . . .

Eichinger, Otto Ger 1922-
O/B 11x8 German Peasant Dum 1/93 450
O/B 11x8 German Peasant Gentleman Dum 1/93 450

Eichinger, Ulrich Aus 20C
O/Pn 11x8 Portraits of Rabbis: Pair Sby 1/93 6,325

Eickelberg, William Hendrik Dut 1845-1920
O/C 21x29 Rotterdam Fishing Village Fre 10/92 4,100

Eilshemius, Louis Michel Am 1864-1941
O/C 44x30 Three Water Nymphs Lou 3/93 2,300
O/M 20x15 The Source 1901 Sby 3/93 1,955
O/M 20x30 Bright Shoreline Sby 9/92 1,760
O/B 12x19 Golden Bough But 12/92 1,650
O/Pa/B 15x24 The Bathers 1910 Sby 3/93 978
O/B 9x18 Landscape with Waterfall 1900 Sby 9/92 935
O/B 19x30 Bathers by a Waterfall 1918 Sby 9/92 770
O/Pa 12x8 Two Nudes Dancing in a Landscape Sby 3/93 . . 748
O/B 18x9 Gray Clouds Sby 3/93 690
O/C 12x9 Nude by a Waterfall Mys 3/93 468
Pe/Pa 7x9 Casadilla Gorge, Ithaca, 1882 Wtf 9/92 350
O/C 9x12 Nude Female in Rocky Landsape Wtf 9/92 300
O/Pa 10x12 Nude Woman Bathing Dum 7/93 300
Pe/Pa 10x8 Study Standing Female Nude 15 Sby 9/92 165
W/Pa 4x4 Young Girl in the Country Mys 3/93 82
Pe/Pa 4x4 Way to Arrogno Lake '87 Eld 8/93 60

Eisele, Christian Am 19C
O/C 22x36 Mountain Lake Hnd 12/92 800

Eisen, Francois Flm 1695-1778
* See 1993 Edition . . . .

Eisendieck, Suzanne Ger 1908-
O/C 24x29 Terrasse a Eze Sby 10/92 4,125
O/C 24x20 Descente Vers la Grande Jatte Sby 2/93 2,415
O/C 24x20 Dimanche aux Tuilleries Hnd 5/93 2,400
O/C 20x24 Au Bord De L'Oise Sby 6/93 1,955
O/C 21x26 Embarcadere San Tomaso Dum 2/93 1,500
O/C 22x25 Femme a sa toilette Chr 5/93 1,380
O/C 18x14 Femme en Robe Raye Sby 2/93 1,265
Medium? 7x5 Rose and Lilacs Ald 5/93 325

Eisenhut, Ferencz Hun 1857-1903
* See 1991 Edition . . . .

Eisenschitz, Willy Fr 1889-1974
O/C 24x29 Les Minimes, La Valette du Var Chr 11/92 4,620

Eisenstat, Ben Am 20C
O/C 27x86 Our Local Heritage Fre 10/92 180

Ekenaes, Jahn Nor 1847-1920
* See 1991 Edition . . . .

Ekvall, Knut Swd 1843-1912
* See 1991 Edition . . . .

El Greco Spa 1540-1614
* See 1992 Edition . . . .

Eldred, Lemuel D. Am 1848-1921
O/C 16x26 View of Coastal Shipping Eld 7/93 5,500
O/C 9x14 Moonlit Homer's Wharf New Beford 1886 Eld 4/93 3,300
O/C 18x31 The Sailing Ship 83 Skn 11/92 1,100

Elger, Louis Am 19C
O/C 20x24 Swan in a Landscape Fre 10/92 150

Ellaerts, Jean-Francois 1761-1848
* See 1990 Edition . . . .

Ellasoph, Paula Am 1895-1983
* See 1990 Edition . . . .

Ellenshaw, Peter Am 20C
* See 1991 Edition . . . .

Ellery, Richard Am 1909-
O/M 18x40 Landscape with Figures Lou 3/93 300

Ellingson, J. Eng 20C
O/B 28x40 Farm Yard Scene Mys 12/92 110

Elliot, Captain Thomas Br a 1790-1800
* See 1992 Edition . . . .

Elliott, Edward Am 20C
P/Pa 19x13 Andrew Jackson; Robert E. Lee: (2) Yng 2/93 . . 175

Ellis, Freemont F. Am 1897-1985
* See 1993 Edition . . . .

Ellis, John Clinton
W/Pa 16x18 Black Touring Car Ih 5/93 1,300

Ellis, Stephen 1951-
O&Pt/C 108x144 Untitled Chr 2/93 4,400

Ellison, J. Milford Am 1909-
W/Pa 25x20 San Diego Harbor '51 Mor 6/93 358

Ellison, Robert
O/C 60x49 Clue #3 66 Sby 2/93 460

Ellsworth, Clarence Am 1885-1961
O/C 24x36 Indians Riding 28 But 6/93 4,888
O/C/B 20x14 Iron Eye Cody But 6/93 2,300
O/Cb 12x9 Dove Eye Dark Cloud Lou 12/92 125
W/Pa 5x8 Crow and Jackdaw Lou 9/92 100
Elmore, Alfred Br 1815-1881
* See 1992 Edition . . . .
Elouis, Jean Pierre Henri Am 1755-1840
* See 1993 Edition . . . .
Elsley, Arthur John Br 1861-
O/C 32x43 Summer Fun 1915 Chr 10/92 77,000
Elvgren, Gil 20C
O/C 36x29 Illustration of Female Nude Sel 4/93 14,000
O/C 36x29 Seated Female Nude Sel 4/93 4,750
Elwell, D. Jerome Am 1857-1912
* See 1993 Edition . . . .
Emerson, Edith Am 1888-
O/Cb 14x11 Woman in Scarf Fre 4/93 70
Emery, James Am 1819-1899
O/C 22x32 Sailing in Maine Under Pink Clouds Brd 2/93 . . . 2,860
O/C 14x20 Fishing on the Maine Coast 82 Brd 2/93 962
Emms, John Br 1843-1912
O/C 24x20 Two Border Collies Sby 6/93 4,025
Emrich, Harvey 1884-
O&R/C 13x16 Men on Camels Passing Onlookers Ilh 11/92 . 125
Ende, Edgar
* See 1992 Edition . . . .
Ender, Thomas Aus 1793-1875
W/Pa 22x14 View of Mellau Sby 1/93 8,338
Engard, Robert Oliver Am 1915-
* See 1992 Edition . . . .
Engel, Johann Friedrich Ger 1844-
* See 1993 Edition . . . .
Engel, Jules Am 1915-
G/Pa 14x21 Facade But 10/92 1,320
Engelhardt, George Ger 1823-1883
* See 1993 Edition . . . .
Englander, Arnold Am 20C
W/B 14x24 Cowboy and Horses in Desert 1923 Wlf 9/92 . . . 350
Englehardt, Edna Palmer Am 20C
* See 1992 Edition . . . .
Engler Am 19C
O/C 11x15 Hunting Dogs in a Landscape Mys 3/93 990
English, Frank F. Am 1854-1922
W/Pa 19x28 Landscape of a Country Lane Ald 5/93 3,950
W/Pa 15x31 The Return Home Chr 12/92 3,850
W&G/Pa 15x30 Harvest at Sunset Fre 4/93 2,900
W/Pa 22x35 Homeward Bound Wlf 5/93 1,300
English, Mark Am 20C
P/Pa 20x14 Lady with a Parasol Hnd 12/92 100
Enjolras, Delphin Fr 1857-
O/C 29x21 Le Boudoir Sby 5/93 16,100
Enneking, John Joseph Am 1841-1916
O/C 30x22 Flowers in a Garden 97 Chr 12/92 66,000
O/C 22x30 The Duck Pond, Autumn 91 Skn 3/93 14,300
O/C 18x26 Potato Harvesting 77 Skn 5/93 9,350
O/C 25x30 Shady Brook Skn 3/93 6,600
O/B 12x14 Baker Chocolate Factory Skn 3/93 4,675
O/C 18x24 Passing Clouds 09 Chr 3/93 4,600
O/C 20x24 Autumn in the Woods Skn 11/92 4,400
O/C 14x18 Figures Working in Fields 83 Skn 5/93 4,400
O/C 7x11 Twilight Chr 9/92 4,400
O/C 22x30 Hillside Before a Storm 97 Brd 8/93 4,180
O/C 24x33 Old Woman Sewing 1883 Yng 5/93 4,000
O/C 18x24 Snow Scene, New England 06 Skn 11/92 3,960
O/C 18x24 Spring Lambs 92 Skn 3/93 3,850
O/C 20x24 Blue Mountains Skn 11/92 3,300
O/C/B 12x14 Snow Scene Chr 9/92 3,300
O/C 16x22 European Street Scene '85 Wes 3/93 2,640
O/C 14x18 Stream with a Wooden Bridge 02 Skn 5/93 . . . 2,420
O/C 12x16 Along the Neponset Lou 9/92 1,900
O/Pn 6x7 Neponset River 1903 Skn 3/93 1,540
O/B 10x8 Late Afternoon, Mystic Village 1927 Skn 5/93 . . . 1,430
O/Pn 15x14 Wagon Road in Winter Skn 3/93 1,430
O/C 16x24 Landscape with Cottages Sby 3/93 1,380

O/B 6x9 Two Travelers 1873 Eld 11/92 440
Enneking, Joseph Eliot Am -1946
O/B 8x10 Red Barns Skn 9/92 550
Ennis, George Pearce Am 1884-1936
O/C 25x28 A Rising Fog Fre 10/92 1,300
O/C 36x30 End of Fisherman's Day Fre 4/93 1,150
O/C 36x30 End of the Fisherman's Day Doy 11/92 1,100
O/B 14x14 The Ledges 1923 But 12/92 880
W/Pa 16x20 Cutler Cove, Maine, 1923 Brd 8/93 798
Enriquez, Carlos Cub 1901-1957
O/C 24x20 Pelea De Gallos Sby 5/93 8,625
W,G&P/Pa 16x20 Caballos 55 Chr 11/92 3,300
Enser, John F. Am 20C
O/Pn 12x15 Landscape with Buildings Eld 11/92 220
O/B 16x12 New England Farm Scene Eld 11/92 66
Ensor, James Bel 1860-1949
* See 1993 Edition . . . .
Ensor, John
O/C Var Three Paintings Eld 8/93 220
Enwright, J. J. Am 20C
O/C 24x36 Near Bass River, Cape Cod Ald 9/92 450
O/C 24x20 Harbour Scene Mys 3/93 385
O/C 24x30 The River in Winter Ald 9/92 350
O/C 20x26 Harbor View Rockport Slo 4/93 325
O/C 20x26 A Gloucester Dock Ald 9/92 225
O/C 20x27 The Wharf in Winter Ald 9/92 175
Epp, Rudolf Ger 1834-1910
O/C 29x33 Grandmother's Birthday '79 Hnd 10/92 31,500
H/Pa 12x10 Portrait of a Man 83 But 5/93 690
Epperly, Richard Am 20C
O/C 20x16 Market Day, Orleans, France 42 Hnd 3/93 300
Eppink, Norman Am 1906-
* See 1991 Edition . . . .
Epstein, Henri Pol 1892-1944
O/C 24x29 Nature Morte 1930 Chr 11/92 1,870
Epstein, Jacob Br 1880-1959
G/Pa 22x17 Roses Doy 11/92 3,080
W&Pe/Pa 18x23 Reclining Nude Chr 11/92 2,860
G/Pa 17x22 Epping Forest Doy 11/92 2,200
G/Pa 17x22 Epping Forest, Spring Doy 11/92 2,200
Pe/Pa 20x15 Portrait Head of Young Girl Chr 5/93 920
W&G/Pa 12x9 Standing Figures But 5/93 690
Epstein, Jehudo Pol 1870-1946
* See 1992 Edition . . . .
Erdman, Otto Ger 1834-1905
* See 1993 Edition . . . .
Erfmann, Ferdinand
* See 1992 Edition . . . .
Erichsen, Thorvald Nor 1868-1939
* See 1992 Edition . . . .
Erman, H. J. Ger 19C
P/Pa 22x17 Pasha with One of His Harem Hnd 12/92 100
Ermels, Johann-Franciscus Dut 17C
* See 1991 Edition . . . .
Erni, Hans Sws 1909-
* See 1993 Edition . . . .
Ernst, Jimmy Am 1920-1984
O/C 50x47 The Silent Place '57 FHB 5/93 8,500
G/Pa 23x17 Abstract in Greys 51 Chr 12/92 2,860
G,W&I/Pa 22x34 Untitled 1954 Chr 12/92 1,980
O/M 14x11 Yesterday and Tomorrow 1963 FHB 5/93 1,700
G/Pa 18x22 Untitled 67 Sby 10/92 1,540
Ernst, Max Fr 1891-1976
O&L/Pn 13x9 Demain Chr 11/92 99,000
O/B 5x4 Microbe Chr 11/92 24,200
G&W/Cd 4x5 Untitled Sby 10/92 19,800
Ernst, Rudolf Aus 1854-1920
O/Pn 16x10 Studying the Koran Chr 10/92 24,200
O/Pn 19x14 The Dance of Salome Sby 2/93 23,000
O/Pn 18x15 The Beggar Sby 10/92 19,800
O/C 29x73 Odalisque Avec Puttis Sby 5/93 9,200
Eroli, Erulo It 1854-1916
* See 1993 Edition . . . .
Erte Fr 1892-1990
G/B 16x12 Harper's Bazaar Cover Sby 2/93 35,650

G&Pe/Pa 11x15 Decor Design Cosi Fan Tutte Sby 6/93 ... 5,750
G&Pe/Pa 15x11 Perspective 1934 Sby 6/93 4,888
G&Pt/Pa 18x11 Porteuse De Lanterne 1919 Sby 2/93 4,888
G&Gd/Pa 11x8 Costume: Venetian Lord 1923 Sby 10/92 .. 4,675
G&Pe/Pa 15x11 Costume: Combination 1925 Sby 10/92 ... 3,960
G/Pa 13x9 Les Travaux D'Hercule 1934 Sel 12/92 3,500
G&Gd/Pa 10x5 Costume: Feminine Planet 1917 Sby 10/92 . 3,300
G/Pa 15x11 Costume Design for L'Algue Sby 6/93 3,105
G/Pa 13x10 La Chaleur Les Nuages 1926 Hnd 12/92 3,000
G&Gd/Pa 15x11 Costume Design Sby 10/92 2,750
G/Pa 5x9 Decor Design World of Beauty Sby 6/93 2,530
G&Pe/Pa 15x11 Le Masque Du Canard Sby 6/93 2,185
G/Pa 15x11 Costume Wonder-World Photo 1964 Sby 2/93 . 2,070
G,I&Gd/Pa 16x11 Costume Chin. Gentleman 1924 Sby 6/93 1,955
G&Gd/Pa 15x11 Costume for Zizi Jeanmaire Sby 6/93 1,840
G,I&Pe/Pa 15x11 Costume Girls De Montmartre Sby 6/93 .. 1,840
G/Pa 10x7 La Poule Dum 1/93 1,800
G/Pa 17x12 Fine Feathers Make Fine Birds Lou 3/93 1,500
W&G/Pa 17x13 Model with Plumed Headdress Dum 1/93 .. 1,500
Erubellin, J. Fr 19C
  * See 1990 Edition
Escobar, Vincente
  * See 1992 Edition
Escobedo, Eberto Cub 1919-
  * See 1993 Edition
Escudier, Charles Jean Auguste Fr 1848-
  O/C 26x39 Enfants Pechant Sby 2/93 14,950
Esner, Arthur L. Am 1902-
  * See 1993 Edition
Esposito, Gaetano It 1858-1911
  * See 1991 Edition
Espoy, Angel Am 1869-1962
  O/C 20x24 California Wildflowers But 3/93 3,300
  O/C 30x40 Mountain Landscape Lou 6/93 2,250
  O/C 26x36 Flowered Field But 3/93 2,200
  O/C 24x36 Pacific Coast at Sunset But 3/93 2,200
  O/C 15x23 Cattle Grazing Wildflowers But 6/93 1,840
  O/C 25x30 Breaking Waves But 10/92 1,760
  O/C 22x16 Yosemite Fisherman But 3/93 1,760
  O/C 20x24 Flowered Hillside Mor 2/93 1,100
  O/C 20x16 Fisherman's Cove Slo 4/93 850
Essig, George Emerick Am 1838-1926
  O/C 11x18 A Beached Sailboat Chr 12/92 1,100
  W/Pa 14x26 Sailboats in Port Fre 10/92 375
  W/Pa 14x25 Apple Blossom by a White House Fre 10/92 ... 210
Este, Florence Am 20C
  O/C 40x47 River Landscape Dum 10/92 1,300
Estes, Richard Am 1936-
  O/M 19x17 Andy Capp Chr 11/92 33,000
  O/M 48x30 Storelights Sby 11/92 27,500
Esteve, Augustin Spa 1753-1809
  * See 1990 Edition
Estorach, Antonio Salvador C. Spa 1847-1896
  * See 1993 Edition
Etcheverry, Hubert-Denis Fr 1867-1950
  * See 1993 Edition
Etienne, Charles Fr 19C
  O/Pn 6x8 Girl Feeding the Ducks Wes 3/93 770
Etnier, Stephen Am 1903-1984
  O/C 13x21 Bibber's Boat Shed 67 Brd 8/93 3,850
  O/C 30x40 New England Harbor Scene Sby 3/93 3,220
Etting, Emlen Am 1905-
  * See 1993 Edition
Etty, William Br 1787-1849
  O/B/M 20x26 Ariadne Chr 5/93 9,200
  O/B 21x14 Seated Study of Nude But 5/93 1,725
  O/B/C 16x24 Reclining Male Nude Skn 3/93 1,320
Eugen, Prins Swd 1865-1947
  * See 1992 Edition
Eustace, Philippe Fr 20C
  O/B 67x36 Standing Nude Chr 5/93 6,900
Evan, Joseph Am a 1857-1898
  * See 1993 Edition

Evans, Bernard Walter Eng 1848-
  W/Pa 8x10 Knarsebro, Yorkshire 1903 Slo 5/93 200
Evans, Bruce Am 20C
  * See 1992 Edition
Evans, De Scott Am 1847-1898
  O/C 43x24 Still Life Daffodils in a Brass Urn 1885 Doy 5/93 3,300
Evans, Donald Am 20C
  * See 1992 Edition
Evans, J. R. Am 19C
  O/B 21x16 Dressing for the Ball 1894 Eld 4/93 302
Evans, Jessie Benton Am 1866-1954
  O/C 20x24 Southwestern Scene Wes 10/92 412
  O/Pn 10x14 Western Landscape Slo 5/93 70
Eve, Jean Fr 1900-1968
  O/C 15x22 Le Guilvinec: Plage du Steir 1959 But 5/93 ... 4,600
  O/C 20x26 Automne: Vetheuil But 5/93 4,025
Evergood, Philip Am 1901-1973
  O/C 30x40 Holocaust or It's Black Outside Chr 5/93 ... 14,950
  O/Cb 21x18 The Success Team Sby 9/92 8,250
  O/C/Pn 31x23 The New Birth 43 Sby 9/92 7,150
  C,Y&W/Pa 22x16 Three Mythological Figures Sby 3/93 ... 3,565
  O/C 25x18 Sacrifice of the Queen 1969 Wes 5/93 3,300
  H/Pa 34x28 Portrait of a Lady Skn 11/92 1,980
  O/C 14x20 Siegfried and the Rhine Maidens Sby 9/92 ... 1,650
  I&S/Pa 25x19 Debate Goldwater and LBJ 1964 Skn 11/92 .. 275
Eversen, Adrianus Dut 1818-1897
  * See 1993 Edition
Eversen, Johannes Hendrik Dut 1906-
  O/C 23x19 Still Life Oysters and Wine Bottle 1957 Wlf 9/92 1,600
Evrard, Adele Flm 1792-1889
  O/Pn 31x24 Hare and Grapes 1820 Doy 5/93 2,310
Evrard, Paula Bel 1876-1927
  * See 1990 Edition
Ewing, Athol L. Am 1880-1936
  O/C 22x20 Parrots & Floral Mor 2/93 400
Exter, Alexandra Rus 1884-1949
  G/Pa 20x26 Euripide-Bacchantes Sby 2/93 3,450
  G/Pa 20x26 Euripide-Bacchantes Sby 2/93 3,450
  G/Pa 13x10 Woman with a Harp Sby 6/93 2,070
  G/Pa 13x10 Abstract Woman Sby 6/93 1,725
Eyden, William A. Am 1859-1919
  O/C 12x16 Wooded Wintry Landscape Sel 4/93 170
Eyden, William Arnold (Jr.) Am 1893-
  O/C 24x36 Indiana Landscape Hnd 10/92 450
Eytel, Carl Am 1862-1925
  * See 1992 Edition
Ezdorf, Christian Ger 1801-1851
  * See 1993 Edition
Fa Presto It 1634-1705
  O/C 51x60 Crucifixion of Saint Peter Sby 5/93 48,875
Fabbi, Alberto It 1858-1906
  * See 1990 Edition
Fabbi, Fabbio It 1861-1946
  * See 1993 Edition
Faber, W. C. Am 20C
  O/C 14x20 Meadow Landscape Sel 4/93 525
Fabian, G. N.
  O/B 13x19 Cows by Ocean Ald 9/92 150
Fabien, Louis Fr 1925-
  O/C 38x58 Baigneuse L'Etang Dore 66 Hnd 3/93 2,800
  O/C 29x39 Monte-Carlo le jour 76 Chr 11/92 1,870
  O/C 29x39 Monte-Carlo, La Nuit 77 Chr 2/93 1,650
Fabre, Auguste-Victor Fr 1882-1939
  * See 1993 Edition
Fabres y Costa, Antonio Spa 19C
  * See 1993 Edition
Fabris, Pietro It 19C
  * See 1990 Edition
Fabris, Pietro It a 1754-1792
  * See 1993 Edition
Facchinetti, Carlo It 1870-
  W/B 11x8 Judith and Holofernes 1859 Wlf 3/93 500
Faccini, Pietro It 1562-1602
  O/Cp 18x14 Saint Jerome in Wilderness Chr 1/93 33,000
  K,PI&S/Pa 10x8 The Raising of Lazarus Chr 1/93 3,080

96

Fachinetti, Carlo   It 1870-
O/C 35x28 The Happy Family Chr 2/93 13,750
O/C 31x23 Maternita Sby 2/93 9,488
Fader, Fernando   Arg 1882-1935
* See 1993 Edition . . . .
Faed, John   Br 1820-1902
* See 1993 Edition . . . .
Faed, Thomas   Br 1826-1900
O/C 24x16 The Harvest 1881 Chr 10/92 6,600
Fagan, Betty Maude Christian   Fr 19C
O/C 41x29 Lustre en Crystal Chr 10/92 2,090
Faggiano, A. M.
MM&L/C 54x92 La Storia in Cielo Sby 10/92 275
Fairley, Barker   Can 1887-1986
O/B 11x14 Hills Near Eugenia 1975 Sbt 5/93 1,672
O/B 20x16 Portrait Leonard Hutchinson 1976 Sbt 5/93 968
Fairman, James   Am 1826-1904
O/C 20x36 Mts. Madison and Adams 1870 Chr 3/93 . . . 27,600
O/C 23x36 Sunlight on the Coast Chr 9/92 5,500
O/C 26x57 New England Village Brd 2/93 4,840
O/Pn 9x13 Bay of New York Skn 3/93 660
Faivre, Justin   Am 1902-
W/Pa 21x30 Boats at Rest Mor 11/92 450
MM/Pa 9x12 On the Farm Mor 2/93 175
Fajon, Rose Jeanne   Fr 1789-
* See 1993 Edition . . . .
Falciatore, Filippo   It a 1728-1768
* See 1993 Edition . . . .
Falcone, Aniello   It 1600-1658
* See 1993 Edition . . . .
Falconer, Ian
* See 1992 Edition . . . .
Falconer, John M.   Am 1820-1903
O/B 16x12 The Reaper Maiden 1876 Yng 2/93 1,700
Falconet, Pierre Etienne   Fr 1741-1791
* See 1991 Edition . . . .
Faldi, R.
O/B 17x14 Floral Still Life 1854 Eld 8/93 110
Falero, Luis Riccardo   Spa 1851-1896
O/C 14x28 The Minstral's Dance Chr 5/93 9,200
Falk, R.   19C
O/C 12x9 Peasant Woman Sel 12/92 275
Falls, Charles B.   Am 1874-1960
O/M 8x7 Hatian Idyl Eld 8/93 302
Falter, John Philip   Am 1910-1982
O/M 20x24 Illustration Family Drinking Beer Sel 4/93 110
Fanfani, Enrico   It 19C
O/C 49x36 Arrival at the Monastery But 11/92 6,600
O/C 29x37 The Lesson Slo 4/93 650
Fangor, Wojciech   20C
O/C 80x80 M-36 1969 Sby 2/93 1,495
Fantin-Latour, Ignace Henri J.   Fr 1836-1904
O/C 20x25 Vase de Fleurs: Dahlias Sby 11/92 . . . . 1.1M
O/C 19x15 Vase de Fleurs-Reine Marguerites 72 Sby 5/93 266,500
O/C 19x17 Dahlias Sombres 75 Sby 5/93 255,500
Fantin-Latour, Victoria Dubour   Fr 1840-
* See 1993 Edition . . . .
Farasyn, Edgard   Bel 1858-1938
* See 1990 Edition . . . .
Farasyn, L.   Bel 1822-1899
* See 1992 Edition . . . .
Farber, Henry   Am 1843-1903
* See 1993 Edition . . . .
Farber, Manny   Am 20C
* See 1992 Edition . . . .
Farenghi, G.   It 19C
* See 1992 Edition . . . .
Farina, Isidoro   It 19C
* See 1991 Edition . . . .
Farinato, Paolo   It 1524-1606
* See 1992 Edition . . . .
Farley, Richard Blossom   Am 1875-
O/C 16x12 Nude at Sunset Fre 10/92 850

Farm, Gerald   Am 1935-
* See 1990 Edition . . . .
Farndon, Walter   Am 1876-1964
O/B 14x18 The Morning Stroll Skn 9/92 1,650
Farnham, Ammi Merchant   Am 1846-1922
* See 1993 Edition . . . .
Farnsworth, Alfred V.   Am 1858-1908
W&G/Pa 10x17 Grazing Cattle on Hillside 1903 But 3/93 . . . 770
W/Pa 12x20 Coastal-Boats Off Rocky Pt. 1904 Mor 6/93 . . . 715
Farnsworth, Jerry   Am 1895-1983
* See 1992 Edition . . . .
Farnum, Herbert Cyrus   Am 1886-
O/B 16x13 Arab Market Scene Mys 12/92 660
O/Cb 7x12 Landscape in Holland Skn 11/92 468
Farny, Henry F.   Am 1847-1916
W/B 10x6 Ukchekehaskan Minneconjue Sioux Sby 12/92 . 16,500
Pl/Pa 15x9 Indian Brave with Rifle '97 Sby 5/93 14,950
Farquharson, David   Eng 1839-1907
* See 1993 Edition . . . .
Farquharson, Joseph   Eng 1846-1935
O/C 20x24 Flowering Herbaceous Borders Sby 5/93 25,300
Farre, Henri   Am 1871-1934
* See 1992 Edition . . . .
Farrer, Henry   Am 1843-1903
W/Pa 24x37 Close of a Grey Day 1887 Sby 3/93 14,950
W/Pa 18x25 Evening Sail 1900 Sby 12/92 8,250
Farrer, Thomas Charles   Am 1840-1891
* See 1992 Edition . . . .
Farsky, Oldrich   Am 20C
O/Pn 15x8 Cardinal Arranging Flowers Hnz 5/93 625
Farsky, Otto   Am 20C
* See 1993 Edition . . . .
Fasce, F.   It 19C
* See 1990 Edition . . . .
Fassett, Truman E.   Am 1885-
* See 1990 Edition . . . .
Fat, Dulcie Foo   Can 1946-
O/C 48x61 Pacific Wildflower 1984 Sbt 5/93 5,500
Faugeron, Adolphe   Fr 1866-
* See 1991 Edition . . . .
Faulkner, Charles   Br a 1890-1900
* See 1993 Edition . . . .
Faulkner, Frank   Br 20C
MM/C 72x72 Ariadne 1983 Sby 6/93 3,450
Faulkner, John   Irs 1803-1888
W/Pb 23x40 A Breezy Morning Chr 5/93 1,150
Faure, Elisabeth
* See 1992 Edition . . . .
Fautrier, Jean   20C
* See 1993 Edition . . . .
Favai, Gennaro   It 1882-1958
O/Pn 28x35 Santa Maria Della Salute at Night Chr 5/93 . . . 2,300
Favard, L.   Fr 20C
* See 1993 Edition . . . .
Fave, Paul   Fr 20C
* See 1993 Edition . . . .
Favelle, R.   Con 19C
O/C 24x36 Skaters on a Frozen Pond 1864 Chr 5/93 1,840
Favory, Andre   Fr 1888-1937
* See 1991 Edition . . . .
Favretto, Giacomo   It 1849-1887
O/C 28x20 Signora a Passeggio in Piazza Slo 7/93 6,500
Fay, Joe   Am 1950-
MM/Pn 48x56 Gunfight at the O.K. Corral 1987 But 4/93 . . . 805
MM/Pa 30x45 Grizzly and Cowboy 1987 But 4/93 690
MM/Pa 30x45 Red Bear 1987 But 4/93 690
MM/Pa 30x45 Urban Coyote with Fish 1987 But 4/93 690
Fay, Joseph   Ger 1813-1875
* See 1992 Edition . . . .
Fayard, R.   Fr 20C
* See 1992 Edition . . . .
Febvre, Edouard   Fr 20C
* See 1992 Edition . . . .
Fechin, Nicolai   Am 1881-1955
O/C 20x16 Still Life with Flowers 1945 Sby 12/92 55,000

O/Pa 9x12 River Sunset Brd 2/93 495
W/Pa 10x14 River Landscape 92 Mor 6/93 385

FitzGerald, Lionel Lemoine   Can 1890-1956
O/B 20x16 Women Working in Field Sbt 5/93 8,360
O/C/B 11x14 Sunlit Forest Sbt 11/92 5,280
O/B 10x8 Birch Woods Sbt 11/92 1,760

Fitzpatrick, Arthur   Br 19C
O/C 20x16 The Storekeeper 1870 But 11/92 1,650

Fitzpatrick, Daniel Patrick   Am 1891-1969
Br,I&Y/Pa 9x20 Hand Beckoning Uncle Sam Ih 11/92 600

Fitzsimmons, Arthur J.   Am 1909-
O/M 24x20 Portrait of an Indian Sel 12/92 475

Fix-Masseau, Pierre Felix   Fr 1869-1937
* See 1992 Edition . . . .

Fjaestad, Gustav Edolf   Swd 1868-1948
* See 1990 Edition . . . .

Flack, Audrey   1931-
* See 1993 Edition . . . .

Flagg, H. Peabody   Am 1859-1937
O/C 12x16 Two Landscapes 1912 Skn 5/93 715
O/Cb 8x10 Spring Landscape 1927 Slo 4/93 50

Flagg, James Montgomery   Am 1877-1960
W,G&Pe/Pb 9x29 Study for a Boxing Mural 44 Sby 12/92 . . 7,150
Pl/Pa 22x23 Man and Woman Shaking Hands Ih 11/92 . . 1,400
W,Pe&I/Pa 9x11 Man/Goat at Railroad Station 1948 Ih 5/93 . 950
S/Pa 21x27 French Chef Hnz 5/93 800
Pl/Pa 21x27 Woman Startled by Man Ih 5/93 700
C&P/Pa 17x14 Bust of Woman "Garda Olesen" Ih 5/93 600
W&Pl/B 12x14 Taxi to the Lombardy 1947 Sby 9/92 550
H/Pa 8x10 Sandy '32 Hnz 5/93 160

Flameng, Francois   Fr 1856-1923
* See 1993 Edition . . . .

Flamm, Albert   Ger 1823-1906
* See 1991 Edition . . . .

Flanagan, John R.   Am 1895-1964
W/Pa 11x9 Slain Man in the Desert Ih 5/93 750

Flandrin, Hippolyte Jean   Fr 1809-1864
* See 1992 Edition . . . .

Flannigan, Lucy Agnes   Am a 1900-
W/Pa 30x20 The Italian Villa Skn 3/93 522

Flavelle, Geoff H.   Eur 20C
W/Pa 13x28 Sailboats on Horizon Yng 2/93 150
W/Pa 20x30 Fall Landscape Dum 1/93 100
W/Pa 19x30 River Landscape Sel 12/92 100
W/Pa 10x14 River Landscape FHB 6/93 80

Flavin, Dan   Am 1933-
I&Pe/Pa 17x22 Untitled (Two Drawings) 1972 Sby 2/93 . . 5,750

Flechemuller, Jacques   1945-
* See 1992 Edition . . . .

Fleck, Joseph A.   Am 1893-1977
O/C 24x20 Girl with Mantilla 1933 Hnd 3/93 5,200
O/M 12x16 First Snow--Taos Chr 9/92 2,200
W/Pa 15x16 Southwestern Still Life '47 Hnd 5/93 150

Flegel, Georg   Ger 1563-1638
* See 1992 Edition . . . .

Fletcher, Aaron Dean   Am 1817-
O/C 28x24 Portraits Gentlemen Lady: Pair 1841 Sby 9/92 . . 1,760

Fletcher, Edwin   Br 1857-1945
O/C 20x30 Shipping on the Thames Sel 12/92 500

Fletcher, George   Can 1941-1987
O/B 24x36 Autumn Road, Lake Kilarney Sbt 5/93 616

Fleury, Albert Francois   Am 1848-1925
O/C 27x42 Afternoon Tea in the Garden Skn 11/92 17,600

Fleury, Fanny Laurent   Fr 1848-
O/C 58x36 Lady in a Blue Satin Gown Chr 10/92 8,800

Fleury, Francois-Antoine Leon   Fr 1804-1858
O/C 40x32 Peasant Cart Mountain Path 1839 Doy 5/93 . . . 5,225

Flieher, Karl   Aus 1881-1958
O/B 5x7 Alpine Village Mys 12/92 605

Flinck, Govaert   Dut 1615-1660
O/Pn 16x23 Landscape with a Tower Sby 1/93 112,500

Flint, Sir William Russell   Br 1880-1969
W/Ab 12x16 Abigail, A New Model 1964 Sby 5/93 34,500

G/Pa 14x25 Dancer Adriana Otero/Seville 1936 Sby 10/92   18,700
W/B 20x27 A Mirror in the Sands 1937 Sby 5/93 18,400
W/Pa 15x22 Fountain at Frascati Chr 2/93 9,350

Flipart, Giuseppe   1721-1797
* See 1993 Edition . . . .

Floch, Joseph   Am 1894-1977
* See 1993 Edition . . . .

Flores, Leonardo   Per 17C
O/C 31x45 El Matrimonio del Rey David Chr 11/92 15,400

Floris, Frans   Dut 1519-1570
* See 1993 Edition . . . .

Floris, J.   Spa 20C
O/Pn 12x6 Flamenco Dancer 98 Hnd 12/92 200

Florsheim, Richard   Am 1916-
O/B 13x9 Yellow Clouds Mys 12/92 330

Flouest   Fr a 1789-1791
* See 1993 Edition . . . .

Flynn, Dianne   Br 20C
O/C 20x24 Early Training Sby 6/93 3,738

Foerster, Emil   Am 1822-1906
* See 1992 Edition . . . .

Foerster, Herbert   Am 20C
O/C 12x16 Maine Coast, Nova Scotia (2) Fre 10/92 110

Fogg   Am 20C
O/Pa Size? Young and Old Man: Two 1944 Wlf 5/93 175

Folinsbee, John Fulton   Am 1892-1972
O/B 8x10 Waterfront Town Ald 9/92 1,900
O/B 10x14 Indian Point Ald 9/92 900
O/B 13x10 Landscape Ald 9/92 650
O/C 20x16 13. Kisky Adams Ald 5/93 250

Folks, I. E.   Am 20C
O/M 8x10 Texas Bluebonnets Lou 3/93 100

Foltz, J. G.   Am 20C
W/Pa 12x18 In the Mountains Yng 2/93 175

Fon, Jade   Am 1911-1983
W/Pa 15x21 Bay Fog But 3/93 2,090
O/C 32x48 Carmel Landscape Mor 6/93 1,760

Fonda, Harry Stuart   Am 1864-1942
* See 1992 Edition . . . .

Fong, Lai   Chi 19C
O/C 25x34 Ship County of Roxburgh 1893 Eld 7/93 3,520
O/C 25x35 Ship County of Roxburgh 1892 Eld 7/93 1,650

Fonseca, Gonzalo   Uru 1922-
O/B 17x14 Constructivo Con Grafismo 50 Sby 5/93 9,200

Fonseca, Reynaldo   Brz 1925-
O/C 29x40 Mae E Criancas Jantando 1976 Sby 5/93 13,800
O/C 39x32 Menina com Cachorro e Mulher 1984 Chr 11/92 12,100

Font, Constantin   Fr 1890-
O/C 46x58 Allegory of Youth and Age 1919 Sby 1/93 3,450

Fontaine, E. Joseph   Am 20C
O/C 24x30 Public Garden, Boston Skn 5/93 2,640
O/C 22x30 Winter Walk/Public Garden 1988 Skn 5/93 . . . 2,640

Fontaine, Gustave   Fr 19C
* See 1993 Edition . . . .

Fontaine, Pierre-Francois-Leo.   Fr 1762-1853
* See 1992 Edition . . . .

Fontaine, Victor   Bel 1837-1884
O/C 24x19 Floral Still Life But 5/93 2,185
O/C 37x23 Flowers in Blue and White Vase Chr 2/93 . . . 1,375

Fontana, Lavinia   1552-1614
O/C 36x28 Portrait of a Lady Wearing Black Chr 1/93 6,600

Fontana, Lucio   It 1899-1968
W&I/Pa 24x16 Concetto Spaziale '48 Sby 5/93 5,750

Fontana, Prospero   It 1512-1597
* See 1993 Edition . . . .

Fontebasso, Francesco   It 1709-1769
O/C 37x50 Family of Darius Before Alexander Sby 1/93 . . 90,500

Foote, Mary Hallock   Am 1847-1938
* See 1992 Edition . . . .

Foote, Will Howe   Am 1874-1965
O/Cb 12x16 Two: Taxco and Mexican Church Skn 9/92 . . . 330

Foppiani, Gustavo   It 20C
* See 1993 Edition . . . .

Forain, Jean Louis   Fr 1852-1931
O/C 11x22 Apres La Danse Sby 10/92 11,000
P&C/Pa/B 24x20 L'Atelier Sby 10/92 9,625
I,S&G/Pa 11x7 Chanteuse Sby 2/93 4,600
W&Y/Pa 6x3 Man in Evening Dress 1898 Sby 2/93 3,335
Pl/Pa 8x5 L'Entr'Acte Sby 2/93 2,875
W&C/Pa 10x9 Le Divan Sby 2/93 2,300
I/Pa 9x10 Le Ministere Berthelot Sby 2/93 2,070
I/Pa 14x10 Vite Ma Fille, Leve Toi Sby 6/93 1,380
K&Y/Pa/B 14x9 Woman Seated in a Cafe Sby 10/92 1,320
I&Y/Pa 15x20 L'Accouchement Sby 6/93 1,035
I&Y/Pa 10x16 The Man of Letters Sby 2/93 920
I&W/Pa/B 12x20 ...Bouge Pas...Elle Va Nous L'Dire Sby 10/92 825
I/Pa/B 18x11 Ca N'te Va Pas? Sby 10/92 660
I&S/Pa/B 13x10 I N'y Pas a Dire Sby 10/92 660
Pe/Pa 16x10 Study of a Ballerina Sby 10/92 440
K/Pa 18x15 Three Drawings Chr 5/93 207
K/Pa 12x7 Four Drawings Chr 5/93 184
Forbes, Charles Stuart   Am 1860-1926
* See 1992 Edition . . . .
Forbes, Helen K.   Am 1891-1945
* See 1993 Edition . . . .
Forbes, John Colin   Can 1846-1925
O/C 13x18 Moonlight, Toronto Harbour Sbt 5/93 1,100
Forbes, Kenneth Keith   Can 1892-1980
O/C 51x41 Portrait Eola B. Hammell Sbt 5/93 2,200
Forbes, Stanhope   Irs 1857-1947
* See 1993 Edition . . . .
Forcella, N.   It 19C
O/C 28x18 The Old Carpet Seller Chr 5/93 10,350
Ford, F.   Br 19C
W/Pa 13x20 View of the Tames Sel 4/93 200
Ford, Henry Chapman   Am 1828-1894
* See 1992 Edition . . . .
Ford, Ruth Van Sickle   Am 1897-
W/Pa 28x21 Children Playing, Haiti Hnz 5/93 60
W/Pa 28x21 Old Red Barn Hnz 5/93 60
Foreau, Henri   Fr 1866-1938
W/Pa 8x11 Figures and Ox-Drawn Cart Wes 10/92 220
Forg, Gunther   1952-
Ph 106x47 28 Ottobre, Marina Dimassa 86 Sby 11/92 . . . 22,000
O/Me 95x63 Untitled (#119-88) 88 Sby 10/92 19,800
W&Pg/Pa 12x9 Untitled 87 Chr 2/93 14,850
A/Pn 48x27 Untitled 1987 Chr 11/92 12,650
A/Pn 106x49 Untitled Sby 2/93 11,500
Ph 111x52 Rom Chr 11/92 11,000
O/Me 48x27 Bleibild 21/88 88 Sby 5/93 9,200
A/C 103x63 Untitled 90 Chr 2/93 8,800
Ph 110x52 Rom Sby 5/93 8,050
A/Wd 24x79 Farbfeld 1986 Chr 2/93 7,700
Ph 106x47 Gardone Sby 2/93 6,900
Formis, Achille B.   It 1832-1906
* See 1993 Edition . . . .
Formozov, Valerian   Rus 1921-
O/C 20x15 Portrait of Kolesnik 1958 Sel 4/93 220
O/C 25x18 Forest Scene '57 Sel 4/93 130
O/B 19x32 On the Mola Bank 1975 Sel 4/93 110
O/C 28x20 Natasha 1964 Sel 4/93 90
Forrestall, Thomas De Vany   Can 1936-
Et/Pn Public Beach 1976 Sbt 5/93 3,520
Et/Pn The Holiday 1974 Sbt 5/93 3,520
Et/Pn Dog, Girl and Beach 1979 Sbt 5/93 2,640
Et/B 24x36 The Old Wing 1965 Sbt 11/92 2,640
W/Pa 15x20 Summer Home, New Brunswick Sbt 11/92 . . . 1,408
Forsner, Leopold   Con 19C
* See 1993 Edition . . . .
Forst, Miles
O/C 35x24 The Sorceress 57 Sby 2/93 345
Forster, George   Am a 1860-1890
O/C 25x30 Still Life with Fruit 1886 Sby 5/93 32,200
Forster, John Wycliffe Lowes   Can 1850-1938
O/C 11x16 The Artist Reading Sbt 11/92 1,672
Forsythe, Clyde Victor   Am 1885-1962
O/M 19x28 Landscape-Near Shoshone 1950 Mor 2/93 2,500

Forte, Luca   It 18C
* See 1991 Edition . . . .
Fortescue, William Banks   Br 1850-1924
O/C 37x29 Madame Butterfly 88 Chr 5/93 9,775
Fortescue-Brickdale, Eleanor   Br 1871-1945
* See 1992 Edition . . . .
Forti, Eduardo   It 19C
O/C 29x10 Mediterranean Street Scene Fre 10/92 250
Forti, Ettore   It 19C
O/C 23x40 Le Depart Du Maitre de Maison Chr 5/93 20,700
O/C 17x26 A Suprise Visitor Chr 5/93 16,100
O/C 29x11 Sapho Sby 5/93 7,188
Fortin, Marc-Aurele   Can 1888-1970
* See 1993 Edition . . . .
Fortunato, P.   It 20C
O/C 23x31 Tabletop Still Life Apples Book Slo 4/93 400
Fortune, Euphemia Charlton   Am 1885-1969
* See 1993 Edition . . . .
Fortuny Y Carbo, Mariano   Spa 1838-1874
W/B 11x8 Playing the Mandolin 1869 Chr 2/93 3,520
Fortuny Y De Madrazo, Mariano   Spa 1871-1949
* See 1990 Edition . . . .
Fortuny Y Marsal, Mariano   Spa 1838-1874
Pl&S/Pa 13x9 Servant; and Study Chr 10/92 1,320
Foschi, Pier Francesco Di Jac.   It 1502-1567
O/Pn 25x21 Lady, half length Chr 10/92 7,700
Fossi, E.   It 19C
O/B 8x6 Cupid Playing the Tambourine Wlf 9/92 500
Foster, Alan   Am 1892-
O/C 26x21 The Dance Sby 9/92 4,400
Foster, Alice C.   Am 1873-
* See 1993 Edition . . . .
Foster, Ben   Am 1852-1926
O/C/C 30x36 Landscape Mor 6/93 3,300
O/C 24x24 Wooded Landscape; Marsh: Pair But 12/92 . . . 1,100
Foster, G. H.   Am 19C
* See 1993 Edition . . . .
Foster, Hal   Am 1892-1982
Pl/Pa 34x23 Sunday Comic "Prince Valiant" Ilh 5/93 2,900
Foster, Robert   Am 1895-
Cs/Pa 17x22 Wary Courier; Man Held at Gunpoint Ilh 11/92 . 200
Foster, Will   Am 1882-1953
* See 1993 Edition . . . .
Fouace, Guillaume Romain   Fr 1827-1895
O/C 22x28 Nature Morte 1890 Chr 10/92 8,800
Foubert, Emile   Fr -1910
* See 1991 Edition . . . .
Foujita, Tsuguharu   Jap 1886-1968
O/C 16x10 La Chatelaine et sa Fillette 62 Sby 11/92 . . . 181,500
O/C 14x11 Young Girl in the Artist's Studio Sby 11/92 . . 110,000
O/C 11x9 Olive 1951 Sby 11/92 104,500
G&Pl/Pa 12x19 Les Danseuses Sby 5/93 21,850
Pl/Pa 11x8 La Ronde Chr 11/92 2,090
Fould, Consuelo   Fr 1862-1927
* See 1992 Edition . . . .
Foulkes, Llyn   Am 1934-
* See 1991 Edition . . . .
Foullon, Lucille   1775-1865
* See 1993 Edition . . . .
Fourie, Albert Auguste   Fr 1854-
O/Pn 11x14 Jeune Baigneuse Dans Le Parc But 5/93 2,300
Fournier, Alexis Jean   Am 1865-1948
O/C 26x40 Hollyhocks in Garden, Bungle House Chr 9/92 . 41,800
O/C 15x22 Venice 13 Chr 3/93 6,325
O/B 6x10 Wooded Landscape Sby 3/93 2,645
Fournier, Paul   Can 1939-
O&A/C 48x66 Blue Mushroom '73 Sbt 11/92 1,144
Fowler, Daniel   Can 1810-1894
W/Pa 18x24 Fallen Tree 1880 Sbt 11/92 2,640

Fowler, Evangeline Am 1885-1934
O/C 22x28 Distant Peaks Skn 3/93 605
Fowler, Frank Am 1852-1910
* See 1991 Edition
Fowler, Helen Am 20C
O/C 16x30 Southern Sea 1959 Lou 12/92 100
Fowler, Robert Br 1853-1926
* See 1992 Edition
Fowler, Trevor Thomas Am 1830-1871
* See 1991 Edition
Fowler, William Am
* See 1992 Edition ....
Fox, Edwin M. Eng a 1830-1870
* See 1992 Edition ....
Fox, J. Fr 19C
O/Pn 10x7 The Giggling Girl Hnz 5/93 700
Fox, John Richard Can 1927-
O/C 30x24 The Cloister, Florence Sbt 5/93 1,496
O/C 24x30 Inlet Sbt 11/92 572
Fox, Robert Atkinson Am 1860-1927
O/C 10x16 Cows in a Pasture Dum 5/93 2,750
O/C 9x17 Cattle by a Stream Fre 10/92 450
Fox, Terry
Ph 24x36 The Labyrinth: Nine 1973 Sby 11/92 2,750
Fragiacomo, Pietro It 1856-1922
* See 1993 Edition ....
Fragonard, Alexandre Evariste Fr 1780-1850
* See 1990 Edition ....
Fragonard, Jean-Honore Fr 1732-1806
* See 1993 Edition ....
Fragonard, Theophile-Evariste Fr 1806-1876
* See 1993 Edition ....
Frampton, Edward Reginald Br 19C
* See 1992 Edition ....
Francais, Francois Louis Fr 1814-1897
O/C 22x19 Wooded Forest 1882 Chr 2/93 1,100
France, Eurilda Loomis Am 1865-1931
O/C 13x22 Coastal France Brd 8/93 632
O/C 15x18 Garden and Olive Tree, France Brd 8/93 632
O/C 15x22 View Across the Wall Brd 8/93 495
France, Jesse Leach Am 1862-1926
O/C 12x18 The Wharf on the Pond Skn 5/93 1,430
O/B 10x12 Venice Brd 2/93 440
Frances Y Pascual, Placido Spa 1840-
* See 1990 Edition ....
Frances, Esteban 20C
* See 1992 Edition ....
Franceschini, Baldassare 1611-1689
O/C 57x91 Bacchus with Putti Sby 5/93 4,888
Franceschini, Marcantonio It 1648-1729
O/C 49x38 The Penitent Magdalene Chr 10/92 33,000
Francesco, Carlo 1609-1669
O/C 74x90 Man Being Escorted to Gallows Chr 1/93 24,200
Franchere, Joseph Charles Can 1866-1921
* See 1993 Edition ....
Franchi, T* It 19C**
* See 1993 Edition ....
Francia, Giacomo It 1486-1557
* See 1993 Edition ....
Francini, Mauro
* See 1992 Edition ....
Francis, John F. Am 1808-1886
O/C 11x13 Still Life with Currents 1866 Sby 12/92 26,400
Francis, Sam Am 1923-
O/C 48x40 Silvio Set One 1963 Sby 5/93 288,500
A/C 72x84 Untitled 1977 Chr 11/92 176,000
A/C 84x120 Untitled No. 7 Chr 2/93 132,000
A/C 87x110 Untitled 1974 Hnd 5/93 105,000
A/C 72x48 Having to do with the Whale 1986 Sby 11/92 . 82,500
G/Pa 71x37 Untitled Sby 5/93 79,500
A/Pa 26x58 Untitled Sby 11/92 68,750
A/Pa 72x36 Around Us Day and Night Chr 11/92 60,500

O/C 27x32 My Fairly Furry Green Angel 1973 Sby 5/93 .. 57,500
A/Pa 72x36 Son of Fire Sby 11/92 55,000
A&O/C 42x34 Untitled 73 Sby 5/93 41,400
A/Pa 24x18 Untitel 1978 Chr 11/92 36,300
A/Pa/C 48x64 Untitled Chr 11/92 35,200
W/Pa 10x22 Untitled 1957 Chr 11/92 33,000
A/Pa 15x18 Untitled Sby 11/92 33,000
A/Pa 22x30 Untitled 1970 Chr 11/92 23,100
A/Pa 19x14 Untitled Sby 11/92 15,400
A/Pa 30x22 Untitled Sby 10/92 9,900
A/C 7x5 Untitled 1985 Sel 12/92 6,500
Francis, Thomas E. Br -1912
W/Pa 10x14 Village with Horsecart Fre 4/93 400
Francisco, John Bond Am 1863-1931
O/C 16x20 California Mountains But 10/92 2,750
O/C 16x20 View Near Pasadena But 3/93 2,475
O/C 16x22 Sunset Wtf 3/93 2,200
Francisque 1666-1723
O/C 28x22 Figures Before a Roman Marble Tomb Sby 5/93 13,225
Franck, Albert Jacques Can 1899-1973
O/B 24x30 St. George Street at Sussex '63 Sbt 11/92 9,680
O/Pn 19x24 The Good Old Days '35 Sbt 11/92 2,376
O/M 10x8 Floral Still Life 1937 Lou 6/93 200
Francken, Frans (the Younger) Flm 1581-1642
O/Cp 27x34 The Building of the Tower of Babel Sby 1/93 . 34,500
O/Pn 21x30 The Road to Calvary Sby 1/93 25,875
O/Pn 31x58 Ways Attaining Immortality 1610 Chr 1/93 .. 20,900
Franco, Giovanni Battista It 1510-1580
* See 1992 Edition ....
Franco, Siron Brz 1947-
* See 1993 Edition ....
Francois, Guy Fr 1578-1650
* See 1992 Edition ....
Francois, Pierre Joseph Bel 1759-1851
* See 1991 Edition ....
Francucci, Innocenzo 1485-1548
O/Pn 38x30 Madonna and Child w/Infant St. John Chr 5/93 81,500
Frandzen, Eugene M. Am 1893-1950
O/C 25x30 Mountainous Landscape Hnd 5/93 1,100
Frangiamore, Salvatore Br 20C
* See 1993 Edition ....
Frank, Gerald A. Am 1888-
* See 1993 Edition ....
Frank, Joseph Ger 20C
* See 1993 Edition ....
Frank, Leo E. Am 20C
* See 1993 Edition ....
Frank-Will Fr 1900-1951
O/B 16x20 Market Scene Wtf 9/92 200
Franke, Albert Ger 1860-1924
* See 1992 Edition ....
Frankenstein, Godfrey N. Am 1820-1873
* See 1993 Edition ....
Frankenthaler, Helen Am 1928-
O/C 54x70 Yellow Clearing Sby 5/93 200,500
O/C 48x109 February's Trun Sby 11/92 79,750
A/C 34x27 Dusk Chr 10/92 46,200
A/C 17x29 Covent Garden Study 1984 Chr 10/92 22,000
O/Pa 17x14 April 1 Sby 10/92 8,250
A/Pa 18x24 Emerson Series III Chr 11/92 7,150
Frankl, Franz Ger 1881-
* See 1992 Edition ....
Franquelin, Jean Augustin Fr 1798-1839
* See 1990 Edition ....
Franquinet, Eugene Am 1875-1940
O/C 30x25 Yellow Cannas But 6/93 2,875
Franz, Ettore R. It 1845-1907
* See 1993 Edition ....
Franz, Otto D. Ger 1871-
O/Pw 33x39 Repose at the Summit But 11/92 1,760
Franzen, August Am 1863-1938
* See 1990 Edition ....
Franzig-Gluzing Ger 20C
O/C 29x48 Marine Scene with Tall Ships 1930 Sel 9/92 ... 400

Frappa, Jose Fr 1854-1904
O/C 33x21 Fille aux Oranges Sby 10/92 3,960
Frasconi, Antonio Am 1919-
W/Pa 20x26 Warwick Mine Fre 4/93 375
Fraser, Alex (the Senior) Br 1786-1865
* See 1990 Edition . . . .
Fraser, Alexander Br 20C
O/C 20x24 The Evening Meal Chr 10/92 1,540
Fraser, Charles Am 1782-1860
* See 1993 Edition . . . .
Fraser, Thomas Douglass Am 1883-1955
O/C 12x14 Cypresses in Landscape 1912 Mor 6/93 2,475
Fratella, Paulo
O/B 16x20 Grape Arbor Ald 5/93 300
Frazer, Harland Am a 1930-1939
O/B 14x21 Explorers Ih 11/92 1,200
Frazetta, Frank Am 1928-
Pl/Pa 16x24 Sunday Comic "Johnny Comet" Ih 11/92 3,750
Pl/Pa 18x14 Sinister Couple Embrace Ih 5/93 1,500
Freckleton, Harry Br 1890-1979
O/C 30x25 Clifton Woods, Notts Hnd 12/92 425
O/C 25x20 The Harbour Wall Hnd 5/93 425
Freddie, Frederik Wilhelm C. Dan 1909-
* . . . .
Fredericks, Ernest Am 1877-1927
O/C 22x28 Autumn Landscape Hnd 10/92 300
O/C 24x30 Golden Sunlit Valley Sel 4/93 225
O/C 16x20 Autumn Landscape Wes 5/93 220
Fredriks, Jan Hendrik 1751-1822
* See 1993 Edition . . . .
Freeman, Don Am 1908-1978
Y&G/Pa 24x32 Impression of Congressional Hearing Slo 4/93   450
Freer, Frederick Warren Am 1849-1908
O/C 24x19 The Old Letter Sby 3/93 5,175
Freezor, George-Augustus Br a 1861-1879
* See 1990 Edition . . . .
Freilicher, Jane 1924-
* See 1993 Edition . . . .
Freiman, Lillian Can 1908-1986
* See 1992 Edition . . . .
Freminet, Martin Fr 1567-1619
* See 1991 Edition . . . .
French, Alice Helm Am 1864-
O/C 24x18 Portrait of Young Girl Mys 3/93 440
French, Frank Am 1850-1933
O/C/B 10x8 Fog in the Mountains Lou 9/92 50
French, Jared Am 1905-
* See 1993 Edition . . . .
Frequenez, Paul Leon Fr 1876-
* See 1991 Edition . . . .
Frere, Charles Theodore Fr 1814-1888
O/Pn 13x19 Au Bord de la Ville Sby 10/92 8,800
Frere, Pierre Edouard Fr 1819-1886
O/B 13x17 Bird Catchers 1869 Hnd 6/93 4,600
Frerichs, William Charles A. Am 1829-1905
O/C 30x46 Skating in Winter Chr 12/92 15,400
O/C 30x50 Shooting Birds in a River Gorge 1878 Sby 5/93   13,800
O/C 60x36 The Swing Sel 9/92 2,500
Frey, Johann Jakob Sws 1813-1865
* See 1993 Edition . . . .
Frey, Johann Wilhelm Aus 1830-
W&I/Pa 8x11 View of Vienna Chr 2/93 1,100
Freyberg, Conrad Ger 1842-
* See 1991 Edition . . . .
Friberg, Arnold Am 1913-
* See 1993 Edition . . . .
Fried, Pal Hun 1893-1976
O/C 30x24 Intermission Sby 6/93 2,013
O/C 24x30 Ballerina Lou 9/92 1,100
O/C 30x24 Simone Lou 9/92 1,100
O/C 30x24 Maxine Wes 3/93 1,045
O/C 24x30 Carmen Wtf 4/93 1,000
O/C 24x30 Woman on Paris Street Lou 12/92 900

O/C 30x24 At the Opera Sel 2/93 800
O/C 24x30 Fishing Lou 9/92 800
O/C 24x30 Rowing on an Autumn Day Lou 9/92 800
O/C 24x30 Parisian Girl Lou 3/93 700
O/C 30x24 Female Nude Sby 6/93 690
O/C 24x30 Two Ballerinas Sby 2/93 575
O/C 30x24 Flamenco Sel 4/93 300
Friedeberg, Pedro It 1937-
* See 1993 Edition . . . .
Friedenthal, David Am 20C
W/Pa/B 59x31 The Wounded Bird But 4/93 1,150
Friedlander, Friedrich Aus 1825-1901
O/Pn 23x31 Words of Reason Doy 5/93 10,450
Friedman, Arnold Am 1879-1946
* See 1993 Edition . . . .
Friedrich, M. G.
O/C 24x12 Sailboat at Sea Wtf 9/92 450
Frielicher, Jane Am 1924-
* See 1990 Edition . . . .
Friend, Washington F. Can 1820-1886
W/Pa 10x14 Little Falls; Lake: Pair Sbt 11/92 2,860
Frier, Harry Br 1849-1919
* See 1993 Edition . . . .
Fries, Charles Arthur Am 1854-1940
O/C 24x36 Afternoon Desert-Palm Springs Mor 2/93 3,500
O/C 24x36 Green Pastures 1937 But 10/92 1,320
O/C 10x14 In the Eucalyptus Grove Mor 2/93 950
Frieseke, Frederick Carl Am 1874-1939
O/C 32x32 On the Beach Chr 12/92 396,000
O/B 11x10 Dressing Sby 12/92 25,300
O/B 24x20 The Satin Slip Chr 9/92 22,000
Friesz, Emile-Othon Fr 1879-1949
O/C 29x24 La Jardiniere Devant la Fenetre Chr 10/92 16,500
O/C 36x29 Le Marche de Toulon 31 Chr 10/92 16,500
O/C 26x21 Nu Sby 10/92 8,800
Frigerio, R. It 20C
O/C 12x16 An Unwelcome Advance Slo 4/93 475
Friis, Frederick Trap Am 1865-1909
O/C 26x24 Florence, Piazza S. Lorenzo Chr 9/92 4,400
O/C 13x10 Artist in His Atelier Lou 9/92 1,600
Frind, August Aus 1852-1924
* See 1990 Edition . . . .
Frink, Elizabeth 1930-
W/Pa 30x22 Male Nude 62 Chr 2/93 1,100
Fris, Jan 1627-1672
O/Pn 19x25 Still Life Stoneware Jug, Roll Sby 5/93 21,850
Frisch, Johannes Christoph Ger 1738-1815
O/C 18x30 An Arab Caravan Chr 2/93 1,540
Frison, Johan 1882-1961
O/C 28x24 Les Pavots et Luminaire 1941 Chr 11/92 2,750
Fristrup, Niels Dan 1837-1909
* See 1991 Edition . . . .
Frith, William Powell Br 1819-1909
O/C 34x44 Sleep 1873 Chr 10/92 13,200
O/C 13x16 Hogarth Before Gov of Calais 1850 Sby 10/92 . . 6,600
Fritzel, Wilhelm Ger 1870-
* See 1991 Edition . . . .
Fromentin, Eugene Fr 1820-1876
O/C 79x54 Centaures et Centauresses Sby 2/93 20,700
Froschl, Carl Aus 1848-1934
* See 1993 Edition . . . .
Frost, Arthur Burdett Am 1851-1928
R,W&G/Pb 26x17 A Shot at a Pheasant 1901 Sby 3/93 . . 17,250
W,G&R/Pa/B 18x26 Political Talk Chr 5/93 7,475
G&R/Pa 20x15 On the Site Chr 5/93 1,150
G&R/Pa 13x11 Men Around Coal-Burning Stove Ih 11/92 . . . 950
G&W/Pa 12x9 Woman in an Interior Lou 12/92 500
Frost, Francis Shedd Am 1825-1902
* See 1993 Edition . . . .
Frost, George Albert Am 1843-
O/C 28x40 Living in the Arctic 1882 But 6/93 2,875
Frost, John (Jack) Am 1890-1937
O/C 30x36 Near Lone Pine, California 1924 But 3/93 35,200
O/Pn 24x28 Pool at Sundown '23 But 3/93 27,500

Frost, William Edward   Br 1810-1877
* See 1993 Edition ....

Fruhmesser, Joseph   Ger 1927-
O/C 40x36 Bavarian Village Scene Dum 4/93 300

Fry, John H.   Am 1861-1946
* See 1992 Edition ....

Fry, Rowena   Am 20C
* See 1992 Edition ....

Fuchs   20C
O/C 29x39 Snow Scene Dum 8/93 450

Fuechsel, Herman   Am 1833-1915
O/C 15x30 Fishing on the Lake Chr 3/93 8,050
O/C 11x20 On the Lake Chr 12/92 1,870
O/C 31x22 The Cataract 1895 Sby 9/92 1,540

Fuertes, Louis Agassiz   Am 1874-1927
G/Pa/B 10x15 Lesser Whistling Teal Doy 11/92 4,950
G/Pa/B 11x15 Muscovy Duck with Mate Doy 11/92 4,950
G/Pa/B 11x15 White Face Tree Duck 1906 Doy 11/92 4,125
Pl/Pa 3x6 Three Birds at Doorstep 1895 Lou 12/92 150

Fuger, Friedrich Heinrich   1751-1818
* See 1993 Edition ....

Fuller, Alfred
O/B 8x10 Clean Swept Ald 9/92 160

Fuller, Arthur D.   Am 1889-1966
O/B 22x34 Canoeing in Rapids 1924 Ald 5/93 9,000

Fuller, Charles B.   Am 1821-1893
* See 1993 Edition ....

Fuller, George   Am 1822-1884
* See 1993 Edition ....

Fuller, Richard Henry   Am 1822-1871
O/C 15x26 Landscape with Fisherman on a Pond Sby 9/92 . 2,640
O/Pn 8x12 Cottage in a Landscape Sby 9/92 1,540

Fulleylove, John   Br 1845-1908
O/C 18x29 Women Picking Fruit 1875 Wtf 4/93 2,100
W/Pa 9x6 An Arab Farmer 1901 Chr 5/93 1,380

Fulop, Karoly   Am 1898-1963
W&P/Pa/B 14x18 Lake Echoes But 10/92 550

Fulton, David   Br 1850-
* See 1992 Edition ....

Fulton, Fitch Burt   Am 1879-1955
O/C 25x30 Grazing in the Yard But 10/92 2,475

Fulton, Hamish   1946-
Ph/B 36x95 Walk to the Summit 1985 Chr 11/92 24,200
Ph/B 29x63 Blue Stack Mtns of Donegal 1982 Chr 10/92 . 14,300
Ph/B 31x96 Sunrise 1982 Chr 2/93 11,000
Ph/B 44x51 River Rock 1987 Chr 11/92 9,350

Fulwider, Edwin   Am 1914-
O/C 24x30 The Vanishing American Sby 9/92 14,300

Fungai, Bernardino   It 1460-1516
* See 1992 Edition ....

Furini, Francesco   It 1604-1646
* See 1991 Edition ....

Fusaro, Jean   1925-
* See 1993 Edition ....

Fuseli, Henry   1741-1825
K,Pl&S/Pa 15x12 Fallen Horseman Attacked Chr 1/93 ... 22,000

Fussell, Charles Lewis   Am 1840-1909
W&G/Pa 20x24 Spring Blossoms 1902 Sby 5/93 11,500

Fussli, Johann Heinrich   1741-1825
K,Pl&S/Pa 15x12 Fallen Horseman Attacked Chr 1/93 22,000

Fyt, Jan   Flm 1609-1661
* See 1992 Edition ....

Gabani, Giuseppe   It 1849-1899
W&H/Pa 24x38 Desert Scene with Horsemen Skn 11/92 ... 1,980
W&G/Pb 21x30 An Arab Procession Chr 2/93 1,760

Gabriel, F.   Fr 20C
O/Pn 20x16 Still Life Grapes, Peaches & Plums Sby 1/93 .. 5,175
O/Pn 20x16 Still Life Flowers in an Urn Sby 1/93 3,450
O/Pn 20x16 An Ornate Still Life in Niche Chr 2/93 2,420
O/Pn 20x16 An Ornate Still Life on Table Chr 2/93 2,420

Gabriel, Francois   Fr 19C
O/Pn 20x16 Floral Still Life But 11/92 2,200
O/B 8x10 Still Life Flowers Yng 5/93 650

Gabriel, H. M.   Fr 19C
O/C 27x22 Dutch Flower Seller Hnd 9/92 300

Gabrini, Pietro   It 1856-1926
O/C 35x47 The Birthday Feast Dum 4/93 7,500
O/C/M 40x26 Fisherman at Dusk Chr 10/92 5,500
W/Pa 25x38 Bringing in the Day's Catch Chr 10/92 3,850
O/C 21x31 Boating in the Lagoon Wes 5/93 3,300
W/Pa 29x20 He Loves me He Loves me Not Chr 10/92 .. 2,200

Gadbois, Louis   -1826
W&Cw/Pa 10x13 Alleys of a Park with Ladies Chr 1/93 ... 1,320

Gael, Barent   Dut 1620-1703
* See 1993 Edition ....

Gaertner, Carl Frederick   Am 1898-1952
* See 1993 Edition ....

Gage, George William   Am 1887-1957
O/B 30x39 Armed Robbery at the Oil Well Ih 5/93 850

Gagen, Robert Ford   Can 1847-1926
W/Pa 13x19 Fishing Village, Fundy: Pair 1909 Sbt 11/92 ... 528
W/Pa 9x13 Monhegan Island, Maine Sbt 11/92 352

Gagliardo, Bartolomeo   1555-1626
K&Pl/Pa 7x7 Saint Francis in Prayer Chr 1/93 2,200

Gagni, P.   Fr 20C
O/Cb 8x11 Cafe de la Paix, Paris Slo 4/93 275
O/Cb 8x11 Marche aux Fleurs, Paris Slo 4/93 250
O/Cb 8x11 Porte St. Denis, Paris Slo 4/93 250

Gagnon, Clarence Alphonse   Can 1881-1942
O/C 24x32 Village in Winter, Poully, Switzer. Sbt 11/92 .. 44,000
W&P/Pa 25x37 Apres la Tempete Sbt 5/93 11,880
O/B 6x9 Moonlight 1946 Sbt 5/93 3,520
O/Pn 5x7 La Riviere Vefsna, Norvege 1934 Sbt 5/93 ... 1,760

Gaines, Charles   20C
* See 1992 Edition ....

Gainsborough, Thomas   Eng 1727-1788
O/C 30x25 Portrait Thomas Nuthall Sby 1/93 54,625
O/C 30x25 Portrait Ralph Leycester Dum 3/93 40,000

Gaiper, T. E.   Con 19C
* See 1993 Edition ....

Gaiser, J.   19C
O/C 30x24 Tavern Courtship 1871 Doy 5/93 2,200

Gaisser, Jacob Emmanuel   Ger 1825-1899
O/Pn 9x7 The Mystery Kerchef Chr 2/93 2,420

Gaisser, Max   Ger 1857-1922
* See 1991 Edition ....

Galan, Julio   LA 20C
O&L/C 20x26 El Juego 84 Chr 11/92 7,150

Galantiere, Nancy   Fr 20C
* See 1992 Edition ....

Galbraith-Cornell, Elizabeth   Can 1916-
O/C 15x20 Morning Perce Sbt 11/92 264

Gale, Dennis   Can 1828-1903
W/Pa 6x9 Falls of Montmorency: Pair Sbt 11/92 1,056
W/Pa 6x9 Moonlight Sleigh Ride Sbt 11/92 880

Gale, William   Br 1823-1909
O/Pn 12x9 Harem Beauty with Dove 64 But 11/92 3,850

Galer, Ethel Caroline Hughes   Br 20C
* See 1993 Edition ....

Galgiani, Oscar   Am 1903-
O/C 25x30 Mountain Landscape '56 Mor 6/93 1,650

Galien-Laloue, Eugene   Fr 1854-1941
G/Pa 8x12 Quai des Celestins Sby 2/93 14,950
G/Pa 8x12 Place de la Republique Sby 2/93 11,500
G/Pa 8x12 Paris Quai with View of Notre Dame Chr 2/93 . 11,000
G/Pa 8x13 Paris Street in Autumn Chr 10/92 11,000
G/Pa 8x13 Paris Street in Winter Chr 10/92 11,000
G/Pa 7x12 Snowy Paris at Twilight Doy 5/93 11,000
G/Pa 8x13 Autumn Evening in Paris Chr 10/92 8,800
W&G/Pa 9x13 La Madeleine Chr 10/92 8,800
G/Pb 8x12 Place de La Republique in Snow Chr 2/93 ... 8,800
O/C 18x26 View of Naples Sby 5/93 8,050
W&G/Pa 8x11 Flower Stalls along the Seine Slo 5/93 8,000
W&G/Pa 12x7 Place Vendome Chr 10/92 7,920
G/Pa 10x17 Paris Street in Winter Hnd 6/93 6,800
O/C 20x26 Bringing Home the Catch Chr 10/92 6,600
O/Pn 6x9 La Gare de L'Est Sby 2/93 5,175
G/Pa/B 9x12 Sur le boulevard Skn 3/93 3,025

Gall, Francois   Fr 1912-1945
O/C 18x11 Devant la Coiffeuse Doy 11/92 8,800
O/C 11x9 Aux Deux Magots Chr 11/92 6,600
O/C 18x15 Jeune femme en rouge Chr 11/92 6,600
O/C 11x18 Eugenie a la Terrace Du Cafe Sby 6/93 5,750
O/C 24x20 Jeune Femme au Cafe Doy 5/93 5,225
O/C 9x16 Deauville Chr 5/93 4,830
O/C 16x13 Ballerine Chr 2/93 4,400
O/C 11x9 Nature Morte and La Plage: Two Doy 5/93 3,740
O/C 9x11 Figures on a Beach Sby 2/93 3,738
O/C 20x24 Le Pont des Arts a Paris Sby 6/93 3,450
O/B 9x13 Plage a Ostende Chr 11/92 3,300
O/C 10x18 Quai de la Seine Sby 10/92 3,300
O/C 11x18 Le Pont Neuf a Paris Sby 6/93 3,163
O/C 9x11 Cafe Interior Sby 2/93 2,990
O/C 9x11 Jeune Femme Dans le Pres Sby 2/93 2,875
O/C 11x9 Femme se Coiffant Chr 2/93 2,860
O/C 9x11 Femme en Rouge Chr 2/93 2,750
O/C 11x9 Danseuse Assise Chr 2/93 2,420
O/C 22x26 Dans Le Parc Chr 5/93 2,300
O/C 9x11 La Plage Chr 5/93 2,300
O/B 18x13 Eugenie a la Robe Rouge Sby 6/93 1,150
O/C 11x9 Lady Seated at Her Vanity FHB 6/93 500
Gallagher, Michael   Am 20C
   * See 1992 Edition ....
Gallagher, Sears   Am 1869-1955
W/Pa 10x7 Man with Red Kerchief Yng 5/93 375
W/Pa 10x7 Portrait of an Old Salt Mys 3/93 275
Gallait, Louis   Bel 1810-1887
   * See 1992 Edition ....
Galland, Pierre Victor   Fr 1822-1892
   * See 1992 Edition ....
**Gallard-Lepinay, Paul Char E.   Fr
842-1885**
   * See 1993 Edition ....
Gallatin, Albert Eugene   Am 1882-1952
O/C 16x12 Composition 1938 Chr 9/92 7,700
Gallegos Y Arnosa, Jose   Spa 1859-1902
O/Pn 15x24 Flower Market 1893 Sby 5/93 107,000
O/Pn 15x10 Venetian Canal Scene Chr 5/93 27,600
Galli, Giuseppe   It 1866-1953
   * See 1993 Edition ....
Galli, Riccardo   It 1869-1944
O/Pn 14x19 Shepherd and his Flock Chr 5/93 1,380
O/Pn 10x6 Piggyback Fre 4/93 1,100
Galli, S.   20C
O/C 21x28 Elderly Woman '74 Dum 12/92 400
Galliani, Omar
   * See 1992 Edition ....
Galliari, Gasparo   It 1760-1818
   * See 1993 Edition ....
Gallis, Pieter   a 1661-1683
   * See 1993 Edition ....
Gallo, Vincent   1961-
O&H/St 36x57 Three Days in April Chr 11/92 2,310
Gallon, Robert   Br 1845-1925
   * See 1991 Edition ....
**Galofre Y Gimenez, Baldomero   Spa
849-1902**
   * See 1993 Edition ....
Galvan, Jesus Guerrero   Mex 1910-1970
C/Cd 31x23 Retrato de Annette 1944 Sby 11/92 10,450
W/Pa 21x15 Peasant Woman with Basket 1940 But 4/93 .. 9,200
O/C 32x47 Murcielago 1963 Chr 11/92 8,800
Gamarra, Gregorio   Per 17C
O/C 48x41 Assumption of the Virgin Chr 11/92 15,400
Gamarra, Jose   Urg 1934-
O/C 35x45 Les Missionnaires De L'Impossible '62 Sby 5/93 11,500
Gamba, Enrico   It 1831-1883
   * See 1993 Edition ....
Gambartes, Leonidas   Arg 1909-1963
   * See 1993 Edition ....
Gambino, Giuseppe
O/C 27x39 Paesaggio Sicilia 1957 Sby 2/93 518

Gamble, John Marshall   Am 1863-1957
O/C 20x30 Morning Mists (Wild Lilac) But 3/93 22,000
O/C 12x16 Wildflowers Near Litton Springs 1904 But 3/93 . 9,350
O/C/B 14x10 Hillside with Lupines But 3/93 7,700
O/M 16x24 California Gold But 10/92 3,575
G/Pb 9x9 Poppies and Lupines But 3/93 2,475
O/B 13x16 Spring Landscape But 10/92 2,090
Gamble, Roy C.   Am 1887-1972
O/C 20x16 Autumnal Landscape w/Tall Tree 1915 Sel 12/92 . 625
O/B 14x11 Farm House Dum 12/92 325
O/C 19x15 Camping 1923 Dum 1/93 275
W/Pa 9x12 Nurse Attending a Soldier '18 FHB 5/93 150
Gammell, Robert Hale Ives   Am 1893-
   * See 1993 Edition ....
Gampenrieder, Karl   Ger 1860-
   * See 1990 Edition ....
Ganbault, Alfred-Emile   Fr 19C
   * See 1993 Edition ....
Gandolfi, Gaetano   It 1734-1802
O/C 63x47 Jacob Stealing Isaac's Blessing Sby 1/93 ... 145,500
K/Pa 13x15 Pluto, Proserpine w/Charon 1798 Chr 1/93 .. 26,400
Gandolfi, Mauro   1764-1834
K/Pa 7x9 Three Girls, Bust Length Chr 1/93 39,600
Gandolfi, Ubaldo   It 1728-1781
   * See 1992 Edition ....
Gannam, John   Am 1897-1965
G/B 15x21 Man and Horse in Corral Ih 11/92 1,800
Ganne, Yves   Fr 20C
O/C 26x36 Nature Morte a la Cafetiere 58 Sby 10/92 1,540
Ganso, Emil   Am 1895-1941
O/C 14x21 Sleeping Nude Sby 9/92 5,225
C&K/Pa 16x23 Reclining Nude Sby 9/92 1,430
C&P/Pa 19x13 Reclining Nude 29 Chr 9/92 1,045
O/B 18x15 Bouquet of Flowers 37 Chr 12/92 605
Y/Pa 16x21 Reclining Female Hnd 3/93 500
W/Pa 15x21 Winter Landscape with Figures Lou 9/92 375
Ganter, Bernard   Fr 1903-
O/C 48x59 Winter Landscape 78 But 10/92 9,350
Gantner, Bernard   1928-
O/C 35x51 Reflets Dans La Riviere Chr 5/93 11,500
O/C 32x40 Maisons de Haute Saone 1972 Chr 11/92 6,600
Ganz, Edwin   Sws 1871-
   * See 1993 Edition ....
Garabedian, Charles   20C
   * See 1990 Edition ....
Garaud, Gustave Cesar   Fr 1847-1914
O/Pn 10x13 Outing by the River Chr 5/93 6,900
Garay Y Arevalo, Manuel   Spa 19C
   * See 1991 Edition ....
Garbell, Alexandre   Fr 1903-1970
   * See 1992 Edition ....
Garber, Daniel   Am 1880-1958
O/C 28x30 Along the Delaware Chr 12/92 71,500
O/C 13x18 Landscape Sel 12/92 1,200
Garburini, G.   It 19C
O/B 13x9 Fishermen Beside a Mill Sel 9/92 200
Garcia Y Mencia, Antonio   Spa 1850-
O/C 29x23 The Musical Party 1874 Sby 2/93 29,900
Garcia Y Ramos, Jose   Spa 1852-1912
   * See 1990 Edition ....
**Garcia Y Rodriguez, Manuel   Spa
1863-1925**
O/B 11x14 Mercato al Aire Libre 1919 Sby 10/92 13,750
Garcia Y Valdemoro, Juan   Spa 19C
O/C 30x40 Casa de Campo 1886 But 11/92 1,320
Garcia, Domingo   PR 1920-
   * See 1993 Edition ....
Garcia, Joaquin Torres   Uru 1874-1949
   * See 1993 Edition ....
Garcia-Sevilla, Ferran
   * See 1992 Edition ....
Garden, William Fraser   Eng 1856-1921
W/Pa 8x11 Stone Bridge into a Village '89 Wes 12/92 2,200
Gardeur, Charles   Bel 19C
O/C 28x35 Wedding Scene Hnd 5/93 1,000

Gardiner, Frank Joseph Henry   Eng 1942-
* See 1992 Edition . . . .
Gardner, J. S.
O/C 7x11 Old Topsail 1870 Eld 11/92   523
Gardner, L. L.
O/C 13x16 Still Life Cake and Wine Glass 1882 Eld 11/92 . .   275
Garet, Jedd   Am 1955-
A/C 73x57 She 1987 Sby 6/93 4,600
Gargallo, Pable   1881-1934
Pl/Pa/B 5x8 L'Eternelle Mediterranee 30 Chr 5/93 1,380
Gargiollo, A.   It 19C
W/Pa/B 21x29 Harem Scene 1892 But 11/92 5,500
Gargiulo, Domenico   It 1612-1679
O/C 25x20 Abraham and the Three Angels Chr 1/93 18,700
**Gargiulo, Domenico & Codazzi   It
1612-1679**
* See 1993 Edition . . . .
Garibaldi, Joseph   Fr 1863-
* See 1991 Edition . . . .
Gariot, Paul Cesaire   Fr 1811-
* See 1992 Edition . . . .
Garland, Charles Trevor   Br a 1874-1901
* See 1991 Edition . . . .
Garman, Ed   Am 1914-
* See 1992 Edition . . . .
Garnier, Jules Arsene   Fr 1847-1889
* See 1992 Edition . . . .
Garnsey, Julian Ellsworth   Am 1887-
W/Pa 13x10 California Landscape 1925 Slo 4/93   175
W/Pa 14x17 Tropical Foliage Slo 4/93   100
W/Pa 14x11 Yosemite, El Capitan Slo 4/93   100
W/Pa 17x14 Towers of the Alhambra 1927 Slo 4/93   80
Garrett, Edmund   Am 1853-1929
O/C 30x25 Peacocks in the Garden But 12/92 3,300
O/C 20x24 Stag Hounds, Somerset Village Yng 2/93 1,000
Garrido, Eduardo Leon   Spa 1856-1906
O/Pn 22x16 The Sketchbook Sby 2/93 24,150
O/Pn 18x15 Elegante, Place de la Concorde Sby 2/93 . . 23,000
O/Pn 22x18 A Song for the Lady Chr 2/93 16,500
O/Pn 8x11 A Lady Reading Chr 10/92 12,100
Garyson, Marvin   Am 19C
O/C 18x24 Bavarian Scene Lou 12/92   100
Gascars, Henri   Fr 1634-1701
* See 1992 Edition . . . .
Gaskell, George Arthur   Br a 1871-1900
* See 1993 Edition . . . .
Gaspard, Leon Schulman   Am 1882-1964
O/B 49x34 Twining Canyon 1954 Chr 12/92 231,000
O/C/B 10x8 Soldiers in the Snow 1911 Sby 9/92 11,000
O/Cb 18x15 King of the Sky Chr 12/92 4,180
Gaspari, Antonio
* See 1991 Edition . . . .
Gasparo, Oronzo   Am 1903-
O/Pa 19x24 My Kitchen 1940 Wlf 12/92   400
Gasser, Henry Martin   Am 1909-1981
W/Pa 15x23 The Hoffman House Sby 3/93 2,530
W&H/Pa 22x30 Houses in the Country Sby 3/93 2,300
O/C 20x28 Gloucester Harbor Fre 4/93 1,600
W&Pe/Pa 23x31 Town Covered in Snow Sby 9/92 1,430
W/Pa 22x31 Winter Harbor Sby 9/92 1,320
W/Pa 19x24 Rural Town Scene Chr 12/92 1,210
W&Pe/Pa/B 22x15 Summer Afternoon in Rome Sby 3/93 . . 1,150
W/Pa 10x8 Night Market Chr 5/93   978
W&Pe/Pa/B 19x24 The Walk Home Sby 9/92   770
W/Pa 30x16 Valley Springtime Fre 4/93   750
W/Pa 8x10 Two Works Wes 12/92   715
W/Pa 8x10 Morning Walk, Venice Lou 12/92   700
W/Pa 10x14 Return to the Mines Yng 2/93   600
G/B 18x23 Bay Road Skn 11/92   495
W/Pa 7x9 Rural Landscape Lou 3/93   275
Pe/Pa 13x20 Gloucester Fre 4/93   180
Gassies, Jean Bruno   Fr 1786-1832
* See 1992 Edition . . . .
Gassner, L.   Am 19C
* See 1993 Edition . . . .

Gast, John   Am a 1870-1879
* See 1993 Edition . . . .
Gatch, Lee   Am 1902-1966
O&L/C 39x25 Corridor 60 Sby 3/93 1,95
O/C/Pn 7x32 The Lamb Sby 3/93 1,49
Gatta, Saverio Della   It -1829
* See 1993 Edition . . . .
Gattorno, Antonio   Cub 1904-1980
G&Pl/Pa/B 18x20 Agricultores 1935 Chr 11/92 3,96
Gaucher, Yves   Can 1933-
A/C 30x30 Square Dance '64 Sbt 11/92 2,20
Gaudfroy, Fernand   Bel 1885-1964
* See 1993 Edition . . . .
Gaudier-Brzeska, Henri   1891-1915
Pl/Pa 15x10 Nu Assis Chr 5/93   36
Gauermann, Friedrich   Aus 1807-1862
* See 1993 Edition . . . .
Gauffier, Louis   Fr 1761-1801
* See 1991 Edition . . . .
Gaugengigl, Ignaz-Marcel   Am 1855-1932
* See 1993 Edition . . . .
Gauguin, Paul   Fr 1848-1903
O/C 13x16 Jacinthe et pommes Chr 11/92 148,50
P,C&W/Pa/B 9x12 Etude de Tetes Tahitiennes Sby 5/93 . 134,50
Y/Pa 8x7 Chaumieres en Bretagne Sby 5/93 4,60
Gaul, William Gilbert   Am 1855-1919
O/C 25x30 Cold Comfort on the Outpost Chr 12/92 27,50
O/C 18x24 A Meeting of the Elders Chr 5/93 13,80
O/C/B 12x16 The Boatbuilder Sby 9/92 4,40
W/Pa 10x7 Civil War Soldiers: Pair Hnd 10/92   95
Gauley, Robert David   Am 1875-1943
O/C 37x30 Helene and Blanquito 1920 But 12/92 1,98
Gaulli, Giovanni Battista   1639-1709
K,Pl&Br/Pa 10x8 The Martyrdom of a Royal Saint Chr 1/93 30,80
Gaume, Henri Rene   Fr 1834-
O/C 10x18 Woman on Hillside 1960 Wlf 5/93 1,90
**Gauthier, Joachim George   Can
1897-1988**
O/C 30x36 Baie Finn Range '36 Sbt 5/93 2,64
O/B 30x36 Cloudy Landscape with River Sbt 5/93 1,76
W/Pa 12x15 Northern Landscape Sbt 5/93   61
**Gauthier-D'Agoty, Jacques-F.   Fr
1710-1781**
* See 1992 Edition . . . .
Gautier, G.   Fr 20C
O/C 22x15 Standing Cavalier Dum 4/93 1,60
Gautier, Leon   Fr 19C
O/C 32x25 An Elegant Lady Seated on Ledge Chr 2/93 . . . 2,42
O/C 17x21 French Artist's Studio Dum 11/92 1,10
Gauvreau, Pierre   Can 1922-
* See 1992 Edition . . . .
Gavagnin, Giuseppe   It 19C
* See 1990 Edition . . . .
Gavarni, Paul Sulpice G.   Fr 1804-1866
Pe/Pa 10x9 A Charlatan Chr 10/92   55
Gaw, William Alexander   Am 1891-1973
W/Pa 16x20 Old Wharf, Pittsburgh But 10/92 3,02
Gay, August   Am 1890-1949
* See 1993 Edition . . . .
Gay, Edward B.   Am 1837-1928
O/C 20x16 Winter Scene 1879 Sby 3/93 2,99
O/C/M 17x27 Sheep Grazing Chr 5/93 1,95
O/Cb 10x14 A Quiet Pond 1906 Chr 12/92 1,43
O/Pn 5x14 Haying Scene Mys 12/92 1,26
O/C 15x21 Resting by a Brook Chr 5/93 1,09
O/C 18x24 Late November Landscape Fre 10/92   70
I/Pa 6x10 Where Seas and Meadow Meet Yng 5/93   12
Gay, George Howell   Am 1858-1931
W/Pa 16x39 Surf at Northampton, LI Sby 12/92 3,85
W&G/Pa 13x32 Rolling Tide Doy 5/93 1,32
W/Pa 14x27 Landscape with Stream Lou 9/92 1,00
W/Pa/B 15x34 Seascape Sby 9/92   66
W/Pa 12x22 House on a Plain Ald 3/93   27
W/Pa 10x20 Seascape Mys 3/93   24
W/Pa 14x26 Fall Landscape Wlf 4/93   15

W/Pa 11x21 Fall Landscape with Stream Wlf 4/93 100

Gay, Walter   Am 1856-1937
O/C 96x87 Charity 1889 Sby 5/93 27,600
O/Pn 22x18 Interior, Chateau du Breau Chr 5/93 9,200
W&G/Pa 15x11 The Mantel Sby 9/92 7,975
W&Pe/Pa 15x11 Library, Chateau du Breau Chr 9/92 4,620
O/B 22x18 Blue and White Wares Sby 9/92 4,400
O/C 22x18 Still Life Blue & White Porecelain Chr 5/93 4,370
O/C 36x26 Man and Machine Sby 3/93 2,875

Gay, Winkworth Allen   Am 1821-1910
O/B 8x12 Rocky Coast, Sailing Vessels 1872 Skn 9/92 825
O/Pn 15x11 Girl in Dutch Costume Sel 4/93 270

Gaylor, Samuel Wood   Am 1883-
W&Pe/Pa 11x16 Central Park, New York 1918 Chr 3/93 . . . 1,380

Gaze, Harold   20C
Pl&W/Pa 14x12 Fairy on Swing 1947 But 12/92 1,760
W&Pl/Pa 13x10 Water Fairies 1942 But 12/92 1,760
Pl&W/Pa 13x10 Flowers (3) 19 But 12/92 1,100

Gazzera, Romano
* See 1992 Edition . . . .

Gebhardt, Wolfgang Magnus   a 1730-1750
* See 1992 Edition . . . .

Gebler, Friedrich Otto   Ger 1838-1917
* See 1990 Edition . . . .

Gechtoff, Leonid   Am 20C
Pe&P/Pa 29x24 Vase of Flowers '33 Fre 4/93 775
P/Pa 24x30 The Red Mosque, Cairo '40 Fre 4/93 650
P/Pa 20x18 Floral Still Life Eld 8/93 88

Gechtoff, Sonia
* See 1993 Edition . . . .

Gedlek, Ludwig   Aus 1847-
* See 1991 Edition . . . .

Geertz, Julius   Ger 1837-1902
O/C 10x8 Des Madchen Und Ihr Puppe 84 Sby 1/93 6,325

Geets, Willem   Bel 1838-
* See 1990 Edition . . . .

Geibel, Casimir   Ger 1839-1896
O/C 26x40 Ploughing the Fields Chr 10/92 6,050

Geiger, Richard   Aus 1870-1945
* See 1993 Edition . . . .

Geirnaert, Jozef   Bel 1791-1859
O/Pn 15x11 Woman Playing the Lute Wes 3/93 2,970

Geisel, Theodor "Dr. Seuss"   Am 1904-1991
* See 1993 Edition . . . .

Gelbel, Casimir   Ger 1839-1896
* See 1991 Edition . . . .

Geldorp, George   1595-1665
O/C 47x35 Portrait of Boy with Dog 1617 Sby 5/93 31,050

Gelena, Giovanni   It 20C
W/Pa 13x19 On the Grand Canal Venice Hnd 5/93 650

Gelerdts, Flore   Bel 19C
* See 1991 Edition . . . .

Gelibert, Gaston   Fr 1850-
* See 1993 Edition . . . .

Gelibert, Jules-Bertrand   Fr 1834-1916
* See 1993 Edition . . . .

Gellee, Claude   Fr 1600-1682
* See 1992 Edition . . . .

Geller, Johann Nepomuk   Aus 1860-1954
O/C/B 23x30 Market Square, Misfrau Chr 2/93 19,800

Gemito, Vincenzo   It 1852-1929
* See 1992 Edition . . . .

Gen-Paul   Fr 1895-1975
O/C 36x23 Violoniste Chr 11/92 9,900
G/Pa/B 19x25 Aux Courses Chr 5/93 4,025
G/Pa 20x26 La Caleche Chr 11/92 2,860
G/Pa/B 19x25 Aux Courses Chr 5/93 2,070
Pl/Pa 16x12 Two Drawings Chr 5/93 920

Gence, Robert   18C
O/C 79x56 Portrait of a Gentleman 1713 Sby 1/93 46,000

Gendall, John   Br 1790-1865
O/C 43x60 London with St. Paul's Cathedral Chr 5/93 . . . 36,800

Genin, Lucien   Fr 1894-1958
O/C 24x29 Marseilles Chr 5/93 5,175

G&K/Pa/B 14x16 Le Moulin Rouge Chr 11/92 1,760
W,G&C/Pa/B 13x16 Notre Dame de Paris Chr 11/92 1,760
W,G&C/B 11x14 Le Pantheon Chr 11/92 1,650
G,W&K/Pa 8x10 Two Watercolors Chr 5/93 1,380
G,W&K/Pa 8x10 Two Watercolors Chr 5/93 1,380

Genis, Rene   Fr 1922-
O/C 37x24 Rue de Bonifacio Sby 10/92 3,575
O/C 46x29 Le Traghetto Venise Sby 10/92 3,025
O/C 15x22 Soir de Croisiere (Mer Egee) Skn 3/93 2,475
O/C 26x18 Le Nuage But 5/93 1,725
O/C 22x15 La Barque Bleue Sby 2/93 1,093

Genisson, Jules Victor   Bel 1805-1860
* See 1991 Edition . . . .

Genn, Robert   Can 1936-
O/C 30x34 West Boat Haven 1978 Sbt 11/92 1,540

Gennari, Benedetto   It 1633-1715
O/C 74x54 Venus Embracing Cupid Sby 1/93 54,625

Genoves, Juan   1930-
O/B 25x20 El Juego de Agedrez 1955 Chr 2/93 1,650

Genth, Lillian   Am 1876-1953
O/C 16x20 Corner Cafe Chr 9/92 9,350
O/C 23x18 Nude Wading by a Stream Chr 12/92 2,860
O/C 29x24 Looking Out the Window Chr 12/92 2,420
O/C 24x20 Portrait of a Woman 37 Hnd 5/93 375

Gentilini, Franco
* See 1992 Edition . . . .

Gentz, Karl Wilhelm   Ger 1822-1890
* See 1993 Edition . . . .

Geoffroy, Henry Jules Jean   Fr 1853-1924
* See 1992 Edition . . . .

George, Frances   Con 19C
O/C 21x26 Dinnertime Chr 2/93 1,320

Georges, Jean Louis   Fr -1893
* See 1993 Edition . . . .

Georges-Michel, Michel   Fr
* See 1993 Edition . . . .

Georgi, Edwin   Am 1896-
W&G/B 27x21 Illustration Intentions Complicated Skn 5/93 . 1,320
W&G/B 22x30 Illustration Redbook Magazine 1954 Skn 5/93 . 770

Georgi, Friedrich Otto   Ger 1819-1874
* See 1991 Edition . . . .

Gerard, Marguerite   Fr 1761-1837
* See 1993 Edition . . . .

Gerard, Paul   Fr 20C
O/C 30x24 Lacing Her Shoe Sel 4/93 300

Gerard, Theodore   Bel 1829-1895
O/Pn 23x35 Rustic Connoisseurship 74 Sby 5/93 27,600
O/Pn 28x21 The Embroidery Lesson 1864 Chr 5/93 18,400
O/Pn 24x29 The House of Cards 1869 Chr 10/92 17,600

Gerasch, August   Aus 1822-
O/Pn 15x12 Caught Playing Hookey Skn 11/92 2,310

Gericault, Theodore   Fr 1791-1824
* See 1991 Edition . . . .

Gerig, Bruce L.   Am 20C
C/Pa 33x33 Still Life with Monkies 1966 Sel 9/93 125

Germain, Jacques   Fr 20C
* See 1991 Edition . . . .

Gerome, F.
O/Cb 10x12 Paris Street Scene, St. Denis Dum 12/92 300

Gerome, Francois   Fr 20C
O/C 24x30 Place du Chatelet, Paris Wes 12/92 2,090
O/C 24x30 La Place de la Concorde a Paris Hnd 9/92 600
O/C/B 8x10 Notre Dame Lou 12/92 500
O/C 24x30 Porte St. Denis a Paris Hnd 9/92 225

Gerome, Jean-Leon   Fr 1824-1904
O/C 38x55 La Reception de Conde a Versailles Sby 5/93 . . 800,000
O/C 29x24 Le Retour de la Chasse Sby 2/93 277,500
O/C 28x22 Marcus Botsaris Sby 2/93 266,500
O/Pn 18x30 Louis XVI et Moliere 1862 Sby 2/93 101,500
O/C 24x40 Polyphemus and the Ship of Acts Sby 10/92 . . 27,500
O/C 21x17 Le Jour Du Jugement Dernier 61 Sby 2/93 24,150
O/C 6x9 Chestnut Throughbred Sby 1/93 3,450

Gerry, Samuel Lancaster   Am 1813-1891
O/C 18x34 Road to the Mountains Chr 3/93 11,500
O/C 20x30 Mt. Washington Vista 185* Chr 9/92 11,000

O/C 22x18 Shepherd Girl with Sheep Hnd 10/92 1,000
O/C 20x14 The Wooded Stream Skn 11/92 990
O/C 10x16 Landscape Near Medfield Yng 5/93 950
W,G&H/Pa 9x12 Lake Shore, Early Autumn Skn 9/92 770
O/B 9x14 Cattle Watering Yng 5/93 500

Gerson, Wojciech   Pol 1831-1901
O/Ab 11x10 Alpine Landscape FHB 6/93 250

Gervais, Lise   Can 1933-
* See 1992 Edition . . . .

Gervais, Paul Jean   Fr 1859-1936
O/C 64x87 Hommage/Bijouterie Francaise 1883 Sby 5/93 . 31,050
O/C 16x13 Jeune Fille Lisant Le Figaro 1888 Sby 1/93 . . . 4,600

Gervex, Henri   Fr 1852-1929
* See 1992 Edition . . . .

Gerzso, Gunther   Mex 1915-
O/C 29x21 Personaje--Paisaje 64 Chr 11/92 41,800
O/C 15x18 Rojo, Azul y Amarillo 66 Chr 11/92 41,800
A&Sd/M 28x36 Naranja-Azul-Verde 79 Sby 11/92 33,000

Gesmar, Charles
W&Pt/Pa 12x15 A Mistinguett 17 Sby 10/92 2,200
W&Pe/Pa 13x9 Two Costume Designs: Travesti Sby 10/92 . 1,100
W,Pe&Gd/Pa 22x15 Costume Flapper & Zinnia Sby 10/92 . . . 990

Gesner, Abelard & Fernand, P.   Hai
* See 1993 Edition . . . .

Gessi, Francesco-Giovanni   It 1588-1649
* See 1992 Edition . . . .

Gevers, Rene   Fr 1869-1944
* See 1993 Edition . . . .

Geyling, Rudolf   Aus 1838-1904
O/C 63x40 Parsifal and the Rhine Maidens But 11/92 8,250

Geza, Vastagh   Fr 20C
O/C 26x56 A Cat Nap Sby 2/93 4,888

Gherardini, Alessandro   It 1655-1726
* See 1993 Edition . . . .

Gherardini, Giovanni   It 1654-1725
* See 1993 Edition . . . .

Ghezzi, Pier-Leone   It 1674-1755
K&PI/Pa 12x8 Portrait of Venetian Cleric Chr 1/93 3,850

Ghiglion-Green, Maurice
* See 1992 Edition . . . .

Ghirlandaio   1452-1525
T/Pn 10x16 The Pieta, with Saints Chr 1/93 66,000

Ghisolfi, Giovanni   It 1632-1683
O/C 31x47 Soldiers Looting a Tomb Chr 1/93 18,700

Giachi, E.   It 19C
O/C 33x22 The Flirtation Sby 5/93 8,050

Giacomelli, Vincenzo   It 1841-1890
* See 1993 Edition . . . .

Giacometti, Alberto   Sws 1901-1966
O/C 73x32 Caroline Sur Fond Blanc 1961 Sby 5/93 . . . 354,500
O/C 36x29 L'Atelier 1961 Sby 5/93 189,500
Pe/Pa 20x13 Portrait de James Lord 1954 Sby 11/92 . . . 35,200
I/Pa 14x10 Chez le Coiffeur Sby 10/92 3,850

Giacometti, Giovanni   It 1868-1934
I/Pa 8x5 Etude de Tetes Sby 10/92 3,850

Giacomotti, Felix Henri   Fr 1828-1909
* See 1992 Edition . . . .

Giallino, Angelos   It 1857-
* See 1991 Edition . . . .

Giambono, Michele   It 1420-1462
* See 1993 Edition . . . .

Giampetrino   It 1493-1540
O/Pn 28x22 Saint Mary Magdalen Sby 10/92 22,000

Giani, Felice   It 1760-1823
T/Pa/C 33x45 Agamemnon's Refusal to Liberate Sby 10/92 17,050

Giani, Hugo   It 20C
* See 1992 Edition . . . .

Gianlisi, Antonio (the Younger)   1677-1727
O/C 39x34 Tompe L'Oeil Still Life Flowers Sby 1/93 85,000

Giannetti, Raffaele   It 1837-1915
* See 1993 Edition . . . .

Gianni   It 19C
W/Pa 7x16 Monk Overlooking the Amalfi Coast Lou 6/93 . . . 225

Gianni, G.   It 1829-1885
* See 1992 Edition . . . .

Gianni, Gerolamo   It 1837-
O/C 8x27 Grand Harbor, Malta 1875 Chr 10/92 7,70

Gianni, Gian   It 19C
G/Pa 16x8 Italian Street Scene Mys 3/93 19
W/Pa 20x13 Amalfi Dum 5/93 12

Gianni, Y.   It 20C
G/Pa 5x13 Porto a Venezia Wes 5/93 77
W&G/Pa 7x10 Bay of Naples Fre 4/93 25

Gianpetrino   It a 1520-1540
* See 1993 Edition . . . .

Gianquinto, Albert
O/C 41x26 Donna Con Bianba Sby 2/93 86

Giaquinto, Corrado   It 1703-1765
* See 1991 Edition . . . .

Giarardin, Frank J.   Am 1856-1945
O/C 20x30 Cathedral Peaks-Yosemite Valley Mor 6/93 41

Giardiello, Giuseppe   It 20C
* See 1993 Edition . . . .

Gibbezi, Jas.   Am 19C
O/C 10x5 Young Boy with Hobby Horse Mys 12/92 24

Gibbs, Leonard James   Can 1929-
A/B 28x17 Distant Call Sbt 5/93 3,08
W/Pa 22x26 Laura's Summer 91 Sbt 11/92 88

Gibbs, T. Bunny   Am 20C
O/C 48x24 Portrait of a Young Girl Chr 5/93 1,26

Gibney, Luke   Am 1894-1960
O/Cb 20x24 Seascape with Figure But 10/92 42

Gibran, Kahlil   Am 1883-1931
Pe&S/Pa 22x28 Two Children with Flowers 1968 Eld 8/93 . . 24

Gibson, Charles Dana   Am 1867-1944
PI/Pa 21x23 Two Women in Interior Ih 5/93 6,00
C/B 23x15 An Air of Elegance Chr 12/92 3,08

Gibson, James Brown   Eng 1888-
O/C 14x20 On Loch Chon Sel 9/92 27

Gibson, Thomas   Br 1680-1751
O/C 71x45 Portrait of Bridget Sby 5/93 6,03

Gide, Francois Theophile E.   Fr 1822-1890
O/C 59x79 The Storyteller Hnd 10/92 21,00
O/C 20x24 Soldier's Return Home Chr 10/92 2,20

Gies, Joseph W.   Am 1860-1935
O/C 21x17 Cavaliers Rolling Dice 86 Chr 5/93 2,99
O/B 8x12 Sailboat in Harbor Dum 9/92 32

Giesen   Am 20C
O/B 20x22 Argosy Magazine-Western Scene Mys 12/92 66

Giet, Alfred   Bel 20C
O/B 25x21 Spring Landscape Sel 4/93 67

Gifford, Charles Henry   Am 1839-1904
O/C 34x55 Returning to Port 1877 Chr 9/92 15,40
O/C 24x18 When the Tide is Out 1886 Eld 4/93 9,35
O/C 13x18 Light Through the Clouds '87 Skn 11/92 7,15
O/C 13x18 March Island, New Bedford Harbor Eld 4/93 . . . 4,95
O/C 9x14 Lake Scene with Mountain and Fog 1878 Eld 8/93 3,30
O/C 9x14 Sailing Off the Cliffs 1884 Skn 3/93 2,97
O/Pn 10x8 Fisherman in Small Boat Eld 7/93 2,53
O/C 12x17 American Steam-Sail Yacht Eld 7/93 2,31
O/C 9x13 Still Life Peaches 1902 Sby 3/93 1,38

Gifford, James   Eng 19C
* See 1991 Edition . . . .

Gifford, John   Br 19C
O/C 30x25 The Day's Bag Chr 2/93 1,65

Gifford, Robert Swain   Am 1840-1905
O/C 20x40 Cove Road, Naushon Island Sby 12/92 13,20
O/C 28x50 Seascape 1872 Sby 3/93 8,05
O/C 15x25 Two Figures with Baskets 1881 Sby 3/93 2,76
O/C 14x25 Brown Meadows Sby 9/92 2,53
O/C/B 27x44 Landscape with Windblown Trees But 12/92 . 2,47
O/C 29x24 Sunset Behind the Trees But 6/93 1,61
W/Pa 7x17 Fisherman in a Creek 1879 Eld 8/93 1,21
W&G/Pa 6x16 A Sandy Coast Chr 12/92 27

Gifford, Sanford Robinson   Am 1823-1880
O/C 14x30 Morning on the Hudson 1866 But 12/92 550,00
O/C 8x14 Sunset at Catania, Sicily Chr 5/93 28,75
O/C 8x13 Sketch of Mansfield Mountain Chr 12/92 26,40

O/C 5x8 A Home in the Woods Sby 5/93 12,650
O/C 16x12 Rider and Horse by a Gate Mys 12/92 12,540
O/B 6x5 North of Saratoga and Near Saratoga Chr 12/92 . 12,100

Gignon, Louis Fr
  * See 1992 Edition . . . .

Gignous, Eugenio It 1850-1906
  O/C 40x28 Montagna Annevata Sby 2/93 6,900

Gignoux, Francois Regis Am 1816-1882
  O/C 14x20 Autumn on the Hudson 1858 Chr 12/92 22,000
  O/C 27x40 Hudson River Valley 1849 Sby 12/92 13,200
  O/C 11x13 View The Jungfrau Lake Thun Sby 9/92 1,870

Gihon, Clarence M. Am 1871-1929
  O/B 6x7 Village Church, France Yng 2/93 150

Gilbert & George Am 20C
  L/B 32x44 Concord 1981 Chr 11/92 10,450
  L/B 54x39 Patriotic Pup 1981 Chr 2/93 8,250
  MM/Pb 52x38 Boadicea Attacking Westmin. 1981 Sby 10/92 6,600

Gilbert, Arthur Br 1815-1895
  O/C 10x14 Windsor Castle Sby 1/93 2,185

Gilbert, Arthur Hill Am 1894-1970
  O/C 24x30 Path Through the Trees But 3/93 6,050
  O/C 21x24 Spring, Monterey But 10/92 4,950
  O/C 25x30 Landscape Mor 11/92 1,800
  O/Cb 12x16 Distant Silo Mor 2/93 1,500
  O/C/B 20x16 Landscape Dum 8/93 1,500
  O/Ab 11x14 Green Pastures Mor 2/93 1,200
  O/Cb 16x20 Cloudy Day But 6/93 1,150
  O/B 12x16 Carmel Coast Dum 3/93 700

Gilbert, C. Allan Am 1873-1929
  P/C 40x15 Standing Woman Holding Rose Ih 5/93 2,500
  C&K/Pa 21x24 Woman Playing Piano Ih 11/92 650

Gilbert, Henry
  Pe&W/Pa 10x8 Full Length Portrait 1838 FHB 6/93 550

Gilbert, John Graham 1794-1866
  O/C 50x40 Portrait Mrs. Oswald of Scotston 1855 Sby 1/93 2,070

Gilbert, Lionel
  G/Pa 16x13 Man at Door in Dungarees Ih 5/93 1,700

Gilbert, Rene Joseph Fr 1858-1914
  O/C 29x23 The Red Parasol 1891 Chr 5/93 16,100

Gilbert, Sir John Br 1817-1897
  O/C 48x72 Scene Shakespeare's Henry VI Sby 5/93 9,200

Gilbert, Terence J. 20C
  * See 1991 Edition . . . .

Gilbert, Thomas Br 19C
  O/C 12x16 Lymington River: A Misty Morning Sby 1/93 . . . 1,495

Gilbert, Victor Gabriel Fr 1847-1933
  O/C 20x28 Flower Vendor Dum 5/93 65,000
  O/Pn 15x20 Le Panier de Cerises Sby 5/93 13,800
  O/C 59x42 Portrait de Jeune Fille 1881 Sby 2/93 12,075

Gilchrist, William Wallace Am 1879-1926
  * See 1990 Edition . . . .

Gildor, Jacob Isr 1948-
  O/C 22x18 Femme au Chapeau 1987 Hnd 9/92 150

Gile, Selden Connor Am 1877-1947
  O/B 18x22 South Bay South Bay But 10/92 6,600
  O/C/B 12x16 Boats and Houses Near Benecia But 6/93 . . . 3,450
  O/C/B 9x12 High Sierras But 6/93 1,840
  W/Pa 9x12 Working Women '32 But 6/93 1,380
  O/Cb 12x18 Mount Tamalpais '13 But 10/92 1,320
  O/C 9x13 Coastal Steamer 1989 Lou 9/92 1,200
  O/C 11x14 Marin County Mountains But 10/92 1,100
  O/Cb 12x16 Coastal Mor 11/92 600

Giles, Howard Am 1876-1955
  * See 1992 Edition . . . .

Gill, Colin
  P/Pa 17x13 Bernard Shaw Sby 2/93 518

Gill, Eric Br 1882-1940
  Pe/Pa 14x10 Female Nude '31 Hnd 9/92 1,500
  Pe/Pa 15x11 Kneeling Female Nude 32 Hnd 9/92 750

Gill, Frederick James Am 1906-1974
  O/C 19x26 Winter Landscape with Farm '47 Fre 10/92 350

Gillemans, Jan Pauw (the Elder) Flm 1618-1675
  * See 1993 Edition . . . .

Gillemans, Jan Pauwel (the Younger) Flm 1651-1704
  O/Pn 9x7 Still Life Grapes, Peaches, Nuts Sby 10/92 11,000

Gillespie, Gregory Am 1936-
  * See 1992 Edition . . . .

Gillig, Jacob Dut 1636-1701
  * See 1990 Edition . . . .

Gillis, Marcel
  * See 1992 Edition . . . .

Gilman, Ester Am 20C
  Pl/Pa 18x11 Reclining Nude Hnd 12/92 190

Gilmore, Ethel M Am 20C
  O/C 25x30 December FHB 6/93 50

Gilot, Francoise Fr 1921-1986
  O/C 51x35 Mother and Child Sby 6/93 2,588
  W/Pa 25x19 Claude and Paloma Skn 11/92 1,650

Gilpin, Sawrey Br 1733-1807
  O/C 34x42 Chestnut Hunter in Landscape 1778 Sby 6/93 . 13,800
  O/C 12x15 In for the Kill Chr 6/93 1,265

Gilsoul, Victor Olivier Bel 1867-
  * See 1993 Edition . . . .

Gimignani, Giacinto It 1611-1681
  * See 1992 Edition . . . .

Gina Am 20C
  W&G/Pa 8x12 Three Southern Folk Scenes 1950 Wlf 3/93 . . 650
  W&G/Cd 11x14 Southern Negro Church Scene Wlf 3/93 . . . 325
  W&G/Pa 11x14 Folk Scene with Slaves 1951 Wlf 3/93 225

Giobbi, Edward Am 1926-
  O&C/C 60x60 Day After Day #2 1967 Dum 6/93 1,600

Gioja, Belisario It 1829-1906
  W/Pa 26x20 A Garden Party Slo 4/93 2,000
  W/Pa 17x13 Two Women Washing Clothes Eld 8/93 1,650
  W/Pb 16x25 A Game of Cards Chr 5/93 1,495

Giordano, Felice It 1880-1964
  O/C 32x47 Harbor of Capri, North Sida Chr 2/93 6,600
  O/C 18x21 Harbor of Fishing Village Sby 1/93 4,025
  O/C 22x29 Fishing Boats in a Harbor Swk 5/93 2,200
  O/C 29x46 Harbor Along the Italian Coast Hnd 12/92 1,500
  O/Cb 20x24 Market Scene Sby 2/93 1,265
  O/C 20x24 Seascape, Capri, Italy Hnd 5/93 800

Giordano, Luca It 1634-1705
  O/C 51x60 Crucifixion of Saint Peter Sby 5/93 48,875
  O/C 38x29 Saint Paul the Hermit Chr 1/93 31,900
  O/C 35x26 The Madonna and Child Chr 1/93 18,700
  K,Br&S/Pa 12x12 Rest on the Flight into Egypt Chr 1/93 . . 13,200

Giorinotto It 20C
  O/C 12x18 Venice at Sunset Hnd 9/92 225

Giovannini, Vancenzo It 1816-1868
  * See 1993 Edition . . . .

Girardet, Eugene Alexis Fr 1853-1907
  O/C 30x40 Moroccan Coffee House Sby 5/93 33,350

Girardet, Jules Fr 1856-
  * See 1993 Edition . . . .

Girardet, Karl Sws 1813-1871
  * See 1993 Edition . . . .

Girardin Hai 20C
  * See 1993 Edition . . . .

Girardin, Frank J. Am 1856-1945
  O/Pn 16x20 Leupin and Wild Mustard Dum 5/93 550

Giraud, Pierre Francois Eugene Fr 1806-1881
  W/Pa 13x21 The Old Mill Chr 10/92 550

Girona, Julio Cub 1914-
  * See 1993 Edition . . . .

Gironella, Alberto Mex 1929-
  * See 1993 Edition . . . .

Girones, Ramon Antonio Pichot Spa 1872-1925
  * See 1993 Edition . . . .

Girotto, Napoleon It 19C
  W/Pa 15x10 Old Man with a Pipe Hnd 10/92 200

Giroud, Paul Fr 20C
  O/C 24x32 Rue de Paris Chr 5/93 575

Gisbert, Antonio Spa 1835-1901
  * See 1993 Edition . . . .

Gissing, Roland   Can 1895-1967
O/Cb 20x24 Bar Harbor, Maine Wlf 4/93 1,100
O/Cd 19x14 Yoho Valley Mountains, B.C. Canada Wlf 4/93 . 1,000
Gisson, Andre   Fr 1910-
O/C 24x36 Lake Landscape FHB 3/93 2,500
O/C 20x24 Summer in the Park Dum 8/93 2,500
O/C 20x16 Blue and Purple Flowers Sby 2/93 2,415
O/C 20x16 A Pair of Paintings: Paris Chr 11/92 2,200
O/C 20x24 Mother and Child by Lake Sby 2/93 2,185
O/C 16x20 Beach Scene with Figures, Sailboats Dum 1/93 . 2,000
O/C 24x30 Mother and Child Summer Landscape Sby 10/92 . 1,870
O/C 24x36 Rue de Paris Chr 11/92 1,870
O/C 24x30 Still Life with White Vase Sby 2/93 1,840
O/C 24x30 Les Champs Elysees Chr 11/92 1,760
O/C 11x14 Paris Street Scene Dum 7/93 1,750
O/C 24x36 Parisian Street Scene Slo 5/93 1,500
O/C 12x16 The Little Rose Sby 2/93 1,495
O/C 20x16 Still Life White and Blue Vases Sby 2/93 1,380
O/C 24x12 Vase of Flowers Sby 2/93 1,380
O/C 12x23 Girl in Boat Wlf 9/92 1,300
O/C 20x16 Floral Still Life Hnz 5/93 1,200
O/C 20x16 Nu se coiffant Hnd 9/92 1,200
O/C 24x20 Floral Still Life Hnd 10/92 1,100
O/C 16x20 Two Nudes in a Landscape Sby 10/92 1,100
O/C 11x14 Parisian Street Scene Wlf 9/92 1,050
O/C 12x16 Young Girl in Pink Bonnet Lou 12/92 1,000
O/C 20x16 Nude Sby 6/93 920
O/C 12x24 Paris Scene Hnd 10/92 900
O/C 9x12 Dans le Pre Hnd 3/93 800
O/C 24x20 Floral Still Life Hnd 3/93 800
O/C 12x24 Paris Scene Hnd 10/92 800
O/C 12x24 Arc de Triomphe Hnd 9/92 750
O/C 12x24 Palace de la Concorde Hnd 9/92 750
O/C 12x24 Paris Street Scene Hnd 3/93 700
O/C 12x24 Paris Street Scene Hnd 3/93 500
O/C 16x12 Female Figure Sel 2/93 475
Giusto, Faust   It 19C
* See 1991 Edition . . . .
Glackens, William James   Am 1870-1938
O/C 18x24 Outdoor Swimming Pool Chr 12/92 154,000
O/C 24x18 Stroll in the Park Chr 9/92 115,500
O/C 20x15 Flower Study Sby 5/93 74,000
O/C 12x15 The Canal at Bayshore Chr 5/93 39,100
O/C 18x15 Girl in Yellow Dress Sby 5/93 23,000
O/Cb 13x16 Roses and Persimmons Chr 9/92 19,800
P/Pa/B 12x16 The Gazebo, Hartford Chr 3/93 14,950
O/Pn 9x11 Feressy with Pink House Chr 9/92 14,300
Br,I&Cw/Pa 13x17 The Castaway Brokers Chr 9/92 4,180
Pe,I&G/Pa 15x22 Soldiers Embarking for Cuba Chr 12/92 . 1,650
C&I/Pa 7x9 The Dispute Chr 12/92 1,650
C/Pa 10x7 In the Kitchen Chr 12/92 1,100
I/Pa 9x8 Man Gesturing Chr 12/92 770
W/Pa 10x14 Extensive Landscape Hnz 5/93 325
Glaman, Eugene Fish   Am 1873-1956
Pe/Pa 5x10 Resting Sel 12/92 170
Glarner, Fritz   Am 1899-1972
* See 1993 Edition . . . .
Glasco, Joseph   1925-
* See 1993 Edition . . . .
Glaser, David   Am 20C
O/C 21x24 The Pool Room Sby 9/92 2,200
Glass, James William   Br 1825-1857
O/C 69x95 Richard, Coeur de Leon 1854 Sby 2/93 71,250
Glatter, Armin   Hun 1861-1916
O/B 13x16 Coastal Village Wes 3/93 358
Glauber, Jan   Dut 17C
* See 1991 Edition . . . .
Glauber, Johannes   Dut 1646-1726
* See 1991 Edition . . . .
Gleason, Joe Duncan   Am 1881-1959
O/B 12x10 Near Lake Arrowhead Mor 2/93 950
G&W/Pa 6x9 Santa Cruz Mission Eld 8/93 88
Gleeson, Gerald Collins   Am 1915-1986
W&I/Pa 18x24 Two City Views 81 Skn 5/93 357

Gleeson, W.   Br 19C
O/B 14x11 Chickens Dum 12/92 75
Gleich, John   Ger 1879-
* See 1993 Edition
Gleitsman, Raphael   Am 1910-
W/Pa 20x25 Railroad Yard Wlf 5/93 2,900
O/B 16x19 Still Life Wlf 5/93 2,700
Gleizes, Albert   Fr 1881-1953
G/Pa 10x7 Composition Abstraite 24 Sby 5/93 20,700
G/B 13x8 Composition 30 Sby 10/92 15,400
Glendening, Alfred Augustus (Jr.)   Br 1861-1907
O/C 20x30 Looking Across Hindhead, Surrey But 5/93 . . . 2,784
Glessing, T. B.
O/C 30x40 Mill and Castle Ald 5/93 125
Glew, E. L.   Am 1817-1870
O/C 31x25 Lieutenant General Winfield Scott 1865 Fre 10/92 1,800
Glicker, Benjamin C.   Am 1914-
O/M 48x30 The Clown FHB 5/93 350
O/C 18x22 Old Mariner's Church FHB 5/93 75
Glindoni, Henry Gillard   Br 1852-1913
* See 1993 Edition
Glintenkamp, Hendrik   Am 1887-1946
Pe/Pa 9x5 Figure Studies, New York Views: Six Sby 9/92 . . . 660
Gloag, Isobel Lilian   Br 1865-1917
O/C 30x25 Still Life Fuschia in Urn Sby 2/93 3,680
Gloutchenko, Nicholai P.   O
* See 1993 Edition
Gluckmann, Grigory   Rus 1898-
O/Pn 11x10 Danseuse Assise Chr 11/92 3,300
Glura, Maes   Con 19C
* See 1993 Edition
Gnoli, Domenico   It 1933-1970
* See 1992 Edition
Gober, Robert   Am 1954-
Pt/Cot 14x27 Untitled (51D) Chr 11/92 11,000
Pe/Pa 14x11 Untitled Sby 5/93 9,200
H/Pa 8x11 Untitled 1984 Chr 10/92 7,700
Pe/Pa 17x20 Untitled, 1984 '85 But 10/92 3,300
Gobert, Pierre   1662-1744
O/C 54x41 Portrait of a Lady as Venus Chr 1/93 19,800
Gobis, Giuseppe   It 18C
* See 1991 Edition
Godard, Gabriel   Fr 1933-
O/C 36x29 Rentree des Classes 60 Sby 10/92 1,430
Godbold, Samuel Berry   Br a 1842-1875
* See 1993 Edition
Godchaux   Con 19C
* See 1991 Edition
Godchaux, Roger   Fr 1878-
* See 1990 Edition
Godman, A. C.   Am 20C
O/Cb 20x24 New York Harbor Slo 4/93 1,600
Godot, F.   Con 20C
O/M 16x21 Parisian Winter Scene Slo 7/93 80
Godward, John William   Eng 1858-1922
* See 1993 Edition
Goebel, Carl   Aus 1824-1899
* See 1992 Edition
Goebel, Rod   Am 20C
* See 1992 Edition
Goeller, Emily Shotwell   Am 1887-1965
* See 1993 Edition
Goenuette, Norbert   Fr 1854-1894
* See 1991 Edition
Goerg, Edouard Joseph   Fr 1893-1969
O/Pa/C 18x13 Enfants/Jardin Luxembourg 1952 Chr 5/93 . 3,450
Goetsch, Gustaf   Am 1877-1969
O/B 10x8 Interior of Artist's Studio Sel 2/93 310
P/Pa 12x15 Snowy Winter Scene Sel 2/93 190
O/Cb 14x18 The Big Wave '55 Sel 2/93 110
Goff, Lloyd Lozes   Am 1917-1983
* See 1993 Edition
Goings, Ralph   Am 1928-
O/C 45x52 Yellow Ford Camper 69 Sby 11/92 66,000

Goissert, F. Ger 20C
O/C 11x16 Three Landscapes Lou 3/93 225
Goitia, Francisco Mex 1882-1960
O/C 18x22 Costa De Cataluna 1906 Sby 5/93 40,250
Gold, Albert Am 1906-
* See 1990 Edition . . . .
Goldbeck, Walter Dean
O/C 28x49 Abroad in the Chalmer Car Dum 9/92 3,250
Goldberg, B. H. Am 19C
O/Pn 26x20 The Scholar Fre 4/93 550
Goldberg, Fred F. Am 20C
* See 1992 Edition . . . .
Goldberg, Glenn Am 20C
* See 1991 Edition . . . .
Goldberg, Michael Am 1924-
O/C 48x44 The Other Sunday Afternoon '60 Chr 11/92 . . . 18,700
O/C 74x78 Land's End 1959 Hnd 5/93 9,500
O/B/M 14x11 Untitled Chr 2/93 2,640
O/Pa 14x11 The Moment Sby 6/93 2,185
Goldberg, Regina Seiden Can 1897-
O/B 9x12 Harbour Scene Mys 3/93 110
Goldberg, Reuben Lucieus Am 1883-1970
* See 1993 Edition . . . .
Golden, Rolland Am 20C
Y/Pa 4x6 Woman; The Ideal (2) Lou 6/93 150
Goldstein, Jack Am 1945-
A/C 78x90 Untitled Sby 2/93 3,450
A/C 96x36 Untitled Chr 5/93 2,300
A/C 84x110 Untitled Chr 11/92 1,760
A/C 84x96 Untitled '86 Chr 11/92 1,400
Gollings, William Elling Am 1878-1932
O/C 30x20 The Passing of Time 1910 Sby 9/92 8,525
O/B 12x18 The Roundup But 6/93 4,888
O/B 7x10 The Wide Open Plains Lou 6/93 450
Golovin, Alexander
W&Gd/Pa 16x11 Two Costume Designs Sby 6/93 920
Golub, Leon Am 1922-
A/C 121x171 White Squad III Chr 11/92 49,500
O/C 120x85 Horsing Around IV Sby 11/92 25,300
A/L 24x64 Three Heads 1988 Sby 5/93 17,250
A/L 98x79 Assassins II 1970 Chr 10/92 9,350
A/C 46x44 Head VI 1964 Sby 5/93 9,200
Golubov, Maurice
* See 1992 Edition . . . .
Gomez Y Gil, Guillermo Spa 19C
* See 1992 Edition . . . .
Gomez, Paul Pierre Fr 19C
* See 1992 Edition . . . .
Gonne, Christian Friedrich Ger 1813-1906
* See 1992 Edition . . . .
Gontcharova, Nathalie Rus 1881-1962
O/C 41x27 Les Arbres en Fleur Sby 5/93 17,250
S/Pa 16x15 Fleurs Chr 5/93 1,380
Gonzales, Eva 20C
* See 1990 Edition . . . .
Gonzales, Jeanne Guerard Fr 1868-1908
* See 1992 Edition . . . .
Gonzalez, Carmelo Cub 1920-
* See 1993 Edition . . . .
Gonzalez, Juan Antonio Spa 1842-1914
O/C 16x12 Naturaleza Muerta Sby 1/93 4,600
Gonzalez, Julio Spa 1876-1942
I&S/Pa 10x6 Maternite 1906 Sby 6/93 4,600
Gonzalez, Maximiliano Cub 1926-
O/C 33x27 Mujer Abstracta 1949 Sby 11/92 7,150
Gonzalez, Xavier Am 1899-
A/C 23x32 Wellfleet, 1963 Eld 8/93 550
Good, Leonard Am 1907-
O/C 20x26 Bathers '31 Lou 12/92 1,000
Good, Samuel S. Am 1808-1885
* See 1993 Edition . . . .
Goodall, Frederick Br 1822-1904
O/C 33x48 The Swing 1854 Doy 5/93 26,400
O/C 53x36 Already He Knew God as His Father Sby 10/92 25,300

O/C 57x39 Rachel and her Flock 1874 Chr 10/92 15,400
O/C 32x72 Shepherdess and Her Flock Hnd 3/93 6,800
Goode, Joe 1937-
O/B 48x45 Ocean Blue #43 1989 Chr 2/93 4,180
Goode, John Br 19C
O/C 18x24 Horse in a Stall 1858 Sby 1/93 1,380
Goodman, Bertram Am 1904-1988
T/Pn 78x92 The Evolution of Tools (3) 1934 Chr 9/92 . . . 24,200
I,Pe&W/Pa 21x13 The Chess Players Sby 3/93 920
W&I/Pa 22x15 The Prodigy Sby 3/93 690
Goodman, Brenda Am 1943-
O&MM/Pa 41x30 Magician, No. 1 FHB 3/93 1,250
O/C 64x48 Untitled #9 '79 FHB 3/93 1,200
O,Pe&Wx/Pa 41x30 Heart '76 FHB 3/93 1,000
O/C 56x40 Untitled (Lotus Painting) '81 FHB 3/93 950
Goodman, Maud Br a 1860-1938
O/C 36x20 Young Queen and Her Court 92 Sby 5/93 . . . 7,475
Goodman, Sidney Am 1936-
O/C 36x50 Afternoon 1971 Sby 2/93 3,450
Goodnough, Robert Am 1917-
O/C 48x48 Going Ashore X 63 Chr 2/93 3,850
O/C 57x57 Abstraction 61 Sby 2/93 3,738
O/C 39x18 Cowboy Chr 11/92 3,520
L/B 33x15 Standing Figure Sby 2/93 2,875
O/C 27x34 The Tree Chr 11/92 1,980
A&O/C 48x78 RZY 1986 Hnd 3/93 1,800
O/C 20x24 Untitled 60 Chr 2/93 1,650
O/C 32x26 Seated Girl Sby 2/93 1,495
O&A/C 34x56 Untitled 1976 Sby 6/93 575
Goodwin, Albert Br 1845-1932
* See 1993 Edition . . . .
Goodwin, Arthur Clifton Am 1866-1929
O/C 30x36 Arlington St., Boston Chr 5/93 21,850
O/C 21x27 Mystic River Docks Chr 12/92 16,500
O/C 22x28 Louis Kronberg in his Studio Skn 5/93 11,000
O/C 32x36 Winter Snow Scene Mys 3/93 5,060
O/C 38x42 Ship at Full Sail Chr 5/93 3,450
O/C 25x30 Landscape with House and Pond Hnd 10/92 . . 2,000
O/C 19x26 Rainy Day, Boston Brd 8/93 1,540
P/Pa 12x17 A Street Scene 1895 Skn 5/93 715
P/Pa 18x22 New England Landscape Hnd 5/93 500
P/Pb 16x20 Sundown Skn 3/93 468
W/Pa 14x18 The Mill Pond Hnd 5/93 400
P/Pa 9x10 Autumn Wes 3/93 358
Goodwin, Philip Russell Am 1882-1935
O/C 24x33 Their Lucky Day Chr 9/92 20,900
W/Pa 6x8 Men in Canoe Meeting Moose Ih 11/92 1,700
Goodwin, Richard Labarre Am 1840-1910
* See 1993 Edition . . . .
Goossens, Josse Ger 1876-1929
* See 1993 Edition . . . .
Gorbatoff, Constantin Rus 1876-
O/Pn 16x19 Evening on the Lake 1935 Skn 11/92 770
Gorchov, Ron Am 20C
O/L 42x30 Acrobat 1980 FHB 3/93 3,750
O/C 48x78 Fifth Vision of the Queen 1959 Sby 2/93 1,610
O/L 41x39 Constant 1978 FHB 3/93 1,500
O/L 18x18 Nostalgia 1978 FHB 3/93 1,200
Gorder, Levon Am 20C
* See 1992 Edition . . . .
Gordigiani, Michele It 1830-1909
O/C 43x32 The Flower Girl Hnd 12/92 6,800
Gordin, Sidney Am 20C
H&Cp/Pa 8x5 Pair of Drawings Sby 3/93 1,495
Gordon, Sir John Watson Sco 1788-1864
* See 1993 Edition . . . .
Gore, Ken Am 1911-
O/B 20x24 The Woods Yng 5/93 425
Gore, William Henry Br 20C
* See 1990 Edition . . . .
Gorelick, B. 20C
O/C 22x28 Tabletop Still Life with Fish Slo 4/93 200
Gori, Alessandro 17C
* See 1992 Edition . . . .

Gorky, Arshile Am 1904-1948
P&P/Pa 17x23 Untitled Sby 11/92 159,500
O/C 10x14 Still Life Tablecloth, Bowl But 4/93 25,875
O/Cb 15x8 Abstraction Sby 2/93 23,000
Gorman, R. C. Am 1933-
* See 1993 Edition . . . .
Gorson, Aaron Henry Am 1872-1933
O/C 35x46 Morning (Pittsburgh) Sby 3/93 9,775
Gorstkin-Wywiorski, Michael Pol 1861-1926
O/Pn 17x11 Soldiers on Horseback Chr 5/93 2,530
Gorter, Arnold Marc Dut 1866-1933
O/C 28x36 Autumn Dum 12/92 3,500
Gortzius, Geldorp Dut 17C
* See 1990 Edition . . . .
Gosse, Nicolas Louis Francois Fr 1787-1878
* See 1993 Edition . . . .
Gosselin, Ferdinand Jules A. Fr 1862-
* See 1993 Edition . . . .
Gotlieb, Jules Am 1897-
O/B 21x38 Painting Images on Cave's Wall Ih 5/93 650
Gottlieb, Adolph Am 1903-1974
O/C 48x36 Fringe 1967 Chr 11/92 189,200
O&E/C 84x41 Pink, Blue, Black 1957 Sby 5/93 90,500
O/C 48x36 Gray Bars 1973 Sby 11/92 55,000
O/C 48x60 Nocturnal Beams 1954 Sby 11/92 49,500
A/Pa/C 40x30 Orange and Lavender #72 1970 Chr 11/92 . . 41,800
A/Pa 19x24 Untitled 1967 Chr 11/92 19,800
A/Pa/C 24x19 Untitled #6 1967 Sby 10/92 19,800
A/Pa 19x24 Untitled 1979 Chr 10/92 13,200
Gottlieb, Harry Am 1895-
O/C 39x16 Side Wheeler on the Hudson Doy 11/92 770
Gottlieb, Leopold Pol 1833-1934
* See 1992 Edition . . . .
Gottwald, Frederick Carl Am 1860-1941
* See 1993 Edition . . . .
Gotuzzo, Leopoldo Brz 1887-1983
* See 1993 Edition . . . .
Gotzloff, Carl Ger 1799-1866
* See 1993 Edition . . . .
Goubaud, Innocent-Louis Fr 1780-1847
* See 1993 Edition . . . .
Goubie, Jean Richard Fr 1842-1899
O/C/B 24x36 Choosing the Best Hunter 1878 Chr 2/93 . . . 28,600
Gould, Alexander Carruthers Eng 1870-1948
O/C 25x30 Hunting Scene Skn 3/93 2,200
Gould, Chester Am 1900-1987
P/Pa 18x27 Sunday Comic "Dick Tracy" Ih 11/92 750
Gould, John F. Am 1906-
W/Pa 16x22 Looking at Christmas Creche Ih 5/93 400
Gould, John Howard Can 1929-
MM 16x10 Old Actor Sbt 5/93 660
Gounder, Grant Am 20C
O/M Size? Peter Pan '33 Fre 10/92 160
Goupil, Jules Adolphe Fr 1834-1890
* See 1993 Edition . . . .
Gourgue, Jacques Enguerrand Hai 1930-
O/M 20x30 Sleeper Chr 11/92 3,960
O/M 24x30 Under the Cool Trees Skn 9/92 1,210
O/M 20x23 Outside the Station Skn 3/93 1,045
Gourgue, Jean Enguerrand Hai 20C
* See 1993 Edition . . . .
Gouvrant, Gerard Fr 1946-
* See 1992 Edition . . . .
Gow, Andrew Carrick Br 1848-1920
O/C 30x25 News from the Front 1877 Sby 10/92 8,800
O/Pn 17x24 Military Procession in Desert 1893 Chr 5/93 . . 8,050
Gow, Mary L. Br 1851-1929
* See 1991 Edition . . . .
Gowing, Louis D.
O&R/C 21x14 Couple in Colonial Dress Ih 11/92 125

Goya Y Lucientes, Francisco J. Spa 1746-1828
* See 1992 Edition . . . .
Grabach, John R. Am 1880-1981
O/C 42x48 Connecticut River in Winter Chr 5/93 18,400
O/C 36x42 Trolley & Clearing the Snow: Double Sby 9/92 . . 5,500
O/C 27x33 Snow in the Woods Chr 12/92 3,300
O/Pn 8x10 Mending Nets Sby 3/93 2,990
Grabar, Ygor Rus 1872-
* See 1993 Edition . . . .
Grabone, Arnold Ger 1896-1981
O/C 24x31 Alpine Chalet Wes 10/92 330
Grabwinkler, Paul Aus 1880-
* See 1990 Edition . . . .
Graciot, L. Con 19C
O/C 15x21 Arab Encampment Slo 4/93 350
Graeb, Karl George Ger 1816-1884
* See 1990 Edition . . . .
Graecen, Edmund Am 1877-1949
P/Pa 10x11 Flowering Trees by a Lake Sby 3/93 920
Graf, Carl C. Am
* See 1990 Edition . . . .
Graf, Paul Edmund Swd 1866-1903
O/C 18x24 Hunters in Winter Landscape 93 Sby 1/93 3,335
Graffione 1455-1527
* See 1992 Edition . . . .
Graham, Charles Am 1852-1911
* See 1991 Edition . . . .
Graham, Dan
* See 1992 Edition . . . .
Graham, Donald Am 20C
* See 1990 Edition . . . .
Graham, Ed
W&G/Pa 20x15 Football Players on Bench Ih 11/92 350
Graham, John Am 1881-1961
P/Pa 9x12 The Bull Fight Incident Sby 3/93 805
Graham, Peter Br 1836-1921
* See 1991 Edition . . . .
Graham, Robert
Pe/Pa 12x15 Reclining Female Nude 1989 Sby 2/93 2,070
Graham, Robert Alexander Am 1873-1946
* See 1993 Edition . . . .
Graham, Robert Macdonald 20C
* See 1990 Edition . . . .
Gran, Daniel 1694-1757
O/C 41x32 Saint Sebastian with Three Cherubim Sby 5/93 . 10,350
Granacci, Francesco It 1477-1543
* See 1991 Edition . . . .
Grandmaison, Orestes Nicholas Can 1932-
O/B 20x24 House in the Woods Sbt 11/92 792
Grandy, Julia Selden
O/C 20x22 Port Scene 1938 Ald 9/92 75
Graner Y Arrufi, Luis Spa 1867-1929
O/C 24x33 Sunset over the Hudson River 1923 Chr 10/92 . 10,450
O/C/B 25x33 Lake in Central Park 1923 Chr 2/93 6,600
O/B 22x44 Chinese Lantern But 12/92 3,300
Grant, Blanche Chloe Am 1874-1948
* See 1992 Edition . . . .
Grant, Charles Henry Am 1866-1939
O/C 31x34 No. 2, Lake George Lou 6/93 2,000
Grant, Clement Rollins Am 1849-1893
O/C 20x30 Fisherman's Family Chr 9/92 8,250
W,G&H/Pb 8x9 Quietude/An Interior View Skn 9/92 1,100
Grant, Duncan
* See 1993 Edition . . . .
Grant, Dwinnell Am 1912-
L/Pa 9x11 Pair Collages 41 Sby 3/93 1,725
L/Pa 9x11 Contrathemis 2811 41 Sby 9/92 1,320
Grant, Frederic M. Am 1886-1959
O/C 30x30 Garden Flowers Sby 3/93 4,888
O/Ab 8x10 Landscape with Figures FHB 6/93 400
Grant, Gordon Am 1875-1962
O/C 40x50 Sail and Steam Sby 3/93 7,188

O/C 24x32 Mission Accomplished, USS Saratoga But 6/93 . 2,875
O/C 24x36 With a Good Wind Dum 3/93 2,750
O/C 24x36 U.S.S. Alabama 1944 But 6/93 2,300
W/Pa 15x21 Harbor Scene with Boats Eld 7/93 1,155
W/Pa 10x14 Schooner in Port Yng 5/93 600
W/Pa 19x16 Two-Masted Schooner Eld 11/92 385
W/Pa 13x14 Couple with Guns in Woods 1902 Ih 11/92 . . . 375
P/Pa/B 28x22 Infantryman 1943 Wes 12/92 165
C/Pa 16x12 Winking Man Yng 5/93 100

Grant, J. Jeffrey   Am 1883-1960
O/B 14x16 Fisherman at the Docks Hnd 9/92 200

Grant, James   Am 1924-
MM/C 56x56 Black Dot But 4/93 920

Grant, Sir Francis   Eng 1803-1878
* See 1993 Edition . . . .

Grant, Vernon   Am 1902-1990
* See 1993 Edition . . . .

Grant, William James   Br 1829-1866
* See 1990 Edition . . . .

Gras, Francisco   Spa 20C
* See 1990 Edition . . . .

Grasdorp, Willem   Dut 1678-1723
* See 1990 Edition . . . .

Grass, Carl Gotthard   1767-1814
* See 1993 Edition . . . .

Grassi, Nicola   1662-1748
O/C 12x15 Saint John the Baptist Fortelling Sby 10/92 . . . 13,200

Grasso, Doris
O/B 22x28 B. Beverly General Store Ald 3/93 325

Grau, Enrique   Col 1920-
C,P&Y/Pa 38x26 Boy with Bees '67 Wes 5/93 6,600

Grau-Sala, Emile   Spa 1911-1975
O/C 24x29 Au Cirque 1964 Chr 2/93 28,600
O/C 35x28 Balerines 1969 Chr 11/92 26,400
O/C 24x29 Gens du Voyage 65 Chr 5/93 25,300
O/C 22x26 La Conversation Chr 5/93 21,850
O/C 21x26 Child with Bird Sby 2/93 19,550
O/C 21x26 Trois Femme Dans le Jardin 1959 Doy 11/92 . . . 15,400
O/C 20x26 Painting and a Drawing 1954 Chr 11/92 14,300
O/C 26x20 Mere et Enfant Sby 6/93 11,500
O/C 23x14 Jeune Fille aux Fruits 61 Chr 11/92 8,250
O/C 11x14 Les Musiciens Chr 11/92 6,600
O/C 11x9 Portrait of Young Woman 37 Sby 6/93 3,450

Grauer, William C.   Am 1896-
W/Pa 21x28 Horses Wlf 5/93 325

Gravelot, Hubert-Francois   Fr 1699-1773
* See 1992 Edition . . . .

Graves, Abbott Fuller   Am 1859-1936
O/C 20x24 Poppies Chr 5/93 28,750
O/C 20x24 Poppies Chr 12/92 28,600
O/C 13x16 Spring Blossoms/A Street Scene Skn 11/92 . . . 15,400
O/C 14x20 Roses Chr 3/93 13,800
O/Cb 14x18 Pool with Swimming Boats Skn 3/93 9,350
O/C 24x20 Sunset on the Yacht Skn 11/92 5,500
O/C 14x20 Bouquet of Pink Roses Skn 11/92 4,400
O/C 16x20 Home from the Market/Jamaican Scene Skn 3/93 . 3,300
O/C 10x14 Market/Jamaican Village Skn 3/93 2,475
O/C 9x12 The Gazebo Brd 2/93 2,090

Graves, Morris   Am 1910-
O/M 9x16 Peaches Sby 3/93 4,888
Pe&K/Pa 17x24 Bird Back Into Its Shell Sby 3/93 4,600
I/Pa 10x19 Untitled 54 Skn 11/92 4,400
O/C 22x20 Flowers in an Urn 33 Doy 11/92 3,850
PI&S/Pa 24x15 Stork But 6/93 3,450
T&I/Pa 9x14 A Slice of Fruit 73 Sby 9/92 2,200
O/C 15x15 House in a Landscape But 4/93 1,725

Graves, Nancy   Am 1940-
A&O/C 64x88 Calipers, Legs, Lines '79 Chr 2/93 7,700

Gray, Cleve   Am 1918-
A/C 69x67 Waimea (Square) 71 Chr 11/92 3,300

Gray, Eileen   Am 20C
* See 1990 Edition . . . .

Gray, Henry Percy   Am 1869-1952
W&Pe/Pa/B 20x27 Summer Pasture Chr 3/93 17,250
O/C/B 15x19 Sand Dunes Along Monterey Coast But 6/93 . 10,350
W&/Pa 10x14 California Oaks But 3/93 9,350
O/C 16x20 Monterey Cypress But 6/93 8,625
W/Pa 16x20 Rocky Coast But 10/92 7,700
W/Pb 10x14 Footpath Through Oaks But 10/92 7,150
W/Pa 10x13 A Field of Daisies But 3/93 6,050
O/C/B 10x14 Pacific Lighthouse But 10/92 6,050
W/Pa 10x14 Green Valley But 10/92 5,500
W/Pa 10x8 Old Oak Tree 1910 But 10/92 5,225
W/Pa 14x10 Cypress Tree Along the Cliffs But 10/92 4,675
W/Pa 10x14 Oaks and Clouds But 10/92 4,675
W/Pa 10x14 Cypress Tree But 3/93 4,400
W/Pa 12x15 A Bend in the River But 6/93 4,312
W/Pa 11x14 California Poppy Field But 3/93 4,125
W/Pa 12x16 Cattle Ranch But 10/92 3,575
PI/Pa 8x11 Crashing Waves 94 But 6/93 3,162

Gray, Henry Peters   Am 1819-1877
* See 1991 Edition . . . .

Gray, Jack L.   Can 1927-1981
O/C 36x60 The Salt Bankers--Schooner Alcala Chr 5/93 . . 34,500
O/C 24x36 Lobsterman Pulling Pots Doy 11/92 7,150
O/C 30x50 Off the Gimlet 56 Chr 5/93 4,600
O/C 24x36 Fishermen in Choppy Seas Chr 5/93 2,300
O/M 23x18 Harbor at Twilight Doy 11/92 990
W,G&H/Pa 21x28 Grand Banks Doryman Skn 5/93 880

Gray, John   Br 19C
* See 1992 Edition . . . .

Gray, Mary   Am 1891-1964
O/C 20x16 New England Fireplace But 12/92 1,100

Graziani, Ercole   It 1688-1765
K,PI&S/Pa 11x8 Madonna, Child w/Infant Baptist Chr 1/93 . 1,210

Graziano, F.   Am 20C
O/C 20x16 Lilies of the Field 1921 Sby 3/93 1,610

Greacen, Edmund William   Am 1877-1949
O/C 25x30 Spray of Flowers in Blue Vase 1940 Mys 3/93 . . 5,500
O/B 16x12 New York Harbor 1915 Chr 9/92 3,080
O/C/B 16x12 Nude Study #2 1917 But 6/93 1,265

Greacen, Nan   Am 1909-
* See 1993 Edition . . . .

Greason, William   Am 1884-
O/C 41x34 Autumnal Landscape Dum 3/93 800

Greatorex, Eleanor Elizabeth   Am 1854-
O/C 11x9 Mere Poulain Knitting 1894 Wes 3/93 715

Greatorex, Eliza Pratt   Am 1820-1897
* See 1993 Edition . . . .

Greatorex, Katherine Honora   Am 1851-
* See 1990 Edition . . . .

Greaves, Walter   Br 1846-1930
* See 1993 Edition . . . .

Greco, Gennaro   It 1663-1714
O/C 18x33 Coastlines w/Capriccio Views: Pair Chr 1/93 . . 77,000

Greco, Simon
G/Pa 12x16 19 C. Wall Street Ih 11/92 375

Green, Albert Van Nesse   Am 20C
* See 1992 Edition . . . .

Green, Bernard I.   Am 1887-1951
O/C 30x25 Portrait of a Black Woman Wes 10/92 715

Green, Charles   Br 1840-1898
O/B 16x21 Girl Seated by the Hearth 1885 Hnd 9/92 2,000

Green, Charles Edwin Lewis   Am 1844-
O/C 8x12 View of a Fishing Village Skn 9/92 2,640

Green, Edward M.   Am a 1920-1929
P/Pa 11x9 Forest Interior Mor 11/92 100

Green, Elizabeth Sheppen   Am 1871-1954
* See 1993 Edition . . . .

Green, Frank Russell   Am 1856-1949
O/Pn 9x12 The Road to Nemours Hnd 12/92 250

Green, George   20C
* See 1991 Edition . . . .

Green, James   Am 20C
W&G/Pa 23x28 Harbor Scene Sel 9/92 125

Green, James   Br 1771-1834
W&G/Pa 23x16 Standing Gentleman and Dog But 5/93 1,380

Green, Roland   Br 1896-1972
* See 1992 Edition . . . .

Green, William Bradford   Am 1871-1945
O/B 16x20 Beach Yng 5/93 300
Greenaway, Kate   Br 1846-1901
* See 1992 Edition ....
Greenbaum, Joseph   Am 1864-1940
O/B 8x11 Atmospheric Landscape Mor 11/92 1,000
Greene, Albert Van Nesse   Am 1887-
O/C 26x32 Houses by a Pond in Winter Chr 12/92 3,080
O/C 8x10 Waterfront Ald 5/93 650
Greene, Balcomb   Am 1904-
O/C 62x56 Daybreak Sby 6/93 4,600
O/C 42x54 The Parisians Chr 12/92 2,200
Greene, Gertrude   Am 1911-1956
* See 1992 Edition ....
Greene, J. Barry   Am 1895-1966
O/C 22x18 Seated Woman 1930 Hnd 3/93 850
Greenleaf, Jacob I.   Am 1887-1968
O/C 16x20 Woodland Pond Yng 2/93 700
O/B 16x20 Covered Bridge, Winter Yng 5/93 600
O/B 16x20 Summer Landscape Yng 5/93 125
Greenman, Frances   Am 1890-1982
* See 1992 Edition ....
Greenwood, Joseph H.   Am 1857-1927
O/C 30x42 An Autumnal Scene 98 Skn 11/92 2,475
O/Pn 10x16 Field on the Ridge, Autumn 17 Skn 9/92 1,100
O/Pn 10x6 Tree/A Touch of Autumn 99 Skn 9/92 1,100
O/B 10x14 Landscape '18 Lou 12/92 600
O/B 5x9 The Passing Front Skn 11/92 302
Greer, J. T.   Am 19C
* See 1992 Edition ....
Greer, James Emery   Am -1948
O/B 16x20 Farm by the Water Yng 5/93 225
O/B 12x16 Late Summer in the Hills Yng 2/93 175
Gregor, Harold   Am 1929-
O&A/C 60x84 Illinois Landscape #43 1980 Chr 5/93 3,220
O&A/C 60x84 Illinois Landscape #43 1980 Chr 11/92 550
Gregori, Luigi   Am 1819-1883
O/Pn 12x8 Young Boy with Goat Fre 4/93 1,450
Gregory, C. F.   Aut 1815-1885
* See 1992 Edition ....
Gregory, Charles   Br 19C
* See 1991 Edition ....
Greil, Alois   Aus 1841-1902
* See 1993 Edition ....
Greiner, Otto   Ger 1869-1916
* See 1993 Edition ....
Greitzer, Jack   Am 1910-
* See 1990 Edition ....
Grel, Schmit
* See 1992 Edition ....
Grell, Louis Frederick   Am 1887-
O/C/B 58x58 Man with Dog Hnd 9/92 475
W&G/Pa 25x37 Opera Scene Hnd 5/93 200
Gremke, Henry Diedrich   Am 1860-1939
* See 1993 Edition ....
Grenie, B.   Fr 20C
O/C/B 29x39 Seated Nude Hnd 3/93 2,200
Gresly, Gabriel   Fr 1712-1756
* See 1992 Edition ....
Gretzner, Harold   Am 1902-1977
W/Pa 19x23 Golden Gate Bridge Mor 11/92 950
W/Pa 20x29 Chinatown Street Scene Mor 6/93 825
W/Pa 18x25 Lake Merritt-Oakland Mor 2/93 800
Greuvenbroeck, Alessandro   a 1717-1724
* See 1991 Edition ....
Greuze, Jean-Baptiste   Fr 1725-1805
* See 1993 Edition ....
Grevenbroeck, Orazio   1678-
* See 1993 Edition ....
Grey, Steve   Am 1952-
O/C 24x30 New Orleans Street Musicians Lou 3/93 600
O/C 24x30 Restoration Jazz Band Lou 9/92 600
Gribble, Paul S.   Am 20C
O/C 20x30 Mountain Leveller 81 Hnd 12/92 250

Gridland, H.   Con 19C
* See 1993 Edition ....
Griff, M. Edward   20C
O/C 19x23 Bridge over Canal Yng 2/93 130
Griffany, J.   Br 19C
O/C 64x45 Woman Strolling Sby 10/92 8,800
Griffier Theelder, Jan (the Elder)   Dut 1652-1718
O/Pn 17x18 River Landscape with Mountains Sby 10/92 . 46,750
Griffier, Jan (the Younger)   -1750
O/C 17x23 Mountainous River Landscape Sby 10/92 .. 25,300
Griffin, Charles Gerald   Am 1864-1945
O/C 10x14 Luminous Sunset Landscape Eld 8/93 1,100
Griffin, De Lacy   Am 20C
O/C 18x24 Scene Near Cresson, PA Slo 7/93 1,550
Griffin, Thomas B.   Am 1858-
O/C 20x30 Morning Along the River Skn 9/92 1,650
O/C 30x40 Gray Sky, White Waters Sby 3/93 1,380
O/C 20x30 Mt. Washington 05 Sby 9/92 1,320
O/C 10x14 Two Landscapes Skn 9/92 1,320
O/C 10x14 River and the Mist Skn 5/93 440
O/C 16x24 Stream through the Hills Chr 12/92 440
O/C 14x19 Landscape with Stream Fre 4/93 375
Griffin, Walter   Am 1861-1935
O/C 24x32 Blue Fishing Nets Wtf 12/92 3,000
Griffin, William Davenport   Am 1894-
* See 1993 Edition ....
Griffith, Grace Allison   Am 1885-1955
W/Pa 19x15 Sunrise, Marin County 23 But 6/93 1,840
Griffith, Louis Oscar   Am 1875-1956
O/C 10x14 On the Hill Hnz 5/93 600
Griffith, William Alexander   Am 1866-1940
O/C 20x24 California Hills 1936 Mor 6/93 2,200
P/L 26x19 Laguna Landscape '24 But 3/93 1,540
O/C 12x20 At Laguna But 10/92 1,100
Griggs, Samuel W.   Am 1827-1898
* See 1992 Edition ....
Grigoriev, Boris   Rus 1886-1939
O/C 21x29 The Farm Chr 10/92 5,500
Grillon, Roger Maurice
O/C 19x23 The Bathers Sby 10/92 1,100
Grimaldi, Giovanni Francesco   It 1606-1680
* See 1992 Edition ....
Grimelund, Johannes Martin   Nor 1842-1917
* See 1993 Edition ....
Grimm, Paul   Am 1892-1974
O/C 43x60 San Jacinto Mor 11/92 11,000
O/C 38x50 Etchings of the Elements Mor 11/92 5,500
O/C 20x24 Los Angeles Harbor But 6/93 3,450
O/C 24x30 Colorful Sand Dunes 1960 But 3/93 2,200
O/C 24x30 Colorful Sand Dunes 1961 But 3/93 2,200
O/Cb 18x24 Under the Sun 1947 But 3/93 2,090
O/Cb 12x16 Mountain Landscape Mor 6/93 1,760
O/B 18x24 Desert Colors Slo 5/93 1,700
O/Cb 20x25 Box Canyon and Smoke Trees 1963 Chr 12/92 . 1,320
O/C 28x36 Sierra Grandeur-Palisades Glacier Mor 6/93 .. 1,210
O/C 26x40 Lone Smoke Tree 1962 But 6/93 1,150
O/C 28x36 Colorful Desert Mor 6/93 1,045
O/B 16x20 Garden in the Desert Mor 11/92 900
O/C 20x40 California Mor 2/93 750
O/C 18x24 Desert Scene Mys 12/92 715
O/C 24x30 Mt. Rainier Mor 2/93 700
O/B 20x16 Mountainous Lake Mys 12/92 660
O/M 20x24 Tujunga Canyon Mor 2/93 600
O/M 12x16 Sycamores Mor 6/93 522
Grimmer, Abel   Flm a 1592-1614
* See 1992 Edition ....
Grimshaw, Arthur F.   Br 1868-1913
* See 1993 Edition ....
Grimshaw, John Atkinson   Br 1836-1893
O/C 24x43 A Manor House in the Autumn 1884 Sby 10/92 79,750
O/C 24x36 Fish Landing, Whitby Sby 5/93 48,875
O/B 11x17 Stapleton Park, Near Pontefract 1877 Sby 5/93 16,100

Grinnell, Roy   Am 1934-
* See 1993 Edition . . . .

Grips, Charles Joseph   Bel 1852-1920
* See 1993 Edition . . . .

Grips, Jean Charles   Bel 19C
* See 1993 Edition . . . .

Gris, Juan   Spa 1887-1927
O/C 22x13 La Bouteille de Bordeaux Sby 11/92 . . . . 2.2M
O/C 32x21 Carafe et Livre 20 Sby 11/92 412,500
O/C 24x20 Guitare et Raisins 1921 Chr 11/92 286,000
G,Br&Pl/Pa 17x21 Leda Chr 11/92 66,000
G/Pa 6x7 Nature Morte Sby 5/93 60,250
Pe/Pa 12x19 Nature Morte a la Nappe Sby 5/93 32,775
Pe/Pa 12x9 Etude de Violon Sby 5/93 31,050

Grison, Francois & Save, G.   Fr 1845-1914
O/C 112x59 The Hunting Party 1874 Sby 10/92 15,400
O/C 112x63 The Tavern 1874 Sby 10/92 15,400

Grison, Francois Adolphe   Fr 1845-1914
O/Pn 11x9 Le Amateur But 5/93 4,600

Griswold, Casmir Clayton   Am 1834-1918
* See 1993 Edition . . . .

Gritchenko, Alexis   Rus 1883-1963
* See 1990 Edition . . . .

Gritten, Henry C.   Br 1818-1873
O/C 24x18 Fountain in Village Square Chr 5/93 2,300

Grob, Conrad   Sws 1828-1904
* See 1990 Edition . . . .

Groenewegen, Adrianus Johannes   Dut 1874-1963
W/Pa/B 13x10 Village Square with Figures Sby 1/93 1,380

Groenewegen, K. L.   Dut 19C
W/Pa 12x19 Pastoral Scene Dum 1/93 650

Groll, Albert Lorey   Am 1866-1952
O/C 12x16 Lava Beds, Laguna, NM Sby 9/92 1,540
W/Pa 8x10 Desert Landscape Wes 12/92 440

Grolleron, Paul Louis Narcisse   Fr 1848-1901
O/Pn 11x14 Preparing for Battle Sby 10/92 5,225
O/Pn 11x8 French Infantryman 1883 Slo 7/93 1,400

Gromaire, Marcel   Fr 1892-1971
O/C 26x32 Le Montagnard 1964 Chr 10/92 38,500
W&Pl/Pa/B 17x13 Commercant Mediterran 1929 Chr 10/92 . 8,800
W&Pl/Pl/Pa/B 12x9 Au port 1941 Chr 11/92 7,920
W,G&Pl/Pa 17x13 Le Violoncelliste 1931 Chr 5/93 5,175
W&I/Pa 13x10 Nature Morte/Cuisine 1927 Doy 5/93 1,210
I&S/Pa/B 10x8 Nude 1952 Sby 6/93 1,035
Pl/Pa 9x7 Portrait of a Man 1925 Sby 2/93 805
Pl/Pa 17x14 Femme Assise 1925 Chr 11/92 462

Gronland, Theude   Ger 1817-1876
* See 1990 Edition . . . .

Grooms, Red   Am 1937-
O/Wd&Me 36x7 Man in Field Sby 10/92 13,200
G/Pa 29x43 Jean-Louis-Scherrer 77 Sby 5/93 12,650
W/Pa 24x18 Conch Cleaners '83 Chr 2/93 4,950
W&Fp/Pa 11x14 Black and White Maine Cows 77 Sby 2/93 3,335

Grooth, Georg Christoph   1716-1749
O/C 34x27 Portrait Elegant Nobleman Sby 10/92 6,600

Gropeanu, Nicole
P/B 9x13 Nurses with Infants Sby 2/93 1,840

Gropper, William   Am 1897-1977
O/Pn 12x12 Waiter Sby 3/93 2,415
O/M 14x18 The Politician FHB 5/93 2,250
C&P/Pa 21x26 The Jurist Sby 3/93 1,725
W&I/Pa 11x17 Woman Reading Chr 12/92 1,540
G/Pa 14x17 Torch Song Sby 3/93 1,265
T&O/Pn 12x10 The Jurist Sby 9/92 1,100
O/C 20x16 The Spotter 1942 Sby 3/93 1,093

Gros, Antoine Jean (Baron)   Fr 1771-1835
O/C 72x90 David Playing Harp for Saul 1822 Chr 5/93 . . 222,500
PeCS&Bc/Pa 13x19 Andromaque Slo 7/93 2,000

Gros, Baron Jean Louis   Fr 1793-1879
* See 1990 Edition . . . .

Grose, Daniel C.   Am a 1860-1890
O/C 12x18 Hudson River Valley View Skn 3/93 660
O/C 12x20 Winter Landscape Eld 11/92 385

Gross, Chaim   Am 1904-1991
W/Pa 23x34 Figure on a Pier 1947 Hnd 12/92 1,500
H&W/Pa/B 22x14 The Music Maker But 4/93 1,495
W&Pe/Pa 15x23 A Bird in Flight 1948 Sby 9/92 1,045
I/Pa 12x8 Acrobats 1949 Chr 5/93 920
Pe&W/Pa 14x11 Three Rabbis Sby 9/92 825
W,I&Pe/Pa 15x23 The Gossips 1950 Sby 9/92 660
Pe&W/Pa 20x13 A Female Nude: Double-Sided Sby 3/93 . . . 633
W/Pa 9x15 Diving Off the Bridge (2) 1929 Chr 12/92 440
W&Pe/Pa 11x15 Reclining Female Nude 54 Sby 9/92 330
W&I/Pa 13x4 Two: Dancing, Nude 72 Skn 9/92 330
W/Pa 13x21 Cabin in Landscape '19 Hnd 10/92 250
W/Pa 10x7 Elderly Couple Mys 3/93 192
W/Pa 8x16 Provincetown Beach Scene Mys 12/92 165
W/Pa 7x25 Provincetown Beach Scene Mys 12/92 165

Gross, Earl   Am 20C
W/Pa 23x18 Street Cafe, Ibiza Hnz 5/93 50

Gross, George
O/B 24x20 Woman Skinny-Dipping Ilh 11/92 1,400
G/Pa 12x9 Woman Leaving Room Ilh 11/92 500

Grossman, Edwin Booth   Am 1887-1957
O/C 27x35 Still Life 13 Skn 3/93 2,090

Grossman, Nancy   1940-
W&L/Pa 36x54 Formal - Blue Double Painting 76 Sby 2/93 . 4,888
W&L/Pa 26x20 Pastel #11 76 Sby 2/93 4,025
Y&S/Pa 19x26 Two Drawings '75 Chr 11/92 1,650
Y&S/Pa 40x26 Tether '73 Sby 6/93 1,150

Grosvenor, Robert   20C
* See 1991 Edition . . . .

Grosz, August Ignate   Fr 1847-1917
I&W/Pa 9x12 After the Battle Slo 4/93 250

Grosz, George   Am 1893-1959
W/Pa 19x25 Auf dem Markt Chr 11/92 35,200
W&Pl/Pa 13x9 Street Scene in Marseille 1929 Sby 5/93 . . 34,500
W/Pa 24x17 Nedicks Sby 5/93 25,300
W&S/Pa 11x16 Street Scene Sby 11/92 24,200
Pl/Pa 15x12 Eingeruckt Chr 11/92 23,100
W&Pe/Pa 25x18 Man with a Whip Sby 11/92 23,100
W&I/Pa 19x25 Strassenszene Chr 11/92 19,800
W/Pa 17x22 The Fight 34 Sby 5/93 17,250
W/Pa 19x15 Stickmen in Blue Sby 5/93 16,100
W/Pa/B 19x26 Spanish Civil War 34 Sby 10/92 11,000
Pl/Pa 17x22 Figuren in der Strasse Chr 10/92 9,350
Pl/Pa 25x19 Deutsches Bordel Chr 10/92 8,800
W/Pa 16x20 Beim Rhein-Wein Sby 10/92 6,600
K/Pa 22x14 Nude with a Straw Hat Chr 5/93 6,325
W/Pa 16x20 Beteuder, or Prayer 1931 Dum 3/93 6,000
Br&I/Pa 22x18 Sitzende Frau Waffenschieber Sby 10/92 . . 5,775
Pl&G/Pa 11x9 Lola Sby 10/92 5,500
W/Pa 15x22 Bavarian Woods Chr 11/92 4,400
Br&I/Pa 21x16 Stehende Frau Chr 5/93 4,400
W/Pa 15x20 Reclining Nude Sby 10/92 4,125
Pe/Pa 23x18 Passers By Sby 2/93 4,025
W/Pa 18x24 Driftwood on the Beach Dum 6/93 3,500
Br&I/Pa 18x12 Untitled Sby 10/92 3,300
W/Pa 24x20 The Wendelstein 1952 Chr 11/92 2,750
C/Pa 25x18 Back of Woman in a Long Skirt 38 Sby 3/93 . . 2,645
Pl/Pa 11x9 Sitzender Akt Chr 11/92 1,980
W/Pa 19x15 New England Beach Sby 3/93 1,380

Groth, John   Am 1908-
W/Pa 30x63 The Quorn-Gassing Luicestershire Dum 10/92 . . 300

Grove, Maria   Dan 19C
* See 1990 Edition . . . .

Grover, Dorothy   Am 1908-1975
* See 1991 Edition . . . .

Grover, Oliver Dennet   Am 1861-1927
O/C 24x30 Serving Breakfast on the Terrace 1913 Chr 12/92 3,850
O/C 14x10 Illinois River Landscape 1899 Hnd 5/93 450

Groves, Hannah Cutler   Am 1868-1952
O/C 16x20 Jersey Shore Fre 10/92 275

Grubacs, Carlo   Ger 19C
* See 1992 Edition . . . .

Gruber, Francis   Fr 1912-1948
* See 1991 Edition . . . .

Gruger, Frederic R. Am 1871-1953
* See 1993 Edition . . . .
Grun, Jules Alexandre Fr 1868-1934
* See 1991 Edition . . . .
Grunenwald, Jakob Ger 1822-1896
* See 1990 Edition . . . .
Grunewald, Isaac Swd 1889-1946
* See 1993 Edition . . . .
Grunsten, Harry N. Can 1902-
O/B 24x28 Bridge at Weston Sbt 11/92 968
Gruppe, Charles Am 1928-
O/B 10x12 Gray Morning in the Harbor Yng 5/93 225
Gruppe, Charles Paul Am 1860-1940
O/C 25x30 Winter Dream Lou 9/92 4,500
O/C 22x29 Twilight/A Canal View Skn 3/93 3,575
O/C 25x39 Cow and Herder Skn 3/93 3,300
O/C 24x30 Under October Skies Sby 9/92 1,650
O/Ab 16x12 The Bath in the Catskills Dum 12/92 1,500
W/Pa 18x14 The Return Home Chr 5/93 1,150
W/Pa 10x13 Three Works Wes 12/92 1,100
O/C 25x30 Oct. Bass Rocks Mass. Skn 3/93 880
O/C 12x16 Summer Landscape with Stream Sby 3/93 690
O/Cb 8x10 Sunlit Hillside Skn 3/93 468
W/Pa 10x14 Beached Schooner Yng 5/93 425
W/Pa 10x14 Digging for Clams '90 Wlf 4/93 350
C/Pa 12x18 Sketches Made in Holland 1896 Wes 12/92 192
Gruppe, Emile Albert Am 1896-1978
O/C 25x30 Spring Chr 12/92 15,400
O/C 30x25 Motif No. 1, Rockport Chr 12/92 8,250
O/C 30x40 Fall Sky Brd 8/93 4,950
O/C 20x24 Harbor Scene at Sunset Wes 12/92 4,950
O/C 25x30 Vermont Covered Bridge Yng 2/93 4,500
O/C 25x30 Winter River Mor 2/93 4,000
O/C 30x36 Jeffersonville, Vermont Chr 9/92 3,080
O/C 30x32 A Winter Stream Chr 5/93 2,760
O/C 16x20 Evening, Gloucester Chr 3/93 2,760
O/C 16x20 Gloucester Port Fre 4/93 2,600
O/C 18x20 Fishermen and Seagulls at Dock Yng 5/93 2,000
O/C/B 12x16 Winter View But 12/92 1,900
O/C 20x24 Covered Bridge, Vermont Sby 3/93 1,840
O/C 20x18 Woods in Snow Yng 5/93 1,800
O/Cb 12x14 Winter Landscape Sby 9/92 1,760
O/Cb 16x20 The Boathouse Chr 5/93 1,725
O/C 18x24 Fishing from Bass Rocks Lou 3/93 1,625
O/B 12x16 Landscape with Oak Tree But 6/93 1,610
O/C 24x20 Gloucester Morning 1960 Skn 9/92 1,540
O/C 25x30 Birch Trees in New England Hnd 3/93 1,500
O/C 16x20 Passing Bass Rocks Brd 8/93 1,430
O/C/B 12x16 Autumn Landscape 1927 But 6/93 1,265
O/Pn 9x8 Nude Bathing Wes 3/93 1,100
O/B 16x12 River's Edge, Autumn Doy 11/92 1,045
O/B 16x12 Morning Gloucester Eld 11/92 990
O/B 16x12 Autumn Woods Yng 5/93 900
O/Cb 20x24 Rocks and Surf, Cape Ann Skn 5/93 880
O/B 20x24 River Landscape Yng 2/93 700
O/Cd 16x20 Dominica, British West Indies Wes 10/92 605
Gruppe, Virginia Helena Am 1907-
W/Pa 10x14 Six Works Wes 12/92 330
Grust, F. G. Dut 20C
O/C 30x25 Feeding the Chickens But 11/92 3,300
Grust, Theodor Ger 1859-
* See 1992 Edition . . . .
Grutzner, Eduard Ger 1846-1925
* See 1992 Edition . . . .
Gsell, Laurent Fr 1860-1944
* See 1993 Edition . . . .
Guaccimanni, Vittorio It 1859-1938
O/Pn 14x10 Street Urchin '87 Wes 12/92 660
Guardabassi, Guerrino It 1848-
W/Pa 21x14 The Connoisseur Hnd 5/93 950
Guardi, Antonio & Guardi, F. It 1698-1730
* See 1992 Edition . . . .
Guardi, Francesco It 1712-1793
O/C 33x51 Rialto Bridge, Venice But 5/93 409,500
O/C 22x28 Palazzo Ducale, Venice Sby 1/93 277,500

PI,S&K/Pa 12x21 Grand Canal Chr 1/93 77,000
K,PI&S/Pa 5x7 Campo with Lagoon in Distance Chr 1/93 . . 9,900
Guardi, Francesco & Guardi, A. It 1712-1793
* See 1992 Edition . . . .
Guardi, Giacomo It 1764-1835
O/C 11x14 Island of San Giorgio in Alga Chr 1/93 37,400
O/C 6x9 Lake Scene; River Scene: Pair But 5/93 34,500
Guardi, Giovanni Antonio It 1698-1760
* See 1993 Edition . . . .
Guarino, Salvatore Anthony Am 1882-
* See 1993 Edition . . . .
Guayasamin, Oswaldo Ecu 1919-
O/C 51x20 Violinista Sby 11/92 33,000
O/C 16x24 Cabeza Sby 5/93 13,800
O/Pa 22x30 Desnudo Sby 11/92 9,025
G/Pa 24x19 Mujer Sby 11/92 7,425
G/Pa 15x22 Caballos Y Figuras En La Selva Sby 5/93 2,760
Guccione, Piero
O/C 33x36 Tre Movimenti Del Mare 1977 Sby 10/92 35,750
Gude, Hans Frederick Nor 1825-1903
O/C 11x20 Sunset 1875 Wes 10/92 4,070
O/C 19x26 Fishermen Hauling in Their Nets Doy 5/93 3,960
Gudin, Jean Antoine Theodore Fr 1802-1880
O/C 6x10 Beached Boats Mys 12/92 522
Gue, David John Am 1836-1917
O&R/C 9x14 Boathouse, South Lake, Catskill Wes 5/93 962
O/C 16x24 Seascape Dum 5/93 500
Gueldry, Ferdinand Joseph Fr 1858-
O/C 22x29 Way of the Coastguards 1919 Chr 10/92 11,000
Guerin, Armand Fr 1913-
O/M 24x29 Seine with the Eiffel Tower Sby 6/93 1,035
Guerin, Charles 1875-1939
O/C 40x32 La Glace Chr 5/93 3,220
Guerin, Jules Am 1866-1946
* See 1993 Edition . . . .
Guerrero, Luis Garcia 20C
* See 1991 Edition . . . .
Guerrero, Manuel Ruiz Spa 19C
O/C 22x32 Pelota Vasca Sby 10/92 7,150
Guerreschi, Giuseppe It 1925-1985
O/C 47x31 Ciclista 954 Hnz 5/93 1,900
Gues, Alfred Francois Fr 1833-
O/C 20x16 Patching up the Doll Chr 2/93 1,320
Guey, Fernand Fr 1877-
* See 1993 Edition . . . .
Guglielmi, O. Louis Am 1906-1956
O/C 30x24 The Persistent Sea No. 2 Chr 5/93 46,000
O/C 40x18 Red to Black 54 Sby 3/93 3,450
MM/Pa 20x18 Building 47 But 10/92 1,540
Guida, William Am 20C
O/C 24x36 Native American in Winter Ald 3/93 475
Guidi, Giuseppe It 1881-1931
* See 1991 Edition . . . .
Guidobono, Bartolomeo 1654-1709
O/C 48x35 Crucifixion with the three Marys Chr 10/92 . . . 11,000
Guigou, Paul Fr 1834-1871
* See 1993 Edition . . . .
Guillaume, Albert Fr 1873-1942
O/Pn 21x26 La Sortie Sby 2/93 8,625
Guillaume, Louis Mathieu D. Am 1816-1892
* See 1993 Edition . . . .
Guillaumin, Armand Fr 1841-1927
O/C 21x29 Bord de Riviere 1905 Sby 11/92 66,000
O/C 26x32 Crozant Sby 11/92 44,000
O/C 32x32 La vallee de la Sedelle Chr 11/92 38,500
O/C 32x44 Les rochers rouges a Agay 95 Chr 10/92 30,800
O/C 32x26 Le Modele Sby 5/93 23,000
O/C 21x26 Paysage Sby 10/92 19,800
O/C 15x18 Nature Morte a L'Houx Sby 2/93 17,250
K/Pa 19x12 Une Paysanne a Breuillet 96 Chr 5/93 1,495
Guillemet, Jean-Baptiste A. Fr 1843-1918
O/C 22x29 Route en Plein Champ Sby 10/92 5,500

116

Guilleminet, Claude   Fr 1821-1860
* See 1993 Edition . . . .
Guillermo, Juan   Spa 1916-1968
* See 1993 Edition . . . .
Guillery, Gilbert   Fr 1906-
O/B 24x18 Construction Worker Drinking Water Dum 8/93 . .   300
O/B 27x22 Cowboy Kneeling by Horse Dum 8/93   250
Guillet-Saguez, A.   Fr 19C
* See 1992 Edition . . . .
**Guillonet, Emile Octave Denis   Fr
1872-1967**
O/C 18x22 Interior Scene 64 But 10/92   5,225
Guillou, Alfred   Fr 1844-1926
O/C 37x48 The Fishermen Sby 10/92   8,800
Guinart, Francisco   Spa 20C
* See 1993 Edition . . . .
Guipon, Leon   Am 1872-1910
O/Cb 30x18 Gentleman and the Fisherman Fre 10/92   325
Guliuny, E*   Con 20C**
O/C 26x36 Spring Landscape with Village Sby 1/93   6,900
Gumery, Adolphe-Ernest   Fr 1861-
* See 1992 Edition . . . .
Gundelach, Matthaus   1566-1654
O/C 31x38 Adam and Eve in the Garden Sby 10/92   5,500
Gunn, Archie   Am 1863-1930
O/C 22x15 Cherries in Danger 1863 But 5/93   7,475
Pe/Pa 22x17 Girl with Teddy Bear Ih 11/92   800
Gunn, Edwin H.   Am 1876-1940
O/B 14x14 Fisherman and Building Eld 8/93   440
Gunther, Georg   Ger 1886-
O/C 24x20 Tabletop Still Life '38 Wes 10/92   385
Gunther, Julius   Ger 1830-
O/C/B 16x20 Waterfall 1882 Hnd 12/92   1,500
Gurvich, Jose   Uru 1927-1974
O/C Size? Bajo Relieve 58 Sby 5/93   10,925
O/B 14x17 Paisaje Constructivista '62 Sby 5/93   7,475
O/B 23x17 Constructivo con Barco y Avion 1952 Sby 11/92   7,150
Gussow, Bernard   Am 1881-1957
O/B 30x23 The Window Dum 7/93   2,250
W/Pa 8x13 Beach Scene Mys 3/93   275
Gustafson, Sven
* See 1992 Edition . . . .
Gustin, Alfred   Am 19C
H&W/Pa 7x11 Four Views of Colombia Sby 5/93   805
Guston, Philip   Am 1912-1980
O/C 76x102 As It Goes Sby 5/93   442,500
O/C 71x78 Stranger 1964 Chr 11/92   110,000
O/Pa/M 26x37 Untitled Sby 11/92   68,750
G/Pa 30x40 Pink Light 1963 Chr 11/92   44,000
O/Pa 20x28 Untitled '71 Chr 11/92   41,800
Br&I/Pa 14x17 Alone '70 Chr 11/92   33,000
Gute, Herbert Jacob   Am 1908-1977
* See 1993 Edition . . . .
Guthrie, W. D.   Br 19C
O/C 18x26 Fallen Roses 1907 Chr 10/92   770
O/B 16x24 Roses 1907 Yng 2/93   200
Gutierrez, Jose L.
* See 1992 Edition . . . .
Gutierrez, Oswaldo   Cub 1917-
* See 1993 Edition . . . .
Gutman, Nathan
* See 1992 Edition . . . .
Gutmann, Bernhard   Am 1869-1936
O/C 33x37 Wood Block Printer 1932 Skn 9/92   440
Guttuso, Renato   It 1912-
* See 1993 Edition . . . .
Guy, Francis   Am 1760-1820
* See 1993 Edition . . . .
Guy, Seymour Joseph   Am 1824-1910
O/C 24x20 The Haunted Cellar (Who's Afraid) Sby 5/93 . .   43,125
**Guyan-Goepp, Maximilienne   Fr
1868-1903**
W/Pa 14x10 Portrait Woman on the Beach Wlf 5/93   400
Guyot, Georges Lucien   Fr 1885-1973
O/Pn 10x12 Floral Lou 9/92   275

Guyp, Benjamin Gerritsz.   Dut 1612-1652
* See 1990 Edition . . . .
Guys, Constantin   Fr 1802-1892
I&W/Pa 12x19 La Caleche Dum 8/93   1,200
Guzzardi, Giuseppe   It -1914
O/C 10x9 Reading Newspaper/Candlelight 1882 Mys 12/92 .   2,090
Gwathmey, Robert   Am 1903-1988
O/C 38x30 Yellow Tables Chr 12/92   6,600
G/Pa 12x14 Darning and Strumming Chr 5/93   2,415
Pe/Pa 17x11 Study for Homo Sapiens Chr 5/93   1,955
Gyngell, Albert E.   Eng 20C
O/C 16x12 Figures in a Spring Landscape 1892 Slo 5/93 . . .   650
**Gysbrechts, Cornelis Norbertus   Dut a
17C**
* See 1992 Edition . . . .
Gysbrechts, Franciscus   Dut a 1674-
* See 1992 Edition . . . .
Gyselinckx, Joseph   Bel 19C
* See 1991 Edition . . . .
Gysels, Pieter   Flm 1621-1690
* See 1991 Edition . . . .
Gysis, Nicholas   Gr 1842-1901
O/C 30x21 Boy with Cherries '88 But 11/92   37,400
Haacke, Hans   20C
* See 1993 Edition . . . .
Haag, Carl   Ger 1820-1915
* See 1992 Edition . . . .
Haag, Jean Paul   Fr 19C
* See 1993 Edition . . . .
Haaland, Lars Laurits   Nor 1855-1938
O/C 22x32 Shipping Off a Rocky Coast 1905 Chr 5/93   6,900
Haanen, Casparis   Dut 1778-1849
* See 1990 Edition . . . .
Haapanen, John Nichols   Am 1891-
O/C 11x13 Fruit Yng 2/93   225
Haas, Richard
* See 1992 Edition . . . .
Haas, Siegfried   Am 20C
* See 1993 Edition . . . .
Hacker, Arthur   Eng 1858-1919
* See 1993 Edition . . . .
Hacker, Dieter   Ger 1942-
O/C 79x79 Tivoli 1982 Chr 5/93   4,025
O/C 71x48 Frau mit Tod 88 Chr 5/93   1,610
A&K/Pa 60x40 Der Spiegel 88 Chr 5/93   575
Hacker, Horst   Ger 1842-1906
* See 1992 Edition . . . .
Haddock, Arthur E.   Am 1895-1980
O/B 14x10 Canyon de Chelly 1951 Eld 4/93   165
Haddon, Arthur Trevor   Eng 1864-1941
* See 1993 Edition . . . .
Hader, Elmer Stanley   Am 1889-1973
O/C 31x23 Moonlight, Paris '12 Sby 9/92   5,500
Hadfield, Scott   Am 20C
E/Wd 48x39 Eire (Spirit of the War Dead) 1983 Skn 5/93 . . .   825
Haelszel, Johann-Baptist   Ger 1712-1777
* See 1990 Edition . . . .
Haenigsen, Harry   Am 1900-1991
Pl/Pa 12x11 Four Gag Cartoons Ih 5/93   300
Hafner, Carl   Ger 1814-1873
* See 1993 Edition . . . .
Hagarty, Clara Sophia   Can 1871-1958
P/Pa 11x14 View of Seine River, Paris '26 Sbt 11/92   1,320
Hagarty, James   Br a 1762-1783
* See 1991 Edition . . . .
**Hagborg, August Wilhelm N.   Swd
1852-1925**
O/C 26x20 Oyster Gatherer Fisherman Doy 11/92   6,600
Hageman, Victor Charles   Bel 19C
O/C 41x44 Figural Composition Chr 10/92   3,300
Hagemann, Oskar N.   Am 20C
O/B 16x13 Floral Still Life 1927 Hnd 10/92   375
Hagemans, Paul   Bel 1884-1959
O/B 23x27 Still Life Flowers Sby 1/93   2,300

Hagen, Walter   Am 1910-
O/Pn 13x17 Landscape with Pond Fre 4/93 325
Hagerup, Nels   Am 1864-1922
O/C 20x30 High Tide But 10/92 2,090
O/C 24x36 Seascape and Sunset But 3/93 1,870
O/C 14x24 Sand Dunes along the Coast But 3/93 1,100
O/C 24x36 Sunrise Over a Calm Sea 1920 Wes 5/93 660
O/C 12x21 Coastal Mor 6/93 550
O/C 14x21 Sunset Coastal Mor 6/93 522
Haghe, Louis   Bel 1806-1885
* See 1993 Edition . . . .
Hagny, J.   Am 19C
* See 1993 Edition . . . .
**Hague, J. Edward Homerville H.   Br a
1885-1903**
O/C/B 16x12 College Chapel and City Wall Sel 4/93 70
Hahn, Georg   Ger 1841-1889
* See 1990 Edition . . . .
Hahn, William   Am 1829-1887
O/C 18x26 In the Storm But 3/93 9,350
O/Pn 12x9 Entrance to the Mission 1869 But 6/93 2,300
O/C 14x19 Bull 1880 But 6/93 1,840
Hahs, Philip B.   Am 1853-1882
O/C/B 12x16 Olden Time 1880 Fre 10/92 7,750
O/B 10x18 First Step Fre 10/92 5,750
O/C/B 17x25 The Reverie 1882 Fre 10/92 5,250
O/B 16x12 Faggot Gatherer in Winter Fre 10/92 800
W/Pa 13x9 Seated Man with a Shoe 1882 Fre 10/92 700
Haig, Axel Herman   Eng 1835-1921
* See 1992 Edition . . . .
Haigh-Wood, Charles   Br 1856-1927
* See 1993 Edition . . . .
**Haines, Frederick Stanley   Can
1897-1960**
O/B 20x26 Winter Country Road Sbt 5/93 2,200
O/B 12x15 Rapids on South River 1936 Sbt 11/92 2,024
O/C 15x18 Watching the Flock Sbt 5/93 1,320
O/B 15x12 Autumn Landscape Sbt 11/92 880
Hajak, Hans   Ger 19C
O/B 20x29 Cows in a River Hnd 12/92 350
Hake, Otto   Am 1876-
* See 1993 Edition . . . .
Halauska, Ludwig   Ger 1827-1882
* See 1990 Edition . . . .
Hale, Lillian Westcott   Am 1881-1953
O/C 30x25 Agnes and Her Cat Chr 5/93 48,300
Hale, Philip Leslie   Am 1865-1931
O/C 36x24 At the Piano Sby 3/93 4,600
Haley, Robert Duane   Am 1892-1959
* See 1990 Edition . . . .
Hall, Edith Emma Dorothea   Am 1883-
O/C 24x28 Old Carriage Factory Fre 4/93 300
O/Cb 10x14 Harbor Scene Lou 9/92 60
Hall, Frederick   Br 1860-1948
* See 1990 Edition . . . .
Hall, George Edward   Am 19C
O/C 12x18 Early Evening, Peach Point, Mass. Skn 5/93 770
Hall, George Henry   Am 1825-1913
O/C 24x19 Young Girl in Red Cape 1887 Chr 12/92 2,420
O/C 32x39 The Dream 1884 Wlf 3/93 2,200
Hall, Harry   Br 1814-1882
O/C 32x48 Champions, Lord Lyon & Elland 1867 Chr 2/93 30,800
O/C 28x36 Dunbar's Bay Filly "Tormentor" 1866 Sby 6/93 . 10,350
Hall, Henry   Br 19C
O/C 12x20 Highland Cattle in Winter Fre 4/93 775
Hall, J. D.
O/C 38x38 Jan/Bubbles-Just Like Sisters 1982 Sby 10/92 . 9,350
Hall, Mary   Am 20C
O/M 23x32 Carnival Wlf 12/92 800
Hallberg, J. Henry   Am 19C
O/C 25x30 Coastline Fre 4/93 450
Halle, Noel   Fr 1711-1781
* See 1993 Edition . . . .

Halle, Samuel Baruch   Fr 1824-1889
* See 1992 Edition . . . .
Hallett, Hendricks A.   Am 1847-1921
P/Pa 10x17 Two 17th Century Sailing Ships Yng 2/93 150
Halley, Peter   1953-
A/C 69x192 Alphaville Sby 5/93 96,000
A/C 77x138 Two Cells with Circulating Conduit Chr 11/92 . 82,500
A/C 73x124 Rectangular Prison w/Smokestack Sby 5/93 . 68,500
A/C 56x41 The Light of Reason 1983 Chr 11/92 41,800
Hallowell, Robert   Am 1886-1939
W/Pa 18x23 Cuban Landscape '29 Hnz 5/93 325
Halpert, Samuel   Am 1884-1930
W/Pa 15x11 Fruit Bowl '14 Sby 12/92 9,900
Halpin, Warren   Br 20C
P/Pa 23x20 Wee Willie '36 Chr 6/93 345
Hals, Dirck   Dut 1591-1656
* See 1991 Edition . . . .
Hals, Frans   Dut 1580-1666
* See 1992 Edition . . . .
Hals, Harmen-Franz   Dut 1611-1669
* See 1990 Edition . . . .
Halsall, William Formby   Am 1841-1919
O/C 22x30 Golden Gate, Lompoc But 3/93 2,750
Halswelle, Keeley   Br 1832-1891
O/C 16x23 Gathering Clouds Chr 10/92 1,870
Hambidge, Jay   Am 1867-1924
O/B 26x17 Made Me Green Tea Fre 10/92 150
Hambleton, Richard   1954-
A/C 62x96 Rainy Season in the Tropics Chr 11/92 550
Hambourg, Andre   Fr 1909-
O/C 32x39 Soleil, Sur la Plage Sby 2/93 18,975
O/C 11x18 Brume Legere de Matin Sby 6/93 10,350
O/C 11x18 Temps Couvert Septembre, Deauville Chr 11/92 . 9,900
O/C 11x14 Place St. Marc 61 Doy 11/92 7,700
O/C 11x14 Temps Calme 1964 Chr 5/93 7,475
O/C 26x32 La Plage a Trouville 1951 But 5/93 6,900
O/C 6x11 Deauville, temps doux sur le port Chr 11/92 . . . 6,050
O/C 5x9 Le Beau Temps a Deauville But 5/93 5,750
O/C 5x9 Soleil dans brume legere Chr 11/92 3,300
Hambridge, Jay   Am 1867-1924
V/Pa 9x7 Brer Rabbit Story 1908 Mys 3/93 110
Hamel, Adolphe   Ger 1820-
* See 1993 Edition . . . .
Hamilton, Edgar Scudder   Am 1869-1903
O/C 10x8 Figure Study Chr 5/93 345
O/B 16x24 California Coast Slo 4/93 275
Hamilton, Edward Wilbur Dean   Am 1862-
* See 1991 Edition . . . .
Hamilton, F. A.   Am 20C
O/C 30x40 Still Life Fruit Orientalia Slo 5/93 450
O/C/B 17x14 Street Scene Slo 5/93 150
Hamilton, Gavin   1723-1798
O/C 67x48 Hygieia Chr 5/93 40,250
Hamilton, Gawen   Br 1697-1773
* See 1990 Edition . . . .
Hamilton, Hamilton   Am 1847-1928
O/C 28x18 The Farewell 1887 Sby 9/92 30,800
O/C/M 30x20 Woman with a Fan Chr 12/92 4,180
O/C 20x27 Mist Rising Over the Mountains 1879 Fre 10/92 . 2,600
Hamilton, James   Am 1819-1878
O/C 10x22 New York Tidelands Chr 9/92 7,700
O/C 12x20 Action The Monitor The Merrimac 1874 Sby 9/92 5,500
O/Pn 8x14 Marshes, Atlantic City But 6/93 4,025
O/C/B 9x17 Ships under the Sunset But 6/93 2,300
O/C 20x36 Shipwreck at Sunset Doy 11/92 1,650
O/C 9x14 Ship in a Stormy Sea at Sunset Fre 10/92 1,500
Hamilton, John McClure   Am 1853-1939
O/C 36x48 Woman by a Window Fre 10/92 5,000
O/C 36x60 Gentleman at Desk with Globes Fre 10/92 2,000
O/C 43x36 Young Girl with Flowers Fre 10/92 2,000
O/C 42x57 Portrait of a Gentleman Fre 10/92 1,700
O/C 63x50 My Mother 1914 Fre 10/92 1,600
O/C 75x39 Gentleman in a Top Hat Fre 10/92 850
P/Pa 21x18 Seated Woman 1914 Fre 4/93 850
O/C 75x38 Man in Top Hat Fre 4/93 800

O/C 50x40 Portrait of a Boy Fre 10/92 800
K/Pa 19x15 Portrait Colonel E. M. Horne 1919 Fre 10/92 . . . 550

Hamilton, Karl William Aus 1668-1754
* See 1991 Edition . . . .

Hamilton, Rupert
W/Pa 7x10 Roping Steer Eld 8/93 121

Hamlin, Edith Am 1902-
O/Cb 30x15 Nude with Bowl of Grapes Lou 6/93 525

Hammer, Hans Jorgen Dan 1815-1882
* See 1992 Edition . . . .

Hammer, Johann J. Am 1842-1906
O/C 29x46 In the Garden 1880 Brd 8/93 5,060
O/C 18x12 Pier, Gloucester Harbor Skn 5/93 715

Hammershoi, Vilhelm Dan 1846-1916
* See 1991 Edition . . . .

Hammerstad, John Olson Am 1842-1925
O/B 16x22 Ship Off Rocky Coast Dum 2/93 500

Hammond, Arthur J. Am 1875-1947
W/Pa 8x11 Western Desert Landscape 1935 Yng 2/93 200

Hammond, Jane Am 1950-
O/C 72x54 Untitled (21.79) 1988 FHB 3/93 5,750
O/C 30x24 Untitled (60.79.37) 1988 FHB 3/93 500

Hammond, John A. Can 1843-1939
O/B 14x17 Birch Trees 1927 Sbt 11/92 1,056

Hammond, Robert John Br a 1882-1911
O/C 18x24 View in Surrey 1910 But 5/93 2,875

Hammons, David
I/Pa 40x47 The Wine Leading the Wine Sby 11/92 7,150
I/Pa 25x19 American Costume Sby 5/93 5,750

Hamon, Jean-Louis Fr 1821-1874
O/B 13x10 Cupid at the Gate 1868 Wlf 3/93 5,000

Hampton, John W. Am 1918-
* See 1993 Edition . . . .

Hamwi, Richard 20C
L/Pa 7x7 Feathers Light (Four) Slo 4/93 225

Hamza, Johann Ger 1850-1927
* See 1993 Edition . . . .

Hancock, Charles Br 1793-1855
O/C 30x25 Thomas Oldacre/Favorite Hound 1827 Chr 6/93 . 8,050

Hancock, Mildred L. Br a 1890-1893
O/C 51x31 Spirit of the Summit Sby 5/93 9,200

Hand, I. Eng 19C
* See 1992 Edition . . . .

Hanke, August Aus 20C
* See 1992 Edition . . . .

Hankey, William Lee Br 1869-1950
O/C 20x24 Honfleur at Full Tide Skn 3/93 7,700
O/C 29x36 Church of St. Wilfran Chr 2/93 5,500
W/Pa 14x10 Study for "The Forgotten Village" Wes 12/92 . . 1,320
W/Pa 9x14 Figure Working in a Field Hnd 6/93 600
W/Pa 10x4 Woman Standing in a Field Hnd 6/93 600

Hankins, A. P.
O/C 20x26 Rocks Ald 9/92 75

Hankins, Abraham Am 20C
O/C 24x20 Card Game '39 Fre 4/93 575

Hanna, David Am 1941-1981
* See 1993 Edition . . . .

Hanna, Thomas King Am -1916
* See 1991 Edition . . . .

Hanna, Thomas King (Jr.) Am 1872-1951
O/C 11x15 Grandma's House Lou 12/92 800

Hannah, Duncan 20C
O/C 51x54 City Lights 1984 Sby 2/93 2,415

Hanneman, Adriaen Dut 1601-1671
* See 1991 Edition . . . .

Hannig, Henry C. Am 20C
O/C 24x18 Contemplation Hnz 5/93 100

Hannot, Jan Dut 17C
* See 1991 Edition . . . .

Hanoteau, Hector Fr 1823-1890
O/C 31x35 Shepherdess Tending Goats Sel 12/92 1,200

Hanriot, Jules Armand Fr 1853-1877
* See 1993 Edition . . . .

Hansen, Armin Am 1886-1957
O/C 30x40 Fishing Boats But 10/92 60,500

O/C/B 15x19 Between Tides But 3/93 24,200
O/B 20x35 Waiting for the News But 3/93 22,000
O/C 34x40 Three Fishermen Hauling in Nets But 10/92 . . . 17,600
O/B 18x22 Return of the Fishing Fleet But 3/93 12,100
O/C 40x54 Landing of Father Serra But 10/92 11,000
O/C/B 10x47 Monterey Fiesta But 3/93 11,000
O/B 16x19 The Conversation; Coastal Scene:Dbl But 6/93 . . 9,775
O/B 10x14 Wind in Mast Tops; Coastal: Double But 3/93 . . 9,350
O/B 10x14 Winter Morning But 3/93 8,800
O/B 10x14 Men Beaching a Dory: Double Mor 6/93 7,700
O/M 12x17 Man in Rowboat; After Storm: Double But 10/92 6,050
W/Pa 13x19 Boatyard Mor 6/93 5,225
O/B 10x14 Fisherman's Quay But 6/93 4,600
O/B 7x7 Hauling in the Nets But 3/93 3,025
O/Pn 6x7 Pulling a Rowboat Ashore But 6/93 1,610

Hansen, Ejnar Am 1884-1965
O/C 22x18 Vase of Roses But 3/93 4,125
O/B 16x20 Magnolia But 6/93 690
O/Pb 19x14 Still Life Flowers '35 Lou 6/93 600
O/C/Pw 18x22 Flowers in Blue Vase Mor 11/92 550
W/Pa 15x20 Adobe Mission Mor 11/92 250

Hansen, Herman Wendelborg Am 1854-1924
* See 1993 Edition . . . .

Hansen, John F. Dan a 1900-1920
* See 1992 Edition . . . .

Hanson, James Am 20C
O/C 60x84 Myself in an Unusual Situation 1983 Skn 5/93 . . 1,650

Hanson, Oscar Rabe
G/Pa 20x13 Onrushing Knights on Horseback Ih 5/93 1,000

Hanson, Peter Am 1821-1887
* See 1993 Edition . . . .

Hanson, R. Con 20C
* See 1992 Edition . . . .

Hansteen, Nils Severin Lynge Nor 1855-1912
* See 1992 Edition . . . .

Hantai, Simon 1922-
* See 1993 Edition . . . .

Haquette, Georges Jean Marie Fr 1854-1906
O/C 30x44 Too Young for the Trip Doy 11/92 7,425
O/C 40x59 Hauling in the Catch But 5/93 6,900
O/C 26x20 Fisherman's Wife Doy 5/93 5,775

Harcourt, George Br 1868-1947
O/C 72x91 Muriel, Cynthia, George Perkins 1900 Sby 2/93 37,375

Hardenbergh, Gerard R. 19C
* See 1993 Edition . . . .

Hardie, Robert Gordon Am 1854-1904
* See 1992 Edition . . . .

Hardime, Pieter Flm 1677-1758
* See 1993 Edition . . . .

Harding, G. P. Eng 19C
W/Pa 6x5 King James V of Scotland 1842 Hnd 5/93 300

Hardman, John Eng 19C
* See 1991 Edition . . . .

Hardwick, Alice Roney Am 1876-
W/Pa 14x20 Sand Dunes Slo 7/93 200

Hardwick, Melbourne H. Am 1857-1916
O/C 25x22 The Toy Boat 1913 Skn 5/93 880
O/C 26x20 Portrait of Dutch Weaver Eld 8/93 550
W/Pa 18x24 Fisherfolk Chr 5/93 368

Hardy, Dudley Br 1865-1922
* See 1993 Edition . . . .

Hardy, Frederick Daniel Br 1826-1911
* See 1993 Edition . . . .

Hardy, Heywood Br 1843-1933
O/C 36x48 The Meet Chr 10/92 30,800
O/C 20x31 The Stirrup Cup Chr 5/93 13,800
O/C 20x30 Breaking Cover Hnd 12/92 9,500
O/C 20x30 Fox Hunt Hnd 12/92 4,700

Hardy, James (Jr.) Br 1832-1889
O/C 34x47 The End of the Day 81 Sby 6/93 60,250
O/C 32x44 The Day's Catch 77 Sby 6/93 48,875

Hardy, Jeremiah P.   Am 1800-1887
  * See 1993 Edition . . . .
Hardy, Thomas   Br a 18C
  * See 1993 Edition . . . .
Hardy, Thomas Bush   Br 1842-1897
  W&G/Pa 13x20 Harbour's Mouth, Boulogne 1877 Chr 10/92 2,200
Hare, Channing Weir   Am 1899-1976
  O/M 34x24 Louis MacNeil... 1951 Skn 3/93 715
  O/C 40x34 Portrait Lili Damita 1944 Skn 11/92 715
  O/C 40x34 The Dancer Skn 11/92 550
  O/C 30x25 Still Life with Carnations Skn 3/93 440
Hare, David
  * See 1992 Edition . . . .
Hare, John Knowles   Am 1882-1947
  C/Pa 24x18 Industrial Scene Yng 2/93 175
Hare, Julius   Br 1859-1932
  * See 1992 Edition . . . .
Hare, Richard Clark   Am 1906-
  W/Pa 11x15 Locomotive Slo 7/93 325
  W/Pa 10x13 Landscapes: Pair Slo 4/93 190
Hare, St. George   Br 1857-
  * See 1990 Edition . . . .
Haring, Keith   Am 1958-1990
  A/Pls 118x120 Untitled 82 Sby 11/92 60,500
  A/C 60x60 Untitled 1985 Sby 5/93 57,500
  A/Pls 84x86 Untitled 1983 Chr 11/92 52,800
  A/Pls 73x73 Untitled 84 Sby 2/93 37,375
  A/C 30x30 Untitled 1984 Sby 11/92 24,750
  A&I/Pa 38x50 Untitled Sby 2/93 23,000
  A/Pn 45x48 Untitled 81 Chr 10/92 22,000
  E&Fp/Pn 45x48 Untitled 81 Chr 2/93 19,800
  E/Me 43x43 Untitled 1982 Chr 2/93 19,800
  Br&I/Pa 38x50 Untitled 81 Chr 11/92 15,400
  A/C 91x59 Untitled Chr 10/92 14,300
  Br&I/Pa 48x34 Untitled 84 Chr 11/92 14,300
  I/Pa 41x45 Untitled 1981 Sby 5/93 13,800
  Br&I/Pa 51x21 Untitled 84 Chr 11/92 11,000
  Br&I/Pa 20x26 Untitled 88 Chr 10/92 8,800
  Br&I/Pa 20x26 Untitled 88 Chr 11/92 7,700
  Br&I/Pa 20x26 Untitled 88 Chr 10/92 7,150
  I/Pa 23x29 Untitled 1983 Sby 2/93 6,900
  Br&I/Pa 39x27 Marilyn Monroe Chr 11/92 6,050
  Pl&E/Wd 12x15 Untitled 1984 Chr 5/93 4,025
  G,Br&I/Pa 20x25 Untitled '89 Chr 11/92 3,850
  Br&I/Pa 25x19 Anti-Missile Demonstration 83 Chr 11/92 . . . 3,520
  Br&I/Pa 25x19 Anti-Missile Demonstration 83 Chr 11/92 . . . 3,520
  P/C 8x8 Wolf and Man 83 But 4/93 2,300
  Fp&Pe/Pa 11x8 Phone Card #2 (New Years) 87 Sby 10/92 1,980
Haring, Keith & L.A. 2   Am 20C
  E&Mk/St 23x48 Untitled 82 Sby 11/92 20,900
Haring, Keith & Martin Roy   Am 20C
  * See 1993 Edition . . . .
Harlamoff, Alexei Alexeiewitsc   Rus 1842-
  O/C 47x34 Young Girl with Flowers Chr 5/93 85,000
  O/C 26x20 Innocence 1889 Chr 5/93 29,900
Harles, Victor J.   Am 1894-1975
  * See 1993 Edition . . . .
Harlow, George Henry   Eng 1787-1819
  O/C 30x25 Portrait of a Young Lady Sby 10/92 8,525
  C&Sg/Pa 8x7 Portrait of a Gentleman Sby 5/93 2,300
Harmer, Alexander F.   Am 1856-1925
  * See 1993 Edition . . . .
Harmon, Annie   Am 1855-1930
  O/C 24x16 Nilouette Falls, Yosemite But 3/93 1,980
Harmon, Fred   Am 1902-1982
  * See 1991 Edition . . . .
Harnden, William   Am 1920-1983
  O/M 30x24 The Pink House Sby 9/92 1,760
  O/B 23x29 Still Life Oriental Statue Wlf 3/93 225
Harnett, William Michael   Am 1848-1892
  O/C 10x8 Still: Jug, Bread, Newspaper 1881 Sby 12/92 . . 57,750
  Pe/Pa 6x5 Portrait of a Woman 76 Chr 4/93 1,650
Harney, Paul E.   Am 1850-1915
  O/Por 10x7 Allegorical Female Semi-Nude Figure Sel 9/92 . . . 550

Harper, J.   Aus 19C
  O/C 16x12 Man and Woman Watching Doves Hnd 9/92 600
Harper, William St. John   Am 1851-1910
  * See 1991 Edition . . . .
Harpignies, Henri Joseph   Fr 1819-1916
  O/Pn 16x23 St. Rive (Yonne) 1906 Chr 5/93 18,400
  O/C 28x48 Stream in Landscape 1888 Chr 10/92 11,000
  W/Pa 11x14 Un Parc sur la Seine a Paris 92 Sby 5/93 . . . 10,925
  O/Pn 18x13 Sundown on the River Loire 1905 Sby 10/92 . . 8,800
  O/C 15x22 Arbres au bord de la Riviere Chr 5/93 8,050
  W&Pe/Pa 21x15 Les Chasseurs a L'Aube 83 Sby 5/93 . . . 5,750
  W&Pe/Pa 8x11 Vue de la Baie De Menton 99 Sby 5/93 . . . 4,600
  W&Pe/Pa 12x18 Vieux Chenes de Breteau 1885 Sby 5/93 . 4,025
  W&Pe/Pa 10x7 Commissariat de Police 85 Sby 5/93 3,450
  O/Pn 16x21 Twi-light Landscape with Figure '90 Slo 4/93 . . 2,750
  K/Pa 15x21 Wooded River Landscape Chr 5/93 2,530
  W&Pe/Pa 5x7 Group of Paintings (3) 1908 Sby 5/93 2,300
  O/C 9x13 Bridge and Figure at River's Edge 1888 But 5/93 . 1,495
Harrer, Hugo Paul   Ger 1836-1876
  * See 1992 Edition . . . .
Harriet, Fulchran Jean   Fr 1778-1805
  * See 1991 Edition . . . .
Harrington, George W.   Am 1833-1911
  O/C 12x16 Landscape Eld 8/93 495
Harris, Charles Gordon   Am 1891-
  O/C 25x30 Mountain Farm Yng 2/93 600
Harris, Charles X.   Am 1856-
  O/Pn 8x11 The Decision 1884 Sby 5/93 47,150
Harris, Edwin   Br 1901-
  * See 1991 Edition . . . .
Harris, F. H. Howard   Eng 19C
  O/C 22x33 Bustling Marketplace in Granada Chr 2/93 1,980
Harris, Lawren Stewart   Can 1885-1970
  O/B 12x15 Isolation Peak Sbt 11/92 114,400
  O/C 49x49 Form, F71 Mount Ann-Alice 1943 Sbt 5/93 . . . 83,600
  O/B 11x14 In the Ward, Toronto 1917 Sbt 11/92 70,400
  O/Pn 10x14 Trees and Snow Sbt 11/92 70,400
  O/B 12x16 Mountain Form Sbt 11/92 39,600
  O/Pn 12x15 Snow Squalls Sbt 5/93 30,800
  O/B 11x14 Maligne Lake, Jasper Park Sbt 5/93 28,160
  O/Pn 11x14 Lismer Lake, Algoma Sbt 5/93 26,400
  O/Pn 11x14 Lake Superior, Pic Island Sbt 11/92 22,880
  O/Pn 8x6 Late Afternoon, Winter '12 Sbt 5/93 5,280
  O/C 39x50 Landscape, Circa 1963 Sbt 11/92 4,180
  Pe/Pa 8x10 Arctic Shore - No. 2 Sbt 5/93 1,760
Harris, Robert   Can 1849-1919
  O/C 25x20 Portrait Artist's Brother 1884 Sbt 5/93 3,520
  O/C 12x16 Houses and Forest Sbt 11/92 968
Harris, Robert George   Am 1911-
  O/C 18x19 Woman, Hands on Hips Ilh 11/92 850
Harris, Robert M.   a 1930-1939
  O/Cb 18x24 Landscape Mor 11/92 550
  W/Pa 10x14 California Farm Scene Lou 12/92 60
Harris, Sam Hyde   Am 1889-1977
  O/C 24x30 Blue Shadows But 10/92 6,600
  O/Cb 16x20 At Ease But 10/92 3,575
  O/Cb 20x24 Desert Wash But 10/92 2,750
  O/C 22x28 Landscape - Parts Dept. Mor 11/92 2,500
  O/C 24x30 Desert Sentinels But 10/92 2,090
  O/C/B 16x20 Cottonwood Tree But 3/93 1,210
  O/C 16x20 Barn in Landscape Mor 2/93 1,200
  O/C 20x24 Landscape Mor 2/93 600
Harrison, Alexander
  O/C 22x36 Sunset Ald 9/92 650
Harrison, Allen
  O/Pn 80x48 Inverness #271 1984 Sby 10/92 1,760
Harrison, B.   Am 19C
  O/C 15x12 Head of a Lady Hnd 12/92 110
Harrison, Birge   Am 1854-1929
  O/C 20x24 A Trout Pond Chr 12/92 1,320
  O/Cb 14x11 A Village Street at Moonlite 1907 Chr 5/93 . . . 748
Harrison, George L.   Br a 1878-1883
  O/C 26x20 The Courtship Sby 1/93 2,645
Harrison, John Cyril   Br 1898-1985
  * See 1992 Edition . . . .

120

Harrison, Thomas Alexander Am 1853-1930
O/C 28x40 Falls at Montigny, France 1901 Chr 5/93 2,990
Harrowing, Walter Br a 1877-1904
O/C 22x27 Beagles at Peterborough Show 1889 Chr 6/93 . . 4,370
Harsh, Fred Dana Am
* See 1992 Edition . . . .
Harshe, Robert Bartholow Am 1879-
* See 1992 Edition . . . .
Hart, Claudia 1955-
O,H&Cp/C 78x56 Untitled Chr 10/92 3,850
Hart, James MacDougal Am 1828-1901
O/C 14x23 View of Farmington, CT 1866 Sby 9/92 13,200
O/C 14x23 River, Farmington, Connecticut Sby 12/92 8,800
O/C 9x16 New Russia, Essex County But 6/93 4,025
O/C 12x10 Landscape Chr 5/93 3,450
O/C 5x8 Cows Watering Chr 9/92 2,860
O/C 11x7 The Watering Hole Lou 9/92 1,550
O/B 10x17 Farm with Field of Wheat Yng 5/93 1,400
Hart, Kevin Pro Aut 1928-
O/B 29x33 Early Settlers Prison Camp 1968 Mys 3/93 . . 1,540
Hart, William Howard Am 1863-1964
* See 1993 Edition . . . .
Hart, William M. Am 1823-1894
O/C 18x14 In the Berkshires 1873 Chr 5/93 10,350
O/C 37x28 Heldenberg Mountain 1849 Doy 11/92 8,250
O/C 25x21 Cows Watering by a River 1883 Sby 3/93 . . . 5,175
O/C 11x15 Craigy Barns 1850 Chr 9/92 3,300
O/B 8x8 Wooded Landscape 1876 Dum 11/92 2,000
O/C 11x16 Forest Landscape Wes 5/93 1,870
O/C 8x11 Cows Drinking by a River 1887 Sby 3/93 1,840
O/C 9x12 Cattle by a Stream Lou 3/93 1,800
O/C 8x10 Man with Two Cows by Stream 1872 Lou 3/93 . . 1,800
O/B 9x15 Autumn Brd 8/93 1,210
Hartigan, Grace Am 1922-
O/C 21x24 Rain King '65 Chr 11/92 2,750
Hartinger, Anton Aus 1806-1890
O/Pn 21x16 Still Life Flowers, Butterfly 1834 Sby 10/92 . . 23,100
Hartley, Marsden Am 1878-1943
O/C 47x40 Abstraction Sby 12/92 . . . . 1.155M
O/B 28x22 Abelard Ascending Sby 12/92 60,500
O/Pn 21x13 Seashells on a Violet Cloth 1929 Sby 3/93 . . 33,350
O/C 21x32 Peppers Sby 12/92 30,800
O/C 24x20 Still Life Blue Bottle, Oranges 1928 Sby 12/92 . . 28,600
O/M 20x28 Roofs and Woods Sby 12/92 22,000
O/C 9x11 Fish and Lemons Sby 12/92 10,450
Hartman, Bertram Am 1882-1960
O/C 32x39 Connecticut Apple Tree 1936 Sby 3/93 1,610
W/Pa 21x14 New York Skyline Chr 12/92 1,100
Hartmann, Ludwig Ger 1835-1902
O/Pn 16x37 Die Pferdeaustellung Sby 5/93 71,250
Hartrath, Lucie Am 19C
* See 1990 Edition . . . .
Hartrick, A. S. Am 1864-1950
W&Pe/Pa 17x11 Constable Carrying Girl Ih 11/92 375
Hartson, Walter C. Am 1866-
W/Pa 10x17 After the Harvest 96 Chr 5/93 345
Hartung, Hans Ger 1904-1989
O/C 11x14 T 1966-E40 '66 Sby 10/92 19,800
Hartwell, Nina Rosabel Am 19C
* See 1990 Edition . . . .
Hartwich, Herman Am 1853-1926
* See 1992 Edition . . . .
Hartwick, George Gunther Am a 1845-1860
* See 1993 Edition . . . .
Hartwig, Heinie Am 1937-
O/M 12x24 Indian Encampment Wes 5/93 990
O/M 12x24 Break in the Sky Fre 4/93 750
O/Pn 5x7 Pair: Indian Encampments Sel 2/93 550
O/Pn 12x16 Land of the Free Fre 10/92 525
O/Pn 12x18 Indian Burial Site Sel 9/92 475
O/M 12x18 The Campsite in Winter Wes 10/92 440
O/Pn 12x16 The Way It Was Fre 10/92 350
O/B 5x7 Western Landscapes: Two Sel 9/92 350

O/M 5x7 Camp and Camping: Two Wes 10/92 330
O/M 21x27 Mountain Landscape Sel 2/93 225
Harvey, George Am 1800-1878
O/C 25x19 Autumn Chr 9/92 30,800
Harvey, George W. Am 1836-1920
O/C 16x24 Haystacks in Winter Slo 4/93 1,800
Harvey, George Wainwright Am 1855-
* See 1993 Edition . . . .
Harvey, Gerald Am 1933-
* See 1990 Edition . . . .
Harvey, Henry T. Br 20C
O/C 28x38 On the Old Canal Chr 5/93 518
Harwood, James Taylor Am 1860-1940
* See 1990 Edition . . . .
Has, H. a 1517-1548
* See 1993 Edition . . . .
Hasbrock, C* A* Am 20C
O/C 25x30 Sailing on a Mountain Lake Wes 10/92 220
Hasbrouck, DuBois Fenelon Am 1860-1934
O/C 30x30 Apple Trees But 12/92 3,575
O/C 11x14 Dreamy Days Wes 5/93 358
W/Pa 11x30 Farm by a Stream Yng 2/93 175
Hasch, Carl Aus 1834-1897
* See 1993 Edition . . . .
Hasegawa, Kiyoshi Jap 1891-
* See 1991 Edition . . . .
Haseltine, Charles Field Am 1840-
O/B 14x18 Meadow Landscape with Figures 1905 Slo 4/93 . 750
Haseltine, William Stanley Am 1835-1900
O/C 26x71 Temple of Fusano '81 Sby 9/92 29,700
O/C 20x31 On the Beach, Capri Chr 5/93 17,250
O/C/B 20x32 Bay at Dawn 1869 Sby 3/93 5,175
O/C 25x71 Canal at Castel Fusano Chr 5/93 3,450
W/B 22x15 Castel Fusano, Ostia Sby 9/92 2,750
G,W&P/B 22x29 Farmhouse in Bavaria Chr 5/93 805
W,Pl&Pe/B 18x22 Sorrento 1888 Chr 5/93 575
Hassam, Frederick Childe Am 1859-1935
O/C 34x34 The Room of Flowers 1894 Sby 5/93 . . . . . 5.5025M
W&G/Pa 14x18 Horse Drawn Cabs at Evening Chr 12/92 . . 825,000
O/C 26x20 Sunny Morning, Villiers-le-Bel Chr 5/93 552,500
O/C 25x31 Couch on the Porch, Cos Cob 1914 Sby 5/93 . . 508,500
P/C 18x22 Horse Drawn Cabs, New York 1891 Chr 5/93 . . 387,500
O/C 32x28 Boys Marching By 1918 Chr 5/93 222,500
O/C 27x27 Moonrise at Sunset 1900 Sby 5/93 222,500
O/C 25x30 October Haze, Manhattan 1910 Sby 12/92 . . . 159,500
W/Pa 19x18 Veranda of the Old House 1912 Chr 5/93 . . . 112,500
O/Pn 5x12 Across the Common, Winter Sby 5/93 107,000
O/C 16x22 Moonlight Isles of Shoals 1899 But 6/93 74,000
P/B 18x22 Old Brush House, Cos Cob 1902 Chr 5/93 . . . 74,000
W&Pe/Pa 17x12 A Venetian Regatta 1891 Chr 12/92 71,500
G&R/B 11x14 World's Fair, Chicago Chr 12/92 60,500
O/C 22x24 Brook in Branchville, CT 1907 Sby 12/92 57,750
O/C 10x14 Autumn Twilight Chr 12/92 44,000
O/C 12x16 The Quiet Stream Chr 5/93 25,300
W&C/Pa/B 9x7 Flags, Columbus Circle 1918 Chr 9/92 . . . 20,900
W/Pa 16x19 Harper's Ferry 2nd 1926 Sby 12/92 17,600
I,Pe&W/Pa 4x5 Isles of Shoals Daybook, 1901 Sby 5/93 . . 17,250
W/Pa/B 12x18 Impression 86 Chr 9/92 8,250
Pl&Pe/B 14x11 European Street Scene 1883 Sby 12/92 . . . 6,600
Hasselbach, Wilhelm Ger 1846-
* See 1992 Edition . . . .
Hastings, T. Mitchell Am 20C
* See 1992 Edition . . . .
Hatfield, Joseph Henry Am 1863-1928
O/C 18x24 Road at Sunset Yng 2/93 1,900
Hathaway, George M. Am 1852-1903
O/Ab 7x13 The Forest City in Portland Harbor 1894 Brd 8/93 3,410
O/Ab 8x15 Portland Headlight from Cushings Is Brd 8/93 . . 1,210
O/B 6x10 Seascape with Ships Yng 9/93 900
O/Pn 6x10 Schooner Approaching Coast Eld 7/93 825
O/C 15x20 Seascape Yng 2/93 190
Hatvany, Baron De Ferencz Hun 1881-
O/C 29x43 A Reclining Nude 16 Chr 5/93 4,830

Hau, Eva Rus 19C
  * See 1991 Edition . . . .
Haughton, Moses Br 1734-1804
  * See 1993 Edition . . . .
Haun, Robert
  O/B Var Adventures of Yankee Doodle (4) Eld 8/93 275
  O/C Size? Various Cultures Eld 8/93 99
Hausch, Alexander Fiodorovich Rus 1873-
  * See 1990 Edition . . . .
Hauschild, Maximilian Ger 1810-1895
  W/Pa 14x10 Figure on the Steps Fre 4/93 350
Hauschka, Carola Spaeth Am 1883-1948
  P/Pa 9x12 My Garden Mys 3/93 165
Hauser, John Am 1858-1913
  G/Pa 17x12 Study for the Hostiles Hnd 12/92 850
Hausmann, Gustav Ger 1827-1899
  * See 1992 Edition . . . .
Havard, James Am 1937-
  A/C 66x67 Drink the Juice of the Stone 75 Sby 10/92 . . . 15,400
Havell, Robert (Jr.) Am 1793-1878
  * See 1990 Edition . . . .
Havell, William Br 1782-1857
  W/Pa 18x13 Landscape with Figures Hnz 5/93 330
Havenith, Hugo Eng 1853-
  * See 1992 Edition . . . .
Havret, Pierre 20C
  O/B 15x9 Iris Slo 4/93 750
Hawgood, Belle Am 20C
  O/C 11x15 A Flowery Garden Wlf 3/93 275
  O/C 9x10 Garden Scene with Birdbath Wlf 3/93 175
Hawksley, Dorothy Am 20C
  * See 1993 Edition . . . .
Hawley, Hughson Am 1850-1936
  * See 1992 Edition . . . .
Haworth, Bobs Cogill Can 1900-1988
  G&W/Pa 21x25 Cape Breton, Nova Scotia 1960 Sbt 11/92 . . . 704
  W/Pa 14x21 Boats & Wharf, Belle Anse 1953 Sbt 11/92 352
  W/Pa 19x25 Church in the Village Sbt 5/93 264
Haworth, Peter Can 1889-1986
  G/B 30x24 Abstract - The Kitchen Sbt 11/92 704
  W/Pa 14x22 Two War Ships Docked Sbt 5/93 528
  W/Pa 16x23 Aliford Bay, Charlottes, B.C. 1943 Sbt 11/92 . . . 352
Hawthorne, Charles Webster Am 1872-1930
  * See 1993 Edition . . . .
Haxton, Elaine Alys Aut 1909-
  W&H/Pa/B 14x14 The Farm Family 1933 Skn 9/92 1,320
Hay, Bernard Br 1864-
  O/Pn 24x41 View of Capri 1909 Sby 1/93 3,450
  O/C 28x17 Bridge of Sighs Chr 5/93 1,150
Hay, Peter Alexander Br 20C
  * See 1992 Edition . . . .
Hayden, Charles H. Am 1856-1901
  * See 1990 Edition . . . .
Hayden, Edward Parker Am -1922
  O/C 22x30 Orchard in Bloom 1890 Skn 9/92 1,430
Hayden, Henri Fr 1883-1970
  O/C 40x29 Femme a la rose 1909 Chr 11/92 24,200
Hayden, S. C.
  O/C 8x10 Shipping Off Shore Eld 11/92 165
Hayes, Claude Con 20C
  W/Pa 16x21 Taming the Horses Chr 2/93 715
Hayes, Edwin Irs 1819-1904
  O/C 11x18 Fishing Boats on Choppy Waters Dum 8/93 . . . 1,200
Hayllar, Edith Br 1860-1948
  * See 1990 Edition . . . .
Hayllar, James Br 1829-1920
  * See 1992 Edition . . . .
Hayllar, Jessica Br 1858-1940
  * See 1990 Edition . . . .
Hayman, Francis 1708-1776
  * See 1992 Edition . . . .
Haymann, Ernest Con 19C
  O/Pn 5x4 Villager with Oxen Slo 7/93 250

Hays, Barton S. Am 1826-1914
  O/C 10x14 Roses Hnd 6/93 1,100
Hays, George Arthur Am 1854-
  O/Pn 10x12 Cows by the River Mys 3/93 908
  O/C 9x12 Landscape with Two Cows Skn 11/92 440
  O/C 38x31 Gentleman with a Beard 1896 Eld 8/93 138
Hays, William Jacob Am 1830-1875
  * See 1991 Edition . . . .
Hayter, Stanley William Br 1901-1988
  O/C 29x36 Spray 1963 But 10/92 5,500
  Pl&P/Pa 13x10 Abstract Drawings (Two) 55 But 4/93 1,035
  P&Gd/Pa 24x20 Untitled Sby 6/93 1,035
Hayward, Joshua Henshaw Am 19C
  * See 1992 Edition . . . .
Hazard, Arthur Merton Am 1872-1930
  O/C 25x20 Woman in Yellow Dress 17 But 12/92 3,025
  W/Pa 20x25 Dolphins Off Pier '20 Mor 2/93 200
Hazard, Garnet Can 1903-
  W/Pa 18x22 Winter Landscape; Sill Life (2) Sbt 5/93 1,408
Hazard, James Eng 1748-1787
  * See 1993 Edition . . . .
Hazelton, Mary Brewster Am 1868-1953
  * See 1991 Edition . . . .
Heade, Martin Johnson Am 1819-1904
  O/C 16x21 Hummingbird and Passion Flowers Sby 5/93 . 354,500
  O/C/B 12x10 Hummingbirds Guarding an Egg Chr 3/93 . 222,500
  O/C/B 13x11 Ruby Throats with Apple Blossoms Chr 3/93 96,000
  O/C 18x15 Still Life Flowers in Silver Vase 1874 Sby 3/93 68,500
  O/C 20x12 Roses in a Transparent Vase Chr 9/92 44,000
  Pe/Pa 9x12 The Housley Sketchbook 1858 Sby 5/93 . . . 27,600
  O/C 20x12 Roses in a Crystal Goblet Chr 5/93 26,450
  O/Ab 12x8 Rose Brd 8/93 25,300
Healy, George Peter Alexander Am 1813-1894
  * See 1993 Edition . . . .
Heard, Joseph Br 19C
  * See 1992 Edition . . . .
Heath, J. Eng 19C
  O/C 20x36 The Day's Bag 70 Slo 4/93 300
Heatherington, Margaret Lyons Am 20C
  Pe/Pa 8x11 Illustrations: Two Hnz 5/93 60
  Pe/Pa 11x10 The Girl Who Ran For President: Two Hnz 5/93 . 60
  Pe/Pa Var Illustrations: Five Hnz 5/93 50
  Pe/Pa 6x9 Illustrations: Two Hnz 5/93 50
  Pe/Pa 15x10 Tree House, For Child Life Hnz 5/93 45
Heaton, Augustus G. Am 1844-1931
  * See 1991 Edition . . . .
Heberer, Charles Am 19C
  O/C 44x32 After Rubens Sby 3/93 1,035
Hebert, Adrien Can 1890-1967
  O/C 43x27 Man with Harmonica 1924 Sbt 11/92 1,760
Hebert, Antoine Auguste Ernest Fr 1817-1908
  * See 1992 Edition . . . .
Hebert, Jules Fr 1812-1897
  O/Pn 17x13 Off to War Chr 2/93 715
Hecht, Victor David Am 1873-1931
  * See 1990 Edition . . . .
Heckel, Erich Ger 1883-1970
  W&C/Pa 20x24 Die Brucke Bei le Puy 26 Sby 2/93 12,650
Heda, Gerrit Willemsz. Dut 1642-1702
  * See 1991 Edition . . . .
Heda, Willem Claesz. Dut 1594-1680
  * See 1992 Edition . . . .
Hedley, G* Br 19C**
  O/C 28 dia Still Life with Fruits Sby 1/93 1,150
Heeks, Willy
  O/C 84x74 Untitled 87 Sby 2/93 6,325
Heeremans, Thomas Dut 1641-1699
  * See 1993 Edition . . . .
Heffer, Edward A. Br 19C
  W/Pa 10x20 Fisherman in Landscape 1890 FHB 3/93 200
Hefferick Dut 20C
  O/C 16x23 Cows at Waterside Hnd 9/92 190

Heffner, Karl   Ger 1849-1925
O/C 47x66 Thames River with Windsor Castle Chr 5/93 . . 34,500
O/C 28x38 Sunset on the River Chr 10/92 6,050
O/C 19x30 Pond at Dusk Fre 4/93 1,700

Hegenbart, Fritz   Ger 1864-
O/Pn 19x13 Gustav Pisko 94 Hnd 10/92 1,000

Heicke, Joseph   Aus 1811-1861
* See 1993 Edition . . . .

Heiland, Maximillian   Ger 1855-
O/C 25x33 Afternoon on the Danube Fre 4/93 1,800

Heilbuth, Ferdinand   Ger 1826-1889
* See 1992 Edition . . . .

Heilmann, Mary   1940-
* See 1993 Edition . . . .

Heilmayer, Karl   Ger 1829-1908
O/C 21x37 Fishing in a Cove 1897 Chr 2/93 2,750

Heim, Harry   Am 20C
O/C 32x48 Five Portraits Hnd 9/92 500

Heimbach, Wolfgang   Ger 1615-1678
* See 1992 Edition . . . .

Hein, Einar   Dan 1875-
O/C 35x53 View of a Fjord Sby 1/93 1,150

Heine, Frederick W.   Am 1845-1921
O/C 49x22 French Peasant Girl Hnd 10/92 850

Heine, W.   Ger 19C
O/C 42x61 Travellers in an Exotic Landscape 1859 Chr 2/93 13,200

Heinefetter, Johann   Ger 1815-1902
O/C 21x32 Traveler Alpine Cottages 1886 Doy 5/93 3,080

Heinisch, Karl Adam   Ger 1847-1923
O/Pn 6x9 The Ferry 78 Chr 5/93 6,900

Heinrichs, Eduard   Ger 1884-
O/C 27x37 Forester's Farmhouse Dum 1/93 400

Heinsbergen, A. B.   20C
O/C 18x24 Snow in Carennac Chr 5/93 345

Heinzman, Louis   Am 1905-1982
* See 1993 Edition . . . .

Heise, Wilhelm
* See 1993 Edition . . . .

Heiss, Johann   Ger 1640-1704
O/C 30x34 Antiochus and Stratonica Sby 5/93 2,990

Heitland, Wilmont Emerton   Am 20C
* See 1990 Edition . . . .

Heitmuller, Louis   Am 1863-
* See 1992 Edition . . . .

Hekking, Joseph Antonio   Am a 1859-1885
O/C 17x26 House by the Falls Skn 11/92 3,575
O/C 10x14 Deer by a River Skn 9/92 3,300
O/C 24x36 Mountain Lake w/Fishermen Hnd 9/92 750

Hekking, Willem   Dut 1796-1862
* See 1992 Edition . . . .

Hekking, William M.   Am 1885-
W/Pa 8x8 Promenade 1924 Sby 9/92 55

Helck, Clarence Peter   Am 1897-
* See 1993 Edition . . . .

Helck, Peter   Am 1893-1988
G/Pa 9x10 Truck Parked, Train Approaching Ih 5/93 800

Held, Al   Am 1928-
A/C 72x109 Pan North VIII 86 Sby 5/93 51,750
A/C 18x14 Untitled 60 Sby 5/93 11,500
W&Pe/Pa 17x24 Hudson 15 Sby 5/93 6,900
W&H/Pa 18x24 Hudson 6 89 Chr 2/93 6,600

Held, John (Jr.)   Am 1889-1958
Pl&W/Pa 7x8 Three Illustrations Ih 11/92 1,500
Pl&W/Pa 9x14 Three Dancing Couples Ih 5/93 800

Heldner, Knute   Am 1884-1952
O/B 43x48 The Mining Accident Sby 9/92 2,750
O/C 18x22 Landscape by Lake Mor 11/92 750

Helfferich, Willem   Dut 20C
* See 1991 Edition . . . .

Heliker, John Edward   Am 1909-
* See 1993 Edition . . . .

Helion, Jean   Fr 1904-1987
* See 1993 Edition . . . .

Heller, Eugenie M.   Am 19C
* See 1991 Edition . . . .

Helleu, Paul Cesar   Fr 1859-1927
P/L 42x39 Camara Sby 2/93 51,750

Helsby, Alfredo   Chl 1862-1936
* See 1993 Edition . . . .

Heming, Arthur Henry Howard   Can 1870-1940
O/B 15x9 Wilderness Adventure '04 Sbt 11/92 1,100

Hemon, Jean-Marie   18C
O/Pn 7x11 River Landscapes with Figures Chr 5/93 8,625

Hemsley, William   Eng 1819-1893
* See 1993 Edition . . . .

Henderson, Charles Cooper   Eng 1803-1877
O/C 13x24 The Kennel Cart Chr 6/93 2,760

Henderson, Elyot   Am 1908-1975
O/C Size? Two Paintings: Nudes Yng 2/93 175
O/C Size? Two Paintings: Nudes Yng 2/93 175
O/C 20x32 Girl Lying Prone Yng 5/93 100
O/C 22x28 Model Reading Yng 5/93 90
O/C 28x22 Seated Nude Yng 5/93 80
O/C Size? Two Paintings: Nudes Yng 2/93 80

Henderson, James   Can 1871-1951
O/Pn 12x14 Edge of the Lake Hnd 10/92 1,200

Henderson, Joseph Morris   Sco 1863-1936
* See 1990 Edition . . . .

Henderson, William Penhallow   Am 1877-1943
P/Pa 7x5 Lady in Black and an Orange Cloak Chr 12/92 880

Hendriks, Gerardus   Dut 19C
* See 1991 Edition . . . .

Hendriks, Willem   Dut 1828-1891
O/C 24x20 Reflections at Laren Chr 10/92 2,860

Henner, Jean Jacques   Fr 1825-1905
O/Pn 11x8 Red Haired Beauty Chr 2/93 4,400
O/Pn 14x8 Standing Nude Chr 2/93 3,850
O/C 23x31 Reclining Nude Hnd 10/92 3,800
O/Pn 10x8 Red Haired Beauty Chr 5/93 3,680
O/Pn 14x10 Portrait Woman with Red Hair But 5/93 2,588
O/Pn 9x13 A Draped Nude Chr 5/93 2,300
O/Pn 11x9 Ideal Head Sby 10/92 2,200

Hennessey, Frank Charles   Am 1894-1941
P/Pa/B 16x20 Early Spring Across the Valley Sbn 9/92 660

Hennings, Ernest Martin   Am 1886-1956
O/C 30x36 Pueblo Village Sby 3/93 71,250

Henningsen, Frants Peter   Dan 1850-1908
* See 1991 Edition . . . .

Henri, Florence   20C
* See 1991 Edition . . . .

Henri, Robert   Am 1865-1929
O/C 24x20 Skipper Mick Chr 12/92 346,500
O/C 41x33 The Failure of Sylvester 1914 Chr 5/93 332,500
O/C 24x20 Girl With Big Hat Chr 5/93 134,500
O/C 28x20 Portrait of Katie McNamara Sby 5/93 118,000
O/C 24x21 Little Girl in Red Chr 12/92 99,000
O/C 32x26 Matta Moana Chr 12/92 99,000
O/C 32x26 Lillian But 12/92 55,000
O/C 24x20 Laughing Boy (Jobie) 1910 Sby 5/93 43,125
O/C 32x26 Lajartigo 1924 Sby 12/92 37,400
O/C 15x19 Ship in the Bay Sby 12/92 24,200
O/C 20x24 Gray Dunes Sby 5/93 8,050
O/Pn 4x6 Old House and Woman But 12/92 3,850
W/Pa 12x17 Seated Nude Chr 12/92 3,080
I/Pa 6x8 Artist, Dancing Before Degas Brd 8/93 2,640
Pl,Y&P/Pa 20x13 Portrait of Marjorie Organ Wes 3/93 . . . 2,640
Pl/Pa 5x6 Woman Dum 11/92 1,200
Pe/Pa 10x7 Two Drawings Wes 5/93 990
C/Pa 8x11 L'Amour Brd 8/93 880
I&S/Pa 6x9 Mountains and Sea Slo 4/93 600
Pl/Pa 9x11 Five Drawings Wes 10/92 495

Henrichsen, Carsten   Dan 1824-1897
O/C 20x28 View of Helsingor Castle 1858 But 5/93 1,725

Henrici, John H.   Am 1839-
O/C 30x20 Two Boys But 6/93 1,150
Henrion, Armand Francois Jos.   Fr 1875-
O/Pn 7x6 Laughing, Crying Clowns: Pair Sby 2/93 . . . 4,600
O/Pn 7x6 The Serious; Smoking Clown: Pair Sby 5/93 . . . 4,025
O/C 11x9 Clown But 5/93 2,300
Henriques, J.   Con 20C
O/M 28x17 Abstract Landscape '55 Wes 5/93 248
Henry, D. M.   Br 19C
 * See 1993 Edition . . . .
Henry, Edward Lamson   Am 1841-1919
O/C 17x25 Unexpected Visitors 1909 Chr 12/92 38,500
O/C 10x17 Leaving Home Sby 9/92 20,900
O/B 9x7 At Home with a Good Book '72 Sby 5/93 17,250
O/Pn 8x6 At the Well '80 Sby 12/92 16,500
O/C 7x11 On the James River, Virginia 1864 Sby 5/93 . . . 12,650
W/Pa 25x20 Sunday Morning 1886 Sby 5/93 12,650
O/Pa/B 7x6 In the Glow, Sunset 1872 Sby 9/92 12,100
W&G/Pa 7x5 Preparing for the Outing '76 Sby 12/92 . . . 11,000
O/B 6x5 China Cupboard 73 Chr 9/92 6,500
W/Pa 8x13 Haying Doy 5/93 3,190
Henry, George   Eng 1858-1943
O/C 16x24 Donkey, Terrier and Cat Slo 7/93 2,800
Henry, Harry Raymond   Am 1882-1974
O/C 16x20 Through the Trees But 10/92 3,300
O/C 30x40 Evening Glow But 10/92 1,650
Henry, J.
O/C 27x35 Cows in a Stream Wlf 9/92 450
Henry, Paul   Irs 1877-1958
 * See 1993 Edition . . . .
Henry, William H.   Eng 19C
W/Pa 18x23 Carribean Landscape 1958 Eld 8/93 55
Hensel, Stephen Hopkins   Am 1921-1979
O/C 22x36 Reflection '47 Sby 9/92 3,575
O/M 50x24 Clowns 50 Skn 11/92 1,430
O/M 24x10 Saltimbanque 47 Skn 11/92 1,045
O/C 24x20 A Deception 45 Skn 3/93 440
O/C 40x24 Nostalgia 1951 Skn 3/93 440
Henseler, Ernst   Ger 1852-
 * See 1993 Edition . . . .
Henshall, John Henry   Br 1856-
 * See 1990 Edition . . . .
Henshaw, Glenn Cooper   Am 1881-1946
 * See 1993 Edition . . . .
Hensley, Jackson   Am 20C
 * See 1993 Edition . . . .
Henstenburg, Anton   1695-1781
Bc/V 11x17 Stag Beetle and Other Insects Chr 1/93 15,400
Henstenburgh, Herman   1667-1726
 * See 1992 Edition . . . .
Henton, George Moore   Br 1861-1924
O/C 15x23 The School Yard, Eton 1894 Sby 1/93 1,495
Henwood, Thomas   Br a 1842-1859
 * See 1991 Edition . . . .
Hepner, Charles I.
O/C 20x30 Winter Landscape with Houses 1914 Ald 5/93 . . . 250
Hepworth, Barbara   Br 1903-1975
 * See 1992 Edition . . . .
Herald, W. F.   Sco 1868-1922
P/Pa 21x26 Young Woman Herding Cows Hnd 12/92 900
Herberer, Charles   Am 19C
 * See 1990 Edition . . . .
Herbert, John Rogers   Br 1810-1890
O/C 43x49 Praying Before Battle 1866 But 5/93 1,150
Herberte, Edward Benjamin   Br 1857-1893
O/C 12x18 The Hunt (Pair) 1881 But 5/93 5,462
Herbin, Auguste   Fr 1882-1960
 * See 1993 Edition . . . .
Herbo, Leon   Bel 1850-1907
O/Pn 26x21 Boy with a Statue Wes 10/92 1,320
Herbst, Frank C.   Am 20C
 * See 1992 Edition . . . .
Herdle, George Linton   Am 1868-1922
W/Pa 11x18 Dutch Canal Scene Hnd 10/92 400

Herdman-Smith, R.   Br 1879-
W/Pa 15x11 Narrow Street, Algiers Fre 4/93 400
Hergeshimer, Ella Sophonisba   Am 1873-1943
O/B 16x20 Industrial Buildings Slo 4/93 500
Herget, H.   Am 20C
O/Cb 10x16 Native American Scene Skn 11/92 605
Herkomer   Br 19C
 * See 1992 Edition . . . .
Herland, Emma   Fr 1856-1947
 * See 1990 Edition . . . .
Herman, Sali   Sws 1898-
 * See 1993 Edition . . . .
Hermann, Leo   Fr 1853-1927
O/Pn 10x8 The Cardinal But 5/93 3,450
Hermann, Ludwig   Ger 1812-1881
 * See 1991 Edition . . . .
Hermanns, Heinrich   Ger 1862-1942
 * See 1991 Edition . . . .
Hermans, Charles   Bel 1839-1924
 * See 1993 Edition . . . .
Hermansen, Olaf August   Dan 1849-1897
 * See 1992 Edition . . . .
Hernandez, Daniel   Per 1856-1932
O/B 9x12 South American Landscape 26 Chr 2/93 1,045
Hernandez, Manuel   1928-
 * See 1991 Edition . . . .
Hernandez, Sergio   Mex 1957-
 * See 1993 Edition . . . .
Hernandez-Chevalo, M.   Am 20C
O/C 16x20 Southwest Landscape w/Buildings 1920 Sel 9/92 . 240
Herold, Georg   20C
A&MM/C 60x48 Black Beluga Sby 11/92 8,250
A/C 81x98 Kathedrale II Sby 2/93 5,750
Herpfer, Carl   Ger 1836-1897
 * See 1993 Edition . . . .
Herpin, Leon Pierre   Fr 1841-1880
 * See 1990 Edition . . . .
Herran, Saturnino   Mex 1887-1918
H/Pa/B 24x18 Estudio, Figuras Y Manos Sby 5/93 10,350
Herrera, Francisc (the Younger)   Spa 1622-1685
 * See 1990 Edition . . . .
Herrick, Arthur R.   Am 1897-1970
O/C 25x30 Autumn Comes to Rockport 1942 Skn 9/92 . . . 468
Herrick, Mary P.   Am 1856-1935
O/C 20x26 House in Atmospheric Landscape Mor 6/93 . . . 220
Herriman, George   Am 1880-1944
Pl&W/Pa 14x11 Krazy Kat Characters Ih 5/93 13,000
Pl/Pa 4x20 Daily Comic "Krazy Kat" Ih 11/92 2,100
Herring, Benjamin (Jr.)   Br 1830-1871
O/C 9x14 Over the Brook; Over the Fence (2) Chr 2/93 . . . 2,420
Herring, John Frederick (Jr.)   Br 1815-1907
O/C 14x20 Horses Chickens Pigs: Pair Sby 6/93 28,750
O/C 16x24 The Farmyard Sby 6/93 21,850
O/C 12x18 Horses and Farmyard Animals: Pair Sby 6/93 . 13,800
O/C 22x33 Noonday Rest Sby 6/93 9,200
O/Pn 10x12 Mare and Foal in Landscape 1853 Chr 10/92 . . 7,700
O/C 15x24 Horses and Cattle in Barnyard Sby 6/93 7,475
O/B 6 dia Fox Hunting: Three Sby 6/93 6,900
O/C 15x21 A Sussex Farmyard Chr 10/92 4,180
O/C 16x16 Cows Watering at Pond But 5/93 3,162
O/C 16x16 Horses Watering in Stable But 5/93 2,588
O/B 7x8 Over the Brook Chr 10/92 1,870
Herring, John Frederick (Sr.)   Br 1795-1865
O/C 35x44 The Baron's Charger Chr 5/93 134,500
O/C 34x44 Conversation in the Stable Sby 6/93 34,500
O/C 28x36 Inheritress 1846 Sby 6/93 27,600
O/C 22x30 Dark Hunter in River Landscape 1832 Sby 6/93 . 20,700
O/Pn 13 dia Best Friends 1848 Sby 6/93 12,075
O/Pn 14x18 The Proud Mother 1852 Sby 6/93 12,075
O/C 16x16 Contentment 1848 Chr 10/92 8,800

Herring, John Jr. & Shayer, W.   Br 1815-1907
O/Pn 5x7 Coaching Scenes: Five 1880 Sby 6/93 14,950
Herrmann, Hans   Ger 1858-1942
* See 1993 Edition . . . .
Herrmann, Leo   Fr 1853-
O/C 10x7 Cardinal's Correspondence Skn 11/92 770
Herter, Albert   Am 1871-1950
O/C 22x20 Lady in a Kimono '94 Sby 5/93 14,950
W/Pa 15x9 Two Women on Stairs Sby 3/93 11,500
O/C 24x20 Beatrice Chr 9/92 1,650
Herterich, L. V.
O/B 28x39 Hunters on Horseback Dum 4/93 300
Herve, Jules Rene   Fr 1887-1981
O/C 26x32 Le Marche Aux Fleurs Hnd 3/93 10,000
O/C 26x32 Les bouquinistes Chr 11/92 6,600
O/C 26x32 Pres du lac Chr 11/92 5,500
O/C 18x22 Place de la Concorde Sby 2/93 4,600
O/C 15x18 La Lecon de Ballet Hnd 3/93 4,400
O/C 18x22 Place de la Concorde Wes 10/92 3,850
O/C 13x16 Children at Play Sby 10/92 3,080
O/C 13x16 Enfants a la Fenetre Chr 11/92 3,080
O/C 24x29 Dans la Foret Chr 5/93 2,300
O/C 18x22 Paris Sby 2/93 2,070
O/C 13x16 Children With Toy Boats Hnd 10/92 1,900
O/C 13x16 Fountain in Paris Sby 2/93 1,840
O/C 8x10 The Ballet Studio Wlf 12/92 750
Herzog, Hermann   Am 1832-1932
O/C 18x24 Summer Afternoon on the Pond Chr 5/93 46,000
O/C 24x22 Artist in a Wooded Landscape Chr 5/93 29,900
O/C 24x28 Relaxation Chr 12/92 24,200
O/B 17x14 Bears by a Cataract 1874 Sby 3/93 24,150
O/C 17x13 Sunlight Reflections Chr 3/93 14,950
O/C 14x17 Fly Fishing Chr 3/93 13,800
O/Pn 11x15 Fishing by the Lumber Mill 1872 Chr 9/92 . . . 10,450
O/C 15x18 Florida Live Oaks with Deer Sby 12/92 9,900
O/C 22x30 Coast Near Portland, Maine But 6/93 6,325
O/C 16x22 Fishing Boats But 5/93 5,462
O/C 16x22 Plowing Sby 3/93 4,830
O/C 20x28 Canal Leading to Alpine Lake Chr 5/93 4,600
O/C 20x16 Norwegian Fjord Mor 6/93 2,750
O/C 18x14 Beached Fishing Boats Sby 9/92 1,760
Heseltine, Jane   Am 20C
O/C 56x40 Two Figures on Horseback But 10/92 4,400
Hess, Marcel   Bel 1878-
* See 1993 Edition . . . .
Hesse, Eva   Am 1936-1970
WYPe&L/Pa 23x28 Untitled 1963 Chr 2/93 16,500
O/C 44x32 Untitled 1957 Sby 10/92 14,300
Hesselius, John   Am 1725-1778
* See 1990 Edition . . . .
Hessemer   Am 20C
A/C 24x36 Green Boat 70 Hnd 6/93 375
Hetzel, George   Am 1826-1906
* See 1992 Edition . . . .
Heubler, Douglas   20C
* See 1993 Edition . . . .
Heuer, R.   Am 19C
O/B 9x12 Moonlit Seascape Hnd 9/92 275
Heuliant, Felix Armand   Fr 1834-
* See 1990 Edition . . . .
Heward, Efa Prudence   Can 1896-1947
O/Pn 14x12 Boy at Fence Sbt 5/93 2,420
O/Pn 12x14 Near Cowansville 1944 Sbt 5/93 1,760
O/Pn 12x14 The Settler's Cabin 1931 Sbt 5/93 1,672
O/Pn 14x12 Village Church Sbt 5/93 1,144
Hewins, Amasa   Am 19C
* See 1992 Edition . . . .
Hewins, Philip   Am 1806-1850
* See 1993 Edition . . . .
Hewton, Randolph Stanley   Can 1888-1960
O/C 28x23 Portrait Audrey Buller, 1921 Sbt 11/92 4,840
O/C 20x24 St. Lawrence South Shore 1928 Sbt 11/92 2,640
O/C 20x24 Autumn, Eastern Townships Sbt 5/93 1,980

Hey, Paul   Ger 1867-1952
* See 1993 Edition . . . .
Heyd, Conrad   Am 1837-1912
O/C 30x25 Portrait Lou 12/92 300
Heyden, E.   Ger 1907-
O/C 28x24 Mounted Hunters Dum 6/93 400
Heydendahl, Friederich Joseph   Ger 1844-1906
* See 1993 Edition . . . .
Heyer, Arthur   Ger 1872-1931
O/C 20x28 Two Angora Cats Watching a Bee Chr 2/93 . . . 2,200
Heyl, Marinus   Dut 1836-1931
* See 1992 Edition . . . .
Heyligers, Gustaaf A. F.   Dut 1828-1897
* See 1992 Edition . . . .
Heyligers, Hendrik   Dut 1877-1915
* See 1993 Edition . . . .
Heyn, August   Ger 1837-
* See 1990 Edition . . . .
Heywood, Tom   Br a 1882-1913
* See 1992 Edition . . . .
Hibbard, Aldro Thompson   Am 1886-1972
O/C 30x34 Southern Vermont '24 Sby 3/93 10,925
O/Cb 18x20 Chocorua Mountain, NH Skn 5/93 4,400
O/C 28x37 Sugaring Shack Lou 6/93 3,750
O/Cb 17x20 Mountain Snow Scene Skn 5/93 2,970
O/Cb 17x21 Vermont Mountains/Winter Skn 9/92 2,970
O/Cb 19x23 Mt. Mansfield Skn 11/92 2,860
O/C 17x21 A Winter Brook Chr 5/93 2,760
O/Cb 17x20 Stream in Winter Skn 11/92 2,310
O/C 22x32 Rushing Winter Stream Wes 12/92 1,980
O/C 24x30 Winter Up Country Eld 8/93 1,980
O/B 18x26 Monhegan Island Yng 5/93 1,700
O/Cb 18x24 Afternoon Monterey Skn 3/93 935
O/C 18x16 Snow Drifts Eld 8/93 770
O/B 10x14 Venice Fishing Village Eld 8/93 440
Hibel, Edna   Am 1917-
O/B 30x40 Girl in a Field with a Lamb Hnz 5/93 3,500
O/Pn 14x11 Young Girl Dum 8/93 1,400
T&H/Wd 18x15 Elderly Couple at Market Wlf 5/93 400
Hicks, David   Am 20C
O/C 46x46 Furrowed Fields Slo 4/93 950
Hicks, Edward   Am 1780-1849
* See 1992 Edition . . . .
Hicks, George Elgar   Br 1824-1914
* See 1991 Edition . . . .
Hicks, Thomas   Am 1823-1890
O/C 91x76 Portrait James Van Dyke Dum 5/93 4,250
O/C 23x29 After 20 Years Sby 3/93 2,990
Hiddemann, J.   Ger 19C
O/C 28x21 Young Girl Fishing with Dog Chr 2/93 19,250
Hider, Frank   Br 19C
O/C 18x14 Coastal Scene Hnd 10/92 450
Hidley, Joseph   Am 1830-1872
* See 1992 Edition . . . .
Hieneman, T. V.   Dut 20C
O/C 21x26 Gorkum, Holland Chr 10/92 2,860
Hierle, Louis   Fr 19C
* See 1993 Edition . . . .
Higgins, Eugene   Am 1874-1958
O/B 8x6 Baby, Holding Hands, Asleep Chr 5/93 1,495
O/C 15x19 On the Road to North Plains Mys 3/93 935
O/C 16x20 The Poor Fisherman Mys 3/93 880
O/C 12x16 Street Scene at Night Chr 5/93 633
O/C 12x16 Artist's Farmhouse Lou 3/93 600
O/B 6x10 Wagon Train Mys 12/92 412
O/Pa 21x16 Figures in State of Exhaustion Eld 8/93 385
Pe&C/Pa 6x6 Girl; Four Figures: Two Lou 12/92 68
C/Pa 14x11 Two Peasants in a Field Eld 8/93 55
Higgins, George Frank   Am a 1855-1885
O/C Size? Forest Interior Mys 3/93 220
Higgins, Victor   Am 1884-1949
W/Pa 16x23 Cottonwood Trees in Winter Chr 3/93 18,400
W/Pa 16x23 Hondo Road, Taos Chr 3/93 18,400
W/Pa 15x21 Adobe and Windmill Sby 12/92 15,400

Highmore, Joseph Br 1692-1780
 * See 1992 Edition . . . .
Hilaer, R. Con 19C
 * See 1992 Edition . . . .
Hilaire, Camille Fr 1916-1988
 O/C 29x36 Concours Hippique 1963 Wlf 9/92 13,500
Hilaire, Jean-Baptiste 1753-1822
 K&S/Pa 10x15 Three Camels at Rest Chr 1/93 7,700
Hildebrand, Ernst Ger 1833-1894
 * See 1993 Edition . . . .
Hildebrandt, Eduard Ger 1818-1969
 * See 1991 Edition . . . .
Hildebrandt, Howard Logan Am 1872-1958
 O/Cb 8x10 Two Beach Scenes Skn 3/93 1,210
 O/C 30x24 Floral Still Life Yng 5/93 1,100
Hilder Am 20C
 O/B 20x15 Stormy Seascape 1926 Wlf 4/93 350
Hiler, Hilaire Am 1898-1966
 W/Pa 15x17 Abstract Lou 3/93 500
 W/Pa 18x15 Abstract Lou 3/93 500
 W&G/Pa 7x10 Dancing Sailor Wlf 3/93 200
Hilgers, Carl Ger 1818-1890
 O/C 21x29 Eine Hollandische Sby 1/93 8,338
Hill, Arthur T. Am 1868-1929
 O/Pn 9x14 Figure and Cattle Skn 9/92 605
Hill, Carl G. 1884-1973
 O/C 18x24 Haying 1942 Doy 11/92 1,650
Hill, Edward Rufus Am 1852-1908
 O/C 48x16 Giant Redwoods But 3/93 1,650
 O/C 14x23 Washing in the River But 3/93 1,650
Hill, Howard Am a 1860-1870
 O/C 26x38 Grouse Family Skn 9/92 2,750
Hill, J. H.
 W/Pa 21x17 Janetta Falls 18?? Ald 3/93 125
Hill, James John Br 1811-1882
 O/C 25x36 Young Boy on Horseback 71 Chr 10/92 5,500
 O/C 20x24 The Lazy Shepherd 1878 Sby 1/93 3,220
 O/C 23x30 Mare and Colt in Farmyard 1869 Lou 12/92 . . . 1,600
Hill, John Henry Am 1839-1922
 W&H/Pa 10x14 The Pear Tree 1895 Skn 5/93 2,200
Hill, John William Am 1812-1879
 W/Pa 9x14 River Landscape '61 Sby 12/92 16,500
 W/Pa 16x14 Landscape Figure in Woodlands 1869 Sby 9/92 990
Hill, Polly (Clarence)
 G/Pa 14x15 Man with Tophat Ih 11/92 325
Hill, Roswell S. Am 1861-1907
 * See 1993 Edition . . . .
Hill, Thomas Am 1829-1908
 O/C/B 16x24 Yosemite Valley But 3/93 18,700
 O/C 22x15 Yosemite Landscape But 3/93 17,600
 O/C 24x20 Yosemite Valley fr Inspiration Pt 1901 But 10/92 15,400
 O/C 46x30 Fremont Grove But 3/93 14,300
 O/C 22x15 Woods with Red Fox 1868 But 10/92 11,000
 O/B 14x21 Mountain Scene But 3/93 10,450
 O/Pn 8x24 Hunter at Sunset But 10/92 7,700
 O/C 14x21 Mount Shasta from Castle Lake But 10/92 7,700
 O/Pa/B 13x21 Cathedral Spires, Yosemite But 10/92 4,125
Hilliard, William Henry Am 1836-1905
 O/C 12x16 Pine Pond, Kennebunk, Maine 1883 Brd 8/93 . . 2,420
 O/C 14x19 Landscape Mys 3/93 1,870
 O/C 34x24 Woman by a Mill Yng 2/93 400
Hillingford, Robert Alexander Br 1825-1904
 * See 1993 Edition . . . .
Hills, Anna Althea Am 1882-1930
 O/C 20x30 Desert Landscape 1914 Mor 6/93 4,675
 O/B 7x10 Live Oaks & Sycamores 1918 Mor 2/93 2,750
 O/Cb 14x21 Old Cypress Near Carmel 1922 But 10/92 2,750
 O/Cb 10x14 When the Tide is Out But 3/93 1,980
Hills, Laura Coombs Am 1859-1952
 P/Pb 13x11 Snow Berries Skn 9/92 8,250
 P/Pa 14x11 Petunias in a Blue Vase Wes 5/93 1,045
Hillsmith, Fannie Am 1911-
 * See 1991 Edition . . . .

Hillyer, William Am 19C
 O/C 30x25 Portrait Martha and Ann Warfield 1834 Fre 4/93 . 4,500
Hilton, John W. Am 1904-1983
 * See 1992 Edition . . . .
Hilverdink, Edouard Alexander Dut 1846-1891
 O/B 9x12 Amsterdam Canal Scene Yng 2/93 1,400
 O/C 20x17 Village Street in Winter 1866 Chr 10/92 1,320
Hinchley, Edith Mason Eng 1870-
 W/Pa 11x7 Springtime, Wallasey 1906 Wes 10/92 440
Hinckley, Thomas Hewes Am 1813-1896
 O/C/C 29x36 Boy/Animals in Landscape 1843 But 12/92 . . 3,850
 O/C 25x30 Portrait of a Terrier 1870 Sby 6/93 2,760
Hind, William George R. Can 1833-1888
 O/Pa 10x13 Self-Portrait in Landscape Sbt 5/93 15,840
Hine, Charles Am 1821-1871
 * See 1991 Edition . . . .
Hines, Theodore Eng 19C
 O/C 20x30 Windsor Wes 10/92 1,540
Hinkle, Clarence K. Am 1880-1960
 O/C 20x24 Still Life Persimmons But 6/93 5,750
 O/C 36x30 Pomagranites Mor 6/93 4,675
 O/C 30x36 Artist's Studio, Santa Barbara But 10/92 3,300
 O/Cb 11x14 Pont Marie, Paris Mor 6/93 1,100
 W/Pa 11x15 Day at the Pier Mor 6/93 715
 W/Pa 15x19 Landscape Mor 11/92 325
 S/Pa 13x15 Santa Barbara Channel 1948 Mor 11/92 250
Hinman, Charles Am 1932-
 * See 1993 Edition . . . .
Hintermeister, Henry (Hy) Am 1897-1972
 O/C 26x24 Dog's Best Friend Chr 3/93 3,680
 O/C 22x30 Boy Fishing from Dock Ih 5/93 2,000
Hinterreiter, Hans Sws 1902-
 * See 1993 Edition . . . .
Hinton, Walter Haskell
 O/Cb 14x17 Moose Wading Ih 5/93 1,600
Hinz, Johann Georg 1630-1688
 O/C 30x25 Wine, Wineglass, Sliced Orange 1656 Chr 1/93 14,300
Hippolyte-Lucas, Marie Felix Fr 1854-1925
 * See 1992 Edition . . . .
Hiraga, Kamesuke Jap 1890-1971
 O/C 21x25 Plomar'ch 1933 But 10/92 2,475
Hiremy-Hirschl, Adolph Aus 1860-1933
 * See 1991 Edition . . . .
Hirsch, Alphonse Fr 1843-1884
 * See 1990 Edition . . . .
Hirsch, Joseph Am 1910-1981
 O/C 24x29 Nude and Picture Book Chr 3/93 17,250
 O/C 30x24 Self-Portrait Sby 3/93 7,475
 O/C 24x12 The Nickel Chr 9/92 3,520
 C&l/B 30x20 Studio Sby 9/92 1,100
 Bp/Pa 12x16 The Dispute Sby 9/92 880
 W/Pa 19x28 Bombing Raid Wlf 4/93 420
 Pe/Pa 9x11 Construction Sites Wlf 9/92 170
 Pe/Pa 9x11 Jungle Scenes Wlf 9/92 150
Hirsch, Stefan Am 1899-
 * See 1991 Edition . . . .
Hirschfeld, Al Am 1903-
 W/Pa 17x13 The Jazz Player Chr 5/93 1,380
Hirsh, Alice Am 1888-1935
 O/C/B 8x10 Manhattan Skyline; Wash. Sq.: Pair But 12/92 . 1,870
Hirshberg, Carl Am 1854-1923
 O/C 44x35 The Veteran 1893 Sby 9/92 6,600
Hirst, Claude Raguet Am 1855-1942
 W/B 8x10 A Book of Poems Chr 9/92 13,750
 O/C 9x14 Still Life Fruit Sby 9/92 5,500
Hirt, Heinrich Ger 1727-1796
 * See 1991 Edition . . . .
His, Rene Charles Edmond Fr 1877-
 O/C 20x30 A Meandering River Chr 10/92 1,650
Hispanus, Johannes Spa 16C
 * See 1991 Edition . . . .
Hitchcock, David Howard Am 1861-1943
 * See 1991 Edition . . . .

Hitchcock, George   Am 1850-1913
O/C 27x46 The Dunes, Holland 1892 Sby 5/93 28,750
O/C 24x25 Woman in Field of Flowers 89 Chr 12/92 4,620
W&Pe/Pa 21x14 Sailing in Choppy Waters 1880 Sby 3/93 . 1,035
Hitchcock, Lucius Wolcott   Am 1868-1942
* See 1993 Edition . . . .
Hittell, Charles Joseph   Am 1861-1938
O/C 12x19 Bringing Home a Buck 1893 But 10/92 4,400
O/C 9x15 Piute Wickiups 1903 But 3/93 2,090
O/C/B 11x15 Grand Canyon of the Colorado But 10/92 1,540
Hoare, William   1706-1792
O/C 29x23 Portrait Richard, Earl of Cavan Sby 5/93 4,313
Hobart, Clark   Am 1880-1948
O/C 21x30 Monterey Bay But 10/92 11,000
O/C/B 50x40 Portrait Miss Helene Maxwell 1917 But 3/93 . 6,050
Hobbs, George Thompson   Am 1846-1929
O/C 16x20 Landscape with Old House Fre 4/93 225
Hobby, Carl F.   Am 1886-1964
O/C 11x13 The Campsite Mor 11/92 350
Hoch, Hannah   Ger 1889-1979
* See 1993 Edition . . . .
Hock, Daniel   Aus 1858-1934
O/C 21x41 Overdoor/Cherub and Flowers 1904 But 11/92 . 4,400
Hocker, Trew   Am 1913-
O/M 30x40 Rock Quarry Scene FHB 6/93 140
Hockney, David   Am 1937-
A/C 84x120 Henry Geldzahler &Christopher Scott Sby 11/92 . 1.1M
MM 72x86 Piscine on Sprayed Blue Paper 78 Sby 5/93 . 321,500
MM 32x50 Gregory in the Pool 78 Chr 11/92 33,000
Pe/Pa 26x20 Gregory 1975 Sby 5/93 31,050
L/B 40x62 Walking in the Zen Garden 1983 Chr 11/92 . . . 14,300
I/Pa 7x5 Untitled: Pair of Drawings 87 Sby 2/93 11,500
P&I/Pa 17x14 Air Mail '76 Sby 5/93 10,925
I/Pa 17x14 George Harris III 1966 Sby 5/93 7,475
Ph&L 26x19 The Skater, New York 1982 Hnd 5/93 5,000
L/B 47x57 The Graffitti Palace 1982 Chr 10/92 4,400
Hode, Pierre   Fr 1889-1942
* See 1992 Edition . . . .
Hodebert, Leon Auguste   Fr 1852-1914
O/C 38x46 The Bathers 1880 Chr 10/92 13,200
Hodel, Ernst   Sws 1881-1955
* See 1993 Edition . . . .
Hodgdon, Sylvester Phelps   Am 1830-1906
* See 1991 Edition . . . .
Hodges, Merrett   Br 1891-1961
O/C 36x32 Tragedy 1932 Hnd 10/92 700
Hodgkin, Howard   Am 1932-
* See 1993 Edition . . . .
Hodgson, Sylvester Phelps   Am 1830-1906
O/C 18x12 Rocky Stream with Fisherman 77 Hnd 5/93 350
Hodgson, Thomas Sherlock   Can 1924-
* See 1991 Edition . . . .
Hodicke, K. H.   20C
* See 1991 Edition . . . .
Hodson, Samuel John   Br 1836-1908
W&G/Pa 13x18 Gathering Wildflowers 1873 Chr 2/93 1,320
Hoeber, Arthur   Am 1854-1915
O/C 25x40 Landscape at Twilight Chr 12/92 4,400
O/C 22x32 Beach at Concarneau Chr 3/93 3,680
O/C/B 22x32 Farm Scene with Pond Hnd 12/92 2,000
O/C 16x22 Summer Landscape/Conn. Yng 2/93 550
Hoeffler, Adolf   Ger 1825-1898
* See 1990 Edition . . . .
Hoeniger, Paul   Ger 1865-1924
* See 1991 Edition . . . .
Hoet, Gerard   Dut 1648-1733
* See 1993 Edition . . . .
Hofbauer, Ferdinand   Aus 1801-1864
* See 1991 Edition . . . .
Hofel, Johann Nepomuk   Ger 1786-1864
* See 1990 Edition . . . .
Hofer, Carl   Ger 1878-1955
G&W/Pa 24x19 Paar mit gelber Fahne Chr 11/92 7,700

Hoff, Carl Heinrich   Ger 1838-1890
O/C 30x36 The Card Game Chr 5/93 14,950
Hoffbauer, Charles   Am 1875-1957
* See 1993 Edition . . . .
Hoffler, Othmar   Ger 20C
O/B 12x10 Seated Ballerina Hnd 12/92 550
Hoffman, Frank B.   Am 1888-1958
O/C 30x24 Western Couple in Field Ih 5/93 1,300
Hoffman, Harry Leslie   Am 1871-1964
* See 1993 Edition . . . .
Hoffman, Helen   Am 20C
O/C 26x30 Over the Fence Wlf 4/93 350
Hoffman, John   Am 20C
O/C 34x61 Wagon Train Chr 9/92 9,900
Hoffmann, Clara   Am 20C
O/C 14x22 Arranging Flowers 1895 Chr 5/93 8,050
Hoffmann, Gary David   Am 1947-
O/C 12x9 Woman in Long White Dress Yng 2/93 650
Hoffmeister, Adolf   1902-1973
PI&L/Pa 20x14 Three Collages Chr 5/93 2,300
Hofman, Hans O.   Am 1893-
* See 1993 Edition . . . .
Hofmann, Ansen
O/C 28x39 The Chess Game FHB 3/93 2,500
Hofmann, Earl Francis   Am 20C
O/C 16x20 Manhattan & Brooklyn Bridge 1955 Sby 9/92 770
Hofmann, Hans   Am 1880-1966
O/C 84x52 Exabundantia 64 Chr 11/92 363,000
O/C 48x36 Flowers of the Mind 65 Chr 11/92 220,000
O/Pn 25x20 Bouquet 51 Chr 11/92 94,600
O/Pn 24x30 Durbilant Equilibrium 1954 Chr 11/92 82,500
W/Pa 11x9 Untitled Sby 5/93 74,000
O/Pw 25x31 Sunrise Over the Dunes 40 Sby 5/93 57,500
G/Pa 18x24 Untitled 43 Sby 5/93 36,800
Y&Fp/Pa 14x17 Untitled 42 Chr 11/92 14,300
O/M 17x14 Sacrifice Sby 5/93 13,800
I&Y/Pa 24x19 Untitled Sby 5/93 13,800
I&Y/Pa 24x19 Untitled Sby 5/93 12,650
I&Y/Pa 24x19 Untitled Sby 5/93 12,075
Y,Br&I/Pa 11x14 Untitled Chr 11/92 7,150
I/Pa 14x11 Untitled 1952 Sel 12/92 4,500
I/Pa 11x9 Untitled Sby 10/92 3,850
I/Pa 11x9 Untitled 33 Sby 10/92 3,300
I/Pa 11x9 Untitled: A Pair of Drawings 33 Sby 10/92 3,080
C/Pa 32x26 Untitled Chr 11/92 2,200
Hoger, Rudolf A.   Aus 1876-1928
O/C 32x51 The Picnic Sby 1/93 3,450
Hoguet, Charles   Fr 1821-1870
O/C 11x14 Preparing the Meal by the Hearth 1864 Chr 10/92 2,640
Hohenberg, Josef Wagner   Ger 1870-
O/C 30x40 Company of Cavaliers Hnd 3/93 5,600
Hohnberg, Josef Wagner   Con 1811-
* See 1992 Edition . . . .
Hohnstedt, Peter Lanz   Am 1872-1957
O/C 24x31 Summer Landscape Mor 2/93 450
Hoin, Claude Jean Baptiste   Fr 1750-1817
* See 1990 Edition . . . .
Hoit, Albert Gallatin   Am 1809-1856
* See 1990 Edition . . . .
Hokinson, Helen   Am 1893-1949
PI&S/Pa 10x11 Women Talking in Theatre Ih 5/93 275
Holbech, Niels Peter   Dan 1804-1889
* See 1990 Edition . . . .
Holberton, W.   Am 19C
O/C 12x20 Trout on a River Bank 1897 Eld 4/93 138
O/C 14x20 Brown Trout 1897 Eld 4/93 110
Holbrook, Hollis   Am 1909-
T/M 16x20 Train Station Sby 9/92 3,575
O/B 16x18 Church in a Winter Landscape Fre 10/92 100
Holcomb, Dal
G/Pa 15x15 Sailor and WAVE Ih 5/93 650
Holden, Raymond J.   Am 1901-
W&G/Pa 12x9 Winter Day Yng 5/93 200
Holding, Henry James   Eng 1833-1872
O/C 34x50 Fisherfolk by a Stormy Shore 1863 Chr 10/92 . 2,860

Holdredge, Ransome G.   Am 1836-1899
O/C 22x36 Indian Encampment But 10/92 3,850
O/C/C 30x50 Mountain Indian Encampment Mor 2/93 3,250
O/C 17x13 The Wooded Road But 6/93 2,875
O/C 20x30 Indian Encampment But 6/93 2,300
O/C 21x44 Figures on the Bank But 6/93 1,495
Holdstein, H. V.   Am 20C
W/Ab 15x11 Industrial Flats '35 Wtf 4/93 175
Holdstock, Alfred Worsley   Can 1820-1901
P/Pa 14x21 Grand Falls, Nameanken River Sbt 5/93 704
Holfeld, Hippolyte Dominique   Fr 1804-1872
* See 1993 Edition ....
Holgate, Edwin Headley   Can 1892-1977
O/C 21x26 Melting Snow - Morin Heights Sbt 11/92 14,960
Holiday, Gilbert   Br 1879-1937
* See 1991 Edition ....
Holings, Clark   Am 20C
* See 1990 Edition ....
Holl, Frank   Br 1845-1888
* See 1991 Edition ....
Holland, Francis Raymond   Am 20C
* See 1990 Edition ....
Holland, J.
W/Pa 14x28 Millpond Landscape with Fishermen Eld 8/93 ... 55
Holland, James   Br 1799-1870
* See 1992 Edition ....
Holland, John   Br 19C
* See 1992 Edition ....
Holland, Tom   Am 1936-
MM/Al 18x32 Mola 87 Chr 5/93 2,300
MM/Pa 35x46 62nd St. Seris, #48 78 But 4/93 920
Holliday, Frank   20C
* See 1993 Edition ....
Holloway, Edward Stratton   Am 1939-
* See 1992 Edition ....
Hollyer, Maud   Br a 1900-1910
W/Pa 19x29 English Country Manor Hnd 3/93 1,300
Holman, Bill   Am 1903-
P/Pa 11x24 Sunday Comic "Smokey Stover" Ih 5/93 375
Holme, Lucy D.   Am 20C
O/C/B 21x26 Flowers Fre 4/93 300
Holmes, A. C.   Br 20C
* See 1993 Edition ....
Holmes, Basil   Br 20C
O/C 21x27 Landscape Woman and Dog Hnd 9/92 1,000
Holmes, Dwight C.   Am 1900-
* See 1992 Edition ....
Holmes, George Augustus   Br -1911
O/C 26x22 Live and Let Live Chr 5/93 10,350
Holmes, Ralph William   Am 1876-1963
O/Cb 16x20 Houses in Hazy Landscape Mor 6/93 1,100
O/Ab 18x23 Landscape Mor 2/93 850
O/C 24x28 Green Hills Mor 6/93 770
O/M 18x20 Landscape Mor 6/93 715
Holmes, S. R.   Am 19C
C/Pa 17x26 Winter Sunday in New England Eld 4/93 220
Holmes, William Henry   Am 1846-1933
W/Pa 15x22 Girl Sitting on Hillside Chr 12/92 7,700
W,G&Pe/B 10x15 Playing on the Hillside Chr 5/93 7,475
W/Pa 16x30 Beach Stroll Brd 8/93 4,400
W/Pa 16x19 Landscape with Figures and Cows Slo 5/93 ... 950
W/Pa 3x4 Christmas, 1924 1924 Brd 8/93 468
W/Pa 10x15 Out in Maryland 1917 Slo 5/93 350
W/Pa 10x15 Jamaican Women Along Path Slo 4/93 250
Holmstedt, J.   Scn 20C
O/C 32x48 Fishing Village Near a Fjord But 11/92 2,475
Holsoe, Carl Vilhelm   Dan 1863-1935
O/C 22x18 Girl Standing on Balcony But 5/93 23,000
Holsoe, Eilsa   Dan 19C
* See 1993 Edition ....
Holson, B.   Am 20C
O/C 18x24 The Clipper "Highflyer" at Sea Hnd 5/93 500

Holst, Laurits   Dan 1848-1934
* See 1992 Edition ....
Holt, Geoffrey   Am 1882-1977
* See 1993 Edition ....
Holty, Carl Robert   Am 1900-1973
W&H/Pa 10x8 Three Drawings 45 Sby 3/93 5,463
G,I&H/Pa 11x14 817 Variations A-B (2) Sby 3/93 4,025
O/C/M 36x24 Abstract Blue, Green, Red 1948 Chr 12/92 .. 2,200
O/C 47x36 Flamenco 1948 Sby 3/93 2,185
O/C 24x30 Duneland 1947 Sby 9/92 1,650
O/M 30x40 Dunes 40 Sby 3/93 1,380
Holyoake, Rowland   Eng a 1880-1911
O/Pn 13x10 The Date Dum 8/93 2,000
Holyoke, William   Br 1834-1894
O/Pb 25x18 Rustic Conversation Dum 9/92 7,000
Holzer, Jenny   Am 1950-
E/Me 21x23 Untitled Chr 2/93 3,850
Al 3x10 Untitled Chr 2/93 1,430
Al 8x10 Untitled (Survival Series) Chr 5/93 1,380
Holzer, Joseph   Aus 1824-1876
* See 1990 Edition ....
Holzhuber, Franz   Am a 1850-
* See 1993 Edition ....
Homa, R.   It 19C
O/C 31x18 Woman Painting an Urn Wtf 9/92 1,300
Homer, Winslow   Am 1836-1910
O/C 24x39 The Unruly Calf 1875 Sby 12/92 .... 1.21M
O/C 14x22 Uncle Ned at Home 1875 Chr 5/93 992,500
O/C 16x23 Looking Out to Sea 1872 Sby 5/93 706,500
O/C 9x14 The Noon Recess 1873 Chr 5/93 607,500
W/Pa 14x21 Deep Sea Fishing 1894 Sby 5/93 255,500
W,Pe&Pl/Pa 13x19 Daydreaming 1880 Chr 5/93 200,500
C&G/Pa 17x8 Girl on a Swing '79 Sby 5/93 76,750
Pe/Pa 8x11 The Bicycle Messenger Sby 9/92 6,050
Pe/Pa 5x7 Gulf Stream Sailing Vessel Sby 9/92 1,320
Hondius, Gerrit   Am 1891-1970
O/C 30x40 Fruit Stalls, New York City Skn 9/92 550
Honegger, Gottfried   20C
* See 1993 Edition ....
Honore, Paul   Am 1885-1956
O/M 20x48 Astronomer with Telescope, Globe '33 Dum 4/93 . 300
Hood, George W.   Am 1869-1949
O/Pa 18x12 Knight and Troubador Walking 1909 Ih 5/93 .. 2,600
Hooks, Mitchell   Am 1923-
W/Pa 24x12 Woman Before Mirror Ih 5/93 300
Hooper, John Horace   Br a 1877-1899
O/C 12x20 Winter Landscape with Figures Sby 1/93 1,150
Hooper, Parker Morse   Am 19C
W/Pa 10x14 Field of Wild Carrots Duxbury, MA 1896 Yng 2/93 125
Hoopes, Florence & Margaret   Am 20C
W/Pa 6x8 Sewing Lesson, The Gift (2) Fre 10/92 300
W/Pa 6x8 Sunday Service, Camp Fire (2) Fre 10/92 300
Hope, James   Am 1818-1892
O/C 20x36 7th Maine Regiment at Antietam Brd 8/93 8,250
Hope, Thomas H.   Am -1926
* See 1991 Edition ....
Hopkin, Robert   Am 1832-1909
O/C 28x40 Isle of Arran 1871 Sby 3/93 3,450
O/C 30x25 Forest Landscapewith a Waterfall 1880 Sby 3/93 3,100
O/C 30x40 Small Boat Mountainous Shoreline Dum 4/93 .. 3,000
O/C 29x52 Mount Marcy, Essex Co., NY 1877 Dum 1/93 .. 2,550
O/C 24x17 Sailing Ship Dum 3/93 1,800
O/C 14x20 Loch Striven Dum 1/93 1,500
O/C 14x16 Art for the Night Dum 4/93 1,100
O/C 20x16 Sailing Ship on Choppy Water 1908 Dum 7/93 . 900
W/Pa 23x32 Sailing Ships in Harbor Dum 4/93 800
W/Pa 21x19 The Stormy Sea Hnd 10/92 800
O/C 12x16 Evening Dum 7/93 400
O/C 17x14 Ships off the Great Cliffs Skn 9/92 400
W/Pa 10x14 Sailing Ships on Seas Dum 12/92 300
W/Pa 10x22 Fishing Boats on Sea Dum 12/92 300
W/Pa 9x19 Dawn Over the Coast Yng 2/93 100
Hopkins, Arthur   Eng 1848-1930
* See 1993 Edition ....

Hopkins, Budd Am 1931-
* See 1993 Edition ....
Hopkins, James R. Am 1877-1969
O/C 30x25 Cynthia Chr 9/92 6,050
Hopkins, Peter Am 1911-
* See 1992 Edition ....
Hopkins, Robert Am 20C
* See 1992 Edition ....
Hopkinson, Charles Sydney Am 1869-1962
W/Pa 13x10 Tree by the Water Yng 5/93 425
Hopper, Edward Am 1882-1967
W/Pa 16x22 Gloucester Houses Sby 12/92 330,000
W/Pa 14x20 Vermont Sugar House Sby 12/92 148,500
O/C 18x14 Portrait of an Artist Sby 3/93 23,000
Hoppner, Sir John Br 1758-1810
* See 1993 Edition ....
Horacio Mex 1912-1972
O/C 24x18 Young Girl with Tea Tray Chr 11/92 7,480
O/C 24x18 Rocha Galarza Holding Her Doll Sby 6/93 7,475
O/C 24x18 Retrato del Nino Horacio Rentoria Chr 11/92 .. 6,600
O/C 24x18 Nina con Canasta de Frutas Chr 11/92 5,500
O/C 24x18 Nina con Perros Chr 11/92 5,280
O/C 24x18 Nino con Sus Gatos y Perro Doy 5/93 4,290
O/C 24x18 Nina con Cesta de Roses Doy 5/93 4,180
O/C 24x18 Nina con Conejo Doy 5/93 4,180
Hordyk, Am 1899-1958
O/C 21x26 Rue de Vaugirard '32 Fre 10/92 225
Horemans, Jan Josef Flm 1682-1759
* See 1991 Edition ....
Horlor, George W. Br a 1849-1891
* See 1993 Edition ....
Hornbrook, Richard Lyde Eng 1783-1865
I,S&W/Pa 9x12 Entrance to Bonaparte's House Slo 7/93 900
Hornby, Lester George Am 1882-1956
W/Pa 12x17 Bass Rocks Yng 2/93 125
Hornel, Edward Atkinson Br 1864-1933
* See 1992 Edition ....
Horny, Franz Ger 1798-1824
W,Bc&H/Pa 13x9 Asters, Grapes, Walnut Sby 5/93 27,600
Horowitz, Leopold Hun 1838-1917
* See 1993 Edition ....
Horschelt, Theodore Ger 1829-1871
* See 1990 Edition ....
Horsley, John Calcott Br 1817-1903
* See 1992 Edition ....
Horst, Franz Aus 1862-1950
O/B 16x22 At the Fountain Sby 10/92 4,950
Horst, Gerrit Willemsz. Dut 1612-1652
* See 1992 Edition ....
Horter, Earl Am 1881-1940
W/Pa 18x23 House in Landscape Fre 4/93 700
I&G/Pa 8x10 Coal Pockets Sby 5/93 575
Horton, William Samuel Am 1865-1936
C/Pa 8x10 Women and Children, St. Ives Chr 5/93 575
P/Pa 10x8 City Scene Mys 12/92 110
Hoschede-Monet, Blanche Fr 1865-1947
* See 1990 Edition ....
Hosiasson, Phillipe Fr 1898-1978
O/C 57x45 Contre-espace 1955 Chr 11/92 4,400
O/C 32x26 Confluences 56 Sby 10/92 3,300
O/C 11x14 Two: Tetes devant une fenetre 45 Skn 9/92 440
Hosking, J. Maurice Am 19C
W/Pa 20x10 Mountainous Landscape Wtf 4/93 60
Hoskins, Gayle Porter Am 1887-1962
O/C 40x29 Mounted Cowboy Pointing Gun Ilh 11/92 3,750
O&R/C 36x24 Opening the Door to the Hold Ilh 11/92 350
Hosmer, Billy Price Am
O/C 36x24 Victorian Rose Sel 4/93 900
Houben, Henri Bel a 1885-1898
* See 1993 Edition ....
Houghton, M. Eng 19C
W/Pa 4x5 North Side of Ross's Bay 1839 Slo 7/93 400
Housser, Yvonne McKague Can 1898-
O/B 25x31 Spring in the Park 1941 Sbt 5/93 12,320

Houston, Georges Br 1869-1947
* See 1993 Edition ....
Hovenden, Thomas Am 1840-1895
O/C 21x14 The Sunday Painter 1886 Skn 11/92 24,200
O/C 37x25 Portrait of a Seated Lady 1883 Slo 7/93 1,200
Howard, Bertram K. Am 1872-
* See 1993 Edition ....
Howard, E. D. Am 19C
O/C 18x30 Landscape Hnd 12/92 100
Howard, Hugh Huntington Am 1860-1927
W/Pa 8x14 Sunset Scene Eld 8/93 138
Howard, Humbert Am -1990
W&Pe/Pa 5x6 Head Learning Fre 4/93 100
Howard, John Langley Am 1902-
Et/Pn 20x32 Night Fishing No. 2 1937 But 10/92 8,250
O/C 20x16 Mother and Child 1931 But 10/92 3,300
W/Pa 15x22 Paul Masson Winery 1946 But 6/93 2,875
O/B 16x23 Still Life with Pomegranates 1981 But 3/93 1,920
O/B 30x24 Night Fishing No. 1 1937 But 10/92 1,870
O/C 20x24 Gathering Wood '56 But 10/92 1,760
A/C 21x28 Rocks Under the Water But 10/92 495
A/Pa 20x29 Forest (Mountain - Green and Rozy) But 10/92 .. 440
A/Pa 16x24 Red with Blue Seed But 10/92 440
Howard, M. Maitland Br 20C
* See 1992 Edition ....
Howe, William Henry Am 1846-1929
O/C 20x29 Cattle Grazing '82 Sel 4/93 850
O/C 20x30 Cattle Grazing 85 Sby 3/93 690
O/C 20x30 Geese in a Landscape Sel 9/92 325
Howell, Felicie Waldo Am 1897-1968
* See 1992 Edition ....
Howell, Henry a 1660-1720
O/C 24x29 Trompe L'Oeil of a Letter Rack 1702 Sby 5/93 .. 17,250
Howell, Peter Am 20C
O/C 24x31 Track from the Dairy Boxes Sby 6/93 3,738
Howes, Kenneth Br 1924-
* See 1992 Edition ....
Howitt, John Newton Am 1885-1958
O/C 24x20 Deer in Autumn Wilds Slo 4/93 130
Howitt, William Samuel Br 1765-1822
* See 1992 Edition ....
Howland, Alfred Cornelius Am 1838-1909
O/Pn 10x12 Solitude Skn 9/92 440
O/Pn 10x12 Young Woman Sleeping Mys 3/93 440
Howland, George Am 1865-1928
O/Pn 7x12 Nymph Couchee sur un Lit de Fleurs Wtf 4/93 .. 1,500
O/C 25x30 Twilight Reflections Skn 9/92 468
Howland, John Dare Am 1843-1914
* See 1993 Edition ....
Hoyland, John Br 1934-
* See 1992 Edition ....
Hoyos, Ana Mercedes Col 1942-
O/C 78x39 Mis Americas 91 Chr 11/92 41,800
O/C 39x39 Bazurto 91 Chr 11/92 30,800
Hoyt, Edith Am 1894-
* See 1990 Edition ....
Hozendorf, Johann-Samuel 1694-1742
* See 1993 Edition ....
Hsu, Ti-Shan 20C
* See 1993 Edition ....
Hubacek, William Am 1866-1958
* See 1993 Edition ....
Hubbard, Harlan
* See 1992 Edition ....
Hubbard, Richard William Am 1816-1888
* See 1991 Edition ....
Hubbard, Whitney Myron Am 1875-
O/Ab 6x8 Winter Afternoon, Greensport, LI Slo 5/93 400
Hubbell, Henry Salem Am 1870-1949
* See 1993 Edition ....
Huber, * 18C**
O/C 23x27 Adoration of the Golden Calf Sby 1/93 6,900
Huber, Arnold Sws 1873-1953
O/C 18x21 Children by Shrine Near Water Mill Yng 2/93 200

Huber, Leon Charles Fr 1858-1928
O/C 15x29 Cat by a Basket Chr 10/92 3,850
O/C 15x18 Still Life Peaches in Basket Sby 1/93 2,070
O/C 15x18 Still Life with Peaches Wes 10/92 1,100
Hubert, Louise Stephanie Fr 20C
O/C 29x39 The Red Hat 1907 Chr 5/93 1,610
Hubner, Carl Wilhelm Ger 1814-1879
O/C 42x34 The Letter 1865 Sby 2/93 10,638
O/C 25x31 Proposal of Marriage 1853 Chr 10/92 7,150
Hudson, Charles Bradford Am 1865-1939
O/C 32x54 Sunset San Jacinto But 10/92 5,500
Hudson, Eric Am 1864-1932
  * See 1993 Edition . . . .
Hudson, Grace Carpenter Am 1865-1937
O/C 20x14 Chu-Bome: The Orphan '17 Sby 12/92 26,400
O/C 10x8 Thurlow 09 But 6/93 17,250
O/C 15x12 Little Papoose x7 Chr 12/92 14,300
O/B 8x7 Near Ukiah But 3/93 3,575
O/Pb 12x8 Plume at Matu; Stream: Pair But 10/92 3,025
O/B 5x6 Portrait of a Dog 1898 But 6/93 1,495
O/C 14x9 Stream; Landscape; Vines: (3) 1959 But 6/93 . . . 1,380
O/B 9x7 Poppies near Ukiah But 3/93 1,320
O/B 11x10 Russian River But 6/93 1,150
Pe&W/Pa 11x9 Artist's Mother; Man: Pair But 6/93 115
Hudson, Henry John Br 1881-1910
  * See 1991 Edition . . . .
Hudson, John Bradley Am 1832-1903
W/Pa 9x20 Autumn on the Coast of Maine Brd 8/93 495
Hudson, Muriel Am 1890-1959
O/B 16x20 Houses in Landscape Mor 11/92 700
Hudson, Thomas Br 1701-1779
O/C 49x39 Portrait of a Lady 1751 Sby 5/93 9,200
O/C 46x42 Elizabeth, Daughter of Viscount 1733 Sby 5/93 . 5,175
Hudson, Thomas Bradford Am 20C
  * See 1991 Edition . . . .
Hue, Jean-Francois 1751-1823
O/C 45x58 Landsape in Roman Campagna 1787 Sby 1/93 41,400
Huebler, Douglas
Ph&L 36x28 Site Sculpture Project 1968 Sby 11/92 4,950
Ph/Pb 28x35 Variable Piece #64 1971 Sby 2/93 4,888
Ph&P/B 31x31 Variable Piece, #99, Israel 1973 Sby 5/93 . . 4,025
Huet, Christophe Fr a 1735-1759
  * See 1993 Edition . . . .
Huet, Ernestine Am 19C
  * See 1991 Edition . . . .
Huet, Jean Baptiste Fr 1745-1811
O/C 41x58 Venus Reclining Rrom the Rear Sby 1/93 . . . 211,500
O/C 42x50 Cow and Her Calf in Barn Sby 5/93 19,550
Huet, Paul Fr 1803-1869
W/Pa 6x15 Children Playing on the Beach Chr 5/93 1,840
Huggins, M. W. Am 20C
O/C 20x32 Still Life with Books and Steins FHB 3/93 95
Huggins, William John Br 1820-1884
  * See 1993 Edition . . . .
Hughes, Edward John Can 1913-
W/Pa 20x24 Maples, Cowichan Bay Road 1973 Sbt 5/93 . . 5,808
W/Pa 20x24 Parliament Buildings, Ottawa Sbt 5/93 3,600
Hughes, Edward Robert Br 1851-1914
  * See 1991 Edition . . . .
Hughes, Edwin Br 1851-1904
  * See 1993 Edition . . . .
Hughes, Eliza Ball Am 1892-
W/Pa 9x13 Mt. Kineo House, Moosehead Lake Hnd 12/92 . . 160
Hughes, George Am 1907-
O/B 16x15 Couple Standing in Front of Mirror Ih 11/92 325
Hughes, George H. Can a 1832-1861
  * See 1992 Edition . . . .
Hughes, J. T. Br 19C
O/C 40x27 Calle E Canali, Venice Yng 2/93 500
O/C 16x24 Harvest Landscape Ald 9/92 155
Hughes, Talbot Br 1869-1942
  * See 1992 Edition . . . .
Hughes, William Br 1842-1901
  * See 1993 Edition . . . .

Hughto, Daryl Am 1943-
A/C 66x99 Slippin' and Slidin' 1976 Sby 2/93 3,450
Hugo, F. Am 19C
  * See 1993 Edition . . . .
Hugo, Jean Fr 1894-1984
T/Pn 19x24 Nocturne Chr 11/92 14,300
O/C 21x26 Scene de Campagne 40 Chr 11/92 8,800
Hugo, Victor Fr 1802-1885
Var 6x9 An Album Chr 5/93 18,400
Pl/Pa 2x5 Landscape 1842 Chr 5/93 1,610
W/Pa 9x10 Landscape with Chateau 1868 Lou 3/93 800
Huguet, Victor Pierre Fr 1835-1902
  * See 1992 Edition . . . .
Huilliot, Pierre-Nicolas Fr 1674-1751
  * See 1992 Edition . . . .
Hulbert, Katherine Allmond Am -1937
  * See 1993 Edition . . . .
Huldah, Cherry Jeffe Am 20C
O/C 31x23 La Femme au Cafe 195 Hnd 3/93 1,200
O/C 16x20 Floral Lou 3/93 800
O/B 12x16 Landscape with Houses Lou 6/93 150
Hulings, Clark Am 1922-
  * See 1990 Edition . . . .
Hulk, Abraham (Jr.) Eng 1851-1922
O/C 40x30 Gumshall Lane, Surry Hnz 5/93 700
O/C 40x30 Boys Fishing Fre 4/93 600
Hulk, Abraham (Sr.) Dut 1813-1897
O/C 24x42 Mooring at the End of the Day Sby 5/93 13,225
Hulk, Johannes Frederik Dut 1829-1911
O/C 24x36 Boats on a Village Canal Chr 10/92 6,050
Hulk, John Frederick Dut 1855-1913
  * See 1991 Edition . . . .
Hullenkremer, Odon
O/B 16x12 Pinyan Girl Dum 2/93 225
Hulme, Frederick William Br 1816-1884
O/C 14x25 Faggot Gatherer in Stormy Landscape Chr 10/92 1,980
Hulme, James Am 1900-1958
O/C 18x24 Lake Cumo Fre 4/93 350
Hulsmann, H. 19C
O/C 21x24 Two Dogs with Bird 1891 Sel 12/92 800
Hulsmann, Howard Am 20C
O/C 12x20 Sunny Landscape 1904 Hnz 5/93 350
Hultberg, John
O/C 50x68 Great Empty Sky 1962 Sby 2/93 1,840
Humblot, George Fr 20C
  * See 1992 Edition . . . .
Humblot, Robert Fr 1907-1962
  * See 1992 Edition . . . .
Humborg, Adolf Aus 1847-1913
O/Pn 19x16 The Wine Connoisseurs 83 Chr 5/93 11,500
O/Pn 17x24 Cleaning Out the Wine Cellar Sby 5/93 8,625
O/C 26x30 The Missed Step 83 Hnd 10/92 5,800
O/Pn 11x9 Ein Guter Tropfen But 5/93 1,380
Humphrey, David 1955-
  * See 1993 Edition . . . .
Humphrey, Jack Weldon Can 1901-1967
W/Pa 15x22 Cargo Boat; City: Double 1940 Sbt 11/92 1,140
W/Pa 14x20 Market Slip and King Street 1930 Sbt 11/92 . . 1,050
Humphrey, Maud Eng 19C
W/Pa 16x13 Young Girl with Violets 89 Slo 4/93 25
Humphrey, Ralph Am 1932-1990
A/C 60x60 Leo for Beth 1971 Sby 10/92 3,300
A/Pa 45x31 Untitled 85 Chr 2/93 1,320
C&K/Pa 30x22 Untitled Chr 2/93 1,100
Humphrey, Walter Beach Am 1892-1966
O/C 36x27 Standing Nude with Red Hair Ih 11/92 2,900
G/Pa 16x16 Antony and Cleopatra Ih 11/92 55
Humphreys Br 19C
O/C 22x31 Toronto Sby 1/93 1,380
Humphries, Jacqueline 1960-
O/L 16x16 Untitled Chr 2/93 1,870
O/L 16x16 Untitled 1990 Chr 2/93 1,760
Hundertwasser, Friedensreich 20C
W&A/Pa 15x28 Sommerhaus 1952 Sby 5/93 40,250

Hunn, Thomas a 1878-1908
W/B 11x14 Pilgrams Path from St. Martha's Chr 5/93 161
Hunnley, Jas.
O/C 16x12 On Harvey's Lake 1873 Dum 6/93 60
Hunt, Arthur Ackland Br a 1881-1913
W&Pe/Pa 12x9 Young Girl with Flowers 1875 Hnd 10/92 . . . 200
Hunt, Bryan Am 1947-
Os/Pa 30x23 The Waterfall Sby 2/93 2,875
H/Pa 85x34 Bridal Veil Sby 10/92 1,650
MM/Pa 30x22 Untitled 88 Chr 2/93 1,100
Hunt, Charles Br 1803-1877
O/C 24x20 Three Children Playing Sby 1/93 4,600
O/C 25x30 Puppy's Mealtime 84 Chr 10/92 4,400
Hunt, Edgar Br 1876-1953
* See 1992 Edition . . . .
Hunt, Edward Aubrey Br 1855-1922
O/C 30x50 Feeding the Geese 1883 Skn 11/92 2,475
O/Pn 4x6 Moorish Farrier, Tangiers Sby 1/93 1,035
Hunt, Esther Anna Am 1885-1951
W/Pb 11x8 Young Girl with Flowers But 6/93 575
Hunt, Henry Br 19C
O/B 10x12 The Conversation 92 Chr 10/92 1,100
Hunt, L. J. Am 20C
O/C 18x26 Lilacs Hnz 5/93 400
Hunt, Lynn Bogue Am 1878-1960
W/Pa 8x10 Four Ducks in Flight Ih 11/92 500
Hunt, Reuben Br 1879-1962
O/Pn 10x8 Fowl Friends Lou 9/92 350
Hunt, Thomas L. Am 1882-1938
O/Pa 8x10 Boat in a Harbor But 3/93 3,025
O/C 24x29 Winter Corn Field 1914 But 6/93 2,875
Hunt, W. S.
P/Pa 15x25 Point Judith, RI Eld 8/93 77
Hunt, Walter Br 1861-1941
* See 1992 Edition . . . .
Hunt, William Henry Eng 1790-1864
W&G/Pa 11x16 Still Life Assorted Fruits & Nuts Chr 10/92 . 2,200
W/Pa 18x30 Decoy Pipe on Fratton Broad 1873 Chr 2/93 . . 132
Hunt, William Holman Br 1827-1910
* See 1991 Edition . . . .
Hunt, William Morris Am 1824-1879
O/C 13x15 Out in the Cold 1864 Chr 3/93 4,600
C/Pa 10x16 View of Ipswich, Massachusetts Sby 3/93 1,035
Hunten, Emil Ger 1827-1902
* See 1992 Edition . . . .
Hunter, Clementine Am 1887-1988
O/Pa 15x11 Still Life with Flowers 1940 Sby 9/92 2,750
O/Cb 16x20 Baptism Sby 9/92 2,530
O/B 16x24 Saturday Night at the Honky Tonk Lou 3/93 . . . 2,250
O/B 17x26 Nativity Scene Lou 3/93 1,800
Hunter, Frederick Leo Am 1862-1943
O/B 9x14 Landscape Mys 3/93 165
Hunter, George Leslie Br 1877-1931
* See 1992 Edition . . . .
Hunter, Isabel Am 1878-1941
O/C 24x30 White Sands and Birches, California Hnd 10/92 . 2,600
O/Cb 13x10 Young Lady Mor 11/92 550
Hunter, Philippa Can 1928-
* See 1992 Edition . . . .
Huntington, Daniel Am 1816-1906
O/C 28x50 On the Connecticut River 1870 But 12/92 13,200
O/C 14x20 Travelers Amongst Ruins 184? Wes 10/92 440
Huntington, Dwight W. Am 19C
* See 1990 Edition . . . .
Huot, Charles Edouard Can 1855-1930
* See 1991 Edition . . . .
Hupe, Martial Fr 19C
. . . .
Huppert, E. A. 19C
O/B 12x9 Child Wearing a Pink Bonnet Sel 4/93 45
Hurd, Michael Am 20C
* See 1992 Edition . . . .
Hurd, Peter Am 1904-1984
O/C 16x20 Sketch at Bitter Lake 1928 But 12/92 2,090
W/Pa 19x29 Heavy Weather Sby 3/93 1,725

Hurt, Louis B. Br 1856-1929
O/C 24x36 Highland Cattle 1888 Sby 6/93 4,888
Huston, William Am a 1880-1889
O/C 20x38 Sailboats Off the Coast 1874 Fre 4/93 3,250
Huszar, Vilmos
* See 1993 Edition . . . .
Hutchens, Frank Townsend Am 1869-1937
* See 1993 Edition . . . .
Hutchinson, Robert Gemmell Br 1855-1936
* See 1993 Edition . . . .
Hutchison, Donald C. Am 1869-1954
O/C 27x21 At the Helm Mys 12/92 522
Hutty, Alfred Am 1878-1954
* See 1993 Edition . . . .
Huygens, Francois Joseph Bel 1820-1876
O/C 31x16 Still Life of Roses in Vase Sby 1/93 2,300
Huys, Modeste Bel 1875-1932
O/C 22x29 Vers Les Champs Sby 10/92 35,750
Huysmans, Jan Baptist Flm 1654-1716
* See 1992 Edition . . . .
Hyde, William Henry Am 1858-1943
O/C 25x14 Rag Picker Mys 3/93 330
Hyler, Hilaire Am 1898-1966
W/Pa 16x13 Abstract Lou 12/92 1,000
Hynd, Frederick S. Am 1905-1964
* See 1993 Edition . . . .
Hyppolite, Hector Hai 1889-1948
* See 1993 Edition . . . .
Iaccarino, Ralph Am 20C
W/Pa 44x67 Clearing in Tambor '82 FHB 6/93 1,300
W/Pa 44x67 A Clearing in Tambor Hnd 5/93 650
Iacovleff, Alexandre Rus 1887-1938
K/Pa 30x23 Japanese Wrestler 1917 Dum 2/93 1,200
Ianelli, Arcangelo Brz 1922-
O/C 51x40 Untitled 1980 Chr 11/92 5,500
Ibanez, Manuel Ramirez Spa 1856-1925
* See 1993 Edition . . . .
Ibbetson, Julius Caesar Eng 1759-1817
O/C 28x36 Ruined Abbey with Milkmaid Chr 5/93 4,600
Icart, Louis Fr 1888-1950
O/C 17x29 Au Bord de L'Eau Sby 10/92 25,300
O/Pn 24x20 Les Cygnes Sby 2/93 19,550
Icaza, Ernesto Mex 1866-1935
O/C 29x40 Cola en Campo Abierto 1913 Sby 11/92 60,500
O/C 29x40 Manganeando a Cuesta 1913 Sby 11/92 60,500
O/C/M 16x23 El Arreo 1910 Chr 11/92 38,500
O/C 24x38 Toreando Un Toro Embolado 1921 Sby 5/93 . . 34,500
Igler, Gustav Hun 1842-1908
O/C 36x27 The Patient Pet 85 Chr 10/92 24,200
Ignatiev, Alexander Am 1913-
W&G/Pa 20x29 Commercial Fishermen, San Pedro Mor 6/93 1,650
W/Pa 21x27 Street w/Old Mission-Bunker Hill LA Mor 6/93 . 495
O/Ab 18x22 Commercial Fishing Boats Mor 2/93 475
W/Pa 22x28 The Castle House-Bunker Hill Mor 6/93 385
MM/Pa 11x15 Fisherman's Return Mor 6/93 358
Il Baciccio It 1639-1709
K,Pl&Br/Pa 10x8 Martyrdom of a Royal Saint Chr 1/93 . . . 30,800
Il Bagnacavallo It 1484-1542
* See 1993 Edition . . . .
Il Bolognese It 1606-1680
* See 1992 Edition . . . .
Il Borgognone It 1621-1675
O/C 37x50 Military Skirmish Sby 10/92 20,900
Il C. Tempesta It 1637-1701
* See 1990 Edition . . . .
Il Canaletto It 1697-1768
* See 1992 Edition . . . .
Il Cavaliere Calabrese It 1613-1699
O/C 46x67 The Feast of Absalom Chr 1/93 49,500
O/C 24x19 An Old Man, Woman and Boy Sby 10/92 25,300
Il Cecco Bravo It 1601-1661
* See 1992 Edition . . . .

Il Cigoli It 1559-1613
O/C 36x29 Adoration of the Shepherds Sby 5/93 8,050
Il Cosci It 1560-1631
* See 1993 Edition ....
Il Flammenghino It 1575-1640
* See 1992 Edition ....
Il Francia It 1450-1517
* See 1990 Edition ....
Il Gaetano It 1549-1598
* See 1990 Edition ....
Il Garofalo It 16C
* See 1991 Edition ....
Il Genovese It 1545-1639
* See 1993 Edition ....
Il Giovane, Palma It 1544-1628
K,Pl&S/Pa 10x8 Studies of Six Bearded Heads Chr 1/93 .. 15,400
K,Pl&S/Pa 10x13 Venus and Adonis Chr 1/93 9,350
Il Guercino It 1591-1666
Pl&S/Pa 12x9 Executioner Holding Head St. John Chr 1/93 85,800
Pl/Pa 10x7 Mars, His Sword Drawn Chr 1/93 52,800
O/C 26x22 Mary Magdalene Contemplating Nails Chr 1/93 49,500
Pl/Pa 10x8 Woman Turned to the Left Chr 1/93 30,800
Pl/Pa 10x16 Hilly Landscape with Huntsman Chr 1/93 ... 12,100
K/Pa 12x8 Saint Jerome in Penitence Chr 1/93 12,100
Il Lissandro It 1667-1749
* See 1993 Edition ....
Il Lucchese It 1605-1675
* See 1993 Edition ....
Il Maltese It a 1650-1680
* See 1993 Edition ....
Il Mascacotta It 1663-1714
O/C 18x33 Coastlines w/Capriccio Views: Pair Chr 1/93 .. 77,000
Il Mastelletta It 1575-1655
O/C 15x18 The Flight into Egypt Sby 10/92 9,350
Il Mecarino It 1486-1551
* See 1993 Edition ....
Il Mercanti It 1657-1734
* See 1992 Edition ....
Il Pitocchetto It 1698-1767
O/C 24x20 Young Woman Holding a Mask Sby 5/93 10,925
Il Poppi It 1544-1597
* See 1992 Edition ....
Il Portoghese It 17C
* See 1990 Edition ....
Il Sassoferrato It 1609-1685
K/Pa 5x8 Hands Joined in Prayer Chr 1/93 3,520
Il Semolei It 1510-1580
* See 1992 Edition ....
Il Spagnoletto It 1555-1626
K&Pl/Pa 7x7 Saint Francis in Prayer Chr 1/93 2,200
Il Tempesta It 1637-1701
* See 1992 Edition ....
Il Tintoretto (Domenico) It 1560-1635
* See 1993 Edition ....
Il Tintoretto (Jacopo) It 1518-1594
* See 1993 Edition ....
Il Todeschini It a 1706-1736
O/C 29x24 Laughing Boy Holding Paper & Garlic Sby 1/93 11,500
Il Veronese It 1528-1588
* See 1993 Edition ....
Il Viterbese It 1610-1662
* See 1993 Edition ....
Il Volterrano It 1611-1689
O/C 57x91 Bacchus with Putti Sby 5/93 4,888
Illes, Aladar Edvi Hun 1870-1911
G/Pa 9x12 Garden Entrance Slo 4/93 750
Illies, Arthur Ger 1870-1952
* See 1993 Edition ....
Ilsted, Peter Vilhelm Dan 1861-1933
* See 1990 Edition ....
Imai, Toshimitsu Fr 1926-
* See 1992 Edition ....
Imhof, George R. Am 1911-1983
O/C 29x36 Reclining Nude '53 Fre 10/92 225

Imhoff, Joseph A. Am 1871-1955
O/C/B 31x47 The Camoufleurs Chr 12/92 55,000
O/C/B 32x26 Abiqui But 12/92 2,200
O/C/B 44x34 Mother with Baby in Cradle But 12/92 2,200
W/Pa/B 22x19 Portrait of an Indian Sby 3/93 920
Immendorf, Jorg 1945-
* See 1993 Edition ....
Imparato, Girolamo It a 1573-1621
O/C 51x39 Adoration of the Shepherds Sby 5/93 24,150
Indiana, Robert Am 1928-
O/C 10x8 Grass 62 Sby 11/92 14,300
Indoni, Filippo It a 1870-1884
O/C 30x25 Genre Scene Dum 5/93 12,000
W/Pa 29x20 Courtship But 5/93 3,162
W/Pa/B 22x15 The Dancers But 5/93 2,875
W/Pa 17x13 Courtship in the Fields Wlf 3/93 1,400
W/Pb 20x13 A Peasant Woman Chr 10/92 990
W/Pb 20x13 Peasant Woman on a Path Chr 10/92 990
Induno, Domenico It 1815-1878
* See 1991 Edition ....
Induno, Girolamo It 1827-1890
* See 1993 Edition ....
Ingelrans, Paul-Leon-Henri Fr a 1893-1920
* See 1993 Edition ....
Ingermann, Keith
O/M 5x4 Basket with Marigolds '60 Wlf 9/92 95
Ingham, Elizabeth H. Am 20C
* See 1992 Edition ....
Ingle, John S. Am 1933-
W/Pa 60x40 Still Life Watermelon and Palm Sby 12/92 ... 42,900
Inglis, J. J.
O/Ab 11x12 Winter Landscape Dum 8/93 150
Inglis, John Irs 1867-
O/C 24x20 Country Lane in Springtime Sby 1/93 3,738
Ingres, Jean Auguste Dominique Fr 1780-1867
H/Pa 13x9 Portrait of a Lady 1834 Sby 2/93 222,500
Pe&K/Pa 12x10 Study for Moliere Chr 10/92 8,800
Inman, George Am 1825-1894
O/B 8x12 City Coastline But 10/92 935
Inman, Henry Am 1801-1846
* See 1992 Edition ....
Inman, John O'Brien Am 1828-1896
* See 1993 Edition ....
Innerst, Mark Am 1957-
G&A/Pa 6x9 View of Brooklyn 1985 Chr 11/92 7,700
Inness, George Am 1825-1894
O/C 48x79 Evening 1868 Sby 5/93 184,000
O/Pn 12x18 Shepherd in a Landscape Sby 5/93 82,250
O/C 10x16 Winter Evening, Montclair Sby 5/93 74,000
O/C 30x45 Sunset, Etretat 1892 Sby 12/92 71,500
O/C 24x36 George Inness's Home, Tarpon Springs Sby 5/93 63,000
O/C 45x40 Sunset, Golden Glow 1893 Sby 12/92 38,500
O/C 20x30 Campagna, From the North 1874 Chr 5/93 ... 36,800
O/C 15x25 Visionary Landscape Sby 12/92 20,900
O/C 10x15 Albano, Italy Hnz 5/93 5,000
Inness, George (Jr.) Am 1853-1926
O/C 20x24 A Walk at Sunset Skn 5/93 2,970
O/C 12x18 Marsh Scene Chr 12/92 2,860
O/B 9x8 A Walk in the Country But 12/92 2,475
Innocenti, Camilio It 1871-1961
* See 1991 Edition ....
Innocenti, Guglielmo It 19C
* See 1990 Edition ....
Insley, Albert Babb Am 1842-1937
O/C 14x20 Grainstacks Skn 9/92 935
O/C 14x20 Summer Landscape Slo 5/93 800
O/C 10x14 New England Landscape Skn 3/93 412
Inukai, Kyohei Am 1934-
O/C 20x17 Portrait of Kate Wes 5/93 550
Ipcar, Dahlov Am 20C
O/C 24x20 Still Life With Decoys Brd 2/93 341
Ipsen, Ernest Ludwig Am 1869-1934
O/C 14x20 Still Life with Teapot '92 Chr 3/93 2,070

Iriarte   Spa 1621-1685
* See 1991 Edition . . . .
Irish, D.   19C
W/Pa 20x15 Children with Cart Wlf 4/93   90
Irolli, Vincenzo   It 1860-1942
* See 1993 Edition . . . .
Irvine, Wilson Henry   Am 1869-1936
O/C 24x36 Gloucester Harbor Chr 3/93   19,550
O/C 29x36 Snow Bound Brook Chr 9/92   12,100
O/C 24x27 Morning in the Harbor Skn 11/92   10,450
O/C 22x28 Sylvan Vista Brd 8/93   5,775
O/C 24x27 Spring Waves, Monhegan Island Hnd 5/93   4,400
O/C 12x16 New England Landscape Hnd 5/93   2,000
W/Pa 14x17 Autumn Lake Hnd 5/93   500
Irwin, Robert   20C
* See 1993 Edition . . . .
**Isabey, Louis Gabriel Eugene   Fr
1803-1886**
O/C 10x15 Plage de Normandie Sby 5/93   6,900
O/C 15x12 Mere en Atours Avec Deux Fillettes 59 Sby 2/93   5,750
O/C 17x24 Launching Fishing Boat Sby 1/93   4,888
O/C 25x37 The Wreck Chr 5/93   4,830
O/B 7x5 Village Scene Brd 5/93   1,840
**Isenbart, Marie Victor Emile   Fr
1846-1921**
O/C 18x26 Vallee de Lion Chr 10/92   4,620
Isenberger, Eric   Am 1902-
* See 1992 Edition . . . .
Isenbrant, Adriaen   Flm a 1510-1551
* See 1992 Edition . . . .
Isham, Samuel   Am 1855-1914
* See 1993 Edition . . . .
Iskowitz, Gershon   Can 1921-1988
O/C 42x38 Deep Lilac No. 2 1977 Sbt 11/92   8,360
Isolda   Brz 1924-
* See 1992 Edition . . . .
Israel, Daniel   Aus 1859-1901
O/Pn 7x9 Harem Girls Reading Chr 10/92   7,700
O/B 4x5 Lesson in the Koran Chr 2/93   4,620
Israels, Isaac   Dut 1865-1934
O/C 30x20 Female Nude Dum 5/93   7,500
Israels, Josef   Dut 1824-1911
O/C 13x20 Pancakes But 5/93   36,800
O/C 26x21 Young Mother and Children Chr 5/93   27,600
O/C 14x22 On the Dunes Sby 2/93   20,700
O/Pn 13x18 Girl Seated on the Dunes 1866 Hnd 10/92 . . .   10,000
O/Pn 12x18 Woman in a Barn Interior Chr 10/92   8,800
O/Pn 13x18 Hauling in the Net Hnd 10/92   8,400
O/C 23x18 An Old Man Chr 5/93   8,050
W&G/Pa 14x10 Homewards Sby 10/92   5,775
W/Pa 24x17 Seated Woman by a Window Chr 10/92   1,870
Issupoff, Alessio   Rus 1889-1957
O/C 40x27 In the Garden Sby 2/93   36,800
**Istvanffy, Gabrielle Rainer   Hun
1865-1964**
O/C 20x24 Two Cats on Alert Yng 2/93   1,500
O/C 16x20 The Chase Sby 6/93   1,380
O/C 20x24 Two Cats Playing w/Basket Flowers Yng 2/93 . . .   600
Itami, Michi   20C
* See 1991 Edition . . . .
Itaya, Foussa   Fr 1919-
* See 1993 Edition . . . .
Iturria, Ignacio   Uru 1949-
O/C 67x77 Cutlery Chr 11/92   13,200
O/C 40x47 Otro Gol Chr 11/92   12,100
Ivanowski, Sigismund   Am 1875-1944
O/C 41x57 The Sculptress Caroline Ball Wes 5/93   1,870
Iverd, Eugene   Am 1893-1938
* See 1993 Edition . . . .
Ives, H. S.   20C
* See 1992 Edition . . . .
Ives, Percy   Am 1864-1928
O/C 32x26 Girl Seated with Oranges Dum 7/93   8,000
Iwill, Joseph   Fr 1850-1923
O/C 12x10 Grand Canal, Venice Chr 2/93   1,650

Izquierdo, Maria   Mex 1906-1950
O/M 36x26 Autorretrato 40 Sby 5/93   140,000
O/C 24x30 Los Peregrinos 45 Chr 11/92   82,500
O/C 21x17 Malabarista 45 Sby 11/92   82,500
Jackman, Oscar Theodore   Am 1878-1940
* See 1992 Edition . . . .
Jackman, Reva   Am 1892-
O/C 21x25 Summer Hills Mor 6/93   880
Jackman, Theodore   Am 20C
* See 1992 Edition . . . .
**Jackson, Alexander Young   Can
1882-1974**
O/C 32x40 Smoke Fantasy, 1932 Sbt 5/93   79,200
O/C 16x20 Islands - Georgian Bay 1920 Sbt 11/92   22,880
O/C 25x32 Diamond Lake 1964 Sbt 5/93   8,800
O/Pn 8x11 Summer, Georgian Bay Sbt 5/93   6,160
O/Pn 9x11 St. Sauveur 1930 Sbt 5/93   5,940
O/Pn 10x14 Silver Mine, Contact Lake 1938 Sbt 5/93 . . .   5,720
O/Pn 11x14 Eastman, Quebec 1958 Sbt 5/93   5,280
O/Pn 9x11 Light and Shadow Sbt 5/93   4,840
O/B 9x11 The Yellow House Sbt 11/92   4,400
O/Pn 9x11 St. Hilarion, Quebec 1928 Sbt 11/92   3,960
O/Pn 11x14 Gargantua Beach, Lake Superior 1957 Sbt 5/93   3,740
Jackson, Elbert McGran   Am 1896-1962
O&R/C 16x23 Hulking Man Threatening Woman Ih 5/93 . .   1,200
O/C 24x20 Two Men at Back of Army Truck Ih 11/92   500
**Jackson, James Randolph   Aut
1886-1975**
* See 1993 Edition . . . .
Jackson, John   1778-1831
O/C 30x25 Portrait William Pitt the Younger Sby 10/92   2,475
Jackson, John Edwin   Am 1875-
C&K/Pa 22x18 Customs Officers Arriving Passenger Ih 11/92   500
Jackson, Lee   Am 1909-
O/M 8x6 Dance Contestants Fre 10/92   325
Jackson, Oliver   Am 1935-
A&W/Pa 48x43 Untitled, 1984 84 But 10/92   2,750
Jackson, Robert Scott   Am 20C
P/Pa 24x34 Nature's Palette Brd 8/93   1,018
Jackson, William Franklin   Am 1850-1936
O/C/B 12x18 Poppies and Lupines But 6/93   4,312
O/C/B 8x11 High Sierra But 3/93   2,090
Jackson, William Henry   Am 1843-1942
* See 1993 Edition . . . .
Jacob, Alexandre   Fr 1876-
* See 1992 Edition . . . .
Jacobi, Annot Kriger Menzel
G/Pa 14x16 Sunflowers Ald 5/93   65
Jacobi, F. C.   18C
* See 1993 Edition . . . .
Jacobi, M. M.   Eng 19C
O/C 12x10 Woman Outside a Mansion 1891 Wes 10/92   440
Jacobi, Otto Reinhold   Can 1814-1901
O/Pn 11x9 Along the River 1861 Sbt 11/92   1,056
Jacobs, Adolphe   Bel a 1887-1910
* See 1991 Edition . . . .
Jacobs, Helen   Am 1888-1970
W/Pa 14x10 Princess in Cavern of Jewels Ih 5/93   4,250
W/Pa 15x9 Girl Dancing with Elf Ih 5/93   2,000
Pl/Pa 12x8 Forest Scene Ih 11/92   475
Jacobs, John Emmanuel   Eng 19C
O/C 40x23 Clad in Scarlet Honours Bright 1880 Slo 7/93 . . .   650
Jacobs, Micheal
O/C 16x24 Forest Scene Ald 9/92   175
Jacobsen, Antonio N.   Am 1850-1921
O/C 29x59 The American Leaving New York 1884 Sby 5/93 43,125
O/B 24x48 Schooner Orlando V. Wooten in NY Doy 5/93 . .   17,600
O/C 25x40 Liner "St. Paul" Picking Up Pilot 1898 Eld 7/93 . .   8,800
O/B 16x24 U.S.S. Constitution 1916 Slo 7/93   6,500
O/C 14x22 Comanche 1904 Sby 6/93   6,325
O/C 22x36 Steamboat W. Whilldin/Cadwalader 1890 Fre 4/93 5,750
Jacobsen, Sophus   Nor 1833-1912
* See 1993 Edition . . . .
Jacobsz., Lambert   1598-1636
* See 1992 Edition . . . .

Jacomin-Vigny, Alfred-Louis   Fr 1842-1913
  * See 1991 Edition ....
Jacopo Del Casentino   It a 14C
  * See 1993 Edition ....
Jacot, Don   Am 1949-
  G/B 11x12 Looking Down Wabash, Chicago, 1990 FHB 3/93   1,100
  G/B 12x17 View at Belle Isle '86 FHB 3/93   1,000
Jacovacci, Francesco   It 1838-1908
  O/C 51x115 Last Day/Venetian Republic 1888 Sby 10/92 .   13,200
Jacovleff, Alexandre   Fr 1887-1938
  O/C 16x39 Sleeping Girl 1929 Doy 11/92   4,675
Jacquart, Lucie   Bel 1882-1956
  O/C 15x21 Still Life Roses, Pottery Sel 12/92   550
Jacque, Charles Emile   Fr 1813-1894
  O/Pn 19x47 Les Moutons Dans le Sous-Bois Sby 10/92 ..   24,200
  O/C 26x32 A Shepherdess and her Flock Chr 5/93   20,700
  O/Pn 8x7 Ferme a Barbizon Chr 5/93   16,100
  O/C 20x24 Woman Herding Sheep into Barn But 5/93 ...   3,738
Jacque, Emile   Fr 1848-1912
  * See 1993 Edition ....
Jacquet, Gustave Jean   Fr 1846-1909
  O/C 24x20 Woman Wearing an Elegant Hat Chr 2/93   2,420
  W&Pe/Pa/B 20x14 Lady with Carafe Sby 1/93   1,380
Jacquette, Yvonne   20C
  * See 1991 Edition ....
Jacquin, Victorine   Fr 19C
  * See 1991 Edition ....
Jaeckel, Henry   Ger 19C
  O/C 18x30 Town in the Italian Alps Brd 2/93   3,250
Jaeckel, Herman   Ger 19C
  * See 1993 Edition ....
Jafe, Myriam   Am 20C
  O/C 26x18 Rose D'Inde 1969 Slo 5/93   50
Jakobs, Paul Emil   Ger 1802-1866
  * See 1991 Edition ....
Jamar, Armand Gustave Gerard   Bel 1870-1946
  * See 1993 Edition ....
Jambor, Louis   Am 1884-1955
  O/C/M 30x30 With Basket of Fish Dum 7/93   1,750
  O/C 24x20 The Butter Churners Yng 5/93   1,000
James, Charles
  * See 1992 Edition ....
James, David   Br a 1881-1898
  * See 1993 Edition ....
James, Ezra   Am 1768-1836
  O/C 30x25 Portrait of Ellen Tree Hnd 10/92   1,000
James, Frederic   Am 1845-1907
  W&Pe/Pa 20x16 Olympia 55 Sby 3/93   460
  W/Pa 5x15 Snowy Rural Townscape Sel 4/93   375
James, Frederick   Am 1857-1932
  P/Pa 12x8 At the Piano 1881 Fre 4/93   260
James, Gilbert   a 1895-1926
  W/Pa 12x14 Arabic Men with Horses Passing Ih 11/92 ..   650
James, John W.   Am 1873-
  * See 1993 Edition ....
James, Richard S.   Eng 19C
  * See 1992 Edition ....
James, William   Br a 1754-1771
  O/C 29x49 Riva Degli Schiavoni, Venice Sby 5/93   79,500
  O/C 23x38 Grand Canal, Venice Sby 10/92   38,500
Jameson, Middleton   Br -1919
  O/C 48x74 La Fille Pecheur 1887 Sby 5/93   18,400
Jamin, Paul Joseph   Fr 1853-1903
  O/C 32x52 Returning Home 189* But 5/93   978
Jamison, Philip   Am 1925-
  W/Pa 20x29 The Old Barn Ald 5/93   425
  W/Pa 10x15 Street Corner Fre 10/92   350
  W/Pa 20x14 House with Dock by the Shore Fre 10/92 ...   250
Jance, Paul Claude   Fr 1840-
  * See 1993 Edition ....
Janco, Marcel   Fr 1895-1984
  O/M 24x34 The Procession Chr 5/93   18,400

Janesch, Albert   Aus 1889-
  * See 1990 Edition ....
Janet, Adele   Fr -1877
  W/B 13x10 Tulips 1843 Chr 5/93   6,325
Janousek, Frantisek   20C
  * See 1991 Edition ....
Janowitz, Joel   Am 20C
  * See 1993 Edition ....
Jansem, Jean   Fr 1920-
  O/C 51x77 Still Life Sby 6/93   28,750
  O/C 52x35 La Fille au Chale Sby 10/92   19,800
  O/C 29x36 Danseuse au Bandeau Blanc Chr 11/92   18,700
  O/C 52x35 La Fille au Chale Sby 6/93   17,250
  O/C 36x29 Isabelle Chr 5/93   16,100
  O/C 32x29 Trois Enfants 64 Chr 11/92   10,450
  O/Pa/C 20x26 Nature Morte aux Fruits But 5/93   6,900
  O/C 36x26 Seated Boy But 11/92   6,050
  O/C 18x15 Trois Femmes Assises Chr 2/93   4,950
  O/Pa/C 10x14 Danseuse en Jaune Chr 11/92   3,520
  Pl&Br/Pa 16x26 L'Atelier Chr 5/93   2,300
  I,S&W/Pa 26x20 Seated Woman Sby 2/93   2,300
Jansen, Alfred   1903-1981
  * See 1993 Edition ....
Jansen, Johan Laurents   Dan 1800-1856
  O/C 17x20 Wine, Grapes and a Wreath 1834 Chr 5/93   5,750
Jansen, Joseph   Ger 1829-1905
  O/C 20x27 Figures Fishing by Moonlight Fre 10/92   2,200
Jansen, Willem George F.   Dut 1871-1949
  * See 1993 Edition ....
Janson, Johannes   Dut 1729-1784
  O/B 14x17 Pastoral Milkmaid 1768 Wlf 12/92   600
Janssens, Abraham Van Nuyssen   Flm 1575-1632
  * See 1992 Edition ....
Janssens, Hieronymous   Dut 1624-1693
  * See 1991 Edition ....
Janssens, Pieter   Bel 19C
  O/Pn 16x13 Fruit and Vegetables on Table '62 Wes 12/92   11,000
Janssens, Victor Emile   Ger 1807-1845
  * See 1993 Edition ....
Janssens, Victor Honore   1658-1736
  O/Pn 12x17 Venus Reclining in a Landscape Chr 10/92 ..   4,950
Jansson, Alfred   Am 1863-1931
  O/C 27x30 Country Landscape 1923 Lou 12/92   800
Jansson, Eugene   Swd 1862-1915
  * See 1992 Edition ....
Japy, Louis Aime   Fr 1840-1916
  * See 1993 Edition ....
Jardines, Jose Maria   Spa 1862-
  O/C 19x26 Parisian Street Scene Chr 5/93   7,475
  O/C 13x21 Villa by a Country Road Wes 3/93   2,860
Jarrett, Charles A.
  O/C 26x51 Man in Suit Drinking Glass of Beer Ih 11/92   800
Jarvis, John   Am 20C
  * See 1992 Edition ....
Jarvis, John Wesley   Am 1780-1840
  * See 1993 Edition ....
Jarvis, W. Frederick   Am 1868-
  * See 1993 Edition ....
Jaudon, Valerie   Am 1945-
  O&Pg/C 90x98 Egypt River 1980 Sby 5/93   11,500
  O/C 60x60 Isola 1977 Chr 5/93   8,625
  H/Pa 25x25 Untitled '76 Chr 11/92   1,100
Javier, Maximino   Mex 20C
  * See 1993 Edition ....
Jawlensky, Alexej   Ger 1864-1941
  * See 1993 Edition ....
Jaxon, J. Q.
  Pl/Pa 17x13 Corpse Surrounded by Spectres 1921 Ih 11/92   1,300
Jazet, Paul Leon   Fr 1848-
  O/Pn 11x7 French Cavalry Trumpeter 1879 Sby 5/93   2,875
Jean, Simon Saint   Fr 1808-1860
  * See 1993 Edition ....

Jeanneret, Charles Edouard   Fr 1887-1965
* See 1993 Edition . . . .

Jeaurat, Etienne   Fr 1699-1789
O/Pn 12x9 Modest & Frivolous Woman: Pair Sby 1/93 . . . 46,000

Jefferson, P.   Am 20C
O/C 24x36 Crashing Surf, New England Slo 4/93 600

Jefferys, Charles William   Can 1869-1951
O/B 8x10 Village by the Water Sbt 5/93 1,540

Jegorev, Andrei   Rus 20C
G/Pa 12x18 Sleigh Ride Wes 12/92 935

Jelinek, Fr. A.   Czk 20C
W/B 5x5 Horse and Trainer Wes 5/93 468

Jenkins, Paul   Am 1923-
A/C 77x160 Phenomena Comstock Lode II 1974 Sby 2/93   46,000
A/C 64x48 Fortune Wheel 1967 Sby 10/92 14,300
O/C 47x77 Phenomena Southern Turn 1983 Sby 2/93 9,775
O/C 38x18 The Riddle 1958 Chr 11/92 4,400
W/C 46x46 Phenomena, Hadrian's Wall 1979 But 4/93 2,875
A/C 16x20 Phenomenon Red Arrested 1965 Sby 6/93 2,300
W/Pa 31x43 Phenomena Druid Mtng Place 1982 Chr 11/92   2,200
W/Pa 31x23 Phenomena Spellbound 6 1964 Sby 10/92 . . . 2,200
W/Pa 31x43 Untitled Chr 11/92 2,200
W/Pa 31x43 Phenomena Prism Sentinels Chr 11/92 1,870
W/Pa 44x31 Phenomena Stately Stance But 4/93 1,840
W/Pa 31x43 Phenomena W Range 1982 Sby 6/93 1,840
W/Pa 22x30 Untitled Sby 10/92 1,650
W/Pa 30x22 Phenomena Cleopatra Fan 1975 Sby 6/93 . . . 1,610
O/C 24x18 Amber Vessel '58 Hnd 9/92 1,400
W/Pa 30x42 Phenomenon Jade Pass 1975 Sby 6/93 1,380
W&I/Pa 22x31 Phenomenon Signing Torture 1965 Sby 6/93   1,265
O/C 16x10 Untitled 1962 Sby 2/93 690
W/Pa 29x21 Abstraction Wlf 12/92 500

Jenkins, Wilfred   Br 19C
* See 1992 Edition . . . .

Jenney, Neil   Am 1945-
A&H/C 59x83 Stop and Spades 1970 Chr 11/92 176,000
O/Wd 33x79 Formation #2 Sby 11/92 137,500
Medium? 61x85 Man and Beast 1970 Sby 10/92 115,500
A/C 58x58 Herd and Flock Chr 10/92 82,500
A/C 59x77 Plowed and Plower 1969 Chr 11/92 82,500

Jennings-Brown, H. W.   Br 19C
* See 1990 Edition . . . .

Jensen, Alfred   Am 1903-1981
O/C 72x72 Mayan Mat Patterns Structure Sby 11/92 71,500
O/C 50x72 Earth, Moon, Sun and Venus 1968 Chr 11/92 . 30,800
O/C 50x46 Structures Male vs. Female 1963 Sby 5/93 . . . 26,450
O/C 70x44 Acrobatic Rectangle; Per Eight 1967 Sby 5/93 . 16,100
O/C 55x110 The Parthenon, Athens 1970 Chr 11/92 15,000

Jensen, Bill   Am 1945-
* See 1993 Edition . . . .

Jensen, Carl Milton   Dan 1855-
O/C 45x74 Two on the Wing/Marsh View 1912 Skn 3/93 . . 7,700

Jensen, George   Am 1878-
O/B 30x30 Winter Landscape Dum 4/93 900

Jensen, Johan Laurentz   Dan 1800-1856
* See 1993 Edition . . . .

Jensen, Oluf   Dan 1864-1923
* See 1993 Edition . . . .

Jensen, Robert   Am 1922-
W/Pa 21x29 Work Boats at Rest Mor 2/93 500

Jerichau, Holger Hvitfeldt   Dan 1861-1900
* See 1991 Edition . . . .

Jerres, Antony   It 19C
O/C/B 16x13 The Grape Pickers But 11/92 2,200

Jess
* See 1991 Edition . . . .

Jessup, Robert   Am 20C
O/C 48x48 Making Bread 1983 Hnd 12/92 1,200

Jettel, Eugen   Aus 1845-1901
* See 1992 Edition . . . .

Jettmar, Rudolf   Pol 1869-1939
* See 1992 Edition . . . .

Jimenez Y Aranda, Jose   Spa 1837-1903
O/C/M 20x31 Venerdi Santo: Far Penitenza 1874 Sby 5/93   60,250
O/C 14x11 Gentleman Reading a Book Sby 2/93 8,050

Jimenez Y Aranda, Luis   Spa 1845-1928
O/C 32x22 La Provende Des Poules Sby 2/93 8,913

Jimenez Y Fernandez, Federico   Spa 1841-
W/Pa 8x5 Outside the Mosque 1907 Chr 5/93 460

Jimenez Y Martin, Juan   Spa 1858-
O/Pn 9x16 In the Harem Chr 10/92 18,700

Joanovitch, Paul   Aus 1859-
O/C 38x57 The Old, Old Story 1894 Chr 5/93 60,800

Jochmus, Harry   Ger 1855-1915
* See 1991 Edition . . . .

Johannenson   Swd 20C
O/C 10x15 Cottage by the Bay Fre 10/92 900

Johannesen, J.   Nor 1934-
O/C 54x42 Still Life Sunlit Houses '18 Fre 4/93 900

Johansen, John Christian   Am 1876-1964
O/C 30x40 Piazza San Marco, Venice 1908 Sby 3/93 8,625

Johansson, Stefan   Swd 1876-1955
* See 1992 Edition . . . .

Johns, Jasper   Am 1930-
O/C 54x45 0 Through 9 '61 Chr 11/92 . . . . 2.31M

Johnson, Avery Fischer   Am 1906-
W/Pa 15x23 Sailboats in Harbor Dum 11/92 200
W/Pa 17x23 Ocean Freighter Dum 11/92 125
W/Pa 15x22 Sailboat Dum 11/92 125
W/Pa 14x21 Town Ald 9/92 110

Johnson, Clarence   Am 1894-1981
O/C 33x39 Spring Trees Fre 10/92 1,200

Johnson, David   Am 1827-1908
O/C 21x30 Upper Twin Lakes/Rockies '65 Chr 12/92 . . . 121,000
O/C 16x26 Lake George 1870 Sby 5/93 40,250
O/C 12x20 Warwick, Orange County 74 Chr 12/92 22,000
O/C 19x15 Joyceville, Connecticut 1881 Sby 5/93 8,050
O/C/Pn 12x17 Road-Side, New Rochelle, NY 1884 Chr 12/92 6,050
Pe/Pa 13x19 Landscapes: Fifteen Drawings Sby 9/92 5,225
Pe/Pa 10x17 Landscapes: Fifteen Drawings Sby 9/92 5,225
Pe/Pa 12x18 Landscapes: Fifteen Drawings Sby 9/92 4,675
Pe/Pa 12x17 The Artist at Lake George Brd 2/93 1,650
Pe/Pa 10x17 Walk by Jervis McEntee's Cottage Brd 2/93 . . 1,650
Pe/Pa 10x14 Landscape Brd 2/93 1,320
Pe/Pa 13x18 Three Drawings 59 Sby 9/92 1,320
Pe&G/Pa 12x18 Three Drawings 79 Sby 9/92 1,320
H/Pa 12x18 Fifteen Drawings Sby 3/93 1,035
H/Pa 13x19 Fifteen Drawings Sby 3/93 978

Johnson, Edward   Am 1911-
* See 1993 Edition . . . .

Johnson, Frank Tenney   Am 1874-1939
O/C 25x19 An Evil Omen 1930 Sby 12/92 38,500
O/B 24x30 Spring Roundup 1938 But 12/92 38,500
O/B 13x10 Standing Guard 1936 Sby 12/92 19,800
O/M 12x9 At Evening 1933 Sby 5/93 13,800
O/M 12x9 Sunset Shadows 1933 Sby 5/93 11,500
W/Pa 30x21 Rider on Horseback But 6/93 9,200
O/Cb 20x16 Canyon Creek 1931 Chr 5/93 6,900
O/B 12x15 Along the Yellowstone Sby 9/92 3,850

Johnson, Gordon   Am 1924-1989
G/Pa 20x18 Piano Lesson Torture Ilh 3/93 1,900

Johnson, H.   Br 18C
* See 1993 Edition . . . .

Johnson, Harry   Eng 20C
O/B 8x10 Marsh Landscape Wes 3/93 550

Johnson, J. William   Am 19C
* See 1991 Edition . . . .

Johnson, Jonathan Eastman   Am 1824-1906
O/B 12x9 The Chimney Sweep 1863 Chr 5/93 145,500
O/C 12x20 Boy in the Maine Woods Sby 12/92 93,500
O/B 13x22 Sugar Camp Sby 12/92 63,250
O/B 7x11 Nantucket School Philosophy 76 Chr 12/92 44,000

Johnson, Larry   Am 20C
A/Al 73x30 Seated Woman, 1968 But 10/92 1,100

135

Johnson, Lester   Am 1919-
O/C 68x60 Emerging Crowd 1970 Sby 2/93 14,950
O/C 66x60 Untitled Sby 5/93 13,800
O/C 60x50 City Women (Ochre) Chr 11/92 9,900
O/C 28x28 Four Men with Hats 1970 Sby 2/93 7,763
O/Pa 40x26 Figure in Silhouette 1960 Sby 2/93 2,530
O/C 20x30 Dusk 1962 Sby 2/93 2,300
O/C 22x28 Park Scene Sby 2/93 2,185
O/Pa 40x27 Head of a Man Sby 6/93 1,840
Johnson, M.   Am 20C
O/B 18x24 Study with Figures Sel 12/92 80
Johnson, Marshall   Am 1850-1921
O/C 25x30 Gaff Rigged Cat Boat Doy 5/93 11,550
O/C 18x14 Two Sailing Vessels Passing Eld 11/92 1,045
Johnson, P.   Am 20C
O/C 28x26 Young Spanish Girl 27 Hnd 5/93 300
Johnson, Robert   Aut 1890-1964
* See 1993 Edition . . . .
Johnson, Sidney Yates   Br 19C
* See 1992 Edition . . . .
Johnston, Alexander   Br 1815-1891
* See 1993 Edition . . . .
Johnston, Frances-Anne   Can 1910-1987
O/B 16x12 Still Life Wine and Fruit Sbt 5/93 528
Johnston, Frank Hans   Can 1888-1949
O/B 12x16 Winter Solitude on Northern River Sbt 11/92 . . 16,720
O/M 26x40 Children of the Wilds Sbt 11/92 13,200
G/Pa 20x15 Autumn Landscape Sbt 5/93 12,100
O/B 25x30 Hour of Enchantment Sbt 11/92 3,960
O/B 18x21 Winter Sun on the Wye Sbt 11/92 3,740
O/C 24x20 River in Spring '11 Sbt 11/92 3,520
O/Pn 16x20 Early Snow Sbt 5/93 2,860
G/Pa 10x14 Lilloet, B.C. Sbt 5/93 1,980
O/B 12x14 Great Bear Lake '39 Sbt 5/93 1,760
O/B 12x16 Serenity Sbt 5/93 1,320
G/Pa 8x6 Moonlight Sbt 11/92 880
G/Pa 10x14 Tree in a Landscape Sbt 11/92 792
Johnston, John R.   Am 19C
* See 1993 Edition . . . .
Johnston, R. L.   Am 20C
O/Cb 20x16 Blossom Trees and Sheep Fre 10/92 130
Johnston, Reuben Le Grande   Am 1850-1918
O/Pn 14x18 Flock in a Country Meadow Wes 10/92 522
O/B 20x16 Sheep in a Meadow Slo 4/93 450
G/Pa 10x13 Farmyard Mys 12/92 248
Johnston, Ynez   Am 1920-
* See 1993 Edition . . . .
Johnstone, Henry James   Br 1835-1907
* See 1991 Edition . . . .
Johnstone, John Young   Can 1887-1930
O/Cb 5x7 Snowy Street Chr 12/92 1,430
Joli, Antonio   It 1700-1777
O/C 10x30 View of Messina from Sea Sby 1/93 54,625
Jolivard, Andre   Fr 1787-1851
* See 1992 Edition . . . .
Jolyet, Philippe   Fr 1832-1908
* See 1993 Edition . . . .
Joncherie, Gabriel Germain   Fr 1824-
O/C 18x15 La Chaufferette Aux Oeufs 1842 Chr 5/93 1,610
Jones, Adrian   Br 1845-1938
O/C 24x36 Mare and Foal But 5/93 2,300
Jones, Allan   Am 1937-
* See 1993 Edition . . . .
Jones, Amy   Am 1899-
O/C 24x30 St. Marks, Venice 1973 Hnd 5/93 950
Jones, Bradley
* See 1992 Edition . . . .
Jones, C.   Am 20C
W/Pa 17x25 Bridge and Castle 1973 Hnd 12/92 150
W/Pa 15x20 Harbor Scene Hnd 12/92 150
Jones, Charles   Eng 1836-1892
* See 1993 Edition . . . .

Jones, Daniel Adolphe Robert   Bel 1806-1874
* See 1990 Edition . . . .
Jones, F. Eastman   Am 19C
* See 1992 Edition . . . .
Jones, Francis & Jones, Hugh   Am 1857-1932
O/C/B 48x96 Threshing Grain Hnd 5/93 8,00
Jones, Francis Coates   Am 1857-1932
O/C 36x30 Friends Chr 12/92 38,50
P/Pa/B 13x16 Lady with a Lyre Chr 3/93 13,8
O/Pn 13x9 Mother and Child 88 But 6/93 2,3
Jones, Hugh & Jones, Francis   Am 1848-1927
O/C/B 48x96 Threshing Grain Hnd 5/93 8,00
Jones, Hugh Bolton   Am 1848-1927
O/C 12x23 Cows by a Stream Sby 3/93 10,92
O/C 24x40 Spring Landscape Sby 9/92 8,80
O/C 14x20 Sun Raked Forest Path Doy 5/93 4,40
O/C 16x22 Stream/A Spring Landscape Skn 5/93 3,19
O/C 20x25 Summer Landscape Sby 9/92 2,0
W/Pa 12x15 Quiet Stream But 6/93 1,1
Jones, Jessie Barrows   Am 1865-1944
W/Pa 10x13 Brooklyn Bridge Hnd 5/93 . . . . 3(
Jones, Joe   Am 1909-1963
W/Pa 15x21 Beach Scene Hnd 12/92 35
Jones, Lawrence A.   Am 20C
W&H/Pa 14x18 Beach/Jackson Park, Chicago 1946 Skn 3/93 16
Jones, Mildred   Am 1899-1991
O/B 16x20 The Prize Winner 1956 Yng 2/93 1
Jones, Paul   Br a 1856-1888
* See 1992 Edition . . . .
Jones, Samuel John Egbert   Br a 1820-1849
* See 1993 Edition . . . .
Jones, William   a 18C
O/C 61x36 Portrait of a Young Girl 1749 Chr 10/92 15,40
Jones, William F.   Am 1815-
O/C 31x25 Young Woman with Letter 1849 Hnd 5/93 . . . . . . 7(
Jonge   Dut 20C
O/C 24x30 Man with Team of Oxen Hnd 3/93 55
Jongkind, Johan Barthold   Dut 1819-1891
O/C 12x9 Embouchure Avec Quelques Voiliers 62 Sby 2/93 16,10
W&Cw/Pa 5x10 La Cote de St. Andre 1878 Chr 2/93 3,8
Jonnevold, Carl Henrik   Am 1856-1930
O/C 18x22 Late Afternoon But 6/93 . . . . 8(
Jonniaux, Alfred   Bel 1822-
* See 1991 Edition . . . .
Jonson, Cornelis   Dut 1593-1661
* See 1990 Edition . . . .
Jonson, Raymond   Am 1891-1982
O/C 35x41 Cliff Dwellings #4 '28 Chr 12/92 88,00
O/C 23x31 Canyon De Chelly 1928 Sby 5/93 63,0
O/B 20x16 Abstract with Pink and Black 50 Chr 12/92 3,5
Jonzen, Basil
O/M 20x24 Flowers and Fruit Sby 6/93 . . . . 4(
Joostens, Paul   20C
* See 1990 Edition . . . .
Jopling, Louise   Br 1843-
* See 1992 Edition . . . .
Jordaens, Hans   Dut 1616-1680
* See 1992 Edition . . . .
Jordaens, Jacob   Flm 1593-1678
* See 1993 Edition . . . .
Jordan, N.   Br 19C
O/C 29x40 Cleopatra 1893 But 5/93 1,1
Jordan, Rudolf   Ger 1810-1887
* See 1992 Edition . . . .
Jorgensen, Christian A.   Am 1860-1935
O/C/B 24x44 Yosemite Valley '09 But 3/93 4,4
O/C 15x26 San Francisco Bay Mys 12/92 3,1
O/C 15x26 By the Bay 1917 But 6/93 3,1
W/Pa/B 15x11 California in the Mariposa Grove Sby 9/92 . . . 9
W/Pa 15x10 House Along Cliff's Edge But 6/93 6
W/Pa 16x10 Mexican Woman in a Doorway 91 But 6/93 . . . 5

Joris, Pio It 1843-1921
* See 1993 Edition . . . .
Jorn, Asger Dan 1914-1973
O/C 22x26 Den Lille Famille Octopus 1953 Sby 5/93 23,000
Joseph, Albert Fr 1868-1952
O/C 19x26 Paysage d'hiver en Creuse 1905 Chr 11/92 2,200
Joseph, Jacques Francois Fr
* See 1991 Edition . . . .
Joseph, Jasmin Hai 20C
* See 1992 Edition . . . .
Joseph, Julian Am 20C
* See 1991 Edition . . . .
Josephi, Isaac A. Am 1934-
W/Iv 4x3 Miniature Portrait of a Lady 1901 Eld 4/93 440
Jouas, Charles Fr 1866-1942
W/Pa 27x36 Building the Paris Metro Chr 2/93 5,500
Joullin, Amedee Am 1862-1917
O/C 16x30 Marsh at Sunset, Mt. Tamalpais But 3/93 4,950
Jourdain, Roger Joseph Fr 1845-1918
* See 1993 Edition . . . .
Jourdan, Adolphe Fr 1825-1889
* See 1992 Edition . . . .
Jourdan, Jacques Jean Raoul Fr 1880-1916
O/C 65x73 Afternoon Tea Sby 5/93 11,500
Jourdeuil, Louis Marie Adrien Fr 1849-1907
* See 1992 Edition . . . .
Jousset, Claude Fr 1935-
O/C 20x24 Harbor Scene Dum 4/93 1,000
Jouvenet, Jean Fr 1644-1717
* See 1993 Edition . . . .
Joy, George Williams Eng 1844-1925
* See 1993 Edition . . . .
Joy, Thomas Musgrave Br 1812-1866
O/C 30x25 Charing Cross to Bank Omnibus Sby 5/93 . . . 17,250
O/C 28x37 The Barber of Seville 1861 Sby 2/93 4,600
Juarez, Jose Mex 1642-1698
* See 1990 Edition . . . .
Juarez, Roberto 20C
* See 1992 Edition . . . .
Judd, Donald Am 1928-
* See 1993 Edition . . . .
Judson, Minnie Lee Am 1865-1938
O/C 25x30 Landscape with Begonias Sby 9/92 1,430
Judson, William Lees Am 1842-1928
O/C 30x50 Live Oaks at Sunset Mor 6/93 4,125
O/C 30x50 View of Grand Canyon But 6/93 4,025
O/C/C 30x50 Live Oaks at Sunset Mor 6/93 1,100
O/C 15x25 Oak Glen But 10/92 990
W/Pa 13x21 Harbour View 1878 Sbt 11/92 836
O/C 18x24 Sunset in a Clearing But 6/93 748
O/C 15x18 Sichel Moon But 6/93 575
W/Pa 12x19 Gathering Leaves But 6/93 460
P/Pa 7x9 Eucalyptus Coastal Mor 2/93 450
Juel, Jens 1745-1802
O/C 29x23 Portrait of a Lady 1778 Chr 1/93 16,500
Juergens, Alfred Am 1866-1934
* See 1993 Edition . . . .
Jules, Mervin Am 1912-
* See 1993 Edition . . . .
Julien, Joseph Bel 19C
O/C 20x28 Maidservant with Cows Slo 5/93 2,750
Jullian Fr 20C
W/Pa 22x30 Female Figures Afloat Mys 12/92 715
Jund, Carl Ove Julian Dan 1857-1936
* See 1990 Edition . . . .
Jung, Charles Jacob Am 1880-1940
* See 1992 Edition . . . .
Jungblut, Johann Ger 1860-1912
* See 1993 Edition . . . .
Jutsum, Henry Br 1816-1869
O/C 12x18 Landscape Near Windsor Castle Wlf 9/92 500
Jutz, Carl Ger 1838-1916
* See 1993 Edition . . . .

Juvin, Juliette
* See 1992 Edition . . . .
Kacere, John Am 1920-
O/C 38x78 Allison 83 Sby 10/92 14,300
Kadar, Bela Hun 1877-1955
G/Pa 12x19 Landscape Houses Figures Sby 6/93 1,380
Pe/Pa 6x8 Horses and Figures in a Landscape Sby 10/92 . . . 550
Kader, Abel Am 1852-1940
W/Pa 17x14 Winter Visit Yng 5/93 150
Kadlacsik, Laszlo Hun 1925-1989
O/Pn 22x18 Still Life with Sunflowers But 10/92 5,500
Kaelin, Charles Salis Am 1858-1929
O/C 25x30 Woods in Winter Wes 3/93 6,710
O/C 10x14 Seascape Wlf 12/92 1,000
Kaelin, Martin Am 1926-
O/C 30x40 Mummer's Parade Fre 10/92 500
O/C 32x43 City in the Rain Fre 10/92 475
O/C 40x42 Globe Theater Boardwalk Fre 10/92 450
Kaemmerer, Frederik Hendrik Dut 1839-1902
O/C 10x6 The Bride Hnd 10/92 2,800
Kaercher, Amalie Ger 19C
O/C 17x20 Still Life Flowers on Ledge 1859 Sby 5/93 . . . 20,700
Kahill, Joseph B. Am 1882-
O/C 12x16 Maine Foliage Brd 8/93 220
Kahler, Carl Aus 1855-
O/Ab 12x14 White Cat on a Red Cushion Eld 8/93 1,320
Kahlo, Frida Mex 1910-1954
* See 1993 Edition . . . .
Kahn, Max Am 1903-
O/C 32x37 Return at Evening, #4 1971 Hnd 6/93 425
O/C 26x32 Yellow Cliffs Hnd 6/93 425
Kahn, Wolf Am 1927-
O/C 24x30 Mr. Hamilton's Heifer's Sby 3/93 5,175
Kalish, Lionel Am 20C
O/B 10x14 Along a Village Street Sby 3/93 2,415
Kalla-Priechenfried, J. Ger 19C
* See 1993 Edition . . . .
Kallemeyer, Minnie Can 20C
O/C 26x33 At Dock, Halifax, Nova Scotia FHB 3/93 300
Kallmorgen, Friedrich Ger 1856-1924
* See 1992 Edition . . . .
Kallos, Paul
O/C 36x29 Untitled 55 Sby 6/93 1,380
Kalraet, Abraham 1642-1722
O/Pn 20x26 Cavaliers Halted Before an Inn Chr 5/93 17,250
Kalwinski, Igor Con 20C
O/B 22x19 Girl with Pink Ribbon Lou 6/93 100
Kammerer, Frederik Hendrik Dut 1839-1902
* See 1992 Edition . . . .
Kandinsky, Wassily Rus 1866-1944
W&Pl/Pa/B 13x19 Zwei Bewegungen 1924 Chr 11/92 . . . 550,000
G&W/Pa 20x13 Grun Im Kreis 27 Sby 5/93 222,500
I&S/Pa 8x17 Untitled 18 Sby 11/92 41,250
Kane, John Am 1860-1934
* See 1992 Edition . . . .
Kann, Frederick I. Am 1886-1965
* See 1992 Edition . . . .
Kantor, Morris Am 1896-1974
* See 1993 Edition . . . .
Kantor, Tadeusz Pol 1915-
* See 1992 Edition . . . .
Kapp, Albert Am 20C
O/B 16x20 Blessing of the Fleet Yng 2/93 200
Karasz, Ilonka Am 1896-
Pe&G/Pa 19x12 Paddock at Belmont Raceway Ih 11/92 . . . 1,300
Karatsonyi, Andrew Am 20C
O/C 16x20 Bustin' a Bronco 1909 Brd 2/93 1,100
Karfiol, Bernard Am 1886-1952
O/C 35x46 Virginie by the Sea (Ogunquit) Brd 8/93 8,525
O/C 36x27 Forest With Two Nudes Brd 8/93 4,125
W&I/Pa 10x12 Two Seated Women Sby 5/93 920
MM/M 24x20 Woman with Red Hair Fre 4/93 425
O/B 16x12 Nude Yng 2/93 400

Kargl, Rudolph   Aus 1878-1942
W/Pa 9x12 Bel Halthum (Walzmann) Mys 3/93 420
Karlovszky, Bertalan   Hun 1858-
O/C 32x42 Teaching the Dog New Tricks Chr 5/93 29,900
Karlovszky-Berci   Hun 19C
* See 1992 Edition . . . .
Karpoff, Ivan
* See 1992 Edition . . . .
Kase, Paul G.
O/B 9x12 Landscape Ald 9/92 150
Kass, Deborah   20C
A/C 63x84 His 1987 Chr 5/93 1,035
Kasyn, John   Can 1926-
O/B 24x18 King Street in Parkdale Sbt 5/93 3,960
O/B 12x10 Approaching Evening, Toronto Sbt 5/93 1,144
O/B 10x8 Old House in Weston Sbt 11/92 1,100
W/Pa 7x5 On Sherbourne St. North Sbt 11/92 660
W/Pa 7x5 Behind Sackville Street Sbt 5/93 572
W/Pa 7x5 Backyard in Snow Sbt 11/92 484
W/Pa 6x8 Stucco House '74 Sbt 5/93 352
Kato, Kentaro   Am 1889-1926
O/C 24x30 Tidal Pool in Gloucester 1920 But 12/92 1,540
Katz, Alex   Am 1927-
O/C 96x72 Ada with Glasses Chr 11/92 77,000
O/C 43x47 Salute #4 Sby 5/93 34,500
O/M 12x12 Ada 66 Sby 5/93 14,375
O/M 20x16 Ada in the Woods 84 Sby 10/92 13,750
O/M 9x12 Alex and Ada 80 Chr 10/92 9,900
O/M 13x12 Study for Peter and Lauren 88 Sby 5/93 9,775
O/M 12x14 Vincent at Window 84 Sby 10/92 7,700
O/B 20x16 Maine Woods Brd 8/93 1,980
Katz, Ethel   Am 1898-1975
W/Pa 15x22 Manhattan; Brooklyn: Pair Lou 6/93 225
Katz, Hilda   Am 1909-
W&G/Pa 40x28 Grapes of Thorns 1940 Mys 3/93 358
Kaub-Casalonga, Alice   Fr 1875-
O/C 71x79 An Afternoon of Sewing Chr 2/93 10,450
Kauffman   Con 19C
* See 1992 Edition . . . .
Kauffman, Craig
* See 1992 Edition . . . .
Kauffmann, Hugo Wilhelm   Ger 1844-1915
O/Pn 15x18 Musical Talent 97 Sby 5/93 82,250
O/Pn 10x8 Old Man with a Pipe Chr 2/93 8,800
Kaufman, Isidor   Aus 1853-1921
* See 1992 Edition . . . .
Kaufmann, A. or R.   Con 20C
O/Pn 6x4 Shepherdess with Flock Autumn Slo 4/93 625
Kaufmann, Adolf   Aus 1848-1916
O/C 25x39 Along the Country Lane 1897 Sby 10/92 5,500
Kaufmann, Ferdinand   Am 1864-1942
O/C 25x30 Carriers of Commerce But 3/93 4,400
O/B 12x16 Cargo Ships in Harbor Mor 6/93 1,980
O/B 12x16 Street Motif-Pasadena, CA Mor 6/93 1,210
O/Cb 20x16 Male Figure Study 1937 Mor 2/93 700
Kaufmann, Isidor   Aus 1853-1921
O/Pn 17x21 Discussing the Talmud Sby 10/92 176,000
O/Pn 20x15 Young Woman in the Synagogue Sby 10/92 . . . 110,000
O/Pn 14x11 Young Chassidic Boy Sby 2/93 76,750
O/Pn 9x12 Young Rabbi with Blue Tallis Sby 2/93 68,500
O/Pn 5x7 Portrait of a Rabbi Sby 2/93 24,150
Kaufmann, Karl   Aus 1843-1901
O/Pn 12x8 Santa Maria Della Salute Chr 5/93 4,025
O/C 18x27 River Landscape by Moonlight 1891 Sby 1/93 . . 2,875
O/Pn 12x19 Canal Scene, Venice But 11/92 1,650
O/Pn 17x7 Entrance to the Grand Canal Sby 1/93 1,035
Kaula, Lee Lufkin   Am 1865-1957
O/C 29x24 Still Life Gladiolas and Lilies 1917 Skn 3/93 . . . 1,320
Kaula, William Jurian   Am 1871-1953
O/C 32x39 Over the Pond But 12/92 9,350
O/B 24x29 View Through Trees Brd 2/93 3,300
O/B 18x23 Hill Top Haying New Ipswich, NH Skn 5/93 . . . 2,860
O/B 18x21 Sugaring Time Brd 8/93 2,090
W&G/B 21x27 Peterboro Hills, New Hampshire Brd 2/93 . . . 1,870
O/B 10x13 Coastal Scene Mys 3/93 1,485

O/B 21x25 Foothills, Spring Brd 8/93 1,320
O/C 15x18 Across the Meadow, Afternoon Skn 11/92 990
O/B 10x13 Landscape Mys 3/93 990
O/B 18x15 Pond and Meadow Brd 8/93 990
O/B 11x13 The Wooden Bridge Brd 8/93 990
O/B 8x10 Mountain Snow Brd 2/93 330
O/B 8x11 Landscape Mys 3/93 302
Kaulbach, Hermann   Ger 1846-1909
O/Pn 25x19 The Jester's Audience Sby 10/92 46,750
O/Pn 9x7 A Lady with a Book Hnd 5/93 4,400
Kaupisch, Leonard   Ger 1878-
P/Pa 9x13 Pair of Mountain Scapes Hnd 9/92 200
Kavanaugh, Marion   Am 1876-1954
* See 1992 Edition . . . .
Kavel, Francois Martin   Fr 20C
O/C 32x24 Seated Elegant Lady Chr 2/93 4,620
Kawakubo, Masana   Jap
W&Pe/Pa 19x13 Pagoda Sby 10/92 1,100
Kawara, On   1933-
A/C 10x13 8.0KT.1976 Chr 2/93 24,200
Rs/Pa 4x6 I Got Up At... 1973 Sby 10/92 12,100
Kayanowk, J.   Con 20C
* See 1992 Edition . . . .
Kaye, Otis   Am 1885-1974
O/Pn 30x25 U.S. Musical Notes Sby 9/92 101,200
O/Pn 15x19 Gun Fight O. Kaye's Corral Sby 9/92 52,250
O/Pn 7x10 Pennies Make Dollars Chr 9/92 18,700
Pe/Pa 2x6 Two Dollar Bill 1953 Sby 9/92 2,750
Kayn, Hilde   Am 1906-1950
O/C 36x28 Two Girls Sby 9/92 1,540
Kearfott, Robert   Am 1890-
O/C 22x22 Old Adobe, Monterey 1920 But 6/93 4,025
Kearns, Jerry   20C
* See 1990 Edition . . . .
Keelhoff, Frans & Verboeck., E   Bel 1820-1893
* See 1993 Edition . . . .
Keener, Anna   Am 1895-
O/C 26x32 Western Landscape Brd 8/93 4,400
Keffer, Frances   Am 1881-1953
O/B 11x14 Autumn Landscape Mor 2/93 700
Kehoe, Patrice   Am 1952-
O&L/C 79x94 Overend Over 1982 Slo 4/93 700
Keil, Bernardt   Dan 1624-1687
O/C 35x27 Two Women Making Lace Sby 10/92 14,300
Keinholz, Ed   Am 1927-
* See 1992 Edition . . . .
Keirincx, Alexander   Flm 1600-1652
* See 1991 Edition . . . .
Keiserman, Franz   Sws 1765-1833
* See 1990 Edition . . . .
Keith, Dora Wheeler   Am 1857-1940
* See 1992 Edition . . . .
Keith, William   Am 1839-1911
O/C 14x21 Near the Russian River 76 But 3/93 16,500
O/Pn 22x26 A Woodland Path But 6/93 8,050
O/C 24x18 Sierra Landscape 78 But 6/93 6,900
O/C 10x15 Figures on Mountainous Path But 6/93 5,750
O/C 22x27 Golden Sunset But 10/92 4,950
O/Pn 20x26 Storm Clouds 02 But 6/93 4,888
O/C 20x14 Hiking the Trail But 3/93 4,675
O/C 24x36 Evening Chr 5/93 4,025
O/C 24x36 Wooded Landscape with Cattle 190? Mor 6/93 . 3,575
O/B 13x15 Wooded Interior But 10/92 3,300
O/C 25x30 Under the Oak Tree But 10/92 3,025
O/C 18x27 Landscape with Trees and Women Dum 9/92 . . 3,000
O/C 18x28 Forest Clearing with Buildings '85 Lou 12/92 . . 2,700
O/C 38x38 Bright Sky at Sunset Hnd 5/93 2,600
O/Pn 6x10 Pastoral Landscape But 3/93 2,475
O/C 19x29 Autumn But 10/92 2,200
O/C 16x26 California Sunset Brd 8/93 1,430
O/Pn 5x9 Inlet on a Cloudy Day But 6/93 1,380
W/Pa 10x17 San Francisco Bay '88 But 6/93 1,380
O/C 13x16 Morgan's Hill Doy 11/92 1,100
O/B 11x14 Landscape with Pond Hnd 9/92 700

O/C 15x11 California Landscape Chr 5/93 575
O/C 30x25 Portrait of a Woman Lou 3/93 550

Keller, Adolphe   20C
* See 1990 Edition . . . .

Keller, Arthur Ignatius   Am 1866-1924
O/Cb 18x23 Woman in Crowd of Children Ilh 11/92 1,000
O&R/C 21x40 Crowd Aboard Sinking Ship Ilh 11/92 900
W&G/Pa 21x14 Caravan Rescuing a Damsel Chr 12/92 550

Keller, C.   Ger 19C
O/C 23x12 Mountain Landscape Hnd 3/93 400

Keller, Edgar Martin   Am 1868-1932
O/Pw 12x16 In the Boat Yard Mor 2/93 700

Keller, Ferdinand   Ger 1842-1922
* See 1993 Edition . . . .

Keller, Henry G.   Am 1870-1949
W/Pa 11x15 Elsass Wlf 9/92 750
W/Pa 15x20 Seascape Wlf 9/92 750
W/Pa 15x20 Afternoon, Foot of the Wetterstein Wlf 9/92 400
W/Pa 20x14 Canyon Landscape Wlf 5/93 400
O/C 18x24 Still Life Wlf 12/92 325
O/C 16x20 Mountainous Landscape Wlf 9/92 200
O/B 7x11 View of Cleveland 1902 Wlf 5/93 175

Keller-Reutlingen, Paul W.   Ger 1854-1920
* See 1993 Edition . . . .

Kelley, Mike   1954-
A/Pa 49x36 Double Hierarchy: Two Sby 11/92 11,000
A/Pa 24x32 Garbage Drawing #37 Chr 2/93 3,850
A/Pa 24x32 Garbage Drawing #67 Chr 2/93 1,980

Kelly, Ellsworth   Am 1923-
O/C 112x115 Blue White 1980 Chr 11/92 209,000
O/C 34x13 Brooklyn Bridge '58 Chr 2/93 55,000
Pe/Pa 10x13 Oak (Two Drawings) 1986 Sby 5/93 9,200
H/Pa 12x9 Sea Grapes 1988 Sby 5/93 9,200
Pe/Pa/B 13x10 Untitled, No. 3, 4, 5 Sby 10/92 8,250
I/Pa 12x6 2 Flower Drawings 1989 Sby 5/93 6,325
Pe/Pa/B 10x13 Branchs of Leaves 86 Sby 10/92 5,500
H/Pa 45x40 Untitled Chr 10/92 2,860

Kelly, James P.   Am 1854-1893
O/B 17x13 Needlepoint Chr 9/92 3,850

Kelly, Leon   Am 1901-
O/C 19x25 Seated Nude Fre 4/93 425
Pe/Pa 31x22 The Moon Man 1954 Hnd 5/93 100

Kelly, Robert George Talbot   Eng 1861-1934
W/B 21x29 Village Along the Nile 1912 Chr 2/93 1,980

Kelly, Sir Gerald   Br 1879-1972
* See 1990 Edition . . . .

Kelpe, Paul   Am 1902-1985
* See 1991 Edition . . . .

Kemble, Edward Windsor   Am 1861-1933
Pl/Pa 14x11 Two: Stevedore; The Apple Sel 2/93 150

Kemeny, Nandor   Hun 1885-
* See 1993 Edition . . . .

Kemm, Robert   Br -1885
O/C 20x24 Clamming Chr 5/93 5,175

Kemmer, Hans   Ger a 1495-1554
* See 1990 Edition . . . .

Kemp-Welch, Lucy
G,W&C/Pa 56x37 Women's Work at the Great War Sby 6/93 . 805

Kendall, William Sergeant   Am 1869-1938
O/C 21x21 Autumn Landscape Sby 3/93 4,888
O/C 21x21 Autumn Landscape with Tree Shadows Sby 3/93 4,600
O/Pn 16x13 Tongues of Fire Sby 3/93 1,035

Kennedy, Cecil   Br 1905-
* See 1992 Edition . . . .

Kennedy, David Johnston   Am 1817-1898
* See 1993 Edition . . . .

Kennedy, John William   Am 1903-
O/C 30x36 New York Skyline Sby 9/92 2,200

Kennington, Thomas Benjamin   Br 1856-1916
* See 1991 Edition . . . .

Kensett, John Frederick   Am 1816-1872
O/C 10x17 Beach at Newport Sby 12/92 104,500

O/C 18x24 A Passing Shower 1848 Chr 5/93 43,700
O/C 10x18 Along the Shore Sby 12/92 33,000
O/C 14x24 Late Summer Chr 3/93 23,000
O/C 13x16 Mist Over the Lake 69 Chr 9/92 19,800
O/C 12x16 Mountain Vista Wes 3/93 10,450
Pe/Pa 10x14 Lake George Sby 9/92 1,210
Pe/Pa 5x8 Steamship by the Shore '68 Sby 9/92 935

Kent, Rockwell   Am 1882-1971
O/C 20x30 Tug, Barges, Men on Hudson 1904 Brd 8/93 . . 28,600
O/C 28x38 Maine Coast Hnd 9/92 28,000
S/Pa 6x10 Holsteinborg, Godhaven Chr 12/92 3,080
S/Pa 6x10 Gabthaab Fiord and Disco Chr 12/92 2,740
Pe/Pa 10x8 Four Drawings Brd 8/93 633
Pe/Pa 5x4 Three Sketches Brd 8/93 572
Pe/Pa 5x8 Fishermen Brd 8/93 187
Pe/Pa 5x6 Horse-Drawn Wagon Brd 8/93 165

Kenyon, Henry R.   Am -1926
* See 1993 Edition . . . .

Keokkeok, Johannes Hermanus B.   Dut 1840-1912
* See 1992 Edition . . . .

Kepes, Gyorgy   Am 1906-
* See 1993 Edition . . . .

Kerg, Theo   1909-
O/C 18x22 Construction d'un Barrage Chr 11/92 550

Kerkam, Earl   Am 1890-1965
O/B 17x14 Three Works Sby 3/93 2,070
G&P/Pa 18x14 Figure with Blue Sby 2/93 575
G&P/Pa 18x15 Seated Figure Sby 2/93 575

Kerling, Anna E.
* See 1991 Edition . . . .

Kern, Hermann   Hun 1839-1912
O/C 14x20 Repairing the Bassoon 1900 Sby 2/93 7,475

Kernan, Joseph F.   Am 1878-1958
O/C 30x24 The Slugger Hnd 10/92 5,900
O/C 28x22 Trout Fisherman Emerging Ilh 5/93 5,000
O/C 22x20 Old Salt Sewing Sails Ilh 11/92 3,750
O/C 28x22 Snowball Fight Hnd 10/92 2,500
O/C 30x24 Turkey in the Straw Hnd 10/92 2,500
O/C 26x21 Model Ship Builder Hnd 10/92 1,900
O/C 13x12 Golfers Hnd 10/92 800

Kerr, Illingworth Holey   Can 1905-1989
O/B 12x16 Jack Pines, French River 1975 Sbt 11/92 792

Kerr, Vernon   Am -1982
O/M 20x16 Mendocino Headlands Mor 6/93 660
O/C 24x36 Quietude Mor 6/93 550

Kerrn, Hansine Sophie Joachimi   Dan 1826-1860
* See 1990 Edition . . . .

Ketteman, Erwin   Ger 1897-1971
O/C 24x32 Winterabend Bei Berchtesgaden Wes 10/92 1,430

Kettle, Tilly   Br 1735-1786
* See 1993 Edition . . . .

Keulemans, Johannes Gerardus   Dut 1842-1878
* See 1992 Edition . . . .

Kever, Jacob Simon Hendrick   Dut 1854-1922
O/C 19x23 Interior Genre Scene Dum 9/92 2,000

Kevorkian, Jean   Fr 1933-
O/C 24x29 Le Port de Douarnenez Doy 11/92 2,200
O/C 24x29 St. Mammes Doy 11/92 2,200

Key, Adraien Thomasz   Dut 1544-1590
O/C 41x31 Gentleman, Standing 1564 Chr 1/93 66,000

Key, John Ross   Am 1837-1920
O/C 18x38 Mt. Dixville - Franconia Plain '73 Skn 9/92 8,250
O/C 25x30 Monteray Bay, California Doy 11/92 3,850
O/B 14x21 World's Columbian Exhibition Hnd 10/92 2,800
Pe/Pa 15x25 Mountain Road 76 But 6/93 1,150

Key, William   1520-1568
* See 1993 Edition . . . .

Keyse, Thomas   1722-1800
O/C 15x11 Trompe L'Oeil London Gazette 1762 Sby 10/92 . 7,700

Keyser, Frederick Rudolph   Am 20C
O/C/B 38x47 Gladiolas on a Table Sby 9/92 2,640

Kezdi, E. Kovacs   Hun 20C
O/C 16x20 Parisian Street Scene Slo 5/93   500
Khnopff, Fernand   Bel 1858-1921
  * See 1992 Edition . . . .
Kick, Cornelis   1635-1681
O/C 24x19 Tulip, Snowball, Roses, Carnations Chr 5/93 . . 23,000
Kidder, Harvey   Am 1918-
  * See 1993 Edition . . . .
Kieczynski, Bodhan   Pol 1850-1916
  * See 1991 Edition . . . .
Kiederich, Paul Joseph   Ger 1809-1850
  * See 1991 Edition . . . .
Kiefer, Anselm   Ger 1945-
O/Bu 72x46 Birke (Birch) Chr 11/92 209,000
MM 34x46 Bruch Der Geffase Sby 5/93 200,500
MM 95x67 Lichtung (Clearing) Sby 11/92 181,500
O/Bu 26x37 How to Paint for Pleasure Chr 11/92   85,800
W/Pa 17x22 Margarethe Sulamit Sby 11/92   38,500
A&Ph 23x32 Gilgamesch 1981 Chr 11/92 26,400
A&Ph 23x31 Des Malers Atelier 1981 Chr 11/92 25,300
Ph 25x37 Das Goldenes Haar, Margarete Sby 5/93 17,250
Kienholz, Edward   Am 1927-
  * See 1992 Edition . . . .
Kiesel, Conrad   Ger 1846-1921
  * See 1992 Edition . . . .
Kiessling, Johann Paul Adolf   Ger 1836-1919
O/C 47x71 Europa Chr 5/93 36,800
Kihn, W. Langdon   Am 1898-1957
  * See 1993 Edition . . . .
Kikoine, Michel   Fr 1892-1968
O/C 29x19 Still Life Sby 6/93 4,600
Kilbourne, Samuel A.   Am 1836-1881
  * See 1993 Edition . . . .
Kilburne, George Goodwin   Br 1839-1924
W&H/Pa 9x12 In the Garden Sby 2/93 7,188
Killgore, Charles P.   Am 20C
  * See 1991 Edition . . . .
Kilpatrick, Aaron Edward   Am 1872-1953
O/C 20x30 Near Eagle Rock 1912 But 3/93 3,300
O/C 24x30 Oaks, Chorro Valley 1926 But 6/93 3,162
Kilvert, Benjamin Sayre Cory   Am 1881-1946
O/C 35x42 Blessing of the Fleet Lou 9/92 300
Kimball, Charles F.   Am 1835-1907
O/C 12x18 Houses Stroudwater River, Portland Brd 2/93 . . 4,180
O/C 10x16 Probably Stroudwater 1876 Brd 8/93 1,210
O/C 22x16 The Clearing 1878 Skn 11/92 770
Kimler, Wesley   Am 1953-
O/C 58x48 Untitled, 1987 But 10/92 2,750
Kinder, Maria Liszt   Am 1902-
O/C 25x30 Bass Rocks Yng 5/93 300
Kinder, Milton Robert   Am 1907-
W/Pa 11x15 Five Unframed Watercolors '79 Lou 12/92 175
Kindleberger, David   Am a 1900-1905
  * See 1992 Edition . . . .
Kindon, Mary Eliva   Br a 1881-1919
O/C 24x16 Portrait of Gentleman with Terrier Eld 8/93 . . . 1,100
King, Albert F.   Am 1854-1934
O/C 18x24 Still Life Peaches, Blueberries Skn 9/92 6,050
O/C 18x24 Still Life Apples and Grapes Skn 11/92 2,750
O/C 14x20 Apples by an Overturned Basket Wes 5/93 2,310
O/C 18x24 Grapes and Apples Wes 5/93 2,200
O/C/B 10x13 View Across the Field Slo 4/93 500
King, Charles Bird   Am 1786-1862
  * See 1992 Edition . . . .
King, Francis Scott   Am 1850-
  * See 1992 Edition . . . .
King, George W.   Am 1836-1922
O/C 18x30 Near Lake George, New York Lou 6/93 800
King, Haynes   Br 1831-1904
  * See 1993 Edition . . . .
King, John Yeend   Br 1855-1924
O/C 24x36 Waiting for the Ferry Fre 10/92 8,250
O/C 51x49 The Expected Arrival Sby 2/93 8,050

King, Mary
O/C 18x32 Pastoral Scene with Cows Grazing Eld 8/93 . . . 8(
King, Paul   Am 1867-1947
O/C 32x40 Harbor Scene Brd 2/93 . . . . 5,5(
O/C 18x22 Winter Landscape with Cabin Lou 6/93 . . . . . . 1,0(
King, William B.   Am 1880-1927
C/Pa 19x29 Man Kneeling at Woman's Bedside Ih 5/93 . . . . 4(
Kingman, Dong   Am 1911-1985
W/Pa 31x22 100 Fishermen Sby 3/93 . . . . 6,9(
W/Pa 22x30 Under the East River Drive 1956 Sby 9/92 . . . 4,2(
W/Pa 14x21 Figures Along a Beach 40 But 3/93 . . . . 2,7(
W&Pe/Pa 22x15 Lands End Light 36 But 3/93 . . . . 2,4(
W/Pa 16x23 Church at 15th Street 47 Sby 3/93 . . . . 1,8(
W/Pa 16x22 Pennsylvania Avenue 45 Sby 3/93 . . . . 1,4(
W/Pa 14x21 New York Buildings Mor 6/93 . . . . 1,4(
W/Pa 12x10 Grant Avenue But 6/93 . . . . 1,3(
W/Pb 20x29 Cornfields 40 Chr 12/92 . . . . 1,1(
W/Pa 19x25 The Parade Doy 11/92 . . . . 9(
Kingman, Eduardo   20C
  * See 1993 Edition . . . .
Kingsbury, Edward R.   Am -1940
O/B 8x10 Late Afternoon Yng 2/93 . . . . 1(
Kinkade, Thomas   Am 20C
O/B 24x30 Yosemite Clearing 1982 But 3/93 . . . . 3,0(
Kinley, Peter   Br 20C
  * See 1992 Edition . . . .
Kinnaird, Frederick Gerald   Br a 1864-1881
  * See 1993 Edition . . . .
Kinnaird, Henry J.   Br a 1880-1920
W/Pa/Cd 15x21 Cornfield Near Arundel Sby 1/93 . . . . . . 1,8(
W&G/Pa 14x21 A Sussex Cornfield Skn 6/92 . . . . 1,6(
O/C 16x24 Sheep on a Country Path Hnz 5/93 . . . . 6(
Kinnaird, J. G.
O/C 24x19 Girl with Lilacs Dum 9/92 . . . . 1,5(
Kinnell, K.   Am 20C
O/C 24x36 Wild Horses Fleeing the Storm 1966 Sby 3/93 . . 9(
Kinney, Margaret West   Am 1872-
O/Pn 15x18 Paris Park Scene Night 05 But 6/93 . . . . 2,8(
Kinsey, Alberta   Am 1875-1955
O/B 16x12 Summer Fragrance Wlf 5/93 . . . . 4(
Kinson, Francois Joseph   Flm 1771-1839
  * See 1992 Edition . . . .
Kinzel, Josef   Aus 1852-1925
  * See 1990 Edition . . . .
Kipness, Robert   Am 1931-
O/C 34x36 Landscape with House Hnd 3/93 . . . . 1,0(
Kippenberger, Martin   20C
  * See 1993 Edition . . . .
Kirafly, Verona A.   Am 1893-1925
O/C 30x25 Still Life 1936 Slo 5/93 . . . . 4(
Kirberg, Otto   Ger 1850-1926
  * See 1992 Edition . . . .
Kirby, Rollin   Am 1875-
Y&I/Pa 19x16 Tomorrow May Be Too Late Hnz 5/93 . . . . 5(
Kirchner, Ernst Ludwig   Ger 1880-1938
G&W/Pa 14x19 Paar in einer Landschaft 1919 Chr 11/92 . 63,80(
Kirchner, Eugen   Ger 1865-
O/C 30x40 Hauling Logs Lou 9/92 . . . . 1,0(
Kirchner, Otto   Ger 1887-1960
O/M 10x7 Character Studies Two Men: Pair Sel 9/92 . . . . 1,6(
O/M 10x7 Portrait of a Cardinal Seated Sel 9/92 . . . . . . 50(
Kirk, Frank C.   Am 1889-1963
O/C 30x30 A Studio Corner Chr 5/93 . . . . 1,3(
O/Cb 20x20 Autumn Landscape Slo 7/93 . . . . 15(
Kirkeby, Per   1938-
O/C 59x39 Billedtavel II Sby 11/92 . . . . 16,50(
Kirkpatrick, J. L.   Br 19C
O/C 16x12 Gallery at Seville Hnd 10/92 . . . . 60(
Kirnbock, R.   Con 19C
  * See 1993 Edition . . . .
Kirsch, Max E.
  * See 1993 Edition . . . .

Kischka, Isis Fr 1908-1974
O/C 20x8 Le Navire Ecole Sby 2/93 978
Kisling, Moise Pol 1891-1953
O/C 22x15 La Fillette Sby 5/93 61,900
O/C 29x21 Nu Assis Sby 11/92 60,500
O/C 15x22 Sanary Sur Mer 1937 Sby 10/92 46,750
O/C 16x13 Portrait de Jeune Fille Chr 10/92 39,600
O/C 9x6 Jeune Fille Chr 10/92 29,700
O/C 16x13 Portrait de jeune femme Chr 11/92 24,200
O/C 16x22 Les Fruits Sby 2/93 24,150
O/C 10x8 Tete de Femme Sby 10/92 14,300
W/Pa/B 11x15 Environs de St. Tropez 1917 Sby 10/92 8,800
Pe/Pa 20x13 Portrait de Femme Chr 5/93 3,450
Kissonergis, Ioannis Grk -1963
W/Pa 14x22 Peasants in a Rocky Landscape Chr 5/93 1,725
Kitaj, Robert B. 20C
O/C 30x24 Little Slum Picture Sby 5/93 51,750
Kitajima, Asaichi Jap 1877-1947
* See 1992 Edition . . . .
Kitchell, Hudson Mindell Am 1862-1944
O/C 40x60 River Landscape with Trees 1917 Sby 3/93 . . . 1,495
O/C 25x30 Golden Glow Yng 2/93 1,100
O/C 25x30 Wooded Landscape Yng 5/93 900
O/C 18x14 Moonlight Hnz 5/93 850
O/C 31x25 Woods Landscape Dum 1/93 550
Kittelsen, Theodor Nor 1857-1914
W/Pa 13x13 Farmhouse by a Wooded Path Chr 10/92 2,860
Klaerskou, Frederick Dan 1805-1891
* See 1990 Edition . . . .
Klaus, Joseph Bel 19C
* See 1990 Edition . . . .
Klee, Paul Sws 1879-1940
O/S 14x17 Gleitendes 1930 Chr 11/92 550,000
WG&Pl/Pa/B 19x12 Abstractions Maske 1924 Sby 11/92 . . 495,000
W&Pl/Pa 8x5 Gondel 1918 Chr 11/92 187,000
W/L/B 5x5 Revier Eines Katers 1919 Sby 5/93 51,750
G&Pe/Pa/B 13x8 Ohne Titel Chr 11/92 33,000
Y/Pa 12x8 Drang Vor Der Wanderung Sby 11/92 17,600
Pl/Pa/B 6x9 Toter wird abgeholt 1924 Chr 11/92 16,500
Kleemann, Ron Am 1937-
A/C 90x70 Erection Site Chr 2/93 1,100
Klein, Pat Am 20C
MM/C 72x96 Yellow Room, 1981 1981 But 4/93 1,265
Kleinert, Josef Edgar Aus 1859-
O/C 22x18 The Botanist Chr 5/93 2,070
Kleinschmidt, Paul Ger 1883-1949
* See 1991 Edition . . . .
Kleitsch, Joseph Am 1881-1931
O/C 18x24 Parenting Joys Mor 2/93 950
Klempner, Ernest Am 1867-1962
O/C 33x26 Young Lad 1932 Fre 4/93 325
Klever, Julius Sergius Rus 1850-1924
* See 1993 Edition . . . .
Kley, Heinrich Ger 1863-1945
Pl/Pa 15x11 Study Monkey, Man, and Beast Hnd 9/92 400
Kleyn, Lodewyk Johannes Dut 1817-1897
* See 1991 Edition . . . .
Klimley, Stan Am
G/Pa 9x20 High School Students Dancing Ih 11/92 450
G/Pa 14x14 Family at Restaurant Ih 5/93 400
Klimsch, Eugen Johann Georg Ger 1839-1896
* See 1993 Edition . . . .
Klimt, Gustav Aus 1862-1918
Pe/Pa 23x15 Portrait of a Woman Sby 5/93 40,250
Kline, Franz Aus 1910-1962
O/Pa 24x19 Warm Black and White '57 Sby 5/93 145,500
I/Pa 10x7 Untitled (Study for Leda) Sby 5/93 46,000
I/Pa 9x11 Untitled Sby 2/93 34,500
Br&I/Pa 18x21 Untitled Chr 11/92 24,200
O/Pn 17x18 Untitled Sby 5/93 19,650
I/Pa 8x11 Untitled Sby 10/92 6,600
G/Pa 10x9 Untitled 46 Chr 11/92 4,180
Br,I&G/Pa 11x8 Untitled Chr 11/92 3,300
I/Pa 15x13 Untitled Chr 2/93 825

Kline, L. A. Am 19C
O/C 11x9 Rabbi 1898 Hnd 9/92 50
Kling, Wendell
G/Pa 17x13 Couple in Forest Ih 5/93 800
Klingender, Louis Henry Weston Br 1861-
* See 1993 Edition . . . .
Klinkenberg, Johannes Karel C. Dut 1852-1924
O/Pn 23x16 A Dutch Canal Scene Chr 10/92 13,200
Klinker, Orpha Am 1891-1964
O/M 24x30 Desert Road, Monument Valley Lou 6/93 525
O/Cb 20x24 California Mountainside Mor 6/93 330
Klopper, Zan D. Am 1870-
O/C 22x40 The Violin Hnd 9/92 1,400
Kloss, Gene Am 1903-
O/C 24x30 Midwinter Moonlight Hnd 3/93 3,600
Kluge, Constantine Fr 1912-
O/C 32x46 Le Quai Conti Sby 2/93 7,188
O/C 32x51 Pont Des Arts Sby 2/93 7,188
O/C 29x46 L'Isle de la Cite et l'Institut Sby 6/93 5,175
O/C 24x29 Le Rond Point Sby 2/93 3,738
O/C 21x24 Parisian Street But 5/93 3,450
O/C 29x46 Le Chateau D'Ermenonville Sby 2/93 3,335
O/C 24x30 Le Marche Aux Fleurs Sby 10/92 3,025
O/C 24x30 Parisian Street Scene Sby 2/93 2,875
O/C 18x22 Marche Aux Fleurs Sby 2/93 2,415
O/C 24x36 La Vienne et L'Issoire But 11/92 1,870
O/C 24x29 Les Bateaux de Peche Hnd 10/92 1,800
Klumpe, Anna Elisabeth Am 1856-1942
* See 1992 Edition . . . .
Kluyver, Pieter Lodewyk Dut 1816-1900
O/Pn 13x18 Winter in Holland But 11/92 9,900
Klyn, J.
O/C 17x20 Dutch House Along River 1854 Dum 8/93 550
Knapp, Charles Wilson Am 1823-1900
O/C 28x46 Early Autumn Chr 12/92 11,000
O/C 20x36 Pastoral Landscape Brd 2/93 4,840
O/C 14x22 A Rocky Coast Chr 9/92 3,300
O/C 20x36 River Landscape with Fisherman Fre 10/92 . . . 2,700
Knaths, Karl Am 1891-1971
O/C 30x45 Aboriginal Chr 3/93 4,600
O/C 30x36 Duck-Decoy 1970 Sby 3/93 1,725
W/Pa 22x29 Still Life Wlf 12/92 325
Knaus, Ludwig Ger 1829-1910
O/Pn 7x6 A Young Girl Sby 2/93 11,213
O/C 10x8 Portrait of Young Girl Sby 5/93 4,888
O/Pn 8x12 Tavern Brawl Chr 5/93 3,450
O/Pn 6x5 Bearded Man Smoking a Pipe 1890 Wes 3/93 . . . 825
Knebel, Franz (Jr.) Sws 1809-1877
* See 1992 Edition . . . .
Knee, Gina Am 1898-
* See 1991 Edition . . . .
Knell, William Adolphus Br -1875
O/C 19x25 French Smugglers Chr 5/93 3,220
Kneller, Johann-Zacharias 1644-1702
* See 1993 Edition . . . .
Kneller, Sir Godfrey Eng 1648-1723
O/C 40x50 Portrait The Lord Euston 1685 Hnd 10/92 9,000
O/C 91x58 Portrait of a Nobleman Sby 5/93 3,450
Knerr, Harold H. Am 1883-1949
Pl/Pa 22x17 Sunday Comic "Katzenjammer Kids" Ih 11/92 . 1,200
Knight, Charles Robert Am 1874-1953
O/C 24x65 Blackfoot Star Lore: Three Studies Sby 9/92 . . 5,500
O/B 7x10 Hopeland 1921 Yng 5/93 200
Knight, Dame Laura Br 1877-1970
* See 1991 Edition . . . .
Knight, Daniel Ridgway Am 1839-1924
O/C 22x18 The Gardener's Daughter Chr 5/93 36,800
O/C 22x18 Brittany Girl Overlooking Stream Sby 5/93 34,500
O/C 22x18 Lovely Thought Chr 12/92 33,000
O/C 32x26 At the Water's Edge Chr 5/93 21,850
O/C 33x26 Apple Blossoms in Normandy Sby 9/92 16,500
W/Pa 25x19 Laundering by the River Sby 9/92 8,800
W,G&Pe/Pa 14x10 The Water Carrier Sby 9/92 5,500
O/Pn 10x7 French Woman at River 1876 Mys 12/92 1,760

W/Pa 13x9 Gardener and the Net Mender Hnd 9/92 1,400
Pl/Pa 13x6 Peasant Woman Chr 10/92 990

Knight, Louis Aston   Am 1873-1948
O/C 26x32 Flowers by the River Sby 3/93 10,063
O/C 32x26 Meandering River at Sunset Chr 10/92 9,350
O/C 33x46 La Seine Pres De Paris Sby 5/93 9,200
O/C 28x46 Riverside Path Hnd 3/93 8,400
O/C 26x32 The Thames at Streatley Doy 11/92 7,975
O/C 22x18 Spring Blossoms Sby 9/92 4,125
O/C 19x22 A Farmhouse Sby 9/92 1,980
O/C 10x13 Houses by a River Yng 5/93 1,100

Knight, William Henry   Br 1823-1863
O/C 24x19 The Traveling Grinder But 11/92 1,980

Knikker, Jan   Dut 1889-1957
O/B 16x20 Dutch Village Dum 5/93 300

Knikker, Jan Simon   Dut 1911-
O/C 24x12 Canal Scene Mys 3/93 275

Knip, Nicolaas Frederik   1742-1809
O/C 22x30 Still Life Tulips, Roses 1789 Sby 10/92 8,250

Knip, William Alexander   Dut 1883-1967
O/C 16x20 Thun, Lechateau Sel 12/92 700

Knochel, Hans   Czk 1850-
O/C 24x30 The Scale Tester Chr 2/93 1,650

Knoebel, Imi   1940-
A/Pa/Cd 47x39 Untitled 88 Sby 2/93 4,313

Knoop, August   Ger 1856-1900
* See 1992 Edition . . . .

Knopp, Imre   Hun 20C
* See 1992 Edition . . . .

Knott, Arthur Harold   Am 1883-1977
O/B 16x20 Santa Lucia Hills Mor 6/93 550

Knowles, Dorothy   Can 1927-
O/C 36x40 Storm Clouds '64 Sbt 11/92 2,640
O/C 27x35 Landscape Sbt 11/92 1,936

Knowles, Elizabeth McGillivray   Can 1866-1928
O/B 8x6 Blue Woods Sbt 11/92 264

Knowles, Farquhar McGillivray   Can 1859-1932
O/B 20x16 Hauling Wood Sbt 11/92 1,496

Knowles, George Sheridan   Br 1863-1931
O/C 22x16 Ready for a Walk 1908 Sby 10/92 10,450
O/C 22x30 Polishing the Brass Chr 10/92 4,950

Knox, John   Br 1778-1845
* See 1993 Edition . . . .

Knox, L. Rebecca   Am 20C
O/C 10x15 Day's End Brd 2/93 275

Knox, S. Harry   Am 19C
* See 1993 Edition . . . .

Knox, Susan Ricker   Am 1874-1960
O/C 39x30 Mother and Child Mys 12/92 385
W/Pa 8x11 Josefina Brd 2/93 220

Knox, Wilfred   Br 20C
O/C 28x42 Yacht "Sceptre" Eld 11/92 440

Kobayashi, Milton   Am 1950-
W/B 17x27 The Bathers 1979 Sby 12/92 4,950

Kobell, Wilhelm   Ger 1766-1855
* See 1991 Edition . . . .

Koberling, Bernd   1938-
O/Bu 33x43 Resting Cormorant 80 Chr 11/92 2,200

Koch, John   Am 1909-1978
O/C 40x50 Still Life at Dusk Sby 12/92 308,000
O/C 25x30 The Accident No. 2 68 Chr 5/93 129,000
O/C 26x40 Listeners, Setauket '72 Chr 5/93 51,750
O/C 24x20 Mr./Mrs. Joseph Lasky at Home '53 Sby 5/93 . 12,650
O/C/M 19x24 Eating Dinner Chr 5/93 3,910
Pe/Pa 5x11 Study of Child's Head Eld 8/93 110

Koch, Ludwig   Aus 1866-1934
* See 1990 Edition . . . .

Koch, S.   20C
O/Pn 7x5 Mischievous Kittens Slo 5/93 275

Kocher, Fritz   Am 1904-1973
O/C 23x32 Cottonwoods - 1940 '40 Mor 11/92 275

Kockert, Julius   Ger 1827-1918
O/C 12x14 Kahnfahrt auf dem Starnberger See Hnd 10/92 . 8,500

O/C 39x31 Johannes Feuer Sby 10/92 5,225

Koehler, Henry   Am 1927-
O/C 20x24 Jockeys Belmont Paddock 1961 Sby 6/93 17,250
O/C 20x30 Three Jockey Studies 1986 Sby 6/93 9,200

Koehler, Paul R.   Am 1866-1909
P/Pa 16x23 Landscape Mys 12/92 275

Koehler, Robert   Am 19C
* . . . .

Koekkoek, Barend Cornelis   Dut 1803-1862
W&Pl/Pa 6x8 Harbor Scene Lou 12/92 425

Koekkoek, H. & Van Leemputten   Dut 1843-1890
O/C 24x20 Heading Home Doy 5/93 4,840

Koekkoek, Hendrik Barend   Dut 1849-1909
* See 1993 Edition . . . .

Koekkoek, Hendrik Pieter   Dut 1843-1890
* See 1993 Edition . . . .

Koekkoek, Hermanus (Jr.)   Dut 1836-1909
* See 1993 Edition . . . .

Koekkoek, Hermanus (Sr.)   Dut 1815-1882
* See 1993 Edition . . . .

Koekkoek, Hermanus Willem   Dut 1867-1929
* See 1993 Edition . . . .

Koekkoek, Jan Hermanus   Dut 1778-1851
* See 1993 Edition . . . .

Koekkoek, Jan Hermanus Barend   Dut 1840-1912
* See 1992 Edition . . . .

Koekkoek, Marianus Adrianus   Bel 1833-1904
* See 1993 Edition . . . .

Koekkoek, Willem   Dut 1839-1895
O/Pn 16x13 Village Street Sby 5/93 12,650

Koelman, Jan   Dut 19C
W/Pa/B 11x8 Italian Peasant Woman Chr 5/93 1,955

Koen, Irma Renee   Am -1974
O/C 16x20 Rain in Valley; Golden Rain (2) Hnd 9/92 900
O/C 16x20 Market at Etla Hnd 9/92 650
O/C 20x24 White Mountains Hnd 9/92 475
O/B 12x12 Little Fantasy Hnd 9/92 170

Koeniger, Walter   Am 1881-1945
O/C 32x32 Winter Landscape Chr 12/92 12,100
O/C 21x24 River in Winter But 12/92 2,200
O/C 24x30 Stream in Winter Landscape Hnd 10/92 1,700
O/Ab 12x16 Early Winter Landscape Eld 8/93 440

Koerner, Henry   Am 1915-
O/C 22x27 Vineyards and Mountains 1960 Sby 9/92 550

Koerner, William Henry D.   Am 1878-1938
O/C 28x40 Make Believe 1930 Sel 12/92 2,400
O/C 28x40 Masqueraders 1930 Sby 3/93 2,070

Koester, Alexander Max   Ger 1864-1932
O/C 29x37 Zwei Madchen am Stickrahmen Chr 2/93 55,000
O/C 21x32 Enten Gehen Sby 5/93 54,625

Koets, Roelof   Dut 1592-1655
* See 1990 Edition . . . .

Koffermans, Marcellus   Dut 16C
* See 1990 Edition . . . .

Kogan, Moisey   1924-
O/C 35x48 Village Festival Chr 2/93 2,090

Kogan, Nina   Rus 1887-1942
* See 1991 Edition . . . .

Kogl, Benedict   Ger 1892-1969
* See 1993 Edition . . . .

Kohlmeyer, Ida   Am 1912-
* See 1991 Edition . . . .

Kohn, Irma   Am 20C
* See 1993 Edition . . . .

Kohn, W. Loengdan   Am 20C
O/C 22x36 Indian Brave in a Blizzard '41 Wes 10/92 412

Koken, Gustav   Ger 1850-1910
 * See 1993 Edition . . . .
Kokoschka, Oskar   Aus 1886-1980
 Pl/Pa 21x15 Studien zu 'Frau in Blau' 1920 Chr 10/92 . . . 24,200
Kolar, Jiri   Czk 1914-
 L/B 18x13 Seven Untitled Collages (Butterfly) 69 Chr 5/93 . 5,750
 L/B 10x14 Eleven Untitled Collages (Car) 80 Chr 5/93 5,175
Kolbe, Ernst   Ger 1876-1945
 * See 1992 Edition . . . .
Kolbe, Georg   Ger 1877-1947
 * See 1993 Edition . . . .
Kolesnikoff, Sergie   Rus 1889-
 O/C 18x26 Rocky Outcrop Chr 2/93 110
Kolitz, Louis   Ger 1845-1914
 * See 1991 Edition . . . .
Kollack, Mary   Am 1840-
 * See 1992 Edition . . . .
Koller, Wilhelm   Aus 1829-1884
 O/Pn 31x41 Faust and Mephistopheles Sby 10/92 27,500
Kollner, Augustus   Am 1813-
 * See 1993 Edition . . . .
Kollwitz, Kathe   Ger 1867-1945
 C/Pa 19x26 Bildhauer Opanos Sby 5/93 17,250
 C/Pa 17x19 Zwei Sitzende Frau Sby 2/93 6,900
Kolsenikoff, Sergei   Rus 1889-
 * See 1990 Edition . . . .
Komar & Melamid   20C
 O/C 84x60 Stalin With Hitler's Remains Chr 10/92 19,800
 O/C 72x47 Natasha with the Bust of Stalin Chr 5/93 16,100
Komoski, Bill   20C
 A/C 47x32 Untitled 86 Chr 2/93 1,100
Konchalovsky, Piotr   Rus 1876-1956
 O/C 15x19 Still Life Mys 12/92 220
Koninck, Philips   Dut 1619-1688
 * See 1991 Edition . . . .
Koning, Roeland   Dut 19C
 * See 1992 Edition . . . .
Kono, Micao   Jap 20C
 * See 1991 Edition . . . .
Kontopoulos, Alex
 O/B 31x47 Figures 1953 Sby 6/93 12,650
Kool, Sipke   Dut 1836-1902
 O/Pn 9x12 Lady Spinning Wool Slo 4/93 575
Kool, Willem Gillesz.   Dut 1608-1666
 * See 1990 Edition . . . .
Koons, Jeff   1955-
 * See 1993 Edition . . . .
Kopman, Benjamin   Am 1887-1965
 O/B 10x8 Evening Yng 5/93 300
 O/C 24x32 Road Through a Village Yng 2/93 100
Koppel, Gustave   Aus 1839-1905
 * See 1992 Edition . . . .
Koppenol, Cornelis   Dut 1865-1946
 O/B 20x28 Children Playing at the Beach Fre 10/92 1,400
Korab, Karl   1937-
 O/C 43x99 Komposition Chr 11/92 9,350
Korecki, Wiktor   20C
 O/C 24x36 Winter Landscape Yng 2/93 800
Kornbeck, Peter   Dan 1837-1894
 * See 1993 Edition . . . .
Korovine, Constantin   Rus 1861-1939
 O/C 24x20 Still Life with Red Roses Sby 10/92 3,300
 O/M 16x20 Winter Scene Chr 5/93 1,725
Kosa, Emil (Jr.)   Am 1903-1968
 O/C 26x40 Everlasting Hills But 10/92 15,400
 O/B 24x36 Towards Evening But 6/93 8,625
 O/C/B 25x36 One Enchanted Evening But 3/93 6,600
 O/C 24x30 By the River Mor 6/93 5,500
 O/C 24x36 Cottonwoods Mor 2/93 4,000
 W/Pa 21x27 Ranch Near Big Pine But 3/93 3,575
 O/M 24x32 Landscape Mor 6/93 2,250
 W/Pa 21x27 Landscape "Hermosa" Mor 6/93 2,200
 W/Pa 22x30 The White House of Peace Mor 6/93 1,650
 W/Pa 18x24 California Coastal Scene Lou 12/92 1,500
 W/Pa 15x22 California Coastal Mor 2/93 1,000

 W/Pa 11x16 Marina Scene Lou 3/93 600
Kosa, Emil (Sr.)   Am 1876-1955
 O/C 28x31 Floral Arrangement Mor 11/92 2,250
 O/C 17x20 Boats in Harbor Mor 11/92 1,200
Koscianski, Leonard   1952-
 O/C 96x144 Head to Head '84 Chr 11/92 4,400
Kossak, Jerszy   Pol 1890-1963
 * See 1992 Edition . . . .
Kossoff, Leon   20C
 * See 1993 Edition . . . .
Kossuth, Egon Josef   Czk 1874-
 * See 1992 Edition . . . .
Kost, Frederick   Am 1861-1923
 O/Pn 13x16 Sunset on the James Mys 3/93 275
Kostabi, Mark   Am 1961-
 O/C 96x72 Everymanhole 1985 Chr 2/93 4,400
 O/C 48x36 Primary Light 1989 Chr 2/93 3,850
 O/C 54x70 The Balinese 2-Step 1989 Chr 2/93 3,520
 O/C 40x26 Globalicism 1990 Chr 11/92 3,080
 O/C 48x36 Two Cultures (Hojo) 1990 Chr 11/92 3,080
 O/C 40x40 Revenge of the Deer 1986 Chr 2/93 2,860
 O/C 72x48 Young But I'm Not Green 1988 Chr 11/92 2,200
 O/C 70x70 Reader and Rider 1987 Hnd 12/92 2,000
Kostabi, Mark/S. Rockefeller
 * See 1992 Edition . . . .
Kosuth, Joseph   Am 20C
 MM/Ph 72x90 Word, Sentence, Paragraph Sby 11/92 55,000
 Ph 47x47 Titled (Art as Idea as Idea) 1967 Sby 11/92 20,900
Koszkol, Jeno   Hun 1868-
 W&Pe/Pa 16x20 Arab Market Scene Sby 1/93 489
Kotarbinski, Vasili Aleksand.   Rus
1849-1921
 O/C 29x25 Teasing the Swan Chr 5/93 2,990
Kotasz, Karoly   Hun 1872-
 O/C 16x20 Female Figures in a Field Dum 2/93 1,100
 O/C 16x19 Landscape Hnd 9/92 850
Kotlarevsky, Paul
 O/C 26x40 Harvest Sby 6/93 12,075
 O/C 26x40 Industry Sby 6/93 6,900
Kotschenreiter, Hugo   Ger 1854-1908
 O/C 19x13 Hunter and Monk with Game Wlf 3/93 4,000
Kotschmiester, G.   Ger 20C
 * See 1992 Edition . . . .
Kounellis, Jannis   1936-
 O/Pa/L 56x79 Untitled 61 Sby 5/93 63,000
 T/Pa 27x39 Untitled 61 Chr 10/92 24,200
 I/Pa 27x39 Untitled Sby 11/92 15,400
Koupal, Marie   Hun 20C
 O/C 27x22 Idleness 1883 Hnd 10/92 300
Kovacs   Hun 20C
 O/C 20x16 Notre Dame de Paris Lou 6/93 350
Kovalchick, Janet
 W/Pa 13x19 Boats Ald 9/92 125
Kovner, Saul   Am 1904-
 O/C 20x24 View from Central Park 1947 Lou 6/93 1,100
Kowalski, Leopold Franz   Fr 1856-
 * See 1991 Edition . . . .
Kozlow, Richard   Am 1926-
 A/M 30x22 Paradise FHB 6/93 80
Krabansky, Gustave   Fr a 1876-1897
 * See 1991 Edition . . . .
Kraemer, Peter   Ger 1857-1941
 * See 1991 Edition . . . .
Krafft, Carl R.   Am 1884-1938
 O/C 40x52 Autumn Landscape Hnd 3/93 4,500
 O/C 16x20 Haywagon Wes 5/93 1,540
Krafts, Michel   Con 19C
 O/C 22x18 Cleopatra Wlf 3/93 1,100
Kraike, Jane   Am 20C
 O/C/B 28x36 Awaiting Their Destination 1946 But 6/93 2,300
Kramer   Am 20C
 A/Pa 7x7 Four Primitives Hnd 5/93 275
Kramer, Johann Victor   Aus 1864-
 O/C 85x157 At the Well Sby 10/92 22,000

Kramer, Konrad Am 1888-
* See 1993 Edition . . . .
Kramskoy, Ivan Nikolaevich Rus 1837-1887
P/Pa 7x4 Portrait of the Artist '87 Yng 2/93 300
Krasner, Lee Am 1911-
O,Y&L/Pa 20x26 Untitled '75 Chr 5/93 5,750
Kratke, Charle-Louis Fr 1848-1921
O/C 15x22 Hunter and Dogs 1879 Hnd 3/93 2,000
Kratke, Marthe Fr 1884-
O/C 15x22 Still Life Daisies & Oriental Vase Chr 10/92 550
Kratochvil, Stephen Am 1876-
* See 1993 Edition . . . .
Kraus, Georg Melchior Ger 1737-1806
* See 1991 Edition . . . .
Kraus, Jan Pol 1760-
* See 1991 Edition . . . .
Krause, Emil A. Br 1891-1914
W/Pa 13x20 Evening Annandale Lake Fre 4/93 650
Krauskopf, Bruno 1892-1960
O/B 22x28 Nu Allonge Chr 11/92 5,280
Br,I&G/Pa 20x27 Boat on Beach; Lake: Two Chr 2/93 3,850
G&W/Pa 17x23 Le Pont Chr 11/92 2,200
Krawiec, Harriet Am 1894-1968
O/C 30x34 Floral Still Life Hnz 5/93 650
O/C 22x26 Still Life Flowers and Bird Hnz 5/93 100
Krawiec, Walter Am 1889-
O/C 30x40 Horse Corral in Winter Hnz 5/93 825
Kray, Wilhelm Ger 1828-1889
O/C 60x47 Spring, Autumn, Winter (3) But 5/93 12,650
O/C 20x18 Maternity Sby 10/92 3,850
Krebs, Lloyd L. Am 1874-1943
O/C 25x30 Painted Canyon 1923 Mor 11/92 225
Krehm, William Am 1901-1968
O/Cb 12x16 Desert Floor #2 Mor 11/92 200
Kremegne, Pinchus Rus 1890-1981
O/C 16x13 Tete De Femme Sby 2/93 1,840
Kremer, Petrus Flm 1801-1888
* See 1993 Edition . . . .
Krenn, Edmund Aus 1846-1902
O/Pn 15x11 Entertaining the Baby Chr 10/92 2,640
Kretchmer, Richard Am 20C
O/C 20x24 Summer at Givet 1988 Hnd 12/92 450
O/C 20x24 Vendee Harvest 1988 Hnd 12/92 350
O/C 10x14 Two Girls in Field of Flowers Hnd 12/92 110
Kretzinger, Clara Josephine Am 1883-
* See 1991 Edition . . . .
Kretzschmer, Johann-Hermann Ger 1811-1890
* See 1992 Edition . . . .
Kreyder, Alexis Joseph Fr 1839-1912
O/C 22x18 Bouquet of Flowers Chr 5/93 5,750
O/C 19x29 Apple Blossoms, Lilac: Pair Doy 11/92 2,420
Kricheldorf, Carl Ger 1863-
* See 1992 Edition . . . .
Krieghoff, Cornelius David Can 1815-1872
O/C 20x24 Bilking the Toll Gate 1857 Sbt 11/92 145,200
O/C 13x18 Hitching Up Sbt 11/92 70,400
O/C 14x21 Gentleman's Cutter Sbt 5/93 39,600
O/C 11x15 Indian Encampment Sbt 11/92 26,400
O/C 12x16 Night Encampment Sbt 11/92 21,120
O/C 12x17 River Gorge, Autumn Sbt 11/92 20,240
O/C 14x21 Indian Encampment Sbt 11/92 14,080
O/C 13x18 Moonlight - Salmon Fishing Sbt 5/93 14,080
O/B 12x10 Woman with Basket Sbt 11/92 10,560
O/C/Pn 14x12 Portrait Young Woman Sbt 5/93 4,400
Kriehuber, Fritz Aus 1800-1876
* See 1992 Edition . . . .
Kriesche, F. (Jr.) Am 1920-
W/Pa 16x20 Swans Hnz 5/93 70
Krippendorf, William H. Am 20C
O/C 25x30 Floral Still Life Wlf 9/92 350
Krischke, Franz Aus 1885-1960
O/C 24x20 Still Life Clock and Globe Dum 1/93 800

Krohg, Christian Nor 1852-1925
* See 1992 Edition . . . .
Kroll, Leon Am 1884-1974
O/Pn 23x14 The Bather, Folly Cove, Cape Ann Wlf 9/92 . . 35,000
O/C 25x30 Still Life Window Ledge '33 Chr 5/93 21,850
O/C 16x24 Interior with Nude (Isabel) 1966 Chr 3/93 8,050
O/C 27x34 Mother, Child and Nursemaid Mys 3/93 2,860
O/C 20x16 Girl with Guitar Sby 3/93 2,410
O/Pa/B 11x8 Portrait of Woman 1923 Dum 1/93 1,600
Y/Pa 17x13 Seated Nude Chr 12/92 1,540
O/C 18x15 The White Veil Skn 11/92 715
P/Pa 11x18 Nude Lou 9/92 600
P/Pa 17x12 Standing Nude Figure Brd 8/93 550
P/Pa 10x17 Nude Sby 3/93 460
C&P/Pa 18x12 Portrait of a Young Girl Chr 5/93 460
C/Pa 17x13 Bust Portrait of Young Woman Yng 2/93 275
Y/Pa 13x10 Head of a Young Woman Skn 11/92 220
Kronberg, Louis Am 1872-1964
O/C 30x22 Dancer in Green with Fan 1905 Chr 9/92 . . 9,900
O/C 61x40 Judith 1906 Sby 10/92 8,800
O/C 24x20 Young Ballerina Holding a Parrot 1901 Chr 5/93 . 4,600
P/Pa 9x17 The Ballet/A Fan Design Skn 3/93 880
O/C 16x10 Ballet Dancer Mys 3/93 550
Kronberger, Carl Aus 1841-1921
O/Pn 8x6 Portrait of a Tyrolean Man Chr 5/93 12,650
O/Pn 13x10 An Unpleasant Surprise Sel 9/92 3,700
Krondorf, William Am 20C
W/Pa 15x19 Three Landscapes Lou 9/92 200
Kropff, Joop Dut 1892-
O/C 15x22 Paris Street Scene Lou 3/93 275
Kroy, A. Fr 20C
O/C 19x22 Landscape with Stone Wall '30 Hnd 9/92 100
Kroyer, Peder Severin Dan 1851-1909
* See 1993 Edition . . . .
Krueger, Gustav Am 20C
O/C 48x72 Girl with Cupids Dum 11/92 1,200
Kruger, Barbara Am 1945-
Ph 99x41 Two Photographs Chr 5/93 18,400
Ph 73x49 We Are Not Made For Each Other Chr 2/93 16,500
Ph 40x50 You Construct Intricate Rituals 1981 Chr 5/93 . . 10,350
Ph 52x63 Untitled (Raw Material) Chr 5/93 5,520
Ph 48x48 Untitled (Image D) blue and white Chr 10/92 . . . 4,400
Kruger, Richard Am 1880-
O/C 25x30 Church by Moonlight Hnz 5/93 350
Kruse, Alexander Zerdini Am 1890-
* See 1993 Edition . . . .
Kruseman, Frederik Marianus Dut 1816-1882
O/C 20x27 River Landscape w/Farmhouse 1876 Chr 5/93 . 20,700
Kruseman, Jan Theodor Dut 1835-1895
* See 1991 Edition . . . .
Krushenick, Nicholas Am 1929-
* See 1991 Edition . . . .
Kuba, Ludvik Czk 1863-1956
* See 1990 Edition . . . .
Kudlatz Am 20C
W/Pa 18x29 Horses in the Stable '70 Wlf 9/92 275
Kudriashev, Ivan 1896-1972
G&W/Pa 7x14 Composition Chr 11/92 3,960
Kuehne, Max Am 1880-1968
O/M 26x30 Still Life Chr 12/92 18,700
O&Pe/M 34x40 Interior Flowers & Turquoise Chair Chr 5/93 16,100
O/C 20x24 View of Gloucester '25 Sby 12/92 11,000
O/C/B 18x15 The Calle del Angel, Granada 1915 Chr 5/93 . 7,475
O/C 24x20 Vase of Flowers Brd 8/93 7,425
O/C 20x24 Still Life: Flowers and Fruit Chr 3/93 5,750
O/C/M 24x20 Still Life Flowers 1919 Sby 9/92 3,300
O/B 15x12 Flowers in a Ceramic Pitcher Doy 5/93 1,760
O/Pn 12x16 Front Beach Sandy Bay, Rockport Wes 10/92 . 1,430
Kugler, J. Ger 20C
O/C 24x36 Forest Landscape Dum 6/93 120
Kuhlmann, Edward Am 1882-1973
* See 1993 Edition . . . .
Kuhn, Robert Am 1920-
Cs/B 15x32 Leopard Stalking Sby 6/93 10,925

Kuhn, Walt Am 1877-1949
O/C 60x40 Clown with Drum 1942 Sby 12/92 308,000
O/C 25x30 Apples with Salmon Cloth 1935 Sby 12/92 . . 59,400
O/C 33x40 Woman Reclining on Rock Chr 9/92 27,500
O/C 24x14 Anemone 192* Sby 12/92 15,400
W/Pa 21x13 Horn of Plenty 1937 Sby 12/92 14,300
G&I/Pa 15x12 Carnival Girl 1943 Sby 9/92 2,420
I&Y/Pa 8x6 Showgirl on Horseback Sby 3/93 1,150
Kuhnen, Pieter Lodewyk Bel 1812-1877
* See 1992 Edition . . . .
Kuhnert, Wilhelm Ger 1865-1926
* See 1993 Edition . . . .
Kuitca, Guillermo Arg 1961-
A/C 51x79 Tres Noches 1985 Chr 11/92 35,200
A/C 55x76 Man Sby 5/93 34,500
O/C 52x80 Siete Ultimas Canciones Sby 11/92 33,000
A/C 79x79 Hamburg Chr 11/92 24,200
A/C 48x59 La Cabeza del Amante Sby 5/93 20,700
A/C 55x55 Un Taller Para el Joven Kuitca 1985 Sby 11/92 17,600
Kulb, B. Ger 19C
O/C 26x37 In the Alps Hnd 5/93 1,000
Kulik, Karl
* See 1991 Edition . . . .
Kulyk, Karen Gay Can 1950-
W/Pa 24x18 View of the Tuilleries '80 Sbt 5/93 264
Kummer, Julius Herman Ger 1817-1872
O/C 28x51 Alpine Landscape with Animals 1870 Sel 12/92 . 1,000
O/C 28x51 Alpine Landscape with Animals 1870 Sel 2/93 . . 800
O/C 12x16 German Landscape Dum 3/93 700
Kunc, Milan 1944-
A/C 42x48 Early Morning Rhapsody 1983 Chr 11/92 7,150
A/C 89x63 Psychedelic Afternoon 1983 Chr 11/92 7,150
A/C 73x95 Untitled (Drawing Room) Chr 5/93 5,520
Kuniyoshi, Yasuo Am 1893-1953
W&I/Pa 15x12 Maine Landscape '23 Sby 12/92 23,100
Pe/Pa 16x13 Cafe 34 Chr 5/93 19,550
O/C 14x20 Landscape 32 Chr 9/92 8,800
C/Pa 12x8 Sketch for War Poster 42 Chr 5/93 1,380
Kunstler, Mort Am 1931-
O/C 25x34 Roger's Rangers/Lake Champlain 82 Hnd 10/92 1,500
Kuntz, Roger
* See 1991 Edition . . . .
Kunz, Ludwig Adam Aus 1857-1929
O/Pn 19x26 Objects Arranged on Tablecloth Chr 5/93 3,450
Kuper, Yuri 1940-
MM/Pw 79x79 Mappa Chr 11/92 16,500
Kupetzky, Jan 1667-1740
* See 1992 Edition . . . .
Kurelek, William Can 1927-1977
MM 14x14 Hay Raking on the Prairies '75 Sbt 11/92 26,400
MM 39x32 Russian Thistles Migrating Sbt 5/93 24,640
MM/B 20x30 Blizzard in Manitoba '67 Sbt 5/93 17,600
Et/B 24x30 Carrying Water to Haying Crew Sbt 11/92 . . . 13,200
MM/B 48x37 Prairie Strawpile on Ukrainian '72 Sbt 5/93 . . 13,200
MM 23x10 The Cook 1973 Sbt 11/92 12,320
MM 40x28 It is an Enemy of Mine 1975 Sbt 11/92 9,680
MM/B 14x14 Boy's Summer, Thunderstorm '74 Sbt 11/92 . 8,800
MM/B 24x30 Glimpse of Mount Robson '72 Sbt 5/93 7,920
MM 24x24 Irish Wake in Montreal '76 Sbt 11/92 7,480
MM/B 13x19 Prairie Winter Mishap '70 Sbt 11/92 6,160
MM/B 12x6 Our Manitoba Farm Today '73 Sbt 11/92 4,840
Et/B 19x14 Fallen Boy in Hay Rake Sbt 11/92 4,620
MM/B 7x18 Divine Love and Natural Love 1964 Sbt 11/92 . 3,520
O/B 20x17 Alcoholism '75 Sbt 11/92 3,300
Kurtz, Elaine Am 1928-
A/C 72x72 White Spectrum Series 1979 Slo 4/93 600
Kusama, Yayoi
O/C 29x24 No B.B.B. 1960 Sby 10/92 11,000
Kushner, Robert 1949-
G,W&Y/Pa 90x22 Can Can Chr 11/92 6,600
Kuss, Ferdinand Aus 1800-1886
* See 1993 Edition . . . .
Kuwasseg, Carl Joseph Fr 1802-1877
* See 1992 Edition . . . .

Kuwasseg, Charles E. (Jr.) Fr 20C
O/C 12x20 Sailboat in a Harbor Hnd 12/92 750
Kuwasseg, Charles Euprhasie Fr 1838-1904
O/C 10x13 Two: Bustling River Town 1871 Chr 10/92 . . . 19,800
O/C 10x13 Montpelier 1869 Slo 4/93 3,750
O/C 25x21 Mountains and Village 1882 Fre 10/92 2,200
Kuwayama, Tadaaki
A/C 72x60 Untitled 1974 Sby 6/93 7,475
Kuypers, Cornelis Dut 1864-1932
O/Pn 9x16 Haystack in a Barnyard Wes 10/92 1,650
O/C 12x23 River Landscape with Cattle Hnz 5/93 1,300
Kvapil, Charles Bel 1884-1958
C/Pa/B 26x19 Nu de dos Chr 11/92 440
Kynast, A. Ger 19C
O/C 22x27 Interior of Wine Cellar Sel 9/92 1,050
L'Aine, Moreau Fr 1740-1806
I,S&W/Pa 9x14 Classical Garden at Versailles Slo 7/93 750
L'Engle, Lucy Brown Am 1889-
* See 1993 Edition . . . .
L'Engle, William Am 1884-1957
* See 1990 Edition . . . .
L'Huillier, Jacques Fr 1867-
* See 1993 Edition . . . .
L'Orbetto It 1578-1649
O/C 55x39 Ecce Homo Sby 1/93 41,400
La Farge, John Am 1835-1910
W,G&Pe/Pa 12x10 Masked Dancer of No 1886 Chr 9/92 . 18,700
W/Ab 9x10 Fishing Party in Canoes, Samoa Sby 12/92 . . 12,100
W/Pa 15x11 Statue of Oya-Jiso 1886 Sby 9/92 8,250
W/Pa 15x10 Study for "The Dawn" Sby 12/92 7,700
O/C 16x12 Margaret Mason Perry La Farge Skn 5/93 3,300
La Fontaine, Thomas Sherwood Br 1915-
* See 1991 Edition . . . .
La Forest, Wesner
* See 1992 Edition . . . .
La Gatta, John Am 1894-1976
* See 1992 Edition . . . .
La Pira It 20C
G/Pa 8x12 Bay of Naples Wes 3/93 2,640
La Salle, Charles Am 1894-1958
* See 1991 Edition . . . .
La Thangue, Henry Herbert Br 1859-1929
* See 1992 Edition . . . .
La Touche, Gaston Fr 1854-1913
P/Pa 40x39 Spirits of the Night 1897 But 5/93 17,250
La Volpe, Alessandro It 1820-1893
O/C 27x52 Costa Napoletana Sby 10/92 11,000
Laballe, John Am 1898-
W/Pa 28x20 Along the Morne Hnd 10/92 250
Labor, Charles Fr 1813-1900
* See 1990 Edition . . . .
Laborde, Charles
W&I/Pa/B 11x9 L'Orgueil Sby 10/92 1,320
Laborne, Edme Emile Fr 1837-1913
O/C 39x52 La Place du Marche en Provence Sby 10/92 . . 29,700
Lacasse, Joseph
O/C 66x45 Untitled 1959 Sby 6/93 6,900
Lach, Andreas Aus 1817-1882
* See 1993 Edition . . . .
Lachaise, Eugene A. Am 1857-1925
* See 1991 Edition . . . .
Lachaise, Gaston Am 1882-1935
Pe&I/Pa 24x19 Male Nudes Sby 9/92 6,600
Pe/Pa 24x18 Male Nude Sby 9/92 4,675
Pe/Pa 19x12 Seated Nude Chr 5/93 4,370
Pe/Pa 24x19 Standing Nude Sby 9/92 4,125
Br,I&Pe/Pa 18x12 Head Chr 9/92 3,520
Lachance, Georges Am 1888-
O/C 28x32 Ship in Harbor Sel 12/92 950
Lachman, Harry B. Am 1886-1974
O/C 18x22 Chemin Azay Le Rideau Sby 3/93 6,900
O/C 20x24 Rougemont 14 Hnd 3/93 3,000
O/Pn 11x14 Grey Day, Brittany Lou 9/92 1,200

Lack, Stephen   Can 1946-
  * See 1992 Edition . . . .
LaCoste, Charles   Fr 20C
  O/C 21x18 Roses in an Oriental Vase Mys 3/93 495
LaCour, Janus Andreas Barthol. Dan 1837-1909
  * See 1993 Edition . . . .
Lacretelle, Jean Edouard   Fr 1817-1900
  * See 1990 Edition . . . .
Lacroix De Marseille   Fr 1720-1790
  O/C 41x57 Mediterranean Harbors: Pair 1776 Sby 1/93 . . 123,500
  O/C 45x64 Coastline w/Figures Standing Chr 1/93 33,000
  O/C 11x17 Shipwreck Stormy Seas Sby 1/93 9,488
  O/C 8x10 Mediterranean Harbour Scene Sby 5/93 9,200
Lacroix, Eugene   Am 19C
  * See 1993 Edition . . . .
Lacroix, Paul   Am a 1858-1869
  O/C/B 29x39 Nature's Bounty Chr 3/93 25,300
Lacy, Alec   Am 20C
  W/Pa 14x17 River; New York Harbor: Two Slo 4/93 125
Ladell, Edward   Br 1821-1886
  * See 1993 Edition . . . .
Laezza, Giuseppi   It a 1877-1903
  O/M 24x49 View of Bay of Naples Sby 1/93 13,225
Lafage, Raymond   1650-1684
  K&Pl/Pa 16x21 Fall of the Rebel Angels Chr 1/93 440
Lafaguays   20C
  O/C 20x24 Danseuse Sel 4/93 300
LaFarge, John   Am 1835-1910
  O/C 8x10 Male Figure Playing Lute Mys 3/93 5,775
Lafon, Henri   Fr 19C
  * See 1993 Edition . . . .
Lafore, W. V.   Fr 19C
  O/C 20x30 Title? Fre 10/92 375
Lafrensen, Nicolas   Fr 1737-1807
  * See 1993 Edition . . . .
Lagage, Pierre-Cesar
  * See 1992 Edition . . . .
Lagar, Celso   1891-1966
  * See 1993 Edition . . . .
Lagarde, A. G.   Con 19C
  * See 1993 Edition . . . .
LaGatta, John   Am 1894-1977
  O/C 37x28 Two Fashionable Women Ih 5/93 5,500
  O/B 24x29 Cowgirls Ih 11/92 4,000
Lagneau   Fr
  * See 1991 Edition . . . .
Lagoni, Luigi   It 20C
  O/C 16x20 Venetian Canal Fre 10/92 1,350
Lagrange, Jacques   Fr 1917-
  * See 1992 Edition . . . .
Lagrenee, Jean Jacques   Fr 1739-1821
  * See 1993 Edition . . . .
Lagrenee, Louis-Jean-Francois   Fr 1725-1805
  O/Pn 12x15 Sarah Presenting Hagar to Abraham Sby 1/93 48,875
Lahuerta, Genaro   Spa 1905-
  O/B 16x13 Altea-VIII Dum 12/92 2,250
Laib, Wolfgang   1959-
  MM 24x32 Pollen Chr 11/92 7,700
Laing, Jamson   Br 19C
  O/Pn 10x16 Loading the Hay Wagon But 11/92 935
Laissement, Henri Adolphe   Fr 1854-1921
  O/C 29x40 News from the Front Sby 10/92 17,600
Lajos, Brucke Ludwig   Hun 1846-1910
  O/C 20x14 Peasant Girl in Landscape Slo 4/93 475
Lalanne, Eugene Georges   Fr 19C
  C/Pa 11x9 Fishing From River Bank Skn 9/92 302
Laloue, Eugene Galien   Fr 1854-1941
  W&G/Pa 7x12 Place Vendome Wlf 12/92 5,500
  W&G/Pa 7x12 Notre Dame Wlf 12/92 5,000
Lam, Wifredo   Cub 1902-1982
  O/L 20x24 Diablos 1945 Chr 11/92 242,000
  O/Bu 44x32 Femme Cheval 1966 Chr 11/92 176,000
  C&P/Pa 30x21 Sans Titre 1969 Sby 5/93 31,625

  C&P/Pa 30x22 Tres Figuras 1969 Chr 11/92 30,800
  H,I&W/Pa 19x25 Le Cheval Enchante 1945 Sby 5/93 29,900
  C&Y/Pa 28x20 Diablo 1970 Chr 11/92 17,600
  O/C 14x18 Sans Titre 1974 Sby 11/92 16,500
Lama, Giulia   1681-1747
  * See 1993 Edition . . . .
Lamasure, Edwin   Am 1866-1916
  W/Pa 17x34 La Laguna, Venice Wes 5/93 825
  W/Pa 21x30 Country Morning Landscape Wes 10/92 660
  W/Pa 8x11 Sunset and Moonrise: Two Wes 10/92 412
  W/Pa 11x14 Autumn & Mountain: Two 1902 Wes 10/92 . . . 358
Lamb, Frederick Mortimer   Am 1861-1936
  O/C 34x41 Haunt of the Oriole Skn 11/92 1,870
  O/Cb 19x24 The Old Apple Tree Chr 5/93 1,035
  P/Pa/B 16x22 Haying Scene in New England Skn 5/93 935
  O/B 17x14 Autumn Landscape Yng 5/93 550
  O/Pb 10x12 Sail Boats Lou 6/93 350
  W/Pa 10x14 Man Plowing in Landscape 1902 Slo 4/93 . . . 300
  W/Pa 14x21 Game Birds Mys 12/92 148
Lamb, Matt   Am 20C
  A/C 59x83 Abraham, Martin and John Hnd 3/93 3,400
Lamb, R. G.
  O/C 10x14 Barnyard Scene Eld 8/93 412
Lambdin, George Cochran   Am 1830-1896
  O/Pn 20x12 Spring Blossoms 1875 Chr 3/93 11,500
  O/Pa 16x12 Yellow Rose Study 77 Sby 3/93 4,025
Lambert, B.   Fr 20C
  O/C 14x27 River Scene Mys 12/92 104
Lambert, C. Bel 20C
  O/B 16x19 Dutch Interior Genre Scene Dum 8/93 1,200
Lambert, Eugene   Fr 1825-1900
  O/C 13x16 Kittens at Play Mys 12/92 3,960
Lambert, George   Br 1710-1765
  * See 1993 Edition . . . .
Lambert, Georges   Fr 1919-
  * See 1992 Edition . . . .
Lambert, Louis   Fr 19C
  O/C 18x15 Fishing Boats Unloading Chr 10/92 1,320
Lambert, R.   19C
  O/C 10x14 Herder with Sheep Slo 7/93 300
Lambert, Theodore Roosevelt   Am 1905-1960
  * See 1992 Edition . . . .
Lambert-Rucki, Jean   Fr 1888-1967
  G&C/Pa 13x10 Figure on Stilts 1928 Sby 10/92 1,760
Lambinet, Emile Charles   Fr 1815-1877
  O/C 11x19 Wooded River Scene Chr 10/92 1,870
Lambrechts, Jan Baptist   Flm 1680-1731
  O/C 25x19 Couple Drinking Tea Chr 10/92 14,300
Lamme, Arie Johannes   Dut 1812-1900
  * See 1993 Edition . . . .
LaMore, Chet Harmon   Am 1908-
  * See 1993 Edition . . . .
LaMotte, Bernard   Fr 1903-
  O/C 36x34 Along the Seine Sby 6/93 920
Lampi, Giovanni Battista   It 1807-1857
  * See 1991 Edition . . . .
Lamplough, Augustus Osborne   Br 1877-1930
  * See 1992 Edition . . . .
Lamy, Pierre Desire Eugene   Fr 1855-1919
  * See 1990 Edition . . . .
Lancerotto, Egisto   It 1848-1916
  * See 1993 Edition . . . .
Lancon, Edouard Michel   Fr 1854-
  * See 1991 Edition . . . .
Lancret, Nicolas   Fr 1690-1743
  K/Pa 6x6 Seated Man Leaning Forward Chr 1/93 22,000
Landaluze, Victor Patricio   Cub 1828-1889
  O/C 14x8 El Encuentro Chr 11/92 13,200
  O/C 22x16 Nino con Cabra 1886 Sby 11/92 13,200
  W&Pe/Pa/B 16x14 Plaza; Dia de Reyes (2) Chr 11/92 . . . 13,200
  H,Pl&W/Pa 11x8 Tomando Agua Sby 5/93 5,750

Landeau, J***   Fr 19C
O/C 19x14 Flirtation 84 Sby 1/93 1,725
Landelle, Charles Zacharie   Fr 1812-1908
O/C 24x20 Study Les Femmes de Jerusalem Chr 2/93 . . . 38,500
Landi, Ricardo Verdugo   It 19C
* See 1990 Edition . . . .
Landini, Andrea   It 1847-
* See 1992 Edition . . . .
Landini, Jacopo   It a 14C
* See 1993 Edition . . . .
Landis, John   Am 1805-
* See 1993 Edition . . . .
Landseer, Charles   Br 19C
* See 1990 Edition . . . .
Landseer, Sir Edwin Henry   Br 1802-1873
O/C 74x93 Alpine Mastiffs Reanimating 1820 Sby 6/93 . 525,000
O/C 52x88 The Ptarmigan Hill Sby 6/93 310,500
o/Pn 39x49 Refreshment Sby 6/93 222,500
Lane, Fitz Hugh   Am 1804-1865
* See 1993 Edition . . . .
Lane, Leonard C.   Can 20C
* See 1992 Edition . . . .
Lanfair, Harold E.   Am 1898-1981
W/Pa 13x20 Industrial Scene Mor 11/92 425
Lanfranchi, Alessandro   It 1662-1730
* See 1992 Edition . . . .
Lanfranco, Giovanni   It 1582-1647
* See 1993 Edition . . . .
Lang, Annie Traquair   Am 1885-1918
O/Pn 6x10 Venetian Piazza Skn 3/93 1,430
Lang, James   Am 20C
O/B 27x20 Birds in a Winter Landscape Sel 9/92 325
Lang, Louis   Am 1814-1893
O/C 17x21 The Bird's Nest 1853 Sby 5/93 8,625
O/C 21x16 Girl Eating Cherries Fre 4/93 950
Langendijk, Dirk   Dut 1748-1805
* See 1990 Edition . . . .
Langendyk, Jan Anthonie   Dut 1780-1818
* See 1993 Edition . . . .
Langer, Olaf Viggo Peter   Dan 1860-1942
* See 1993 Edition . . . .
Langeveld, Frans   Dut 1877-1939
* See 1992 Edition . . . .
Langevin, Claude   Can 1942-
O/C 16x20 St. Jean De Matha, Laurentides 1982 Sbt 11/92 . 1,408
O/C 24x30 La Basse Cour, Notre Dame Des Monts Sbt 5/93 1,320
O/C 20x24 Rue Principale Sbt 5/93 1,232
Langley, Edward   Am 1870-
O/B 18x24 Desert Scene Lou 3/93 525
Langley, William   Eng 19C
O/C 12x10 Highland Castle by a Lake Wes 10/92 495
Langlois, Jerome Martin   Fr 1779-1838
* See 1991 Edition . . . .
Langlois, Mark W.   Br 19C
O/C 30x25 Tavern Scene Wlf 12/92 2,500
O/C 21x17 The Flute Concert Hnd 10/92 1,800
Langworthy, William H.   Am 19C
* See 1992 Edition . . . .
Lanman, Charles   Am 1819-1895
* See 1992 Edition . . . .
Lansdale, N. M.
W/Pa 21x28 Seascape Ald 9/92 115
Lansil, Walter Franklin   Am 1846-1925
O/C 22x36 The Grand Canal, Venice 1895 Yng 5/93 4,000
O/B 7x9 In the Gulf of Venice 1917 Skn 3/93 302
Lanskoy, Andre   Rus 1902-1976
O/C 29x24 Composition Sby 5/93 18,400
Lantier, Lucien Louis Bernard   Fr 1879-
O/Pn 35x46 Dinner at Maxim's Sby 5/93 37,375
Lantz, Paul   Am 1908-
* See 1992 Edition . . . .
Lanyon, Ellen   Am 20C
O/B 20x16 The Clown Chr 12/92 1,100
Lanza, Giovanni   It 1827-
* See 1993 Edition . . . .

Lapira, ***   It 19C
* See 1992 Edition . . . .
Laporte, George Henry   Am 1799-1873
* See 1993 Edition . . . .
Laporte, Georges   Fr 1926-
O/C 15x22 Fishing Harbor Wes 3/93 385
Lapostolet, Charles   Fr 1824-1890
* See 1993 Edition . . . .
Lara, Edwina   Br 19C
O/C 16x24 Unloading the Catch Fre 4/93 700
Lara, Georgina   Br 19C
O/C 10x18 Farm Scene Wlf 12/92 1,200
Lara, William   Br 19C
O/C 12x24 Resting Beside the Path Hnz 5/93 650
Larche, Francois Raoul   Fr 1860-1912
* See 1992 Edition . . . .
Lareuse, Jean   Fr 1925-
W&G/Pa 10x14 At the Beach Slo 5/93 325
Larionov, Mikhail   Rus 1881-1964
G/Pa 18x12 Personnage Marche Funebre Sby 2/93 10,350
O/C/B 28x24 Nature Vivante 1900 Chr 10/92 6,600
Larraz, Julio   Cub 1942-
O/C 40x60 Cazador (The Hunter) 85 Chr 11/92 44,000
O/C 30x24 Sobre la Lune 88 Sby 11/92 14,300
Larrinaga, Mario   Am 1895-1979
O/B 30x24 Gilded Ghetto (San Francisco) But 6/93 1,495
Larsen, Adolf Alfred   Dan 1856-1942
* See 1993 Edition . . . .
Larsen, W.   Eng 20C
O/C 16x20 Up for the Hunt Hnz 5/93 250
Larsson, Carl   Swd 1853-1919
* See 1992 Edition . . . .
Larwin, Hans   Aus 1873-1938
O/Cb 18x14 Hospital in Russian Church 1915 Hnd 3/93 400
O/B 13x11 War Ruins in Italy 1918 Hnd 3/93 275
Lascano, Juan   Arg 1947-
* See 1993 Edition . . . .
Lascari, Salvatore   Am 1884-
O/C/B 33x38 Touch of the Southwest But 12/92 1,650
Lascaux, Elie   20C
O/C 18x24 On the Riviera 35 Sby 10/92 1,760
Lasellaz, Gustave Francois   Fr 1848-1910
* See 1993 Edition . . . .
Laske, Oskar   Aus 1841-1911
G/Pa 16x21 April in the Danube Valley Doy 5/93 6,050
G/Pa 21x16 Dormant Fields Near Vienna Doy 5/93 4,675
G/Pa 15x21 Krakowitz Castle Doy 5/93 3,080
Lasker, Jonathan   1948-
A/C 59x71 A Time for the World Sby 2/93 17,250
O/C 30x24 Terse Psyche 1989 Chr 11/92 12,100
Lassalle, Fr 1810-
O/Pn 12x9 The Faggot Gatherers Sby 10/92 2,640
Lassen, Hans August   Ger 1857-
* See 1993 Edition . . . .
Lassonde, Omer T.   Am 1903-1980
O/C 18x13 Village Church Yng 2/93 225
O/C 15x18 Flowers in Bowl Yng 2/93 200
O/C 18x20 Village Path Yng 2/93 200
Latapie, Louis   1891-1972
O/C 37x29 Les Trois Graces 65 Chr 2/93 2,750
Lataster, Ger
* See 1992 Edition . . . .
Latham, Barbara   Am 1896-1976
* See 1992 Edition . . . .
Latham, Rose O'Neill   Am 1875-1944
Pl/Pa 18x24 People at the Beach Ih 11/92 900
Lathrop, Francis Augustus   Am 1849-1909
* See 1993 Edition . . . .
Lathrop, Ida Pulis   Am 1859-1937
O/C 20x23 Peacock Feather, Print and Photo Chr 5/93 . . . 14,950
Lathrop, William Langson   Am 1859-1938
O/M 16x20 Rocky Shore, Lloyd's Harbor Doy 5/93 2,420
O/C 12x16 Marsh Grass Gatherers Skn 3/93 1,320
O/C 14x20 The Marsh Grass Gatherer Ald 3/93 825

Latimer, Lorenzo Palmer Am 1857-1941
W/Pa 14x10 California Redwoods But 6/93 2,875
W/Pa 7x10 Landscape Mor 11/92 750
W/Pa 13x24 In the Sandhills, San Francisco 1894 But 6/93 . . 575
Latoix, Gaspard Am 20C
* See 1993 Edition . . . .
Latortue, Franklin Hai
* See 1993 Edition . . . .
Latortue, Phillipe Hai 20C
* See 1992 Edition . . . .
Latouche, Claude Gaston Fr 20C
W/pa 15x21 Chiens de Meute Sby 6/93 1,955
Latouche, Gaston Fr 1854-1913
O/Pn 30x31 Soiree Chez Un Artiste Sby 2/93 18,400
Latour, D. Fr 19C
O/B 11x4 Rendez-vous Wlf 12/92 500
Lattard, Phillip Am 19C
* See 1990 Edition . . . .
Lauder, Charles James Br 1841-1920
* See 1991 Edition . . . .
Laudy, Jean Dut 1877-1956
O/C 24x32 White and Pink Roses Chr 2/93 5,500
Laufman, Sidney Am 1891-
* See 1992 Edition . . . .
Lauge, Achille Fr 1861-1944
* See 1992 Edition . . . .
Laugee, Georges Fr 1853-
O/C 15x22 The Shepherdess Chr 2/93 4,950
Laur, Marie Yvonne Fr 1879-
O/Pn 15x18 Motherly Love Sby 1/93 5,175
O/Pn 15x18 Afternoon Tea Sby 1/93 4,600
Laurence, Sydney Am 1865-1940
O/C 24x20 Morning Sunlight, Mt. McKinley 1929 Sby 3/93 . 19,550
O/C 21x26 Early Evening, Mt. McKinley Chr 9/92 16,500
O/C 20x24 Northern Lights, Cape Homer Wes 10/92 11,000
O/C 16x20 Ship in Full Sail Mys 12/92 9,350
O/C 36x52 Safe in Gloucester Harbor Hnd 3/93 7,500
O/B 8x18 Rocky Beach Scene Chr 12/92 1,100
Laurencin, Marie Fr 1883-1956
O/C 29x24 L'infante Chr 11/92 242,000
O/C 22x18 Turquerie 1937 Chr 11/92 231,000
O/C 20x24 Deux Jeunes Filles Sby 2/93 167,500
O/C 16x13 Autoportrait au chapeau Chr 11/92 82,500
O/C 15x18 Jeune fille a la guitare Chr 11/92 82,500
W&PI/Pa 6x6 Jeune Fille a l'Evantail Sby 11/92 33,000
W&Pe/Pa 13x10 Deux Femmes Sby 11/92 29,700
W&Pe/Pa/B 15x11 Les Trois Graces Sby 5/93 26,450
O/C 18x15 Tulipes 1940 Sby 2/93 26,450
W/Pa/B 11x15 Trois jeunes filles Chr 11/92 24,200
W&PI/Pa 15x11 L'elegante au foulard Chr 11/92 22,000
W/Pa/B 12x10 Deux jeunes filles Chr 11/92 19,800
W&Pe/Pa 4x4 De Femme au Chapeau Sby 2/93 8,050
O/Pa/C 16x13 Vase de Tulipes et Pivoines Sby 2/93 6,900
Pe/Pa 9x13 Femmes au Bord de L'Eau 1931 Sby 2/93 . . . 2,875
Pe/Pa 10x8 Female Nude from the Back Sby 10/92 2,640
Laurens, Henri Fr 1885-1954
* See 1993 Edition . . . .
Laurens, Jean Paul Fr 1838-1921
O/C 47x36 La Separation de Berthe Et Robert Sby 5/93 . . 16,100
Laurens, Jules Joseph Augustin Fr 1825-1901
* See 1992 Edition . . . .
Laurent, Ernest Joseph Fr 1859-1929
O/C 19x26 Nu Etendu sur un Lit Sby 5/93 34,500
Laurent, Felix Fr 1821-1908
* See 1991 Edition . . . .
Laurent, Jean Pierre Fr 20C
O/C 15x22 Port at Breton Slo 4/93 250
Laurenti, Cesare It 1854-
* See 1993 Edition . . . .
Lauret, Francois Fr 1820-1868
* See 1993 Edition . . . .
Lauritz, Jack Am 20C
O/C 24x26 Landscape Mor 2/93 550

Lauritz, Paul Am 1889-1975
O/B 16x20 Landscape Mor 6/93 2,475
O/C/B 18x26 Entrance to Zion National Park But 3/93 2,200
O/C 20x24 Morain Mountain Chr 5/93 2,070
O/C 28x36 Clouds Building Above the Desert But 6/93 1,725
O/C/B 24x34 Grant's Pass, Oregon But 3/93 1,650
O/C 20x32 Crashing Surf Mor 6/93 1,320
W/Pa 21x24 Mountain Stream But 6/93 1,265
O/C 22x26 Sierra Landscape Mor 6/93 1,210
W/Pa 20x29 Icy River But 6/93 1,035
O/C/B 20x25 Landscape Mor 2/93 850
O/Cb 20x24 High Sierras Lone Pine But 6/93 748
W/Pa 14x19 Landscape Mor 6/93 715
O/Pw 14x18 Carmel Coast Mor 6/93 660
O/C 20x24 Seascape Mor 2/93 600
O/Cb 12x14 The High Sierras Mor 11/92 475
Lauvray, Louis Alphonse Abel Fr 1870-1950
O/C 15x21 Paysage a la Riviere Doy 11/92 1,650
Laux, August Am 1847-1921
O/C 10x14 Chickens in a Barnyard Sby 3/93 5,463
O/C 10x14 Strawberries Brd 8/93 4,400
O/C 11x14 Wild Berries Lou 3/93 3,600
O/C 10x14 Chickens Feeding Chr 12/92 2,750
O/C 10x14 Basket of Cherries, Raspberries (2) Wlf 3/93 . . 2,700
O/C 11x16 Basket of Cherries Chr 12/92 2,200
O/B 7x9 Rooster with Chickens Sby 9/92 2,090
O/C 10x14 Chickens, Roosters, Ducks Chr 12/92 1,430
O/C 20x11 Bouquet of Grapes '94 Fre 4/93 1,200
Lavagna, Francesco a 18C
O/C 29x38 Still Life Flowers in Sculpted Urn Sby 10/92 . . 18,700
Lavalle, John Am 1896-
* See 1993 Edition . . . .
LaValley, Jonas Joseph Am 1858-1930
O/C 17x22 A Wooded Brook Chr 5/93 1,840
O/C 20x14 An Autumn Stream Chr 5/93 1,265
Lavery, Sir John Br 1856-1941
O/Cb 10x14 On the Hills, Tangiers Chr 10/92 10,450
O/Ab 20x10 Portrait of Mr. Mehta 1931 Sby 5/93 5,175
Lavielle, Eugene Antoine S. Fr 1820-1889
* See 1992 Edition . . . .
Laville, Joy Br 1923-
* See 1993 Edition . . . .
Lavin, Robert Am 1919-
O/C 24x36 Smelting Plant Against Dark Sky Chr 12/92 880
Lavreince, Nicolas Fr 1737-1807
* See 1993 Edition . . . .
Law, Anthony Can 20C
* See 1993 Edition . . . .
Law, Harry V. Am 20C
W/Pa 15x12 Mythological Scene Mys 12/92 110
Law, Margaret M. Am 20C
T/B 20x16 Cotton Pickers '21 Sby 9/92 1,320
Lawless, Carl Am 1894-1934
* See 1993 Edition . . . .
Lawley, John Douglas Can 1906-1970
* See 1992 Edition . . . .
Lawrence, Edna W. Am 1898-
* See 1991 Edition . . . .
Lawrence, Jacob Am 1917-
T/M 24x30 Northbound '62 Sby 9/92 68,750
Lawrence, Sir Thomas Br 1769-1830
O/C 36x33 Portrait Fanny and Jane Hamond Sby 5/93 . . 277,500
Lawrence, Sydney Am 1865-1940
O/B 10x8 Old Cache But 6/93 6,900
Lawrence, William Goadby Br
* See 1991 Edition . . . .
Lawrie, A.
O/Pn 12x10 The Waiting Young Page Ald 3/93 350
Laws, Arthur J. Am 1894-1960
* See 1992 Edition . . . .
Lawson, Cecil Gordon Br 1851-1882
O/C 8x10 Ducks in Landscape Sby 1/93 1,380
Lawson, Ernest Am 1873-1939
O/C 20x24 Reflections of Spring Chr 9/92 33,000

O/C 18x21 Inwood, Upper Washington Heights Sby 5/93 . 27,600
O/C 9x16 Boat on a Lake Sby 12/92 13,200
O/C 12x16 The Brook, Segovia Sby 9/92 12,100
O/C 16x20 Winter, Spuytin Duyvil Sby 5/93 10,350
O/C/B 9x12 Spring Planting Chr 3/93 7,475
O/C 12x14 The Frozen Pool Skn 9/92 4,400

Lawson, Thomas 1951-
O/C 66x96 The View from the Berghof Chr 11/92 2,860

Layton Am 20C
G/B 25x12 Wade Gallery Wtf 9/92 650

Lazelle, Blanche Am -1956
W/Pa 9x7 Abstract 1931 Mys 12/92 110

Lazerges, Jean Baptiste Paul Fr 1845-1902
O/C 20x24 The Bedouin at Night 1899 Dum 1/93 3,000

Lazerges, Jean Raymond H. Fr 1817-1887
O/C 29x23 Man Gathering Straw 1884 Sby 5/93 8,338

Lazo, Eberto Escobedo Cub 1916-
O/C 36x42 Paisaje Cubano 1951 Chr 11/92 7,150

Lazzari, Pietro Am 1898-1979
I/Pa 16x12 Windy Day, Priests, Piazza 1962 Slo 7/93 125

Lazzell, Blanche Am 1878-1956
W/Pa 22x18 Abstraction 1973 Wtf 12/92 2,400

Lea, Wesley Am 20C
* See 1992 Edition . . . .

Leader, Benjamin Williams Br 1831-1923
O/C 29x41 Sunset in the Highlands 1886 Sby 5/93 11,500
O/C 24x37 Jungfrau Mountains 1901 Chr 10/92 8,800

Lear, Edward Br 1812-1888
Pl&W/Pa 15x22 Dubrovnik, Yugoslavia 1866 Sby 2/93 21,850

Lear, George
O/C 16x16 Landscape 1931 Ald 9/92 400

Lear, John Am 20C
* See 1992 Edition . . . .

Leaver, Noel H. Br 1889-1951
W/B 10x14 An Arab Village Chr 2/93 2,860
W/B 11x8 Arab Street Scene Sby 1/93 805
W/Pa 10x7 Alpine Landscape Slo 7/93 600

Leavers, Lucy Ann Br a 1887-1898
O/C 36x50 Barnyard Friends Chr 2/93 8,800
O/C 34x49 Three Against One Chr 2/93 8,800

Leavitt, Edward Chalmers Am 1842-1904
O/C 14x18 Pansies 1885 Chr 12/92 14,300
O/C 20x12 Wedgewood & Flowers (2) Mys 3/93 5,280
O/C 20x12 Still Life Vase, Roses, Geraniums 1876 Chr 12/92 3,850
O/C 9x13 A Rocky Shore Eld 11/92 66

Leavitt, John Faunce Am 1905-1974
W/Pa 21x28 U.S. Clipper "Dreadnaught" Eld 7/93 1,430

LeBarbier, Jean-Jacques It 1738-1826
* See 1991 Edition . . . .

LeBas, Gabriel Hippolyte Fr 1812-1880
W/Pa 11x19 Landscape Lou 6/93 150

Lebas, Leonie Fr 20C
O/Pn 10x13 Figures along the Seine Slo 5/93 450

Lebasque, Henri Fr 1865-1937
O/C 36x44 Le jardin Chr 11/92 78,100
O/C 20x24 Jeune Femme Aux Fleurs Sby 5/93 68,500
O/C 25x32 La Baie de Toulon Sby 11/92 52,250
O/C 22x15 Deux Jeunes Femmes Sby 11/92 36,300
O/C 18x21 Femme et Enfant Devant Une Table Sby 11/92 35,750
O/C 19x23 Le jardin de l'artiste au Cannet Chr 11/92 33,000
O/C 29x22 Jeune Fille a La Colombe Sby 5/93 31,625
O/C 21x18 Fleurs Dans Un Vase Sby 11/92 30,800
O/C 22x18 Jardin a Saint Tropez Sby 5/93 25,875
O/C 20x24 La Robe Rose 1920 Hnd 10/92 17,000
O/C 19x22 Figure Dans Jardin au Pradet 1923 Doy 11/92 . 14,300
O/C 19x17 Jeune Femme Dans Un Transat Sby 5/93 14,300
O/C 11x14 Nature Morte aux Peches Sby 10/92 11,000
O/C 18x15 L'enfant au turban Chr 10/92 9,350
O/Pa/L 20x24 Femme au Collier de Perles Doy 5/93 8,360
O/Pn 10x14 Bord de Mer Sby 10/92 6,600
O/C 18x21 Dans Les Tranchees 1917 Sby 10/92 5,500
O/B 16x13 Jeune Fille Assise Sby 10/92 5,500

W/Pa 10x18 La Regate Sby 2/93 5,463
O/C 18x15 Running Child Sby 2/93 4,313
Pe&K/Pa 15x10 Jeune Fille en Bleu Chr 2/93 3,520
W,K&Pl/Pa 9x12 Vue du Baie Chr 5/93 2,530
Y/Pa 11x10 Etude de Jeune Femme Doy 5/93 880

Lebduska, Lawrence H. Am 1894-1966
O/C 20x24 Prancing Horses 56 Sby 9/92 1,760

Lebedev, Vladimir Am 1910-1991
O/B 10x16 Martha's Vineyard Yng 5/93 500
O/B 12x16 Misty Point, Block Island 1967 Fre 4/93 200
O/B 12x16 Stone Barn, Block Island 1967 Fre 4/93 150

Lebel, Edmond Fr 1834-1909
I/Pn 16x11 Carrying Hay 1871 Chr 2/93 1,430

Lebenstein, Jan
* See 1992 Edition . . . .

LeBeuze, G. Fr 20C
O/C 15x25 Waiting at La Charcuterie 1943 Hnd 12/92 1,300

Lebourg, Albert Fr 1849-1928
O/C 20x29 Barques Devant Saint-Gingolph Sby 11/92 . . . 26,400
O/C 18x24 Le Parc du Petit Trianon Sby 2/93 21,850
O/C 22x29 Bord de Seine Sby 5/93 17,250
O/C 16x26 Evening Landscape But 5/93 9,200
W&K/Pa 15x22 Pont sur Seine 1898 Chr 5/93 4,025

Lebret, Frans Dut 1820-1909
O/C 23x30 Fetching Water for the Animals Skn 11/92 2,640

Lebret, Frans & J. Portielje Bel 1820-1909
* See 1992 Edition . . . .

LeBrocquy, Louis 1916-
* See 1993 Edition . . . .

Lebrun Con 19C
O/C 46x35 Girl with Baskets of Flowers 1844 Chr 5/93 . . . 1,610

LeBrun, Christopher 1951-
O/C 96x90 Region 83 Chr 11/92 8,800

Lebrun, Guillaume Charles Fr 1825-1908
O/C 40x25 The Love Token Sby 2/93 34,500

Lebrun, Marcel Fr 19C
* See 1992 Edition . . . .

LeBrun, Marie Louise E. V. Fr 1755-1842
* See 1992 Edition . . . .

LeBrun, Rico Am 1900-1964
Pl&P/B 18x25 Fall of the Centurion 1948 But 4/93 1,840

LeBrunne, A.
O/C Size? Musical Interlude Dum 10/92 700

Lecamus, Jules Alexandre Fr 1814-1878
* See 1991 Edition . . . .

Lechat, Albert Eugene
Pe&W/Pa 11x18 Place Du Marche 1904 Sby 2/93 575

Lechner, Hans H. Aus 20C
O/B 13x10 Snow Covered Chalet Hnd 3/93 200

Leclaire, Victor Fr 1830-1885
* See 1991 Edition . . . .

LeClerc Des Gobelins Fr 1734-1785
* See 1993 Edition . . . .

LeClerc, Sebastien Jacques Fr 1734-1785
* See 1993 Edition . . . .

Lecomte Du Nouy, Jean Jules A. Fr 1842-1923
O/Pn 19x15 Demosthene S'Exerce deux femmes1870 Sby 2/93 33,800

Lecomte, Paul Emile Fr 1877-1950
O/C 24x30 La Descente a Varenne Hnd 3/93 1,500

Lecomte, Valentine Fr 1872-
* See 1992 Edition . . . .

Lecomte, Victor Fr 1856-1920
* See 1993 Edition . . . .

Lecomte-Vernet, Charles Emile Fr 1821-1900
O/C 50x34 Oriental Beauty 1871 Hnd 3/93 25,000

Lecoque, Alois Am 1891-1981
O/C 18x24 Charbon et Bois Sby 6/93 1,350
O/M 16x20 Rue St. Julien le Pauvre, Paris Sby 10/92 880
G/Pa 19x23 Montmartre Brd 8/93 798
G/Pa 19x23 The Courtyard Brd 8/93 798

LeCorbusier   Fr 1887-1965
  * See 1993 Edition . . . .
Ledesma, Gabriel Fernandez   Mex 1900-1983
  O/C 20x25 Los Guantes Negros 1940 Sby 11/92 25,300
Ledieu, Philippe   Fr 19C
  O/C 10x15 Chasse aux Perdrix (2) Yng 2/93 1,500
Leduc, Fernand   Can 1916-
  G/B 14x14 Project #10 '73 Sbt 11/92 1,056
Leduc, Ozius   Can 1864-1955
  Pe/Pa 16x13 Study of Contemplative Man Sbt 5/93 836
Ledward, Gilbert   Br 1888-
  C/Pa 25x15 Female Torso 1936 Hnd 5/93 325
Lee, Bertha Stringer   Am 1873-1937
  O/C 24x16 Moonlight-Golden Gate Park Mor 6/93 825
  O/B 7x9 Flowered Coastal Mor 11/92 300
Lee, Catherine   1950-
  * See 1992 Edition . . . .
Lee, Doris Emrick   Am 1905-1983
  * See 1993 Edition . . . .
Lee, Joseph   Am 1827-1880
  * See 1993 Edition . . . .
Lee, Manning Del   Am 1894-1980
  W&R/Pa 17x13 Pirates Boarding Ship Ih 5/93 1,200
Lee, Robert E.   Am 1899-
  * See 1990 Edition . . . .
Lee, Robert J.   Am 1921-
  O/C 28x34 Sailing Ships at Dock Yng 2/93 200
Lee, Sydney   Br 1866-1949
  O/Pn 6x9 Landscape with Tower Hnd 10/92 550
Lee-Hankey, William   Br 1869-1952
  O/C 20x24 St. Valery Sur Somme But 5/93 8,625
Leech, Conrad   Am 20C
  O/C 26x18 Lady at the Piano Hnd 12/92 450
Leeke, Ferdinand   Ger 1859-
  O/C/B 33x52 Nude on Rock 1926 But 11/92 2,200
Leemans, Antonius   Dut 1631-1673
  * See 1990 Edition . . . .
Leempoels, Jef   Bel 1867-
  * See 1991 Edition . . . .
Lees, John   Am 1943-
  O/C 18x22 Landscape M.S.A.C. '78 FHB 3/93 1,500
Leeteg, Edgar   Am 20C
  * See 1993 Edition . . . .
Lefebvre, Jules Joseph   Fr 1835-1911
  O&H/Pa/Pn 9x5 The Slave Market 1876 Sby 10/92 1,980
Lefeuvre, Jean   Fr 1882-
  * See 1990 Edition . . . .
Lefevre, Adolphe Rene   Fr 1834-
  O/Pn 9x7 Faust and Margarite Leaving Church Chr 10/92 . . 4,620
Lefevre, Jean   Fr 1916-
  * See 1993 Edition . . . .
Lefevre, Robert Jacques F.   Fr 1755-1830
  * See 1991 Edition . . . .
Lefler, Franz   Czk 1831-1898
  * See 1993 Edition . . . .
Lefort, Jean   Fr 1875-1954
  * See 1993 Edition . . . .
LeFranc, J.   20C
  O/C 11x14 L'Elle a Quimperle Slo 4/93 250
Legacheff, Anton   Rus 1798-1865
  * See 1992 Edition . . . .
Leganger, Nicolay Tysland   Am 1832-1894
  * See 1992 Edition . . . .
Legat, Leon   Fr 1829-
  O/C 46x35 Le Plaisir de la Peche Chr 10/92 35,200
  O/C 23x19 Poultry and Figures Fre 4/93 10,000
Legeay, Jean-Laurent   Fr 1710-1786
  * See 1993 Edition . . . .
Leger, Fernand   Fr 1881-1955
  O/C 18x26 Nature Morte 31 Chr 11/92 165,000
  G&I/Pa 26x20 Mere et Enfant Sby 11/92 96,250
  G&I/Pa 26x20 Les Deux Amoureux Sby 11/92 82,500
  W/B 12x9 Nature Morte 25 Chr 11/92 66,000

Br,I&W/Pa 17x13 Le Mecanicien Sby 5/93 54,625
G/Pa 14x17 Femme et Fleur Sby 5/93 40,250
I/Pa 25x19 L'Ouvrier Accoude 50 Sby 5/93 34,500
W,Br&Pl/Pa 22x17 Femme debout Chr 11/92 28,600
O/C 13x10 Atelier de Fernand Leger Sby 11/92 25,300
Pe/Pa 7x9 Les Joueurs de Cartes Sby 5/93 11,500
G,Pl&Pe/Pa 5x4 A L'Amitie Franco-Americaine Sby 10/92 . . 7,700
Legge, Russell
  * See 1993 Edition . . . .
Leggett, Alexander   Eng 19C
  * See 1993 Edition . . . .
Legout-Gerard, Fernand Marie E   Fr 1856-1924
  O/C 45x57 Pardon de Sainte Anne de la Palud Sby 5/93 . . 26,450
  O/Pn 22x18 Retour des Pecheurs a Concarneau Chr 2/93 . . 8,800
  O/C 26x22 A Busy Harbor Chr 10/92 7,700
  P/Pa 20x26 Port at Bretagne Dum 7/93 2,400
Legrain, Pierre   Fr 20C
  * See 1990 Edition . . . .
Legrand, Alexandre   Fr 1822-1901
  * See 1992 Edition . . . .
Legrand, Jenny   Am 20C
  * See 1991 Edition . . . .
Legueult, Raymond-Jean
  W&Pe/Pa 19x26 La Belle Odalisque 68 Sby 2/93 3,450
LeHarve, Montardier   Fr a 1812-1848
  W/Pa 25x29 Ship Mayesville of Philadelphia Eld 7/93 4,620
Lehman   Ger 19C
  O/C/B 20x26 Family Scene Hnd 9/92 275
Lehmann, Karl Ernest R. H. S.   Fr 1814-1882
  K/Pa 9x10 Drapery, Hand and Head Studies Sby 2/93 4,025
Lehmbruck, Wilhelm
  * See 1992 Edition . . . .
Leibl, Wilhelm Maria Hubertus   Ger 1844-1900
  * See 1991 Edition . . . .
Leibovitz, Freda
  W/Pa 14x19 New Orleans - Canal Street 1940 Ald 5/93 95
Leickert, Charles Henri Joseph   Bel 1818-1907
  O/C 25x40 Busy Dutch River Village 66 Chr 10/92 41,800
Leigh, William Robinson   Am 1866-1955
  O/C 25x30 Zuni Pottery Maker 1907 Chr 12/92 165,000
Leighton, Edmund Blair   Br 1853-1922
  * See 1992 Edition . . . .
Leighton, J. C.   Eng 19C
  O/C 45x35 Old Friends Doy 11/92 3,080
Leighton, Kathryn W.   Am 1876-1952
  O/C 25x30 California Mountain Trail Hnd 10/92 3,000
Leighton, Lord Frederic   Br 1830-1896
  O/C 24x20 Antigone Chr 5/93 90,500
Leighton, Lucille   Am 20C
  O/B 32x16 The Lantern Shop Hnz 5/93 90
Leighton, Nicholas Winfield S.   Am 1847-1898
  * See 1993 Edition . . . .
Leighton, Scott   Am 1849-1898
  O/C 24x36 Farm and Its Livestock Sby 6/93 12,850
  O/C 24x36 St. Julian Sby 6/93 11,500
  O/C 27x44 The Three Veterans Brd 2/93 4,180
  O/C 24x18 Ready for the Hunt Sby 9/92 1,980
Leistikow, Walter   Rus 1865-1908
  * See 1993 Edition . . . .
Leith-Ross, Harry   Am 1886-1973
  O/C 24x32 Spell of the Spring Fre 10/92 6,250
  O/C 22x32 Country House with Figures Fre 10/92 5,250
  O/B 10x8 Landscape Ald 9/92 5,250
  O/B 10x8 Cows in the Pasture Ald 3/93 1,900
  O/B 8x10 Spring Landscape Skn 11/92 935
  W/Pa 12x16 Ocean Beach Fre 10/92 325
Lejeune, Eugene   Fr 1818-1894
  O/C 17x28 An Overturned Wagon Fre 4/93 6,500
Leleux, Adolphe Pierre   Fr 1812-1891
  * See 1993 Edition . . . .

Leloir, Alexandre Louis Fr 1843-1884
O/C 38x78 The Trumpeter 1870 But 11/92 12,100
Leloir, Jean-Baptiste Auguste Fr 1809-1892
 * See 1990 Edition . . . .
Leloir, Maurice Fr 1853-1940
 * See 1993 Edition . . . .
LeLong, Pierre Fr 1908-
O/Pa/B 29x24 La Repetition, 1958 Lou 3/93 150
Lelong, Rene Fr 20C
 * See 1992 Edition . . . .
Lelong, V* Fr 19C**
O/C 22x16 Maiden in Barn Sby 1/93 3,335
Lely, Sir Peter Br 1618-1680
 * See 1992 Edition . . . .
Lemaire, Madeleine Jeanne Fr 1845-1928
 * See 1993 Edition . . . .
Lemaire, Marie Therese Fr 1861-
 * See 1992 Edition . . . .
Lemaitre, Hernando
 * See 1992 Edition . . . .
Lemaitre, Maurice
O/C/B 14x19 Boats and Fishnets Sby 2/93 863
LeMaitre, Nathaniel Fr 1831-1897
O/C/B 21x25 Landscapes with Figures: Pair 1856 FHB 5/93 . 400
Leman, Jacques Edmond Fr 1829-1889
O/Pn 21x30 Moliere Posant Chez Mignard 1861 Sby 10/92 . 7,975
Lembeck, Jack Am 1942-
A/C 48x38 Automated Playthings 1990 Chr 5/93 1,150
Lemeunier, Basile Fr 1852-
 * See 1990 Edition . . . .
Lemieux, Annette 1957-
O&L/C 72x54 Finger Painting on Yellow Pages 88 Chr 11/92 6,600
Lemieux, Jean-Paul Can 1904-1990
O/C 16x12 Portrait of a Nun 1967 Sbt 11/92 15,840
O/C 18x14 Serenitie Sbt 11/92 7,480
Lemmen, Georges Bel 1865-1916
O/Pn 11x14 La Meuse, Caucher du Soleil Sby 11/92 88,000
O/Pn 20x16 Les Jonquilles Sby 5/93 17,250
P/Pa 23x19 Nu a L'Atelier Sby 5/93 17,250
O/Pn 9x7 Portrait of Jacques Lemmen 02 Sby 10/92 8,525
O/B 15x18 Nature Morte au Citron Sby 2/93 8,050
P/Pa 20x19 Young Woman Sleeping 1901 Sby 10/92 6,600
O/Pn 8x10 Le Sommeil 1900 Sby 10/92 4,675
W&Y/Pa 11x10 Madame Lemmen 1907 Sby 10/92 1,980
K&P/Pa 18x24 Femmes Avec Une Colombe 1913 Sby 10/92 1,650
W&Y/Pa 10x11 Woman Reading a Book 1908 Sby 10/92 . . 1,320
K&C/Pa 15x12 Etude de Deux Femmes 99 Sby 10/92 825
Lemmens, Theophile Victor E. Fr 1821-1867
 * See 1993 Edition . . . .
Lemmi, Angiolo It 19C
 * See 1993 Edition . . . .
LeMoine, Elisabeth Fr a 1783-
 * See 1991 Edition . . . .
Lemoine, Marie-Victoire Fr 1754-1820
O/C 24x19 Portrait Madame Genlis 1781 Sby 1/93 40,250
LeMolt, Phillipe Fr 1895-
O/C 18x24 Port Breton Slo 5/93 475
LeMore, Paul Fr 20C
 * See 1992 Edition . . . .
LeMoyne, Francois Fr 1688-1737
K/Pa 10x8 Saint John the Baptist Preaching Chr 1/93 3,080
Lenepveu, Jules Eugene Fr 1819-1898
 * See 1993 Edition . . . .
Lengo Y Martinez, Horacio Spa -1890
O/C 47x22 Unrequited Love: Pair Sby 5/93 17,250
Lenoir, Charles Amable Fr 1861-
O/C 18x13 La Bain Wes 10/92 9,350
Lenoir, Simon-Bernard Fr 1729-1791
 * See 1993 Edition . . . .
Lenpen, A. Con 20C
 * See 1992 Edition . . . .

Lens, Bernhard (the Younger) Dut 1682-1740
 * See 1991 Edition . . . .
Lens, Cornelis a 1738-
O/C 22x21 Tulip, Narcissi, Roses, Snowballs Chr 10/92 . . . 8,800
Lenson, P. Eng 20C
O/C 8x10 Summer Sheep Grazing 1908 Slo 4/93 160
Lenz, Norbert Am 20C
O/M 55x36 Birds Wtf 5/93 425
O/M 30x50 Pyramid Landscape Wtf 5/93 400
Leon Y Escosura, Ignacio Spa 1834-1901
 * See 1992 Edition . . . .
Leon, Angel Acosta Cub 1932-
O/C 31x58 Sin Titulo 64 Chr 11/92 16,500
Leon, Ernesto
 * See 1992 Edition . . . .
Leon, Noe Col 1907-
 * See 1991 Edition . . . .
Leonard, Ruth Am 1955-
O/C 60x72 Cliffside Highway 1984 FHB 3/93 1,000
O/C 26x39 Slow Fires of Autumn 1983 FHB 3/93 950
Leonardi It 19C
 * See 1992 Edition . . . .
Leone, R. Fr 20C
O/C 20x28 Coastal Scene with Fishing Boats FHB 6/93 . . . 500
Leoni, Ottavio Maria It 1587-1630
K/Pa 7x6 Portrait of a Noblewoman Chr 1/93 3,520
Leonori, R. G. L. Am a 19C
O/C 14x18 Snow Scene Chr 9/92 3,850
Leontus, Adam Hai 20C
 * See 1992 Edition . . . .
Leopold-Levy Fr 1886-1966
O/C 13x18 Mountainside in Provence Wes 3/93 1,100
LePersan, Jean Raffy Fr 1920-
O/C 17x21 Theatre de l'Atelier a Montmartre Chr 11/92 . . . 1,760
LePho Fr 1907-
O/C 24x29 Femmes aux Fleurs Chr 11/92 2,640
O/C 32x26 Vase de Fleurs au Fond Bleu Chr 2/93 1,210
O/C 24x29 Bouquet aux Pivoines Chr 11/92 880
O/C 13x10 Girl Amid Blossoms Sby 2/93 748
O/C 20x26 Fleurs Hnd 5/93 600
Lepicie, Michel Nicolas B. Fr 1735-1784
 * See 1993 Edition . . . .
Lepine, Joseph
 * See 1992 Edition . . . .
Lepine, Stanislas Fr 1835-1892
O/Pn 6x9 Au Bord de la Riviere Sby 5/93 12,650
O/Pn 6x9 Unloading on the Seine Embankment Doy 5/93 . . 8,800
LePoittevin, Eugene Modeste E. Fr 1806-1870
O/Pn 12x18 Family Fishing Off the Coast Wtf 3/93 2,600
O/C 15x18 An Allegorical Scene Chr 2/93 1,980
Lepri, Stanislao It 1905-
 * See 1993 Edition . . . .
Leprin, Marcel Fr 1891-1933
 * See 1992 Edition . . . .
Leprince, August-Xavier Fr 1799-1826
 * See 1991 Edition . . . .
Leprince, Jean-Baptiste Fr 1734-1781
O/C 18x21 Tarquin and Lucretia Sby 5/93 57,500
O/C 16x13 A Lady, Seated: Pair 1766 Chr 1/93 41,800
LeProu Fr 19C
O/Pn 9x17 Picnic on the Banks of a River Sel 9/92 1,700
Leray, Prudent Louis Fr 1820-1879
 * See 1992 Edition . . . .
Lerin, Giralt Am 20C
O/C 36x24 Religious Gathering Sel 2/93 100
Lerner, Leslie Am 1949-
T/Cd 9x11 El Pate Muerto But 4/93 460
Leroux, Auguste Fr 1871-1954
O/C 70x53 The Reflection Chr 5/93 21,850
Leroux, Gaston Veuvenot Fr 1854-
 * See 1992 Edition . . . .
Leroux, P. Fr 19C
I&S/Pa 6x5 Young Napoleon and Josephine Hnd 10/92 . . . 375

LeRoy, Gustave Jules   Fr 1833-1865
O/C 29x37 The Curious Kitten Chr 2/93 16,500
O/C 18x22 Grandeur Dechue But 5/93 4,600
LeRoy, Harold   Am 20C
* See 1993 Edition . . . .
**LeRoy, Paul Alexandre Alfred   Fr
1860-1942**
* See 1990 Edition . . . .
LeSage, Henriette Gabrielle   Fr 20C
W/Pa 14x10 Breath of Fresh Air Slo 4/93 225
LeSauteur, Claude   Can 1926-
* See 1992 Edition . . . .
LeSeyeux, Jean
W&Pe/Pa 14x10 Costume Design Eye of Partridge Sby 10/92   990
LeSidaner, Henri   Fr 1862-1939
O/C 24x29 La Terrasse, Gerberoy Sby 11/92 49,500
O/C 18x22 Neige a Guimcamp Sby 5/93 43,125
O/C 17x23 La Chaumiere, Etaples 1893 Sby 2/93 20,700
O/B 13x18 Le Pont, Automne, Gisors Sby 2/93 20,700
P/Pa 25x19 Canal Sous la Neige a Beauvais Sby 10/92 . . 14,300
O/Pn 11x14 L'Eglise Treguier Sby 2/93 12,075
O&K/Pa 15x8 Le Vieux Faune Chr 2/93 990
Lesieur, Pierre   Fr 1922-
* See 1993 Edition . . . .
Leslie, Alfred   Am 1927-
O/C 58x44 Portrait of Mikey Besch 1990 Chr 5/93 2,760
O&L/M 9x17 Untitled Sby 2/93 575
Leslie, Charles   Br 1840-
O/C 30x50 Extensive Highlands Landscape 1885 Mys 12/92 . 798
Leslie, Charles Robert   Br 1794-1859
O/C 30x51 The Highlands 1881 Sby 1/93 5,175
Leslie, Edward   Am 1891-1960
O/C 24x30 Marin Landscape 1928 But 6/93 1,840
Lesrel, Adolphe Alexandre   Fr 1839-1921
* See 1993 Edition . . . .
Lessieux, Ernest   Fr 1849-1925
W/Pa 18x11 Alger - Mosque Sidi Abderhaman Brd 2/93 330
Lessing, Carl Friedrich   Ger 1808-1880
O/C 24x45 Huss before Council of Constance Chr 2/93 . . . 4,620
LeSueur, Eustache   Fr 1616-1655
K&S/Pa 10x14 David Dancing Before Ark Covenant Chr 1/93 16,500
Lesur, Henry Victor   Fr 1863-
O/Pn 18x22 An Afternoon Flirtation Chr 10/92 4,950
Letendre, Rita   Can 1929-
A/C 26x32 Lutte, Ramat Gan '63 Sbt 5/93 2,640
O/C 12x14 Chevauchee '61 '61 Sbt 11/92 1,056
Lethbridge, Julian   1947-
A&Pt/L 27x21 Untitled 1988 Chr 2/93 5,500
H&G/Pa 13x10 Untitled 89 Chr 2/93 2,860
H&G/Pa 18x12 Cobweb 88 Chr 2/93 1,760
Lettwill, J.   Am 20C
O/C 24x36 Girls in a Meadow by a Lake Sby 3/93 575
Letuaire, Pierre   Fr 1799-1884
* See 1992 Edition . . . .
Leullier, Felix Louis   Fr 1811-1882
* See 1992 Edition . . . .
Leutze, Emanuel Gottlieb   Am 1816-1868
Pe/Pa 13x10 Study Washington Crossing Del. 1851 Sby 9/92 6,600
Leuus, Jesus   Mex 20C
O&Sd/B 24x12 Mother and Child 1947 But 10/92 1,045
LeVa, Barry   Am 1941-
E&L/C 60x61 Sculpture Activities: Green 1986 Chr 11/92 . . 4,620
I/Pa 9x11 Distribution and Density Price 1968 Sby 11/92 . . 2,750
Leve, Frederic Louis   Fr 1877-
* See 1991 Edition . . . .
Levee, John Harrison   Am 1924-
O/C 51x64 April IV, 1959 59 Sby 6/93 690
Leveille, Andre   Fr 1880-1963
* See 1993 Edition . . . .
Levene, Sherrie   Am 20C
* See 1991 Edition . . . .
Lever, Richard Hayley   Am 1876-1958
O/C 50x60 Summer St. Ives Harbor, Cornwall Sby 5/93 . . 40,250
O/C 25x30 Lower Manhattan Chr 12/92 33,000
O/C 24x30 Anchored Ships at St Ives, Cornwall Chr 3/93 . 14,950

O/C 18x24 Smeaton's Pier, St. Ives Sby 3/93 14,375
O/C 73x70 View of Gloucester Sby 9/92 14,300
W/Pa 11x16 Gloucester Hills Sby 12/92 9,900
O/C 24x30 St. Ives Chr 3/93 7,475
O/C 20x24 Harbor with Fishing Boats Sby 3/93 5,750
O/C 18x24 Evening in the Harbor Brd 2/93 4,620
O/C 10x13 Central Park Sby 9/92 3,575
O/B 14x18 Covered Bridge Doy 11/92 3,080
W&Pe/Pa 11x15 The Shore Town Chr 3/93 2,645
O/C 7x10 Brittany Beach Scene Mys 12/92 2,640
O/C 14x18 Early Morning, St. Ives Chr 12/92 2,420
O/C 14x22 Sailboat at Dockside Sby 3/93 2,070
O/C 14x18 Rock by the Sea Sby 3/93 1,840
O/M 12x16 Fishing Boat Wes 3/93 1,320
O/Pn 12x16 View of Sheridan Square Sby 9/92 1,210
W/Pa 10x14 Kew Common, London 1900 Wlf 12/92 900
W/Pa 10x14 Kew Common, London Slo 4/93 900
O/Pn 7x10 Street in St. Ives Doy 5/93 715
O/Cb 18x14 Two Paintings Sby 3/93 690
W/Pa 9x13 Still Life Pears and Grapes Fre 4/93 600
W/Pa 16x29 Sunset, East Gloucester, 1913 Lou 9/92 300
Leverd, Rene   Fr 1872-1938
O/C 11x15 Winter View Through the Trees But 11/92 2,750
Levier, Charles   Fr 1920-
O/C 30x40 Le Vieux Pont Sby 2/93 3,738
O/C 40x30 Fleurs Sauvages Chr 11/92 3,410
O/C 30x40 Fleurs a la Fenetre Sby 10/92 3,025
O/C 30x40 Ville en Corse Sby 10/92 3,025
O/C 40x30 Walk Along the Seine Wes 10/92 2,090
A/C 40x30 Femmes dands Un Bar Sel 2/93 1,800
O/C 30x40 L'Atelier Chr 5/93 1,725
O/C 40x30 L'Aube Chr 5/93 1,725
O/C 40x30 Le Cadeau Sby 2/93 1,725
O/C 24x30 Two Paintings Chr 5/93 1,725
O/C 48x24 Fleurs Sauvages Yng 2/93 1,700
O/C 30x40 Port Corse Chr 11/92 1,650
O/C 40x30 Promenade Doy 11/92 1,650
O/C 15x30 Street Scene Lou 3/93 1,500
O/C 30x40 Venise Lou 6/93 1,500
O/C 22x28 Parisian Street in Winter Wes 10/92 1,430
O/C 48x24 Fleurs Sauvages Sel 12/92 1,400
A/C 40x30 Fleurs sur la Table Rouge Sel 2/93 1,400
O/C 40x30 Still Life Hnd 3/93 1,200
O/C 30x40 Avignon 59 Chr 2/93 990
O/C 30x24 Fleurs '61 Wes 12/92 880
O/C 24x29 Village au Perigord Chr 5/93 863
O/C 20x24 Barques Chr 2/93 770
O/C 24x30 Le Port Chr 11/92 660
W/Pa 30x22 Still Life Vase of Flowers Sel 12/92 425
A/C 30x24 Five Figures in Street Scene Sel 2/93 350
A/C 24x30 Still Life Fruit Sel 2/93 300
W/Pa 30x22 The Harbour Hnd 10/92 225
O/Pa 15x30 Fruit and Pitcher on Table Yng 5/93 200
Levin, W.   Am 19C
O/C 10x14 Child's Dance 1903 Hnd 6/93 275
Levine, David   Am 1926-
W/Pa 13x10 Joy Ride '82 Sby 12/92 4,950
Pl/Pa 7x6 General Custer with Dead Native Am. Ih 5/93 700
Levine, David Phillip   Am 1910-
O/B 10x8 Audience Chr 12/92 605
Levine, Jack   Am 1915-
O/C 28x32 Lolita Chr 9/92 33,000
O/C 48x42 David and Goliath Chr 3/93 29,900
O/C 26x32 Lady in the Woods Chr 12/92 26,400
O/C 24x21 Woman in Green Sby 12/92 17,600
O/C 20x27 The Oath Chr 12/92 11,000
O/C 32x26 Portrait of Joan Chr 3/93 10,350
O/C 32x26 Girl with Red Hair Chr 9/92 7,700
W,Pe&G/Pa 11x15 Old City Hall, Boston '83 Sby 12/92 . . 5,225
K/Pa 20x13 Three Drawings '60 Sby 3/93 1,725
Y/Pa 20x13 Two Drawings Sby 3/93 1,610
I/Pa 12x17 Three Drawings Sby 3/93 978
Levine, Sherrie   Am 1947-
Cs&Wx/Wd 24x20 Broad Stripe #1 Chr 11/92 14,300
A/Wd 21x17 Gold Knot #1 1985 Chr 2/93 12,100

Cs/Wd 47x27 Untitled (Mr. Austridge: 2) Chr 11/92 12,100
Ph 20x16 Untitled Chr 2/93 2,420
W&H/Pa 14x11 After Henri Matisse 1983 Chr 2/93 2,200
Ph 10x8 After Walker Evans 1987 Chr 11/92 1,980
W,G&Pe/Pa 13x11 After Joan Miro 1984 Sby 10/92 990
W&Pe/Pa 14x11 Volucelle 1984 Sby 10/92 990

Levis, Maurice   Fr 1860-1902
* See 1993 Edition ....

Levison, Nanna   Scn 20C
O/C 28x18 Afternoon's Pastime 1917 Sby 2/93 6,325

Levitan, Isaac Ilyitch   Rus 1860-1900
* See 1993 Edition ....

Levoiger, A. J. P.   Dut 1853-1952
* See 1990 Edition ....

Levow, Irving   Am 1902-
O/C 16x24 Handball Players 1939 Chr 5/93 1,265
O/C 16x24 Handball Players 1934 Lou 12/92 600

Levy, Alexander O.   Am 1881-1947
* See 1993 Edition ....

Levy, Beatrice S.   Am 1892-1974
O/C 10x14 Guadaloupe Church, Santa Fe 20 But 6/93 920

Levy, Henri Leopold   Fr 1840-1904
O/C 71x78 Mercury Sby 5/93 9,775

Levy, Henry L.   Am 1868-
O/C 34x26 Portrait of a Gentleman 93 Hnd 3/93 200

Levy, James   Eng 19C
W&G/Pa 10x15 Rural Landscapes: Two Slo 5/93 150

Levy, Nat   Am 1896-1984
* See 1993 Edition ....

Levy, Rudolph
* See 1992 Edition ....

Levy, William Auerbach   Am 1889-1964
A/C 20x24 Three Figures Waiting Hnd 12/92 900
Pl/Pa 23x16 Caricature Hnd 12/92 200
C/Pa 12x8 Paula Trueman; Girl Sleeping (2) Hnd 12/92 200

Levy-Dhurmer, Lucien   Fr 1865-1953
O/C 39x26 La Bourrasque (The Gust of Wind) Sby 2/93 . 112,500

Lew, August Wilhelm   Ger 1819-1897
* See 1990 Edition ....

Lewandowski, Edmund D.   Am 1914-
G&Pe/B 20x30 White Barn, Wisconsin 1960 Chr 3/93 3,680

Lewezuk, Margaret   20C
O/C 28x20 The Gate 84 Chr 11/92 110

Lewis, Archie Henry   Am 20C
O/C 30x26 Ridin' Kid from Tonque River Sby 3/93 690

Lewis, Charles James   Br 1830-1892
* See 1992 Edition ....

Lewis, Edmund Darch   Am 1835-1910
O/C 30x50 Morro Castle, Havana Harbor 1869 Sby 11/92 . 24,200
O/C 11x20 Seascape, Jersey Coast 1876 Sby 9/92 14,300
O/C 24x42 By the Mill Stream 1876 Chr 3/93 8,050
O/C 14x22 Yachts Racing/Committee Boat 1875 Eld 7/93 . 5,280
G,W&Pe/Pa 10x21 Moored in an Inlet 1896 Chr 9/92 3,850
G/Pa/B 10x21 Narragansett Bay 1891 Chr 3/93 2,990
O/C 15x26 Cattle by the Lake 1886 But 12/92 2,750
O/C 24x20 Fisherman Along Chester Creek 1867 Chr 12/92 . 2,750
W,Pe&G/Pa 10x21 Sailing Off the Rocks 1903 Sby 12/92 . 2,750
G/Pa 22x34 Sailboats in a Harbor 1902 Sby 3/93 2,530
G/Pa/B 15x26 Ships Off Point Lookout, NJ Chr 3/93 2,530
O/C 18x30 Lighthouse Amidst the Palms 1874 Chr 12/92 . 2,420
W&G/Pa 15x28 Fishing and Sailing Brd 8/93 2,200
O/C 23x37 Fishing on the Delaware 1874 Fre 4/93 2,200
W&G/Pa 7x15 The Casino 1888 Fre 4/93 1,900
W/Pa 7x15 Figures Walking Through Surf 1892 Fre 10/92 .. 825
W&G/Pa 7x15 Distressed Vessel Along Coast 1888 Fre 4/93 . 700
W&G/Pa 10x21 Rocky Coastal Scene 1899 Eld 11/92 468
W&G/Pa 14x16 Main Stable with a Courtyard 1869 Chr 5/93 . 460
W/Pa 9x19 Sailboats Off Coast 1874 Fre 4/93 450
W&G/Pa 22x33 The Mill Skn 11/92 385
G/Pa 6x12 Landscape Mys 12/92 302
W/Pa 9x20 Oceanscape 1874 Ald 9/92 125

Lewis, Geoffrey   Am 20C
* See 1990 Edition ....

Lewis, Harry Emerson   Am 1892-1958
O/B 24x30 The Old Barn and Corral Mor 6/93 880

O/C 19x14 Man on a Path But 10/92 660
O/Cb 20x24 Sunlit Valley Mor 6/93 660
O/M 24x30 Sierra Landscape Mor 2/93 475
W/Pa 14x10 To the Court of the Moon '39 Mor 2/93 475
O/B 20x24 Landscape Mor 6/93 358

Lewis, Jeanette Maxfield   Am 1894-1982
* See 1993 Edition ....

Lewis, John Frederick   Br 1805-1876
* See 1993 Edition ....

Lewis, Martin   Am 1883-1962
W&Pe/Pa 16x11 Brooklyn Bridge fr Downtown Chr 12/92 .. 1,320

Lewis, Mary Amanda   Am 1872-1953
O/B 10x15 Landscape Mor 2/93 325

Lewis, Percy Wyndham   Br 1882-1957
* See 1991 Edition ....

Lewis, Phillips Frisbee   Am 1892-1930
O/C 20x24 Valley of the Sweet Peas Chr 5/93 17,250
O/C/B 11x14 Green Screen and Old Plants But 6/93 1,495

LeWitt, Jan
O/C 56x44 Promethee 1963 Sby 10/92 715

LeWitt, Sol   Am 1928-
I/Pa 20x70 Geometric Drawing Sby 5/93 34,500
Fp/Pa 17x17 Four Color Drawing 1971 Chr 11/92 11,000
Fp/Pa 17x17 Four Color Drawing with Error 1971 Chr 11/92 . 11,000
H&Pl/Pa 7x20 12345-1 1979 Chr 10/92 9,900
I/Pa 18x24 22 Pieces in 5 Sets 1969 Sby 10/92 8,800
I/Pa 19x35 Plan for Drawing on East Wall 1969 Sby 10/92 . 8,800
I/Pa 14x35 Plan Wall Drawing, Wisc. State 1970 Sby 10/92 . 7,150
Br&I/Pa 15x30 Double Ink Drawing 1982 Chr 11/92 5,280
A/Wd 24x18 Maquette for Chicago Wall Project Chr 5/93 . 2,875
W/Pa 6x8 Untitled 89 Chr 2/93 1,210
W&Pe/Pa 6x8 Untitled 89 Sby 10/92 1,100

Lewy, James   Am 20C
O/C 10x14 Peaches 1898 Hnd 9/92 650
O/B 8x10 Peaches 1891 Hnd 9/92 425

LeYaouane, Alain   Fr 1940-
O/C 72x57 Composition 1972 Hnd 12/92 1,500

Leyendecker, Frank Xavier   Am 1877-1924
O/C 36x26 Athlete Before a Mosaic Sby 3/93 5,175

Leyendecker, Joseph Christian   Am 1874-1951
O/C 21x28 Studies, Football Players Tackling Ih 11/92 4,000
O/C 24x7 Independence Hall and U.S. Capitol Ih 5/93 ... 2,900
O/C/B 15x10 He Giveth His Beloved Sleep Slo 4/93 1,800
Pe/Pa 10x9 Two Drawings Ih 11/92 1,800
O/C 17x14 Cameo Portrait of Woman Ih 11/92 1,500
O/C 11x6 Woman with Praying Hands Ih 5/93 1,000
W/Pa 9x6 Byrnhilda's Immolation Lou 12/92 475

Leyendecker, Paul Joseph   Fr 1842-
O/C 13x10 Two Gentlemen in a Forest 1875 Sby 1/93 460

Leyster, Judith   Dut 1610-1660
* See 1992 Edition ....

Lhermitte, Leon Augustin   Fr 1844-1925
O/C 31x40 Glaneuses en avant Vieilles Meules Chr 10/92 . 99,000
O/C 27x23 Les Pecheurs Sby 10/92 52,250
O/C 34x28 La Ferme de Sombre Sby 10/92 38,500
P/Pa/C 14x18 Glaneuses Pres Des Meules Sby 10/92 19,800
P/Pa 13x17 Le Chemin de L'Ecole Sby 10/92 15,400
P/Pa 9x12 Les Fagoteuses Sby 2/93 7,475

Lhote, Andre   Fr 1885-1962
O/C 16x22 Nu Assis Chr 10/92 33,000
O/Pa/C 26x21 Femme Assise Sby 2/93 24,150
O/C 18x22 La Cote Froide a Mirmande 1950 Sby 10/92 ... 15,400
O/C 14x20 Paysage Sby 2/93 13,800
O/C 22x26 La Maison au Cedre Hnd 10/92 13,000
O/C 22x29 Nature Morte au Pichet 56 Sby 2/93 12,650
O/C 13x22 Bois de Boulogne au Chalant Sby 10/92 6,600
G/Pa 12x15 Landscape 47 Sby 6/93 4,600
G/Pa 12x15 Landscape 47 Sby 6/93 4,600
O/C 11x18 Carrieres de Platre Sby 10/92 3,850
G&Pe/B 10x13 Les Arbres Sby 6/93 3,450
W&H/Pa 10x13 Village Landscape with Figure Skn 5/93 .. 2,750
W&G/Pa/B 12x15 Chantier Naval Chr 5/93 2,530

153

Liang, Yen Wan Chi
  O/C 18x35 Spring Brook Fre 10/92 1,600
Liberi, Pietro It 1614-1687
  * See 1993 Edition . . . .
Liberman, Alexander Am 1912-
  A/C 61x91 Untitled 82 Sby 6/93 3,450
  O,G&C/Pa 30x23 Untitled 76 Sby 10/92 440
Liberti, Carlos
  * See 1992 Edition . . . .
Liberti, F. 18C
  * See 1993 Edition . . . .
Libertino It 1614-1687
  * See 1993 Edition . . . .
Liberts, Ludolfs Rus 1895-1945
  * See 1993 Edition . . . .
Lichtenstein, Roy Am 1923-
  Mg/C 68x48 Girl with Piano 63 Sby 11/92 . . . . 1.815M
  O&Mg/C 50x42 Girl With Tear II '77 Sby 11/92 462,000
  O&Mg/C 100x44 Woman with Flower '78 Chr 11/92 . . . 385,000
  O&Mg/C 36x40 Trigger Finger '63 Chr 11/92 258,500
  O&Mg/C 40x32 Plus and Minus III '88 Sby 5/93 178,500
  O&Mg/C 20x24 Cubist Still Life '74 Sby 11/92 165,000
  O&Mg/C 18x24 Modern Pntg w/Yellow Arc '67 Sby 5/93 101,500
  Mg/C 24 dia Mirror '70 Sby 11/92 66,000
  E/St 23x36 Sunrise 65 Sby 5/93 41,400
  A&L/Pa 26x17 Head V 86 Sby 10/92 38,500
  E/St 35x45 Modern Painting in Porcelain Chr 2/93 26,400
  L 26x28 Untitled 66 Sby 2/93 14,950
  E/Me 3x2 Modern Head Brooch Sby 10/92 3,025
  E/Me 3x3 Modern Head Pendant Chr 11/92 1,650
Licinio, Bernardino It 1489-1560
  * See 1992 Edition . . . .
Lidov, Arthur Herschel Am 1917-
  O/C 24x22 De Glory Road 36 But 6/93 1,150
Lie, Jonas Am 1880-1940
  O/C 35x42 After the Snow Fall '08 Chr 5/93 9,200
  O/C 21x32 Rocky Harbor Sby 9/92 4,950
  O/C 18x24 Harbor with Boats 1919 Sby 9/92 4,400
  O/C 43x51 Winter Stream Chr 5/93 3,680
  O/C 30x25 Windswept Birches Mor 6/93 1,870
  O/C/B 20x16 Harbor Scene Wes 12/92 935
Liebenwein, Maximilian Aus 1869-1926
  * See 1992 Edition . . . .
Lieber, Tom Am 20C
  * See 1992 Edition . . . .
Liebermann, Max Ger 1847-1935
  * See 1993 Edition . . . .
Liebers, A.
  * See 1993 Edition . . . .
Liebmann, Gerhardt Am 20C
  * See 1992 Edition . . . .
Liegeois, Paul a 17C
  O/C 12x17 Peaches and Grapes on a Ledge Chr 10/92 . . 24,200
Lienz, Egger Jules Sws 19C
  O/Pn 14x10 Boy with Spaniel & Peacock 1885 Chr 10/92 . . 1,650
Lievens, Jan Dut 1607-1672
  O/Pn 22x16 Head of Bearded Old Man Chr 1/93 44,000
Lievre, Lucien Fr 1878-
  * See 1993 Edition . . . .
Ligare, David 1945-
  O/C 79x111 Milos (Thrown Drapery) 1980 Chr 11/92 6,600
Ligozzi, Jacopo It 1547-1627
  O/C 54x40 Christ Carrying the Cross Chr 1/93 104,500
Likan, Gustav Con 20C
  Pl&S/Pa 10x13 Artist and Model Hnd 9/92 160
  Pl&S/Pa 11x8 Seated Couple Hnd 9/92 140
Liljefors, Bruno Andread Swd 1860-1939
  * See 1990 Edition . . . .
Liljestrom, Gustave Am 1882-1958
  O/C 20x30 Superstition Mountain But 6/93 1,150
Limouse, Roger Fr 1894-
  * See 1991 Edition . . . .
Lin, Hans Dut a 17C
  * See 1993 Edition . . . .

Linard, Jacques Fr 1600-1645
  * See 1992 Edition . . . .
Lincoln, Ephraim F. Am 20C
  * See 1992 Edition . . . .
Lindau, Dietrich Wilhelm Ger 1799-1862
  * See 1993 Edition . . . .
Lindberg, Arthur Harold Am 20C
  * See 1991 Edition . . . .
Linde, Ossip E. Am -1940
  O/B 8x10 The City of the Doges Mor 11/92 600
Lindemann, C. Con 19C
  O/C 21x16 Eavesdropping 1866 Fre 10/92 850
Lindenmuth, Tod Am 1885-1976
  O/M 24x26 Lifting Fog Fre 10/92 450
  O/B 14x17 The Dunes of Provincetown Ald 9/92 350
  O/B 24x32 Sisters of Saint Joseph Yng 2/93 300
Linder, Harry Am 1886-1931
  P/Pa 24x39 Meandering Brook But 6/93 690
  P/Pa 8x12 Landscape Mor 11/92 150
Linder, P. Br 19C
  * See 1993 Edition . . . .
Linderum, Richard Ger 1851-
  O/C 28x42 Tavern Interior But 11/92 6,600
Lindh, Bror Swd 1877-1941
  * See 1992 Edition . . . .
Lindin, Carl Olaf Eric Am 1869-1942
  * See 1993 Edition . . . .
Lindner, Ernest Can 1897-1988
  * See 1993 Edition . . . .
Lindner, Richard Am 1901-1978
  Cp,W&L/B 17x13 Jacques 1965 Sby 10/92 19,800
  Pl&G/Pa 18x13 Untitled 41 Chr 11/92 4,400
  W/Pa 27x20 Untitled Chr 5/93 2,300
Lindsay, Thomas Corwin Am 1839-1907
  * See 1993 Edition . . . .
Lindstrom, Arvid Mauritz Swd 1849-1923
  O/C 50x30 Sunset Over Winter Forest But 5/93 2,588
Linford, Charles Am 1846-1897
  O/C/B 28x36 Coastal Landscape FHB 6/93 1,000
  O/C 22x30 Elmwood Falls, Pennsylvania Fre 4/93 200
Lingelbach, Johannes Dut 1622-1674
  * See 1992 Edition . . . .
Lingenfelder, E. Ger 19C
  O/Pn 8x6 Pair of Portraits Hnd 3/93 600
Lingke, Albert Muller Ger 1844-
  O/C 35x48 Landscape with Figures Lou 6/93 5,250
Linke, Simon 20C1958-
  O/L 72x72 Gary Stephan, October 1986 Sby 5/93 5,750
Linley, Dora K. Am 20C
  O/C 24x20 Impressionistic Flower Garden Wlf 5/93 475
Linnell, C. L. Br 19C
  O/C 11x13 Donkey in Stable 1803 Hnd 10/92 200
Linnell, John Br 1792-1882
  * See 1993 Edition . . . .
Linnell, William Br 1826-
  O/C 36x50 Vale of Avoe 1880 Chr 2/93 9,900
Linnig, Egidius Bel 1821-1860
  O/C 29x39 The Day's Catch 1849 Sby 5/93 17,250
Linnig, Willem (Snr.) Bel 1819-1886
  O/Pn 12x9 Old Man Filling a Pipe Sby 1/93 3,738
Lins, Adolf Ger 1856-1927
  O/C 40x34 Blowing Bubbles 85 Chr 2/93 17,600
Linson, Corwin Knapp Am 1864-1934
  O/C 40x48 Underwoods - Winter Sunshine 1923 Sby 9/92 . 6,600
  W/Pa 7x12 Four Editorial Illustrations 1898 Ih 11/92 2,500
  O/B 10x8 Winter Afternoon by the Sea 1912 Skn 9/92 1,100
  O/Pn 12x16 Winter Meadows 1910 Skn 3/93 1,045
Linton, Frank Benton Am 1871-1943
  * See 1992 Edition . . . .
Lintott, Edward Bernard Am 1875-1951
  O/C 22x42 Italian Comedy Mys 12/92 495
  O/C 30x24 Mums in an Oriental Vase Mys 3/93 192
Linzoni, P. It 20C
  * See 1992 Edition . . . .

Lipchitz, Jacques Fr 1891-1973
V/Pa 8x11 Deux Figures: Pair Sby 10/92 4,400
Pe&Pl/Pa 17x11 Le Sacrifice Chr 2/93 2,420
Br&Pl/Pa 9x6 Femme Assise Chr 2/93 1,430
Lippert, Leon Am -1950
* See 1991 Edition . . . .
Lippincott, William Henry Am 1849-1920
O/C 11x14 The Cliffs at Etretat 1890 Sby 12/92 13,200
O/C 16x12 Autumn Glow Doy 5/93 1,870
O/Pn 11x14 Just a Few Puffs Chr 3/93 1,725
Lipps, Richard Ger 1857-1926
* See 1993 Edition . . . .
Lipton, Seymour 1903-1986
* See 1993 Edition . . . .
Lira, Pedro Chi 19C
* See 1993 Edition . . . .
Lismer, Arthur Can 1885-1969
O/B/C 13x17 Rocks and Pines, Georgian Bay Sbt 11/92 . . 10,560
O/Pn 12x16 Channel, Georgian Bay 1952 Sbt 5/93 9,680
O/Pn 12x16 Little Lake, Baie Finn Sbt 5/93 9,680
O/B 13x16 Sentinel, Canadian Rockies '22 Sbt 11/92 7,040
O/Pn 12x16 Evening - Georgian Bay Sbt 5/93 6,600
O/C 16x20 Rocky Shore VI '61 Sbt 5/93 4,840
O/B/C 13x16 Water and Rocks Sbt 11/92 3,960
S/Pa 16x12 Tree Study '64 Sbt 5/93 1,144
V/Pa 8x10 Fishing Boats; Long Beach: Two Sbt 11/92 572
V/Pa 8x6 Tree - Georgian Way Sbt 11/92 528
Lissitsky, El Rus 1890-
* See 1991 Edition . . . .
List, Wilhelm Aus 1864-1918
W/Pa 16x12 Trees Reflecting by a Lake Wtf 9/92 500
Litterman, Anne 1956-
O/L 66x48 The Healing of Paloma '92 Chr 11/92 8,250
O/L 66x48 Le Observes Destructive Effect '91 Chr 11/92 . . 7,150
Little, J. Wesley Am 1867-1923
W/Pa 17x24 Cows at the Watering Hole Mys 12/92 220
Little, John Geoffrey C. Can 1928-
O/C 16x20 Avenue des Pins, Montreal 1968 Sbt 5/93 3,740
O/C 24x30 Le Printemps, Quebec '75 Sbt 5/93 3,520
O/C 12x16 Rue Duluth, Coin Laval, Montreal '69 Sbt 11/92 . 2,288
O/C 12x16 Rue Marie Anne, Montreal '72 Sbt 5/93 1,760
Little, Phillip Am 1857-1942
O/C 31x51 Old Fish Weirs 1912 Skn 11/92 1,430
O/C 36x29 The Herring Weirs Sunset 1913 Skn 11/92 1,320
W/Pa 14x20 Rocky Coast Mys 3/93 165
Littlefield, William Horace Am 1902-1969
O/B 20x26 Abstract Landscape Mys 12/92 358
O/B 15x11 Abstract Mys 3/93 302
Litzinger, Dorothea M. Am 1889-1925
O/C 40x42 Pond Lilies and Irises Skn 5/93 2,420
Livemont, Privat Bel 1861-1936
* See 1993 Edition . . . .
Livens, Horace Mann Br 1860-1936
O/C 14x18 Fruit Still Life Hnz 5/93 425
Liz, Domingo 20C
* See 1991 Edition . . . .
Ljuba 20C
* See 1992 Edition . . . .
Llasera Y Diaz, Jose Spa 1882-
O/C 28x23 Carmen 1926 Sby 1/93 2,415
Llona, Ramiro Per 1947-
O/C 69x72 Arquitectura de Desierto 1987 Chr 11/92 19,800
Llorens, Jose Navarro Spa 1867-1923
W/Pa 8x20 Figures and Donkeys on a Street Chr 10/92 . . . 5,500
Llorente, Bernardo German Spa 1680-1759
* See 1993 Edition . . . .
Lloyd, Helen Sharpless Am 20C
O/Cb 22x28 San Fernando Valley 1948 Mor 11/92 1,000
Lloyd, J. C. Br 19C
O/C 33x20 Harem Girl 1902 Wes 12/92 1,210
Lloyd, John Am 20C
O/C 8x10 Winter Afternoon Sel 12/92 100
Lloyd, Thomas Ivester Br 1873-1942
G/Pa 9x14 Check and Hare Hunting: Pair Sby 6/93 2,875

Lloyd, Thomas James Br 1848-1910
O/C 24x21 A Man in a Punt Chr 5/93 2,875
Llull, Jose Pinello Spa 1861-1922
O/Pn 18x22 View of Alcala 1898 Chr 10/92 6,050
O/Pn 18x22 View of Alcala 1898 Chr 5/93 2,875
Lo Scarsellino It 1551-1620
O/C 86x55 Deposition from the Cross Sby 5/93 123,500
Lo Scheggia It 1407-1486
* See 1993 Edition . . . .
Lo Spada It 1520-1589
* See 1993 Edition . . . .
Lo Spadino It 1659-1731
* See 1993 Edition . . . .
Lo Spagna It 1450-1528
O,T&Gd/Pn 13x9 The Madonna and Child Sby 1/93 43,125
Lo Spagnoletto It 1588-1656
O/C 40x32 Portrait Philosopher or Architect Sby 1/93 96,000
Lobbedez, Charles Auguste R. Fr 1825-1882
* See 1992 Edition . . . .
Lobdell, Frank
* See 1993 Edition . . . .
Lobrichon, Timoleon Marie Fr 1831-1914
* See 1991 Edition . . . .
Locatelli, Andrea It 1693-1741
* See 1991 Edition . . . .
Locca, Albert
O/C 22x18 Woman in Red 1958 Sby 2/93 690
Locher, Carl Dan 1851-1915
* See 1992 Edition . . . .
Locher, Thomas 1956-
MM/Pn 27x55 1-11 1987 Chr 10/92 6,600
O/Gl 47x40 1-5 Sby 2/93 5,175
A/Gl 47x40 1-5 Chr 2/93 4,950
A/Gl 24x24 1-7 1987 Chr 5/93 2,875
Lockerby, Mabel Irene Can 1887-
* See 1993 Edition . . . .
Lockman, Dewitt M. Am 1870-1957
O/C 50x40 The Gold Jacket Chr 12/92 4,400
Loder of Bath, James Br a 1820-1860
* See 1991 Edition . . . .
Lodge, Reginald Br a 1881-1892
* See 1993 Edition . . . .
Lodi, Gaetano It a 1850-
* See 1993 Edition . . . .
Loeb, Louis Am 1866-1909
O/B 19x13 Lady Seated by Window Mys 12/92 440
Loeber, Lou Dut 1894-1983
* See 1992 Edition . . . .
Loeding, Hermen Dut 1637-1673
* See 1990 Edition . . . .
Loemans, Alexander F. Am 19C
* See 1993 Edition . . . .
Logan, Maurice Am 1886-1977
W/Pa 21x29 Rocks and Quiet Surf But 6/93 1,495
W/Pa 23x31 Pescadero Coast But 10/92 825
W/Pa 13x19 Marina Mor 6/93 715
W/Pa 22x30 Rigging and Gulls But 10/92 660
W/Pa 22x29 Point Lobos But 10/92 605
W/Pa 22x30 Fishing Boat at Water's Edge (2) But 6/93 . . . 575
W/Pa 13x19 House in Landscape Mor 11/92 475
Logan, Robert Fulton Am 1889-1959
* See 1993 Edition . . . .
Logan, Robert Henry Am 1874-1942
* See 1992 Edition . . . .
Logsdail, William Eng 1859-
* See 1993 Edition . . . .
Lohr, August Ger 19C
W/Pa 12x16 Valle de Mexico/Popocatepetl 1915 Sby 11/92 . 5,500
Loir, Luigi Fr 1845-1916
O/Pn 6x9 Parisian Festival Chr 10/92 14,300
Loiseau, Gustave Fr 1865-1935
O/C 26x32 L'Eure En Ete 1902 Sby 5/93 107,000
O/C 23x28 Maison sur la Cote Normande 1909 Sby 11/92 . 93,500
O/C 29x36 Bord de riviere a l'Automne 1908 Chr 11/92 . . 71,500

O/C 26x36 Etretat, La Pointe de la Batterie 1902 Sby 5/93   54,625
O/C 24x20 Nature Morte aux Fleurs Sby 5/93 43,700
O/Pa/C 18x22 Maison Campagnarde au Bord Sby 5/93 . . 20,700
O/C 13x16 Quai Le Long de la Riviere Sby 5/93 19,550
O/B 15x18 Harengs et Soupiere Sby 5/93 14,950
O/Pa/C 13x16 Rue Animee Sby 2/93 11,500
O/C 20x18 Montmartre Doy 11/92 8,800

Lojacono, Francesco It 1841-1915
  O/C/M 24x39 After the Rainstorm But 5/93 23,000

Lomax, John Arthur Br 1857-1923
  O/C 21x14 The Good Smoke Chr 10/92 1,650

Lomi, Aurelio It 1556-1622
  * See 1990 Edition . . . .

Lommen, Wilhelm Ger 1838-1895
  * See 1990 Edition . . . .

Londer, Ja. Dut 18C
  * See 1992 Edition . . . .

Lone Wolf (James Will. Shultz) Am 1882-1970
  O/C 22x28 Indian Scouts on Horseback 21 Sby 9/92 2,860

Long, Christopher 20C
  * See 1993 Edition . . . .

Long, Edwin Br 1829-1891
  * See 1991 Edition . . . .

Long, Richard 1945-
  MM/B 45x47 Whitechapel Spiral Chr 11/92 17,600
  Pe&Ph/Pa 19x24 Untitled 1969 Sby 11/92 9,900
  MM/Pa 19x15 Untitled Chr 10/92 6,050
  MM/Pa 22x16 River Avon Mud Drawing Sby 5/93 5,750

Long, Stanley M. Am 1892-1972
  W/Pa 10x7 Bucking Bronco Lou 12/92 325
  W/Pa 9x7 Calf Roping Mor 11/92 225
  W/Pa 20x16 Cowboy on Horseback Eld 8/93 165

Long, Ted Am 20C
  O/M 20x24 Squaw Creek '61 Sel 4/93 475

Longhi, Alessandro It 1733-1813
  * See 1992 Edition . . . .

Longhi, Barbara 1552-1638
  O/C/Pn 26x20 Saint Catherine of Alexandria Chr 10/92 . . . 11,000

Longhi, Luca It 1507-1580
  * See 1993 Edition . . . .

Longhi, Pietro It 1702-1785
  * See 1993 Edition . . . .

Longo, Robert Am 1923-
  MM 19x46 Camouflage in Heaven Sby 2/93 2,875
  A/Pa 23x30 Two Paintings 91 Chr 11/92 1,650

Longuet, Alexandre Marie Fr 1805-1851
  W/Pa 9x7 Peasant Woman and a Child Wes 3/93 550

Longuet, Frederic
  O/B 18x22 Along the Canal at Twilight 37 Sby 2/93 1,725

Loomis, Charles Russell Am 1857-1936
  W/Pa 5x10 Mountain Landscape Lou 12/92 250
  W/Pa 11x15 Ships Off the Coast Mys 12/92 165

Loomis, Osbert Burr Am 1813-1886
  O/C 17x21 Watermelon, Cigars and Wine 1866 Sby 9/92 . . 3,300

Loomis, William Andrew Am 1892-1959
  * See 1993 Edition . . . .

Looney, Ben Earl Am 1905-1981
  W/Pa 18x26 Horse and Buggy 1964 Lou 6/93 200

Loos, John Con a 1880-1889
  * See 1992 Edition . . . .

Lopez Y Portana, Vincente Spa 1772-1850
  * See 1991 Edition . . . .

Lopez, Gasparo It 1650-1732
  * See 1993 Edition . . . .

Lopez-Rey
  O/M 32x48 Civil Guard 1943 Sby 10/92 2,860

Loran, Erle Am 1905-
  W&G/Pa 15x19 Caspar, North Coast, 1941 But 6/93 4,025
  O/C 18x28 San Francisco Docks '46 But 10/92 3,850
  G/Pa 15x18 Dark Afternoon, Cove at Albion '40 But 10/92 . 2,090
  W&G/Pa 14x19 Winding Road '41 But 3/93 2,090
  O/C 36x27 Self Portrait '43 But 3/93 1,870
  W&G/Pa 15x22 Coastal View '46 But 6/93 1,840

W&G/Pa 15x22 Houses on the Bank '46 But 6/93 1,725
W/Pa 15x22 Bridge at Elks '45 But 10/92 1,650
T/M 14x24 Old Dam at Elk '47 But 10/92 1,650
W&G/Pa 14x19 Boathouses '40 But 3/93 1,540
G/Pa 15x22 Red Cliffs '48 But 10/92 1,540
W&G/Pa 15x22 Houses by the Pier 46 But 6/93 1,495
W&G/Pa 15x22 Red Cliffs '45 But 3/93 1,430
O/B 13x20 Coastal Scene '45 But 3/93 1,320
G/Pa 13x19 Telegraph Hill, San Francisco '46 But 10/92 . . 1,320
W&G/Pa 15x22 Under the Bridge '48 But 3/93 1,320
W&G/Pa 15x22 The Boatyard But 6/93 1,265
W/Pa 16x23 Jenner '47 But 10/92 1,100
W&G/Pa 15x22 Town on the Shore '46 But 6/93 920
G/Pa 15x22 Relics '49 But 6/93 748
W&G/Pa 15x20 Old Dam at Eld '42 But 6/93 575

Lord, Caroline Am 1860-
  O/C 18x19 Cincinnati Street Scene 1920 Slo 4/93 850

Lorentzen, Christian August 1749-1828
  * See 1991 Edition . . . .

Lorenzi, Francesco 1723-1787
  O/C 23x12 Virgin Appearing to St. Philip Neri Chr 1/93 . . 22,000

Loria, Vincenzo It 1850-
  O/C 22x37 Temple of Paestum at Dusk Chr 5/93 4,830
  W/Pa 21x30 Harbor Scene Hnz 5/93 700
  W/Pa 16x30 Naples Harbor Hnd 5/93 425

Lorjou, Bernard Fr 1908-1986
  O/C 40x40 Romeo et Juliette 1953 Chr 11/92 5,500

Lorrain, Claude Fr 1600-1682
  * See 1992 Edition . . . .

Los, Waldemar Pol 1849-1888
  * See 1991 Edition . . . .

Lossi, T. It 19C
  * See 1993 Edition . . . .

Lossow, Heinrich Ger 1843-1897
  * See 1992 Edition . . . .

Loth, Johann Carl Ger 1632-1698
  * See 1991 Edition . . . .

Lotiron, Robert
  * See 1993 Edition . . . .

Lotti, A. It 19C
  W/Pa 8x11 Roman Charity Slo 5/93 375

Lotto, Lorenzo It 1480-1556
  * See 1990 Edition . . . .

Lotz, Matilda Am 1858-1923
  * See 1993 Edition . . . .

Louderback, Walt Am 1887-1941
  O/C 32x23 Girl and Old Man on Board Ship 1924 Ih 5/93 . . 3,750
  O/C 12x9 Read All About It Skn 3/93 770

Lougheed, Robert Elmer Am 1910-1982
  O/B 24x29 Delivering the Mail Sbt 5/93 2,640
  O/B/M 12x16 Feeding Time Chr 5/93 2,300
  O/M 12x16 White and Pinto Circus Horses Chr 5/93 1,265

Louis, Morris Am 1912-1962
  A/C 100x142 Beth Zayin Chr 11/92 385,000
  A/C 90x24 Infield 1962 Chr 11/92 187,000
  A/C 90x138 Kuf Chr 10/92 110,000

Lourdes, Manuel Guillermo
  * See 1992 Edition . . . .

Loustaunau, Auguste Louis G. Fr 1846-1898
  O/Pn 14x11 La Rencontre Sby 5/93 8,338

Louvrier, Maurice 1878-1954
  * See 1993 Edition . . . .

Louyot, Edmond Ger 1861-1909
  O/C 32x24 Snowy Riverbank Chr 10/92 3,080

Lovatti, E. Augusto It 1816-
  O/C 18x29 Parole Segrete Sby 10/92 13,200

Lovatti, Matteo It 1861-
  * See 1993 Edition . . . .

Lovell, Katherine Adams Am 1877-1965
  O/Bu/B 28x30 Carmel Valley, California Sby 3/93 690
  O/B 12x16 Ogunquit 1942 Yng 5/93 150

Lovell, Tom Am 1909-
  O/C 17x19 Two Bear Cubs in Campsite Ih 11/92 1,600

Loven, Frank W.   Am 1869-1941
O/C 30x40 River Landscape in Winter 1914 Sby 3/93 3,220
Loveridge, Clinton   Am 1824-1902
* See 1993 Edition ....
Loveroff, Frederick Nicholas   Can 1894-1959
O/B 12x14 Farm View, Winter Sbt 5/93 2,024
Loving, J.   Am 19C
O/C 25x39 A Light Breeze 1879 Mys 3/93 990
Lovmand, Christine Marie   Dan 1803-1872
* See 1991 Edition ....
Low, Mary Fairchild   Am 1858-1946
O/B 24x18 Dawn at Gloucester 1925 Chr 5/93 1,380
Low, Will Hicock   Am 1853-1932
* See 1993 Edition ....
Lowe, Agatha   Aus 20C
O/C 37x33 Japanese Still Life 1919 Wlf 9/92 3,800
Lowell, Milton H.   Am 1848-1927
* See 1993 Edition ....
Lowell, Orson Byron   Am 1871-1956
G/Pb 21x26 Dick Telling His Story Sby 3/93 1,035
Pl/Pa 18x28 Gag Cartoon (2) Ih 11/92 850
G/Pa 26x17 Two Victorian Women Ih 5/93 750
Lowith, Wilhelm   Aus 1861-
O/Pn 4x4 Gentleman in His Study 1893 Chr 5/93 2,185
Lowndes, Alan   1921-1978
O/Pa 21x14 Borra 1959 Chr 11/92 880
Loyeux, Charles Antoine Joseph   Fr 1823-1893
* See 1992 Edition ....
Lozano, Manuel Rodriguez   20C
* See 1992 Edition ....
Lozano, Margarita   Fr 1936-
O/C 41x47 Florero con Fondo Lila 90 Chr 11/92 7,700
Lozowick, Louis   Am 1892-1973
Pe/B 14x16 Inca Highway Sby 9/92 880
Lubbers, Bob   Am 1922-
Pl/Pa 19x27 Sunday Comic Strip "Tarzan" Ih 5/93 550
Lubieniecki, Christoffel   Pol 1660-1728
* See 1991 Edition ....
Lucas Y Padilla, Eugenio   Spa 1824-1870
O/Pn 6x10 Dance Around the Fire Chr 10/92 4,620
Lucas Y Villaamil, Eugenio   Spa 1858-1918
O/C 20x26 Procession de Los Reyes Magos Chr 10/92 .. 38,500
O/C 26x37 Senorita Y Duena Sby 2/93 19,550
Lucas, Edward George Handel   Br 1861-1936
O/C 18x14 Primula Chr 5/93 1,725
Lucas, John Seymour   Br 1949-1923
O/C 13x17 The Interrupted Duet Chr 5/93 5,175
Lucas, John Templeton   Br 1836-1880
O/C 70x62 The Rainbow Lou 6/93 4,750
Lucas-Robiquet, Marie Aimee   Fr 1864-
* See 1991 Edition ....
Lucchesi, Giorgio   It 1855-1941
O/C 25x18 Autumnal Still Life 1899 Chr 10/92 13,200
Luce, Maximilien   Fr 1858-1941
O/C 51x63 Baigneuses a Saint-Tropez 1892 Chr 11/92 .. 495,000
O/C 26x36 Camaret, La Digue 95 Sby 11/92 275,000
O/C 21x29 Guinguette au bord de l'Oise 97 Chr 11/92 .. 198,000
O/C 24x31 Paysage 97 Sby 11/92 187,000
O/B/C 9x11 Le Petit Pont, Paris Sby 5/93 26,450
O/C 18x22 Cheval et Chevalier Pres Riviere Sby 10/92 .. 19,800
O/Pa/C 15x18 La Sieste Sby 2/93 18,400
O/B 15x20 Environs de Rolleboise Sby 10/92 13,200
O/Pa/C 10x16 Le Treport, Pecheurs Sur Le Quai Chr 5/93 .. 9,200
O/Pn 14x10 Bessy Sur Cure 1909 Sby 2/93 5,750
C/Pa 9x12 Houses Along the Shore Sby 10/92 440
Lucebert, Jean   Fr 20C
* See 1993 Edition ....
Lucioni, Luigi   It 1900-1988
O/C 18x15 Portrait of a Young Man 30 But 6/93 14,950
O/C 14x16 The Shell '33 Sby 5/93 10,350
O/C 15x16 Classic Greys 1969 Doy 5/93 7,150

O/M 6x8 Vermont 40 Sby 3/93 3,565
O/C 12x18 Vermont Farmland 1933 Chr 3/93 3,450
Luckenbach, Reuben   Am 19C
* See 1991 Edition ....
Luckx, Frans Josef   Bel 1802-1849
* See 1993 Edition ....
Ludekens, Fred   Am 1900-1982
* See 1993 Edition ....
Ludlow, Mike   Am 1921-
G/Pa 18x16 Woman with Unopened Presents Ih 5/93 500
Ludovici, A. (Jr.)   Br 1852-1932
* See 1992 Edition ....
Lueg, Konrad   20C
* See 1993 Edition ....
Luini, Bernardino   It 1475-1532
Frs/Pn 12x11 Head of a Woman Sby 1/93 10,925
Luke, Jane
O/Ab 12x16 Dorset, England Eld 8/93 143
Luker, William (Jr.)   Eng 1867-
O/Pa/B 12x15 Dick Stone and Rival Stone: Pair Slo 5/93 .. 2,750
Lukits, Theodore N.   Am 1897-
* See 1992 Edition ....
Luks, George Benjamin   Am 1867-1933
P/Pa 18x29 Market at Dawn 1900 Chr 5/93 19,500
W/Pa 14x20 Autumn Landscape Sby 12/92 7,700
Pe/Pa 9x7 Brownstones, Figures, Crowd (4) Chr 5/93 ... 1,035
C/Pa 10x7 Cape Cod 33 Brd 8/93 550
Pe/Pa 5x5 Drunks Hnd 9/92 500
Luminais, Evariste-Vital   Fr 1822-1896
W/Pa 12x9 Huntsmen Crossing a River Chr 6/93 518
Lumpkins, William   Am 20C
* See 1992 Edition ....
Lumsdaine, Leesa Sandys   Am 20C
* See 1992 Edition ....
Luna, Antonio Rodriguez   Mex 1910-
* See 1992 Edition ....
Luna, Justo Ruiz   Spa 19C
* See 1992 Edition ....
Lundberg, August Frederick   Am 1878-1928
* See 1993 Edition ....
Lundberg, M.   Am 20C
W/Pa 21x29 Figure at the Shore Mys 12/92 132
Lunde, Carl D. M.   Scn 19C
O/C 23x37 A Wooded Stream 1912 Chr 10/92 1,760
Lundgren, Charles   Am 20C
O/C 18x24 Sailing Mys 3/93 715
Lundmark, Leon   Am 1875-1942
O/C 25x30 Rocks and Surf Hnd 12/92 425
Lunetti, Tommaso Di Stefano   It 1490-1564
* See 1992 Edition ....
Lungren, Ferdinand   Am 1859-1932
W&Cw/Pa 19x13 Indian Boy on Cliff 91 But 6/93 1,725
Luny, Thomas   Br 1759-1837
O/C 20x27 Entering the Harbor 1805 Chr 10/92 3,300
O/Pn 9x12 View of the Leige Brd 8/93 2,475
O/Pn 10x14 Ship in a Storm 1826 Chr 5/93 1,610
Lupertz, Marcus   1941-
O/B/M 32x43 Jedermann und der Tod Chr 11/92 14,300
Lurcat, Jean   Fr 1892-1966
O/Pn 21x15 Le Coiffeur 30 Chr 11/92 1,980
Lusk, Maria Koupal   Am 1862-
* See 1993 Edition ....
Lussigny, L.   Fr 19C
* See 1992 Edition ....
Luteri, Battista   It 1474-1548
O/C 21x14 The Flight Into Egypt Sby 1/93 31,625
Lutero, Giovanni   It 1517-1548
O/C 32x53 Figures on Country Road Sby 1/93 200,500
Luti, Benedetto   It 1666-1724
* See 1992 Edition ....
Luttichuys, Isaac   1616-1673
* See 1993 Edition ....

Lutz, Daniel Am 1906-1978
  * See 1993 Edition ....

Lux, L. Am 20C
  O/C/B 21x27 Through the Doorway '81 Hnd 10/92 100

Lux, Peter SAf 20C
  O/C 24x36 African Mountain Valley Slo 7/93 375

Luyken, Jan
  * See 1992 Edition ....

Luyten, Jean Henri Bel 1859-1945
  O/C 16x22 Seascape with Ships on Horizon Chr 2/93 1,100

Luyten, Mark 1955-
  MM/C 79x95 Serre Chr 10/92 4,620

Luz, Julius Sws 1868-1892
  O/C 34x19 Peasant Girl with Roses 1889 Slo 7/93 950

Luzzl, Cleto It 20C
  * See 1993 Edition ....

Lyall, Laura Adeline (Muntz) Can 1860-1930
  O/C 21x14 Portrait Young Girl Sbt 11/92 3,960
  W/Pa 10x7 Portrait of a Girl 1927 Sbt 5/93 1,144

Lyford, Philip Am 1887-1950
  * See 1991 Edition ....

Lyle, Byron Br 19C
  * See 1991 Edition ....

Lyman, John Goodwin Can 1886-1967
  I/Pa 12x9 Self Portrait Sbt 5/93 330

Lynch, Albert Per 1851-
  O/C 29x22 Maiden in a Boat But 11/92 17,600
  O/C 24x18 Young Lady Preparing Flowers Sby 5/93 10,350
  P/C 42x34 A Lady with a Fan Sby 2/93 8,050
  O/C 24x20 Young Beauty in a Straw Hat Doy 11/92 6,325

Lyne, Michael Br 1912-1989
  O/C 30x24 Coaching, Top of the Hill Sby 6/93 2,300
  O/C 20x40 "Coursing" Vignettes Sby 6/93 1,150

Lynton, W. S.
  P/Pa 11x30 Shore Views with Shipping '95 Eld 11/92 523

Lyon, Hayes Am 20C
  * See 1992 Edition ....

Maar, Dora 1909-
  * See 1993 Edition ....

Maas, Dirk Dut 1659-1717
  O/C 31x35 William III of England Hunting Sby 1/93 18,400
  O/C 29x41 Turkish Horsemen Sby 5/93 9,200

Maas, Paul Bel 1890-1962
  * See 1993 Edition ....

Maass, David Am 20C
  * See 1993 Edition ....

Mabe, Manabu Brz 1910-
  * See 1993 Edition ....

Mac'Avoy, Edouard 1905-
  O/C 39x20 Capucines et Soleils 61 Chr 11/92 2,200

Macartney, Jack Am 1893-1976
  W/Pa 15x19 Street Scene - Los Angeles Mor 6/93 495

Maccari, Mino 1898-1989
  O/C 20x30 La Cometa Chr 5/93 8,050

Maccio, Romulo Arg 1931-
  O/C 64x51 Al Pie De La Letra 65 Sby 5/93 6,900
  O/C Size? Otra Vez 64 Sby 5/93 3,450

Maccloy, Samuel Br 1831-1904
  * See 1992 Edition ....

MacConnel, Kim 1946-
  G,Br&I/Pa 23x30 Night Owl 84 Chr 11/92 1,760

MacDonald, James Edward Hervey Can 1873-1932
  O/B 8x10 Rapid Near Minden, Ontario '17 Sbt 11/92 17,600
  O/B 9x11 Cathedral Mountain Sbt 5/93 14,080
  O/B 13x16 Apple Orchard, Thornhill '14 Sbt 11/92 11,440
  O/B 8x10 Nasturtiums Sbt 5/93 11,440
  O/B 9x11 Thornhill Fields '29 Sbt 5/93 4,840

MacDonald, Manly Edward Can 1889-1971
  O/C 24x32 Autumn Landscape Sbt 5/93 2,640
  O/B 16x20 Open Stream, Sunnybrook Farm Sbt 11/92 1,376

MacDonald-Wright, Stanton Am 1890-1973
  * See 1992 Edition ....

MacEntyre, Eduardo Arg 1929-
  * See 1990 Edition ....

MacEwen, Walter Am 1860-1943
  * See 1993 Edition ....

MacGilvary, Norwood Hodge Am 1874-1950
  O/C 16x13 Landscape with Seated Nude Sby 9/92 1,320
  O/C 19x8 Nocturnal Nymphs Fre 4/93 950

Machard, Jules Louis Fr 1839-1900
  O/C 47x75 La Reve D'Eros Sby 5/93 23,000

Machen, William H. Am 1832-1911
  O/C 30x25 Game Birds Dum 1/93 1,100

Machiavelli, Zanobi 1418-1479
  * See 1992 Edition ....

MacIntire, Kenneth Stevens Am 1891-1979
  O/B 34x28 Picnic in the Forest Skn 5/93 2,200
  O/B 18x21 Day at the Races Hnd 9/92 250
  W/Pa 18x22 Manners Man 1937 Hnd 9/92 160

Macintosh, Marian T. Am 1871-1936
  * See 1990 Edition ....

Mackay, Edwin Murray Am 1869-1926
  O/C 35x27 Woman Reading Tea Leaves Chr 9/92 11,000

MacKay, Florence Br 19C
  * See 1993 Edition ....

Mackellar, Duncan Br 19C
  O/C 16x22 Fox Hunt Hnd 12/92 950

MacKenzie, Frederick Br 1787-1854
  * See 1993 Edition ....

Mackintosh, Charles Rennie Sco 1868-1928
  * See 1992 Edition ....

MacKnight, Dodge Am 1860-1950
  W&H/Pa 15x21 Orizaba Mountains, Mexico Skn 9/92 1,760
  W/Pa 13x21 Along the Nile Skn 11/92 1,540
  W/Pa 16x23 Lake in the Rockies Skn 3/93 1,430
  W/Pa 17x21 Canyon Passages Skn 9/92 1,320
  W&H/Pa 16x23 Winter-Cape Cod Skn 5/93 1,320
  W/Pa 16x22 Kitchen Interior 18th C. Home Eld 4/93 550
  W&H/Pa 16x22 An Interior (Peasants') Skn 9/92 385

Macky, Eric Spencer Am 1880-1958
  * See 1990 Edition ....

Maclane, Jean Am 1878-1964
  * See 1992 Edition ....

MacLeod, Pegi Nicol Can 1904-1949
  O/C 24x18 Winter View, St. John River Sbt 11/92 3,344
  O/Pn 15x20 Skyscraper Construction Sbt 11/92 1,232

Maclet, Elisee Fr 1881-1962
  O/C 26x32 Bastia, Place de la Galetta Sby 2/93 9,775
  O/C 18x22 Le Moulin et la Tour du Philosophe Chr 11/92 . 8,250
  O/C 24x29 Les moulins Chr 11/92 8,250
  O/C 18x22 Les Stes. Marie de la Mer Sby 2/93 6,325
  O/C 21x29 Landscape with Yellow House Sby 10/92 5,775
  O/B 23x34 La Sacre-Coeur Chr 11/92 5,500
  O/B 22x18 Rue de Mont Cenis Sby 10/92 4,675
  O/B 18x24 View of Paris Sby 6/93 3,738
  O/B 18x24 View of Paris Sby 6/93 3,450
  O/Pa/C 14x11 View of Paris Sby 10/92 3,410

Maclise, Daniel Br 1806-1870
  * See 1993 Edition ....

MacMonnies, Frederick Am 1863-1936
  O/C 18x13 French Nursemaid and Baby Berthe Sby 5/93 . 19,550

MacNeil, Ambrose (DeBarra) Am 1852-
  * See 1992 Edition ....

Macomber, Mary Lizzie Am 1861-1916
  O/B 13x10 Study for Pot of Basil Chr 9/92 2,090
  O/C 18x14 Woman in Red Lou 9/92 1,000

MacPherson, John Havard Am 1894-
  O/C 16x20 Corn Shucks Chr 12/92 1,870

MacPherson, Virginia
  P/Pa 25x20 Deco Lady with Flamingoes '29 FHB 5/93 22

MacRae, Elmer Livingston   Am 1875-1952
O/C 27x22 Girl in White Dress Sby 3/93 6,038
P/L 16x20 Ships off a Coast 1919 Chr 5/93 978
P/S/B 13x10 Clarissa & Twins: 2 Drawings 1906 Sby 3/93 . . 805
Pe/Pa 11x8 Clarissa 1906 Sby 3/93 403
MacRae, Emma Fordyce   Am 1887-1974
O/B 16x12 Yellow Fuchsia Mys 3/93 578
O/B 16x12 Floral Mys 3/93 550
Macrum, George H.   Am 20C
O/C 25x30 The Pile Driver Sby 3/93 3,450
MacWhirter, John   Br 1839-1911
W&Bc/Pa 21x15 Riders in the Beech Avenue Sby 2/93 5,290
Macy, William Ferdinand   Am 1852-1901
O/C 11x25 Marsh Scene with Woodland Border 79 Eld 8/93 . 880
Macy, William Starbuck   Am 1853-1916
O/Pn 9x12 Farmyard Scene Lou 9/92 2,200
Madden, Jan   Eng 1884-
O/C 24x36 At the Pier Skn 11/92 770
Maddersteg, Michael   Dut 1658-1709
* See 1990 Edition . . . .
Madelain, Gustave   Fr 1867-1944
O/C 16x11 Mont Louis Chr 11/92 2,200
Madeline, Paul   Fr 1863-1920
O/C 32x40 Le Moulin Genetin Sur la Creuse Chr 2/93 8,800
O/C 18x22 Le Vieux Pont A Axat Sby 2/93 4,313
Madou, Jean Baptiste   Bel 1796-1877
O/Pn 10x8 Break from Reading 1861 Chr 5/93 3,220
Maella, Mariano Salvador   Spa 1739-1819
* See 1993 Edition . . . .
Maes, Eugene Remy   Bel 1849-1931
O/Pn 9x14 Chickens in a Barnyard 1886 Chr 2/93 6,050
O/Pn 11x14 Hen and Chicks But 11/92 3,850
O/Pn 11x14 Poultry in the Barnyard Doy 5/93 2,860
Maes, Giacomo   It 19C
* See 1992 Edition . . . .
Maes, Nicolaes   Dut 1632-1693
O/C 43x36 Portrait of a Gentleman Chr 1/93 28,600
O/C 17x13 Portrait of a Young Man Sby 1/93 9,775
Maestosi, F.   It 19C
* See 1990 Edition . . . .
Maestri, Michelangelo   It -1812
* See 1993 Edition . . . .
Maffia, Daniel
O/C 50x72 Bengal Tiger in Marsh Dum 9/92 3,000
Magafan, Ethel   Am 1915-
* See 1993 Edition . . . .
Magafan, Jennie   Am 1916-1950
O/C 24x35 Pigs '38 Sby 9/92 3,300
Magaud, Dominique Antoine J.B.   Fr 1817-1899
* See 1991 Edition . . . .
Magee, Alan   Am 20C
* See 1992 Edition . . . .
Magee, James C.   Am 1846-1924
O/Ab 10x13 Riverside Farmhouse 1904 Eld 8/93 495
O/Pn 9x13 Country Path Eld 8/93 440
Maggi, Cesare   20C
* See 1991 Edition . . . .
Maggs, John Charles   Br 1819-1895
O/C 17x30 Mail Coach on Route 1879 Sby 6/93 3,450
O/C 14x26 Coach and Four 187? Sby 1/93 3,163
O/C 14x27 London-Birmingham Run 1874 Sby 1/93 3,163
O/C 24x36 Coach Outside the Inn 1882 Doy 5/93 3,080
Magnasco, Alessandro   It 1667-1749
* See 1993 Edition . . . .
Magne, Desire Alfred   Fr 1855-
* See 1992 Edition . . . .
Magni, Giuseppe   It 1869-1956
O/C 26x20 Mother Playing with Her Baby Wes 12/92 17,600
Magnus, Camille   Fr 1850-
* See 1993 Edition . . . .
Magnussen, Gustaf A.   Am 1890-1957
* See 1993 Edition . . . .
Magnussen, Gustave A.   Am 1868-1944
* See 1993 Edition . . . .

Magonigle, Edith   Am 20C
* See 1992 Edition . . . .
Magrath, William   Irs 1838-1918
O/Pn 14x18 Come to Your Daddy 1897 Slo 7/93 1,400
Magritte, Rene   Bel 1898-1967
O/C 51x64 L'Arc de Triomphe 1962 Chr 11/92 . . . . 1.1M
O/C 18x15 L'Empire des lumieres 1953 Chr 11/92 528,000
O/C 14x18 Souvenir de Voyage (I) 53 Sby 11/92 517,000
G/Pa 16x12 L'Empire des Lumieres Sby 11/92 374,000
G/Pa 15x18 L'Incendie 1947 Chr 11/92 220,000
G/Pa 16x11 Les Liasons Dangereuses Sby 11/92 165,000
G/Pa/B 6x7 Scheherazade Sby 5/93 68,500
Pe/Pa 9x13 L'Aimable Verite Sby 11/92 20,900
Pe/Pa 13x10 La Legende Sby 11/92 17,600
Maguire, Robert
O/Cb 18x14 Man Holding Woman in Orange Ih 5/93 550
Magyar-Mannheimer, Gustav   Hun 1859-
O/Pn/B 16x19 Bridge Over a River Wes 12/92 605
Mahaffey, Noel   Am 1944-
* See 1991 Edition . . . .
Maher, Kate Heath   Am 1860-1946
O/C 14x20 Sonoma Valley But 10/92 1,980
Mahlknecht, Edmund   Aus 1820-1903
* See 1993 Edition . . . .
Maillaud, Fernand   Fr 1863-1948
O/C 26x32 Woman on Terrace Mys 12/92 3,190
O/C 13x16 Country Village Lane Doy 11/92 2,200
Maillol, Aristide   Fr 1861-1944
* See 1993 Edition . . . .
Mainardi, Sebastiano   It 1450-1513
* See 1993 Edition . . . .
Major, Ernest L.   Am 1864-1950
O/Cb 12x14 A Harbor View Skn 3/93 2,200
O/C 26x32 Duck Blind on a Creek Sby 9/92 1,100
Makart, Hans   Aus 1840-1884
* See 1993 Edition . . . .
Makielski, Leon A.   Am 1885-
* See 1993 Edition . . . .
Makovsky, Vladimir Yegorovich   Rus 1846-1920
* See 1991 Edition . . . .
Makowsky, Constantin   Rus 1839-1915
O/B 28x24 Portrait of Russian Girl 1883 Dum 10/92 8,500
O/C 16x13 Modele de Pose Wes 3/93 2,090
Malaine, Joseph-Laurent   Fr 1745-1809
* See 1993 Edition . . . .
Malavine, Philippe   Rus 1869-1939
* See 1990 Edition . . . .
Maldarelli, Federico   It 1826-1893
* See 1990 Edition . . . .
Maldura, Giovanni   It 1772-1849
* See 1993 Edition . . . .
Maleas, Constantin
* See 1993 Edition . . . .
Malet, Albert   Fr 1905-1986
O/C 21x26 Foret en Automne Chr 11/92 1,650
O/M 17x20 Arbres au bord de la riviere Chr 11/92 1,540
Malevich, Kasimir   Rus 1878-1935
* See 1992 Edition . . . .
Malfroy, Charles   Fr 1862-1940
* See 1990 Edition . . . .
Malfroy, Henry   Fr 1895-
O/Pn 9x11 Champs Elysees Sby 6/93 1,380
Malherbe, William   Am 1884-1951
O/C 24x18 Portrait of a Lady in Blue 1918 Sby 9/92 1,320
Mali, Christian Friedrich   Ger 1832-1906
* See 1992 Edition . . . .
Malkine, Georges   Fr 1898-1970
* See 1993 Edition . . . .
Mallet, Jean-Baptiste   Fr 1759-1835
* See 1993 Edition . . . .
Mallo, Maruja   Spa 1910-
* See 1990 Edition . . . .
Malloy, Michael   Am 20C
O/M 24x30 Landscape Mor 11/92 750

Malmstrom, August Swd 1829-1901
* See 1991 Edition . . . .
Malnoir
O/C 24x20 Profile of a Lady FHB 6/93 150
Man Ray Am 1890-1976
* See 1993 Edition . . . .
Manchester, Hope Am 20C
O/C 34x45 Phoenix Hnd 9/92 50
Mancin, Francesca It 1830-1905
* See 1990 Edition . . . .
Mancinelli, Guiseppi It 1817-1875
* See 1991 Edition . . . .
Mancini, Antonio It 1852-1930
* See 1993 Edition . . . .
Mancini, Francesco 1679-1758
O/C 21x17 Madonna and Child Sby 1/93 10,350
Mander, William Henry Eng 1880-1922
O/C 24x18 Landscape Mys 3/93 1,100
Mane-Katz Fr 1894-1962
G&W/Pa 24x20 Arab Mother with Children Chr 5/93 8,050
G/B 22x28 Provincetown Drydock 41 Sby 2/93 3,450
P/Pa 11x9 Study of a Young Girl But 4/93 2,587
Manessier, Alfred Fr 1911-
O/C 18x22 Composition abstraite 55 Chr 11/92 23,100
G&Y/Pa 7x7 Sans Titre Chr 10/92 5,500
Manet, Edouard Fr 1832-1883
* See 1993 Edition . . . .
Mangilli, Ada It 1863-
O/C 80x119 The Pagan Festival 1884 Sby 2/93 36,800
Manglard, Adrien Fr 1695-1760
O/C 19x30 Waterfront at Naples Chr 1/93 77,000
O/C 38x51 Capriccio Southern Port with Ships Sby 5/93 . . 28,750
Mangold, Robert Am 1937-
A&Pe/Pa 39x103 2 Triangles in 3 Rectangles Sby 5/93 . . . 25,300
A,C&Pe/Pa 44x28 Four Color Frame Painting #4 Sby 10/92 19,800
A&H/M 20x20 2 Triangles in Square #3 1975 Chr 11/92 . 17,600
A&H/Pa 30x44 Green Ellipse/Yellow Frame 1988 Chr 2/93 13,750
A&Pe/Pa 28x22 Irregular Aqua Area Sby 5/93 8,050
Y&Pe/Pa 12x12 An Octagonal Within a Circle 1974 Sby 5/93 6,900
A&H/Pa 63x47 Rectangle Within Three Rectangles Chr 5/93 6,900
Mangold, Sylvia Plimack 1938-
A&H/C 61x61 The Test Chr 11/92 3,300
Mangravite, Peppino Am 1896-
O/C 38x34 Sonny's Dream Mys 12/92 935
Manguin, Henri Fr 1874-1943
O/C 36x29 Jeanne a l'ombrelle, Cavaliere Chr 11/92 99,000
O/C 29x24 Dahlias et Fruits Sby 11/92 38,500
O/C 14x11 La Proue a L'Oustalet, Saint-Tropez Sby 2/93 . 19,550
O/C 26x21 Torse de Femme, Marie 1912 Hnd 6/93 11,000
Manheim, Erwin Am 20C
O/B 31x23 Coastal Town 1960 But 6/93 4,600
Maniatty, Stephen G. Am 1910-
O/C 25x30 Ice Bound, Allen House, Deerfield Eld 8/93 . . . 770
Manigault, Edward Middleton Am 1887-1922
O/C 33x27 Windswept Forest Sby 9/92 8,800
Manley, Shirley Am 20C
O/B Size? Mr. Larchmont's Curiosity Wlf 5/93 75
Manley, Thomas R. Am 1853-1938
O/B 18x24 Red House by the River Fre 10/92 750
Mann, Harrington Am 1865-1937
O/C 24x19 Man in a Brown Cap Chr 5/93 863
Mann, Joshua Hargrave Sams Br -1886
* See 1992 Edition . . . .
Manners, William Eng a 1884-1910
O/C 8x12 Running Brook; Along Shore (2) 1906 Chr 2/93 . 3,080
O/C 24x36 Fisherman Beside Stream 1901 Sel 12/92 1,000
Mannheim, Jean Am 1863-1945
O/C 23x19 Fixing her Hair But 3/93 4,675
O/C 41x51 Mountain River But 10/92 4,125
O/M 12x16 After the Rain Mor 2/93 4,000
O/Cb 12x16 Flintridge Mor 2/93 3,250
O/C 20x25 Southern California Coastal Scene But 6/93 2,875
O/B 12x15 Landscape Mor 6/93 2,475
O/B 20x24 Near La Quinta But 10/92 2,200

O/C/B 16x12 Eucalyptus Trees But 3/93 1,650
O/C/B 12x16 Windy Day, Arch Beach But 3/93 1,650
O/B 12x16 View Through the Trees But 3/93 1,430
O/B 24x20 Quince in Blue Vase But 6/93 920
Mannucci, Cipriano A. It 1882-1970
* See 1992 Edition . . . .
Manoir, Irving Am 1891-1982
* See 1992 Edition . . . .
Mansfield, Joseph
* See 1992 Edition . . . .
Mansvelt-Beck, P. Dut 20C
O/B 38x51 Still Life, Chrysanthemums Wlf 12/92 1,800
Mantegani, Roger Arg 1957-
O/C 51x55 Naturaleza Muerta con Calas 90 Chr 11/92 . . . 14,300
Mantegazza, Giacomo It 1853-1920
O/C 20x33 Preparations for the Wedding Chr 10/92 22,000
O/C 33x20 Couple Feeding Chickens Chr 5/93 8,050
O/C 16x10 The Wandering Minstrels Chr 10/92 5,500
Mantelet-Martel, Andre Fr 1876-
* See 1990 Edition . . . .
Manuel, Jorge
* See 1992 Edition . . . .
Manuel, Victor Cub 1867-1969
O/C 12x9 Mulatta Sby 11/92 4,400
O/C 15x12 Mujeres Frente al Rio Chr 11/92 3,190
Br&S/Pa 12x9 Cerca del la Casa; Interior 1928 Chr 11/92 . . 2,750
W/Pa 24x16 Mujer con Paisaje Chr 11/92 2,640
Manzoni, Ignazio It 1799-1888
* See 1993 Edition . . . .
Manzoni, Piero Fr 1933-1963
* See 1990 Edition . . . .
Manzu, Giacomo 1908-1991
Pe&G/Pa 19x25 Painter with Model in Blue Sby 2/93 8,625
Pe/Pa 14x19 Inge (Nude Study) Sby 2/93 5,175
Pl&S/Pa 16x12 Ballerina Sby 2/93 3,220
Manzur, David Col 1929-
P/Pa 20x26 San Jorge 91 Chr 11/92 16,500
Mao It 1575-1625
* See 1993 Edition . . . .
Mapplethorpe, Robert Am 20C
* See 1993 Edition . . . .
Marais, Adolphe Charles Fr 1856-1940
O/C 41x54 Winter Time Chr 10/92 16,500
Marais-Milton, Victor Fr 1872-
* See 1993 Edition . . . .
Marasco, Antonio It 1886-
* See 1991 Edition . . . .
Marble, Arthur D. Am 19C
W/Pa 14x9 Ten Botanical Watercolors 1906 Sby 3/93 4,025
W/Pa 14x9 Ten Botanical Watercolors 1909 Sby 3/93 4,025
Marble, John N. Am 1855-1918
O/C 16x20 Landscape Mys 3/93 165
Marc, Franz Ger 1880-1916
* See 1993 Edition . . . .
Marca-Relli, Conrad Am 1913-
O&L/C 36x36 M-S-7-59 59 Chr 2/93 5,500
A&L/Cb 20x25 S-5-72 (I) 72 Chr 11/92 2,640
L/C 18x16 Untitled Sby 2/93 1,150
Marcel-Clement, Amedee Julien Fr 1873-
* See 1990 Edition . . . .
March Y Marco, Vincente Spa 1859-1914
* See 1993 Edition . . . .
Marchand, Andre 1907-
O/C 16x13 L'Arlesienne Chr 2/93 4,620
Marchand, Andre Fr 1877-1951
O/C 26x32 Les Figues a la Nappe Blanche Sby 10/92 3,850
O/C 18x22 La Nappe Rouge Sby 10/92 2,750
O/C 26x32 Tomates et Aubergines Sby 10/92 2,750
C/Pa 20x26 Nu Assis Chr 11/92 935
O/C 20x24 La Barque Abandonne, Provence Sby 2/93 748
Marchand, Charles Aus 19C
* See 1993 Edition . . . .
Marchand, Jean Hippolyte Fr 1883-1940
* See 1992 Edition . . . .

Marchesini, Alessandro It 1664-1738
* See 1993 Edition . . . .
Marchetti, Ludovico It 1853-1909
* See 1993 Edition . . . .
Marchig, Giannino It 1897-1981
O/B 27x19 Young Woman Resting Wlf 3/93 5,200
Marchioni, Elisabetta It a 17C
* See 1993 Edition . . . .
Marchisio, Andrea It 1850-1927
* See 1993 Edition . . . .
Marchment, M. Eng 19C
O/C 12x24 The Fall Harvest 1892 Hnz 5/93 500
Marcil, Rene Can 1917-
O/Pa 15x22 Reclining Nude '67 Sbt 5/93 1,232
Marcius-Simons, Pinckney Am 1865-1909
* See 1992 Edition . . . .
Marcks, Gerhard
Pe/Pa 17x10 Standing Female Nude Sby 10/92 550
Marcon, Charles 20C
* See 1993 Edition . . . .
Marcoussis, Louis Fr 1883-1941
* See 1993 Edition . . . .
Marden, Brice Am 1938-
C/Pa 41x29 Houston Drawing 3 73 Sby 5/93 17,250
I/Pa 17x14 Untitled #4 73 Sby 5/93 16,100
Br,I&Ss/Cd 6x6 Card Drawing, (Counting) #6 82 Chr 11/92 13,200
Marec, Victor Fr 1862-1920
* See 1993 Edition . . . .
Maresca, M. It 20C
O/C 20x28 Paris at Night Lou 12/92 275
Marescalchi, Pietro It 1520-1589
* See 1993 Edition . . . .
Marevna, (Marie Vorobieff)
* See 1992 Edition . . . .
Margetson, William Henry Br 1861-1940
O/C 60x33 The Stranger 1902 Sby 5/93 40,250
Margitay, Tihamer Pol 1859-1922
O/C 40x56 The Accused Chr 2/93 1,980
Margo, Boris Am 1902-
Pe/Pa 23x20 Untitled Sby 9/92 1,430
Margolis, Nathan Am 20C
O/C 20x26 Inlet Guards '34 Fre 4/93 525
Margulies, Joseph Am 1896-1984
O/C 20x24 Street Scene, Rockport Skn 5/93 1,320
O/C 36x28 Fish Market Yng 5/93 700
O/B 16x12 Laughing Hans '22 Sby 3/93 460
W/Pa 19x14 Harbour Scene Mys 12/92 385
W&H/Pa 14x21 On the Beach, Good Harbor '49 Skn 3/93 . . . 330
W/Pa 17x23 Along Bass Rocks, Cloucester Yng 2/93 275
Mariani, Carlo Maria It 1931-
W&Cp/Pa 39x27 Il Pittore Mancino 83 Sby 10/92 6,600
Mariani, Pompeo It 1857-1927
* See 1993 Edition . . . .
Marieschi, Michele It 1696-1743
* See 1993 Edition . . . .
Marilhat, Prosper Georges A. Fr
1811-1847
O/C 15x24 Egyptian Landscape 1837 Chr 10/92 4,950
O/C 7x14 Windmill and Cottage by the Sea Chr 10/92 2,750
Marin, John Am 1870-1953
W/Pa 14x19 Old Church at Ranchos, NM '30 Sby 12/92 . . . 60,500
W/Pa 17x20 Sea Movement, Maine 1923 Sby 12/92 44,000
W&H/Pa 14x13 Fishing Boat at Eastport 33 Skn 11/92 24,200
W/Pa 13x19 Near Taos, New Mexico 1930 Sby 12/92 . . . 22,000
O/Cb 12x16 Pertaining to West New Jersey '50 Sby 12/92 20,900
W&Pe/Pa/B 14x17 Castorland Landscape 13 Chr 9/92 . . . 16,500
W/Pa 10x12 Sea and Rock, Stonington, Maine 19 Chr 9/92 9,900
Marin, Joseph Charles Fr 1759-1834
* See 1991 Edition . . . .
Marinelli, Vincenzo It 1820-1892
* See 1992 Edition . . . .
Marini, Antonio It 18C
* See 1992 Edition . . . .
Marini, Leonardo It 1730-1789
* See 1991 Edition . . . .

Marini, Marino It 1901-1980
* See 1993 Edition . . . .
Marinus, Ferdinand Joseph B. Bel
1808-1890
* See 1991 Edition . . . .
Mario, Alessandro E. Am 19C
O/C 12x16 Holding Peaches Mys 3/93 495
Maris, Jacob Henricus Dut 1837-1899
O/C 38x30 Moored Sailboat Sby 2/93 17,250
Maris, Willem Dut 1844-1910
* See 1992 Edition . . . .
Marisol 1930-
* See 1993 Edition . . . .
Mark, Lajos
O/C 31x23 Afternoon Tea in the Garden Sby 6/93 2,070
Markart, Hans
* See 1993 Edition . . . .
Markham, Charles Cole Am 1837-1907
* See 1993 Edition . . . .
Markham, Kyra Am 1891-
T/M 24x30 Square Dance Sby 9/92 22,000
Marko, Andreas Aus 1824-1895
O/C 16x26 Cows by a Watering Trough 1884 Chr 2/93 . . . 4,950
Marko, Karl Hun 1822-1891
* See 1993 Edition . . . .
Marko, Karoly (Sr.) Hun 1791-1860
* See 1993 Edition . . . .
Markowicz, Arthur Pol 1872-1934
* See 1992 Edition . . . .
Marks, Henry Stacy Br 1829-1898
* See 1993 Edition . . . .
Marlatt, H. Irving Am 1860-1929
O/C 30x50 Autumn Landscape 1926 Sby 9/92 2,200
Marno, J. Con 19C
* See 1992 Edition . . . .
Marny, Paul Br 1829-1914
W/Pa/B 18x12 Bustling Village Street Chr 2/93 330
Marohn, Ferdinand Fr 19C
W/Pa 15x12 At the Well 1846 Chr 9/93 1,035
Marot, Francois 1666-1719
* See 1993 Edition . . . .
Marple, William L. Am 1827-1910
O/C 12x20 Coming into Shore 76 But 6/93 1,495
O/C 12x20 Waiting for the Ferry 81 But 6/93 920
O/C 7x12 Wooded River Landscape '79 Sel 4/93 330
Marquet, Albert Fr 1875-1947
O/C 20x24 Le Port de la Ponche, Saint-Tropez Sby 5/93 . . 178,500
O/C 24x29 Neige sur Laperlier, Alger Sby 11/92 88,000
O/C 20x24 Les Coteaux de Mericourt Sby 5/93 74,000
Marquez, Roberto
* See 1992 Edition . . . .
Marrel, Jacob Dut 1614-1681
O/Pn 29x24 White Lilies, Roses, Tulips, Irises Chr 1/93 . . . 363,000
Marsano, L. It 19C
* See 1993 Edition . . . .
Marsans, Luis 20C
* See 1991 Edition . . . .
Marsh, Lucille Patterson Am 1890-
* See 1993 Edition . . . .
Marsh, Reginald Am 1898-1954
T/M 24x30 Band Playing by the Hudson '32 Sby 5/93 . . 107,000
T/B 22x30 Palace of Wonders 1947 Chr 9/92 35,200
T/B 20x24 Coney Island 1951 Sby 12/92 28,600
O/B 21x18 Girl on a Carousel Horse: Double Chr 12/92 . . 15,400
O/M 16x12 Woman Walking by a Stoop 1951 Sby 5/93 . . 8,050
O/B 12x9 Two Girls of the Night Chr 12/92 5,500
O/M 10x8 Ladies in Hats Chr 9/92 5,280
O/M 12x9 Out for a Walk 51 Chr 3/93 5,175
W/Pa 14x20 Grain Elevator Sby 12/92 4,400
O/B 8x6 Seated Woman 1951 FHB 5/93 4,000
W&Pe/Pa 14x20 Ship and Scows 1928 Chr 9/92 3,850
O/M 10x8 Walking Down Street: Double 1952 Chr 12/92 . . 3,300
O/Pa/M 10x8 Woman in Yellow Dress Sby 9/92 3,080
Pl/Pa 9x12 Twelve Figure Studies Chr 5/93 1,495
H/Pa 31x22 Grand Windsor Hotel 1946 Sby 3/93 1,380

I&S/Pa 14x11 Circus Sketches Sby 9/92 990
W/Pa 9x12 Three Young Girls 1929 Mys 3/93 770
W/Pa 8x12 Fashion Designs Mys 3/93 440
W/Pa 10x9 Fashion Designs Mys 3/93 412

Marshall, Ben   Br 1767-1835
O/C 28x36 Lord Deerhurst's "Judgement" 1810 Sby 6/93 . 54,625

Marshall, Bruce   Am 20C
O/C 30x40 Charge of the Texas Rangers Sby 3/93 633

Marshall, Charles   Br 1806-1890
O/C 20x30 Kenilworth Castle Sby 1/93 1,380
O/C 12x22 Cottage by the River Dum 1/93 1,200

Marshall, Charles S.   Am 20C
O/C 17x20 Winter Landscape Wtf 5/93 375

Marshall, Frank Warren   Am 1866-1930
W/Pa 16x19 Boats at the Dock Mys 3/93 110

Marshall, Thomas Falcon   Br 1818-1878
* See 1991 Edition . . . .

Marshall, Thomas William   Am 1850-1874
O/C 20x16 Forest Scene 1870 But 6/93 2,875

Martel, Paul
P/Pa 32x24 Shirley Rudman Ald 5/93 195

Martens, Ernest Edouard   Fr 1865-
* See 1993 Edition . . . .

Martens, Willem Johannes   Dut 1838-1895
* See 1990 Edition . . . .

Martin, Agnes   Am 1912-
O&Pe/C 72x72 The Garden 1967 Sby 5/93 244,500
O/C 72x72 Untitled #11 1989 Sby 5/93 167,500
O/C 25x25 David 58 Sby 11/92 29,700
I/Pa 8x8 Untitled Sby 11/92 13,200
W,H&I/Pa 12x12 Untitled 77 Sby 5/93 10,925

Martin, Benito Quinquela   Arg 1890-1977
O/B 20x28 Tarde en La Boca Chr 11/92 22,000
O/B 15x21 Quietud en el Puerto Chr 11/92 8,800
O/B 23x27 Seashore Hnd 10/92 6,400

Martin, David   Br 1737-1798
* See 1993 Edition . . . .

Martin, F.   Spa 20C
O/B 7x11 Gypsies by the Beach Chr 5/93 1,150

Martin, Fletcher   Am 1904-1979
O/C 20x24 Small Businessman Sby 9/92 3,300
O/C 30x16 Woman with a Hat 1956 Sby 9/92 2,420
O/C 20x30 The Blossom 1951 Fre 4/93 1,800
O/B 9x12 Pineapple Sby 9/92 880
Y/Pa 22x17 Seated Nude 39 Sby 9/92 770

Martin, Henri   Fr 1860-1943
O/C 44x35 Le Coin du Village Sby 11/92 85,250
O/C 22x40 Voiles Blanches Dans Le Port Sby 5/93 79,500
O/C 26x32 La Pergola a Marquayrol 1911 Sby 5/93 57,500
O/C 32x21 L'Arbre Sby 11/92 49,500
O/C 29x36 La Vallee du Vert Sby 5/93 46,000
O/C 24x30 Jardinier Dans Son Verger en Fleurs Sby 5/93 . 43,125
O/C 22x27 Meditation 96 Chr 11/92 38,500
O/Pn 22x13 Vase de Fleurs Sby 5/93 36,800
O/Pn 12x16 Scene De Rue Sby 2/93 13,800
O/C 15x18 Les Communiantes 89 Sby 2/93 11,500

Martin, Homer Dodge   Am 1836-1897
O/C 13x24 Lake George Sby 9/92 22,000
O/C 12x20 East Hampton 75 Chr 9/92 6,050
O/C 14x20 Landscape with a Valley Wes 3/93 3,740
W/Pa 9x13 Boulders in the Marsh Brd 8/93 2,750
O/C 12x10 Woodland Scene Eld 8/93 1,540

Martin, J. H.   Am 19C
O&S/B 15x12 Indians on Horseback Sel 9/92 350

Martin, J. R.   19C
* See 1991 Edition . . . .

Martin, Jacques   Fr 1844-1919
* See 1993 Edition . . . .

Martin, John   Eng 1789-1854
* See 1993 Edition . . . .

Martin, Keith   Am 20C
* See 1992 Edition . . . .

Martin, Knox   Am 1923-
O/Pa/C 15x13 Woman Seated Yellow Nose 1972 Sby 2/93 . 4,888

Mg&L/B 20x18 White Point Sby 2/93 2,185
L/Wd 12x10 Untitled 1964 Sby 10/92 1,980

Martin, Maurice   Sws 19C
* See 1993 Edition . . . .

Martin, Thomas Mower   Can 1838-1934
O/C 30x50 Mountain Landscape Sbt 5/93 1,320
O/B 14x21 A Beach View Sbt 11/92 1,056
W/Pa 13x20 Lake in the Rockies Sbt 11/92 616
W/Pa 20x14 Country Road Sbt 5/93 396

Martin, W.   Br 20C
* See 1993 Edition . . . .

Martin-Ferrieres, Jac   Fr 1893-1974
O/C 20x29 Le Pont 21 Chr 10/92 8,800

Martin-Kavel, Francois   Fr 19C
* See 1991 Edition . . . .

Martindale, G. Thomas   Br 19C
* See 1991 Edition . . . .

Martine, Omar   Con 19C
O/C 52x42 Ideal Wtf 5/93 3,000

Martinetti, Angelo   It 19C
* See 1993 Edition . . . .

Martinetti, Maria   It 1864-
W/Pa 23x17 Italian Peasant Hnd 10/92 1,500

Martinez
* See 1992 Edition . . . .

Martinez, Alfredo Ramos   Mex 1872-1946
O/C 28x24 Vendedoras de Flores Chr 11/92 38,500
C&T/Pa/B 30x27 Mujer con Flores Sby 11/92 25,300
C&T/Pa 22x17 Virgen de Guadalupe Sby 5/93 16,100
G&C/Pa/B 22x16 Campesinos Chr 11/92 11,000
W/Pa 20x14 Chalupas en Xochimilco 1898 Sby 5/93 6,325

Martinez, F. F.   Am 20C
P/Pa 29x23 Woman in Black Chr 5/93 115

Martinez, Gonzalo Martinez   Spa 1860-1938
O/C/B 45x18 An Oriental Beggar 89 Sby 10/92 9,350

Martinez, Jose Ignacio Pinazo   Spa 1879-
* See 1991 Edition . . . .

Martinez, Jose Roldin E.   Am 1808-1871
O/C 41x31 Scene in Seville 1856 Mys 3/93 1,870

Martinez, Ricardo   Mex 1918-
O/C 12x10 Cabeza De Mujer Sby 5/93 7,475

Martinez, Xavier   Am 1869-1943
* See 1992 Edition . . . .

Martinez-Pedro, Luis   Cub 1910-
* See 1993 Edition . . . .

Martini, Alberto   It 1876-1954
* See 1990 Edition . . . .

Martini, Simone   It 1284-1334
* See 1992 Edition . . . .

Martino, Antonio Pietro   Am 1902-1989
O/C 40x50 Winter 1929 Ald 9/92 10,000
O/C 25x28 Fall Hillside Ald 3/93 3,500
O/B 14x22 Edge of Town Ald 5/93 1,300
O/C 28x45 Perce, Gaspe Peninsula Yng 5/93 1,200
O/C 16x24 From Cotton Street Fre 4/93 1,050
O/C 24x36 Corner House Fre 4/93 750
O/C 28x46 Perce Fre 10/92 700
O/C 27x45 Vinal Haven Fre 10/92 700
O/Pn 14x21 Along Tower Street Fre 4/93 525

Martino, Edmund   Am 1915-
O/B 12x16 Early Morning Ald 9/92 260

Martino, Giovanni   Am 1908-
O/C 30x40 Abandoned Ald 9/92 2,500
O/C 25x30 Point Pleasant 1931 Ald 5/93 1,300
O/Pn 11x20 Manayunk Trestle, Philadelphia Brd 2/93 990
T&O/B 12x18 Levering Street, Manayunk Fre 10/92 950
O/C 24x36 Child Fishing Ald 5/93 900
W/Pa 17x22 Rooftops Fre 4/93 230

Marx, Ernest Bernhard   Ger 1864-
* See 1993 Edition . . . .

Maryan   20C
* See 1991 Edition . . . .

Mas Y Fondevila, Arcadio   Spa 1850-
* See 1992 Edition . . . .

Mascacotta   1663-1714
   * See 1992 Edition ....
Mascart, Gustaf   Fr 20C
   O/C 26x37 Rivertown with Windmills Chr 2/93 3,300
Mascart, Paul
   O/C 15x22 The Canal of Mons Sby 2/93 690
Masillo   It 1677-1743
   * See 1993 Edition ....
Mason, Barry   Br 1947-
   O/C 24x36 The Wild Ship of the Atlantic But 11/92 ... 5,500
Mason, Mary T.
   O/C 25x30 Siesta on the Rocks Ald 3/93 1,550
   P/Pa 8x12 Man and Woman by Beach Ald 3/93 120
Mason, Roy M.   Am 1886-1972
   W/Pa 16x23 Little Deer Isle Brd 2/93 1,320
   W&G/Pa 11x14 The Tile Yard Lou 3/93 1,100
   O/M 12x16 Chopping Wood Lou 12/92 700
Mason, William Sanford   Am 1824-1864
   * See 1992 Edition ....
Masriera Y Manovens, Francisco   Spa 1842-1902
   O/C 54x46 The Belles of the Ball 1898 Sby 10/92 41,250
Massani, Pompeo   It 1850-1920
   O/C 14x18 Listening to Caruso Lou 3/93 3,600
   O/C 11x8 Self-Portrait Chr 2/93 825
Masse, Jules   Fr 1825-1897
   O/C 41x57 Une Matinee Chez Barras 1864 Sby 2/93 43,700
Massillo   It 18C
   * See 1990 Edition ....
Masson, Andre   Fr 1896-1987
   O/C 11x9 Nature Morte Cubiste Aux Grenades Sby 10/92 . 39,600
   O/C 11x9 Nature Morte Cubiste Aux Dominos Sby 10/92 . 34,100
   I/Pa 15x21 Anthropomorphic Instrument 42 Sby 11/92 ... 17,600
Masson, Henri Leopold   Can 1907-
   W/Pa 11x16 Sailboats Sbt 11/92 440
Mastenbroek, Johann Hendrick   Dut 1875-1945
   * See 1993 Edition ....
Master B B   17C
   * See 1991 Edition ....
Master Leonardesque Female Por   It 16C
   * See 1991 Edition ....
Master of 1310   a 1310-1325
   * See 1993 Edition ....
Master of 1518   It 16C
   * See 1992 Edition ....
Master of 1540s   a 1541-1551
   * See 1993 Edition ....
Master of Almudevar   It a 1473-1500
   * See 1992 Edition ....
Master of Annunc. to Shepherds 1618-1648
   O/C 41x31 Man Playing Mandolin Chr 1/93 165,000
Master of Apollo & Daphne   1480-1510
   * See 1993 Edition ....
Master of Castello Nativity   It 15C
   * See 1992 Edition ....
Master of Female Half   It 16C
   * See 1992 Edition ....
Master of Fiesole Epiphany   15C
   O/Pa 50x26 Saints Sebastian and Roch Sby 5/93 46,000
Master of Frankfort   a 1493-1520
   * See 1993 Edition ....
Master of Greenville Tondo   16C
   * See 1991 Edition ....
Master of Incredulity St. Thom   a 1505-1525
   * See 1993 Edition ....
Master of Johnson Assumption   a 1500-
   O/Pn 31x38 Teh Return of Ulysses Chr 5/93 55,200
Master of Khanenko Adoration   16C
   O/Pn 13x10 Madonna and Child Sby 10/92 22,000
Master of Kress Landscapes   a 1505-1530
   O&T/Pn 41x33 Holy Family Infant St. John Sby 1/93 85,000

Master of Legend St. Ursula   a 1470-1500
   O/Pn 17x11 Madonna and Child Sby 10/92 77,000
Master of Leonardesque   16C
   * See 1993 Edition ....
Master of Magdalene Legend   It a 15C
   * See 1992 Edition ....
Master of Naumberg Madonna   a 1485-1510
   O/Pn 40 dia Holy Family w/Infant St. John Chr 1/93 137,500
Master of Panzano Triptych   It
   * See 1990 Edition ....
Master of Saint Ivo   It a 1400-
   * See 1993 Edition ....
Master of San Miniato   It 15C
   * See 1992 Edition ....
Master of Staffolo   It 15C
   * See 1992 Edition ....
Master of Stories of Helen   It 1440-1470
   * See 1992 Edition ....
Master of the Lathrop Tondo   16C
   O&T/Pn 56x16 Standing Bishop Saint Sby 10/92 16,500
Master of the Rugs   17C
   O/C 37x53 Grapes, Figs, a Melon, Pomegranate Chr 10/92 38,500
Master, Johnson Nativity   It 15C
   * See 1990 Edition ....
Master, Miller Tondo   It 15C
   * See 1990 Edition ....
Masters, Edwin   Br 19C
   O/C 20x30 Rustic English Village Wlf 3/93 3,300
Matania, Fortunino   It 1881-1985
   H&G/B 14x20 Two Drawings for Stage Settings Wlf 3/93 ... 325
Matare, Ewald   1887-1965
   W/Pa 6x9 Kuh Chr 11/92 7,150
Matham, Theodor Dirck   1606-1676
   * See 1992 Edition ....
Mather, John   Br 1848-1916
   W/Pa 8x11 Sketch in Cadzow Forest 1871 Hnd 5/93 900
Mathews, Arthur Frank   Am 1860-1945
   O/C 26x30 Monterey Bay But 10/92 52,250
   O/Pn 12x10 Dutchwoman But 10/92 9,350
   O/Pn 9x11 The Old Dutchman 87 But 10/92 8,250
Mathews, John Chester   Br a 1884-1900
   * See 1992 Edition ....
Mathews, Lucia Kleinhans   Am 1870-1955
   * See 1993 Edition ....
Mathewson, Frank Convers   Am 1862-1941
   O/C 20x26 Roses in Copper Pot Yng 2/93 800
   O/C 7x11 Autumn Flowers '89 Yng 5/93 300
Mathieu, Georges   Fr 1921-
   O/C 46x29 Composition A 58 Sby 2/93 18,400
   W,Pl&G/Pa 31x23 Untitled 59 Chr 11/92 5,280
Mathieu, Paul
   * See 1993 Edition ....
Mathurin, Maurice   Fr 20C
   O/C/B 23x32 Printemps Chr 2/93 550
Matisse, Henri   Fr 1869-1954
   O/C 35x35 Harmonie Jaune 1927 Chr 11/92 .... 14.52M
   O/C 46x32 L'Asie 46 Sby 11/92 .... 11M
   O/C 13x16 La Plage Rouge Sby 11/92 .... 1.375M
   O/C 24x32 Fleurs de Nice Chr 11/92 528,000
   O/C 15x18 Nature Morte au Fruits 1898 Chr 11/92 451,000
   L&G/Pa 14x10 La Danseuse Sby 11/92 341,000
   O/C 15x18 Etretat, la plage, mer noire Chr 11/92 198,000
   Pl/Pa 15x20 Lydia en blouse Roumaine 36 Chr 11/92 ... 165,000
   C/Pa 12x20 Odalisque 1924 Chr 11/92 165,000
   O/C 14x10 Tete de Femme Sby 11/92 143,000
   W/Pa 13x17 Collioure Sby 11/92 115,500
   I/Pa 17x13 Femme au Turban 44 Sby 11/92 63,250
   Pl/Pa 20x15 Femme aux bras leves 41 Chr 11/92 52,800
   I/Pa 20x16 Nature Morte aux Lunettes 45 Sby 11/92 ... 38,500
   K/Pa 21x16 Tete de femme 47 Chr 11/92 33,000
   W&Pe/Pa 7x9 Paysage Cotier, Collioure Sby 2/93 32,200
   Pl/Pa 4x5 Study Poissons Rouges: Interieur Sby 11/92 .. 31,900
   C/Pa/B 13x8 Femme Debout Sby 5/93 16,100

PI&Y/Pa 11x8 Etudes Des Feuilles Chr 5/93 5,175
Matsubara, Kazuo Am 1895-
  O/B 18x22 Chapel Through the Trees 1927 But 3/93 1,430
Matta Chi 1911-
  O/C 45x58 Composicion Chr 11/92 121,000
  H,Y&Pe/Pa 13x19 Psychological Morph. #14 Sby 5/93 . 104,250
  Cp&H/Pa 11x15 Femme Jouant 40 Sby 11/92 82,500
  O/C 69x80 Ecran de la Memoire Chr 11/92 77,000
  O/C 32x38 Upon the Growing Chr 11/92 71,500
  Pe&H/Pa 11x15 Sans Titre 40 Sby 5/93 68,500
  O/C 32x40 Pointe Chr 11/92 63,800
  Pe&H/Pa 10x13 Dialectique Du Paysage 39 Sby 5/93 . . . 34,500
  P/Pa 39x27 Bigne Chr 11/92 6,600
Matta-Clark, Gordon
  * See 1992 Edition . . . .
Matteis, Paolo 1662-1728
  * See 1993 Edition . . . .
Mattern, Alice L. Am 1909-1945
  * See 1993 Edition . . . .
Matteson, Bartow V. Am 1894-
  O/B 32x25 Couple in Boudoir Ih 11/92 475
Matteson, Tomkins Harrison Am 1813-1884
  * See 1991 Edition . . . .
Matthew, Edward
  * See 1991 Edition . . . .
Matthews, Marmaduke Can 1837-1913
  W/Pa 41x31 Birch Tree by Lake Sbt 11/92 3,080
Matthews, Michael Eng 1933-
  O/Pn 9x11 Afternoon at the English Fair Slo 7/93 1,100
Matthews, William F. Am 1878-
  O/C 16x20 Harbour Scene Sel 4/93 400
Matthieu, Cornelis a 1637-1656
  O/C 38x54 River Landscape with Hunters Chr 1/93 8,800
Matto, Francisco Uru 1911-
  O/C 37x26 Ada 53 Sby 11/92 8,800
  T/B 33x21 Constructivo ABCDEFG '60 Sby 5/93 8,625
  T/B 14x17 Cafe Sby 11/92 3,850
Mattson, Henry E. Am 1887-1971
  * See 1992 Edition . . . .
Matulka, Jan Am 1890-1972
  O/C 30x24 Still Life Fruit and Pitchers Sby 3/93 9,200
Maturo, Joseph A. Am 1867-1938
  O/C 36x24 Movie Poster "Heidi" Ih 5/93 10,000
Maufra, Maxime Fr 1861-1918
  O/C 20x26 Coup D'Orage, Quiberon 1903 Sby 2/93 26,450
  O/C 24x29 Automne, foret de Fontainebleau 1909 Chr 10/92 14,300
Maurer, Alfred Henry Am 1868-1932
  G/Pa 22x18 Head of a Woman Sby 12/92 29,700
  O/C 18x24 Still Life Brd 8/93 13,200
  O/B 18x22 Still Life Chr 9/92 11,000
  O/Pa 11x16 Quarry, Shadybrook Chr 9/92 6,600
  G&C/Pa 21x18 Flowers in a Vase 26 Chr 9/92 6,050
  G/Pa 22x18 Vase of Flowers 1926 Chr 9/92 5,500
  O/B 22x18 Woman in a Rust-Colored Dress Chr 9/92 5,500
Maurer, Louis Am 1832-1932
  * See 1991 Edition . . . .
Maurer, Sascha Am 1897-1961
  O/C 23x30 Menemsha Creek, Martha's Vineyard 1937 Eld 4/93 468
Maury, Cornelia Field Am 19C
  O/B 14x15 Harem Hnz 5/93 700
Maury, Francois Fr 1861-1933
  O/C 37x26 A Pond in the Forest But 11/92 1,980
Maury, Georges-Sauveur Fr 1872-
  * See 1991 Edition . . . .
Mauve, Anton Dut 1838-1888
  O/C 26x38 Return of the Flock Chr 10/92 24,200
  W&G/Pa 19x28 Homeward Bound Chr 10/92 11,000
  O/C 12x20 Ploughman and His Horses Sby 5/93 5,175
Max, Peter Am 1937-
  A/C 22x18 Figure Holding an Umbrella Dum 10/92 3,500
  A/C 12x12 Zero Man Hnd 5/93 2,400
Maxence, Edgard Fr 1871-1954
  O/Pn 29x18 Recueillement Sby 5/93 19,550

Maxfield, James Emery Am 1848-
  * See 1990 Edition . . . .
Maxim, David
  * See 1992 Edition . . . .
May, Henrietta Mabel Can 1884-1971
  O/B 20x16 Daffodils Sbt 5/93 2,860
  O/B 30x23 Calla Lillies Sbt 11/92 2,464
May, Ivan Olinsky Rus 1878-1962
  O/C 20x16 Portrait of Bearded Gentleman Eld 4/93 99
May, J. Eur 19C
  O/C 12x18 Figure and Cottages Sel 12/92 750
Mayer, Auguste Etienne Fr 1805-1890
  O/C 42x73 Boats on the Venetian Laguna Chr 2/93 9,350
Mayer, Constance Fr 1775-1821
  * See 1990 Edition . . . .
Mayer, E. Aus 19C
  O/Tn 10x9 The Lesson Chr 5/93 518
Mayer, Frank Blackwell Am 1827-1899
  * See 1990 Edition . . . .
Mayer, Luigi a 18C
  O/C 18x26 Port of Brindisi, Italy Chr 5/93 2,530
Mayer, Peter Bela Am 1887-1993
  * See 1992 Edition . . . .
Mayer, William C. Am 20C
  * See 1991 Edition . . . .
Mayhew, Neil Brooker Am 1876-1940
  O/C 33x23 Landscape Mor 6/93 1,430
Maynard, George Willoughby Am 1843-1923
  O/C 51x39 Soldier of the Revolution 1876 Chr 12/92 8,250
  O/Pn 11x9 Reading by the Fire Chr 3/93 4,600
Maynard, Richard Field Am 20C
  * See 1993 Edition . . . .
Mayo, Williamson Am 20C
  O/M 24x48 Anguar Home '68 Wes 10/92 440
Mayr, Carl Viktor Aus 1881-1975
  O/Pn 36x28 Interior Seated Woman Fre 10/92 200
Maze, Paul Fr 1887-1979
  O/C 21x31 Regatta on Henley-On-Thames Chr 2/93 2,200
Mazot, Angeline Fr 19C
  * See 1990 Edition . . . .
Mazotta, Federico It 19C
  * See 1990 Edition . . . .
Mazzanovich, Lawrence Am 1872-1946
  O/C 32x40 Poplars But 12/92 7,700
  O/C 15x18 Spring Reflections 1908 Skn 9/92 990
Mazzola, Filippo It 16C
  * See 1990 Edition . . . .
Mazzolini, Giuseppe It 1748-1838
  * See 1993 Edition . . . .
Mazzolini, Giuseppe It 1806-1876
  * See 1993 Edition . . . .
Mazzolini, Joseph It 19C
  * See 1990 Edition . . . .
Mazzotta, Federico It 19C
  * See 1993 Edition . . . .
McAfee, Ila Am 1897-
  * See 1993 Edition . . . .
McArdle, Montrose Am a 1930-1940
  O/C 30x24 On the Missouri Sel 4/93 . . . . 15(
McAuliffe, James J. Am 1848-1921
  O/C 22x27 Bay Racehorse Sby 6/93 . . . . 2,30●
McBey, James Br 1883-1959
  O/C 24x18 Crowded Beach by Cliffs 1921 Chr 5/93 . . . . . 4,37●
McBride, Clifford Am 1901-1951
  Pl/Pa 22x16 Two Sunday Comic Strips Ih 5/93 . . . . 80●
  Pl/Pa 22x16 Trying to Take a Bath Ih 5/93 . . . . 50●
McCallion, P. Am 19C
  O/C 12x16 One of the Stern Realities of War 1899 Chr 9/92 5,50●
McCann, Gerald Am 20C
  * See 1992 Edition . . . .
McCarter, Henry Bainbridge Am 1864-1942
  O/C 28x32 Spring Landscape Fre 10/92 . . . . 2,40●
  H/Pa 20x15 Girls by the River Fre 4/93 . . . . 35●

McCarthy, Doris Jean   Can 1910-
O/Pn 12x14 Bullrushes in Snow, Haliburton Sbt 5/93 792
McCarthy, Frank C.   Am 1924-
O/B 19x22 New York Yankee Swinging at Pitch Ih 5/93 . . . 1,000
McCay, Winsor   Am 1869-1934
Pl/Pa 16x9 Father Knickerbocker Tammany Tiger Ih 11/92 . 2,600
McChesney, Clara Taggart   Am 1860-1928
  * See 1993 Edition . . . .
McChesney, Robert   Am 1913-
E&Sd/C 25x45 Arena #64 But 4/93 1,265
McCloskey, James   Am 20C
  * See 1993 Edition . . . .
McCloskey, William J.   Am 1859-1941
  * See 1993 Edition . . . .
McCollum, Allan   1944-
  * See 1993 Edition . . . .
McColvim, J.   Br 19C
O/C 16x8 Italian Water-Bearer Sel 9/92 200
McColvin, John
O/C 22x11 Spring Dum 5/93 600
McComas, Eugene Francis   Am 1886-1982
  * See 1992 Edition . . . .
McComas, Francis John   Am 1874-1938
C/Pa 18x24 Stevenson House, Monterey But 3/93 3,300
W/Pa 7x30 Monterey Bay '98 But 10/92 3,025
W/Pa 8x10 Monterey Houses But 10/92 2,475
W/Pa 14x20 Southwest Landscape 1928 Wes 3/93 550
McConnell, George   Am 1852-1929
O/Cb 12x18 Mountain Landscape 1913 Wlf 4/93 250
O/B 26x38 Surf off Portland Head 1915 Brd 8/93 110
McCord, George Herbert   Am 1848-1909
O/B 12x9 Regatta Near Newburgh, New York Chr 3/93 3,450
O/C 9x14 Cows/Edge of the Watermeadow 1874 Skn 9/92 . 2,530
O/C 12x16 Seaside Village at Sunset Sby 9/92 880
O/C 20x36 Fisherfolk on the Coast Chr 5/93 748
O/C 14x17 Harbour Scene Mys 12/92 688
O/B 10x8 Venice But 12/92 660
McCormick, Evelyn   Am 1869-1948
O/C 20x30 Old Monterey Building Mor 11/92 4,250
McCormick, Howard   Am 1875-1943
  * See 1993 Edition . . . .
McCoy, Wilson   Am 1902-1986
W/Pa 11x15 Sycamore Trees '44 Mor 6/93 412
McCrossan, Mary   Eng -1924
O/C 14x18 Treasury in Moonlight, Tangier Slo 7/93 950
McDermott & McGough   Am 20C
O/C 60x60 The Newspaper - 1912 Chr 2/93 8,250
O/C 71x71 Fear or Faith 1921 Chr 2/93 5,500
O/Me 86x43 The Red Light Chr 2/93 5,500
McDougall, John Alexander   Am 1810-1894
  * See 1993 Edition . . . .
McDowell, William   Br 1888-1950
G/B 10x15 Battle of Midway: Pair Sby 1/93 2,070
McDuff, Frederick   Am 1931-
  * See 1993 Edition . . . .
McEntee, Jervis   Am 1828-1891
O/B 12x20 Gathering Christmas Finery 1877 Chr 9/92 . . . 18,700
O/C 38x30 Late Afternoon Landscape Chr 5/93 11,500
O/B 12x14 My Little Fisher Girl 1875 Chr 12/92 9,900
O/C 7x12 Pause in the Roman Campagna Chr 12/92 8,250
O/C 7x12 Rocks in the Woods Chr 12/92 3,520
O/C/Pa 4x6 A Stag at Eve, Autumn Brd 8/93 2,200
O/C/B 9x13 Sunset 1870 Chr 9/92 2,200
O/C 14x26 Landscape with Small Pond Dum 4/93 2,000
McEvoy, Ambrose
W/Pa 20x14 Head Dum 7/93 3,750
W/Pa 20x13 Melisande Dum 7/93 3,500
McEwan, Walter   Am 19C
O/C/B 8x14 Two Girls Netting Fish Sby 9/92 1,320
McEwan, William   Am 19C
  * See 1990 Edition . . . .

McEwen, Jean Albert   Can 1923-
O/C 50x70 Les Continents Fleuris #18 '74 Sbt 11/92 14,520
O/C 77x81 Elegie Criblee de Bleu '86 Sbt 5/93 13,200
McFee, Henry Lee   Am 1886-1953
  * See 1993 Edition . . . .
McGee, Charles   Am 1924-
O/M 18x29 Female Combing Her Hair '52 FHB 5/93 200
McGeehan, Jessie M.   Br a 1892-1913
G/Pa 15x13 Herons in a Marsh Hnd 5/93 425
McGhie, John M.   Br 1867-1941
  * See 1992 Edition . . . .
McGinnis, Robert E.   Am 1926-
  * See 1993 Edition . . . .
McGlynn, Thomas   Am 1878-1966
O/C 19x21 View of the Coast But 3/93 4,400
McGrath, Clarence   Am 20C
  * See 1990 Edition . . . .
McGrew, Ralph Brownell   Am 20C
  * See 1990 Edition . . . .
McGuiness, Bingham   Br a 1882-1892
  * See 1993 Edition . . . .
McIlhenney, Charles M.   Am 1858-1904
O/C 14x25 Summer Afternoon Sby 9/92 33,000
O/C 18x14 Creek in Winter Landscape Fre 4/93 100
McIver, D.
O/C 13x19 Harbor Scene 1904 Dum 8/93 650
McKain, Bruce   Am 1900-
  * See 1993 Edition . . . .
McKay, Thomas Hill   Am 1875-1941
  * See 1992 Edition . . . .
McKeever, Ian   1946-
O&L/C 98x171 Crossing 86 Chr 11/92 10,450
McLane, Murtle Jean   Am 19C
  * See 1991 Edition . . . .
McLaughlin, John   Am 1898-1976
O/C 48x36 E-1956 1956 Sby 5/93 10,350
McLean, A. M.   Am 19C
O/Tn 10x12 Still Life Apple, Knife, Wineglass 1865 Hnd 6/93 950
McLean, Bruce   1944-
  * See 1993 Edition . . . .
McLean, Richard   Am 1934-
O/C 54x58 Dixie Coast 74 Sby 10/92 17,600
McLellan, Ralph   Am 20C
  * See 1990 Edition . . . .
McManus, George   Am 1869-1954
Pl&W/Pa 22x17 Father Tries to Sneak Out 1912 Ih 5/93 . . . 1,700
Pl/Pa 4x17 Daily Comic "Bringing Up Father" Ih 11/92 . . . 325
McMein, Neysa   Am 1890-1949
P/Pa 36x28 Elegant Woman Seated in Car Ih 11/92 2,600
McNair, William
O/C 30x40 California Landscape 1932 Dum 9/92 2,200
McNeil, George   1908-
A/C 56x68 Palentown Abstractscape 84 Chr 5/93 6,325
O/M 12x15 Torrent 1967 Chr 11/92 715
McPherson, Bill   Am 20C
C/Pa 12x10 Labrador Retriever; Scottie: Pair FHB 6/93 200
P/Pa 10x8 Portrait of a Dog 1937 FHB 6/93 60
McRickard, James P.   Am 1872-
O/B 8x10 Near Indian Head, White Mts., NH Yng 2/93 250
McSwiney, Eugene   Br 1866-
O/C 20x30 Figures by a Stream with a Mill But 11/92 1,430
Meacci, Ricciardo   It 1856-
Gd&W/Pa 11x9 And He Gathers Prayers Wlf 5/93 1,100
W/Pa 10x7 Woman in an Italian Courtyard Wes 3/93 220
Meadows, Edwin L.   Br a 1854-1872
O/C 24x42 Leaving the Village 1867 Hnz 5/93 3,300
O/C 12x22 River Landscape 1858 Sel 12/92 350
Meadows, James   Br 1798-1864
O/C 12x22 Rough Seas 1862 Hnz 5/93 1,400
Meadows, James Edwin   Br 1828-1888
O/C 18x32 Rest During the Harvest 1884 Hnz 5/93 3,400
O/C 23x41 English Countryside 1863 Hnz 3/93 1,200
Meakin, Lewis Henry   Am 1853-1917
O/C 21x33 Mountainous Landscape Sby 3/93 2,070

Mears, Henrietta Dunn   Am 1877-
O/B 6x10 Sailboats   Mor 11/92 375
Mechau, Frank Albert   Am 1903-1946
* See 1992 Edition ....
Medairy, F. F.   Am 19C
W/Pa 17x26 Landscape with Flower Gatherer   Hnd 9/92 70
Medard, Jules Ferdinand   Fr 1855-1925
* See 1993 Edition ....
Meeker, Joseph Rusling   Am 1827-1889
O/C 14x24 Bayou at Lake Maurepas 1887   Sby 12/92 19,800
Meeks, Eugene   Am 1843-
* See 1990 Edition ....
Meerts, Frans   Ger 1836-1896
* See 1991 Edition ....
Meeser, Lilian   Am 1864-
O/B 10x8 Dock Scene   Mys 12/92 385
**Megargee, Lawrence (Lon) A.   Am
1883-1960**
O/C 18x24 Landscape   Mor 2/93 600
Mehigan, S.
Pe/Pa 30x23 Lady Holding a Bird '45   FHB 6/93 150
Pe/Pa 18x14 Cubist Style Portrait with Fruit '48   FHB 6/93 40
Mehring, Howard   Am 1931-1978
A/C 47x54 August   Wes 10/92 605
Mehus, Livio   Flm 1630-1691
* See 1991 Edition ....
Mei, Bernardino   It 1615-1676
* See 1993 Edition ....
Meierhans, Jos.
O/B 24x40 Abstract   Ald 9/92 300
O/C 52x34 Blue and Yellow Design   Ald 9/92 300
Meifren Y Roig, Eliseo   Spa 1859-1940
* See 1993 Edition ....
Meijer, Gerhardus   Dut 1816-1875
O/C 26x21 The Cobbler's Family 1875   Chr 10/92 16,500
Meijer, Jan   Fr 20C
O/C 58x35 Demon Blue 62   Hnd 9/92 70
Meindl, Albert   Aus 1891-1967
* See 1992 Edition ....
Meissel, Ernst   Ger 1838-1895
* See 1991 Edition ....
Meissner, Adolf Ernst   Ger 1837-1902
* See 1992 Edition ....
Meissonier, Jean Charles   Fr 1848-1917
O/C 18x29 The Encampment   Sby 5/93 10,925
O/Pn 8x6 A Cavalier   Hnd 9/92 700
**Meissonier, Jean Louis Ernest   Fr
1815-1891**
O/Pn 9x6 Le Cuirassier   Sby 2/93 3,450
Melancon, Henri   Fr 1876-1960
O/C 16x24 Harbor Town   Yng 5/93 200
**Melbye, Daniel Hermann Anton   Dan
1818-1875**
* See 1992 Edition ....
Melcher, George Henry   Am 1881-1957
O/C 25x30 Point Dume from Malibu Hills   But 6/93 6,900
O/C 9x12 Melcher's Cabin   Lou 6/93 600
Melchers, Frantz   Bel 1868-
* See 1993 Edition ....
Melchers, Julius Gari   Am 1860-1932
O/C 40x30 Child with an Orange   Sby 5/93 82,250
O/C 18x15 Girl Knitting   Sby 5/93 27,600
O/C 23x29 Offertory (Interior of a Church)   Sby 5/93 25,300
O/C 18x22 Early Morning, North River   Sby 3/93 18,400
O/Pn 12x8 After the Ball '84   Sby 9/92 17,600
G&Pe/C 30x27 Madonna of the Fields   Chr 5/93 17,250
Melchoir, Wilhelm   Ger 1817-1860
O/C 29x35 The Day's Catch   Sby 10/92 2,200
Meldolla, Andrea   1522-1563
O&T/Pn 11x20 Perseus Rescuing Andromeda   Sby 5/93 .. 23,000
Melendez, Luis   Spa 1716-1780
* See 1992 Edition ....
Melios, Janis
O/B 10x15 Boats Dock by Beach   Ald 5/93 300

Mellen, Mary Blood   Am 1817-
O/C 22x27 House Portrait   Sby 9/92 4,400
Mellor, William   Br 1851-1931
* See 1993 Edition ....
Melrose, Andrew W.   Am 1836-1901
O/C 30x50 Life on the River   But 12/92 24,750
O/Pn 6x12 The Narrows   Chr 9/92 3,520
O/C 22x27 Tyrolean Landscape 87   Sby 3/93 1,495
Meltsner, Paul R.   Am 1905-
O/Cb 18x24 A Reclining Nude   Chr 5/93 575
Meltzer, Anna E.   Am 1896-
O/C 27x15 The Plumed Hat '44   Skn 9/92 715
Meltzer, Arthur   Am 1893-
O/C 13x14 Verbenas '29   Fre 4/93 1,900
**Menageot, Francois Guillaume   Fr
1744-1816**
* See 1993 Edition ....
**Menard, Marie Auguste Emile   Fr
1862-1930**
P/C 53x34 Nude   Sby 2/93 5,463
Menassier, *A*   16C**
O/C 38x28 Mary Magdalene Skull   Sby 10/92 6,050
Mendenhall, Emma   Am 1873-
W/Pa 14x18 Cafe; Sidewalk Scene; Mountain (3)   Lou 6/93 . 350
W/Pa 14x18 Landscape Near Palmade Majorca   Hnd 6/93 ... 140
W/Pa 12x16 Garden Capell, Antibes   Hnd 9/92 100
Mendenhall, John   Am 1937-
O/C 57x84 Store Window Dining Set   Chr 2/93 1,100
Mendez-Gonzales, Manuel   Spa 19C
* See 1992 Edition ....
Mendieta, Ana   20C
* See 1991 Edition ....
Mendilaharzu, G.   Arg 19C
O/C 16x13 The Feather Duster Shop   Sby 5/93 4,600
Mendjisky, Serge   Fr 1929-
* See 1993 Edition ....
Mendoza   Por 19C
O/C 12x15 Elegant Figures on the Boardwalk   Chr 2/93 3,850
Mendoza, Francisco   Mex 1814-1865
Pl/Pa Var Eight Pen Drawings   Eld 8/93 385
Menegazzi, Carlo   It 19C
W/Pa 15x10 Venice Canal   Yng 2/93 300
Menendez-Pidal, Luis   Spa 1864-
* See 1993 Edition ....
Menker, F.   Con 19C
O/C 16x24 Tiburon '91   But 5/93 3,162
Menkes, Sigmund Joseph   Am 1896-1986
O/C 28x33 Woman Resting   Hnd 3/93 3,600
O/M 14x19 Nature Morte   Chr 5/93 2,875
O/C 24x18 Harlequin and Pierrot   Sby 6/93 2,760
O/C 16x12 New Song   Sby 10/92 2,750
O/B 26x21 Vase de Fleurs   Chr 11/92 1,870
O/C 16x13 Woman Playing a Mandolin   Sby 2/93 1,840
O/C 36x46 Woman Eating Grapes   Fre 10/92 250
Menkman, William
* See 1992 Edition ....
Menotti, V. A.   It 19C
* See 1993 Edition ....
Menta, Edouard   Fr 1858-
* See 1993 Edition ....
Mentor, Will   20C
* See 1993 Edition ....
Menzel, Adolf Friedrich E.   Ger 1815-1905
* See 1993 Edition ....
Menzler, Wilhelm   Ger 1846-
* See 1993 Edition ....
Menzler, Wm.
O/B 9x5 Nude '21   Dum 6/93 400
Mercier, Philippe   Fr 1689-1760
* See 1993 Edition ....
Meredith, John   Can 1933-
O/B 36x24 Dragon City '55   Sbt 5/93 4,840
l/Pa 17x14 Untitled '67   Sbt 11/92 1,848
l/Pa 14x17 Red, Yellow, Blue and Purple '92   Sbt 5/93 1,320
Pe&l/Pa 20x26 Untitled 1988 '88   Sbt 11/92 1,320

Mereiles De Lima, Vitor   LA 1832-1903
  * See 1993 Edition . . . .
Merian, Matthaeus (I)   1593-1650
  K&S/Pa 7x14 Group of Nobles Observing Hunt Chr 1/93 . . . 4,400
Mericourt, Felix   Eur 19C
  O/C 27x39 A Cossack Charge Hnz 5/93 2,200
Merida, Carlos   Mex 1891-1984
  Pol/L 22x15 El Hombre y Su Morada 1961 Chr 11/92 44,000
  O/Pa/M 21x24 Adriana y el Laberinto 1975 Sby 11/92 . . . 30,250
  O/M 24x18 Untitled 1966 Sby 11/92 24,200
  T&I/L 10x13 Cinco Ideas 1939 Sby 11/92 22,000
  O/Pa/M 20x24 Los Tres Reyes Magos 1975 Sby 5/93 . . . 21,850
  T/B 16x12 Composicion Geometrica 1961 Sby 11/92 9,350
  A,Sd&I/B 15x11 Construccion En Rojo 1968 Sby 5/93 9,200
  T/Pa 20x15 Oro y Rojo 1963 Sby 11/92 4,400
Merle, Georges Hugues   Fr 19C
  * See 1992 Edition . . . .
Merle, Hugues   Fr 1823-1881
  * See 1993 Edition . . . .
Merlin, Daniel   Fr 1861-1933
  O/C 18x22 En Famille Chr 10/92 7,700
  O/C 23x29 Kittens at Play Sby 1/93 3,450
Merlino, Silvio   1952-
  ASd&K/Pa/C 49x73 Vulcano Che Dorme 1985 Chr 2/93 . . . 7,700
Merriam, James Arthur   Am 1880-1951
  O/C 30x40 Palm Springs But 6/93 805
  O/C 30x40 Early Morning Colorado Desert Mor 2/93 650
  O/C 20x30 Landscape Hnd 3/93 550
  O/C 28x36 Landscape Mor 2/93 275
Merritt, Anna Lea   Am 1844-1930
  O/C 30x25 The Letter Fre 4/93 750
Mersfelder, Jules   Am 1865-1937
  O/C 21x30 Grazing Cattle in Clearing But 6/93 1,150
Merson, Luc-Olivier   Fr 1846-1920
  * See 1991 Edition . . . .
Mertens, Stella   Fr 1896-1986
  O/C 28x19 Portrait of Jane Harper 1954 Fre 4/93 1,300
  O/C 26x21 Landscape with Yellow Sky 1956 Fre 4/93 700
  I/Pa 15x11 Tree 1953 Fre 4/93 45
Merwart, Paul   Pol 1855-1902
  O/C 62x79 Bacchante aux Raisins 1887 Sby 5/93 17,250
Merz, Gerhard   1947-
  * See 1993 Edition . . . .
Merz, Mario   1925-
  A&O/C 80x96 Pittore in Africa Sby 11/92 44,000
Mesdag, Hendrik Willem   Dut 1831-1915
  O/Pn 9x7 Boat at Sea But 5/93 2,300
Mesgriny, Claude Francois A.   Fr 1836-1884
  * See 1992 Edition . . . .
Mesple, James   Am 20C
  O/Pn 16x20 Classic Landscape 1922 Hnd 9/92 110
Mesples, Paul Eugene   Fr 1849-
  * See 1991 Edition . . . .
Mess, George Jo   Am 1898-1962
  * See 1993 Edition . . . .
Mestrallet, Andre-Louis
  O/B 15x18 Le Vieux Bassin a Honfleur Sby 6/93 920
Mestrovich, Ivan   Yug 1883-1962
  Y/Pa 35x18 Study of a Male Nude 1942 But 10/92 880
Metcalf, Willard Leroy   Am 1858-1925
  O/C 26x29 East Boothbay Harbor '04 Chr 12/92 330,000
  O/C 12x15 The Lily Pond '87 Sby 12/92 126,500
  O/Pn 14x11 Breton Girl 1884 Sby 5/93 24,150
  O/C/C 15x18 Landscape 1884 Chr 3/93 7,475
  P/Pa 10x14 Dance Masks and Trophies Sby 9/92 1,100
Meteyard, Sydney Harold   Br 1868-1947
  O/C 20x30 Portrait of Christina Rossetti Chr 2/93 9,350
Meteyard, Thomas Buford   Am 1865-1928
  * See 1993 Edition . . . .
Methfessel, Adolfo   Arg 1836-1909
  O/B 11x15 Los Chorros de las Escabas Sby 11/92 6,600
Metzinger, Jean   Fr 1883-1956
  O/C 46x29 Joueur de cartes 1920 Chr 11/92 209,000
  O/C 14x11 Nu Au Bateau Sby 5/93 35,650

Meucci, Michelangelo   It 19C
  O/B 34x24 Tropical Birds in Wooded Landscape Sby 5/93 . 10,350
  O/C 45x19 Still Life with Colorful Roses 1889 Chr 5/93 . . . 3,450
  O/C 20x24 Tabletop Still Life Fruit 1868 Slo 5/93 2,250
  O/Ab 12x9 Pair of Still Lifes Songbirds 1871 FHB 5/93 1,800
  O/Pn 9x7 Birds (3) Hnd 10/92 1,700
  O/Pn 13x9 Two Birds Hnd 12/92 950
Meugnier, J.
  * See 1992 Edition . . . .
Meulener, Pieter   Dut 1602-1654
  * See 1992 Edition . . . .
Meunier, R. V.   Fr 19C
  O/C/B 22x13 A Chamber Maid Hnd 6/93 1,100
  O/C/B 22x13 Peasant Woman Playing Lute Hnd 6/93 400
Meurer, Charles Alfred   Am 1865-1955
  O/C 38x30 My Passport 1892 Chr 12/92 40,700
  O/C 15x20 Sheep in a Snowy Landscape Chr 12/92 5,500
Meuris   Bel 19C
  G/Pa 10x15 View of Monte Carlo FHB 5/93 850
Meyer, Albert   Am 19C
  O/C 16x20 Rural Landscape with Cottage: Pair Sel 9/92 . . . 275
Meyer, Emile   Fr 19C
  * See 1992 Edition . . . .
Meyer, Ernest Frederick   Am 1863-1961
  O/B 8x10 Summer Landscape Wes 5/93 358
Meyer, G. A.   Am
  O/Ab 30x44 Autumn in the Berkshires Dum 1/93 250
Meyer, Georges   Fr 19C
  * See 1993 Edition . . . .
Meyer, H.   Br 19C
  * See 1993 Edition . . . .
Meyer, Herbert   Am 1882-1960
  O/C 12x18 Landscape Ald 9/92 275
Meyer, Johann Heinrich Louis   Dut 1806-1866
  * See 1992 Edition . . . .
Meyer, Louis   Dut 1809-1886
  * See 1993 Edition . . . .
Meyer, Louise   Ger 1789-1861
  * See 1990 Edition . . . .
Meyer-Wismar, Ferdinand   Ger 1833-1917
  * See 1992 Edition . . . .
Meyerheim, Hermann   Ger 1840-1880
  O/C 27x38 A Busy Port Town 1895 Chr 10/92 13,200
Meyerheim, Wilhelm Alexander   Ger 1815-1882
  O/C/B 27x38 The Ferry Chr 5/93 10,350
  O/C 25x34 Peasants by a Frozen Pond 1870 Chr 10/92 . . . 9,350
Meyerowitz, William   Am 1898-1981
  O/C 20x25 The West End, Gloucester Lou 9/92 1,500
  O/B 20x24 Red Buildings, Rocky Neck Sby 9/92 1,320
  O/C 27x36 Still Life by a Window Mys 12/92 1,210
  O/C 17x34 Quintet Sby 3/93 978
Meyers, Frank Harmon   Am 1899-1956
  * See 1991 Edition . . . .
Meyers, Harry Morse   Am 1886-1961
  O/C 17x19 Mounted Figure on Horse 1920 Ilh 11/92 550
Meynell, Louis   Am 1868-
  O/C 27x36 Two Autumn Trees and Lake Skn 11/92 468
Meza, Guillermo   Mex 1917-
  * See 1993 Edition . . . .
Mezzera, Rosa   20C
  * See 1990 Edition . . . .
Miahle, Federico   Mex 1800-1868
  * See 1993 Edition . . . .
Michau, Theobald   Flm 1676-1765
  * See 1992 Edition . . . .
Michaud, Leonie   Fr 1873-
  * See 1990 Edition . . . .
Michel, Alfonso   Mex 1897-1957
  O/C 19x17 La Copa Chr 11/92 38,500
Michel, Georges   Fr 1763-1843
  O/C 38x50 Before the Storm Chr 10/92 19,800
  O/C 26x32 Dechargement de la Peche Sby 5/93 5,750
  O/Pn 22x32 Figures Traveling the Road But 11/92 4,950

O/C 21x28 Two Windmills and Approaching Storm Chr 2/93 3,850

Michel, Robert Ger 1897-
 * See 1993 Edition . . . .

Michel, William Con 19C
 O/C/M 21x19 Still Life Fruit and Books 1848 Chr 10/92 . . . 4,400

Michelet, G. C. Fr 20C
 * See 1993 Edition . . . .

Michetti, Francesco Paolo It 1851-1929
 * See 1993 Edition . . . .

Michielsen, Hendrick Evert Dut 1852-1929
 O/M 19x29 Wooded Landscape 1890 But 5/93 2,875

Michl, Ferdinand Czk 1877-
 O/C 12x24 Czechoslovakian Town Slo 5/93 500

Michonze, Gregoire Fr 1902-1982
 O/M 7x20 Les Bastisseurs 60 Sby 10/92 1,430

Middendorf, Helmut Ger 1953-
 G,C,Y&I/Pa 39x28 Blue Head 82 Chr 11/92 2,640

Middleton, Stanley Am 1852-
 O/C 24x20 Woman with a Violin Wtf 9/92 . . . . : . . 750

Mieczkowski, Edwin Am 1929-
 O/B 16x20 Night Street Scene with Buildings Wtf 5/93 600

Mieduch, Dan Am 1947-
 * See 1993 Edition . . . .

Miel, Jan Flm 1599-1663
 * See 1993 Edition . . . .

Mielich, Leopold Alphons Aus 1863-1929
 * See 1993 Edition . . . .

Mieninger, Ludwig
 * See 1992 Edition . . . .

Migliaro, Vincenzo It 1858-1938
 O/Pn 12x17 The Carnival Ball Sby 1/93 10,063

Mignard, Pierre Fr 1612-1695
 * See 1993 Edition . . . .

Mignon, Abraham Ger 1640-1679
 O/C 35x27 Still Life Cockerel, Partridge Sby 1/93 156,500

Mignot, Louis Remy Am 1831-1870
 O/C 12x20 The Day's Departure 60 Chr 12/92 6,050
 O/C 24x36 Mount Cayambe, Ecuador But 6/93 5,175
 O/C 32x42 Sunset on a Mountainous Landscape But 12/92 . 4,675

Mihalovits, Miklos Hun 1887-1960
 O/C 24x36 Reclining Nude Dum 7/93 1,600
 O/C 24x20 Semi-Nude Female Dum 3/93 750
 O/C 24x20 Dancing Ballerina Dum 6/93 350
 O/C 20x16 Christ Holding a Staff Dum 6/93 125

Mijares, Jose Cub 1921-
 O/C 33x44 Arlequines Chr 11/92 14,300
 O/L 25x34 Barcas Chr 11/92 9,900
 O/C 25x18 Mujer en el Balcon 1948 Sby 11/92 3,575
 O/Pa/C 20x27 Verticalidad 1953 Sby 11/92 2,475

Milder, Jay Am 1934-
 O/M 36x47 Subway Figures #2 Sby 2/93 690
 G/Pa 40x26 Still Life with Red Chair 60 Sby 2/93 460

Miles, Don Am 1921-
 O/M 18x24 Women in Taos Mor 6/93 990

Miles, John Christopher Can 1837-1911
 O/C 28x44 Gathering Dulce Sbt 5/93 3,520

Miles, Samuel S. Am 19C
 O/C/C 10x14 River Landscape Mor 6/93 412
 O/C 6x9 Landscape Lou 6/93 100

Miles, Thomas Rose Br 1869-1900
 O/C 24x36 Westerly Galemargyl Pt, Isle of Man Dum 2/93 . 1,200

Milesi, Alessandro It 1856-1945
 * See 1991 Edition . . . .

Milhoff, Mark Am 20C
 A/C 58x49 I am Moriturus 82 Skn 5/93 275

Milich, Abram Adolphe Pol 1884-1964
 * See 1992 Edition . . . .

Miliken, G. Con 19C
 O/C 18x29 Along the River Chr 10/92 880

Millais, John Guille Br 1865-1931
 W&G/Pa 15x20 Death of Frederick Courtney Selous Sel 12/92 1,500

Millais, Sir John Everett Br 1829-1896
 * See 1991 Edition . . . .

Millar, Addison T. Am 1860-1913
 O/C 18x24 The Turkish Vase Sby 10/92 22,000
 O/C 18x14 The Rug Merchant Sby 5/93 9,200
 O/Pn 8x10 The Rug Merchant Sby 3/93 3,565
 O/C 9x11 Still Life with Fruit Lou 9/92 1,450
 O/C 31x39 Interior with Figures Yng 2/93 950

Millar, H. T. Am 20C
 O/C 10x15 Haystacks Fre 4/93 120

Millard, Charles Stuart Can 1837-1917
 * See 1992 Edition . . . .

Millares, Manolo Spa 1926-1972
 * See 1991 Edition . . . .

Miller, Alfred Jacob Am 1810-1874
 O/C 12x10 Indian Scout on Horseback Sby 5/93 112,500
 W/Pa 7x10 Escape from a Grizzly Bear Sby 12/92 33,000
 I&Pe/Pa 7x10 Death of the Elk 62 Sby 12/92 23,100
 O/C 24x20 Portrait of a Young Lady Sby 9/92 1,320

Miller, Barse Am 1904-1973
 W/Pa 14x20 Sunday in Phoenixville 1940 Mor 6/93 1,430
 W/Pa 11x20 Checkers Mor 11/92 800
 O/C 20x30 Freight Station Lou 12/92 500

Miller, Charles Henry Am 1842-1922
 O/C 14x22 Grazing Cows in Wooded Landscape Slo 7/93 . . . 425

Miller, Edith M. Am a 1920-1939
 O/Cb 24x20 Floral Bouquet '29 Mor 11/92 275

Miller, Evylena Nunn Am 1888-1966
 O/B 10x14 Hillside with Trees & Clouds Mor 6/93 1,045

Miller, F. H. Am 19C
 * See 1993 Edition . . . .

Miller, George Br 1827-1853
 * See 1993 Edition . . . .

Miller, Harriette G. Am 20C
 * See 1991 Edition . . . .

Miller, Henry Am 1897-1980
 W/Pa 24x17 Untitled 66 But 10/92 1,320

Miller, John Paul Am 20C
 W/Pa 14x19 Farm in Autumn Slo 4/93 75

Miller, Josef Ger 19C
 * See 1992 Edition . . . .

Miller, Kenneth Hayes Am 1876-1952
 * See 1992 Edition . . . .

Miller, Melvin Am 1937-
 O/C 17x26 Tugboat, "James McAllister" Eld 7/93 660
 O/C 10x12 Baltimore Street Scene Eld 8/93 248

Miller, Mildred Bunting Am 1892-1964
 O/C 28x25 The Garden Yng 2/93 2,500

Miller, Ralph Davison Am 1859-1946
 O/C 30x40 Mountain Landscape Mor 6/93 935
 O/B 12x16 Coastal Mor 2/93 600

Miller, Richard
 MM/C 20x21 Premonition Sby 10/92 165

Miller, Richard Edward Am 1875-1943
 O/C 26x28 The Necklace Chr 12/92 220,000
 O/C 32x26 In the Shadow Sby 5/93 140,000
 O/B 36x38 Bather 1930 Sby 12/92 55,000
 T&G/B 22x19 A Woman Reading Chr 5/93 2,530
 O/B 20x24 Canton China Chr 5/93 1,150

Miller, W. Am 1920-
 O/C 20x24 Under a Bridge Yng 5/93 150

Miller, William Rickarby Am 1818-1893
 O/C 18x24 House in the Country 1858 Sby 3/93 12,650
 O/C 17x14 River Walk Under Castle Point 1873 Chr 9/92 . . 9,350
 W/Pa 8x12 Along the River, Autumn 1892 Sby 9/92 6,875
 W/Pa/B 9x15 Mohawk River, Little Falls 1880 Chr 3/93 . . . 2,300

Milleson, Royal Hill Am 1849-
 O/C 40x54 Gallinas Canyon Sby 3/93 3,335
 O/C 28x22 Before the Storm Lou 3/93 1,100

Millet, Francis Davis Am 1846-1912
 * See 1993 Edition . . . .

Millet, Francois Fr 1851-1917
 P/Pa/C 11x16 Cows Grazing Chr 10/92 2,420

Millet, Francois (II) Fr 1666-1723
 O/C 28x22 Figures Before a Roman Marble Tomb Sby 5/93 13,200

Millet, Jean Francois Fr 1814-1875
 Y/Pa/Pa 12x9 Shepherdess Knitting Chr 5/93 222,500

168

O/Pn 9x13 Swimmers Chr 5/93 55,200
K/Pa 11x14 Peasant Crouching by the Roadside Chr 5/93 . 20,700
C/Pa 9x6 Mere et Enfant Sby 10/92 12,650
Pe/Pa 4x2 Study Woman, Hands (2) Chr 2/93 3,300
Pe/Pa 5x7 Sketch for Autumn Landscape Chr 10/92 2,860
C/Pa 4x4 Study of Figures Sby 1/93 1,265

Millevoix, Fritz Hai 20C
O/C 30x40 Three Owls Lou 9/92 400

Milliere, Maurice Fr 1871-
* See 1991 Edition . . . .

Millman, Edward Am 1907-1964
O/C 20x34 Relics of Pretentious Dreams Mys 12/92 220

Millner, Karl Ger 1825-1894
O/C 20x15 Wandern Im Hoch Alpen: Pair Sby 5/93 11,500

Mills, John Br 19C
O/C 24x26 Boy on a Bay Horse Sby 6/93 6,900

Milne, David Brown Can 1882-1953
O/C 12x16 Village; Dark Hills: Double Sbt 11/92 39,600
O/C 20x18 Leaves in Sunlight 1914 Sbt 5/93 31,680
W/Pa 20x15 Ferris Wheel, Coney Island '12 Sbt 5/93 23,760
O/C 11x14 Last Snowdrift 1936 Sbt 5/93 15,840
W/Pa 15x22 Empty Box 1938 Sbt 5/93 9,680

Milne, John Maclaughlan Br 1885-1957
* See 1992 Edition . . . .

Milroy, Lisa 1959-
O/C 18x24 Untitled '83 Chr 11/92 1,320

Milton, John
* See 1991 Edition . . . .

Milton, Victor Marais Fr 1872-
* See 1993 Edition . . . .

Minaux, Andre Fr 1923-
O/Pn 11x28 Instruments De Jardinage Sel 12/92 750
O/Pn 11x28 Instruments de Jardinage Sel 2/93 300

Mink, David Am 1912-
W/Pa 8x11 Ice Skaters in a Park Setting Wlf 5/93 100

Minor, Robert Crannel Am 1839-1904
O/B 8x12 Autumn Sunset Hnd 12/92 900

Mintchine, Abraham
O/C 20x26 Still Life with Fruit Sby 10/92 6,325

Minter, Marilyn 1948-
E/C 24x36 Handrolling, Cleaning Painting 1988 Sby 2/93 . 6,325
E/Me 24x31 Nine Ways to be a Better Cook 1989 Chr 2/93 . 6,050

Miotte, Jean 1926-
O/C 20x26 En Verite Chr 5/93 1,150

Mira, Alfred S. Am 20C
O/Cb 12x16 View Sheridan Square Sby 9/92 3,300

Miralles, Francisco Spa 1850-1901
O/C 22x26 Elegant Ladies in a Garden Sby 5/93 37,375
O/C 24x20 A Summer's Afternoon Chr 10/92 27,500
O/C 24x20 A Confrontation 1889 Chr 5/93 20,700

Mirella
* See 1992 Edition . . . .

Mirko, Basdella Am 1910-1969
* See 1993 Edition . . . .

Miro, Joachim Spa 20C
O/B 6x9 Paris Street Scene Chr 5/93 2,530
O/Pn 10x6 A Busy Parisian Street Chr 5/93 2,300
O/C 15x21 An Arabian Cavalry Charge 1901 Chr 2/93 2,200
O/C 15x22 Chariot Race Sel 9/92 550

Miro, Joan Spa 1893-1983
O/C 29x6 Personnages, Oiseau, Etoiles 1944 Sby 5/93 . . 101,500
G&I/Pa 9x16 Personnages, Lune Bleue et Etoile Sby 5/93 . 67,400
G&W/Pa 16x25 Les Nobles a la Trappe Sby 5/93 54,050
G&I/Pa 9x8 Chien Aboyant Sby 5/93 51,750
G&W/Pa 16x25 La Nuit, L'Ours: Ubu Roi XI Sby 5/93 50,600
G&W/Pa 16x24 La Guerre: Ubu Roi X Sby 5/93 48,300
G&W/Pa 16x25 Le Massacre du Roi de Pologne Sby 5/93 42,550
Y/Pa 10x8 Composition: Pair Sby 2/93 26,450
G&Y/Cd 13x8 Untitled Sby 11/92 23,100
Y/Pa 7x9 Personnages: Pair Sby 2/93 18,400
Y/Pa 10x8 Personnage Sby 2/93 9,775
Pl/Pa 9x16 L'Arc-En-Ciel Sby 2/93 5,463

Mirou, Anton Flm 1586-1661
* See 1992 Edition . . . .

Mirsky, Samuel
O/B 11x14 Studying by Candlelight Sby 6/93 2,300

Mischeles, Margaret Eng 1871-1924
O/B 10x8 Still Life Flowers and Peaches Fre 10/92 850

Mitchell, Alfred R. Am 1888-1972
O/B 20x16 Beach at Torrey Pines But 10/92 5,500
O/B 16x20 Mammoth Lakes But 3/93 4,950
O/C/C 20x24 High Sierra Mor 11/92 4,750
O/B 8x10 Along Riverbed Creek But 3/93 3,300
O/B 16x20 Desert Canyon But 10/92 3,300
O/B 16x20 Morning Sby 9/92 3,300
O/B 16x20 Mount San Miguel in Fall But 10/92 3,300
O/B 8x10 Sunset, Shadow Lake, Sierras But 3/93 3,300
O/B 7x10 Summer Landscape Mor 6/93 3,025
O/B 8x10 Sierra Meadow But 3/93 2,750
O/B 8x10 Rocky Point But 10/92 2,475
O/B 8x10 Cliffs But 10/92 2,090
O/Ab 8x10 House in Tree Shaded Stream Mor 2/93 2,000
O/B 8x10 La Jolla Rocks But 10/92 1,980
O/C 16x20 Spring Landscape Chr 3/93 1,035
O/B 8x10 San Gregornio Mor 11/92 950

Mitchell, Arthur R. Am 1889-1977
* See 1993 Edition . . . .

Mitchell, G. B. Can 20C
W/Pa Var Native Americans (6) Eld 8/93 440
W/Pa Var Portraits of Native Americans (6) Eld 8/93 440
Pe/Pa Var Five Drawings Eld 8/93 192
W/Pa 8x11 Stony Tribe Indian Stampede 1938 Eld 8/93 . . . 143
W/Pa Var Five Sketches Eld 8/93 132

Mitchell, George Bertrand Am 1872-1966
* See 1993 Edition . . . .

Mitchell, Glen Am 1894-1972
* See 1990 Edition . . . .

Mitchell, James
O/M 14x18 Fishing Schooner in the Fog Eld 7/93 110

Mitchell, Joan Am 1926-1992
O/C 27x26 Untitled Sby 11/92 55,000
O/C 36x29 Untitled Sby 10/92 38,500
O/C 24x20 Untitled Sby 5/93 36,800
O/C 22x18 Untitled '84 Chr 11/92 26,400
K&W/Pa 13x9 Untitled Chr 2/93 14,300

Mitchell, John Campbell Am 1862-1922
* See 1991 Edition . . . .

Mitchell, Lloyd Am a 1930-1939
O/C 14x18 The Barnyard Mor 11/92 150

Mitchell, Philip Br 1814-1896
W/Pa 11x17 Devon Landscape with Steamboat But 11/92 . . . 990

Mitchell, Thomas John Am 1875-
O/B 18x22 Winter Stream '54 Wes 12/92 248

Mitchell, Thomas Wilberforce Can 1879-1958
O/B 12x14 Quebec Farmyard Sbt 5/93 1,056
O/B 12x14 In Rural Quebec Sbt 5/93 968

Mitchnick, Nancy
* See 1992 Edition . . . .

Mitchum, Howard
W/Pa 22x30 Along Commerical, Provincetown 1952 Eld 8/93 165

Mitrecey, Maurice Fr 1869-1894
O/C/M 31x17 Male Academy 1891 Sby 1/93 1,610

Mitsutani, Kunishiro
* See 1993 Edition . . . .

Mizen, Fredrick Kimball Am 1888-1964
O/C 32x25 Vision of Mount Rushmore Ih 11/92 2,500

Modersohn, Otto Ger 1865-1943
* See 1992 Edition . . . .

Modersohn-Becker, Paula 1876-1907
C/Pa/B 10x8 Madchenkopf Chr 11/92 7,700

Modigliani, Amedeo It 1884-1920
O/C 13x10 Tete de Jeune Fille 1916 Chr 11/92 308,000
Pe/Pa 17x10 Les Deux Orphelines Sby 5/93 41,400
Pe/Pa 11x15 Portrait de Paul Guillaume Sby 5/93 22,000
Pe/Pa/B 11x8 Portrait Leopold Zborowski Sby 11/92 18,700

Modra, Theodore B. Am 1873-1930
* See 1991 Edition . . . .

Moeller, Louis Charles   Am 1855-1930
O/C 18x24 Cronies Chr 5/93   29,900
O/C 12x10 The Art Critics Sby 12/92   22,000
O/C 25x32 Discussion in the Library Sby 9/92   8,800
O/C 18x24 The Discussion Sby 9/92   7,700
O/C 16x12 The Violinist Chr 3/93   6,900
Moffett, Ross   Am 1888-1971
O/C 36x30 Portrait of Artist's Wife Mys 12/92   660
Mogan, John William   Am 20C
* See 1993 Edition . . . .
Mogford, John   Br 1821-1885
* See 1993 Edition . . . .
Mogniat-Duclos, B.   Fr 20C
O/C 18x22 River Landscape Lou 3/93   350
Moholy-Nagy, Laszlo   Am 1895-1946
* See 1993 Edition . . . .
Mohr, Albert   Ger 20C
O/C 16x12 Artist at Her Easel Lou 6/93   300
Mohr, Karl   Ger 1922-
* See 1993 Edition . . . .
Mohrmann, John Henry   Am 1857-1916
O/C 23x39 3 Masted Barque "Highland Glen" 1893 Sby 6/93   7,475
Moisand, Marcel Emmanuel   Fr 1874-1903
* See 1992 Edition . . . .
Moitte, Jean Guillaume   Fr 1746-1810
* See 1992 Edition . . . .
Mola, Pier Francesco   It 1612-1666
* See 1993 Edition . . . .
Molarsky, Abram   Am 1883-1951
* See 1993 Edition . . . .
Mole, John Henry   Br 1814-1886
* See 1993 Edition . . . .
Molenaer, Claes   Dut 1630-1676
O/Pn 13x10 House by the River with Fishermen Sby 5/93 . 20,700
O/C 28x25 An Elegant Couple and other Figures Chr 10/92   12,650
O/Pn 10x14 Fisherfolk in Boat Chr 5/93   5,175
Molenaer, Jan Miense   Dut 1610-1668
* See 1993 Edition . . . .
Molet, Salvador   Spa 1773-1836
* See 1990 Edition . . . .
Molin, Pelle   Swd 1864-1896
O/C 12x18 Country Scene with Sheep Herd Hnd 5/93   400
Molinari, Antonio   It -1648
* See 1991 Edition . . . .
Molinari, Antonio   It 1655-1734
* See 1993 Edition . . . .
Molinari, Guido   Can 1933-
* See 1991 Edition . . . .
Moll, Evert   Dut 1878-1955
O/C 24x40 White Three Master in Busy Harbor But 5/93 . . .   4,600
Mollica, Achille   It a 1870-1887
* See 1992 Edition . . . .
Molnar, Fusti
O/C 30x24 Young Girl Sewing Dum 6/93   200
Molnar, Reizes
O/Ab 30x24 Young Girl Dum 6/93   200
Molnar, Y.   Hun 20C
O/C 30x40 Central Park Scene, Budapest Dum 6/93   300
Molsted, Christian   Dan 1862-1930
* See 1992 Edition . . . .
Moltino, Francis   Br 1818-1872
O/C 24x42 Westminster Abbey Houses Parliament Chr 10/92   2,750
Molyn, Pieter   Dut 1595-1661
* See 1990 Edition . . . .
Molyneux, Edward   Am 1896-
G/Pa 12x8 Back of Black Car Ih 5/93   350
Mommers, Hendrick   Dut 1623-1693
* See 1993 Edition . . . .
Mompo, Manuel Hernandez   1927-
O/C 28x35 Dos Musicos 1957 Chr 11/92   8,800
Monaldi, Paolo   It a 1760-
* See 1991 Edition . . . .
Monamy, Peter   Br 1670-1749
O/C 18x26 Warship Battle Scene Ald 5/93   675

Monasterio, Luis Ortiz   Mex 1906-
* See 1993 Edition . . . .
Monchablon, Jean Ferdinand   Fr 1855-1904
O/C 25x20 La Saone au Bas de Lironcourt FHB 6/93   21,000
O/C 15x22 Shepherdess in Pasture 93 But 5/93   16,100
O/C 10x14 Bords de l'Apance Chr 5/93   12,075
Mondrian, Piet   Dut 1872-1944
* See 1993 Edition . . . .
Mondrus, Martin   Am 1927-
* See 1993 Edition . . . .
Monet, Claude   Fr 1840-1926
O/C 40x80 Le Bassin Aux Nympheas 1919 Chr 11/92 . . . .   12.1M
O/C 26x36 Le Palais Decal 1908 Chr 11/92 . . . .   3.08M
O/C 36x36 Printemps a Giverny 1900 Chr 11/92 . . . .   1.76M
O/C 26x36 Paysage a Giverny 1887 Chr 11/92 . . .   330,000
Money, Fred   Fr 1882-1956
* See 1993 Edition . . . .
Monfallet, Adolphe Francois   Fr 1816-1900
* See 1992 Edition . . . .
Monge, Jules   Fr 1855-
* See 1993 Edition . . . .
Monge, Luis   Ecu 1920-
O/C 53x48 Garza/Triangulo Amazonico 1976 Chr 11/92 . .   14,300
Monginot, Charles   Fr 1825-1900
O/C 13x10 Curiousity Leads to Chaos Doy 11/92   1,100
Monje, Luis   Ecu 1925-
* See 1993 Edition . . . .
Monks, John Austin Sands   Am 1850-1917
O/C 18x28 Sheep in a Pasture Dum 6/93   1,300
Monnoyer, Antoine   Fr 1677-1735
O/C 53x38 Flowers in a Sculpted Urn Sby 10/92   19,800
Monnoyer, Jean Baptiste   Fr 1636-1699
* See 1992 Edition . . . .
Monogrammist I.K.   a 16C
* See 1993 Edition . . . .
Monreal, Andres   Chl 20C
O/C 20x16 Still Life with Pitchers and Fruit But 4/93   575
Monsted, Peder Mork   Dan 1859-1941
O/C 16x22 Snowy River Banks 1915 Sby 2/93   10,350
O/C/B 28x46 A Pond in the Forest 1893 But 11/92   7,150
O/C 12x18 Deer by the Forest Brook 1900 Sby 10/92   2,200
Monsu Bernardo   Dan 1624-1687
O/C 35x27 Two Women Making Lace Sby 10/92   14,300
Monsu Desiderio   It 1593-1640
O/C 36x34 Stoning of Saint Stephen Sby 10/92   5,500
Montagny, Elie Honore   Fr -1864
* See 1992 Edition . . . .
Montague, Alfred   Br a 1832-1883
* See 1993 Edition . . . .
Montague, Clifford   Br 19C
* See 1992 Edition . . . .
Montague, F. L.   Am 19C
O&R/C 22x18 Truckee River, Sierra Nevada 1884 Slo 4/93 . .   375
Montani, Carlo   It 1868-1936
O/B 12x19 Washing Clothes 1926 Mys 12/92   330
Monte, Ira   Spa 1918-
O/C 30x40 Tropical Birds with Music Book Hnd 3/93   900
O/C 55x39 Tropical Birds Hnd 3/93   850
O/C 41x30 Birds Perched in Tree Hnd 3/93   600
O/C 36x48 Water Fowl Hnd 12/92   400
Monteagudo
O/C 32x39 Strikers 61 Dum 8/93   900
Montelatici, Francesco   It 1601-1661
* See 1993 Edition . . . .
Montemezzo, Antonio   Ger 1841-1898
* See 1991 Edition . . . .
Montenegro, Roberto   Mex 1885-1968
O/C 28x28 Autorretrato 1961 Sby 5/93   46,000
O/C 24x28 Dos Mujeres Sby 5/93   16,100
O/C 20x20 Pantera Negra 64 Chr 11/92   11,000
O/M 24x28 Two Figurines 1947 But 10/92   9,900
O/C 28x28 Inditas Cantadoras Chr 11/92   8,800
H&W/Pa 12x10 El Deseo De Volar Sby 5/93   3,450

Montezin, Pierre Eugene   Fr 1874-1946
O/C 26x32 Le pont de Saint-Mammes au soleil Chr 11/92 . 24,200
O/Pn 11x16 Roses et Coupe Bleue Sby 2/93 16,100
O/C 23x28 Maisons au Bord D'Une Riviere Sby 10/92 . . . 13,200
O/Pn 11x15 Nature Morte Roses et au Livre Sby 2/93 8,050
Montfort, Antoine Alphonse   Fr 1802-1884
* See 1991 Edition . . . .
Montgomery, Alfred   Am 1857-1922
O/B 12x16 Sheep in Pasture 1910 Sel 12/92 300
Montgomery, Claude   Am 20C
W/Pa 20x28 Seguin Light Brd 8/93 1,870
Monti, Francesco   It 1646-1712
* See 1993 Edition . . . .
Monti, Francesco   It 1685-1768
* See 1992 Edition . . . .
Monti, R.   Am 19C
O/C 21x32 River Landscape Hnd 5/93 450
O/C 21x32 Mountain Stream Hnd 4/92 400
Monticelli, Adolphe Joseph T.   Fr 1824-1886
O/C 21x40 La Fete Florale Sby 10/92 29,700
O/Pn 15x21 La Rencontre Musicale Renaissance Sby 10/92 11,000
Montigny, Jenny   Bel 1875-1937
O/C 19x23 Spring Landscape Dum 5/93 8,000
Montoya, Gustavo   Mex 1905-
O/C 22x18 Young Girl in a Blue Dress But 10/92 4,950
O/C 22x18 Nino Con Sandia Sby 6/93 4,600
O/C 22x18 La Muchacha con Vestido de Amarillo But 4/93 . 4,025
O/C 34x28 Girls on Bicycles 1965 But 10/92 3,575
O/C 22x18 Nina Con Dulce Sby 2/93 2,588
O/C 22x18 Boy and His Toy Sby 2/93 2,185
O/C 22x18 Girl and Her Ukulele Sby 2/93 2,185
Montrichard, Raymond   Am 1887-1937
* See 1992 Edition . . . .
Monvoisin, Raymond Auguste Q.   Fr 1794-1870
* See 1991 Edition . . . .
Moon, Carl   Am 1879-1948
* See 1990 Edition . . . .
Moore, Albert Joseph   Br 1841-1892
O/Pa/C 30x14 Sea Shells 75 Chr 2/93 220,000
P/Pa 15x6 A Bathing Place Sby 10/92 25,300
Moore, Arthur W.   Eng 1840-1913
O/C 38x71 Sheep and Horseless Carriage Lou 6/93 1,100
Moore, B. Charles   Eng 20C
O/B 9x13 Beach Scene Mys 12/92 358
Moore, Barlow   Br 1834-1897
O/C 24x36 Yawl Rigged Yacht Racing Sby 6/93 6,900
Moore, Benson Bond   Am 1882-1974
O/C 22x24 Early Spring on the Anacostia Wes 12/92 1,430
W/Pa 12x15 Canvas Backs Landing on Water Wes 10/92 . . . 550
W/Pa 6x7 Four Landscapes Wes 10/92 248
O/C 18x24 Mallards Over Water Sel 9/92 100
Moore, Edwin Augustus   Am 1858-1925
O/C 12x18 Still Life Fruit Vase of Flowers Sby 9/92 4,400
Moore, Frank Montague   Am 1877-1967
O/B 20x24 Hawaiian Coast 1924 But 6/93 2,585
O/B 12x15 Monterey Coastal Mor 6/93 2,475
Moore, Harry Humphrey   Am 1844-1926
O/Pn 9x6 New Orleans Street Scene Chr 5/93 1,380
Moore, Henry   Br 1831-1895
O/C 54x36 Summer Moonlight 1876 Sby 10/92 3,025
Moore, Henry   Br 1898-1986
WYC&PI/Pa 11x7 Studies for Seated Woman Chr 11/92 . . 24,200
W,C&Y/Pa 11x9 Family Group Sby 5/93 17,250
W,Y&I/Pa 9x7 The Lyre Bird 42 Sby 2/93 4,600
Moore, John   Am 20C
* See 1992 Edition . . . .
Moore, Nelson Augustus   Am 1824-1902
O/C 13x14 Lake George Wes 5/93 1,430
O/C 12x19 Windy Bay/Figure on a Beach Skn 9/92 770
Moore, Robert Eric   Am 1927-
W/Pa 7x10 Maine Otter Trail Yng 5/93 275
Moore, William C.   Br 19C
O/C 25x31 Wonder Hnd 12/92 850

Moormans, Franciscus   Dut 1832-1884
* See 1993 Edition . . . .
Mora, Francis Luis   Am 1874-1940
O/C 30x25 Mercedes 1909 Chr 12/92 16,500
O/Pn 12x16 At the Shore 1912 Chr 3/93 10,925
O/C 25x30 A Family Party, Triana, Sevilla 1908 Sby 12/92 . 9,900
O/C 30x25 Juan and Juanita Chr 9/92 6,600
O/C 18x22 Children on the Beach 1909 Chr 9/92 4,400
O/C 22x32 Roses of Spain Mor 6/93 3,575
W&Pe/Pa/C 14x10 View of the Courtyard Chr 9/92 3,300
O/C 20x14 The Rally on the Hill 1908 Skn 5/93 412
Morado, Jose Chavez   Mex 1909-
* See 1993 Edition . . . .
Moragas Y Torres, Tomas   Spa 1837-1906
* See 1990 Edition . . . .
Morales, Armando   Nic 1927-
O/C 65x51 Trois Nus et Voiture a Cheval 85 Sby 5/93 . . 376,500
O/C 64x51 Foret Tropicale 86 Sby 11/92 231,000
O&Wx/C 58x72 Circo 81 Chr 11/92 220,000
O&Wx/C 49x39 Mujer entrando/Espejo II 82 Chr 11/92 . . . 99,000
O&Wx/C 26x32 Naturaleza Muerta con Queso 76 Chr 11/92 66,000
O/C 24x20 Naturaleza Muerta Con Mangos '80 Sby 5/93 . 49,450
O&Wx/C 22x18 Mujer Desvistiendose 78 Sby 11/92 45,100
O&Wx/Pa 23x30 Banistas 81 Chr 11/92 30,800
G/Pa 21x34 Mujer Dormida 79 Sby 11/92 27,500
C&Pe/Pa/Pa 21x27 En el Circo 80 Chr 11/92 24,200
P/Pa 19x23 Still Life Humero Guanabana '83 Sby 5/93 . . . 20,700
MM&L/C 80x58 Composicion Abstracta Sby 5/93 16,100
P/Pa 17x24 Dos Figuras 81 Sby 11/92 10,450
O/Pa 6x9 Naturaleza Muerta 85 Sby 5/93 6,325
O/C 15x24 Paisaje Maritimo Con Barco '63 Sby 5/93 4,025
Morales, Dario   Col 1944-1988
H/Pa 12x15 Torso 78 Sby 5/93 5,463
H/Pa 12x15 Torso 78 Sby 5/93 5,175
Morales, Eduardo   Cub 1868-1938
O/C 23x31 La Volanta 1912 Chr 11/92 6,600
Morales, Rodolfo   Mex 1881-1968
O/C 48x59 Untitled Chr 11/92 30,800
O/C 24x28 Untitled Sby 11/92 12,100
O/M 17x32 Paisaje y Figuras 1966 Sby 11/92 7,700
Moralt, A.   Ger 19C
O/C 11x20 Lake Scene with Boatman Hnd 3/93 850
Moran, Edward   Am 1829-1901
O/C 41x64 The Shipwreck 1866 Sby 5/93 63,000
O/C 28x41 Little Sailors, Rockaway Beach Chr 12/92 26,400
O/C 14x22 Early Dawn, New York Harbor Sby 5/93 21,850
O/C 37x28 Moonlight on the Thames But 6/93 18,400
O/C 17x24 The Harbor at Sunset Sby 5/93 16,500
O/C 62x45 Cliffs in a Storm Sby 9/92 14,300
O/C 30x48 Off Atlantic Highlands Chr 12/92 12,100
O/C 30x50 Children Crabbing 1890 Sby 3/93 11,500
O/C 12x20 Ships in Harbor Sby 9/92 7,150
O/C 23x42 Mid-Ocean Fre 10/92 5,750
W/B 18x24 New York From the Channel Sby 9/92 3,850
O/C 16x24 Resting in the Field Sby 3/93 3,738
O/C 12x18 Sailing Vessels Before a Storm Skn 9/92 2,640
O/C 25x22 Ships on High Seas Chr 5/93 2,300
P/Pa 8x10 Ships in Harbor Lou 12/92 1,500
H&K/Pa 13x15 Village Church, Florida Skn 5/93 110
Moran, Edward Percy   Am 1862-1935
O/C/B 22x35 The Minuet Slo 5/93 4,450
O/C/M 22x35 The Minuet Sby 3/93 3,220
O/C 30x20 Waiting in the Garden Chr 5/93 2,530
Moran, Leon   Am 1864-1941
O/C 9x15 Pair of Landscapes 87 Sby 3/93 1,840
O/C 14x18 Anticipation and Bean Night: Two Hnd 6/93 . . . 850
O/C 19x34 Garden with Red Flowers Sby 9/92 605
Moran, Peter   Am 1841-1914
O/C 18x14 Luminous Forest Interior Slo 5/93 1,900
O&R/B 12x27 Cows by the Shore Sby 9/92 1,650
Moran, Thomas   Am 1837-1926
W/Pa 20x16 Castle Butte, Green River 1900 Sby 12/92 . 264,000
O/C 30x45 Icebergs in Mid-Atlantic 1909 Sby 5/93 222,500
O/C 31x46 Cloud/Sunshine on Montauk 1898 But 12/92 . . 88,000
O/C 10x12 Under Red Wall, Grand Canyon 1917 Chr 3/93 85,000

W&Pe/Pa 15x22 Castle Butte, Green River 1894 Chr 5/93 . 79,500
O/C 18x28 Venice: Reminisce Vera Cruz 1886 Sby 12/92 . 55,000
O/C 20x25 The Bathing Hole 1913 Chr 12/92 52,800
O/Pn 8x13 Green River, Wyoming Sby 12/92 49,500
O/C 14x20 Entrance Grand Canal, Venice 1906 Chr 12/92 . 44,000
O/C 10x14 A Rustic Bridge--Easthampton 1905 Chr 5/93 . 36,800
O/Pn 14x20 A Summer Shower 1878 Chr 5/93 25,300
O/C 21x17 The Bathers Sby 5/93 25,300
W/Pa 9x14 Green River '79 Sby 9/92 22,000

Morandi, Giorgio   It 1890-1964
O/C 11x16 Natura Morta 1946 Chr 11/92 297,000
O/C 8x14 Nature Morta But 4/93 244,500
O/C 8x10 Natura Morta, 1957 But 4/93 140,000
W/Pa 7x11 Natura Morta Chr 11/92 38,500
W/Pa 6x8 Natura Morta Chr 11/92 35,200
Pe/Pa 11x8 Natura Morta 1932 Chr 11/92 17,600
Pe/Pa 7x10 Nature Morta, 1959 But 4/93 13,800

Morandini, Francesco   It 1544-1597
* See 1992 Edition

Morang   Ger 20C
O/B 24x30 Sailboats at Sea Hnd 6/93 300

Morang, Alfred   Am 1901-1958
W&Pl/Pa 11x9 Ginger 54 But 6/93 1,380

Morang, Dorothy   Am 1906-
* See 1993 Edition

Moras, Walter   Ger 1856-1925
* See 1993 Edition

Morcillo, Gabriel   Spa 20C
* See 1993 Edition

Mordey, J.   Eng 20C
O/Pa/B 13x9 The Old Mill Grancetown 1806 Slo 4/93 1,100

Moreau, Adrien   Fr 1843-1906
O/C 51x79 Le Bac 1884 Sby 2/93 48,875

Moreau, Charles   Fr 1830-
O/B 21x18 A Glass of Wine Wlf 12/92 2,500

Moreau, Chocarne   Fr 19C
* See 1990 Edition

Moreau, Gustave   Fr 1826-1898
* See 1993 Edition

Moreau, Louis-Gabriel   Fr 1740-1806
I,S&W/Pa 9x14 Classical Garden at Versailles Slo 7/93 750

Moreau, Max   Fr 20C
O/C 39x32 Woodcutter Wlf 5/93 600

Moreelse, Paulus   Dut 1571-1638
* See 1993 Edition

Morel, Jan E. & Van Severdonck   Dut 1835-1905
O/C 24x34 Shepherd with Family and Flock 1872 Sby 5/93 . 8,050

Morel, Jan Evert   Dut 1777-1808
* See 1992 Edition

Morel, Jan Evert (II)   Dut 1835-1905
O/C 26x36 Along the Country Lane Sby 10/92 8,800

Morel, Jean Baptiste   1662-1732
O/C 22x16 Still Lifes Tulips, Roses, Poppies Sby 5/93 . . 28,750

Morelli, Domenico   It 1826-1901
* See 1993 Edition

Moret, Henry   Fr 1856-1913
O/C 21x29 Bord de Mer Sby 5/93 23,000

Moretti, R.   It 17C
* See 1993 Edition

Moretto, Alesandro Bonvicino   It 1498-1554
* See 1992 Edition

Morgan, Frederick   Br 1856-1927
O/C 51x38 Steady Sby 10/92 71,500
O/C 26x19 Grandfather's Birthday Sby 5/93 26,450

Morgan, Mary DeNeal   Am 1868-1948
O/B 22x18 Cypress Trees Monterey Coast But 3/93 3,850
G/Pb 14x18 Sand Dunes near Carmel But 3/93 3,025
O/B 24x24 Spring Rain But 10/92 2,475
G/Pa 11x10 Cypress Trees on the Coast But 6/93 2,070
O/Pa/B 8x8 Carmel Garden But 3/93 1,430
O/B 8x10 Atmospheric Landscape Mor 6/93 1,320
G/B 11x15 Monterey Coastal Mor 6/93 825
P/Pa 11x14 Monterey Coastal Mor 6/93 770

G/B 16x20 Near Palm Springs, CA Mor 6/93 770
G/Pa 5x6 Garden Cottage Mor 11/92 700
O/Ab 5x7 Monterey Coastal Mor 2/93 425

Morgan, Tom   Am 20C
O/B 8x9 Shepherdess and Her Flock '92 Slo 4/93 110

Morgan, William   Am 1826-1900
* See 1993 Edition

Morgenstern, Frederick Ernst   Ger 1853-1919
* See 1993 Edition

Morgenstern, Karl Ernst   Ger 1847-1928
O/C 15x20 Shipping in a Calm Chr 2/93 1,650

Morimura, Yasumasa   1951-
Ph/Pn 94x47 Dublonnage: Dancer II Chr 2/93 6,050

Morisot, Berthe   Fr 1841-1895
W&Pe/Pa 7x9 Le Bois de Boulogne Sby 2/93 10,350
Pe/Pa 11x8 Jeune Fille Assise Sur Une Echelle Sby 10/92 . 6,600
Pe/Pa/B 8x10 Jeune Fille Assise Sby 6/93 2,415

Morisset, Francois Henri   Fr 1870-
* See 1993 Edition

Morland, George   Br 1763-1804
O/C 20x26 Winter Landscape w/Figures Skating Chr 5/93 . 23,000
O/C 28x35 The Wreck, Isle of Wight Sby 10/92 9,900
O/C 29x37 'The Smugglers'or'Jack at Capstan' Chr 10/92 . 5,500
O/C 26x31 The Shipwreck Chr 10/92 3,520
O/C 18x22 Sailors Carousing But 5/93 2,300
O/Pn 12x14 Stable Interior But 11/92 880

Morley, Malcolm   Am 1931-
A/C 64x84 SS Amsterdam in Rotterdam 1966 Sby 11/92 440,000
O/C 20x27 Onsettant Moie 74 Sby 5/93 57,500
O/C 30x21 San Miguel of Allende Postcard Sby 11/92 . . . 27,500
A&Ss/C 9x12 HMS Hood 1964 Chr 11/92 7,700
W/Pa 15x23 Untitled Chr 11/92 6,600
W/Pa 21x25 Untitled Chr 5/93 3,450
W/Pa 12x16 Untitled 76 Sby 10/92 3,300
W/Pa 12x16 Untitled 73 Sby 5/93 1,955

Morley, Robert   Br 1857-1941
O/C 25x31 By the Fireside Sby 6/93 17,250

Morlon, Paul Emile Antony   Fr 19C
O/C 53x76 Scandalous Behavior Chr 10/92 11,000

Mormile, Gaetano   It 1839-1890
* See 1993 Edition

Morot, Aime Nicolas   Fr 1850-1913
* See 1993 Edition

Morphesis, Jim
* See 1992 Edition

Morren, Georges   Bel 1868-
* See 1992 Edition

Morrice, James Wilson   Can 1865-1924
* See 1993 Edition

Morris, Fred   Eng 20C
P/Pa 10x13 Two Horse Portraits Chr 6/93 460

Morris, George   Am
* See 1992 Edition

Morris, George Ford   Am 1873-1960
O/Pa 10x14 Horses and Collies: Two Works '57 Wes 5/93 . 248
O/B 10x12 A Bay in Spring Hnz 5/93 220

Morris, George L. K.   Am 1905-1975
* See 1993 Edition

Morris, J.   Br 19C
O/C 36x27 The Day's Bag Chr 2/93 1,320

Morris, John   Am 20C
O/B 16x20 The Devil or the Deep Blue Sea 1907 But 10/92 . 1,540

Morris, John Floyd   Am 20C
* See 1993 Edition

Morris, Kathleen Moir   Can 1893-1986
O/Pn 12x14 House by the River Sbt 5/93 4,180

Morris, Kyle   Am 1918-1979
* See 1990 Edition

Morris, Philip Richard   Eng 1833-1902
* See 1991 Edition

Morris, Robert   Am 1931-
Pe/Pa 9x36 Untitled 63 Sby 10/92 4,950
I/Pa 21x28 Untitled 1966 Sby 2/93 1,840

Morrison, Kenneth M. Br 20C
  * See 1992 Edition . . . .
Morrisroe, Mark   1959-
  Ph 20x16 Three Photographs 1986 Chr 11/92 . . .   1,100
  Ph 20x15 Two Photographs 83 Chr 11/92   880
Morrow, Raymond   Am 19C
  O/C 26x40 Winter Skating Scene Slo 7/93   1,000
Morse, George F.   Am 19C
  O/B Size? Landscape Mys 3/93   165
Morse, J. B.   Am a 1875-1890
  O/C 17x28 Landscape, Morris County, NJ Wes 3/93   2,860
  O/C 18x30 Coast of Maine Eld 4/93   440
  O/C 16x20 Landscape with Pond Eld 4/93   330
Morse, Samuel F. B.   Am 1791-1872
  O/C 24x20 Junius Brutus Booth as Brutus Wes 5/93   4,950
  O/Pn 5x4 Portrait of a Man in a Top Hat 1840 Sby 9/92 . . .   1,980
Mortelmans, Frans   Bel 1865-1936
  * See 1992 Edition . . . .
Mortlock   Br 20C
  O/B 76x40 Portrait of Duke of Windsor Hnd 10/92   2,800
Morton, Andrew   Br 1802-1845
  K&W/Pa 15x11 Three Female Portraits 1831 Hnd 3/93   700
Morviller, Joseph   Am a 1855-1870
  O/C 14x20 Skating on the Pond 66 Chr 5/93   8,050
  O/C 14x22 Winter Landscape 1864 Sby 3/93   2,760
Mosca, August   Am 20C
  O/C 48x34 Boy on Bicycle 1957 Fre 4/93   5,500
Moseley, R S**   Eng 20C**
  O/Pn 9x11 Three Dogs Wes 3/93   990
Moser, Richard   Aus 1874-
  * See 1993 Edition . . . .
Moser, Wilfrid
  * See 1993 Edition . . . .
Moses, Anna Mary R. (Grandma)   Am 1860-1961
  O/M 24x30 In the Springtime 1944 Chr 5/93   79,500
  O/M 18x24 Canada 1958 Sby 3/93   29,900
  O/M 16x20 Home of John Brown 1943 Chr 3/93   23,000
  T/M 18x24 The Thrashers 1954 Chr 5/93   21,850
  O&MM/B 12x16 Sleet Storm 1957 Skn 11/92   14,300
  O/M 9x10 Through the Bridge 1944 Chr 9/92   9,900
Moses, Ed   Am 1926-
  * See 1993 Edition . . . .
Moses, Forrest   Am 1893-1974
  * See 1993 Edition . . . .
Moses, Mary Wade   Am 19C
  O/C 20x16 The Lovers Fre 4/93   475
Moses, Thomas G.   Am 1856-1934
  * See 1993 Edition . . . .
Moses, Walter Farrington   Am 1874-1947
  O/C 25x30 Sycamores and Live Oak Lou 3/93   800
  O/C 25x30 Landscape Mor 6/93   770
  O/C 25x30 Mojave Desert in Bloom Mor 4/93   600
Moskowitz, Robert   Am 1935-
  L&P/t/C 54x40 Untitled 1962 Sby 11/92   22,000
  O&L/C 51x40 Untitled 1962 Sby 2/93   8,625
  MM&L/C 25x25 Untitled 1961 Sby 5/93   8,050
Mosler, Henry   Am 1841-1920
  O/C 63x93 Requiem Slo 4/93   2,500
Mossa, Gustave Adolf   Fr 1883-1971
  * See 1993 Edition . . . .
Mosset, Olivier   1944-
  A/C 24x25 Untitled Chr 11/92   1,760
Mostaert, Gillis (the Elder)   1534-1598
  O/Pn 54x81 David Freeing Ahinoam/Abigail 1625 Chr 10/92   22,000
Mostyn, Tom   Br 1864-1930
  O/C 18x29 Mediterranean Seaside Arbor But 11/92   1,100
Mote, George William   Br 1832-1909
  * See 1991 Edition . . . .
Motherwell, Robert   Am 1915-1991
  A/C 78x30 Splurge #2 1974 Chr 11/92   77,000
  O/C 78x30 Full Tide 1976 Chr 11/92   71,500
  O/Pa 12x15 A Spanish Elegy 1960 Chr 11/92   66,000
  A,Pa&L/B 40x27 Die Spinnerin 76 Chr 11/92   63,800
  I/Pa 12x15 Splatter Sby 11/92   35,750

O&L/B 20x16 Gauloises with Red and Green 71 Sby 5/93   34,500
  A/Pa 27x21 Untitled 75 Chr 11/92   24,200
  A&I/Pa 22x17 Untitled Sby 10/92   23,100
  A&L/Cb 20x16 Scarlet and Gauloises #15 1972 Chr 11/92   22,000
  I&Pe/Pa 12x14 Untitled Sby 10/92   6,050
Mottet, Jeanie Gallup   Am 1884-1934
  O/C 27x23 Woman Sewing in the Veranda Mys 3/93   1,320
Mottez, Victor Louis   Fr 1809-1897
  * See 1991 Edition . . . .
Mouchot, Ludovic   Fr 1846-1893
  * See 1993 Edition . . . .
Mouillot, Marcel   Fr 1889-
  O/C 22x26 Port Du Havre Dum 12/92   1,700
Moulin, Charles Lucien   Fr 19C
  * See 1993 Edition . . . .
Mount, Shepard Alonzo   Am 1804-1868
  * See 1993 Edition . . . .
Mount, William Sidney   Am 1807-1868
  O/B 9x14 Cracking Nuts 1856 Chr 3/93   33,350
  Pl&S/Pa 11x16 Chopping Down the Tree 1844 Chr 3/93 . .   14,150
Mowbray, Henry Siddons   Am 1858-1928
  O&Gd/C 24x48 Myth of Proserpine: Study Sby 3/93   11,500
Mower, Martin   Am 1870-1960
  W/Pa 26x19 Meeting of the Waters 1903 Fre 4/93   825
Moyaert, Nicolas   Dut 1592-1655
  * See 1990 Edition . . . .
Mucha, Alphonse Maria   Czk 1860-1939
  C/Pa 16x26 Stained Glass: Joan of Arc 1898 Hnd 9/92   900
Muchen, William Henry   Am 1832-1911
  * See 1992 Edition . . . .
Mucke, Carl Emil   Ger 1847-1923
  O/M 6x5 The First Born But 5/93   2,588
Muckley, William Jabez   Br 1837-1905
  O/C 24x16 The Orange Tree 1880 Sby 10/92   3,025
Mueller, Carl   Am 20C
  W/Pa 19x14 Midday Rendez-vous Fre 10/92   110
Mueller, Otto   Ger 1874-1930
  Y,Br&I/Pa 14x20 Liegende frau Chr 11/92   88,000
Mueller, Stephen   Am 20C
  * See 1992 Edition . . . .
Mueller, W.   Ger 19C
  O/C 29x23 Praying Before a Grotto 1842 Fre 4/93   1,300
Muendel, George   Am 1871-
  * See 1993 Edition . . . .
Muenier, Jules Alexis   Fr 1863-1942
  * See 1991 Edition . . . .
Muhl, Roger   Fr 1929-
  O/C 32x26 Fruits Sby 10/92   4,675
  O/C 39x32 Fleurs Chr 5/93   4,025
  O/C 24x29 Nature Morte au Pot Gris 1961 Chr 5/93   2,300
  O/C 11x9 Hiver Sby 2/93   460
Muhlenfeld, Otto   Am 1871-1907
  * See 1991 Edition . . . .
Muhlig, Bernhard   Ger 1829-1910
  * See 1992 Edition . . . .
Muhlig, Hugo   Ger 1854-1929
  O/Pn 9x14 Guarding the Herd Chr 5/93   32,200
  O/Pn 11x8 The Farmyard Sby 10/92   11,000
Muhlstock, Louis   Can 1904-
  O/C 30x26 Autumn, Mount Royal Sbt 5/93   748
Mulard, Francois Henri   Fr 1769-1850
  * See 1993 Edition . . . .
Mulhaupt, Frederick John   Am 1871-1938
  O/B 8x10 Evening, Wheeler's Wharf/Gloucester Skn 5/93 . .   2,090
  O/C 12x16 Sailing Ship '10 Sel 4/93   1,100
  O/Pn 8x9 Rural Landscape 1910 Sel 4/93   425
  O/B 9x11 Shore of Darkness, Dusk 09 Skn 5/93   385
Mulholland, Sydney A.   Br 19C
  W/Pa 13x24 Fishing Boats in the Harbor Wlf 9/92   325
  W/Pa 11x23 A Memory of Scotland Lou 9/92   275
Mulier, Pieter (II)   Dut 1637-1701
  * See 1992 Edition . . . .
Mulier, Pieter (the Elder)   Dut 1615-1670
  * See 1992 Edition . . . .

Muller, Carl   Ger 20C
  * See 1993 Edition . . . .
Muller, Charles   Br 19C
  O/C 22x36 Sheep in Extensive Landscape Sby 1/93   1,495
Muller, Charles Louis   Fr 1815-1892
  O/C 9x7 Interesting Reading Wlf 3/93   850
  O/C 32x26 Charlotte Corday Slo 4/93   575
Muller, Charles Louis   Fr 1902-
  * See 1993 Edition . . . .
Muller, Erich   Ger 1888-1972
  O/C 25x33 View of Old Berlin 1911 Wes 5/93   1,980
Muller, Franz   Ger 1843-1929
  * See 1992 Edition . . . .
Muller, Fritz   Ger 1897-
  O/M 10x7 Peasant Man Smoking; Man w/Pipe (2) Chr 2/93 .   770
  O/B 10x7 The Wine Drinker Dum 5/93   650
  O/M 10x7 Gentleman Holding Glass of Wine Sel 4/93   275
Muller, Jan   Am 1922-1958
  C&G/Pa/B 25x19 Untitled Chr 11/92   2,200
Muller, Leopold Carl   Ger 1834-1892
  O/C 28x47 The Blind Beggar 1879 Chr 5/93   51,750
Muller, Moritz   Ger 1841-1899
  * See 1992 Edition . . . .
Muller, William James   Br 1812-1845
  * See 1993 Edition . . . .
Muller-Kaemfh, E.   Ger 19C
  O/B 8x10 Interior Scene Lou 9/92   225
Muller-Stersuel   Ger 20C
  O/C 24x36 Beached Boats by a River Mys 12/92   385
Mulley, Oskar   Aus 1891-1949
  O/C 33x44 Small Village in the Alps 1943 Wlf 9/92   3,000
Mullholland, St. John   Br 19C
  * See 1992 Edition . . . .
Mullican, Matt   Am 1951-
  A&O/C 96x48 Untitled (green elements) Chr 10/92   11,550
  MM 102x34 Untitled '84 Sby 6/93   4,025
  O/Pa 14x24 Untitled Sby 6/93   2,300
Mullin, Willard   Am 1902-1978
  Pl&H/Pa 18x14 Giants' Third Base Position Ih 11/92   800
Mulvany, Thomas James   Irs 1779-1845
  * See 1993 Edition . . . .
Munakata, Shiko   20C
  * See 1990 Edition . . . .
Munari, Cristoforo   It 1667-1720
  * See 1991 Edition . . . .
Munch, Edvard   Nor 1863-1944
  O/C 20x18 Norskt Varlandskap Sby 11/92   55,000
Munger, Gilbert Davis   Am 1836-1903
  * See 1993 Edition . . . .
Munier, Emile   Fr 1810-1885
  O/C 32x39 The Favorite Pets 1885 Chr 5/93   96,000
  O/C 11x9 Deux Filles Avec Un Panier 1895 Sby 10/92 . . .   16,500
  O/C 27x22 La Lettre Sby 5/93   13,225
Munierdo, B.   20C
  O/C 29x16 Testing the Waters Slo 4/93   225
Munkacsy, Mikaly   Hun 1844-1900
  * See 1992 Edition . . . .
Munninger, Ludwig   Ger 20C
  O/C 30x40 Alpine Winter Landscape Dum 12/92   3,500
  O/C 40x30 Winter Mountain Landscape Dum 7/93   3,250
Munnings, Sir Alfred James   Br 1878-1959
  O/C 40x47 A Winner at Epsom Sby 6/93   354,500
  O/C 50x40 The Whip: Trevelloe Wood Sby 6/93   310,500
  O/C 32x28 Dragoon Guard: Pair Sby 6/93   288,500
  O/Pn 15x26 The Saddling Paddock, Cheltenham Sby 6/93   255,500
  O/Pn 17x24 'Black Speck' 'Knight's Ar' 1940 Doy 5/93 . .   33,000
  O/Pn 16x24 Black Speck & Southern Hero 1940 Doy 5/93 .   33,000
Munoz   Spa 19C
  O/Pn Size? Courtyard Scene Mys 12/92   358
Munoz Y Lucena, Tomas   Spa 1860-1942
  * See 1991 Edition . . . .
Munoz, Alberto   Spa 20C
  O/C 24x36 Pelea de Gallos But 4/93   546

Munoz, Godofredo Ortega
  * See 1993 Edition . . . .
Munoz-Vera, Guillermo   Chi 1949-
  * See 1990 Edition . . . .
Munro, Hugh
  * See 1993 Edition . . . .
Munter, Gabriele   Ger 1877-1963
  O/B 13x16 Am Stamberger See 08 Chr 11/92   236,500
  O/B 13x18 Staffelsee Chr 11/92   104,500
Munthe, Ludwig   Nor 1841-1896
  O/Pn 26x22 Winter Twilight 91 Chr 10/92   16,500
  O/B 6x8 An Evening Landscape 1871 Chr 2/93   550
Muntz, Johann Heinrich   1727-1798
  * See 1992 Edition . . . .
Muraton, Euphemie   Fr 1840-
  O/C 20x29 Nature Morte aux Fruits 1883 Sby 5/93   7,188
Muray, Nickolas   Am 1892-1965
  * See 1992 Edition . . . .
Murch, Walter Tandy   Am 1907-1967
  O/C 14x14 Still Life with Lemons and Potato Sby 5/93 . . .   23,000
  G/Pa 10x14 Girders and Factory Sby 9/92   1,210
  G/Pa 11x14 I-Beam & Tower Sby 9/92   1,100
Murillo, Bartolome Esteban   Spa 1618-1682
  * See 1993 Edition . . . .
Murphy, Catherine   Am 20C
  * See 1990 Edition . . . .
Murphy, Herman Dudley   Am 1867-1945
  O/C 30x25 White Roses Skn 3/93   8,800
  O/C 20x27 The Surf Chr 9/92   8,250
  O/C 36x48 Path Through Landscape But 12/92   3,300
  O/C 20x27 Winter Landscape Eld 11/92   2,860
  O/Cb 19x14 Seascape with Sun Behind Clouds Chr 12/92 .   2,640
  O/C/B 7x9 In Summer Sby 3/93   633
  O/B 12x16 Mango Trees Skn 3/93   522
  O/Pn 16x20 Mountain Lake Fre 4/93   500
  O/Pn 20x16 Moorish Arch Fre 4/93   450
  O/B 8x10 The Fire on the Beach Eld 11/92   330
  O/B 6x10 Evening Seascape Eld 11/92   220
  O/B 11x8 The Valley Eld 11/92   220
  W/Pa 20x14 Woman in Green Dress '90 Yng 5/93   200
  O/B 12x16 Swamp Scene Eld 11/92   138
  W/Pa 20x14 Portrait of a Woman Eld 11/92   88
Murphy, John Francis   Am 1853-1921
  O/C/B 16x22 Late Fall Landscape 1920 Lou 9/92   6,000
  O/C 8x12 Landscape with Sunset 1904 Chr 9/92   4,400
  W/B 7x14 Tonalist Landscape 1866 Sby 3/93   4,140
  O/C 16x22 Aback From the Highway 1891 Sby 3/93   4,025
  O/Pn 4x10 Woodland Interior Sby 9/92   3,520
  O/C 16x22 Day in October 1904 Chr 3/93   3,220
  O/C 19x26 Golden Hues of Autumn Chr 12/92   3,080
  O/C 10x14 Golden Landscape But 12/92   2,200
  O/C 8x10 Twilight But 12/92   1,870
Murray, Elizabeth   Am 1940-
  K/Pa 23x30 Walk 1981 Chr 11/92   20,900
  K/Pa 22x26 Star Cup '82 Chr 11/92   17,600
  P/Pa 29x48 Which Way Sby 5/93   13,800
  C/Pa 42x30 Big and Small 75 Sby 10/92   9,900
  P/Pa 14x24 Wave 1984 Sby 10/92   7,700
Murray, Elizabeth   Br 1815-1882
  W&G/Pa 30x24 Middle Eastern Genre Scene Skn 11/92   825
Murray, F. Richardson   Am 20C
  * See 1990 Edition . . . .
Murray, H.   Eng a 1850-1860
  W&Cw/Pa 13x18 Arrival of the Pact (3) Chr 5/93   4,600
  W&Pe/Pa 12x18 Tracking the Scent: Pair Sby 6/93   1,725
Murray, John   Am 20C
  * See 1991 Edition . . . .
Murry, Jerre   Am 1904-
  * See 1992 Edition . . . .
Muschamp, Francis Sydney   Br 1829-1929
  O/C 20x30 The Piano Lesson 1879 Sby 2/93   28,750
  O/C 20x30 Fortune Telling 1895 Chr 5/93   23,000
Music, Antonio   It 1909-
  O/C 13x16 Donne con Cavallini 1950 Chr 10/92   82,500

O/C/B 10x13 Cavallini Sby 10/92 63,250
W/Pa 13x19 Cavalli 1951 Doy 5/93 17,600
G/Pa 14x19 Tre Cavalli 1952 Hnd 3/93 10,500
W/Pa 14x19 Cavalli 1950 Hnd 3/93 9,000
Y/Pa 7x5 Horse and Rider Wes 10/92 578

Musin, Auguste   Bel 1852-1920
O/C 32x26 Ships on the Escaut River, Holland Chr 2/93 . . . 2,090

Musin, Francois Etienne   Bel 1820-1888
O/C 18x22 Beached Sailboat Sby 1/93 4,025

Musmeci, G.   It 20C
W/Pa 22x13 Neapolitan View Sel 12/92 120

Muss-Arnoldt, Gustav   Am 1858-1927
  * See 1991 Edition . . . .

Musselman, Darwin   Am 20C
O/C 20x24 Industrial Fresno '46 Sby 9/92 1,650

Mussini, Luigi   It 1813-1888
  * See 1993 Edition . . . .

Muter, Marie-Mela   Fr 1886-1967
  * See 1992 Edition . . . .

Muzzioli, Giovanni   It 1854-1894
  * See 1992 Edition . . . .

Myers, Bob   Am 20C
  * See 1990 Edition . . . .

Myers, Frank Harmon   Am 1899-1956
O/C 24x32 Coast Route But 10/92 2,750
O/C/B 6x8 Fishing Boats But 3/93 1,980
O/C 20x24 The Bullfight Sby 3/93 1,380
O/Cb 12x16 Dyeing Nets, Brittany But 6/93 862

Myers, Harry   20C
O/M 16x20 In the Park Doy 11/92 1,650

Myers, Jerome   Am 1867-1940
O/C 25x30 In the Old Quarter Chr 9/92 16,500
O/B 16x22 The Wooden Indian 1918 Sby 5/93 8,625
O/C 24x16 Around Street Shrine, Little Italy Sby 9/92 2,640
W,Pe&I/Pa 11x9 The Orange Box Sby 3/93 1,380
P&C/Pa 9x12 Two Drawings Sby 3/93 863

Mygatt, Robertson K.   Am 1861-1919
O/B 5x7 Ships Near a Headland '07 Yng 5/93 225

Mytens, Jan   Dut 1614-1670
  * See 1992 Edition . . . .

Naager, Franz   Ger 1870-
O/Cd 18x14 Artist's Studio 1922 Wlf 5/93 500
O/Cb 27x19 Scene from "Die Zauberflote" 22 Skn 9/92 495

Nabert, Wilhelm Julius August   Ger 1830-1904
  * See 1990 Edition . . . .

Nachtmann, Franz Xaver   Ger 1799-1846
  * See 1993 Edition . . . .

Nadejen, Theodore   Am 1889-1974
W/Pa 12x16 Fruit Sellers: Pair Lou 6/93 150

Nadelman, Elie   Am 1882-1946
PI/Pa 12x5 Standing Nude Sby 3/93 1,380

Nadin, Peter   1954-
  * See 1993 Edition . . . .

Naegele, Charles Frederick   Am 1857-1944
O/C 16x34 Prospect Pond, Brooklyn Chr 3/93 5,750

Nagel, Andres   20C
MM&O/Pls 75x52 Mercury Sby 5/93 12,650

Nagy, Peter   20C
O/C 36x36 End of the Whole Imaginary 86 Sby 6/93 920

Nahl, Charles Christian   Am 1818-1878
O/C 22x28 The Chase But 10/92 9,900
O/Pn 16x9 Flowers in Memorial 1862 Dum 7/93 750

Nahl, Perham Wilhelm   Am 1869-1935
  * See 1993 Edition . . . .

Naiveu, Matthys   1647-1721
O/Pn 17x13 Portrait of a Gentleman Sby 1/93 1,725

Nakagawa, Hachiro   Jap 1877-1922
  * See 1990 Edition . . . .

Nakamura, Kanzi   Jap 20C
  * See 1993 Edition . . . .

Nakamura, Kazuo   1926-
O/C 40x50 Blue Reflections 2, 1967 '67 Sbt 5/93 3,300

Nakamura, Naondo
T/Pa/M 21x15 Young Daughter and Cat 56 Sby 2/93 2,185
T/Pa/M 11x11 Crouching Female Nude Sby 2/93 1,380

Nakian, Reuben   Am 1897-1986
I/Pa 14x17 Europa and the Bull Wes 5/93 715
I/Pa 8x11 Abstraction 1954 Slo 7/93 400

Nallard, Louis Armand   1918-
G&Wx/Pa 19x23 Composition Abstraite Chr 11/92 418

Nalsh, John George   Br 1824-1905
  * See 1991 Edition . . . .

Nanteuil, Charles Gaugiran   Fr 1811-
  * See 1991 Edition . . . .

Napoletano, Filippo   It 18C
  * See 1991 Edition . . . .

Nardi, Enrico   It 1864-
  * See 1992 Edition . . . .

Nardone, Vincent Joseph   Am 1937-
  * See 1992 Edition . . . .

Narvaez, Francisco
  * See 1992 Edition . . . .

Nash, Joseph   Br 1808-1878
W&G/Pa 13x20 Drawing Room at Levens Hall Chr 2/93 . . . 1,760

Nash, Manley K.   Am 20C
O/C 60x84 The Founding of St. Louis '25 Sel 4/93 2,400

Nash, Willard Ayer   Am 1898-1943
  * See 1992 Edition . . . .

Nasmyth, Alexander   Eng 1758-1840
  * See 1993 Edition . . . .

Nasmyth, Patrick   Br 1787-1831
  * See 1992 Edition . . . .

Nason, Gertrude   Am 1890-1969
  * See 1992 Edition . . . .

Nason, Pieter   1612-1690
O/C 35x27 Portrait of a Gentleman half length Chr 10/92 . . 9,350

Nast, Thomas   Am 1840-1902
G,I&Pe/Pa 26x19 Robber and the Robbed Chr 12/92 1,430
PI/Pa 8x7 Four Animated Liquor Bottles Ih 11/92 1,300

Natkin, Robert   Am 1930-
A/C 59x108 Untitled 1980 Sby 10/92 9,900
A/C 89x79 Field Mouse Chr 11/92 8,800
A/C 78x71 Apollo 1968 Chr 2/93 7,700
A/C 50x64 Untitled Sby 10/92 5,500
A/C 50x49 Untitled FHB 3/93 5,500
O/C 48x72 Apollo Series 1964 Sel 12/92 3,750
A/B 30x26 Untitled 1969 Sby 10/92 2,090
A/C 49x54 Apollo with Red Stripe Hnd 6/93 1,300
A/C 8x27 Untitled 1976 Chr 11/92 880
A/Pa 22x26 Untitled 1969 Chr 11/92 880

Natoire, Charles-Joseph   Fr 1700-1777
K/Pa 8x7 Head of a Girl Chr 1/93 8,250
K/Pa 16x16 A Putto Chr 1/93 4,950

Nattier, Jean Marc   Fr 1685-1766
  * See 1993 Edition . . . .

Nauer, Ludwig   Ger 1888-
O/C 20x24 Gathering in a Tavern Chr 2/93 2,750

Nauman, Bruce   Am 1941-
A,Os&H/Pa 63x80 Study for Dream Passage 84 Chr 11/92 . . 99,000
C/Pa 24x35 Drawing for Malice 1980 Chr 2/93 28,600
I&Pe/Pa 30x40 Diamond Mind Circle 75 Sby 5/93 13,800
Pe&W/Pa 23x29 Chamber w/Video, Audio 72 Sby 10/92 . . . 8,800

Naumann, Carl Georg   Ger 1827-1902
  * See 1990 Edition . . . .

Navarra, Pietro   18C
O/C 24x18 Still Life Grapes, Melon, Figs Sby 1/93 17,250

Navarro Y Llorens, Jose   Spa 1867-1923
O/C/B 11x14 Ladies in Hats on the Beach Sby 2/93 17,250
O/C/Cd 11x14 Sailboats Near the Shore Sby 2/93 14,950

Navez, Francois Joseph Navez   Bel 1787-1869
  * See 1991 Edition . . . .

Naviet, Joseph   Fr 1821-1889
  * See 1991 Edition . . . .

Navone, Edoardo   It 19C
W/Pa 27x19 Travelling Minstrels, Rome Wlf 3/93 1,100

Neagle, John   Am 1796-1865
O/C 30x25 Portrait of Mrs. Dale 1844 Eld 8/93 1,100
Neagle, John   Br 20C
O/B 18x30 Oxford - 36. Shire Lou 3/93 300
Nebel, Otto   1892-1973
O/Pa 17x15 Ermutigend 1968 Sby 6/93 1,955
W,K&Pl/Pa 9x6 Abstract Composition 1965 Chr 2/93 1,760
O/Pa 13x9 Hohengrade 1968 Sby 6/93 1,610
O/Pn 8x16 Im Warmen Geborgen 1955 Sby 6/93 1,610
O/Pa 10x13 Reich in Sich 1968 Sby 6/93 1,495
O/Pa 7x14 Die Frue Singt 1968 Sby 6/93 1,150
Neder, Johann Michael   Aus 1807-1882
* See 1992 Edition . . . .
Neebe, Louis Alexander   Am 1873-
O/C 36x40 On the Beach Hnd 5/93 4,600
Neebe, Minnie Harms   Am 1873-
O/C 24x18 Anchored-Provincetown Hnd 3/93 500
Neefs, Pieter (the Elder)   Flm 1578-1656
O/Pn 18x27 Cathedral Interior with Figures Sby 1/93 60,250
**Neefs, Pieter (the Younger)   Flm
1620-1675**
O/Pn 21x26 Interior of a Gothic Cathedral Chr 10/92 33,000
Neel, Alice
O/C 40x40 Portrait of Bill White '71 Chr 5/93 17,250
**Neergaard, Hermania Sigvardine   Dan
1799-1874**
O/C 26x25 A Lily Pond 1855 Sby 10/92 55,000
Neff, Edith   Am 20C
* See 1992 Edition . . . .
Neggessi, Peter   Hun 20C
O/C 38x50 In the Library Hnd 9/92 275
Negretti, Jacopo   It 1544-1628
O/C 50x68 Venus and Cupid Slo 10/92 33,000
K,Pl&S/Pa 10x8 Studies of Six Bearded Heads Chr 1/93 . . 15,400
K,Pl&S/Pa 10x13 Venus and Adonis Chr 1/93 9,350
Nehlig, Victor   Fr 1830-1910
* See 1993 Edition . . . .
Neil, Thomas   Br 19C
O/C 22x16 Windsor Castle 1905 Fre 4/93 150
Neillot, Louis   Fr 1898-1973
C&W/Pa/B 13x19 French Landscapes (Three) But 4/93 575
Neilson, Charles Peter   Am a 1890-1910
* See 1993 Edition . . . .
**Neilson, Raymond Perry Rodgers   Am
1881-1964**
O/C 36x28 Girl Beside a Fence Hnz 5/93 500
Neiman, Leroy   Am 1927-
W/Pa 23x17 Sammy Davis, Jr. and Bill Cosby '83 Lou 6/93   5,000
Neimann, Edmund John   Br 1813-1876
* See 1993 Edition . . . .
Nel-Dumouchel, Jules   Fr 19C
* See 1991 Edition . . . .
Nelson, Ernest Bruce   Am 1888-1952
P/Pa 20x24 Rocky Coastal Scene Wtf 4/93 700
Nelson, Ernest O.   Am 19C
* See 1991 Edition . . . .
Nelson, George Laurence   Am 1887-1978
* See 1992 Edition . . . .
Nelson, Joan   Am 1958-
O/Wd 16x16 Untitled (#197) 1988 Sby 11/92 12,100
Et&MM/M 40x48 Untitled 1984 Sby 5/93 8,050
Et/M 24x26 Untitled 1984 Sby 11/92 4,400
Nelson, Roger Laux   Am 20C
* See 1991 Edition . . . .
Nelson, W.   Eng 20C
O/B 11x13 American Clipper Ship Off Coast Slo 4/93 225
Neme, Clarel   Uru 1926-
* See 1992 Edition . . . .
Nemethy, Albert   Am
O/C 40x30 A Victorian Winter Sby 9/92 2,970
Neogrady, Laszlo   Hun 1900-
O/C 24x30 Winter Forest with a Frozen Stream Chr 2/93 . . 3,300
O/C 31x37 Snowy Winter Stream Chr 10/92 1,870
O/C 24x30 Promenade by the River Sby 1/93 1,380
O/C 24x30 Feeding the Ducks Chr 2/93 1,320

O/C 23x31 Mountains in Snow Yng 5/93 750
W/Pa 16x24 Woman with Bouquet seated in Woods Wtf 12/92 650
O/C 24x36 Alpine Village in Moonlight Sel 9/92 500
Neogrady, Laszlo (Antal)   Hun 1861-1942
O/C 36x24 Winter Landscape Lou 12/92 2,000
G/B 18x27 After a Day of Skating Chr 5/93 1,725
O/C 24x30 Winter Mountain Landscape Slo 5/93 550
Nepote, Alexander   Am 1913-1986
O/C 70x32 Waterfall But 10/92 1,100
Nerly, Friedrich   It 1824-1919
* See 1991 Edition . . . .
Nesbitt, Lowell   Am 1933-
A/C 36x36 Red Violet Monochrome Flowers 1981 Sby 10/92 3,300
A/C 52x72 Peach and Grapes 78 Sby 10/92 1,760
A/C 34x22 Three Yellow Tulips '90 Sby 2/93 1,380
Nessi, Marie-Lucie
* See 1992 Edition . . . .
**Nesterov, Mikhail Vasillevich   Rus
1862-1942**
* See 1990 Edition . . . .
Netscher, Caspar   1635-1684
O/C 21x24 Couple with Their Two Children Sby 1/93 60,250
O/C 21x18 Portrait Lady with Pet Spaniel 1675 Sby 5/93 . . 20,700
O/C 32x25 Portrait of Queen Mary Stuart II 1676 Chr 5/93   13,800
Netscher, Constantyn   Dut 1669-1722
O/C 17x14 Young Girl with her Spaniel Wes 12/92 13,200
Nettleton, Walter   Am 1861-1936
* See 1992 Edition . . . .
Neubauer, H.
* See 1992 Edition . . . .
Neuberger, Klara
* See 1992 Edition . . . .
Neuhaus, Karl Eugen   Am 1879-1963
O/C 35x38 Cerra Obispo But 6/93 3,737
Neuhuys, John Albertus   Dut 1844-1914
O/C 51x42 The Sewing Lesson Chr 10/92 19,800
O/C 19x15 Feeding the Baby Porridge Chr 5/93 2,760
O/C/B 18x15 Interior Mother and Two Children Wes 3/93 . . 1,540
Neuman, Carl   Am 1858-1932
* See 1993 Edition . . . .
Neuman, Robert   Am 1926-
* See 1992 Edition . . . .
Neumann, Alexander   Ger 1831-
* See 1993 Edition . . . .
Neumann, Johan Jens   Dan 1860-1940
* See 1990 Edition . . . .
Neumann, Prof. Carl   Dut 1833-1891
* See 1992 Edition . . . .
Neuquelman, Lucien   Fr 1909-
* See 1992 Edition . . . .
Neuschul, Ernest
* See 1992 Edition . . . .
Neustatter, Ludwig   Ger 1829-1899
* See 1990 Edition . . . .
Nevelson, Louise   Am 1900-1989
Pe/Pa 8x5 Untitled: Pair Sby 6/93 1,495
Nevin, I. M.   Am 19C
W/Pa 11x15 Battle Scene 1856 Hnd 12/92 225
Newell, George Glenn   Am 1870-1947
* See 1993 Edition . . . .
Newell, Henry C.   Am a 1865-1885
* See 1993 Edition . . . .
Newell, Hugh   Am 1830-1915
O/C 29x25 The American Sportsman Skn 9/92 8,250
O/C 18x24 The Harvesters Chr 10/92 3,080
O/C 16x20 The Frugal Meal Lou 3/93 950
Newell, Peter   Am 1862-1924
G&R/Pa 12x7 Couple Sitting on Haystack Ilh 11/92 375
Newman, Barnett   Am 1905-1970
* See 1991 Edition . . . .
**Newman, Benjamin Tupper   Am
1859-1940**
O/B 16x20 Campfire by Lakeside 1937 Sby 9/92 1,320
Newman, George A.
O/C 26x36 Farm and Bridge Ald 9/92 500

176

O/B 16x20 Cavern Run Bridge, Bucks County Ald 9/92 175

Newman, Henry Roderick   Am 1833-1918
W/Pa 16x12 Japanese Pagoda 1897 Sby 9/92 7,700
W/Pa 14x20 Venice, La Dogana 1894 Yng 2/93 5,500

Newman, John   1936-
* See 1993 Edition . . . .

Newman, John   1952-
* See 1993 Edition . . . .

Newman, Joseph   Am 1890-
O/B 12x16 Lady in Garden Lou 12/92 175

Newman, Robert Loftin   Am 1827-1912
O/C 10x14 Good Samaritan 1886 But 6/93 3,737

Newmarch, Strafford   Br a 1866-1874
O/B 9x12 Three New Jersey Landscapes Mys 3/93 495

Newton, Richard (Jr.)   Am 20C
O/C 72x24 Over Fence: 4 Panelled Screen 1927 Sby 6/93 . 10,350

Ney, Lloyd Raymond   Am 1893-1964
* See 1993 Edition . . . .

Neyland, Harry A.   Am 1877-1958
O/C 17x14 La Pianiste Eld 8/93 880

Neymark, Gustave Mardoche   Fr 1850-
* See 1993 Edition . . . .

Neyts, Gillis   Flm 1623-1687
* See 1992 Edition . . . .

Nibbs, Richard Henry   Eng 1816-1893
W/Pa 20x30 Rottingdean-Sussex Fre 10/92 850

Niblett, Gary   Am 1943-
* See 1990 Edition . . . .

Nibrig, Ferdinand Hart   Dut 1866-1915
* See 1992 Edition . . . .

Nice, Don   1932-
* See 1993 Edition . . . .

Nicholas, Benvenueto   It 1848-1900
O/C 20x28 Venetian Scene Mys 12/92 1,100

Nicholas, Thomas Andrew   Am 1934-
O/M 14x20 Two: Peaks and Valleys; The Road Skn 3/93 . . . 935
W/Pa 9x12 Winter Pond Yng 5/93 400

Nicholl, Charles Wynn   Irs 1831-1903
* See 1990 Edition . . . .

Nicholls, Burr H.   Am 1848-1915
* See 1993 Edition . . . .

Nicholls, Rhoda Holmes   Am 1854-1930
* See 1991 Edition . . . .

Nichols, Carroll L.   Am 1882-
O/Pn 11x11 Blue Ice, Buck's County 1934 Lou 9/92 700

Nichols, Dale   Am 1904-
O/C 24x40 Death in the Wheatfields 1937 Sby 5/93 20,700
O/C 24x30 Winter Landscape with a Barn 1935 Sby 3/93 . 10,925
O/C 30x40 Black Birds and Evening Star Chr 12/92 8,250
O/C 30x40 The Last Log Chr 5/93 3,450
P&C/Pa 17x26 The Red Barn at Night 1959 Chr 12/92 880

Nichols, Edward H.   Am 1819-1871
O/Cb 12x22 Landscape Lake Waramaug: Two Sby 9/92 . . . 2,310

Nichols, Henry Hobart   Am 1869-1962
O/Cb 13x16 Rockport Winter But 12/92 1,760

Nichols, William   Am 20C
* See 1990 Edition . . . .

Nicholson, Ben   Br 1894-1982
G,W&Pe/B 7x11 Untitled Sby 5/93 37,375

Nicholson, Charles W.   Am 1886-1965
O/B 12x16 Sand Verbenas in Coachella Valley Mor 2/93 200
O/M 10x12 Desert in Bloom Mor 11/92 150

Nicholson, Edward Horace   Am 1901-1966
O/Cb 24x18 Lady with Umbrella Mor 6/93 2,200
O/C 26x26 Moonlight in Morro Bay But 3/93 2,090
O/C 16x20 Mountain Landscape Mor 11/92 400
W/Pa 11x15 Houses and Boatdock Mor 6/93 248

Nicholson, George Washington   Am 1832-1912
O/Pn 5x9 On the Delaware Water Gap Chr 9/92 3,300
W&G/Pa 11x15 Bahamian Scene Sby 12/92 2,750
O/C 12x20 A River Barge Chr 5/93 2,530
O/Pn 16x12 Barnyard in the Snow Sby 9/92 1,210
O/Pn 9x9 Boats Cottages Along the Coast Sby 9/92 935

O/B 11x14 Coastal Scene Mys 12/92 825
O/Pn 16x12 Fishermen and Boat on Shore Eld 7/93 660
O/Pn 10x12 Fishermen and Boat Eld 7/93 605

Nicholson, Lillie Mae   Am 1884-1964
O/B 14x11 Cabin in the Woods, Yosemite But 10/92 660
O/B 12x16 Weeping Willow at Pond But 10/92 550
O/Cb 16x12 Woodland Scene Mor 6/93 440

Nicholson, W.
O/Pn 23x19 Boys in Ocean Cave Ald 5/93 500

Nickele, Isaac   a 1660-1703
O/C 13x11 Interior of St. Bavo's, Harrlem (2) Chr 1/93 . . . 11,000

Nickerson, Reginald E.   Am 1915-
O/C 21x36 The B. R. Woodside Wlf 5/93 2,500
O/C 29x35 Childe Harold Sel 12/92 2,200
O/C 24x39 American Bark "John Worster" Hnd 10/92 2,000
O/C 20x28 Gloriana and Viatore Sel 12/92 1,430

Nickolaus, August Wilhelm   Swd 1852-1925
* See 1990 Edition . . . .

Nicol, Erskine   Br 1825-1904
O/C 30x25 The Pet Rabbit Skn 3/93 1,100

Nicoll, James Craig   Am 1846-1918
O/C 18x30 On Cape Elizabeth, Maine Sby 3/93 4,600
O/C 24x40 California Coast Skn 3/93 880
O/C 13x21 Seascape 1881 Wes 10/92 825

Niczky, Eduard   Ger 1850-1919
O/C 14x11 Lady in Feathered Hat 1882 Hnd 3/93 4,000

Nielsen, Amaldus Clarin   Nor 1838-1932
* See 1992 Edition . . . .

Nielsen, Jack
* See 1992 Edition . . . .

Niemann, Edmund John   Br 1813-1876
O/C 30x50 Runny Mede and Windsor 1871 Hnd 6/93 11,500
O/C 28x36 View Near Richmond Chr 2/93 3,850
O/C 24x36 North Hallerton 1876 Chr 10/92 2,750

Niemann, Edward H.   Br a 1863-1867
O/C 24x42 Cottages by a Stream Chr 2/93 2,090

Niemeyer, John Henry   Am 1839-1932
* See 1990 Edition . . . .

Nierman, Leonardo   Mex 1932-
O/B 49x36 Cosmic Abstraction Sby 6/93 2,300
A/B 16x24 Bird in Flight Hnd 9/92 1,200
A/B 16x24 Volcanic Fury Hnd 9/92 1,200
A/B 24x31 Abstract Composition Hnd 12/92 850
O/B 24x32 Composition '64 Hnd 9/92 800
O/B 24x32 Cosmic Flame '63 Wlf 9/92 600
O/M 32x24 Cosmic Ignition 76 Hnd 6/93 600
A/M 16x24 Space Fury '66 Wlf 9/92 600
O/M 15x23 Solar System '64 Wes 12/92 522
O/M 24x16 Jungle Bird Hnd 6/93 375
W/Pa 15x11 Paper Illusion Hnd 12/92 200

Nieto, Rodolfo   Mex 1936-1988
* See 1993 Edition . . . .

Nightingale, Basil   Eng 1864-1940
O/C 36x60 Gentry's New Horsepower 1902 Sby 6/93 9,200
W&C/Pa 28x40 Celebrated Belvoir Gambler Sby 6/93 2,185
Pe&W/Pa 24x29 Celebrated Belvoir Gambler Sby 6/93 . . . 1,725
C/Pa/B 17x22 Lord Lonsdale's Big Jump 1912 Wes 10/92 . . 412

Nignet, Georges   Fr 1926-
O/C 30x40 Le Marine du Fleurs au Monffetard Doy 11/92 . . 3,520
O/C 30x40 Girls on the Beach Fre 4/93 1,600
O/C 24x36 Le Rivage du Brittany Fre 10/92 1,600
O/C 24x36 L'Eglise du Seine Fre 10/92 1,500

Nikoff, Alexis Matthew Podcher   Am 1886-1933
* See 1992 Edition . . . .

Nilson, Johann Esaias   1721-1788
* See 1993 Edition . . . .

Nilsson, Gladys
A/C 20x28 Semisighmetricall Sby 6/93 2,185

Nino, Carmelo   Ven 1951-
* See 1991 Edition . . . .

Nisbet, Marc   Am 20C
A/Pn 12x13 Afternoon Sky Wlf 4/93 450

Nisbet, Robert Hogg   Am 1879-1961
O/C 30x36 View of Connecticut Valley Fre 10/92 5,000
O/C 19x15 Winter Landscape at Dusk Wes 5/93 660
Y/Pa 8x10 People at the Beach Mys 12/92 550
W/Pa 4x6 Farmer Plowing Yng 2/93 200
Nishisawa, Luis   Mex 1926-
W/Pa&I/Pa 24x36 Pair: Tlayacapan; Tepoztlan 89 Chr 11/92   9,900
Nissl, Rudolph   Aus 1870-1955
* See 1992 Edition . . . .
Nivert, Georgette   Fr 20C
O/C 26x21 Street Scene Lou 12/92 225
O/C 26x21 Woman Playing Mandolin Lou 12/92 200
Nivet, A.   Fr 19C
O/Pn 7x10 Dance of the Innocents Skn 9/92 1,430
Noble, John Sargeant   Br 1848-1906
O/C 40x61 In the Lap of Luxury 1881 Sby 6/93 48,300
Noble, Thomas S.   Am 1835-1907
* See 1993 Edition . . . .
Noe, Luis Felipe   Arg 1933-
L&Fp/Pa 14x17 Sin Titulo 65 Sby 5/93 1,150
Noel, Alexandre-Jean   Fr 1752-1834
O/C 20x34 Paris with Notre Dame Sby 1/93 32,200
Noel, Danielle   Fr 20C
G/Pa 16x8 Girl in Interior Lou 3/93 150
Noel, Georges   Fr 1924-
* See 1992 Edition . . . .
Noel, John Bates   Br
O/C 18x14 Gypsy Camp; Woods (2) Fre 4/93 850
Noel, Jules Achille   Fr 1815-1881
W/Pa 11x18 Shipping in a Storm 1876 Chr 5/93 1,955
Noel, Peter Paul Joseph   Fr 1789-1822
O/Pn 17x22 The Uninvited Guest 1821 Chr 2/93 12,100
Noguchi, Isamu   Am 1904-
H/B 17x11 Seated Nude Sby 2/93 5,175
Noland, Kenneth   Am 1924-
A/C 70x70 Blue Horizon 1963 Chr 11/92 93,500
A/Pa 73x37 Untitled Chr 2/93 60,500
A/C 53x101 Via Fall 1969 Chr 11/92 44,000
A/C 93x48 April in Balance 1971 Chr 11/92 26,400
A/C 77x67 Knit 1978 Sby 10/92 18,700
A/C 96x24 Up 1967 Chr 2/93 15,400
Nolde, Emil   Ger 1867-1956
W/Pa 18x14 Floral Composition Sby 11/92 104,500
W/Pa 13x19 Sonnenblumen Sby 5/93 76,750
W/Pa 11x9 Kopf Eines Jungen Sby 5/93 8,050
Nolf, John Thomas   Am 1872-1955
O/C 16x20 Valley and Seas at San Diego 1925 Hnd 10/92 . . 300
Nollekens, Josef Frans   Flm 1702-1748
* See 1992 Edition . . . .
Nolpe, Pieter   Dut 1613-1652
* See 1991 Edition . . . .
Nonnenbruch, Max   Ger 1857-1922
* See 1991 Edition . . . .
Nonnotte, Donat   Fr 1708-1785
* See 1990 Edition . . . .
Nooms, Reinier   Dut 1623-1664
* See 1992 Edition . . . .
Noortig, Jan   17C
* See 1993 Edition . . . .
Nordalm, Federico   Nic 1949-
O/C 39x36 Calabazas 1991 Chr 11/92 6,600
Nordell, Carl   Am 1885-
* See 1993 Edition . . . .
Nordenberg, Bengt   Swd 1822-1902
* See 1990 Edition . . . .
Nordenberg, Carl Henrik   Swd 1857-1928
O/C 32x36 The Game of Checkers Chr 2/93 19,800
Nordfeldt, Bror Julius Olsson   Am 1878-1955
O/C 38x24 Fire Lilies in a Clay Pot Chr 12/92 33,000
O/C 26x32 New Mexico Landscape Chr 3/93 20,700
O/C 48x34 White Vase Chr 12/92 16,500
O/B 22x32 Low Tide 1945 Chr 12/92 13,200
O/B 26x32 At the Swimming Hole Mys 12/92 5,280
W/Pa 15x22 Trees and Sunlight Sby 12/92 5,225

O/C 34x42 Sunflower Pods '43 Sby 9/92 4,400
W/Pa/B 14x20 Mountainside Chr 9/92 3,520
W&Pe/Pa 15x22 High Country Farm Chr 9/92 2,420
Nordhausen, August Henry   Am 1901-
* See 1993 Edition . . . .
Norman, Irving   Am 20C
H/Pa 23x37 The Bridge, 1946 But 4/93 747
Normann, Adelsteen   Nor 1848-1918
O/C 20x24 The Lake Dum 8/93 1,500
Normil, Andre   Hai 20C
O/M 36x48 Earthly Paradise Sby 10/92 4,620
Norris, S. Walter   Am 1868-
O/C 24x30 Harbor Grouping Fre 4/93 3,100
North, John William   Br 1842-1924
O/C/B 37x51 Landscape with Sheep 1889 Doy 11/92 17,600
Northcote, James   Am 1822-1904
* See 1993 Edition . . . .
Northcote, James   Eng 1746-1831
* See 1990 Edition . . . .
Northleach, J. Miles   Eng 19C
* See 1990 Edition . . . .
Norton, William Edward   Am 1843-1916
O/C 12x16 On the Dunes-Holland Sby 3/93 3,450
O/C 16x24 Coastal Scene '74 Lou 3/93 3,000
O/C 18x40 Leaving the Ship Behind Sby 3/93 1,380
Norwell, Graham Noble   Can 1901-1967
O/C 20x24 Winter Landscape Sbt 11/92 2,464
W/Pa 14x19 Laurentian Village Sbt 4/93 616
Nosworthy, Florence E.   Am 1872-1936
W/Pa 16x15 Children Frolicking at Easter Ih 11/92 775
Noterman, Zacharias   Bel 1820-1890
O/Pn 24x32 Les Deux Chiens Sby 1/93 8,050
O/Pn 18x15 Monkeys Drinking: Pair 1875 Sby 5/93 6,900
O/Pn 8x6 Morning Shave; Reading the Paper -2 Chr 5/93 . . 4,370
Nott, Raymond   Am 1888-1948
O/M 25x30 Desert Landscape Hnd 3/93 700
P/Pa 19x23 Sailboats Mor 2/93 475
Nourse, Elizabeth   Am 1859-1938
* See 1992 Edition . . . .
Nousveaux, Edouard Auguste   Fr 1811-1867
O/C 21x29 Istanbul Across the Bosphorus 1860 Sby 10/92 . 2,750
Novo, Stefano   It 1862-
W/Pb 16x8 The Fruit Seller Chr 5/93 437
Novotny, Elmer L.   Am 1910-
* See 1993 Edition . . . .
Novros, David   Am 1941-
* See 1991 Edition . . . .
Nowak, Ernst   Aus 1853-1919
* See 1993 Edition . . . .
Nowak, Franz   Aus 20C
O/Pn 8x6 Fruit and Porcelain Urn Chr 5/93 2,300
Nowak, Leo   Am 20C
* See 1993 Edition . . . .
Nowey, Adolf   Con 19C
O/Pn 10x8 Lamb with Ducks and Peacock (2) Chr 5/93 . . . 1,840
Noyer, Denis Paul   Fr 1940-
O/C 18x22 Montmartre 68 Hnd 5/93 160
O/C 20x26 Le Bateau Bleu 1969 Hnd 5/93 150
Noyer, Philippe-Henri   Fr 1917-
* See 1993 Edition . . . .
Noyes, George Loftus   Am 1864-1951
O/C 25x30 Early Spring Chr 12/92 22,000
O/C 18x24 The Pond Brd 8/93 4,180
O/Cb 15x14 Along the Grand Canal Skn 3/93 4,125
O/B 14x15 Harbor Gloucester Skn 5/93 3,520
O/B 11x9 The Market Square Skn 9/92 1,540
O/C 13x18 Lowland Landscape Sby 9/92 1,320
O/Cb 8x10 Winter Hillside Fre 4/93 1,241
O/B 14x15 Floral Still Life Ald 9/92 650
O/B 13x15 Autumn Landscape Hnd 10/92 325
Nudersher, Frank B.   Am 1880-1959
O/C 37x30 Sunset in the Ozarks Sel 9/92 4,600
O/C 7x9 Saint Louis Riverfront Sel 4/93 2,000
O/C 80x98 The Founding of St. Louis 1937 Sel 4/93 1,900

O/B 18x16 Autumnal Missouri Landscape Sel 9/92 450
O/Cb 16x14 Cowboy in Western Landscape Sel 12/92 250

Nunamaker, Kenneth   Am 1890-1957
O/C 12x15 Spring Thaw Brd 8/93 2,090
O/C 12x15 Barn in Winter Landscape Wlf 4/93 1,050

Nussio   It 20C
O/C 36x58 Visti da Sori, Genova 1927 Sby 1/93 2,300

Nutt, Jim   Am 1938-
A/C 59x49 I've Seen This Before 74 Sby 11/92 14,300

Nuvolone, Carlo Francesco   It 1608-1665
O/C 37x47 Angel Appearing to Mary Magdelene Sby 5/93 . 13,800

Nuvolone, Panfilo   1609-1669
O/C 74x90 Man Being Escorted to Gallows Chr 1/93 24,200

Nybo, Povl Fris   Dan 1869-
* See 1993 Edition . . . .

Nye, Edgar Hewitt   Am 1879-1943
O/C 24x30 Summer Landscape 1912 Wes 3/93 660
W/Pa 17x20 Mountain Landscape '22 Lou 3/93 125

Nye, M.
* See 1992 Edition . . . .

Nyholm, Arvid Frederick   Am 1866-1927
O/C 27x22 Portrait of Woman Seated Sel 12/92 900

O Lusitano   1699-1778
K/Pa 10x18 Saint Francis Entering the Church Chr 1/93 . . 1,045

O'Brien, Lucius Richard   Can 1832-1899
W/Pa 20x26 Cove on Coast of Gaspe 1883 Sbt 5/93 10,120
W/Pa 15x22 Waterfall '73 Sbt 5/93 2,200
W/Pa 16x11 Still Life of Roses 1896 Sbt 5/93 1,584
W/Pa 13x18 Boating on a River 1898 Sbt 5/93 1,408
W/Pa 14x20 Coastal Scene Sbt 5/93 792

O'Conner, James Arthur   Irs 1792-1841
O/C 19x24 Hunter in Wooded Landscape Sby 1/93 2,990

O'Connor, John   Irs 1830-1889
* See 1992 Edition . . . .

O'Conor, Roderick   Irs 1860-1940
* See 1991 Edition . . . .

O'Donnell, Hugh   20C
* See 1991 Edition . . . .

O'Gorman, Juan   Mex 1905-1982
W&H/Pa 7x10 Cuernavaca 1929 Sby 11/92 4,400

O'Higgins, Pablo   Mex 1904-
G/Pa 9x14 Dos Mujeres 1934 Sby 11/92 3,575

O'Keeffe, Georgia   Am 1887-1986
O/C 40x14 Ritz Tower, Night Chr 12/92 . . . . 1.21M
O/C 18x12 Three Pears Sby 12/92 176,000
O/C 10x7 Red Gladiola in White Vase 1928 Chr 12/92 . . 154,000
O/C 18x12 Cannas Sby 12/92 143,000

O'Kelly, Aloysius   Irs 1853-
O/C 20x14 Street Scene, Cairo Skn 9/92 4,675

O'Kelly, Mattie Lou   Am 1907-
* See 1991 Edition . . . .

O'Neil, Henry Nelson   Br 1817-1880
* See 1991 Edition . . . .

O'Neill, Daniel   Br 20C
* See 1992 Edition . . . .

O'Neill, George Bernard   Br 1828-1917
O/C 20x17 Grandma's Attorney Chr 2/93 4,400

O'Neill, Raymond Edgar   Am 1893-1962
* See 1993 Edition . . . .

O'Neill, Rose   Am 1875-1944
C&Pe/Pa 19x15 Mother with Babies: Pair Sby 9/92 2,750
Br&I/Pa 13x19 Couple Seated Ih 5/93 600

O'Shea, John   Am 1876-1956
O/C 30x36 Corsair But 10/92 6,600
O/B 20x24 Golden Hills But 3/93 3,575
O/C 36x31 Banana Blossoms But 6/93 3,450
O/C 25x30 California Hills But 10/92 3,300
O/C 25x30 Flowering Hills But 10/92 3,300
O/C 25x30 Grand Canyon No. 2 But 10/92 3,300
O/C 25x30 Shadows But 10/92 3,025
O/C 25x30 Barren Hills But 3/93 2,475
O/C 30x36 Cypress Trees But 10/92 2,475
O/C 30x36 Seascape But 10/92 2,475
O/C 25x30 Flowering Orchard But 6/93 2,300
O/C 25x30 Fruit Trees But 3/93 1,870

W/Pa 23x29 Ocean Through Trees, Point Lobos But 10/92 . 1,870
O/C 25x30 Autumn Reflections But 10/92 1,760
W&G/Pa 22x30 Seascape But 6/93 1,725
W/Pa 22x30 Cypress Trunks and Forest But 10/92 1,650
O/C 25x30 Lush Foliage But 10/92 1,650
O/B 32x40 Violence But 6/93 1,380
O/C 25x30 Hideaway But 10/92 1,320
O/C 25x30 Early Spring, Arizona But 10/92 1,045
W/Pa 30x22 Portrait of a Man But 6/93 1,035
O/C 25x30 Arizona Desert But 6/93 920
MM/Pa 12x15 Portrait: Red Head, Blue Eyes Mor 2/93 750
P/Pa 15x11 Man in Armchair Mor 11/92 650
W/Pa 30x22 Portrait of a Woman But 6/93 575
MM/Pa 15x10 Seated Man Mor 6/93 358

Oakes, Frederick   Am
* See 1991 Edition . . . .

Oakes, Minnie F.   Am a 1891-
* See 1993 Edition . . . .

Oakes, Wilbur L.   Am 1876-
* See 1991 Edition . . . .

Oakley, Thornton   Am 1881-1953
O/C 53x29 News Vendor on Broadway 1905 Chr 12/92 . . 55,000
O/C 30x20 Boy Sitting on Barge Ih 11/92 900
W/Pa 6x9 Avila 1935 Fre 10/92 160

Oakley, Violet   Am 1874-1961
Y/Pa 15x10 Women Playing Cello 1924 Fre 10/92 900
W/Pa 15x11 Off Gibralter Mys 3/93 275

Oberhauser, Emanuel   Ger 19C
* See 1991 Edition . . . .

Obermoser
O/B 16x20 Boat and Stream Ald 9/92 175

Obermuller, Franz   Aus 1869-1917
O/B 7x6 Woman with Red Kerchief Yng 2/93 900

Obersteiner, Ludwig   Aus 1857-
* See 1993 Edition . . . .

Oberteuffer, George   Am 1878-1940
O/C 44x52 View of Notre Dame Chr 12/92 7,700
O/C 18x20 Rockport Harbor Brd 8/93 5,500

Oberteuffer, Karl Amiard   Am 1908-
W&H/Pa 15x22 Two Massachusetts Views Skn 5/93 522

Obin, Antoine   Hai 1929-
O/M 20x24 Meeting of General Toussaint But 4/93 575
O/M 20x24 Un Coin du Cap-Haitien Sby 2/93 575

Obin, Philome   Hai 1892-
O/M 24x30 Le Marche de Limbe 1957 Chr 11/92 25,300
O&Pe/M 24x30 Marriage Chr 11/92 7,700
O/M 20x24 Une Haitien au bas du Limbe Chr 11/93 6,600
O/M 12x8 The Hunter Chr 11/92 2,860

Obin, Seneque   Hai 1893-1977
O&H/M 24x30 L'Amour De Calvaire 63 Sby 5/93 14,950
O/M 24x30 Funeraille Maconnique Sby 5/93 9,200
O/M 17x18 The Way to the Market Chr 11/92 4,180
O/B 24x20 On the Road to Market Skn 9/92 935

Obregon, Alejandro   Spa 1920-
O/C 32x37 Sin Titulo Chr 11/92 52,800

Ocampo, Isadoro   Mex 1902-
G/Pa 20x14 Figure with Baskets But 4/93 2,185

Ochtervelt, Jacob   Dut 1635-1682
* See 1991 Edition . . . .

Ochtman, Leonard   Am 1854-1935
O/C 30x40 Approaching Storm 1899 Chr 12/92 13,200
I/Pa 4x6 Close of an August Day (2) Yng 5/93 125

Ockert, Carl   Ger 1825-1899
O/C 11x16 Chasing Ducks at River's Edge Mys 3/93 440

Odie, Walter M.   Am 1808-1865
* See 1993 Edition . . . .

Odierna, Guido   It 1913-
O/C 24x36 Mediterranean Post Hnd 3/93 500
O/C 27x39 Blue Grotto Isle of Capri Dum 11/92 450
O/C 28x39 Fishing Boats at Dusk Hnz 5/93 300

Oehlen, Albert   1954-
O&Pls/C 79x78 Loves Body 85 Chr 2/93 24,200
O&MM/C 75x51 Untitled 84 Chr 11/92 22,000
O&MM/C 75x103 Guernica 84 Sby 11/92 9,900
O&E/C 75x75 Blick Durch Den Stier Sby 2/93 8,050

Oehmichen, Hugo   Ger 1843-1933
* See 1993 Edition . . . .
Oehring, Hedwig   Ger 1855-
O/Pn 15x12 The Conversation Sby 10/92 4,950
**Oertel, Johannes Adam Simon   Am
1823-1909**
* See 1992 Edition . . . .
Ogden, Frederick D.   Am 19C
O/C 24x32 Lincoln Memorial Mys 3/93 1,045
Ogilvie, John Clinton   Am 1836-1900
* See 1993 Edition . . . .
Ogilvy, Charles   Eng 1832-1890
* See 1993 Edition . . . .
Oguiss, Takanori   Jap 1900-
* See 1992 Edition . . . .
Ohtake, Tomie   Jap 1913-
* See 1990 Edition . . . .
Okada   Am 20C
O/C 18x24 Harbor Hnd 10/92 200
Okada, Kenzo   Am 1902-
* See 1993 Edition . . . .
Okamura, Arthur   Am 1932-
W&G/Pa 24x18 Untitled '66 But 10/92 495
O&Wx/C 18x21 Bird Wave '65 Wes 3/93 440
O/C 18x21 Bird Wave '65 Hnd 9/92 350
Olalla, Francisco Garcia Santa
O/C 28x39 Columbus Before Spanish Court 1894 Chr 11/92 55,000
Oldenburg, Claes   Am 1929-
Y&W/Pa 17x12 Monument for Grant Park 67 Sby 11/92 . . 25,300
W,H&Y/Pa 30x20 Cotello Ship, From Above '85 Chr 11/92 . 9,900
W&Pe/Pa 15x22 Drainpipe 66 Sby 10/92 8,250
W&Y/Pa 10x9 Teabag in Landscape '85 Chr 10/92 5,500
A&L/Cb 5x7 Untitled 1985 Chr 11/92 1,650
Y&K/Pa 22x15 Untitled '84 Chr 2/93 1,320
Pe/Pa 4x6 Sketch Sleeping Man, Baked Potato Sby 10/92 . . . 990
Oldfield, Otis   Am 1890-1969
O/C 58x45 La Penupienne Sby 9/92 13,200
Olinsky, Ivan G.   Am 1878-1962
O/C 60x36 The Old Fashioned Gown 1913 Sby 5/93 90,500
O/C 36x30 Two Young Women 1914 Sby 5/93 36,800
O/B 7x9 Girl Reclining on Pillow 1916 Dum 1/93 4,500
P&C/Pa 22x20 Seated Nude with Yellow Cloth Sby 3/93 748
W/Pa/B 14x10 Nude by a Stream 1902 Sby 9/92 605
Olinsky, Tosca   Am 1909-1984
* See 1992 Edition . . . .
Oliphant, Patrick   Am 1935-
Pl/Pa 8x15 Reporting Pollution's Damage Ih 5/93 375
Olitski, Jules   Am 1922-1964
A/C 88x80 Passion of Beverly Torrid 1963 Sby 11/92 . . 82,500
A/C 44x36 Dead Ringer 1963 Sby 10/92 22,000
A/C 98x15 Overtone One 1970 Chr 10/92 9,350
A/C 95x68 Fourth Daughter 1973 Chr 11/92 8,250
A/C 31x67 Grand Universe 83 Sby 10/92 6,050
A/C 84x28 Eminent Domaine-2 1974 Sby 10/92 5,500
A&E/C 68x49 Halcyon 88 Chr 5/93 4,830
A/C 30x20 Thalass Mystery-9 1978 Chr 2/93 2,860
Olive, Jacinto   Spa 1896-1967
* See 1991 Edition . . . .
Oliveira, Nathan   Am 1928-
A/Pa 36x28 Untitled Figurative Painting 2 Sby 2/93 4,888
Pe/Pa 18x20 Untitled 64 Sby 10/92 2,640
Oliver, Archer James   Eng 1774-1842
O/C 48x66 The Middleton Family Eld 8/93 16,500
Oliver, Myron   Am 1891-1967
* See 1992 Edition . . . .
Oliver, Thomas Clarkson   Am 1827-1893
O/C 12x18 Ships at Sea/Boston Harbor 79 Skn 5/93 1,320
O&R/B 17x27 Sailing Vessels in a Stiff Breeze 1892 Skn 9/92 330
Oliver, William   Br 1805-1853
O/C 43x39 The New Shawl Sby 2/93 6,900
Olivera, Nathan   Am 1928-
* See 1992 Edition . . . .
Olivetti, Luigi   It 19C
W/Pa 20x14 Baskets of Oranges Chr 2/93 825

Olivier, Michel-Barthelemy   Fr 1712-1784
* See 1992 Edition . . . .
Oller, Francisco   Am 1833-1917
* See 1991 Edition . . . .
Olleros y Quintana, Blas   It 1851-1919
O/C 31x26 A Roman Spectacle Chr 10/92 7,150
Ollivier, Michel Barthelemy   Fr 1712-1784
* See 1993 Edition . . . .
Olmsted, Elsie L.   Am
O/Pn 7x10 Eastham Dunes, Cape Cod Eld 8/93 77
Olson, Joseph Olaf   Am 1894-1979
O/C 16x19 Gloucester Harbor Fishing Boats Chr 12/92 1,980
**Ommeganck, Balthasar Paul   Flm
1755-1826**
O/Pn 15x20 Cows, Donkey, Goat in Meadow 1810 Chr 2/93 4,400
Onderdonk, Julian   Am 1882-1922
O/C 25x30 Winter Morning Guadaloupe River But 6/93 . . 28,750
O/C 25x30 Shinnecock 1906 Chr 5/93 18,400
O/Pn 9x6 Early Spring Morning 1909 Eld 8/93 4,510
O/Pn 4x6 Landscape 1908 Wes 10/92 825
**Onderdonk, Robert Jenkins   Am
1853-1917**
* See 1992 Edition . . . .
Ongania, Umberto   It 20C
W/Pa 8x13 St. Mark's Square, Venice: Pair But 11/92 1,980
Onley, Toni   Can 1928-
* See 1993 Edition . . . .
Onslow-Ford, Gordon   20C
* See 1992 Edition . . . .
Opdenhoff, George Willem   Dut 1807-1873
* See 1993 Edition . . . .
Operti, Albert Jasper   Am 1852-1922
* See 1992 Edition . . . .
Opfer, Gustav   Ger 1876-
* See 1993 Edition . . . .
Opie, John   Br 1761-1807
* See 1992 Edition . . . .
Oppenheim, Dennis   Am 1938-
Ph/Pb 22x13 Reading Position 2nd Degree Burn 70 Sby 2/93 6,325
Opsomer, Isidore   Bel 1878-1967
* See 1992 Edition . . . .
Orange, Maurice Henri   Fr 1868-1916
O/Pn 13x10 Un Tambour de L'Infanterie 1901 Sby 10/92 . . 4,400
Orchardson, Sir William Q.   Br 1832-1910
* See 1992 Edition . . . .
Ord, Joseph Blays   Am 1805-1865
* See 1990 Edition . . . .
**Ordinaire, Marcel & Courbet, G   Fr
1848-1896**
* See 1992 Edition . . . .
Ordonez, Sylvia   Mex 1957-
* See 1990 Edition . . . .
Ordway, Alfred T.   Am 1819-1897
O/C 30x36 Woodland Stream Slo 5/93 1,100
O/C 14x18 Spring Landscape Mys 3/93 358
Organ, Marjorie   Am 1886-1931
Pl/Pa 9x7 Head of a Man, Children: Two Wes 10/92 192
Orizzonte   Dut 1662-1749
O/C 29x24 Two Figures Conversing by Pool Sby 1/93 . . . 28,750
O/C 19x15 Landscape with Figures Conversing Sby 10/92 . 13,200
Orlando, Felipe   Cub 1911-
O/C 22x28 Woman in a Yellow Dress Wes 3/93 1,430
O/Cb 9x12 Woman with a Cat Wes 12/92 715
Orlik, Emil   Czk 1870-1932
Pe/Pa 9x12 Study of a Girl Hnd 9/92 400
**Orlovsky, Vladmir Donatovitch   Rus
1842-1914**
* See 1993 Edition . . . .
Orozco, Jose Clemente   Mex 1883-1949
O/C 26x32 Acordada Sby 11/92 374,000
O/Pa/Pn 20x13 Rosana Chr 11/92 77,000
O&Pl/Pa 20x17 Prometheus 45 Sby 11/92 66,000
O/C 20x16 El Elevado Chr 11/92 48,400
O/C 15x14 La Prostituta Sby 11/92 27,500
T,G&H/Pa 15x10 Mujer 1946 Sby 11/92 13,200

C/Pa 26x14 Figura Sby 5/93 4,600
H/Pa 9x14 Manos Sby 11/92 2,750
Orpen, William Newenham Montag   Br 1878-1931
  * See 1990 Edition . . . .
Orr, Alfred Everitt   Am 1886-
  C/B 24x18 Portrait of a Gentleman '23 Sby 9/92 220
Orr, Elliot   Am 1904-
  O/Cb 10x14 Cape Cod Study 1934 Sby 9/92 330
Orr, Eric   Am 20C
  * See 1992 Edition . . . .
Orr, George P.   Am
  O/C 12x16 Lobstermen's Huts 1944 Fre 4/93 700
Orr, Louis   Am 1879-1961
  W&H/Pa 12x18 Fishing Boats Anchored Near Shore Skn 9/92   220
Orr, W.
  O/Pw 18x24 A Clipper Ship 1940 Eld 7/93 66
Orselli, Arturo   It 19C
  * See 1992 Edition . . . .
Ortega, Charles   1925-
  O/Cb 16x20 Paysage Chr 11/92 1,100
Ortkens, Aert   Dut 16C
  * See 1990 Edition . . . .
Ortlieb, Friedrich   Ger 1839-1909
  O/C 27x33 Feeding the Rabbits Chr 10/92 14,300
Ortlip, Aimee E.   Am 1888-
  O/C 31x36 Spring Flowers '27 Slo 4/93 650
Ortmans, Francois Auguste   Fr 1827-1884
  O/C 23x33 Deer in a Clearing 1855 Chr 5/93 6,900
Ortner, F.   Aus 19C
  O/C 21x15 Laughing Peasant Hnd 6/93 650
Osborne, S. M.   Am 19C
  * See 1992 Edition . . . .
Osnaghi, Josefine   Aus a 1890-1920
  O/Pn 8x10 Still Life Candelabra, Fan, Flowers Sby 1/93 . . . 1,380
Ossorio, Alfonso   Am 1916-1990
  W&Wx/B 18x10 The Garden 1950 Chr 11/92 4,180
Ostersetzer, Carl   Ger 19C
  O/Pn 10x13 Discussion and Persuasion (2) 1906 Chr 2/93 . 4,950
  O/C 19x12 Man Playing a Clarinet FHB 3/93 1,400
Osthaus, Edmund Henry   Am 1858-1928
  O/C 24x36 Two Pointers Sby 3/93 34,500
  O/C 24x36 Setter and a Pointer Sby 3/93 28,750
  O/C 18x22 Setters on Point Sby 6/93 13,225
  W/Pa 23x31 King of the Game Birds Sby 3/93 7,475
  W/Pb 21x30 Two English Setters on Point Sby 9/92 5,500
  O/C 21x17 English Setter Sby 6/93 4,025
Ostroumova-Lebedeva, Anna P.   Rus 1871-1955
  W/Pa 12x16 Park Near St. Petersburg Autumn 1931 Yng 2/93   700
Osver, Arthur   Am 1912-
  O/C 69x58 Flight 1970 Hnd 6/93 500
  O/C 13x14 Autunno FHB 3/93 60
Otero, Alejandro   Ven 1921-
  * See 1993 Edition . . . .
Otis, Amy   Am 20C
  O/C 18x24 Landscape with Stone Wall Fre 4/93 70
Otis, Bass   Am 1784-1861
  O/C 36x27 Portraits William & Eliza Hillegas Fre 10/92 3,800
Otis, George Demont   Am 1879-1962
  O/C 30x36 Cabin by the Sea But 10/92 15,400
  O/C 24x30 The Arroyo But 10/92 6,600
  O/C 27x42 Sanchez Adobe Ranch But 6/93 5,750
  O/C 24x30 Eucalyptus Landscape Mor 11/92 5,500
  O/C 24x30 Lagunitas But 10/92 5,500
  O/C 20x26 Noon Light But 10/92 4,400
  O/B 16x20 Inverness #8 Mor 6/93 2,750
  O/B 12x16 Pacific Waters Mor 11/92 700
Ott, Jerry   Am 20C
  * See 1992 Edition . . . .
Ott, Sabina   1955-
  * See 1992 Edition . . . .
Otte, Carel   Br 20C
  O/C 17x20 House in Terraced Landscape Fre 4/93 375

Otte, William Louis   Am 1871-1957
  O/B 26x36 Coachella Valley 1927 But 10/92 13,200
  O/C 30x40 Eucalyptus Dum 1/93 9,500
Ottesen, Otto Didrik   Dan 1816-1892
  O/C 10x8 Still Life Roses and Lilacs 1853 Sby 10/92 7,700
Ottini, Pasquale   It 1580-1630
  * See 1992 Edition . . . .
Ottmann, Henri   Fr 1877-1927
  * See 1992 Edition . . . .
Otto, Carl   Ger 1830-1902
  O/C 23x20 Still Life Assorted Flowers Fruits 1869 Chr 2/93   11,000
Oudinot, Achille   Fr 1820-1891
  * See 1993 Edition . . . .
Oudot, Roland   Fr 1897-1981
  O/C 24x32 The White Cottage Sby 2/93 4,313
  O/C 29x46 Chateau de Monblanc a Maussanne Sby 2/93 . . 2,990
  O/C 26x32 Stone Farm House Doy 11/92 2,200
  O/C 15x24 Automne aux Mesnuls Chr 5/93 1,725
  O/C 24x36 Hennequeville Sby 2/93 1,725
  O/Pn 10x14 Evening River Scene Hnz 5/93 725
Oudry, Jacques-Charles   Fr 1720-1778
  * See 1991 Edition . . . .
Oudry, Jean Baptiste   Fr 1686-1755
  * See 1992 Edition . . . .
Oulton, Therese   1953-
  * See 1993 Edition . . . .
Ouren, Karl   Nor 1882-1943
  O/C 39x58 Snowy Village by a Lake Hnd 9/92 800
Outcault, Richard F.   Am 1863-1923
  * See 1993 Edition . . . .
Outin, Pierre   Fr 1840-1899
  * See 1991 Edition . . . .
Ouvrie, Pierre Justin   Fr 1806-1879
  W/Pa 9x6 Figures by a Church Mys 3/93 165
Ovens, Jurgen   Ger 1623-1678
  * See 1993 Edition . . . .
Oviedo, Ramon   LA 1927-
  O/C 40x50 Areito Chr 11/92 7,150
Owen, Robert Emmett   Am 1878-1959
  O/C 30x40 Long Shadows of Winter Doy 5/93 3,850
  O/C 30x36 Landscape Lou 3/93 1,950
  O/C 20x24 Summer Meadow/Conway Skn 3/93 605
  O/C 20x24 Crawford Notch Skn 3/93 550
  O/C 16x20 Farmhouse in Winter Dum 8/93 550
  O/C 24x36 Three Clowns Hnd 6/93 100
Owen, Samuel   Br 1768-1857
  W&Pe/Pa 6x9 Fleet in Full Sail Chr 10/92 715
Ozenfant, Amedee   Fr 1886-1966
  O/C 69x59 La belle vie 1929 Chr 11/92 38,500
Paalen, Wolfgang   Mex 1905-1959
  O/Pa 18x11 Mujer Sby 11/92 9,900
Pacecco De Rosa   It 1600-1654
  * See 1992 Edition . . . .
Pach, Walter   Am 1883-1958
  W/Pa 10x14 Aquarium 1914 Sby 9/92 880
Pachaubes
  * See 1993 Edition . . . .
Pacheco, Maria Luisa   Bol 1919-
  * See 1992 Edition . . . .
Pacher, Ferdinand   Ger 1852-1911
  * See 1991 Edition . . . .
Pacioni, Celestino   Am 20C
  O/Cb 14x16 Before and After Hnz 5/93 325
  O/C 8x10 White Zinnias Hnz 5/93 170
  O/Cb 8x10 Orange Flowers Hnz 5/93 110
  O/Cb 8x10 Still Life Hnz 5/93 110
Padilla, J.
  * See 1992 Edition . . . .
Padina, Alex Moser   20C
  O/C 18x25 European City Scene 1952 FHB 6/93 40
Padriant, Jules   19C
  O/C 18x28 Fisherman Along Shore Slo 4/93 425
Padura, Miguel   Cub 1957-
  O/C 23x32 Acorn Squash Chr 11/92 10,450

Page, Edward A.   Am 1850-1928
O/C 14x20 Fishing Boat on Shore Eld 11/92 1,210
Page, Marie Danforth   Am 1869-1940
* See 1993 Edition
Page, W.   Am 19C
O/B 9x11 Western Desert Landscape Eld 4/93 132
Page, Walter Gilman   Am 1862-1934
* See 1992 Edition
Page, William   Br 1794-1872
* See 1992 Edition
Pagels, Herman J.   Ger a 1876-1935
* See 1992 Edition
Pages, Jules Eugene   Am 1867-1946
O/Cb 10x7 End of Day in Chinatown But 3/93 2,090
Pages, Jules Francois   Am 1833-1910
* See 1993 Edition
Pagliacci, Aldo   It 1913-
O/C 12x10 La Visita '68 Hnd 12/92 500
Paice, George   Eng 1854-1925
O/C 9x12 The Rook '08 Slo 5/93 750
Pail, Edouard   Fr 1851-
* See 1992 Edition
Pailier, Henri   Fr 19C
* See 1991 Edition
Pain, Robert Tucker   Eng a 1863-1877
* See 1993 Edition
Pajetta, Pietro   It 1845-1911
O/C 26x43 Il Vendita Vino 1886 Chr 10/92 52,800
Pajou, Augustin   Fr 1730-1809
* See 1992 Edition
Palacios, Alirio   Ven 1944-
MM/Pa/Pn 72x30 Aparicion Magica 1 1989 Chr 11/92 ... 20,900
Paladino, Mimmo   It 1948-
A/L 48x36 Untitled 1983 Sby 5/93 34,500
A,Wx&L/B 29x41 Untitled 1985 Chr 11/92 30,800
O/Pa 28x40 Untitled 1982 Sby 5/93 23,000
A/Pa/C 36x71 Untitled 1980 Chr 11/92 17,600
Ph 41x38 Le Immagini Sono Riflessi 75 Sby 11/92 8,800
Palamedes, Anthonie   Dut 1601-1673
* See 1993 Edition
Palamedesz., Palamedes   Dut 1607-1638
O/Pn 20x48 Cavalry Battle Sby 5/93 33,350
O/C 26x33 A Cavalry Skirmish But 5/93 1,725
Palanquinos Master   15C
* See 1993 Edition
Palanti, Giuseppe   It 1881-1946
* See 1993 Edition
Palermo, Blinky   Am 20C
* See 1993 Edition
Palin, William Mainwaring   Br 1862-1947
* See 1991 Edition
Palizzi, Filippo   It 1818-1899
* See 1992 Edition
Palizzi, Giuseppe   It 1813-1888
* See 1993 Edition
Palko, Franz-Xaver-Karl   1724-1767
* See 1991 Edition
Palladino, Mimmo
* See 1992 Edition
Pallares Y Allustante, Joaquin   Spa 19C
O/Pn 15x23 Parisian Street Scene Chr 5/93 7,475
O/Pn 11x9 Tieing her Shoe Lace Chr 10/92 1,540
Pallentine, A   It 20C**
O/C 20x30 Venetian Scene Wes 10/92 825
Pallissat, C.   Fr 19C
* See 1992 Edition
Palm, Anna Sofia   Swd 1859-1924
W&G/Pa 11x17 Ship Flying French Flag Skn 9/92 522
Palma Il Giovane, Jacopo N.   It 1544-1628
O/C 50x68 Venus and Cupid Sby 10/92 33,000
Palmaroli Y Gonzalez, Vicente   Spa 1834-1896
* See 1993 Edition
Palmeiro, Jose
* See 1992 Edition

Palmer, Harry Sutton   Eng 1854-1933
W/Pa 11x14 Pair: River Landscape '89 Sel 4/93 1,950
Palmer, Herbert Sidney   Can 1881-1970
O/C 20x24 Haliburton Road Sbt 11/92 3,740
O/C 22x17 Road to Haliburton Sbt 5/93 2,860
O/B 17x14 Sunshine and Shadow Sbt 5/93 1,320
O/B 6x8 October Morning Sbt 5/93 880
O/Pn 6x9 Humber Valley 1912 Sbt 5/93 792
Palmer, Lynwood   Eng 1868-1941
O/C 20x36 An Open Coach Sby 6/93 2,990
Palmer, Pauline   Am 1865-1938
O/C 16x20 Autumn Landscape Hnd 5/93 1,600
O/B 19x15 The Garden Gate Hnd 12/92 1,200
O/M 16x12 P-Town (Provincetown) Sby 3/93 690
W/Pa 10x13 Rainy Day Near Burlington, Wisc. Hnd 3/93 . 250
Palmer, Walter Launt   Am 1854-1932
O/C 24x16 Farmyard with Blue Snow at Sunset Eld 8/93 . 15,400
O/C 25x30 Winter Thaw Doy 11/92 13,200
O/C 21x28 Venetian Boats Chr 5/93 8,050
G,W&Pe/Pa 23x17 September Sby 3/93 4,600
P/Pa 13x18 Lake in the Early Fall 1884 Fre 10/92 3,000
P/Pa 13x17 The Lagoon, Venice 1893 Brd 2/93 2,310
Palmer, William   Br 1763-1790
* See 1991 Edition
Palmer, William Charles   Am 1906-1987
* See 1992 Edition
Palmerton, Don F.   Am 1899-1937
O/C 18x24 Eucalyptus-Montecito 1935 Mor 11/92 800
O/C 12x16 Yachting off Los Angeles 1936 But 6/93 575
Palmezzano, Marco   It 1458-1539
* See 1992 Edition
Palmieri, Frank   Am 20C
O/B 16x20 Child at the Beach Hnd 10/92 150
Paltronieri, Pietro   It 1674-1741
* See 1990 Edition
Palusen, Erich   Ger 1932-
O/C 23x29 European Flower Market Dum 5/93 1,300
Panabaker, Frank Shirley   Can 1904-1992
O/C 24x30 Red Heads Sbt 11/92 1,980
O/B 20x24 Stream in Winter, Dundas Sbt 5/93 1,760
Pancoast, Henry Boller   Am 1876-
* See 1992 Edition
Pancoast, Morris Hall   Am 1877-1963
O/B 8x10 Rocks Off Shore Yng 5/93 90
Pancorvo, Alberto   Col 1956-
* See 1991 Edition
Panerai, F. Ruggero   It 1862-1923
O/B 5x7 View of Florence Chr 10/92 2,640
Panini, Francesco   It 1725-1794
* See 1992 Edition
Panini, Giovanni Paolo   It 1691-1765
O/C 28x36 Roman Ruins w/Alexander the Great Chr 1/93 . 60,500
O/C 28x51 Roman Ruins with Trajan's Column Chr 1/93 . 55,000
Pannini, Francesco   It a 1790-
* See 1992 Edition
Pansas, F.   Spa 20C
O/C 32x26 Lady with a Mantilla and a Fan Chr 10/92 1,650
Pansing, Fred   Am 1844-1916
* See 1993 Edition
Panunzi, Sebastiano   It 19C
O/C 9x14 A Sunday Outing Chr 10/92 3,850
Panza, Giovanni   It 19C
* See 1993 Edition
Paoletti, Antonio Ermolao   It 1834-1912
* See 1992 Edition
Paoletti, Silvio D.   It 1864-1921
* See 1993 Edition
Paolillo, Luigi   It 1864-
* See 1992 Edition
Paolini, Giulio   20C
* See 1993 Edition
Paolini, Pietro   It 1605-1682
* See 1993 Edition
Paolo, Giovanni   It 1691-1786
* See 1990 Edition

Paone, Peter   Am 1936-
Bc/lv 3x3 The Red Jacked 67 Fre 10/92 280
Papaluca, L.   It 20C
O/C 23x30 Ship at Sea Mys 3/93 330
Papart, Max   Fr 1911-
* See 1993 Edition
Pape, Emile   Hun 1884-
* See 1992 Edition . . . .
Pape, Eric   Am 1870-1938
O/C 36x58 Artist's Home, Gloucester Sby 9/92 15,400
P/Pb 38x26 The Mexican Dancer 1914 Skn 9/92 2,750
O/Pn 5x9 Sunset at Sea Skn 5/93 2,200
G/Pa 15x11 Rip Van Winkle Legend Sleepy Hollow Ih 5/93 . . 2,000
O/Pn 5x9 Sunset Over Water Skn 11/92 1,650
P/Pa 24x18 Bust of Beautiful Woman 1912 Ih 11/92 1,600
O/C 17x23 Still Life Peppers, Onions, Pitcher 1901 Skn 3/93 1,100
C&K/Pa 34x20 The Mexican Cowboy Skn 11/92 990
Pape, Friedrich Edouard   Ger 1817-1905
* See 1990 Edition . . . .
Papperitz, Fritz Georg   Ger 1846-1918
* See 1992 Edition . . . .
Papsdorf, Richard   20C
* See 1992 Edition . . . .
Paqueau, Gaston   Fr 19C
O/C 32x23 Parisiennes au Cafe 1886 Sby 2/93 16,100
Paradise, Phillip   Am 1905-
W/Pa 18x28 Casita Vieja Mor 6/93 1,650
O/C 21x28 California Coast Hnd 5/93 1,100
Paramonov, Vasilii   Rus 1923-
O/C 24x32 Lilacs 1985 Sel 4/93 650
O/B 14x20 Birch Tree Forest 1975 Sel 4/93 100
Parcy, Sidney Richard   Br 1821-1886
* See 1990 Edition . . . .
Parigi, Giulio   a 1568-1635
K&Pl/Pa 8x11 Landscape with Farm (2) Chr 1/93 1,320
Paris   Am 19C
O/C 16x12 Girl Seated in Haystack 1878 Lou 12/92 600
Paris, Alfred Jean Marie   Fr 1846-1908
* See 1993 Edition . . . .
Paris, Walter   Am 1842-1906
W/Pa 13x20 East Gloucester 1885 Slo 5/93 3,250
Park, David   Am 1911-1960
O/C 40x36 Tea 56 Sby 10/92 107,250
H/Pa 9x12 Untitled 1955 Chr 11/92 3,080
Pe/Pa 17x14 Untitled Sby 2/93 2,588
Pe/Pa 17x14 Untitled Sby 2/93 2,530
G/Pa 12x10 Four Untitled Works Chr 11/92 1,760
G/Pa 8x3 Female Nude Mys 3/93 1,045
Park, John Anthony   Br 1888-1962
* See 1992 Edition . . . .
Parker, Agnes Miller   Am 20C
* See 1993 Edition . . . .
Parker, Bill   Am 20C
* See 1991 Edition . . . .
Parker, Cushman   Am 1882-1940
* See 1993 Edition . . . .
Parker, George Waller   Am 1888-1957
* See 1992 Edition . . . .
Parker, Henry H.   Br 1858-1930
O/C 24x36 Silent Waters But 11/92 7,700
O/C 24x36 Landscape with Cows Sby 10/92 7,150
O/C 24x36 The Thames at Cleeve Hnd 6/93 4,600
Parker, Henry Perle   Br 1795-1873
O/Pn 21x18 Young Woman Picking Flowers But 5/93 1,840
Parker, John Adams   Am 1829-1905
* See 1991 Edition . . . .
Parker, Lawton S.   Am 1868-1954
O/C/B 20x13 Lady Seated in Landscape Hnd 3/93 8,000
O/Cb 16x20 Field with Trees But 12/92 1,650
Parker, Ray   Am 1922-
* See 1992 Edition . . . .
Parkhurst, Thomas   Am 1853-1923
* See 1993 Edition . . . .
Parks, Walter C.   Am 20C
O/Pn 22x16 The Balloons Mys 3/93 385

Parlo, Percy   Fr 1890-
O/C 15x14 Seated Nude 1912 Sby 6/93 920
O/B 14x17 Au Bois de Fontainbleau 1910 Dum 5/93 375
Parr, James Wingate   Am 20C
W/Pa 21x29 Boston Street Scene Winter Eld 11/92 1,210
Parra, Carmen
* See 1992 Edition . . . .
Parra, Gines   Spa 1895-1960
O/C 19x23 Figures in a Landscape But 4/93 1,150
Parrish, David   Am 1939-
* See 1991 Edition . . . .
Parrish, Maxfield   Am 1870-1966
O/Pn 30x24 Cinderella 1913 Chr 12/92 187,000
O/M 23x19 The Old Glen Mill 1950 Chr 12/92 89,100
O/M 16x14 Deep Valley 1946 Chr 3/93 57,500
O/Pa 17x12 Botanical Gardens at Padua Chr 5/93 43,700
O/Pb 6x8 From Phoebus Halzaphron: Pair 1901 Sby 9/92 . 23,100
W/Pa 14x11 Jack Sprat 1919 Dum 9/92 3,500
Parrish, Steven Windsor   Am 1846-1938
O/M 20x28 Tide-Water Landscape Skn 5/93 880
Parrocel, Charles   Fr 1688-1752
* See 1990 Edition . . . .
Parrott, F. W.   Sco 19C
W/Pa 28x40 Highland Scene Deer Hunter 1855 Sel 12/92 . . 450
Parrott, William   Br 1813-1869
O/C 29x48 View of Naples with Fisherfolk 1845 Chr 10/92 19,800
Parrott, William Samuel   Am 1844-1915
O/B 8x7 Oregon River-Blue Mountain Mor 2/93 800
Parshall, Dewitt   Am 1864-1956
* See 1993 Edition . . . .
Parshall, Douglass   Am 1899-
O/B 16x20 Mountain Lake #2 Mor 11/92 425
O/B 6x8 Hope Ranch 1930 Mor 11/92 275
Parsons, Beatrice   Eng 1870-1955
W/Pa 10x7 Water Garden, Pleasaunce Sby 2/93 3,163
Parsons, Charles R.   Am 1821-1910
W/Pa 10x18 Coastal Dunes '04 Slo 5/93 110
Parsons, Marion Randall   Am 1878-1953
O/B 16x20 House with Cactus But 10/92 2,200
O/B 16x20 Old Ranch House But 3/93 1,650
Parsons, Orrin Sheldon   Am 1866-1943
O/B 16x20 Adobe Houses, Sante Fe Chr 5/93 4,140
Parsons, P. B.   Am 20C
Pe/Pa 11x7 Mother and Children Hnd 9/92 70
Partington, Richard Langtry   Am 1868-1929
O/C 30x44 Sunset at Point Lobos w/Schooner But 3/93 . . . 4,400
O/C 24x36 Glimpse of Monterey Bay 1914 But 3/93 3,300
Parton, Arthur   Am 1842-1914
O/C 24x34 Cows in a Marsh Ald 3/93 1,800
O/C 14x18 Out on the Pond Skn 11/92 1,540
O/C 18x24 Clearing in a Landscape Slo 5/93 850
Parton, Ernest   Am 1845-1933
O/C 21x32 The Sommer Valley Chr 9/92 3,850
O/C/C 26x36 The Young Fisherman But 12/92 2,200
Parturier, Marcel   1901-1976
O/C 21x26 Honfleur Chr 5/93 2,875
Pascal, P B**   Con 19C**
O/C 36x26 Meryem La Danseuse 1887 Sby 2/93 8,050
Pascal, Paul   Fr 1832-1904
G/Pb 12x18 Arab Encampment Along the Nile 1900 Sby 1/93 690
G/Pa 7x12 Camel Riders 1904 Wlf 9/92 450
Pascal, Paul B.   Fr 1867-
G/Pa 18x26 An Arab Encampment 1900 Hnz 5/93 1,300
Paschke, Ed   Am 1939-
O/C 50x96 Essernia '84 Chr 11/92 16,500
O/C 27x24 Red Float 71 Sby 5/93 9,200
Pascin, Jules   Fr 1885-1930
O/C 29x32 Le Cirque Sby 5/93 90,500
O/C 32x25 Deux Jeunes Filles Sby 2/93 77,300
O/C 32x25 Portrait D'Hermine David Sby 11/92 55,000
O/b 24x19 Femme Nue Dans Un Fauteuil Sby 11/92 48,400
O/B 18x22 Le client indecis Chr 11/92 44,000
P&C/Pa/B 28x22 Jeune Femme Sous Un Parasol Sby 10/92 . 8,800
Pe/Pa 19x15 Deux Femmes Allongees Sby 5/93 6,325

I&W/Pa 17x12 Jeune Fille 1921 But 4/93 3,162
K&Fp/Pa 15x12 Nu Assis Chr 2/93 2,860
Pe/Pa 6x8 Groupe d'Hommes Chr 2/93 2,750
Pl,W&Pe/Pa 6x8 Les Mariniers Chr 5/93 2,530
C/Pa 14x20 Two Female Reclining Nudes Sby 10/92 2,200
Pl/Pa 8x16 Dans le parc Chr 11/92 1,650
W/Pa 10x14 Four Negroes Wes 3/93 1,650
W&Pl/Pa 10x9 Deux Femmes Chr 5/93 1,380
I/Pa 13x9 Seated Woman Sby 10/92 1,100
Pl&W/Pa 5x8 Trois Musiciens Chr 11/92 1,045
W/Pa 15x12 Seated Nude Hnd 10/92 850
Pl/Pa 9x12 Figures by a Rocky Cliff 31 Sby 2/93 690
Pl/Pa 12x15 Family Group Lou 6/93 200
Pl/Pa 12x15 Family Group Lou 12/92 200

Pascutti, Antonio   Aus 19C
O/C 25x19 The Lacemakers But 11/92 6,600
Pasinelli, Lorenzo   1629-1700
O/C 19x16 The Annunciation Chr 1/93 8,250
Pasini, Alberto   It 1826-1899
O/C 12x9 The Fruitmarket 1886 Sby 2/93 68,500
O/Pn 9x15 Mounted Arab Warriors Sby 5/93 23,000
Paskell, William   Am 1866-1951
W/Pa 10x14 Cottages at Dawn Yng 5/93 325
Pasmore, Daniel   Br 1829-1891
   * See 1993 Edition . . . .
Pasmore, Victor   Br 1908-
   * See 1992 Edition . . . .
Passante, Bartolomeo   1618-1648
O/C 41x31 Man Playing Mandolin Chr 1/93 165,000
Passey, Charles H.   Br a 1883-1885
O/C 28x36 A Lane, Boxhill, Surrey Dum 1/93 1,200
Passot, Nicolas   1521-
   * See 1993 Edition . . . .
Pastega, Luigi   It 1858-1927
   * See 1993 Edition . . . .
Pasternacki, Vetold   Am 1897-
O/C 18x23 Landscape with Town '38 Dum 3/93 300
Pasternak, Leonid Ossipovitch   Rus 1862-1945
   * See 1993 Edition . . . .
Pastina, Ed   It 19C
   * See 1993 Edition . . . .
Pata, Cherubin   Fr 19C
   * See 1990 Edition . . . .
Pata, Cherubin & Courbet, G.   Fr 19C
O/C 17x20 Le Puits Noir a Ornans Chr 5/93 28,750
Patel, Pierre Antoine (II)   Fr 1605-1676
   * See 1993 Edition . . . .
Pater, Jean-Baptiste   Fr 1695-1736
O/C 19x22 Mlle Dangeville as Thalia Sby 5/93 387,500
Paterson, Caroline   Br a 1878-1892
   * See 1993 Edition . . . .
Paterson, R. F.   Am 20C
Pe/Pa 11x16 The Yacht "Hurricane" Mys 12/92 165
Patino, Virgilio   Col 1947-
O/C 79x51 La Sabana Chr 11/92 11,000
Patkin, Izhar   1955-
O/Me 73x53 Southern Momento Chr 11/92 6,600
A&Gd/Me 48x36 Pansy, Rose, Others 87 Chr 11/92 5,500
Patrois, Isidore   Fr 1815-1884
O/Pn 12x14 In the Atelier 57 Chr 10/92 6,050
Pattein, Cesar   Fr a 1882-1914
   * See 1993 Edition . . . .
Patten, George   Br 1801-1865
   * See 1991 Edition . . . .
Patterson, Charles Robert   Am 1878-1958
   * See 1992 Edition . . . .
Patterson, Howard Ashman   Am 1891-
   * See 1992 Edition . . . .
Patterson, Margaret Jordan   Am 1867-1950
W/Pa/B 11x9 Two: Fountain; Wild Flowers '26 Skn 3/93 880
G&C/Pa 10x14 Villa in Ravello Slo 4/93 420
W,G&H/Pa 14x17 The Long Ridge 1927 Skn 3/93 385
W&G/Pa 7x10 Verdant Hill/Summer Skn 11/92 358

W/Pa 10x13 The Coastal Village Skn 3/93 302
Patterson, Russell   Am 1896-1977
W/Pa 17x10 Standing Showgirl Ih 11/92 1,100
Pl/Pa 15x23 Two Sunday Comic "Mamie" Ih 11/92 700
Pl/pa 13x9 Two Women in Dressing Room Ih 5/93 450
A/C 12x24 Reclining Nude Ih 11/92 325
Pattie, E. E.   Am 19C
P/Pa/C 16x20 Still Life Hnd 9/92 375
Pattison, James W.   Am 1844-1915
   * See 1992 Edition . . . .
Pattison, Robert J.   Am 1898-1981
   * See 1991 Edition . . . .
Patty, William Arthur   Am 1889-1961
O/C 10x12 Landscape Mor 2/93 450
Paul, John   Br 19C
   * See 1993 Edition . . . .
Paul, Joseph   Eng 1804-1887
   * See 1993 Edition . . . .
Paulman
O/C 20x30 Woman Walking by Marsh Ald 3/93 900
Paulman, Joseph   Con 19C
O/C 12x16 Mother and Child Dum 4/93 1,250
Paulsen, N. Chr.   Dan 19C
   * See 1993 Edition . . . .
Paulucci, Enrico
   * See 1993 Edition . . . .
Paulus, Francis Petrus   Am 1862-1933
   * See 1993 Edition . . . .
Paus, Herbert   Am 1880-1946
G/Pa 19x12 Man Pouring Molten Steel Foundary Ih 11/92 . 3,750
Pavesi, Pietro   It 19C
   * See 1992 Edition . . . .
Pavil, Elie Anatole   Fr 1873-1948
   * See 1993 Edition . . . .
Pavlosky, Vladmir   Am 20C
W&H/Pa 17x23 Sorting the Nets Skn 11/92 412
Pawla, Frederick Alexander   Am 1877-1964
O/C 30x36 Point Lobos But 3/93 3,025
Pawley, James   Br a 1854-1869
   * See 1993 Edition . . . .
Pawliszak, Waclaw   Pol 1866-1905
O/C 38x61 The Falcon Hunt 1897 Sby 10/92 11,000
Paxson, Edgar Samuel   Am 1852-1919
G/Pa 16x20 Buffalo Hunt Chr 9/92 15,400
O/C 40x26 Trail, Head of Bitter Root River 1917 Chr 3/93 . . 5,750
W,G&Pe/Pb 12x10 Portrait of Indian 1908 But 12/92 2,750
Pe/Pa 20x15 Indians Hunting Buffalo: Pair 1901 Sel 9/92 . . . 250
Paxson, Ethel Easton   Am 1885-1982
O/B 24x30 Vermont Woods 1940 Yng 5/93 150
Paxton, Elizabeth V. O.   Am 1877-1971
   * See 1990 Edition . . . .
Paxton, William McGregor   Am 1869-1941
O/C 36x36 Together Chr 9/92 24,200
O/C 45x36 Nellie and Phryne Chr 12/92 20,900
C/Pa 7x6 Portrait of Alice Trask Chr 5/93 920
Payne, Charlie Johnson   Br 1884-1967
   * See 1990 Edition . . . .
Payne, David   Br 19C
   * See 1992 Edition . . . .
Payne, Edgar Alwyn   Am 1882-1947
O/C 40x50 Navahos Sby 12/92 60,500
O/C 30x40 Summit Lake But 10/92 27,500
O/C 24x28 Tuna Boats But 10/92 27,500
O/C 29x29 Boats in Harbor Mor 6/93 18,700
O/C 29x29 The Orange Sail But 6/93 18,400
O/C 20x24 Harbor Twilight But 6/93 17,250
O/C 34x34 Near Mt. Whitney Chr 5/93 16,100
O/C 24x28 Fishermen's Holiday But 3/93 15,400
O/C 20x24 The Miner Peaks Iceberg Lake But 3/93 13,200
O/C 28x34 High Sierra Scene But 10/92 11,000
O/C 15x47 Summer Landscape 24 But 3/93 11,000
O/C 14x14 Lowering the Sails But 10/92 10,450
O/C 20x24 On the Canal, Chioggia But 3/93 9,900
O/C/B 16x20 Return of the Fishing Fleet But 3/93 9,900

184

O/C 25x30 Sailboats But 10/92 9,900
O/C/B 16x12 Palisades Glacier But 6/93 6,325
O/Cb 10x14 Afternoon Shadows Mor 6/93 4,675
O/Cb 11x14 Fisherman's Return But 10/92 4,400
O/B 10x12 ? Lake Mor 11/92 4,000
O/Cb 10x14 High Sierra Mor 11/92 3,750
O/B 10x14 Sierra Lake But 10/92 3,575
O/Cb 12x10 Brittany Boats But 10/92 3,300
O/Cb 13x16 Brittany Village But 10/92 3,300
O/Cb 7x10 Village of San Gervais 1922 But 10/92 3,300
O/Cb 8x10 Along the Trail Mor 11/92 2,250
O/Cb 6x8 High Sierra Mor 11/92 1,200
W/Pa 16x23 Sailboats Wlf 5/93 1,100
O/Cb 16x12 Nude in Studio But 6/93 920
O/Ab 20x24 Brittany Boats Mor 2/93 550

Payne, Elsie Palmer   Am 1884-1971
G/Pa 12x14 Mountains in Rain; Sierras: (3) But 10/92 3,300
O/C 24x20 White Flowers But 6/93 1,955
P/Pa 20x25 Floral Still Life Lou 6/93 800

Payne, William
W/Pa 5x7 ...bury House - Devon Ald 5/93 205

Payzant, Charles   Am 1898-1980
W/Pa 19x25 Going Home Mor 6/93 1,100
W/Pa 12x19 Rural House in Landscape Mor 6/93 715
W&G/Pa 13x19 California Farm Scene But 6/93 575

Peak, Bob   Am 1928-1992
G&Pe/Pa 22x23 Two Advertisements Ih 11/92 800

Peale, Anna Claypoole   Am 1791-1878
   * See 1992 Edition . . . .

Peale, Charles Willson   Am 1741-1827
O/C 36x27 Maskell Ewing & Portrait Fre 10/92 90,000
O/C/M 26x22 Portrait of Colonel John Cox Chr 12/92 26,400
O/C 36x27 Portrait of Jane Hunter Fre 10/92 9,250

Peale, Harriet Cany   Am 1800-1869
   * See 1993 Edition . . . .

Peale, James   Am 1749-1831
   * See 1993 Edition . . . .

Peale, Margaretta   Am 1795-1882
   * See 1991 Edition . . . .

Peale, Mary Jane   Am 1827-1902
   * See 1991 Edition . . . .

Peale, Raphaelle   Am 1774-1825
O/C 26x22 Portrait of Artemas Ward 1795 Chr 9/92 7,150

Peale, Rembrandt   Am 1778-1860
O/C 36x29 George and Martha Washington: Pair Sby 5/93 299,500
O/C 29x25 Angel, After Correggio Chr 9/92 8,800
O/B 21x17 Portrait Provost Marshall Fre 4/93 6,500
O/C 25x20 Captain Jonathan Ashe Sby 9/92 4,400
O/C 24x20 Portrait of a Lady Slo 4/93 4,000
O/B/M 20x17 Head of a Young Girl Chr 12/92 3,520

Peale, Rubens   Am 1784-1864
   * See 1993 Edition . . . .

Peale, Sarah Miriam   Am 1800-1885
   * See 1992 Edition . . . .

Peale, Titian Ramsey   Am 1799-1885
   * See 1991 Edition . . . .

Pearce, Charles Sprague   Am 1851-1914
O/C 24x29 The Blue Umbrella 1890 Chr 9/92 12,100
O/C 13x10 Portrait of a Lady Sby 3/93 2,070

Pearlmutter, Stella   Am 20C
O/C 56x84 Spring Flowers '75 Sel 12/92 2,800
O/C 29x39 Zinnias '75 Sel 12/92 475
O/C 55x84 Yellow Flowers '75 Sel 12/92 450
O/C 24x20 Roses Sel 12/92 375

Pearlstein, Philip   Am 1924-
O/C 84x60 Male and Female Models Chr 10/92 46,200
O/C 48x60 Female Models Seated in Chairs 72 Chr 11/92 . 22,000
W/Pa 29x41 Male and Female on Navajo Blanket Sby 2/93 10,350
O/C 26x22 Reclining Nude 65 Chr 11/92 7,150
Br&I/Pa 29x41 Untitled 76 Chr 11/92 5,500
O/C 43x49 The Seven Hills of Rome Lou 3/93 4,000

Pears, Dion   Br 20C
W/Pa 29x37 Monte Carlo Race Lou 6/93 450

Pearson, C. & Wainwright, T.   Br 1805-1891
W&S/Pa 15x28 Cattle Resting/Sheep: Pair 1881 Doy 5/93 . . 3,190

Pearson, Cornelius   Am 1805-1891
W/Pa 7x12 Cows in River Landscape 1887 But 5/93 690

Pearson, Marguerite Stuber   Am 1898-1978
O/C 25x30 The Punch Bowl Chr 12/92 20,900
O/C 36x30 Tapestry and Brocade Chr 12/92 15,000
O/C 25x30 Silver Moon Roses Chr 3/93 6,900
O/C 29x35 Still Life with Brass Bowl Chr 3/93 4,830
O/C 28x24 Lady in Blue 24 Brd 8/93 2,310
O/B 10x8 Still Life Brd 2/93 1,320
O/Cb 16x14 Boats at Harbor Skn 5/93 770
O/B 12x16 Coastal Scene Yng 2/93 400
O/C 8x7 Roses Mys 12/92 138

Pease, Ray   Am 1908-
O/B 25x19 Three Couples in Living Room Ih 11/92 1,400

Pebbles, Frank M.   Am 1839-1928
O/C 11x15 The Old Schoolhouse 1910 Yng 5/93 100

Pecault, C. E.   Fr 19C
   * See 1992 Edition . . . .

Pechaubes, Eugene   Fr 1890-1967
O/C 19x22 The Horse Race Chr 5/93 2,300

Peche, Dale   Am
O/B 12x16 San Francisco Treat Wlf 12/92 1,150

Pecheur, Emile   Fr 19C
   * See 1991 Edition . . . .

Pechstein, Max   Ger 1881-1955
O/C 28x32 Abend in den Pyreneen 1921 Hnd 10/92 52,000
W&C/Pa 14x19 Sitzendes Madchen Chr 11/92 7,700

Peck, Orrin M.   Am 1860-1921
   * See 1991 Edition . . . .

Pecrus, Charles Francois   Fr 1826-1907
O/Pn 16x25 Sancho But 5/93 4,600

Peczeley, Antal
O/C 23x31 Peasant Girls Embroidering Dum 6/93 250
O/C 16x20 Bucju Dum 6/93 200
O/C 16x20 Muteremben Dum 3/93 175

Pedersen, Finn   1944-
O/C 21x27 Ansigter '68 Sby 5/93 3,450

Pedersen-Mols, Niels   Dan 1859-
   * See 1991 Edition . . . .

Pediaso, Manuel
O/C 33x28 Retratro De Una Mujer 1865 Sby 5/93 4,600

Pedrini, Giovanni Pietro Rizzo   It 1493-1540
O/Pn 28x22 Saint Mary Magdalen Sby 10/92 22,000

Pedro, Luis Martinez   Cub 1910-
Pl&W/Pa 23x17 Hombres Atrapando Pajaros 41 Sby 5/93 . 10,350

Pedulli, Federigo   It 1860-
   * See 1993 Edition . . . .

Peel, James   Br 1811-1906
   * See 1993 Edition . . . .

Peel, Paul   Can 1860-1892
O/C 24x38 Children Fishing 1881 Sbt 11/92 72,600
O/C 18x15 Resting '92 Sbt 11/92 48,400
O/C 58x40 La Jeunesse 1891 Sbt 11/92 44,000
O/C 15x22 Dejeuner 1884 Sbt 11/92 31,680
O/C 16x13 Study of a Lady in Bonnet Sbt 5/93 23,760

Peelor, Harold   Am 1856-1940
   * See 1993 Edition . . . .

Peeters, Bonaventur (the Elder)   Flm 1614-1652
O/Pn 23x32 Harbor Scene Approaching Storm Sby 5/93 . . 46,000

Peeters, E.   Am 19C
   * See 1992 Edition . . . .

Peeters, Jan   Flm 1624-1680
   * See 1993 Edition . . . .

Pegg, James Dean   Am 20C
O/C 20x16 Untitled Still Life 85 Hnd 5/93 130

Pegurier, Auguste   1856-1936
O/C 20x26 La voile blanche Chr 11/92 2,080

Peirano, *   17C**
   * See 1993 Edition . . . .

Peirce, Gerry
W/Pa 7x11 Mother and Child Seated FHB 3/93 30
Peirce, H. Winthrop   Am 1850-1936
I/Pa 8x13 Woman in Field of Grain Yng 5/93 150
Peirce, Waldo   Am 1884-1970
O/C 23x37 Bathers in Brook #2 66 Sby 3/93 2,300
O/C 25x30 Beach at Truro, Cape Cod 54 Sby 9/92 935
W/Pa 11x16 University Olives, U. of Arizona 53 Brd 2/93 . . . 275
W/Pa 11x13 Haying 53 Brd 2/93 154
Peiser, Kurt   Bel 1887-1962
O/C 20x16 Lady and Gentleman 1917 FHB 3/93 300
Peixotto, Ernest Clifford   Am 1869-1940
O/C 31x25 Lake Como, Italy But 6/93 2,300
Pelaez, Amelia   Mex 1897-1968
H/B 22x28 Autorretrato 1935 Chr 11/92 18,700
G/Pa 24x34 Naturaleza Muerta 60 Sby 5/93 13,800
O/C 27x16 Florero 61 Chr 11/92 10,450
O/C 12x14 Silla 67 Sby 5/93 6,325
G/Pa 15x20 Sin Titulo Sby 5/93 2,300
Pelcynski, Adam   Con 20C
O/B 24x20 Swan in Summer Pond 1915 Slo 4/93 400
Pelham, Gene
O/C 35x27 City Dwellers Moving to the Country Ih 11/92 . . 1,600
Pelham, Thomas Kent   Eng 19C
  * See 1991 Edition . . . .
Pellan, Alfred   Can 1906-
  * See 1993 Edition . . . .
Pellegrini, Riccardo   It 1863-1934
  * See 1993 Edition . . . .
Pelletier, Pierre Jacques   Fr 1869-1931
  * See 1993 Edition . . . .
Pellew, John   Am 1903-
O/C 34x27 Saturday Night in Astoria 1947 Yng 5/93 1,300
O/M 20x28 Summer Headlands Skn 11/92 358
Pelliciotti, Tito   It 1872-1943
  * See 1993 Edition . . . .
Pellicerotti, Frederico   It 19C
  * See 1992 Edition . . . .
Pelouse, Leon Germain   Fr 1838-1891
O/C 16x24 Farm Along the River Sby 1/93 1,840
Pels, Albert   Am 1910-
O/C 36x30 Dancing to the Accordian 1942 Ald 3/93 1,800
O/C 25x25 Hotsy Totsy Night Club Ald 5/93 900
O/C 20x24 Jazz Trio 1939 Ald 5/93 750
O/C 19x15 The Card Player Ald 3/93 500
Peltier   Con 19C
O/C 26x36 Park Scene 1913 Wes 5/93 770
Pelton, Agnes   Am 1881-1961
O/Pn 30x24 Still Life with Gladiolas Wlf 9/92 3,250
O/C 20x24 Desert Blossoms Sby 3/93 2,415
W/Pa 20x30 Poppies Wlf 4/93 2,100
W/Pa 24x25 Rubrum Lilies Wlf 9/92 500
W/Pa 24x36 Cattleya Orchids Mor 2/93 450
Peluso, Francesco   It 1836-
O/Pn 15x8 Two Gypsy Women Wes 12/92 1,980
Pena, Angel   Ven 1949-
  * See 1992 Edition . . . .
Penck, A. R.   Ger 1939-
Dis/C 79x118 Another R. T. 83 Sby 11/92 93,500
O/C 28x32 Gehieme Wege Sby 5/93 51,750
Dis/C 79x110 Untitled Chr 11/92 46,200
A/Pa/C 20x25 Untitled 81 Chr 11/92 24,200
O/C 44x37 Untitled 1969 Sby 5/93 20,700
O/C 20x39 The Black Lion Chr 2/93 18,700
A/Pa 21x33 Untitled 80 Chr 11/92 9,350
A/Pa 21x33 Untitled 80 Chr 11/92 8,800
O/Pa 25x34 Adler Und Tanzer I Sby 2/93 5,750
Fp/Pa 17x12 Untitled (Dani) Chr 11/92 1,650
Os/Pa 17x23 Untitled Chr 5/93 1,150
Penfield, Anna   Am 19C
  * See 1991 Edition . . . .
Penfield, Edward   Am 1866-1925
W&I/Pa 7x10 Washington's Coach Ih 5/93 3,500
Penfold, Frank C.   Am a 1880-1890
  * See 1992 Edition . . . .

Penley, Aaron Edwin   Br 1807-1870
W/Pa 7x9 Scottish Highlands 1887 But 5/93 1,035
Pennachini, Domenico   It 1860-
O/C 19x31 News from Afar Chr 10/92 8,800
Pennell, Joseph   Am 1860-1926
W/Pa 11x13 Brooklyn Bridge, Lighting Up Sby 12/92 6,325
G/Pa 14x18 The Whitehouse Chr 5/93 2,875
G/Pn 12x16 New York Harbor Sby 3/93 1,955
W/Pa 7x10 The Heroes After Zeppelin Explosion Sby 12/92 . 1,870
G&I/Pa 13x16 The Small Dome '88 Sby 9/92 1,760
W/Pa 10x12 Cityscape Dum 6/93 1,750
W/Pa 10x12 Cityscape Dum 6/93 1,500
Pe&W/Pa/B 7x10 New York Skyline Sby 9/92 1,430
PI&Pe/Pa 13x15 Old Levee Stream, Presq. 1882 Sby 9/92 . 1,210
PI/Pa 14x10 Views of London Chr 12/92 990
Penney, Fred D.   Am 1900-1988
O/Cb 24x36 Springtime in the Desert Mor 2/93 350
O/Cb 12x16 Coastal Mor 6/93 220
Pennoyer, Albert Sheldon   Am 1888-1957
O/C 25x30 From the Peaks Down Chr 5/93 4,830
O/C 18x24 House for Sale Skn 9/92 550
Penny, Edward   Br 1714-1791
  * See 1991 Edition . . . .
Penny, Edwin   Br 19C
G/Pa 30x21 Red Grouse Sby 6/93 4,313
Pent, Rose Marie   Am -1954
O/C 20x16 Flowers in a Bowl Yng 5/93 125
Peoli, Juan Jorge   Spa 19C
  * See 1993 Edition . . . .
Peploe, Samuel John   Br 1871-1935
O/C 18x16 Pink Roses in a White Vase Doy 11/92 20,900
Pepper, George Douglas   Can 1903-1962
  * See 1993 Edition . . . .
Peppercorn, Arthur D.   Br 1847-1926
O/C 16x27 Cows Under Cloudy Skies Skn 11/92 825
Peraire, Paul Emanuel   Fr 1829-1893
  * See 1993 Edition . . . .
Perboyre, Paul Emile Leon   Fr 19C
  * See 1993 Edition . . . .
Percy, Sidney Richard   Br 1821-1886
O/C 28x60 Landscape with Haymaking 69 Sby 5/93 40,250
O/C 24x36 Highland Landscape with Cattle 1884 Chr 10/92 12,100
O/C 11x18 On the Conway, North Wales 1878 Sby 1/93 . . 4,025
O/C 12x20 Figure Near a Highland Lake 79 But 11/92 . . . 3,025
O/C 12x22 Scottish Countryside Scene 1867 Dum 4/93 . . 2,000
Percy, W.
W/Pa 15x13 Portrait of a Gentleman 1879 FHB 3/93 100
Percy, William   Br 1820-1903
W/Pa 8x6 Portrait Mrs. William Crowther Wlf 3/93 50
Pereda, Antonio   1608-1678
O/C 40x20 Saint Lawrence Sby 1/93 40,250
Perehudoff, William   Can 1919-
A/C 14x17 Arcturus #9 1972 Sbt 5/93 1,320
Perez, Alonso   Spa a 1893-1914
O/Pn 23x29 Rainy Day in Spring Hnz 5/93 7,750
O/C 29x24 The Arriving Coach Hnz 5/93 5,750
Perigal, Arthur   Br 1816-1884
O/C 17x26 Landscape: Two 1865 Sby 1/93 2,875
Perignon, Alexis Joseph   Fr 1806-1882
  * See 1990 Edition . . . .
Perignon, Alexis-Nicolas   1726-1782
K,W, Bc/Pa 8x12 Rotunda/Triumphal Arch 1776 Chr 1/93 . . 5,500
Perilli, Achille   1927-
A&MM/C 12x14 La Materia Delle Pietra 60 Chr 2/93 6,600
Perillo, Gregory   Am 1932-
  * See 1993 Edition . . . .
Perkin, Isabelle L.   Br a 1888-1928
O/C 18x24 Still Life Kittens and Lobster 1896 Skn 9/92 . . . 2,750
Perkins, Granville   Am 1830-1895
O/C 16x20 Rocky Stream Sby 9/92 935
Perkins, Mary Smyth   Am 1875-1931
  * See 1993 Edition . . . .
Perkins, Parker S.   Am 1862-
O/C 20x24 Crashing Surf Slo 5/93 225

Perlasca, Martino   Sws 1860-1899
* See 1993 Edition . . . .
Perlin, Bernard   Am 1918-
T/Pa 18x28 Study for Criminal Court 1961 Yng 5/93 1,400
T/Pa 20x26 Textile Inspection Yng 5/93 800
Perrault, Leon Jean Basile   Fr 1832-1908
O/C 55x78 La Baigneuse 1875 Sby 2/93 107,000
Perre, Henri   Can 1828-1890
W/Pa 12x17 Figures on Country Road '78 Sbt 5/93 748
Perret, Aime   Fr 1847-1927
* See 1993 Edition . . . .
Perrey, Leon Auguste   Fr 1841-1900
* See 1992 Edition . . . .
Perrier, Emilio Sanchez   Spa 1855-1907
* See 1992 Edition . . . .
Perrigard, Hal Ross   Can 1891-1960
O/Pa 18x23 Canadian Ship 47 Eld 7/93 440
Perrin, Francois Nicolas A. F.   Fr 1826-1888
* See 1993 Edition . . . .
Perrine, Van Dearing   Am 1869-1955
* See 1993 Edition . . . .
Perron, Charles   1880-1935
* See 1992 Edition . . . .
Perron, Charles Clement F.   Fr 1893-1950
* See 1990 Edition . . . .
Perroneau, Jean-Baptiste   Fr 1715-1783
* See 1990 Edition . . . .
Perry, Enoch Wood   Am 1831-1915
O/B 12x15 Chinese Family '63 Sby 3/93 18,400
O/B 13x16 Chinese Children in a Garden '63 Sby 3/93 . . 13,800
O/C 20x16 Girl Carrying Water '82 Yng 2/93 4,750
O/C 14x10 Woman in Doorway Mys 12/92 412
Perry, Frank Chester   Am 1859-
O/C 20x24 Moonlit River Scene Mys 12/92 220
O/C Size? Old Homestead Mys 3/93 165
O/B 14x20 New England Summer Landscape Slo 4/93 150
Perry, J.
O/C 12x16 Still Life Peaches Dum 11/92 200
Perry, Lilla Cabot   Am 1848-1933
O/C 40x30 The Pink Rose 1910 Chr 12/92 35,200
O/C 40x30 Scent of Roses Chr 12/92 28,600
O/C 18x15 The Red Tunic/Portrait Edith Perry '88 Skn 5/93 . 5,500
Pertgen, Karl Maria   Ger 1881-
* See 1991 Edition . . . .
Pes, H. H.   Spa 19C
O/Pn 10x5 Spanish Dancer Fre 10/92 375
Pescheret, Leon   Am 1892-1961
* See 1992 Edition . . . .
Peske, Jean   Fr 1880-1949
* See 1992 Edition . . . .
Pesne, Antoine   Fr 1683-1757
* See 1990 Edition . . . .
Peterdi, Gabor   Am 1915-
* See 1993 Edition . . . .
Peterelle, Adolphe   Fr 1874-1947
O/C 24x20 Kneeling Female Nude Sel 2/93 225
Peters, Anna   Ger 1843-1926
O/C 30x42 Wildflowers in a Forest Hollow Doy 5/93 29,700
Peters, Carl William   Am 1897-1980
O/C 25x30 At the Wharf-Fair Pont Dum 2/93 2,500
O/C 40x36 Torpedoed Sby 9/92 1,320
O/C 16x20 Village in Winter Yng 5/93 1,200
O/C 25x30 Winter Landscape Ald 9/92 1,050
Peters, Charles Rollo   Am 1862-1928
O/C 35x25 Dusk Sby 9/92 8,800
O/C 19x25 Evening Reflection But 3/93 7,150
O/C 10x14 Nocturne on Monterey Coast But 3/93 7,150
O/C 16x24 Crescent Moon But 10/92 4,125
O/C 21x25 Nocturne But 3/93 2,750
O/C 16x24 Adobe at Night But 6/93 2,588
O/Pn 11x14 Fishing Boats in Creek 1894 But 6/93 2,588
O/B 9x11 Fishing Boats and Clam Diggers 1888 But 6/93 . . 1,955
O/C 19x25 Nocturne on the Monterey Coast 1906 But 6/93 . . 920

Peters, Matthew William   Irs 1741-1814
* See 1993 Edition . . . .
Peters, Pieter Francis   Dut 1818-1903
O/C 22x27 Watermill by a Lake Chr 10/92 3,520
Peters, Pietronella   Dut 1848-1924
* See 1991 Edition . . . .
Petersen, Edvard Frederik   Dan 1841-1911
* See 1990 Edition . . . .
Petersen, Einar   Am 1885-1986
O/C 32x26 View from Garden But 10/92 1,980
Petersen, John Eric Christian   Am 1839-1874
* See 1991 Edition . . . .
Petersen, L. C.   Am 20C
O/C 27x20 Portrait of an American Indian '05 FHB 6/93 525
Petersen, Martin   Am 1870-1943
O/B 22x18 New York Street Scene Hnd 9/92 600
Petersen, Sophus   Dan 1837-1904
O/C 16x14 Still Life Pewter Vase, Oranges 1895 Chr 10/92 . 1,320
Peterson, Heinrich A.   Br 19C
* See 1993 Edition . . . .
Peterson, Jane   Am 1876-1965
O/C 32x32 Quiet Harbor Chr 12/92 38,500
G&C/Pa 18x24 Docks at Gloucester Wes 12/92 16,500
G&C/B 24x18 Crowded Street in Venice Chr 12/92 15,400
O/C 30x40 Floral Still Life Skn 11/92 10,450
O/Cb 24x30 Florida Trees and Sand Skn 5/93 7,700
O/C 24x30 Still Life with Zinnias Sby 12/92 7,700
O/C 17x17 Dock Scene Wes 12/92 6,600
O/C 24x24 Petunias Chr 9/92 6,050
G,W&C/Pa 18x24 Low Library at Columbia Univ. Chr 9/92 . 5,500
O/C 30x24 Orchids 1943 Chr 9/92 5,500
G&C/Pa 18x24 The Palisades, New York Chr 3/93 4,600
G&C/Pa 18x24 Vancouver Water Front Wes 12/92 4,400
O/C 30x24 Zinnias Snapdragons and Marigolds Slo 7/93 . . 4,250
O/C 30x24 A Vase of Zinnias Chr 3/93 4,025
O/C 32x32 Bouquet of Roses Hnd 3/93 2,000
W&I/Pa 14x21 Florida Beach and Palms Skn 5/93 1,980
O/C 24x24 The Trade Winds Sby 9/92 1,980
O/B 18x18 Stage Fort Beach Lou 12/92 1,350
O/B 11x14 Evening Glow Wes 5/93 1,320
W/B 24x27 Evening, Volendam, Holland Wes 12/92 605
Peterson, Perry   Am 1908-1958
W/Pa 15x10 Woman Sitting on Garden Bench Ih 11/92 200
Peterson, Roland   Am 1926-
O/C 14x18 Figure on the Beach 1969 But 10/92 3,575
Petham, G*** K***
O/C 14x24 The School Room 1852 Sby 1/93 4,025
Pether, Abraham   Br 1756-1812
O/C 16x21 Landscape with Shepherds Sby 1/93 2,875
Pether, Henry   Br 19C
* See 1991 Edition . . . .
Petit, Alfred   Fr -1895
* See 1992 Edition . . . .
Petit, C.   Bel 19C
O/Pn 11x8 Little Girl with Lamb 1881 Hnd 10/92 1,400
Petit, Eugene   Fr 1839-1886
O/C 12x16 Flushing Pheasants: Pair Sby 6/93 4,600
Petit-Gerard, Pierre   Fr 1852-
* See 1991 Edition . . . .
Petiti, Filiberto   It 1845-1924
* See 1993 Edition . . . .
Petitjean, Edmond   Fr 1844-1925
* See 1993 Edition . . . .
Petitjean, Hippolyte   Fr 1854-1929
* See 1993 Edition . . . .
Peto, John Frederick   Am 1854-1907
O/Ab 6x9 Still Life Mug, Pipe, Crackers Sby 5/93 46,000
O/Pn 5x9 Still Life Pipe, Book, Matches Sby 9/92 17,600
O/C 22x16 Still Life Bulletin Board Chr 12/92 13,200
O/C 8x6 My Pipe and Mug 84 But 6/93 12,650
Petrini, Giuseppe Antonio   It 1677-1759
* See 1992 Edition . . . .

Petter, Franz Xaver   Aus 1791-1866
   * See 1991 Edition . . . .
Pettibone, Shirley
   O/C 24x24 Spring Pond-Charlottesville 1972 Sby 10/92 . . . 3,080
   A/C 26x34 Shoreline-Brighton Beach 1973 Sby 2/93 1,380
Pettitt, Charles   Br 19C
   * See 1990 Edition . . . .
Pettoruti, Emilio   Arg 1892-1971
   O/Pn 41x28 El Cantante 1930 Chr 11/92 220,000
   O/B 11x14 Costruzione Antica 1916 Sby 11/92 77,000
   O/C 32x24 Verano 1969 Chr 11/92 22,000
   O/B 7x9 Bodegon Sby 11/92 17,600
   Br&I/Pa 8x10 Cuadernos de Musica 1919 Chr 11/92 12,100
Petty, George   Am 1894-1975
   * See 1993 Edition . . . .
Petua, Leon Jean   Fr 1846-1921
   * See 1990 Edition . . . .
Pevsner, Antoine   20C
   * See 1993 Edition . . . .
Pew, Gertrude L.   Am 1876-
   * See 1993 Edition . . . .
Peyfuss, J. Karl   Aus 19C
   O/C 21x17 Classical Figures in Garden Sel 9/92 550
Peyraud, Frank Charles   Am 1858-1948
   O/C 18x24 Light through the Trees '95 Hnd 9/92 1,150
   O/B 12x16 River Landscape Hnd 5/93 1,000
Peyrol-Bonheur, Juliette   Fr 1830-1891
   * See 1993 Edition . . . .
Peyton, Bertha Menzler   Am 1871-1950
   W&G/Pa 19x23 Fishermen Loading Ice But 12/92 1,980
Pezant, Aimard Alexandre   Fr 1846-
   O/C 32x26 Vaches Au Paturage Sby 2/93 6,325
Pezzuti, P.   It 19C
   * See 1992 Edition . . . .
Pfaff, Judy   20C
   * See 1990 Edition . . . .
Pfeiffer, Gordon Edward   Can 1899-1983
   * See 1993 Edition . . . .
Pfeiffer, Heinrich H. (Harry)   Am 1874-1960
   O/C 24x30 Village Bandstand Slo 4/93 250
Pfeiffer, Wilhelm   Ger 1822-1891
   O/C 30x26 The Long Journey Sby 10/92 5,225
Pflug, Christiane Sybille   Can 1936-1972
   * See 1993 Edition . . . .
Pflug, Johanes Baptiste   Ger 1785-1866
   * See 1991 Edition . . . .
Pforr, Johann Georg   Ger 1745-1798
   O/Pn 20x28 Riders Tending Their Horses 1790 Chr 10/92 . 82,500
Phelan, Charles T.   Am 1840-
   O/C 16x20 The Spring Flock 1905 Skn 9/92 770
   O/C 12x16 Sheep in a Landscape Mys 3/93 742
Phelps, Edith Catlin   Am 1879-1961
   O/C 26x19 Landscape with Carriage Lou 3/93 1,200
Phelps, William Preston   Am 1848-1923
   O/C 30x50 Pasture White Mountains Brd 8/93 4,950
   O/C 10x14 Landscape with Cows at Rest Skn 3/93 1,540
   O/C 16x30 Longhorns at Pasture Late Afternoon Skn 5/93 . . 550
Philipp, Robert   Am 1895-1981
   O/C 37x50 Olympia Chr 9/92 8,800
   O/C 20x26 Siesta Sby 9/92 4,400
   O/C 36x30 Friends Chr 3/93 4,370
   O/C 24x48 In Central Park 1977 Chr 12/92 3,520
   O/C 20x30 Port of Weehawken Chr 3/93 2,760
   O/C 25x19 Woman in Contemplation Chr 5/93 2,760
   O/C 31x25 Woman in Red Seated 1947 Chr 12/92 2,420
   O/C 45x22 Still Lifes Flowers and Fruit: Pair Sby 9/92 2,200
   O/C 18x15 Young Girl Reading Mys 12/92 2,200
   O/C 20x12 The White Hat Sby 9/92 1,540
   O/C 20x16 Black Haired Girl 1965 But 6/93 1,150
   O/C 31x26 Friends 1960 But 6/93 1,150
   O/C 14x12 Self-Portrait with Black Hat Sby 3/93 1,150
   O/M 17x14 Young Girl in a Bonnet Chr 5/93 1,150
Philippe, Auguste Salnave   Hai
   * See 1993 Edition . . . .

Philippeau, Karel Frans   Dut 1825-1897
   * See 1993 Edition . . . .
Philippoteaux, Henri Felix E.   Fr 1815-1884
   O/C 56x80 Invasion des Gaules/Romains 1855 Chr 10/92 . 71,500
   O/C 27x20 Arabian Street Scene Dum 10/92 13,000
Philippoteaux, Paul Dominique   Fr 1846-
   * See 1993 Edition . . . .
Phillip, John   Br 1817-1867
   O/C/Pn 23x18 Little Fisher Friends Sby 6/93 2,185
Phillipe-Auguste, Salnave   Hai 20C
   * See 1992 Edition . . . .
Phillips
   O/C 12x9 Sheep Herding 1901 Ald 3/93 650
Phillips, Bert Greer   Am 1868-1956
   O/Cb 9x12 Taos Indian with His Horse Sby 12/92 16,500
   O/B 14x14 Taos Indian and Pony Sby 9/92 13,200
   O/B 16x20 Cottonwoods after Rain 1925 Yng 2/93 5,500
   O/C/B 12x16 Song to the Moon But 12/92 3,575
Phillips, Charles   Br 1708-1747
   * See 1993 Edition . . . .
Phillips, Coles   Am 1880-1927
   G/Pa 22x16 Woman in Black Ih 5/93 14,000
Phillips, Dorothy Sklar   Am 20C
   * See 1991 Edition . . . .
Phillips, Gordon   Am 1927-
   O/C 35x42 Sadie's Back in Town Sby 9/92 7,150
Phillips, James March   Am 20C
   W/Pa 8x10 Barn in Landscape Mor 11/92 200
Phillips, Marjorie   Am 1895-
   * See 1993 Edition . . . .
Phillips, Peter   1939-
   * See 1993 Edition . . . .
Phillips, Robert J.   Am 20C
   W&G/Pa 9x14 The Junk Collector Chr 5/93 460
Phillips, S. George   Am -1965
   O/B 25x30 Beachscape Ald 9/92 2,000
   O/C 24x28 November Day Ald 5/93 1,400
   O/C 20x30 Ducks Flying Over Lake Ald 9/92 850
Phillips, Thomas   Br 1770-1845
   * See 1993 Edition . . . .
Phillips, W. E.
   * See 1993 Edition . . . .
Phillips, Walter Joseph   Can 1884-1963
   * See 1993 Edition . . . .
Philpot, Glyn   Br 1884-1937
   * See 1992 Edition . . . .
Philppeau, Karel Frans   Dut 1825-1897
   * See 1991 Edition . . . .
Phippen, George   Am 1916-1966
   O/C 24x36 Headed for the Trap Chr 9/92 4,400
   O/C 25x30 Brahman Bull Eld 4/93 350
Piacenza, Armodio   It 20C
   O/Pn 20x16 3 Oils 1964 Hnd 12/92 1,300
Piazzetta, Giovanni Battista   It 1683-1754
   K/Pa 16x12 Allegory Reign Pope Benedict XIV Chr 1/93 . . 12,100
Piazzoni, Gottardo   Am 1872-1945
   * See 1993 Edition . . . .
Picabia, Francis   Fr 1878-1953
   O/C 26x32 L'Eglise De Montigny Sby 5/93 112,500
   G/Pa/B 21x17 Composition Sby 5/93 46,000
   W,K&Pe/Pa 26x20 Visages Chr 11/92 41,800
   I,Pl&Pe/Pa 9x11 Sirenes Sby 5/93 10,350
   C/Pa 17x13 Model Sby 2/93 2,185
Picabia, Marie   Fr 20C
   G/Pa 13x18 Still Life with Trout 1955 Fre 4/93 325
Picart, Bernard   1673-1733
   K/Pa 10x16 A Reclining Nude 1730 Chr 1/93 6,050
Picasso, Pablo   Spa 1881-1973
   O/C 36x29 Femme Dans Un Fauteuil 32 Sby 11/92 . . . . . 2.86M
   O/C/Pn 32x26 Guitare et journal Chr 11/92 . . . . 2.2M
   O/B 20x13 Danseuse Espagnole Chr 11/92 . . . . 1.32M
   O/C 65x38 Homme a la Pipe 68 Sby 11/92 . . . . 1.21M
   O/C 20x16 Iris Jaunes 1901 Chr 11/92 935,000
   O/C 39x32 Femme Assise 1943 Chr 11/92 825,000

O/Pn 5x9 La Conversation 1900 Chr 11/92   462,000
O/Pn 38x51 Le Peintre et Son Modele 1964 Chr 11/92 . .   385,000
O/C 15x19 Le peintre et son modele 65 Chr 11/92   264,000
Pe&S/Pa 14x9 Femme Dubout Tenant Sby 11/92   220,000
O/C 8x11 Verre, paquet de tabac Chr 11/92   137,500
W&G/Pa/B 13x10 Arlequin a le Guitare 1916 Sby 11/92 .   121,000
l/Pa 11x16 Le Peintre et Son Modele 70 Sby 5/93   79,500
Y&Pe/B 11x9 Tete 71 Chr 11/92   77,000
Pe/Pa 12x9 Tete de femme Chr 11/92   66,000
O/Pn 6x9 Le port de Malaga Chr 11/92   61,600
Pl/Pa 14x10 Femme nue assise 25 Chr 11/92   46,200
Pl/Pa 14x10 Etude Pour Les Trois Graces Sby 5/93   43,125
Pe/Pa 10x8 Jeune Femme Au Panier 98 Sby 5/93   43,125
O/Pa 4x5 Portrait l'oncle Baldomers Chiara Chr 11/92 . . .   35,200
O/Pa 4x5 Nature Morte Chr 11/92   33,000
Y,Fp&l/Pa 7x7 Mousquetaire 68 Sby 5/93   26,450
O/Por 15 dia Vinos del Rivero 94 Chr 11/92   24,200
l/Pa 8x12 Etude Pour Un Journal: Double Sby 5/93   24,150
Fp/Pa 11x8 Tete d'homme 69 Chr 10/92   15,400
Y/Pa 10x8 Tete de Singe and L'Oiseau: Pair Sby 5/93 . . .   10,350
Pl/Pa 6x9 La Victorieuse 55 Sby 10/92   8,800
Y/Pa 10x8 Singe Sby 5/93   8,050
Pl/Pa 6x10 La Chevre 53 Chr 10/92   6,050
Fp/Pa 9x7 Visage 66 Sby 2/93   5,175
Bp&MM/Pa 7x5 Santa Claus 61 Chr 11/92   4,400
Pl/Pa 14x10 L'Oeil 1954 Chr 5/93   4,370

Picci, Pio
O/C 20x15 Woman with Flowers and Man Ald 3/93   4,300

Piccillo, Joseph   Am 20C
H&C/Pa 35x29 Study of a Horse 1981 But 4/93   977

Pichette, James   Fr 1920-
* See 1992 Edition . . . .

Pichler, Adolf   Hun 1835-1905
* See 1991 Edition . . . .

Pichot, Emile Jules   Fr 1857-
* See 1993 Edition . . . .

Pichot, Ramon   Spa 1925-
O/C 33x26 Chica en Amarillo Doy 5/93   2,750

Picken, George   Am 1898-
W/Pa 17x11 Cabbage Pickers Mys 3/93   110

Pickenoy, Nicolas Elias   Dut 1590-1656
* See 1992 Edition . . . .

Pickens, Lucien Alton   Am 1917-
T/M 13x9 Child Waving Flag 45 Sby 9/92   1,760

Pickering, Bernard   Can 1903-
O/B 12x10 Autumn 1928 Sbt 5/93   396

Pickering, J. L.   Am 19C
* See 1992 Edition . . . .

Pickersgill, Frederick Richard   Br 1820-1900
* See 1990 Edition . . . .

Pickhardt, Carl E. (Jr.)   Am 1908-
O/C 32x21 Nightclub Sby 9/92   2,750

Picknell, William Lamb   Am 1854-1897
O/C 28x36 Annisquam Landscape Sby 5/93   20,700

Picot, Francois Edouard   Fr 1786-1868
* See 1990 Edition . . . .

Picou, Henri Pierre   Fr 1824-1895
O/C 40x30 Ronde de Mai 1873 Sby 10/92   27,500
O/C 24x32 Venus Sby 10/92   27,500
O/C 32x24 At the Fountain 1880 Sby 10/92   24,200
O/C 24x32 Clipping Cupid's Wings Sby 2/93   11,213
O/C 24x31 The Fortune Teller 1872 But 11/92   3,025

Pieler, Franz Xaver   Aus 1879-1952
O/Pn 31x23 Tulips, Wild Roses, Dahlias: Pair Sby 2/93 . . .   40,250

Pierce, Charles Franklin   Am 1844-1920
O/C 14x18 Autumn Landscape with Cows Skn 5/93   4,675
MM/C 11x15 Winter in New Hampshire Brd 2/93   1,430

Pierce, Lucy   Am 1887-1974
* See 1993 Edition . . . .

Pierre, Andre   Hai 20C
* See 1992 Edition . . . .

Pierre, Jean-Baptiste-Marie   Fr 1713-1789
O/C 13x16 Sculptor's Studio 1756 Sby 5/93   189,500

Pierre, Laureus   Hai 20C
* See 1992 Edition . . . .

Pieters, Evert   Dut 1856-1932
O/C 48x36 The Sewing Lesson Sby 10/92   20,900
O/C 43x35 Maternite Sby 5/93   10,638
O/C 36x48 Mother and Child at Seashore But 5/93   9,200

Pietsch, Ed   19C
O/B 20x15 Cabins in Mountain Landscape Slo 4/93   100

Piette, Ludovic   Fr 1826-1877
* See 1990 Edition . . . .

Piffard, Harold Hume   Br a 1895-1899
* See 1990 Edition . . . .

Pignon, Edouard   Fr 1905-
O/C 29x24 La Femme en Bleu 1945 Sby 10/92   17,600
O/C 37x29 La Moisson a Pilacciano 58 Sby 6/93   9,200
O/B 14x24 Abstract Composition 54 Sby 2/93   2,875
l,C&W/Pa 15x22 Abstract Figural '42 Slo 4/93   2,750
W/Pa 12x15 Study of Men Working 1952 Slo 4/93   1,400

Pignoni, Simone   1614-1698
O/C 46x60 Andromeda Sby 1/93   19,550

Pignoux   Fr 19C
* See 1992 Edition . . . .

Pigott, Marjorie   Can 1904-1990
W/Pa 22x14 June Blossoms Sbt 5/93   660
W/Pa 21x20 Hazy Day Sbt 5/93   484
W/Pa 21x29 Whispering Pines Sbt 5/93   484
W/Pa 17x23 Wintry Morning 1967 Sbt 11/92   484

Piguet, Rodolphe   Sws 1840-1915
* See 1992 Edition . . . .

Pihnnero, H.   It 19C
* See 1992 Edition . . . .

Pike, John   Am 1911-1979
W&G/Pa 38x29 Rakam's World Wes 10/92   660

Pike, William   Br 1846-1908
W/Pa 13x10 Hawking; Stepping Stone: Pair 87 But 11/92 . . .   825

Piletti, Arturo   It 20C
O/B 20x17 Boy with Instrument Slo 4/93   175

Pillement, Jean   Fr 1728-1808
O/C 24x34 Tagus, Portugal w/Ships: Pair 1790 Sby 5/93 .   167,500

Pilot, Robert Wakeham   Can 1898-1967
O/C 13x17 View of Kingston from Fort Henry Sbt 5/93 . . .   7,260
O/C 18x24 Harbour Scene, Newfoundland Sbt 5/93   6,600
O/C 18x22 Early Spring, Val Morin '46 Sbt 5/93   6,440
O/C 20x24 Melting Snow '38 Sbt 5/93   5,280
O/B 8x11 Skating Rink, Porte St. Louis 1964 Sbt 11/92 . .   3,520
O/Pn 8x11 Ottawa River Seigneury Club 1936 Sbt 11/92 . .   1,980
O/Pn 5x7 Winter Harbour Scene Sbt 11/92   1,848
Pe/Pa 8x10 Street Scene, Montreal '21 Sbt 5/93   660

Pils, Isidore Alexandre August   Fr 1813-1875
K/Pa 12x18 Military Studies: Four Chr 5/93   920
K/Pa 13x14 Study of Hands; Arm: (2) Chr 10/92   605

Pilters, Joseph   Ger 1877-1957
O/C 18x23 The Lily Pond Sby 2/93   14,950

Piltz, Otto   Ger 1846-1910
* See 1991 Edition . . . .

Pimentel, Rodrigo Ramirez   Mex 1945-
* See 1992 Edition . . . .

Pinal, Ferdinand   Fr 1881-1958
* See 1992 Edition . . . .

Pincemin, Jean-Pierre   1944-
* See 1993 Edition . . . .

Pinchart, Emile Auguste   Fr 1842-1930
O/C 32x24 The Rendezvous Chr 10/92   1,650

Pinchon, Jean Antoine   Fr 1772-1850
* See 1992 Edition . . . .

Pinchon, Robert Antoine   Fr 1886-1943
O/C 26x32 Nature Morte au Service a Cafe Chr 2/93   7,150

Pinel, Gustave Nicolas   Fr 1842-1896
* See 1990 Edition . . . .

Pinelli, Bartolomeo   It 1781-1835
* See 1992 Edition . . . .

Pinggera, H.   Con 19C
O/C 23x31 Birthplace Friedrich von Schiller Hnd 9/92   1,100

Pingret, Edouard Henri T. Fr 1788-1875
O/C 39x32 Autorretrato 1852 Sby 5/93 85,000
Pinqqera, H. Con 19C
* See 1993 Edition . . . .
Pinto, Alberto Por 19C
* See 1993 Edition . . . .
Pinto, Angelo Am 1908-
O/C 12x15 Trapeze Performer '34 Lou 3/93 1,000
Piola, Domenico It 1627-1703
* See 1993 Edition . . . .
Piot, Adolphe Fr 1850-1910
O/C 26x20 Young Beauty with Roses Sby 5/93 8,913
O/C 18x15 Girl with a Red Shawl Chr 10/92 6,600
P/Pn 18x15 June Chr 5/93 1,725
Piotrowski, Antoni Pol 1853-1924
* See 1990 Edition . . . .
Piper, Jane Am -1992
O/B 5x10 Arrangement of Fruit Fre 4/93 500
Piper, John Br 1903-1992
G&Pl/Pa 18x21 Shankin, Isle of Wight Eld 8/93 1,760
Pipo, Emanuel Ruiz Spa 1928-
O/M 14x11 Pair of Paintings '66 Chr 5/93 1,840
Pippel, Otto Ger 1878-1960
O/C 29x39 Am Bade Chr 5/93 3,450
Pippin, Horace Am 1888-1946
* See 1990 Edition . . . .
Pirie, George Br 1863-1946
* See 1991 Edition . . . .
Pisa, Alberto It 1864-1936
W/Pa 13x19 The Flower Cart Fre 10/92 3,400
Pissarro, Camille Fr 1830-1903
O/C 21x26 Soleil Couchant au Valhermeil 1880 Chr 11/92 . 1.045M
O/C 21x26 Stamford Brook Common 1897 Chr 11/92 . . 770,000
O/C 18x15 Henri IV, Arbres en Fleurs 1901 Sby 5/93 . . 189,500
G/S 11x22 Paysage Avec Deux Paysannes Sby 11/92 . . . 110,000
O/C 9x11 Vue des bassins 1902 Chr 11/92 110,000
P/Pa/B 20x13 Paysan au sarrau bleu Chr 11/92 66,000
P/Pa 12x9 Le Pre a Eragny Sby 11/92 41,250
W&Pe/Pa/B 7x10 Regents Park Sby 11/92 38,500
Pt/Cer 8x8 La recolte des pommes de terre Chr 10/92 . . . 22,000
W&Pe/Pa 7x5 Portobello Road Sby 11/92 17,600
H/Pa 14x7 Rio De Maiquetia Sby 5/93 17,250
C&K/Pa 6x9 La Rue St. Vincent, Montmartre 1860 Sby 5/93 16,100
Y/Pa 9x7 Causerie Dans Les Champs Sby 11/92 12,650
Y/Pa 9x7 Paysanne au Marche Sby 11/92 11,550
Pl&S/Pa 5x4 Paysanne Versant Une Cuvette Sby 2/93 9,775
Pe&W/Pa 8x6 Paysanne Gardant Des Cochons Sby 10/92 . . 9,350
Pe&W/Pa 6x4 Marche a la Volaille Sby 10/92 8,250
Pl&Pe/Pa 6x4 Deux Pissarro Sby 2/93 7,188
Pe/Pa 9x7 Personnages Causant Sby 10/92 6,600
I/Pa 7x11 Feuille D'Etudes Sby 10/92 4,400
C&S/Pa 6x4 Paysanne Sby 10/92 4,125
S&Pe/Pa 6x4 Peasants Walking Through Village Sby 2/93 . . 3,335
Pe/Pa 11x15 Etude d'arbre Chr 10/92 3,300
C/Pa 3x6 Giverny, Rue Des Arguillieres Sby 6/93 2,530
Pe/Pa 10x6 Scene De Village Sby 10/92 2,200
K/Pa 7x9 Trois Paysannes Chr 11/92 1,430
Pe/Pa 8x5 Danseuse Javanaise Sby 10/92 990
C/Pa 4x7 Landscapes: Two Drawings Sby 10/92 880
Pe/Pa 9x10 Three Donkeys Hnz 5/93 725
Pissarro, H. Claude Fr 1935-
O/C 18x22 Entree du village Chr 11/92 10,450
O/C 22x26 L'Allee de Sully Sby 2/93 10,063
O/C 18x22 Yachts a Deauville Sby 2/93 8,625
O/C 20x24 Felicie Avec Ses Moutons Sby 2/93 8,050
O/C 21x29 Le Port de Vannes Chr 5/93 8,050
O/C 22x26 Pont des St. Peres, Bonjour Doy 5/93 7,975
O/C 22x26 La Petite Kalia et sa Mere Doy 11/92 7,700
O/C 26x32 Le Champ-Placy Chr 5/93 7,475
O/C 20x24 Le Pain de Sucre Sby 6/93 7,475
O/C 20x24 La Normandie sous la Neige Chr 11/92 7,150
O/C 20x24 Varangeville Sby 6/93 6,900
O/C 21x26 Le Pont de Montaubon Sby 10/92 6,875
O/C 26x32 Le Mont St. Michel Chr 2/93 6,600
Pe/Pa 8x6 Man Working Doy 5/93 6,600

O/C 20x24 Le Bouquet Orange Sby 2/93 6,325
O/C 26x32 Le Clocher d'Exmes pres d'Argentan Chr 5/93 . . 5,750
O/C 21x26 Le Grand Poirier Du Mesnil Sby 6/93 5,750
O/C 18x22 La Barque Chr 11/92 5,500
O/C 19x22 La Plaine Du Cher A Blere Dum 12/92 5,500
O/C 22x26 Celine et Estelle au Verger Sby 10/92 5,225
O/C 18x22 Etude Pour L'Etoile Doy 11/92 5,225
O/C 20x24 Le Parc D'Urville 07 Sby 6/93 5,175
O/C 20x24 Le bouquet d'orchidees Chr 11/92 4,400
O/C 18x22 Le Tramway Jaune Sby 10/92 4,400
O/C 21x26 Les Hauts Vents en Hiver Doy 5/93 4,400
O/C 18x22 Le Verger de Tracy Sby 10/92 4,070
P/Pa 14x19 Avenue a Bruxelles Doy 11/92 3,080
O/C 13x16 Moisson a la Faurie Sby 10/92 3,080
P/Pa 14x19 Champs Elysee Doy 11/92 2,860
P/Pa 15x20 La route de Belleme Chr 11/92 2,640
K/Pa 10x15 Le Village du Petit-Autun Chr 2/93 2,420
P/Pa 14x20 Neige a Criqueville-Saint-Leger Chr 11/92 2,200
P/Pa 14x20 Les Bateaux Chr 11/92 1,980
O/C 8x10 Beninze Chr 2/93 1,760
O/C 8x10 Notre Dame Chr 2/93 1,760
O/C 8x10 Le Petite du Pere de Michele Nadeau Chr 5/93 . . 1,380
Pissarro, Lucien Fr 1863-1944
* See 1992 Edition . . . .
Pissarro, Paul Emile Fr 1884-1972
O/C 21x26 La Saulee du Roule Sby 2/93 4,600
P/Pa 8x11 L'Ete Doy 11/92 2,200
P/Pa 8x11 Paysage a Normandie Doy 11/92 2,200
P/Pa 8x12 Landscape Sby 6/93 1,840
O/C 15x18 Landscape with Stream Lou 12/92 1,600
O/B 15x18 Trees Sby 6/93 920
W&K/Pa 8x11 Two Watercolors Chr 11/92 715
Pissis, Amaro Fr a 1810-1850
* See 1993 Edition . . . .
Pistoletto, Michelangelo It 1933-
* See 1992 Edition . . . .
Pitt, William Br a 1853-1890
* See 1993 Edition . . . .
Pittman, Hobson Am 1899-1972
O/C 31x25 The Poet Sby 3/93 2,645
O/B 24x45 Clare in the Azalea Garden But 12/92 2,200
Pittoni, Giovanni Battista It 1687-1767
* See 1993 Edition . . . .
Pitz, Henry Clarence Am 1895-1976
W/Pa 20x30 The Ravine 1965 Yng 2/93 350
C/Pa 22x14 Courtier and Monk Reading Ih 11/92 175
W/Pa 19x30 The Ravine Mys 12/92 138
Pla Y Gallardo, Cecilio Spa 1860-
* See 1993 Edition . . . .
Pla Y Rubio, Alberto Spa 1867-
* See 1992 Edition . . . .
Planas, Juan Battle Spa 1911-1966
* See 1993 Edition . . . .
Planson, Andre Fr 1898-
* See 1993 Edition . . . .
Plaschke, Moriz Ger 1818-1888
O/C 16x14 Children Playing in Field Sby 1/93 2,415
Plaskett, Joseph Francis Can 1918-
P/Pa 20x26 Fields and Mountains, Mexico 1978 Sbt 5/93 . . . 396
Plassan, Antoine Emile Fr 1817-1903
O/Pn 11x8 Woman Reading and Child But 11/92 4,400
Plathner, Hermann Ger 1831-1902
* See 1993 Edition . . . .
Platt, Charles Adams Am 1861-1933
O/C 20x25 A Dutch River Sby 3/93 9,200
Plauzeau, Alfred Fr 1875-1918
O/C 22x26 Crossing the Stream Fre 10/92 2,300
Player, William H. Br a 1858-1884
* See 1993 Edition . . . .
Pleissner, Ogden Minton Am 1905-1983
O/C 23x24 Evening on the River Chr 3/93 41,400
W&Pe/Pa 15x22 Got One Chr 3/93 20,700
W/Pa 16x23 Gnarled Juniper Sby 12/92 11,000
W/Pa 9x12 Woodcock Shooting Sby 3/93 10,063
W&G/Pa 12x15 Local Stores of Bonneville, WY But 12/92 . . 4,400

Plisson, Henri   Fr 1908-
O/C 30x40 La Grande Jetee Sby 10/92   20,900
Ploquin, Gaston   Fr 20C
   * See 1990 Edition . . . .
Plumb, Henry Grant   Am 1847-1936
O/B 9x11 Bank of the Chenango (2) Mys 3/93   330
Plummer, Elmer G.   Am 1910-1987
W/Pa 15x23 Rail Cars in Eucalyptus Landscape Mor 2/93 . . .   750
Plummer, S. J.
O/M Size? Two Men on Horses Eld 8/93   55
Plummer, William H.   Am 19C
O/C 12x20 Fruit & Wine Bottle Mys 3/93   110
Plumot, Andre   Bel 1829-1906
O/C 32x27 The Donkey Ride 1876 Sby 1/93   12,075
O/C 24x36 Cattle, Sheep, Goat Resting 1869 Chr 10/92 . . .   8,250
Podchernikoff, Alexis M.   Am 1886-1933
O/C 40x30 Twilight 1926 But 6/93   4,312
O/M 10x12 Eucalyptus Landscape Mor 6/93   4,125
O/C 33x26 Cattle Grazing Mt. Tamalpais 1933 But 3/93 . . .   3,850
O/M 10x12 Cattle Watering Mor 6/93   2,090
O/C 30x40 Path Through a Landscape But 3/93   1,980
O/C 20x30 Woman in Pastoral Landscape But 3/93   1,870
O/C 28x22 Eucalyptus Mor 2/93   1,700
O/Pn 8x11 Sand Dunes But 6/93   1,495
O/C 20x24 Figures in Wooded Landscape Mor 2/93   1,300
O/C 16x24 Landscape Mor 2/93   1,100
O/B 9x12 Carmel Mission-Near Monterey Mor 2/93   1,000
O/C 20x28 Figures & Cattle Wooded Landscape Mor 6/93 . .   990
O/M 12x14 Cows in Landscape Mor 11/92   950
O/Pn 6x8 Flowered Hillside Mor 2/93   700
O/C 14x18 Mountain Landscape Wlf 9/92   700
O/B 8x10 Spring Landscape Wlf 9/92   700
O/Pn 6x9 Cabin in Landscape Mor 11/92   650
O/Pn 9x10 Landscape Mor 11/92   550
O/Cb 9x12 Coastal Mor 11/92   475
Poerson, Charles   Dut 1653-1725
   * See 1990 Edition . . . .
Poggioli, Marcel Dominique   Fr 1882-
   * See 1992 Edition . . . .
Poilpot, Theophile & Du Paty,L   Fr 1848-1915
   * See 1993 Edition . . . .
Poiret, Paul   Fr -1844
   * See 1991 Edition . . . .
Poirier, Anne and Patrick
   * See 1992 Edition . . . .
Poisson, Louverature   Hai 1914-1985
O/M 31x25 Mambo Conducting Ceremony Sby 5/93   5,175
O/C/B 20x16 Voodoo 1958 But 4/93   805
Poitevin, Auguste Flavien   Fr 19C
   * See 1990 Edition . . . .
Pokitonov, Ivan   Rus 1851-1924
O/Pn 7x11 Horseman in a Landscape 89 Chr 10/92   8,800
Poleo, Hector   Ven 1918-
Cs/C 29x36 Prelude 1966 Chr 11/92   52,800
Cs/C 15x18 La Machine Calcinee 1971 Chr 11/92   18,700
Poliakoff, Serge   Fr 1906-1969
O/C 29x24 H.S.T. Composition Sby 2/93   74,000
G/Pa 19x25 Untitled Chr 11/92   25,300
Polidori, Giancarlo   It 20C
W/Pa 21x14 Shoemaker at Work But 11/92   1,210
Polke, Sigmar   Ger 1941-
A&O 71x59 Untitled (Sommerbilder I, II, III) Sby 5/93 . . .   453,500
O&Pt/C 102x79 Untitled (Heads at Skylight) Sby 11/92 . .   176,000
O&Ph 24x37 Quetta 74 74 Chr 11/92   84,700
A&Pt/F 35x89 Untitled Sby 5/93   74,000
O,Sd&MM/L 79x103 Untitled 90 Chr 11/92   66,000
G,W&E/Pa 39x27 Untitled Chr 11/92   38,500
MM 12x17 Uri Geller Empfangt Sby 5/93   32,200
A&MM/Pa 25x33 Untitled 71 Sby 5/93   31,625
Pollak, August   Aus 1838-
   * See 1992 Edition . . . .
Pollard, James   Br 1792-1867
   * See 1990 Edition . . . .

Pollentine, Alfred   Br a 1861-1880
O/C 19x30 Canal in Venice Sby 1/93   1,380
O/C/B 12x20 View of the Rialto Bridge, Venice Chr 2/93   880
Pollet, Jean   Fr 1929-
O/C 29x21 Nature Morte aux Champignons Lou 3/93   450
Pollet, Victor Florence   Fr 1811-1882
   * See 1993 Edition . . . .
Pollock, Jackson   Am 1912-1956
O&E/Pa/B/C 23x31 #6, 1948: Blue, Red, Yellow Chr 11/92 .   1.98M
O&E/C/M 17x9 Untitled 1947 Chr 11/92   275,000
Polo, Roberto
   * See 1993 Edition . . . .
Pomeroy, Florence   Am 1889-
O/B 19x24 Still Life Lou 9/92   500
O/C 18x24 Circus Performer Lou 9/92   300
O/C 24x20 Still Life Lou 12/92   300
Ponce De Leon, Fidelio   Cub 1895-1949
O/C 44x38 Despues del Ensayo Chr 11/92   82,500
Pondel, Friedrich   Ger 1830-
O/Pn 8x6 Portrait Young Woman Skn 11/92   715
Ponsen, Tunis   Am 1891-1968
O/C 26x30 Landscape at Edgebrook Hnd 10/92   1,800
O/Cb 12x15 Boats on a Lake Mor 6/93   440
Pont, A.   Fr 20C
Y/Pa 9x6 Five Color Crayon Drawings Hnd 5/93   300
Pontormo   It 1494-1556
   * See 1990 Edition . . . .
Pooke, Marion Louise   Am 20C
O/C 21x17 Young Lady Dum 6/93   550
O/C 20x16 Young Lady Dum 6/93   500
Poole, A.   Br 20C
O/C 30x22 Spring Landscape Fre 4/93   500
Poole, Burnell   Br 20C
O/C 20x17 J. P. Morgan's Yacht "Graviling" 1922 Sby 6/93 .   3,450
Poole, Eugene Alonzo   Am 1841-1912
O/C 22x30 Grazing in the Meadow 1912 But 12/92   825
Poole, Horatio Nelson   Am 1884-1949
O/C 37x43 Castaic Lake 1927 But 3/93   3,300
Poole, Miss Narcissa   Am 19C
C&K/Pa 15x22 View on the Ohio 1851 Slo 7/93   375
Poole, Paul Falconer   Br 1807-1879
O/Pn 13x10 Pensive Moment 1865 Chr 2/93   1,650
Poons, Larry   Am 1937-
A/C 41x25 Little Cobalt 1972 Sby 10/92   8,250
A/C 118x39 Broken Summer 69 Sby 5/93   7,475
Poor, Henry Varnum   Am 1888-1970
O/C 35x37 Self Portrait with Family 1914 But 6/93   1,380
O/C 24x20 Black Walnut Tree Lou 3/93   1,000
O/C/Pn 8x12 Still Life with Fruit and Nuts Skn 3/93   275
Poore, Henry Rankin   Am 1859-1940
O/C 20x30 Horses Hauling Logs Mys 12/92   2,970
O/C 28x36 The Long Day Sby 3/93   1,265
O/C 14x20 Cow in a Winter Landscape Fre 10/92   850
O/B 12x16 Horse and Carriage Ald 9/92   550
Pope, Alexander   Am 1849-1924
O/C 20x45 Thanksgiving Still Life 83 Doy 11/92   2,420
O/C 10x8 Portrait of a Spaniel 1890 Skn 9/92   1,430
O/C 16x20 Jumping Small Mouth Bass Skn 3/93   1,045
Pope, Gustav   Br a 1852-1895
   * See 1991 Edition . . . .
Pope, Thomas Benjamin   Am -1891
   * See 1992 Edition . . . .
Popelin, Gustave Leon Antoine   Fr 1859-
   * See 1991 Edition . . . .
Popova, Liubov   Rus 1889-1924
Y/Pa 5x8 Linear Composition 5 x 5 = 25 Sby 6/93   3,738
Popovich, Milosh
O/C 25x37 Ducks 32 Dum 9/92   500
Poray, Stanislaus   Am 1888-1948
   * See 1993 Edition . . . .
Porcellis, Jan   Dut 1584-1632
O/Pn 15x18 Dutch Shipping Sby 1/93   46,000
Porcellis, Julius   Dut 1609-1645
O/C 27x37 Dutch Shipping in Stormy Sea 1639 Chr 5/93 .   11,500

Porpora, Paolo It 1617-1683
* See 1993 Edition . . . .
Portaels, Jean Francois Bel 1818-1895
* See 1992 Edition . . . .
Porter, Charles Ethan Am 1850-1923
O/C 20x24 Still Life Fruit, Nuts and Vessel Sby 9/92 3,410
Porter, Fairfield Am 1907-1975
O/C 60x48 July 1970 Brd 2/93 83,600
O/C 36x36 Big House, Great Spruce Head Chr 5/93 66,300
O/C 24x28 South Meadow, Afternoon 1970 Brd 8/93 50,600
W/Pa 22x30 Interior, Looking Out Brd 8/93 29,700
O/C 19x21 Still Life on a Mirror 66 Brd 8/93 26,400
O/Pn 18x22 Late Afternoon, Winter 1974 Sby 5/93 24,150
W/Pa 16x20 The Trail 1974 Brd 8/93 7,975
W/Pa 12x16 View Toward Peaks Island 69 Brd 8/93 3,850
W/Pa 16x12 Wildflowers in the Rocks 75 Brd 8/93 3,850
Porter, John J. Am a 1850-
* See 1993 Edition . . . .
Porter, Katherine Am 1941-
O/C 64x95 Southern Persia II 1970 Chr 10/92 5,500
A/C 73x132 Evening of the Day Chr 5/93 2,300
Porter, Maud Br a 1888-1908
O/C 20x16 The Winning Hand 1897 Sby 10/92 3,850
Portielje, Edward Antoon Bel 1861-1949
* See 1993 Edition . . . .
Portielje, Gerard Bel 1856-1929
O/C 18x23 The Card Game 1896 Sby 10/92 44,000
O/C 20x27 A Rainy Day Chr 10/92 17,600
O/Pn 16x22 Card Playing in the Tavern 1879 Sby 10/92 . . 16,500
O/Pn 11x14 Over Easy Doy 5/93 11,000
O/B 16x13 Mother and Daughter Dum 3/93 1,250
Portielje, Jan Frederik Pieter Dut 1829-1895
O/C 30x23 Playtime Sby 1/93 10,350
O/Pn 12x9 A Spanish Beauty Sby 5/93 6,325
Portinari, Candido Brz 1903-1962
O/C 16x13 Natureza Morta com Flores 1941 Chr 11/92 . . . 26,400
Portocarrero, Rene Cub 1912-
T&W/Pa 20x15 Interior del Cerro 43 Sby 11/92 22,000
H,G&O/Pa 23x29 Danza 5/93 Sby 5/93 20,700
O/C 24x20 Catedral 62 Chr 11/92 17,600
O/C 28x18 Catedral 66 Chr 11/92 17,600
P/Pa 23x15 Figuras Danzantes 48 Chr 11/92 8,250
P/Pa 20x24 Arte Abstracto 1948 Sby 11/92 7,700
O&P/C 20x16 Mujeres 48 Sby 6/93 6,900
O/C 27x20 Catedral 63 Chr 11/92 6,600
Br&I/Pa 14x11 Figuras Para Una Mitologia (2) 43 Sby 5/93 . 5,175
P/Pa 16x18 Figura con Cetro 1948 Sby 11/92 4,675
O/Pa/M 12x19 Ciudad 1954 Sby 5/93 3,450
W/Pa 11x15 Flores 1943 Chr 11/92 2,970
W,G&I/Pa 15x11 Composicion Abstracta 1952 Sby 11/92 . . 2,420
Posen, Steven Am 1939-
* See 1991 Edition . . . .
Possart, Felix Ger 1877-1928
O/C 32x24 Market Scene, Alexandria But 11/92 3,300
Possner, Hugo Am a 20C1920-1929
O/Cb 11x16 Flowered Hillside 1926 Mor 2/93 125
Post, Frans Dut 1612-1680
* See 1993 Edition . . . .
Post, George Booth Am 1906-
W/Pa 18x23 Wharfs Mor 6/93 1,210
W/Pa 18x23 House on Hill-San Francisco Mor 6/93 660
W/Pa 18x23 Ships in Harbor Mor 6/93 550
Post, Pieter Jansz Dut 1608-1669
* See 1992 Edition . . . .
Post, William Merritt Am 1856-1935
O/C 16x24 The Walk Home Chr 3/93 3,680
O/C 28x36 Autumn in the Hills Ald 9/92 3,250
O/C 25x30 Early Autumn Ald 9/92 1,900
O/C 25x30 Sun has Gone to Rest Sel 12/92 1,600
O/Pa/C 20x30 Autumn Landscape with Cows Lou 12/92 . . 1,200
O/C 20x16 Fall Landscape Lou 6/93 1,100
Postiglione, Salvatore It 1861-1906
O/C 39x19 Courting Scene Mys 3/93 1,980

Pothast, Bernard Dut 1882-1966
O/C 48x28 Mother and Children Sby 5/93 37,375
O/C 30x26 Blowing Bubbles Chr 10/92 26,400
O/C 25x30 Motherhood Doy 11/92 18,700
O/C 26x31 Morning with the Children Chr 2/93 17,600
Pott, Laslett John Br 1837-1898
* See 1992 Edition . . . .
Potter, Mark Am 20C
T/Pa 23x41 Roxbury Window 1961 Eld 4/93 275
Potter, Philip Am 19C
O/C 21x36 Walk to Church in Mountains Wlf 4/93 1,700
Potter, W. C.
* See 1993 Edition . . . .
Potthast, Edward Henry Am 1857-1927
O/B 12x16 Children at Play on the Beach Chr 12/92 115,500
O/C 24x30 At the Beach Chr 5/93 85,000
O/B 12x16 Landscape by the Shore Sby 12/92 29,700
O/C 12x16 Waiting for Sunrise, Yonkers Chr 12/92 15,400
O/B 16x12 The Bather Chr 5/93 11,500
O/C 12x16 Gloucester Harbor Chr 3/93 7,475
O/B 12x16 Coastal Cliffs Brd 2/93 2,420
W&G/B 9x15 Rough Sea Wlf 9/92 500
Potucek, Eva Am 20C
* See 1992 Edition . . . .
Pougny, Jean Fr 1894-1956
* See 1992 Edition . . . .
Pousette-Dart, Richard Am 1916-
W&I/Pa 18x12 Composition #3 Sby 10/92 16,500
A/M 42x48 Untitled 1950 Skn 11/92 8,250
Poussin, Etienne De Lavalle 1733-1793
K,PI&S/Pa 6x9 David Ordains Priests Chr 1/93 440
Poveda, Carlos 1940-
* See 1990 Edition . . . .
Powell, Ace Am 1912-1978
* See 1991 Edition . . . .
Powell, Arthur James Emery Am 1864-1956
O/C 29x41 Clipper Ship at Full Sail Sby 3/93 2,300
Powell, Charles Martin Br -1824
* See 1990 Edition . . . .
Powell, Lucien Whiting Am 1846-1930
O/C 30x40 The Grand Canyon 1909 Wes 10/92 5,060
O/C 20x20 Venetian View 1905 Slo 4/93 3,750
O/C 24x36 View of Grand Canal, Venice Chr 12/92 1,650
W/B 17x26 Sunset Over the Coliseum 1910 Wes 3/93 . . . 660
W/Pa 17x28 Nile Boats 1910 Wes 12/92 385
W/Pa 20x30 Forest Stream 1905 Yng 5/93 375
Powell, William E. Br 1878-
W/Pa 10x13 Tower Bridge, London 26 Brd 8/93 1,760
Pradilla Y Ortiz, Francisco Spa 1848-1921
O/C/Pn 4x7 Summer's Day at the Beach Chr 10/92 8,800
Prampolini, Enrico It 1894-1956
MM/B 22x29 Magic of the Stratosphere But 10/92 16,500
Pratella, Attilio It 1856-1932
O/Pn 9x14 Neapolitan Fishing Scene Wes 12/92 20,900
O/Pn 9x14 Day at the Beach Chr 2/93 13,200
O/Pn 9x13 Rainy Street Scene, Paris But 11/92 8,800
O/Pn 9x14 Fisherfolk on a Quay Chr 10/92 6,600
O/Pn 9x14 A Neapolitan Market Chr 10/92 4,400
O/Pn 9x14 Hauling in the Nets Doy 5/93 4,400
O/Pn 9x14 Hauling in the Nets Chr 10/92 3,300
O/Pn 9x14 Preparing for the Day Doy 5/93 2,860
Pratella, Paolo It 1892-
* See 1992 Edition . . . .
Pratt, Henry Cheever Am 1803-1880
* See 1993 Edition . . . .
Pratt, Mary Frances Can 1935-
MM 20x26 Study of a Swan '90 Sbt 1/92 2,200
Pratt, William Br 1855-1897
O/C 27x40 Harvesters Resting 1930 Chr 5/93 7,475
Prax, Valentine Henriette 1899-1981
O/C 26x32 Still Life Ship, Sea Shell, Globe Sby 2/93 1,150
Preisler, Johann Justin Ger 1698-1771
Sg/Pa 5x4 Head of Medusa Hnd 3/93 250

Prell, Hermann   Ger 1854-1922
  * See 1990 Edition ....
Prell, Walter   Ger 1857-
  * See 1993 Edition ....
Prendergast, Charles   Am 1868-1948
  * See 1990 Edition ....
Prendergast, Maurice Brazil   Am 1859-1924
  W&Pe/Pa 13x22 May Day, Central Park Sby 12/92 418,000
  W&Pe/Pa 16x12 Old Mosaics, St. Marks, Venice Sby 12/92 269,500
  W&Pe/Pa 14x20 New England Beach Scene Chr 12/92 . . 200,000
  WGP&Pe/Pa 16x18 New England Village Sby 5/93 112,500
  W&Pe/Pa 15x12 Charles Street, Boston Sby 5/93 79,500
  W&Pe/Pa 11x8 The Dancers Sby 5/93 51,750
  W/Pa/B 9x12 On the Beach Chr 9/92 27,500
  W/Pa 10x14 Summer Day Sby 12/92 19,800
Prentice, Levi Wells   Am 1851-1935
  O/C 9x15 Still Life with Raspberries Chr 5/93 39,100
  O/C 12x10 Apples and Tree Trunk 1891 Chr 12/92 28,600
  O/C 12x18 Still Life Baskets of Plums Sby 3/93 18,400
  O/C 9x15 The Watering Hole Doy 11/92 2,750
  O/C 7x5 Lake Ald 9/92 155
  O/C 8x6 Creek Ald 9/92 120
Prescott, Victor L.   20C
  G/Pa 16x20 Venetian Canal 1922 Slo 5/93 300
Presser, Josef   Am 1907-
  * See 1992 Edition ....
Pressmane, Joseph   Fr 1904-1967
  O/C 18x15 La Cathedrale 55 Chr 5/93 2,300
Preston, Alice   Am 1888-
  O/B 11x9 Wedding; Sorceress: (2) Mys 12/92 1,760
Preston, James M.   Am 1874-1962
  O/C 18x24 Industry Landscape; View Town: Dbl Sby 3/93 . 1,035
Preston, Jessie Goodwin   Am 20C
  O/C 20x24 White House, Provincetown Brd 8/93 1,100
Preston, May Wilson   Am 1873-1949
  O/C 50x36 Woman With Fan Sby 3/93 17,250
Prestopino, Gregorio   Am 1907-1984
  O/C 36x25 Scrub Woman Sby 3/93 3,450
  O/M 8x6 Figure: Mother Sby 3/93 1,035
Preti, Mattia   It 1613-1699
  O/C 46x67 The Feast of Absalom Chr 1/93 49,500
  O/C 24x19 An Old Man, Woman and Boy Slo 10/92 25,300
Preusser, Robert Ormerod   Am 1919-
  O/C 34x48 Circular & Angular Equivalence 1941 Sby 9/92 . 8,800
  O/C 48x34 Dark & Light Equivalence 1941 Sby 9/92 ... 6,600
  I&Pe/B 18x14 Abstract Compositions: Two Sby 9/92 770
Prevost   Fr 19C
  O/C 24x20 Fisherman and Clamdigger Slo 5/93 850
Prevost, Jean-Louis (the Younger) 1760-1810
  O/C 16x13 Still Life Flowers in a Basket 1795 Sby 1/93 . . 57,500
Prevot   Fr 19C
  W/Pa 19x13 Forest Stream with Deer Hnd 3/93 130
Preyer, Emilie   Ger 1849-1930
  O/C 11x14 Still Life Pomegranate, Peach, Plum Chr 10/92 . 44,000
  O/C 8x10 Still Life Grapes and Peaches Sby 5/93 28,750
  O/C 9x12 Still Life Plums and Peaches 187* Sby 5/93 .. 18,400
  O/C 9x11 Still Life Peaches, Grapes, Walnut Chr 10/92 ... 16,500
Preyer, Johann Wilhelm   Ger 1803-1889
  * See 1992 Edition ....
Prezzi, Wilma Maria   Am 1915-1964
  * See 1993 Edition ....
Price, Addison Winchell   Can 1907-
  O/Pn 11x14 Autumn Trees Sbt 11/92 396
Price, Alan   Am 20C
  * See 1992 Edition ....
Price, Clayton S.   Am 1874-1950
  * See 1993 Edition ....
Price, Garrett   Am 1896-1979
  * See 1993 Edition ....
Price, George   Am 1901-
  Pl&W/Pa 11x15 Man Having Microphone Pulled Away Ih 5/93 850
Price, Norman M.   Am 1877-1951
  Pe/Pa 10x8 Women Watching Jester in Woods Ih 11/92 . 2,000

Price, William Henry   Am 1864-1940
  O/C 30x36 Crashing Waves But 6/93 1,150
Pricert, Raphael   20C
  O/C 24x29 Place Du Tertre Montmartre Sel 4/93 700
Prichard, G. Thompson   Am 1878-1962
  O/C 25x30 Arab Scene Dum 4/93 1,900
Prichett, Edward   Br 19C
  * See 1993 Edition ....
Priechenfried, Alois   Ger 1867-1953
  O/B 5x4 The Old Scholar Hnd 9/92 425
Priestman, Bertram   Br 1868-1951
  O/C 16x20 Horse-Drawn Plow '95 Dum 4/93 1,300
Priking, Franz   Ger 1927-1979
  * See 1993 Edition ....
Prince, Richard   1949-
  Ph 39x56 3 Man's Hands with Watches 1980 Chr 11/92 . 60,500
  Ph 87x48 Untitled Chr 11/92 31,900
  A/C 56x48 Untitled 88 Sby 11/92 27,500
  A&Ss/C 96x75 Two Leopard Joke Sby 5/93 26,450
  Ph 24x20 Untitled (Cowboys) 1986 Chr 10/92 16,500
  Ph 86x47 Three Girlfriends, One w/Motorcycle Sby 5/93 . 14,950
  A,H&Ss/C 70x48 Song 2120 S. Michigan 1989 Chr 11/92 . 14,300
  Ph 23x15 Cowboys 1986 Sby 5/93 8,050
  Ph 24x20 Untitled 86 Chr 10/92 2,640
  Ph 23x16 Untitled 1983 Sby 5/93 2,300
  Pl/Pa 7x12 Joke 86 Chr 11/92 880
Prince, William Meade   Am 1893-1951
  Pe&G/Pa 14x18 Two Women Arguing Ih 11/92 1,100
  O&R/C 22x20 Eskimo Boy Ice-Fishing with Dog Ih 5/93 .. 600
Princeteau, Rene   Fr 1844-1914
  * See 1990 Edition ....
Pringle, James Fulton   Am 1788-1847
  * See 1992 Edition ....
Pringle, William   Br a 1834-1858
  * See 1992 Edition ....
Prins, Benjamin   Dut 1860-1934
  O/C 40x32 Admiring the Jewel Chr 10/92 4,950
Prins, Johan Huibert   Dut 1757-1806
  * See 1992 Edition ....
Prins, Pierre Ernest   Fr 1838-1913
  O/C 14x12 Nature Morte aux Dessert et Vin But 11/92 .. 4,125
Prinsep, Valentine Cameron   Br 1836-1904
  * See 1993 Edition ....
Prinz, Bernhard
  * See 1992 Edition ....
Prior, William Mathew   Am 1806-1873
  * See 1992 Edition ....
Pritchard, George Thompson   Am 1878-1962
  O/C 25x36 Gathering Kelp Mor 2/93 2,750
  O/C 25x30 Canal in Cairo Hnd 12/92 1,500
  O/C 25x30 Arab Street Scene Dum 8/93 1,400
  O/C 25x30 Cattle by Stream Mor 6/93 1,100
  O/C 25x30 Cottage in Eucalyptus Landscape Mor 2/93 1,000
  O/C 20x24 Sailboats at Rest-Gloucester Mor 2/93 1,000
  O/C 18x24 Sunset on the River Wes 3/93 935
  O/C 21x25 Quiet Stream But 3/93 825
  O/C 24x28 Landscape Hnd 3/93 350
  W/Pa 17x23 Coastal Landscape in Fog: Pair Eld 4/93 ... 165
Pritchard, J. Ambrose   Am 1858-1905
  * See 1992 Edition ....
Pritchett, Edward   Br a 1828-1864
  O/C 36x56 The Doge's Palace and Piazzetta Chr 5/93 ... 39,100
  O/C 12x19 A View of Venice Chr 5/93 6,900
Pritchett, Samuel   Eng 1827-1907
  * See 1993 Edition ....
Probst, Thorwald   Am 1886-1948
  O/C 30x40 Grand Canyon Mor 10/92 6,600
Procaccini, Giulio Cesare   1570-1625
  K/Pa 7x12 Two Men Seated on a Rock Chr 1/93 10,450
Procter, Burt   Am 1901-1980
  * See 1993 Edition ....
Prohias, Antonio   Am 20C
  I/Pb 14x17 Two Images for Spy vs. Spy Skn 5/93 440

Proiss, Friedrich Anton Otto   Ger 1855-
* See 1990 Edition
Pron, Louis Hector   Fr 1817-1902
* See 1991 Edition
Proom, Al   Am 1933-
O/B 20x16 Lilacs But 12/92 2,750
Proschwitzky, Frank   Br a 1883-1889
* See 1993 Edition ....
Prosdocini, Albert   It 1852-
W/Pa 18x31 Fishing Boats on a Lagoon But 11/92 1,980
W/Pa 13x24 View of the Grand Canal Chr 2/93 1,320
W/Pa 22x15 Family Interior Scene Mys 12/92 632
W/Pa 12x7 Canal Scene Wes 3/93 550
W/Pa 5x10 Italian Coast Hnd 10/92 200
Prossalendi, Pavlo   Grk 1857-1894
O/C 36x29 An Arab Coffee House 90 Chr 5/93 34,500
Prout, Samuel   Eng 1783-1852
W/Pa 17x15 Frontal View of a Cathedral Chr 10/92 1,100
W/Pa 8x11 Italian River Town Hnz 5/93 325
W/Pa 8x5 Worshipping Before Religious Facade Hnz 5/93 .. 225
Provis, Alfred   Eng 19C
O/C 9x13 Interior Scene Hnd 5/93 600
Provost, Jan   Dut 1462-1529
* See 1991 Edition ....
Prucha, Gustave   Aus 1875-
O/C 20x28 Romantic Sleigh Ride Chr 10/92 1,100
Prud'hon, Pierre Paul   Fr 1758-1823
K/Pa 10x12 Nemesis and Themis Slo 7/93 2,000
Pruitt-Early   Am 20C
Ph 31x21 The Artists in Their Studio Chr 11/92 1,100
Pruna, Pedro   Spa 1904-1977
O/C 36x26 Arlequin 60+ Chr 11/92 17,600
O/Pn 18x15 Retrato de Mujer 37 Chr 2/93 4,950
O&Wx/B 16x13 Grand dos a la cire Hnd 10/92 1,500
Pseudo-Boltraffio   16C
* See 1992 Edition ....
Pucci, Albert John   It 20C
O/C 47x23 Gondola Hnd 5/93 375
Puig, V.   Spa 20C
* See 1992 Edition ....
Puig-Roda, Gabriel   Spa 1865-1919
* See 1993 Edition ....
Pujol De Gustavino, Clement   Fr 19C
* See 1991 Edition ....
Pujol, Paul   Fr 19C
* See 1993 Edition ....
Pulicino, Alberto   1719-
O/C 22x25 View of Valetta with Ships Sby 5/93 14,950
Puligo, Domenico   It 1492-1527
* See 1990 Edition ....
Puller, John Anthony   Br a 1821-1866
O/C 10x8 The Toy Boat; The Sweep (2) Sby 2/93 2,875
Pullinger, Herbert
W/Pa 13x18 Ships Ald 9/92 225
Pulzone, Scipione   It 1549-1598
* See 1990 Edition ....
Pummil, Robert   Am 1936-
* See 1990 Edition ....
Purdy, Donald   Am 1924-
* See 1993 Edition ....
Purvis, William G.   Am 1870-1924
O/B 5x7 Landscape Mor 11/92 550
O/B 7x10 Landscape Mor 11/92 500
Pushman, Hovsep   Am 1877-1966
O/M 35x26 Music of Serenity Chr 3/93 23,000
O/M 27x21 Still Life, Wilted Rose Chr 9/92 16,500
O/Pn 26x20 Still Life with Seated Buddha Dum 7/93 13,000
O/Pn 19x15 Still Life with Seated Buddha Dum 7/93 10,000
O/Pn 23x15 Autumn Solitude Hnd 5/93 7,000
Puskas, John
E/Cp 12x9 Abstracts of Musical Instrument 1950 Wlf 5/93 .. 525
Putative Jan De Cock   Dut 16C
* See 1991 Edition ....
Puthuff, Hanson   Am 1875-1972
O/C 24x30 Breath of Azure But 10/92 11,000

O/C 18x24 Oaks and Mountain Grandeur But 10/92 10,450
O/C/B 12x16 Desert Mountain But 10/92 6,050
O/C/B 12x16 House and Fall Trees But 10/92 4,675
O/C/B 16x20 Rocky Landscape But 6/93 3,450
O/B 12x16 Landscape Mor 11/92 3,250
O/B 8x10 Landscape Mor 2/93 1,900
Putz, Leo   Ger 1869-1940
* See 1990 Edition
Putz, Michel Richard   Con 19C
O/C 79x39 The Peacock Throne Sby 2/93 11,500
Puy, Jean   Fr 1876-1960
* See 1993 Edition ....
Puytlinck, Christoffel   Dut 1640-1670
* See 1993 Edition ....
Pycke, Francois   Bel 1890-1922
* See 1992 Edition ....
Pye, Fred   Am 1882-
G/Pa 12x10 Near the Opera '53 Yng 2/93 200
Pyle, Aaron G.   Am
* See 1992 Edition ....
Pyle, Howard   Am 1853-1911
O&R/B 10x12 Nun and Monk with Chalice Ih 11/92 11,000
Pynacker, Adam   Dut 1622-1673
* See 1992 Edition ....
Pyne, James Baker   Br 1800-1870
O/Pn 11x16 View in Venice But 5/93 1,725
Qua, Sun   Chi 19C
* See 1990 Edition ....
Quadrone, Giovanni-Battista   It 1844-1898
O/Pn 8x6 Il Filosofo 1870 Sby 10/92 14,300
Quaedvlieg, Carl Max Gerlach   Dut 1823-1874
* See 1992 Edition ....
Quaglia, Carlo   It 1907-1970
* See 1992 Edition ....
Quaglio, Franz   Ger 1844-1920
* See 1993 Edition ....
Quartararo, Riccardo   It 15C
* See 1993 Edition ....
Quartley, Arthur   Am 1839-1886
O/C 15x22 The Old Wreck 80 Brd 8/93 10,780
O/C 26x20 Morning, Raritan Bay 1881 Chr 3/93 4,945
Quaytman, Harvey   Am 20C
* See 1991 Edition ....
Quellinus, Erasmus (the Younger)   Flm 1607-1678
* See 1993 Edition ....
Quentel, Holt   20C
Pg/C 110x102 Blue 4 (Selvedge) 1988 Sby 10/92 3,300
Querena, Luigi   It 1860-1890
* See 1992 Edition ....
Querfurt, August   Ger 1696-1761
O/C 13x17 Military Escort; Messengers (2) Chr 10/92 ... 12,100
Quest, Charles F.
* See 1993 Edition ....
Quigley, Edward B.   Am 1895-
O/C 28x40 The Green Hand '38 Sel 9/92 1,100
Quignon, Fernand Just   Fr 1854-
O/C 15x22 Hilly Landscape with Steeple Chr 2/93 990
Quincy, Edmund   Am 1903-
* See 1992 Edition ....
Quinlan, Will J.   Am 1877-
O/C 24x20 Snowscene Mys 3/93 495
Quinones, Lee   1960-
A/C 60x52 The Bitch Chr 11/92 1,100
Quinsa, Giovanni   It a 1641-
* See 1991 Edition ....
Quintana, Manuel   Ven 1920-
O/C 22x18 Floral Still Life FHB 6/93 100
Quinton, Alfred Robert   Br 20C
* See 1993 Edition ....
Quinton, Clement Henri   Fr 1851-
O/C 17x26 The Greeting Chr 5/93 2,530
O/C 18x29 Farmer with Two Horses Lou 9/92 1,100

Quinton, H.   Br 19C
O/C 18x24 Silvertail and Dairymaid: Pair 1897 Sby 6/93 . . .   4,025
Quirt, Walter   Am 1902-
  * See 1990 Edition
Quizet, Alphonse   Fr 1885-1955
O/M 20x26 Rue a Montmartre Sby 6/93   4,600
O/C 18x22 Landscape with Village Sby 10/92   4,125
O/M 8x10 Vues de Seine: Pair Doy 5/93   1,430
G/Pa/B 9x13 Village in the Snow Sby 2/93   575
Raaphorst, Cornelis   Dut 1875-1954
O/C 16x20 Inquisitive Kittens Sby 10/92   9,350
Raaphorst, Wilheimus   Dut 1870-1963
O/C 20x24 Mealtime Fre 10/92   625
Rabkin, Leo   Am 1919-
W&G/Pa 23x25 Purple Burning Through '62 Wes 10/92   275
Rabuzin, Ivan   1919-
A/C 20x25 Village 1981 Chr 11/92   2,640
Rachmiel, Jean   Am 1871-
  * See 1992 Edition
Rackham, Arthur   Br 1867-1939
PVPa 6x7 Demons in Belfry; Old Witch: Two Sby 10/92 . . .   7,150
PVPa 7x10 St. George of Merry England Chr 10/92   990
Racoff, Rotislaw   Rus 20C
O/M 14x11 Au Bord de la Seine: Pair 53 Sby 6/93   1,035
Rae, John   Am 1882-
  * See 1992 Edition
Raeburn, Sir Henry   Sco 1756-1823
O/C 35x27 Portrait William J. Napier, Capt. 1818 Sby 5/93 .   14,950
O/C 30x25 Portrait Mrs. Jean Craufurd Sby 1/93   4,600
Raffael, Joseph   Am 1933-
  * See 1992 Edition
Raffaelli, Jean Francois   Fr 1850-1924
O/Pn 12x11 L'Heure Du The Sby 2/93   29,900
O/C 15x18 Seine with a View of the Pont Neuf Chr 10/92 . .   7,700
O/Pn 7x6 Village Street Scene Chr 2/93   6,600
O/Pa/C 20x24 Le Sculpteur et Son Modele Sby 1/93   2,070
Raffalt, Ignaz   Aus 1800-1857
  * See 1992 Edition
Raggi, Giovanni   It 1712-1794
  * See 1993 Edition
Raggio, Giuseppe   It 1823-1916
  * See 1993 Edition
Ragione, Raffaele   It 1851-1925
  * See 1993 Edition
Ragusa, Giovanni   It 20C
O/C/Wd 65x41 Untitled (Portrait) But 10/92   1,045
O/C/B 62x26 Untitled (Portrait) But 10/92   990
O/C 72x48 Untitled 86 But 10/92   825
Rahon, Alice   Fr 1916-1987
O/C 47x71 El Viento 54 Chr 11/92   13,200
O/M 31x26 Untitled Sby 11/92   7,150
T/Clx 14x24 Pajaro Chr 11/92   7,000
Raibolini, Francesco Di Marco   It 1450-1517
  * See 1990 Edition
Raimondi, Roberto   It 1877-
O/C 33x22 The Roman Antiquarian But 11/92   5,500
W,H&G/Pa 21x14 Interior Courtship Scene Skn 9/92   660
Rain, Charles   Am 1911-
  * See 1991 Edition
Rainer, Arnulf   1929-
Os/Ph 20x24 Untitled Sby 11/92   9,900
O,Os&Y/Ph 24x20 Untitled Chr 2/93   8,800
Raleigh, Henry   Am 1880-1944
S/Pa 13x18 Man and Woman at Gate Ih 5/93   850
Ralli, Theodore Jacques   Grk 1852-1909
  * See 1990 Edition
Ramah, Henri Francois R.   Bel 1887-1947
O/Pn 24x21 At the Fish Market But 5/93   1,610
Rame, E.   Eur 19C
  * See 1992 Edition
Ramel, Pierre   Fr 20C
O/C 18x22 Pipes et Oiseaux Hnz 5/93   100
Ramenghi, Bartolomeo   It 1484-1542
  * See 1993 Edition

Ramon, A. A.   Am a 1930-1939
  * See 1993 Edition
Ramondi, R.   It 19C
W/Pa 21x14 Spinning Yarn Fre 4/93   850
Ramos, Alvaro Delgado   1922-
  * See 1993 Edition
Ramos, Domingo   Cub 1894-
O/C 24x30 Paisaje de Vinales 1953 Chr 11/92   9,900
O/C 16x15 Paisaje 1921 Chr 11/92   6,600
Ramos, L. C.   Con 20C
O/C 37x58 Dinner on Fishing Boat 45 Hnd 3/93   800
Ramos, Mel   Am 1935-
O/C 30x26 Crime Buster Chr 11/92   33,000
Rampazo, Luciano   Fr 1936-
O/C 26x36 St. Maria Della Salute Doy 11/92   5,775
O/C 26x36 Parisian Boulevard Doy 11/92   2,200
Ramsay, Allan   Br 1713-1784
  * See 1991 Edition
Ramsdell, Mary Louise   Am 1883-1970
O/B 20x16 January Thaw Eld 8/93   55
W/Pa 15x21 Shore Scene with Buildings Eld 8/93   55
Ramsey, Milne   Am 1847-1915
O/C 32x47 Alpine Waterfall Chr 3/93   4,600
Ranc, Jean   Fr 1674-1735
O/C 57x44 Portrait of a Gentleman Chr 10/92   24,200
Randolph, Lee F.   Am 1880-1956
  * See 1993 Edition
Ranftl, Johann Matthias   Aus 1805-1854
O/Pn 8x5 Holding a Doll 1849 Chr 2/93   6,050
Ranger, Henry Ward   Am 1858-1916
O/C 28x36 Harbor at Sunset, Noank 1907 Sby 5/93   16,100
O/B 12x18 Sailboats in a Stormy Cove Sby 9/92   3,300
O/C 18x26 The Road into Town Skn 11/92   2,475
O/B 12x16 Landscape Lyme, Connecticut 1911 Sby 9/92 . .   2,310
O/C 17x12 Bearded Man with Hat Fre 4/93   150
Ranney, William T.   Am 1813-1857
  * See 1992 Edition
Ransom, Fletcher C.   Am 19C
W&R/Pa 15x19 Reading the Will 1906 Ih 5/93   450
Ranson
G&Pe/Pa 12x10 Two Costume Designs Sby 10/92   880
Ranson, Paul   Fr 1864-1909
  * See 1990 Edition
Raphael   It 1483-1520
K&PVPa 5x5 Woman, Bust Length Chr 1/93   39,600
Raphael, Joseph M.   Am 1869-1950
O/C 27x26 House in a Clearing But 6/93   23,000
O/B 11x14 80 and Still on the Job But 6/93   3,162
Raphael, Mary F.   Br a 1896-1915
  * See 1992 Edition
Raphael, William   Br 1833-1914
  * See 1993 Edition
Rapp, ***
O/C 29x37 Vue sur la Seine et Gennevilliers Sby 10/92 . . .   1,980
Rapp, Joh Rudolf   Sws 1827-1903
  * See 1993 Edition
Rapp, Lois   Am
W/Pa 14x19 Paphiopedilum Callosum (4) 87 Ald 3/93   425
W/Pa 20x30 Barn in Spring Mill, PA Ald 3/93   400
Rasch, Heinrich   Ger 1840-1913
  * See 1992 Edition
Raschen, Henry   Am 1854-1937
  * See 1992 Edition
Raser, J. Heyl   Am 1824-1901
O/C 18x30 Reading, Pennsylvania Eld 4/93   3,300
Rasinelli, Roberto   It 19C
O/C 22x15 A Message of Love Chr 10/92   5,500
Raskin, Joseph   Am 1897-1981
O/C 20x24 Pulling Ashore, East Gloucester Lou 6/93   1,000
Rasmussen, Georg Anton   Nor 1842-1914
  * See 1993 Edition
Raspis, Francesco   18C
  * See 1992 Edition
Rast   Dut 19C
W&G/Pa 13x10 Two Hunting Dogs Wtf 9/92   175

Rathbone, John   1750-1807
* See 1993 Edition . . . .
Ratterman, Walter G.   Am 20C
O/C 28x22 Romantic Couple Outdoors Ih 11/92 1,000
Rattner, Abraham   Am 1895-1978
O/C 39x32 Temptation of St. Anthony Sby 3/93 9,200
O/M 16x13 Descent from the Cross Sby 9/92 1,540
G/Pa 18x12 Woman by a Table Wes 12/92 660
Rau, Emil   Ger 1858-
Rau, William   Am 1874-
* See 1993 Edition . . . .
Rauch, Johann Nepomuk   Aus 1804-1847
* See 1993 Edition . . . .
Raudnitz, Albert   Ger 19C
* See 1992 Edition . . . .
Raul, Josephine G.   Am 20C
O/C 30x25 Metal & Glass Mor 2/93 1,000
Raupp, Karl   Ger 1837-1918
* See 1992 Edition . . . .
Rauschenberg, Robert   Am 1925-
O&Ss/C 84x60 Press 1964 Sby 11/92 . . . . 1.1M
MM/S 18x18 Untitled Chr 11/92 770,000
A/L 81x81 Lichen (Salvage Series) 1984 Sby 5/93 60,250
A,Slt&L/Wd 74x97 Crystal Still 80 Sby 10/92 55,000
E/Al 126x97 Garden Stretch 88 Chr 2/93 46,200
Slt&L/Pa 31x46 Mobile Crypt 79 Chr 11/92 41,800
A&Slt/C 89x35 Slipper (Salvage Series) 84 Chr 10/92 . . . 38,500
MM 98x75 Rush IV (Cloister Series) 80 Sby 5/93 37,950
A/Cp 96x48 Five Wise Men Chr 10/92 22,000
Slt&L/F 66x35 Untitled (Hoarfrost Series) 75 Sby 5/93 . . . 20,700
Slt&A/Pa 11x9 Untitled 87 Chr 10/92 12,100
MM&L 42x66 Bottle Cap, Airport Series 1974 Dum 11/92 . . 3,000
Rauscher, Theo   Ger 1931-
O/C 20x24 European Landscape Dum 6/93 550
Ravier, Auguste Francois   Fr 1814-1895
* See 1993 Edition . . . .
Ravinov, P.   Rus 20C
O/C 30x58 Lady in a Rowboat Chr 5/93 1,610
Ravlin, Grace   Am 1885-
O/B Size? Mexican Woman and Monument Valley Wlf 5/93 . . 100
Raymond, Alex   Am 1909-1956
Pl/Pa 6x20 Daily Comic "Rip Kirby" 55 Ih 5/93 325
Rayner, Louise   Br 1829-1924
* See 1993 Edition . . . .
Rayo, Omar   20C
* See 1991 Edition . . . .
Rayski-Kietlicz, Konstantine   1910-1976
O/B 20x16 Abstract, The Dance 1959 Sbt 5/93 528
Rea, Louis Edward   Am 1868-
* See 1991 Edition . . . .
Read, Thomas Buchanan   Am 1822-1872
* See 1993 Edition . . . .
**Ready, William James Durant   Br
1823-1873**
O/C 36x63 European Coastal Scene at Dusk 1866 Sel 12/92 3,500
Realfonso, Tommaso   It 1677-1743
* See 1993 Edition . . . .
**Ream, Carducius Plantagenet   Am
1837-1917**
* See 1993 Edition . . . .
Ream, Morston C.   Am 1840-1898
O/C 27x22 Still Life Fruit and Fish Bowl Sby 3/93 4,715
O/C 30x25 Still Life Fruit Sby 3/93 3,105
Reaser, Wilbur Aaron   Am 1860-1942
O/B 23x28 Oakland Harbor 1903 But 10/92 4,950
P/C/B 38x67 Butternut Valley, N.W. N.Y. State Sby 3/93 . . . 3,450
Rebay, Hilla   Am 1890-1967
O/C 43x30 Untitled Sby 10/92 4,400
O/C 50x37 Andantino 1945 Sby 2/93 3,738
O/C 82x78 To Cheer 1949 Sby 10/92 3,300
O/C 51x42 Embrace 1945 Sby 10/92 3,025
W,Pe&L/Pa 10x15 Cosmic Center Sby 10/92 1,870
O/C 23x43 Untitled Chr 3/93 1,725
W/Pa 7x11 Intermezzo 1948 Sby 10/92 1,540

Pe&H/Pa 12x16 Green 44 Sby 2/93 1,265
W&I/Pa 14x11 Composition No. 14 Sby 2/93 920
Rebeyrolle, Paul   Fr 20C
* See 1992 Edition . . . .
Rebolledo, Benito Correa   Chi 1880-1964
* See 1992 Edition . . . .
Rebry, Gaston   Can 1933-
O/C 18x24 Lake Castor, Quebec 1992 Sbt 5/93 1,584
Rebull, Santiago   Mex 1829-1902
* See 1992 Edition . . . .
Recco, Giuseppe   It 1634-1695
* See 1993 Edition . . . .
Reckless, Stanley L.   Am 1892-
* See 1992 Edition . . . .
Redein, Alexander   Am 1912-1965
O/C 25x36 Barren Landscape Slo 4/93 50
Redelius, Frank   Am 20C
* See 1993 Edition . . . .
Reder-Broili, Franz   Ger 1854-1918
O/C 24x37 Duck Shooting Chr 2/93 1,100
Redfield, Edward Willis   Am 1869-1965
O/C 38x50 The Grey Veil Chr 12/92 88,000
O/C 32x40 The Breeze Chr 5/93 68,500
O/C 26x32 The Toymaker's Home Chr 3/93 68,500
O/C 21x26 Garden, Boothbay Harbor 1924 Hnd 3/93 . . . 50,000
O/C 26x32 Meadow Brook Sby 5/93 28,750
O/C 23x32 Horse and Carriage in Winter Chr 12/92 20,900
O/C 32x26 Forest Lane Through the Birches Ald 9/92 . . . 15,000
Redig, Laurent Herman   Bel 1822-1861
* See 1993 Edition . . . .
Redin, Carl   Am 1892-1944
O/C/B 12x16 New Mexico Landscape Sby 9/92 1,320
Redmond, Alec
O/C 23x18 Woman with Smoking Gun Ih 5/93 2,200
Redmond, Frieda V.   Am 20C
W/Pa 15x22 Nasturtiums Slo 5/93 200
Redmond, Granville   Am 1871-1935
O/C 16x20 California Wildflowers But 3/93 41,250
O/C 33x71 Bringing the Flock Home '03 Sby 12/92 30,800
O/C/M 19x13 Sailboats at Catalina Island '05 Mor 11/92 . . 9,500
O/C 24x30 Shadow of Storm, Menlo Park 1911 But 10/92 . . 9,350
O/C/B 8x10 Stream and Wildflowers But 10/92 9,350
O/C 14x18 Landscape Mor 11/92 8,500
O/C 16x20 Sunset Menlo, Morn San Mateo 1912 Mor 6/93 . . 7,700
O/B 11x14 Catalina Moonlight But 6/93 7,475
O/B 11x14 Lion's Head, Catalina Island 1918 But 6/93 . . . 7,475
O/B 10x14 Sunny Lagoon But 10/92 6,600
O/M 11x14 Catalina Island 1920 Mor 11/92 6,500
O/C 8x12 Landscape Mor 2/93 5,500
O/C 9x12 Sunrise But 10/92 5,225
O/C/C 12x18 River Landscape Mor 2/93 4,750
O/B 9x12 Study by Moonlight, Golden Gate 1916 Chr 12/92 3,300
O/C 14x18 Landscape with Woods Dum 9/92 3,000
Redmore, Henry   Br 1820-1887
* See 1993 Edition . . . .
Redon, Odilon   Fr 1840-1916
O/Gl 15x13 Peintures Decoratives: Pair Sby 5/93 20,700
Redoute, Pierre Joseph   Fr 1759-1840
* See 1990 Edition . . . .
Redwood, Allen Carter   Am 1834-1922
* See 1992 Edition . . . .
Reed, D. C.   Br 19C
* See 1992 Edition . . . .
Reed, David
A/C 12x82 Untitled 1979 Sby 11/92 8,800
Reed, Marjorie   Am 1915-
O/C 24x30 Back Country Run-Off Mor 2/93 2,500
O/C 24x36 Vallecito Station-Midnite Stop Mor 2/93 2,500
O/B 12x16 Two Works 1969 Wes 3/93 688
O/Cb 8x10 Butterfield Stage Apache Pass Mor 2/93 400
O/Cb 4x8 Race of the Stage Lines Mor 6/93 275
Reedy, Leonard H.   Am 1899-1956
O/M 25x30 Battle on the Plain Sby 3/93 2,185
Reeves, Richard Stone   Am 20C
* See 1993 Edition . . . .

Regagnon, Albert   1874-1961
  * See 1993 Edition . . . .
Regamey, Frederic   Fr 1849-1925
  O/Pn 16x13 Avant Le Duel Sby 2/93 10,925
Reggianini, Vittorio   It 1858-1924
  * See 1993 Edition . . . .
Regnault, Jean Baptiste   Fr 1754-1829
  * See 1990 Edition . . . .
Regnier, Nicolas   Flm 1590-1667
  * See 1993 Edition . . . .
Rehn, Frank Knox Morton   Am 1848-1914
  O/C 16x28 Long Beach, New York Sby 3/93 2,300
  O/C 16x24 Gondola on a Back Canal in Venice Chr 12/92 . . 1,210
  O/C 16x28 Sunset at Crescent Beach Slo 5/93 950
Reich, Albert   Ger 1881-
  O/Pn 17x20 River Landscape Wes 5/93 605
Reichardt, Ferdinand   Am 1819-1895
  * See 1993 Edition . . . .
Reichert, Carl   Aus 1836-1918
  O/B 16x12 Play Fellows 1901 Sby 2/93 17,825
  O/Pn 8x16 Horses at the Fence Chr 2/93 4,400
  O/C 11x9 Poodle in the Andes 1869 But 11/92 3,850
Reichmann, Josephine Lemos   Am 1864-1939
  O/B 12x14 Drying the Sail Mor 6/93 605
Reid, Flora MacDonald   Br a 1879-1929
  * See 1990 Edition . . . .
Reid, George Agnew   Can 1860-1947
  O/C 25x42 Trees and Lake 1922 Sbt 5/93 880
Reid, Henry Logan   Am 19C
  O/B 14x12 Grand Canyon Scene Hnd 12/92 140
Reid, Robert   Am 1862-1929
  O/C 27x31 The Brook Chr 12/92 44,000
  O/C 13x16 Watching the Boats Skn 3/93 16,500
  O/Pa/Pn 26x20 The Bather Chr 12/92 14,300
Reid, Robert Payton   Br 1859-1945
  * See 1993 Edition . . . .
Reider, Marcel   Fr 1852-
  * See 1993 Edition . . . .
Reiffel, Charles   Am 1862-1942
  O/B 17x20 Ballast Point, California 1930 Chr 5/93 19,500
  O/C 28x32 Connecticut Landscape Mys 3/93 9,350
  O/B 20x24 Banner Gorge, 1932 1932 But 6/93 6,900
  O/B 12x16 Connecticut Street Scene Mor 6/93 5,225
  O/B 12x18 The Prospectors 1941 But 3/93 4,400
  O/Cb 9x12 Sailboats at Sea Wlf 4/93 1,700
  O/B 6x7 Harbour Scene Mys 3/93 825
Reinagle, Philip   Br 1749-1833
  * See 1992 Edition . . . .
Reinagle, Richard Ramsay   Br 1775-1862
  * See 1991 Edition . . . .
Reindel, Edna   Am 1900-1990
  O/C 12x10 Still Life with Fig and Pomegranate FHB 5/93 . . . 800
  W/Pa 12x19 Head Hnd 9/92 50
Reindel, William George   Am 1871-1948
  O/C 14x18 Passing Snow 1913 Slo 7/93 450
  W/Pa 10x10 Tree in Landscape: Two 1921 FHB 3/93 80
  W/Pa 14x22 Birch Trees in Landscape 1918 FHB 3/93 . . . 50
Reinhardt, Ad   Am 1913-1967
  O/C 32x40 Untitled 48 Sby 5/93 54,625
Reinhardt, Louis
  O/C 23x34 Barnyard Scene Dum 3/93 1,000
Reinhardt, Ludwig Louis   Ger -1870
  * See 1992 Edition . . . .
Reinhardt, Siegfried   Am 1925-1984
  A/M 18x72 Abstract Composition 1954 Sel 12/92 2,700
  O/M 11x17 Wash Day 1955 Skn 9/92 1,210
  A/B 36x24 Self Portrait 1981 Sel 4/93 1,100
Reinhart, Benjamin Franklin   Am 1829-1885
  O/C 34x44 Portrait Normanda Workman Larwill 1870 Wlf 3/93 650
Reinhold, Friedrich (the Younger)   Aus 1814-1881
  * See 1991 Edition . . . .

Reisman, Philip   Am 1904-
  * See 1993 Edition . . . .
Reisner, Martin Andreas   Am 1798-1862
  O/C 36x47 Gathering of Indians 1860 Chr 3/93 13,800
Reitzel, Marques   Am 1896-1963
  * See 1992 Edition . . . .
Relli, Conrad Marca   20C
  L/C 21x28 Untitled Sby 10/92 6,050
Rembrandt Van Rijn, Harmensz.   Dut 1606-1669
  O/Pn 9x7 Head of a Bearded Man Sby 1/93 5,175
Remfry, David
  * See 1992 Edition . . . .
Remington, Frederic Sackrider   Am 1861-1909
  I,S&G/Pa 18x23 The Three Prospectors Sby 12/92 82,500
  I,G&S/Pa 18x18 Commanche on Horseback Sby 5/93 37,950
  PI&S/B 15x15 Besieged By the Utes Chr 3/93 18,400
  PI/Pa 9x11 Moose Head from Song of Hiawatha Chr 9/92 . . 6,050
  PI/Pa 12x9 A Trip Up Country Wlf 9/92 2,400
Remisoff, Nicolai   Am 1887-
  * See 1993 Edition . . . .
Remmey, Paul   Am 20C
  W,G&Pe/B 22x30 Sea Isle Dock '46 Sby 3/93 748
Remy, Jean
  O/C 20x24 Paris Street Scene Dum 6/93 500
Renard, Paul   Fr 20C
  * See 1993 Edition . . . .
Renart   Am 20C
  O/C 24x30 Flowers in a Vase Hnd 9/92 150
Renaudin, Alfred   Fr 1866-
  * See 1993 Edition . . . .
Rendon, Manuel   Fr 1894-
  O/C 36x26 Visage De Femme Sby 5/93 12,650
Rene, Peter   Fr 20C
  O/B 16x12 Reflet des Eaux Fre 4/93 110
Reniatzen
  O/C 22x17 Barnyard Pigs Ald 5/93 325
Renieri, Nicola   Flm 1590-1667
  * See 1993 Edition . . . .
Renner, Paul Freidrich August   Ger 1878-
  O/C 29x21 Woman with Black Panther 1923 Wlf 9/92 . . . 1,700
Renninger, Katharine Steele   Am 20C
  O/C 17x15 Barge Club Fre 10/92 170
Renoir, Pierre-Auguste   Fr 1841-1919
  O/C 19x23 La Lecture 1917 Chr 11/92 . . . . 2.09M
  O/C 25x21 Baigneuse Assise Vue Profil 1913 Chr 11/92 . . 1.705M
  O/C 10x10 Leontine lisant Chr 11/92 . . . . 1.045M
  O/C 49x26 Le Jeune Garcon au Chat Sby 11/92 797,500
  O/C 16x13 Nature Morte Aux Anemones 1901 Chr 11/92 . . 605,000
  P/Pa 24x17 Femme a L'Ombrelle Sby 11/92 495,000
  O/C 13x16 Gerbe D'Anemones Sby 11/92 330,000
  O/C 13x16 Bretagne, Arbres Rochers 1893 Chr 11/92 . . . 308,000
  O/C 13x12 Vase de Fleurs Sby 11/92 231,000
  O/C 10x13 Paysage de Bretagne Sby 5/93 189,500
  O/C 8x13 Etude de baigneuse Chr 11/92 170,500
  P/Pa/C 18x12 Faune or Silene Dansant: Pair Sby 11/92 . . 104,500
  P/Pa 18x13 Jean Renoir a Deux Ans 1895 Doy 5/93 104,500
  O/C 9x10 Etude de Roses Sby 11/92 96,250
  O/C 12x15 Nu Dans Un Paysage Sby 11/92 93,500
  O/C 7x11 Paysage Sby 5/93 77,300
  O/C 8x16 Paysage Sby 5/93 74,000
  O/C 10x13 Arbres, fond mer, esquisse tete Chr 11/92 . . . 66,000
  O/C/Pn 6x3 Tete De Femme Sby 10/92 36,300
  O/C 6x10 Etudes de Femmes et Petit Paysage Sby 10/92 . . 33,000
  G&W/Pa 5x5 Les Deux Arbres Sby 11/92 33,000
  Pe&C/Pa 12x16 Portrait of the Artist's Son Sby 10/92 . . . 16,500
  W&PI/Pa 7x5 Etude de Feuilles Sby 10/92 6,050
Renouf, Emile   Fr 1845-1894
  * See 1990 Edition . . . .
Renoux, Andre   Fr
  * See 1993 Edition . . . .
Renoux, Charles Calus   Fr 1795-1846
  * See 1990 Edition . . . .

Repin, Ilya Efimovich   Rus 1844-1930
O/C 39x25 Scene of Government Overthrow But 5/93 34,500
O/C/B 16x12 The Cossack Girl '89 Sby 2/93 10,350
Reppen, John Richard (Jack)   Can 1933-1964
O/B 24x16 Abstract Composition '63 Sbt 5/93 968
Reschi, Pandolfo   Pol 1643-1699
* See 1993 Edition ....
Resnick, Milton   Am 1917-
O/C 80x60 Straw 81 Chr 2/93 14,300
O/C 63x37 Untitled 1969 Sby 2/93 11,500
O/C 44x40 Time 1 1984 Chr 5/93 7,475
O/Pa/M 32x20 Untitled Sby 10/92 7,150
O/Cd 40x30 Skow 1981 Sby 2/93 1,150
Resnikoff, I.
* See 1993 Edition ....
Rethel, Alfred   Ger 1816-1859
* See 1990 Edition ....
Rethore, *   Fr 20C**
W&G/Pa 19x25 Two Works '60 Wes 3/93 358
Rettegi, S. W.   Eur 20C
* See 1993 Edition ....
Rettig, Heinrich   Ger 1859-1921
* See 1992 Edition ....
Reusswig, William   Am 1902-1978
T/B 23x24 The Raid to Kill Rommel '54 Skn 5/93 770
Pl&W/Pa 21x11 Hanging a Man on Horseback Ih 5/93 425
Reuterdahl, Henry   Am 1871-1925
O&G/Pa 18x12 Naval Scene Mys 3/93 412
Reverchon, Victor Bachereau   Fr 1842-
O/Pn 9x6 Walk in a Garden Chr 2/93 715
Reveron, Armando   Ven 1890-1954
T&O/B 37x25 Autorretrato 33 Chr 11/92 88,000
G/Pa/B 33x24 Retrato de Mujer Chr 11/92 60,500
C,K&P/Pa 26x19 La Enfermera 57 Sby 5/93 32,200
C&P/Pa 38x38 Mujer Ante El Espejo Sby 5/93 25,875
Revesz, Imre Emerich   Hun 1859-
O/C 30x47 The Jewelry Merchant 1883 Sby 5/93 8,625
Revolg
W,G&Pe/Pa 15x11 Costume Design German Star Sby 10/92 1,100
Reyes, Juan Cruz   Mex 20C
W/Pa 26x25 Untitled Wlf 5/93 300
Reyher, Max   Am 1862-1945
* See 1993 Edition ....
Reyna, Antonio   Spa 1859-1937
O/C 14x29 Venetian Canal Scene Chr 2/93 28,600
O/C 14x29 Venice from the Laguna Chr 2/93 18,700
O/C 14x29 A Venetian Canal Chr 2/93 17,600
O/C 10x20 A Venetian View Chr 2/93 5,500
O/B 3x6 A Beach Scene Chr 10/92 2,090
Reynolds, Charles H.   Am 20C
* See 1993 Edition ....
Reynolds, Frank   Br 1876-1953
H/Pa 6x5 Illustrations: Three Hnz 5/93 200
Reynolds, J. F.   Am 20C
O/C 18x28 Fruit and Wine Bottle 1896 Mys 3/93 770
O/C 18x28 Still Life Pineapples and Lemons 96 Skn 11/92 . 660
Reynolds, Sir Joshua   Br 1723-1792
O/C 30x25 Portrait of a Lady Chr 5/93 51,750
O/C 30x26 Portrait of Sir Brooke Boothby Chr 10/92 .. 26,400
O/C 50x39 Portrait of a Man Sby 5/93 7,188
Reynolds, Wade
* See 1993 Edition ....
Reynolds, Wellington Jarard   Am 1869-
O/Pn 20x30 Lake Sunrise Hnd 9/92 500
O/Pn 20x30 Beach Sunset Hnd 9/92 375
Rhodes, Charles Ward   Am -1905
O/B 20x10 Souvenir d'Ete 1894 Yng 2/93 1,100
Rhodes, John   Eng 1809-1842
* See 1992 Edition ....
Rhomberg, Hanno   Ger 1820-1869
* See 1993 Edition ....
Rhys, Oliver   Ger 19C
* See 1992 Edition ....

Riba-Rovira, Francois
* See 1992 Edition ....
Ribak, Louis   Am 1902-1972
O/Pa 14x19 Iron Workers Mys 12/92 412
Ribaud, Francois   Fr 19C
O/C/Pn 19x26 Preparing for Conflict Sby 1/93 1,610
Ribera, Pierre   Fr 1867-1932
O/C 24x49 Le Jour de Marche a San Gabriel Sby 11/92 . 30,800
Ribot, Germain Theodore   Fr 1825-1893
* See 1993 Edition ....
Ribot, Theodule Augustin   Fr 1823-1891
O/C 37x29 Le Chasseur Sby 10/92 33,000
O/C 10x8 Young Peasant Girl Sby 5/93 9,200
O/C 29x24 Portrait of M. Cardon Chr 10/92 8,800
O/B 18x13 Brittany Shepherd, Half-Length Chr 5/93 .. 8,050
O/C 26x18 Jeune Fille a la Cruche Sby 5/93 4,600
O/C 29x24 Portrait D'Homme Sby 5/93 4,600
O/C 18x15 Somber Moment Chr 2/93 1,100
Ricardi, G.   It 19C
* See 1992 Edition ....
Riccardi, C. C.   Am 20C
O/B 20x24 Fishing Boats Fre 4/93 240
Ricchi, Pietro   It 1605-1675
* See 1993 Edition ....
Ricchiardi, Giovanni   -1820
* See 1993 Edition ....
Ricci, Alfredo   It 1864-1889
W/Pa 10x23 Villa Medici Fountain Hnd 3/93 900
Ricci, Arturo   It 1854-
* See 1993 Edition ....
Ricci, Pio   It 1850-1919
O/C 20x15 Courting Sby 5/93 6,325
Ricci, Sebastiano   It 1659-1734
O/C/Pn 32x26 Rest on Flight into Egypt Chr 1/93 74,800
Ricciardelli, Gabrielle   a 1745-1777
O/C/M 39x52 Peasant Family and Their Flock Chr 1/93 . 26,400
Ricciardi, Caesare A.   Am 1892-
O/C 24x30 Boats at Dock 59 Hnd 12/92 350
O/C 24x30 Boats at Dock '56 Hnd 9/92 325
O/C 16x20 Houses by River Ald 3/93 275
O/B 12x16 Winter Landscape Ald 5/93 150
O/C 25x29 Floral Bouquet Ald 5/93 65
Ricciardi, Oscar   It 1864-1935
O/Pn 11x7 Marketplace in Naples Chr 10/92 2,090
Riccio, L. F.   It 19C
O/C 10x8 Mother and Children But 11/92 1,650
Riccke, George   Am 19C
O/C 10x14 Three Sheep Hnd 12/92 160
Rice-Pereira, Irene   Am 1907-1971
G/Pa 40x26 Descent of Dove 1965 Chr 5/93 1,150
Rich, John Hubbard   Am 1876-1954
O/C 16x20 Still Life Fruit, Jug, Goblet But 3/93 3,800
Richard, Edna Vergon   Am 1890-1985
* See 1993 Edition ....
Richard, Jacob
O/C 28x30 Winter Creek Landscape 1940 Ald 3/93 1,900
Richard, P.   Fr 19C
* See 1993 Edition ....
Richard, R.   Br 19C
W/Pa 14x21 Figures Along the Coast Fre 10/92 ... 325
Richard, Rene-Jean   Can 1895-1982
O/B 14x18 Lac Dans Les Laurentides Sbt 5/93 ... 1,320
Richard, Will   Am 20C
* See 1993 Edition ....
Richard-Putz, Michel   Fr 1868-
* See 1990 Edition ....
Richards, F. T.   Am 1864-1921
* See 1993 Edition ....
Richards, Frederick DeBourg   Am 1822-1903
O/C 18x30 On the Juniata Eld 4/93 962
Richards, L.   Br 1878-
O/C 24x16 Lane Near Frigate; Country Lane (3) But 5/93 .. 4,600

198

**Richards, Thomas Addison   Am
1820-1900**
 * See 1993 Edition ....
Richards, W.   Eng 19C
 O/C 20x30 Glen Shiel, Ross,... Yng 2/93 400
Richards, William Trost   Am 1833-1905
 O/C 23x44 Atlantic Seascape 1870 Sby 5/93 90,500
 O/C 13x23 Snow Storm, Atlantic City 1872 Chr 3/93 40,250
 O/C 24x20 The Arched Bridge 1869 Sby 3/93 29,900
 W&G/Pa 23x37 Fisherman on the Shore 1879 Sby 12/92 . 28,600
 O/C 41x32 Path Through the Mountains 1858 Chr 12/92 . 28,600
 O/C 25x42 Portsmouth Light and Buoy 1875 Sby 3/93 20,700
 W/Pa 11x16 On the Beach-Moonlight 1875 Sby 5/93 ... 11,500
 W&G/Pa 5x9 Along the Shore 1873 Sby 9/92 11,000
 W&Pe/Pa/B 9x15 Along the Jersey Coast 1871 Chr 12/92 . 9,350
 W,G&Pe/Pa 8x13 Point Judith 1871 Chr 9/92 7,700
 O/C 20x30 Near Philadelphia 1854 Sby 9/92 7,150
 O/B 9x16 Breaking Waves, Late Afternoon 07 Skn 9/92 .. 3,630
 W/Pa 12x24 Crashing Waves on the Rocks Chr 12/92 ... 3,080
 O/C/B 9x16 The Tide Comes In Chr 12/92 2,750
 O/Pn 8x15 Birdstacks, Scotland Doy 11/92 2,420
 O/C/B 9x16 Waves Crashing on a Rocky Coast Chr 12/92 . 2,200
 O/B 5x7 St. Katherine's Island, Wales Brd 8/93 1,980
 W/Pa 14x26 Far Rockaway 1901 Hnd 12/92 1,900
 O/B 5x8 Landscape, Scotland Brd 8/93 1,540
 W/Pa 11x23 Coast and Rocks Fre 10/92 1,300
 W&G/Pa/B 14x10 A Rocky Stream Chr 12/92 1,100
 O/B 9x16 Rocky Coast Wes 10/92 1,100
Richardson, Constance   Am
 O/B 17x23 East Arlington '37 Dum 2/93 1,125
Richardson, Daniel   Br 19C
 O/C 51x70 Still Life Game Birds, Rabbit, Fish Hnd 3/93 ... 9,600
Richardson, Jonathan (Sr.)   Br 1665-1745
 * See 1993 Edition ....
Richardson, Louis H.   Am 1853-1923
 O/C 8x10 Marsh Scene Mys 12/92 358
Richardson, Mary Curtis   Am 1848-1931
 O/C 38x27 Mother and Child But 3/93 5,500
Richardson, Mary Neal   Am 1859-1937
 * See 1993 Edition ....
Richardson, Sam   Am 20C
 O/B 24x22 Crated II Hnd 5/93 750
Richardson, Thomas Miles (Jr.)   Br 1813-1890
 * See 1991 Edition ....
Richardson, Volney A.   Am 1880-
 O/C 9x12 Still Life with Lilacs 1907 Wes 5/93 660
Richardt, Ferdinand   Am 1819-1895
 O/C 14x20 Santa Cruz Mountains But 10/92 2,090
 O/C 18x28 Niagra Above the Falls Hnd 10/92 1,800
 O/C 9x13 Country Road with Figures But 10/92 1,210
Richenburg, Robert   Am 1917-
 * See 1993 Edition ....
Richer, Ira   20C
 E,Y&L/Wd 54x46 Bark 1982 Chr 11/92 1,650
Richert, Charles Henry   Am 1880-1974
 W&C/Pa 8x12 Tracks in the Snowy Woods Sby 9/92 83
Richet, Leon   Fr 1847-1907
 O/C 18x24 A Summer Morning Chr 10/92 12,100
 O/C 15x22 Church by the Sea Chr 5/93 9,775
 O/Pn 23x18 Genre Scene with Young Girl 1878 Skn 11/92 . 8,800
 O/C 17x26 Paysanne Pres D'Un Etang Sby 2/93 8,338
 O/C 15x22 Village Beside a Lake Chr 5/93 8,050
 O/C 15x22 Route Dans la Campagne Sby 2/93 6,038
 O/Pn 18x22 Figure beside a Pond Chr 2/93 5,500
 O/C 12x18 Au Bord de la Riviere Sby 5/93 4,600
Richir, Hermann Jean Joseph   Bel 1866-1942
 G/B 35x20 Paths Together They Have Trod Doy 5/93 3,850
Richley, Rudolf
 * See 1992 Edition ....
Richmond, Agnes M.   Am 1870-1964
 O/C 19x24 Nymph at Water's Edge Fre 4/93 2,000
Richmond, Thomas (Jr.)   Br 1802-1874
 * See 1993 Edition ....

Richter, Adrian Ludwig   Ger 1803-1884
 * See 1993 Edition ....
Richter, Edouard Frederic W.   Fr 1844-1913
 O/C 48x32 Harem Beauties Sby 2/93 17,250
 O/C 25x16 A Harem Beauty 1884 Sby 10/92 7,150
Richter, Gerhard   Ger 1932-
 O/C 79x63 Untitled (554/1) 1984 Chr 11/92 269,500
 O/C 89x79 Besen Sby 11/92 242,000
 O/C 27x29 Mouth (Briditte Bardot's Lips) '63 Sby 11/92 .. 88,000
 O/C 32x26 Untitled (608-3) 1986 Chr 11/92 85,800
 O/C 28x40 Untitled (607-1) 1986 Chr 11/92 71,500
 O/L 44x40 Untitled #678-2 1988 Sby 11/92 66,000
 A/C 32x26 Untitled 592-2 1986 Sby 2/93 46,000
 A/C 32x26 Untitled 618-1 1986 Sby 2/93 34,500
 O/C 11x16 Untitled 72 Sby 11/92 15,400
 O/C 18x15 Roehren (Tubes) Sby 5/93 10,925
 O/Pa/C 16x16 Fingermalereien 71 Chr 2/93 8,800
 A/Ph 24x25 Untitled (Candle) 1989 Chr 5/93 7,475
 O/Pa 16x16 Fingermalereien 71 Chr 11/92 7,150
 W/Pa 7x10 Untitled 88 Chr 2/93 7,150
 A/Vy 12x12 Bach, The Goldberg Variations Sby 2/93 5,750
 O&Ph/Cd 4x6 Untitled 88 Chr 11/92 4,400
Richter, Guido Paul   Ger 1859-1941
 * See 1990 Edition ....
Richter, Hans Rudolf   Aus 1920-
 O/C 10x8 Gentleman Playing a Mandolin Dum 4/93 600
 O/C 10x8 Holding a Glass of Beer Dum 4/93 550
 O/C 10x8 Through His Glasses at Magazine Dum 4/93 ... 550
Richter, Henry L.   Am 1870-1960
 O/C 16x20 Winter Stream But 12/92 1,650
 W/Pa 14x18 Landscape Mor 11/92 1,600
 O/C 20x34 Saddleback Mountain-Tustin Mor 6/93 1,320
 O/C 10x8 Woman in Green Dress Mor 11/92 70
Richter, Ilse   Aus 20C
 W/Pa 17x12 Four Costume Designs Hnd 3/93 140
 W/Pa 17x12 Ten Costume Designs Hnd 3/93 130
Richter, Johann   Swd 1665-1745
 * See 1991 Edition ....
Richter, Leopoldo   20C
 * See 1991 Edition ....
Richter, Wilmer S.   Am 20C
 O/B 12x15 Winter Farm Scene Hnz 5/93 60
Rico Y Ortega, Martin   Spa 1833-1908
 O/C 29x18 Gondoliers on a Venetian Canal Chr 10/92 ... 35,200
 O/C 19x30 A Venetian Afternoon Sby 10/92 33,000
 O/Pn 14x9 A Venetian Canal Scene Sby 10/92 22,000
 O/C 15x27 River Landscape Sby 5/93 11,500
 O/C 22x18 A Sunlit Piazza Chr 2/93 4,400
Ridell, Annette Irwin   Am a 1920-1939
 * See 1993 Edition ....
Rider, Arthur Grover   Am 1886-1975
 O/C 30x33 Breezy Day on the Beach Mor 6/93 38,500
 O/C 19x25 Pulling in the Fishing Boats But 6/93 5,750
 W/Pb 8x10 Bringing Home the Catch But 10/92 1,980
 W/Pa 8x10 Balancing the Sail But 10/92 1,760
 O/C 16x21 Near Laguna But 3/93 1,100
Riedel, H.   Ger 19C
 O/Pn 19x12 Wine Taster Slo 4/93 950
Rieder, Marcel   Fr 1852-
 * See 1993 Edition ....
Riegen, Nicolaas   Dut 1827-1889
 * See 1993 Edition ....
Rieger, Albert   Aus 1834-1905
 * See 1992 Edition ....
Riemer   Am 20C
 O/C 23x32 Birch Trees Dum 8/93 85
Riemers, Gosta   20C
 P/Pa 22x30 California Landscape FHB 6/93 125
Riesenberg, Sidney G.   Am 1885-
 O&R/C 32x22 The Fight Sby 9/92 1,100
 O/C 30x21 Woodsman Hooking Up Dogsled Ih 5/93 750
Riesener, Henri Francois   Fr 1767-1828
 * See 1991 Edition ....

Rifka, Judy   20C
  * See 1991 Edition . . . .
Rigaud, Hyacinthe   Fr 1659-1743
  * See 1991 Edition . . . .
Rigaud, John Francis   Br 1742-1810
  * See 1990 Edition . . . .
Rignano, Vittorio   It 1860-1916
  O/C 27x16 Monk Illustrating a Manuscript Chr 2/93 1,320
Rigolot, Albert Gabriel   Fr 1862-1932
  * See 1993 Edition . . . .
Rijlaarsdam, J.   Dut 1821-
  O/C 24x20 Lady and Gentleman Outside Cafe Slo 4/93 100
Rikelme, Claudio   20C
  * See 1991 Edition . . . .
Riley, Arthur (Art) I.   Am 1911-
  W/Pa 22x28 Surf Fisherman on Rocky Coast Mor 6/93 1,650
Riley, Bridget   Br 1931-
  A/C 91x91 Chant 2 '67 Chr 11/92 33,000
  G&H/Pa 32x50 Blue, Green, Red Twisted '75 Chr 11/92 . . . 5,500
  H&I/Pa 30x33 Fine Line Open Disk Study 75 Chr 11/92 . . . 3,300
  Br,I&H/Pa 22x30 Study for Intake '64 Chr 11/92 2,200
  G/Pa 16x18 Blue, Turquoise w/Ochre on Grey 72 Chr 11/92 1,430
Riley, John   Eng 1646-1691
  O/C 30x25 Portrait Martha Baker Chr 1/93 5,500
Riley, Kenneth Pauling   Am 1919-
  G/M 19x15 Hunter, Woman and Child Ih 5/93 800
Rimbert, Rene   Fr 20C
  * See 1991 Edition . . . .
Rinaldi, Claudio   It 19C
  * See 1992 Edition . . . .
Rindin, V. F.
  G/Pa 16x12 Costume Designs for Clowns 1947 Sby 10/92 . 1,100
Rindisbacher, Peter   Am 1806-1834
  * See 1993 Edition . . . .
Rines, Frank M.   Am 1892-
  O/B 12x16 Autumn Day Yng 2/93 425
Ring, Ole   Dan 1902-1972
  * See 1993 Edition . . . .
Riopelle, Jean Paul   Can 1924-
  O/C 21x26 Le Puits Hante 57 Sby 10/92 49,500
  O/C 22x18 Sur Les Graviers Chr 11/92 22,000
  O/Pa/C 31x23 Gerardmer 58 Sby 10/92 20,900
  O/C 16x9 Untitled Chr 10/92 13,200
  O/C 11x9 Untitled (PM 34) Chr 2/93 10,450
  I/Pa 10x14 Untitled, 1953 Sbt 11/92 8,800
Rioult, Louis Edouard   Fr 1790-1855
  * See 1993 Edition . . . .
Rip, Willem Cornelius   Dut 1856-1922
  * See 1993 Edition . . . .
Ripamonti, Carlos Pablo   Arg 1874-1968
  O/C 50x70 Amores 1943 Doy 5/93 8,525
  O/C 61x30 Emboscan en Noche Doy 5/93 5,280
Ripari, Virgilio   It 1843-1902
  O/C 16x20 Gondola in the Canal Wlf 3/93 500
Ripley, Aiden Lassell   Am 1896-1969
  W/Pa 14x19 Bass Rocks, Cape Ann Skn 5/93 2,200
  W/Pa 14x20 The Guides' Cabin Skn 3/93 1,650
  W,H&G/Pa 13x18 An Italian Harbor Skn 3/93 935
  W/Pa 14x21 Spring Plowing 49 Chr 5/93 920
  W/Pa 14x20 Southern Street Scene Yng 2/93 700
Ritchie, John   Br a 1858-1875
  * See 1993 Edition . . . .
Ritman, Louis   Am 1889-1963
  O/C 26x32 Sunday Boating on Epte River 1917 Hnd 12/92 120,000
  O/C 32x26 Garden in Giverny 1914 Chr 12/92 110,000
  O/C 32x40 Quietude, Sun Spots Sel 12/92 25,000
  O/C 42x51 Interior Hnd 3/93 18,000
  O/C 26x32 Grazing Cattle Hnd 12/92 4,200
  O/Pn 18x15 The White Corsage Lou 6/93 2,250
  O/Pn 13x16 A Seated Woman Chr 5/93 1,380
  O/C 14x14 Still Life Chr 5/93 575
  O/C 14x14 Still Life with Apples Lou 9/92 250
Ritschel, William P.   Am 1864-1949
  O/C 40x50 Misty Shores, California 1927 Sby 12/92 . . . 82,500
  O/C 25x30 Moonbeams Sby 3/93 26,450

O/C 32x47 Kelp Gathering, Maine But 10/92 15,400
O/Pn 30x25 Girl From Bali-Java Mor 6/93 9,900
G/Pa 26x34 Return of the Fishing Fleet But 6/93 7,475
O/C 21x18 Two Boats along the Bay But 6/93 5,175
P&W/Pa 25x21 Dutch Countryside Scene Dum 2/93 950
W/B 25x29 Fishing Boats, Katwyk, Holland Wes 5/93 852
Rittenberg, Henry R.   Am 1879-1969
  * See 1991 Edition . . . .
Ritter, Caspar   Ger 1861-1923
  * See 1991 Edition . . . .
Ritter, Louis   Am 1854-1892
  W&Pe/Pa 11x15 Amalfi '89 Chr 3/93 3,220
Ritter, Paul   Am 1829-1907
  * See 1992 Edition . . . .
Rivas, Antonio   It 19C
  * See 1993 Edition . . . .
Rivelli, Con 20C
  O/C 18x30 Seascape 1842 Hnd 3/93 900
Rivera, Diego   Mex 1886-1957
  O/C 50x36 Nina en Azul y Blanco 1939 Chr 11/92 . . . 770,000
  O/C 30x24 Retrato de Maria Felix 1948 Chr 11/92 . . . 148,500
  O/C 48x35 Portrait of Helen N. Starr 1951 Chr 11/92 . . 88,000
  W/Pa 15x11 Cargador 1956 Sby 5/93 63,000
  W/Pa 20x15 Vendedora de Flores 41 Chr 11/92 60,500
  W/Pa 19x22 Arboles 1937 Chr 11/92 49,500
  W/Pa 15x11 Mujer Cargando Flores 1954 Sby 11/92 . . . 38,500
  W&K/Pa 7x11 El Bocadillo Chr 11/92 30,800
  W/Pa 16x12 Young Girl Kneeling '49 Dum 5/93 27,500
  Br,I&Pe/Pa 24x19 Retrato de Ann Harding Chr 11/92 . . . 24,200
  W/Pa 15x11 Llendo Al Mercado 46 Sby 5/93 21,850
  Pe/Pa 15x11 Mother and Child '26 But 4/93 20,700
  W&Pe/Pa 12x19 Montanas en Sonora 31 Chr 11/92 . . . 19,800
  Sg&H/Pa 12x9 Nino 35 Skn 3/93 19,800
  W/Pa 15x11 Woman Carrying Basket 1948 But 4/93 . . . 17,250
  W/Pa 15x11 Woman Carrying Basket 48 But 4/93 17,250
  C&W/Pa 16x11 Mujer con Alcatrazes Sby 11/92 16,500
  W/Pa 16x11 Nina Con Canasta Sby 6/93 12,650
  C/Pa 25x19 Lavanderas 25 Sby 10/92 7,150
  Br&I/Pa 16x11 Mujer y Nino 47 Chr 11/92 6,600
  Pe/Pa 8x5 Three Drawings Sby 6/93 3,738
  C/Pa 14x9 Head Studies: Three Drawings 23 Sby 10/92 . . 3,300
  I&S/B 8x10 Arbol Cerca de las Casas But 4/93 2,300
  H/Pa 10x8 Cabeza 20 Sby 5/93 2,300
Riveros, Jorge   Col 1934-
  * See 1991 Edition . . . .
Rivers, Larry   Am 1923-
  W/Pa 8x10 Three Queens 61 Sby 2/93 10,350
  Y&H/Pa 11x11 Natural Camels III '80 Chr 10/92 6,050
  H,Y&K/Pa 35x29 Banker Called Rothschild '83 Chr 5/93 . . . 5,750
  H&L/Pa 13x16 Untitled Chr 2/93 3,520
  Pe/Pa 8x8 Webster Sby 10/92 2,750
Rives, Frances E.   Am 1890-1968
  * See 1991 Edition . . . .
Riviere, Briton   Eng 1840-1920
  O/C 32x45 Confederates 1892 Doy 11/92 3,300
  O/C 42x53 Rizpah 1886 Sby 2/93 2,300
Riviere, Henri   Fr 1864-1951
  * See 1993 Edition . . . .
Riviere, William   Br 1806-1876
  O/C 42x66 Riding Out the Storm Sby 6/93 8,050
Rivoire, Francois   Fr 1842-1919
  * See 1993 Edition . . . .
Rix, Julian   Am 1850-1903
  O/C 29x60 A Mountain Lake Fre 10/92 9,000
  O/C 18x28 California Oaks But 3/93 8,800
  O/C/B 30x50 High Country Indian Encampment 83 But 3/93 6,600
  O/C 30x40 Sunny Day Near the Bay 1898 But 6/93 5,750
  O/B 42x32 Sunset Brd 2/93 4,400
  O/C 20x12 Wooded Path 77 But 6/93 4,312
  O/C 36x54 Road Through a Forest Sby 3/93 2,300
  O/C 25x42 Autumn Scene 78 But 3/93 2,200
  O/C 21x28 Ship Returning at Sunset Wes 12/92 1,760
  O/Pn 11x8 Sunset 76 But 12/92 1,760
Robaudi, Alcide Theophile   Fr 19C
  * See 1992 Edition . . . .

Robb, Elizabeth B. Am 20C
  * See 1991 Edition . . . .
Robb, J. E. Am 19C
  * See 1991 Edition . . . .
Robb, William George Br 1872-
  O/C 13x30 The Summer Ball Skn 3/93 1,650
Robbe, Henri Bel 1807-1899
  * See 1991 Edition . . . .
Robbe, Louis Marie Dominique Bel 1806-1887
  * See 1993 Edition . . . .
Robbecke, Moritz Friedrich Ger 1857-1916
  O/C 34x46 Christmas Lore 94 Chr 10/92 5,500
Robbins, Ellen Am 1828-1905
  W/B 20x25 Lincoln Boat House 1890 Sby 12/92 3,850
Robbins, Horace Wolcott Am 1842-1904
  * See 1993 Edition . . . .
Robert, Alexandre Nestor N. Bel 1817-1890
  O/C 45x34 Jeune Fille Pensive 1878 Sby 5/93 13,800
Robert, Hubert Fr 1733-1808
  O/C 21x26 Tomb Jean-Jacques Rousseau 1802 Sby 5/93 . 63,000
  O/C 64x39 Washerwomen at a Pool Sby 5/93 63,000
Robert, Jean Con 20C
  O/C 24x36 Landscape Lou 9/92 250
Robert, Marius Hubert Fr 20C
  O/C 24x32 Les Martigues Hnd 10/92 300
Roberti, Fernando Di Roberto It 1786-1837
  G/Pa/Pb 13x18 La Villa Reale, Real Casino: Pair Chr 5/93 . . 8,050
Roberts, Alice T. Am 20C
  O/C 30x22 The Model Fre 10/92 50
Roberts, David Sco 1796-1864
  O/C 34x24 Moorish Tower on the Bridge Sby 10/92 22,000
Roberts, Edwin Thomas Br 1840-1917
  O/C 30x25 Mother and Child Dum 5/93 2,500
Roberts, Morton Am 1927-1964
  W/Pa 22x28 Boats at Pierside 1959 Ih 11/92 550
Roberts, Nathan B. Am 19C
  O/B 12x18 Red Bank, Delaware River Chr 9/92 3,520
Roberts, Thomas E. Eng 1820-1901
  * See 1992 Edition . . . .
Roberts, Thomas Keith (Tom) Can 1909-
  O/B 16x22 Rain - Grand Allee Sbt 5/93 1,760
  O/B 12x18 Park Street Sbt 5/93 748
  O/Pn 8x10 Credit Valley Sbt 5/93 616
Roberts, Thomas William Aut 1856-1931
  * See 1993 Edition . . . .
Roberts, William Goodridge Can 1904-1974
  * See 1993 Edition . . . .
Robertson, Charles Eng 1844-1891
  * See 1990 Edition . . . .
Robertson, Percy Br 1868-1934
  * See 1993 Edition . . . .
Robertson, Sarah Margaret A. Can 1891-1948
  * See 1992 Edition . . . .
Robie, Jean Baptiste Bel 1821-1910
  O/Pn 24x18 Still Life with Roses, Syringas Chr 5/93 57,500
  O/Pn 28x20 Bouquet de Roses Hnd 10/92 20,000
  O/C 28x20 Floral Still Life But 11/92 6,600
Robin, Michel Fr 1930-
  O/C 23x28 Le Port Doelan Dum 4/93 2,100
Robins, Thomas Sewell Br 1814-1880
  * See 1991 Edition . . . .
Robinson, Albert Henry Can 1881-1956
  O/C 12x18 Victoria Square, Montreal 1909 Sbt 5/93 6,600
  O/Pn 9x11 Cote Des Neiges 1930 Sbt 11/92 5,500
Robinson, Charles Dormon Am 1847-1933
  O/C 12x18 Sidewheeler in San Francisco Bay But 3/93 7,150
  O/C 12x18 Mt. Tamalpais But 3/93 4,950
  O/C 28x38 Mt. Tamalpais But 6/93 4,312

  O/C 16x22 Flowering Dunes But 10/92 2,750
  O/Pn 5x9 Wildflowers Along the Coast But 6/93 1,955
Robinson, Florence Vincent Am 1874-1937
  W/Pa 14x19 Place de la Concorde Slo 7/93 2,000
  W/Pa Var Ten Works Wes 3/93 358
Robinson, H. W. Am 19C
  O/C 20x16 Chrysanthemums 1896 Brd 8/93 990
Robinson, Hal Am 1875-1933
  O/C 28x35 Dunes with Ocean Beyond Sby 9/92 1,760
  O/C 30x36 Creek Landscape Ald 5/93 1,600
  O/C 12x10 Open Gate Mys 12/92 440
Robinson, Theodore Am 1852-1896
  O/C 22x18 Girl Sewing Chr 5/93 101,500
  O/C 13x9 Girl in Red at the Piano Chr 3/93 17,250
Robinson, Thomas Am 1834-1888
  O/C 36x29 Herder with Cows and Sheep Skn 11/92 2,090
Robinson, Walter 20C
  E/C 36x36 Rapture, Remorse 1985 Chr 11/92 550
Robinson, William Br 1835-1895
  C&W/B 13x20 The Old Bridge 1878 Sby 1/93 805
Robinson, William Heath Eng 1872-1944
  * See 1992 Edition . . . .
Robinson, William S. Am 1861-1945
  * See 1993 Edition . . . .
Robinson, William T. Am 1852-1934
  * See 1993 Edition . . . .
Robus, Hugo Am 1885-1964
  Pe/Pa 10x12 Shaded Forms and Untitled Chr 12/92 220
Robusti, Domenico It 1560-1635
  * See 1993 Edition . . . .
Robusti, Jacopo It 1518-1594
  O/C 68x104 Holy Family with Infant St. John Sby 5/93 . . 101,500
Rocca, Michele It 1670-1751
  O/C 20x39 Bacchus and Ariadne Sby 5/93 10,925
Rocchi, F. It 19C
  W/Pa/B 15x21 Bringing the Horses in Chr 10/92 1,540
Roche, A. Br 19C
  O/C 5x11 Coach and Four on Open Road Chr 5/93 805
Rochegrosse, Georges Antoine Fr 1859-1938
  O/C 28x44 Nu Au Repos Sby 10/92 22,000
Rock, Geoffrey Allan Can 1923-
  * See 1993 Edition . . . .
Rockburne, Dorothea Can 1934-
  O/Pa 14x17 Untitled 70 Chr 2/93 550
Rockenschaub, Gerwald 1952-
  O/L 10x16 Untitled 85 Chr 11/92 1,100
Rockwell, Cleveland Am 1837-1907
  O/C 10x20 Rowing Across the River 1877 But 6/93 9,200
  O/Cd 6x11 Moonlit Landscape Wlf 12/92 2,100
Rockwell, Mary Chauplin Am 20C
  O/C 37x29 In Her Riding Habit Brd 2/93 1,320
Rockwell, Norman Am 1894-1978
  O/C 35x28 Happy Skiers on a Train Sby 5/93 134,500
  O/C 34x27 Jazz It Up with a Sax Sby 12/92 132,000
  O/C 43x34 The Convention (Hat Check Girl) Sby 5/93 . . 101,500
  O&Pe/Pb 30x31 Boy & Shopkeeper Sby 3/93 68,500
  O/C 15x13 Old Man and Boy: Halloween Sby 12/92 60,500
  O/C 30x19 Gramercy Park Chr 12/92 57,200
  O/C 22x18 Soldier Darning Socks Ih 11/92 55,000
  O/C 17x11 Study for Harvest Moon Sby 3/93 31,050
  W/B 12x10 Dance on a Music Box Chr 12/92 19,800
  O&R/C 23x36 Wolf, The Watchdog 1918 Chr 9/92 14,300
  Pe/Pa 18x17 Man, Boy in Church 1961 Ih 11/92 11,000
  O&Pe/C 23x29 At the Jewellers Chr 12/92 10,120
  O&R/C 23x36 Wolf, the Watchdog 1918 Chr 3/93 9,775
  Pe/Pa 17x14 A Christmas Prayer Chr 3/93 7,150
  C&Pe/Pa 9x14 Soldier at Machine Gun Ih 5/93 4,750
  O/C 18x16 Man Seated at Desk Ih 5/93 3,750
  Pl/Pa 4x9 Dog in Topcoat and Hat Ih 5/93 2,300
Rocle, Marius R. Am 1897-1967
  O/C 36x40 Shorty Shoeing Silver Mor 2/93 7,500
Roda, Antonio Spa 1921-1970
  O/C 51x77 Flores No. 16 87 Chr 11/92 13,200

Rodde, Michel Fr 1913-
  * See 1991 Edition . . . .
Rodetti, A* It 19C**
  O/B 16x24 Venetian Canals: Pair Sby 1/93 2,645
Rodin, Auguste Fr 1840-1917
  W/Pa 10x8 3 Watercolors Lou 6/93 1,675
  W/Pa 9x6 3 Watercolors Lou 6/93 800
  Pe&S/Pa 17x12 Figure Resting on One Leg Lou 9/92 800
  W/Pa 10x6 3 Watercolors Lou 6/93 650
  Pe&S/Pa 18x12 Standing Figure Lou 9/92 550
  Pe/Pa 11x8 Mother with Two Children Lou 12/92 525
  W/Pa 11x8 3 Watercolors Lou 6/93 500
  Pe&W/Pa 17x11 Female Figure Lou 12/92 500
  Pe&W/Pa 13x10 Standing Male Lou 12/92 500
  Pe/Pa 17x12 Kneeling Figure Lou 9/92 450
  Pe&S/Pa 18x12 Leaning Figure Viewed from Rear Lou 9/92 . 450
  Pe&W/Pa 10x16 Female in Prone Position Lou 12/92 425
  Pe&W/Pa 18x12 Seated, Standing Female: Two Lou 12/92 . 425
  Pe&W/Pa 12x9 Cambodian Dancer Lou 12/92 375
  Pe&W/Pa 15x10 Standing Female Lou 12/92 375
  W/Pa 15x10 Standing Female Lou 12/92 350
  Pe&W/Pa 14x10 Standing Female Lou 12/92 350
  Pe/Pa 15x10 Standing Female Lou 12/92 250
Rodolphe, Gustave Clarence Fr 19C
  * See 1991 Edition . . . .
Rodon, Francisco 1934-
  * See 1992 Edition . . . .
Rodriguez, Mariano Cub 1912-1990
  Pl/Pa 18x23 Baile 47 Sby 6/93 2,300
Roe, Clarence Br -1909
  O/C 12x35 Highland Landscape at Dusk Sby 1/93 1,380
  O/C 20x30 Mountainous Lake Chr 5/93 518
Roe, Frederick Rushing Br 1887-1947
  O/C 25x30 Gypsy Camp Lou 9/92 1,200
Roedig, Johannes Christian Dut 1750-1802
  * See 1993 Edition . . . .
Roelofs, W. & Verboeckhoven, E Dut 1822-1897
  O/C 19x30 A Summer's Day Chr 10/92 35,200
Roelofs, Willem Dut 1822-1897
  O/Pn 8x12 Wooded Clearing Chr 5/93 805
Roepel, Coenraet Dut 1678-1748
  * See 1993 Edition . . . .
Roerich, Nicholaj Konstantinov Rus 1874-1947
  O/C 19x39 Figure with Pan Pipes and Bears 1919 But 10/92 2,475
Roesch, Kurt Am 1905-
  O/C 24x34 Insects But 6/93 1,035
Roesen, Severin Am a 1848-1871
  O/C 30x25 Floral Still Life Sby 5/93 48,875
  O/C 25x30 Still Life with Pilsner Glass Chr 9/92 30,800
  O/Pn 20x16 Still Life with Fruit Sby 3/93 28,750
  O/Pn 16x20 Still Life Strawberry Basket Chr 12/92 27,500
  O/C/M 40x50 Still Life Fruit, Glass of Water FHB 6/93 . . . 25,000
  P/Pa 22x26 Still Life Fruit, Bird's Nest Sby 5/93 21,850
  O/C/B 6x9 Still Life Dum 11/92 6,000
  O/C/B 6x9 Still Life Dum 11/92 5,500
  O/C/B 6x9 Still Life Dum 11/92 4,000
Roesler, Ettore Franz It 1845-1907
  * See 1991 Edition . . . .
Roessler, Walter Rus 20C
  O/Pn 10x7 Tyrolean Peasants Chr 10/92 1,760
Roffiaen, J & Verboeckhoven, E Bel 1820-1898
  O/C 17x15 An Alpine Farm Scene 1851 Chr 10/92 6,600
Roffiaen, Jean Francois Bel 1820-1898
  * See 1992 Edition . . . .
Roger, Augustin Fr 19C
  * See 1992 Edition . . . .
Rogers, Annette Perkins Am 1841-1920
  O/C 17x21 Dunes at East Gloucester Skn 11/92 440
Rogers, Charles A. Am 1848-1918
  O/C 24x16 San Gabriel Mission '06 Mor 11/92 350

Rogers, Franklin Whiting Am 1854-
  O/C 20x24 Sunrise Over the Salt Marsh Skn 5/93 660
Rogers, Otto Donald Can 1935-
  * See 1993 Edition . . . .
Rogers, William Eng 19C
  * See 1992 Edition . . . .
Rohde, H. Am 19C
  O/C 31x26 Catskill Mountain Landscape Sby 3/93 1,380
Rohlfs, Christian Ger 1849-1938
  H&G/Pa 19x16 Study of a Seated Nude But 4/93 7,475
Rojas, Elmar LA 1938-
  O&A/C 71x69 Un Dia Fiesta en el Campo 91 Chr 11/92 . . 33,000
Roje, Arsen
  A/C 75x72 Break In 1984 Sby 10/92 2,970
Roland Dut 19C
  O/B 6x9 Wash Women; Landscape: Two Fre 4/93 1,100
Rolfe, Alexander F. Br a 1839-1871
  * See 1992 Edition . . . .
Rolfe, Helen G. Am 20C
  O/C 30x25 Woman in Blue Hat Yng 5/93 250
Rolfe, Henry Leonidas Br 1847-1881
  W&Pe/Pa 10x14 Ships Sailing off the White Cliffs Chr 10/92 1,320
Rolle, August H. O. Am 1875-1941
  * See 1992 Edition . . . .
Rollins, J. Am 20C
  O/C 23x31 Autumn Blossoms Brd 2/93 990
Rollins, Nona Bickford
  G&P/Pa 19x15 Santa and Reindeer Airborne Ih 11/92 350
Rollins, Tim Am 1955-
  * See 1992 Edition . . . .
Rollins, Tim & K.O.S. 20C
  A&MM/C 105x48 F451: The Scarlet Letter 87 Chr 11/92 . 11,000
  O&Mk/Pa/L 32x32 Nature Theater of Oklahoma Sby 11/92 . 8,800
  A&K/Pa/C 32x32 Nature Theatre of Oklahoma VII Chr 11/92 8,800
  Gd,W&Pe/Pa 8x5 Amerika: Two Drawings 86 Sby 10/92 . . 2,200
  Pe&Pt/Pa 8x5 Untitled Sby 5/93 1,150
  A/Pa/C 10x8 Whiteness of Whale (Study IV) 85 Chr 11/92 . 770
Rollins, Warren Eliphalet Am 1861-1962
  O/C 10x14 Indians Camping on the Prairie 1891 Chr 5/93 . 4,600
  O/C 14x17 Indians and Teepee Sby 9/92 4,125
  O/C/B 18x14 Spirit Song But 10/92 1,980
  O/C/B 11x6 Navajo Weaver But 6/93 1,265
  O/C 12x20 Desert Scene with Figure Eld 8/93 715
  O/Cb 8x15 The Sea-Calif Mor 11/92 400
Rolshoven, Julius C. Am 1858-1930
  O/B 16x12 Rainmaker Sby 12/92 8,250
  O/C 33x26 Castanets Hnd 10/92 4,200
Romagnoli, Giovanni It 1893-1976
  O/C 31x27 Girl Eating Fruit 1924 Hnd 5/93 13,000
Romako, Anton Aus 1832-1889
  * See 1993 Edition . . . .
Roman, A. Am 20C
  MM/Pa 8x6 New Orleans Scene Lou 6/93 125
Romanach, Leopoldo Cub 1862-1951
  O/C 36x48 Guajiros 1922 Chr 11/92 33,000
  O/C 26x51 La Casa de los Amos Chr 11/92 20,900
Romanelli, Giovanni Francesco It 1610-1662
  * See 1993 Edition . . . .
Romano, Guilio It 1499-1546
  I/Pa 8x15 Roman Court Scene Hnz 5/93 37
Romano, Umberto Am 1905-1984
  * See 1992 Edition . . . .
Romanovsky, Dimitri Am 20C
  * See 1993 Edition . . . .
Romans, Charles J. Am 1893-1973
  O/C 25x30 Sunflowers FHB 6/93 10
Rombouts, Gillis 1630-1678
  O/Pn 23x19 Village Scene with Church Tower Sby 10/92 . . 5,50
Romero Y Escalante, Juan De S. Spa 1643-1695
  * See 1992 Edition . . . .
Romero, Carlos Orozco Mex 1898-
  O/C 18x24 Valle de Mexico 1944 Sby 11/92 26,40
  O/C 19x25 Caminantes Sby 5/93 13,80

W/Pa 11x10 Mujer Sby 11/92 6,050
G/Pa 13x10 Paisaje Metafisico I 1931 Chr 11/92 6,050
G/Pa 10x9 Pescador 1929 Sby 5/93 2,300
PVPa 13x10 Hombre Con Latigo Sby 5/93 1,955

Romieu, Leon Edouard Fr 19C
* See 1992 Edition . . . .
Romiti, Romano It 1906-1951
* See 1992 Edition . . . .
Romney, George Br 1734-1802
O/C 31x26 Portrait of a Lady Chr 1/93 38,500
O/C 30x25 Portrait of Sir Thomas Frankland Sby 10/92 . . . 17,050
O/C 30x25 Portrait Mrs. Richard Tickell Chr 1/93 13,200
PVPa 5x7 Studies for Portrait of Lady Chr 1/93 3,080
Romo, Jose Luis 20C
* See 1993 Edition . . . .
Romulo, Teodulo Mex 1943-
* See 1990 Edition . . . .
Ronald, William Smith Can 1926-
O/C 78x60 The Doctor 74 Sbt 5/93 4,180
W/Pa 17x19 Abstract Composition '56 Sbt 11/92 1,496
W/Pa 22x30 Lilli Palmer '81 Sbt 5/93 704
Ronay, J. L. Con 19C
* See 1993 Edition . . . .
Rondel, Frederick Am 1826-1892
O/C 29x40 The Unexpected Visitor 1859 Sby 9/92 2,420
O/C 6x10 River Landscape in Autumn Sby 3/93 1,955
Rondel, Henri Fr 1857-1919
O/C 26x22 Young Woman in Diaphanous Gown But 5/93 . . 3,450
O/C 26x22 Red Haired Beauty Chr 10/92 2,420
Ronmy, Guillaume Frederic Fr 1786-1854
* See 1991 Edition . . . .
Ronner-Knip, Henriette Dut 1821-1909
O/Pn 14x21 Contentment 1900 Chr 10/92 35,200
O/Pn 9x13 Kittens 93 Sby 5/93 28,750
Rook, Ada D.
W/Pa 19x23 Central Park Zoo Eld 8/93 66
Roos, Philipp Peter Ger 1657-1706
O/C 68x98 Shepherd Resting with Flock Chr 5/93 46,000
O/C 38x58 Shepherd Cows Sheep Dogs Sby 1/93 6,900
Roosenboom, Albert Fr a 1865-1875
O/C 17x26 A Day at the Beach Sby 5/93 14,950
O/C 18x15 Watching the Goldfish But 5/93 2,300
Roosenboom, Margarete Dut 1843-1896
* See 1993 Edition . . . .
Roosenboom, Nicholas J. Dut 1808-1880
O/Pn 5x7 Skaters on a Frozen River Chr 2/93 5,500
Roosevelt, Jae Am 20C
A/C 34x36 Spring Garden '83 Slo 4/93 150
Root, Robert Marshall Am 1863-
O/B 28x48 Shelbyville Park 1929 Hnd 12/92 850
Ropp, Roy M. Am 1888-
O/C 18x36 California Landscape Lou 6/93 900
Rosa, Salvator It 1615-1673
PVPa 3x3 The Head of an Angel Chr 1/93 990
Rosal, Ottone It 1895-1957
* See 1991 Edition . . . .
Rosam, Walter Alfred Ger 1883-1916
* See 1993 Edition . . . .
Rosati, Albert It 19C
W/Pa 19x29 In the Harem Chr 5/93 2,530
Rosati, E. It 20C
O/C 24x20 An Italian Peasant Girl Chr 10/92 1,210
Rosati, Giullio It 1858-1917
* See 1992 Edition . . . .
Rosch, Ludwig Aus 1865-1908
O/C 25x36 Wildflowers Shaded by Trees Chr 2/93 3,080
Rose, Carl Am 1903-1971
W/Pa 13x10 Fraternity Initiate at Restaurant Ih 5/93 600
Rose, Guy Am 1867-1925
O/C/B 24x29 Twin Lakes, Eastern Sierras But 3/93 77,000
O/C 20x24 Sunrise in Early Sunlight But 6/93 48,875
Rose, Herman Am 1909-
* See 1991 Edition . . . .
Rose, Iver Am 1899-1972
O/M 18x24 Woman Artist in Studio Lou 3/93 1,050

Rose, Julius Ger 1828-1911
* See 1993 Edition . . . .
Rose, Manuel Uru 1887-1961
O/C 55x62 La Familia del Artista 1936 Sby 5/93 46,000
O/C 32x24 La Paica y el Garado Sby 11/92 7,700
Rose, William Am 1909-
G&W/Pa 20x30 Distraught Senorita Ih 5/93 250
Rose, William S. Br 1810-1875
O/C/B 19x26 Giving the Child a Bath 74 Chr 10/92 1,540
Roseboom, A. Dut 19C
O/Pn 19x26 Skaters on Frozen Pond 1855 Chr 5/93 2,760
Roseland, Harry Herman Am 1868-1950
O/C 28x40 Coney Island '33 Sby 12/92 52,250
O/C 20x31 Reading Tea Leaves 10 Chr 12/92 28,600
O/C 25x32 An Important Letter 98 Chr 12/92 26,400
O/C 22x30 "He loves me..." Chr 3/93 21,850
O/C 20x30 Reading the Crystal 1906 Chr 9/92 17,600
O/C 22x28 The Chess Game Chr 5/93 16,100
O/C 14x20 Tending the Fire 1906 Chr 3/93 8,625
O/C 14x20 Paying the Rent Lou 3/93 8,000
O/B 8x10 Mother and Child Hnd 3/93 4,600
O/Ab 8x11 Her Favorite Flower Sel 9/92 3,500
O/C 10x14 The Fortune Teller Skn 9/92 2,860
O/C 14x20 Cabin Interior Hnd 10/92 950
Rosell, A.
O/C 30x22 Young Girl with St. Bernard 1907 Dum 2/93 . . . 2,000
Rosell, Alexander Br 19C
* See 1993 Edition . . . .
Rosen, Charles Am 1878-1950
* See 1993 Edition . . . .
Rosen, Ernest T. Am 1877-1926
* See 1993 Edition . . . .
Rosen, Jan 19C
* See 1991 Edition . . . .
Rosenberg, James N. Am 1874-1970
P/Pb 21x19 Adirondack Landscape 64 Skn 5/93 220
O/B 14x17 Adirondack Landscape Mys 12/92 192
O/B 24x30 Mt. Hurricane Mys 12/92 165
Rosenquist, James Am 1933-
O/C 78x198 Earth Revolves at Night Sby 11/92 319,000
O/C/Pn 75x114 Untitled 1988 Chr 11/92 231,000
O/C 58x58 Win House This Christmas 1964 Chr 11/92 . . 132,000
O/C 60x35 Paint Brush 1964 Chr 11/92 83,600
O/C 43x55 Fiery Flowers Hrs Sby 5/93 57,500
L&MM/Pa 28x74 Star Way 74 Sby 10/92 12,100
Rosenthal, Albert Am 1863-1939
O/C 50x35 Portrait Mrs. H. Bryan Owsley 1910 Chr 12/92 . 15,400
Rosenthal, Doris Am 1895-1971
C&P/Pa 17x14 Mexican Children Slo 5/93 100
Rosenthal, Toby Edward Am 1849-1917
O/C 45x72 A Seminary Alarmed, Mills College But 12/92 . 33,000
Rosenthalis, Moshe
* See 1992 Edition . . . .
Roshardt, Walter 1897-1966
G&K/Pa/M 40x28 Ein Junges Madchen 1950 Chr 5/93 . . . 978
Rosier, Amedee Fr 1831-
* See 1992 Edition . . . .
Rosierse, Johannes Dut 1818-1901
O/Pn 23x18 The Night Market Sby 2/93 6,900
O/C 15x11 Boys with Bird's Nest Hnd 10/92 2,200
Roslin, Alexandre Swd 1718-1793
* See 1992 Edition . . . .
Rosner, Charles Am 20C
* See 1992 Edition . . . .
Rosofsky, Seymour Am 20C
O/C 34x42 Parking Lot Hnd 10/92 3,200
P/Pa 19x25 Man with Bandaged Foot Hnd 10/92 600
Ross, Alvin Am 20C
* See 1993 Edition . . . .
Ross, James Am 20C
W/Pa 14x18 Seaside November Fre 10/92 800
W/Pa 19x28 Philadelphia Fre 10/92 500
W/Pa 18x23 Winter Mist Fre 10/92 500
W/Pa 21x29 Morning Glow Fre 4/93 400
W/Pa 13x19 Valley Oasis Fre 4/93 375

W/Pa 18x23 Daylight on Nightlight Fre 4/93 350
W/Pa 19x23 Harborside Fre 10/92 300
W/Pa 19x27 Independence Hall Fre 4/93 300
W/Pa 13x19 Sea Watch Fre 10/92 180
Medium? 13x20 Walk Through the Sand Dunes Fre 10/92 . . 150

Ross, Joseph Halford   Br 1866-
* See 1992 Edition . . . .
Ross, Robert Thorburn   Sco 1816-1876
* See 1993 Edition . . . .
Rossano, Federico   It 1835-1912
O/C 25x36 Le Printemps 1877 Sby 5/93 29,900
Rosseau, J. J.   Eur 19C
* See 1992 Edition . . . .
Rosseau, Percival Leonard   Am 1859-1937
O/C 22x19 Best of Friends Sby 6/93 5,750
O/C 13x28 On Point Lou 6/93 1,600
Rosseletti, Rosso   It 19C
O/C 15x12 General Lafayette 1777 Hnd 12/92 725
Rosselli, Bernardo   It 1450-1526
T/Pn 28x16 Madonna, Child, Infant St. John 1762 Sby 10/92 46,750
Rosselli, Cosimo   It 1439-1507
* See 1990 Edition . . . .
Rossert, Paul   Fr 1851-1918
W/Pa 9x14 The Vigil Hnd 10/92 700
Rossetti, Dante Gabriel   Br 1828-1882
* See 1991 Edition . . . .
Rossetti, Luigi   It 1881-1912
* See 1992 Edition . . . .
Rossi, Alberto   It 1858-1936
O/C 21x9 The Orange Seller '98 Wlf 12/92 1,100
Rossi, Alexander M.   Br 19C
* See 1993 Edition . . . .
Rossi, Enrico   It 1856-1916
O/Pn 18x15 An Elegant Young Lady Chr 5/93 3,220
Rossi, G*   It 19C**
O/C 35x48 Still Life of Flowers Sby 1/93 4,025
Rossi, Lucio   Fr 1846-1913
W/Pa 15x20 Le Prestidigitateur Sby 10/92 3,300
W&G/Pa 14x9 The Assassin Sby 5/93 2,760
Rossi, Luigi   Sws 1853-1923
O/C 42x67 Figures and Animals in a Barn Chr 2/93 60,500
O/C 29x25 Peasant Family 1870 But 5/93 5,462
Rossi, Nicola Maria   It 1699-1755
* See 1992 Edition . . . .
Rossi, Pasqualino   It 1641-1725
* See 1992 Edition . . . .
Rossier, Rudolf   Aus 1864-
* See 1991 Edition . . . .
Rossignol, Lily   Fr 20C
* See 1993 Edition . . . .
Rossiter, Thomas Prichard   Am 1818-1871
O/C 17x28 Muses and Graces 1859 Chr 9/92 5,280
Rossier, Rudolf   Aus 1864-
* See 1993 Edition . . . .
Rostad, Thorbjorg   20C
O/C 25x28 Still Life by the Lake Slo 4/93 125
Roszezewski, Henri Dominique   Fr 19C
O/Pn 14x11 Aiguiere d'Agathe Sby 2/93 2,875
Rota, G.   It 19C
O/Pn 11x14 Young Boy with a Basket of Fruit But 11/92 . . 3,575
Rotari, Pietro Antonio   It 1707-1762
P/Pa/C 18x14 Young Woman Holding a Fan Sby 5/93 . . . 51,750
O/C 17x13 Peasant Girl in White Scarf Sby 1/93 5,175
Rotella, Mimmo   It 1918-
L/C 30x23 Untitled 1960 Chr 2/93 6,050
L/B 9x7 Untitled 60 Chr 2/93 5,280
Roth, Andreas   Am 20C
* See 1992 Edition . . . .
Rothaug, Alexander   Aus 1870-1946
* See 1992 Edition . . . .
Rothaug, Leopold   Am 1868-
O/C 20x28 Diana the Huntress 1899 Chr 10/92 2,860

Rothbort, Samuel   Am 1882-1971
O/C/B 8x25 Coney Island But 12/92 1,650
Rothenberg, Susan   Am 1945-
O/Pa 30x23 Untitled Sby 5/93 14,950
C/Pa 31x22 Untitled (Mondrian) 1985 Chr 11/92 11,000
O/Pa 25x23 Untitled 85 Chr 11/92 4,180
Rothenstein, Sir William   Br 1872-1945
* See 1990 Edition . . . .
Rothermel, Peter Fred   Am 1817-1895
O/C 24x20 The Beggar Girl 18? Sby 3/93 3,450
Rothko, Mark   Am 1903-1970
O/C 90x59 Dark Over Light 1954 Chr 11/92 . . . . 1.21M
O/C 70x60 Brown, Black & Blue 1958 Sby 11/92 . . . . . . 1.1M
O/C 79x69 Untitled 1957 Chr 11/92 . . . . 1.1M
O&Mg/C 68x38 Black Stripe 57 Sby 5/93 882,500
O/Pa/C 70x41 Untitled 1969 Sby 5/93 332,500
A/Pa/C 78x59 Untitled '69 Sby 11/92 297,000
O/C 18x15 No. 9 Sby 11/92 99,000
Rotta, Antonio   It 1828-1903
O/C 25x21 Canine Casualty Finds Home (2) 1866 Chr 5/93 43,700
O/C 56x73 Venetian Water Fete 1863 But 5/93 43,125
O/Pn 9x6 Peasant Girl; Peasant Girl: Pair Sby 1/93 14,375
Rottenhammer, Hans (the Elder)   Ger 1564-1625
* See 1992 Edition . . . .
Rottman, Mozart   Hun 1874-
* See 1992 Edition . . . .
Rottmanner, Alfred   Ger 20C
O/C 24x19 Watering the Garden Chr 2/93 660
Rottmayr, Johann Franz Michael 1654-1730
* See 1993 Edition . . . .
Rouan, Francois   1943-
* See 1993 Edition . . . .
Rouault, Georges   Fr 1871-1958
Pac&C/Pa/C 13x8 Hommes de peine Chr 11/92 50,600
O&Lh/Pa/C 12x14 Saint Jean Baptiste Chr 11/92 39,600
O,G&W/Pa 18x12 En Pensant a l'Abbe Pierre Sby 11/92 . . 38,500
Roubaud, Franz   Rus 1856-1928
O/C 28x40 Fording the River Chr 10/92 6,600
Rouby, Alfred   Fr 1849-
* See 1990 Edition . . . .
Rougeron, Jules James   Fr 1841-1880
O/C 39x32 Deux Jeunes Filles Sby 2/93 8,913
O/C 32x15 Woman with Umbrella But 5/93 8,625
O/C 36x29 Un Ecrivain Public (sic) Espagnol Brd 2/93 5,500
Rouland, Orlando   Am 1871-1945
* See 1993 Edition . . . .
Roulle, Lucien   Fr 20C
O/C 24x29 Blues Number 2 Hnd 5/93 400
Roumegous, Auguste Francois   Fr 19C
* See 1992 Edition . . . .
Rousseau, Alain   Fr 1926-
O/C 18x15 Fleurs au Jardin Dum 8/93 2,200
Rousseau, Helen   Am 1898-
O/B 20x24 Section House But 10/92 4,950
O/B 30x34 Campground But 10/92 4,675
O/B 25x30 Southern California Street Scene But 10/92 3,850
Rousseau, Henri   Fr 1844-1910
O/Pn 17x21 Arab Horsemen 1907 Dum 6/93 15,000
Rousseau, Henri Emilien   Fr 1875-1933
O/C 26x22 Arabs Falconing on Horseback But 11/92 10,450
Rousseau, Marc   Fr 20C
O/C 18x23 Street Scene Hnd 9/92 170
Rousseau, Marguerite   Bel 1888-1948
* See 1993 Edition . . . .
Rousseau, Phillipe   Fr 1816-1887
O/C 11x14 Les Chiens But 5/93 3,738
O/C 18x13 Arcadian Scene with Courting Couple Hnd 12/92 . 800
Rousseau, Theodore Etienne   Fr 1812-1867
O/C 40x34 Coucher de Soleil Sby 2/93 123,500
O/Pa/C 9x12 Pont Dans Lejura Sby 5/93 29,900
O/C 9x10 Bord de L'Oise Sby 10/92 8,800
O/Pn 9x12 Coucher de Soleil Sby 5/93 8,625

O/C 11x13 Au Bords de la Loire Sby 10/92 7,700
O/C 16x26 Road with a Figure at Sunset Fre 10/92 . . 4,250
Roussel, B.   Fr 19C
O/C 16x21 Two Bird Dogs Hnz 5/93 190
O/C 16x20 Two Dogs Hnz 5/93 180
Roussel, Ker-Xavier   Fr 1867-1944
* See 1993 Edition . . . .
Roussel, Pierre   Fr 1927-
* See 1991 Edition . . . .
Rousset, Jules   Fr 1840-
* See 1992 Edition . . . .
Roux Family   Fr 19C
W/Pa 17x22 Barque Vigo 1862 Brd 8/93 3,300
Roux, Paul   Fr 1840-1918
W/Pa 7x10 Landscape with Cottage 1914 Hnd 6/93 . . . 160
Rowbotham, Charles   Eng 1823-1895
W/Pa 10x7 Italian Girl Mys 3/93 275
Rowe, Ernest Arthur   Br -1922
* See 1992 Edition . . . .
Rowes, B. J.   Am 19C
O/C 18x26 River Landscape Sel 9/92 375
Rowland, Benjamin (Jr.)   Am 1904-
O/C 20x24 Noon Day Sun on the Delta Fre 4/93 1,100
Rowlandson, George Derville   Br 1861-
* See 1993 Edition . . . .
Rowlandson, Thomas   Eng 1756-1827
W,I&S/Pa 8x11 Marital Love Chr 10/92 1,760
S&Pe/Pa 6x8 Sleeping Beauties Chr 10/92 1,430
Roy, Alix   Hai
* See 1993 Edition . . . .
Roy, Marius   Fr 1833-
O/Pn 13x18 The Mess Sby 2/93 5,175
Roy, Martin & Keith Haring   Am 20C
* See 1993 Edition . . . .
Roy, Pierre   Fr 20C
* See 1992 Edition . . . .
Roy, Tine   20C
O/C 40x48 Autumn Landscape with Lake Dum 1/93 60
Roybet, Ferdinand   Fr 1840-1920
O/Pn 17x13 Young Arab Chr 2/93 9,900
O/Pn 32x25 Portrait of a Cavalier Sby 2/93 4,370
O/C 29x20 Girl Bathing Fre 4/93 1,400
Royle, Herbert   Eng 1870-1958
* See 1992 Edition . . . .
Rozaire, Arthur D.   Can 1879-1922
* See 1992 Edition . . . .
Rozen, George
O/C 20x16 Cowboy with Rifle Ih 11/92 1,600
Rozen, Jerome   Am a 1933-
O/Cb 12x16 Harbor Late Afternoon/Calif Skn 9/92 1,540
Rozier, A.   Fr 19C
O/Pn 17x12 Venice, The Piazzetta Hnd 10/92 2,000
Rubbiani, Felice   1677-1752
O/C 23x38 Still Lives (4) Chr 1/93 77,000
Rubbiani, Felice & Velani, F.   It 1677-1752
* See 1993 Edition . . . .
Ruben, Franz Leo   Aus 1843-1920
* See 1991 Edition . . . .
Rubens, Sir Peter Paul   Flm 1577-1640
O/Pn 28x21 Head of a Bearded Man Chr 5/93 354,500
Rubert, F. S.   Am 19C
O/C 22x32 Fisherman at River Bank 1892 Mor 6/93 275
Rubin, Michael   Am
* See 1993 Edition . . . .
Rubin, Reuven   Isr 1893-1974
O/C 26x32 Jaffa Harbor Sby 5/93 75,100
O/C 25x32 Safed Sby 5/93 68,500
O/C 29x36 Springtime in Galilee Sby 2/93 50,600
O/C 26x32 Valley of Sharon Sby 10/92 35,750
O/C 13x10 The Flute Player Sby 5/93 20,700
O/C 15x18 Springtime in Galilee Chr 10/92 18,700
O/C 13x10 Biblical Vision Sby 10/92 8,800
Pl&S/Pa/B 31x21 In the Negev 1960 Chr 11/92 6,600
G&I/Pa 30x21 Crowning of the Torah Sby 10/92 3,575
I,S&W/B 30x22 Musicians of Safed Sby 10/92 3,300

I/Pa 25x19 Mother and Child Skn 11/92 1,650
Rude, Olaf   Dan 1866-1957
* See 1991 Edition . . . .
Rude, Sophie (Nee Fremiet)   Fr 1797-1867
* See 1991 Edition . . . .
Ruelas, Julio   Mex 1870-1907
* See 1991 Edition . . . .
Ruf, Don Louis   Am 20C
O/C 16x20 Mexican Street Scene Lou 6/93 300
Ruff, Thomas   1958-
Ph 83x65 Untitled 1988 Sby 2/93 11,500
Ph 83x65 Untitled 1988 Sby 11/92 9,900
Ph 81x63 Untitled (Ralph Muller) 1986 Chr 11/92 9,900
Ph 83x65 Untitled 1988 Chr 11/92 6,600
Ph 83x65 Untitled 1988 Sby 10/92 5,500
Ph 82x70 Untitled 1989 Chr 11/92 2,530
Ph 16x12 Two Untitled Photographs 1988 Chr 11/92 . . . 2,200
Rugendas, Johann Moritz   Ger 1802-1858
W/Pa 8x12 Fiesta a San Miguel Arcangel Sby 11/92 41,250
O/C/Pn 9x12 Pueblo 1838 Chr 11/92 28,600
Ruiz, Antonio   Mex 1897-1964
* See 1993 Edition . . . .
Ruiz, Tomasso   Spa 18C
* See 1993 Edition . . . .
Ruiz, Yamero   Am a 1890-1910
* See 1993 Edition . . . .
Ruiz-Pipo, Manolo   Spa 1929-
* See 1992 Edition . . . .
Rundt, Hans Hinrich   1660-1750
* See 1993 Edition . . . .
Rungius, Carl Clemens Moritz   Am 1869-1959
O/C 30x45 The Old Man of the Mountains Sby 5/93 29,900
O/C 30x36 Rocky Mountain Landscape Chr 3/93 23,000
O/C 24x32 Bear in the Mountains Chr 5/93 13,800
O/C 12x16 Bighorn Sheep, Nigel Pass 1919 Chr 5/93 13,800
O&R/C 18x14 Two Moose on Promontory Sel 12/92 2,900
Ruoppolo, Giovanni Battisa   It 1629-1693
* See 1991 Edition . . . .
Ruscha, Ed   Am 1937-
A/C 62x138 Light (Part I) Sby 2/93 112,500
O/C 84x138 Study of Friction and Wear 1983 Chr 11/92 . . . 71,500
A/Pa 60x40 True Lady Sby 11/92 30,250
Pg/B 40x60 Nice Destiny 1989 Chr 11/92 23,100
Pg/Pa 23x29 You and Me 83 Sby 11/92 17,600
O/C 20x24 Wire 1972 Chr 5/93 16,100
Gp/Pa 23x14 1984 1967 Sby 2/93 14,950
MM 36x40 Do You Think She Has It? 1974 Sby 10/92 . . . 13,200
Pg/Pa 23x29 Small, Med., Large Companies 1983 Sby 2/93 12,650
P/Pa 23x29 S-Sea of D-D-Desire '79 Sby 10/92 12,100
E,A&L/B 17x35 Study for Light Chr 11/92 12,100
Pg/Pa 22x29 Various Things That Hurt 1976 Chr 11/92 . . 12,100
E,A,H&L/B 17x35 Study for Light Chr 11/92 9,350
Gp/Pa 14x23 Act Sby 5/93 9,200
Ruschi, Francesco   It 1610-1661
* See 1992 Edition . . . .
Rusinol, Santiago   Spa 1861-1931
* See 1993 Edition . . . .
Russ, C. B.   Am a 1860-1920
* See 1993 Edition . . . .
Russ, Robert   Aus 1847-1922
* See 1991 Edition . . . .
Russell, Charles Marion   Am 1864-1926
O&R/B 19x25 The Making of a Warrior 1898 Chr 12/92 . . 77,000
W/Pa 7x5 Indian with Rifle Chr 9/92 7,700
Russell, George Horne   Can 1861-1933
* See 1993 Edition . . . .
Russell, Gyrth   Am 1892-1970
* See 1992 Edition . . . .
Russell, John   Br 19C
* See 1993 Edition . . . .
Russell, John   Br 1745-1806
* See 1993 Edition . . . .
Russell, John Wentworth   Can 1879-1959
O/C/B 13x16 Gathering Hay 1910 Sbt 11/92 968

Russell, Marion   Am 20C
W/Pa 14x11 Nuremburg Church 1892 Mys 3/93 412
Russell, Mary   Am 19C
O/C 15x22 Tabletop Still Life of Fruit Slo 7/93 350
Russell, Morgan   Am 1886-1953
O/C 20x20 Infantry Maneuvers Chr 12/92 1,760
O/C 16x13 Untitled Sby 3/93 1,265
Pe/Pa 14x13 Three Bathers 1940 Sby 9/92 1,210
Russell, Walter   Am 1871-1963
O/C 29x36 At the Seashore 98 Chr 12/92 77,000
Russell, William George   Am 1860-
W/Pa 6x8 Cottage by a Lake: Pair Eld 4/93 143
Russolo, Luigi   It 20C
* See 1991 Edition . . . .
Rust, Johna Adolph   Dut 1828-1915
O/C 12x17 Shipping in the Estuary Chr 10/92 3,080
O/Pn 10x13 Fishing Boats by the Shore Chr 2/93 1,210
Ruthenbech, Reiner   20C
* See 1993 Edition . . . .
Rutledge, Ann   Am 1890-
W/Pa 25x31 Magnolias Mor 2/93 100
Ruvolo, Felix   Am 1912-
* See 1993 Edition . . . .
Ruysch, Anna Elisabeth   a 1680-1741
O/C 14x12 Still Life Peaches, Grapes 1685 Sby 1/93 28,750
Ruysch, Rachel   Dut 1664-1750
* See 1993 Edition . . . .
Ruysdael, Jacob Salomonsz.   1630-1681
O/Pn 20x27 Landscape with Cattle Resting Sby 5/93 18,400
Ruytinx, Alfred   Bel 1871-
* See 1992 Edition . . . .
Ryan, Anne   Am 1889-1954
MM/M 17x14 Gray and White Collage Sby 5/93 7,475
L/Pa 7x5 Untitled Collage Chr 3/93 3,450
Ryan, Patrick   19C
* See 1991 Edition . . . .
Ryan, Tom   Am 1922-
* See 1990 Edition . . . .
Ryback, Issachar   Rus 1897-1935
* See 1993 Edition . . . .
Ryckaert III, David   Flm 1612-1661
* See 1993 Edition . . . .
Ryckaert, Marten   1587-1631
O/Cp 8x11 Landscape w/Hunters by Stream 1622 Sby 5/93 79,500
Ryder, Chauncey Foster   Am 1868-1949
O/Pn 10x13 The Beach Skn 11/92 6,050
O/C 30x36 Extensive Mountainous Landscape Chr 5/93 . . . 3,450
O/C 24x20 On the Mountain Side Skn 11/92 3,300
W/Pa 14x18 The Farm Brd 2/93 2,860
O/B 7x9 Hilly Landscape Mys 3/93 1,045
O/C/B 12x16 Mountain Landscape Wes 10/92 770
O/B 6x9 Topsfield Hnd 12/92 650
O/Pn 6x9 Surf and Rocks Skn 3/93 605
Ryder, H. O.
O/C 18x24 Landscape Study 1899 FHB 6/93 50
Rygaard, Thorvald   Scn 20C
O/C 14x21 Country Road 1918 Lou 12/92 250
Ryland, Henry   Br 1856-1924
O/Pn 20x9 Arch Angel 87 Sby 10/92 7,150
Ryland, Robert Knight   Am 1873-1951
* See 1993 Edition . . . .
Ryman, Robert   Am 1930-
O/Pls 19x19 Surface Vale Sby 5/93 40,250
Rynecki, Moses
W/Pa 14x20 Cafe Scene; Accordianist: Two 1934 Sby 6/93   1,955
Ryott, J. R.   Br a 1810-1860
* See 1993 Edition . . . .
Rysbrack, John Michael   1693-1770
K,Pl&S/Pa 8x5 Women Carrying a Basket Chr 1/93 1,210
Saal, Georg Otto   Ger 1818-1870
* See 1992 Edition . . . .
Saari, Peter
MM/C 79x42 Untitled: Wall Relief '86 Sby 6/93 6,325
Sabatini, I.   It 19C
* See 1991 Edition . . . .

Sabatini, Raphael   Am 1898-
O/C 16x20 Coulter Street Fre 4/93 850
Sabbatini, Andrea   It 1487-1530
* See 1991 Edition . . . .
Sabbatini, Lorenzo   It 1530-1576
* See 1993 Edition . . . .
Saboia, Jose   Brz 1949-
O/C 14x11 Grupo De Musicos Sby 5/93 3,105
Saccaro, John   Am 1913-1981
O/B/M 5x10 Space Continuum But 4/93 862
Sachs, R.   Ger 19C
O/Pn 10x8 Serenading with a Mandolin Chr 10/92 1,540
Sacks, B.   Br 19C
P/Pa 31x21 Elegant Lady with Dog Hnd 3/93 1,500
Sacks, Joseph   Am 1887-1974
* See 1993 Edition . . . .
Sadee, Philippe   Dut 1837-1904
* See 1991 Edition . . . .
Sadler, W.   Br 20C
O/Pn 10x12 The New Punch Hnz 5/93 250
Sadler, Walter Dendy   Br 1854-1923
O/C 38x50 Chorus Gentlemen Chr 5/93 25,300
Sadock, Vuna   Am 20C
I/Pa Size? Abbie Hoffman Hnd 5/93 50
Saenz, Antonio Lopez   Mex 1936-
* See 1993 Edition . . . .
Saftleven, Cornelis   1607-1681
O/Pn 15x23 Cardplayers in Tavern Interior Sby 5/93 13,800
Saftleven, Herman   Dut 1609-1685
* See 1993 Edition . . . .
Sage, Cornelia Bentley   Am 1876-1936
O/C 14x10 Autumn Scene Mys 3/93 440
Sagrestani, Giovanni Camillo   1660-1730
O/C 17x12 Two Turks Playing a Game Sby 5/93 4,600
Sailmaker, Isaac   1633-1721
* See 1992 Edition . . . .
Sain, Edouard Alexandre   Fr 1830-1910
* See 1993 Edition . . . .
Saint Andre, Berthome   Fr 1905-1977
O/C 24x20 Simone Devant La Glace Sby 2/93 2,415
Saintin, Jules Emile   Fr 1829-1894
O/C 36x26 A Visit to the Glove Maker 1872 Chr 5/93 29,900
Saintpierre, Gaston Casimir   Fr 1833-1916
* See 1991 Edition . . . .
Sakai, Kazuya   Arg 1927-
* See 1993 Edition . . . .
Sala Y Frances, Emilio   Spa 1850-1910
O/C 8x6 Man with a Moustache Chr 5/93 1,150
Sala, Juan   Spa 1867-1918
* See 1993 Edition . . . .
Sala, Paolo   It 1859-1924
O/C 40x50 The Pretty Maid Sby 2/93 34,500
W/Pa 14x21 Canale Grande Chr 10/92 5,280
W&Cw/Pa/Pb 11x18 Riding in the Park Chr 5/93 4,830
W/Pa 13x20 Canal Grande-Venezia Slo 4/93 2,250
W/Pa 13x20 Panorama de Venezia Slo 4/93 2,250
Sala, Ventura Alvarez   Spa 1871-
* See 1991 Edition . . . .
Salabet, Jean   Fr 20C
* See 1993 Edition . . . .
Salanson, Eugenie Marie   Fr a 1864-1892
* See 1993 Edition . . . .
Salas, Antonio   Ecu 1795-1860
O/C 16x14 Yndio Yumbo Sby 5/93 5,175
Salazar, Carlos   Col 1956-
* See 1992 Edition . . . .
Salazar, Ignacio   Mex 1947-
* See 1990 Edition . . . .
Saleh, Radeaa Sarief Bastaman   Jav 1814-1880
O/C 48x65 Figures in an Exotic Landscape 1867 Chr 10/92 55,000
Salemme, Attilio   It 20C
O/C 13x20 Untitled '44 Sby 10/92 2,640

Sales, Francesco
  O/C 24x18 Portrait of a Toreador 52 Sby 2/93 1,610
Salieres, Paul Narcisse   Fr 19C
  * See 1993 Edition . . . .
Salinas Y Teruel, Augustin   Spa 1862-1915
  * See 1992 Edition . . . .
Salinas, Juan Pablo   Spa 1871-1946
  O/C 28x51 La Vernissage Chr 5/93 79,500
  O/C 16x26 Valuation of Jewels Chr 5/93 48,300
  O/C 16x26 The Recital Chr 5/93 42,550
Salinas, Porfiro   Am 1910-1972
  * See 1993 Edition . . . .
Salini, Tommaso   It 1575-1625
  * See 1993 Edition . . . .
Salle, David   Am 1952-
  A/C 48x72 Unexpectedly, Missed Cousin 1980 Sby 5/93 . 107,000
  A,O&MM/C 98x205 Poverty Is No Disgrace Sby 11/92 . . . 104,500
  A&Y/C 46x72 Express Vague Humanism 3 1980 Chr 11/92 . 35,200
  A&O/C 30x44 American Glass V 1987 Sby 10/92 18,700
  W/Pa 18x24 Untitled 84 Sby 5/93 12,650
  W&H/Pa 18x24 Untitled 1987 Chr 11/92 8,800
  H/Pa 19x26 Untitled 90 Chr 11/92 1,100
Salles, Jules Wagner   Fr 1814-1898
  * See 1992 Edition . . . .
Salmon, Robert   Am 1775-1842
  O/C 18x24 Rough Seas 1802 Sby 6/93 34,500
  O/Pn 20x31 Two Vessels Off Greenock 1820 Sby 12/92 . . 27,500
  O/C 34x22 Royal Navy Brig at Liverpool 1813 Doy 5/93 . . 22,000
  O/C 16x24 Coastal View Near Greenock 1825 Sby 3/93 . . 12,650
  O/B 8x10 View of Holy Head Sby 3/93 5,175
  O/C 7x10 Moonlight Smugglers 1840 Sby 9/92 2,970
Salmson, Hugo F. & Schoenfels   Swd 1843-1894
  * See 1992 Edition . . . .
Salome   Ger 1954-
  A/C 77x53 Jeansboys II 87 Chr 2/93 5,500
Salome and Castelli   Ger 20C
  A/C 95x158 Funambule Sby 5/93 17,250
Salt, John   Br 1937-
  * See 1993 Edition . . . .
Saltini, Pietro   It 1839-1908
  O/C 25x20 Woman in Green Hat Dum 10/92 1,500
Saltmer, Florence A.   Eng a 1882-1908
  O/C 14x21 Watching Boats Hnd 9/92 1,500
Salvi, Giovanni Battista   It 1609-1685
  K/Pa 5x8 Hands Joined in Prayer Chr 1/93 3,520
Salviati, Francesco   1510-1563
  O/Pn 25x21 Portrait of a Young Boy Sby 5/93 25,875
Salvo   1947-
  O/Pn 24x12 Untitled 85 Chr 11/92 3,520
Samara, Helga   Ger 1941-
  O/C 20x16 Still Life Dum 2/93 550
  O/B 9x12 Still Life Dum 7/93 450
  O/B 9x12 Floral Still Life Dum 8/93 400
  O/B 9x12 Still Life Dum 6/93 375
Samaras, Lucas   Am 1936-
  P/Pa 12x9 Untitled - August 14, 1961 Sby 5/93 16,100
  K/Pa 13x10 Untitled 74 Chr 10/92 11,000
  P/Pa 12x9 Untitled - February 16, 1961 Sby 5/93 8,050
  P/Pa 12x9 Untitled - August 14, 1961 Sby 5/93 6,900
  P/Pa 12x9 Untitled - Early November 1961 Sby 5/93 6,900
  Ph 3x3 Phototransformation (11/1/73) 73 Sby 5/93 6,325
  Ph 3x3 Phototransformation (10/25/73) 73 Sby 5/93 5,750
  Ph 3x3 Phototransformation (9/8/76) 76 Sby 5/93 4,888
  Ph 3x3 Phototransformation (4/4/76) 76 Sby 5/93 4,600
  Ph 3x3 Phototransformation (7/31/76) 76 Sby 5/93 4,600
  Ph 3x3 Phototransformation (4/4/76) 76 Sby 5/93 4,025
Sambrook, Russell   Am 20C
  O/C 20x32 Woman Hanging Santa's Suit Ih 11/92 3,750
Sambusetti   It 19C
  W/Pa 26x39 The Jester Fre 4/93 1,600
Sammann, Detlef   Am 1857-1938
  O/C 18x24 Coastal Through Trees 1915 Mor 2/93 350

Sammons, Carl   Am 1886-1968
  O/C 20x26 Carmel Coast 1945 Mor 11/92 3,750
  O/Cb 12x16 Yucca, Palm Springs But 10/92 3,575
  O/Cb 12x16 Smoke Trees, Palm Springs But 10/92 3,300
  O/C 24x30 Silver Lake But 3/93 2,750
  O/C 20x24 San Jacinto But 3/93 2,200
  O/Cb 12x16 Wild Flowers, Palm Springs But 6/93 1,725
  O/Cb 12x16 Mattole River, Humboldt County 1953 But 3/93 1,650
  O/Cb 12x16 Cotton Woods - Palm Springs 1945 Mor 11/92 1,600
  O/C 20x26 Laquinta Canyon But 6/93 1,380
  O/C 6x8 Hope Ranch - Santa Barbara Mor 11/92 1,100
  O/B 11x15 Point Lobos Mor 2/93 850
  O/C 6x8 Mt. Jacinto-Palm Springs Mor 11/92 800
  O/Cb 6x8 Landscape Mor 6/93 770
  O/Cb 14x20 June Lake-High Sierra Calif Mor 2/93 650
  O/Cb 6x8 Landscape Mor 6/93 605
  O/B 6x8 17 Mile Drive-Carmel by the Sea Mor 2/93 550
  P/Cd 8x12 Landscape Mor 2/93 550
  O/C 12x18 Beach Scene 1929 Lou 6/93 250
Sample, Paul Starrett   Am 1896-1974
  A/C 20x31 Community of Newark, Vermont Sby 3/93 4,600
  W&I/Pa 13x10 Family Outing But 6/93 2,588
  W&G/Pa 10x14 Expedition Pinware River Labrador Skn 3/93 1,870
  G/Pa 14x19 Man and Woman on a Boat '43 Wtf 9/92 900
  W&Pe/Pa 13x11 Working w/Construction Pulley '43 Wtf 9/92 . 500
  W&Pe/Pa 11x13 Army Men in Jeeps '43 Wtf 9/92 450
  W&Pe/Pa 10x13 Soldiers Working on Airplanes '42 Wtf 9/92 . 400
  W&Pe/Pa 11x13 Soldiers Fixing Pier in Hawaii '42 Wtf 9/92 . 350
  W&Pe/Pa 9x11 Portrait of a Hawaiian Woman 1943 Wtf 12/92 125
  W/Pa 11x15 Winter Landscape Hnz 5/93 90
  W&Pe/Pa 10x14 Village Church, Hawaii '44 Wtf 12/92 60
Sampson, A.   Eur 19C
  O/C 20x16 Mountain Landscape Slo 5/93 275
Sampson, Alden   Am 1853-
  O/C 20x16 River Landscapes (2) Fre 4/93 500
Sampson, James Henry   Eng a 1869-1879
  O/C 20x36 Ships along the French Coast Slo 5/93 3,750
Samuels, Daniel   Br 1917-
  O/M 16x24 Siesta Brd 8/93 578
Sanborn, Percy A.   Am 1849-1929
  * See 1993 Edition . . . .
Sanchez, Edgar   Ven 1940-
  A/C 47x47 Rostro, Imagen 3003 Chr 11/92 10,450
Sanchez, Edward   Spa 19C
  O/C 21x26 Spanish Garden Chr 10/92 3,300
Sanchez, Emilio   Cub 1921-
  O/C 70x50 Large Doorway Sby 5/93 11,500
Sanchez, Enrique   Mex 1940-
  * See 1991 Edition . . . .
Sanchez, Juan   Am 20C
  A/C 72x48 Untitled Hnd 12/92 100
Sanchez, Tomas   Cub 1948-
  A/C 44x60 Ojo de las Aguas 87 Chr 11/92 66,000
  A/C 32x40 Bosque y Laguna en Noche Clara 88 Chr 11/92 38,500
  W/Pa 7x17 Paisaje Cubano 80 Chr 11/92 5,280
Sanchez-Perrier, Emilio   Spa 1855-1907
  O/Pn 16x11 Three Men Fishing on a River 82 Chr 5/93 . . 13,800
  O/B 10x5 The Fruit Sellers 84 Sby 5/93 8,625
Sand, Maximilien E.   Am 19C
  O/C 24x20 Woman with a Fan 1883 Sby 3/93 2,070
Sanderson-Wells, John   Br 1872-1955
  * See 1992 Edition . . . .
Sandham, J. Henry   Can 1842-1912
  O/C 18x27 Indian Camp on River Sbt 11/92 5,940
  O/C 12x16 Man Carrying Driftwood Sbt 5/93 1,320
  O/Cb 10x14 Gathering Wood/A Coastal Skn 11/92 1,100
  W/Pa 14x9 Oriental Musician Sbt 11/92 352
Sandhurst, G.   Br 19C
  * See 1993 Edition . . . .
Sandler, Al   Am 20C
  O/C 12x16 Cuban Dance Lou 3/93 200
Sandor, Mathias   Am 1857-1920
  O/C 24x20 Rock Formations/Southwestern View Skn 11/92 . . 935
Sandorfi, Istvan   20C
  * See 1991 Edition . . . .

Sandrucci, Giovanni It 19C
O/C 26x21 A Taste of Wine Chr 5/93 5,750
Sandzen, Birger Am 1871-1954
O/M 14x12 Landscape 1929 Mor 6/93 6,050
W/Pa 10x15 Hutchinson Bend Hills, Kansas Wes 3/93 1,760
W/Pa 9x12 Rocks and Trees Hnd 9/92 900
Sanger, Grace H. C. Am 1881-
O/C 28x18 Still Life with Flowers Eld 8/93 275
SanGiovanni, A* It 18C**
* See 1993 Edition . . . .
Sani, Alessandro It 19C
O/C 36x28 La Famiglia Sby 2/93 44,850
O/Pn 15x19 The Maid Sby 2/93 8,050
O/C 20x25 Disputed Change Sby 2/93 5,463
O/C 12x16 Question of Taste Sby 1/93 2,300
O/C/B 16x13 A Rare Vintage 1882 Hnd 10/92 1,800
O/C 15x12 Monk Cleaning Fish Dum 5/93 850
O/C 15x12 Benedictine Monk Cleaning Fish FHB 3/93 300
Sani, David It 20C
O/C 25x20 The Love Letter Chr 5/93 9,200
O/C 24x30 Just Like Grandpa Chr 5/93 6,325
O/C 13x10 Testing the Wine Wes 12/92 935
Sanin, Fanny 20C
* See 1991 Edition . . . .
Sankowsky, Itzhak Am 1908-
O/M 36x48 Figure in Red Fre 4/93 275
H&Pe/Pa 15x11 Abstract 1940 Fre 4/93 180
O/M 40x31 Flowers and Fruit 1974 Fre 4/93 140
Sansalvadore, Piero It 1892-1955
O/Pn 7x9 Combe Martin, North Devon Wes 5/93 385
O/Pn 7x9 Criccieth: Early Morning Wes 5/93 358
Sant, James Br 1820-1916
I/Pa 4x7 Interior of the Royal Academy Slo 7/93 600
Santerre, Jean Baptiste Fr 1658-1771
* See 1991 Edition . . . .
Santhy, M. D.
O/C 9x11 Expressionist Tree under Night Sky Wlf 12/92 . . . 300
Santini, A.
W/Pa 16x20 Interior Depicting Two Gentlemen Sel 12/92 . . . 275
Santini, D.
W/Pa 8x12 Pair: Roman Ruins Sel 2/93 100
Santomasso, Guiseppe It 1907-
C&K/Pa 20x14 Untitled 48 Chr 2/93 990
Santoro, Francesco Raffaello It 1844-
* See 1993 Edition . . . .
Santoro, Rubens It 1859-1942
* See 1993 Edition . . . .
Santry, Daniel Am 1867-1951
O/Cb 25x31 The Shore in Autumn Skn 3/93 495
Sanvitale, Giovanni It 1935-
O/Pa 12x16 Rabbits Dum 1/93 2,000
O/B 12x16 Rabbits Dum 6/93 1,750
O/B 12x16 Horses and Colt in Pasture Dum 3/93 900
O/B 9x12 Still Life Dum 3/93 800
O/Pa 9x12 Stillife Dum 1/93 800
Sanz, Bernhard Lukas 1650-1710
* See 1993 Edition . . . .
Sanzio, Raffaello It 1483-1520
K&Pl/Pa 5x5 Woman, Bust Length Chr 1/93 39,600
Sapp, Allen Can 1929-
* See 1993 Edition . . . .
Saret, Alan 1944-
Pe&Y/Pa 11x21 Circle-Branch Circle Sby 2/93 1,380
H&Y/Pa 30x44 New Grass Ensoulment 1988 Chr 2/93 1,320
Sargeant, Geneve Rixford Am 1868-1957
* See 1992 Edition . . . .
Sargent, Dick Am 1911-1978
* See 1993 Edition . . . .
Sargent, J. Ford Am 20C
W/Pa 16x30 Stormy Landscape Wlf 9/92 350
Sargent, John Singer Am 1856-1925
O/C 24x20 Portrait of Teresa Gosse Chr 12/92 242,000
O/C/B 17x17 Portrait Major George Conrad Roller Chr 5/93 . 79,500
W&G/Pa 14x21 Above Lake Garda Chr 12/92 55,000
O/C 25x30 At Calcot Near Reading Sby 5/93 35,650

O/C 37x25 Portrait Mrs. Colin Hunter 1896 Sby 5/93 31,625
W/Pa 14x9 The Sphinx Sby 5/93 19,550
W/Pa 19x15 Jupiter Beseeching Eros Sby 5/93 13,800
W/Pa 19x15 Three Nudes with Cupid Sby 5/93 13,800
Pe/Pa 6x9 Study of Three Swan Sby 3/93 4,888
Pe/Pa 12x15 Study of Cows and Rocks Sby 3/93 2,300
Pe/Pa 3x3 Two Drawings Sby 3/93 920
H/Pa 17x41 Study for a Frieze Skn 9/92 440
P/Pa 13x17 Study of a Woman Lou 9/92 200
Sargent, Paul Turner Am 1880-1946
O/C 20x16 Fall Landscape Lou 6/93 300
O/C/B 10x12 Forest Sunlight 1933 Hnd 5/93 300
Sargent, Walter Am 1868-1927
* See 1992 Edition . . . .
Sarka, Charles N. Am 1879-1960
Pl/Pa 21x25 Aged Warriors on Swan Boat Ih 5/93 250
Sarkisian, Sarkis Am 1909-1977
O/C 34x27 Oriental Boy '34 Dum 10/92 1,500
O/C 16x21 Female with Carnation 35 Dum 7/93 1,100
Sarkissian, Paul 20C
* See 1990 Edition . . . .
Sarluis, Leonard
O/C 40x30 Portrait of Nude Woman 1931 Sby 6/93 2,300
Sarnoff, Arthur Am 1912-
* See 1993 Edition . . . .
Sarri, Egisto It 1837-1901
* See 1992 Edition . . . .
Sartain, William Am 1843-1924
* See 1993 Edition . . . .
Sartelle, Herbert Am 1885-1955
* See 1993 Edition . . . .
Sarthou, Maurice Elie
O/C 52x38 Taureaux en Camargue Sby 10/92 880
Sarto, Lucia It 1950-
O/C 16x20 Floral Still Life Dum 8/93 1,800
Sartorio, Giulio Aristide It 1860-1932
P/Pa/B 10x23 Pine Grove, The Royal Palace 1892 Chr 2/93 6,050
P/Pa 9x23 Il Tevre alla Margliana 1892 Chr 2/93 4,400
P&G/Pa 10x22 Tivoli from the Roman Plain 1892 Chr 2/93 . 4,400
P/Pa/B 10x24 Il Tevre a Grotta Rossa 1892 Chr 2/93 2,200
Sartorius, Francis Br 1734-1804
* See 1993 Edition . . . .
Sartorius, John Nost Br 1759-1828
O/C 15x18 On the Scent Chr 6/93 4,370
Sato, Key Jap 1906-
* See 1993 Edition . . . .
Sato, Tadashi Am 1923-
* See 1993 Edition . . . .
Satterlee, Walter Am 1844-1908
O/C 36x21 Peasant Girl Wes 3/93 302
Sattler, Hubert Aus 1817-1904
* See 1992 Edition . . . .
Sauer, Walter Bel 1889-1972
* See 1991 Edition . . . .
Sauerwein, Frank Peters Am 1871-1910
O/C 12x18 The Blizzard 1909 But 12/92 3,850
O/Cb 12x10 Chief Red Feather Fre 4/93 1,250
W/Pa 12x9 Vista Point Wes 5/93 468
Saufelt, Leonard Fr 19C
* See 1991 Edition . . . .
Saul, Peter Am 1934-
* See 1991 Edition . . . .
Saunders, Norman Am 1906-1988
G/Pa 15x22 Trail of Covered Wagons Ih 5/93 1,300
Saunders, Raymond Am 1934-
MM&L/Ab 48x44 Valentine But 10/92 6,050
Saunier, Noel Fr 1847-1890
* See 1992 Edition . . . .
Saura, Antonio Spa 1930-
O/C 51x38 Amaplo 1959 Chr 11/92 38,500
G&L/Pa 25x35 Untitled Sby 5/93 8,050
Saurfelt, Leonard Fr 20C
O/C 8x16 Market Scene 1878 Chr 2/93 2,200
O/C 13x18 Garden Party Wes 5/93 660

Sautry, Daniel   Am 20C
O/C 16x20 Landscape Hnd 9/92 150
Sauvage, Piat Joseph   Flm 1744-1818
* See 1990 Edition . . . .
Sauvageot, Charles Theodore   Fr 1826-1883
O/C 35x57 Shepherd & His Flock in Open Field Chr 2/93 . . 3,520
Sauwin, P.   Am 19C
O/B 9x11 Still Life with Peaches 62 Sby 3/93 1,955
Sauzay, Adrien Jacques   Fr 1841-1928
* See 1991 Edition . . . .
Savage, Anne Douglas   Can 1897-1971
O/Pn 12x14 Cottage at St. Hilaire Sbt 5/93 4,620
Savage, Eugene Francis   Am 1883-1978
* See 1992 Edition . . . .
Save, Gaston G. & Grison, F.   Fr 1844-1901
O/C 112x59 The Hunting Party 1874 Sby 10/92 15,400
O/C 112x63 The Tavern 1874 Sby 10/92 15,400
Savelieva, Valentina   Rus 20C
* See 1993 Edition . . . .
Savery, Jacob   Dut 1565-1603
* See 1990 Edition . . . .
Savery, Roelandt Jacobsz   Flm 1576-1639
O/Pn 12x19 Tower and Buildings by Waterfall Chr 5/93 . . 40,250
Savini, Alfonso   It 1836-1908
* See 1991 Edition . . . .
Savinio, Alberto   It 1891-1952
* See 1993 Edition . . . .
Savry, Hendrick   Dut 1823-1907
O/C 33x52 Young Shepherdess Chr 2/93 12,650
Sawtelle, Mary Berkeley   Am 1872-
O/C 39x36 Alice by the Sea Sel 9/92 9,000
Sawyer, Clifton Howard   Am 1896-1966
* See 1993 Edition . . . .
Sawyer, Helen Alton   Am 1900-
O/Cb 7x10 Study for Fruit and Jugs Skn 3/93 330
W/Pa 15x20 Marsh Scene Mys 3/93 192
Sawyers, Martha   Am 1902-1988
O/C 35x24 Three People Drinking From Coconuts Ih 11/92 . . 400
Sawyier, Paul   Am 1865-1917
W/Pa/B 16x26 Frankfort Bridge Sby 9/92 8,800
Saxlide, Carl R.   Am 20C
* See 1991 Edition . . . .
Sayre, Fred Grayson   Am 1879-1939
O/C 21x24 California Foothills But 10/92 9,350
O/C 20x24 Dancing Girl Sby 3/93 4,600
O/M 12x15 California Landscape Sby 3/93 1,725
O/C 20x24 Landscape Mor 11/92 1,100
Saz-Bernharb, G.   Ger 20C
O/C 24x18 Evergreen Trees Hnd 9/92 50
Scaffai, Luigi   It 1837-
* See 1993 Edition . . . .
Scala, Vincenzo   It 19C
O/C 40x65 Peasants by Wooded Stream Chr 2/93 6,050
Scalbert, Jules   Fr 1851-
* See 1993 Edition . . . .
Scalella, Jules   Am 1895-
O/C 30x36 New Hope Canal Fre 10/92 2,400
O/C 25x30 Winter Day But 12/92 1,650
Scanlan, Robert Richard   Br -1876
* See 1993 Edition . . . .
Scarlett, Rolph   Am 1889-1984
O/C 48x56 Largo Sby 9/92 8,800
O/C 48x48 Nocturne Sby 9/92 4,675
Scarsellino, Ippolito   It 1551-1620
O/C 86x55 Deposition from the Cross Sby 5/93 123,500
Schaan, Paul   Fr 20C
O/Pn 14x11 Napoleon 1912 Chr 2/93 1,870
O/Pn 14x11 Napoleon 1912 Skn 9/92 990
Schaefels, Lucas   Bel 1824-1885
* See 1993 Edition . . . .
Schaeffer, August   Aus 1833-1916
* See 1990 Edition . . . .

Schaeffer, Henri   Fr 1900-1975
O/C 16x20 Paris Street Scene Wes 10/92 2,310
Schaeffer, J. S.   Am 19C
O/C 20x24 Farm House '87 Eld 4/93 1,650
Schaeffer, Mead   Am 1898-1980
O/C 24x50 Man w/Trenchcoat Amidst Eskimos Ih 11/92 . . 6,500
O/C 38x31 He Received Two Dozen Lashes 25 Skn 3/93 . . 5,500
O/C 32x26 George Washington Greeted Ih 5/93 2,200
O/C 30x42 Paradise Poachers Chr 12/92 2,200
Schafer   Am 20C
P/Pa 20x20 Landscape Mor 2/93 375
Schafer, Frederick Ferdinand   Am 1839-1927
O/C 30x50 Bear Lake in the Wasatch Mountains Sby 3/93 . 4,888
O/C 20x36 Coast Near Monterey, California But 10/92 3,300
O/C 12x20 Cypress Point, Monterey Bay But 10/92 3,300
O/C 30x50 Mt. Hood from Hood River But 3/93 3,300
O/C 30x50 View of Mount Tamalpais 1880 But 10/92 3,025
O/C 20x36 Pastoral Landscape But 3/93 2,750
O/C 20x36 Olympic Mountains, Washington But 10/92 2,090
O/C 12x10 Tropical Sunset But 3/93 880
O/Pb 13x19 Mountain Landscape Lou 12/92 350
Schafer, Henry Thomas   Br a 1873-1915
W,Pl&G/Pa 40x29 Toledo Cathedral, North Transept Chr 2/93 3,300
O/B 10x7 Frankfort 1881 Hnd 12/92 800
O/B 10x7 Dortrecht, Holland 1881 Hnd 12/92 700
Schaffer, H.   Ger 19C
* See 1992 Edition . . . .
Schalcken, Godfried   1643-1706
O/C 29x25 Portrait of a Gentleman 1704 Sby 10/92 6,600
Schaldack, William J.   Am 1896-
W/Pa 11x13 Western Landscape Hnd 9/92 50
Schall, Jean Frederic   Fr 1752-1825
* See 1993 Edition . . . .
Schamann   Am 20C
O/C 29x23 Autumn Landscape Hnd 12/92 200
Schamberg, Morton Livingston   Am 1881-1918
* See 1993 Edition . . . .
Schanker, Louis   Am 1903-1981
W&I/B 7x23 Mural Study for WNYC, 1937 Chr 5/93 4,370
G&H/B 9x20 North Wall 38 Sby 3/93 2,645
W&I/Pa 15x20 Workers and Abstract Chr 5/93 1,265
Scharf, Kenny   Am 1958-
A&O/C 48x60 Tangello Purple Tempelo 85 Chr 11/92 . . . 26,400
A,O&Pt/C 115x88 Balanca Precoriosex 85 Sby 2/93 16,100
MM/C 72x77 Retchmess Chunky Chunky 1985 Sby 6/93 . . 8,625
O/C 32x24 Greenoright Over Bluepoint 84 Sby 6/93 4,600
Scharff, William Dan 1866-1959
O/C 30x40 Rocky Seashore Hnd 6/93 600
Scharl, Josef   Ger 1896-1954
* See 1991 Edition . . . .
Scharp, Henri   Con 19C
* See 1992 Edition . . . .
Schary, Saul   Am 1904-1978
O/C 28x22 Portrait of Arshile Gorky Chr 9/92 2,750
O/C 20x24 Extensive Landscape Mys 3/93 275
O/C 16x20 Rolling Hills Chr 12/92 220
O/C 12x15 Extensive Landscape Mys 3/93 110
Schattenstein, Nikol   Am 1877-1954
* See 1992 Edition . . . .
Schatz, Daniel Leon   Am 1908-
* See 1992 Edition . . . .
Schauss, Ferdinand   Ger 1832-1916
* See 1993 Edition . . . .
Schawinsky, Xanti
O/C/M 44x88 Reclining Nude '58 Sby 10/92 10,725
O/M 8x72 Untitled 56 Sby 10/92 2,970
Schedone, Bartolomeo   It 1570-1615
* See 1992 Edition . . . .
Scheerboom, Andries   Dut 1832-1880
* See 1992 Edition . . . .
Scheffer   Fr 19C
O/Tn 10x8 Jeune Novice Wlf 5/93 350

Scheffer, Ary Fr 1795-1858
* See 1992 Edition ....
Scheffer, Jack Am 20C
O/C 16x20 Three Figures on a Bridge Lou 3/93 110
Scheffer, Robert Aus 1859-
* See 1992 Edition ....
Scheffers, Glen C. Am 19C
* See 1992 Edition ....
Scheffler, Rudolf Am 1884-1973
O/C 84x66 Max Schmeling 1929 Sby 12/92 19,800
Scheggini Da Larciano, Giovan. It 1455-1527
* See 1992 Edition ....
Scheiber, Hugo Hun 1873-1950
G&W/Pa/B 21x20 Man on a Park Bench Chr 11/92 2,090
O/B 18x20 Head of a Man Smoking a Pipe Sby 6/93 1,495
G,W&K/Pa 20x14 The Cellist Chr 5/93 1,495
G&K/Pa 27x22 Silhouettes at a Window Chr 11/92 1,430
Scheibl, Hubert 1951-
O/C 59x59 Untitled 1985 Chr 10/92 7,150
Schelfhout, Andreas Dut 1787-1870
O/Pn 12x16 Moored on the Beach Sby 10/92 27,500
O/C 22x34 Boats at Low Tide 61 Sby 5/93 6,900
Schell, Susan Gertrude Am 1891-1970
* See 1992 Edition ....
Schenau, Johann Eleazar Zeizig Ger 1737-1806
O/C 12x9 Girls Watching a Boy Playing Sby 10/92 6,600
Schenck, August Friedrich A. Dan 1828-1901
* See 1993 Edition ....
Schenck, William
Pt/C 132x72 Wyoming Plus XV '72 Sby 2/93 4,313
Scherrewitz, Johan Dut 1868-1951
O/C 13x20 Horses and Drawn Cart Hnd 3/93 4,400
Scheuerer, Julius Ger 1859-1913
O/Pn 3x7 Poultry Feeding and Ducks by Stream Chr 10/92 . 4,400
Scheuerer, Otto Ger 1862-1934
O/Pn 5x6 Ducks Wading; Chickens Feeding (2) Chr 5/93 . 5,750
Scheyerer, Franz 1770-1839
O/C 23x29 Figures Resting; Fisherfolk: Pair Chr 5/93 20,700
Schiavo, Paolo It 1397-1478
* See 1993 Edition ....
Schiavone, Andrea It 1522-1563
O&T/Pn 11x20 Perseus Rescuing Andromeda Sby 5/93 .. 23,000
Schiavoni, Natale It 1777-1858
O/C 150x111 La Visita de Pastori 183* Sby 10/92 28,600
Schiele, Egon Aus 1890-1918
Pe/Pa 18x10 Bildnis Eines Madchens 1913 Sby 11/92 ... 71,500
Schier, Franz Ger 1852-1922
* See 1993 Edition ....
Schiertz, August Ferdinand Ger 1804-1878
* See 1993 Edition ....
Schilder, Andrei Nicolajevitch Rus 1861-
* See 1990 Edition ....
Schille, Alice Am 1869-1955
* See 1993 Edition ....
Schindler, A. Zeno Am 1813-1880
* See 1992 Edition ....
Schindler, Emil Jakob Aus 1842-1892
O/Pn 10x13 Partie; Moonlit Landscape 1887 Chr 10/92 ... 7,150
Schindler, Thomas 20C
* See 1990 Edition ....
Schiodte, Harald Valdemar I. Dan 1852-1924
* See 1990 Edition ....
Schirek, J. Hemingway Am 19C
W/lv 3x3 Girl with Bonnet and Scarf Hnd 3/93 300
Schivert, Victor Rom 1863-
O/C 20x16 Two Women (2) Fre 10/92 280
Schjelderup, Leis Nor 19C
* See 1993 Edition ....
Schleich, Robert Ger 1845-1934
O/Pn 5x7 The Horse Market Sby 5/93 4,888

Schleisner, Christian Andreas Dan 1810-1882
O/C 25x20 Pulling a Tooth But 5/93 2,185
Schlenker, Barbara Am 20C
O/C 25x36 Urban Landscape Hnd 5/93 100
O/C 25x36 Urban Landscape Hnd 6/93 60
Schlesinger, Felix Ger 1833-1910
O/Pn 5x8 Rabbits Feeding Chr 5/93 8,050
Schlesinger, Henri-Guillaume Fr 1814-1893
O/C 25x20 Young Girl with Opera Glasses 1882 Hnd 10/92 5,000
Schlesinger, Karl Ger 1825-1893
* See 1993 Edition ....
Schlimarski, Heinrich Hans Aus 1859-
O/Pn 13x10 The Young Beauty Skn 11/92 1,045
Schluckmuller 20C
O/C 9x7 Pair: Character Studies of Two Men Sel 2/93 325
Schmid, Erich Con 20C
O/C 32x26 Street Scene at Night Chr 2/93 715
Schmid, Richard Am 20C
O/C 24x36 Manhattan, City Dawn Sby 9/92 3,575
Schmid, Rudolf Am 1896-
O/B 40x46 Construction Site 1929 Wes 3/93 1,430
Schmid, Rudolf & Bing, V. Am 1896-
O/B 43x41 Telephone Workers 1929 Wes 3/93 1,018
Schmidt Con 19C
* See 1993 Edition ....
Schmidt, Albert H. Sws 1883-1970
* See 1991 Edition ....
Schmidt, Carl Am 1885-1969
O/C 40x50 Indian Shepherdess with Flock But 12/92 2,750
O/C 38x48 Mammoth Lake But 12/92 2,750
O/C 30x32 Sheep Grazing But 12/92 2,750
O/C 38x48 The Roundup But 12/92 2,750
O/B 30x36 Trees Dum 8/93 1,100
O/C 32x30 The Old Chapel-San Juan Mission Mor 11/92 . 950
O/Pn 30x36 Desert Scene Dum 2/93 800
O/B 16x24 Sycamores with Mountains Dum 8/93 600
Schmidt, Carl Am 1909-
* See 1992 Edition ....
Schmidt, E. Allan Ger 19C
* See 1993 Edition ....
Schmidt, E. Trier Br a 1879-1903
* See 1993 Edition ....
Schmidt, Elmer G. Am a 1920-1939
O/C 26x30 Monterey Coastal Mor 2/93 200
Schmidt, H. A.
O/C 10x12 Impressionistic Tree Wlf 12/92 275
Schmidt, Hans Wilhelm Ger 1859-
O/C 48x65 The Kill 1896 Chr 2/93 17,050
Schmidt, Karl Am 1890-1962
* See 1993 Edition ....
Schmidt, Oscar F. Am 1892-1957
G/Pa 22x8 Couple at Table Ih 11/92 750
Schmidt, Peter Ger 17C
Pl&H/Pa 12x9 Drawing But 5/93 402
Schmidt-Rottluff, Karl Ger 1884-
* See 1992 Edition ....
Schmied, Th. Dut 19C
O/C 29x39 On the Look Out Hnd 3/93 700
Schmitz, Ernst Ger 1859-1917
* See 1993 Edition ....
Schmutzler, Leopold Aus 1864-1941
O/C 38x30 Flower Girl Dum 10/92 600
Schnabel, Julian Am 1951-
O/V 108x84 Untitled Sby 11/92 187,000
MM/Wd 108x84 Nighttime Rhonda Chr 11/92 165,000
O/V 120x108 Some Peaches Chr 11/92 110,000
O&MM/Wd 60x48 Untitled Chr 11/92 71,500
O&MM/Wd 84x56 Portrait of Patrick Sby 5/93 57,500
O&Wx/C 76x63 Series of Small Crosses 77 Chr 11/92 ... 35,200
O/Pn 25 dia Christ in the Bay of Naples II 1987 Chr 11/92 16,500
O/Pa 48x38 Untitled Chr 10/92 14,300
O,Pe&L/Pa 60x40 Untitled (Divan) Sby 2/93 8,625
O,Y&H/Pa 106x67 Rhonda Chr 2/93 8,250

W/Pa 43x30 Drawings in the Rain Sby 10/92 6,050
Os/Pa 24x36 Untitled 1979 Sby 2/93 690

Schnakenberg, Henry Ernest Am 1892-1970
O/C 45x66 A Place to Swim Sby 3/93 1,150
O/C 14x10 Portrait of a Lady 31 Hnd 5/93 275

Schneider, G. Eng 19C
O/C 24x48 Twilight, Herd at Rest 1888 Slo 4/93 2,300

Schneider, Otto Henry Am 1865-1950
O/C/M 12x15 Construction of Boulder Dam Lou 9/92 450

Schneider-Blumberg, Bernhard Ger 1881-
O/Cb 14x18 The Music Lesson 19 Skn 9/92 990

Schneider-Blumberg, Ernst Am 20C
O/C 13x17 Two Boys (Music Lesson) Fre 4/93 650

Schneir, Jacques Am 1898-1988
H/Pa 11x17 Woman with Feline '27 But 4/93 977

Schnelle, William G. Am 1897-
O/C 30x39 Woman in an Interior Chr 3/93 2,760

Schneller, P. Am 20C
O/C 20x24 Winter Scene Mys 3/93 220
O/C 20x24 Winter Scene Mys 3/93 220

Schnetz, Jean Victor Fr 1787-1870
* See 1992 Edition . . . .

Schodl, Max Aus 1834-1921
* See 1990 Edition . . . .

Schoenberger, E. Am 20C
O/M 22x28 WPA Style Fighting Devils 1940 Fre 4/93 350

Schoenfeld, Flora Am 20C
* See 1991 Edition . . . .

Schoettle, L. Aus 19C
O/C 23x31 Love's Dream Hnd 12/92 2,200

Schoffstall, Don Am 20C
W/Pa 15x32 Geese in Flight Yng 5/93 175

Schofield, Walter Elmer Am 1867-1944
O/C 30x36 McLegrenow Farm 20 Chr 12/92 36,300
O/C 30x36 The Outer Harbor, Polperro Chr 12/92 18,700
O/B 33x39 Fall Woodland Ald 9/92 7,000
O/C 24x20 Forest Scene with Creek Hnd 10/92 4,400
O/B 17x20 Autumn Lake Scene Mys 12/92 2,200

Scholder, Fritz Am 1937-
A/C 80x68 Hollywood Indian #5 73 Sby 5/93 14,375
A/C 50x40 Monster Love #10 1986 Chr 11/92 8,800
A,Br&V/Pa 15x11 Indian with White Feather Chr 11/92 3,300

Scholz, Max Ger 1855-1906
* See 1992 Edition . . . .

Schommer, Francois Fr 1850-1935
O/Pn 18x15 Portrait of a Seated Woman 1894 But 11/92 . . 1,210

Schon, Andreas
O/C 79x99 Dover Sby 5/93 11,500
O/C 55x79 Benevent 89 Sby 2/93 5,750

Schonborn, Anton Am -1871
* See 1992 Edition . . . .

Schonieber, Gustav Ger 1851-1917
* See 1991 Edition . . . .

Schoonover, Frank Earle Am 1877-1972
O/C 30x38 The Trooper Shifted Both Hands 26 Chr 12/92 . . 14,300

Schopin, Frederic Henri Ger 1804-1880
* See 1991 Edition . . . .

Schoppe, Julius Ger 1795-1868
O/C 31 dia The Fortune Teller 1858 Hnd 10/92 4,000

Schotanus, Petrus 17C
O/Pn 23x31 Barnyard Fowl Sby 1/93 5,175

Schotel, Jan Christianus Dut 1787-1838
* See 1992 Edition . . . .

Schouman, Aert Dut 1710-1792
* See 1990 Edition . . . .

Schoumann, Martinus Dut 1770-1848
* See 1990 Edition . . . .

Schouten, Henri Bel 1864-1927
* See 1993 Edition . . . .

Schrader, Julius Friedrich Ger 1815-1900
* See 1993 Edition . . . .

Schrag, Julius Ger 1864-
O/C 10x12 Farm Under Stormy Sky Skn 11/92 825

Schramm, Viktor Rom 1865-1929
* See 1992 Edition . . . .

Schranz, Anton Ger 19C
* See 1991 Edition . . . .

Schreckengost, Viktor Am 1906-
W/Pa 21x29 Abundance Wtf 5/93 425

Schreiber, Charles Baptiste Fr -1903
O/Pn 9x6 L'Auteur Favori 1896 Wtf 3/93 1,800
O/Pn 12x7 A Divine Serenade Skn 9/92 1,320

Schreiber, Georges Am 1904-1977
* See 1993 Edition . . . .

Schreyer, Adolf Ger 1828-1899
O/C 45x68 Lone Arab on Horseback Sby 5/93 32,200
O/C 34x59 Wallachian Horsemen in the Snow Chr 10/92 . 16,500

Schreyvogel, Charles Am 1861-1912
* See 1992 Edition . . . .

Schroder, Albert Friedrich Ger 1854-1939
O/Pn 10x13 Man with a Pipe Sby 1/93 3,450

Schroff, Alfred Hermann Am 1863-1939
* See 1992 Edition . . . .

Schubauer, Fredrich Leopold Ger 1795-1852
O/Pn 13x16 El Rapto de Trinidad Salcedo Sby 5/93 23,000

Schuch, Carl Aus 1846-1903
O/C 41x30 Fisherman at an Alpine Stream Sby 5/93 6,900

Schucker, James W. Am 1903-
W/Pa 5x8 Indians on the Warpath Lou 9/92 125

Schuffenecker, Claude Emile Fr 1851-1934
O/C 32x40 Travailleurs au Champ Sby 5/93 18,400

Schufried, Dominik Aus 1810-
O/Pn 14x18 Peasant Family 1860 Hnd 9/92 1,000

Schultz, Carl Ger 19C
O/Pn 8x12 Sheep in a Landscape But 11/92 550

Schultz, Erdmann Ger 1810-
O/C 14x18 Still Life Vase of Roses, Cabbage Chr 10/92 . . . 8,800

Schultz, George F. Am 1869-
O/C 24x36 Seascape Hnd 10/92 750
O/C 13x17 Marine Lands Ald 3/93 175

Schultz, Gottfried Ger 1842-
* See 1992 Edition . . . .

Schultzberg, Anshelm Leonhard Swd 1862-1942
* See 1993 Edition . . . .

Schultze, Robert Ger 1828-
O/C 26x40 Lago Maggiore (Bei Locarno) Sby 1/93 3,450

Schulz, Adrien Fr 1851-1931
* See 1992 Edition . . . .

Schulz, Charles M. Am 1922-
Pl/Pa 15x23 Sunday Comic "Peanuts" Ih 11/92 4,750
Pl/Pa 16x22 Sunday Comic "Peanuts" Ih 5/93 2,300
Pl/Pa 5x27 Daily Comic "Peanuts" 54 Ih 5/93 1,200
Pl/Pb 6x27 Peanuts Daily Strip 1969 Skn 11/92 330

Schulz, Robert E. Am 1928-1978
O/B 16x14 Man Behind Fence, Group in Front Ih 11/92 375

Schulze, Andreas 1955-
* See 1993 Edition . . . .

Schumacher, William Emile Am 1870-1931
O/Cb 12x16 On the East River Lou 3/93 300

Schurr, Claude Fr 1921-
* See 1992 Edition . . . .

Schuster, Donna Am 1883-1953
O/C 30x25 Anemones But 10/92 3,300
O/B 16x20 Near Los Feliz, Los Angeles But 10/92 2,475
O/C 16x12 Palace of Fine Arts Mor 6/93 2,090
O/C 30x28 Sierra Mountain Lake But 10/92 1,650
O/B 12x16 Landscape Mor 11/92 1,500
W/Pa 14x18 Boats at the Harbor Mor 6/93 1,320
W/Pa 19x14 Sailboats at Pan Pacific Exhibit. Mor 2/93 900
W&Pe/Pa 21x15 Mexico But 6/93 690
W&Pe/Pa 17x13 Rigging But 6/93 575

Schuster, Joseph Aus 1873-1945
* See 1992 Edition . . . .

Schuster, Karl Maria   Aus 1871-1953
  * See 1993 Edition . . . .
Schuster, Ludwig   Aus 1820-
  * See 1992 Edition . . . .
Schutte, Thomas   1954-
  O/C 36x18 Schwabisch Hall 1980 Chr 5/93 2,070
Schutz, Christian Georg   Ger 1718-1791
  O/Cp 19x24 Landscape with Travellers 1775 Chr 1/93 . . . 60,500
Schutze, Wilhelm   Ger 1840-1898
  O/C 30x36 Genre Scene Children and Kittens Skn 5/93 . . 71,500
  O/C 16x13 Mending Kitty's Paw Sby 10/92 25,300
Schuyff, Peter   1958-
  A/C 96x66 Untitled 84 Chr 10/92 5,500
  A/L 90x61 Untitled Chr 5/93 4,600
  O/C 75x75 Untitled 86 Chr 2/93 3,080
  A/L 33x24 Untitled 85 Chr 11/92 2,090
  A/C 34x24 Untitled Sby 10/92 1,760
Schuyler, Remington   Am 1887-1955
  O/C 31x25 Fending Off the Enemy Sby 3/93 2,185
Schwabe, Heinrich August   Am 1843-1916
  * See 1992 Edition . . . .
Schwacha, George
  O/B 25x30 Landscape Ald 9/92 200
Schwanfelder, Charles Henry   Br 1774-1837
  * See 1993 Edition . . . .
Schwartz, Albert G.   Ger 1833-
  * See 1991 Edition . . . .
Schwartz, Andrew Thomas   Am 1867-1942
  O/M 40x52 Landscape/Houses by River 1911 Chr 3/93 . . 19,550
Schwartz, Davis F.   Am 1879-1969
  O/C 32x40 California Landscape Mys 3/93 935
Schwartz, Manfred   Am 1909-1970
  C&P/Pa 12x10 Untitled Slo 7/93 200
Schwartz, Robert   Am 20C
  W/Pa 15x13 Soprano Abbandonato 1979 But 10/92 2,090
Schwartz, William S.   Am 1896-1977
  O/C 40x30 Solitude 1936 Sby 9/92 7,700
  Pe/Pa 10x9 Self-Portrait 1926 Hnd 5/93 900
Schwartzkopf, Earl   Am 1888-
  O/C 36x30 Landscape with Cabin Lou 6/93 900
Schwarz, Alfred   Ger 1833-
  * See 1992 Edition . . . .
Schweninger, Karl   Aus 1818-1887
  * See 1992 Edition . . . .
Schweninger, Karl (Jr.)   Aus 1854-1903
  O/Pn 21x32 Halcyon Days: Pair 80 Sby 10/92 13,750
Schweninger, Rosa   Aus 1849-
  * See 1990 Edition . . . .
Schwitters, Kurt   Ger 1887-1948
  * See 1993 Edition . . . .
Scialoja, Toti   1914-
  O/C 22x30 Sorpresa 58 Chr 2/93 2,090
Scifoni, Anatolio   It 1841-1884
  * See 1993 Edition . . . .
Scilla, Agostino   It 1639-1700
  * See 1992 Edition . . . .
Scognamiglio, Cavalier Antonio   It 19C
  O/C 15x19 Arabs Praying But 11/92 3,850
Scognamiglio, E.   It 19C
  * See 1993 Edition . . . .
Scoppetta, Pietro   It 1863-1920
  * See 1993 Edition . . . .
Scorrano, Luigi   It 1842-1924
  * See 1992 Edition . . . .
Scorzelli, Eugenio   It 1890-1958
  O/Cb 12x16 Nuvoli di Primavera Chr 2/93 605
Scott, Adam Sheriff   Can 1887-1980
  O/C 24x20 Inuit Woman Sbt 5/93 1,056
Scott, Benton   Am 1907-
  O/C 10x8 Moulin la Gallette Lou 12/92 75
Scott, Campbell   Sco 20C
  O/C 24x36 Landscape with Lake Sel 4/93 300

Scott, Clyde   Am 1884-1959
  * See 1993 Edition . . . .
Scott, Edwin   Am 20C
  * See 1993 Edition . . . .
Scott, Emily   Am 1832-1915
  O/C 14x11 Flowers in a Vase Yng 2/93 275
Scott, Frank Edwin   Am 1863-1929
  O/Pn 14x11 A Grey Parisian Day Sby 9/92 935
Scott, Henry   Eng 1911-
  O/C 28x42 Sundown, Clipper South Australian Slo 4/93 . . 12,000
  O/C 20x30 The Ship Thomas Steven in Open Sea But 5/93 . 2,300
Scott, John   Am 1907-
  * See 1991 Edition . . . .
Scott, John White Allen   Am 1815-1907
  * See 1993 Edition . . . .
Scott, Julian   Am 1846-1901
  O/C 12x20 Major General William F. Smith 1882 Chr 12/92 . 3,520
Scott, Katherine   Am 1871-
  * See 1992 Edition . . . .
Scott, Peter   Br 20C
  * See 1993 Edition . . . .
Scott, Walt   Am 20C
  * See 1993 Edition . . . .
Scott, William   20C
  * See 1992 Edition . . . .
Scribner, Elizabeth   Am 20C
  O/C 28x22 Floral Mys 12/92 258
Scully, Sean   Br 1946-
  O/C 96x108 Now 1987 Sby 11/92 99,000
  O/C 112x93 Dark Face 86 Chr 11/92 93,500
  O/L 96x96 Sound 87 Sby 5/93 79,500
  O/C 74x72 After Life 89 Chr 11/92 60,500
  O/C 60x60 Once Over 1986 Sby 11/92 55,000
  K/Pa 29x41 Untitled 89 Chr 11/92 20,900
  P/Pa 48x60 Untitled 7.9.90 90 Sby 10/92 20,900
  C&K/Pa 30x23 Untitled 84 Sby 10/92 8,800
Seager, Edward   Am 1809-1886
  Pe/Pa 8x10 Four Works 1845 Wes 10/92 330
  P/Pa 21x17 Portrait of Robert Seager 1846 Wes 10/92 . . . 192
  C/Pa 33x28 Portrait of a Gentleman Wes 10/92 110
Seager, Sarah   1958-
  E/Pa 31x41 The Participation of Letters: Ba Chr 2/93 110
  E/Pa 35x43 The Participation of Letters: Hah Chr 2/93 . . . 110
Seago, Edward   Br 1910-1974
  O/B 12x16 Dutch Waterways Near Leiden Wlf 1/92 10,000
Sealy, Allen Culpepper   Br 1850-1927
  O/C 21x26 Racehorse with Jockey Up 1905 Sby 6/93 8,338
Seanche, Bertel H.   Scn 20C
  P/Pa/B 20x21 Village by the Sea in Winter 24 Chr 2/93 . . . 418
Searing   Am 1938-
  O/C 24x36 Parisian Street Scene Dum 8/93 275
Searle, Ronald   Br 1920-
  W,I&C/Pa 8x19 Ghostly Rider Hnd 5/93 425
Sears, Benjamin Willard   Am 1846-1905
  * See 1993 Edition . . . .
Sears, Taber   Am 1870-
  * See 1992 Edition . . . .
Sease, Mary Shecut   Am 20C
  O/C 28x20 Still Life Lou 3/93 250
Sebes, Pieter Willem   Dut 1830-1906
  * See 1992 Edition . . . .
Sebire, Gaston   Fr 1920-
  O/C 21x26 La Plage Chr 2/93 3,850
  O/C 29x36 La Tente Bleue Chr 2/93 3,850
  O/C 38x58 Printemps Normand Sby 2/93 2,990
  O/C 22x26 Fin de Journee Doy 11/92 2,200
  O/C 64x51 La Sacre-Coeur Chr 11/92 1,100
Seboth, Josef   Aus 1814-1883
  * See 1991 Edition . . . .
Sedgley, Peter
  * See 1992 Edition . . . .
Sedlacek, Stephan   Ger 20C
  O/C 26x36 Serious Songs/Genre Scene Skn 9/92 825
Seeger, Hermann   Ger 1857-
  * See 1991 Edition . . . .

Seel, Adolf   Ger 1829-1907
* See 1990 Edition . . . .
Seery, John   Am 1941-
O/C 33x68 Snow in Summer 1985 FHB 6/93 800
A/C 46x57 Summer Afternoon 1990 Hnd 5/93 700
O/C 33x68 Snow in Summer 1985 Hnd 5/93 650
Segal, George   Am 1924-
P/Pa 18x12 Untitled 64 Sby 2/93 3,163
Segantini, Giovanni   It 1858-1899
* See 1992 Edition . . . .
Segar, Elzie Crisler   Am 1894-1938
O/C 23x20 Art Reacts to Life But 12/92 1,650
Pl&Pe/Pa 5x21 Daily Comic "Popeye" Ih 5/93 1,600
Pl/Pa 6x21 Daily Comic, Popeye Ih 11/92 1,000
Segar, Sir William   Br 17C
* See 1990 Edition . . . .
Segner, E. B.
O/C 42x32 Woman Giving Sugar to Horse Ih 11/92 750
Segovia, Andres   Spa 1929-
* See 1992 Edition . . . .
Segrelles, Jose   Spa 1885-
W/Pa 10x6 The Pit of Despair 1929 Mys 12/92 248
Segui, Antonio   Arg 1934-
O/C 32x40 The Christ Child Detail Sby 11/92 7,700
Sehring, Adolf   Rus 1930-
* See 1991 Edition . . . .
Seibels, Carl   Ger 1844-1877
O/C 12x17 Cows Watering Chr 10/92 2,640
Seibert   Am 20C
O/C 16x20 Forest Stream Yng 5/93 150
Seifert, Alfred   Czk 1850-1901
O/Pn 12x10 A Young Lady Holding Violets Chr 5/93 2,990
Seignac, Guillaume   Fr 1868-1926
O/C 69x38 Confidence Sby 10/92 49,500
O/C 38x69 L'Abandon Sby 2/93 40,250
O/C 41x33 Grecian Maiden But 5/93 28,750
O/C 26x21 Nymphe Avec Puttis Sby 10/92 24,750
O/C/B 60x34 Classical Maiden with Lyre Wlf 12/92 20,000
Seignac, Paul   Fr 1826-1904
O/Pn 14x11 Greens for a Bunny Sby 10/92 11,550
Seiler, Carl Wilhelm Anton   Ger 1846-1921
O/Pn 6x4 Gentleman Reading 1889 Sby 5/93 3,680
Seiler, Joseph Albert   Aus a 1848-
* See 1993 Edition . . . .
Seitz, Alexander Maximilian   Ger 1811-1888
* See 1990 Edition . . . .
Seitz, Anton   Ger 1829-1900
O/Pn 8x4 The Artist's Studio 72 Chr 2/93 1,760
Seitz, Georg   Ger 1810-1870
* See 1991 Edition . . . .
Sekine, Yoshio   20C
* See 1992 Edition . . . .
Seligmann, Kurt   Sws 1900-1961
O/C 48x59 Exorcist 54 Sby 11/92 55,000
O/M 44x33 Noctambulation 1942 Sby 5/93 31,050
Pt/Gl 20x16 Sous Verre Automne Sby 10/92 5,500
W,G&P/Pa 19x27 Four Costume Studies 1947 Sby 10/92 . . 2,200
Selinger, Jean Paul   Am 1850-1909
O/C 20x14 Waterfall in the White Mountains Skn 3/93 550
Sell, Christian   Ger 1831-1883
* See 1993 Edition . . . .
Sellaer, Vincent   Flm a 1538-1544
* See 1993 Edition . . . .
Selmercheim-Desgrange, Jean 1877-1958
O/Cb 23x18 Vase de fleurs Chr 10/92 5,500
Selous, Henry Courtney   Br 1811-1890
* See 1992 Edition . . . .
Seltzer, Olaf Carl   Am 1877-1957
G&Pe/Pa 12x9 Indian Brave Chr 5/93 11,500
G&Pe/Pa 14x11 Portrait of a Plains Indian 1906 Chr 5/93 . . 7,475
Seltzer, William S.   Am
* See 1990 Edition . . . .

Semenowsky, Eisman   Fr 19C
O/Pn 13x10 Two Exotic Beauties: Pair Chr 5/93 11,500
O/Pn 15x22 The Harem Terrace Sby 2/93 8,050
Semple, Joseph   Irs 19C
* See 1993 Edition . . . .
Senat, Prosper Louis   Am 1852-1925
W/Pa 18x12 Bermuda Street Scene Eld 8/93 1,100
O/Cb 28x20 Capri Pergola Brd 2/93 688
Senet-Perez, Rafael   Spa 1856-1927
O/Pn 15x22 Grand Canal with the Rialto Bridge Chr 10/92 . . 23,100
O/C 20x12 A Venetian Side Canal Sby 2/93 23,000
Sennhauser, John   Am 1907-1978
* See 1993 Edition . . . .
Sepeshy, Zolton L.   Am 1894-1970
O/C 36x42 In the Taos Desert 1926 Dum 9/92 5,000
O/C 36x31 Mountain Landscape with Village Dum 2/93 . . 2,250
T/B 23x27 Wake of a Steamer Dum 2/93 2,250
W/Pa 16x20 Landscape Scene Dum 2/93 800
W/Pa 13x20 Indians at Water Dum 5/93 700
T/B 15x21 Northern Michigan Beach Scene FHB 6/93 625
W/Pa 13x20 Mexico Dum 7/93 500
Serbaroli, Ettore (Hector)   Am 1886-1951
O/Cb 12x16 Landscape Lou 12/92 50
Serisawa, Sueo   Am 1910-
O/M 11x9 Jeannie '42 Sby 6/93 1,150
G/B 12x10 Pauline '43 Sby 6/93 805
Serpan, Iaroslav   1922-1976
* See 1993 Edition . . . .
Serra Y Auque, Enrique   Spa 1859-1918
* See 1993 Edition . . . .
Serra, Ernesto   It 1860-
O/C 26x18 Spanish Beauty Sby 1/93 1,150
Serra, Richard   Am 1938-
I/Pa 33x49 Untitled Sby 10/92 37,400
Pts/L 81x81 Left Corner Square to the Floor Sby 11/92 . . 33,000
Os/Pa 38x50 Elevator Chr 2/93 20,900
Serrano, Andres   1950-
Ph 45x64 Blood & Soil Chr 10/92 8,250
Ph 65x45 Black Mary Chr 10/92 7,150
Ph 46x33 Female Bust 89 Sby 5/93 6,325
Ph 45x33 Black Jesus Sby 2/93 4,600
Serrano, Manuel Gonzalez   Mex 1917-1948
* See 1992 Edition . . . .
Serres, Dominic   Br 1722-1793
W/Pa 16x12 British Man-of-War But 11/92 1,320
Serres, John Thomas   Br 1759-1825
* See 1993 Edition . . . .
Serri, Alfredo   It 1897-1972
* See 1992 Edition . . . .
Serrure, Auguste   Flm 1825-1903
* See 1991 Edition . . . .
Serveau, Clement   Fr 1886-1972
O/C 26x20 Still Life Pitcher, Vase, Flowers 45 Sby 10/92 . . 2,200
Servieres, Eugenie M. H. L.   Fr 1786-
O/C 39x30 The Sleeping Poet 1818 But 5/93 16,100
Sessions, James   Am 1882-1962
W/Pa 24x28 Drying the Sails Chr 12/92 1,320
W/Pa 14x18 Walking on the Beach Hnd 5/93 1,000
W/Pa 23x33 Farm Jeeps Pulling Wagons Dum 11/92 600
W/Pa 21x29 Rough Crossing Wlf 12/92 450
Sether, Gulbrand   Am 1869-
O/C 15x17 Pale Dawn Wlf 9/92 425
Seton, J. T.   Eng 18C
O/C 30x25 Lord Pitfour 1776 Dum 2/93 1,200
O/C 29x25 Lady Pitfour 1776 Dum 2/93 1,100
Settanni, Luigi   Am 1909-1984
* See 1993 Edition . . . .
Seurat, Georges   Fr 1859-1891
Pe/Pa 9x13 Ulysse et les pretendants 1876 Chr 10/92 . . . 14,300
Severini, Gino   It 1883-1966
* See 1993 Edition . . . .
Sevilla, Ferran Garcia   1949-
* See 1993 Edition . . . .

Sewell, Amos Am 1901-1983
O/B 28x26 Family Scene (Post Cover) Hnd 10/92 1,200
Sewell, Robert van Vorst Am 1860-1924
O/C 20x34 Rocky Coast Skn 9/92 935
Sexton, Frederick L. Am 1889-
O/B 12x16 New England Village in Winter Hnd 5/93 350
Seydel, Eduard Gustav Ger 1822-1881
* See 1993 Edition ....
Seyffert, Leopold Gould Am 1887-1956
O/C 82x40 Mrs. Henry Clews Sby 3/93 4,600
Seyler, Julius Ger 1873-1958
* See 1991 Edition ....
Seymour, George L. Br a 1876-1888
O/Pn 13x10 An Elegant Lady in Side Profile Chr 2/93 3,520
O/C/Pn 20x12 Allahu Akbar Hnd 10/92 2,200
Seymour, James Br 1702-1752
O/C 29x36 Racehorse with Jockey 1752 Sby 6/93 68,500
Seymour, Samuel Am 1797-1882
* See 1993 Edition ....
Seyssaud, Rene Fr 1867-1952
O/B 12x20 Paysage Chr 11/92 4,180
Shabunin, H. A. Rus 19C
* See 1992 Edition ....
Shadbolt, Jack Leonard Can 1909-
O/B 13x16 Valley Behind Patras 1961 Sbt 11/92 3,696
Shafer, S. P. Am 19C
O/C 17x24 Pointers in Autumn Dum 5/93 900
Shahn, Ben Am 1898-1969
G/Pa 30x20 Brick Factory Sby 12/92 13,200
O/C 24x32 Picnic, Prospect Park Chr 9/92 8,800
O/Pa 11x13 Still Life Flowers and Fruit Sby 3/93 2,875
W/Pa 18x23 House in Woods Sby 3/93 2,185
W/Pa 11x14 Landscape with Houses and Trees Sby 3/93 . . 1,380
W/Pa 17x25 Figures by the River Chr 12/92 1,320
Shalders, George Br 1826-1873
* See 1991 Edition ....
Shane, Frederick Am 1906-
Pe/Pa 14x11 Study Musicians; Builders: Pair But 12/92 990
Shanker, Louis Am 20C
O/Pn 23x14 Evolvement: Double Sby 9/92 660
Shanks, M. L. Can 19C
W/Pa 14x6 Dike Lands of Nova Scotia Dum 3/93 85
**Shannon, Charles Haslewood Br
1865-1937**
* See 1993 Edition ....
**Shannon, Sir James Jebusa Br
1862-1923**
O/C 56x45 Portrait of a Lady 1907 Chr 10/92 23,100
Shapiro, Joel Am 1941-
C&K/Pa 21x16 Untitled Sby 10/92 9,350
A/C 11 dia Untitled 67 Chr 11/92 1,100
Shapland, John Br -1929
O/C 72x42 Orpheus and Euridyce Hnd 10/92 1,500
Shapleigh, Frank Henry Am 1842-1906
O/C 21x36 Conway Valley from Mt. Willard 1877 Skn 5/93 . 2,970
O/C 10x16 Marshes, Barnstable 1878 Skn 9/92 2,090
O/C 22x34 Kenilworth Castle Eld 8/93 990
O/C 17x32 European Landscape with Church 1869 Eld 8/93 . 880
Share, H. Pruett Am 1853-1905
O/C 11x15 Pastoral Scene Wes 5/93 770
Sharp, Dorothea Eng 1874-1955
O/C 20x30 Feeding the Chickens Wlf 4/93 6,200
Sharp, Joseph Henry Am 1859-1953
O/C 18x26 Big Medicine Camp Chr 3/93 79,500
O/C 20x30 Indians Returning to Winter Camp Chr 12/92 . . 77,000
O/C 20x24 The Drummer in Firelight Chr 5/93 68,500
O/B 16x20 Palm Springs, California Sby 5/93 25,300
O/C/B 24x36 Indian Encampment Hnd 12/92 21,000
O/B 16x20 Desert, Palm Springs, California Sby 5/93 18,400
O/C 15x20 Crow Camp Sby 12/92 13,200
O/C 25x30 Floral Still Life Sby 12/92 13,200
O/C 20x30 Winter Afternoon Sby 5/93 12,650
O/C/B 8x10 Valley Landscape But 6/93 5,175
O/C 16x20 Waimanalo Bay, Honolulu But 12/92 4,400
O/C 12x18 Sand Dunes, Laguna, New Mexico But 12/92 . . 3,850

O/C 20x16 Bright Angel Creek, Grand Canyon But 12/92 . . . 3,300
O/Pn 9x13 Sunset Over the Marshes Mys 3/93 962
Sharp, Louis Hovey Am 1875-1946
* See 1993 Edition ....
Sharp, William Am 1900-1961
O/C 28x18 Manhattan Rooftops Sby 9/92 715
O/C 29x17 Musical Instruments Sby 9/92 715
O/C 18x27 Factory on the Road to the Bridge Sby 3/93 460
O/C 21x24 Treeroots and Fisherman 35 Sby 3/93 460
Sharpe, James Am 1936-
* See 1992 Edition ....
Shattuck, Aaron Draper Am 1832-1928
O/B/B 11x19 White Mountains, NH Sby 9/92 4,675
O/C 19x31 Landscape with Cows and Sheep 76 Skn 3/93 . 3,850
Shaw, Annie Cornelia Am 1852-1887
* See 1992 Edition ....
Shaw, Arthur Winter Br 1869-1948
O/C 11x18 Homeward Bound Sby 1/93 2,875
O/C 21x17 By Candlelight Chr 2/93 1,100
Shaw, Austin 19C
O/C 19x24 Portrait of a Woman Dum 4/93 800
Shaw, Charles Green Am 1892-1974
O/B 20x16 Composition Sby 9/92 15,400
O/C 28x24 Abstraction Sby 3/93 7,475
O/Cb 9x12 Abstraction 1941 Sby 3/93 5,175
O/Cb 9x12 Bathers on the Beach Chr 5/93 1,725
O/B 23x20 Composition Hnd 6/93 1,000
O/B 20x18 Composition Hnd 6/93 1,000
O/B 16x12 Today is Soon Ago Mys 3/93 825
Shaw, Harry Hutchinson Am 1897-1989
* See 1993 Edition ....
Shaw, Jim 20C
H,K,C&I/Pa 14x11 Two Untitled Drawings Chr 11/92 2,200
Shaw, John Byam Eng 1872-1919
* See 1993 Edition ....
Shaw, Joshua Am 1777-1860
* See 1993 Edition ....
Shaw, Sydney Dale Am 1879-1946
O/B 20x16 Picnic in the Woods Yng 5/93 550
O/C 16x20 Autumn View with Cottage Skn 3/93 412
Shawhan, Ada Romer Am 1865-1947
* See 1993 Edition ....
Shayer, Charles & Shayer, H. Br 19C
* See 1993 Edition ....
Shayer, Henry & Shayer, C. Br 19C
* See 1993 Edition ....
Shayer, William (Jr.) Eng 1811-1892
O/C 36x30 Resting Beside the Path Hnz 5/93 2,300
Shayer, William (Sr.) Eng 1788-1879
O/Pn 24x20 Gypsies Near Shirley Sby 10/92 6,600
O/C 19x27 Fisherfolk by the Sea, Southampton But 11/92 . . 3,300
**Shayer, William & Herring, Jr. Br
1811-1892**
O/Pn 5x7 Coaching Scenes: Five 1880 Sby 6/93 14,950
Shearer, Christopher H. Am 1840-1926
O/C 22x36 Deer by a Stream 1894 Fre 10/92 1,200
O/C 22x36 Creek Landscape Ald 3/93 600
Shearer, Victor
O/C 15x25 Seascape 1934 Ald 9/92 275
O/C 20x30 Landscape 1942 Ald 5/93 175
Shed, Charles Dyer Am 1818-1893
* See 1993 Edition ....
Shee, Sir Martin Archer Irs 1769-1850
O/C 93x60 Portrait of a Gentleman and his Dog Sby 10/92 17,600
Sheeler, Charles Am 1883-1965
O/C 25x33 California Industrial 1957 Chr 12/92 220,000
Pe/Pa/B 6x5 Rose 1920 Chr 12/92 11,000
Pe&Y/Pa 7x11 Untitled (Yachting) Chr 9/92 11,000
Sheets, Millard Owen Am 1907-1989
W&Pe/Pa 22x30 Horses at Patzquaro 1965 Sbt 3/93 9,350
W/Pa 30x22 The Plumeria Tree But 10/92 9,350
O/C 18x21 Bridge of Espalion, France 1929 But 3/93 8,250
O/C 20x22 Dockworkers 26 But 6/93 6,900
W/Pa 22x30 Noonday, San Xavier Mor 2/93 5,500
O/C 15x18 Fishing Boats 1926 But 6/93 5,175

214

W/Pa 21x29 Date Palms Mor 6/93 3,300
W/Pa 14x11 The Cockfight, Burma '44 Wlf 12/92 500
Sheffers, P. Winthrop   Am 1893-1949
O/C 30x25 Guardian of Valley, Yosemite Dum 6/93 375
Shepherd, J. Clinton   Am 1888-1975
O/C 32x28 Beachwear of the Future Ih 11/92 550
**Sheppard, Peter Clapham   Can
1882-1965**
O/C 48x35 Old New York Sbt 11/92 6,600
Sheppard, Warren W.   Am 1858-1937
O/C 16x26 Venetian Canal Sby 3/93 3,738
O/C 20x30 Seascape at Sunset Sby 3/93 2,300
O/C 18x36 Sailboats in the Moonlight 1884 Chr 12/92 1,650
O/C/B 12x15 Sailing at Sunset Hnd 3/93 850
Sheridan, John E.   Am 1880-1948
* See 1993 Edition
Sheringham, George   Br 1884-
* See 1992 Edition . . . .
Sherman, Cindy   Am 1954-
Ph 28x53 Untitled (#90) 1981 Chr 11/92 20,900
Ph 73x49 Untitled #140 1985 Chr 10/92 19,800
Ph 8x10 Untitled (#55) 1980 Chr 11/92 19,800
Ph 8x10 Untitled (Film Still #38) 1978 Chr 2/93 19,800
Ph 8x10 Untitled Film Still #49 Sby 5/93 17,250
Ph 40x30 Untitled #123 1983 Sby 5/93 16,100
Ph 49x30 Untitled 1982 Chr 2/93 15,400
Ph 8x10 Untitled 1979 Sby 2/93 14,950
Ph 45x30 Untitled #112 Sby 5/93 14,950
Ph 8x10 Untitled (Film Still #40) 1977 Chr 10/92 13,200
Ph 50x32 Untitled (#217) Chr 11/92 11,000
Ph 72x48 Untitled (#174) Chr 11/92 10,450
Ph 8x10 Untitled #27 1979 Sby 5/93 8,625
Ph 30x40 Untitled 1983 Chr 5/93 5,750
Ph 40x30 Untitled 1986 Chr 11/92 2,750
Sherman, G.   Am 20C
O/C 24x20 World's Fair; Ferris Wheel (2) Chr 12/92 6,600
Sherman, Pamela   Am a 1860-
W/Pa 13x10 Sixty-Eight Botanical Zoological Sby 9/92 . . . 1,980
W/Pa 12x8 Thirteen Botanical Watercolors Sby 9/92 1,870
Shermund, Barbara   Am 1910-1978
G/Pa 17x13 Woman Playing Cymbals Ih 5/93 1,500
Sherrin, Daniel   Br a 1895-1915
O/C 20x30 Lake at Sunrise Wlf 5/93 2,000
O/Cb 35x48 Mountain Landscape Wlf 5/93 1,800
Sherrin, David   Br 1868-
O/C 24x36 Twilight But 5/93 3,162
Sherrin, John   Br 1819-1896
G/Pa 12x16 Still Life, Plum Branches Wlf 12/92 2,200
Sherwood, Mary Clare   Am 1868-1943
O/C 14x12 Harvest Time But 12/92 1,210
**Sherwood, Vladimir Osipovich   Rus
1832-1897**
* See 1990 Edition . . . .
Sherwood, William A.   Can 1875-1951
* See 1991 Edition . . . .
Shikler, Aaron   Am 1922-
* See 1993 Edition . . . .
Shilling, Arthur   Can 1941-1986
O/B 18x24 Clotheslline Sbt 11/92 1,584
Shinn, Everett   Am 1876-1953
P/Pa/B 11x15 Rooftop Cafe 1925 Chr 5/93 66,300
W,G&Pe/Pa 18x24 The Soiree 1905 Chr 5/93 34,500
P/B 19x26 Alley Cat 1933 Chr 12/92 28,600
P&W/Pa 9x14 Fleishman's Bread Line 1900 Sby 12/92 . . . 25,300
P/Pa/B 18x12 After the Performance 1934 Chr 9/92 24,200
O/C 16x20 The Ballet 1943 Sby 9/92 19,800
K/Pa 12x17 Woman Looking in Mirror 1904 Chr 12/92 4,400
W&Pe/B 10x14 A Village in Winter 1940 Sby 9/92 3,080
W,I&C/B 17x22 The Golden Lancet, Act I 1934 Sby 3/93 . . 2,875
W/Pa 17x11 Quarrel: Landless & Drood 1941 Chr 12/92 . . 2,200
G/Pa 10x15 Winter Scene with Coach 1941 Hnd 10/92 . . . 2,000
Y/Pa 14x8 Girl with Skirt over her Head Chr 12/92 1,760
Y/Pa 13x8 A Woman Dressing Chr 5/93 1,495
W&Pe/Pa 11x13 Simeon with Christ Child 1945 Sby 3/93 . . 1,495
W/Pa 13x11 Study of a Head 1909 Chr 5/93 920

C/Pa 12x17 Woman in a Landscape 1907 Sby 3/93 920
P/Pa 8x9 Lawyer's Office 1905 Lou 6/93 700
Y/Pa 14x8 Standing Female Figure 1906 Chr 5/93 403
Shinoda, Toko   1913-
* See 1992 Edition . . . .
Shipley   Br 20C
O/C 30x24 Three Dogs Hnd 3/93 550
Shirey, S.   Am 1939-
P/Pa 11x16 Beach Umbrellas Eld 8/93 138
P/Pa 10x15 Peonies Eld 8/93 138
Shirlaw, Walter   Am 1838-1909
* See 1992 Edition . . . .
Shishkin, Ivan Ivanovitch   Rus 1831-1898
O/C/B 16x12 Flowers in the Woods 1895 Wes 3/93 5,060
Shoemaker, Vaughn   Am 1902-1991
PI/Pa 17x14 Two Editorial Cartoons Wes 3/93 578
PI/Pa 17x13 Two Cartoons Wes 5/93 138
Shokler, Harry   Am 1896-
O/C 24x40 NYC 9th Ave & 17th to 19th 1936 Sby 9/92 . . . 2,310
Short, Frederick Golden   Am 20C
* See 1991 Edition . . . .
Shoup, Charles   Am 20C
* See 1990 Edition . . . .
Shulz, Ada Walter   Am 1870-1928
O/C 34x32 Portrait Francis with Stephen Hnd 12/92 17,000
O/C 24x27 Washing Hnd 3/93 16,000
O/C 24x27 Return From a Visit Skn 9/92 12,100
O/B 22x18 Two Sisters Hnd 5/93 7,000
Shulz, Adolph Robert   Am 1869-1963
O/B 16x18 Houses in a Landscape Mys 3/93 1,760
Shurtleff, Roswell Morse   Am 1838-1915
O/C 12x16 Autumn But 12/92 2,200
Shuster, William   Am 1893-1969
O/C/C 20x24 Storm Clouds 25 But 12/92 3,575
**Siberechts, Guiellimus Jan   Flm
1627-1703**
* See 1992 Edition . . . .
Sichel, Harold M.   Am 1881-1948
O/C 18x24 California Hills 42 But 3/93 3,575
O/C 16x24 Grazing under the Trees 46 But 3/93 1,760
Sicilia, Jose Maria   1954-
O/C 64x65 Flor 85 Chr 11/92 35,200
O/C 98x102 Hiver 1984 Chr 11/92 30,800
A,Wx&Pg/L 102x75 Tulips Chr 11/92 24,200
A/C 32x96 Red Flower 1986 Sby 10/92 16,500
A/C 36x36 Black Flower 86 Sby 10/92 13,200
Sickert, Walter Richard   Br 1860-1942
* See 1992 Edition . . . .
Sickles, Noel   Am 1910-1982
G/Pa 13x10 Kidnapping Man on Steps of Mansion Ih 5/93 . 250
Siebert, Edward Seimar   Am 1856-1944
PWPe&C/Pa Var Sketchbook/Scrapbook (73) Wes 12/92 . . 468
O/B 9x11 Woodland Stream 1907 Lou 12/92 450
CPPe&W/Pa Var Sketchbook/Scrapbook (48) Wes 12/92 . . 330
Sieger, Rudolph   Ger 1867-1925
O/Pn 29x19 Still Life Peonies, Oriental Vase 1916 Sby 10/92 8,800
Siegert, August   Ger 1786-1869
* See 1992 Edition . . . .
Siegert, August Friedrich   Ger 1820-1883
O/C 11x9 Reading the Daily News Wlf 3/93 2,200
Siegfried, Edwin   Am 1889-1955
P/Pa 25x37 Stinson's Beach But 3/93 2,475
P/B 20x24 Sunrise on the Nevada Desert But 10/92 990
P/B 21x17 Eucalyptus Tree Golden Gate Park 1943 Mor 2/93 750
P/Pb 20x30 Indian in Tepee 1929 Lou 3/93 200
Siegriest, Louis   Am 1899-1989
O/M 23x27 Back of "C" Street-Virginia City '50 Mor 2/93 . . 1,700
MM/M 12x16 Utah Landscape But 4/93 1,150
MM/B 10x14 Aguacaliente 1959 But 10/92 990
W/Pa 7x10 A View in Martinez '33 But 10/92 550
Siegriest, Lundy   Am 1925-
O/C 16x20 Petaluma Breaking Cart 1977 But 3/93 2,750
O/C 16x20 Bass Run, Martinez 1979 But 3/93 2,475
O/C 16x20 China Camp, Summer 1977 But 3/93 1,870
O/C 8x10 Surf and Cliffs But 3/93 1,760

MM/Pn 48x48 Desert Cliffs '71 But 10/92 1,650

Siemer, Christian   Am 1874-1940
O/C 24x30 Sierra Landscape '37 Mor 2/93 850

Siemiradzki, Hendrik   Pol 1843-1902
O/C 31x61 Sunny Afternoon at the Well Chr 5/93 29,900

Sieurac, Henry   Fr 1823-1863
O/C 23x31 A Poetry Reading 1862 Wlf 3/93 1,400

Sievers, R.   Dut 1929-
O/C 27x31 Floral Dum 5/93 4,500
O/C 27x31 Floral Still Life Dum 7/93 3,500

Siewert-Miller, Elizabeth   Am 20C
O/C 38x48 Fancy of the Winds Hnd 9/92 30

Sigler, Hollis   Am 20C
* See 1991 Edition

Signac, Paul   Fr 1863-1935
O/Pn 6x9 Asnieres (La Barque Du Passeur) Sby 5/93 68,500
W&Pe/Pa 11x17 Port de Saint Malo Sby 5/93 23,000
I&S/Pa/B 18x22 Bateaux Dans le Canal Sby 11/92 20,900
W,G&Y/Pa 10x17 Paimpol 1927 Sby 11/92 18,700
W,G&C/Pa/B 10x16 Le Puy 1912 Sby 11/92 17,600
W&C/Pa 6x4 La Cathedrale a Quimperle 00 Sby 11/92 . . . 14,850
W,G&Y/Pa 11x18 Lezardrieux 1927 Sby 11/92 13,200
G&W/Pa/B 8x6 Overschie 1906 Chr 5/93 8,625
W,I&Pe/Pa 5x6 Bateau a Voiles Sby 10/92 3,850
C/Pa/B 8x12 Harbor View, Honfleur Sby 10/92 3,575
W&H/Pa 5x6 Samois II But 5/93 3,162
W&C/Pa 4x7 Port de Toulon 34 Sby 10/92 1,980

Signni, G.   It 20C
W/Pa 7x10 Neapolitan Harbor Scene Sel 9/92 150

Signorelli, Luca   It 1441-1523
* See 1991 Edition

Signoret, Charles Louis Eugene   Fr 1867-1932
O/C 22x32 Fishing Boat at Sunset Chr 5/93 2,530

Signorini, Giuseppe   It 1857-1932
* See 1993 Edition

Sigriste, Guido   Sws 1864-1915
O/Pn 10x7 News From the Front Sby 1/93 1,840

Silberhorn, Tibor   Am 20C
O/C 20x36 Dispatch to General Washington Sby 3/93 460

Silbert, Max   Fr 1871-
O/C 10x14 Family Seated for Dinner But 5/93 1,610

Sillens, Herman   Dan 19C
* See 1992 Edition

Sillett, James   Br 1764-1840
* See 1990 Edition

Silva, Benjamin   Brz 1927-
* See 1993 Edition

Silva, Francis Augustus   Am 1835-1886
O/C 18x30 On the Hudson Near Haverstraw '72 Sby 3/93 . 184,000
O/C 24x44 October on the Hudson Chr 5/93 101,500
O/C 12x24 Approaching Storm '71 Sby 5/93 79,500
O/C 24x44 Midsummer's Twilight '81 Sby 12/92 57,750
O/C 42x58 Autumn New England Coast 86 Chr 12/92 35,200
O/C 9x18 View from the Hudson River 70 But 6/93 24,150
O/C 20x36 Along the Shore Chr 5/93 20,700
O/C 8x16 Beach at Long Branch, New Jersey Chr 9/92 . . . 19,800
O/C 9x18 Gloucester Dawn Chr 5/93 16,100
W/Pa 29x21 Crashing Surf Fre 4/93 3,000

Silva, William Posey   Am 1859-1948
O/B 12x16 Rocky Shore But 10/92 7,150
O/C 25x30 Magnolias on the Asa(?) 1925 Mor 11/92 2,250
O/B 11x14 Springtime, Carmel Shore But 6/93 1,725
O/B 11x14 Springtime Carmel Shore Mys 3/93 1,430
O/C/B 14x18 Cliff Path, Point Lobos Wes 10/92 825

Silvani, Ferdinando   It 1823-1899
* See 1992 Edition

Silvari, F.   It 19C
O/Pn 11x7 Family at Piazza San Marco Wlf 5/93 50

Silverman, Burton   Am 1928-
W,G&Pe/B 24x14 Woman in a Beach Hat '82 Sby 12/92 . . . 3,850

Simbari, Nicola   It 1927-
O/C 32x40 Sails on the Riviera Sby 2/93 12,650
O/C 32x36 Boy on a Bicycle at the Beach Sby 2/93 8,338
O/C 24x32 Sunny Walk Chr 5/93 6,900

O/C 27x39 Balcone in Amalfi '61 Sel 4/93 5,750
O/C 32x40 Fence Chr 5/93 5,175
O/C 20x24 Girl in a Shawl Hnd 3/93 4,600
O/C 40x24 Woman at Flower Mart 64 Hnd 10/92 4,400
O/C 21x32 Ishia 65 Sby 10/92 3,850
O/C 41x41 La Romana Lou 3/93 3,000
O/C 26x32 Wall in Sorrento Chr 5/93 2,530
O/C 39x36 The Flower Stall 62 Chr 11/92 2,420
O/C 24x30 Fabienne Sby 2/93 2,300
O/C 48x36 Palm Tree 64 Sby 10/92 1,980
O/C 22x14 Flower Vendor 63 Sby 10/92 1,430
O/C 16x8 Marina of Sicilia Sby 6/93 920
O/C 19x17 Still Life Crab, Bottle and Guitar 66 Skn 3/93 385

Simboli, Raymond   Am 1894-1964
* See 1993 Edition

Sime, Sidney Herbert   Am 20C
* See 1991 Edition

Simensen, Sigvald   Nor -1920
O/C 32x55 Winter Village Chr 2/93 330

Simkhovitch, Simka   Am 1893-1949
* See 1993 Edition

Simmler, Wilhelm   Ger 1840-1914
* See 1992 Edition

Simmons, Edward Emerson   Am 1852-1931
* See 1992 Edition

Simmons, Laurie   1949-
Ph 84x48 Walking Hourglass 1989 Chr 11/92 8,800

Simon, Eugene
O/C 16x20 Outside Church Service 1919 Ald 9/92 145
O/C 12x16 Mountain Landscape Ald 9/92 75

Simon, Hermann Gustave   Am 1846-1895
W/Pa 12x18 Pointer on Point Sby 6/93 1,495

Simon, Lucien   Fr 1861-1945
O/C 40x60 La Belle Jacquetta But 5/93 6,900

Simon, Pincus Marcius   Am 19C
O/C 42x29 Maidens Descending a Staircase Chr 5/93 2,530

Simon, Tavik Frantisek   Czk 1877-1942
O/C 21x29 Barges in Winter Chr 2/93 2,420

Simon, Yohanan
O/C 15x18 Ambiance Flamboyante 1969 Sby 10/92 2,200

Simonelli, Giuseppe   It 1650-1710
* See 1992 Edition

Simonet, Augustin   Fr 19C
* See 1991 Edition

Simonetti, Amedeo Momo   It 1874-1922
* See 1993 Edition

Simonetti, Andres   It 20C
* See 1993 Edition

Simonetti, Attilio   It 1843-1925
W/Pa 15x22 The Seraglio Sby 5/93 6,900

Simonetti, Ettore   It 19C
O/C 26x36 The Rug Merchant Sby 10/92 26,400

Simoni, Cesare   It 19C
* See 1993 Edition

Simoni, Gustavo   It 1846-
O/C 42x29 In the Courtyard Chr 5/93 21,850
W/Pa 14x11 Woman in Garden by Villa 78 Sby 1/93 1,955

Simoni, Scipione   It a 1891-1898
* See 1993 Edition

Simonidy, Michel   Rom 1870-1933
O/C 27x13 Summer 1901 Sby 10/92 8,800

Simonin, Victor   1877-1946
O/C 32x23 Pichet d'Anemones 1915 Chr 2/93 1,650

Simonini, Francesco   It 1686-1753
* See 1993 Edition

Simons, Michiel   Dut a 1648-1673
* See 1992 Edition

Simonsen, Niels   Dan 1807-1885
* See 1990 Edition

Simonson, David   Ger 1831-1896
* See 1990 Edition

Simony, Stefan   Aus 1860-
* See 1992 Edition

Simpkins, Ronald   Can 1942-
* See 1992 Edition . . . .
Simpson, Charles Walter   Br 19C
* See 1991 Edition . . . .
Simpson, David
* See 1992 Edition . . . .
Simpson, Maxwell Stewart   Am 1896-
O/C 40x26 Baron Benners 1947 Fre 4/93 2,100
Simpson, W* H***   Br 1866-1886**
O/C 44x55 Beechwood Winter Sby 1/93 4,313
Sinclair, Irving   Am 1895-1969
O/C 54x78 The Poker Game 44 Chr 9/92 7,700
Sinclair, Olga   20C
* See 1992 Edition . . . .
Sinding, Otto Ludvig   Nor 1842-1909
O/C 30x42 Twilight After the Rain 75 Chr 5/93 6,900
Sinet, Andre   Fr 1867-
* See 1993 Edition . . . .
Singer, Burr   Am 1912-
* See 1992 Edition . . . .
Singer, Clyde   Am 1908-
O/Cb 26x22 Kiosk 1968 Wtf 5/93 750
O/C 16x20 Conversation in the Rain '50 Wtf 5/93 600
O/Cb 18x34 After the Shower '49 Wtf 5/93 550
O/M 12x15 Landscape Lou 12/92 250
Singer, William H. (Jr.)   Am 1868-1943
* See 1991 Edition . . . .
Singier, Gustave   Fr 1909-
* See 1993 Edition . . . .
Singleton, Henry   Br 1766-1839
* See 1993 Edition . . . .
Sinibaldi, Jean Paul   Fr 1857-1909
* See 1993 Edition . . . .
Sinibaldo, Toroi   It 19C
O/Pn 14x10 The Flirtation Chr 10/92 2,090
Siqueiros, David Alfaro   Mex 1896-1974
Prx/Pn 32x24 El Padre de la Primera Victima 61 Sby 5/93 . 68,500
Prx/Pw 31x24 Relacion entre la Objetividad 1971 Chr 11/92 28,600
A/Pn 35x16 La Vie 65 Sby 11/92 27,500
Px&G/B/Pn 15x20 Cabeza de Mujer Sby 5/93 23,100
O/B/M 18x13 Tormenta 63 Sby 11/92 12,100
W&Pe/Pa 30x22 Boceto Para Una Piscina 1967 Sby 5/93 . . 4,888
I&G/Pa 13x17 Tres Danzadoras 61 But 4/93 4,312
P/Pa 12x8 Portrait of a Woman Sby 10/92 1,980
Siqueiros, Jose Alfaro
* See 1991 Edition . . . .
Sirani, Elisabetta   1628-1665
O/C 35x29 Cleopatra Chr 5/93 46,000
O/Pn 28x19 Young Saint John the Baptist Sby 1/93 43,125
Sironi, Mario   It 1885-1961
G&Pe/Pa 7x10 Piccolo Bozzetto di Un Paessaggio Chr 5/93   5,750
G/Pa/C 11x9 Il Bevitore Sby 2/93 4,140
Sisley, Alfred   Fr 1839-1899
O/C 21x29 Ferme Aux Sablons, en Soleil 85 Chr 11/92 . . 605,000
O/C 22x29 Le Matin a Moret en Mai 86 Sby 11/92 550,000
O/C 18x25 La Seine a Suresnes Sby 11/92 385,000
Sisson, Laurence P.   Am 1928-
O/M 6x11 Surf and Rocks '63 Skn 3/93 220
W&I/Pa 21x28 Two Men on a Beach 1968 Skn 9/92 192
Sisson, Richard   Irs -1767
O/C 30x25 John and Cornelia King: Pair 1756 Hnd 5/93 . . 1,000
Sitzman, Edward R.   Am 1874-
* See 1993 Edition . . . .
Sivard, Robert   Fr 20C
O/M 16x12 Coiffure 1966 Wes 10/92 1,045
Sjamaar, Pieter Geerard   Dut 1819-1876
* See 1992 Edition . . . .
Sjoholm, Charles   Swd 1933-
O/C 21x26 The Circus Sel 12/92 150
Sjostrom, G. J.
* See 1992 Edition . . . .
Skarbina, Franz   Ger 1849-1910
* See 1993 Edition . . . .
Skeaping, John Rattenbury   Br 1901-1980
* See 1993 Edition . . . .

Skelton, Red   Am 20C
* See 1992 Edition . . . .
Skilling   Am 20C
O/C 48x60 A Monkey and a Dog Hnd 10/92 900
Skipworth, Frank Markham   Br 1854-1929
* See 1993 Edition . . . .
Sklar, Dorothy   Am 20C
O/B 25x30 Savoy Hotel But 10/92 1,045
O/B 30x36 The Blanket Sellers '62 But 6/93 862
W/Pa 13x20 Children in City Street Scene '44 Mor 6/93 . . . 660
W/Pa 13x19 Laguna Shore II '46 Mor 2/93 650
W/Pa 17x22 Los Angeles-Outfit Cars Mor 6/93 605
W/Pa 14x21 Los Angeles-Outfit Cars & Tunnel '50 Mor 6/93 . 605
W/Pa 16x21 Boatyards '47 Mor 6/93 412
W/Pa 16x21 Ripple 53 Mor 6/93 330
W/Pa 13x20 Sunday Morning 46 Mor 11/92 300
Skou, Sigord   Am -1929
* See 1992 Edition . . . .
Skovgaard, Johan Thomas   Dan 1888-
* See 1992 Edition . . . .
Skredswig, Christian Eriksen   Dan 1854-1924
* See 1993 Edition . . . .
Slade, Caleb Arnold   Am 1882-1961
* See 1993 Edition . . . .
Sloan, John   Am 1871-1951
O/Pn 16x20 Landscape, Sante Fe Chr 9/92 24,200
O/C 24x20 Pink and Blue Sby 5/93 19,550
O/C 9x11 Gray Day (Billings Mansion) '08 Sby 5/93 12,650
T&O/B 20x15 Nude on Harp Chair Chr 5/93 6,325
Sloan, Junius R.   Am 1827-1900
O/B/B 7x11 The Break in the Clouds 1877 Hnd 5/93 400
Sloane, Eric   Am 1910-1985
O/M 36x46 Fishing Season Sby 5/93 19,550
O/M 22x28 Pennsylvania Barn Sby 3/93 10,350
O/M 20x29 October Barn Sby 5/93 8,625
O/M 15x11 Father Sky Sby 3/93 5,175
O/B 24x25 Bittersweet Season Chr 12/92 4,620
O/M 24x32 Vermont September Sby 3/93 4,600
O/B 30x40 Farm Landscape Ald 9/92 4,000
O/C 47x65 Cumulus Clouds 1946 Sby 9/92 3,575
O/M 20x23 On the Water Chr 3/93 3,450
O/Cb 20x27 Cloud Painting 1939 Sby 9/92 2,530
O/B 26x22 Planes Over the City Mys 12/92 1,320
P/Pa 21x16 Night and Day 1942 Fre 4/93 1,300
O/Cb 25x30 Landing Strip Through Clouds Fre 4/93 1,200
P/Pa 21x16 Cumulonimbus at 10,000 Feet 1942 Fre 4/93 . . 1,100
P/Pa 12x20 Republic Thunderbolt Fre 4/93 650
O/Cb 25x30 P47 Republic Fre 4/93 625
Sloane, George   Br 20C
* See 1993 Edition . . . .
Sloane, Marian Parkhurst   Am 1875-1955
O/C 30x40 Spring Skn 3/93 880
Slobodkina, Esphyr   Am 1914-
O/C 13x16 Houses Sby 3/93 4,600
Slocombe, Frederick Albert   Br 1847-
* See 1990 Edition . . . .
Sloman, Steven   Am 20C
A/C 56x81 French Ultramarine 1975 FHB 3/93 300
Slott-Moller, Harald   Dan 1864-1937
* See 1993 Edition . . . .
Slusser, Jean Paul   Am 1886-
P/Pa 24x19 Four Pastel Drawings Lou 9/92 450
Small, Frank O.   Am 1860-
* See 1993 Edition . . . .
Smart, Jeffrey   Nz 20C
O/B 32x24 Radar Station Dum 7/93 17,000
Smart, John   Br 1838-1899
O/C 22x36 The Island Pool on the Orchy 1889 Chr 10/92 . . 1,650
Smedley, William Thomas   Am 1858-1920
W&R/Pa 10x13 Couple in Drawing Room 1890 Ilh 5/93 400
Smeers, Frans   Bel 1873-
* See 1992 Edition . . . .
Smets, Louis   Dut 19C
O/C 23x31 Skaters on a Frozen River 1865 Sby 10/92 4,950

Smillie, George Henry   Am 1840-1921
O/C 9x17 Pigeon Cove 1861 But 12/92 6,600
O/C 9x6 Path to the Meadow Fre 4/93 1,400
W/Pa 11x17 Venetian Scene 1900 Ald 3/93 450
O/B 9x11 Maine Coast Landscape Ald 9/92 300
Smillie, James David   Am 1833-1909
* See 1992 Edition ....
Smirnoff, Fedor   Fr 20C
O/C 24x15 French Street Scene Slo 4/93 60
Smit, Derk   Am 20C
O/C 20x24 Winter Scene Hnd 3/93 725
**Smith of Chichester, George   Eng
1714-1776**
* See 1993 Edition ....
Smith, A.   Am 20C
O/C 18x24 Mountainous Snowy Winter 1925 Sel 9/92 250
Smith, Albert E.   Am 1862-1940
* See 1993 Edition ....
Smith, Alexis   1949-
* See 1993 Edition ....
Smith, Alice Ravenel Huger   Am 1876-
* See 1993 Edition ....
Smith, Andrew
W/Pa 10x15 Black Buick Roadster Dum 7/93 40
Smith, Archibald Cary   Am 1837-1911
* See 1990 Edition ....
Smith, Carlton A.   Eng 1853-1946
W/Pa 31x50 The Three Sisters 1902 Chr 10/92 12,100
Smith, Charles Alexander   Can 1864-1915
O/C 22x18 Lady Reading '88 Sbt 11/92 3,740
O/C 20x24 Boys in the Field Sbt 11/92 1,584
O/C 20x26 The Shepherd '88 Sbt 5/93 1,320
O/C 18x13 Man in a Field '88 Sbt 11/92 1,056
O/C 24x30 Farm in Springtime Sbt 5/93 880
Smith, Charles Augustus   Am 20C
* See 1993 Edition ....
Smith, Charles L. A.   Am 1871-1937
O/C 30x50 Rocky Coastal Scene But 10/92 550
Smith, Dan   Am 1865-1934
* See 1993 Edition ....
Smith, David   Am 1906-1965
E/Pa 18x12 A Sketch For Sculpture Chr 10/92 5,500
Smith, De Cost   Am 1864-1939
O/C 30x24 Native American Scene 1890 Skn 11/92 18,700
O/C 45x34 Signal 1909 Chr 12/92 3,520
Smith, Erik Johan   Am 20C
W/Pa 18x23 Street Scene, Key West 1934 Slo 5/93 375
Smith, Ernest Browning   Am 1866-1951
O/C/C 36x45 Mountain Landscape Mor 6/93 1,430
O/C 30x36 Early Moonrise-Mount Cahuenga 1919 Mor 6/93 .. 1,320
O/C 24x30 California Mountains Dum 3/93 1,200
O/B 16x20 Landscape Mor 2/93 1,200
O/C/C 30x36 Big Sky Landscape Mor 6/93 1,100
O/C 18x24 Coastal Landscape Mor 6/93 1,100
O/C/C 28x36 Farm House 1922 Mor 6/93 1,100
O/Cb 12x16 Coastal Mor 2/93 900
O/C/B 16x20 Gray Morning-Annandale 1914 Mor 6/93 770
O/Cb 11x14 Landscape Mor 11/92 750
O/C 16x20 Landscape Mor 2/93 750
Smith, F. Carl   Am 1868-1955
O/C 25x30 Boats at Dock Mor 11/92 1,700
O/B 12x16 On the Moors-North Shore Mor 2/93 425
O/M 12x16 Gloucester Landscape Mor 2/93 350
O/B 20x16 Mountain Village Mor 11/92 300
Smith, Francis Drexel   Am 1874-1956
* See 1992 Edition ....
Smith, Francis Hopkinson   Am 1838-1915
G/Pa 17x23 Elegant Ladies 1906 Sby 3/93 9,200
W,C&G/Pa/B 18x27 River View Sby 12/92 7,700
W&G/Pa 20x12 Canal Scene, Venice Sby 12/92 7,150
G/Pa 12x21 A Venetian Piazza Sby 3/93 4,600
G&Pe/Pa 14x22 Dock Scene But 12/92 3,575
G&W/B 18x24 Holland Canal Scene Sby 3/93 3,335
W&G/Pa/B 18x26 Sailboats in a Calm Sea Sby 9/92 2,970
W&Pe/Pa 23x13 In the Shadow of a Palace But 12/92 1,760

W,G&I/Pa 12x18 Street in Marianao 81 Sby 3/93 1,380
W/Pa 9x12 Coastal Village '80 Lou 6/93 1,200
Smith, Frank Anthony   Am 1939-
A/C 45x55 Flag '80 Slo 4/93 475
Smith, Frank Vining   Am 1879-1967
O/C 28x36 Ship on the High Seas Sby 3/93 3,335
O/C 28x36 Fleeing Bears, Campers Approaching Ih 5/93 .. 1,200
Smith, Frederick Carl   Am 1868-1955
O/Cb 12x16 Landscape Lou 12/92 200
Smith, Gean   Am 1851-1928
O/C 16x24 Artful and his Trainer 1904 Chr 3/93 2,875
Smith, George Melville   Am 1879-
T/Pn 24x43 Land Yields Her Increase Sby 9/92 3,300
Smith, Gordon   Can 1937-
* See 1992 Edition ....
Smith, Gordon Appelby   Can 1919-
* See 1993 Edition ....
Smith, Graham
W/Pa 15x22 Pair: Cheltenham Gold Cup 1950 Dum 10/92 . 2,000
Smith, H.   Ger 19C
O/C 7x9 The Good Book and A Good Drink: Two Hnz 5/93 .. 700
Smith, Harry Knox   Am 1879-
W&Y/Pa 15x11 Venice; Opulence (2) 1926 Chr 12/92 990
Smith, Hassel   Am 1915-
* See 1992 Edition ....
Smith, Henry Pember   Am 1854-1907
O/C 14x20 A Day in September Sby 9/92 3,575
O/C 20x28 Mid-Summer Morning Sby 9/92 3,300
O/C 10x15 Small New England House on River Chr 9/92 .. 3,080
O/C 14x20 Lakeside Cottage Lou 3/93 3,000
G&Pe/Pa/B 12x17 Seascape 1883 Sby 9/92 2,090
O/C 20x14 Venetian Canal Wlf 3/93 1,200
Smith, Hugh Bellingham   Br 20C
O/C 24x18 Portrait of G. H. Martin, Esq. Hnd 10/92 300
Smith, Hughie Lee   Am 1910-
O/C 24x18 Two Figures on a Rooftop Dum 2/93 4,750
O/C 24x32 The Hill 1963 Dum 2/93 3,500
O/M 8x12 Man with Sail Boats in Background '54 Dum 2/93 2,900
O/B 24x29 Landscape Dum 11/92 2,400
W/Pa 11x15 Deserted Beach 58 Dum 9/92 1,400
Smith, J. Wells   Br 19C
O/C 12x10 Apple Seller; Fisherman: Two 1878 Lou 9/92 ... 600
Smith, Jack Martin
* See 1992 Edition ....
Smith, Jack Wilkinson   Am 1873-1949
O/B 12x16 High Sierra Mor 11/92 1,500
O/Ab 14x12 Pikes Region Colorado Wlf 12/92 400
Smith, Jeremy   Can 1946-
* See 1993 Edition ....
Smith, Jerome Howard   Am 1861-1941
O/C 30x48 Cowboys & Horses at Watering Hole Mor 2/93 . 1,400
Smith, Jessie Willcox   Am 1863-1935
G&C/B 19x26 Jack and Jill Chr 5/93 18,400
W&I/Pb 15x19 Out on the Lawn There Arose such Skn 3/93 . 412
Smith, John Brandon   Br a 1850-1900
O/C 18x14 Landscape with Waterfall 1855 Dum 4/93 2,000
Smith, John Christopher   Am 1891-1943
O/C 24x30 Green Landscape Near Salinas But 10/92 1,650
O/B 13x16 Landscape Near Salinas But 10/92 1,540
O/C 24x20 Poinsettias and Fruit Mor 6/93 495
Smith, John Warwick   Br 1749-1831
W/Pa 14x20 Travellers Hnz 5/93 280
Smith, Joseph Lindon   Am 1863-1950
* See 1993 Edition ....
Smith, Julia Benedict   Am 20C
O/C 30x25 Cabin Through the Grove 1930 Skn 9/92 248
Smith, Kiki   1954-
* See 1993 Edition ....
Smith, Lawrence Beall   Am 1909-
* See 1992 Edition ....
Smith, Leon Polk   Am 1906-
* See 1993 Edition ....
Smith, Letta Crapo   Am 1862-1921
* See 1990 Edition ....

Smith, Mary   Am 1842-1878
  * See 1992 Edition . . . .
Smith, Miriam Tindall   20C
  * See 1991 Edition . . . .
Smith, Mortimer L.   Am 1840-1896
  O/C 18x26 Smugglers Cove Hnd 10/92   9,000
Smith, Ray   1959-
  O/Pn 36x48 Untitled 1989 Chr 11/92   11,000
  A/C 51x50 Pancho 1986 Sby 2/93   5,750
Smith, Richard   Br 1931-
  O/C&Me 65x93 After HL But 10/92   1,100
  O/C&Me 78x11 Keyring But 10/92   1,100
  O/C&Me 94x72 Mask II But 10/92   1,045
Smith, Rosamond Lombard   Am 20C
  * See 1991 Edition . . . .
Smith, Rupert Jasen
  * See 1992 Edition . . . .
Smith, Russell   Am 1812-1896
  O/C 12x18 Northern Lights 1880 Ald 9/92   170
Smith, Thomas Lochlan   Am 1835-1884
  O/C 24x20 Landscape with Fisherman Sby 9/92   2,860
Smith, Wallace Herndon   Am 1901-
  O/C 25x30 The Finish Sel 12/92   4,000
  O/C 27x36 Notre Dame Sel 12/92   1,400
Smith, Walter Granville   Am 1870-1938
  W/Pa 17x29 Resting at the Inn 1896 Yng 5/93   2,750
  O/C 16x20 The Hillside Yng 2/93   2,250
  O/C 12x16 The Sunset Sby 9/92   1,210
  O/B 6x9 Hillside Mor 2/93   1,000
  O/C 16x12 The Locket Brd 2/93   770
  W&Pe/B 10x13 The Fly Fisherman 1930 Sby 3/93   633
  Pe/Pa 6x7 Portrait of John Sloan 1928 Brd 8/93   66
Smith, William Collingwood   Br 1815-1887
  W/Pa/B 8x11 Italianate Village by a River Chr 10/92   660
Smith, William Russell   Am 1812-1896
  W/Pa 13x19 Open Ocean Yng 5/93   350
Smith, Xanthus Russell   Am 1839-1929
  O/C 15x21 Cottage/Herding Livestock 1898 Sby 3/93   1,725
  O/C 7x10 Figures Along the Road Fre 10/92   750
  O/B 8x11 Seascape Brd 8/93   660
  W/Pa 6x9 View from Artist's House, Maine Brd 8/93   632
Smith-Hald, Frithjof   Nor 1846-1903
  O/C 18x30 Bergen Winter Landscape Wtf 3/93   3,000
Smithers, Collier   Br 20C
  * See 1993 Edition . . . .
Smithers, Herbert H.   Am 1871-1960
  W/Pa 7x9 California Sketchbook Mor 6/93   110
Smithson, Robert   Am 1938-1973
  Pe/Pa 24x19 Earth Mirror 68 Sby 5/93   7,475
  Y/Pa 14x17 Mirror Thicket 69 Sby 10/92   7,150
  Cp&/Pa 14x17 Mirror Thicket 69 Sby 10/92   6,050
  Pe/Pa 19x24 Floating Island, Barge 71 Sby 5/93   5,750
  Pl/Pa/B 24x18 Untitled 62 Sby 2/93   1,725
Smits, Jacob   Dut 1855-1928
  * See 1993 Edition . . . .
Smits, Johann Gerard   Dut 1823-1910
  O/C 32x23 Market Day Sby 5/93   5,750
Smolen, Frank   Am 1900-
  O/B 14x18 Simon Kehl's Barn Wtf 12/92   200
Smoot, Ella Rose   Am 19C
  O/C 12x18 Red and White Grapes 1897 Slo 4/93   150
Smyth, James
  O/Ab 11x15 Village Near Edinburgh Eld 8/93   143
Smythe, Edward Robert   Br 1810-1899
  O/C 30x25 Gypsy Camp Hnd 12/92   3,000
Smythe, Ernest   Am 20C
  W/Pa 16x20 In Flander's Fields Mor 2/93   350
Smythe, Minnie   Eng 19C
  * See 1992 Edition . . . .
Smythe, Thomas   Br 1825-1906
  O/C 17x24 Fishing at Ipswich But 11/92   6,050
  O/C 20x30 Woodland Harriers Chr 6/93   5,750
Snayers, Pieter   1592-1666
  O/Pn 19x25 Military Skirmish Sby 1/93   23,000

Snead, Louise W.   Am 19C
  W/Pa 15x12 Woman in White Eld 8/93   605
Snelgrove, Walter   Am 1924-
  O/C 54x80 Landscape But 10/92   3,025
Snell, Henry Bayley   Am 1858-1943
  O/C 10x12 Rocky Harbor Ald 9/92   400
Snell, James Herbert   Eng 1861-1935
  * See 1992 Edition . . . .
Snoeyerbosch, Cornelius Johann   Dut 1891-1955
  * See 1993 Edition . . . .
Snow, E. Taylor
  O/B 8x12 Landscape Ald 5/93   145
Snowman, Isaac   Isr 1874-
  O/C 30x25 Lady with Small Bouquet Hnd 5/93   3,000
Snyder, A.   Am 19C
  O/C 10x15 Still Life Grapes and Apples Fre 10/92   1,050
Snyder, Ann L.   Am 20C
  O/B 16x14 Floral Still Life Mor 11/92   250
Snyder, Joan   Am 1940-
  MM/Pn 36x20 Cantana Number 2 88 Chr 11/92   5,280
  O,A&Pe/Pb 24x32 Untitled 71 Sby 6/93   748
Snyder, Peter Etril   Can 1944-
  O/B 12x16 In His Father's Footsteps 1981 Sbt 5/93   1,320
Snyder, William Henry   Am 1829-1910
  O/C 26x46 Fence and Fallen Trees Wtf 3/93   1,700
Snyder, William McKinley   Am 20C
  O/C 10x14 Beech Grove Yng 5/93   650
Snyders, Frans   Flm 1579-1657
  * See 1993 Edition . . . .
Snyers, Pieter   Flm 1681-1752
  O/Cp 8x7 Flowers in Vase, Snake and Reptile (2) Chr 5/93 57,500
Soggi, Niccolo   It 1474-1552
  * See 1992 Edition . . . .
Soglow, Otto   Am 1900-1975
  Pl/Pa 14x20 Sunday Comic "Little King" Ih 11/92   375
  Pl/Pa 20x12 Trapeze Artists Advertising Dental Ih 5/93   200
Sohler, Alice Ruggles   Am 1880-
  * See 1990 Edition . . . .
Sohn, August Wilhelm   Ger 1830-1899
  O/C 17x13 Lady in Black Sby 10/92   2,640
Solana, Jose Guiterrez   Spa 1885-1945
  * See 1991 Edition . . . .
Soldi, Andrea   It 1703-1771
  * See 1990 Edition . . . .
Soldi, Antenore   It 1844-1877
  * See 1992 Edition . . . .
Soldi, Raul   Arg 1905-
  P/Pa 40x27 Arlequines 52 Chr 11/92   12,100
Soler, Antonio   19C
  * See 1993 Edition . . . .
Soliday, Tim   Am 20C
  * See 1992 Edition . . . .
Solimena, Francesco   It 1657-1747
  * See 1993 Edition . . . .
Solman, Joseph   Am 1883-
  * See 1993 Edition . . . .
Solneck, Franz   19C
  * See 1992 Edition . . . .
Solomon, Abraham   Br 1824-1862
  * See 1990 Edition . . . .
Solomon, Simeon   Br 1840-1905
  K&Pe/Pa 17x13 How Beautiful is Death 1884 Chr 10/92 . . .   3,080
Solomon, Solomon Joseph   Eng 1860-1927
  * See 1991 Edition . . . .
Solomon, Syd   Am 1917-
  O/B 36x36 Sea Call Hnd 3/93   450
Soltau, nee Suhrlandt, Pauline   Ger 1833-1902
  * See 1993 Edition . . . .
Somerscales, Thomas   Br 1842-1927
  * See 1991 Edition . . . .
Somerset, Richard Gay   Br 1848-1928
  * See 1992 Edition . . . .

Sommer, Charles A. Am 1829-1894
O/C 21x36 Storm Across the River Valley Doy 5/93 7,150
Sommer, Otto Am a 1851-1868
O/C 34x49 Cows in Mountainous Landscape 1873 Sby 1/93 3,450
Sommer, William Am 1867-1949
O/B 20x24 Village Road Wlf 5/93 5,100
W/Pa 16x20 Family Portrait Wlf 5/93 4,600
O/B 31x23 Boy with Green Face Wlf 5/93 3,800
O/B 20x16 Boy with Green Apple 1928 Wlf 5/93 3,500
O/B 20x24 Plumed Trees and The Red Barn Wlf 5/93 . . . 3,500
O/B 20x26 Trees Lake Antlers Wlf 5/93 2,700
O/B 19x23 Snow Scene 1928 Wlf 5/93 2,000
W&Pe/Pa Size? Seated Boy 1930 Wlf 12/92 650
Pl/Pa 3x5 Nude Women with Dog Wlf 5/93 625
W&Pl/Pa 12x20 Decorative Cows Wlf 9/92 550
W&I/Pa 12x19 Grazing Cows Wlf 12/92 450
I&Y/Pa 16x10 Standing Female Nude 1921 Wlf 5/93 325
I&Y/Pa 10x16 Crouching Female Nude Wlf 5/93 300
W&I/Pa 11x15 Horse in Barn Door 1940 Wlf 5/93 225
G&W/Pa 5x3 Grandma Reading Newspaper Wlf 5/93 200
I&Y/Pa 15x7 Woman with Fan Wlf 5/93 125
Son, Johannes Fr 1859-
* See 1992 Edition
Sonderland, Fritz Ger 1836-1896
* See 1992 Edition
Sonn, A. H.
Pl/Pa 14x11 Christmas Day in Old York Ald 3/93 50
Sonnenschmidt, Max Am 1864-
O/C 14x18 Indiana Landscape Hnd 3/93 150
Sonnenstern, Friedrich Schrode 20C
* See 1991 Edition
Sonntag, William Louis Am 1822-1900
O/C 20x36 Mountain Landscape, New York 69 Chr 3/93 . . 21,850
O/C 26x36 Autumn Morn, Western Virginia 1856 Sby 5/93 18,400
O/C 40x55 White Mountain Landscape 1881 Sby 5/93 . . 17,250
O/C 20x31 Conestoga Wagon Chr 9/92 12,100
O/C 12x20 Fishing on a Mountain Lake Sby 9/92 11,000
O/C 21x35 Landscape with Waterfall Dum 5/93 10,000
O/C 12x20 River View Sby 9/92 9,900
O/C 7x11 Eagle Cliff, New Hampshire Sby 5/93 8,050
O/C 21x35 Waterfall, Snow Covered Peak 185? Yng 2/93 . 7,500
O/C 20x36 Adirondak Landscape 1868 Chr 5/93 6,325
O/C/M 19x32 View of the White Mountains 1866 Sby 9/92 5,500
O/C 10x12 River Landscape Sby 3/93 5,175
O/C 14x20 Fishing Near the Old Mill Sby 3/93 4,600
Sonntag, William Louis (Jr.) Am 1870-
* See 1993 Edition
Sonrel, Elizabeth Fr 1874-1953
W,G&Pe/Pa 13x20 Castle and Allegorical Figures Hnd 9/92 . . 700
WGI&Pe/Pa 13x20 Feeding the Pheasants Hnd 9/92 700
W,Pe&G/Pa 12x20 Feeding the Birds Chr 2/93 550
W,K&G/Pa 12x19 Floating Nymphs by a Castle Chr 2/93 . . . 550
Soper, Thomas James Br 19C
O/C 19x27 On the Arun, Sussex Hnd 12/92 275
Sorbi, Rafaello It 1844-1931
O/C 24x40 Departure of the Hunting Party 1926 Sby 2/93 107,000
Soreau, Isaac 1604-1638
O/Pn 14x21 Grapes on Pewter Plate Chr 1/93 88,000
Sorel, Edward Am 1929-
Pl&W/Pa 16x20 Prince Charles and Lady Diana Ih 11/92 . . . 850
Sorel, Paul 20C
W/Pa 38x26 Woman with Red Hair 1960 Sel 9/92 275
Sorensen, Carl Frederick Dan 1818-1879
* See 1991 Edition
Sorgh, Hendrick Maartensz Dut 1611-1670
O/Pn 18x23 Kitchen Interior Sby 10/92 8,800
Soriano, Juan Mex 1920-
O/C 52x40 Apolo con Peces 87 Chr 11/92 24,200
G/B 24x24 Banistas 45 Chr 11/92 19,800
W&Pe/Pa 16x27 Sin Titulo 37 Chr 11/92 15,400
W&Pe/B 22x14 Estudio para Mural 49 Chr 11/92 12,100
Pl/Pa 12x16 Gatos 73 Sby 5/93 1,150
Soriano, Rafael Mex 1920-
O/C 50x60 El Hechizo de La Noche Chr 11/92 18,700

Sorolla Y Bastida, Joaquin Spa 1863-1923
O/C 16x22 Ninos en el Mar: Estudio Sby 5/93 178,500
O/C 54x40 Retrato De D. Diego De Alvear 1903 Sby 2/93 . 79,500
O/Pn 8x13 Fishing Port at San Sebastian 190 Chr 10/92 . . 41,800
O/C/Pn 4x5 Beach: Seated Woman, Fisherman Chr 2/93 . . 31,900
O/Pa/B 4x8 Estudio de Barcas Sby 10/92 27,500
O/C 42x36 Lydia Beekman Hibbard 1911 Sby 10/92 22,000
Sother, J. K. Am 20C
O/C 16x20 Coastal Scene Fre 10/92 230
Soto, Jesus Rafael Ven 1923-
Pt/Me 83x43 Nucleo Central 1969 Sby 11/92 33,000
Sotomayor Y Zaragoza, Fernando Spa 1875-1960
O/C 22x22 Figures in a Church Chr 10/92 27,500
Sotomayor, Antonio Bol 1904-
W/Pa 5x8 Indian Women Washing Yng 5/93 400
Sotter, George William Am 1879-1953
O/B 10x12 Oceanscape Ald 9/92 3,200
O/Cb 10x12 Massachusetts Coast Fre 10/92 2,600
O/B 7x9 Day Break in the Pine Wood Country Ald 9/92 . . . 1,400
Sottocornola, Giovanni It 1855-1917
* See 1991 Edition
Soubre, Charles Bel 1821-1895
O/C 29x39 The Flax Harvest 1866 Chr 5/93 5,750
Soucek, Karel Czk 1915-
* See 1992 Edition
Soulacroix, Joseph Frederic C. Fr 1825-1879
O/C 39x26 The Cavalier's Kiss Sby 10/92 27,500
O/C 21x15 Le Coffret Aux Bijoux Sby 10/92 9,350
Soulages, Pierre Fr 1919-
O/C 38x51 Untitled 58 Chr 10/92 97,900
S&I/Pa/C 22x15 Etude 1958 Skn 5/93 11,000
Soulen, Henry James Am 1888-1965
O/C 28x32 Bridal Procession But 12/92 2,750
O/C 28x28 Presentation of the Royal Child But 12/92 . . . 2,750
O/C 30x26 The Gypsy Camp Skn 11/92 2,200
Soulies, Paul Fr a 1850-1859
* See 1992 Edition
Souplet, Louis Ulysse Fr 1819-1878
* See 1991 Edition
Souter, John Bulloch Br 1890-1972
* See 1993 Edition
Soutine, Chaim Rus 1894-1943
O/C 24x22 Femme en Rouge Sby 11/92 165,000
Soutner, Theodore Fr 19C
* See 1992 Edition
Souverbie, Jean 1891-1981
O/C 29x36 Les Baigneuses Chr 5/93 8,625
Souza-Pinto, Jose Guilio Por 1855-
* See 1992 Edition
Sowers, Robert
O/C 40x50 Picnic in the Park 86 Sby 2/93 1,725
A/C 40x50 Untitled 88 Sby 10/92 1,650
Soyer, Isaac Am 1907-
O/C 30x25 The Waitress Chr 12/92 14,850
Soyer, Moses Am 1899-1974
O/C 20x16 Seamstresses Lou 12/92 8,000
O/C 25x20 Burlesque Dancer Chr 12/92 6,050
O/C 20x24 Still Life with Violin and Vase '36 Lou 9/92 4,000
O/Cb 18x16 Seated Dancer in Red Chr 5/93 3,680
O/C 20x18 Seated Girl Reading Magazine Sby 3/93 3,565
O/C 20x16 David Burliuk Sketching Wife 1944 FHB 5/93 . . 3,500
O/C 20x16 Dancer and Teacher '44 Lou 6/93 3,100
O/C 24x18 Girl in Red Sweater Sby 5/93 2,400
O/C 14x11 Young Girl '29 Lou 3/93 2,050
O/C 20x16 Nude in Profile Sel 4/93 1,900
O/C 20x10 Dancer in Red Skirt Sby 5/93 1,870
O/C 20x10 Pink Ballet Dancer Chr 5/93 1,840
O/C 20x11 Two Standing Women Chr 12/92 1,760
O/Pa/C 20x15 Young Man in Blue Shirt Chr 12/92 1,320
O/C 16x12 Half Draped Woman Chr 5/93 1,265
O/C 12x9 Self-Portrait 66 Sby 3/93 1,265
O/C 16x12 Portrait Woman in Red Sby 9/92 1,210

O/C 16x12 Female Nude Sel 4/93 1,000
O/C 25x20 The Flutist Chr 5/93 575
P/Pa 10x8 Seated Ballerina Slo 4/93 500
W&Pe/Pa 10x13 Resting Model Fre 4/93 280

Soyer, Raphael   Am 1899-1987
O/C 32x26 Getting Dressed Chr 5/93 16,100
O/C 68x40 Sarah Jackson Sby 3/93 14,375
O/C 30x20 Karen Conrad, Ballerina Sby 12/92 ... 14,300
O/C 36x24 Roommates Chr 9/92 13,200
O/Ab 9x7 Self-Portrait 1941 Dum 1/93 7,000
O/C 14x10 Seated Female Nude Sby 3/93 5,750
O/C 16x12 Undressing Chr 5/93 3,680
O/C 16x12 Girl in Green Sby 9/92 2,750
O/C 20x16 Seated Girl Sel 4/93 2,200
O/Pn 20x24 Still Life Sby 9/92 2,200
W&I/Pa 10x8 Four Watercolors Sby 3/93 2,185
O&Pe/C 10x8 Nude Studies But 12/92 2,090
G&Pe/Pa 15x11 Seated Woman in Red Sby 3/93 2,070
O/C 9x12 Woman in Purple Sby 3/93 2,000
O/C 8x10 Reclining Female Nude Sby 3/93 1,725
Pe/Pa/B 14x10 Self Portrait 1964 Chr 5/93 1,725
O/C 13x10 Two Nudes Doy 11/92 1,650
Pe/Pa 14x11 Self-Portrait; Rebecca: Two Sby 3/93 .. 1,265
I&S/Pa 14x9 Standing Female Sby 9/92 1,210
Pe&W/Pa 19x13 Woman Reclining on a Sofa Sby 3/93 .. 978
W&H/Pa 16x12 Meeting w/Zosin in Front of Library Skn 3/93 935
W&Pe/Pa 16x21 An Artist's Model Chr 12/92 880
P&C/Pa 19x15 Seated Female Nude 1972 Sby 9/92 .. 660
I/Pa 9x7 Seated Woman Lou 6/93 500
I/Pa 10x7 Seated Nude Hnd 12/92 325
I/Pa 9x7 Nude on a Bed Hnd 12/92 300

Spada, Lionello   It 1576-1622
   * See 1991 Edition ....
Spadaro, Micco   It 1609-1675
O/C 25x20 Abraham and the Three Angels Chr 1/93 18,700
Spadaro, Micco & Codazzi, V.   It 1612-1679
   * See 1993 Edition ....
Spadino (Jr.)
   * See 1991 Edition ....
Spangenburg, George   Am 1907-1964
   * See 1993 Edition ....
Sparks, Will   Am 1862-1937
O/C 24x36 Spanish House 1931 But 10/92 5,500
O/C 16x22 La Purisima Concepcion But 3/93 4,125
O/C 10x14 Harbor at Dusk 1910 But 3/93 3,850
O/B 9x12 Adobe at Twilight But 3/93 3,575
O/B 9x8 Nocturne 1911 But 3/93 3,575
O/B 12x18 The Old Farmhouse 1908 But 10/92 2,750
O/C 6x9 House in Moonlight But 6/93 1,955
O/C 10x14 Interior with Fireplace But 6/93 1,955
O/Pn 9x12 Woman in Front of Adobe But 6/93 1,955
O/Pn 9x13 Moonlight, Chinese Camp But 6/93 1,380
Sparre, Richard   Am 20C
A/C 19x23 Tower on the Lily Estate Eld 11/92 440
Spat, Gabriel   Am 1890-1967
O/B 7x14 Elegant Figures Along the Dock Chr 12/92 ... 1,980
O/Cb 13x16 Bois de Boulogne Autrefois Fre 4/93 1,300
O/Cb 9x13 Courses a Saint-Cloud Hnd 9/92 1,300
I&G/Pa 11x8 Horse Racing Scene Slo 4/93 1,000
O/Cb 6x8 Backstage (Group of Jockeys) Slo 5/93 ... 950
O/Cb 5x10 Courses a Longchamps Hnd 9/92 850
O/Cb 4x5 At Home, Au Restaurant: Two Slo 5/93 ... 600
Spaulding, Henry Plympton   Am 1868-
G/Pb 29x19 March of the Red Cross Flags 1918 Skn 5/93 . 2,860
Spear, Ruskin   Br 1911-
   * See 1991 Edition ....
Spear, Thomas Truman   Am 1803-1882
O/C/B 13x13 Shylocke and Porche 1861 Slo 7/93 475
Speckaert, Hans   -1577
   * See 1993 Edition ....
Speer, J. A.
   * See 1992 Edition ....
Speer, Wil   Am 20C
   * See 1992 Edition ....

Speicher, Eugene E.   Am 1883-1962
O/C 17x13 Still Life with Flowers 1947 Chr 12/92 4,180
O/C 38x32 Seated Nude Sby 9/92 2,860
O/C 19x14 Yellow and Red Tulips Lou 12/92 1,800
O/C 19x24 Rural Street Lou 9/92 1,500
O/C 18x22 Rural Landscape Lou 6/93 950
Speight, Francis   Am 1896-1989
O/C 25x30 Factories Near Manayunk 1927 Fre 10/92 ... 3,100
Spelman, John A.   Am 1880-
O/C 32x36 Autumn River Landscape 30 Sby 3/93 2,185
O/C 28x32 Vacation Days 27 Hnd 10/92 1,300
O/C 24x27 Morning Mist 28 Hnd 3/93 850
O/C 22x26 The Surf Hnd 9/92 225
Spence, Thomas Ralph   Eng 1855-
O/C 20x33 Idle Moments 1878 Doy 11/92 4,675
Spencelayh, Charles   Br 1865-1958
O/C 30x20 The New Pet Chr 2/93 8,800
Spencer, A.   Br 19C
O/C 24x36 Hills in Summer Yng 5/93 375
Spencer, F. R.
O/C 35x28 Dean Richmond Ald 3/93 200
Spencer, Howard Bonnell   Am 1871-1967
   * See 1992 Edition ....
Spencer, John C.   Am 19C
O/C 20x16 Still Life Grapes, Peaches 1916 Skn 9/92 ... 1,210
W&P/Pa 10x15 Roses 1915 Yng 2/93 175
Spencer, Lilly Martin   Am 1822-1902
O/B 18x14 Little Piggy Went to Market 1857 Sby 5/93 .. 20,700
Pe&K/Pa 20x15 Old Man Playing w/Two Children Wes 12/92 605
Spencer, Robert S.   Am 1879-1931
O/C 30x36 Hilltown Chr 12/92 38,500
O/C 16x12 Woman Hanging Clothes Chr 3/93 10,925
Spencer, Stanley   Br 1891-1959
   * See 1992 Edition ....
Sperlich, Sophie   Ger 19C
O/Pn 9x11 Cats and Broom But 5/93 2,875
Sperling, Heinrich   Ger 1844-1924
   * See 1990 Edition ....
Sperling, Johann Christian   1691-1746
   * See 1993 Edition ....
Sperman, L.   Am 20C
   * See 1993 Edition ....
Spero, Nancy
   * See 1992 Edition ....
Spey, Martinus   1777-
   * See 1993 Edition ....
Spicuzza, Francesco J.   Am 1883-1962
   * See 1991 Edition ....
Spielmann, Viktor   Sws 1769-1848
W/Pa 10x13 Midday on the Piazza San Marco 1839 Chr 2/93 660
Spielter, Carl Johann   Ger 1851-1922
   * See 1990 Edition ....
Spiers, Harry   Am 1870-1947
G/B 25x20 Woodland Quietude Skn 9/92 660
G/Pa 14x20 Mouth of the Flume 1912 Yng 5/93 200
Spinelli, Luca   It 1350-1410
   * See 1991 Edition ....
Spinetti, Mario   It a 1881-1905
O/C 24x40 The Entrance to the Salon Sby 2/93 6,440
Spinks, Thomas   Br 19C
   * See 1993 Edition ....
Spiridon, Ignace
   * See 1991 Edition ....
Spiro   Bel 20C
O/C 31x25 Le Fate est Fini Fre 4/93 400
O/C 32x25 Hommage a Brueghel '55 Fre 4/93 375
Spiro, Georges   Fr 1909-1948
O/M 18x15 Still Life Flowers in Blue Vase Sby 2/93 ... 1,610
O/C 24x19 Surrealistic Horse and Rider '59 Wes 12/92 .. 990
Spitzer, Walter   Pol 1927-
O/C 21x26 Dejeuner Sur L'Herbe 57 Chr 2/93 2,200
O/C 26x21 Jeune Fille avec sa Poupee 65 Chr 11/92 ... 1,210
Spitzweg, Carl   Ger 1808-1885
   * See 1992 Edition ....

221

Spizzini, Luigi   Am 20C
W/Pa 11x9 Cabin Through the Trees Fre 4/93 70
Spode, Samuel   Br a 1825-1858
O/C 36x28 Matadore and Prize Cow: Pair Sby 6/93 6,750
Spohler
O/Pn 11x9 Dutch Canal and Street Ald 3/93 4,500
Spohler, Jan Jacob   Dut 1811-1879
* See 1991 Edition . . . .
**Spohler, Jan Jacob Coenraad   Dut
1837-1923**
O/C 26x37 Windmills on Dutch Canal Chr 2/93 3,300
O/Pn 10x8 Dutch Canal Scene Chr 10/92 2,200
O/Pn 12x16 Skaters on a Frozen Lake Chr 2/93 1,320
**Spohler, Johannes Franciscus   Dut
1853-1894**
* See 1992 Edition . . . .
Spohn, Clay   20C
* See 1992 Edition . . . .
Spoldi, A.
Pe/C 83x57 Da "Ubu Re" di Alfred Jarry 1978 Sby 10/92 . . 1,045
Spolverini, Ilario   It 1657-1734
* See 1992 Edition . . . .
Sprague, Howard F.   Am a 1871-1899
* See 1993 Edition . . . .
Sprinchorn, Carl   Am 1887-1971
O/Cb 12x16 Boulder in the Woods 1939 Sby 9/92 660
W,G&Pe/Pa 12x9 Nude Brd 8/93 578
O/M 15x8 Dahlia 1935 Brd 8/93 550
Spring, Alfons   Ger 1843-1908
O/Pn 21x28 The Card Game Sby 10/92 6,600
O/Pn 10x8 Artist Painting in Studio Mys 3/93 2,750
Springer, Cornelius   Dut 1817-1891
O/C 24x31 Along the Canal 44 Sby 2/93 51,750
O/Pn 10x8 De Poort in Buuren by Zomer 1865 Chr 2/93 . . 22,000
Spruance, Benton   Am 1904-1967
* See 1993 Edition . . . .
Spruce, Everett Franklin   Am 1907-
O/B 16x20 Little Canyon Lou 6/93 1,350
Squires, C. Clyde   Am 1883-1970
* See 1992 Edition . . . .
St. Brice, Robert   Hai 20C
* See 1993 Edition . . . .
St. Clair, Norman   Am 1863-1912
W/Pa 14x18 Coastal Mor 6/93 825
St. John, J. Allen   Am 1872-
* See 1993 Edition . . . .
St. John, Terry   Am 20C
O/M 12x16 Point Richmond 1987 But 4/93 1,380
O/M 11x14 Benecia from Martinez 1988 But 4/93 1,150
O/M 11x14 Rodeo Beach 1986 But 4/93 1,150
O/M 12x16 Contra Costa Ranch 1986 But 4/93 1,092
O/M 11x14 Clusters of Oaks 1980 But 4/93 1,035
O/M 12x14 Santa Cruz Beach 1987 But 4/93 747
Stacey, Anna Lee   Am 1865-1943
* See 1993 Edition . . . .
Stacey, John F.   Am 1859-1941
O/C 30x40 Footpath Through the Meadow But 10/92 2,750
O/C 25x30 Spring Meadow 1927 But 10/92 2,750
O/C 25x30 Haystacks But 10/92 1,870
O/C 14x18 Landscape with Pond Hnd 6/93 450
Stacey, Walter S.   Br 1846-1929
O/C 56x44 Prince Edward and his Dog 1882 Chr 10/92 . . . 4,400
Stachiewicz, Piotr   Pol 20C
K/Pa/B 18x24 A Crowned Madonna Chr 2/93 1,320
**Stachouwer, Jacobus Nicolaas   Dut
1822-1895**
O/C 32x37 Les Moissonneurs Sby 5/93 7,763
Stackhouse, Robert   1942-
Br,I&W/Pa 16x20 Corcran Model #2 73 Chr 11/92 330
Stackpole, Ralph   Am 1885-1973
* See 1991 Edition . . . .
Stademann, Adolf   Ger 1824-1895
O/C 24x40 Frozen Winter Landscape Chr 10/92 7,700
O/B 12x18 Skaters on a Frozen Pond Chr 2/93 4,620

Stagliano, Arturo   It 1870-1936
* See 1990 Edition . . . .
Stahl, Benjamin Albert   Am 1910-1987
* See 1993 Edition . . . .
Stahr, Paul C.   Am 1883-1953
* See 1993 Edition . . . .
Stallaert, Joseph   Bel 1825-1903
O/C 49x38 Maternity Sby 2/93 21,850
Stammel, Eberhard   Ger 1833-1906
* See 1993 Edition . . . .
Stamos, Theodoros   Am 1922-
O/C 56x52 Delphic Sunbox #1 1968 Sby 10/92 16,500
A/C 60x60 Infinity Field Lefkada Series 1980 Sby 2/93 . . 14,950
A/C 46x28 Infinity Field, Lefkada Series 1980 Chr 10/92 . . 13,200
O/C 56x52 Untitled Chr 11/92 9,900
O/C 18x52 Channel 1958 Sby 2/93 9,775
A/C 50x30 Infinity Field, Lefkada Series 1982 Chr 5/93 . . 9,775
A&Pe/Pa 22x22 Transparent Sun Box Sby 6/93 3,450
A/C 14x90 Long Yellow--Sun Box Chr 11/92 2,750
O/C 40x30 Casablanca Wes 5/93 2,640
A/C 17x69 Delphic Sun-Box 1968 Sby 2/93 2,300
A/Pa 30x22 Untitled 1973 Chr 2/93 1,320
Stan, Walter   Am 1917-
* See 1993 Edition . . . .
Stancliff, J. W.   Am 1814-1891
O/Pn 11x19 Coney Island '76 Chr 9/92 3,850
Standard   1657-1720
K,Br&S/Pa 11x7 Portrait of Seated Cavalier Chr 1/93 1,870
Standing, A. W.   Eng 20C
W/Pa 14x21 Caldwell Coach 1910 Mor 5/93 100
Stanfield, Clarkson   Br 19C
W/Pb 8x11 The Shipwreck Chr 10/92 440
Stanfield, George Clarkson   Br 1828-1878
* See 1993 Edition . . . .
Stanfield, William Clarkson   Br 1793-1867
* See 1993 Edition . . . .
Stanley, A.
W/Pa 8x11 View of Capetown, South Africa Dum 8/93 30
Stanley, John   Am 1914-
Pl/Pa 6x20 "Little Lulu" Ih 5/93 375
Stanley, John Mix   Am 1814-1872
O/C 8x10 Scouting Party 1864 Sby 5/93 57,500
Stannard, Emily   Br 1803-1885
O/Pn 13x18 Tulip, Roses, Primroses, Grapes Chr 5/93 6,325
Stannard, Henry Sylvester   Br 1870-1951
W/Pa 14x19 Queen Adelaide's Garden Chr 10/92 1,540
W/Pa 20x14 Return of the Flock Hnd 10/92 350
Stannard, Lilian   Br 1884-
* See 1993 Edition . . . .
**Stannard, Theresa Sylvester   Br
1898-1947**
W/Pa 20x30 Landscape with Cottage Dum 3/93 3,500
O/C 20x30 Landscape with Cottage Hnd 5/93 1,700
Stanton, Penrhyn   Am 20C
P/Pa 18x12 Pastels of Nudes Dum 7/93 1,250
Stanwood, Franklin   Am 1856-1888
* See 1993 Edition . . . .
Stanzione, Massimo   It 1585-1656
O/C 82x70 Martyrdom of Saint Lawrence Chr 1/93 154,000
Stappers, Julien   Bel 19C
* See 1991 Edition . . . .
Stark, James   Br 1794-1859
O/C 18x24 Landscape with Cowherds Hnd 12/92 2,000
Stark, Karl
G/Pa 25x19 Gladiolas in a Pitcher 1970 Sby 6/93 920
Stark, Melville F.   Am 1904-
O/C 30x36 Evening Farmscape Ald 9/92 400
Starkweather, William   Am 1879-1969
O/C 29x36 Old Henri and his Grandson 1908 Chr 9/92 6,600
O/C 30x37 Connecticut Children 1921 Wes 3/93 1,870
O/B 11x14 Hudson River from 14th Street 1919 Wlf 9/92 . . 1,550
Starn Twins   Am 1961-
Ph&L 108x79 The Stark Portrait Chr 11/92 17,600
MM 105x105 Yellow Plant No. 3 90 Chr 5/93 10,350
Ph 10x6 Ian Churchill (Yellow Striped) 86 Chr 11/92 880

222

Starrett, Henrietta
　Pe&W/Pa 15x11 Men Focus on Woman 1931 Ilh 11/92 200
Stead, Fred　Br 1863-1940
　* See 1993 Edition ....
Steadman, Ralph　Am 1936-
　I&W/Pa 21x28 Cartoon, Man Dreaming Ilh 11/92 1,100
Stearns, Junius Brutus　Am 1810-1885
　* See 1991 Edition ....
Stebbins, Roland Stewart　Am 1833-1974
　O/C 21x25 Family on a Porch Hnd 5/93 650
Steele, Daniel　Am 19C
　* See 1993 Edition ....
Steele, Edwin　Br 1850-
　* See 1992 Edition ....
Steele, J.　Am 19C
　O/B 6x9 One Silver Dollar Slo 5/93 600
Steele, Juliette　Am 1909-1980
　* See 1993 Edition ....
Steele, Theodore Clement　Am 1847-1926
　O/C 14x22 Seascape 1903 Sby 9/92 5,775
　O/C 22x32 Rural Landscape 1908 Sby 9/92 5,500
Steele, Thomas Sedgwick　Am 1845-1903
　* See 1992 Edition ....
Steell, David George　Br 1856-1930
　* See 1993 Edition ....
Steell, Gourlay　Sco 1819-1894
　O/C 40x50 Clydesdale Mare 1860 Sby 6/93 9,200
Steen, Jan　Dut 1626-1679
　* See 1992 Edition ....
Steenks, Gerard L.　Am 1847-1926
　O/C 18x30 Lobster Salad Chr 5/93 16,100
Steer, Philip Wilson　Br 1860-1942
　* See 1992 Edition ....
Steffani, Luigi　It 1827-1898
　* See 1992 Edition ....
Stehlin, Caroline　Am 1879-1954
　O/C 30x16 The Flowered Kimono Chr 5/93 8,050
Steichen, Edward　Am 1879-1973
　* See 1991 Edition ....
Stein, Georges　Fr 20C
　O/C 15x22 Le Marche aux Fleurs '10 Sby 2/93 8,050
Stein, Leo　Am 20C
　O/C 15x20 House in the Forest 1923 Lou 3/93 100
Steinach, Anton　Sws 1819-1891
　* See 1992 Edition ....
Steinberg, Saul　Am 1914-
　MM/Pa 28x23 The Sketchbook Table 1974 Chr 11/92 24,200
　MM/Wp 20x26 The Egypt Notebook 1973 Chr 10/92 19,800
　W,Cp&I/Pa 29x23 Landscapes with Palaces 65 Chr 11/92 . 18,700
　MM/Pn 26x20 Four Tiles 1988 Chr 2/93 17,600
　I&Rs/Pa 23x29 Gallery 1966 Sby 5/93 14,950
　W,I&Rs/Pa 23x29 Six Sunsets 1972 Chr 11/92 13,200
　Pl&Y/Pa 19x25 Techniques 1966 Chr 10/92 13,200
　Pl&Br/Pa/B 12x18 Lion 1950 Chr 2/93 6,600
　Pl/Pa 15x20 Untitled Chr 11/92 6,600
　Pl/Pa 12x9 Self Portrait 1946 Chr 11/92 6,050
　I&Y/Pa 23x29 Untitled 1960 Sby 5/93 5,750
　Pl&Rs/Pa 20x26 Authentic Certification Chr 2/93 5,500
　I/Pa 12x18 Untitled Sby 10/92 5,500
　Pl/Pa 14x18 Woman Sewing Ilh 5/93 1,700
　H&Y/Pa 12x9 "E" 60 But 4/93 1,610
Steiner, Emmanuel　Sws 1778-1831
　O/Cp 16x12 Still Life w/Flowers & Nest 1815 But 11/92 ... 1,650
Steiner, Johann Nepomuk　1725-1793
　* See 1993 Edition ....
Steinlen, Theophile Alexandre　Fr 1859-1923
　C&K/Pa 10x9 Normandy Women Sby 10/92 1,100
　Y&H/Pa 14x19 Monkey and Bull: Double Sby 2/93 690
　Pl/Pa 6x10 Le Chemineau Wlf 9/92 200
Steinmetz-Noris, Fritz　Ger 1860-
　* See 1992 Edition ....
Steir, Pat　1940-
　O/C 24x120 Beautiful Painting Sby 11/92 13,200
　O&H/C 72x108 Cellar Door Chr 11/92 10,450

O/C 36x35 Untitled (Wave Series) Chr 10/92 8,250
Stella　1679-1748
　O/C 49x62 Holy Family Saint Anne & Angel Sby 1/93 14,375
Stella, Frank　Am 1936-
　A/C 105x105 Sacramento Mall Proposal #2 Sby 5/93 .. 310,500
　Pg&H/C 55x53 Sketch Red Lead 1964 Chr 11/92 198,000
　Pt/C 84x42 Window Sketch '69 Sby 5/93 112,500
　Pt/C 84x42 Window Sketch '69 Sby 11/92 99,000
　Pt/C 23x23 Cato Manor 1965 Sby 5/93 90,500
　Pt/C 101x110 Tuftonboro III Sby 5/93 85,000
　A/C 108x108 Flin Flon No. XII '70 Chr 10/92 66,000
　MM&L/B 61x88 Kagu 80 Sby 11/92 60,500
　Pt/C 21x21 Rabat Sketch 1965 Sby 5/93 25,300
　A&MM/Pb 31x27 Felsztyn (Sketch) 73 Sby 10/92 17,600
　A&L/Pb 33x30 Kozangrodek 73 Sby 10/92 15,400
　A&L/B 32x30 Olyka (Sketch) 73 Sby 5/93 12,650
　Pe/Pa 17x22 Untitled 66 Sby 2/93 12,650
　L/B 20x20 The Last Cubist Collage 1959 Sby 5/93 11,500
　Y,A&L/Pa 33x27 Nasiek '73 Chr 5/93 10,350
　G&Fp/Pa 21x39 Balboa Island '70 Chr 11/92 6,600
Stella, Joseph　Am 1877-1946
　O,Br&I/C 19 dia Italian Scenery: A Tondo 1910 Chr 5/93 .. 25,300
　O/C 25x18 Portrait of Helen Walser 1940 Sby 3/93 16,100
　W/Pa 10x7 Abstraction Sby 12/92 15,400
　O/C 11x14 In the Bronx Zoo Chr 9/92 11,550
　P&Y/Pa 19x25 Abstraction Sby 9/92 11,000
　O/C/B 23x15 Belltower Chr 3/93 10,350
　O&Pe/C/B 13x10 Diana and the Stag Chr 3/93 8,625
　P/Pa 19x25 Night Sby 3/93 7,475
　C&Sp/Pa 11x9 Lily Chr 9/92 7,150
　P/Pa 24x19 Squash Chr 5/93 5,520
　Y&Pe/Pa 7x4 Flower Study Chr 9/92 4,950
　P&Y/Pa 25x19 Hillside Village, Provence Sby 9/92 3,850
　W/Pa 10x12 Reading the Paper Chr 12/92 3,850
　Y&Pe/Pa 14x10 Bird on a Rose Sby 3/93 3,738
　O/C 11x15 Still Life Tropical Flowers Sby 3/93 3,738
　G&W/Pa 19x25 Barbados: Tropical Trees 1937 Sby 3/93 . 2,645
　Sp&Y/Pa 14x11 Study White Flower Sby 3/93 2,070
　P/Pa 19x8 Still Life Lou 3/93 1,900
　Pe/B 14x15 Portrait of a Young Woman Sby 3/93 1,840
　Pe&Y/Pa 9x12 Sleeping Cat Sby 9/92 1,760
　O/C 7x12 Vesuvius Wes 5/93 1,760
　W&C/B 15x12 Woman in Side Profile 1947 Chr 5/93 1,610
　Pe&K/Pa 7x6 A Man and a Woman (2) Chr 5/93 1,150
　W/Pa 7x5 Sunflower in a Blue Vase Wes 10/92 1,025
　Pe/Pa 8x5 Four Drawings Sby 3/93 920
　Pe/Pa 7x4 Study of a Man and Skyline: Two Sby 9/92 770
Stelzner, Heinrich　Ger 1833-1910
　O/Pn 14x10 Scholar at Work 1883 Chr 10/92 2,200
Stephan, Gary　Am 1942-
　A/C 90x48 St. Martin and the Begger 1981 Chr 2/93 550
　A/Pn 81x47 Untitled '72 Chr 11/92 330
Stephens, Alice Barber　Am 1858-1932
　* See 1993 Edition ....
Stephens, James　Am 1961-
　O/C 56x56 Tyrone, (The Spaghetti Eater) 1990 FHB 3/93 .. 1,100
　O/C 27x25 Rust Hut 1987 FHB 3/93 650
Stephon, A.
　O/C 22x27 French Parlor Scene Dum 2/93 600
Steppe, Romain　Bel 1859-1927
　* See 1992 Edition ....
Stern, Bernard　20C
　O/C 72x72 Fruit Crates Sby 2/93 8,050
　A&O/Pa 42x30 Have Fun in Manhattan Sby 6/93 2,070
Stern, Ignaz　1679-1748
　O/C 49x62 Holy Family Saint Anne & Angel Sby 1/93 14,375
Stern, Lionel　Am 20C
　O/Cb 20x16 The Chemist Wes 3/93 385
Stern, Max　Ger 1872-1943
　* See 1993 Edition ....
Sternberg, Harry　Am 20C
　* See 1991 Edition ....
Sterne, Maurice　Am 1878-1957
　O/Pa 17x13 Taos Indian Chr 3/93 7,475
　O/Pn 24x32 By the Sea, Provincetown 1946 Sby 9/92 935

O/C 15x10 Standing Female Nude at Sink FHB 6/93 600
Br,I&G/Pa 13x10 Cafe Olympia 1905 Eld 8/93 121
Sterner, Albert   Am 1863-1946
O/C 28x24 Harold Reading Sby 3/93 2,300
O/C 28x20 Morning Bath 1902 Sby 3/93 2,070
O/C 26x20 The Green Hat 1918 Sby 3/93 978
O/C 24x20 Nude with Purple Cloak Sby 3/93 690
Sterner, Harold   Am 20C
G/B 15x11 Artist at an Easel Sby 3/93 805
R&O/B 20x13 Eclipse and Obelisk Sby 3/93 690
G/B 11x9 Two Gouaches Sby 3/93 460
Stettheimer, Florine   Am 1871-1944
O/C 36x26 My Birthday Eyegay 1929 Chr 12/92 66,000
Stevaerts   Dut 1601-1673
   * See 1993 Edition . . . .
Stevaerts   Dut 1607-1638
   * See 1993 Edition . . . .
Stevens, A. P.   Am 1900-
O/C 16x12 Nighttime Fishing Scene Eld 4/93 330
Stevens, Agapit   Bel 19C
O/C 43x28 Carmen But 5/93 4,600
Stevens, Aime   Bel 1879-
   * See 1990 Edition . . . .
Stevens, Alfred   Bel 1823-1906
O/C 37x23 L'Etude du role 88 Chr 2/93 165,000
O/C 29x24 L'Inde a Paris: Le Bibelot Exotique Sby 2/93 . 107,000
O/C/Pn 27x8 L'Automne 1874 Chr 10/92 22,000
O/Pn 10x14 Sail Ships Sby 10/92 2,200
O/C 25x17 North Sea Moonlight Fre 4/93 2,000
Stevens, Dorothy Austin   Can 1888-1966
O/B 13x16 Saguenay Country Sbt 11/92 616
Stevens, George   Br 19C
   * See 1992 Edition . . . .
Stevens, John Calvin   Am 1855-1940
   * See 1993 Edition . . . .
Stevens, Lawrence   Am 20C
O/C 24x36 Farm in Winter Yng 2/93 275
Stevens, Marjorie   Am 1902-
W/Pa 17x21 Victorian House Mor 2/93 325
Stevens, Pieter   Ger 1567-1624
   * See 1991 Edition . . . .
Stevens, S. W.
O/C 12x18 New Hampshire Brook Scene Eld 8/93 110
Stevens, William Lester   Am 1888-1969
O/C 36x40 Rockport Morning, Autumn Skn 9/92 3,080
O/C 24x30 Boats at the Docks, Gloucester Skn 5/93 2,750
T,P&C/Pa 16x20 Snow Covered Harbor Sby 9/92 1,870
O/B 12x14 Old White Church Mys 12/92 1,595
O/Cb 11x13 Gloucester Harbor Skn 5/93 1,320
O/Cb 20x24 Country Road, Winter 1904 Skn 3/93 1,210
G/B 15x18 View Across the Fence 1920 Sby 9/92 1,210
O/C 24x30 Gloucester Coastal Scene Mys 3/93 1,045
O/C 16x20 Boats in Harbor Yng 5/93 375
W/Pa 20x29 Winter Town Landscape Ald 9/92 250
Stevers   Dut 1601-1673
   * See 1993 Edition . . . .
Steward, Seth   Am 1844-1927
   * See 1993 Edition . . . .
Steward, W. L.
O/C 15x22 Trout Taking a Fly 1920 Eld 4/93 330
Stewart, David (Sir)   Br 1772-1829
W,H&Pl/Pa 7x5 Four Peruvian Watercolors Sby 5/93 920
Stewart, Frank Algernon   Br 1887-1945
   * See 1990 Edition . . . .
Stewart, John A.   Br 19C
W/Pa 9x28 The Meynell Sby 6/93 3,163
Stewart, Julius   Am 1855-1919
O/Pn 6x5 Self-Portrait 86 Chr 12/92 6,600
O/C 26x20 Study from a Chinese Temple 72 Skn 9/92 5,500
Stewart, Robert W.
O/B 30x33 Ailing Woman in Bed Ih 5/93 900
Stezaker, John   20C
Ph/B Var Please Take One 1976 Sby 5/93 2,300
Stick, Frank   Am 1884-1966
   * See 1990 Edition . . . .

Stiepevich, Vincent G.   Rus 1841-1910
W/Pb 20x29 Serenading a Harem Beauty Chr 5/93 6,325
O/C 28x20 Harem Girls Admiring a Swan Chr 5/93 5,175
O/C 30x20 Elegant Lady Feeding Doves Hnd 6/93 2,800
O/C 24x16 Ladies on a Country Outing Sby 3/93 1,610
Stifter, F.
O/C 34x55 18th C. Viennese Music Room Dum 9/92 4,500
Stifter, Mortiz   Aus 1857-1905
O/Pn 19x13 Un Regard Hnd 10/92 2,900
Stilke, Hermann Anton   Ger 1803-1860
   * See 1991 Edition . . . .
Still, Clyfford   Am 1904-1980
   * See 1991 Edition . . . .
Stiller, Vic   Am 20C
O/C 29x36 Expressionist Still Life 1954 Eld 8/93 110
Stirling, Dave   Am 1889-1971
O/B 12x16 View in Estes Park Yng 2/93 175
O/B 20x26 Alpine Sunset Hnz 5/93 140
Stocklin, Christian   1741-1795
   * See 1993 Edition . . . .
Stocks, Minna   Ger 1846-1928
O/C 17x23 Puppies and Crow Skn 11/92 2,530
Stoddard, Alice Kent   Am 1893-1976
   * See 1992 Edition . . . .
Stoiloff, Constantin   Rus 1850-1924
O/B 13x19 Russian Calvary Charge But 11/92 4,125
Stoitzner, Constantin   Aus 1863-1934
O/C 24x32 Monks Reading in a Library Chr 5/93 2,530
Stojanow, C. Pjotr   Rus 19C
   * See 1993 Edition . . . .
Stojanow, O.   Con 20C
   * See 1992 Edition . . . .
Stokes, Adrian   Eng 1854-1935
O/B 15x20 The Teign Near Teignmouth Yng 5/93 500
Stokes, L.   Br 19C
O/C 18x30 Highland Landscape with Fisherman Sel 12/92 . . . 250
Stolker, Jan   1724-1785
   * See 1993 Edition . . . .
Stoll, Rolf   Am 1892-
O/Pn 16x11 Aphrodite Wlf 5/93 1,800
O/C 41x29 Abstract Wlf 5/93 1,000
O/C 29x41 Abstract Wlf 5/93 900
O/B 35x29 Portrait of a Seated Woman '52 Wlf 5/93 350
O/B 18x14 Floral Still Life Wlf 5/93 200
Stoltenberg, Donald   Am 1927-
O/C 30x40 Cityscape Skn 11/92 330
Stoltz, David
W&C/Pa 40x30 Untitled (2) 80 Sby 2/93 920
Stomer, Mathias   Flm 1600-1650
O/C 40x54 Christ/Woman Taken in Adultery Sby 1/93 . 123,500
O/C 37x48 The Vision of Saint Jerome Chr 1/93 49,500
Stone, Anna Belle   Am 1874-1949
O/B 25x25 Floral Still Life Mor 2/93 375
Stone, Marcus   Br 1840-1921
   * See 1992 Edition . . . .
Stone, Marland   Am
   * See 1993 Edition . . . .
Stone, Richard
Pe&W/Pa 12x22 Girl with Books Ih 11/92 350
Stone, Robert   Br 19C
O/Pn 6x13 The Meet: Four Sby 6/93 4,888
Stone, Seymour Millais   Am 1877-
O/B 20x15 The Visit Chr 5/93 4,600
Stone, Thomas Albert   Can 1897-1978
O/C 30x36 Pioneer Homestead Sbt 5/93 1,408
O/B 9x11 Mill Pond; Village: Pair 1923 Sbt 11/92 836
Stone, William R.   Br 19C
O/C 18x26 Reflections on a Pond 1886 Chr 10/92 1,320
Stoopendaal, Mosse   Swd 1901-1948
   * See 1992 Edition . . . .
Stoops, Herbert Morton   Am 1888-1948
O/C 36x40 Captain John Smith and Pocahontas Ih 11/92 . . 4,250
O/C 24x36 Greeting on the Plain Sby 3/93 1,955
O/C 24x16 Male and Female Warriors Ih 5/93 1,100

Storck, Abraham Jansz. Dut 1635-1710
* See 1993 Edition ....
Storck, Adolf Eduard Ger 1854-
O/C 41x30 Forest Interior with Fox Sby 1/93 1,380
Storck, Jacobus Dut 1641-1687
* See 1992 Edition ....
Storer, Charles Am 1817-1907
O/C 30x23 Choice Orchids 1897 Dum 1/93 1,100
Storie, Jose Bel 1899-
* See 1991 Edition ....
Storm, J. Kinnard
W/Pa 14x20 Huntress with Bow 1899 Eld 8/93 99
Storrs, John Henry Bradley Am
1885-1956
* See 1993 Edition ....
Story, George Henry Am 1835-1923
O/B 10x8 The Letter 78 Skn 3/93 1,430
Story, Julian Russel Am 1850-1919
* See 1992 Edition ....
Stout, Myron 1908-1987
* See 1993 Edition ....
Strachan, Claude Br 1865-1929
* See 1992 Edition ....
Stradanus Dut 1523-1605
* See 1992 Edition ....
Strain, Daniel J. Am -1925
* See 1993 Edition ....
Strain, Frances Am 1898-1962
O/C 15x18 Apple Orchard 1930 Hnd 5/93 160
Strang, Ray C. Am 1893-1957
* See 1993 Edition ....
Stranover, Tobias Czk 1684-1724
* See 1993 Edition ....
Stratton, P. Herring Am 20C
O/C 18x22 Horse Grooming Mys 3/93 330
Straus, Meyer Am 1831-1905
O/C 20x24 Still Life with Fruit 1884 But 6/93 1,035
O/C 30x20 After the Hunt 1877 But 6/93 805
Strauss, Raphael Am a 1859-1897
* See 1990 Edition ....
Strawbridge, Anne West Am 1883-1944
* See 1990 Edition ....
Strayer, Paul Am 1885-
O/C 28x36 Battle at Covered Wagons Ih 5/93 1,300
O/C 31x24 Men Fishing Brd 8/93 578
O/C 27x34 Indian Encampment with Coyotes Hnz 5/93 425
O/Cb 24x18 "Mr. Chapman, Please Be Seated" Hnd 9/92 ... 100
Strean, Maria Judson Am 20C
G/lv 5x3 Portrait of Miss Wicks Sby 3/93 1,725
Streator, Harold Am 1861-1926
O/C 19x23 Garden Vista Wlf 3/93 2,300
Streckenbach, Max Thomas Ger
1865-1936
O/C 27x23 Still Life with Flowers But 5/93 3,450
O/C 20x28 Still Life with Flowers in Vase But 5/93 3,450
Street, Robert Am 1796-1865
O/C 60x41 Portrait Two Young Boys 1839 But 12/92 6,600
O/C 30x25 Portrait of John Sexton 1836 Chr 5/93 920
Stretton, Philip Eustace Br a 1884-1919
* See 1993 Edition ....
Strevens, John Am 1902-
O/C 29x26 Haying Scene Mys 12/92 1,210
Strindberg, August Swd 1849-1912
* See 1992 Edition ....
Stringer, Francis Br a 1760-1772
* See 1992 Edition ....
Strisik, Paul Am 1918-
* See 1993 Edition ....
Strobel, Mickey
I&W/Pa 13x10 Seaport Characters and Violinist Ih 5/93 300
Strobel, Oscar Am 1891-1967
W/Pa 14x18 Flowering Cactus Hnz 5/93 150
Stroebel, Johann Anthonie B. Dut
1821-1905
O/Pn 36x27 A Visit to the Apothecary Sby 10/92 8,800

Strohling, Peter Eduard Rus 1768-1826
* See 1991 Edition ....
Strombotne, James
* See 1992 Edition ....
Strong, Elizabeth Am 1855-1941
O/C 20x30 Tilling the Fields 1910 But 3/93 2,750
O/C 60x41 English Setter with Roses But 6/93 1,955
Strong, Joseph D. Am 1852-1899
* See 1990 Edition ....
Strong, Maud Am 20C
O/C 12x16 Flower Garden Slo 5/93 250
Strong, Ray Am 1905-
O/B 24x48 Landscape Mor 11/92 1,200
Stroobant, Francois Bel 1819-1916
O/C 28x38 Monks Taking Lunch 1842 Sby 1/93 3,738
Strozzi, Bernardo It 1581-1644
O/C 69x63 La Cuoca: Maid Plucking Goose Chr 5/93 ... 376,500
Struck, Herman G. Am 1887-1954
* See 1991 Edition ....
Struth, Thomas 1954-
Ph 17x22 Two Photographs 1988 Chr 10/92 4,180
Strutt, Alfred William Br 1856-1924
O/C 18x25 Attack and Defeat: Pair Sby 6/93 10,063
G&W/Pa/B 7x10 The Fairies Dance Sby 1/93 1,150
Strutzel, Leopold Otto Ger 1855-1930
* See 1993 Edition ....
Stry, Irene Am 20C
O/B 5x6 Three Miniature Harbor Scenes Yng 5/93 175
Stuart, Charles Br a 1880-1904
* See 1993 Edition ....
Stuart, E. Warren Am 19C
O/C 22x36 Swiss Lake Yng 2/93 225
Stuart, Gilbert Am 1755-1828
O/C 29x24 Portrait of George Washington Sby 5/93 310,500
O/Pn 26x21 Moses and Elizabeth Wheeler: Pair Sby 5/93 . 57,500
O/Pn 29x24 Portrait Sir Edward Thornton Sby 3/93 11,500
Stuart, James Everett Am 1852-1941
O/C 18x30 Fishing Camp on Columbia 1884 Chr 12/92 ... 1,980
O/C 36x52 Cloudy Day, Yosemite Valley But 10/92 1,650
O/C 7x11 Headwaters of the Yellowstone 1904 Mor 6/93 ... 385
Stuart, Jane Am 1814-1888
* See 1991 Edition ....
Stuart, R. James
O/Pn 22x31 Fortune Teller & Woman in Nightclub Ih 11/92 . 2,100
Stuart, Raymond J. Am
* See 1993 Edition ....
Stubbs, George Br 1724-1806
O/Pn 33x31 "Trentham" with William South Up Sby 6/93 .. 23,000
Stubbs, W. F. Am
* See 1993 Edition ....
Stubbs, William Pierce Am 1842-1909
O/C 25x40 Schooner "Benjamin Hale" Eld 7/93 7,260
O/C 24x36 The Bark "Penobscot" Eld 7/93 4,290
Stuber, D. B. Am 20C
O/Pn 10x7 Sunset Hnd 6/93 225
Stuber, Dedrick B. Am 1878-1954
O/C 25x30 Ships of Sentiment But 10/92 8,250
O/B 16x18 Quiet Morning But 10/92 6,050
O/C 25x30 Afterglow Mor 6/93 5,225
O/B 20x24 A Silvery Bay But 6/93 3,450
O/C/B 16x20 Tujunga Hills But 3/93 2,090
O/C/B 16x20 Field and Clouds But 3/93 1,650
O/B 12x16 Summer Landscape But 3/93 1,320
O/B 12x16 Farmhouse But 6/93 1,265
Stuempfig, Walter Am 1914-1970
O/C 30x26 Man in a Doorway Chr 5/93 2,530
O/C 8x10 Two Boys Sby 9/92 1,650
Stuhmuller, Karl Ger 1858-1930
O/Pn 14x22 Rural Village Sby 2/93 13,800
O/B 14x23 Winter Market Scene Sel 12/92 8,750
Stull, Henry Am 1851-1913
O/C 16x20 Racehorse with Jockey Up 1896 Sby 6/93 5,175
O/C 18x24 Portrait of a Gray Colt 1881 Sby 3/93 4,888
O/C 12x19 Heads Apart 1893 Skn 3/93 2,750
O/C/B 18x23 Bay in a Paddock 1889 Wes 10/92 1,540

Stull, John DeForest   Am 1910-1972
O/C 10x8 Girl with Parrot '70 Slo 7/93   300
Sturtevant, Elaine   Am 1926-
O&H/C 54x53 Lichtenstein's Happy Tears 1967 Chr 11/92   18,700
SpSs/C 22x22 Study for Warhol Flowers 65 Chr 2/93   4,400
Stuven, Ernst   Ger 1660-1712
* See 1992 Edition . . . .
Styka, Adam   Fr 1890-1959
O/C 29x35 Gathering Water Sby 1/93   10,350
O/Ab 18x22 Egyptian Sunrise Sby 2/93   9,200
O/C 22x29 Hot Rocks Hnz 5/93   1,300
Styka, Jan   Fr 1858-1925
* See 1993 Edition . . . .
Styka, Tade   Fr 1889-
O/B 18x27 Lion 1904 But 11/92   4,400
O/C 36x28 Portrait Dikran Kelekain Doy 11/92   2,420
Suba, Miklos   Am 1880-1944
C/Pa 16x19 Dead End 1936 Sby 9/92   715
Sugai, Kumi   Jap 1919-
* See 1993 Edition . . . .
Suger, Zsuzsanna   Hun 1939-
O/B 5x7 Interior Scene: Pair Dum 2/93   450
O/B 5x7 Interior Scene Dum 4/93   300
Sughi, Alberto   It 1928-
O/C 20x23 Sala d'Attesa '58 Lou 12/92   2,400
O/C 10x16 Bambini Nella Strada Romana 62 But 4/93   1,610
Suhrlandt, Carl   Ger 1828-1919
* See 1993 Edition . . . .
Sullivan, Edmund J.   Am 1861-1933
Pl/Pa 15x10 Two Drawings Urging Peace 19 Ih 11/92   450
Sullivan, William Holmes   Br -1908
* See 1990 Edition . . . .
Sullivant, Thomas S.   Am 1854-1926
Pl/Pa 13x20 Gag Cartoon Ih 11/92   900
Pl/Pa 10x16 Giraffe Craning Neck Ih 5/93   800
Sully, Jane Cooper   Am 1807-1877
* See 1993 Edition . . . .
Sully, Robert Matthew   Am 1803-1855
* See 1993 Edition . . . .
Sully, Thomas   Am 1783-1872
O/C 69x51 Interior of the Capuchin Chapel 1821 Sby 5/93   37,950
O/C 30x25 Girl Leaning at a Window Sby 5/93   16,100
O/C 30x25 Portrait Levi Fletcher 1830 Sby 12/92   14,300
O/C 35x40 Mrs. Caleb Newbold and Son 1813 Chr 5/93 . .   13,800
W/Pa 11x11 Mother with Her Children 1831 Sby 12/92 . . .   8,250
O/C 15x13 Portrait of a Young Lady Sby 9/92   7,150
O/C 24x19 Portrait of Master Graham: Sketch Hnd 3/93 . .   1,800
O/Pn 9x7 An Elegant Lady in White Chr 12/92   990
O/B 25x21 Bust of a Young Woman Hnd 6/93   800
Sultan, Altoon   1948-
* See 1993 Edition . . . .
Sultan, Donald   Am 1951-
MM/M 96x96 Quinces 1989 Sby 11/92   71,500
MM/M 96x96 Double Chinese Vase 1990 Sby 10/92   49,500
O&MM/M 97x49 Streetlight - Blue Streetlight 1982 Chr 2/93   38,500
MM/M 97x96 Migs, June 18, 1984 1984 Chr 2/93   33,000
O&MM/Wd 13x13 Three Pears 1984 Sby 11/92   28,600
O&MM/Wd 13x14 Cherries 1987 Sby 11/92   19,800
C/Pa 50x38 Black Lemons April 30 1985 1985 Chr 2/93 . .   15,400
C/Pa 50x38 Black Tulip, Nov 8 1983 1983 Chr 11/92   11,000
MM/Wd 12x12 Dominoes Nov 30 1989 1989 Sby 10/92 . .   11,000
MM/Wd 12x12 April 27, 1979 1979 Chr 5/93   9,200
C/Pa 60x48 Three Lemons 1987 Sby 10/92   7,700
C/Pa 50x38 Black Lemon Aug 29, 1984 1984 Sby 2/93 . . .   4,600
I/Pa 15x15 Three Lemons April 5, 1985 1985 Sby 2/93 . . .   2,300
Pe&W/Pa 14x11 Iris March 31, 1987 1987 Sby 2/93   690
Summer, A.   Aus 20C
O/C 9x6 Honorable Pastor and A Prayer (2) Chr 2/93   1,650
Summers, Alick D.   Eng 1864-1938
* See 1992 Edition . . . .
Summers, Ivan   Am 20C
O/B 10x12 Bass Rocks, East Gloucester Sel 4/93   260
Summers, P H**   Am 19C**
O/C 24x42 River Landscape St. John's Newfound Wes 3/93   1,870

Summers, Robert   Am 1940-
* See 1990 Edition . . . .
Sundblom, Haddon Hubbard   Am 1899-1976
O/C Size? Two Workers Driving a Spike Ih 5/93   4,000
W&G/Pa 19x14 Fisherman in a Rocking Chair Lou 3/93 . . .   1,100
Sunyer Y Myro, Joaquin   Spa 1875-1956
O/C 18x15 On the Balcony Sby 6/93   7,475
Surdi, Luigi   It 1897-1959
* See 1993 Edition . . . .
Surrey, Phillip Henry Howard   Can 1910-
W&P/Pa 10x15 Crossing Sherbrooke & Bishop Sbt 11/92 .   1,056
Survage, Leopold   Fr 1879-1968
O/B 11x14 Homme dans la ville Chr 11/92   10,450
G&Pe/Pa 13x10 Two Women 30 Sby 10/92   4,125
G/Pa 20x25 Bird and Hand 31 Sby 2/93   4,025
O/C 8x11 L'oiseau 27 Chr 11/92   3,850
W/Pa 9x7 Floral Still Life Sby 10/92   2,090
Susemihl, Johann Theodor   Ger 1772-
O/C 7x9 Shooting Scenes: Four Sby 6/93   8,050
Susenier, Abraham   1620-
* See 1992 Edition . . . .
Sustris, Friedrich   1540-1599
* See 1993 Edition . . . .
Sustris, Lambert   1515-1591
* See 1993 Edition . . . .
Sutcliffe, Lester   Eng 19C
O/C 20x30 Ships at Sea Wes 5/93   770
O/C 20x30 Ships and Gull Ald 3/93   700
Sutherland, Graham   Br 1903-1980
* See 1993 Edition . . . .
Sutz, Robert
G/Pa 16x30 Chinatown Street 1976 Dum 11/92   250
Suydam, James Augustus   Am 1819-1865
* See 1991 Edition . . . .
Suzor-Cote, Marc-Aurele De Foy   Can 1869-1937
Pe/Pa 11x9 Nude with Hand Mirror Sbt 11/92   1,056
Svendson, Charles C.   Am 1871-1959
* See 1992 Edition . . . .
Svendson, Svend   Am 1864-1934
O/Cb 24x18 Snowy Winter Landscape Sel 9/92   600
O/C 30x22 Winter Wood, Late Afternoon Skn 9/92   495
O/C 28x18 Snowy Winter Landscape Sel 12/92   300
O/C 28x22 Nocturnal Wooded Landscape Sel 12/92   250
Swaine, Francis   Br 1740-1782
* See 1991 Edition . . . .
Swan, John Macallan   Br 1847-1910
* See 1991 Edition . . . .
Swane, Sigurd   Dan 1879-
* See 1993 Edition . . . .
Sweeney, Dan   Am 1880-1958
W/Pa 12x20 Aftermath of Swordfight Ih 5/93   450
Sweerts, Michael   Dut 1624-1664
* See 1991 Edition . . . .
Swengel, Faye
O/B 17x20 River Village Ald 9/92   2,500
Swertschkow, Nicolas Gregorov.   Rus 1817-1898
I,S&G/Pa 6x11 Troika Slo 7/93   375
Swieszewski, Alexander   Pol 1839-1895
* See 1992 Edition . . . .
Swift, Clement N.   Am 19C
O/B 17x21 Genre Scene with Pigs Skn 9/92   880
Swiggett, Jean   Am 1910-
* See 1993 Edition . . . .
Swinnerton, James Guilford   Am 1875-1974
O/C 18x24 Desert Landscape Mor 11/92   700
Pl/Pa 10x10 Comics "Mr Jack" "Little Jimmy" (2) 26 Ih 11/92   450
O/Cb 14x12 Desert Canyon '10 Slo 7/93   400
O/Cb 12x16 Virgin River - Utah Mor 11/92   375
Swoboda, Rudolph (the Younger)   Aus 1859-1914
O/C 37x22 Indian Selling Shawls Chr 5/93   19,550

Swope, Kate Francis   Am 20C
O/C 29x29 Mother and Child Lou 12/92 650
Swope, Vance H.   Am 1879-1926
O/C 30x32 A Rocky Coast Hnd 9/92 1,300
Sword, James Brade   Am 1839-1915
O/C 20x36 Gypsy Encampment Sby 3/93 5,635
O/C 18x30 Landscape with Sheep Eld 8/93 1,650
Swords, Cramer   Am 20C
* See 1992 Edition ....
Sychkov, Th.   Rus 20C
* See 1993 Edition ....
Syer, John   Br 1815-1885
W/Pa 10x8 Mother w/Children on Country Lane FHB 3/93 ... 425
Sylvester, Frederick Oakes   Am 1869-1915
* See 1993 Edition ....
Syme, John   Sco 1795-1861
* See 1992 Edition ....
Symington, James   Am 1841-
W/Pa 6x4 Standing Nude Yng 5/93 150
Symons, George Gardner   Am 1863-1930
O/C 25x30 Near Springfield, Massachusetts Sby 5/93 28,750
O/C 40x50 Moon and Morning Light Hnd 10/92 23,000
O/B 11x14 River Scene But 6/93 4,025
O/B 7x9 Winter Landscape But 10/92 3,575
O/C 11x9 Connecticut Landscape But 3/93 3,300
O/Pn 6x9 Summer Morning Mor 6/93 2,200
O/C 15x21 Van Cortland Park, Bronx Chr 5/93 1,955
O/B 4x6 Landscape House & Stream Mor 11/92 1,500
O/C 18x20 Red Flowers Lou 6/93 1,400
Szantho, Maria   Hun 1898-1984
O/C 24x30 Reclining Nude Dum 7/93 500
O/C 24x36 Venus Hnd 5/93 375
Szasz, Paul
* See 1992 Edition ....
Szemerei, Bela M.   Hun 20C
O/C 15x13 Two Hasadic Boys Wtf 3/93 475
Szoog, L.   Am 20C
O/C 16x20 Market Scene Mys 3/93 165
Szule, Peter   Hun 1886-1944
O/C 32x24 The Letter Sby 1/93 3,738
O/C 24x30 Man Smoking Pipe Dum 7/93 175
Szyk, Arthur   Am 1894-1951
Pl&W/Pa 10x5 Nazi Wrapped in Sheep Skin 44 Ih 11/92 ... 1,400
G/Pa 9x7 In the Synogogue Chr 5/93 805
Taaffe, Phillip   1955-
A,I&L/Pa/L 111x111 Brest 1985 Chr 11/92 41,800
L&A/C 96x19 Queen of the Night 1985 Chr 11/92 33,000
A&L/C 82x29 Phantastiche Gebete II 1987 Chr 11/92 30,800
A,I&L/Pa/L 42x47 Untitled Chr 2/93 26,400
W,G&Wx/Pa 17x22 Untitled 1988 Chr 11/92 2,640
O/Pa 28x28 Untitled 1990 Chr 2/93 1,540
Y&W/Pa 14x17 Two Untitled Drawings 88 Chr 11/92 1,320
O&E/Pa 22x34 Untitled 1987 Chr 5/93 1,150
Tabaesi, C.   It 20C
O/C 28x39 A Fishermen's Trio Hnz 5/93 300
Tack, Augustus Vincent   Am 1870-1949
O&Gd/C 44x36 Untitled Sby 5/93 33,350
G/B 48x48 Sketch "The High Command" Sby 9/92 7,150
O/C 53x33 Portrait of Robert Tack Hnd 10/92 2,800
O/C 36x29 Little Miss Ross Hnd 12/92 2,200
O/C 28x25 Girl in Fancy Bonnet Hnd 3/93 1,700
G&Pe/B 22x30 Sketch of Justice Frank Murphy Sby 9/92 ... 330
Tackett, William   Am a 1950-1970
* See 1992 Edition ....
Tafuri, Clemente   It 1903-1971
* See 1990 Edition ....
Tafuri, Raffaele   It 1857-1929
* See 1993 Edition ....
Tag, Willy   Ger 1886-
* See 1993 Edition ....
Taggart, B.   Am 20C
A/C 20x22 Green 78 Hnd 5/93 160
Tait, Arthur Fitzwilliam   Am 1819-1905
O/C 20x31 The Challenge 1877 Chr 12/92 33,000

O/B 9 dia Trying for Meal Noontime Meal: Pair Chr 5/93 .. 25,300
O/C 18x22 Escaped 1883 Sby 6/93 17,250
O/C 18x27 The Twa Dogs 1897 Sby 6/93 14,950
O/B 10x14 Six Chicks and a Ladybug 1864 Wes 5/93 13,200
O/Pa/B 7x9 Spaniel and Canvas Back Duck 1864 Chr 3/93 . 11,500
O/C/M 10x14 Cows Fording a Stream 65 Chr 5/93 9,200
O/C 14x22 The Barnyard 1900 Dum 6/93 8,000
O/C 14x22 Farm Yard 1861 Sby 3/93 6,613
O/C 10x16 Deer in the Woods Sby 9/92 6,600
O/Pn 12x16 The Barnyard 1871 Chr 12/92 5,500
O/C 12x18 Sheep and Chickens in Barn Yng 2/93 4,750
O/B 10x14 A Summer Day '98 Sby 3/93 2,875
O/B 8x10 Portrait of Black Labrador 1860 Sby 6/93 2,760
O/C 18x24 A Cow and Her Calves 96 Sby 9/92 2,530
O/Pn 12x10 Cow Watering 99 Chr 5/93 1,955
Takashima, Y.   Am 20C
* See 1993 Edition ....
Takis, Nicholas   Am 1903-
O/C 19x26 Charleston-at-Dusk Sel 4/93 525
Tal-Coat, Pierre Jacob   Fr 1905-1985
O/C 35x51 Untitled Sby 2/93 24,150
Talbot, F. A.   Am 20C
W/Pa 13x20 Landscape Mys 3/93 27
Talbot, Hattie Crippen   Am 1878-1944
O/C 22x18 Landscape with House 1928 Lou 6/93 150
Talcott, Allen Butler   Am 1867-1908
O/Pn 18x24 Connecticut Landscape Mys 12/92 2,640
Taliaferro, Alfred Charles   Am 1905-1969
Pl/Pa 6x19 Daily Comic "Donald Duck" Ih 5/93 350
Talwinski, Igor   Pol 1907-
O/C 24x20 Nude with a Rose Wes 3/93 385
Tamayo, Rufino   Mex 1899-1991
O&Sd/C 51x77 Mujer en Extasis 73 Sby 11/92 .... 1.485M
O&Sd/C 79x250 La Tierra Prometida 63 Sby 11/92 825,000
O/C 26x40 The Sleepwalker 54 Sby 11/92 495,000
O&Sd/C 32x40 Dos Cabezas 67 Sby 11/92 385,000
O&Sd/C 31x37 Torso 78 Sby 5/93 332,500
O&Sd/C 18x26 Pareja 73 Sby 11/92 220,000
O,Sd&C/C 20x14 Cabeza en Blanco 70 Sby 11/92 85,250
O&Sd/C 24x18 Hombre con Sombrero 65 Chr 11/92 71,500
G/Pa 19x13 Banistas 38 Sby 11/92 49,500
G/Pa 11x8 Hombre con Tronco 34 Chr 11/92 41,800
W&H/Pa 9x8 Mujer de Espaldas Sby 5/93 34,500
H&Y/Pa 10x13 Sandias 68 Chr 11/92 28,600
H&Cp/B 10x12 Mujer 67 Sby 11/92 11,000
H&Cp/Pa 12x9 Mujer Sentada Sby 11/92 8,250
Tamburini, Arnaldo   It 1843-
O/C 13x10 Monk with Bowl of Soup Sby 1/93 2,300
O/C 36x28 Eucalyptus Trees 14 Chr 5/93 748
Tamson, George M.   Ger 1873-1939
O/Pn 7x14 River Landscape Wes 12/92 522
Tanabe, Takao   1926-
O/C 32x64 More Flags 1962 Sbt 11/92 1,408
Tanaka, Akira   Jap 1918-
O/C 29x40 Two Women Sby 6/93 6,038
Tanguy, Yves   Fr 1900-1955
G/Pa 3x10 Sans titre Chr 11/92 68,200
Tannahill, Mary H.   Am 20C
O/C 24x18 Still Life Pears, Grapes, Plant Sby 9/92 1,320
Tanner, Henry Ossawa   Am 1859-1937
* See 1993 Edition ....
Tanner, Louis   Ger 19C
* See 1992 Edition ....
Tannert, Volker
* See 1992 Edition ....
Tanning, Dorothea   Am 1912-
O/C 51x38 Still in the Studio 1979 Sby 2/93 6,900
Tanoux, Adrien Henri   Fr 1865-1923
O/C 29x24 The Harvesters 1907 Sby 1/93 8,625
O/C 24x18 An Elegant Lady Resting 1903 Chr 2/93 4,180
O/C 22x15 An Oriental Beauty Sby 1/93 4,025
O/C 29x24 Beauty with Embroidered Robe 1903 Doy 5/93 . 3,300
Tansey, Mark   1949-
O/C 58x160 Four Forbidden Senses 1982 Sby 11/92 ... 165,000
O/C 36x78 Action Painting 1981 Chr 11/92 110,000

H/B 12x15 Chess Game 1982 Chr 10/92 29,700
O/C 15x12 Pleasure of the Text 1986 Chr 11/92 24,200
Tanzi, Leon Louis Antoine   Fr 1846-1913
* See 1990 Edition . . . .
Tapies, Antoni   Spa 1923-
MM/Pb 41x30 Materia I Negre Sobre Carto Rosat Sby 5/93   23,000
Pt&L/Pa 25x19 X and Hair Sby 5/93   17,250
O&L/Pa 20x25 Untitled Sby 11/92   16,500
Pe&Pt/Pa 22x30 Two 'I' Sby 5/93   5,463
Tapiro Y Baro, Jose   Spa 1830-1913
O/C 10x16 Winding River Chr 10/92   1,320
Tappert, Georg   Ger 1880-1957
* See 1991 Edition . . . .
Taraval, Guillaume-Thomas   Fr 1701-1750
* See 1991 Edition . . . .
Taraval, Hugues   Fr 1729-1785
* See 1993 Edition . . . .
Tarbell, Edmund C.   Am 1862-1938
O/C 25x30 Mother and Child in Pine Woods Chr 5/93 . .   442,500
O/C 49x37 My Daughter Josephine 1915 Wes 12/92 . . .   150,000
O/C 25x21 Study for On Bosn's Hill Sby 5/93   13,800
Tarenghi, Enrico   It 1848-
W/Pb 30x22 A Game of Chess Chr 10/92   3,850
Tarini, G*   It 19C**
O/C 16x20 Monks Playing Cards Sby 1/93   2,875
Tarkay, Itzchak   Isr 1935-
* See 1993 Edition . . . .
Task, J. S.   Am 20C
O/C 9x18 Child with Chickens Sel 9/92   170
Tassel, Jean   Fr 1608-1667
* See 1992 Edition . . . .
Tate, Gayle Blair   Am 1944-
O/Pn 10x14 Time is Money Chr 3/93   4,600
O/Pn 10x8 Money to Burn Chr 3/93   3,680
Tauber-Arp, Sophie   1889-1943
* See 1993 Edition . . . .
Taubert, Bertoldo   Fr 20C
O/C 13x16 Les Amis Hnz 5/93   275
Taubes, Frederick   Am 1900-1981
O/C 19x25 Summer Lou 12/92   1,350
Taunay, Nicolas Antoine   Fr 1755-1830
O/Pn 12x17 The Departure of the Prodigal Son Chr 10/92 .   33,000
Taurelle, B.
O/C 46x35 Nu a la Serviette Rouge Sby 6/93   1,265
Tauszky, David A.   Am 1878-1972
O/C 30x25 Nudes Art Deco Setting Mor 2/93   1,500
Tauzin, Louis   Fr a 1867-1914
O/C 24x18 Wooded Park Landscape Sby 1/93   2,588
Tavella, Carlo Antonio   It 1668-1738
* See 1993 Edition . . . .
Tavernier, Jules   Am 1844-1889
P/Pa/B 25x47 Red Cloud's Cup 1881 Sby 3/93   2,300
Tavernier, Paul   Fr 1852-
* See 1992 Edition . . . .
Tayler, Albert Chevallier   Eng 1862-1925
* See 1993 Edition . . . .
Taylor of Bath, John   Br 1735-1806
* See 1991 Edition . . . .
Taylor, D.   Am 20C
O/C 23x35 Schooner at Sea Hnd 9/92   850
O/C 24x36 American Three-Masted Schooner Slo 4/93   800
Taylor, Edward   Br 1828-1906
W/Pa 9x7 Blond Girl Fre 4/93   550
Taylor, Edward R.   Br 1838-1911
* See 1991 Edition . . . .
Taylor, Ernest Archibald   Sco 1874-
W/Pa 12x5 Design for a Stained Glass Window Chr 2/93 . . .   440
Taylor, Frank Walter   Am 1874-1921
* See 1992 Edition . . . .
Taylor, Grace Martin   Am 1903-
* See 1992 Edition . . . .
Taylor, Henry Weston   Am 1881-
C&W/Pa 24x16 Trio at Doorway Ih 11/92   175
Taylor, Leonard Campbell   Eng 1874-1963
O/Pn 28x23 Woman Spinning But 5/93   13,800

Taylor, Richard   Am 1902-1970
H/Pa 17x14 Look Better With Clothes On Skn 3/93   522
Taylor, W. F.
O/B 12x16 Comfort Road 1957 Ald 9/92   600
Tchelitchew, Pavel   Am 1898-1957
G/Pa/B 14x11 Skull 44 Sby 11/92   6,050
I/Pa 17x11 Man in Top Hat with Fan Sby 10/92   5,775
G/Pa 14x11 Study of a Male Nude 40 Sby 10/92   2,860
S/Pa 12x8 Portrait of a Dancer 1931 Sby 6/93   2,300
I/Pa 10x14 On the Beach Sby 6/93   2,185
P/Pa 133x10 Space Composition Sby 6/93   1,725
I&S/Pa 8x11 Leaf Children: Pair of Drawings Sby 10/92 . . .   1,650
I&S/Pa 11x8 Eye Sby 10/92   1,210
S/Pa 17x12 Skull Face Sby 2/93   1,035
I&S/Pa 12x17 Two Drawings Sby 2/93   690
Pe/Pa 8x11 Allegorical Scene 32 Chr 11/92   440
I&S/Pa 11x15 The Horned Man Sby 2/93   403
I/Pa 10x13 Figure and Landscape Study 38 Sby 2/93   345
Te Gempt, Bernard   Dut 1826-1879
* See 1992 Edition . . . .
Teague, Donald   Am 1897-
W&Pe/Pa 20x30 White Walls in Andalusia But 3/93   12,100
W&Pe/Pa 17x23 Range Talk Chr 9/92   9,350
W/Pa 15x17 Siesta Time But 10/92   2,475
O/B 18x28 Illustration for Bois D'Arc 45 Hnd 12/92   1,500
Tedeschi, Petrus   1750-1805
* See 1993 Edition . . . .
Teed, Douglas Arthur   Am 1864-1929
O/C 34x72 Rocky Beach Landscape Sby 3/93   3,450
O/C 28x37 Middle Eastern Courtyard 1921 Dum 12/92   3,000
O/C 42x36 Middle Eastern Street Scene 1929 Dum 9/92 . . .   3,000
O/C 16x20 Mosque Scene 1920 Dum 9/92   1,500
O/C 14x11 The Minarets 1896 Skn 9/92   715
Teel, Raymond   Am a 1940-1949
* See 1992 Edition . . . .
Teichel, Franz   Ger 19C
O/Pn 9x15 Woman Breast Feeding Hnd 12/92   475
Tejada, J. Moreno   Spa 19C
* See 1993 Edition . . . .
Teles, Jose Jeronimo (Jr.)   Brz 1851-1908
* See 1991 Edition . . . .
Telkessy, Valeria   Hun 1870-
* See 1992 Edition . . . .
Telser, A.   Aus 19C
O/C 24x12 Letter and The Chambermaid: Pair Hnd 5/93 . . .   900
Temple, T.   Br a 1865-1871
* See 1992 Edition . . . .
Ten Cate, J.   Dut 20C
O/C 16x24 Village Scene Lou 3/93   275
Ten Compe, Jan   Dut 1713-1761
* See 1993 Edition . . . .
**Ten Kate, Herman Frederik C.   Dut
1822-1891**
O/Pn 24x37 Toast to the Bride and Groom Chr 10/92   16,500
O/Pn 21x26 Family at Table Dum 9/92   5,500
O/Pn 13x16 The Artist's Studio Sby 5/93   4,600
W/Pa 9x13 The Matters at Hand 1850 Doy 5/93   1,320
Ten Kate, Johan Mari   Dut 1831-1910
W&G/Pa 16x21 Two Shepherd Girls Sby 1/93   4,025
**Ten Kate, Johannes Marinus   Dut
1859-1896**
O/C 24x31 Fisherfolk with Their Catch Chr 2/93   11,000
**Teniers, David (the Younger)   Flm
1610-1690**
K/Pa 5x7 Demon Instructing Three Demons Chr 1/93 . . .   2,860
Teniswood, George F.   Br a 1856-1876
* See 1992 Edition . . . .
Tennant, John F.   Br 1796-1872
O/C 26x42 Autumn Sunset on the Thames Chr 5/93   18,400
Tenre, Charles-Henry   Fr 1864-1926
* See 1990 Edition . . . .
Tepper, Saul   Am 1899-1987
O/C 27x11 Seated Couple, Lawyer Standing Ih 11/92   1,400
O/C 34x23 Foreign Legion Slo 4/93   1,000

Teptmeier, K. Ger 20C
O/C 15x22 Bowl of Roses Hnd 9/92 600
Terbrugghen, Hendrick Dut 1587-1629
  * See 1992 Edition
Terechkovitch, Constantin Rus 1902-1978
  * See 1993 Edition ....
Terenghi, Enrico It 1848-
W&H/Pa 29x21 Morning Prayers/Mosque Skn 3/93 2,475
Terpning, Howard A. Am 1927-
  * See 1992 Edition
Terraire, Clovis Frederick Fr 19C
  * See 1993 Edition ....
Teruz, Orlando Brz 1902-1984
  * See 1991 Edition
Terwesten, Matthaus Dut 1670-1757
  * See 1993 Edition
Tessari, Romolo It 1868-
  * See 1993 Edition ....
Tessari, Vittorio It 1860-
W/Pb 10x8 Peasant Woman Chr 5/93 1,150
Testa, Pietro It 1611-1650
O/C 39x54 Birth and Infancy of Achilles Chr 1/93 55,000
Teye
  * See 1992 Edition
Teyssen, George Frederick Dut 1873-1955
O/C 24x32 Dutch Farm Slo 7/93 250
Thackeray, William Makepeace Br 1811-1863
Pl/Pa 10x8 Mr. Boz, Tinto, Mac, Prout 1836 Hnd 5/93 425
Thalinger, E. Oscar Am 1885-1965
O/M 22x24 The 10:14 Sby 9/92 2,090
Tharrats, Juan Josep Spa 1918-
  * See 1993 Edition ....
Thaulow, Frits Nor 1847-1906
O/C 16x20 Monongahela River, Pittsburgh Sby 2/93 24,150
Thayer, Abbott Handerson Am 1849-1921
O/C 21x17 The Philosopher Chr 5/93 253
Thayer, Ethel Randolph Am 1904-
  * See 1992 Edition
Thayer, Polly Am 1904-
  * See 1993 Edition
The Perea Master a 16C
  * See 1991 Edition
The Torralba Master 15C
  * See 1993 Edition
The Villalobos Master a 15C
  * See 1993 Edition
Theiss, John W. Am 1863-
W/Pa 9x13 House in Landscape Mor 11/92 600
Theotokopoulos, Domenikos 1540-1614
  * See 1992 Edition
Therkildsen, Michael Dan 1850-1925
O/C 26x20 The Letter Sby 2/93 8,913
Theron, Pierre Fr 1918-
O/C 17x21 Juin en Ie de France '50 Yng 2/93 250
Therrien, Robert 1947-
O&T/C 48x66 Untitled (Dog Dish) Sby 11/92 13,200
MM&T/Pa/B 20x17 No Title Chr 2/93 2,420
Thevenet, Louis Bel 1874-1930
O/C 16x20 Musical Still Life 1927 Wes 12/92 8,800
Thevinin, A. H. Con 19C
  * See 1992 Edition
Thibault, A. 20C
O/C 24x18 Tabletop Floral Still Life Slo 4/93 300
Thibesart, Raymond 1874-1968
O/C 10x13 Homme avec Cheval Chr 11/92 880
Thiebaud, Wayne Am 1920-
O/C 17x20 Hot Dog and Mustard 61 Sby 5/93 68,500
W&C/Pa 7x14 Cake Slices Chr 11/92 19,800
Cp/Pa 21x21 River Pond Study 1970 But 4/93 13,800
Br,I&H/Pa 10x10 Cake Chr 5/93 4,600
W&Pe/Pa 18x24 San Francisco Bay But 4/93 2,587

Thiebault, Henri Leon Fr 1855-
  * See 1991 Edition ....
Thieblin, Reine Josephine Fr 19C
  * See 1992 Edition
Thiele, Alexander Ger 1924-
O/C 16x24 Ducks Wlf 9/92 300
O/C 15x23 Five Ducks Wlf 9/92 300
Thielens, Gaspard 1630-1691
  * See 1991 Edition
Thieme, Anthony Am 1888-1954
O/C 30x36 79th Street Boat Basin, NYC 1935 Chr 5/93 ... 43,700
O/C 31x36 Rooftops, Gloucester Chr 12/92 22,000
O/C 30x36 Patio Mediterreaneo Chr 5/93 19,550
O/C 30x36 Rockport Landscape Chr 9/92 16,500
O/C 30x36 Harbor Scene Brd 2/93 15,400
O/Cb 16x20 Boats at Dock, Holland Chr 9/92 8,800
O/Cb 20x24 Sails Up Chr 3/93 8,050
O/C 30x37 The Blue Door Ald 5/93 8,000
O/B 25x30 Boats in Harbor Lou 12/92 6,500
O/C 30x36 The Old House, Rockport Brd 8/93 5,500
O/Cb 12x16 New York Subway Chr 5/93 4,025
O/C 32x32 Gaff-Rigged Trawler Heading Out Wes 12/92 . 3,850
O/C 30x36 Drying Sails But 12/92 3,575
O/C 30x25 Autumn Pastorale Brd 8/93 2,970
O/C 31x25 Morning Light Doy 5/93 2,750
O/C/B 14x18 Mexican Street But 12/92 2,475
O/Cb 16x20 Vessels in a Harbor But 12/92 2,475
O/Cb 16x20 Docked Sailboats Chr 5/93 2,300
O/C 25x30 Covered Bridge/Autumn Skn 11/92 1,540
O/C/B 12x16 Lowering the Sails But 12/92 1,540
O/Cb 12x16 Mexican Landscape Skn 11/92 1,320
O/Cb 12x16 Day's End/A Harbor View Skn 5/93 1,045
O/Pn 8x10 In the Dinghy Skn 5/93 852
O/Cb 12x16 Surf and Rocks Brd 8/93 578
Thierriat, Augustin Alexandre Fr 1789-1870
  * See 1992 Edition ....
Thirion, Charles Victor Fr 1833-1878
  * See 1992 Edition
Tholen, Willem Bastian Dut 1861-1931
O/C 23x15 Midday on a Busy City Street 94 Chr 10/92 ... 13,200
Thom, James Crawford Am 1835-1898
O/Ab 10x21 Ducks at Sunset Dum 1/93 550
Thomas, Alma Woolsey Am 1896-1978
  * See 1992 Edition
Thomas, Howard Am 1899-
  * See 1992 Edition
Thomas, Melina Fr 19C
O/C 67x39 Little Girl Playing with a Hoop Chr 10/92 ... 3,520
Thomas, Paul Am 1859-
  * See 1992 Edition
Thomas, Stephen Seymour Am 1868-1956
O/Pn 11x14 Sheep; Boats; Low Tide: Four Oils But 6/93 ... 2,070
Pe/Pa 7x4 Pair of Sketchbooks But 6/93 1,265
O/C 9x6 Portraits: Three Oils 1892 But 6/93 1,150
O/C 20x16 Self Portrait But 6/93 920
O/C 11x14 First Studio in Paris 1892 But 6/93 862
G/B 14x18 Grassy Dunes '50 Wes 5/93 302
O/Pn 10x14 Opalescent Sea - Carmel 1943 Mor 11/92 200
Thomassin, Desire Ger 1858-1933
O/C 22x30 The End of the Hunt Chr 5/93 9,200
O/C 20x16 Townspeople on Pond Ald 5/93 5,000
O/Pn 10x7 Rural Village Road Sby 2/93 4,140
Thomire, Pierre Phillipe Fr 1751-1843
I&W/Pa 5x5 Design for a Mustard Pot Slo 7/93 900
Thompson Am 19C
O/C 10x18 Ships at Sea Fre 10/92 500
Thompson, Alfred Fr a 1862-1876
  * See 1992 Edition
Thompson, Alfred Wordsworth Am 1840-1896
  * See 1992 Edition
Thompson, Bob Am 1937-1966
T/Pa 26x40 Golden Nude '60 Chr 2/93 4,400

T/Pa 26x40 Provincetown Beach Scene '60 Chr 2/93 4,400

Thompson, Cephas Giovanni   Am 1809-1888
O/C 30x25 Portrait of a Lady Slo 7/93 6,000

Thompson, George A.   Am 1868-1938
O/C 21x18 Mill River Falls Hampden 1920 Mys 12/92 990

Thompson, J. Arthur   Am 20C
O/C 20x25 Countryside in Spring Brd 8/93 660

Thompson, Jerome   Am 1814-1886
O/C 36x52 Youth 1874 Sby 5/93 18,400
O/C 36x52 Old Age 1874 Sby 5/93 16,100

Thompson, Leslie P.   Am 1880-1963
O/C 35x30 Woman Reading a Book 1916 Skn 5/93 2,420

Thompson, Michael   Can 1954-
* See 1991 Edition . . . .

Thompson, Walter Whitcomb   Am 1881-1948
O/B 12x16 Harbour Scene Mys 3/93 495

Thomsen, August Carl Vilhelm   Dan 1813-1886
* See 1993 Edition . . . .

Thomsen, Pauline   Dan 1858-1931
* See 1992 Edition . . . .

Thomson, E. W.   Br 1770-1847
W/B 6x5 Lady Wearing Summer Bonnet 1826 Sby 1/93 . . . 1,495

Thomson, G. F.   Br 19C
* See 1992 Edition . . . .

Thomson, George   Can 1868-1965
O/B 10x14 Thomson's Nieces Picnicing Sbt 11/92 1,936

Thomson, Henry Grinnell   Am 1850-1939
* See 1993 Edition . . . .

Thomson, Tom   Can 1877-1917
O/Pn 8x11 In Petawawa Gorges, Spring 1916 Sbt 5/93 . . . 74,800
O/B 9x11 Giant's Tomb - Georgian Bay Sbt 11/92 72,600
O/C/Pn 9x14 Lake Scugog Sbt 5/93 15,840

Thorburn, Archibald   Sco 1860-1935
* See 1993 Edition . . . .

Thorenfeld, Anton Erik C.   Dan 1839-1907
* See 1992 Edition . . . .

Thornley, William   Fr 1857-
O/C 10x16 Views of St. Michael's Mount (2) Chr 2/93 4,400
O/C 14x12 Ships Entering a Harbor Chr 2/93 880

Thornton, Mildred Valley   Can 1890-1967
O/B 20x16 Ambrose Derrick 1943 Sbt 11/92 1,408

Thorp, J.   20C
O/C 24x20 Figure in Horse Drawn Cart Sel 4/93 1,200

Thors, Joseph   Br 1822-1890
O/C 36x29 Forest Interior Sby 1/93 1,380
O/C 10x16 Country Lane Sby 1/93 1,035
O/C 8x12 Cottage in Landscape Hnd 12/92 800

Thorsen, Lars   Am 1876-
O/C 24x30 Topsail Sch. Yacht Gression Skn 11/92 1,100

Thouron, Henry Joseph   Am 1851-1915
O/C 10x8 A Favorite Summer Pastime 1873 Wes 12/92 715

Thrash, Dox   Am 1892-1965
W/Pa 18x13 Seated Nude Fre 10/92 100

Thrasher, Leslie   Am 1889-1936
O/C 20x17 Three Children Fixing Clock Ih 5/93 2,600

Thuma, Marilyn   Am 20C
* See 1993 Edition . . . .

Thurber, James Grover   Am 1894-1961
* See 1993 Edition . . . .

Tiarini, Alessandro   It 1577-1668
O/C 33x26 The Ecstasy of St. Teresa But 11/92 6,050

Tiepolo, Giovanni Battista   It 1696-1770
K/Pa 8x6 Head of a Youth Chr 1/93 24,200
K,Pl&W/Pa 5x5 Angel Turning Heads of Men Chr 1/93 . . . 17,600
K,Pl&S/Pa 9x6 Draped Bearded Man Chr 1/93 12,200

Tiepolo, Giovanni Domenico   It 1727-1804
K,I&S/Pa 19x15 The Disrobing of Christ Chr 1/93 35,200
Pl&S/Pa 9x12 Nessus and Deianeira Chr 1/93 14,300
Pl&S/Pa 10x7 Rinaldo Abandoning Armida Chr 1/93 7,150

Tiepolo, Lorenzo Baldissera   It 1736-1776
* See 1993 Edition . . . .

Tiffany, Louis Comfort   Am 1848-1933
O/C 24x36 Pushing Off the Boat, Sea Bright 87 Chr 9/92 . 60,500
G&W/Pa/B 20x29 Family Group with Cow Chr 9/92 55,000
O/C 13x12 View from a Mosque Chr 9/92 24,200
G&Pe/Pa 13x10 Islamic Door Chr 9/92 13,200
W,Pl&G/Pa 10x7 Aswan, Nile '08 Chr 9/92 12,100
O/C 9x25 Carriage Waiting Beside a Wall Chr 9/92 12,100
W&G/Pa 15x10 Arabian Subject Sby 12/92 11,550
W,G&Pe/Pa 13x15 Old Shops in Geneva Chr 9/92 7,700

Tigani, Bill   Am 20C
W/Pa 13x16 House in a Field 1986 Yng 5/93 150

Tilche, O.   Con 19C
W/Pa 10x20 Middle Eastern Desert Camp: Pair But 11/92 . 1,100

Tilgner, F.   Bel 19C
O/C 13x11 Mother and Daughter at Baby Cradle Hnd 5/93 . 1,000
O/C 13x8 Girl and Chicken Lou 6/93 300

Tillemans, Peter   Bel 1684-1734
O/C 42x51 Young Squire on Horseback Sby 6/93 36,800

Tilton, John Rollin   Am 1833-1888
O/C 19x30 La Ronda, Spain Chr 12/92 1,760

Timmermans, Louis   Fr 1846-1910
* See 1993 Edition . . . .

Timmins, William   Am 20C
W,G&Pe/Pa 15x17 Gutierrez Adobe, Monterey But 3/93 . . . 1,650

Timmons, Edward J. F.   Am 1882-1960
O/C 24x30 San Juan Capistrano Hnd 9/92 750

Ting, Wallasse   1929-
W/Pa 23x31 Untitled 66 Chr 11/92 935

Tingeler, Johannes Willem   1746-1811
O/Pn 10x14 Landscape w/Figures Skating 1788 Chr 5/93 . 11,500

Tinguely, Jean   Sws 1925-1991
* See 1993 Edition . . . .

Tinoco, Carmen Montilla   Ven 1936-
* See 1993 Edition . . . .

Tintoretto   It 1518-1594
O/C 68x104 Holy Family with Infant St. John Sby 5/93 . . 101,500

Tintoretto   It 1560-1635
* See 1993 Edition . . . .

Tippert   Br 19C
O/C 15x22 Highland Cattle Hnd 12/92 150

Tiratelli, Aurelio   It 1842-1900
* See 1992 Edition . . . .

Tironi, Francesco   It 18C
* See 1991 Edition . . . .

Tischbein, Johann (the Elder)   Ger 1722-1789
* See 1993 Edition . . . .

Tisi, Benvenuto   It
* See 1991 Edition . . . .

Tissot, James Jacques Joseph   Fr 1836-1902
O/C 85x43 L'Orpheline (Orphan) Chr 2/93 . . . . 2.97M
O/C 58x40 La Mondaine (Woman of Fashion) Sby 2/93 . 1.9825M
O/C 58x42 Sans Dot (Without Dowry) Sby 2/93 882,500
O/C 44x27 Study for "Le Sphinx" Sby 2/93 882,500
O/C 22x15 L'Escalier 1869 Sby 5/93 415,000
O/C 26x18 L'Esthetique (Au Louvre) Sby 5/93 222,500
O/C 42x28 Jeune Femme Chantant a l'Orgue Chr 2/93 . . 110,000
P/Pa 15x11 Spanish Woman Yng 5/93 1,200

Titcomb, Mary Bradish   Am 1856-1927
O/C 30x36 Marblehead Harbor Sby 5/93 19,550

Titian   It 1488-1576
* See 1992 Edition . . . .

Title, Christian   Am 20C
* See 1991 Edition . . . .

Tito, Diego Quispe   Ecu 17C
O/C 48x65 Holy Family w/St. John the Baptist Chr 11/92 . 18,700

Tittle, Walter Ernest   Am 1883-1966
O/C 20x30 Central Park Sby 9/92 1,100
O/B 16x20 Nude Mys 12/92 138
O/C Size? Portrait of the Artist Mys 12/92 138
O/C 32x26 Woman in Spanish Garb Mys 12/92 110

Tobey, Mark   Am 1890-1976
T/Pa 12x8 White Writing Sby 11/92 23,100
T/B 23x9 Modern Saint But 10/92 8,800

G/Pa 8x7 Untitled 66 Chr 11/92 8,800
PI&G/Pa 6x8 Untitled 54 Chr 2/93 8,250
T/B 7x11 Radiations '57 Sby 11/92 4,400
I/Pa 23x34 Space Ritual #10,1957 But 10/92 4,400
T/Pa 6x5 Totem #2 '53 Sby 11/92 3,850
Medium? Size? White Lights/Bahai: Double 1936 Sby 2/93 . 3,220
G/Pa 4x6 Untitled 63 Chr 10/92 2,420
T/Pa 7x5 Strange Cloud Sby 2/93 1,840
T/Pa 8x14 Beaver 55 Skn 3/93 1,100
I/Pa 11x10 Symbolist Pictograph Letter Sby 2/93 920
PI&W/Pa/B 9x5 Three Men in an Interior But 4/93 402
Tobiasse, Theo Fr 1927-
O/C 26x21 Le Berger et L'Enfant 62 Sby 2/93 11,500
O/C 16x16 N'Oublie Jamais Que tu es Prince 79 Sby 2/93 . 9,775
O/C 24x29 Le Fou Traine Une Ombre Humain 75 Chr 2/93 . 8,250
O/C 11x14 Des Yeux Qui N'Ont 79 Sby 2/93 7,475
O&PI/Pa/M 20x27 Venise et la Bicyclette 67 Chr 5/93 6,325
G/Pa 20x27 Je ne Trouve Plus au Ciel Lumiere Sby 10/92 . 3,300
Tobin, George T. Am 1864-1956
W/Pa 12x9 Two Magazine Cover Comprehensives Ih 11/92 1,400
Tocque, Louis Fr 1696-1772
* See 1993 Edition . . . .
Todd, Henry George Br 1847-1898
* See 1991 Edition . . . .
Todhunter, Francis Am 1884-1963
O/C 24x30 Boats, Old Sausalito But 6/93 4,312
O/C 24x30 Little Church at Tiburon But 6/93 4,312
O/C 24x30 Ignacio Ranch But 10/92 4,125
O/C 24x30 The Straits But 10/92 3,850
O/C 24x30 The Old Lyford Place But 6/93 2,875
O/C 24x30 Mill Valley Composition But 10/92 2,750
O/C 24x30 Marin Hills But 6/93 2,588
O/C 20x26 Greenbrae But 10/92 2,475
O/C 24x30 Approaching Fog But 6/93 2,300
O/C 24x30 Mountain Framhouse But 6/93 1,955
O/C 24x30 Tom Nune's Ranch But 6/93 1,955
O/C 24x30 Looking North But 10/92 1,430
W/Pa 21x28 Tiburon But 10/92 1,320
O/C 24x30 Catholic Church, Mill Valley But 10/92 1,100
W/Pa 18x20 Small House at Martins But 10/92 935
Todt, Max Ger 1847-1890
* See 1992 Edition . . . .
Toeschi, G. It 19C
* See 1993 Edition . . . .
Tofani, Oswaldo 1849-1915
G&R/Pa 16x22 Florentine Street Scene Ih 11/92 1,000
Tofano, Edouard It 1838-1920
W/Pa 26x19 Summer Refreshment Chr 2/93 8,800
Toffoli, Louis Fr 1907-
* See 1992 Edition . . . .
Toft, Peter Petersen Dan 1825-1901
* See 1993 Edition . . . .
Tojetti, Domenico Am 1806-1892
* See 1990 Edition . . . .
Tojetti, Virgilio It 1851-1901
* See 1993 Edition . . . .
Tol, Claes Nicolas Jacobsz Dut a 1634-1636
* See 1992 Edition . . . .
Toledo, Francisco Mex 1940-
O&PI/C 40x51 El Perro Ladra 74 Chr 11/92 264,000
G,W&PI/Pa 9x7 El Cuento del Coyote y Conejo Chr 11/92 . 99,000
O&Sd/C 38x50 Sapo Chr 11/92 93,500
G&I/Pa 22x30 Yuze Sby 11/92 82,500
O&Sd/C 31x43 Toro Sby 5/93 74,000
W,G&PI/Pa 11x15 Pareja y Lobos (Recto) Chr 11/92 30,800
G/Pa 13x9 La Ronda Chr 11/92 24,200
G&W/Pa 11x15 Sin Titulo Chr 11/92 19,800
W,G&PI/Pa 10x11 El Conejo y el Colibri Chr 11/92 16,500
G&PI/Pn 11x15 Iguanas Y Cactus Sby 5/93 14,375
W,PI&Br/Pa 11x8 Escorpiones y Telas de Arana Chr 11/92 . 14,300
W/Pa 10x13 El Cangrejo (Femme Au Crabe) Sby 5/93 . . . 13,800
W,G&PI/Pa 10x13 Mujer en un Bote Chr 11/92 13,200
W&H/Pa 10x12 No te Metas en Enredos Sby 11/92 13,200
W&G/Pa 7x11 Chango III Sby 11/92 8,250

W/Pa 31x25 Composition Sby 6/93 6,900
W&I/Pa 23x30 Visage Sby 6/93 4,313
G&I/Pa 10x12 Untitled Sby 2/93 2,588
W/Pa 17x26 Composition: Double '59 Wes 10/92 1,320
W/Pa 20x12 Untitled Sby 10/92 1,100
Tollant, R. H. Am 20C
O/C 44x30 Mountain Landscape Estes Park 1912 Sel 4/93 . 1,450
Tolman, Stacy Am 1860-1935
O/C 20x24 Winter Scene Mys 12/92 440
Tom of Finland Am 20C
* See 1992 Edition . . . .
Tomalty, Terry Can 1935-
O/B 12x16 St. Basile; St. Patrick Street: (2) '79 Sbt 5/93 704
Tomanek, Joseph Czk 1889-
O/C 63x63 Feeding the Deer 28 Chr 5/93 12,650
O/C 25x30 Garden Party Hnd 10/92 400
Tomaso, Rico Am 1898-1964
O/C 38x18 Couple on Lawn Ih 11/92 1,600
Tomba, Casimiro It 1857-1929
* See 1993 Edition . . . .
Tominz, Alfredo It 1854-1936
* See 1990 Edition . . . .
Tomlin, Bradley Walker Am 1899-1953
O/C 34x22 Man Painting But 12/92 5,500
W/Pa 10x16 Concarneau 1926 Fre 4/93 700
Tommasi, Adolfo It 1851-1933
* See 1993 Edition . . . .
Tommasi, Paolo 20C
O/C 25x32 Album of a City Slo 5/93 425
Tommaso It 16C
* See 1993 Edition . . . .
Tonsberg, Gertrude Martin Am 1902-1973
O/C 24x20 Marlboro Street, Boston Skn 5/93 990
Tooker, George Am 1920-
* See 1993 Edition . . . .
Toorenvliet, Jacob Dut 1635-1719
* See 1993 Edition . . . .
Topham, Frank William Warwick Br 1838-1924
O/C 51x81 Home After Service 1879 Sby 2/93 68,500
O/C 51x79 Messenger of Good Tidings 1882 Chr 10/92 . . 46,200
O/C 14x20 Young Neapolitans at the Well 1877 Sby 2/93 . . 5,750
Toran, Alphonse T. Am 1898-
O/B 20x24 Blossom and Reflections Skn 9/92 275
Toras, A. Am 20C
O/C 27x20 Seated Nude Wlf 3/93 350
Tordi, Sinibaldo It 1876-1955
* See 1991 Edition . . . .
Tordia, Radish Rus 1936-
* See 1992 Edition . . . .
Torgerson, William Am 19C
* See 1991 Edition . . . .
Torinana, F.
O/C 32x24 Fortune Teller Dum 3/93 1,100
Torr, Helen Am 1886-1967
C/Pa 14x10 Flower in a Landscape Chr 5/93 7,475
O/B 24x19 Still Life Mechanical Man Sby 2/93 6,000
Torre, Nicolas Andres Mex 17C
O/Cp 8x6 Madona del Rosario Sby 11/92 7,150
Torres, Augusto Spa 1913-1992
O/B/M 24x31 El Mundo Del Hombre Sby 11/92 8,800
O/C 25x25 Constructivo Sby 5/93 4,600
Torres, Horatio 20C
O/B 17x34 Puerto Sby 5/93 13,800
Torres, Jose Samano
* See 1992 Edition . . . .
Torres-Garcia, Joaquin Uru 1874-1949
O/B/C 31x40 Figuras Universales 42 Sby 11/92 209,000
O/C 20x24 Constructivo con Cielo Azul 30 Sby 11/92 . . . 192,500
T/B 32x21 Artefacto en Blanco y Negro 38 Sby 11/92 . . 187,000
O/Pn 28x14 Constructivo con Pescado 31 Sby 11/92 . . . 181,500
O/C 35x21 Constructivo con Figuras Extranas Sby 11/92 . 170,500
Pt/Wd 16x16 Forma Policromada 31 Sby 11/92 110,000
O/C 18x26 Naturaleza Muerta 41 Chr 11/92 93,500

O/Wd 9x6 Constructiva en Madera 32 Sby 11/92 88,000
O/Wd 17x12 Grafismo Inciso con Figuras 30 Sby 11/92 . . 82,500
VWd 17x11 Constructivo en Madera Incisa 32 Sby 11/92 . 71,500
O/B 14x13 Naturaleza Muerta 30 Chr 11/92 71,500
Pt/Wd 8x12 Sin Titulo 1927 Sby 11/92 66,000
O/Wd 17x8 Madera Planos de Color 29 Sby 11/92 63,250
O/Wd 8x14 Pez A.A.C. 39 Sby 11/92 46,200
O/B 14x20 Naturaleza Muerta 24 Chr 11/92 22,000
O/B/Cb 12x19 El Compadrito 24 Chr 11/92 17,600
Pe&Y/Pa 10x13 Rosario-Espana 1918 Chr 11/92 17,600
Cp/Pa 10x13 Pesca Salada 1919 Sby 11/92 12,100
I&H/Pa 7x6 Sin Titulo 33 Sby 11/92 9,900
PI/Pa 8x6 Composicion Abnoy 32 Sby 11/92 6,600
Torrey, Charles Am 1859-1921
 * See 1990 Edition . . . .
Torrey, Elliot Bouton Am 1867-1949
 O/C 30x24 Girl by a Boat Wlf 9/92 1,300
 O/C 30x24 Bathers Ald 9/92 1,050
 O/B 15x12 Portrait of a Young Girl Mor 11/92 650
 O/C 25x30 Seascape Mor 6/93 605
Torrey, George Burroughs Am 1863-1942
 * See 1993 Edition . . . .
Torri, Flaminio It 1621-1661
 O/C 26x20 Saint Mary Magdalene Fre 10/92 5,250
Torricelli, Giovanni Antonio It 1716-1781
 I&S/Pa 10x7 Study of an Ornate Ceiling Slo 7/93 1,000
Torriglia, Giovanni Battista It 1858-1937
 * See 1991 Edition . . . .
Torrini, E. It 19C
 O/C 15x10 Blacksmith at Anvil Slo 7/93 1,100
Torrini, Pietro It 1852-
 * See 1993 Edition . . . .
Toscani, Giovanni Di Francesco It 1370-1430
 * See 1991 Edition . . . .
Tosini, Michele 1503-1577
 O/Pn 38x30 Virgin and Child w/Infant St. John Sby 1/93 . . 68,500
Tossey, Verne Am 1920-
 G/Pa 13x11 Boy Reading Magazine Ih 5/93 700
 O/Pn 19x13 Woman Concealing Fugitive Ih 11/92 650
Touchemolin, Alfred Fr 1829-1907
 O/C 25x21 An Alsatian Beer Garden Wlf 3/93 800
Toudouze, Edouard Fr 1848-1907
 * See 1991 Edition . . . .
Toulmouche, Auguste Fr 1829-1890
 O/C 18x13 News from Afar Chr 2/93 9,350
 O/C 20x14 Contemplation 1872 Sby 10/92 7,150
Toulouse-Lautrec, Henri de Fr 1864-1901
 O,G&Y/B 24x15 Elles - La Glace a Main 96 Sby 11/92 . . 330,000
 O/C 24x20 Tete D'Homme Chr 11/92 330,000
 Cer 20x11 Yvette Guilbert Sby 2/93 50,600
 Y/Pa 5x7 Portrait-Charge Sby 10/92 5,225
Toussaint, Fernand Bel 1873-1955
 * See 1992 Edition . . . .
Toussaint, Louis Ger 1826-1879
 O/C 22x18 The Souvenir Seller Skn 5/93 2,420
Toussaint, Pierre Joseph Bel 1822-1888
 O/C 18x13 The Soloist Skn 9/92 1,430
Tousseau, Theodore Fr 1812-1867
 * See 1990 Edition . . . .
Tovar, Ivan Czk 20C
 * See 1990 Edition . . . .
Towle, H. Ledyard Am 1890-
 * See 1992 Edition . . . .
Town, Harold Barling Can 1924-1991
 O/C 29x29 Hommage to Turner, #4 '60 Sbt 11/92 1,496
Towne, Charles ((of Liverpool)) Br 1763-1840
 O/B 11x13 Stallions in Wooded Landscape 1808 Sby 6/93 15,525
 O/C 12x16 Pointers in Landscape 1820 Sby 6/93 7,188
 O/C 10x12 Dapple Grey Hunter 1827 Chr 6/93 3,680
Towne, Charles ((of London)) Br 1781-1854
 O/C 20x25 Hunter in a Landscape 1827 Hnd 10/92 8,400

Townley, Charles Br 1746-1800
 * See 1993 Edition . . . .
Townsend, Diane 20C
 * See 1991 Edition . . . .
Townsend, Ernest Am 1893-1945
 O/B 14x19 Winter Scene Mys 3/93 220
Tracy, John M. Am 1844-1893
 O/C 22x44 Erin II and Biddy Sby 6/93 13,800
 O/C 36x60 Driving a Covered Wagon But 3/93 4,400
 O/C 10x14 At the Point Skn 5/93 2,750
 O/C 16x24 Setter Fre 10/92 1,700
Tracy, Scogin Am 19C
 O/C 13x21 Road to the Ocean Hnd 5/93 275
Traquair, Phoebe Anna Irs 1852-1936
 * See 1991 Edition . . . .
Travis, Olin Herman Am 20C
 O/C 20x27 Hill Top Ozarks Hnd 3/93 500
Travis, Paul Am 1891-1975
 O/B 30x25 Winter 1965 Wlf 5/93 550
 C/Pa 13x20 Mangebuttu Child Congo 1927 Wlf 5/93 100
 C/Pa 13x20 Mangebuttu Mother and Child 1927 Wlf 5/93 . . . 100
 P/Pa 24x37 Three Studies 1946 Wlf 12/92 80
Trazzini, Angelo It 19C
 * See 1993 Edition . . . .
Treasure, Frank R. Am 1863-1937
 O/B 14x16 Cattle on Path Yng 2/93 150
Trebilcock, Paul Am 1902-
 * See 1992 Edition . . . .
Trebutien, Etienne Leon Fr 1823-1871
 O/C 81x49 Still Life Flowers and Cherub 1866 Sby 5/93 . . 24,150
Tredupp, Charles Am 1864-1936
 O/B 10x13 Landscape with Windmill Wlf 5/93 175
Treganza, Ruth C. Robinson Am 1877-
 * See 1993 Edition . . . .
Trego, J. K.
 O/C/B 10x12 Horse 1881 Ald 3/93 275
Treiman, Joyce Am 1922-
 * See 1992 Edition . . . .
Trenholm, William Carpenter Am 1856-1931
 * See 1990 Edition . . . .
Trevisani, Francesco It 1656-1746
 * See 1993 Edition . . . .
Trickett, W. Wasdell Am 20C
 * See 1992 Edition . . . .
Triebel, Carl & Von Rentzel, A Ger 1823-1885
 * See 1993 Edition . . . .
Trinka, Randi Am 20C
 O/C 56x56 Untitled '77 Slo 4/93 1,500
Trinquesse, Louis Roland Fr 1746-1800
 * See 1992 Edition . . . .
Tripet, Alfred Fr 19C
 * See 1991 Edition . . . .
Tripp, Wilson B. Evan Am 1896-
 * See 1993 Edition . . . .
Triscott, Samuel Peter Rolt Am 1846-1925
 W/Pa 14x11 Part of My Garden, Monhegan Brd 8/93 825
Trivas, Irene
 * See 1992 Edition . . . .
Trockel, Rosemary 1952-
 O/Pa 7x5 Untitled (Skull) 84 Chr 5/93 2,990
Troger, Paul Aus 1698-1762
 * See 1992 Edition . . . .
Trombadori, Francesco It 1886-1961
 O/C 26x32 Paura della Pittura But 4/93 1,610
Tromp, Jan Zoetelief Dut 1872-1947
 * See 1993 Edition . . . .
Trompiz, Virgilio It 20C
 * See 1992 Edition . . . .
Troppa, Girolamo It 1636-1706
 * See 1991 Edition . . . .
Trotter, Newbold Hough Am 1827-1898
 O/C 24x36 Coyote and Startled Deer Eld 4/93 1,760

O/B 10x16 Horses in Pasture Eld 8/93 935

Troubetzkoy, Prince Pierre   Am 1864-
  * See 1991 Edition . . . .

Trouillebert, Paul Desire   Fr 1829-1900
  O/C 19x22 Canoeing on a River Sby 10/92 24,200
  O/C/Pn 26x32 Fisherman on the Bank Chr 2/93 24,200
  O/C 69x47 The Snake Charmer Chr 10/92 24,200
  O/C 13x18 On the Banks of the Seine Chr 10/92 16,500
  O/C 18x22 The Mill House 70 Sby 3/93 16,100
  O/C 13x18 Landscape Man Cutting Grass Chr 5/93 11,500
  O/C 24x17 Woman Walking Along a Riverbank Chr 5/93 . 11,500
  O/Pn 27x20 Deux Pecheurs dans une Barque Chr 5/93 9,775

Trova, Ernest   Am 1927-
  A/C 67x67 Study for Falling Man 63 Chr 2/93 4,180
  A/B 25x36 Untitled Hnd 5/93 400

Troye, Edward   Am 1808-1874
  O/C 25x30 American Eclipse 1834 Chr 9/92 16,500

Troyon, Constant   Fr 1810-1865
  O/C 64x91 Clairiere dans la Foret Chr 5/93 222,500
  O/Pn 23x30 Horses Near a Fountain Chr 5/93 34,500
  O/C 22x29 Cattle Watering Sby 5/93 9,200
  P/Pa 10x15 Figures Resting in Shade of Tree Chr 10/92 . . 4,400
  O/Pn 11x8 Le Ane But 5/93 2,070
  Pe/Pa 9x7 Head of a Maiden Chr 5/93 1,725
  O/Pn 13x10 View of the Marketplace But 5/93 1,150

Truchet, Abel   Fr 1857-1918
  O/C 32x51 Sheep and Cow Herd Ald 5/93 250

Trudeau, Garry   Am 1948-
  P&/Pa 5x15 Boopsie is Following Elvis Ih 5/93 650

True, David   Am 20C
  * See 1993 Edition . . . .

Truesdell, Gaylord Sangston   Am 1850-1899
  * See 1992 Edition . . . .

Trumbull, John   Am 1756-1843
  O/Pn 4x3 General Otho Holland Williams of MD Eld 11/92 39,600

Trupheme, Auguste Joseph   Fr 1836-1898
  * See 1991 Edition . . . .

Truphemus, Jacques   Fr 20C
  * See 1993 Edition . . . .

Truxa, Anna   Ger 1899-1945
  W/Pa 6x9 Four Costume Designs 1917 Hnd 3/93 275
  W/Pa 13x7 Four Designs 1925 Hnd 3/93 225
  Pe/Pa 18x11 Woman Reading 1916 Hnd 3/93 170
  W/Pa 12x10 Three Watercolors Hnd 3/93 130
  W/Pa 12x10 Three Watercolors Hnd 3/93 100
  W/Pa 16x11 Three Watercolors Hnd 3/93 100
  W/Pa 17x10 Three Watercolors Hnd 3/93 70

Tryon, Benjamin F.   Am 1824-
  * See 1992 Edition . . . .

Tryon, Dwight William   Am 1849-1925
  O/Pn 20x30 Evening Fog 1905 Chr 12/92 44,000
  O/Pn 20x13 Chrysanthemums 1890 Chr 3/93 11,500
  P/Pa 10x7 Landscape 1913 Dum 12/92 1,300

Tschacbasov, Nahum   Am 1899-1984
  O/C 12x9 Bird Cage Wes 5/93 330
  O/C 12x9 Puppet Clown '57 Sel 4/93 70

Tschaggeny, Charles Philogene   Bel 1815-1894
  * See 1991 Edition . . . .

Tschaggeny, Edmond Jean Baptis   Bel 1818-1873
  * See 1990 Edition . . . .

Tselmardinos, Dimitrios
  O/C 50x36 Untitled 75 Sby 6/93 920

Tsingos, Thanos   1914-1965
  * See 1993 Edition . . . .

Tubach, Allan K.   Am 20C
  A/B 48x48 Reflection in a Yellow Skn 5/93 770

Tucker, Allen   Am 1866-1939
  O/C 28x34 Fir Tree Shadows 1911 Chr 12/92 20,900
  O/C 24x20 In the Garden 1909 Sby 3/93 18,975
  O/C 30x25 Winter Landscape 1911 Sby 9/92 8,800
  O/C 20x24 Claypit Creek Sby 3/93 3,565
  O/C 25x30 Foot Hills 1913 Doy 11/92 2,200

  O/C 24x20 Baker's Island 1913 Sby 9/92 1,650
  O/C 25x34 The Deserted Garden 1937 Sby 9/92 1,650
  W&C/Pa 20x14 Maple Trees 1930 Sby 3/93 1,150
  W/Pa 14x20 Toward Evening Hnd 5/93 550
  W/Pa 14x20 Desert Landscape Hnd 5/93 500
  P/Pa 8x6 Autumn Home 1920 Lou 9/92 150

Tucker, Edward   Eng 1847-1910
  W/Pa 5x8 Shipwreck Slo 4/93 275

Tudgay, F. J.   Am 19C
  * See 1993 Edition . . . .

Tudgay, Frederick   Br a 1850-1877
  * See 1991 Edition . . . .

Tudgay, J. K. E.   Br 19C
  O/C/Pn 26x37 Clipper Bark, Wildfire, Sailing Chr 2/93 7,700

Tufts, Florence Inglesbee   Am 20C
  O/C 17x12 The Makeshift Garden Brd 2/93 1,320

Tuke, Henry Scott   Br 1858-1929
  O/C 16x12 French Barque 1918 Sby 5/93 11,500
  O/Pn 16x12 The Gully 1918 Sby 5/93 7,475

Tulloch, William Alexander   Am 1887-
  O/C 40x54 Modern Amazons Chr 5/93 2,530

Tunnard, John   Br 1900-
  * See 1991 Edition . . . .

Tupnell, E.   Br 20C
  W/Pa 15x21 American Ship "Oracle" Eld 7/93 495

Turcato, Giulio   It 1912-
  * See 1993 Edition . . . .

Turchi, Alessandro   It 1578-1649
  O/C 55x39 Ecce Homo Sby 1/93 41,400

Turnbull, William   20C
  * See 1992 Edition . . . .

Turner of Oxford, William   Br 1789-1862
  * See 1992 Edition . . . .

Turner, C. E.   Br 20C
  * See 1993 Edition . . . .

Turner, Charles Henry   Am 1848-1908
  O/C/B 8x20 Little Boar's Head - Hampton 1890 Brd 8/93 . . 1,210
  O/C 14x10 White Mountain View '87 Yng 2/93 475
  O/B 21x17 Mother and Child Yng 2/93 350
  O/C 17x12 Mountain Brook Yng 2/93 300
  O/C 12x17 Wood Bridge 1902 Yng 2/93 275
  O/C 42x30 Girl in White 1890 Yng 2/93 250
  O/C 17x12 Waterfall 1904 Yng 2/93 225
  O/C 52x30 Colonial Coquette '85 Yng 2/93 200
  O/C 34x42 Market at Stathagen Yng 2/93 200
  O/C 10x8 Woman in White Yng 5/93 150
  P/Pa 22x15 Lady in a Pink Bonnet '99 Yng 2/93 90
  O/C 24x14 Woman in White Yng 2/93 60

Turner, Charles Yardley   Am 1850-1918
  O/C 17x13 Woman in Black Yng 2/93 700
  C/Pa 18x15 Portrait An Old Man 1878 Lou 3/93 350

Turner, Francis Calcraft   Eng 1782-1846
  * See 1990 Edition . . . .

Turner, George   Br 1843-1910
  * See 1993 Edition . . . .

Turner, Helen M.   Am 1858-1958
  O/C 16x24 Autumn Forest But 12/92 2,200

Turner, Janet   Am 20C
  W/Pa 22x14 Drift Roots Lou 6/93 550

Turner, Joseph Mallord William   Br 1775-1851
  S/Pa 5x10 Loch Lomond Hnz 5/93 525

Turner, Ross Sterling   Am 1847-1915
  W/Pa 14x20 Seascape Lou 6/93 1,200
  W/Pa 12x18 View of Venice 83 Skn 5/93 1,100
  W&G/Pa/B 19x13 Le Asuncion 98 Skn 3/93 605

Turner, W.   Br 19C
  O/C 14x18 Portrait of "Broomieknowe" 1881 Hnd 3/93 2,200

Turner, William L.   Eng 1867-1936
  O/Pn 11x16 Falcon Crag and Derwentwater Wes 10/92 605

Turney, Winthrop   Am 1884-1965
  O/C 32x28 The Barber Shop Sby 9/92 4,125

Turquaud, Helen E.
  O/B 9x12 On the Champs-Elysees Ald 9/92 175

Tusquets Y Maignon, Ramon It -1904
  * See 1992 Edition . . . .
Tuttle, Avel C. Am 20C
  W/Pa 18x14 Paris Street Scene 1898 Mys 12/92 165
Tuttle, George Am 20C
  O/C 24x20 Rocky Mountain Scene Hnd 10/92 100
Tuttle, Richard Am 1941-
  W&Pe/Pa 36x30 Untitled Sby 10/92 4,400
  Br&I/Pa 14x11 Two Untitled Drawings 1974 Chr 2/93 3,300
  E/Pa 7x7 Untitled Chr 10/92 3,300
  H&W/Pa 12x9 Portland Works, Group II Chr 5/93 2,070
  H&W/Pa 12x9 Portland Works, Group II Chr 5/93 2,070
  H&W/Pa 12x9 Portland Works, Group II Chr 5/93 1,955
Tuttle, Ruel Crompton Am 1866-
  W,G&H/Pa 18x13 Paris Street Scene '98 Skn 3/93 275
Tutundjian, Leon 1905-1968
  Pl/Pa 13x10 Composition 1927 Chr 11/92 1,100
Tuxen, Laurits Am 1853-1927
  O/C 27x37 Children Playing 18 But 6/93 1,725
Twachtman, John Henry Am 1853-1902
  O/C 30x30 Niagara Gorge Chr 5/93 68,500
  O/C 14x24 New York Harbor 79 Chr 12/92 28,600
  O/C 9x15 Venetian Canal 1878 Hnd 3/93 11,000
Twelvetrees, Charles Am
  G/Pa 14x11 Boy and Dog Fishing in Gutter Ih 11/92 1,700
Twining, Yvonne Am 1907-
  * See 1990 Edition . . . .
Twombly, Cy Am 1929-
  O,Y&Pe/C 46x69 Untitled 1956 Sby 11/92 . . . . 2.145M
  MM/Pa 69x134 Naxos 82 Chr 11/92 302,500
  E&Os/Pa 28x34 Roman Note 1970 Sby 5/93 63,000
  Pe&I/Pa 13x14 Untitled (Delian Ode Series) 1961 Sby 5/93 60,250
  W,Os&H/Pa 30x22 Protea 83 Chr 11/92 49,500
  Pe&P/Pa 39x28 Gladdings: Love's Causes Sby 2/93 . . . 20,700
Tworkov, Jack Am 1900-
  * See 1993 Edition . . . .
Tyler, Bayard Henry Am 1855-1931
  O/C 16x20 Mist on the Mountain Lou 6/93 900
  O/C 19x23 Afternoon Sun, Cape Cod 1915 Brd 8/93 742
Tyler, James Gale Am 1855-1931
  O/C 28x40 Rounding the Lighthouse Brd 8/93 3,410
  O/C 30x25 Under Sail by Moonlight 1882 Sby 3/93 3,163
  O/C 30x42 Evening Full Sail Chr 5/93 2,185
  O/C/B 24x36 The Bay Hnd 12/92 1,700
  O/C 30x25 Moonlight Sailing Dum 2/93 1,400
  O/C 17x14 Clipper Ship at Sea Wlf 9/92 1,300
  O/C 30x25 Clipper in the Moonlight Chr 12/92 990
  W/Pa 15x24 Shipwreck of St. Paul Wlf 9/92 250
Tyler, William Richardson Am 1825-1896
  * See 1993 Edition . . . .
Tyson, Carroll Am 1878-1956
  P/Pa 24x19 Ballet Class 1927 Fre 4/93 1,400
Tytgat, Edgard Bel 1879-1957
  * See 1991 Edition . . . .
Ubeda, Augustin Spa 1925-
  O/C 32x40 Composicion Chr 11/92 2,860
  O/C 26x32 Untitled Sby 10/92 1,760
Ubertini, Francesco It 1497-1557
  * See 1991 Edition . . . .
Uecker, Gunther 20C
  MM/Pn 39x26 Untitled '64 Sby 5/93 35,650
Ufer, Walter Am 1876-1936
  O/C/Al 50x50 Builders of the Desert Chr 12/92 242,000
  O/C 25x25 Noon Shadows Chr 5/93 41,400
  O/B 11x12 Street in Taos 1915 Hnd 10/92 7,000
  O/C/M 20x16 Portrait of a Woman Chr 3/93 5,175
Ugalde, Manuel
  * See 1992 Edition . . . .
Uguccione, Irene It 19C
  * See 1992 Edition . . . .
Uhlman, Fred Ger 20C
  O/B 11x16 Die Nonnen Hnd 6/93 850
Ulianoff, Vsevolod Am 1880-1940
  * See 1993 Edition . . . .

Ullmann, Charles Scn 19C
  O/C 29x47 Extensive Landscape Chr 10/92 5,280
  O/C 29x47 An Extensive Landscape 1862 Chr 5/93 3,450
Ulmann, Charles Swd 19C
  * See 1993 Edition . . . .
Ulrich, Charles Frederic Am 1858-1908
  * See 1993 Edition . . . .
Ulrich, Friedrich Ger 1750-1808
  * See 1993 Edition . . . .
Ulysse-Roy, Jean Fr 19C
  * See 1990 Edition . . . .
Umbstaetter, Nelly
  W/Pa 14x10 Four Watercolor Illustrations Eld 8/93 2,530
  W/Pa 9x12 Three Illustrations Eld 8/93 2,420
  W/Pa 10x7 Four Watercolor Illustrations Eld 8/93 1,870
  W/Pa Var Twenty-Five Watercolors Eld 8/93 1,320
  W/Pa 9x6 Three Watercolor Illustrations Eld 8/93 880
Unbereit, Paul Aus 1884-1937
  O/B 13x9 Farmhouse Courtyard Hnd 5/93 300
Unterberger, Franz Richard Bel 1838-1902
  O/C 34x48 Les Pecheurs sur la Terrasse Sby 10/92 46,750
  O/C 33x28 Amalfi-Golfe de Salerne Sby 10/92 36,300
  O/C 26x37 Fisherfolk in the Fjords Chr 2/93 13,200
  O/C 28x23 Drawing in the Catch Sby 10/92 8,800
Upjohn, Anna Milo Am -1951
  O/C 30x34 A Solemn Procession Chr 9/92 6,600
Uppink, Willem 1767-1849
  O/C 114x70 Landscapes: Pair Sby 1/93 35,650
Urban, Humberto Mex 1936-
  * See 1990 Edition . . . .
Urlaub, Georg Anton Abraham 1744-1788
  * See 1990 Edition . . . .
Urquhart, Tony Can 1934-
  O/C 48x40 Landscape on Tapestry 59 Sbt 5/93 1,408
Ursillo, P. T. Am 20C
  Pe/Pa 14x15 Delta Plantation Mississippi Mys 12/92 110
Urueta, Cordelia Mex 1908-
  O/C 55x47 El Barco Perdido 1989 Chr 11/92 19,800
Ury, Lesser Ger 1861-1931
  P/B 20x14 Strassenszene Chr 11/92 41,800
  O/C 16x11 Rendezvous, Capri Sby 5/93 18,400
  O/C 28x39 Joseph in Chains 1919 Chr 10/92 9,900
Usher, Leila Am 1859-1955
  O/C 21x17 Woman in Green '08 Yng 5/93 100
Utrillo, Lucie Valore
  * See 1993 Edition . . . .
Utrillo, Maurice Fr 1883-1955
  O/C 18x23 Le maison a Piliers 1935 Chr 11/92 154,000
  O/C 18x22 Montmartre Chr 11/92 110,000
  O/C 18x22 Rue a Poissy Sby 10/92 110,000
  O/C 16x18 Rue du Mont-Cenis a Montmartre Sby 11/92 . . 71,500
  G/Pa 13x20 Montmartre Chr 11/92 63,800
  G/Pa 19x25 Jardin de Domremy (Vosges) 1937 Chr 10/92 33,000
  G/B 12x9 Montmartre Sby 11/92 22,000
  G/Pb 8x12 Chapelle de Saint-Generi (Orne) 1933 Slo 4/93 18,000
  Pe/Pa/B 10x8 Le Moulin de la Galette 1923 Doy 5/93 1,100
Utz, Thornton Am 1914-
  G/Pa 19x13 Three Women Three Children Ih 5/93 700
V. Gent, Joan B. N.
  O/C 20x16 Bouquet Still Life Ald 5/93 200
Vaarbergh, H. Dut 19C
  O/Pn 8x8 The Chess Game Chr 2/93 770
Vacatko, Ludvig Aus 20C
  O/C 79x63 Gentleman on Horseback Sby 6/93 6,900
Vaccaro, Andrea It 1598-1670
  O/C 39x28 Saint Agatha Chr 1/93 14,300
Vaccaro, Nicola It 1637-1717
  * See 1992 Edition . . . .
Vago, Sandor Am 1887-1950
  O/C 54x44 Self Portrait Lou 6/93 450
Vail, Eugene Am 1857-1934
  O/C 11x9 Still Life Brd 8/93 1,650
Vaillant, Wallerand Dut 1623-1677
  * See 1992 Edition . . . .

Valade, Gabrielle Marie Fr 1709-1787
 * See 1991 Edition . . . .
Valadon, Suzanne Fr 1865-1938
 O/C 40x32 Femme Assise Devant 1929 Sby 5/93 28,750
Valbuena, Ricardo Col 1960-
 * See 1990 Edition . . . .
Valcin, Gerard Hai 20C
 * See 1993 Edition . . . .
Valencia, Manuel Am 1856-1935
 O/C 20x30 Old Customs House, Monterey But 6/93 2,588
**Valenkamph, Theodore V. C. Am
1868-1924**
 O/B 12x18 Full-Rigged Ship at Twilight Eld 7/93 3,410
 O/C 24x36 Wind Power and Steam 1907 Skn 5/93 3,190
 O/C 26x22 Adventure on the High Seas Skn 3/93 935
 O/C 16x20 The River's Mouth 1903 Brd 2/93 908
Valente, Richard Am 20C
 O/M 24x18 House by the Lake '70 Sby 9/92 330
Vallayer-Coster, Anne Fr 1744-1818
 * See 1992 Edition . . . .
Vallee, Etienne Maxime Fr 19C
 * See 1993 Edition . . . .
Vallee, Ludovic Fr
 O/C 18x23 Liseuse Au Jardin 1909 Sby 6/93 4,600
Vallejo, Boris Am 1941-
 * See 1993 Edition . . . .
**Vallejo, Don Francisco Antonio Mex a
1752-1784**
 * See 1993 Edition . . . .
Vallet, Jean Emile Fr -1899
 * See 1993 Edition . . . .
Vallet-Bisson, Frederique Fr 1865-
 * See 1991 Edition . . . .
Vallois, Paul Felix Fr 19C
 * See 1993 Edition . . . .
Vallotton, Felix Sws 1865-1925
 * See 1991 Edition . . . .
Valls, Ernesto Spa 20C
 * See 1993 Edition . . . .
Valmier, Georges Fr 1855-1937
 * See 1992 Edition . . . .
Valtat, Louis Fr 1869-1952
 O/C 25x32 Vase de Soucis et Pommes Sby 11/92 30,250
 O/Bu 18x22 La Chaumiere Sby 2/93 20,700
 O/C 16x10 Fleurs et Anemones Sby 10/92 13,200
 O/C 20x16 Houx et Gui Sby 2/93 12,650
 O/C 12x14 Nature Morte Aux Fraises Sby 2/93 8,625
 O/C 8x10 Bouquet de Fleurs Sby 2/93 6,325
 O/Pn 4x4 Vase de Fleurs Sby 2/93 3,450
 Pe/Pa 13x10 Paysage a Choisel Sby 10/92 1,210
Van Aelst, Pieter Coecke
 * See 1990 Edition . . . .
Van Aelst, Willem Dut 1626-1683
 * See 1993 Edition . . . .
Van Aenvanck, Theodor 1633-1690
 * See 1993 Edition . . . .
**Van Anthonissen, Hendrick Dut
1606-1660**
 * See 1992 Edition . . . .
Van Arden, George Am a 19C
 O/C 15x26 Shooting Quail Chr 9/92 9,900
Van Asch, Pieter Jansz. Dut 1603-1678
 O/Pn 16x24 River Landscape with Travellers Chr 10/92 . . . 9,350
Van Baburen, Dirck Dut 1595-1624
 * See 1993 Edition . . . .
**Van Balen, Hendrik & Brueghel
1575-1632**
 O/Cp 14x18 Allegory of Love Chr 10/92 60,500
**Van Bassen, Bartholomeus Dut
1590-1652**
 * See 1992 Edition . . . .
Van Beers, Jan Dut 1852-1927
 O/C 38x33 Alice Antoinette De La Mar Chr 5/93 29,900
Van Beyeren, Abraham Dut 1620-1690
 * See 1992 Edition . . . .

**Van Bijlert, Jan Harmensz. Dut
1603-1671**
 * See 1992 Edition . . . .
**Van Blarenberghe, Henri-J & LN Fr
1741-1826**
 * See 1992 Edition . . . .
**Van Blarenberghe, Jacques G. Dut
1679-1742**
 * See 1993 Edition . . . .
**Van Blarenberghe, Louis-N & HJ Fr
1716-1794**
 * See 1992 Edition . . . .
**Van Blarenberghe, Louis-Nic. Fr
1716-1794**
 * See 1993 Edition . . . .
Van Bloemen, Jan Frans Flm 1662-1749
 O/C 30x39 Roman Ruins w/Arch of Constantine Chr 10/92 44,000
 O/C 29x24 Two Figures Conversing by Pool Sby 1/93 . . . 28,750
 O/C 19x15 Landscape with Figures Conversing Sby 10/92 . 13,200
Van Bloemen, Pieter Flm 1657-1720
 O/Pn 29x40 Soldiers on Horseback Chr 1/93 14,300
 K,Br&S/Pa 11x7 Portrait of Seated Cavalier Chr 1/93 1,870
Van Bommel, Elias Pieter Dut 1819-1890
 * See 1990 Edition . . . .
**Van Boskerck, Robert Ward Am
1855-1932**
 O/C 25x33 American Farm Scene Hnz 5/93 1,700
 O/C 24x36 Springtime Stream Chr 12/92 1,650
 O/C 12x18 Stream Through the Meadow 1879 Skn 11/92 . . . 880
Van Bredael, Joseph Flm 1688-1739
 O/Cp 7x11 Peasants and Travellers 1597 Chr 5/93 57,500
Van Bredael, Pieter Flm 1629-1719
 * See 1992 Edition . . . .
**Van Brekelenkam, Quiringh G. Dut
1620-1688**
 O/Pn 10x12 Kitchen Interior w/Man Reading 1652 Sby 5/93 6,900
Van Bruell, J. Dut 19C
 O/Pn 10x13 Tavern Scene Sel 12/92 600
Van Buren, Raeburn Am 1891-1987
 Pe/Pa 12x20 Man and Woman Seated at Table 1928 Ilh 11/92 475
**Van Bylandt, Alfred Edouard Dut
1829-1890**
 * See 1993 Edition . . . .
**Van Ceulen, Cornelis Janssens Dut
1593-1664**
 * See 1991 Edition . . . .
Van Chelminski, Jan Pol 1851-1925
 O/Pn 10x14 The Return from the Battle 1878 Chr 10/92 . . . 3,520
Van Cleve, Cornelis Fr 1520-1567
 * See 1990 Edition . . . .
Van Cleve, Joos Dut a 1511-1540
 O/Pn 35x24 Christ on Cross w/Mary, Mary Mag. Sby 1/93 387,500
Van Coppenolle, E. Con 19C
 * See 1993 Edition . . . .
Van Couver, Jan Dut 1836-1909
 O/C 23x35 A Fishing Village Chr 10/92 2,640
**Van Couwenbergh, Christiaan Dut
1604-1667**
 * See 1991 Edition . . . .
Van Craesbeeck, Joos Flm 1606-1661
 O/Pn 12x12 Peasants Brawling in a Tavern Chr 10/92 . . . 4,620
**Van Cuylenborch, Abraham Dut
1620-1658**
 O/Pn 24x33 Grotto with Diana's Nymphs Bathing Sby 1/93 . 7,475
Van Dael, Jan Frans Flm 1764-1840
 K,Pl&S/Pa 45x30 Bouquet, Pineapple on Ledge Chr 1/93 . . 8,250
Van Dalens, Dirk 1600-1676
 O/Pn 23x27 Landscape Latona and Her Children Sby 5/93 . 14,950
Van Dam, Pieter Dut 20C
 O/C 20x28 Figures on the Beach Lou 3/93 500
**Van De Bylandt, Alfred Edouard Eng
1829-1890**
 O/C 18x22 Windmills Near Zuiderzee Slo 7/93 975
Van De Eycken, Charles Bel 1809-
 O/Pn 17x23 Homeward Bound 1847 Chr 10/92 8,800

Van De Roye, Jozef   Bel 1861-
  * See 1992 Edition . . . .
Van De Velde, Pieter   Dut 1634-1687
  O/C 32x48 Shipping Off the Dutch Coast Sby 1/93 14,950
Van De Velde, Willem (II)   Dut 1633-1707
  K/Pa 11x17 English Vessels Becalmed Chr 1/93 990
Van De Venne, Adriaen   Dut 1589-1662
  * See 1992 Edition . . . .
Van De Venne, The Pseudo Adria   17C
  * See 1993 Edition . . . .
Van Delen, Dirck   Dut 1605-1671
  * See 1992 Edition . . . .
Van Den Abeele, Remy   Bel 1918-
  O/C 40x32 Untitled 1967 FHB 3/93 400
Van Den Berg, Willem   Dut 1886-1970
  * See 1992 Edition . . . .
Van Den Berghe, Charles   Bel 1883-1939
  * See 1991 Edition . . . .
Van Den Berghe, Christoffel   Dut a 1617-1642
  * See 1991 Edition . . . .
Van Den Bos, Georges   Bel 1853-1911
  * See 1993 Edition . . . .
Van Den Bosch, Paulus   1615-1655
  O/Pn 22x35 Still Life Roemer, Silver Beaker Sby 1/93 31,050
Van Den Bossche, Balthasar   Flm 1681-1715
  * See 1993 Edition . . . .
Van Den Broeck, Elias   Dut 1650-1709
  O/C 29x22 Nocturnal Landscape Lizard, Snake Sby 1/93 . 17,250
Van Den Bundel, Willem   Dut 1600-1655
  O/Pn 15x24 Travellers on a Path Chr 5/93 14,950
Van Den Daele, Casimir   Bel 1818-1880
  * See 1992 Edition . . . .
Van Den Eycken, Charles   Bel 1859-1923
  O/C 16x20 Jewel Thieves 1899 But 11/92 13,200
  O/C 17x22 Jolie Bouquet 1897 Chr 5/93 9,200
Van Den Hoecke, Jan   Flm 1611-1651
  O/C 47x38 Still Life Basket of Fruit Sby 5/93 90,500
Van Den Vos, Georges   Bel 1853-1911
  O/C 26x36 Two Women in Farmyard Sel 12/92 1,300
Van Der Ast, Balthasar   Dut 1594-1657
  * See 1993 Edition . . . .
Van Der Burgh, Hendrik   Dut 1769-1858
  * See 1993 Edition . . . .
Van Der Croos, Anthonie Jansz.   Dut 1606-1662
  O/Pa 2x3 Fisherman Along the River Chr 5/93 1,955
Van Der Croos, Pieter   Dut 1610-
  * See 1993 Edition . . . .
Van Der Graus   Dut 20C
  O/Pn 12x16 A Dutch Canal Slo 4/93 250
Van Der Haagen, Joris   Dut 1615-1669
  * See 1991 Edition . . . .
Van Der Hamen Y Leon, Juan   Spa 1596-1632
  * See 1991 Edition . . . .
Van Der Heyden, Jan   Dut 1637-1712
  O/Pn 12x17 Village Landscape with Peasants Chr 1/93 . . . 28,600
Van Der Lamen, Christoph J.   Dut 1606-1652
  * See 1992 Edition . . . .
Van Der Lanen, Jaspar   Flm 1592-1626
  O/Pn 19x25 River Landscape with Travellers Chr 5/93 . . . 13,800
Van Der Lisse, Dirck   Dut a 1639-1669
  * See 1993 Edition . . . .
Van Der Marel, A.   Dut 20C
  W/Pb 14x18 Dressing the Baby 1882 Chr 5/93 460
Van Der Meer, Jan   Dut 1665-1722
  K,Br&l/Pa 8x12 Abbey by a Bridge 1704 Chr 1/93 990
Van Der Meide, J. L.   Dut 20C
  O/C 24x36 Venetian Harbor Scene Eld 8/93 770
Van Der Meulen, Edmond   Bel 1841-1905
  * See 1992 Edition . . . .

Van Der Mijn, Hieronymous   Dut 18C
  * See 1992 Edition . . . .
Van Der Myn, Francis   Dut 1719-1783
  O/C 30x25 Portrait of a Lady Chr 5/93 4,025
Van Der Neer, Aert   Dut 1604-1677
  * See 1992 Edition . . . .
Van Der Ouderaa, Pierre Jan   Bel 1841-1915
  * See 1992 Edition . . . .
Van Der Plas, Nicholaas   Dut 1954-
  O/Pn 20x28 Family Beach Scene Wes 5/93 1,980
Van Der Poel, Egbert   Dut 1621-1664
  * See 1993 Edition . . . .
Van Der Pol, Louis   Dut 1896-1982
  O/Pn 10x12 Women and Children at the Beach Dum 8/93 . . . 850
  O/Pn 10x12 Beach Wes 5/93 495
  O/Pn 10x12 Cabanas on the Beach Hnz 5/93 475
  O/B 10x12 Beach Scene Mys 12/92 302
Van Der Poorten, Hendrik Josef   Bel 1789-1874
  * See 1992 Edition . . . .
Van Der Slout-Valmingon, A.   Con 20C
  O/C 34x48 Fisherfolk Returning Home Chr 2/93 4,400
Van Der Stoffe, Jan Jacobsz.   Dut 1611-1682
  * See 1992 Edition . . . .
Van Der Straet, Jan   Dut 1523-1605
  * See 1992 Edition . . . .
Van Der Vaardt, Jan   Dut 1647-1721
  * See 1993 Edition . . . .
Van Der Velde, Hanny   Am 1883-
  O/Cb 18x15 Landscape Hnd 12/92 225
Van Der Ven, W.   Ger 20C
  O/C 16x12 Church on a Winter Evening Hnd 9/92 350
Van Der Venne, Adolf   Aus 1828-1911
  * See 1993 Edition . . . .
Van Der Vin, Paul   Bel 1823-1887
  * See 1992 Edition . . . .
Van Der Weele, Herman Johannes   Dut 1852-1930
  * See 1993 Edition . . . .
Van Der Werff, Adriaen   Dut 1659-1722
  * See 1992 Edition . . . .
Van Der Werff, Pieter   Dut 1665-1722
  * See 1993 Edition . . . .
Van Der Weyde (Jr.)   Am a 1850-
  * See 1993 Edition . . . .
Van Der Weyden, Harry   Am 1868-
  O/B 14x22 After the Gale, Tete de Chien 1926 Hnd 12/92 . . . 450
Van Der Willigen, Claes Jansz.   Dut 1630-1676
  * See 1993 Edition . . . .
Van Dieghem, A*   Dut 19C**
  O/Pn 7x10 Grazing Sheep 1876 Sby 1/93 2,300
Van Dieghem, Jacob   Dut 19C
  O/Pn 7x10 Sheep Grazing 83 Chr 5/93 2,875
Van Diest, Willem   Dut
  O/Pn 16x25 Dutch Shipping in a Calm Sea 1634 Sby 1/93 24,150
Van Doesburg, Theo   Dut 1883-1931
  * See 1993 Edition . . . .
Van Dongen, Kees   Fr 1877-1968
  O/C 26x21 La Geisha Sada Yacco Sby 11/92 770,000
  O/C 22x18 Les Roses Mousses Sby 10/92 60,500
  Y&C/Pa/B 17x13 Tete De Femme Sby 6/93 3,278
Van Dorne, Martin   Flm 1736-1808
  O/C 23x16 Tulip, Roses, Morning Glory 1784 Chr 10/92 . . 25,300
Van Douw, Simon-Johannes   Flm 1630-1677
  * See 1992 Edition . . . .
Van Dyck, A.   Can 20C
  O/C 12x16 Sousbois Lou 3/93 125
Van Dyck, Philip   Flm 1680-1753
  O/C 32x27 Portrait of a Gentleman 1722 Sby 1/93 4,025
Van Dyck, Sir Anthony   Flm 1599-1641
  * See 1991 Edition . . . .

Van Dyn Con 20C
O/C 20x28 Seascape Lou 3/93 150
Van Eertvelt, Andries Flm 1590-1652
* See 1991 Edition . . . .
Van Elk, Ger 1941-
Ph 40x26 Study for Honda Gothic 1986 Chr 10/92 3,300
Van Elten, Hendirk Dirk K. Am 1829-1904
O/C 40x26 The Dunes of Holland Doy 11/92 5,775
O/C 39x30 Woodland Creek Doy 11/92 2,310
O/M 12x22 Children Fishing by an Inlet Chr 12/92 1,980
Van Es, Jacob Flm 1596-1666
* See 1992 Edition . . . .
Van Everdingen, Allart Dut 1621-1675
* See 1993 Edition . . . .
Van Everdingen, Caesar Boetuis Dut a 1617-1678
* See 1990 Edition . . . .
Van Everen, Jay Am 1875-1947
O/C 35x56 Composition Sby 9/92 3,850
Van Falens, Carel Flm 1683-1733
* See 1993 Edition . . . .
Van Gogh, Vincent Dut 1853-1890
Pe&Y/Pa 13x8 Head of a Peasant Woman Sby 11/92 . . . 385,000
Van Gool, Jan Dut 1685-1763
O/Pn 20x30 Peasants with Cattle, Sheep Sby 1/93 10,925
Van Gorder, Luther Emerson Am 1861-1931
O/C 18x24 Flower Sellers Along French Blvd. But 6/93 3,450
O/B 10x8 Dome of the Pantheon Sby 3/93 690
Van Goyen, Jan Dut 1596-1656
O/Pa/Pn 10x15 Fortified House on River 1651 Chr 5/93 . . 40,250
Van Haanen, Remigius Adrianus Dut 1812-1894
O/C 27x36 Fishing Boats at Shore 1846 Sby 5/93 24,150
Van Haarlem, Cornelis C. Dut 1562-1638
* See 1992 Edition . . . .
Van Haarlem, Johan. (the Elder) Dut 1628-1691
* See 1992 Edition . . . .
Van Haensbergen, Jan Dut 1642-1705
* See 1992 Edition . . . .
Van Hagen Ger 19C
O/Pn 8x6 Cavalier Having a Smoke Chr 2/93 715
Van Hamme, Alexis Bel 1818-1875
O/Pn 28x21 Going to Market But 5/93 4,600
Van Hasselt, Willem Dut 1882-1963
O/C 15x18 Springtime on the Canal Sby 2/93 1,840
O/B 15x18 The Farm by the River '27 Sby 2/93 1,610
Van Heemskerk, Egbert (the Younger) Dut 1700-1744
O/C 40x50 Boors Playing a Game Chr 10/92 9,900
Van Heemskerk, Maarten Dut 17C
* See 1991 Edition . . . .
Van Hees, Gerrit Flm a 1650-1670
O/Pn 13x10 Landscape w/Houses and Fishermen Sby 5/93 5,750
Van Honthorst, Gerard Dut 1590-1656
O/Pn 30x23 Portrait of a Gentleman Chr 1/93 8,800
Van Hoogstraten, Samuel Dircks Flm 1627-1678
* See 1993 Edition . . . .
Van Horssen, Winand Bastien Dut 1863-
* See 1993 Edition . . . .
Van Houbraken, Nicola 1660-1723
* See 1992 Edition . . . .
Van Huysum, Jan Dut 1682-1749
O/C 17x20 Italianate Landscape Shepherds:Pair Sby 5/93 . 20,700
Van Huysum, Justus Dut 1659-1716
O/C 38x33 Still Life Peonies, Hollyhocks Sby 5/93 31,050
Van Kalraat, Abraham Dut 1642-1722
* See 1993 Edition . . . .
Van Keirsbilck, Jules Bel 1833-1896
O/C 36x24 The Artist's Studio 1885 Chr 2/93 4,400
Van Kessel, Jan Dut 1626-1679
* See 1993 Edition . . . .

Van Kregten, Fedor Dut 1871-1937
O/C 24x36 Landscape with Figure and Sheep Lou 9/92 800
Van Lach, Ursula 1949-
O/B 20x24 Les Coquelicots de Provence Chr 2/93 3,300
Van Laer, Alexander T. Am 1857-1920
* See 1993 Edition . . . .
Van Leemputten, C. & Koekkoek Bel 1841-1902
O/C 24x20 Heading Home Doy 5/93 4,840
Van Leemputten, Cornelis Bel 1841-1902
O/Pn 14x17 Barnyard Fowl 1865 Chr 2/93 3,080
O/Pn 14x17 Barnyard Fowl 1865 Hnd 9/92 1,200
Van Leemputten, Frans Bel 1850-1914
O/Pn 11x14 Shepherdess Knitting 1884 Wes 3/93 1,540
Van Leemputten, Jef Louis Bel 20C
O/C 20x28 Landscape with Sheep Dum 12/92 1,800
Van Leen, Willem Dut 1753-1825
* See 1993 Edition . . . .
Van Leyden, Aertgen Fut 1498-1564
* See 1991 Edition . . . .
Van Lint, Hendrick Flm 1684-1763
* See 1991 Edition . . . .
Van Loo, Carle Fr 1705-1765
O/C/B 30x18 The Resurrection 1734 Chr 5/93 40,250
Van Loo, Jacob Dut 1614-1670
* See 1993 Edition . . . .
Van Loo, Jules Cesar Denis 1743-1821
* See 1993 Edition . . . .
Van Loo, Louis Michel Fr 1707-1771
* See 1990 Edition . . . .
Van Marcke De Lummen, Emile Fr 1827-1890
O/Pn 30x38 The Young Shepherd Boy Sby 2/93 6,038
O/C 15x21 Study of a Cow Chr 5/93 3,680
O/C 15x21 Cow in Landscape Chr 5/93 2,300
Van Marcke De Lummen, Marie Fr 1856-1935
O/C 32x26 Le Troupeau des Vaches Sby 2/93 9,200
Van Mastenbroek, Johann H. Dut 1875-1945
* See 1992 Edition . . . .
Van Mierevelt, Michiel Jans Dut 1567-1641
* See 1992 Edition . . . .
Van Mieris, Frans Dut 1689-1793
* See 1991 Edition . . . .
Van Mieris, Frans (the Elder) Dut 1635-1681
* See 1993 Edition . . . .
Van Mieris, Willem Dut 1662-1747
O/Pn 4x5 Horseman in Foreground Sby 5/93 14,375
Van Mierveldt, Michael Dut 1567-1641
O/Pn 28x23 Portrait of Frederick Henricksz. 1633 Sby 10/92 5,500
Van Millett, George Am 1864-
* See 1992 Edition . . . .
Van Minderhout, Hendrik Dut 1632-1696
* See 1993 Edition . . . .
Van Montfoort, Anthonie B. Dut 1532-1583
* See 1992 Edition . . . .
Van Mulders, Camille Con 19C
O/C 46x32 Vase de Fleurs et Lilas Sby 5/93 14,950
Van Musscher, Michiel Dut 1645-1705
* See 1992 Edition . . . .
Van Mytens, Martin (II) Swd 1695-1770
* See 1993 Edition . . . .
Van Nieulandt, Willem Dut 1584-1636
* See 1993 Edition . . . .
Van Noort, Adrianus Cornelis Dut 1914-
O/C 28x44 Under the Rainbow Umbrella Hnd 9/92 3,000
O/Pn 12x18 Two Girls Under Umbrella Hnd 9/92 1,600
O/Pn 12x16 The Bay and His Blue Shovel Hnd 9/92 1,500
O/Pn 12x16 Searching for Clams Hnd 9/92 1,400
O/Pn 12x16 Playful Children in July Hnd 9/92 1,300
O/Pn 8x11 Beach Scene Hnz 5/93 1,200

Van Notti, Henry   Am 1876-1962
O/B 14x18 Under the Brooklyn Bridge Yng 5/93 300
Van Nuyssen, Abraham Janssens
1575-1632
   * See 1992 Edition . . . .
Van Oosten, Isaak   Flm 1613-1661
   * See 1992 Edition . . . .
Van Oostsanen, Jacob Cornelisz   Dut
1470-1533
O/Pn 39x31 The Crucifixion: Panel of Triptych Sby 1/93 . 607,500
Van Orley, Barent   Dut 1492-1542
   * See 1991 Edition . . . .
Van Orley, Hieronymus (III)   Dut a 1652-
   * See 1992 Edition . . . .
Van Orley, Richard   Flm 1663-1732
K/Pa 9x14 Allegory Victory Crowning Peace Chr 1/93 825
Van Os, Georgius Jacobus J.   Dut
1782-1861
O/Pn 4x6 Still Lifes Flowers, Fruit on Ledge 47 Sby 10/92 . 9,900
Van Os, J.   Dut 20C
O/B 9x9 Figures at the Beach Yng 5/93 350
Van Os, Jan   Dut 1744-1808
O/Pn 31x23 Still Life Flowers and Fruit: Pair Sby 5/93 . . 607,500
Van Ostade, Adriaen Jansz   Dut
1610-1685
   * See 1993 Edition . . . .
Van Ostade, Isaac   Dut 1621-1649
   * See 1993 Edition . . . .
Van Oudenhoven, Joseph   Flm 19C
O/C 22x26 A Stop to Pick Wild Flowers Chr 10/92 1,650
Van Patten, James
A/C 48x64 Pond 1987 Dum 9/92 3,500
A/C 48x64 Bear Mountain For Now 1985 Dum 9/92 2,800
Van Peag, J.   Dut 19C
O/C 34x46 Horse Cart by the Sea Fre 4/93 1,150
Van Plattenberg, Mattias   Flm 1608-1660
   * See 1993 Edition . . . .
Van Poelenburgh, Cornelis   Dut
1586-1667
   * See 1992 Edition . . . .
Van Pol, Christian   Dut 1752-1813
   * See 1990 Edition . . . .
Van Raden, Marinus   Dut 1832-1879
O/C 10x18 Figures on Donkeys 1870 Dum 3/93 1,500
Van Ravesteyn, Dirck De Quade   Dut 16C
   * See 1990 Edition . . . .
Van Ravesteyn, Jan Anthonisz.   Dut
1570-1657
O/C 29x24 Lady, half length 1659 Chr 10/92 9,350
Van Roekens, Paulette   Am 1896-
O/C 12x14 The Swan Boat 1957 Sby 9/92 2,090
Van Roestraten, Pieter Gerrits   Dut
1630-1700
   * See 1991 Edition . . . .
Van Roose, Ch.   Bel 20C
   * See 1992 Edition . . . .
Van Royen, Willem Frederik   Ger
1654-1723
O/C 25x20 Opium Poppies, Tulips, Snowballs Chr 1/93 . . 66,000
Van Ruysdael, Salomon   Dut 1600-1670
   * See 1991 Edition . . . .
Van Ruysdael, Salomon Jacobsz.   Dut
1629-1681
O/Pn 20x27 Cattle Resting by Stream Chr 5/93 33,350
Van Ryder, Jack   Am 1898-1968
O/M 15x12 Near Casa Grande, Arizona Lou 6/93 375
Van Rysselberghe, Theo   Bel 1862-1926
O/Cb 18x15 Tulipes and Capucines Sby 2/93 19,550
Van Ryswyck, Edward   Bel 19C
O/C 47x63 Nature Morte au Melon Sby 10/92 8,800
O/C 20x28 Peonies on a Mossy Bank Chr 10/92 2,640
Van Schendel, Petrus   Bel 1806-1870
O/Pn 9x8 Hearing the News by Candlelight 1853 Chr 10/92   2,090

Van Schooten, Floris Gerritsz   Dut a
1605-1655
O/Pn 16x22 Still Life Strawberries, Silver Cup Sby 1/93 . . 33,350
Van Schrieck, Otto Marseus   Dut
1619-1678
   * See 1990 Edition . . . .
Van Seben, Henri   Bel 1825-1913
O/Pn 20x15 Chilly Winter Afternoon Chr 2/93 1,650
O/Pn 5x4 Young Girl Carrying Twigs Mys 3/93 715
Van Severdonck, Franz   Bel 1809-1889
O/Pn 8x9 White Draught Horse 1859 Skn 3/93 2,640
O/C 16x20 Cows on a Path Chr 2/93 2,420
O/Pn 7x10 Sheep and Chickens 1875 Wlf 3/93 2,300
O/Pn 7x10 Poultry Feeding with Ducks 1889 Chr 5/93 1,840
O/Pn 7x10 Farm Pastorale Brd 2/93 1,760
Van Severdonck, Franz & Morel   Bel
1809-1889
O/C 24x34 Shepherd with Family and Flock 1872 Sby 5/93 . 8,050
Van Slingelandt, Pieter   Dut 1640-1691
O/Pn 9x7 Portrait Lady in a Satin Gown 1683 Sby 10/92 . . 8,800
Van Sloun, Frank   Am 1879-1938
O/C 20x16 In the Park But 3/93 4,125
Van Sluys, Theo   Bel 19C
   * See 1993 Edition . . . .
Van Soelen, Theodore   Am 1890-1964
   * See 1992 Edition . . . .
Van Somer, Hendrick   Dut 1615-1684
   * See 1990 Edition . . . .
Van Son, Joris   Flm 1623-1667
O/Pn 18x24 Still Life Grapes, Pears, Ming Dish Sby 10/92   15,400
Van Spaendonck, Cornelis   Dut
1756-1840
   * See 1990 Edition . . . .
Van Spaendonck, Gerard   Fr 1746-1822
   * See 1990 Edition . . . .
Van Steenwyck, H. (the Younger)   Dut
1580-1649
O/Cp 3x3 Fame w/Horn; Mercury w/Putti: Pair Sby 10/92 . . 6,050
Van Streeck, Juriaen   Dut 1632-1687
   * See 1992 Edition . . . .
Van Stry, Abraham   Dut 1753-1826
O/C 20x24 Herdsmen and Cattle Wes 10/92 1,870
Van Stry, Jacob   Dut 1756-1815
   * See 1993 Edition . . . .
Van Strydonck, Guillaume   Bel 1861-1937
   * See 1990 Edition . . . .
Van Swanenburg, Isaac Claesz.   Flm
1537-1614
O/Pn 32x25 Portrait Adriana Vrancken Paets 1593 Sby 10/92 9,075
Van Swanevelt, Herman   Dut 1600-1655
   * See 1993 Edition . . . .
Van Tilborch, Gillis   Flm 1578-1623
   * See 1991 Edition . . . .
Van Utrecht, Adriaen   Flm 1599-1652
O/Pn 39x27 Iris, Tulips, Roses, Columbine 1642 Chr 5/93 134,500
Van Valkenborch, Martin   Flm 1535-1612
   * See 1991 Edition . . . .
Van Veen, Pieter   Dut 1563-1629
   * See 1992 Edition . . . .
Van Veerendael, Nicolaes   Flm 1640-1691
   * See 1990 Edition . . . .
Van Velde, Bram   Dut 1910-
   * See 1990 Edition . . . .
Van Velde, Geer   Dut 1898-
   * See 1993 Edition . . . .
Van Vittel, Gaspar   1653-1736
K,Pl&S/Pa 8x16 View of the Badia Fiesolana Chr 1/93 . . . 33,000
Van Vliet, Hendrik   Dut 1611-1675
   * See 1992 Edition . . . .
Van Vogelaer, Karel   Dut 1653-1695
O/C 26x21 Still Life Poppies, Anemones Sby 5/93 10,925
Van Vries, Roelof   Dut 1631-1681
O/C 25x19 Travellers on a Road Sby 10/92 34,100
Van Vucht, Gerrit   Dut 1610-1699
   * See 1992 Edition . . . .

Van Walscapelle, Jacob   Dut 1644-1727
* See 1993 Edition . . . .
**Van Waning Stevels, Marie   Dut
1874-1943**
O/C 21x17 Still Life with Primroses But 11/92   550
**Van Waning, Cornelis Antonie   Dut
1861-1929**
O/C 19x23 Harbor Scene Slo 4/93   1,400
Van Wittel, Gaspar   Dut 1653-1736
O/C 22x44 View of Vaprio and Canonica Chr 5/93   123,500
Van Woensel, Petronella   1785-1839
* See 1993 Edition . . . .
**Van Wyngaerdt, Anthonie J.   Dut
1808-1887**
* See 1993 Edition . . . .
**Van Wyngaerdt, Petrus Theo.   Dut
1816-1893**
* See 1993 Edition . . . .
Van Young, Oscar   Am 1906-
* See 1992 Edition . . . .
Van Zandt   Ger 20C
O/C 22x14 Construction '55 Hnd 9/92   200
Van Zandt, William   Am 20C
* See 1993 Edition . . . .
Van Zevenberghen, Georges A.   Bel 1877-
* See 1990 Edition . . . .
Vander Salm, Wilhelmus   1918-1965
O/B 16x24 Figures on Beach Dum 6/93   1,100
Vanderbanck, John   1694-1739
* See 1993 Edition . . . .
Vanderhoof, Charles A.   Am 1853-1918
W/Pa 8x10 Chickens in Barnyard Yng 2/93   150
Vanderlyn, John   Am 1775-1852
* See 1992 Edition . . . .
Vanetti   It 19C
O/C 28x20 Floral Still Life Hnz 5/93   575
Vannini, Ottavio   It 1585-1643
* See 1992 Edition . . . .
Vannutelli, Scipione   It 1834-1894
* See 1993 Edition . . . .
Vanter, Wilhelm Vander   Dut 19C
* See 1992 Edition . . . .
**Vantongerloo, Frans Joseph   Bal
1882-1965**
* See 1991 Edition . . . .
Vantongerloo, Georges   Bel 1886-1965
O/C 41x59 Landscape with Cows 1927 Hnd 5/93   2,000
**Vantore, Erik Mogens Christian   Dan
1895-**
* See 1992 Edition . . . .
Vanvitelli, Gaspare   Dut 1653-1736
O/C 22x44 View of Vaprio and Canonica Chr 5/93   123,500
K,Pl&S/Pa 8x16 View of the Badia Fiesolana Chr 1/93 . . .   33,000
Varese, Edgard   Fr 1888-1965
* See 1992 Edition . . . .
Vargas, Alberto   Am 1926-1983
* See 1993 Edition . . . .
**Varley, Frederick Horsman   Can
1881-1969**
O/Pn 12x15 Between Trenton and Belleville 1940 Sbt 5/93 .   8,800
O/B 12x15 Low Coulds, Kootenay Lake Sbt 5/93   4,840
H/Pa 18x12 Portrait Phillip Surrey's Mother 1937 Sbt 5/93 . .   528
Varo, Remedios   Spa 1908-1963
O/M 34x41 La Tejedora de Verona Chr 11/92   528,000
Pl&G/Pa 13x9 Personaje Sby 11/92   23,100
Vasarely, Victor   Fr 1908-
A/C 48x48 Katax 1970 Chr 10/92   19,250
A/Wd 33x32 Chelloe Sby 2/93   11,500
O/Wd 13x13 Beryel-Alx-2 1964 Sby 10/92   7,700
L/B 7x6 Untitled (Green) Sby 2/93   3,163
Vasari, Giorgio   It 1511-1574
* See 1991 Edition . . . .
Vasarri, Emilio   It 19C
* See 1993 Edition . . . .

Vassilieff, Marie   Rus 1884-1957
* See 1991 Edition . . . .
Vassilieff, Nicolai   Am 1892-1970
O/C 24x20 Still Life Maroon Tablecloth Chr 5/93   2,530
Vassiliev, Oleg
O/C 95x59 Untitled Sby 11/92   7,150
**Vauchelet, Theophile Auguste   Fr
1802-1873**
* See 1992 Edition . . . .
**Vauthier, Pierre Louis Leger   Fr
1845-1916**
O/C 15x18 Les Loges 92 Sby 2/93   7,475
Vavra, Frank   Am 1898-1967
* See 1993 Edition . . . .
**Vazquez Y Ubeda, Carlos   Spa a
1889-1907**
* See 1992 Edition . . . .
Vecellio, Tiziano   It 1488-1576
* See 1992 Edition . . . .
Vedder, Elihu   Am 1836-1923
O/C 9x9 Feeding the Pigs Chr 12/92   3,520
C&K/Pa 16x12 Sleep Chr 9/92   2,860
P&K/Pa 8x13 Study for Government Sby 3/93   1,725
C&P/Pa 8x13 Middle Eastern Views: Four 1890 Sby 9/92 . .   1,210
C&Cp/Pa 8x13 Seven Drawings Sby 3/93   575
Vega Y Munoz, Pedro   Spa 19C
* See 1990 Edition . . . .
Veillon, Auguste-Louis   Fr 19C
* See 1991 Edition . . . .
Velasco, Jose Maria   Mex 1840-1912
O/B 18x14 Platanilla 1883 Sby 11/92   126,500
O/Pa 6x10 Paisaje Sby 11/92   68,750
O/Cd 4x6 Paisaje Sby 11/92   20,900
**Velasquez, Eugenio Lucas   Spa
1817-1870**
O/C 15x19 La Coronada Chr 10/92   14,300
O/C 24x18 Alcala de Henares-Madrid 1855 Chr 10/92 . . .   8,800
O/C 27x20 La Coronela Chr 10/92   8,250
Velasquez, Jose Antonio   LA 1906-1985
O/C 20x27 San Antonio Oriente 1965 Chr 11/92   3,300
O/C 21x29 San Antonio de Orient 1951 Sby 2/93   3,220
Velier, E.   Fr 19C
* See 1993 Edition . . . .
**Vellani, Francesco & Rubbiani   It
1688-1768**
* See 1993 Edition . . . .
Velten, Wilhelm   Rus 1847-1929
O/Pn 9x13 The Horse Market Chr 2/93   23,100
Vely, Anatole   Fr 1838-1882
O/Pn 18x12 Courting Scene 1874 Slo 4/93   1,100
Venard, Claude   Fr 1913-
MM/C 45x58 L'Aeroplane Chr 2/93   4,400
O/C 38x38 Still Life Sby 10/92   3,850
O/C 40x40 Still Life Chairs, Table, Flowers Sby 10/92   2,970
O/C 38x46 Port Croix Sel 12/92   2,600
O/C 51x38 Femme sur la Plage Chr 11/92   2,420
O/C 30x30 La Cale de Bandol Sby 6/93   2,300
O/C 39x39 Canal St. Martin Chr 5/93   2,185
O/C 40x40 La Lampe a Petrole Sby 2/93   2,070
O/C 38x51 Canal St. Martin Chr 5/93   1,955
O/C 40x40 Pond Under Snow 57 Sby 10/92   1,760
O/C 31x58 Sacre-Coeur Chr 5/93   1,725
O/C 14x16 Still Life Sby 10/92   1,210
O/C 22x18 Composition a la Cafetiere Sel 9/92   800
O/C 16x13 Still Life with Melons Sby 6/93   690
Venneman, Charles   Bel 1802-1875
* See 1993 Edition . . . .
Ventnor, Arthur   Br 20C
* See 1993 Edition . . . .
**Verbeeck, Pieter Cornelisz.   Dut
1610-1654**
* See 1993 Edition . . . .
Verbeet, Gijsberta   Dut 1838-1916
* See 1993 Edition . . . .

Verboeckhoven, E & Keelhoff, F   Bel 1798-1881
* See 1993 Edition . . . .
Verboeckhoven, E & Roffiaen, J   Bel 1798-1881
O/C 17x15 An Alpine Farm Scene 1851 Chr 10/92   6,600
Verboeckhoven, E. & Roelofs, W   Bel 1798-1881
O/C 19x30 A Summer's Day Chr 10/92   35,200
Verboeckhoven, E. & Verwee, L.   Bel 1798-1881
O/C 32x45 Shepherdess in a Landscape 1858 Chr 2/93 . .   16,500
Verboeckhoven, Eugene Joseph   Bel 1798-1881
O/Pn 28x34 The Horse Yard 1854 Sby 6/93   50,600
O/Pn 25x31 Sheep in a Manger 18?8 Sby 10/92   11,550
O/Pn 11x16 Sheep in a Stall 1828 Sby 5/93   8,625
O/C 16x15 Head of a Sheep 1847 Sby 1/93   3,450
O/C 14x21 Shepherd with his Flock 1878 Chr 5/93   3,450
O/Pn 14x18 Sheep Grazing Wes 3/93   1,760
Verboeckhoven, Louis   Bel 1802-1889
O/C/B 37x47 Sailing Ships in Choppy Seas Chr 5/93   17,250
O/Pn 10x16 Ships on Stormy Seas Chr 5/93   2,990
Verbruggen, Gaspar (the Elder)   Dut 1635-1687
O/C 19x16 Still Life Flowers in an Urn Sby 1/93   17,250
O/C 27x22 Marigolds, Snowballs, Roses Chr 10/92   12,100
Verbrugghen, Gaspar (the Younger)   Dut 1664-1730
O/Pn 18x20 Classical Female Figure Sby 5/93   10,350
Verbuecken, J.   Con 19C
* See 1993 Edition . . . .
Verburgh, Dionijs   Dut 1655-1722
* See 1993 Edition . . . .
Verdaguer, Dionisio Baixeras   Spa 1862-
* See 1992 Edition . . . .
Verdier, H.   Fr 19C
O/Pn 12x18 Peasants on a Hilly Landscape Chr 10/92   2,640
O/Pn 15x20 The Cavalier's Card Game Hnd 10/92   1,550
Verdier, Jules V.   Fr 1862-
O/C 26x32 Making Cannon Balls 1892 Fre 10/92   400
Verdilham, Mathiew   Eur 20C
C/Pa 9x10 Sortie Hnd 12/92   130
Verdun, Raymond Jean   Fr 19C
* See 1992 Edition . . . .
Verelst, John   Flm a 1698-1734
* See 1992 Edition . . . .
Verelst, Pieter   Dut 1618-1671
* See 1993 Edition . . . .
Verelst, Simon Pietersz   Dut 1644-1721
O/C 30x25 Irises, Poppies, Roses, Tulips Chr 1/93   28,600
Vergez, Eugene   Fr 19C
O/C 14x21 Beach with Trees and Boats Sby 1/93   2,588
Verhaecht, Tobias   Flm 1561-1631
O/Pn 20x27 Mountainous River Landscape Sby 1/93   85,000
Verhas, Frans   Bel 1827-1897
* See 1993 Edition . . . .
Verheyden, Francois   Am 1880-
O/B 12x16 Overlooking a Harbor Yng 2/93   325
Verheyden, Francois   Bel 1806-1890
* See 1993 Edition . . . .
Verhoesen, Albertus   Dut 1806-1881
O/C 16x20 Various Fowl: Pair 1876 Sby 1/93   9,488
O/Pn 5x7 Spaniel Resting 1873 Fre 10/92   2,600
O/Pn 5x7 Poultry in a Landscape Fre 10/92   1,800
O/B 9x11 Cows in a Pasture 1846 Wtf 12/92   1,700
Verkolje, Nicolaes   1673-1746
O/Pn 14x17 The Finding of Moses Sby 1/93   28,750
Verlat, Charles Michel Maria   Bel 1824-1890
* See 1990 Edition . . . .
Verlot, O.   Fr 20C
* See 1992 Edition . . . .

Vermehren, Johan Frederick N.   Dan 1823-1910
* See 1990 Edition . . . .
Vermeulen, Andreas   Dut 1821-1884
* See 1991 Edition . . . .
Vermeulen, Andries   1763-1814
* See 1993 Edition . . . .
Vermeulen, M.   Dut 20C
O/Pn 9x12 Skaters on Frozen River: Pair Sby 10/92   3,575
Vermeylen, D.   Bel 19C
O/C 18x24 Landscape with Reflecting Pond Sel 9/92   325
Vermorcken, Frederic Marie   Bel 1860-
O/C 18x14 Reading in the Afternoon Sun 1893 Chr 10/92 . .   4,180
Verne, Alfred   Am 1850-1910
* See 1992 Edition . . . .
Verner, Elizabeth O'Neill   Am 1883-
* See 1993 Edition . . . .
Verner, Frederick Arthur   Can 1836-1928
O/C 16x26 Bison - Morning 1916 Sbt 5/93   14,080
O/C 16x24 Buffalo - Evening '19 Sbt 5/93   14,080
W/Pa 21x29 Ojibbawa Wigwams - Lake 1919 Sbt 11/92 . .   10,560
W/Pa 12x24 Ojibbawas, Lake Huron Sbt 11/92   6,600
O/C 27x22 Portrait of Charles Dickens Sbt 5/93   3,080
W/Pa 12x24 Buffalo Grazing 1893 Sbt 11/92   2,640
W/Pa 13x20 Canadian Elk Sbt 11/92   2,640
W/Pa 15x22 Buffalo 1900 Sbt 5/93   1,980
W/Pa 13x20 English Cottage Landscape 1890 Sbt 5/93 . .   1,584
G&W/Pa 4x10 Shoreline with Indians and Canoes Chr 5/93 .   1,380
W/Pa 13x20 Shepherd's Cottage, Dorset 1895 Sbt 11/92 .   1,320
O/C/B 7x10 Country Path at Sunset 1890 Sbt 5/93   1,144
W/Pa 14x10 Study of a Tree Stump Sbt 11/92   572
Vernet, Antoine Charles Horace   Fr 1758-1836
* See 1993 Edition . . . .
Vernet, Claude Joseph   Fr 1714-1789
* See 1993 Edition . . . .
Vernet, Horace   Fr 1789-1863
O/C 40x51 The Boar Hunt 1835 But 11/92   495,000
O/C 18x22 Le Dernier Grenadier de Waterloo Sby 10/92 .   34,100
O/C 13x10 Portrait John B. Church 1821 Chr 2/93   3,300
Vernier, Emile Louis   Fr 1829-1887
* See 1992 Edition . . . .
Vernier, J.   Fr 20C
O/C 21x26 A Fishing Port 92 Chr 5/93   1,380
Vernon, Della   Am 1876-1962
O/C 36x24 The Ox Train But 3/93   2,090
Vernon, Emile   Fr 19C
O/C 36x24 Starlight Sby 2/93   34,500
O/C 18x15 The Cherry Bonnet 1919 Sby 10/92   25,300
O/C 24x20 Pink Carnations Chr 1/93   9,900
O/C 36x26 Lady Carrying Pink Roses Sby 1/93   3,450
Veron, Alexander Rene   Fr 1826-1897
O/C 31x45 Promeneur au Bord de L'Eau Sby 10/92   20,900
O/C 32x46 Figures in a Punt 1858 Chr 5/93   17,250
O/C 31x46 Les Lavandieres Sby 10/92   15,950
O/C 31x46 Le Vieux Parc de Montleveque Sby 5/93   13,800
O/C 17x22 Paysage de Riviere Sby 2/93   4,945
Veronese   It 1528-1588
* See 1991 Edition . . . .
Verpoeken, Hendrik   Dut 1791-1869
* See 1990 Edition . . . .
Verschaffelt, Edward
* See 1991 Edition . . . .
Verschuring, Hendrik   Dut 1627-1690
* See 1992 Edition . . . .
Verschuur, Wouterus   Dut 1812-1874
O/Pn 8x11 King Charles Spaniels by a Fire Chr 10/92   4,620
Vertes, Marcel   Fr 1895-1961
O/C 69x66 Trois Enfants Chr 2/93   6,050
O/C 21x29 Two Paintings Chr 5/93   2,530
O/C 30x24 Jeune Femme a la Harpe Chr 11/92   1,650
G/Pa 14x10 Harpers Fashion Lady 33 Hnd 5/93   170
Vertin, Pieter Gerard   Dut 1819-1893
O/Pn 14x11 Dutch Street Scene Fre 10/92   3,900

Vertunni, Achille It 1826-1897
O/C 24x43 Bestie Vicino del Lago Sby 10/92 5,500
Verveer, Elchanon Dut 1826-1900
* See 1992 Edition . . . .
Verveer, Salomon Leonardus Dut 1813-1876
* See 1990 Edition . . . .
Verwee, L. & Verboeckhoven, E. Bel 1807-1877
O/C 32x45 Shepherdess in a Landscape 1858 Chr 2/93 . . 16,500
Verwee, Louis Pierre Bel 1807-1877
* See 1992 Edition . . . .
Vesin, Jaroslav Fr. Julius Bul 1859-1915
O/C 22x29 Im Kreuzfeuer Sby 5/93 11,500
Vespignani, Renzo It 1924-
* See 1992 Edition . . . .
Vester, Willem Dut 1824-1871
* See 1990 Edition . . . .
Veyrassat, Jules Jacques Fr 1828-1893
O/C 19x24 Forest of Fontainebleau Chr 5/93 25,300
O/Pn 6x4 L'Eglise du Village Hnd 6/93 950
Vezin, Charles Am 1858-1942
* See 1993 Edition . . . .
Viale, Pedro Blanes Uru 1878-1926
O/C 52x45 Sol y Sombra Sby 11/92 192,500
O/C 54x34 Glicina de la Quinta de Castro 1922 Sby 5/93 . 85,000
Vianelli, Achille It 1803-1894
O/C 23x15 Il Studio Da Pittura Sby 10/92 6,600
Viard, Georges Fr a 1831-1848
* See 1991 Edition . . . .
Vibert, Jean Georges Fr 1840-1902
O/C 11x14 Game of Chess Chr 2/93 3,950
O/Pn 5x4 Valet de Chambre Fre 4/93 2,700
W/Pa 5x3 Cardinal in Profile 1880 Chr 2/93 1,320
Vicente, Esteban Spa 1904-
O/C 68x57 Spring 1972 Sby 6/93 10,350
Vickers, Alfred Br 1786-1868
O/B 8x12 Village on Water; Walk by Pond: (2) Chr 2/93 . . . 990
O/C 12x25 Activity Along the Coast 1854 Fre 10/92 250
Vickers, Alfred H. Br a 1853-1907
O/C 10x14 Along the River Chr 5/93 2,530
O/Pn 11x9 Figures in Country Landscape Wes 5/93 660
Vickery, Charles Am 20C
O/C 12x16 Seascape Hnd 10/92 600
Vickrey, Robert Am 1926-
Et/M 23x18 Vaudeville Figure Chr 12/92 12,100
Victors, Jacobus Dut 1640-1705
* See 1992 Edition . . . .
Vidal, A. It 20C
* See 1993 Edition . . . .
Vidal, Louis Fr 1754-1805
O/Pn 28x41 Still Life Flowers and Fruit Sby 10/92 7,425
Vidal, Margarita Hahn Am 20C
O/M 18x13 Golden Poem 1960 Skn 9/92 440
Viegers, Bernard Dut 1886-1947
* See 1993 Edition . . . .
Vieira Da Silva, Maria Helena Fr 1908-
* See 1993 Edition . . . .
Vigee, Louis 1715-1767
P/Pa/C 22x18 Girl Holding A Giamblette Sby 5/93 14,950
Vigee-Lebrun, Marie Louise Fr 1775-1842
* See 1991 Edition . . . .
Vighi, Coriolano It 1846-1905
P/Pa 20x25 Sailboats at Sunset 1904 Chr 10/92 2,860
Vignaud, Jean 1775-1826
O/C 26x22 Portrait of a Lady 1809 Chr 5/93 4,600
Vignet, Henri Fr 1857-1920
* See 1993 Edition . . . .
Vignoles, Andre Fr 1920-
O/C 35x46 Chemin vers Montfort-L'Amaury Chr 11/92 3,850
O/C 26x32 Les bles fleuris Chr 11/92 2,640
Vignon, Claude Fr 1593-1670
* See 1993 Edition . . . .
Vignon, Victor Fr 1847-1909
* See 1993 Edition . . . .

Vigny, Andre Fr
* See 1992 Edition . . . .
Vila Y Prades, Julio Spa 1873-1930
* See 1993 Edition . . . .
Vilato, Javier Fr 1921-
O/C 38x51 La Maison Dans Le Fond Wes 3/93 990
Vilia, Carlos Am 1936-
MM/C 83x72 Bedspread '84 But 10/92 770
Villa, Hernando G. Am 1881-1952
* See 1993 Edition . . . .
Villacres, Cesar Ecu 1880-
O/C 22x35 Mountainous Landscape Sby 6/93 1,380
O/C 30x25 Parisian Market Scenes: Pair Sby 6/93 1,150
Villanueva, Leoncio Per 1936-
* See 1991 Edition . . . .
Villegas Y Cordero, Jose Spa 1848-1922
O/C 44x28 The Siesta 1874 Sby 2/93 332,500
O/C 63x34 Le Fumeur Oriental 1875 Sby 5/93 299,500
O/Pn 16x24 View of the Piazza San Marco Chr 10/92 93,500
O/Pn 5x9 Paisaje Rocoso '19 Sby 10/92 2,475
Villegas Y Cordero, Ricardo Spa 1852-
* See 1991 Edition . . . .
Villegas, Armando
* See 1992 Edition . . . .
Villon, Jacques Fr 1875-1963
C/Pa 10x13 Seated Nude Woman Sby 10/92 3,300
Pe&W/Pa/B 10x15 Sur le Plage, Le Treport 05 Chr 11/92 . . 2,860
Pl/Pa/B 8x10 Femme au Chapeau Chr 2/93 1,760
O/Pa 10x7 La Palette du Peintre 59 Chr 5/93 920
Pl/Pa 11x10 Portrait de Femme 61 Chr 11/92 825
Vinall, Joseph Williams Topham Br 1873-
* See 1992 Edition . . . .
Vinay, Jean Fr 1907-
O/C 9x10 Vallee du Gresivaudan FHB 5/93 500
Vincent, Harry Aiken Am 1864-1931
O/B 8x10 Canal Dock Wlf 12/92 500
Vinci, Guidi It 19C
W/Pa 15x20 Figures Along the River 1885 Fre 10/92 325
Vinciata
O/Pn 26x14 Helena Child of Italy Sby 10/92 550
Vinckboons, David Fr 1576-1629
O/Pn 10x13 Peasant Feast 1606 Sby 1/93 134,500
Vine, J. Br 19C
O/C 18x24 Prize-Winning Hereford 1854 Hnd 6/93 1,800
Vinea, Francesco It 1845-1902
O/C 53x36 Tea Time Tease Chr 10/92 22,000
O/C 18x28 Il Giardino Botanico 1884 Sby 2/93 4,600
Viner, B. Am 20C
W/Pa 8x14 Country Church 1900 Yng 5/93 125
Vines, Roberto Spa 20C
* See 1993 Edition . . . .
Vinton, Frederick Porter Am 1846-1911
O/C 14x24 Across the Hay Meadow 1886 Skn 9/92 7,700
O/C 30x24 Portrait Spanish Woman Skn 9/92 4,125
O/C 16x10 Gate Way in Toledo Skn 9/92 880
Vinton, John Rogers Am 1801-1847
* See 1993 Edition . . . .
Viollet Le Duc, Victor Fr 1848-1901
* See 1992 Edition . . . .
Viollier, Jean
O/C 13x22 Conversation II 1957 Sby 2/93 1,840
Viry, Paul Alphonse Fr 19C
* See 1993 Edition . . . .
Visconti, Alphonse Adolfo Fr 1850-1924
* See 1991 Edition . . . .
Viski, Janos Hun 1891-
O/C 24x30 Galloping Horses Dum 7/93 350
O/C 24x30 Galloping Horses Dum 7/93 325
Viski, Jean Am 20C
O/C 12x31 Wild Horses Sby 3/93 920
Vitali, E. It 19C
* See 1993 Edition . . . .
Viteri, Alicia
* See 1992 Edition . . . .

Vitturi, I. It 19C
O/C/B 51x39 Saint Gerome Translating 1899 Hnd 5/93 500
O/C/B 51x39 Saint Jerome Translating Bible 1899 Hnd 9/92 . 500
Vivancos, Miguel-Garcia Spa 1895-1972
O/C 15x18 Nature Morte et Marine '63 Slo 4/93 1,000
Vivarini, Antonio It 1445-1503
  * See 1991 Edition . . . .
Vivian, Calthea Campbell Am 1857-1943
O/C 21x15 #18-Moonlight-Pacific Grove Mor 6/93 935
Vivin, Louis Fr 1861-1936
  * See 1991 Edition . . . .
Vizzini, Andrea
MM/B 24x32 Interno Teoretico 1982 Sby 2/93 2,300
MM/Pn 38 dia Interno T. Concavalli di S. Marco Sby 2/93 . . 1,380
Voelcker, Gottfried Wilhelm Ger 1775-1849
  * See 1992 Edition . . . .
Vogel, E. Con 20C
O/C 24x36 Beach Scene Lou 9/92 350
Vogel, Valentine Am -1966
O/C 40x50 Little Red School House '41 Sel 4/93 350
O/C 25x30 Allegorical Subject, Female Nude Sel 12/92 160
Vogler, Hermann Ger 1859-
  * See 1993 Edition . . . .
Voirin, Leon Joseph
  * See 1991 Edition . . . .
Voiriot, Guillaume Fr 1713-1799
  * See 1990 Edition . . . .
Voisard-Margerie, Adrien Fr 19C
  * See 1991 Edition . . . .
Volaire, Pierre Jacques Fr 1729-1802
  * See 1993 Edition . . . .
Volk, Stephen A. Douglas Am 1856-1935
O/C 14x17 Water Lily Chr 3/93 2,300
O/B 13x7 Girl with Lamb 1923 Dum 8/93 425
Volkers, Emil Ger 1831-1905
O/C 23x34 Hungarian Nomads Chr 5/93 3,680
Volkert, Edward Charles Am 1871-1935
O/B 9x12 Spring Ploughing Chr 5/93 1,610
O/C 25x31 Winter Morning Lou 6/93 1,500
O/B 12x16 Plowing the Hill Hnd 10/92 950
Volkhart, Max Ger 1848-1935
O/C 29x42 Courtship 67 Sby 10/92 6,050
Volkmar, Charles Am 1841-1914
  * See 1993 Edition . . . .
Vollerdt, Johann Christian Ger 1708-1769
O/C 24x29 Hilly Landscape with Figures 1759 Sby 1/93 . . 24,150
Vollmar, Ludwig Ger 1842-1884
  * See 1992 Edition . . . .
Vollmer, Grace L. Am 1884-1977
  * See 1993 Edition . . . .
Vollmering, Joseph Am 1810-1887
  * See 1993 Edition . . . .
Vollon, Alexis Fr 1865-1945
O/C 20x24 Vue de la Seine, Paris Sby 5/93 18,400
O/C 17x13 Woman Sewing Chr 5/93 1,725
Vollon, Antoine Fr 1833-1900
O/C 19x23 Still Life with Gilt Ewer But 11/92 7,150
O/B 8x14 Shipping Along a River But 5/93 4,888
Vollweider, Johann Jacob Ger 1834-1891
  * See 1991 Edition . . . .
Voltz, Friedrich Johann Ger 1817-1886
O/C 14x20 Study of a Cow Sby 10/92 3,575
O/Cb 9x11 At Rest in the Field Skn 9/92 1,045
Von Amerling, Friedrich Ritter Aus 1803-1887
  * See 1993 Edition . . . .
Von Baldaugh, Anni Am 1881-1953
O/C 14x14 Girl in Blue Mor 6/93 2,475
Von Baranya, Gustov Lorincz Hun 1886-1938
  * See 1991 Edition . . . .
Von Bartels, Hans Ger 1856-1913
  * See 1993 Edition . . . .

Von Bergen, Carl Ger 1853-
O/C 27x25 The Inquisitive Child Sby 5/93 15,525
Von Blaas, Eugen Aus 1843-1932
O/C 30x40 Flirtation 1887 Chr 10/92 38,500
Von Blaas, Julius Aus 1845-1922
O/Pn 14 dia Feeding at the Post 1890 Sby 6/93 3,220
O/C 24x29 Bay in Loose Stall 1886 Doy 5/93 2,200
Von Bochmann, Gregor (the Elder) Ger 1850-1930
O/Pn 7x10 Cow Pulling a Plow Wes 10/92 3,190
Von Bosse, Georg Am 20C
O/C 12x17 Woman in Garden Lou 12/92 100
Von Bremen, Johann Georg Meyer Ger 1813-1886
O/C 20x16 Mittagsruhe 1866 Sby 10/92 42,900
O/C/B 21x16 Appealing to Higher Authority 1863 Doy 5/93 38,500
O/C 17x14 Rechnendes Madchen 1866 Sby 2/93 29,900
O/C 15x12 Kehr Wieder 1872 Sby 2/93 27,600
O/Pn 8x6 Young Girl Knitting 1851 Sby 5/93 21,850
O/Pn 7x6 Young Shepherdess in Thought 1867 Chr 10/92 19,800
O/Pn 6x5 The New Doll 1876 Chr 2/93 8,800
O/Pn 6x5 Auf Der Hohe 1876 Sby 2/93 7,475
Von Burkel, Heinrich
O/Pn 14x18 Hay Wagon with Poachers Dum 5/93 37,500
Von Chelminski, Jan Pol 1851-1925
  * See 1993 Edition . . . .
Von Chlesbowski, Stanislaus Pol 1835-1884
O/C 20x16 The Sentry 1860 Chr 2/93 9,900
Von Defregger, Franz Ger 1835-1921
O/C 37x29 Der Zitherspieler auf der Alm 1876 Sby 10/92 115,500
O/B 13x9 Portrait of an Old Man But 11/92 9,900
Von Demuth, Anni Aus 1866-
  * See 1993 Edition . . . .
Von Destouches, Johannes Ger 1869-
O/B 27x37 Pansies in a Basket Chr 5/93 3,450
Von Eckenbrecher, Themistocles Ger 1842-1921
  * See 1991 Edition . . . .
Von Faber Du Faur, Otto Ger 1828-1901
  * See 1990 Edition . . . .
Von Ferraris, Arthur Hun 1856-
  * See 1992 Edition . . . .
Von Gegerfelt, Wilhelm Swd 1844-1920
O/C 27x38 Fishing on the Laguna 83 Chr 10/92 12,100
O/C 34x52 Washerwomen by a River 76 Chr 5/93 2,990
Von Gietl, Josua Ger 1847-1922
  * See 1992 Edition . . . .
Von Grutzner, Eduard Ger 1846-1925
  * See 1990 Edition . . . .
Von Gunten, Roger Sws 1933-
P&G/Pa 13x13 Lunarina Esmeralda '57 Hnd 9/92 50
Von Hamilton, Ferdinand-Philip Ger 1664-1750
O/Pn 10x13 Goose, Poultry in Landscape 1746 But 11/92 . . 3,025
Von Hassler, Carl Am 1887-1962
O/C 20x26 Autumn and Winter: Two Wes 10/92 2,310
Von Hoermann, Theodor Aus 1840-1895
  * See 1991 Edition . . . .
Von Huctenburgh, Jan Dut 1646-1753
  * See 1992 Edition . . . .
Von Janda, Hermine Aus 1854-
O/Pn 15x19 Still Life Spring Blossoms 1895 Sby 1/93 4,888
Von Jawlensky, Alexej Ger 1864-1931
  * See 1993 Edition . . . .
Von Kaulbach, Friedrich August Ger 1822-1903
  * See 1990 Edition . . . .
Von Kaulbach, Friedrich August Ger 1850-1920
O/C 23x23 Portrait of Young Lady Sby 5/93 9,775
O/C 39x29 Woman Carrying Fruit Sby 1/93 8,330
Von Keller, Albert Sws 1844-1920
  * See 1993 Edition . . . .

Von Klever, Julius Sergius Rus 1850-1924
  * See 1992 Edition . . . .
Von Kobell, Wilhelm A. W. Ger 1766-1855
  * See 1993 Edition . . . .
Von Kowalski-Wierusz, Alfred Pol 1849-1915
  I&W/Pa 7x11 Embarking a Troika 1911 FHB 6/93 600
Von Kreuznach, Konrad Faber Ger 16C
  * See 1990 Edition . . . .
Von Lenbach, Franz Seraph Ger 1836-1904
  O/B 28x26 Oval Portrait of a Child 1903 Sel 9/92 19,000
  O/C 20x15 Portrait of Ludwig II Sby 1/93 4,025
Von Luerzer, F.
  O/C 28x48 Elk on the Cloquet River 1909 Eld 4/93 660
  O/C 28x48 Elk on the Shores of Lake Jackson 1910 Eld 4/93 660
Von Madarasz, Gyula Aus 1858-
  * See 1990 Edition . . . .
Von Marr, Carl Ger 1858-1936
  * See 1993 Edition . . . .
Von Max, Gabriel Cornelius Czk 1840-1915
  O/C 24x19 Far Away Thoughts Chr 10/92 4,620
  O/C 19x15 Young Widow Wlf 3/93 400
Von Menzel, Adolf Ger 1815-1905
  * See 1991 Edition . . . .
Von Muhlenen, Max Sws 1903-1971
  * See 1992 Edition . . . .
Von Muller, Emma Aus 1859-
  O/Pn 11x8 Portrait of Girl Holding Book Sel 12/92 300
Von Pausinger, Clemens Ger 1855-1936
  P/Pa 37x27 Portrait Maria Jeritza 1937 Fre 4/93 850
Von Perbandt, Carl Am 1832-1911
  O/C 19x25 Artist's Children Painting 73 But 3/93 10,450
Von Piloty, Karl Theodor Ger 1826-1886
  * See 1993 Edition . . . .
Von Poschinger, Richard Ger 1839-1915
  O/C 23x33 Harbor with Figures Sby 1/93 2,415
Von Rentzel, August & Triebel Ger 1810-1891
  * See 1993 Edition . . . .
Von Reth, Caspar Ger 1858-1913
  * See 1991 Edition . . . .
Von Scheidel, Franz Anton Aus 1731-1801
  * See 1992 Edition . . . .
Von Schmidt, Harold Am 1893-1982
  O/C 30x50 Tugboat Annie Gets the Works 1934 Sby 3/93 . 5,750
  O/C 28x35 The African Warriors Sby 9/92 3,300
  O/C 30x50 Tugboat Annie Gets the Works 1954 Fre 10/92 . 1,800
  G/B 25x14 Robbers Roost 1930 Wlf 12/92 800
Von Schneidau, Christian Am 1893-1976
  O/C 46x40 Summertime But 6/93 6,325
  O/C 30x40 Sunset & Fish Boat at Wharf Mor 2/93 600
Von Schrotter, Alfred Aus 1856-
  * See 1993 Edition . . . .
Von Schwind, Moritz Aus 1804-1871
  * See 1992 Edition . . . .
Von Sedelmayer, Ferdinand Ger 19C
  * See 1992 Edition . . . .
Von Stuck, Franz Ger 1863-1928
  O/Pn 23x20 Weibliches Portrat Sby 2/93 9,200
Von Szankowski, Boleslaw Pol 1873-
  * See 1992 Edition . . . .
Von Tamm, Franz Werner 1658-1724
  O/C 67x48 Still Life Flowers in Landscape Sby 1/93 . . . 31,625
Von Thoren, Otto Karl Kasimir Aus 1828-1889
  O/Pn 21x32 Horses in a Field But 5/93 5,750
Von Volkmann, Hans Richard Ger 1860-1927
  * See 1993 Edition . . . .
Von Wedig, Gottfried 1583-1641
  * See 1993 Edition . . . .

Von Werner, Anton Alexander Ger 1843-1915
  * See 1992 Edition . . . .
Von Wichera, Raimund Aus 1862-1925
  * See 1992 Edition . . . .
Von Wiegand, Charmion Am 1900-1983
  O/C 12x9 Modern Minuet 194? Brd 8/93 12,100
Von Wierusz-Kowalski, Alfred Pol 1849-1915
  O/Pn 14x10 The Mountain Pass Sby 2/93 19,550
  O/C 20x25 The Happy Return Sby 2/93 13,800
Von Zugel, Heinrich Ger 1850-1941
  O/C 24x32 Schafhirte auf Wiese 1894 Sby 10/92 35,750
  O/C 24x37 On the High Road 1905 Sby 5/93 20,700
Vonck, Elias Dut 1605-1652
  O/Pn 29x37 Still Life Game on Table Sby 1/93 5,750
Vonck, Jan Dut 1630-1660
  * See 1993 Edition . . . .
Vonnoh, Robert William Am 1858-1933
  O/C 24x30 Pleasant Valley, Lyme Chr 12/92 60,500
  O/C/B 26x21 Moist Weather (France) 1890 Chr 12/92 . . . 33,000
  O/C 30x36 The Orchard Sby 12/92 33,000
  O/C 24x30 Monarch of the Valley But 6/93 13,800
Voogd, Hendrick Dut 1768-1839
  * See 1992 Edition . . . .
Voorhees, Clark Greenwood Am 1871-1933
  O/C 23x30 Campfire under the Trees Chr 5/93 1,495
Voorhout I, Johannes 1647-1773
  * See 1993 Edition . . . .
Vorobieff, Marie (Marevna)
  * See 1992 Edition . . . .
Voroshilov Rus 19C
  O/C 35x21 Troika But 11/92 19,800
Vos, Hubert Am 1855-1935
  O/C 40x60 Dutch Family in an Interior '91 Wes 12/92 825
Voss, Carl Leopold Ger 1856-1921
  * See 1990 Edition . . . .
Voss, Frank Brook Am 1880-1953
  O/C 14x16 Bay Hunter in the Stable 1936 Sby 6/93 4,313
Vostell, Wolf 20C
  * See 1993 Edition . . . .
Vouet, Simon Fr 1590-1649
  K&S/Pa 13x8 Assumption of the Virgin Chr 1/93 28,600
Vrancx, Sebastian Flm 1573-1647
  O/Pn 19x30 Village Landscape with Travellers Chr 5/93 . . 51,750
Vrancx, Sebastian & De Momper Flm 1573-1647
  * See 1993 Edition . . . .
Vreedenburgh, Cornelis Dut 1880-1946
  * See 1993 Edition . . . .
Vrolyk, Adrianus Jacobus Dut 1834-1862
  O/C 14x10 City Street Scene Fre 4/93 1,200
Vroom, Hendrik Cornelisz Dut 1566-1640
  * See 1993 Edition . . . .
Vuillard, Edouard Fr 1868-1940
  O/B/Pn 17x26 Madame Vuillard a Table Sby 11/92 . . . 440,000
  O/B/Pn 18x24 Mme Vuillard Salle Manger 1903 Chr 11/92 286,000
  P&C/Pa 9x12 Madame Vuillard Dans Interieur Sby 10/92 . . 27,500
  O/C 18x14 La Table de Salle a Manger Sby 10/92 25,300
  Br&I/Pa 8x10 Interieur Chr 11/92 24,200
  W&I/Pa 9x6 Programme de Theatre Sby 10/92 10,450
  Pl/Pa 6x3 Femme Assise Devant Une Fenetre Chr 5/93 . . . 4,830
  Pe/Pa 5x5 Interieur au Clos Cezanne Sby 11/92 4,125
  Pl/Pa 5x2 Femme au Chapeau Chr 5/93 863
Vysekal, Edouard Antonin Am 1890-1939
  O/C 11x14 The Back of the House Sby 9/92 7,150
  O/C/B 11x14 Japanese Nursery But 6/93 3,738
Vysekal, Luvena Am 1873-1954
  O/B 22x24 M. Washington Geranium Mor 11/92 1,100
Vytlacil, Vaclav Am 1892-1984
  T/B 24x18 Table Top Abstraction 1938 Chr 12/92 3,080
  T/B 17x27 Beach and Boats 1947 Chr 12/92 2,420
  T/Pa 22x32 Fishing Nook 1947 Chr 5/93 1,150
  T/B 12x17 Beach No. 3 1946 Chr 12/92 825

Wachtel, Elmer Am 1864-1929
O/C 30x40 Mt. San Antonio, California But 3/93 18,700
O/C 16x20 Topanga Canyon But 10/92 14,300
O/C 10x7 Landscape Mor 11/92 3,500
W/Pa 11x16 Wooded River Landscape Chr 5/93 633
Wachtel, Marion Kavanaugh Am 1875-1954
O/C 25x30 Sycamores-Millard Canyon 1943 Mor 2/93 . . . 27,500
O/C 30x40 Matilaja Canyon Mor 2/93 25,000
O/C 20x26 Pasadena Mountain View Mor 11/92 25,000
O/C 22x28 After the Storm-Mt. San Antonio Mor 2/93 22,500
O/C 20x26 Laguna Coastal Mor 2/93 15,000
W/Pa 18x24 View of Sierras But 6/93 11,500
O/C 14x18 House in Landscape Mor 2/93 8,500
O/C 13x17 California Coastal/Landscape Mor 6/93 7,700
O/C 20x16 High Sierras But 3/93 7,700
O/C/B 14x18 Sycamores in Landscape Mor 6/93 5,500
W/Pa 9x23 Still Life - Yellow Roses Mor 2/93 3,000
G/B 14x17x23 The Monterey Coast Wes 3/93 1,100
Wadsworth, Wedworth Am 1846-1927
* See 1992 Edition . . . .
Wagemans, P. G. A. Con 19C
O/C 16x32 Ships in a Harbor Chr 10/92 1,320
Wagner, Ferdinand Ger 1847-1927
* See 1992 Edition . . . .
Wagner, Fred Am 1864-1940
O/C 29x36 Philadelphia Waterfront in Winter Fre 10/92 6,250
O/C 20x26 Red Barn in Norristown Fre 10/92 1,200
P/Pa 13x17 Tug Boat Philadelphia Waterfront Fre 10/92 850
O/C 30x20 Philadelphia Port Fre 10/92 750
P/Pa 11x13 Boats in Dry Dock Fre 10/92 700
P/Pa 23x18 Ships in a Harbor Sby 9/92 550
P/Pa 7x9 Mill in Winter Fre 10/92 475
P/Pa 3x9 Schukyill in Winter Fre 10/92 275
P/Pa 7x9 Winter Landscape Fre 4/93 190
Wagner, Fritz Ger 1896-1939
O/B 10x8 Fruhstuck Fre 10/92 550
Wagner, Fritz Sws 1872-
O/B 10x8 Pipe Smoker Dum 2/93 650
Wagner, Jacob Am 1852-1898
* See 1991 Edition . . . .
Wagner, Wilhelm Aus 1887-
O/C 23x56 The Race Fre 4/93 1,000
Wagner, Wilhelm Georg Dut 1814-
* See 1992 Edition . . . .
Wagoner, Harry B. Am 1889-1950
O/C/B 6x8 Indian Village, Sunset: Two Wes 10/92 1,100
O/C 20x30 Vagabond Clouds, Palm Springs Wes 10/92 990
Wahlberg, Alfred Swd 1834-1906
O/C 39x28 Bois de Hetres, A Durehaven 1874 Sby 2/93 . . . 6,900
Wahlberg, Ulf Swd 1938-
MM/C Size? Landscape Wtf 12/92 1,000
Wahlqvist, Ehrnfried Swd 1815-1895
* See 1991 Edition . . . .
Wainewright, Thomas Francis Eng 19C
* See 1992 Edition . . . .
Wainwright, I. Br 19C
O/C 18x24 After the Hunt: Two Quails 1866 Hnd 5/93 1,300
Wainwright, John Br 19C
* See 1992 Edition . . . .
Wainwright, T. & Pearson, C. Br 19C
W&S/Pa 15x28 Cattle and Sheep: Pair 1881 Doy 5/93 3,190
Wainwright, William John Br 1855-1931
* See 1991 Edition . . . .
Wakhevitch, Georges 20C
* See 1993 Edition . . . .
Walbourn, Ernest Br 1872-
O/C 16x24 Ducks by a Pond Chr 10/92 2,860
Walcott, Harry Mills Am 1870-1944
* See 1991 Edition . . . .
Walde, Alfons 20C
* See 1991 Edition . . . .
Waldek, H.
* See 1992 Edition . . . .

Waldmuller, Ferdinand Georg Aus 1793-1865
O/C 20x27 Landscape Shepherd Presenting 1823 Sby 5/93 . 68,500
Waldo, J. Frank Am 19C
O/C 20x36 Island Park, Lake Winnebago 1875 Chr 5/93 . . 29,900
Waldo, Samuel & Jewett, W. Am
* See 1993 Edition . . . .
Waldo, Samuel Lovett Am 1783-1861
* See 1993 Edition . . . .
Waldorp, Antoine Dut 1803-1866
O/Pn 12x18 Shipping in an Estuary Chr 2/93 4,050
O/Pn 12x18 Sailing on the Canal Wes 10/92 3,080
O/Pn 19x27 Setting Out to Sea 1856 Chr 2/93 1,540
O/Pn 8x10 Shipping in an Estuary Chr 5/93 1,380
Walenta, Edmund Am 19C
* See 1992 Edition . . . .
Wales, Susan Makepeace Larkin Am 1839-1927
W&Pe/Pa 20x14 Interior of a Greenhouse Sby 9/92 1,430
Walker, Chuck Am 20C
* See 1992 Edition . . . .
Walker, E. B. Br 19C
W/Pa 13x16 Relaxing by the Fire Hnz 5/93 140
Walker, Frederick R. Am 20C
* See 1992 Edition . . . .
Walker, Henry Oliver Am 1843-1929
* See 1992 Edition . . . .
Walker, Horatio Can 1858-1938
W/Pa 14x11 The Bee Keeper Sbt 11/92 2,112
O/B 19x15 Portrait of a Lady 1889 Sbt 11/92 1,760
Walker, J. Edward Am a 1920-1929
O/C 12x18 Sand Dunes Lou 12/92 70
Walker, James Am 1819-1889
O/C 20x51 Battle Scene Chr 12/92 4,400
Walker, James Alexander Br 1841-1898
* See 1993 Edition . . . .
Walker, John Am 1931-
O&Rs/C 84x66 Autumn Figure 1985 Sby 10/92 13,200
C&K/Pa 30x23 Oceanic Study III 88 Chr 11/92 1,100
Walker, John Law Am 1899-
O/C 26x32 Pima Fair (Night) 1957 But 3/93 2,200
O/C 33x34 The Santa Clara in Spring 1958 Slo 5/93 850
Walker, Robert Hollands Br 20C
W&G/Pa/B 8x15 Breezy Day on the Mersey Skn 3/93 522
Walker, William Aiken Am 1838-1921
O/C 12x20 Bringing in the Cotton Chr 12/92 28,600
O/C 12x20 Blue Fish Chr 12/92 10,450
O/B 10x13 Southern Homestead But 12/92 8,800
O/B 9x12 Laundry Day Chr 12/92 8,250
O/B 6x12 Wash Day Sby 3/93 6,900
O/B 12x9 Cotton Pickers Chr 3/93 5,750
O/B 8x4 Man with Pipe Chr 3/93 4,600
O/B 8x4 The Fruit Vendor Chr 3/93 4,600
O/C 7x4 New Smyrna Beach, Florida Chr 3/93 4,370
Walkowitz, Abraham Am 1880-1965
W,Pl&Pe/Pa 14x9 Isadora Duncan: Three Chr 5/93 6,900
W&C/Pa 22x15 At the Opera Chr 3/93 5,750
W,I&Pe/Pa 8x3 Isadora Duncan Dancing: Seven Sby 9/92 . . 4,125
W&H/Pa 12x18 Figures in a Landscape 1915 Sby 3/93 2,070
W&Pe/Pa 12x10 Two Drawings 1906 Sby 3/93 1,725
W,Pe&I/Pa 14x9 Two Watercolors Sby 3/93 1,725
G&Pe/Pa 14x12 A Group of Women 1904 Sby 9/92 1,540
W&I/Pa 7x3 Isadora Duncan: Pair Watercolors Sby 9/92 880
I&Pe/Pa 5x7 Bathers in a Rocky Grotto 1905 Sby 9/92 825
Pe/Pa 11x14 Abstract Dancer 1913 Sby 3/93 518
O/B 16x10 Seated Dancer Mys 12/92 330
Wall, A. Bryan Am -1937
O/B 8x9 Two Works Wes 5/93 330
Wall, Sue Am 20C
A/C 16x14 Front Porch Wtf 5/93 600
Wall, W. C. Am 19C
* See 1992 Edition . . . .
Wall, William Allen Am 1801-1885
* See 1991 Edition . . . .

Wall, William Guy Am 1792-1864
* See 1992 Edition . . . .
Wallace, Lucy Am 1884-
O/Cb 16x12 Moonlight Rendevous Skn 9/92 495
Wallenn, Frederick D. Br a 1880-1920
Pe&W/Pa/Pn 10x23 Women of Antiquity 1904 Sby 2/93 . . . 2,760
Waller, Samuel Edmund Br 1850-1903
* See 1991 Edition . . . .
Walraven, Jan Dut 1827-1874
O/C 26x22 Blowing Bubbles Sby 2/93 4,600
Walseth, Niels Dan 20C
O/C 26x22 Afternoon Rest by Mountainside Chr 2/93 495
Waltensperger, Charles E. Am 1871-1931
O/C 14x12 Girl with Goat Dum 4/93 550
Walter, Martha Am 1875-1976
O/B 14x18 Pink and Purple Group Chr 12/92 28,600
O/Cb 14x18 Chairs at Brighton Beach Chr 12/92 26,400
O/B 14x18 Crowded Beach Chr 12/92 24,200
O/B 15x18 Biarritz Beach Sby 9/92 17,600
O/Cb 15x18 Quadro-Flamenco Chr 9/92 13,200
O/Cb 15x18 French Beach Scene Chr 3/93 12,650
O/C 32x24 Seated Child in a Cape Sby 9/92 8,800
O/Cb 15x18 Mid-France Sby 9/92 7,150
O/B 20x16 Italian Mother and Children Sby 3/93 6,613
O/Cb 18x15 Baby in a Blue Dress Sby 9/92 4,950
O/Cb 15x18 Crab Sale Chr 9/92 4,950
Walter, Otto Aus 19C
* See 1993 Edition . . . .
Walters, Emile Am 1893-
* See 1993 Edition . . . .
Walters, George Stanfield Br 1838-1924
O/C 13x20 Estuary Sby 1/93 1,840
W/Pa 13x20 Boats at Dawn 1888 But 5/93 920
W&Cw/Pa 12x19 Shipping off the Coast 1880 Chr 2/93 605
Walters, Samuel Br 1811-1882
* See 1992 Edition . . . .
Walther, Charles Am 1879-1938
* See 1991 Edition . . . .
Walton, Edward Arthur Eng 1860-1922
* See 1992 Edition . . . .
Walton, Henry Am 1746-1813
* See 1990 Edition . . . .
Walton, Henry Br 20C
O/C 20x30 Capel Curig, North Wales Chr 10/92 880
Walton, William Am 1843-1915
G/Pa 18x23 Tugs Wes 10/92 330
Wandesforde, Juan Am 1817-1902
* See 1993 Edition . . . .
Wappers, Gustave, Baron Bel 1803-1874
* See 1993 Edition . . . .
Ward, Alfred Br a 1880-1929
O/B 35x26 Lady French Sel 12/92 510
Ward, Charles Caleb Can 1831-1896
* See 1993 Edition . . . .
Ward, Edmund F. Am 1892-1991
O/C 30x23 Boy and Giant Having Breakfast Ih 11/92 3,750
O/Pn 14x12 Mother Tying Scarf Around Boy's Ih 11/92 . . . 1,400
O/C 30x36 Reviving a Fallen Man Mys 3/93 750
O/C 24x33 Bearded Man Being Wrestled into Car 24 Ih 5/93 . . 650
C&W/Pa 19x26 Man Being Arrested in Nightclub Ih 11/92 . . 600
W/Pa 25x12 Bank Teller Line Mys 3/93 522
W/Pa 23x9 Jockey Mys 3/93 522
W/Pa 18x9 The Liar Mys 3/93 412
Ward, J. Stephen Am 1876-
O/C 30x40 Trees of Bishop Mor 11/92 1,000
O/C 16x20 Houses in Winter Landscape Mor 2/93 800
O/C 24x30 Sierra Lake Lou 3/93 600
Ward, James Br 1769-1859
* See 1991 Edition . . . .
Ward, John Can 1948-
* See 1993 Edition . . . .
Ward, Martin Theodore Br 1799-1874
O/C 25x30 Foxhole Sby 6/93 1,955
Ward, William (Jr.) Can -1935
O/C 16x20 Red Sails Skn 9/92 385

Wardle, Arthur Br 1864-1949
O/C 29x37 The Tiger Pool Sby 2/93 85,000
O/C 15x21 Hunter with Brace of Setters Sby 6/93 7,763
W&G/B 35x27 Young Lady and Dogs 1890 Sby 6/93 1,840
O/B 11x14 Topsy Sby 6/93 1,725
Warhol, Andy Am 1928-1987
I&SpSs/C 81x224 Marilyn X 100 1962 Sby 11/92 . . . . . . 3.74M
ISs/C 84x96 Double Marlon 1966 Sby 11/92 935,000
SpSs/C 31x34 Race Riot 64 Chr 11/92 627,000
SpSs&Y/C 70x54 Old Telephone Sby 5/93 552,500
Gd&Ss/C 18 dia Marilyn '62 Chr 11/92 352,000
SpSs/C 54x43 Marilyn 1986 Chr 11/92 275,000
I&SpSs/C 30x30 Five Deaths (Red) Sby 11/92 258,500
SpSs/C 36x28 Four Marilyns 86 Chr 11/92 181,500
Ss/Pa 40x30 Suicide 1964 Sby 11/92 132,000
I&SpSs/C 50x42 Mao 73 Sby 11/92 126,500
SpSs/C 36x28 Four Marilyns 1979 Sby 10/92 121,000
SpSs/C 84x70 Russell Means 1976 Sby 11/92 110,000
SpSs/C 20x16 Jackie Sby 11/92 82,500
SpSs/C 16x14 One Green Marilyn Sby 11/92 82,500
SpSs/C 18x14 Multicolored Marilyn 1979 Sby 10/92 77,000
I&SpSs/C 18 dia Round Jackie Sby 11/92 66,000
SpSs/C 74x60 Shadow Sby 11/92 63,250
ASs/C 50x40 Portrait of Princess Diana Sby 5/93 57,500
Pg&MM/C 48x50 Oxidation Painting 1978 Sby 11/92 55,000
SpSs/C 20x16 Jackie 64 Chr 11/92 44,000
SpSs/C 20x16 Jackie 64 Chr 10/92 38,500
SpSs/C 18x14 One Grey Marilyn Chr 10/92 38,500
SpSs/C 22x22 Blackglama 85 Sby 11/92 35,750
I&SpSs/C 22x22 Flowers 1964 Chr 2/93 33,000
O&P/C 15x15 Truman Capote Chr 10/92 24,200
SpSs/C 20x16 Dollar Sign 83 Sby 5/93 20,700
I&SpSs/C 20x16 Jackie (Blue) 64 Chr 2/93 19,800
SpSs/C 20x16 Campbell's Soup Can 81 Sby 5/93 19,550
SpSs/C 20x20 Campbell's Chicken Rice 1986 Sby 5/93 . . 18,400
SpSs/C 16x20 Gun 81 Chr 11/92 17,600
SpSs/C 16x16 Man Ray 1978 Sby 2/93 17,250
SpSs/C 16x12 Shoe Chr 10/92 16,500
I&SpSs/C 20x20 Chicken Noodle Soup Box 86 Chr 2/93 . . 15,400
SpSs/C 5x5 Flowers 64 Chr 11/92 15,400
I&SpSs/C 11x14 Roll Over Mouse 83 Chr 5/93 14,950
SpSs/C 7x7 7-cent Airmail Stamp 1962 Chr 11/92 14,300
SpSs/C 5x5 Untitled 64 Sby 11/92 14,300
SpSs/C 10x20 Album of a Mat Queen 1963 Chr 11/92 13,200
SpSs/C 5x5 Flowers 64 Chr 11/92 12,100
A/Pa 11x9 Self-Portrait Sby 11/92 9,900
Ph 8x2 Two Photo-Booth Self-Portraits Chr 11/92 9,900
A/C 5x5 Untitled 64 Sby 10/92 9,900
I&SpSs/C 14x11 Poinsettia Flowers 1982 Chr 2/93 8,250
SpSs/C 14x11 Untitled 83 Sby 5/93 8,050
I&SpSs/C 5x5 Flowers 64 Chr 2/93 7,150
SpSs/C 11x14 Blue Valentine 1982 Sby 2/93 6,900
SpSs/C 14x11 Shadows Chr 10/92 6,600
SpSs/C 26x20 Poinsettia 82 Sby 10/92 6,050
Ss&C/Pa 18x24 Untitled 1980 Chr 5/93 5,750
SpSs/C 9x9 Untitled 86 Chr 11/92 5,500
SpSs/C 11x14 Caution 82 Chr 11/92 5,280
Pe/Pa 23x31 Untitled 81 Sby 2/93 5,175
I&L/Pa 13x8 Four Drawings Sby 6/93 4,025
PV/Pa 24x18 Tom 'n' Jerry Recipe Sby 6/93 3,163
PV/Pa 29x23 Young Woman with Halo of Birds Sby 6/93 . . . 2,300
I/Pa 23x29 Red and Pink Rose Garland Sby 6/93 2,070
Sp/V 15x18 Christmas T-Strap Sby 10/92 990
I/Pa 29x23 Times Fashion Special Sby 6/93 690
PV/Pa 23x29 Waterzoie Recipe Sby 6/93 690
Warner, Everett Longley Am 1877-1963
* See 1993 Edition . . . .
Warner, Mary Loring Am 20C
O/C 25x45 Newport Marshes Brd 2/93 6,380
Warner, Neil Walker Am 1891-1970
O/C 34x40 Echoes from a Cherry Garden Sby 3/93 4,255
O/C 30x26 The Gold Scarf But 3/93 2,200
O/Cb 12x16 House in Eucalyptus Landscape Mor 11/92 . . . 1,500
O/C 25x30 Zinnias in Yellow Bowl Mor 11/92 650

Warren, *** Am 19C
O/C 10x8 Young Boy Modelling with Clay 1866 Sby 9/92 . . 1,980
Warren, Henry Am 1794-1879
O/C 22x28 Delaware Near Trenton Fre 4/93 425
Warren, Melvin C. Am 1920-
* See 1990 Edition
Warshawsky, Abel George Am 1883-1962
O/C 26x40 California Landscape But 6/93 6,325
O/C 26x32 View of the Village But 3/93 6,050
O/C 26x22 French Village; Woman: Double But 3/93 4,125
O/C 18x22 Isle aux Mornes 30 But 3/93 2,475
O/C 18x22 The Open Door Lou 9/92 2,250
O/Cb 35x48 Reclining Nude Vase of Flowers Wtf 4/93 1,900
O/Cb 16x13 Floral Still Life Wtf 4/93 800
Warshawsky, Alexander Am 1887-1945
O/C 24x30 Hollywood Hills But 6/93 2,300
O/C 25x32 Portrait of a Breton Woman Wtf 12/92 1,650
O/C 21x25 Figure on a Country Lane 1911 Wtf 12/92 850
Waschmuth, Ferdinand Fr 1802-1869
* See 1991 Edition
Washburn, Cadwallander Am 1866-1965
W/Pa 13x15 Flower Garden Lou 3/93 600
Washburn, Mary Nightingale Am 1861-1932
O/C 24x20 Flora 1917 Skn 9/92 1,320
Washburn, Roy Engler Am 1895-
C/Pa 25x15 Male & Female Nudes: Pair '16 FHB 3/93 340
Washington, Georges Fr 1827-1910
* See 1992 Edition
Waslaske, Ida
O/C 22x28 Apple Blossoms Ald 3/93 275
Wasmuller, J. H. Am 19C
* See 1991 Edition
Wasson, George Savary Am 1855-1932
* See 1993 Edition
Watelet, Charles Joseph Bel 1867-1954
O/C 61x48 Elegant Lady in White 1930 Chr 10/92 6,600
Watelet, Louis Etienne Fr 1780-1866
* See 1993 Edition
Watelin, Louis Fr 1838-1905
* See 1993 Edition
Waterhouse, John William Br 1849-1917
W/Pa 15x10 Touchstone, The Jester Sby 5/93 3,163
Waterman, Marcus A. Am 1834-1914
O/C 25x31 High Beach, Provincetown Skn 11/92 1,760
O/C 20x30 Clearing in a Woods Lou 6/93 825
O/C 36x46 Figures in Middle Eastern Costume 1886 Fre 10/92 475
O/C 24x20 Roman Statesman Mys 3/93 165
Waters, George W. Am 1832-1912
O/C 26x42 Hudson River Landscape '76 Dum 6/93 2,300
Waters, Susan Am 1823-1900
O/C 28x42 Sheep in a Landscape Sby 3/93 1,725
Watkins, Catherine Am 1861-1947
O/B 10x8 St. George - France Mor 11/92 250
Watkins, Franklin C. Am 1894-1972
O/C 28x36 Son My Son 1946 Dum 11/92 1,700
Watkins, William Reginald Am 1890-
O/C 25x30 Four Masted Schooner 1938 Wes 5/93 440
W/Pa 21x27 The Eldray Mayin, Cambridge Slo 5/93 375
Watlin, V. Am 20C
O/C 9x12 Watering Cows Slo 4/93 160
Watrous, Harry Willson Am 1857-1940
O/C 24x18 Solitaire Sby 12/92 8,800
O/Pn 17x22 A Drawn Game Sby 5/93 5,750
O/C 19x14 Lady Nicotine Sby 3/93 5,750
O/Pn 7x6 An Old Score Chr 5/93 2,070
Watson
O/C 12x16 Pastoral Landscape with Cattle Eld 11/92 358
Watson, Adele Am 1875-1947
* See 1993 Edition
Watson, Amelia Am 1856-1934
W/Pa 10x15 Southport North Carolina Scene Mys 3/93 302
Watson, Charles A. Am 1857-1923
O/B 6x8 A Hazy Morning Eld 7/93 88

Watson, Charles H. R. Irs 20C
* See 1992 Edition
Watson, Edward Facon Br 19C
* See 1992 Edition
Watson, Homer Ransford Can 1855-1936
O/C 18x24 Figures in a Forest Glade Sbt 11/92 5,280
O/C 14x18 Country Landscape with Sheep '88 Sbt 5/93 . . . 4,400
O/B 17x16 Riders in a Forest Sbt 11/92 3,520
O/C 10x15 Summer Storm Sbt 5/93 2,200
O/B 13x17 Landscape - Hespeler Sbt 5/93 1,320
O/B 7x10 Doon Woods Sbt 5/93 1,144
Watson, Howard N.
W/Pa 14x19 Betsy Ross' House Ald 5/93 425
W/Pa 11x15 Philadelphia Art Museum Ald 5/93 300
W/Pa 10x13 Street Harbor Scene Ald 5/93 95
Watson, Jessie N. Am 1870-1963
* See 1993 Edition
Watson, John Dawson Eng 1832-1892
* See 1992 Edition
Watson, P. 19C
O/C 29x48 Town View Dum 12/92 550
Watson, Robert Am 1923-
* See 1993 Edition
Watson, Robert Br 20C
O/C 20x29 Highland Cattle 1901 Hnd 3/93 2,400
O/C 22x36 Highland Landscape with Sheep 1906 FHB 6/93 1,800
Watson, Walter J. Br 1879-
O/C 20x29 Near Beddgelert, North Wales But 11/92 1,980
Watson, William (Jr.) Br -1921
O/C 24x37 Cattle Watering in a Stream 1901 But 11/92 . . . 7,700
O/C 24x36 Highland Cattle 1919 But 5/93 6,900
O/C 24x36 Morning in Highland 1909 Chr 2/93 5,500
Watson-Gordon, Sir John Eng 1790-1864
* See 1991 Edition
Watteau, Jean-Antoine Fr 1684-1721
* See 1993 Edition
Watts, Frederick Waters Br 1800-1862
* See 1992 Edition
Watts, George Frederick Br 1817-1904
* See 1992 Edition
Watts, William Clothier Am 1869-1961
O/C 30x36 Haze After Storm But 6/93 2,875
W/Pa 24x20 Normandie Wtf 5/93 700
W/Pa 30x20 Arch of Titus Wtf 4/93 375
Watzelhan, Carl Ger 1867-1942
* See 1990 Edition
Waud, Alfred R. Am 1828-1891
Pe&Cw/Pa 6x10 Office of Freedmen's Bureau 65 Chr 12/92 1,100
Waugh, Frederick Judd Am 1861-1940
O/C 30x40 Breaking Seas Sby 3/93 17,250
O/C 30x40 Still Life Skn 3/93 9,350
O/C 18x36 Family Gathering 1892 Sby 3/93 8,050
O/C 29x36 Little Harbor, Bailey's Island 1903 Sby 3/93 . . . 8,050
W/Pa/B 15x21 Looking West, St. Ives Sby 12/92 7,700
O/M 25x30 Coast Under Heavy Surf Sby 9/92 7,150
O/M 28x36 Gale from the West Chr 9/92 6,600
O/M 20x24 Lively Surf Sby 3/93 6,325
O/M 30x40 Rain, Clouds, and Sea Brd 8/93 4,180
O/M 28x36 Maine Coast Slo 7/93 4,000
O/M 16x20 Crashing Surf Wes 5/93 1,980
O/Pn 7x8 Nocturnal Seascape Mys 3/93 1,540
O/B 23x30 Coming Day Hnd 10/92 800
O/B 12x16 Barbados Wes 5/93 770
O/M 23x28 Crashing Waves Lou 6/93 700
Waugh, Samuel Bell Am 1814-1885
O/C 24x20 Portrait of Jennie Thompson 1869 Eld 8/93 495
Wauters, Camille Bel 1856-1919
* See 1993 Edition
Wauters, Constant Bel 1826-1853
O/Pn 15x12 The Conversation Sby 5/93 4,888
Way, Andrew John Henry Am 1826-1888
* See 1993 Edition
Way, Charles Jones Can 1834-1919
W/Pa 19x29 Alpine Landscape Sbt 5/93 1,232

**Weatherbee, George Faulkner   Am
1851-1920**
  * See 1990 Edition . . . .
Weaver, Thomas   Br 1774-1843
  * See 1990 Edition . . . .
Webb, Boyd
  Ph 60x48 Enzyme Sby 2/93   5,175
Webb, Charles Meer   Br 1830-1895
  O/C 37x50 Reading the News 1887 Chr 10/92   9,900
Webb, James   Br 1825-1895
  O/C 18x30 Seeking Shelter from Storm 1855 Chr 5/93   5,520
Webb, Paul   Am 1902-
  G&W/Pa 15x17 Man Running to Outhouse Ih 5/93   175
Webb, Robert   Am 20C
  O/C 16x12 Desert Landscape Hnd 9/92   100
Webb, Thomas   Am 20C
  O/C 39x18 The Last Dance Skn 11/92   1,430
Webb, William Edward   Br 1862-1903
  O/C 37x51 Charles III, Baron of Southampton Sby 6/93 . .   36,800
Webber, Charles T.   Am 1825-1911
  O/C 33x16 Girl Picking Flowers Hnd 3/93   5,200
Webber, W. B.
  O/C 30x50 Rescue at Sea Dum 2/93   2,500
Webber, Wesley   Am 1841-1914
  O/C 30x50 Near North Head, Grand Manon Chr 3/93 . . .   13,800
  O/C 37x26 Ship at Moonlight Chr 5/93   1,150
  O/C 14x20 Rest on a Stroll Autumn Foliage Brd 2/93   1,100
  O/C 26x36 Sailing by Moonlight Sby 9/92   1,100
  O/C 22x36 Indian Point Penobscott Bay Skn 9/92   935
  O/C 16x26 Water Lilies Yng 5/93   875
  O/C 15x25 Venetian Scene Hnz 5/93   475
  O/C 18x30 Moonlight Harbor Hnz 5/93   400
Weber   Fr 20C
  O/C 18x21 Paris Street Scene Hnd 6/93   100
Weber, Alfred Charles   Fr 1862-1922
  O/Pn 13x9 Sip of White Wine Chr 10/92   6,050
  O/Pn 11x14 A Game of Checkers But 11/92   2,475
  W/B 15x10 A Cardinal Singing at the Piano Chr 2/93   880
Weber, Carl   Am 1855-1925
  W/Pa 23x36 Sheep Grazing Under Apple Blossoms Chr 12/92   715
  W/Pa 12x24 Sheep in Spring Landscape Sel 9/92   400
  W/Pa 15x23 Flock of Sheep Grazing Sel 2/93   200
Weber, Charles Philipp   Am 1849-
  O/B 13x17 A Wooded Stream Chr 5/93   1,035
**Weber, Gottlieb Daniel Paul   Ger
1823-1916**
  O/C 21x30 Castle on Mountainside 1863 Sby 1/93   5,750
Weber, M*   Ger 19C**
  * See 1993 Edition . . . .
Weber, Maris   Ger a 1876-
  * See 1993 Edition . . . .
Weber, Max   Am 1881-1961
  T/C 21x18 Interior with Men 1919 Sby 12/92   99,000
  O/C 18x15 Among the Trees 1911 Sby 5/93   46,000
  O/B 49x38 Good News '44 Sby 3/93   26,450
  O/B 8x5 Primitive Head Chr 5/93   19,550
  T/B 11x9 Women in a Garden 11 Chr 5/93   14,950
  O/Cb 14x11 Still Life 1910 Chr 3/93   10,350
  W&P/Pa/B 18x24 Sleep 1938 Sby 3/92   8,800
  W/Pa 12x9 Resting Women 1912 Sby 3/93   4,313
  C/Pa/C 25x19 The Drawing Class Sby 3/93   1,725
Weber, Otis S.   Am 19C
  O/C 12x22 Moonlight, Leity Point, MA 1881 Lou 6/93   600
  O/C 26x40 Sailing off Shore Yng 2/93   450
  W/Pa 18x29 Seascape Lou 3/93   200
Weber, Otto   Ger 1832-1888
  * See 1992 Edition . . . .
Weber, Paul   Am 1823-1916
  O/C 11x15 Mountain Landscape with River 1855 Sby 5/93 .   8,050
  O/C 10x8 Cottage on Cliff; Beach Scene: (2) Mys 12/92 . .   1,540
Weber, Philip   Am 1849-
  * See 1992 Edition . . . .
Weber, Sarah S. Stilwell   Am 1878-1939
  * See 1993 Edition . . . .

Weber, Theodore F.   Fr 1838-1907
  O/C 13x22 Les Jetees de Trouville But 11/92   9,350
  O/C 24x36 Shipping in Choppy Seas Chr 10/92   7,700
  O/C 11x8 Fisherman with Boats: Two Hnd 3/93   4,200
  O/C 18x28 Shipping off a Jetty Chr 10/92   3,080
Weber-Ditzler, Charlotte   Am 1877-1958
  W/Pa 30x28 Seated Couple Ih 5/93   350
Webster, E. Ambrose   Am 1869-1935
  O/C 30x20 Webster House, Bradford Street '31 Sby 3/93 . .   5,750
Webster, Herman Armour   Am 1878-1970
  O/C 25x20 Still Life with a Vase Sby 9/92   275
Webster, J.   Eng 19C
  O/C 28x34 Mischievous Dog with Lovers Wlf 3/93   1,100
Webster, Thomas   Br 1800-1886
  O/C 8x10 Young Boy Resting on Haystack Hnd 5/93   300
Webster, Walter   Am 1878-1959
  O/C 30x25 Young Girl in Pink Ballet Costume Ih 11/92 . . .   3,000
Weege, William   Am 20C
  Pa 48x48 Untitled '77 But 10/92   1,045
  MM 29x29 Untitled 78 Hnd 5/93   350
Weekes, Henry   Br a 1849-1888
  * See 1992 Edition . . . .
Weekes, Herbert William   Br a 1864-1904
  O/C/B 14x12 Pet Dogs: Pair 79 Sby 5/93   11,500
Weeks, Edwin Lord   Am 1849-1903
  O/C 40x32 The Rajah's Favorite Chr 2/93   132,000
  O/C 57x75 The Buddhist Temple 1905 Sby 12/92   110,000
  O/C 29x20 Before a Mosque '83 Sby 5/93   37,950
  O/C 56x74 A Fete Day at Bekanir Chr 5/93   36,800
  O/C 22x18 Indian Scene Chr 2/93   33,000
  O/C 20x30 Muttra 88 Chr 10/92   26,400
  O/C 24x19 Promenade on an Indian Street Chr 5/93   25,300
  O/C 18x13 An Arab Scene Chr 2/93   11,000
Weeks, James   Am 1922-
  * See 1993 Edition . . . .
Weenix, Jan Baptist   Dut 1621-1663
  O/C 32x28 Elegant Woman Standing Sby 1/93   28,750
Wegener, Gerda   Dan 1883-1931
  * See 1993 Edition . . . .
Wegener, P.   20C
  K/Pa 15x11 Portrait Chr 5/93   368
Weger, Marie   Am 1882-
  O/C 30x26 Flowers and Bust of Napoleon Yng 5/93   200
Wegman, William   Am 1943-
  Ph/B 26x45 At Desk, 3 Chr 11/92   4,620
  Br,I&G/Pa 14x11 Dog Paints Man 85 Chr 11/92   2,860
  I/Pa 14x11 Two Untitled Drawings 89 Chr 10/92   2,750
  Ph 14x11 Bow and Arrow, Arrow and Bow (2) Sby 2/93 . .   2,300
  W&I/Pa 11x14 Sled Dogs 83 Sby 10/92   1,100
  W&Fp/Pa 11x14 Rene is Serving 82 Chr 2/93   880
Wegner, Erich   Ger 1899-
  * See 1992 Edition . . . .
Weidenaar, Reynold   Am 20C
  O/M 6x16 Dust to Dust 1962 Wes 3/93   440
Weidenbach, Augustus   Am a 1853-1869
  O/C 30x46 Southern Landscape with Figures Slo 7/93   3,750
Weidner, Carl A.   Am 19C
  O/C 20x16 Reading Lesson 1891 Fre 10/92   550
Weigall, Arthur Howes   Eng -1877
  * See 1991 Edition . . . .
Weiland, Johannes   Dut 1856-1909
  O/C 53x42 The New Doll 1901 Chr 2/93   9,900
Weindorf, Arthur   Am 1885-
  * See 1993 Edition . . . .
Weiner, Lawrence   20C
  * See 1993 Edition . . . .
Weingaertner, Hans   Am 1896-1970
  O/Pn 20x18 White Cats with Birds Fre 10/92   325
Weinles, F.   20C
  O/C 31x43 Service for Yom Kippur Dum 1/93   10,000
Weinrich, Agnes   Am 1873-1946
  O/B 14x11 Still Life with Lady Slipper Skn 9/92   715
  W/Pa 14x11 Cubist Still Life Sby 3/93   575
  W/Pa 10x14 Fruit on a Table Mys 12/92   495
  W&H/Pa 10x10 Landscape Skn 9/92   468

W/Pa 9x8 Shade Trees Skn 5/93 440
P,I&H/Pb 9x6 Still Life with Pears Skn 9/92 220

Weir, John Ferguson   Am 1841-1926
O/C 30x25 Japanese Iris Sby 9/92 12,650
O/C 20x33 Isola Madre, Lago Maggiore 1885 Chr 3/93 6,325
O/B 9x12 Cows in Pasture Hnd 10/92 1,400

Weir, Julian Alden   Am 1852-1919
O/C 17x11 Chalice, Japanese Bronze, Red Taper Sby 5/93 40,250
O/C 34x27 The Birches 1903 Chr 12/92 38,500
O/C 27x23 Cora Chr 5/93 17,250
O/C 39x31 Follower of Grolier Sby 5/93 14,950
W/Pa 6x7 Branchville, Connecticut Sby 12/92 8,800
O/C 20x24 Caroline Clark Marshes Dum 1/93 4,000
O/C 39x29 Portrait George Piano 1872 Sby 3/93 1,380

Weir, Robert Walter   Am 1803-1889
W&Pe/Pa 10x13 Fir Trees and A Cottage: Pair Sby 9/92 495
Pe/Pa 13x18 Rural Landscapes: Three Sby 9/92 385

Weis, John Ellsworth   Am 1892-
O/C 25x30 Village Street in the Snow Eld 8/93 1,320
O/C 26x32 Still-Life of Flowers Wlf 9/92 600

Weisbuch, Claude   Fr 1927-
O/C 46x35 Portrait of a Seated Man 71 Sby 2/93 4,313
O/C 39x32 Portrait of a Clown Sby 6/93 4,025
O/C 46x35 Seated Man Sby 6/93 3,738
O/C 21x26 Portrait of a Man Sby 6/93 3,220
O/C 58x45 Femme Nue Debout Chr 2/93 3,080
O/C 32x26 Portrait of a Man 68 Sby 2/93 2,415
O/C 20x24 The Clown Sby 6/93 2,070

Weisenborn, Rudolph   Am 1881-
G/B 37x23 Head 42 Hnd 12/92 3,600
O/C 33x20 Portrait of Mrs. Kutner 1951 Hnd 5/93 1,000
P/Pa 25x19 Abstract Head 1948 Hnd 5/93 950
C/Pa 25x19 Mrs. Louis Kutner with a Book 1951 Hnd 5/93 . . 550
O/Cb 20x16 Untitled 52 Hnd 5/93 450

Weisman, Joseph   Am 1906-1977
W/Pa 13x15 Old Dairy Farm C.1930 Mor 6/93 468
W/Pa 11x16 Old Barn-Arroyo Seco, Pasadena, CA Mor 6/93 . 358

Weisman, William H.   Am 19C
O/C 14x17 Mountain Dam Brd 8/93 742
O/C 20x42 Moonlit Surf Skn 9/92 330

Weiss, Johann Baptist   Ger 1812-1879
* See 1993 Edition

Weiss, Jose   Br 1859-1929
O/C 24x40 Verdant Landscape Chr 5/93 5,520
O/C 14x20 On the River Arun, Sussex Sby 1/93 1,725
O/B 11x14 Pastoral Landscape Wes 10/92 578

Weisse, Rudolf   Sws 1846-
O/B 19x13 Nubian Guard Sby 5/93 20,700

Weissenbruch, Jan Hendrik   Dut 1824-1903
W/Pa 12x18 Canal Scene Hnd 12/92 5,000
O/B/Pn 10x17 Canal Scene Hnd 12/92 2,800

Weissenbruch, Willem Johannes   Dut 1864-1941
* See 1993 Edition . . . .

Weisz, A.   Fr 1868-
O/C 27x21 Portrait Young Girl Fre 10/92 3,800

Welch, Ludmilla P.   Am 1867-1925
O/C/B 12x20 Grazing above the Bay But 3/93 1,430

Welch, Thaddeus   Am 1844-1919
O/C 20x36 San Geronimo Valley But 3/93 14,300
O/C 14x36 Grazing on the Coast 96 But 6/93 9,775
O/C 22x36 Cattle in Landscape 1918 Mor 11/92 9,000
O/C 10x18 Marin County Landscape But 6/93 2,588

Welk, Allen   Am 20C
G/B 17x23 Man on Horseback in Forest Wlf 12/92 175

Welling, James   1951-
Ph 5x4 Bushing--Starry Night 80 Chr 10/92 5,280
O/C 52x52 Untitled 1986 Chr 5/93 3,450
Ph/B 19x23 Untitled (HC 79) 1982 Chr 5/93 2,875
O/C 52x52 Untitled Sby 6/93 1,380

Welliver, Neil   Am 1929-
O/C 60x60 Vicky II '73 Chr 2/93 9,350

Wells, J. S. Sanderson   Br 1872-1955
* See 1993 Edition . . . .

Wendel, Theodore   Am 1857-1932
P/Pa/B 21x26 View from the Boathouse 96 Skn 11/92 990

Wendelborg, Herman   Am 1854-1924
O/C 24x36 Riders of the Plains Dum 2/93 2,500

Wendt, William   Am 1865-1946
O/C 25x30 The Bay Road 1930 Sby 3/93 51,750
O/C 28x36 Houses Along the Coast But 10/92 49,500
O/C 30x40 Ranch in the Valley But 10/92 38,500
O/C 30x36 The Malibu But 10/92 30,250
O/C 25x30 San Luis Obispo Landscape But 3/93 26,400
O/C 30x36 Quiet Brook 1923 But 3/93 25,300
O/C 32x36 On the Heights 1906 But 3/93 24,200
O/C 24x36 Dusk, California But 6/93 21,850
O/C 25x30 Midsummer 1928 But 10/92 20,900
O/C 18x28 Modjeska Canyon Mor 6/93 20,900
O/C 24x32 View over the Trees 1914 But 3/93 20,900
O/C 25x30 Spring 1916 But 10/92 19,800
O/C 24x32 Landscape Mor 11/92 19,000
O/C 28x36 Atmospheric Landscape Mor 2/93 17,000
O/C 19x23 Moonlight Landscape Mor 11/92 16,000
O/C 21x36 Afternoon's Golden Light But 3/93 15,400
O/C 24x20 Mountain Road But 3/93 15,400
O/C 28x36 Arroyo Seco But 6/93 13,800
O/C 20x36 California Landscape Mys 12/92 11,000
O/C 30x48 Woman by a Lake 95 But 10/92 11,000
O/C 14x18 Landscape - Rolling Hills Mor 11/92 7,000
O/B 10x14 Rocky Coast 1918 But 3/93 5,500

Wenger, John   Am 1887-1976
O/B 24x20 The Music Room Sby 3/93 1,495
W/Pa 15x21 Fantasia I 1946 Eld 8/93 99

Wenglein, Josef   Ger 1845-1919
* See 1993 Edition . . . .

Wenzell, Albert Beck   Am 1864-1917
O/C 26x20 Couple in Outdoor Restaurant But 6/93 1,265

Werenskiold, Erik Theodor   Nor 1855-1936
* See 1992 Edition . . . .

Weretshchagin, Piotr Petrovitc   Rus 1836-1886
* See 1991 Edition . . . .

Werner, Carl Friederich H.   Ger 1808-1894
O/Pn 23x19 Temple Ruins on the Nile 1867 Sby 5/93 5,750

Werner, Hermann   Ger 1816-1905
O/C 24x28 Stopping for a Drink 1876 Sby 2/93 8,913

Werner, Joseph (the Younger)   Sws 1637-1710
* See 1992 Edition . . . .

Wertheimer, Gustav   Aus 1847-1904
* See 1993 Edition . . . .

Wescott, Paul   Am 1904-1970
O/B 12x20 Friendship Sloop Ald 5/93 2,100
O/C 26x46 Pine Trees by the Shore Wes 3/93 1,320

Wesselmann, Tom   Am 1931-
MM/C 44x77 Great American Nude #89 1967 Chr 11/92 . . 165,000
O&L/Pn 56x56 Sill Life #14 1962 Chr 11/92 148,500
O/Al 60x90 Still Life with Abstract Painting Sby 5/93 68,500
O/C/B 30x51 Reclining Stockinged Nude No. 2 Sby 5/93 . . 57,500
E/St 70x78 Still Life Wildflowers, Fruit, Hat Sby 10/92 . . . 55,000
O/C 24x24 Great American Nude #6 + 23 84 Sby 5/93 . . 41,400
Pe&Lq/Pa 12x11 Great American Nude 65 Sby 11/92 . . . 18,150
O/C 16x15 Study for Smoker 1975 Sby 5/93 17,250
Lq,H&L/B 26x41 Blonde on the Beach 84 Chr 11/92 11,000
Lq&H/B 14x18 Woman in Green Blouse 85 Chr 5/93 9,200
Pe/Pa 5x6 Study for Nude Aquatint 76 Sby 2/93 6,900
Bp&Cp/Pa 4x6 Long Delayed Nude 73 Sby 10/92 5,500
Lq&H/B 4x9 Beautiful Kate #29 91 Chr 11/92 5,280
G&Pe/Pb 4x9 Beautiful Kate 92 Sby 2/93 5,175
Pe/Pa 4x4 Study for Helen Nude 81 Sby 2/93 4,025
Pe/Pa 11x9 Study for "Claire's Valentine" 69 Sby 2/93 . . . 2,185

Wessels, Glenn   Am 1895-1982
W&G/Pa 19x26 The Ferris Wheel But 10/92 1,540

Wessley, Anton   Aus 1848-
* See 1990 Edition . . . .

Wesson, Robert Shaw   Am 1902-1967
O/B 18x24 Country Lane Yng 5/93 450

248

O/B 18x24 Autumn Yng 5/93 400

West, Benjamin   Am 1738-1820
O/C 13x17 Hannah Presenting Samuel to Eli 1800 Sby 5/93   37,375
O/C 51x23 Adoration of the Kings 1794 Sby 5/93   34,500
K&P/Pa 5x9 Two Women Before Chieftain Chr 1/93   1,210

West, Michael
O/C 17x25 Untitled Sby 2/93   1,725

West, Raphael Lamar   Br 1769-1850
* See 1992 Edition

West, Samuel   Irs 1810-1867
O/C 37x29 Portrait of Two Sisters 1856 Chr 5/93   13,800

Westall, Richard   Eng 1765-1836
O/Cp 13x10 The Bird Nest Slo 7/93   1,900

Westchiloff, Constantin   Rus 1880-1945
O/C 27x36 Maine Dum 3/93   1,100
W&G/Pa 25x31 Spring Thaw on the Volga Brd 8/93   880

Westerbeek, Cornelis   Dut 1844-1903
* See 1993 Edition

Westermann, H. C.   Am 1922-
Bp/Pa 11x14 Untitled 76 Chr 11/92   1,100

Westin, Frederik   Swd 1782-1862
O/C 26x21 Portrait of King Oscar II Sby 1/93   4,313

Westmacott, S.   Am 19C
O/C 21x26 Niagara Falls 1857 Eld 4/93   1,430

Wetherill, B.
O/C 21x16 Caught! Dum 1/93   350

Wetherill, Elisha Kent Kane   Am 1874-1929
O/C 21x22 Mountainous Village Chr 12/92   1,100

Wetmore, Mary M.   Am 20C
O/Cb 8x10 Dutch Girl Knitting Mor 2/93   650

Wex, Willibald   Ger 1831-1892
O/C 26x37 Landscape with Rushing Stream '72 Fre 4/93 . .   2,200
O/C 26x38 Landscape with Figures Fre 4/93   1,700

Weyl, Max   Am 1837-1914
O/C 26x33 Rock Creek Park Slo 4/93   5,500
O/C 29x23 Spring Birches Slo 7/93   1,800
O/C 20x15 Birches, Late Autumn Slo 7/93   800
O/C/M 16x20 Spring Landscape with Apple Trees Wes 10/92   770
O/C 18x24 Sun Settles over the Marshes Mys 12/92   742
O/C 11x17 Path by the Potomac Wes 12/92   550
O/C 11x15 The Ploughed Fields 98 Skn 5/93   522
O/C 16x20 Landscape Dum 5/93   500

Whale, Robert Reginald   Can 1805-1887
O/C 21x35 Ferry Dock, Grand River Sbt 5/93   5,280

Whalley, J. K.   Br 19C
* See 1993 Edition

Wheatley, Francis   Eng 1747-1801
O/C 22x18 Coming from Market Sby 1/93   6,900
O/C 24x20 Portrait of a Young Lady Chr 5/93   4,370

Wheatley, G. H.
O/Cb 12x16 Full Sail Sel 12/92   280

Wheeler, Alfred   Br 1852-1932
* See 1993 Edition

Wheeler, Clifton
O/B 18x24 The Clearing Ald 9/92   475

Wheeler, J., Sen. of Bath   Eng 19C
* See 1993 Edition

Wheeler, John Alfred   Eng 1821-1903
O/C 20x24 Ladas Sby 6/93   4,888

Wheeler, Stewart
W/Pa 18x25 Beached Fishing Boats Ald 5/93   350
W/Pa 17x23 Tugboats Ald 5/93   300
O/B 11x13 Houses Ald 5/93   125
Y/Pa 17x9 Abstract City Ald 5/93   75
W/Pa 23x17 People in Garden Ald 5/93   75
W/Pa 13x9 White Palace Barbers Ald 5/93   75

Wheeler, William R.   Am 1832-1894
* See 1992 Edition

Wheelock, Mabel L.   Am 20C
G/Pa 19x15 Female Painting en Plein Air 1919 FHB 5/93 . .   1,000

Wheelwright, N. H.   Br 19C
W/Pa 11x17 The Fox Hunt 1887 Fre 4/93   650

Wheelwright, Rowland   Br 1870-1955
* See 1990 Edition

Wheelwright, W. H.   Br a 1857-1897
O/C 28x36 The White Horse 1858 Sby 6/93   5,175

Whipple, Seth Arca   Am 1855-1901
* See 1991 Edition

Whistler, James Abbott McNeill   Am 1834-1903
K&P/Pa 8x12 Giudecca-Winter: Grey and Blue Sby 5/93 . .   54,625
W/Pa 8x5 The Sands, Dieppe Sby 12/92   49,500
W/B 7x9 Mouth of the River Chr 12/92   16,500
Pl/Pa 7x5 Westpoint Cadets Sby 9/92   4,675
C/Pa 11x8 Seated Woman Hnz 5/93   410

Whitaker, Frederic   Am 1891-
W/Pa 16x22 The Inlet Slo 4/93   110

Whitaker, George William   Am 1841-1916
O/C 10x16 Still Life Pears, Grapes and Plums 97 Sby 3/93 .   1,380
O/C 13x20 Figure on a Path '97 Yng 5/93   1,200
O/C 22x28 Hay Wain Crossing a Bridge Skn 5/93   715
O/C 47x23 Forest Interior Mys 12/92   660
O/C 40x27 Forest Interior Mys 12/92   522
O/C 20x24 Early Steamship at Moonlite 96 Chr 5/93   460
O/B 4x6 Figures in a Landscape Mys 3/93   358

Whitaker, William   Am 1943-
* See 1990 Edition

Whitcomb, Jon   Am 1906-1988
W/Pa 14x14 Girl with Three Telephones Ih 5/93   750
G&R/Pa 14x10 Woman Holding a Glass of Beer Ih 11/92 . .   750

Whitcombe, Thomas   Br 1760-1824
* See 1993 Edition

White, A. A.   Am 20C
O/C 9x12 Hoxie House, Sandwich, MA Eld 8/93   248
O/C 12x18 Scorton Creek, East Sandwich, MA Eld 4/93 . . .   138

White, C. H.   Am 19C
O/C 27x22 Portrait of Mrs. R. Holmes White 1893 Hnd 10/92   150

White, Edith   Am 1855-1946
* See 1993 Edition

White, Edwin   Am 1817-1877
O/C/Pa 8x6 The Door is Shut 1875 Brd 2/93   248

White, Gabriella Antoinette   Am a 1880-1915
* See 1993 Edition

White, George   Am 1826-1872
* See 1993 Edition

White, George Harlow   Can 1817-1888
O/C 24x30 Boy and His Dog 1863 Sbt 5/93   1,408

White, Henry Cook   Am 1861-1952
* See 1991 Edition

White, Janet   Am 20C
O/C 50x34 Girl with Crocuses Fre 4/93   850

White, John   Br 1851-1933
* See 1992 Edition

White, Orrin A.   Am 1883-1969
O/C 22x28 Landscape Mor 2/93   9,000
O/C 26x32 Valley Landscape But 3/93   8,800
O/C 25x30 Brown Hillside Chr 5/93   4,370
O/C 24x24 Sierra Stream Mor 2/93   4,250
O/C 18x24 Arroyo Landscape Mor 11/92   4,000
O/C 24x22 Hillside Landscape But 3/93   3,575
O/C/B 20x24 Landscape with Stream Mor 6/93   3,575
O/B 12x16 Arroyo Landscape Mor 2/93   3,575
O/C 24x22 The Fiesta Mor 6/93   1,760
O/M 9x12 Landscape Mor 11/92   1,500
O/B 20x24 California Coast But 10/92   880

White, Robert   Am 20C
* See 1993 Edition

White, Thomas Gilbert   Am 1877-1939
* See 1990 Edition

White, Wade   Am 1909-
O/C 14x19 Sun and Wind 37 Sby 9/92   3,850

White, William   Am 1888-
O/C 32x34 Ships Docked in Harbour Sel 4/93   350

Whitefield, Edward   Am 1816-1892
O/C 14x18 Among the Berkshire Hills, Lee, MA Eld 4/93 . . .   1,980
O/B 10x14 Falls at Ithaca, New York Eld 4/93   220

Whitehead, Frederick William   Eng 1853-1938
* See 1990 Edition ....
Whiteley, T. J.   Am 19C
O/C 17x22 Still Life Fruit on Table: Pair 1892 Sel 9/92 825
Whiteside, Brian   Am 20C
O/C 24x36 Polo Match, Palm Springs Sby 6/93 1,840
Whiteside, Frank Reed   Am 1866-1929
* See 1992 Edition ....
Whitford, Richard   Br 19C
O/C 20x24 A Bay Stallion 1873 Chr 2/93 1,045
Whiting, Henry W.   Am 19C
O/C 14x24 Mist Lifting Off the Lake Doy 5/93 3,300
Whitmore, Coby   Am 1913-1988
* See 1993 Edition ....
Whittaker, James   Eng 1828-1876
* See 1990 Edition ....
Whittaker, John Barnard   Am 1836-1926
* See 1993 Edition ....
Whittemore, William John   Am 1860-1955
W/Pa 21x17 Portrait of a Young Girl 1903 Sby 9/92 2,475
Whittredge, Thomas Worthington   Am 1820-1910
O/C 14x22 Platte River Sby 12/92 33,000
O/B 10x15 View of the Hudson River Hnd 6/93 7,600
O/C 8x11 Under the Trees Sby 5/93 6,613
Whorf, John   Am 1903-1959
W/Pa 22x31 Trap Fishermen '53 Chr 12/92 9,900
W/Pa 30x39 Night-Time Boating Scene Eld 11/92 4,950
W/Pa 20x28 Returning Home Sleigh Ride Skn 9/92 3,410
W/Pa 20x24 Fishing Boat in Harbor 37 Hnd 5/93 3,400
W/B 22x30 Notre Dame Chr 3/93 3,220
W/Pa 15x21 Spring Comes to Parnal Street Chr 5/93 ... 2,990
W/Pa 15x23 The Dark Bow Brd 8/93 2,530
W&H/Pa 14x18 View with Bathers Skn 9/92 2,200
W/Pa/B 11x15 Street by Night Sby 3/93 1,725
W/Pa 14x21 Birches in Winter But 6/93 575
W/Pa 10x14 Snowy Landscape Yng 5/93 300
Wicar, Jean Baptiste   1762-1834
O/L 30x25 Officer of the Queen's Regiment Sby 1/93 ... 17,250
Wichera, Raimund   Aus 1862-
* See 1990 Edition ....
Wicker, John T.   Am 1860-1931
O/M 32x24 Two Nude Ladies at a Stream FHB 5/93 325
Widdas, Richard Dodd   Br 1826-1885
* See 1991 Edition ....
Wider, Wilhelm   Ger 1818-1884
* See 1990 Edition ....
Widerberg, Frans
O/C 36x26 Father Carrying Child Sby 2/93 6,440
O/C 35x39 Kuinne Sby 2/93 2,415
Widforss, Gunnar   Am 1879-1934
W/Pa 17x14 Grand Canyon But 3/93 11,000
W/Pa 16x22 Sunlight on Grand Canyon 1924 But 3/93 ... 11,000
W/Pa 20x18 Grand Canyon 1929 Sby 3/93 10,925
W/Pa 18x14 Merced River, Yosemite 1921 But 3/93 7,150
W/Pa 13x17 Rocky Coastline 1920 But 3/93 3,850
W/Pa 13x18 Old Houses, Stockholm 1915 Mor 6/93 990
Widgery, Frederick John   Br 1861-1942
G/Pa 10x14 The Moors Brd 2/93 660
Wieden, Wenzeslaus   Bel 1769-1814
Pt/Gl 20x26 Great Admiral Nelson Ships 1812 Eld 7/93 .. 46,200
Wiegand   Am 20C
O/C 24x30 Still Life '67 Hnd 5/93 200
Wiegand, Gustave Adolph   Am 1870-1957
O/C 20x24 Winter Landscape Sby 9/92 880
O/C 16x12 Autumn Landscape Sby 9/92 770
O/C 16x36 Lake in Autumn Skn 3/93 605
O/C 16x12 Landscape with Stream Dum 4/93 550
O/C 14x18 Farm Wagon in Landscape Dum 1/93 400
Wieghorst, Olaf   Am 1899-1988
O/C 14x12 Cheyenne Sentry 1977 Sby 12/92 17,600
O/C 30x36 On the Lookout Chr 3/93 5,750
Pe/Pa 6x8 Mare and Foal Sby 3/93 2,933

Wierusz-Kowalski, Alfred Von   Pol 1849-1915
* See 1991 Edition ....
Wiesenthal, Franz   Hun 1856-
O/C 31x24 Broken Doll Buggy 1893 But 11/92 11,000
Wiesner, Hella   Ger a 1910-
* See 1991 Edition ....
Wiggins, Carleton   Am 1848-1932
O/C 16x28 In the Palisades 1871 Chr 12/92 7,700
O/C 20x24 Sheep Grazing 1918 Sby 9/92 1,980
O/C 29x36 Evening on the Farm Chr 12/92 990
O/C 12x16 The Prize Bull Skn 3/93 605
Wiggins, Guy Carleton   Am 1883-1962
O/C 30x25 Fifth Avenue Winter Sby 9/92 25,300
O/C 35x30 Winter's Day at the Library Chr 9/92 24,200
O/C 25x30 Winter Along Central Park Sby 12/92 22,000
O/C 25x30 Washington Arch 1930 Wes 5/93 18,700
O/C 30x25 Red X Week, Winter Chr 3/93 18,400
O/C 28x24 Mid-Town Storm FHB 6/93 16,500
O/C 20x24 Washington Square in Winter Chr 5/93 16,100
O/Cb 12x9 Midtown, New York Sby 5/93 11,500
O/B 12x16 Central Park Skyline 1936 Sby 9/92 9,900
O/C 16x20 City Snowstorms 1934 Sby 3/93 8,913
O/Cb 5x3 Fifth Avenue and 26th Street 1927 Chr 3/93 .. 8,625
O/Cb 13x9 Christmas Eve at Old Trinity Doy 11/92 7,975
O/C 25x30 Quiet Day, Essex, Connecticut Sby 3/93 ... 6,900
O/B 8x10 5th Avenue at 42nd Street Sby 9/92 6,050
O/Cb 12x16 New York Skyline Sby 9/92 5,775
O/Cb 10x8 West Side, New York City Wes 12/92 5,500
O/C 12x16 Fifth Avenue Blizzard Chr 12/92 4,400
O/B 10x8 Broadway in Snow Chr 12/92 3,520
Wigle, Archie Palmer   Am 20C
* See 1993 Edition ....
Wigmana, Gerard   1673-1741
O/Pn 21x16 Female Nude Asleep on Bed Sby 1/93 10,638
Wiig, S.
O/C 25x34 Landscape Ald 9/92 85
Wijsmuller, Jan Hillebrand   Dut 1855-1925
* See 1991 Edition ....
Wilake, W.   Ger 20C
O/M 27x32 The Rhine Valley Fre 4/93 225
Wilcox, Frank   Am 1887-1964
W/Pa 10x14 Still Life with Apples Wlf 5/93 400
W/Pa 18x24 Frontiersman in Ambush Wlf 5/93 125
Wilcox, R. D.   Am 20C
O/C 27x39 Sunset over the Sea 1932 Wlf 9/92 900
Wilcox, William H.   Am 1831-
* See 1992 Edition ....
Wilda, Charles   Aus 1854-1907
* See 1992 Edition ....
Wilde, John   Am 1919-
O/M 10x12 Myself as Anatomist 47 Chr 9/92 3,850
Wildens, Jan   Flm 1586-1653
O/C 48x74 Figures and Cows by a River Sby 1/93 40,250
Wilder, Tom
* See 1993 Edition ....
Wiles, Irving Ramsay   Am 1861-1948
O/Pn 10x13 Along the Shore Sby 9/92 30,800
O/C 11x9 Thoughtful Chr 3/93 16,100
Wiles, Lemuel M.   Am 1826-1905
O/C 9x15 St. Helena, Valley of Genesee 1868 Chr 5/93 . 14,950
O/C 14x24 Hudson--West Point 1872 Chr 9/92 14,300
O/C 24x40 Coast of the Pacific 1881 But 3/93 4,675
Wiles, Walter G.   SAf 20C
O/M 19x25 Overlooking the Breakers Slo 7/93 750
Wiley, William T.   Am 1937-
W&P/Pa 14x11 Adore Well Open '73 But 10/92 2,750
W&/Pa 18x15 Open Conclusion, 1972 1972 But 4/93 ... 1,380
MM/C/B 11x14 Doodle '62 But 10/92 1,210
Fp/Pa 29x23 Untitled 1984 But 10/92 770
Wilford, Lauren F.
W/Pa 14x20 Soldier Meets Leprechaun Ald 5/93 240
Wilhelm, Roy   Am 1895-1954
W/Pa 19x29 Foley Cove Wlf 5/93 325

W/Pa 18x24 Beached Wtf 5/93 300
W/Pa 18x24 Early Evening Wtf 5/93 300
Wilke, Hannah   20C
  * See 1991 Edition . . . .
Wilkie, Robert D.   Am 1828-1903
  O/B 4x5 Sunset, Rockport, Mass. Yng 5/93 175
Wilkinson, Arthur Stanley   Br 20C
  * See 1992 Edition . . . .
Wilkinson, Ellen   Am 20C
  W/Pa 14x20 Kitchen Interior 1897 Mys 3/93 275
Wilkinson, H. R.   Br a 1907-1908
  W/Pa 8x10 Coastal Scenes: Pair Sel 9/92 150
**Wilkinson, Thomas Harrison   Can
1847-1929**
  W/Pa 22x15 Figures Beneath Natural Bridge Slo 4/93 400
  W/Pa 12x16 Village Scene Sbt 5/93 308
Willaert, Ferdenand   Bel 1823-1905
  O/C 33x45 Canal in Venice Fre 10/92 2,500
Willaert, Adam   Dut 1577-1664
  O/Pn 18x27 Fisherfolk Unloading Catch Sby 10/92 25,300
Willaerts, Isaac   Dut 1620-1693
  * See 1990 Edition . . . .
Willcock, George Barrell   Br 1811-1852
  * See 1993 Edition . . . .
Wille, Johann Georg   Ger 1715-1808
  * See 1992 Edition . . . .
Wille, Pierre Alexandre   1748-1821
  K&S/Pa 6x5 Portrait of an Old Man 1774 Chr 1/93 1,320
Willemart, Louise   Fr 1863-
  O/C 18x15 An Elegant Lady with Pink Rose Chr 2/93 2,420
Willems, Florent   Bel 1823-1905
  * See 1992 Edition . . . .
Willems, L.   Dut 19C
  O/Pn 10x11 The Music Lesson Slo 5/93 500
Willemsens, Abraham   a 1627-1672
  O/Pn 21x30 Sportsman Asking His Way Chr 1/93 33,000
Willenech, Michel   Fr -1891
  O/C 15x25 Houses Along a River Slo 4/93 725
Willet, G.   Am 19C
  O/C 14x10 Landscape with Fisherman Hnd 10/92 550
Willett   Am 20C
  O/C 26x32 Forest Clearing Hnd 9/92 250
Willey, Philo Levi "Chief"   Am 1886-
  O/M 16x20 Winter Landscape 1975 Slo 5/93 175
  O/M 16x20 Landscape with House, Trees 1975 Slo 5/93 95
Willia   Sco 19C
  * See 1992 Edition . . . .
William   Hun
  O/B 12x16 Floral Still Life Dum 4/93 750
William, John Haynes   Br 19C
  * See 1990 Edition . . . .
Williams   Am 20C
  O/C 36x26 Portrait Lou 12/92 50
Williams, Albert Henry   Br 20C
  O/Pn 12x16 Thatched Cottage Hnd 5/93 1,000
Williams, Alfred Walter   Br 1824-1905
  * See 1991 Edition . . . .
Williams, Charles R.   Am 20C
  O/B 6x8 Landscape Mor 2/93 125
Williams, E.   Br 19C
  W/Pa 18x14 Boy in a Hat 1872 Hnd 12/92 350
Williams, Edward Charles   Eng 1807-1881
  O/Pn 9x10 The Old Mill - Dedham Wtf 9/92 475
**Williams, Frederick Ballard   Am
1871-1956**
  O/B 4x6 Landscape: Two Hnz 5/93 400
**Williams, Frederick Dickinson   Am
1829-1915**
  O/C 18x31 Walk along a Country Path 1875 Chr 12/92 3,520
Williams, George A.   Am 1875-1932
  I/Pa 6x9 The Boy Spy Yng 2/93 250
Williams, Gluyas   Am 1888-1982
  PI/Pa 8x8 Man Grows Impatient Ih 5/93 425
Williams, Graham   Br 19C
  O/C 36x25 Landscape Hnd 5/93 450

Williams, Helen   Am 20C
  O/C 16x20 Summer Clouds (North Carolina) Sby 3/93 1,725
Williams, John Haynes   Br 19C
  * See 1992 Edition . . . .
Williams, John L. Scott   Am 1877-1976
  O/B 12x16 Woman on a Ledge Yng 2/93 225
Williams, Mary Belle   Am 1873-1928
  * See 1993 Edition . . . .
Williams, Neil   20C
  * See 1992 Edition . . . .
Williams, Paul A.   Am 1934-
  O/C 20x16 Summer Rapture Lou 3/93 1,650
  O/C 12x9 Reve Wes 10/92 1,430
  O/C 12x9 Wildflowers Wes 10/92 1,210
  O/C 19x15 Summer Rapture Sel 9/92 700
Williams, Penry   Br 1798-1885
  O/C 24x36 River Landscape at Sunset Chr 2/93 5,500
Williams, Sheldon   Am 19C
  W&G/Pa 13x23 Masked Highwayman 1878 Hnd 12/92 150
Williams, Terrick   Br 1860-1936
  * See 1992 Edition . . . .
Williams, Virgil   Am 1830-1886
  O/B 10x13 Shepherd Boy 65 But 3/93 1,540
Williams, Walter   Br 1835-1906
  O/C 31x25 Wharfedale 1876 Sby 5/93 6,900
  O/C 6x9 Coastline Scenes of Wales: Pair Dum 6/93 1,700
Williamson, John   Am 1826-1885
  O/C 22x16 Trout Brook, Bushkill, New York 82 Chr 3/93 . . . 5,750
  O/C 14x24 Landscape with Mountains and River Sby 3/93 . 2,530
**Williamson, William Henry   Eng
1820-1898**
  O/B 6x11 Ships Off Dover Yng 5/93 1,000
  O/C 10x18 Sailing Off the Cliffs of Dover 1882 Wes 3/93 . . . 880
Williot, P.   Bel 19C
  O/C 22x33 Ships on Stormy Seas 1874 Chr 10/92 1,650
Willis, A. V.   Br 19C
  * See 1993 Edition . . . .
Willis, Henry Brittan   Eng 1810-1884
  * See 1993 Edition . . . .
Willis, Thomas   Am 1850-1912
  O/C 22x30 Depicting a Sailing Vessel Eld 7/93 1,718
  MM&O/C 22x32 Clipper Ship Fre 10/92 700
  MM&O/C 22x31 Sailboat Fre 10/92 700
  MM&O/C 15x26 American Steam Yacht Eld 7/93 385
Willmann, Michael Lucas Leo.   1630-1706
  O/Pn 21x15 Christ on the Cross Sby 5/93 8,913
Willroider, Ludwig   Ger 1845-1910
  O/C 40x28 Forest Rain Shower Sby 5/93 20,700
  O/C 17x20 Forest Interior 1871 Sby 10/92 3,575
Wilmarth, Christopher   Am 1943-1987
  * See 1993 Edition . . . .
Wilms, Peter Joseph   Ger 1814-1892
  * See 1993 Edition . . . .
Wilner, Marie   Am 1910-
  * See 1993 Edition . . . .
Wilson   Am 20C
  O/C 35x28 Portrait of a Woman Wtf 4/93 100
Wilson   Eng 19C
  O/C 22x27 Feeding the Calves Slo 7/93 425
Wilson, Ashton   Am 1880-
  O/C 24x20 Peasant Girl in Twilight Yng 2/93 750
Wilson, David Forrester   Br 1873-1950
  * See 1992 Edition . . . .
Wilson, Donald Roller   Am 20C
  O/C 40x32 Full Moon 1976 Sby 5/93 17,250
  O/C 36x30 Jimmy had been instructed 1986 But 4/93 9,200
Wilson, Francis Vaux   Am 1874-1938
  * See 1993 Edition . . . .
Wilson, J. P.   Am 20C
  O/Cb 12x16 Glimpse of the Sea 1940 Skn 9/92 1,100
Wilson, Jane   Am 1924-
  O/C 30x40 Snapdragons and Apples Sby 3/93 1,840
  W/Pa 4x6 Purple Anemones Skn 11/92 165
Wilson, John   Br 1774-1855
  O/C 25x30 Two Figures by a Stream 1843 Sby 1/93 4,025

Wilson, M. B.   Am 19C
* See 1993 Edition . . . .
Wilson, Mary Loomis   20C
* See 1991 Edition . . . .
Wilson, Raymond C.   Am 1906-1972
W/Pa 15x23 Horse Corral But 10/92 550
W/Pa 19x25 Houses in Landscape Mor 2/93 550
W/Pa 18x29 Houses in Landscape Mor 6/93 220
Wilson, Richard   Br 1714-1782
O/C 25x29 Figures in Landscape Mys 12/92 990
Wilson, Ronald York   Can 1907-1984
O/B 24x8 Amorphus Figure #4, 1950 Sbt 5/93 660
O/B 12x9 Striped Skirt Sbt 5/93 396
Wilson, Solomon   Am 1896-1974
O/C 46x41 Province Town Pier Scene Mys 12/92 3,080
O/C 16x12 The White Stump Wes 3/93 275
Wilson, Thomas Walter   Br 1851-
* See 1993 Edition . . . .
Wilson, Virginia F.   20C
O/Pn 8x6 Portrait Lady Gentleman: Pair Slo 5/93 150
Wimar, Carl   Am 1828-1862
O/C 10x12 On the Warpath 1856 Sby 5/93 57,500
Wimmer, Conrad   Ger 1844-1905
O/C 16x21 Return Home of the Hunter Chr 10/92 . . 8,250
Wimperis, Edmund Morison   Br 1835-1900
* See 1993 Edition . . . .
Winchell, Paul   Am 20C
O/C 22x19 Portrait of a Young Girl Wtf 5/93 200
Winck, Johann Amandus   Ger 1748-1817
O/C 13x10 Still Life Rose, Morning Glories Sby 1/93 . . 9,775
Windels, Carl Friedr   Ger 1869-1920
O/Pn 18x15 Docked Fishing Boats 1907 Slo 5/93 350
Windmaier, Anton   Ger 1840-1896
* See 1993 Edition . . . .
Winfield, Rodney   Am 20C
W/M 12x9 Spiritual Marriage Sel 12/92 2,700
Wingate, James Lawton (Sir)   Br 1846-1924
O/C 14x10 Bunny Trail/Scottish Landscape 67 Skn 9/92 330
Wingfield, James Digman   Br -1872
* See 1992 Edition . . . .
Winhart, A.   Ger 19C
O/C 19x15 The Chess Game Mys 12/92 715
Winner, William E.   Am 1815-1883
* See 1992 Edition . . . .
Winslow, Sylvia   Am 20C
O/Pn 19x24 Evening at the Mojave Desert 1945 Fre 4/93 . . . 350
Winter, Alice Beach   Am 1877-1970
O/C 16x30 Pink Flowers Fre 4/93 750
Winter, Andrew   Am 1892-1958
O/C 14x20 Maine Lighthouse Brd 2/93 1,045
Winter, Charles Allan   Am 1869-1942
O/C 26x30 Woman in Red in Landscape Skn 5/93 4,675
O/C 30x26 Diana, Portrait of a Woman Skn 5/93 3,300
O/C 20x24 Landscape with Distant Houses Sby 3/93 . . . 1,265
O/C 20x24 Rocky Coastal View Mys 3/93 275
O/B 10x14 Landscape with House Yng 5/93 200
Winter, Fritz   Ger 1905-1978
* See 1992 Edition . . . .
Winter, Lumen Martin   Am 1908-
O/C 24x38 Thunderhead Hnz 5/93 120
Winterhalter, Franz Zavier   Ger 1806-1873
* See 1991 Edition . . . .
Winters, Robin
* See 1993 Edition . . . .
Winters, Terry   Am 1949-
O/L 87x70 Theophrastus' Garden (1) Chr 2/93 79,200
O/C 46x60 Untitled 1983 Chr 11/92 33,000
W&H/Pa 21x16 Untitled 1986 Chr 5/93 1,955
Wire, Melville T.   Am 20C
O/B 10x14 Scotch Broom and Sage Hnz 5/93 360
Wirsum, Karl   Am 1939-
O/C 27x19 Asparagus Sby 6/93 1,150
I/Pa 18x13 Draw Dick Tracy the Hard Way Hnd 9/92 200

Wisby, Jack   Am 1870-1940
O/C 16x28 Grazing Cows But 3/93 1,980
O/C/B 13x22 Bolinas Landscape But 6/93 1,150
O/C 20x24 Yosemite Valley But 6/93 1,035
Wise, Kurt
O/C 9x12 Deer Grazing Ald 9/92 65
Wisinger-Florian, Olga   Aus 1844-1926
* See 1992 Edition . . . .
Wissing, Willem   1656-1687
* See 1992 Edition . . . .
Wistehuff, Revere F.   Am 1900-1971
O/C 34x24 Two Boys in Front of Church Ih 11/92 1,700
Witherington, William Frederic   Br 1785-1865
* See 1991 Edition . . . .
Withrow, Evelyn A.   Am 1858-1928
W/Pa 3x5 Hazy Coastal Mor 6/93 385
Witkowski, Karl   Am 1860-1910
O/C 24x28 Secrets Sby 3/93 8,625
O/C 24x20 Street Urchins Chr 5/93 8,625
O/C 21x15 Playing a Tune Sel 9/92 7,000
O/C 19x24 Two Boys with Harmonica Chr 9/92 4,400
O/C 22x14 Young Boy Taking a Bite Chr 12/92 3,300
Witters, Nell   Am 20C
O/Ab 18x15 Girl with Doll Lou 3/93 600
O/C 17x13 Portrait of a Girl Hnd 5/93 600
Wittmack, Edgar F.   Am 1894-1956
O/C 30x27 Pilgrim Wondering: Shot Turkey? 1934 Ih 11/92 . 1,300
Wizon, Tod   20C
* See 1993 Edition . . . .
Wodzinski, V. Serge   Am 20C
O/C 24x36 Winter Landscape Hnd 12/92 350
Woelfle, Arthur   Am 1873-1936
* See 1993 Edition . . . .
Wohner, Louis   Ger 1888-
* See 1993 Edition . . . .
Wojnarowicz, David   1954-1992
E,I&L/M 48x72 Untitled 1983 Chr 11/92 11,000
A&L/M 48x48 Map Face 84 Chr 2/93 7,700
A/B 30x22 The Burning House 1982 Sby 10/92 3,300
Wolcott, Harold C.   Am 20C
O/C 13x20 Gathering Maple Syrup Mys 3/93 440
Wolf, Augusto   It 19C
O/C 36x29 Odalisca 1885 Sby 5/93 6,325
Wolf, Franz Xavier   Aus 1896-1989
O/Pn 20x18 Stille Stunde Sby 1/93 2,875
Wolf, Hamilton A.   Am 1883-1967
O/M 48x36 Untitled Abstract Mor 6/93 1,045
O/B 25x19 Automation Mor 6/93 825
Wolf, Joseph   Br 1820-1899
* See 1993 Edition . . . .
Wolfe, Edward   Br 1897-1982
* See 1991 Edition . . . .
Wolff, Gustave   Am 1863-1934
O/C 16x12 Landscape at Dusk Sel 4/93 500
Wolff, Henrik   Dan 19C
* See 1993 Edition . . . .
Wolff, Robert Jay   Am 1905-
* See 1992 Edition . . . .
Wolffort, Artus   1581-1641
* See 1992 Edition . . . .
Wolfle, Franz Xavier   Aus 1896-1989
O/Pn 7x6 Bavarian Gentleman: Three Sby 1/93 2,185
O/B 7x6 Man Smoking a Pipe Dum 8/93 1,200
Wolfson, Irving   1899-
W/Pa 13x19 Lower East Side Markets: Pair Doy 11/92 . . . 605
Wolfson, William   Am 1894-
* See 1993 Edition . . . .
Wollaston, John   Eng a 1738-1775
* See 1993 Edition . . . .
Wollon, William Barnes   Br 1857-1936
O/B 6x12 Boer War 1902 Fre 4/93 900
Wolpert, Elizabeth Davis
O/C 14x20 Country Monolith Ald 5/93 60

Wols (Alfred Otto W. Schulze) 1913-1951
W&P/Pa 11x13 Ohne Titel Chr 11/92 39,600
Wolsky, Milton Am 1916-
G/Pa 7x16 Deep Sea Diver Ih 11/92 225
Wolstenholme, Charles Dean (Jr.) Br 1798-1883
O/C 9x12 Harriers on Scent; and The Kill (2) Chr 6/93 3,450
Wolstenholme, Dean (Sr.) Eng 1757-1837
O/C 12x16 Meet Matching Green; Death-Fox (2) Chr 6/93 . . 11,500
O/C 12x16 View of Hatfield Broad Oak Chr 6/93 7,475
O/C 12x16 Fox Crossing the Country Chr 6/93 6,900
O/C 14x16 Gentleman on his Bay Hunter Chr 6/93 3,450
Wolter, Jan Hendrik Dut 1873-1952
* See 1991 Edition . . . .
Wolters, Charles Am 1936-
A/Pa 26x19 T129/80 Hnd 5/93 100
Woltze, Berthold Ger 1829-1896
* See 1993 Edition . . . .
Wonner, Paul Am 1924-
O/C 22x18 Model by the Studio Window But 4/93 11,500
O/B 10x12 Man in Profile But 10/92 6,050
W/Pa 17x14 Model Leaning Against a Sofa But 4/93 4,600
A&P/Pa 18x17 #5 View with Double Rainbow But 10/92 . . 1,650
W&G/Pa 12x18 Oranges and Lemons But 4/93 1,265
G/Pa 23x30 Untitled But 4/93 1,092
Wontner, William Clarke Br a 1879-1912
O/C 25x21 Young Woman in Shawl Chr 5/93 46,000
Wood, Charles Haigh Br 1856-1927
* See 1991 Edition . . . .
Wood, Edith Am 20C
O/C 20x25 Bearded Gentleman Fre 4/93 100
Wood, George Albert Am 1845-1910
O/B 14x19 Connecticut Landscape Mys 3/93 248
Wood, Grant Am 1891-1942
C,Pe&K/Pa 24x19 Booster 1936 Chr 5/93 112,500
Pe&Cp/B 12x15 Tame and Wild Flowers: Two Chr 5/93 . . . 46,000
O/B 13x15 Autumn View 1926 Slo 4/93 9,000
Wood, Harrie Morgan Am 1902-1974
O/C 27x22 Calla Lily in Clay Pot Lou 6/93 300
Wood, Lewis John Br 1813-1901
O/C/M 22x16 Cathedrals at Rouen, Chartres: Pair Sby 2/93 . 5,060
Wood, Ogden Am 1851-1912
O/C 37x49 Peasants Driving Carts Sel 9/92 4,500
Wood, Robert Am 1889-1979
O/C 25x30 High Tide Mor 6/93 8,250
O/C 30x36 Mountain Landscape Lou 9/92 5,000
O/C 20x24 San Simeon Coast 54 But 6/93 4,600
O/C 25x30 Pacific Shores '44 Mor 2/93 3,250
O/C/B 20x30 Autumn Landscape Dum 11/92 3,000
O/C 25x30 Mountain Landscape Lou 12/92 2,500
O/C 24x29 Sunlight in Mountains Dum 1/93 2,000
O/C 25x30 Mountain Stream Skn 9/92 1,760
O/C 25x30 Mountainous Landscape Mys 12/92 1,760
O/B 12x16 March Wind Mor 11/92 850
O/C 20x30 Autumn Landscape Hnd 9/92 800
O/Cd 8x10 Farm Wlf 5/93 800
O/Cb 12x16 Landscape Lou 9/92 500
Wood, Robert E. Am 1926-1979
W/Pa 30x22 The Tall White Tree 1951 Mor 6/93 495
Wood, Stanley Am 1894-
W/Pa 14x21 Cowboy in Corral 44 Mor 11/92 250
Wood, Thomas Waterman Am 1823-1903
O/C 28x20 Fresh Eggs 1881 Chr 12/92 121,000
O/C 30x20 Neglecting Trade 1883 Chr 3/93 51,750
W/Pa 28x22 The Doubtful Coin 1881 Sby 5/93 25,300
Wood, William John Can 1877-1954
O/C 27x34 Summer's Farewell, Ontario 1933 Sbt 11/92 . . 2,640
O/B 5x7 Barn in Landscape Sbt 5/93 660
O/B 17x23 Landscape 1950 Sbt 5/93 242
Wood, William Thomas Eng 1877-
O/C 12x10 Pink and White Roses 1932 Chr 10/92 1,100
Wood, Worden Am 20C
W&G/Pa 14x21 Aircraft Carrier at Sea Fre 4/93 160
Woodard, Mabel Am 1877-1945
O/M 17x21 Tree Symphony Sel 9/92 1,300

Woodbury, Charles Herbert Am 1864-1940
O/C 17x21 Maine Coastal Landscape Eld 8/93 2,420
W/Pa 12x22 The Wave Yng 5/93 1,800
O/C 20x26 Walking in April Showers Skn 3/93 1,320
W/Pa 15x21 Port de France, Martinique Yng 2/93 850
W&H/Pa 12x17 Village at the Foot of Mountains Skn 11/92 . . 522
O/C 17x22 Hunter's Moon Ald 9/92 350
Woodcock, Hartwell L. Am 1853-1929
O/C 20x16 Winter Snow Scene Mys 3/93 220
Woodcock, Percy Franklin Can 1855-1936
O/Pn 7x12 Paysage Sbt 5/93 1,320
O/Pn 8x11 Willow Tree Near Chateauguay Sbt 11/92 1,320
Woodhouse, H. J. Br 19C
* See 1993 Edition . . . .
Woodhouse, William Br 1857-1935
* See 1993 Edition . . . .
Woods, Henry Br 1846-1921
O/C 28x39 Venetian Fan Seller 1882 Sby 2/93 28,750
O/Pa/Pa 15x18 On the Seashore 1880 Hnd 10/92 1,500
Woodside, John Archibald (Sr.) Am 1781-1852
O/C 25x32 Horse and Trainer Chr 6/93 32,200
Woodward, Mabel May Am 1877-1945
O/C 25x30 Afternoon at the Playground Sby 12/92 27,500
O/C 20x16 The Favorite Doll Chr 12/92 24,200
Woodward, Stanley Wingate Am 1890-1970
O/Ab 16x20 Florida Beach Scene Eld 8/93 1,210
W&H/Pa 11x15 In the Everglades Skn 9/92 302
Woog, Raymond Fr 1875-
* See 1990 Edition . . . .
Wool, Christopher 1955-
Pt&A/Al 72x48 Untitled 1989 Sby 11/92 33,000
Pt/Al 96x72 Untitled (P72) 1988 Chr 2/93 19,800
Pt/Al 72x48 Untitled (P.65) 1988 Chr 11/92 18,150
Pt/Al 72x48 Untitled '86 Chr 11/92 17,600
Pt&MM/Al 48x32 Untitled 87 Sby 10/92 12,100
Pt&A/Al 36x24 Untitled 1989 Sby 10/92 10,450
Pt&A/Al 48x24 Untitled (Study #14) '87 Sby 11/92 . . . 10,450
Pt/Pa 40x26 Untitled 1988 Sby 10/92 4,950
Woolf, Samuel Johnson Am 1880-1948
* See 1993 Edition . . . .
Woolmer, Alfred Joseph Br 1805-1892
* See 1991 Edition . . . .
Woolrych, Francis Humphrey Am 1868-
O/C 40x30 Mother and Child But 6/93 1,150
Woolsey, Carl Am 1902-
* See 1993 Edition . . . .
Wooster, * Am 20C**
O/B 8x10 Still Lifes Fruit: Pair Paintings Sby 9/92 1,320
Wooster, Austin C. Am 19C
O/C 13x18 Still Life: Lemonade, Cake 1903 Sby 3/93 4,888
O/C 14x18 Still Life with Apples 1902 Fre 10/92 1,350
Wootherspoon, William Wallace Am 1821-1888
O/B 10x3 Looking Down Alley (2) Mys 3/93 468
Wootton, John Br 1683-1764
* See 1991 Edition . . . .
Wopfner, Joseph Aus 1843-1927
O/C 34x56 Ave Maria/Lake View Skn 9/92 36,300
O/B 16x23 In the Orchard Sby 10/92 9,350
Wores, Theodore Am 1859-1939
O/C 72x48 Entertainment w/Musicians Sby 12/92 55,000
W/Pa 11x14 Harbor Scene Lou 6/93 850
Worms, Jules Fr 1832-1924
O/C 24x32 Le Nouveau Qui Arrive Sby 10/92 28,600
O/C 18x15 The Connoisseur Sby 2/93 8,913
O/Pn 18x22 The Courtship Chr 5/93 6,900
O/Pn 14x11 Conversation in a Village Square Chr 10/92 . . 2,420
Worster Am 19C
O/B 8x10 Fruit Still Life: Pair Yng 5/93 600
Worth, Thomas Am 1834-1917
* See 1993 Edition . . . .

Worthington, W. G. Br 19C
O/B 8x6 Chickens Dum 12/92 500
Wostry, Carlo It 1865-1943
O/C 25x21 The Grandstand 1898 Sby 5/93 20,700
Wouters, Frans Flm 1614-1658
* See 1993 Edition . . . .
Wouwerman, Philips Dut 1619-1668
O/Pn 16x19 Customs House on River Maas Sby 1/93 . . 442,500
O/Pn 12x15 Interior of a Stable Sby 5/93 14,950
O/Pn 13x16 Travelers/Wagon and Horseback Sby 5/93 . . 10,350
Wouwermans, Pieter Dut 1623-1682
* See 1992 Edition . . . .
Wright, George Br 1860-1942
O/C 7x10 Polo Match Sby 6/93 6,325
O/C 9x13 On the Scent Doy 5/93 5,500
Wright, George Hand Am 1873-1951
* See 1993 Edition . . . .
Wright, Gilbert Scott Br 1880-1958
O/C 12x18 Outside the George Inn Sby 6/93 3,738
Wright, James Couper Am 1906-1969
W&Pe/Pa 14x22 Hills of New Mexico 1934 But 6/93 1,150
W/Pa 21x29 Landscape Near Lake '58 Mor 6/93 275
Wright, John Am a 1860-1869
* See 1992 Edition . . . .
Wright, Joseph Am 1756-1793
* See 1993 Edition . . . .
Wright, Joseph (of Derby) Br 1734-1797
* See 1990 Edition . . . .
Wright, R. Stephens Am 1903-
O/C 30x38 Sailboats Along the Beach But 10/92 2,200
O/C 30x38 Sierra Lake But 10/92 1,320
O/C 30x38 Riding Along the Ridge But 10/92 1,210
Wright, Rufus Am 1832-
* See 1993 Edition . . . .
Wright, Stanton MacDonald Am 1890-1973
O/C 30x24 Cubist Still Life 54 Chr 3/93 21,850
Wright, W. Am 20C
O/C 22x38 White Mountain Landscape Yng 5/93 200
Wrinch, Mary Evelyn Can 1877-1969
* See 1992 Edition . . . .
Wtewael, Joachim Dut 1566-1638
O/C 61x45 Adam and Eve Chr 5/93 717,500
Wtewael, Peter Dut 1596-1660
O/Pn 20x30 Homo Bulla: Boy Blowing Bubbles Chr 5/93 . . . 5,175
Wuchters, Abraham 1610-1682
* See 1993 Edition . . . .
Wuermer, Carl Am 1900-1982
* See 1993 Edition . . . .
Wuerpel, Edmund Henri Am 1866-1958
* See 1992 Edition . . . .
Wunder, Wilhelm Ernst 1713-1787
* See 1993 Edition . . . .
Wunderlich, Paul Ger 1927-
A&Pe/Pa 34x27 Target Figure with Anton 72 Sby 6/93 3,450
Wunnenberg, Carl Ger 1850-1929
* See 1992 Edition . . . .
Wusmuller, J. H. Ger 20C
O/C 16x24 European Village Scene Eld 8/93 1,320
Wuste, Louise Heuser Am 1803-1875
O/C/B 20x16 Woman in a Green Dress 1853 Wes 3/93 . . . 330
Wyant, Alexander Helwig Am 1836-1892
O/C/Pn 37x49 Summer Haunt Sby 5/93 35,650
O/C 20x28 Lake George 1872 Sby 5/93 21,850
O/C 10x14 Autumn Landscape Chr 3/93 4,370
O/C 16x20 A Wooded Landscape Chr 5/93 4,025
O/C 8x14 Figures and Cattle in Landscape '84 Dum 12/92 . 2,100
O/C 12x17 Tonal Landscape with Pond Yng 5/93 1,700
W&G/Pa/B 17x24 Cottage by the Marsh Skn 11/92 1,650
O/C 12x16 Autumnal Wooded Landscape Eld 8/93 770
O/B 10x8 Mountainous Landscape Mys 3/93 385
O/C 12x18 Extensive Landscape Mys 12/92 330
Wyatville, Jeffrey (Sir) Eng 1766-1840
I,S&W/Pa 12x9 Design for a Chandelier Slo 7/93 475

Wydeveld, Arnoud Am a 1855-1862
O/C 24x18 Brook Trout in a Landscape Skn 3/93 1,100
O/C 14x22 Still Life Pineapple, Grapes, Plums Chr 5/93 . . . 1,093
Wyeth, Andrew Am 1917-
W/Pa 22x26 From My Window Sby 12/92 176,000
W/Pa/B 22x30 Rough Pasture Sby 12/92 66,000
W/Pa 18x30 Wagon Blue Wes 5/93 50,600
W/Pa 18x22 The White Skiff Sby 5/93 28,750
G/Pa 11x17 A Winter Scene Skn 3/93 8,800
W,G&Pe/Pa 9x12 The Trail of the Fox Sby 9/92 4,400
Pe/Pa 13x16 Young Lady of Maine Chr 12/92 2,750
Wyeth, Caroline Am 1909-
* See 1993 Edition . . . .
Wyeth, Henriette Am 1907-
* See 1992 Edition . . . .
Wyeth, Jamie Am 1946-
W/Pa 22x30 Coast Guard Anchor 1982 Sby 12/92 34,100
W/Pa 18x22 New Calf Chr 12/92 9,900
MM/Pa 30x22 Eagles, London Sby 5/93 6,900
Wyeth, Newell Convers Am 1882-1945
O/C 24x16 I Ain't Through with You Yet Chr 5/93 27,600
Wyld, William Br 1806-1889
* See 1993 Edition . . . .
Wylie, Robert Am 1839-1877
O/C 22x26 Card Players in Brittany Sby 5/93 46,000
Wyllie, Charles William Br 1853-1923
* See 1992 Edition . . . .
Wyllie, Charlotte Major Br a 1872-1888
O/C 35x26 The Blue Ribbon Sby 10/92 7,700
Wyman, M. A. Am 20C
* See 1993 Edition . . . .
Wynants, Jan Dut 1630-1684
* See 1991 Edition . . . .
Xavery, Jacob 1736-1769
* See 1992 Edition . . . .
Xceron, John Am 1890-1967
* See 1993 Edition . . . .
Ximenes, Ettore It 1855-1927
O/C 20x16 Procession with Altar Boys Fre 4/93 3,000
Xul Solar, Alejandro Arg 1887-1963
W&I/Pa 11x15 Mundo 1925 Sby 5/93 51,750
W,Y&Pe/Pa 14x11 Patria B 1925 Chr 11/92 38,500
Yamagnchi, K. Am 20C
O/C 18x24 River Inlet Hnd 10/92 160
Yankel, Jacques 1920-
* See 1993 Edition . . . .
Yarber, Robert Am 1943-
A/C 72x122 Floaters 1985 Chr 11/92 5,500
Yard, Sydney Janis Am 1855-1909
W&Pe/Pa 11x16 Grazing Sheep 89 But 3/93 2,090
W/Pa 11x15 Figures by the Mill Mor 2/93 1,000
W/Pa 11x8 Sheep Grazing 95 But 6/93 460
Yarz, Edmond Fr 20C
* See 1992 Edition . . . .
Yates, Cullen Am 1866-1945
O/C 12x16 Rocky Coastal Inlet Doy 5/93 2,420
O/C 12x16 Off the Maine Coast Fre 4/93 1,100
Yates, Thomas Br -1796
* See 1991 Edition . . . .
Yates, William Br 19C
O/C 30x50 The Reutrn Home Chr 5/93 2,990
Yatrides, Georges Fr 1931-
O/C 26x20 Street Scene 60 Chr 5/93 1,150
Yeckley, Norman Am 1914-
O/C 25x30 Landscape Mor 2/93 950
Yektai, Manoucher Am 1922-
O/C 32x36 Still Life with Pineapple '68 Dum 6/93 350
Yelland, Raymond Dabb Am 1848-1900
O/C/B 9x12 Landscape with Haystacks But 3/93 2,200
Yens, Karl Am 1868-1945
O/C 38x40 Her Finishing Touches 1921 But 3/93 8,250
O/C 33x36 Her Halloween Party But 6/93 1,840
O/B 10x14 San Gabriel Mission 1912 Mor 6/93 1,540
O/C/B 18x24 In the Sierras 1919 But 6/93 805
G/Pa 8x12 Crucifixion-After Dean Cornwell Mor 11/92 350

Yepes, Tomas   Spa a 1642-1674
* See 1991 Edition ....
Yesteban, Angel Lizcano   Spa 1846-1929
O/C 28x51 At the Well 1889 Sby 10/92 8,525
Yewell, George Henry   Am 1830-1923
* See 1992 Edition ....
Yglesias, Vincent Philip   Eng 1845-1911
O/C 34x45 Durham Castle Wes 10/92 880
Yip, Richard   Am 1919-1981
W/Pa 14x21 San Francisco Bay Mor 2/93 650
Ykens, Frans   1601-1693
O/Cp 16x12 Roses, Carnations, Tuilp: Pair Chr 5/93 66,300
Yoakum, Joseph E.   Am 1886-1973
Fp,Bp&Y/Pa 12x18 Australia Hnd 10/92 1,700
Yohn, Frederick C.   Am 1875-1933
O/B 22x16 Military Officer with Gun Ih 5/93 600
Yokers, Herman (Jr.)   Am 20C
W/Pa 20x29 Farm by the Road 55 Hnd 12/92 150
Yon, Edmond Charles Joseph   Fr 1836-1897
O/C 11x14 Paysage a la Riviere Sby 1/93 1,495
York, William   Am 19C
* See 1993 Edition ....
Yorke, William G.   Am 1817-1883
O/C 25x36 Fishing Schooner "Mary H. Dyer" Eld 7/93 14,850
O/C 26x36 Schooner "Mary E. Douglas" 1875 Eld 7/93 ... 11,000
Yorke, William Howard   Br 1858-1913
* See 1993 Edition ....
Yoshida, Hiroshi   Jap 1876-1950
W/Pa 20x13 Hanging Garden in the Waterway Wtf 4/93 ... 2,500
W/Pa 20x26 Fisherman's Hut 1903 Hnd 9/92 2,400
W/Pa 20x13 Stone Walkway to a Temple Wtf 4/93 1,800
Young, August   Am 1837-1913
* See 1992 Edition ....
Young, Charles Morris   Am 1869-1964
O/C 15x18 Winter Landscape 1916 Chr 9/92 5,500
Young, Florence Upson   Am 1872-
O/C 20x24 Sycamores in Fall Mor 11/92 550
Young, Gordan   Am 20C
* See 1992 Edition ....
Young, Harvey Otis   Am 1840-1901
O/C 29x39 Indian Encampment Chr 12/92 2,420
O/Ab 20x30 Herder with Sheep Slo 7/93 2,250
O/Ab 20x30 Autumn Near Colorado Springs 1900 Slo 7/93 . 1,800
O/B 16x24 The View from a Path Wes 5/93 1,210
O/C 16x20 Figures in Winter '91 Fre 10/92 675
O/B 16x24 Old Trees in Tucson, Arizona Hnd 12/92 325
W/Pa 8x14 Arizona Landscape Eld 8/93 248
Young, Mahonri Mackintosh   Am 1877-1957
K/Pa 17x12 Ballet Dancer Slo 7/93 700
Young, Michael   20C
* See 1993 Edition ....
Young, Murat "Chic"   Am 1901-1973
Pl/Pa 4x18 Daily Comic "Blondie" 30 Ih 11/92 600
Young, William S.   Am a 1850-1870
* See 1993 Edition ....
Youngerman, Jack   Am 1926-
* See 1992 Edition ....
Younglove, Ruth Ann   Am 20C
O/C 24x30 Sierra Hemlock Mor 11/92 100
Yuan, Si Chen   Am 1912-1974
O/B 25x32 Up for Repairs But 10/92 4,950
O/M 18x29 Autumn Mor 6/93 3,850
Yuzbasiyan, Arto   Can 1948-
W/Pa 22x30 Queen Street 1990 Sbt 11/92 2,376
O/C 30x40 Storm, Queen St. East Sbt 11/92 1,496
O/B 12x16 Victorian Houses Sbt 11/92 1,496
Yvon, Adolphe   Fr 1817-1893
* See 1993 Edition ....
Zabaleta, Vladimir   Ven 1944-
* See 1992 Edition ....
Zach, Karl   Am 20C
P/Pa 24x32 House with Geese Lou 6/93 100

Zacharie, Ernest Philippe   Fr 1849-1915
* See 1991 Edition ....
Zachry, H. C.
C/Pa 36x24 North Texas Cowboy Eld 8/93 330
Zack, Leon   Rus 1892-
* See 1992 Edition ....
Zadkine, Ossip   Fr 1890-1967
* See 1993 Edition ....
Zaganelli, Francesco   It 1460-1532
* See 1993 Edition ....
Zahnd, Johann   Sws 1854-1934
O/C 25x45 Peasants Returning from Fields Sby 5/93 9,200
Zais, Giuseppe   It 1709-1784
K,Pl&S/Pa 9x13 River Landscape with Figures Chr 1/93 ... 6,050
Zak, Carel J.   Am 20C
T/Ab 8x10 Autumn by the River Hnz 5/93 100
Zak, Eugene   Pol 1884-1926
O/C 32x26 Young Man with Pointed Hat Sby 10/92 18,700
Zakanitch, Robert   Am 1935-
O&H/Pa 60x48 Lounger I 87 Chr 2/93 825
Zalce, Alfredo   Mex 1908-
O/M 24x32 Llegando al Muelle 1948 Chr 11/92 44,000
Zalopany, Michele   20C
C&P/Pa 74x98 City of the Gods Sby 10/92 3,850
Zamacois Y Zabala, Eduardo   Spa 1842-1871
* See 1993 Edition ....
Zamora, Gimenez   It 19C
O/C 28x39 Roses and Fruit on Marble Ledge Chr 2/93 1,320
Zampagna, D.   Fr 20C
O/C 23x29 Paris Street Scene '59 Hnd 9/92 150
Zampighi, Emiliano   It 19C
* See 1993 Edition ....
Zampighi, Eugenio Eduardo   It 1859-1944
O/C 22x30 First Steps Sby 10/92 25,300
O/C 29x41 A Happy Family Hnz 5/93 25,000
O/C 22x30 Playing in the Kitchen Sby 5/93 24,150
O/C 22x31 Family Concert Hnd 10/92 22,000
O/C 26x36 Grandpa's Visit Hnz 5/93 15,000
O/C 16x14 Friar Playing Violin But 5/93 3,450
O/C 20x26 Grandpa's Visit: A Study Hnz 5/93 3,000
Zanchi, Antonio   It 1631-1722
* See 1992 Edition ....
Zandini   It 19C
* See 1993 Edition ....
Zandomeneghi, Federico   It 1841-1917
O/C 26x32 La Lecture Chr 5/93 629,500
P/Pa 13x8 Seated Woman Hnz 5/93 325
Zang, John J.   Am 19C
* See 1990 Edition ....
Zannoni, Giuseppe   It 1849-1903
O/C 24x16 Children and Poultry Fre 4/93 4,900
Zao-Wou-Ki   Chi 1921-
O/C 29x36 Untitled 50 Sby 5/93 29,900
O/C 32x26 Untitled 67 Chr 10/92 24,200
O/C 15x18 La Poivres Vertes 1952 Wes 10/92 8,800
W&Pe/Pa 10x8 Trees Sby 10/92 3,025
G/Pa 11x8 Mountain and Prairie 50 Sby 10/92 2,640
I&G/Pa 8x11 Two Wolves 50 Sby 10/92 2,420
Zapkus, Kes   Am 1938-
* See 1992 Edition ....
Zaragoza, Fernando Alvared
* See 1991 Edition ....
Zarate   19C
* See 1993 Edition ....
Zardo, Alberto   It 1876-1959
O/Cb 11x16 Sheep Grazing on Hillside Chr 2/93 990
Zaritzky, Joseph   Isr 20C
* See 1991 Edition ....
Zarraga, Angel   Mex 1886-1946
O/C 14x26 Bodegon con Fruta Sby 11/92 26,400
O/C 22x15 Le Vieux Moyer, Biot (A.M.) 1921 Sby 5/93 .. 24,150
O/C 16x13 Malabaristas Sby 11/92 14,300
O/C 46x32 Naturaleza Muerta Slo 4/93 12,000

Zatzka, Hans   Aus 1859-1945
O/C 31x23 The Dream Sel 4/93 7,500
O/C 23x32 The Lover's Dream Sby 10/92 7,480
O/C 32x21 Nymphs Adorning a Statue Wtf 3/93 7,000
O/C 30x25 Still Life with Roses Butterflies But 5/93 5,175
O/C 30x25 Roses, Tulips, Bluebells, Butterfly Chr 5/93 4,830
O/C 30x25 Elaborate Floral Still Life Chr 5/93 4,370
Zeeman   Dut 1623-1664
* See 1992 Edition
Zehme, Werner   20C
Zendel, Gabriel   Fr 1906-
G/Pa 10x12 Still Life with Guitar '52 But 10/92 935
O/C 32x21 Still Life Fruit and Objects 56 Sby 2/93 748
Zenil, Nahum   20C
* See 1992 Edition
Zenisek, Franz   Aus 1849-1916
O/Pn 14x12 Junge Frau Sby 10/92 1,980
Zeno, Jorge   Am 1956-
O/L 60x50 Luna Clara Chr 11/92 9,900
Zerbe, Karl   Am 1903-1972
* See 1993 Edition
Zeverling
O/C 12x18 Rubber Workers: Pair Eld 4/93 248
Zewy, Karl   Aus 1855-1929
* See 1993 Edition
Zezzos, Alessandro   It 1848-1913
W&P/Pa 37x28 La Chitarara But 11/92 4,400
Zick, Januarius   Ger 1730-1797
* See 1993 Edition
Ziegler, Eustace Paul   Am 1881-1969
W/Pa 10x14 Pulling in the Nets But 6/93 2,300
W/Pa 15x11 Climbing the Mast 1944 But 6/93 1,150
O/M 8x10 Mt. Blackburn Alaska 1925 Sel 4/93 1,000
O/C 9x12 Pointe aux Pins, Michigan 1902 Hnd 9/92 800
Ziegler, Henry   Am 1889-
P/Pa Var Five Drawings Eld 8/93 308
Ziegler, Nellie E.   Am 1874-1948
* See 1993 Edition
Ziem, Felix Francois Georges   Fr 1821-1911
O/Pn 25x31 Constantinople Chr 2/93 33,000
O/Pn 22x32 The Grand Canal, Venice Chr 10/92 28,600
O/Pn 17x24 Le Quai Chr 10/92 18,700
O/C 21x31 Le Canal de la Giudecca Doy 5/93 17,600
O/C 16x24 Gondola and the Campanile Wtf 3/93 6,500
O/C 14x22 Venetian Docks Wtf 3/93 5,000
W/Pa 9x12 Les Bateaux Dans le Port Sby 2/93 3,738
Zier, Francois Edouard   Fr 1856-1924
* See 1993 Edition
Zig
W,Pe&Gd/Pa 15x11 Costume Design Fish Sby 10/92 1,210
W,Pe&Pt/Pa 19x12 Costumes Puff & Lipstick Sby 10/92 990
Pe,W&Gd/Pa 15x11 Costumes Goldfish, Fish Gold Sby 10/92 660
W,Pe&Pt/Pa 19x13 Costumes Cigarette Holder Sby 10/92 ... 550
Zille, Heinrich   Ger 1858-1929
I/Pa 4x6 Family Outing Dum 5/93 3,250
Zilotti, Domenico Battisha   It 1887-
O/B 22x35 View of Rialto Bridge Fre 4/93 1,400
Zim, Marco   Am 1880-
* See 1992 Edition
Zimmer, Bernd   1948-
A/C 63x79 Zwieselstein '80 Chr 2/93 2,420
Zimmer, Wilhelm Carl August   Ger 1853-1937
* See 1991 Edition
Zimmerman, Carl   Am 1900-
W/Pa 7x10 Rocky Shorelines Wtf 9/92 250
Zimmerman, Eugene   Am 1878-1935
PI/Pa 14x22 Man Standing at Foot of Bed Ih 11/92 225
Zimmerman, Frederick   Am 1886-1974
* See 1992 Edition
Zimmerman, Karl   Ger 1796-1857

Zimmerman, Reinhard Sebastian   Ger 1815-1893
O/Pn 9x13 Sharing the News Sby 10/92 4,950
Zimmermann, August Albert   Ger 1808-1888
O/C 26x39 mountainous Lake Chr 5/93 7,475
Zimmermann, Ernst   Ger 1852-1901
O/Pn 20x25 Tavern Interior with Figures Sel 12/92 2,300
Zimmermann, Jan Wendel G.   Dut 1816-1887
* See 1993 Edition
Zimmermann, Julius   Ger 1824-1906
O/C 40x61 Frederick II with His Hunting Party 184 Chr 2/93 12,100
Zingg, Jules-Emile   Fr 1882-1942
O/C 15x21 Workers in the Field Wtf 9/92 3,000
Zingoni, Aurelio   It 1853-1922
O/C 41x34 Threading the Needle 1875 Hnd 3/93 5,200
Zinkeisen, Doris Clare   Br 1898-
O/C 20x40 The Carriage Ride But 5/93 3,450
Zinnogger, Leopold   Aus 1811-1872
* See 1992 Edition
Zobel, Fernando   Spa 1924-
* See 1993 Edition
Zoboli, Jacopo   It 1681-1767
* See 1992 Edition
Zocchi, Guglielmo   It 1874-
O/C 11x28 The Young Acrobat But 11/92 4,400
Zoffoli, Andrea   It 19C
W/Pa 20x14 Drink For Man But Not Mule Fre 10/92 500
Zogbaum, Rufus Fairchild   Am 1849-1925
* See 1993 Edition
Zoir, Emil   Swd 1867-1936
* See 1992 Edition
Zona, Antonio   It 1813-1892
* See 1993 Edition
Zopf, J.
O/C 27x42 Landscape Ald 5/93 375
Zorach, Marguerite   Am 1888-1968
* See 1993 Edition
Zorach, William   Am 1887-1966
W/Pa 15x22 Hendricks Head Lighthouse 1947 Brd 8/93 ... 7,150
W&H/Pa 12x9 Landscape Sby 3/93 3,575
W&I/Pa 14x21 Cottages by a Lake Chr 12/92 1,320
W/Pa 15x22 Creek 1954 Wtf 12/92 200
Zorn, Anders   Swd 1860-1920
O/C 26x17 Solnedgong 1910 Sby 5/93 68,500
Zornes, James Milford   Am 1908-
W/Pa 12x18 Our Back Fence 1934 Mor 11/92 1,900
W/Pa 15x23 House in a Landscape 1939 But 3/93 1,870
W/Pa 22x29 Colorado River, Arizona '40 But 6/93 1,092
W/Pa 13x21 Mission in Southwest Landscape Mor 2/93 900
W/Pa 22x29 Commercial Fishing Boat '70 Mor 2/93 750
W/Pa 14x21 Rural Landscape Farmhouse But 6/93 748
W/Pa 22x30 El Salvador '79 But 3/93 715
W/Pa 16x23 River Landscape 1953 Mor 6/93 440
Zorthian, Jirayr Hamparzoom   Am 1912-
O/Pa 16x19 At the Big Game Skn 9/92 880
Zox, Larry   Am 1936-
* See 1992 Edition
Zuber-Buhler, Fritz   Sws 1822-1896
O/C/B 29x24 Maternite Sby 10/92 17,600
O/Pn 13x11 The Bath Chr 10/92 5,280
Zuccarelli, Francesco   It 1702-1788
* See 1992 Edition
Zuccaro, Federico   1540-1609
K/Pa 8x10 Two Female Figures Seated '62 Chr 1/93 6,600
Zucker, Jacques   Am 1900-
* See 1993 Edition
Zucker, Joe   Am 1941-
Fp/Pa 18x24 Three Drawings 77 Chr 5/93 863
Fp/Pa 18x24 Lotsa Junk 77 Chr 2/93 220
Zuckerberg, Stanley   Am 1919-
* See 1993 Edition

Zugel, Heinrich Johann   Ger 1850-1941
   * See 1993 Edition . . . .
Zugno, Francesco   It 1709-1787
   * See 1993 Edition . . . .
**Zuloaga Y Zabaleta, Ignacio   Spa
1870-1945**
   W/Pa 6x4 Bust of a Man Hnd 10/92   450
Zuniga, Francisco   Mex 1913-
   C&P/Pa 28x20 Desnudo Sentado 1978 Sby 5/93   9,200
   C&P/Pa 20x28 Mujer Sentada 1983 Chr 11/92   8,250
   W&H/Pa 26x20 Desnudo Sentado 1969 Sby 11/92   7,700
   W&Y/Pa 11x17 Tres Mujeres 1960 Chr 11/92   7,150
   C&P/Pa 20x28 Dos Mujeres Reposando 1980 Chr 11/92 . .   5,500
   Pe&I/Pa 20x26 Reclining Female Nude 59 Sby 6/93   5,175
   P&C/Pa 18x24 Desnudo 1964 But 4/93   4,887
   P,C&Sg/Pa 20x26 Mujer Dormida 1975 Chr 11/92   4,400
   P/Pa 19x28 Desnudo 1979 Sby 5/93   4,025
   H/Pa 21x27 Seated Female Nude 1974 But 10/92   3,850
   Pl/B 20x26 Desnudo 1964 But 4/93   3,737
   K/Pa 20x26 Desnudo 1972 Sby 2/93   3,105
Zwaan, C.
   O/C 20x24 Dutch Mother with Children Dum 1/93   1,200
Zwann, Cornelisz C.   Dut 1882-1964
   * See 1993 Edition . . . .
Zwara, John   Am 1880-
   O/C 18x24 Snow Scene Lou 3/93   600
Zwengauer, Anton   Ger 1810-1884
   * See 1992 Edition . . . .
Zwillinger, Rhonda   1950-
   O/C 54x79 Bon Voyage Chr 2/93   1,100

ART NOTES

ART NOTES

ART NOTES

ART NOTES